THE ANNUAL OBITUARY 1982

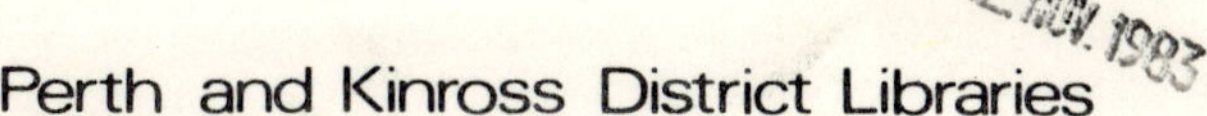

Perth and Kinross District Libraries

REFERENCE LIBRARY

Readers are requested to place books consulted on the Reference tables. Please do not return them to the shelves.

FOR USE ON LIBRARY PREMISES ONLY

THE ANNUAL OBITUARY 1982

Editor
JANET PODELL

Associate Editor
STEVEN ANZOVIN

ST. JAMES PRESS • LONDON

For information, write:
St. James Press, 3 Percy Street, London W1P 9FA
Manufactured in the United States of America

All photographs courtesy of Wide World Photos unless otherwise indicated.

ISSN 0278-1573
ISBN 0-912289-01-5

This book is printed on long-lasting acid-free paper.
The signatures are Smyth-sewn with cotton thread.

CONTENTS

EDITORS' NOTE

The editors wish to thank Howard Batchelor, Alison Brown, Richard Calhoun, Peter Desmond, Betty Donaldson, Adele Fried, Philip Kemp, Jonathan Rogers, Irina Rybacek, Michael Tubridy, and Roland Turner. Special thanks are due to Andrew Kimmens, chief writer, and to Lisa Friedman, editorial assistant and researcher. We are indebted for information and photographs to many families, colleagues, employers, professional organizations, institutional archives, embassies and consulates, and above all to the New York Public Library and the libraries of New York University and Englewood, New Jersey.

—Janet Podell and Steven Anzovin

Alphabetical Index of Entrants

Asterisks indicate entrants from previous volumes or the current volume for whom additional information is given in the Addendum.

Names prefixed with particles—*de, du, al, von,* etc.—are alphabetized as follows: if the particle begins with a letter in uppercase (for example, *De Lullo*), the name is alphabetized under the first letter of the particle. If the particle begins with a letter in lowercase (for example, *de Irujo* or *el-Sadat*), the name is alphabetized under the first letter of the main word. Asian names spelled with the surname first are so alphabetized, without a comma (e.g., *Soong Ching-ling*), but regular alphabetization is used if the entrant adopted the Western custom of placing the surname last (e.g., *Ling, Hung-hsun*).

Index of Entrants By Profession

Asterisks indicate entrants from previous volumes or the current volume for whom additional information is given in the Addendum.

Names prefixed with particles—*de, du, al, von,* etc.—are alphabetized as follows: if the particle begins with a letter in uppercase (for example, *De Lullo*), the name is alphabetized under the initial letter of the particle. If the particle begins with a letter in lowercase (for example, *de Irujo* or *el-Sadat*), the nâme is alphabetized under the first letter of the main word. Asian names spelled with the surname first are so alphabetized, without a comma (e.g., *Soong Ching-ling*), but regular alphabetization is used if the entrant adopted the Western custom of placing the surname last (e.g., *Ling, Hung-hsun*).

Teachers and writers who worked within a particular field of endeavor are grouped with those who practiced the profession. A teacher of ballet, for example, would be listed under "Dancers and Choreographers"; a professor of law would be listed under "Judges, Lawyers, and Criminologists"; and a writer who produced essays on architecture would be listed under "Architects and Planners."

The index is divided into the following categories:

Actors, Actresses, Mimes, and Entertainers

Anthropologists

Archaeologists

Architects and Planners

Art Historians, Collectors, Critics, and Dealers

Artists and Craftsmen

Arts Administrators

Astronomers

Aviators and Astronauts

Biographers and Memoirists

Biologists, Botanists, and Zoologists

Business Executives and Industrialists

Chemists

Children's Writers

Composers, Arrangers, and Songwriters

Criminals

Dancers and Choreographers

Designers

Diplomats

Directors

Dramatists and Scriptwriters

Earth Scientists
(including Geographers, Geologists, Meteorologists, and Oceanographers)

Economists, Financial Specialists, and Bankers

Educationists and Educational Administrators

Engineers and Technologists

Explorers

Farmers, Horticulturists, and Agricultural Researchers

Folklorists

Foundation Administrators

Heads of State, Presidents, Premiers, and Governors General

Historians

Illustrators, Cartoonists, and Animators

Intelligence Agents and Officers

International Affairs Officials

Inventors

Journalists and Editors (including Travel Writers)

Judges, Lawyers, and Criminologists

Labor Leaders

Librarians, Museum Curators, Archivists, and Antiquarians

Linguists, Philologists, and Lexicographers

Literary Scholars (including Critics and Translators)

Management and Industrial Relations Specialists

Mathematicians and Statisticians

Medical Practitioners and Researchers

Military Officers and Strategists

Musical Performers and Conductors

Naturalists

Novelists and Short Story Writers (including Humorists)

Performing Arts Critics and Scholars

Philanthropists

Philosophers

Photographers and Cinematographers

Physicists

Poets

Political Scientists

Politicians

Producers

Psychiatrists and Psychologists

Public and Government Officials

Publishers

Radio and Television Personalities

Religious Figures
(including Clergy, Scholars, and Occultists)

Royalty and Socialites
(including notable spouses of famous people)

Social, Political, and Human Rights Activists

Social Workers

Sociologists and Social Scientists

Sports and Games Figures

THE ANNUAL OBITUARY 1982

JANUARY

ERWIN D(AIN) CANHAM

Newspaper editor

***Born* Auburn, Maine, USA, 13 February 1904**

***Died* Agana, Guam, Mariana Islands, 3 January 1982**

Erwin D. Canham worked for 49 years on the staff of the *Christian Science Monitor*, successively as reporter, columnist, Washington bureau chief, managing editor, and chief editor. Under his guidance the Boston-based newspaper became one of the most respected in the country, especially in the areas of foreign reporting and news analysis. He was also extensively involved in public service, among other offices as the first newspaperman to be elected president of the U.S. Chamber of Commerce (1959) and during the 1970s, after his active years on the *Monitor*, as commissioner of the Northern Mariana Islands in the western Pacific.

An only child, Canham spent his youth learning the newspaper business in the small towns of rural Maine. His father was agricultural editor of the *Lewiston Sun and Journal*, and the boy was taking down news items over the telephone from the age of eight. At 14, because of the manpower shortage during World War I, Canham became a general reporter for the paper. He entered Bates College in Lewiston, where by the end of his third year he was earning the very considerable sum of $100 per week putting out a resort paper in Poland Springs and working as correspondent for eight dailies in Portland, Boston, Philadelphia, and New York.

Upon graduating in 1925, Canham went to work for the *Monitor*. That paper was a natural choice: when he was ten his family had converted from a strict Methodism to Christian Science following his mother's cure from a succession of serious illnesses by a Christian Science practitioner. He worked on the paper only a year before winning a Rhodes scholarship to Oxford University. The *Monitor* gave him a leave of absence, and he spent three years studying in England, where he worked during the long vacations reporting on the sessions of the League of Nations Assembly in Geneva.

Canham returned to the *Monitor* full-time in 1929 and reported from Geneva until 1932, when he became chief of the paper's Washington bureau. He served as general news editor from 1939 to 1941, as managing editor from 1941 to 1945, then as editor until 1964, when the post of editor in chief was created for him. He was editor emeritus from 1974 until his retirement five years later.

The *Monitor* had been started in 1908 at the direction of Mary Baker Eddy, the founder of Christian Science, who was shocked by the sensationalism of the American popular press, which she considered an affront to public morals. The paper's credo was printed in its first anniversary issue, and regularly thereafter: "Whatever is of public importance or affects the public welfare, even though it be news of what is ordinarily reckoned as crime or disaster, is printed in the *Monitor* in completeness sufficient for information without unnecessary embellishment or sensational display. The emphasis, however, is reserved for the helpful, the constructive, the encouraging, not their opposites." These rules were strictly adhered to throughout Canham's tenure. Stories of crime, corruption, scandal, and catastrophe were given short shrift; even medical news was hardly reported at all. Public figures always "passed on" rather than died, and a host of products ranging from coffee to tobacco to medicine were barred from the advertising pages. The paper's accomplishment was to rise above all such editorial restrictions and to report on its chosen subjects with professional thoroughness. Its circulation was never large, especially in Boston, but its national readership included people of influence and discernment, many of whom cared nothing about the religious beliefs of its editors.

Canham was reckoned a hard taskmasker by his employees, who were forbidden to smoke or drink on the *Monitor*'s premises. He would usually enter the paper through the back door, so as to be able to pass through the pressroom and smell the ink. He also had the ability to laugh at himself, as when he took with good grace the incongruous nickname Spike after it was suggested by his friend, the *Monitor* columnist Roscoe Drummond.

Although newspaper reporters have often accepted positions in public service, few have done so to the extent Canham did, or over so long a time. In 1948 he was appointed deputy chairman of the U.S. delegation to the U.N. Conference on Freedom of Information, and was alternate delegate to the U.N. General Assembly in 1949. From 1949 to 1951 he was on the U.S. Commission for Information, part of the National Commission for UNESCO. His government service continued in 1970, when he was appointed to the Presidential Commission on Campus Unrest and later to the board of the Public Broadcasting Service. In 1975, Canham was sent to Saipan as commissioner to supervise a plebiscite in which the voters of the Northern Marianas chose to form a U.S. commonwealth, withdrawing from the Trust Territory of the Pacific Islands. He stayed on as resident commissioner until 1978, and even after a new governor was elected, Canham and his wife divided their time between their homes on Saipan and on Cape Cod, Massachusetts.

In his other public-service positions, Canham was president of the American Society of Newspaper Editors (1948–49), president (1959–60) and chairman of the board (1960–61) of the U.S. Chamber of Commerce, chairman of the Federal Reserve Bank of Boston (1962–67), board member of the National Safety Council (1964–68), and director of the National Bureau of Economic Research. In Boston he was a trustee of the Museum of Fine Arts and from 1968 was president of the board of trustees of the Boston Public Library. In 1966 he served for a year as president of the Christian Science organization. Bostonians of all kinds held him in high regard, and in 1955 he was asked by armed inmates at Charleston State Prison to negotiate with prison officials for the release of 11 hostages.

Courtesy of The Christian Science Monitor

Canham, always considered a quick thinker and writer, was the author and editor during the 1950s and 1960s of several books, some on public affairs, others of a religious or inspirational nature. He received numerous governmental decorations, including an honorary CBE from Britain. He died at the age of 77 after abdominal surgery. A.K.

Parents Vincent Walter C., farmer and newspaperman, and Elizabeth May (Gowell) C. **Married** (1) Thelma Whitman Hart 1930 (d. 1967): Carolyn Dain Paul; Elizabeth Dain Davis. (2) Patience Mary Daltry 1968. **Religion** Family converted to Christian Science from Methodism when he was ten. **Education** Public schs., Lisbon and Auburn, ME; Bates Coll., Lewiston, ME, B.A. 1925; Oxford Univ. (Rhodes Scholarship) 1926–29, B.A., M.A. 1936. **Career** Reporter, *Lewiston Sun and Journal*, ME, high sch. years; newspaper corresp. and ed. of resort mag., coll. years. • With *Christian Science Monitor*, Boston: reporter 1925; corresp., England 1926–30; corresp., Geneva 1930–32; chief of Wash. DC bureau 1932–39; gen. news ed. 1939–41; managing ed. 1942–44; ed. 1945–64; ed. in chief 1964–74; ed. emeritus since 1974. • Radio commentator 1938–39 and 1945–64; moderator, TV program "Starring the Editors," Boston, since 1953; commentator on public affairs, Westinghouse Broadcasting Co., Group W, 1970s. • Deputy chmn., U.S. delegation to U.N. Conference on Freedom of Information 1948; member, U.S. Commn. for Information, U.S. Natl. Commn. for UNESCO 1948–51; U.S. alternate delegate to

U.N. General Assembly 1949; delegate, Intl. Chamber of Commerce, Tokyo 1955; pres. 1959–60, bd. chmn. 1960–61, and exec. cttee. chmn. 1961–62, U.S. Chamber of Commerce; member, Pres.'s Commn. on Campus Unrest 1970; plebiscite commnr. 1975 and resident commnr. 1976–78, North Mariana Islands. **Officer** Pres.: Amer. Soc. of Newspaper Editors 1948–49; Mother Church, First Church of Christ, Scientist, Boston 1966; Boston Public Library 1968; Wash. DC branch, Writers Club. • Dir.: Natl. Manpower Council 1966–70; Keystone Custodian Funds, Inc.; John Hancock Insurance Co.; Natl. Bureau for Economic Research; Resources for the Future, Inc. • Trustee: Robert H. Taft Inst. of Govt.; 20th Century Fund.; Mus. of Fine Arts, Boston; Bates, Simmons, and Wellesley colls. • Other: bd. chmn., Federal Reserve Bank, Boston 1962–67; bd. member, Natl. Safety Council 1964–68; corp. member, Northeastern Univ.; officer, Intl. Fedn. of Newspaper Editors. **Fellow** Amer. Acad. of Arts and Sciences. **Member** Assn. of Amer. Rhodes Scholars; Delta Sigma Rho; Mason, 33°. • Clubs: Gridiron, Natl. Press, and Overseas Writers, Wash. DC; Saturday and Tavern, Boston. **Honors** Chevalier 1946 and officer 1958, Légion d'Honneur, France; officer, Order of Southern Cross, Brazil 1951; comdr., Order of Orange-Nassau, Netherlands 1952; Order of George I, Greece 1954; Grand Distinguished Service Cross, order of Merit, West Germany 1960; Roosevelt Distinguished Service Medal for public service, Theodore Roosevelt Assn. 1961; Columbia Journalism Award, Columbia Univ. Graduate Sch. of Journalism 1962; Key Award, Amer. Soc. of Associated Executives 1962; Vigilant Patriot's Recognition Award, All-Amer. Conference to Combat Communism 1963; CBE, U.K. 1964; Freedom Award, Freedoms Foundn. 1966; Distinguished Service to Journalism Award, Ohio Newspaper Assn. 1968; White Foundn. Award 1968; Grand Silver Badge of Honor, Austria 1968; Pro Merito Medal, Free World Latvian Assn. and Amer. Latvian Assn. 1968; Zenger Award, Univ. of Arizona 1971; Amer. Education Award, Amer. Assn. of School Administrators 1971; Golden Plate Award, Amer. Acad. of Achievement; Wilson Religion in American Life Award 1973; others. • Hon. fellow, Sigma Delta Chi; hon. degrees for univs. of Boston, Yale, Tufts, Temple, Brigham Young, Northeastern, and Suffolk, Bates Coll., others. **Author** (Jtly.) *Awakening: The World at Mid-Century*, 1951; *New Frontiers for Freedom*, 1954; *Commitment to Freedom: The Story of the Christian Science Monitor*, 1958; (ed.) *Man's Great Future*, 1959; *A Christian Scientist's Life*, 1962.

Further reading K.N. Stewart and J. Tebbel, *Makers of Modern Journalism*, 1952; Louis Finkelstein, *Thirteen Americans: Their Spiritual Autobiographies*, 1953.

MARGARET CULKIN BANNING

Novelist and short-story writer

***Born* Buffalo, Minnesota, USA, 18 March 1891**

***Died* Tryon, North Carolina, USA, 4 January 1982**

Margaret Culkin Banning, who began writing novels in the 1920s, was an early feminist whose themes did not become popular material for fiction writers until 50 years later. Although she worked in the genre called, often contemptuously, "women's fiction," she dealt with such issues as the career aspirations, financial independence, sexual mores, religious values, and political activities of women when most writers in the genre limited themselves to stories of romance and family life. "The only possible reason why women should read anything I write," she once said, "might be because I might get a glimmer of truth once in awhile and would pass it right along."

Born in Minnesota, Banning was educated at Vassar College and the Chicago School of Civics and Philanthropy and was a research fellow of the Russell Sage Foundation in 1913. She published her first novel, *This Marrying*, in 1920, and for the next two decades, while she was raising her daughter and son (two other children died in infancy), published novels at the rate of about one a year. During World War II she served on the advisory committee of the Writer's War Board, studied industrial and home conditions in England as a guest of the Ministry of Information, and wrote nonfiction works on the role of women in the defense effort. (She once noted that she had been present at the outbreak of three wars—in London in 1914, Spain in 1936, and Paris in 1939.)

Her novels from the 1940s onward dealt mainly with the problems faced by Roman Catholic protagonists who, like herself, had been divorced and remarried. *Fallen Away* (1951) concerned marriage between people of different religions; *The Vine and the Olive* (1965) examined the dilemma of American Catholic women who want to use contraception; *The Will of Magda Townsend* (1973) was a fictionalized autobiography. Banning also lectured, spoke on radio programs, and published numerous magazine articles, one of which, "Filth on the Newsstands" (*Reader's Digest*, 1952), resulted in her being called to testify before the House Select Committee on Current Pornographic Materials. In all, she wrote 42 books, and contributed more than 400 short stories to such magazines as *Collier's*, *The Saturday Evening Post*, and *Ladies' Home Journal*.

Banning was active in a number of charitable, professional, and civic organizations, including the National Federation of Business and Professional Women's Clubs and the American Council on Education. She maintained homes in Tryon, North Carolina, and Duluth, Minnesota, where she wrote seven hours a day in a room overlooking Lake Superior. She was at work on another novel when she died. J.P.

Born Margaret Culkin. **Parents** William Edgar C. and Hannah (Young) C. **Married** (1) Archibald T. Banning, Jr., lawyer, 1914 (div.): Mary Margaret Banning Friedlander, physicist; Archibald Tanner III, naval officer; William Culkin (d.); Margaret Brigid (d.). (2) LeRoy Salsich, mining exec., 1944. **Religion** Roman Catholic. **Education** Vassar Coll., Poughkeepsie, NY, A.B. (Phi Beta Kappa) 1912; Chicago Sch. of Civics and Philanthropy, certificate 1913; research fellow, Russell Sage Foundn. 1913. **Career** Novelist since 1920; also writer of short stories, articles, and travel books. **Officer** Chmn.: Commn. on Education of Women, Amer. Council on Education; program coordination, Natl. Fedn. of Business and Professional Women's Clubs. • Trustee: Duluth Public Library since 1930; Vassar Coll. 1937–45; St. Paul Inst. of Science; Natl. Fund for Medical Education; Natl. Health and Welfare Retirement Fund. • Dir.: Alworth Memorial Scholarship Fund; Natl. Council of Community Chests of America. • Pres., Duluth chapter, Amer. Assn. of University Women. **Member** Advisory cttee., Writers' Bd., WWII; council, Authors League of Amer. 1948–50; advisory bd., Women's Medical Coll. of Pennsylvania; League of Women Voters; Vassar Coll. Alumnae; Natl. League of Amer. Pen Women; PEN; Republican Party. • Clubs: Arts and Cordon, Chicago; Duluth Woman's and Northland Country, Duluth; Tryon Country and Tryon Riding and Hunt, Tryon, NC; Business and Professional Women's, Pen and Brush, and Cosmopolitan, NYC. **Honors** Hon. member, Junior League, Duluth. **Author** *This Marrying*, 1920; *Half Loaves*, 1921; *Spellbinders*, 1922; *Country Club People*, 1923; *A Handmaid of the Lord*, 1924; *The Women of the Family*, 1926; *Pressure*, 1927; *Money of Her Own*, 1928; *Prelude to Love*, 1929; *Mixed Marriage*, 1930; *The Town's Too Small*, 1931; *Path of True Love*, 1932; *The Third Son*, 1933; *The First Woman*, 1934; *The Iron Will*, 1935; *Letters to Susan*, 1936; *You Haven't Changed*, 1937; *The Case for Chastity*, 1937; *Too Young To Marry*, 1938; *Enough To Live On*, 1939; *Out in Society*, 1940; *Salud: A South American Journal*, 1941; *A Week in New York*, 1941; *Letters from England*, 1942; *Women for Defense*, 1942; *Conduct Yourself Accordingly*, 1944; *The Clever Sister*, 1947; *Give Us Our Years*, 1949; *Fallen Away*, 1951; *A New Design for the Defense Decade*, 1951; *The Dowry*, 1955; *The Convert*, 1957; *Echo Answers*, 1960; *The Quality of Mercy*, 1963; *The Vine and the Olive*, 1965; *I Took My Love to the Country*, 1966; *Mesabi*, 1969; *Lifeboat Number Two*, 1971; *The Will of Magda Townsend*, 1973; *The Splendid Torments*, 1976; *A Place in the Country*, 1979; *Such Interesting People*, 1979. **Contributor** of short stories, articles, and book reviews to literary jrnls. and popular mags.

HANS CONREID
Actor and comedian
***Born* Baltimore, Maryland, USA, 1 April 1915**
***Died* Burbank, California, USA, 5 January 1982**

Character actor Hans Conreid specialized in playing eccentric, often sinister Europeans. He was perhaps best known to American television audiences for his comic portrayal of the irascible Uncle Toonoose on "The Danny Thomas Show" in the 1960s.

Though many viewers thought him to be of European birth, he was born Frank Foster Conreid in Baltimore, and studied acting at Columbia University in New York City. He began his stage career in productions of Shakespeare, but soon moved to radio, where his distinctive voice and faultless diction won him roles with Orson Welles's Mercury Theater troupe. Throughout the late 1930s and early 1940s he played in the popular radio comedies "The Great Gildersleeve," "Life with Luigi," and "My Friend Irma" (he was also in the 1949 film version with Dean Martin and Jerry Lewis). He appeared in more than 100 films, beginning with *Dramatic School* in 1937, and provided memorable voice characterizations—notably Captain Hook in *Peter Pan* (1953)—for several animated films from the Disney studios.

In 1953 Conreid scored a hit with his first Broadway role as the manic sculptor Boris Adzinidzinadze in the Cole Porter musical *Can-Can*, but despite a number of stage successes in the latter part of his career, he was most familiar as a television actor. In addition to his regular role on "The Danny Thomas Show," he hosted "Fractured Flickers," a comedy program in which clips from silent films were overdubbed with incongruous or satiric dialogue. He appeared frequently on "The U.S. Steel Hour," "Stump the Stars," and "The Tony Randall Show." He had just completed a television version of Neil Simon's play *Barefoot in the Park* when he died of a heart attack.
S.A.

Born Frank Foster C. **Married** Margaret: Trilby; Hans III; Alexander; Edith. **Education** Columbia Univ., NYC. **Career** Actor and comedian on stage and radio since ca. 1935; with Mercury Theater radio troupe late 1930s; in films since 1937; on TV since ca. 1955. **Member** (and co-founder) AFTRA. **Stage** *Can-Can*, NYC 1959; *Tall Story*, NYC 1959; *The Absence of a Cello*, NYC 1966; *Generation*, NYC and tour 1967; *Don't Drink the Water*, Miami 1967 and tour 1969–70; *70, Girls, 70*, NYC 1971; *Norman, Is That You?*, tour 1971; *Irene*, NYC 1974; appeared in stock productions of *My Fair Lady*, *The Pleasure of His Company*, *The Second Time Around*, others. **Films** *Dramatic School*, 1937; *Journey into Fear*, 1942; *Crazy Horse*, 1943; *Mrs. Parkington*, 1944; *The Senator Was Indiscreet*, 1947; *My Friend Irma*, 1949; *Big Jim McClain*, 1952; *The Twonky*, 1953; *The 5,000 Fingers of Dr. T.*, 1953; *Peter Pan*, 1953; *Bus Stop*, 1956; *Rockabye Baby*, 1958; *The Patsy*, 1964; *The Brothers O'Toole*, 1973; also appeared in *It's a Wonderful World*, *The Falcon Takes Over*, *Duley*, *The Wife Takes a Flyer*, *Blondie's Blessed Event*, *Nightmare*, *His Butler's Sister*, *Nancy Goes to Rio*, *The Affairs of Dobie Gillis*, *The Birds and the Bees*, *The Cat from Outer Space*, and many others. **Ra-**

dio "The Great Gildersleeve"; "My Friend Irma"; "Life with Luigi"; "Edgar Bergen–Charlie McCarthy Show"; others. **Television** "Danny Thomas Show"; "Fractured Flickers"; "Stump the Stars"; "Great Voices from Great Books"; "Tony Randall Show"; many guest appearances. **Voices** for film and television cartoons.

PAUL (EDWARD) LYNDE

Comedian and actor

***Born* Mount Vernon, Ohio, USA, 13 June 1926**

***Found dead* Beverly Hills, California, USA, 9 January 1982**

Paul Lynde's one-line wisecracks, sardonic sneer, and fussy mannerisms were for 13 years a feature of the daytime television game show "Hollywood Squares." His comedy routine was incorporated intact into numerous television shows and films.

The fifth of six children of a meat store owner, he was, by his own account, a "funny fat kid" whose weight problem made him the butt of family jokes. He studied drama at Northwestern University, worked at odd jobs in New York City for three years while waiting for acting roles, and made his stage debut in a stock production of *Happy Birthday* after losing 80 pounds by going on a strenuous diet. An amateur contest at a New York nightclub started him on a career as a stand-up comedian on the club and hotel circuit. After appearing in the Broadway revue *New Faces of 1952*—his classic routine as Carl Canker, a battered tourist on safari, was called "the funniest bit of the evening" by critic Walter Kerr—he became a regular performer in stock theater productions. His best-known stage role was that of Harry MacAfee, the harassed father of a teenage daughter with a crush on a rock 'n' roll singer, in the 1960 Broadway musical *Bye Bye Birdie*. He repeated the role in the 1963 film version and went on to make several other light comedy films, including the cartoon *Charlotte's Web*, for which he supplied the voice of the rat.

Lynde made his television debut on "The Ed Sullivan Show" with his tourist routine and over the next three decades logged in hundreds of guest appearances on variety and talk shows. During the early 1960s' season he was one of the Kraft Music Hall Players on "The Perry Como Show." From 1965 to 1972 he played the practical joker Uncle Arthur on the series "Bewitched," and followed that with two short-lived situation comedies, "The Paul Lynde Show" (1972–73) and "Temperatures Rising" (1974). On "Hollywood Squares," the game show on which he appeared as a celebrity panelist from 1968 until its cancellation in 1981, he specialized in delivering witty off-the-cuff ripostes to straight questions. (Announcer: "Why are motorcyclists partial to leather?" Lynde: "Because chiffon wrinkles so easily.") Despite his many live performances, Lynde said that he never lost a sense of stage fright that approached nervous collapse.

Courtesy of J. Allen, Public Relations

Lynde died at the age of 55 of a heart attack.

C.M.

Parents Hoy C. L., meat market owner, and Sylvia (Bell) L. **Education** Mount Vernon High Sch., OH, grad. 1944; Northwestern Univ., Evanston, IL, B.S. 1948. **Career** Sales clerk, NYC 1948–51; nightclub debut as comedian 1950, stage debut as actor 1951, TV and film comedian since mid-1950s; actor with Kenley Players, OH since 1960s. **Officer** Chmn., Heart Fund campaign, OH 1971. **Member** SAG; AEA; AFTRA; Acad. of Motion Picture Arts and Sciences; Phi Kappa Sigma. **Honors** Merit of Achievement Award, Northwestern Univ. Alumni Assn. 1970; Gov.'s Award, OH 1971. **Stage** *Happy Birthday*, Corning, NY 1951; *New Faces of 1952*, NYC; (sketch writer and sketch dir.) *New Faces of 1956*, NYC; (sketch writer) *New Faces of 1962*, NYC; *Anything Goes, Dream Girl, Show Boat, A Streetcar Named Desire, Irene, Panama Hattie, Visit to a Small Planet, Desk Set, Season in the Sun, Dig We Must*, and *Once More with Feeling*, stock circuit 1950s; *Bye Bye Birdie*, NYC 1960; summer stock, OH since 1960s. **Films** *New Faces of 1954*; *Bye Bye Birdie*, 1963; *Under the Yum-Yum Tree*, 1963; *Son of Flubber*, 1963; *For Those Who Think Young*, 1964; *Send Me No Flowers*, 1964; *The Glass Bottom Boat*, 1965; *Beach Blanket Bingo*, 1965; *How Sweet It Is*, 1968; (voice) *Charlotte's Web*, 1972; *Hugo the Hippo*, 1978; *Rabbit Test*, 1978; *The Villain*, 1979; others. **Television shows** "Perry Como Show," 1960–62; "Bewitched," 1965–72; "Hollywood Squares," 1968–81; "Dean Martin Presents the Gold Diggers," 1968, 1969; (voice) "Where's Huddles?" cartoon series, 1970; "Paul Lynde Show," 1972–73; "Temperatures Rising," 1974; numerous guest appearances on variety and talk shows and comedy series. **Television movies** *Gidget Grows Up*, 1969; *Gidget Gets Married*, 1972.

JAN SCHILT

Astronomer

***Born* Gouda, The Netherlands, 3 February 1894**

***Died* Englewood, New Jersey, USA, 9 January 1982**

Astronomer Jan Schilt elucidated the motions of stars, refined various means of determining their distance from earth, and improved on previous attempts to measure the density of matter in the galaxy.

Born and raised in Gouda, the Netherlands, Schilt entered the University of Utrecht in 1912. After four years' service with the Royal Dutch Army during World War I, he pursued graduate studies at the University of Groningen under Jacobus Kapteyn, a pioneer in the application of statistical methods to astronomy, and received his Ph.D. in 1924. Some of Schilt's early research on stellar velocities was done in collaboration with his fellow student Jan Oort, who also became a leading figure in twentieth-century astronomy.

Schilt served as an assistant at the Leyden Observatory from 1922 until 1925, when he went to the United States on a fellowship to work at the observatory on Mount Wilson in California. He spent five years teaching astronomy at Yale and joined the faculty of Columbia University in 1931.

At Columbia, Schilt had access to a collection of star photographs dating back to 1868 that had been taken by Lewis Morris Rutherfurd, the founder of Columbia's astronomy department. By comparing Rutherfurd's photographs with his own, he was able to demonstrate in 1935 that the relative positions of the stars in the cluster Pleiades had changed in the intervening 67 years, thus confirming the theory, then not widely accepted, that the cluster is in the process of dispersing. In 1936 he became Rutherfurd Professor of Astronomy at Columbia, as well as chairman of the astronomy department and head of the Rutherfurd Observatory.

In the following years, Schilt devoted much attention to the precise measurement of stellar distances. He pointed out a common observational error in the calculation of parallax (the angular displacement of a star against the background of other stars as seen from the moving earth), by which the distances of nearby stars are determined. Using a new estimate (based on his corrected distance figures) of the number of stars per cubic mile in the Milky Way, Schilt refuted the conclusion of some astronomers that this galaxy is less thickly strewn with stars than other galaxies. He also developed an improved photometer, the light-measuring device used to gauge the apparent luminosity, and thus the distance, of faraway stars.

In 1950 Schilt published his most notable contribution to astronomy. By analyzing the velocities of stars approaching or retreating from the plane of the galaxy, he was able to calculate the period of their oscillation and to estimate the density of matter near the galactic plane. The result was an improvement on the density figure previously arrived at by Oort and others.

Schilt became involved during the 1950s and 1960s in setting up astronomical observing stations in the southern hemisphere, a project in which Columbia and Yale universities cooperated. Observatories under his direction were established in Johannesburg, Canberra, and Argentina. Following his retirement from Columbia in 1962, Schilt served as university representative to the Yale-Columbia Southern Observatory until his death. P.D.

Courtesy of Columbia University

Married Joanna Timmer 1925: Joan Luikart. **Emigrated** to U.S. 1925; naturalized. **Education** Elementary sch., Gouda; Univ. of Utrecht, B.S. 1915; Univ. of Groningen, Ph.D. in astronomy 1924. **Mil. service** Royal Dutch Army 1914–18; U.S. Office of Scientific Research and Development 1941–45. **Career** Asst., Leyden Observatory, the Netherlands 1922–25; fellow, Intl. Education Bd., Mt. Wilson, CA 1925; instr., then asst. prof., Yale Univ. 1926–31. • With Columbia Univ.: assoc. prof. 1931–36; chmn. of astronomy dept., dir. of Rutherfurd Observatory, and Rutherfurd Prof. of Astronomy 1936–62; project chmn., Yale-Columbia Southern Sta., Johannesburg 1948, Canberra 1951–52, Chile and Argentina 1959–61; Rutherfurd Prof. Emeritus and univ. rep. to Yale-Columbia Southern Observatory since 1962. • Delegate: Natl. Research Council 1945–48; Intl. Astronomical Union, England 1925, the Netherlands 1928, Cambridge, MA 1932, Paris 1935, Sweden 1938, Switzerland 1948, Moscow 1958. **Member** Amer. Astronomical Soc.; Sigma Xi; Intl. Astronomical Union. **Honors** Gold Medal, Bachiene Inst., Netherlands 1924; citation for WWII research; kt., Order of Orange-Nassau, Netherlands; hon. degree from Univ. de Cuyo, Argentina; hon. member of Dutch Astronomers' Soc. and Astronomical Soc. of South Africa. **Inventor** of Schilt photometer. **Author** "The Gravitational Force and the Density of Interstellar Matter," in *Astronomical Journal*, May 1950; "Parallax Problems Old and New," in *Astronomical Journal*, Mar. 1954; many other articles in professional jrnls.

JIRO HORIKOSHI
Aeronautics engineer
***Born* Japan, circa 1904**
***Died* Tokyo, Japan, 11 January 1982**

Jiro Horikoshi was the chief designer of the Zero fighter plane that spearheaded the Japanese attack on Pearl Harbor in 1941. He joined Mitsubishi Heavy Industries Ltd., the giant manufacturing conglomerate, in 1927, after studying engineering at Tokyo Imperial University. Mitsubishi sent him to Europe and the United States to study aircraft and warplane design and on his return appointed him chief engineer of a project to develop the first Japanese carrier-based fighter aircraft, the 7-*shi*. Applying his knowledge of Western design and manufacturing techniques to this and subsequent projects, Horikoshi was largely responsible for transforming the derivative Japanese aeronautics industry, which had begun importing airplanes barely 25 years earlier, into one capable of producing original aircraft of high quality.

From the mid-1930s, Horikoshi was assigned to the design of naval warplanes. After he developed the successful 9-*shi* (Type 96) fighter, the Bureau of Aeronautics placed him in charge of Mitsubishi's 12-*shi* fighter design group when Japan invaded China in 1937. The 12-*shi*, known in the West as the Zero or Zeke, was planned by the Navy as a lightweight, easy-to-manufacture fighter; at the request of the pilots who were to fly it, its design emphasized maneuverability and firepower over heavy armor and other safety features. The first successful test flight was held in March 1939. More than 10,000 Zeros in various models were built by Mitsubishi over the course of World War II.

At the beginning of the war, the single-engined Zero, equipped with dual machine guns and 20-millimeter cannon, was far more agile and better armed than any American fighter plane. By 1943, however, the United States had begun to introduce heavily armed and larger-engined fighters, including the Grumman Hellcat, the Chance-Vought Corsair, and the Lockheed Lightning, which were superior to the Zero in range and altitude. Horikoshi's last fighter, the SAM, was meant to offset the defects of the Zero, but was delayed in production and never saw action.

After the war, Horikoshi continued to work for Mitsubishi on the design of commercial aircraft, including the short-range YS-11 passenger plane, manufactured in the early 1960s. He died of pneumonia at the age of 78.

S.A.

Education Tokyo Imperial Univ., engineering degree ca. 1927; studied aircraft design in Europe and U.S. **Career** With Mitsubishi Heavy Industries Ltd.: aircraft engineer 1927–37; chief engineer, 12-*shi* (Zero) project for Japanese Bureau of Aeronautics 1937–45; engineer and designer, commercial aircraft 1950s and 60s. • Prof.: Defense Inst. of Japan; Nippon Univ. **Designer** 7-*shi* carrier fighter plane, mid-1930s; 9-*shi* (Type 96) fighter plane, late 1930s; 12-*shi* (Zeke or Zero A6M) fighter plane, 1940; SAM fighter plane 1944; YS-11 commercial passenger plane 1962; others. **Author** (Jtly.) *The Zero Fighter* (English ed.), 1956.

Further reading Charles Gibbs-Smith, *Aviation, an Historical Survey*, 1970.

SIR KENNETH (WILLIAM DOBSON) STRONG
British and Allied intelligence chief
***Born* 9 September 1900**
***Died* Eastbourne, Sussex, England, 11 January 1982**

Sir Kenneth Strong was the most brilliant and influential director of Allied European intelligence during World War II. From early in 1943 he served under Gen. Dwight Eisenhower as head of G-2, the intelligence section in Allied Force Headquarters, providing the supreme Allied commander with the best available information preparatory to the Allied assault on Hitler's Europe. After the war he was active in Britain's intelligence community as a seasoned advocate of an integrated intelligence service and became the first director general of the Defence Intelligence Staff.

Kenneth William Dobson Strong was the son of Prof. John Strong of Edinburgh University. After attending Montrose Academy, a Scottish public school, he went against his father's wish that he go to university and entered the Royal Military College, Sandhurst. He joined the Royal Scots Fusiliers upon being commissioned in 1920 and spent several years thereafter as a subaltern in Ireland, hunting down wanted members of the Sinn Fein. It was his first experience with intelligence work and, although he never caught anyone of importance, he was placed on the

Sinn Fein's assassination list before his regiment was called home.

From 1925 until 1929, Strong was posted in Germany as intelligence officer for the British occupation force in the Rhineland. His knowledge of German was quickly acquired—he had a formidable aptitude for languages—and he was able to observe at first hand the rise of Nazism and to report on it to the War Office, which, he later recalled, seemed quite unconcerned. After he was moved to Malta in 1930, his intelligence-gathering activities often took him to Sicily, where he once saw Mussolini speak. After a short tour of duty with his regiment at home, he was sent to the War Office as a German intelligence expert, assigned to monitor German military growth. Another sensitive assignment came his way in 1937 when he was appointed military attaché at the British embassy in Berlin, where he was able to develop a personal acquaintance with nearly all the top Nazi political and military leaders. On one occasion he gained information about the size and strength of the German armed forces by jotting down the layout of a military parade sketched out in chalk on the sidewalk by the parade-master.

By then a lieutenant colonel, Strong was brought back to England in August 1940 to take over the German section (MI14) at the War Office, developing an exceptionally qualified team of experts and a thoroughly studied picture of the German High Command's intentions for the coming war. When the United States entered the war in early 1942, the MI14 analysis was accepted by the Americans as the best possible intelligence on German plans, and an integrated Anglo-American intelligence network was established. Strong came to know the American commanders well, and they greatly respected him. He was sent into the field to gain some experience as battalion commander within his regiment, then served briefly as intelligence chief for the British Home Forces under Gen. Sir Bernard Paget. In February 1943, when Gen. Eisenhower, who was shortly to be appointed supreme Allied commander in Europe, asked for the best British intelligence expert available, Strong was sent to Allied Force Headquarters as chief of G-2.

He served Eisenhower with great skill for the rest of the war, distinguishing himself during the Allied campaigns in North Africa, Sicily, Italy, France (where he predicted the Ardennes offensive), and Germany. They remained close the rest of Eisenhower's life, and in 1966 the former president wrote in a letter: "Because of the secret nature of your work over the past many years, only a relatively few people have any conception of the worth of the great contributions you have made to your country and indeed to mine. I, indeed the entire staff, had complete confidence in your findings and conclusions about our enemies. We trusted your judgment implicitly. From your work during that period I, possibly more than any other single individual, was the principal beneficiary. I find myself unable to express the true depth of my obligation to you."

During 1943, Strong was a key Allied negotiator in Lisbon and Sicily for the Italian surrender; he served in the same role during 1945 for the German surrenders at Rheims, France, and finally in Berlin. After the war, while still an officer, he was director general of the political intelligence department at the Foreign Office, and he retired from the army in 1947.

His wartime experiences had convinced Strong that only a unified, centralized intelligence service was suitable for Britain, which had often suffered from divided and divisive intelligence responsibilities. His views prevailed at once within the Ministry of Defence, when he was given the task of organizing the Joint Intelligence Bureau, of which he was director from 1948 to 1964. He served for another two years, after a further consolidation, as the ministry's director general of intelligence. Complete integration of British intelligence, however, was a goal he was never to see, although he firmly and frequently advocated it. He had in mind an organization somewhat like the U.S. Central Intelligence Agency, a "completely independent group . . . within the machinery of the Cabinet Office or, if not there, somewhere close to the levers of power. The constitution and manning of the national staff should be so devised that there is no predominance by any part of it. Its head, who should command universal respect for his intellectual distinction, would need to have direct access to the prime minister of the day and other ministers, and his representatives would be able to attend conferences when policy was being discussed or made." Such a bold project failed perhaps to take sufficient account of long-held and entrenched opinion at the Foreign Office, the senior intelligence service, which steadfastly resisted formal incorporation with military intelligence.

Strong was the author of two well-received books, *Intelligence at the Top* (1968), a professional autobiography, and *Men of Intelligence*

(1970). He was knighted in 1952 and received a KBE on his retirement in 1966. He died of bronchial failure at the age of 81. A.K.

Father John S., prof. **Married** Brita Horridge: one stepson. **Education** Montrose Acad., Angus; Glenalmond; Royal Military Coll., Sandhurst; Camberley Staff Coll. **Career** Second lt., 1st Battalion, Royal Scots Fusiliers 1920; served with Rhineland Army of Occupation 1925–29; with Defence Security Office, Malta and Gibraltar 1930; member, Saar Force 1935; military attaché, Berlin 1937; qualified as interpreter in German, French, Italian, Spanish; lt. col. ca. 1939; staff appointments, then head of German Sect., MI Directorate, War Office 1940; comdr., 4/5 Battalion, Royal Scots Fusiliers 1941; brig. gen. staff and chief of intelligence, Home Forces 1942; chief of intelligence, Allied Forces HQ, Africa, Sicily, Italy, France, Germany 1943–45; member of delegations to armistice negotiations with Italy 1943 and with Germany 1945; dir. gen., Political Intelligence Dept., Foreign Office 1945–47; retired from armed services 1947. • First dir., Jt. Intelligence Bureau 1948–64, and 1st dir. gen. of intelligence 1964–66, Ministry of Defence; consultant and advisor to govts. of Australia, Canada, and U.S. **Officer** Dir., Philip Hill Investment Trust and Eagle Star Insurance Co. 1966–77. **Member** Army and Navy Club. **Honors** OBE 1942; mentioned in dispatches, WWII; C.B. 1945; kt. 1952; KBE 1966; Distinguished Service Medal and Legion of Merit, U.S.; chevalier and officer, Légion d'Honneur, and Croix de Guerre with Palms, France; Order of Red Banner, USSR. **Author** *Intelligence at the Top* (memoirs), 1968; *Men of Intelligence*, 1970.

MARCEL CAMUS

Film director

Born **Chappes, Ardennes, France, 21 April 1912**

Died **Paris, France, 13 January 1982**

The French director Marcel Camus made one memorable film, *Orfeu negro* (1958; released in English-speaking countries as *Black Orpheus*), a modern version of the Greek legend of Orpheus and Eurydice set in Rio de Janeiro during Carnival. It won an Oscar for best foreign film and the Palme d'Or of the Cannes Film Festival and popularized the song "Manhã da Carnaval." But Camus did not develop a distinctive style, and none of his other ten films earned much attention.

The son of a schoolteacher, Camus originally intended to become a teacher of painting and sculpture. During World War II he spent four years in a prisoner-of-war camp in Wismar, Germany, where he directed inmate play productions and discovered, as he later wrote, "the joy of offering a few hours of escape to frustrated and unhappy souls." After his repatriation, his uncle, the filmmaker Roland Dorgelès, introduced Camus to his colleague Henri Decoin, who hired him as an assistant. There followed a period of apprenticeship during which he served as assistant and technical advisor to Jacques Feyder, George Rouquier, Luis Buñuel, Alexandre Astruc, and Jacques Becker. His first film, a short subject entitled *Renaissance du Havre*, was released in 1950. Because he refused to submit his work to government censors, he was unable to direct feature films until 1957, when he adapted for the screen a novel by Jean Hougron, *Mort en fraude* (*Fugitive in Saigon*), about the French war in Indochina. Camus's avoidance of the political issues and his concentration on the "human angle" became trademarks of all his films. "I try to make only love stories," he said. "I try to offer the public my own desire . . . a world of brotherhood." *Fugitive in Saigon* won the gold medal at the Festival of Youth in Moscow.

Black Orpheus, his third feature, was shot during the 1958 Rio Carnival, and the vibrant colors and rhythms of Brazilian street life lent it a remarkable intensity. The modern-day Orpheus, a tram conductor and guitar player, kills his lover Eurydice accidentally as she tries to escape a jealous pursuer and throws himself off a cliff in order to join her in death. The film galvanized critics at the 1959 Cannes Festival and garnered a strong popular following.

Camus was offered a five-year, five-film contract by a production company, but turned it down as too strenuous. He returned to Brazil to make *Os Bandeirantes* (1960) and *Otalia de Bahia* (1976) and to Indochina for *L'oiseau de paradis* (1962), but neither they nor his other films—including one comedy, *Le mur de l'Atlantique* (1970)—achieved much success. During the 1970s he worked mainly in television. He died at the age of 69 following heart surgery. J.P.

Father a schoolteacher. **Married** Lourdès de Oliveira, actress. **Education** Trained as an art teacher. **Mil. service** French Army, POW, WWII. **Career** Painter and sculptor 1930s; art teacher, Charlesville 1938–39 and Paris 1940; technical advisor and asst. to film dirs. c1946–56; film dir. and scenarist 1950–72; TV dir. 1970s. **Film director** (also co-scenarist or adaptor) *Renaissance du Havre*, 1948; *Mort en fraude* (rel. as *Fugitive in Saigon*), 1957; *La semaine sainte à Seville*, 1957; *Orfeu negro* (rel. as *Black Orpheus*), 1958; *Os bandeirantes*, 1960; *L'oiseau de paradis*, 1962; *Le chant du monde*, 1965; *Vivre la nuit*, 1968; *Un été sauvage*, 1969; *Le mur de l'Atlantique*, 1970; *Otalia de Bahia*, 1976. **Television** *La porteuse de pain*, 1973; *Molière pour rire et pour pleurer*, 1973; *Les faucheurs de marguerites*, 1974; *Feminin pluriel*, 1982; *Les amours du mal aimé*; *Ce diable d'homme*.

SEYMOUR (LESTER) HESS
Meteorologist
***Born* New York City, USA, 27 October 1920**
***Died* Tallahassee, Florida, USA, 15 January 1982**

Seymour Hess headed the team that designed the meteorological experiments for the National Aeronautics and Space Administration's Project Viking. Soon after Viking I landed on Mars on 20 July 1976, Hess gave the first Martian weather report from data collected on the planet's surface. "Light winds from the east in the late afternoon, changing to light winds from the southwest after midnight," his bulletin read. "Temperature ranged from −122 degrees Fahrenheit just after dawn to −22. Pressure steady at 7.70."

A native of Brooklyn, Hess graduated from Brooklyn College in 1941. He received his master's degree in 1945 while serving as an officer in the Army Air Corps, and received his Ph.D. in meteorology in 1949 while working at the Lowell Observatory in Flagstaff, Arizona, analyzing photographs of the planets. This assignment marked the beginning of his lifelong interest in planetary atmospheres.

Hess joined the faculty of Florida State University in 1950. He became a full professor in 1953, served for five years as associate dean, twice headed the meteorology department, and in 1978 was named Robert O. Lawton Distinguished Professor of Meteorology. Over the years, visiting professorships and other temporary assignments took him to New York City, Boulder, Colorado, London, and Leningrad.

In 1951, Hess and Hans Panofsky of New York University published a pioneering analysis of the surface features of the planet Jupiter, including the white zones and Great Red Spot, which are believed to mark the presence of vast storms. Hess pointed out that they are regions of high (anticyclonic) pressure and hence are strikingly different from terrestrial storms, which are regions of low (cyclonic) pressure. His *Introduction to Theoretical Meteorology* appeared in 1959, and is still the basic textbook in the field.

When planning began in the 1960s for a Mars mission, NASA asked Hess to head the project's meteorology team. The equipment designed by Hess and his staff for the Viking robot probes was housed inside swinging booms, which extended into the Martian atmosphere after the vehicles landed. As Hess had expected, weather conditions on Mars proved much easier to predict than those on earth, largely because of the scarcity of water (and hence of large-scale precipitation and

Courtesy of Florida State University

evaporation) on the red planet. Even so, there were surprises: although the barometric readings from Viking I dropped steadily during the first month, no storm ever developed.

The amount of data sent back by the Viking landers was voluminous. Hess was still analyzing this information when he died at the age of 61 of complications following surgery. P.D.

Parents Morris J. H. and Rose B. H. **Married** Eugenia E. Legrande 1966: Stephen B.; Robert N.; Barbara Keith; Martha Hillstrom, stepdaughter. **Religion** Jewish. **Education** Brooklyn Coll., B.A. 1941; Univ. of Chicago, M.S. 1945. Ph.D. in meteorology 1949. **Mil. service** First lt., USAAC 1942–46. **Career** Asst. meteorologist 1946–47 and instr. 1947–48, Univ. of Chicago; resident meteorologist, Lowell Observaory, Flagstaff, AZ 1948–50. • With Florida State Univ., Tallahassee: assoc. prof. of meteorology 1950–53; prof. of meteorology since 1953; chmn. of meteorology dept. 1958–63 and 1977–78; assoc. dean, Coll. of Arts and Sciences 1966–71; Lawton Distinguished Prof. 1978–79. • Visiting prof, New York Univ. 1956–58; leader of meteorology science team since 1969 and member of science steering group, Project Viking, NASA; liaison scientist, U.S. Office of Naval Research, London 1971–72; Fulbright Hays Lectr., Leningrad Univ. 1978; visiting scientist, Natl. Center for Atmospheric Research, Boulder, CO 1967; member of study panels on strategy for exploration of Venus and on priorities of space science and applications, Natl. Academy of Sciences. **Officer** Trustee: Natl. Center for Atmospheric Research; Univ. Corp. for Atmospheric Research. **Fellow** Amer. Assn. for Advancement of Science; (also council member) Amer. Meteorological Soc. **Member** Amer. Astronomical Soc.; Amer. Geophysical Union; Royal Meteorological Soc.; exobiology panel, Amer. Inst. of Biological Sciences; Sigmi Xi; Rotary Intl.; Cosmos Club, Tallahassee. **Honors** Medal, NASA 1977; Viking Flight Team Special Award, Amer. Meteorological Soc. 1977. **Author** *Introduction to Theoretical Meteorology*, 1959.

Further reading NASA, *Viking I: Early Results*, 1976; Eric Burgess, *To the Red Planet*, 1978; Victor R. Baker, *The Channels of Mars*, 1982; Michael H. Carr, *The Surface of Mars*, 1982.

RAMÓN J(OSÉ) SENDER
Novelist, essayist, and professor of Spanish literature
***Born* Chalamera de Cinca, Huesca, Aragon, Spain, 3 February 1902**
***Died* San Diego, California, USA, 15 January 1982**

Ramón J. Sender was one of the most distinguished and prolific contemporary authors writing in the Spanish language, producing some 70 novels and short-story collections and 15 volumes of essays, reportage, and criticism. During the 1920s and 1930s he was active in the republican movement. He left Spain in 1937 following the murder of his wife by a

Fascist firing squad and spent the rest of his life in Mexico and the United States. He reclaimed his Spanish citizenship in 1980, three years after the restoration of democracy in Spain, but continued to live in retirement in California, where he had been a professor of Spanish literature.

Sender was born to a farming family in the province of Aragon and attended the institutes of Teruel and Zaragoza while supporting himself as a pharmacist. In the early 1920s he served as a conscript in the Moroccan campaign. He edited the liberal magazine *El Sol* in Madrid from 1925 to 1930, collaborated on the leftist publications *El Socialista* and *La Libertad*, and was twice imprisoned for political activities against the monarchy and the authoritarian government of Primo de Rivera.

His first book, a study of religion and society in Mexico, with a prologue by his friend, the writer Ramón María del Valle-Inclán, appeared in 1928. Two years later he published his first novel, *Imán*, an account of the Moroccan campaign from the viewpoint of a downtrodden and mistreated soldier, which has been compared to Erich Maria Remarque's *All Quiet on the Western Front*. Translations were published in England as *Earmarked for Hell* (1934) and in the United States as *Pro Patria* (1935). The critic Charles L. King wrote in his book on Sender: "One sees in *Pro Patria* the sure hand of Sender the novelist: a direct, sober, verbal style, an impersonal distancing of the author from the work, the same grim—sometimes gruesome—humor present even in his latest novels, the same interweaving of objective and subjective realities to create the novel's own private world, the harshest of realistic detail alongside lyrical and metaphysical fantasy, the flight into delirium and dreams which sometimes cast a surrealistic spell over the action, and the ever-present probing of the ultimate reality, mystery."

Between 1930 and 1936 Sender published another six novels, one of which, *Mr. Witt Among the Rebels* (1936; English ed. 1937), about the Murcian uprising of 1873, won the National Prize for Literature in 1935. During the Spanish Civil War he served the Loyalist forces as a brigade commander and as a major with the general staff (he was reportedly the model for the character Manuel in André Malraux's novel of the war, *Man's Hope*). He came to the United States on a Guggenheim Fellowship in 1942, five years after his escape to Mexico via France, and worked briefly as a translator for MGM in New York before becoming a teacher of Spanish literature, first at the University of New Mexico from 1948 to 1963 and then at the University of Southern California from 1964 until his retirement in 1972.

Though he continued to explore the motives and actions of revolutionaries and to paint what critics called a vivid and authentic picture of Spanish life, the strong realism of Sender's earlier novels was gradually eclipsed by poetic and philosophical elements. In his philosophical novel *The Sphere* (1947; English ed. 1949) he pursued his idea that human beings are of two natures: "the person," meaning the isolated, individual identity, and "the man," the mystical, eternal, and unconscious essence that partakes of divinity. *The Sphere*, like many of his novels, was subjected to several revisions.

Sender's later fiction includes the biographical *Chronicle of Dawn* (1942–71; sections published in English under the title *Before Noon*, 1957), a series of nine novels arranged in three volumes, and some experiments with black humor. His nonfiction works include social commentary, reportage, criticism of Spanish dramatists and philosophers, and collections of lectures. He won the Barcelona Municipal Prize in 1967 for *Chronicle of Dawn* and received the Planeta Prize, Spain's highest literary award, for *In the Life of Ignacio Morel* in 1969. In the 1970s he was nominated for the Nobel Prize in literature.

An edition of Sender's complete works was begun in 1976. A number of novels were still in press at the time of his death of a heart attack. J.P./L.F.

Parents José S., farmer, and Andrea (Garcés) S., teacher. **Married** (1) Amparo Barayon 1933 (d. 1936): Ramón, Jr., musician, b. 1934; Andrea (Sister Benedicta), nun, b. 1936. (2) Florence Hall, prof., 1943 (div. 1963). **Religion** Roman Catholic. **Emigration** Escaped to France 1937; emigrated to Mexico 1939; emigrated to U.S. 1942, naturalized 1946; regained Spanish citizenship 1980. **Education** Colegio de la Sagrada Familia, Reus, Tauste, Catalonia, diploma; Inst. de Teruel; Inst. de Zaragoza, bachillerato 1918; Univ. of Madrid, lic. en fil. y let. 1924. **Mil. service** Infantry officer, Spanish Army, Morocco 1923–25; brigade comdr. and maj. gen. staff, Spanish Republican Army, Spanish Civil War 1936–37. **Career** Worked as pharmacist during sch.

years; collaborated on leftist newspapers *La Libertad* and *El Socialista*; ed., *El Sol* liberal newspaper, Madrid 1925–30; free-lance writer, Spain 1931–36; political activist against Spanish monarchy, imprisoned 1927; lived in Paris, Berlin, Moscow 1933; speaking tour of U.S. as rep. of Spanish republic 1938; free-lance writer, Mexico 1939–41; trans. and adaptor, MGM, NYC 1943–44. • Prof. of Spanish literature: Amherst Coll., MA 1943–44; Univ. of Denver, CO 1946; Univ. of New Mexico 1948–63, prof. emeritus since 1963; Ohio State Univ. 1951; Univ. of California at Los Angeles 1963–64; Univ. of Southern California, L.A. 1964–72, also writer in residence 1968, prof. emeritus since 1972. **Member** Natl. Council of Culture, and Alliance of Intellectuals for Defense of Democracy, Spain 1930s; North Amer. Acad. of the Spanish Language, NYC 1974; Atheneum of Science, Literature, and the Arts, no. 36, Madrid 1975; bd. of advisors, Hispanic Soc. of America, NYC; Alpha Mu Gamma; Intl. Soc. of Arts and Sciences, Berne; Mark Twain Club. **Honors** Medal of Morocco and Mil. Cross of Merit, Spain ca. 1925; Premio Nacional de Literatura, for *Mr. Witt Among the Rebels*, Spain 1935; Guggenheim Fellowship 1942; Premio de Novela, for *Chronicle of Dawn*, City of Barcelona 1967; Planeta Prize, for *In the Life of Ignacio Morel*, Spain 1969; Key of City of Los Angeles 1969; nominated for Nobel Prize in literature 1970s; Gold Apple for outstanding teaching, State of California 1973; Librero de Honor, Ministry of Culture, 9th Natl. Book Fair, Zaragoza 1979; Aragonese of the Year, Zaragoza Press Assn. 1980; Cross of Isabel the Catholic, Spain 1980; hon. member, Spanish Confederated Socs., NYC; hon. degrees from univs. of New Mexico and Southern California. **Fiction** *Imán*, 1930 (trans. as *Earmarked for Hell*, 1934, and *Pro Patria*, 1935); *O.P.: Orden público* [*Public Order*], 1931; *El verbo se hizo sexo (Teresa de Jesus)* [*The Word Made Flesh*], 1931; *Siete domingos rojos*, 1932 (trans. as *Seven Red Sundays*, 1936); *Viaje a la aldea del crimen* [*Voyage to the Village of the Crime*], 1934; *La noche de las cien cabezas* [*Night of a Hundred Heads*], 1934; *Mr. Witt en el cantón*, 1936 (trans. as *Mr. Witt Among the Rebels*, 1937); *El lugar del hombre*, 1939, issued as *El lugar de un hombre*, 1958 (trans. as *A Man's Place*, 1940); *Proverbia de la muerte* [*Omen of Death*], 1939; *Mexicayotl*, 1940; *Epitalamio del prieto Trinidad*, 1942 (trans. as *Dark Wedding*, 1943); *La esfera*, 1947 (trans. as *The Sphere*, 1949); *El rey y la reina*, 1949 (trans. as *The King and The Queen*, 1948); *El verdugo afable*, 1952 (trans. as *The Affable Hangman*, 1954); *Mosén Millán*, 1953, issued as *Réquiem por un campesino español*, 1960 (trans. as *Requiem for a Spanish Peasant*, 1960); *Bizancio* [*Byzantium*], 1956; *Los cinco libros de Ariadna* [*The Five Books of Ariadne*], 1957; *Emen hetan* [*We Are Here*], 1958; *Los laureles de Anselmo* [*The Laurels of Anselmo*], 1958; *Novelas ejemplares de Cíbola*, 1961 (trans. as *Tales of Cibola*, 1964); *La tésis de Nancy* [*Nancy's Thesis*], 1962; *La luna de los perros* [*The Moon of the Dogs*], 1962; *Carolus Rex* [*King Charles II*], 1963; *La aventura equinoccial de Lope de Aguirre* [*The Equinoctial Adventure of Lope de Aguirre*], 1964; *El bandido adolescente* [*The Young Outlaw*], 1965; *Cabrerizas altas* [*Tall Goatherds*], 1965; *La llave y otras narraciones* [*The Key and Other Stories*], 1967; *Las gallinas de Cervantes y otras narraciones parabólicas* [*The Hens of Cervantes and Other Parabolic Tales*], 1967; *Tres novelas teresianas* [*Three Stories of St. Teresa*], 1967; *Las criaturas saturnianas* [*Melancholy Creatures*], 1968; *El extraño señor Photynos y otras novelas americanas* [*The Strange Mr. Photynos and Other American Stories*], 1968; *Novelas del otro jueves* [*Tales of the Unusual*], 1969; *Nocturno de los 14* [*Night of the Fourteen*], 1969; *En la vida de Ignacio Morel* [*In the Life of Ignacio Morel*], 1969; *Tánit*, 1970; *Zu, el ángel anfibio* [*Zu, the Amphibious Angel*], 1970; *La antesala* [*The Anteroom*], 1971; *Relatos frontizeros* [*Reports from the Frontier*], 1970; *El Fugitivo* [*The Fugitive*], 1972; *Túpac Amaru*, 1973; *Una virgen llama a tu puerta* [*A Virgin is Calling at Your Door*], 1973; *Las tres sorores* [*The Three Sisters*], 1974; *Nancy y el bato loco* [*Nancy and the Loony*], 1974; *La mesa de las tres moiras*, 1974; *Cronus y la señora con rabo* [*Cronus and the Lady with a Tail*], 1974; *Nancy, doctora en gitanería* [*Nancy, Doctor of Flattery*], 1976; *Arlene y la gaya ciencia* [*Arlene and Poesy*], 1976; *La efemérides* [*The Ephemeris*], 1976; *El Mechudo y la Llorona* [*El Mechudo and the Mourner*], 1977; *El alarido de Yaurí* [*Yauri's Scream*], 1977; *Gloria y vejamen de*

Nancy [*Exaltation and Abuse of Nancy*], 1977; *Adela y yo* [*Adela and I*], 1978; *El superviviente* [*The Survivor*], 1978; *La mirada inmóvil* [*The Fixed Stare*], 1979; *El pez de oro* [*The Gold Fish*], in press; *Andalucía descubre a Nancy* [*Nancy Discovers Andalucia*], in press; *Reencuentro con Metchell* [*Collision with Metchell*], in press. • Trilogy *Crónica del alba*, 1971: Vol. I. *Crónica del alba*, 1942 (trans. as *Chronicle of Dawn*, 1949); *Hipogrifo violento*, 1954 (trans. as *Violent Griffin*, in *Before Noon*, 1957); *La quinta Julieta*, 1957 (trans. as *The Villa Julieta*, in *Before Noon*, 1957). Vol. II. *El mancebo y los héroes* [*The Youth and the Heroes*], 1960; *La onza de oro* [*The Ounce of Gold*]; *Los niveles del existir* [*Levels of Being*]. Vol. III. *Los términos del presagio* [*The Limits of Foreknowledge*]; *La orilla donde los locos sonríen* [*The Shore Where the Fools Smile*]; *La vida comienza ahora* [*Life Begins Now*]. **Plays** *Hernán Cortés*, 1940; *El diantre* [*The Devil*], 1958; *Comedia del diantre y otras dos* [*Comedy of the Devil and Two Other Plays*], 1967; *Don Juan en la mancebía* [*Don Juan in the Brothel*], 1968; *Donde crece la marihuana* [*Where the Marijuana Grows*], 1973. **Essays and journalism** *El problema religioso en Méjico* [*The Religious Problem in Mexico*], 1928; *Teatro de masas* [*Mass Theater*], 1932; *Casas viejas* [*Old Houses*], 1933; *Carta de Moscú sobre el amor* [*Letter from Moscow on Love*], 1934; *Proclamación de la sonrisa* [*Proclamation of the Smile*], 1934; *Madrid-Moscú*, 1934; *Contraataque*, 1938 (trans. as *The War in Spain*, 1937, and *Counter-Attack in Spain*, 1937); *Unamuno, Baroja, Valle-Inclán y Santayana*, 1955; *Examen del ingenios; los noventayochos* [*Examination of Genius: The Generation of '98*], 1961; *Valle-Inclán y la dificultad de la tragedia* [*Valle-Inclán and the Problem of Tragedy*], 1965; *Ensayos sobre el infringimiento cristiano* [*Essays on Christian Abuses*], 1967; *Ensayos del otro mundo* [*Essays from the Other World*], 1970; *Tres ejemplos de amor y una teoría* [*Three Examples and a Theory of Love*], 1969; *Páginas escogidas* [*Selected Papers*], 1972; *El futura comenzó ayer* [*The Future Began Yesterday*], 1975; *Solanar y lucernario aragonés* [*Bright Places of Aragon*], 1978. **Poetry** *Las imágenes migratorias* [*Fleeting Images*], 1960; *Poesía y memorias bisiestas* [*Poetry and Bissextile Memories*], 1974; *Libro armilar de poesía y memorias bisiestas* [*Ringed Book of Poetry and Bissextile Memories*], 1974. **Other** *Obra completa*, vol. 1, 1976 other vols. to follow. **Contributor** of essays, reviews, and fiction to literary and gen. periodicals. **Interview** M. Peñuelas, ed., *Conversaciones con Ramón Sender*, 1970.

Further reading Sherman H. Eoff, *The Modern Spanish Novel*, 1961; Charles L. King, *Ramón J. Sender*, 1974.

RED SMITH
Sportswriter
Born **Green Bay, Wisconsin, USA, 25 September 1905**
Died **Stamford, Connecticut, USA, 15 January 1982**

Sportswriting, which as a rule tends to be dull, sentimental, and sycophantic, has on occasion been made into something approaching an art form by writers who think the subject of sports worthy of the same serious reflection and precise description as any other aspect of the human condition. Among these writers are Ring Lardner, Grantland Rice, and Red Smith, the Pulitzer Prize-winning columnist for the *New York Times*, whose prose style and powers of observation set a standard for the profession. "Writing is easy," Smith once said. "I just open a vein and bleed."

The son of a wholesale grocer in Green Bay, Wisconsin, Walter Wellesley Smith graduated in 1927 from Notre Dame University and landed a job as a general reporter with the *Milwaukee Sentinel* after applying to some 100 newspapers. The following year he started at the *St. Louis Star* as a copy editor and moved to the sports department after the managing editor and most of the sports staff were fired. He wrote on sports for the *Philadelphia Record* from 1936 to 1945, for the *New York Her-*

ald Tribune from 1945 to 1966, and for its successor, the *World Journal Tribune*, from 1966 until its demise in 1967. His column remained in syndication, and four years later he was hired by the *New York Times*, which had rejected his first job application 44 years earlier. He was the most widely syndicated sports columnist in the country after the death of his close friend Grantland Rice in 1954, and his "Sports of the Times" column appeared in 500 newspapers in 30 different countries.

Smith was equally at home writing about baseball, boxing, fishing, and horse racing—indeed, any sport and its players, owners, rulemakers, and fans (although he was bored by basketball and hockey). He liked to go fishing himself, he once said, because fishing is "an attractive form of masochism." His prose style, famous for its wit, finesse, and erudition, occasionally put one in mind of Mark Twain (a piece he wrote on a boxing match between Joe Louis and Rocky Marciano was anthologized in a college textbook called *A Quarto of Modern Literature*). "Sports is not really a play world," he once remarked. "I think it's the real world. . . . It's no accident that of all the monuments left of the Greco-Roman culture, the biggest is the ball park, the Colosseum, the Yankee Stadium of ancient times. The man who reports on these games contributes his small bit to the record of his time."

Smith frequently discussed controversial issues in his column and directed sharp criticism at those who run the sports establishment, including baseball commissioner Bowie Kuhn and George Steinbrenner, owner of the New York Yankees. He was particularly critical of the International Olympic Committee and its "eighteenth-century" view of sports. Writing from Munich in 1972, he condemned the head of the International Olympic Committee, Avery Brundage (whom he called "Slavery Avery"), for allowing the Olympic Games to continue after Palestinian terrorists slaughtered athletes from Israel, and caustically described the scoring machinations by which corrupt judges were able to cheat winning boxers out of their medals for political reasons. In January 1980 he proposed that the United States boycott the upcoming summer Olympic Games in Moscow to protest the Soviet Union's invasion of Afghanistan. Less than three weeks later, Pres. Carter announced that the United States would boycott the Games.

Smith—who once described himself as a "seedy amateur with watery eyes behind glittering glasses, a receding chin, a hole in his frowzy haircut"—won numerous journalism awards, including the 1976 Pulitzer Prize for distinguished commentary (only the second Pulitzer awarded to a sportswriter). He was the author or editor of ten books, including several collections of his columns, and served as a consultant to dictionaries and encyclopedias. In recent years he suffered from cancer of the colon. His death came a few days after he wrote in the *Times* that he was cutting back from four columns a week to three. J.R.

Courtesy of New York Times

Born Walter Wellesley Smith. **Parents** Walter Philip S., wholesale grocer, and Ida Elizabeth (Richardson) S. **Married** (1) Catherine Cody 1933 (d. 1967): Catherine W. Halloran; Terence Fitzgerald, journalist. (2) Phyllis Warner Weiss, artist, 1968: five stepchildren. **Religion** Roman Catholic. **Education** Public schs., Green Bay, WI; Notre Dame Univ., IN, A.B. 1927. **Career** Reporter, *Milwaukee Sentinel*, WI 1927–28; copy ed. 1928 and sportswriter and rewriter 1928–36, *St. Louis Star*, MO; sportswriter and columnist, *Philadelphia Record* 1936–45. • Sports columnist: *New York Herald Tribune* 1945–66; *World Journal Tribune*, NYC 1966–67; Publishers Newspaper Syndicate 1967–71; *New York Times* since 1971. • Narrator of TV shows on intl. sports. **Member** Soc. of the Silurians;

Players Club, NYC; Louis Norman Newsom Club. **Honors** Journalism award, Natl. Headliners Club 1945; citation, Page One Award Cttee., New York Newspaper Guild 1950; Rice Memorial Award, Sportsmanship Brotherhood of New York 1956; award, Catholic Inst. of the Press 1958; Pulitzer Prize for commentary 1976; hon. degree from Notre Dame Univ.; many other awards and hon. degrees. **Author** (Ed.) *Selected Sports Stories*, 1949; *Out of the Red*, 1950; *Views of Sports*, 1954; *Red Smith's Sports Annual*, 1961; *The Best of Red Smith*, 1963; *Red Smith on Fishing Around the World*, 1963; *This Was Racing*, 1973; *Strawberries in the Wintertime: The Sporting World of Red Smith*, 1974; *Red Smith's Favorite Sports Stories*, 1976; (comp.) *Press Box*, 1980; *To Absent Friends from Red Smith*, 1982; Dave Anderson, ed., *The Red Smith Reader*, 1982. **Interview** John L. Kern, "Red Smith in the Final Innings," in *Writers Digest*, June 1982.

VARLAM (TIKHONOVICH) SHALAMOV
Writer
Born **Vologda, Russia, 18 June 1907**
Died **Moscow, USSR, 17 January 1982**

Varlam Tikhonovich Shalamov was a writer best known in the West for one book, *Kolyma Tales* (1980), a collection of stark, unflinching accounts of the 17 years he spent within the Stalinist Gulag in the horrifyingly brutal slave-labor camps of the Kolyma gold fields.

He began to train as a lawyer in 1926 at Moscow State University, but was arrested in 1929, while still a student, and sentenced to five years in a corrective-labor camp at Solovki, site of a former monastery. The camps during the early 1930s were reasonably administered; the prisoners were well fed and cared for and were even paid for their work, and Shalamov was able to begin publishing his writing in 1932. He was arrested again in 1937 during the Great Purge, just as Stalin was calling for less "coddling" of prisoners and his system of state terror was approaching its greatest excesses, and was sentenced to five years in Kolyma.

Kolyma is a vast stretch of frozen tundra, four times the size of France, in far northeastern Siberia. The Soviets began intensive gold-mining operations there in the early 1930s using the labor of convicts, who were housed in camps under abominable conditions. "In the camp," wrote Shalamov, "it took 20 to 30 days to turn a healthy man into a wreck. Working in the camp mine 16 hours a day, without any days off, with systematic starvation, ragged clothes, sleeping in a torn tent at 60 below zero, did the job." Very few survived: it is estimated that between two and three million people perished in Kolyma.

Shalamov's sentence, along with that of most other political prisoners, was routinely extended in 1942 "until the end of the war." In 1943 he received an additional ten years for having referred to Ivan Bunin, an émigré Russian writer who had won the Nobel Prize in 1933, as a "classic author of Russian literature." Shalamov managed to survive his ordeal chiefly because he had been allowed to take a nursing course in the Siberian city of Magadan, and his paramedical skills were greatly needed. He was released in 1954 after the death of Stalin and the fall of internal security chief Lavrenti Beria and returned to Moscow the next year. It was only then that he began to write his tales.

A most remarkable quality of Shalamov's stories is their narrative tone—resigned, dispassionate, only faintly ironic, and quite unrhetorical—which gives the collection its understated but tremendous power. The more horrifying the subject matter—prisoners eating mice, chopping off their fingers to escape the mines, stealing the underwear from a dead body to trade for food, or bulldozers uncovering mass graves full of frozen corpses—the more restrained and precise the prose. Andrei Sinyavski, himself a survivor of the camps, said of *Kolyma Tales*: "Shalamov is the antipode of all existing camp literature. He leaves us no way out. He seems just as merciless to his readers as life was merciless to him, to the people he portrays. . . . Hence the feeling of genuineness, of the adequacy of the text to the subject. And this is Shalamov's special advantage over other authors. He writes as if he were dead."

The exiled writer Aleksander Solzhenitsyn spoke of his shock "as of meeting a long-lost brother" on first reading Shalamov's accounts of the camps. Solzhenitsyn asked him to co-author *The Gulag Archipelago*, but Shalamov declined, for he was by then too old, greatly weakened by his ordeal, and in ill health.

Kolyma Tales was first published in English in the West in 1980. The book was a collection of 24 tales, selected and arranged by John Glad, the translator, from a much larger body of work. Another collection, *Graphite*, appeared in 1981. In the USSR journal publication of a few of the tales had been permitted in the early 1960s during the cultural thaw under Khrushchev, but that was quickly halted and no collection has ever appeared. Many were circulated in *samizdat*, the Soviet literary underground, before they were sent to the West. In 1972, however, the Soviet weekly *Literaturnaya Gazeta* published a letter from Shalamov denouncing publication of his works abroad. His friends maintained that he had been forced to do this as a condition of being allowed to rejoin the Writers Union, a writer's only source of support in the USSR. Membership in the union allowed him to publish four volumes of poetry since his release from Kolyma.

The Soviet state was involved even in Shalamov's death and burial. He had been forcibly removed from an old people's home and placed in a psychiatric nursing home, and was said to have died of heart failure three days later. He had told friends he wanted a Russian Orthodox funeral but the Writers Union, citing the absence of surviving relatives, gave him a civil one instead. A.K.

Married and divorced. **Religion** Russian Orthodox. **Education** Law studies, Moscow State Univ. 1926–29. **Career** Imprisoned in labor camp at Solovki 1929–34 and in forced-labor camps in Kolyma, Siberia 1937–54; poet and short-story writer since 1932; trans. of poetry from Bulgarian, Kazakh, Chuvash, and other languages. **Member** Writers Union. **Honors** Prize, French Sect., Intl. PEN Club 1981. **Fiction** *Kolymskiye Rasskazy* [*Stories from Kolyma*], 1978 (excerpts trans. as *Kolyma Tales*, 1980, and *Graphite*, 1981); *Ocherki prestupnogo mira* [*Essays on a Criminal World*] (unpublished). **Poetry** *Ognivo* [*Steel*], 1961; *Shelest listev* [*Rustle of Leaves*], 1964; *Doroga i sudba* [*The Road and the Fate*], 1967; *Moskovskiye oblaka* [*Moscow Clouds*], 1972. **Contributor** of stories and poems to *Novy zhurnal* (NYC) and Soviet literary jrnls.

Further reading V. S. Pritchett, "A Sense of the Day," in *The New Yorker*, 3 Nov. 1980; Irving Howe, "Beyond Bitterness," in *New York Review of Books*, 14 Aug. 1980.

JUAN O'GORMAN
Architect and muralist
***Born* Coyoacán, Mexico City, Mexico, 6 July 1905**
***Found dead* Mexico City, Mexico, 19 January 1982**

Juan O'Gorman was the first Mexican architect to design buildings according to the principles of Functionalism, the severely modernist, Bauhaus-influenced style popularized by the Swiss-French architect Le Corbusier. Within 20 years, he had made a complete aesthetic about-face and was advocating an integrated, organic architecture based on the formal and decorative elements of pre-Columbian Aztec structures.

Of Irish and Mexican parentage—his father was a portrait painter—O'Gorman attended Jesuit schools and studied architecture at Mexico's National University from 1922 to 1927. Under the guidance of his mentor José Villagrós García, the first Mexican architect to espouse Bauhaus principles, he built, between 1929 and 1932, what are generally considered the first modernist houses in Mexico, closely following the Functionalist style of Le Corbusier's glass and concrete Parisian villas. These included a house for himself in the San Angell neighborhood of Mexico City and a house and studio for his friend, the muralist Diego Rivera.

During the 1930s, O'Gorman taught design

at the National Polytechnic Institute and built 28 modern public schools for the National Ministry of Education. He also painted a number of major public murals, including three for the old Mexico City Airport (two are now housed in Chapultepec Castle) and one for the public library in Patzcuaro in the state of Michoacán, depicting the history of the Tarascon Indians. O'Gorman's murals, like those of his great contemporaries Rivera, David Siqueiros, and José Orozco, were graphically powerful and politically controversial, combining symbols from the nationalist, anti-Fascist, and populist revolutionary movements. (Twelve murals that he designed in 1940 for the Cultural Association of Jewish Youth in Pittsburgh were rejected because they depicted U.S. settlement houses in an unfavorable light.)

O'Gorman renounced the doctrines of Functionalism in the 1940s and devoted himself almost exclusively to mural and easel painting. Speaking before an assembly at the Palace of Fine Arts in Mexico City in 1950, he said: "I took the architecture of Le Corbusier as a model and that makes me partly responsible for the implanting of Functionalism in our country; it is, at the same time, valid proof of my own lack of talent. . . . The Swiss puritanism of Le Corbusier's architecture is exactly the antithesis to the plastic arts of Mexico, from the antique Anahuac down to the popular expressions of today." He went on to praise the work of the American architect Frank Lloyd Wright, calling it "the contemporary expression of our own tradition."

Courtesy of Sotheby Parke Bernet, Inc.

In 1952, O'Gorman, proclaiming the need for a uniquely Mexican architecture that would integrate traditional decoration with modern forms, returned to building designs as co-builder, with Gustavo Saavedra and Juan Martínez de Velasco, of the National Library of Mexico's massive University City complex, his best-known work. Using millions of colored stone tesserae quarried from sites around the country, he created an elaborate mosaic that covers the library's rectangular stack tower and that depicts the history of Mexico in the graphic style of Mayan and Aztec codices.

In 1956 O'Gorman completed work on another home for himself in a suburb outside Mexico City. It was a perfectly realized union of form with external decoration and a masterpiece of "fantastic architecture." Partly carved from a natural grotto of volcanic rock, the house's curved walls were covered with mosaics and reliefs using motifs from Aztec mythology. The circular stone stairway at its core extended above the roof to form a statue of the rain god Chac Mool, while a mosaic of a feathered serpent formed the balcony railings. The principal purpose of the house, O'Gorman wrote, was to "protest in favor of humanism, perishing in the technological desert of our marvellous civilization." He sold it in 1970 to the sculptor Helen Escobedo, who subsequently had it destroyed, claiming that it was uninhabitable.

Despondent, O'Gorman abandoned architecture and spent his last years painting murals, notably a series for the History Museum at Chapultepec Castle in Mexico City. He developed a heart ailment that kept him from working and committed suicide at the age of 76.

S.A.

Parents Cecil Crawford O., artist, and Encarnación O'Gorman O. **Married** Helen Fowler, sculptor and botanist, 1940: Maria Elena. **Education** Jesuit schs., Mexico City; Natl. Medical Schs.; Sch. of Architecture, Natl. Autonomous Univ. of Mexico, Dip.Arch. 1926; apprenticed to architect Carlos Obregón Santacilia 1927; studied painting with Diego Rivera and others. **Career** Architectural asst., García, Tarditi, and Contreros, Mexico City 1927–29; chief draftsman, office of Carlos Obregón Santacilia 1929–32; head, Dept. of Architecture, Secretariat of Public Education 1932–35; head, Dept. of Bldg. Construction,

Mexico City 1932–39; co-founder of Sch. of Architecture 1932, and prof. of architecture and architectural composition 1932–48, Natl. Polytechnic Inst., Mexico City; in private architectural practice 1934–70; founder, Workers' Housing Study Group 1936; visiting critic, Sch. of Architecture, Yale Univ. 1966. **Member** Liga de Escritores y Artistas Revolucionários ca. 1928; Natl. Coll. of Architects of Mexico 1956; Bolivarian Soc. of Architects, Caracas 1967; Acad. of Arts, Mexico City 1971. **Honors** First prize, La Tolteca Painting Competition, Mexico City 1930; 1st prize for Mexico City, Excelsior Painting Competition 1948; medal of honor, Sch. of Engineering and Architecture, Natl. Polytechnic Inst. 1959; Sourasky Natl. Art Award 1967; Mexican Natl. Art Prize 1972. • Diplomas from City of Morelia 1952, Sch. of Engineering and Architecture of Natl. Polytechnic Inst. 1959, Natl. Inst. of Mexican Youth 1972. **Architect** (all Mexico City) Bank of Mexico reconstruction and SSA Bldg., 1925–28; Lomas House, Chapultepec 1927–28; Diego Rivera House and Studio and Juan O'Gorman House I, 1929–30; Thomas O'Gorman House, 1931; Technical Sch. and 28 primary schs. for Ministry of Education, 1932–34; Julio Castellanos House, Manuel Toussaint House (unfinished), and Frances Toor House, 1934; Sindicato de Electricistras Bldg., 1936; (jtly.) Museo Anahuacalli, 1944–45; (jtly.) Natl. Library, State Univ. of Mexico, Univ. City 1952–53; Juan O'Gorman House II, 1953–56. **Public murals** Public Library, Azcapotzalco 1931; Mexico City Airport 1936–37 (two of three panels now in History Mus., Chapultepec Castle, Mexico City); Xochimilco Public Sch., Mexico City 1939; Cultural Assn. of Jewish Youth, Pittsburgh (unfinished), 1940; Bocanegra Public Library, Patzcuaro, Michoacán 1941; Natl. Library, State Univ. of Mexico, Univ. City 1952–53; Ministry of Communication and Public Works, Mexico City 1952–53; Posada de la Misión Hotel, Taxco 1954–56; History Mus., Chapultepec Castle 1960–61, 1968–79; entrance hall, Centre Interamericano del Seguro Sociál de la Unidad Independéncia, San Jerónimo Lidice 1962–65; Banco Internacionál del Paseo de la Reforma, Mexico City 1962–65; (consultant and supervisor) San Cristobal Park, Santiago, Chile 1962–65; Convention Center Theater, San Antonio, TX 1966–67. **Exhibitions** Palace of Fine Arts, Mexico City 1934, 1948, 1950, 1968; Galerías del Bosque, Chapultepec 1949; City of Morelia, Mexico 1951; Inst. of Mexican Art, 1961; Salon de la Plástica Mexicana, Mexico City 1964; San Fernando Valley State Coll., CA 1964; Yale Univ. 1966; touring exhib., U.S. 1964. **Collections** MOMA; Palace of Fine Arts and Mus. of Modern Art, Mexico City; Philadelphia Mus. of Art; many others. **Author** *El arte util y el arte artístico* [*Applied and Fine Art*], 1932.

Further reading Clive Banford Smith, *Builders in the Sun: Five Mexican Architects*, 1967.

LEOPOLD TREPPER

Head of Soviet spy network

Born **Novy-Targ, Galicia, Austria-Hungary, 23 February 1904**

Died **Jerusalem, Israel, 19 January 1982**

Leopold Trepper directed the field operations of the Soviet Union's extensive espionage network in Nazi-occupied Europe during the early years of World War II. His organization was called the Red Orchestra *(die rote Kapelle)* by the mystified Germans, who spent two and a half years of furious effort trying to track down him and his operatives. He seemed to cooperate with the enemy after his arrest in Paris, but managed to escape his comfortable detention and subsequently aided the French Resistance until the liberation of Paris.

The son of a Jewish shopkeeper in a small town of impoverished rural Galicia, Trepper remembered seeing, when he was ten years old, V. I. Lenin pass through his town under arrest as a Russian spy. He witnessed the reawakening of virulent anti-Semitism in Poland after the country became independent of Austria-Hungary at the end of World War I and soon joined the Hashomer Hatzair, an Eastern European leftist-Zionist organization. For his role in support of a general strike in Cracow he was blacklisted by the authorities, and shortly thereafter decided to emigrate to Palestine.

In the summer of 1924, Trepper and his companions landed at Jaffa. He found work draining marshes, but leftist political organizing was never far from his mind, and he joined the Communist Party of Palestine early in 1925. He was among the founders of Ichud, a faction within the party that advocated class unity between Jewish and Arab workers, and became party secretary for Haifa. The British police force was determined to stem the growth of Communism in the Mandate, and Trepper was constantly harassed, frequently arrested, twice imprisoned, and finally deported to France in late 1929 by the British governor. In Paris he presented himself at party headquarters the day he arrived and was soon given the assignment of starting a Yiddish-language weekly for the large leftist refugee communities in France and Belgium. The arrest of a close comrade as a Soviet spy, however, persuaded French party leaders to send Trepper out of the country; he went to study in the USSR in the summer of 1932. He was accompanied on these travels by his wife, Luba Brodje, like him a leftist refugee from Galicia, whom he had met in Palestine.

The Comintern enrolled him in Marchlevski University, an institution reserved for national minorities. The Soviet Union was in the early years of an intense and brutal effort at farm collectivization, and the cult of personality surrounding Stalin was already well under way. Illustrious old Bolsheviks—Zinoviev, Bukharin, Kamanev—made speeches to the students lauding Stalin and the steps he was taking to transform Soviet society, but the purges soon began and they were swept away. As Trepper watched all this happening around him, he felt his neophyte's zeal becoming hardened by reality, and he began to realize the widening gap between theory and practice in the developing Soviet state.

Trepper escaped the Great Purge of 1936–38 because he was a foreign student, but his relatively extensive party experience in Palestine and France secured him an appointment to the school for foreign espionage run by the GRU, then the chief Soviet spying organization. There he progressed rapidly, mastering the elements of clandestine radio transmission, microdot photography, sabotage, and cryptography. Nazi Germany was the prime target of Soviet espionage, and Western Europe was chosen as the principal locale, primarily because the Gestapo had eliminated almost the entire Communist underground in Germany. Trepper was assigned as resident director of the GRU in Brussels, with a backup office in Paris. He took up his post in March 1939.

Within a year Trepper controlled a spy network covering nearly the whole of Western Europe. The organization lay low during the Nazi invasions of Holland, Belgium, and France, and during the Battle of Britain. In June 1941, Trepper began to mobilize the seven networks he controlled. The Germans attacked the Soviet Union on 22 June, exactly when he had predicted, and the radio transmissions to Moscow began. The intricate five-figure cipher was never fully broken by the Germans, and information of the most sensitive kind got past them unblocked: the German High Command's strategic objectives, the Luftwaffe's operational plans, location of German oil stores, news of Hitler's whereabouts and of tensions between him and the army. Of the 1,500 coded messages sent by the Red Orchestra, Trepper claimed the Germans decoded fewer than 250.

In December 1941, when the Gestapo and the Abwehr discovered the location of Trepper's headquarters in Brussels and raided it, Trepper arrived from Paris just as they were searching the house. With utter aplomb he passed himself off as a fur dealer looking for rabbit skins. Incredibly, the Nazis suspected nothing and let him go. He went into hiding and reorganized the network. German counterespionage redoubled its efforts, however, and in December 1942, Trepper was arrested in his dentist's office in Paris. He agreed to reveal everything to his interrogators, knowing full well that the GRU had established a backup espionage network of whose organization and codes he was completely ignorant. For months he told the Germans all they wanted to know about the Red Orchestra, yet he claimed never to have betrayed his own operatives. In any case, he was treated relatively well, living under house arrest in one of the German-requisitioned mansions on Avenue Foch. He was even permitted to travel about Paris under guard. He escaped in June 1943 while on one of these outings, quickly made contact with Communist groups within the Maquis, and got back in touch with Moscow. He remained at liberty until the Germans were driven from France in May 1945.

That summer he was recalled to Moscow, where he was soon arrested by the NKVD and disappeared for nine years into the Stalinist Gulag. He was released in 1954 after Stalin's death and was repatriated to Poland, where he lived quietly with his family in Warsaw, becoming director of the Cultural Association of Polish Jews. In 1967 anti-Semitism in Poland began to be officially encouraged by the government and his entire family emigrated to Israel. When Trepper was refused permission to leave "for reasons of state," a worldwide campaign was begun on his behalf to persuade the Polish authorities to let him go. He was ultimately released in November 1973, after ten months under house arrest, and spent his last years in Israel working on his memoirs, which appeared in English in 1977 as *The Great Game*. A.K.

Also known by code names Domb, Le grand chef, Gilbert, some dozen others. **Father** a storekeeper. **Married** Luba Brojde, Communist organizer, late 1920s: Michel, b. 1931; Edgar, prof. of Russian literature; Pierre, electronics engineer. **Religion** Jewish. **Emigrated** to Palestine 1924; deported to France 1929; in USSR 1932–39, 1945–late 1950s; repatriated to Poland; emigrated to London 1973, thence to Israel. **Education** Jewish high sch., Vienna and Novy-Targ, Galicia; Univ. of Cracow early 1920s; Marchlevski Univ., Moscow 1932–mid-1930s; spy training with GRU, USSR mid-1930s. **Career** Joined Hashomer Hatzair leftist-Zionist youth movement ca. 1918: branch chief, Novy-Targ, Galicia 1918; elected to natl. leadership 1920; branch chief, Dombrova, Silesia 1921. • Clockmaker's apprentice 1920; worked in iron, steel, and soap plants, political activist, and black marketeer, Silesia 1921–23. • In Palestine 1924–29: marsh drainer 1924; joined C.P. 1925, secty. of Haifa sect. 1928; founder 1925 and secty. 1927, Ichud wing of C.P.; imprisoned 1927, 1928; deported 1929. • In France 1929–32: floor scrubber, freight loader, construction worker, and house painter, Paris 1930–32; active with Jewish sect. of French C.P.; rep. of Jewish immigrant labor to C.P. Central Cttee.; sent by C.P. to study in USSR 1932. • Resident dir., Soviet spy networks in Western Europe, Brussels and Paris 1939–42; arrested and detained by Germans, Paris 1942, escaped 1943; active with French Resistance 1944–45; arrested by NKVD after WWII; imprisoned in Gulag for nine years for allegedly collaborating with Nazi captors; dir. of Cultural Assn. of Polish Jews and publisher, Poland until 1967; under police surveillance 1967–73 and under house artist 1973 until emigration. **Author** *The Great Game* (autobiography; English ed.), 1977.

Further reading Charles Wighton, *The World's Greatest Spies*, 1962; Ronald Seth, *Forty Years of Soviet Spying*, 1965; Gilles Perreault, *The Red Orchestra*, 1968; Harry Rositzken, *The KGB, The Eyes of Europe*, 1981.

SEMYON K(UZMICH) TSVIGUN
Deputy head of KGB
***Born* Ukraine, Russia, 27 September 1917**
***Died* Moscow, USSR, 19 January 1982**

Semyon K. Tsvigun spent virtually his entire adult life as an agent of the KGB, the Soviet secret police. From 1967 he was deputy head of the agency, and thus was probably among the people most responsible for the widespread official repression of all dissident activity during the 1970s. He had close ties to Pres. Leonid Brezhnev: they served together in Moldavia during the early 1950s and Tsvigun was rumored to be married to the sister of Brezhnev's wife, though this was never officially confirmed.

Born into a Ukrainian peasant family in the year of the Bolshevik Revolution, Tsvigun was graduated as a teacher from the Odessa Pedagogical Institute in 1937. He taught for two years thereafter and served as director of an intermediate school in the Odessa region, but left teaching in 1939 to join the Committee of State Security (Komitet Gosudarstvennoy Bezopastnosti, or KGB), becoming a party member a year later. During World War II, Tsvigun probably served in the Red Army, and there is suspicion that he was a member of SMERSH (Smert Shpionam, or Death to Spies), the Soviet military counterespionage organization.

In 1951 he was sent to the Moldavian SSR, on the border of Rumania, as deputy minister of state security. Brezhnev was first secretary of the Moldavian Communist Party from 1950 to 1952. Tsvigun became deputy interior minister in Moldavia (1953–54) and in 1955 moved on to Tadzhikistan, bordering China and Afghanistan in Soviet Central Asia, where he was deputy chief until 1957, then chief of the Committee of State Security until 1963. He was then assigned to a similar post in Azerbaijan, on the Iranian border, from 1963 to 1967. In both Asian posts he was also a member of the Central Committee of the provincial Communist Party.

The KGB had been in eclipse as a power center since Nikita Krushchev's de-Stalinization efforts of 1956–64. On becoming first secretary, Brezhnev apparently determined to put the organization firmly back in the service of the party and the state. Yuri Andropov, a senior party *apparatchik* and Brezhnev associate, was named that year as chairman of the national Committee of State Security, and Tsvigun was brought up from Azerbaijan and installed as Andropov's first deputy chairman.

As civil dissent within the USSR grew during the 1970s, so also did the power and influence of the KGB, which gradually increased its vigilance and reasserted its control over all sectors of society. The security service certainly weakened the dissidents' popular appeal within the country; the movement as a whole would have had a good chance of raising Soviet consciousness had it not been for the KGB's unrelenting campaign of hostility, slander, and violence against leading dissidents. Only a few months before his death, in the September 1981 issue of the journal *Kommunist*, Tsvigun claimed that the dissident movement had finally been eradicated: "As a result of the measures taken by the KGB, carried out in strict conformity with the law and under the leadership of the party organs, despite significant material and moral support from the West, they [the dissidents] have failed to set up a cohesive organization on the basis of anti-Sovietism." In the same article, however, he warned against other forms of subversion in Soviet society, including the emigration movements among Jews, Armenians, and ethnic Germans, the fatal lure of consumerism among large segments of the population, and the continuing attraction for Soviet youth of Western styles and mores.

Tsvigun was promoted to the rank of full general in the Soviet Army in 1978 and in 1981 he was advanced from alternate to full member of the Central Committee of the CPSU. His death followed a long illness. A.K.

Parents peasants. **Married** (reportedly) sister-in-law of Leonid Brezhnev. **Education** Odessa Pedagogical Inst., grad. 1937. **Mil. service** Some sources report WWII service in Red Army and partisan movement; others report WWII participation in SMERSH military counterespionage agency. **Career** Teacher and dir., intermediate sch., Odessa province 1937–39; joined KGB 1939; member CPSU since 1940; deputy minister of interior 1953–54, and deputy chmn. of KGB 1954–55, Moldavian SSR; deputy chief 1955–57 and chief 1957–63, KGB, Tadzhik SSR; member of Central Cttee. and Bureau, Tadzhik C.P. 1958–63; chmn., KGB, Azerbaijan SSR 1963–67; member of Central Cttee., Azerbaijan C.P. 1964–67; 1st deputy chmn. of KGB since 1967; deputy to USSR Supreme Soviet since 1970; candidate member 1971–81 and full member since 1981, CPSU Central Cttee.; full gen., Soviet Army since 1978. **Honors** Hero of Socialist Labor 1977. **Author** of many articles in Soviet publications.

Further reading Peter Deriabin, *Watchdogs of Terror*, 1972; John Barron, *KGB: The Secret Work of the Soviet Secret Agents*, 1974.

MARYA ZATURENSKA
Poet
***Born* Kiev, Russia, 12 February 1902**
***Died* Shelburne Falls, Massachusetts, USA, 19 January 1982**

Marya Zaturenska wrote finely crafted poetry in the idiom of the pre-Raphaelites. She was born in Kiev, Russia, and was brought at the age of eight to New York City, where she attended public school. At 14 she began to work in a factory, although she continued school at night. After a year at Valparaiso University, she received a scholarship to study library science at the University of Wisconsin, from which she was graduated in 1925.

While still in her teens, Zaturenska began publishing poems in *Poetry* and other magazines; her first collection, *Threshold and Hearth*, appeared in 1934, and her second, *Cold Morning Sky*, was awarded the Pulitzer Prize in 1938. Her six subsequent books of poetry included a volume of collected poems (1965). Zaturenska also wrote a biography of the pre-Raphaelite poet Christina Rossetti, edited the poems of Sara Teasdale, and collaborated with her husband, the poet and critic Horace Gregory, on *A History of American Poetry* and on anthologies of religious and romantic verse.

Zaturenska's poems, like those of Rossetti, were metrical, musical, and meditative, with subjects drawn largely from nature and mythology. Arthur Gregor, reviewing her book *Terraces of Light* (1960) in *Poetry*, wrote: "Her theme is always the transcendence of earthly limits—her art is a constant act of devotion. The fabric of her poems is a lyric tone often marvelously inventive; the structure aids the process of emergence from time to timeless, from form to the pure substance of form; the mood is inspiring, haunting, and always in the key of celebration." Other critics, while they spoke with appreciation of the delicacy, restraint, and melodiousness of her lines, suggested that her romanticism kept her from coming to terms with the modern world and made her poetry a static rather than a growing and changing art.

Zaturenska died of heart failure at the age of 80. J.P.

Parents Abram Alexander Zaturensky and Johanna (Lubovska) Z. **Married** Horace Gregory, poet and critic, 1925 (d. 1982): Johanna Elizabeth Ziegler; Patrick Bolton. **Emigrated** to U.S. 1909; naturalized 1912. **Education** Public schs., NYC; Valparaiso Univ., IN (scholarship) 1922–23; Library Sch., Univ. of Wisconsin, Madison (Zona Gale Scholarship), grad. 1925. **Career** Worked in a factory and bookstore and as a newspaper feature writer ca. 1916–22; poet since 1920s; also biographer and ed. of anthologies. **Honors** Reed Memorial Award 1924; Shelley Memorial Award, Poetry Soc. of New England 1935; Guarantors Award 1936 and Glatstein Memorial Award 1973, *Poetry*; Pulitzer Prize, for *Cold Morning Sky*, 1938; hon. degree from Univ. of Wisconsin. **Poetry** *Threshold and Hearth*, 1934; *Cold Morning Sky*, 1937; *The Listening Landscape*, 1941; *The Golden Mirror*, 1944; *Selected Poems*, 1954; *Terraces of Light*, 1960; *Collected Poems*, 1965; *The Hidden Waterfall*, 1974. **Criticism and biography** (with Horace Gregory) *A History of American Poetry, 1900–1940*, 1946; *Christina Rossetti: A Portrait with Background*, 1949. **Editor** (with H. G.) *The Mentor Book of Religious Verse*, 1957; (with H. G.) *The Crystal Cabinet: An Invitation to Poetry*, 1962; *The Collected Poems of Sara Teasdale*, 1966; (with H. G.) *The Silver Swan: Poems of Romance and Mystery*, 1966; (with H. G.) *Selected Poems of Christina Rossetti*, 1970. **Contributor** to *Poetry*, *Republic*, other literary periodicals.

H(UMPHREY) D(AVY) F(INDLEY) KITTO
Professor of classical Greek literature
***Born* Stroud, Gloucestershire, England, 6 February, 1897**
***Died* Bristol, England, 21 January 1982**

H. D. F. Kitto was among the English-speaking world's foremost critics and interpreters of ancient Greek culture and literature. The author of several widely praised books, which have often proven to be as useful to students of literary criticism as to classicists, Kitto took a clear, learned, and forceful approach to his subject that found favor with even the severest and most rarefied scholarly critics as well as with the intelligent reading public.

Humphrey Davy Findley Kitto was born in west-central England, the son of a schoolmaster. He attended the Crypt Grammar School in Gloucester, where the headmaster insisted on his thoroughly learning classical Greek and Latin, and he continued the study of these subjects at St. John's College, Cambridge University. In 1921, having achieved his degree the year before, he went to the University of Glasgow, Scotland, as assistant to the professor of Greek. He later became lecturer in Greek and remained at that university until 1944, when he was himself named professor of Greek at the University of Bristol, a post he held until 1962.

He first began traveling extensively in Greece as an undergraduate, and this familiarity with the modern locus of the classical culture led him to write his first book, *In the Mountains of Greece*, which was published in 1933. His first important contribution to classical studies, however, was *Greek Tragedy: A Literary Study*, a work whose importance was recognized as soon as it was published in 1939, and which was revised and reprinted many times.

The Greeks (1951) was a book of a more general nature, treating the history of ancient Greece through its people's character and ways of thinking. It was first published by Penguin Books and kept in print by them over three decades—more than 30 reprintings in all—as well as being translated into several foreign languages. Many thousands of British students have begun their studies of the classics or of ancient history by reading *The Greeks*.

Kitto's most famous book was probably *Form and Meaning in Drama: A Study of Six Greek Plays and of "Hamlet"* (1956). Here he reached into the English theater for a helpful analogy to his ideas about classical drama. One of the book's chapters compares the dramatic forms of fifth-century Greece and Elizabethan England, and another treats Shakespeare's *Hamlet* at length. His study of *Hamlet*, which he saw as a religious tragedy about the purging of the general corruption in the state of Denmark, was very well received by teachers and students of English literature, and the whole of *Form and Meaning* has generally been regarded as a classic of comparative criticism.

Courtesy of J. K. Comrie

Kitto's other works were *Sophocles, Dramatist and Philosopher* (1958) and verse translations of three of Sophocles' tragedies—*Antigone*, *Oedipus the King*, and *Electra*—which were published in 1962. His last book was *Poiesis: Structure and Thought* (1966), an analysis of the poetic art of Aeschylus, Homer, Sophocles, Pindar, Plato, Thucydides, and Shakespeare. These studies comprised the Sather Classical Lectures, given by Kitto at the University of California, Berkeley, in 1960–61. In addition, he was Ziskind Professor at Brandeis University in 1962–63 and Regents' Professor at the University of California, Santa Barbara, in 1963–64.

Kitto was awarded honorary doctorates by the universities of Aix-Marseille (1961) and Glasgow (1976). He was elected a fellow of the British Academy in 1955 and a fellow of the Royal Society of Literature in 1957.

A.K.

Parents H. D. K., schoolmaster, and Caroline (Findley) K. **Married** Ann K. Kraft, pianist, 1928: John, musician; Jane. **Education** Crypt Grammar Sch., Gloucester; St. John's Coll., Cambridge, B.A. 1920. **Career** Lectr. in Greek, Univ. of Glasgow 1921–44. • With Univ. of Bristol: Wills Prof. of Greek and chmn. of dept. of Greek 1944–62; chmn., Consultative Cttee. on Drama 1955–60; dean of faculty; prof. emeritus since 1962. • Visiting prof., Cornell Univ. 1954 and Brandeis Univ. 1959; Sather Prof., Univ of California 1960–61; Ziskind Prof., Brandeis Univ. 1962–63; Regents Prof., Univ. of California, Santa Barbara 1963–65. **Fellow** FBA 1955; FRSL 1957. **Honors** Hon. degrees from univs. of Aix and Glasgow. **Author** *In the Mountains of Greece*, 1933; *Greek Tragedy*, 1939; *The Greeks*, 1951; *Form and Meaning in Drama: A Study of Six Greek Plays and of "Hamlet"*, 1956; *Sophocles, Dramatist and Philosopher*, 1958; (trans. into English verse) Sophocles, *Three Tragedies: Antigone, Oedipus Rex, and Electra*, 1962; *Poiesis: Structure and Thought, 1966*. **Contributor** John Garrett, ed., *More Talking of Shakespeare*, 1959; Claire Sacks and Edgar Whan, eds. *Hamlet: Enter Critic*, 1960; Whitney J. Oates, ed., *From Sophocles to Picasso: The Present-Day Vitality of the Classical Tradition*, 1962; Quentin Anderson and Joseph Mazzeo, eds., *The Proper Study: Essays on Western Classics*, 1962; Joseph Gassner and Ralph Allen, eds., *Theatre and Drama in the Making*, 1964; numerous articles in classical jrnls.

Further reading M. J. Andersen, ed., *Classical Drama and Its Influence* (festschrift), 1965.

EDWARD (ROLKE) FARBER
Photographer and inventor
***Born* Milwaukee, Wisconsin, USA, 22 July 1914**
***Died* Delafield, Wisconsin, USA, 22 January 1982**

Edward Farber was the inventor of the first portable electronic flash for press photographers. Born in Milwaukee, he began photographing local fires at the age of 12 with a box camera given to him by his father and formed his first company, which manufactured neon lights for small businesses, while still a teenager. After graduating from the University of Wisconsin in 1936, he became a photographer for the *Milwaukee Journal*. The following year he built a dozen battery-operated portable stroboscopic flash units for the newspaper's photographers. These lightweight and simple flash units "stopped the action" much more effectively than the relatively slow and imprecise flash equipment then in use and helped pave the way for the golden age of photojournalism in the 1940s and 1950s.

Farber studied electrical engineering at Northwestern University in the late 1930s and designed flash equipment for the U.S. Army during World War II. After the war, he returned to Milwaukee, where he ran a company that manufactured his electronic flash units; he eventually sold the business to the Graflex Corp. In the late 1950s he was a photographic advisor to the U.S. government on its program of testing intercontinental ballistic missiles at White Sands, New Mexico, and Redstone, Alabama.

In his later years, Farber wrote extensively for photographic magazines, was active in civic planning and development in the Milwaukee area, and exhibited his photographs in local galleries. He died of a heart attack at the age of 67.

S.A.

Father a drugstore owner. **Education** Univ. of Wisconsin, Madison 1936; Northwestern Univ., Evanston, IL late 1930s. **Mil. service** Designed electronic flash equipment for U.S. Army, WWII. **Career** Founded neon lighting co., Milwaukee ca. 1929; staff photographer, *Milwaukee Journal* 1936; founded and headed flash-unit manufacturing co., Milwaukee 1945–54; photographic advisor, U.S. govt. ballistic missile tests, White Sands, NM, and Redstone, AL, 1950s; writer, photography mags.; free-lance photographer. **Exhibitions** Univ. of Wisconsin 1981; others.

EDUARDO FREI (MONTALVA)
President of Chile
***Born* Santiago, Chile, 16 January 1911**
***Died* Santiago, Chile, 22 January 1982**

Eduardo Frei Montalva was the founder and leader of Chile's Christian Democratic Party, which he led to victory in the presidential election of 1964. He served as president of Chile until 1970, when he was succeeded by Salvador Allende Gossens, whose intransigently leftist policies provoked the military right wing into a bloody and destructive coup in 1973, led by Gen. Augusto Pinochet Ugarte. Frei at first supported the coup, but soon came to oppose openly the junta's repressive rule. Unlike many of his former congressional colleagues, however, whom the junta did not hesitate to imprison or murder for speaking out against it, Frei's international reputation seemed to guarantee him a freedom of expression remarkable for Pinochet's Chile up until his death, which occurred just after his 71st birthday, of complications following a hernia operation.

Courtesy of Consuelo Salamé

Frei was born into a middle-class family; his father had emigrated to Chile from Switzerland, and his mother was Chilean. He attended Catholic schools and studied law at the Catholic University in Santiago, from which he graduated near the head of his class in 1933. The following year he was a Chilean delegate to the Congress of University Youth, a Catholic gathering held in Rome. He met Pope Pius XI, Eugenio Cardinal Pacelli (later Pius XII), and Jacques Maritain, the French social philosopher, all of whom were to influence Frei's politics and hence his life's work.

On his return to Chile, Frei and several of his university friends (including Bernardo Leighton, who was later to serve as his vice president, and Radomiro Tomic, the unsuccessful Christian Democratic candidate for president in 1970) started the Movement of Conservative Students, which the powerful Conservative Party at first adopted, then shunned in reaction to its founders' obviously progressive ideas. The movement grew into a political party called the Falange Nacional, and Frei in 1937 ran unsuccessfully for a congressional seat from Tarapacá province, in the desertlike north of the country, where he was directing a newspaper, *El Tarapacá*, in the seaport town of Uquique.

After the election loss, Frei returned to Santiago to practice law and continued to build the Falange. In 1941, while working as a professor of labor law in the Catholic University, he became president of the party, which was later renamed the Christian Democratic Party to avoid association with the fascist ruling party of Spain. He won reelection in 1943 and 1945.

Frei accepted an appointment as minister of public works and communications in the Popular Front government of Pres. Juan Antonio Ríos in May 1946, but resigned the next January following the government's brutal suppression of a workers' demonstration. He won election to the senate in 1949, the first Christian Democrat to do so, and was reelected in 1957 with the largest majority in the country. He became known as a political writer of considerable ability, striving in most of his books to delineate his Christian Democratic political vision, which was grounded in Catholic social doctrine—especially the encyclicals *Rerum novarum* of Leo XIII (1891) and *Quadragesimo anno* of Pius XI (1931)—and which attempted to combat the appeal to workers and peasants of the Socialists and Communists by infusing Christian ethics and social conscience into capitalism. "We are convinced," Frei wrote, "that the Marxist conception of the world is obsolete and that Chileans—and all peoples—need solutions to economic and social problems in accord with a new age of science and technology that will at the same time protect personal rights. Christian Democracy believes that the modern world is in crisis and that only a complete readjustment of society, humanizing capitalism, for instance, can save man from materialism and collectivism. Christian Democracy works for a civilization of work and solidarity with man as its center, rather than the pursuit of monetary gain that has pervaded the bourgeois society." It was a stirring message for Chile, the promise of a progressive center party in a country with a long democratic tradition whose politics were nevertheless chronically polarized between a repressive and oligarchic conservatism and the revolutionary left of students, workers, and peasants.

In the 1958 presidential elections, Frei finished a poor third behind Allende's Socialist-Communist Popular Front and the winner, Pres. Jorge Alessandri. He attributed the loss to his failure to make an alliance with the right, especially the Conservative Party. "After twenty years of fighting," he said, "am I going to give up to the right?" During the early 1960s his party continued its spectacular growth, largely at the right's expense. He won the election of 1964 decisively, gaining a rare absolute majority of the popular vote, and promised in his inaugural address "a profound revolution within liberty and law." His party was in the minority in both legislative houses at his election, but he appealed to the people for "a congress for Frei," and in the March 1965 legislative elections the Christian Democrats won majority control of the deputies and made striking gains in the senate.

After such an auspicious beginning, his administration was an almost unqualified disaster. He pushed through his program of "Chileanization" of the U.S.-owned copper mines—by far the largest industry in Chile—but the 51 percent share taken by the government satisfied no one, least of all important sectors of his own party; Allende nationalized the mines outright as one of his first acts in 1971. Frei's much-vaunted agrarian reform turned into a painful fiasco: by the end of his term only a tiny fraction of the country's peasants had been given their own land—and at a gigantic cost to the treasury. The price of copper fell on the world market and inflation grew steadily worse, harming all Chilean economic sectors. Unprecedented wage settlements given to workers only increased the number of strikes nationwide. Finally, a severe drought of several years' duration brought disaster to Chile's agriculture and caused widespread and prolonged hydroelectric power failures. Confronted by continual electoral gains by the left and a violent resurgence of right-wing nationalism, the Christian Democratic center abruptly collapsed. Barred by the constitution from succeeding himself, Frei watched Tomic, his chosen successor, come in a badly beaten third in the presidential elections of 1970.

Frei halfheartedly led his party into a coalition with Pres. Allende—traditionally his adversary, though parts of their programs were remarkably similar—but quickly found himself disillusioned by the rapid leftward course of the new government. The rightist generals, who had tried a coup late in Frei's administration, were finally successful in September 1973, killing Allende in the process. Frei assented to the coup—one of his most uncharacteristic acts—and undoubtedly regretted it ever afterward. Despite an exceptionally brutal police state and an absolute ban on political activity, he allowed the clandestine use of his law offices as a front for the Christian Democrats. He led the campaign in 1978 against the junta's proposed plebiscite to "reaffirm" its legitimacy, but a continuation of military rule was approved by 67 percent of the voters. In his later years he was an important member of the Brandt commission on international development.

In 1973, before the coup and just as Frei was being elected to another term in the senate, an investigation by the U.S. Senate Foreign Relations Subcommittee on Intelligence revealed that $20 million in U.S. funds had been funneled by the CIA into Frei's 1964 campaign. Frei refused all comment, and though there is good reason to disbelieve some of the allegations, the timing of the announcement could hardly have been worse. For at a time of unprecedented national peril, the story strongly confirmed many Chileans' doubts about the viability and reliability of Frei's political center. A.K.

Parents Eduardo Frei Schlins and Victoria Montalva. **Married** María Ruíz-Tagle 1935: seven children. **Education** Public schs., Santiago; Inst. of Humanities, Santiago; law studies, Catholic Univ. of Chile, grad. 1933. **Career** Law practice, Santiago 1933–35 and from 1937; organizer, youth wing of Conservative Party 1935; ed., *El Tarapacá* newspaper, Uquique 1935–37; co-founder 1938 and pres. 1941–47, Falange Nacional (since 1958 known as Partido Demócrata Cristiano, or Christian Democratic Party); prof. of labor law and economics, Catholic Univ. 1940–45; minister of public works and communications 1946–47; sen. from Atacama and Coquimbo 1949–57, from Santiago 1957; pres. of Chile 1964–70; sen. from Santiago 1973; led opposition to Pinochet junta late 1970s; member, Brandt commn. on intl. development issues late 1970s. **Honors** Literary prize, for *Truth Has Its Hour*, 1956; hon. degree, Catholic Univ. of Chile; GCB, U.K. **Author** *El régimen del salariado* [*The Management of Wage Earners*], 1934; *Chile desconocido* [*Unknown Chile*], 1937; *Aún es tiempo* [*There Is Still Time*], 1942; *La política y el Espíritu* [*Politics and the Spirit*], 1946; *Historia de los partidos políticos chileanos* [*History of the Chilean Political Parties*], 1949; *Sentido y forma de una política* [*Meaning and Form of a Policy*], 1951; *La verdad tiene su hora* [*Truth Has Its Hour*], 1955; *Pensamiento y acción* [*Thought and Action*], 1958; *Chile, 1964–1970*, 1964; (jtly.) *Maritain entre nosotros* [*Maritain Between Ourselves*], 1964; *América Latina tiene un destino* [*Latin America Has a Destiny*], 1967; *Un mundo nuevo: respuesta a una carta* [*A New World: Reply to a Letter*], 1973; *Crisis sin fronteras* [*Crisis Without Borders*], 1974; *Chile y el pacto andino* [*Chile and the Andean Pact*], 1976; *El mandato de la historia y las exigencias del porvenir*, 1976 (trans. as *The Mandate of History and Chile's Future*, 1977); *América Latina: opción y esperanza*, 1977 (trans. as *Latin America, The Hopeful Option*, 1978); numerous pamphlets, articles, essays, and speeches.

Further Reading Jay Kinsbruner, *Chile: A Historical Interpretation*, 1973; John A. Crow, *The Epic of Latin America*, 1980.

RAGINI DEVI

Performer, teacher, and researcher of Indian dances
***Born* Petoskey, Michigan, USA, 18 August circa 1894**
***Died* Englewood, New Jersey, USA, 23 January 1982**

Though American-born, Ragini Devi—born Esther Sherman—not only introduced classical Indian dance to the United States but played a major part in the revival of that ancient art in India itself. The country's dance-drama rituals had long since fallen into disuse when she arrived in India in 1930, but a visit by the ballerina Anna Pavlova the previous year had prompted renewed interest in them. Devi helped to bring them to light again and to popularize them in the West. She was noted for her faithfulness to traditional forms and for the precision with which she executed them.

Not much was known about Indian dance in America in the early 1900s, but the gift of two Sanskrit books on the subject so intrigued Sherman as a teenager that she began an intensive study that was to continue unabated for more than half a century. After her marriage to an Indian chemist, Ramlal Bajpai, she left her hometown in Michigan to live in New York City. There, accompanied by Indian musicians, she gave recitals as Ragini Devi. In 1928 she appeared in *Light of Asia*, a play about the life of Buddha, and published *Nritanjali: An Introduction to Hindu Dancing*, the first book on the subject in English.

Devi and her husband moved to India in 1930; she toured India's major cities as a solo-

Courtesy of Indrani Devi

ist in 1931. After studying the ancient (and all-male) Kathakali dance-drama at the temple of Kerala, she and the Indian dancer Gopindath organized a performance troupe that played at India's universities. She also gave command performances for the maharajas of six states. Her daughter Indrani, who later became a dancer of international repute, remembers that, when she was old enough to join her mother onstage, her first role was that of a golden deer "wrapped in yards and yards of golden cloth."

During the 1938–39 season Devi performed in Paris and London and lectured at the University of London, then moved to New York. She established the India Dance Theatre on West 57th Street and taught and performed there regularly until her return to India in 1948. In 1950 she received a grant from the Rockefeller Foundation to search for and record forgotten dances at village temples and festivals throughout the country. She witnessed eight consecutive dusk-to-dawn performances of the Kathakali dance ritual at a Kerala temple festival and studied the form with the poet Vallathol of Malabar. Her subsequent presentation of these dances provoked great international interest. Her fundamental text *Dance Dialects of India* was published in 1972.

Devi returned to the United States in 1978. The following year, by then in her eighties, she appeared onstage at New York University with her daughter Indrani and her granddaughter Sukanya. To the enthusiastic audience she expressed her happiness at seeing "the pure tradition" handed down through three generations. B.D.

Born Esther Sherman. **Parents** Alexander O. S. and Ida B. (Parker) S. **Married** Ramlal B. Bajpai, chemist, ca. 1921 (d. 1962): Indrani Bajpai Rahman, classical Indian dancer, b. 1930. **Career** Performer, student, teacher, and researcher of Indian dance since 1920s; performed in play *Light in Asia*, NYC 1928; toured India as solo recitalist 1931; co-founder of Kathakali dance-drama troupe, toured India mid-1930s, Paris and London 1938; lectr., Indian univs. 1930s and Univ. of London 1938; founder and teacher, India Dance Theatre, NYC 1940s; dancer and researcher, India 1947–78. **Honors** Rockefeller Foundn. grant 1950; Ford Foundn. grant 1978; citation of honor, Sangeet Natak Akadami, New Delhi 1982. **Author** *Nritanjali, An Introduction to Hindu Dancing*, 1928, rev. as *Dances of India*, 1953; *Dance Dialects of India*, 1972.

ALFREDO OVANDO (CANDIA)
President of Bolivia
Born Cobija, Pando department, Bolivia, 6 April 1918
Died La Paz, Bolivia, 24 January 1982

For much of Bolivia's two centuries of existence as a nation, its politics have lurched between the extremes of left and right. The few popularly elected national governments have only rarely been able to complete their allotted terms, and the military coups that ended them have always spawned others of their kind. The victims of this chronic instability have been the Bolivian people, whose standard of living is among the lowest in the world and whose national economy has remained stagnant for decades. During the 1960s, when Bolivia was following the fashion then current in Latin America for leftist-nationalist military rule, Gen. Alfredo Ovando Candía was among the country's paramount leaders. He served twice as president and during that decade was never far from power.

Born in Pando department in northern Bolivia, Ovando received his primary education in Sucre and his military training at the Colegio Militar del Ejército. He received his commission in 1936, then was sent to the Escuela Superior de Guerra and studied military science with a group sent to Argentina. He moved up gradually within the army's ranks, and was made brigadier general in 1959 and general of division in 1962. He was army chief of staff from 1957, army commander from 1960, and by 1962 was commander in chief of the Bolivian armed forces.

Ovando was a rightist by background and training, yet he supported the successful coup of Victor Paz Estenssoro, whose National Revolutionary Movement came to power in 1952. Over the next decade the armed forces became increasingly dissatisfied with the Paz regime, which they nevertheless allowed to win election twice, the second time in May 1964 with the Air Force commander, Gen. René Barrientos Ortuño, running as vice president. Ovando had been asked by Paz to run as well, but he stood aside in favor of Barrientos. The two generals then led the coup which drove Paz from office the following 4 November. They were sworn in as co-presidents the next day, but Ovando quickly resigned in the face of violent worker-student demonstrations against total military rule. The following month he was promoted to general of the Army.

Ovando was generally supportive of Barrientos, and when the next crisis came in the form of a general strike by tin miners in May 1965, he was again sworn in as co-president to maintain an appearance of unity within the junta. In January 1966, Barrientos resigned to run for election as constitutional president, and Ovando remained as interim chief of state. When Barrientos won the election that August, Ovando returned to his post as commander in chief.

During 1967 the Bolivian army was increasingly occupied with fighting Cuban-backed guerrillas who had chosen Bolivia, with its unstable regimes, as the jumping-

off place for inciting revolutionary change throughout South America. Ovando led the antiguerrilla campaign and in May announced the capture of Régis Debray, the French leftist who was an effective publicist for Castro's revolution. Bolivian soldiers then managed to capture Ernesto "Che" Guevara the following October, and he was promptly murdered on Ovando's orders, after which the guerrillas' challenge ebbed.

In response to more civil unrest in July 1968, Pres. Barrientos declared a state of siege and replaced the civilian cabinet with a military one. During the three months of the state of siege, Ovando declared himself a candidate for the presidential elections of 1970 (Barrientos was ineligible under the 1967 constitution to succeed himself). Ovando was visiting the United States when Barrientos was killed in a helicopter crash in April 1969; had he been at his post, it is generally believed, he would have seized power to prevent the conservative vice president, Luis Adolfo Siles Salinas, from succeeding to the presidency.

Pres. Siles served for barely five months of increasing tension with the military before Ovando took over the presidency. His own rule was rather remarkable: he chose an extremely leftist cabinet, promised the peasants greater efforts toward land reform, and proposed an "ideological confederation" with neighboring Peru, whose new military rulers were showing a compatible political coloration. His most potentially significant act was to nationalize the Bolivian Gulf Oil Company, yet this action was effectively vitiated by his own and succeeding governments.

Pres. Ovando was himself ousted in October 1970 after only a year in office. His more leftist successor was Gen. Juan José Torres. Ovando then served for a year as ambassador to Spain, remaining in that country after 1971, when a rightist junta replaced the Torres regime. He returned from exile in 1979 and pursued business interests in Santa Cruz, Bolivia's second-largest city, until his death of a stomach ailment at the age of 65. A.K.

Parents Máximo O. and Mercedes Candía. **Married** Elsa Elena Omiste Barrón, pres. of Natl. Youth Council: five children. **Emigration** In voluntary exile, Spain 1971–79. **Education** Primary sch., Sucre; Colegio Militar del Ejército, grad. 1936; Escuela Superior de Guerra late 1930s; studied military strategy, Argentina late 1930s. **Career** Commissioned 1936; lt. 1940; capt. 1943; maj. 1948; leader, Movimiento Nacionalista Revolucionario early 1950s; gen. 1959; army comdr. 1960; div. gen. and comdr. in chief of armed forces 1962; gen. of Army since 1964; led coup against Paz govt. 1964; co-pres. of Bolivia 1964 and 1965–66; led coup against Siles govt. 1969; chief of staff, comdr. of army, comdr. in chief of armed forces, and pres. of Bolivia 1969–70; overthrown in military coup 1970; ambassador to Spain 1970–71; in voluntary exile, Spain 1971–79; businessman, Santa Cruz, Bolivia, since 1979. • Formerly: asst. prof., Escuela Superior de Guerra; chief of studies, Escuela de Estado Major; military attaché, Uruguay and Paraguay; dir. of planning, Ministry of Defense.

Further reading John Gunther, *Inside South America*, 1966; Stephen Clissold, *Latin America, New World, Third World*, 1972; John A. Crow, *The Epic of Latin America*, 1980.

MIKHAIL A(NDREYEVICH) SUSLOV
Chief Soviet ideologist
***Born* Shakovskoye, Ulyanovsk province, Russia, 21 November 1902**
***Died* Moscow, USSR, 25 January 1982**

Of all the heirs of Josef Stalin, none held power so long or so securely as Mikhail A. Suslov, the ultraconservative watchdog of ideological purity within the Soviet state and in the Communist movement worldwide. Under the largely collegial system of rule that the USSR has experienced since the fall of Nikita Khrushchev, Suslov was widely believed to be second in power only to Pres. Leonid Brezhnev. His death at age 79 from the aftereffects of a cerebral hemorrhage removed from the center of Soviet power the one man who had been expected to exert a decisive and steadying influence in choosing the successor to Brezhnev, whose increasing feebleness had drawn comment for nearly a decade.

Mikhail Andreyevich Suslov was born into a peasant family in a village of the middle Volga basin. The Bolshevik Revolution broke out when he was 15, whereupon he quickly joined the Young Communist League and became active in the local Committee of the Poor, a Bolshevik organization that requisitioned food from landowning peasants to supply the Red Army and the starving cities. He joined the party at 19 and was sent to a workers' school in Moscow. An excellent student, he made the most of his educational opportunities during the 1920s, completing studies in politics and economics at the Plekhanov Institute of the National Economy (1924–28) and at the prestigious Economics Institute of Red Professors (1928–30). From 1929 to 1931 he taught economics at Moscow University and the Industrial Academy, where Khrushchev was one of his students.

In 1931, having been singled out as reliable by his party superiors, he was appointed to the crucially important joint organization formed by the party's Central Control Commission and the government's People's Commission for Worker and Peasant Inspection, which was used by Stalin to root out dissent in his widening purge of the state and party structures. Millions were exiled, imprisoned, or liquidated throughout the USSR at just the time that Suslov's career within the party was advancing. He helped with purges in the Urals, in the Chernigov section of the Ukraine, and then, during the height of the terror in 1937, as chief of the purge in the city of Rostov, southern Russia, where he became regional party secretary. In 1939 he was appointed first secretary in the Stavropol area of the northern Caucasus. He remained there during World War II, when much of the Caucasus was occupied by the Nazis, and was instrumental in the NKVD's deporting to Siberia of many thousands of members of ethnic minorities whom Stalin suspected of pro-German sympathies. In 1956, Khrushchev declared the charges against these people false and they were allowed to return to their lands. Suslov was elected to the Central Committee of the CPSU in 1941.

In 1944, the Germans having been driven from Soviet soil, Suslov was sent by Stalin to Lithuania. He was charged with eliminating Lithuanian nationalism and achieving the country's political integration with the USSR, which he accomplished by more mass deportations to Siberia. His varied regional expertise and his zealous adherence to party discipline had set him apart as a paragon of orthodoxy, and in 1946 he was recalled to Moscow for service within the central party organization, where he remained for the rest of his life. He was named a national party secretary in late 1947.

His party positions were usually concerned with propaganda, first as director of the Department of Agitation and Propaganda (Agitprop), an organization that enforced domestic ideological correctness, then in 1947 as one of the founders and overseers of the Communist Information Bureau (Cominform), which fostered unity of action and aims among the European Communist parties. He was chief Soviet representative to the Cominform meeting that expelled Yugoslavia in 1948. For one year (1949–50) he was editor of the party newspaper *Pravda*. In 1952, a year before Stalin's death, Suslov, in obvious favor with the dictator, was appointed to the Presidium (now the Politburo), the chief organization in the CPSU.

Suslov's relationship to Khrushchev, whom he was completely unlike in almost every way, has always seemed ambiguous to observers of Kremlin maneuverings. He was instrumental in Khrushchev's assumption of supreme authority in 1957, and later, during the bitter struggles against the "antiparty group" of old Bolsheviks—Malenkov, Molotov, Kaganovitch, Bulganin, and Voroshilov—Suslov sided with the first secretary against their former colleagues and engineered the group's expulsion from the CPSU. Yet he is believed to have opposed many of Khrushchev's initiatives, especially the break in relations with the Chinese, the brief cultural liberalization of the early 1960s, the downgrading of defense and heavy industry as an economic priority in favor of consumer goods, and the rapprochement with Yugoslavia. Finally, Suslov was almost certainly the man most responsible for Khrushchev's ouster in October 1964, preparing the list of charges and speaking against him at the extraordinary session of the Central Committee that removed him from power.

Suslov's authority in party matters was unchallenged from the time of Brezhnev's ascendency. Indeed, as senior member of the Politburo he probably had the chance to become first secretary himself, but realistically stepped aside in favor of the marginally more charismatic Brezhnev, five years his junior in age and considerably more than that in high-level service to the party. He became even more conservative, aloof, and ascetic; non-Communists almost never got to see him, he never gave interviews, and he rarely traveled outside areas of Soviet hegemony. Within that sphere of influence, however, he was viewed as practically infallible. He was a firm opponent of Eurocommunism, the assertion of independence from Moscow by the Western European parties, and resisted any deviation from strict orthodoxy within the Eastern bloc. He was deeply involved in the Warsaw Pact invasion of Czechoslovakia in 1968, the Soviet occupation of Afghanistan in 1979, and the internal crackdown in Poland in 1981, although he was thought to be dismayed by the stark diminution of the Polish party's authority during Gen. Wojciech Jaruzelski's imposition of martial law.

Suslov was last seen in public a month before his death, leading the tributes at Brezhnev's 75th birthday celebration. His funeral was the most elaborate of any since Stalin's, with central Moscow closed for days and thousands of the party faithful bused in from outside the city. The obvious lack of emotion among ordinary Russians was widely reported. He was buried beside Stalin near that part of the Kremlin wall reserved for the highest Communist elite.

The recipient of decorations from nearly every Communist country, Suslov was also awarded all of the USSR's highest honors, including the rarely given Order of the October Revolution. He won the Order of Lenin four times and the Hero of Socialist Labor award twice. His death was followed by weeks of speculation in the West about his successor as ideologist in chief, much of it focusing on Yuri Andropov, the longtime head of the KGB, who would need a period of "sanitizing," as it is generally called, after years of secret-police activity, before he could properly aspire to become first secretary. There is no one, however, at present in the hierarchy who could aspire to Suslov's breadth of command and authority over Communist doctrine and its worldwide implementation. A.K.

Courtesy of Tass from Sovfoto

Parents peasants. **Married** Yekaterina, dir. of dental coll. (d. 1972): one son; one daughter, philologist and historian. **Education** Prechistenko Workers' Faculty, Moscow 1921–24; Plekhanov Inst. of Natl. Economy, Moscow 1924–28; Economics Inst. of Red Professors 1928–30. **Mil. service** Member of military council, northern Caucasian front, and head of Stavropol Regional HQ for partisan forces 1941–45. **Career** Joined Komsomol (Young Communists League), Chvalinsk ca. 1918; member, Cttee. of the Poor ca. 1918–20; lectr., Industrial Acad. and Moscow Univ. 1929–31; deputy to USSR Supreme Soviet from 1937. • With CPSU: joined 1921; exec. post, Central Control Commn. and People's Commn. for Worker and Peasant Inspection 1931–36; regional secty., Rostov-on-Don Regional Cttee. 1937–39; member, Central Auditing Commn. 1939–41; 1st secty., Stavropol Territorial and City Cttee., Northern Caucasus 1939–44; member, Central Cttee. since 1941; chmn., Central Cttee. Bureau, Lithuanian SSR 1944–46; member of Organization Bureau, and lectr. at Soviet Acad. of Sciences, Central Cttee. 1946; dir., Agitprop (Dept. of Agitation and Propaganda) 1946–47; secty. for Agitprop affairs, Central Cttee. 1947–49; natl. party secty. since 1947; cofounder 1947 and dir., Cominform (Communist Information Bureau) 1947; candidate member, Politburo 1948; chief Soviet delegate to Cominform 1948–53; ed., *Pravda* C.P. newspaper 1949–50; member 1950, and full member 1952–53 and since 1955, Presidium (Politburo); reappointed secty. of Central Cttee. 1952; chmn., Foreign Affairs Commn., Council of Nationalities since 1954; 2nd secty. of CPSU since 1964; head of Soviet delegations to congresses of foreign C.P.s. **Honors** Order of Lenin four times, including 1952; Hero of Socialist Labor 1962, 1972; Order of October Revolution 1977; Order of Patriotic War, 1st Class; Hammer and Sickle Gold Medal twice; Order of Sukhe Bator, Outer Mongolia; decorations from German Socialist Unity Party, Czechoslovakia, Bulgaria, others. **Author** [*Selected works*], 1952; [*On the Roads of the Construction of Communism*] (collected speeches), 2 vols., 1977.

Further reading Michel Tatu, *Power in the Kremlin*, 1970; Rodger Swearingen, ed., *Leaders of the Communist World*, 1971.

RUSSEL V(AN ARSDALE) LEE
Physician
***Born* Spanish Fork, Utah, USA, 10 May 1895**
***Died* Portola Valley, California, USA, 27 January 1982**

Russel Lee was a founder of the Palo Alto Medical Clinic, the first group practice in the country, and served on the controversial presidential commission that recommended the enactment of prepaid national health insurance programs (Medicare and Medicaid) funded by the federal government.

Lee's father, a Presbyterian minister, had gone out to Utah in the days of Brigham Young to convert the Mormons to Calvinism. The same quixotic spirit characterized his son, who was at his best when encountering opposition. He studied chemical engineering at Stanford University but switched to medicine on the advice of the eminent bacteriologist Hans Zinsser and completed his medical training in the record time of seven years, in spite of the fact that for three of those years his nights were devoted to running an emergency shipyard hospital. He married Dorothy Womack in his junior year, and their first child was born while he was still an intern. They had four sons and one daughter, all of whom became physicians, and two adopted daughters, both of whom married physicians.

Courtesy of Palo Alto Medical Foundation

In 1924, after practicing briefly in San Francisco, Lee went into partnership in Palo Alto. His local reputation was given a boost after he helped a wealthy invalid over an attack of paroxysmal tachycardia (rapid heartbeat) by pressing on the carotid sinus at the side of her neck. Her son, a San Francisco financier, extolled the virtues of the young doctor far and wide; his practice grew dramatically, and to handle the load he recruited other doctors. In 1930 a large new building was opened to house the Palo Alto Medical Clinic, the first of its kind in the United States devoted to meeting the needs of the immediate community. Lee also persuaded the city council to build a new hospital on land donated by Stanford University; $342,000 was raised and a modern 100-bed facility built.

Despite hostility from neighborhood doctors, and the American Medical Association's insistence that "group practice is nothing but a device for fee-splitting," the Clinic thrived. Lee continued to teach at Stanford Medical School and in 1935 took a sabbatical to study hospitals and medical schools around the world. This knowledge proved invaluable early in World War II when he was called upon to set up and staff Army Air Corps hospitals. From 1943 to 1945 he served as chief of preventive medicine for the Air Corps at the Pentagon, visited every front, and was personal physician to Secretary of War Henry Stimson and Gen. Henry "Hap" Arnold.

Signs of a population explosion were noticeable when Lee returned to Palo Alto after the war, and 20 local specialists were added to the clinic. (By 1973 the enlarged facility was staffed by 130 doctors and 300 other employees.) In 1950 he established the Palo Alto Medical Research Foundation to enable local physicians to pursue research ideas. He took part in the founding of the American Group Practice Association and served for two terms in the AMA House of Delegates as the representative of the Military Medicine Section.

In 1951 Pres. Truman appointed him to the Commission on the Health Needs of the Nation. The commission's report, which was largely Lee's work, eventually led to the enactment of the Medicare and Medicaid programs, feared by many doctors as first steps toward a socialist system of health care. When a resolution condemning the commission's recommendations was introduced in the AMA, Lee led the opposition and won by a four-vote margin.

After some 15 years of shuttling between Washington and California, Lee returned home to reorganize the clinic. Far in advance of his time, he introduced a prepayment plan for elderly patients, formed a council for the care and treatment of retarded children, and built Channing House, an outstanding residential retirement home. Always a maverick, he worked indefatigably along the way for such controversial causes as national health insurance, free drugs for addicts, legal abortion, and legal euthanasia. Once, in the 1930s, he lobbied a venereal-disease-control bill through the California legislature with funds derived from a high-stakes poker game.

Lee was a millionaire from his real estate investments—his holdings included vineyards that produce cabernet sauvignon wine—and he donated 1,500 acres to the city of Palo Alto for the creation of a municipal park. After his retirement from the clinic and from Stanford Medical School in 1960 he was a writer, lecturer, and advisor on international development. He died at the age of 86 after several years of declining health. B.D.

Parents Theodore L., Presbyterian minister and beekeeper, and Anna (Wray) L. **Married** Dorothy Womack 1918 (d. 1972): Richard S., obstetrician; Peter V., internist; Philip R., prof. of environmental medicine; R. Hewlett, surgeon; Margo Lee Paulsen, physician (d. 1973); Jane Langnecker Stratte; Leslie Langnecker Luttgens. **Education** Univ. of California, B.A. 1917; Stanford Medical Sch., S.F., M.D. 1920; intern, San Francisco Hosp. 1917–18. **Mil. service** Pvt., Medical Reserve Corps, U.S. Army, WWI; chief of professional services, Santa Ana Air Corps Hosp. 1941–43; Col., Medical Corps, and chief of preventive medicine, USAAC 1942–45. **Career** Head, emergency hosp., Shaw-Butcher Shipyard, S.F. 1917–20; visiting physician, San Francisco Hosp. 1920; asst. to internist, S.F. 1920–24; private practice, Palo Alto, CA since 1924; founder 1929, dir. 1929–60, and consultant since 1960, Palo Alto Medical Clinic; founding pres., Palo Alto Medical Research Foundn. 1950–60; member, Pres.'s Commn. on Health Needs of Nation 1951; founding pres., Channing House retirement home, Palo Alto since 1964; founder, Children's Health Council, Palo Alto 1960s; with Agency for Intl. Development 1960s–70s; ed., annual geriatric issue, *Medical World News*. • With Stanford Medical Sch., S.F.: teacher of pharmacology 1918–19; medical house officer 1919–20; instr. in medicine 1920–22; clinical instr. in therapeutics 1923–24; assoc. prof. of therapeutics 1924–38; clinical prof. of medicine 1946–60; prof. emeritus since 1960. **Officer** Pres.: (also founder 1936) Amer. Soc. for Control of Venereal Disease; Amer. Assn. of Medical Clinics 1950–61; Palo Alto Medical Soc.; Stanford Medical Alumni; Stanford Alumni Assn. • Chmn.: Palo Alto Community Chest; Palo Alto Planning Commn.; Military Medicine Sect., AMA. • Dir.: (also cofounder) Amer. Group Practice Assn.; California Acad. of Medicine. **Member** AMA House of Delegates 1950–55. • Clubs: Bohemian; Menlo Country; Rotary; Palo Alto Yacht. **Honors** Legion of Merit and army commendations, WWII; Hoover Medal, Stanford Alumni Assn. 1974. **Author** *The Pharmacology of Mercury*, 1921; *Manual of Coccidioidmycosis*, 1943; (jtly.) *Building America's Health*, 1952; *The Role of the Internist*, 1957; "Medicine's Living History" (autobiographical article) in *Medical World News*, 28 Sept. 1973.

PALDEN THONDUP NAMGYAL
Chogyal of Sikkim
***Born* Gangtok, Sikkim, 22 May 1923**
***Died* New York City, USA, 29 January 1982**

Palden Thondup Namgyal was the second son of Sir Tashi Namgyal, chogyal, or king, of the Himalayan country of Sikkim. He was educated in India and was trained as a Buddhist monk. When his elder brother, the crown prince, died, Namgyal, then about 20 years old, entered the government in his stead and oversaw the economic development of the country for the next 22 years while his father remained in semiretirement. After the British withdrew from the Indian subcontinent in 1947, he worked to thwart India's attempts to absorb Sikkim, which had been ruled by the same royal family since the 1600s, and represented his country in negotiations that resulted in Sikkim's becoming a protectorate of India in 1950. Namgyal succeeded to the throne after the death of his father in 1963 and was formally crowned two years later, together with his second wife, Hope Cooke, an American.

During the 1960s, Sikkim was the site of frequent border clashes between China and India. In 1975, following two years of domestic unrest that was instigated, according to some reports, by the government of India, Sikkim was annexed by India as its 22nd state. Namgyal was kept under house arrest until 1979, when he finally recognized Sikkim's annexation and was allowed to travel to New York to see his family. He died there of cancer at the age of 58. J.P.

Parents Sir Tashi N., chogyal of Sikkim, and Kunzang Dechen N. **Married** (1) Sangay Deki Namgyal 1950 (d. 1957): Tenzing (d. 1978); Yangchen; Wangchuk. (2) Hope Cooke 1963 (div. 1980): Palden; Hope Leezum. **Religion** Buddhist. **Education** St. Joseph's Coll. Darjeeling, India; Bishop Cotton Sch., Simla, India. **Career** Crown prince of Sikkim ca. 1941–63; chogyal of Sikkim 1963–75; deposed 1975. **Officer** Pres.: Sikkim State Council 1944–49; Mahabodhi Soc. of the Subcontinent 1953; (also founder) Namgyal Inst. of Tibetology, Gangtok, Sikkim. **Honors** Padma Vibhushan 1954; comdr., Ordre de l'Étoile Noire 1956; hon. maj. gen., Indian Army 1965; Order of Druk Jung Thusay, 1st Class, 1974; col. in chief, Sikkim Guards; OBE, U.K.

Further reading Hope Cooke, *Time Change*, 1980.

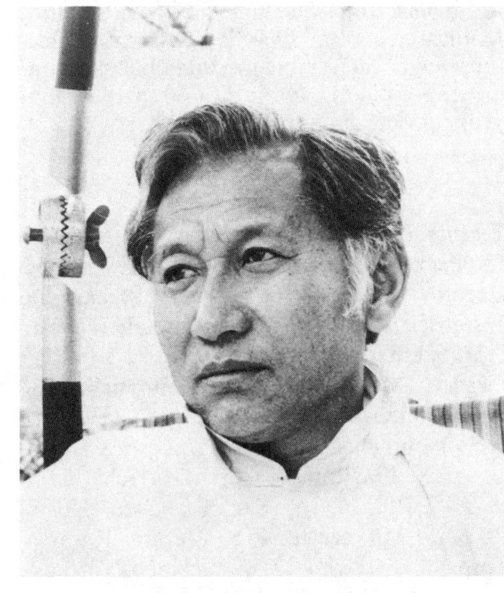

STANLEY (AUGUSTUS) HOLLOWAY
Actor and singer
***Born* London, England, 1 October 1890**
***Died* Littlehampton, Sussex, England, 30 January 1982**

Stanley Holloway, a veteran of the British music hall and theater, will be recorded in theatrical history as the creator of Alfred P. Doolittle, the ebullient dustman of Lerner and Loewe's musical *My Fair Lady*. Holloway's Broadway performance in 1956 made his reputation in the United States, and crowned a 50-year British career that included appearances in vaudeville, films, and Shakespearean drama. He later became still more widely known in the United States for his portrayal of an old-fashioned, straight-laced English butler trying to cope with the chaos of American suburban life in the situation comedy *Our Man Higgins*, produced by ABC television in 1962. Holloway, the supreme stage Cockney, was also a Cockney in real life. He was born in the East End of London, the son of a lawyer's clerk, and began his working life in Billingsgate fish market, whose name has passed into the language as a term for abusive language. It was in this environment that Holloway mastered the idiom that he was to use on the stage 50 years later, but his earliest ambition was to be a singer. He became a church soloist as a child, was performing professionally by the age of ten as Master Stanley Holloway, the Wonderful Boy Soprano, and by the time his voice had matured to a baritone was earning his living as a singer in "concert parties," a then-popular comic entertainment resembling the contemporary revue. Intending to become an opera singer, he had saved enough by 1913 to travel to Milan, where he studied for six months before the outbreak of World War I. During the war Holloway served as an infantryman in the Connaught Rangers, rising to the rank of lieutenant.

In a *New Yorker* article of 1956, Holloway remembered the postwar years as a time of apprenticeship in the music hall, where he performed "two turns a night, six nights a week." His acting style retained a flavor of vaudeville comedy, but by 1919, when he made his London theater debut in *Kissing Time* at the Winter Garden Theatre, he had already begun to extend his range. In 1920 he made a second London appearance in *A Night Out*, and in the following year played his first film role in *The Rotters*, based on a popular farce by H. F. Maltby. None of these parts won him as much acclaim as his performances as a member of the Co-Optimists, a small group of comedians and singers who toured Britain giving concert parties for six years beginning in 1921.

It was at a revival concert party by the Co-Optimists in 1929 that Holloway gave his first recital of a monologue he had written called "Sam, Pick Oop Tha' Musket," featuring Sam Small, a character whose remarks are still quoted in Britain to this day. Small is a Yorkshireman who has been conscripted, much against his will, into the army of the Duke of Wellington, and who, at the Battle of Waterloo, refuses to fight until asked to do so by the Duke himself. Small, like Doolittle, became a national hero, as did another Yorkshire character, Albert Ramsbottom, an odious small boy who figured in a series of monologues written for Holloway by Marriott Edgar. In the final monologue, Albert, who has recently been given "a stick with un 'orse's 'ead 'andle" by his parents, is devoured by a lion at the zoo.

The success of these monologues, which Holloway often performed on the radio, made him one of Britain's most successful comic actors and a frequent choice for cameo roles in films. His film appearances became more frequent during World War II, when he played parts in *The Way Ahead* (1944) and *The Way to the Stars* (1945), and his reputation was firmly established in David Lean's celebrated film *Brief Encounter* (1945), in which he played the principal supporting role of the railroad station guard, Albert Godby. Although never typecast, Holloway almost invariably portrayed in films a bluff and likeable workingman whose common sense and good humor make him an ideally ordinary Englishman. Although increasingly active in films, Holloway continued to appear on the stage and in pantomimes, in which he was often the comic villain. In 1948 he used his gift of lively comic characterization and a Cockney accent to play the gravedigger in Laurence Olivier's film of *Hamlet*, a performance that he repeated on the stage in 1951. His second Shakespearean role came in 1954, when he was cast as Bottom, the "rude mechanical" of *A Midsummer Night's Dream*. This production by the Old Vic Company was given in New York, where Herman Levin, producer of *My Fair Lady*, saw Holloway and chose him for the part of Doolittle.

Courtesy of the Bert Aza Agency

By the time of his debut on Broadway in 1956, Holloway had begun to win an international reputation for *Brief Encounter* and for his roles in the film comedies *The Lavender Hill Mob* (1951) and *The Titfield Thunderbolt* (1953). In the former, perhaps his finest film, he played Pendlebury, a craftsman who manufactures miniature souvenir Eiffel Towers from stolen gold under the direction of a bungling amateur criminal, played by Alec Guinness. His success in *My Fair Lady* eclipsed his previous achievements, however. In adapting George Bernard Shaw's *Pygmalion*, Alan Jay Lerner and Frederick Loewe had given the role of Doolittle greater prominence, making him the epitome of Cockney shrewdness and vitality, and an ideal foil to the suave elocution teacher, Prof. Higgins, played by Rex Harrison. Holloway, portraying Doolittle in classical vaudeville song-and-dance style, had found an ideal vehicle for his talent, and regularly stopped the show with his numbers, "Wiv A Little Bit o' Luck" and "I'm Gettin' Married in the Mornin'." He repeated his performance in the London production of 1958, and again in the Warner Brothers film of 1964.

Holloway was awarded an OBE in 1960, but neither fame nor increasing age slackened his energy, although in his later years he suffered from glaucoma. His autobiography appeared in 1967 and does not describe the last ten years of his active career, which concluded with a tour of Australia and the Far East in *The Pleasure of His Company*, a celebration of Noel Coward. H.B.

Parents George H., law clerk, and Florence (Bell) H., teacher. **Married** (1) Alice May Foran 1912 (d. 1937): Joan Adams, b. 1914; Patricia Smith, b. 1918; John, businessman, b. 1922; Mary, b. 1927. (2) Violet Marion Lane, actress, 1939: Julian, actor and writer, b. 1944. **Religion** Church of England; converted to Roman Catholicism late 1910s; returned to Church of England. **Education** Worshipful Sch. of Carpenters, London; left sch. age 12; studied operatic singing, Milan 1914. **Mil. service** Lt., Connaught Rangers, British Army, France, WWI. **Career** Office boy and clerk, Billingsgate fish market; started singing professionally at age 10 at seaside resorts, town halls, and concert parties; on stage since 1919, with Co-Optimists troupe 1921–27, 1929–30; in films since 1921, on radio since 1923, on TV since 1930s; writer of comedy monologues. **Member** Garrick Club; Green Room Club. **Honors** OBE 1960; special award, Variety Club of Great Britain 1978. **Stage** (all London except as noted) *Kissing Time*, 1919; *A Night Out*, 1920; *Hit the Deck*, 1927; *Song of the Sea*, 1928; *Cooee*, 1929; *Co-Optimists of 1930* and other Co-Optimists shows; *Savoy Follies*, 1932; *Here We Are Again*, 1932; *Three Sisters*, 1934; *Aladdin*, various cities, Christmas seasons since 1934; *All Wave*, 1936; *London Rhapsody*, 1938; *All the Best*, tour 1938; *Up and Doing*, 1940; *Fine and Dandy*, 1942; *Mother Goose*, 1946; *Hamlet*, 1951; *A Midsummer Night's Dream*, Edinburgh Festival and tour of U.S. and Canada 1954; *My Fair Lady*, NYC 1956 and London 1958; *Laughs and Other Events*, solo show, NYC 1960; *Cool Off*, Phila. 1964; *Candida*, Shaw Festival 1970; *Siege*, 1972; *You Never Can Tell*, Shaw Festival 1973; *The Pleasure of His Company*, tour of Australia and Far East 1977; appearances at variety theaters throughout U.K.;

concert tours of Australia, N.Z., South Africa. **Films** *The Rotters*, 1921; *Sing as We Go*, 1934; *Squibs*, 1936; *Cotton Queen*, 1937; *The Vicar of Bray*, 1939; *Major Barbara*, 1940; *This Happy Breed*, 1944; *The Way Ahead*, 1944; *Champagne Charlie*, 1944; *Caesar and Cleopatra*, 1945; *The Way to the Stars*, 1945; *Brief Encounter*, 1945; *Nicholas Nickleby*, 1947; *Hamlet*, 1948; *Noose*, 1948; *Passport to Pimlico*, 1948; *Midnight Episode*, 1950; *The Lavender Hill Mob*, 1951; *The Magic Box*, 1951; *One Wild Oat*, 1951; *Lady Godiva Rides Again*, 1951; *Meet Me Tonight*, 1952; *The Beggar's Opera*, 1952; *The Titfield Thunderbolt*, 1953; *Meet Mr. Lucifer*, 1954; *Fast and Loose*, 1954; *An Alligator Named Daisy*, 1955; *Alive and Kicking*, 1958; *No Love for Johnnie*, 1961; *My Fair Lady*, 1964; *In Harm's Way*, 1965; *Ten Little Indians*, 1965; *The Sandwich Man*, 1966; *Mrs. Brown You've Got a Lovely Daughter*, 1968; *Run a Crooked Mile*, 1969; *What's in It for Harry?*, 1969; *Blanding Castle*, 1969; *The Private Life of Sherlock Holmes*, 1970; *Flight of the Doves*, 1971; *Up the Front!*, 1972; *Journey into Fear*, 1975; more than 30 others. **Television** "The Mikado," 1960; "Our Man Higgins" series, U.S. 1962–63; "Thingumybob," 1968; "Dr. Jekyll and Mr. Hyde," 1975; numerous variety shows and specials. **Author** *Wiv a Little Bit o' Luck* (autobiography), 1967; *Monologues*, 1979. **Recordings** *'Ere's 'Olloway*; *The Elephant Alphabet*.

Further reading Patrick Nicholson, "Our Stanley," in *Sunday Times Magazine* (London), 28 Sept. 1980.

LIGHTNIN' HOPKINS
Blues singer and guitarist
***Born* Centerville, Texas, USA, 15 March 1912**
***Died* Houston, Texas, USA, 30 January 1982**

In his book *The Country Blues*, musicologist Samuel Charters wrote of the blues singer and guitarist Lightnin' Hopkins: "Lightnin', in his way, is a magnificent figure. He is one of the last of his kind, a lonely, bitter man who brings to the blues the intensity and pain of the hours in the hot sun, scraping at the earth, singing to make the hours pass. The blues will go on, but the country blues, and the great singers who created from the raw singing of the work songs and the field cries the richness and variety of the country blues, will pass with men like this thin, intense singer from Centerville, Texas."

Hopkins came from a family of musicians and learned his first blues from an older brother. At the age of eight he built a guitar from a cigar box, a plank, and chicken wire, and got some impromptu lessons from the great bluesman Blind Lemon Jefferson, whom he met at a church picnic. His cousin, the blues vocalist Alger "Texas" Alexander, taught him to sing. Until the mid-1940s, he worked as a farm laborer and as an itinerant musician in the streets, bars, and dance halls of Texas towns, sometimes accompanying his cousin. It was a rough existence, and on more than one occasion he did time in prison farms and road gangs.

His reputation as a blues artist, already considerable in Houston and east Texas, began to widen in 1946, when he and pianist Wilson "Thunder" Smith went to Hollywood at the invitation of a talent scout to cut a record for the Aladdin label. (From this partnership, Hopkins, whose first name was Samuel, derived his professional name.) Between 1947 and 1949 he made a series of singles for Houston's Gold Star label, many of which became hits—"Baby Please Don't Go" sold 80,000 copies. During the next ten years he cut some 200 singles for dozens of companies, including Jax, Sittin' In With, Herald, TNT, Harlem, Ace, Mercury, and Decca, making more recordings than any other blues artist in history. His popularity was due in part to the directness of his approach and the rapport he had with his audience. Unlike most bluesmen, he played guitar without amplification or accompaniment, and his rambling, improvised verses drew more on the hardships and sorrows of his own life (and, by extension, of the lives of his listeners) than on the traditional store of blues material. His guitar, droning rhythmically beneath the lyrics and erupting between verses in a piercing wail, provided dramatic counterpoint to his harsh voice.

Although his singles sold well, Hopkins mismanaged his money and had to struggle to get by. In 1959 he was introduced to white audiences by Samuel Charters, who sought him out and recorded him for the folk-archive label Folkways. The following year, he appeared at Carnegie Hall and the Village Gate in New York City and at the University of California Folk Festival. From then on he alternated between tours of northern cities and the West Coast on the folk music circuit and the familiar dives and joints of Houston's Dowling Street. He made a series of albums (including reissues of his singles), performed on radio shows and television programs, and was featured in several film shorts, including *The Sun's Gonna Shine* (1967) and *The Blues According to Lightnin' Hopkins* (1968), both by Les Blank. In 1977 he toured Europe, appearing at jazz festivals in the Netherlands and Germany.

Hopkins's last professional engagement was at the New York City club Tramps in the fall of 1981, a few months after he underwent surgery for cancer of the esophagus. He died of pneumonia at the age of 69. J.P.

Born Samuel Hopkins. **Parents** Abe H., musician, and Frances Sims. **Married** (1) . . . (2) . . . (3) Antoinette Charles. **Children** Four from first two marriages. **Religion** Baptist. **Education** Left sch. at age 8. **Career** Farm laborer and itinerant blues musician, TX 1920s–40s; did time in Houston County Prison Farm late 1930s; accompanied blues singer Texas Alexander, Houston 1945–50s; began recording 1946; introduced to folk music audiences 1959; frequent performer in concerts, clubs, folk and jazz festivals, and bars, U.S. and Europe until 1981; recorded several hundred singles and numerous albums. **Partial list of albums**—*Lightnin' Hopkins*, 1959; *Lightnin' & the Blues*, 1960; *Autobiography in Blues*, 1960; *Country Blues*, 1960; *Lightnin'*, 1961; *Fast Life Woman*, 1962; *Walkin' This Road by Myself*, 1962; *Blues in My Bottle*, 1962; *Lightnin' Sam Hopkins*, 1962; *Lightnin' & Co.*, 1963; *Smokes Like Lightnin'*, 1963; *Hootin' the Blues*, 1964; *Early Recordings*, 1964; *First Meetin'*, 1964; *Lightnin' Hopkins with His Brothers Joel and John Henry*, 1966; *Berkeley Blues Festival*, 1967; *Lightnin' Hopkins, the Texas Blues Man*, 1968; *The Roots of Lightnin' Hopkins*, 1968; *Ball and Chain*, 1969; *Lightnin' Strikes*, 1972; *Double Blues*, 1972; *Blues Bash*, 1973; *The Blues Giant*, 1973; *Low Down Dirty Blues*, 1974; *L. H. in Berkeley*, 1976; **Film shorts** Les Blank, *The Sun's Gonna Shine*, 1967; Les Blank, *The Blues Accordin' to Lightnin' Hopkins*, 1968; *Sam Lightnin' Hopkins*, PBS-TV 1971; *A Program of Songs by Lightnin' Sam Hopkins*, Univ. of Washington 1971. **Soundtrack** *Blues Like Showers of Rain*, 1970.

Further reading Samuel Charters, *The Country Blues*, 1959; Samuel Charters, *Legacy of the Blues*, 1975.

HELEN M(ERRELL) LYND
Sociologist and educator
***Born* La Grange, Illinois, USA, 17 March 1896**
***Died* Warren, Ohio, USA, 30 January 1982**

Helen Merrell Lynd wrote with her husband, Robert Staughton Lynd, two pioneering classics in the sociology of community development, *Middletown: A Study in American Culture* (1929) and *Middletown in Transition: A Study in Cultural Conflicts* (1937). She was a renowned educator, teaching social philosophy at Sarah Lawrence College, Bronxville, New York, from 1929, the year after its founding, until 1964, when she was named professor emeritus. She was partly responsible for the college's liberal curriculum and unusual grading standards.

Lynd was born in the Middle West and received her primary education there, but traveled East to attend university, graduating Phi Beta Kappa from Wellesley College in Massachusetts in 1919. She taught school for a while in New York City, married in 1921, earned her M.A. from Columbia University in 1922, then entered with her husband upon sociological research. During 1924 and 1925 the Lynds and several assistants lived in Muncie, Indiana—the "Middletown" of both their books—and correlated their observations of the inhabitants' lives painstakingly and without condescension, at the same time recording verbatim their opinions. It was the first scientific study of an American community. Their book, published four years later, was divided into sections on work, family life, education, religion, community and government, and leisure, and provided detailed tables on such specifics as the numbers of books borrowed from the public library and the issues on which parents and children disagreed. It became a classic in the newly developed field of sociology and has remained assigned reading in college sociology courses to this day.

In 1935, six years into the Great Depression, the Lynds returned to Muncie for a follow-up study of how economic hardship had affected the native optimism they had encountered among the residents ten years before. Although they found somewhat greater social and religious tolerance, they also noted a hardening of economic attitudes and an entrenched class distinction based on money. The local capitalist had become a kind of dictator. "Those who . . . skim the cream from the economy," the Lynds wrote, "also control the press, the radio, the movies, and other formal media in diffusion of attitudes and opinions. They are thus in a position . . . to tell a cityful of people living off the skimmed milk of the economy what to believe."

Progressive education was among Lynd's guiding interests throughout her life. Although she also taught at both New York University and Vassar College, Sarah Lawrence and its developing educational philosophy were at the center of her concern for nearly four decades. She helped devise the college's flexible, interdisciplinary curriculum; its much-discussed system of extensive written analyses of student performance in place of grading by letter or number; and the plan by which all students would spend part of each academic year working at off-campus jobs.

Lynd continued her own formal education while teaching, earning her Ph.D. in history from Columbia in 1944. Her dissertation was published in 1945 as *England in the 1880s: Toward a Social Basis for Freedom*, a historical analysis of social change at a time of great material power and societal ferment. Her other books were also well received, and included *On Shame and the Search for Identity* (1958), which approached such psychological concerns as emotional stability, shame, and guilt from an anthropological viewpoint, and *Toward Discovery* (1965), a collection of lectures, essays, and other occasional pieces.

Lynd was a vocal opponent of McCarthyism during the early 1950s, a time when many leftist scholars were dismissed from their university positions, and she wrote articles defending academic freedom in such magazines as the *Nation*. Her son, Staughton Lynd, was a prominent activist against the Vietnam War during the 1960s. A.K.

Born Helen Merrell. **Parents** Edward Tracy M. and Mabel (Waite) M. **Married** Robert Staughton Lynd, sociologist, 1921: Staughton, history prof.; Andrea Lynd Nold. **Religion** Congregationalist; later agnostic. **Education** Wellesley Coll, B.A. (Phi Beta Kappa) 1919; Columbia Univ., M.A. 1922, Ph.D. in history of ideas 1944. **Career** Teacher, private sch., NYC early 1920s; asst. dir., Middletown studies, Inst. of Social and Religious Research 1924–29; prof. 1929–64 and emeritus prof. in social philosophy since 1964, Sarah Lawrence Coll., Bronxville, NY; visiting lectr., Vassar Coll., Poughkeepsie, NY 1930–31; lectr., New York Univ., NYC. • Consultant: Gen. Education Bd.; Rockefeller Foundn.; Academic Freedom Commn., ACLU; Amer. History Assn. **Fellow** Wellesley Coll. **Member** Amer. History Assn.; Amer. Philosophical Assn.; Amer. Assn. of Univ. Professors; Soc. for Psychological Study of Social Problems. **Honors** Squires Prize, Columbia Univ.; hon. fellow, Cowell Coll., Univ. of California at Santa Cruz; hon. degrees from Ripon Coll. and Univ. of California at Santa Cruz. **Author** (with Robert S. Lynd et al.) *Middletown: A Study in American Culture*, 1929; (with R. S. L. et al.) *Middletown in Transition: A Study in Cultural Conflicts*, 1935; *Field Work in College Education*, 1945; *England in the 1880s: Toward a Social Basis for Freedom*,

1945; (jtly.) *Essays in Teaching*, 1948; *On Shame and the Search for Identity*, 1958; *Toward Discovery* (essays), 1965.

Further reading John H. Madge, *The Origins of Scientific Sociology*, 1962; Seymour M. Lipset, *The First New Nation*, 1963.

BARON RITCHIE-CALDER OF BALMASHANNAR

Peter Ritchie Calder
Science writer, journalist, and public servant
***Born* Forfar, Angus, Scotland, 1 July 1906**
***Died* Edinburgh, Scotland, 31 January 1982**

Though Lord Ritchie-Calder never completed secondary school, he was one of the first writers to succeed in making science intelligible and interesting to the general reading public, and he eventually carried on simultaneous careers as a writer and journalist, a world-traveling consultant for the United Nations, a university professor, and a socialist member of the House of Lords. He held an unshakeable belief in the power of technology to provide solutions to famine, war, and other plagues of human society, and his effort to organize international cooperation in scientific ventures—known in the United States as the Calder Plan—led to the founding in 1937 of the British Association's division of social and international relations. H. G. Wells once said of him, "No one has quite the same grasp of modern trends and modern inventions."

Born Peter Ritchie Calder, he was one of four children of a Scottish jute worker and factory manager. He left school at the age of 15, taught himself shorthand, and became a police court reporter for the *Dundee Courier*. During the next 18 years he worked on a succession of newspapers (from 1926 to 1930 on London's *Daily News*, from 1930 to 1941 on the *Daily Herald*). In the course of his work he was sometimes assigned to cover science stories. These piqued his interest, and he began to study science on his own, to befriend scientists, and to write about their work for what was then a mystified public. Thus it happened that he was the first observer present at the Cavendish Laboratory in Cambridge when Sir John Cockcroft and E. T. S. Walton first split the atom. In his first two books, *The Birth of the Future* and *The Conquest of Suffering*, both published in 1934, he sketched recent findings in science and medicine and speculated optimistically about developments to come.

Ritchie-Calder spent the year 1940 as a war correspondent, filing reports on the sufferings of bomb victims in London's East End and provincial cities; his two books of war reportage, *Carry On, London* and *The Lesson of London*, brought about several reforms of Civil Defense policy. He left newspaper work in 1941 to join the political warfare executive of the Foreign Office. In 1944 his home and office were destroyed by bombs and he suffered a brain hemorrhage. After his recovery he served as special advisor to Gen. Eisenhower's Supreme Headquarters.

After the war, Ritchie-Calder returned to journalism, serving as science editor of the *News Chronicle* until 1956 and holding a seat on the editorial board of the *New Statesman* until 1958. Most of his time, however, was spent in the service of the United Nations, for whom he undertook numerous missions to survey educational, economic, and medical problems in troubled or controversial areas—the arid zones of North Africa and the Middle East in 1950, Southeast Asia in 1951 and 1962, the Arctic in 1955, and the Congo in 1960. These trips resulted in a series of books, lectures, and broadcasts. He also served as a delegate to UNESCO, as a member of the U.K. commissions for UNESCO and the World Health Organization, and as a consultant to the Atoms for Peace and the Science and Technology conferences.

Between journeys, Ritchie-Calder continued to write on science and social policy in his distinctive style—"solid nourishment served up as a soufflé," in the words of the *Times Literary Supplement*. In *After the Seventh Day* (1960), published in the United States as *The Inheritors,* he recounted, in a series of short vignettes, the history of the human encounter with the earth and its environment, and imagined the world of the future as a utopia in which technological expertise would supply a peaceful population with unlimited food and resources.

In 1961, Ritchie-Calder began a third career as professor of international relations at Edinburgh University. He taught there for six years. From 1969 to 1972 he was chairman of Britain's Metrication Board, and from 1972 to 1975 he held a senior fellowship at the Center for the Study of Democratic Institutions in Santa Barbara, California.

Ritchie-Calder's three careers fed his social activism. He was a leader in the movement for nuclear disarmament during the 1930s and the early 60s, served as vice president of the Workers' Educational Association from 1958 to 1968, was a member of the executive of the Fabian Society, and stressed in his books the necessity of marshaling human ingenuity to avert political and environmental catastrophe. In all, he was the author of more than 30 widely translated books and more than a thousand articles. He was also a consultant on the production of documentary films about hunger and poverty. In 1966 he was elevated to a life peerage as Baron Ritchie-Calder of Balmashannar. He received the Victor Gollancz Award for service to humanity in 1969.

P.D.

Courtesy of Mabel Ritchie-Calder

Parents David Lindsay C. and Georgina (Ritchie) C. **Married** Mabel Jane Forbes McKail 1927: Fiona Rudd; Nigel, science writer; Angus; Allan; Isla. **Education** Forfar Acad., Scotland, left at age 15; Edinburgh Univ., M.A. 1961. **Mil. service** Dir. of plans, Political Warfare Exec., Foreign Office 1941–44; special advisor, SHAEF 1945. **Career** Reporter: *Dundee Courier* 1922; D. C. Thomson Press 1924–25; *Daily News*, London 1926–30; *Daily Chronicle* 1930; *Daily Herald* 1930–41. • Science ed., *News Chronicle* 1945–56; editorial bd. member, *New Statesman* 1945–58; Burton Prof. of Intl. Relations, Edinburgh Univ. 1961–67; chmn., Metrication Bd. 1969–72; sr. fellow, Center for the Study of Democratic Instns., Santa Barbara, CA 1972–75. • Beard Lectr., Ruskin Coll., Oxford 1957; Danforth Foundn. Lectr., U.S. 1965; visiting prof., Heriot-Watt Univ. 1973; Bentwich Lectr., Hebrew Univ. 1973; Brodetsky Lectr., Leeds Univ. 1973. • Consultant: *World of Plenty* ca. 1945, *World Without End* 1954, other documentary films; U.S. Librarian of Congress 1976; Oxfam. • With U.N.: member, U.K. delegation to UNESCO 1946, 1947, 1966, 1968; special advisor, Famine Conference, Food and Agriculture Org. 1946; desert survey for UNESCO 1950; chief, special mission to Southeast Asia 1951; member, missions to Arctic 1955, Congo 1960, Southeast Asia 1962; member, conferences on Peaceful Uses of Atomic Energy, U.N. Secretariat 1955 and 1958; member, WHO group on mental aspects of atomic energy 1957; consultant ed., Science and Technology Conference, Geneva 1963; member, U.K. Commn. for WHO and U.K. Commn. for UNESCO; exec., U.N. Assn. **Officer** Secty., Viscount Sankey Cttee. on New Declaration of the Rights of Man 1940. • Pres.: Sect. X, council, British Assn. 1955; British Sub-Aqua Club 1971–74; Mental Health Film Council; Natl. Peace Council. • Chmn.: (also founder) Assn. of British Science Writers 1949–55; Chicago Univ. study group on radiation in the environment 1960; advisory cttee. on oil pollution of the sea 1977. • Other: v.p., Workers' Educational Assn. 1958–68; vice chmn., Campaign for Nuclear Disarmament 1960. **Member** Labour Party since 1924; council 1945–60, and co-founder of Social and Intl. Relations of Science Div. 1937, British Assn.; Community Relations Commn. 1968–70; gen. council, Open Univ. since 1969; council, Intl. Ocean Inst. since 1970; exec., Fabian Soc.; Edinburgh Univ. Settlement; Soc. of Visiting Scientists, London; English-Speaking Union. • Clubs: Savile; Scottish Arts; Univ. Staff, Edinburgh; Edinburgh Press; Cosmos, Wash. DC; Century, NYC. **Fellow** Amer. Assn. for Advancement of Science; World Acad. of Arts and Science; FRSA. **Honors** CBE 1945; Kalinga Prize, UNESCO 1960; Jubilee Medal, New York Public Library 1961; created Baron Ritchie-Calder of Balmashannar, life peer, 1966; Gollancz Award 1969; WHO Medical Soc. Medal 1974; hon. degrees from Open and York (Toronto) univs. **Author** *Birth of the Future*, 1934; *Conquest of Suffering*, 1935; *Roving Commission*, 1935; *Lesson of London*, 1941; *Carry On, London*, 1941; *Start Planning Britain Now*, 1941; *Men Against the Desert*, 1951; *Profile of Science*, 1951; *The Lamp Is Lit*, 1951; *Men Against Ignorance*, 1953; *Men Against the Jungle*, 1953; *Science in Our Lives*, 1954; *Science Makes Sense*, 1955; *Men Against the Frozen North*, 1957; *From Magic to Medicine*, 1958; *Medicine and Man*, 1958; *Ten Steps Forward: The Story of WHO*, 1958; *The Hand of Life: The Story of the Weizmann Institute*, 1959; *The Inheritors*, 1960; *Agony of the Congo*, 1961; *Life-Savers*, 1961; *Common Sense About a Starving World*, 1962; *Living with the Atom*, 1962; *World of Opportunity*, 1963; *Two-Way Passage*, 1964; *The Evolution of the Machine*, 1968; *Man and the Cosmos*, 1968; *Leonardo and the Age of the Eye*, 1970; *How Long Have We Got?*, 1972; *The Pollution of the Mediterranean*, 1972; *Understanding Energy*, 1979.

AGNES SLIGH TURNBULL

Novelist

Born **New Alexandria, Pennsylvania, USA, 14 October 1888**

Died **Livingston, New Jersey, USA, 31 January 1982**

Agnes Sligh Turnbull wrote novels that celebrated the virtues of the traditional way of life in her native rural Pennsylvania. The quaintness of her themes and characters were appreciated by a considerable body of readers who found them a comforting alternative to the violence of much modern fiction, and even critics who thought her books shallow and nostalgic noted the skill with which she recreated the details of her admittedly limited world.

Courtesy of Houghton-Mifflin Co.

Of Scottish ancestry, Turnbull grew up in western Pennsylvania, attended teachers college, and taught high-school English until her marriage in 1918. Two years later she published her first story, in the *American Magazine*, and began a six-decade career as a writer. *The Rolling Years*, her first novel, was a three-generation family epic that was popular enough to warrant 36 printings in as many years. "The elements that have given her stories their appeal," wrote Andrea Parkes in a *New York Times* review of *The Golden Journey*, "lie in her unabashed use of sentiment, backstopped with plots full of color and incident." In addition to her 14 novels for adults (some of which appeared in foreign-language editions), she published several books for children and a memoir in diary form. She died at the age of 93. C.M.

Born Agnes Sligh. **Parents** Alexander Halliday S. and Lucinda Hannah (McConnell) S. **Married** James Lyall Turnbull 1918 (d. 1957): Martha Lyall Turnbull O'Hearn. **Religion** Presbyterian. **Education** Washington Seminary, PA; Indiana State Teachers Coll., PA, grad. 1910; Univ. of Chicago 1910–11. **Career** High-sch. English teacher ca. 1911–18; short-story writer and novelist since 1920s. **Honors** Hon. degrees from Westminster Coll. and Indiana Univ. of Pennsylvania. **Member** Authors Guild; Authors League of America; PEN; Phi Beta Kappa; Pi Kappa Sigma; Kappa Delta Pi; Republican Party. **Author** *The Rolling Years*, 1936; *Remember the End*, 1938; *Elijah the Fish-bite* (juvenile), 1940; *Dear Me: Leaves from the Diary of Agnes Sligh Turnbull*, 1941; *The Day Must Dawn*, 1942; *The Bishop's Mantle*, 1947; *The Gown of Glory*, 1952; *The Golden Journey*, 1955; *Out of My Heart* (nonfiction), 1955; *Jed, the Shepherd's Dog* (juvenile), 1957; *The Nightingale*, 1960; *The King's Orchard*, 1963; *Little Christmas*, 1964; *George* (juvenile), 1965; *The Wedding Bargain*, 1966; *Many a Green Isle*, 1968; *The White Lark* (juvenile), 1968; *Whistle and I'll Come to You*, 1970; *The Flowering*, 1972; *The Richlands*, 1974; *The Winds of Love*, 1977; *The Two Bishops*, 1980.

YEFIM (LVOVICH) DZIGAN

Film director

Born **Georgia, Russian Empire, 2 December 1898**

Died **Moscow, USSR, January 1982**

Yefim Lvovich Dzigan was a Soviet film director of the generation of Sergei Eisenstein and Vsevolod Pudovkin who attempted to infuse the dominant tenets of Socialist Realism with new means of cinematic expression, while still serving what few themes were permitted artists under Stalin's rigid regime.

His career began in his native Georgia, where he graduated from film school and learned filmmaking in local studios. His first co-direction effort, with Mikhail Chaiureli, was *First Cornet Streshnev* (1928), about the Civil War of 1918–21. After he directed *God of War* (also known as *The White Rider*) in 1929, he was transferred to the Mosfilm Studios in the capital, where his most famous film, which took years to make, was *My iz Kronshtadta* (1936; *We Are from Kronstadt*). Still occasionally seen in the West, this was an epic treatment of an incident just after the Revolution when Red seamen from the naval base at Kronstadt held the road to Petrograd against superior White forces. It had sweep and historical authenticity about it that set it apart from other similar attempts of the time, and even in the West the film was praised for impressive photography and bold direction. It won the grand prize at the Paris World's Fair in 1937.

Dzigan's scenarist in *Kronstadt* was the playwright Vsevolod Vishnevsky, whose *An Optimistic Tragedy*, about a Red defeat during the Civil War, was a popular and official theatrical success. The published correspondence between Vishnevsky and Dzigan affords a rare glimpse into the workings of Soviet filmmaking at an important time in the history of the country and the industry. A subsequent collaboration between them on another Vishnevsky play, *First Cavalry Army*, a Civil War epic on the same large scale as *Kronstadt*, was halted just before completion in 1939 and never released.

Others of the more than two dozen films made by Dzigan during a 40-year career include the documentary *If War Comes*, of which he was co-director (1938); *Dzhambul* (1953); *Prologue* (1956), about the Revolution of 1905 and one of the first Soviet widescreen films; *Unquenchable Flames* (1964); and *The Iron Flood* (1967). Most of his mature efforts were large-scale historical or biographical epics that glorified the revolutionary spirit and the Soviet state.

His somewhat narrow thematic vision often yielded Dzigan official rewards, from the time that Stalin gave him the coveted State Prize of the USSR in 1941 until he was designated a People's Artist of the USSR in 1969. He was awarded the Order of Lenin, the Order of the October Revolution, and the Order of the Red Banner of Labor. For many years he taught at the All-Union State Institute of Cinematography, and he was the author of two books, including a description of the making of *We Are from Kronstadt*. A.K.

Education B. V. Chaikovsky Motion Picture Sch., grad. 1926. **Career** Actor, Rakhmanov studio; asst. film dir. 1924–28, film dir. since 1928, with Mosfilm Studios since ca. 1930; teacher since 1937, appointed prof. 1965, All-Union State Inst. of Cinematography; member, CPSU since 1943. **Honors** Grand Prize, Paris World's Fair, for *We Are from Kronstadt*, 1937; State Prize of USSR 1941; People's Artist of USSR 1969; Order of Lenin; Order of October Revolution; Order of Red Banner of Labor. **Films** (Jtly.) [*First Cornet Streshnev*], 1928; [*The War God*], 1929; [*Woman*], 1932; *My iz Kronshtadta* (rel. as *We Are from Kronstadt*), 1936; [*If War Comes Tomorrow*] (documentary), 1938; (Jtly.) [*First Cavalry Army*] (unfinished), 1939; (Jtly.) [*Moscow Music Hall*], 1946; [*Dzhambul*], 1953; [*Prologue*], 1956; [*Fatali-Khan*], 1959; [*Unquenchable Flames*], 1964; [*The Iron Flood*], 1967. **Author** *My iz Kronshtadta: Printsipy rezhisserskogo postroeniya filma* [*We Are from Kronstadt: Principles of the Director's Construction of a Film*], 1937; *O rezhisserskom stsenarii*, 1961.

Further reading Jan Leyda, *A History of the Russian and Soviet Film*, 1960.

FEBRUARY

AMZIE MOORE
Civil-rights activist
***Born* Grenada County, Mississippi, USA, 23 September 1912**
***Died* Bolivar County, Mississippi, USA, 1 February 1982**

Amzie Moore was a leader of the National Association for the Advancement of Colored People in Mississippi during the 1950s and one of the prime movers of the black voter registration drives of the 1960s. He graduated from high school in 1932 and taught at the Rosenwald School in Grenada after obtaining a teacher's license from Rust College. In 1942 he was drafted into the army and was stationed outside El Paso, Texas, in special barracks for black soldiers. "We were not allowed to go to the main PX," he told James Forman, author of *The Making of Black Revolutionaries,* in 1962. "We were not allowed to go to the recreational facilities provided for soldiers on the place; we had to ride in the back of the buses from the base into El Paso . . . it was the first time I really knew how evil segregation really was." Moore later served in India, China, and Burma, where he was assigned to give lectures on patriotism to black soldiers to counteract the effects of Japanese propaganda.

Returning to his hometown of Cleveland, Mississippi, after the war, Moore found that local whites, alarmed by photographs in *Newsweek* of white German women sitting in the laps of black servicemen, had formed vigilante groups to terrorize black veterans and were murdering blacks at the rate of one a week. In 1950 he helped organize the Regional Council of Negro Leadership, the first civil-rights action committee based in the Mississippi Delta. Thirteen thousand people came to its first rally. "The purpose of the Regional Council," Moore said, "was to teach Negroes first-class citizenship, the preservation of property, the holding of public office, the changing of the economic standpoint." The motto of the organization was "Don't buy gas where you can't use the rest room." Moore, who now worked for the U.S. Postal Service and owned a gas station, was elected president of the local NAACP chapter in 1955, and raised its membership sevenfold within six months despite the threat of racial violence that followed the U.S. Supreme Court's 1954 decision to desegregate the public schools.

In 1956 Moore initiated a voter registration drive in Cleveland. At his urging, several blacks, with poll tax receipts in hand, tried to vote in the first gubernatorial primary of that year, but were prevented by a contingent of armed whites guarding the ballot box. The next year, the Mississippi legislature enacted a law requiring voters to pass a test of their knowledge of the state constitution, a measure intended to discourage poorly educated blacks. Moore and John Lebouvre, a Catholic priest, set up a "citizenship school" to tutor them, but it was discontinued soon after by Lebouvre's successor. After attending a meeting of the Student Nonviolent Coordinating Committee in Atlanta in 1960, Moore enlisted the organization's help in setting up new and more successful voter registration drives in the state with the assistance of white student civil-rights workers.

In the 1960s Moore was active in the Bolivar County Loyal Democratic Party, the Mississippi Action for Community Education committee, and the Head Start program. After retiring from the Postal Service in 1968, he worked for the National Council of Negro Women and managed a low-income housing project. S.A.

Parents Louis M. and Edna (Person) M. **Married** (1) . . . (div.). (2) Mary Lee 1968. **Children** Seven, including stepchildren. **Religion** Baptist. **Education** Stone Street High Sch., Greenwood, MS, grad. 1932; Rust Coll., Holly Springs, MS, teacher's license. **Mil. service** Staff sgt., U.S. Army 1942–46; served in China, India, and Burma 1944–45. **Career** Teacher, Rosenwald Sch., Grenada, MS; with U.S. Postal Service ca. 1940s–68; gas station owner since 1954; mgr., Turnkey III housing project 1970s. • Civil-rights activist since 1940s; co-founder, Regional Council of Negro Leadership, MS 1950; pres., Cleveland, MS chapter, NAACP 1955; voter registration recruiter 1956–early 60s; chmn. Operation Freedom Cttee. 1950s; organized first Head Start program in Bolivar County, MS 1966; chmn., Bolivar County Loyal Democratic Party 1967–72; bd. chmn., Mississippi Action for Community Education 1967–70; active with Natl. Council of Negro Women 1970s; member, bd. of dirs., Delta Ministry, Natl. Council of Churches of Christ. **Honors** Good Conduct Medal and China-India-Burma Medal, USAAC, WWII. **Interview** Michael Garvey, *An Oral History with Amzie Moore,* 1981.

Further reading James Forman, *The Making of Black Revolutionaries,* 1972; Howell Raines, *My Soul Is Rested,* 1977.

SALLY STANFORD

Mayor of Sausalito, California, and madam
***Born* Baker, Oregon, USA, 5 May 1903**
***Died* Greenbrae, California, USA, 1 February 1982**

Sally Stanford, mayor of Sausalito, California, during the mid-1970s, began her career as one of San Francisco's most famous and flamboyant madams.

She was born Mabel Janice Busby, the daughter of poor potato farmers in Oregon. She eloped at the age of 16 and landed in the state prison shortly thereafter when she cashed a $10 check that her husband had stolen. Paroled after two years, she went to southern California, where she began a bootleg operation. "I learned my arithmetic at the cash register, chemistry I picked up in my bathtub gin experiments, and my customers taught me the rudiments of psychology," she wrote in her 1966 autobiography *Lady of the House.*

In 1924 she moved to San Francisco and opened a hotel. Though it was legitimate, the police arrested her on a charge of operating a brothel. "I didn't set out to be a madam," she wrote, but after her acquittal she decided that "if I was going to have the name, I might as well have the game." Although she changed her first name to Marsha, was married five times, and took the surname Owen from one of the two adopted children whom she raised from infancy, for business purposes she used the name Sally Stanford. Her first establishment, a mansion on posh Russian Hill, was so successful that it was included as a landmark on sightseeing tours. Even more successful was her brothel at 1144 Pine Street. It featured a drawing room with a fountain, a marble bath, and a giant fireplace. The patrons included prominent political figures, businessmen, and diplomats. Stanford was arrested 17 times, but was convicted only twice and was never fined more than $1,500.

A more puritanical climate prevailed in San Francisco after World War II, and Stanford closed her house of prostitution and opened the Valhalla Restaurant in Sausalito, across the Golden Gate. When town officials resisted her efforts to have an electric sign installed, she decided to take a hand in local politics and was elected to the city council in 1972 after five unsuccessful bids. In the 1976 election she received more votes than any other candidate and automatically became mayor for a two-year term. "The people voted for me because they've got common sense," she told *Time* magazine. Her policy for the town, a fashionable writers' and artists' colony, was one of "controlled growth." She was elected to an-

other four-year council term in 1976, served as vice mayor in 1978, and was named vice mayor for life by the council in 1980, by which time she had won the backing of Sausalito's Good Government League. She also held a mail-order ministry from the Universal Life Church in Modesto, California.

Stanford's autobiography was the basis of a 1978 television movie, also called *Lady of the House,* starring Dyan Cannon. She survived 11 heart attacks and died of heart failure at the age of 78. B.B.

Born Mabel Janice Busby; later known as Marsha Owen and Sally Stanford; legally changed name to Sally Stanford 1971. **Parents** potato farmers. **Married** (1) Dan Goodan ca. 1919 (div.). (2) Ernest Spagnoli, lawyer (annulled). (3) Louis Rapp (div.). (4) Robert Livingston Gump 1951 (div.). (5) Robert Kenna, businessman, 1954 (div. 1956). **Children** John D. Owen; Hara Melinda Owen. **Career** Imprisoned for passing bad checks, OR ca. 1919–21; bootlegger, southern CA ca. 1921–24; hotel proprietor, S.F. 1924; madam, S.F. ca. 1925–49; proprietor, Valhalla Restaurant, Sausalito, CA 1950–late 70s. • With City of Sausalito: city councilman 1972–80; mayor 1974–76; vice mayor 1978; vice mayor for life since 1980. • Ordained minister, by mail order, of the Universal Life Church. **Author** *Lady of the House* (autobiography), 1966.

(FRANK) STRINGFELLOW BARR
Educator
***Born* Suffolk, Virginia, USA, 15 January 1897**
***Died* Alexandria, Virginia, USA, 2 February 1982**

As the innovative president of St. John's College in Annapolis, Maryland, from 1937 to 1946, Stringfellow Barr introduced a controversial program of liberal education based on what he called "the hundred best books of European thought in all fields." After leaving St. John's, he served for a decade as president of the Foundation for World Government.

Barr received his bachelor's degree from the University of Virginia in 1916 and stayed on for his master's in history the following year. After army service with an ambulance unit and the Surgeon General's Office (1917–19), Barr won a Rhodes Scholarship and spent two years at Balliol College, Oxford University. He followed his Oxford B.A. with a diplôme from the Sorbonne (1922) and a further year of study at the University of Ghent, Belgium.

From 1924 to 1937 Barr taught modern European history at the University of Virginia, where he was a full professor from 1930 and the editor (1930–34) of the *Virginia Quarterly Review.* His interest in the theory of university education led him to take up a visiting professorship (1936–37) at the University of Chicago, where the president, Robert Hutchins, had formed a committee to investigate the U.S. undergraduate curriculum. In 1937, Barr accepted the presidency of St. John's, a very small liberal arts college; with it went a mandate to restructure the entire four-year course of study.

Barr's program required that every student have by graduation a thorough knowledge of all the hundred-odd books in the program, as well as mastery of two foreign languages, proficiency in mathematics, and at least 300 hours of laboratory science. Some critics felt the program was too restrictive; others, like the eminent educational philosopher John Dewey, while approving it in theory, doubted the ability of most students to master and profit from it. Barr always defended the program vigorously, even taking to CBS radio in 1940 with "Invitation to Learning," whose format was based on the great books.

While president of the Foundation for World Government from 1948 to 1958, Barr attacked the nation-state as the primary evil responsible for the threat of nuclear destruction. Nor had he any faith in such organizations as the United Nations, saying, "To trust any league, alliance, association, or treaty among sovereign nations to outlaw the production or use of atomic bombs is to trust swamps to cease producing mosquitoes."

Barr was a visiting professor of political science at the University of Virginia from 1951 to 1953 and professor of the humanities at the Newark campus of Rutgers University from 1955 to 1964. He then spent three years (1966–69) as a fellow of the Center for the Study of Democratic Institutions in Santa Barbara, California, where he urged educators to show restraint in dealing with campus unrest, then widespread in the United States. He settled in Kingston, New Jersey, after his retirement.

Barr was the author of 11 books, including popular histories of Europe and ancient Greece; *Mazzini: Portrait of an Exile* (1935); a children's book; a cookbook; *Purely Academic* (1958), a satirical novel of college life; and *Voices that Endured: The Great Books and the Active Life* (1971). He died at 84 of pneumonia. A.K.

Parents William Alexander B., Episcopalian minister, and Ida (Stringfellow) B. **Married** Gladys Baldwin 1921 (d. 1974). **Religion** Episcopalian. **Education** Tulane Univ., New Orleans 1912–13; Univ. of Virginia, B.A. 1916, M.A. 1917; Balliol Coll., Oxford (Rhodes scholarship), B.A. 1921, M.A. 1927; diplôme, Sorbonne 1922; Univ. of Ghent, Belgium 1922–23. **Mil. service** Sgt., U.S. Army 1917–19: with ambulance service 1917–18; with Office of Surgeon Gen. 1918–19. **Career** Asst. prof. 1924–27, assoc. prof 1927–30, prof. of modern European history 1930–37, and visiting prof. of political science 1951–53, Univ. of Virginia, Charlottesville; visiting prof. of liberal arts, Univ. of Chicago 1936–37; pres., gov., and member of bd. of dirs., St. John's Coll., Annapolis, MD 1937–46; pres., Foundn. for World Government 1948–58; prof. of humanities, Rutgers Univ., Newark, NJ 1955–64; visiting fellow, New Coll., Hofstra Univ., NY 1966–67; fellow, Center for the Study of Democratic Instns. 1966–69. • Advisory ed. 1926–30 and 1934–37, and ed. 1930–34, *Virginia Quarterly Review;* broadcaster, "Invitation to Learning" radio series 1940; advisory ed., Great Books Series for *Encyclopaedia Britannica* 1944–46. **Member** Authors League; Alpha Tau Omega; Phi Beta Kappa; Raven Soc.; Democratic Party. **Honors** Lindback Award for distinguished teaching 1961; Waite Award, Natl. Inst. of Arts and Letters 1967. **Author** *Mazzini: Portrait of an Exile,* 1935; *The Pilgrimage of Western Man,* 1949; *Let's Join the Human Race,* 1950; *Citizens of the World,* 1952; *Copydog in India* (juvenile), 1955; (jtly.) *The Kitchen Garden Book: Vegetables from Seed to Table,* 1956; *Purely Academic* (novel), 1958; (jtly.) *American Catholics: A Protestant-Jewish View,* 1959; *The Will of Zeus: A History of Greece from the Origins of Hellenic Culture to the Death of Alexander,* 1961; *The Three Worlds of Man* (essays), 1963; *The Mask of Jove: A History of Graeco-Roman Civilization from the Death of Alexander to the Death of Constantine,* 1966; *Voices That Endured: The Great Books and the Active Life,* 1971. **Contributor** to *Atlantic Monthly, Nation, Virginia Quarterly Review,* other periodicals.

JOSÉ ANTENOR PATIÑO
Diplomat and industrialist
***Born* Bolivia, 12 October 1894**
***Died* New York City, USA, 2 February 1982**

The Bolivian diplomat and businessman José Antenor Patiño inherited extensive tin holdings from his father, who made a fortune operating several of his country's largest mines when tin was Bolivia's main export. He was educated in private schools and earned a law degree from the Sorbonne. While running the family mining and metals companies from various residences in Europe and North America, he served as Bolivia's diplomatic minister to Great Britain during World War II and was later chargé d'affaires in Spain. Although Patiño's mines were nationalized during the Bolivian National Revolution of 1952, he continued to manage highly profitable tin works in Canada, Great Britain, and Thailand.

One of the richest men in the world, Patiño

was an avid art collector and traveled frequently between homes in Paris and New York. He died of a heart ailment at the age of 85. S.A.

Father Simon P., mining magnate. **Married** Princess Maria Cristina de Bourbon 1931: Cristina Kurtess. **Education** Private schs., Bolivia; Sorbonne, law degree. **Career** Envoy extraordinary and diplomatic minister to U.K. 1938–42; chargé d'affaires, Madrid. • Pres. and dir.: Patiño Mines and Enterprises Consolidated, Inc.; Patican Co. Ltd.; Consolidated Tin Smelters Ltd.; General Metal Securities Ltd., London. • Dir.: Patiño Enterprises of Canada, Ltd.; British-American Tin Mines Ltd.; British Tin Investment Corp. Ltd.; Tin Industrial and Finance Ltd.; Thailand Tin Mines Ltd. **Honors** Chevalier, Légion d'Honneur, France; gran oficial del Condor de los Andes.

PETER (MASON) OPIE

Scholar of the folklore and folk life of children
Born **Cairo, Egypt, British Empire, 25 November 1918**
Died **West Liss, Hampshire, England, 5 February 1982**

The folklore and folk literature of British children has been collected and made available to the reading public largely through the efforts of Peter and Iona Opie, a husband-and-wife team who, in nearly four decades of field work and historical research, became the leading authorities on the subject.

Peter Opie was born in Cairo, the only son of a major in the Royal Army Medical Corps. He developed a great love of literature while at Eton, and his first book, a schoolboy autobiography entitled *I Want to Be a Success,* was published in 1939. Invalided out of the Army in 1941, he worked for the BBC until 1944, when he and his wife, whom he had married the previous year, had their first child and began their lifelong study of childhood traditions. Their second collaborative work, the classic *Oxford Dictionary of Nursery Rhymes* (1951), provided scholarly histories (including origin, first literary appearance, variants, and parallels in other languages) for more than 500 examples; the next, *The Oxford Nursery Rhyme Book* (1955), was a compendium of traditional lullabies, riddles, ballads, finger games, street cries, charms, and songs. These were followed in 1957 by *Christmas Party Games.*

The Opies' growing reputation among folklorists was clinched with the publication in 1959 of *The Lore and Language of Schoolchildren,* a massive study of every kind of orally transmitted tradition, from puns, tricks, jeers, and superstitions to holiday rites, ghost stories, and secret languages, collected in rural and urban schoolyards throughout England, Scotland, and Wales. The authors found "that traditional lore exists everywhere; that as many, if not more, traditional games are known to city children as to country children; and that children with homes and backgrounds as different from each other as mining community and garden suburb share jokes, rhymes, and songs, which are basically identical."

In 1969, the Opies published *Children's Games in Street and Playground,* the product of ten years of field and archive research, based on reports from 10,000 children aged 6 to 12. In it they demonstrated the remarkable continuity of children's games, showing that those played by modern British children had their counterparts in ancient Pompeii and Rome, and identifying 55 still-popular games in a sixteenth-century painting by Pieter Brueghel. The Opies argued emphatically that games played spontaneously in street and field provide better emotional and psychological resources for children than games controlled by adult supervisors. "In the security of a game [the child] makes acquaintance with insecurity, he is able to rationalize absurdities, reconcile himself to not getting his own way, 'assimilate reality' . . . [and act] heroically without being in danger." On this subject, Opie told an interviewer: "The idea that if you leave a lot of children on an island they will turn savage is the exact opposite of the truth—they would in fact become more civilized."

After their growing accumulation of manuscripts forced the Opies out of their first home, they bought an old farmhouse near the village of Liss, 50 miles southwest of London, and turned eight of its rooms into libraries and a museum. Ten thousand volumes, including a collection of rare eighteenth-century children's books, lined the walls; another wall was devoted to files containing children's accounts of their games. The Opies' index file in 1969 contained over 100,000 cards, and the top floor of the house was packed with 1,500 cartons containing children's clothes, toys, and trinkets. Their literature collection formed the basis of *The Oxford Book of Children's Verse* (1973), *The Classic Fairy Tales* (1974), and *A Nursery Companion* (1980). Each of the ten books on which the Opies collaborated took many years to write—*The Oxford Book of Children's Verse* alone took 21 years—and was financed largely by the authors. The majority of the research was done by Iona, the majority of the writing by Peter.

The Opies' work earned them an international reputation, and the care and scholarship they brought to their work has been recognized by many learned bodies, including Oxford University, which awarded them honorary master's degrees in 1962. Their *Oxford Book of Narrative Verse* was not yet completed at the time of Peter Opie's death.

J.P./B.D.

Parents Philip Adams O., army physician, and Margaret (Collett-Mason) O. **Married** Iona Margaret Balfour Archibald, folklorist, 1943: James; Robert; Letitia. **Education** Eton Coll. **Mil. service** Lt., Royal Fusiliers 1939; comdr., Royal Sussex Regiment 1940–41. **Career** Worked with BBC ca. 1941–44; author from 1939; folklorist since 1944; broadcaster, *The Lore and Language of Schoolchildren* BBC 1960. **Officer** Pres.: anthropology sect., British Assn. for Advancement of Science 1962–63; Folklore Soc. 1963–64. **Honors** Chosen Book Competition, for *The Case of Being a Young Man,* 1946; silver medal, RSA 1953; (with Iona Opie) Coote Lake Research Medal 1960; (with I. O.) European Prize, City of Caorle, Italy, for *The Puffin Book of Nursery Rhymes*, 1964; (with I. O.) Chicago Folklore Prize, for *Children's Games in Street and Playground*, 1970; (with I. O.) hon. M.A., Oxford Univ. **Author** *I Want to Be a Success* (autobiography), 1939; *Having Held the Nettle,* 1945; *The Case of Being a Young Man,* 1946. **Co-author with Iona Opie** (Comp.) *I Saw Esau,* 1947; (ed.) *The Oxford Dictionary of Nursery Rhymes,* 1951; (comp.) *The Oxford Nursery Rhyme Book,* 1955; *Christmas Party Games,* 1957; *The Lore and Language of Schoolchildren,* 1959; (comp.) *The Puffin Book of Nursery Rhymes,* 1963; (comp.) *A Family Book of Nursery Rhymes,* 1964; *Children's Games in Street and Playground,* 1969; *The Oxford Book of Children's Verse,* 1973; *Three Centuries of Nursery Rhymes and Poetry for Children,* 1973; *The Classic Fairy Tales,* 1974; *A Nursery Companion,* 1980; *The Oxford Book of Narrative Verse* (unfinished). **Contributor** to *Encyclopaedia Britannica, Chambers Encyclopedia, New Cambridge Bibliography of English Literature.*

GRIGORY (MIKHAYLOVICH) SHNEERSON
Musicologist
***Born* Yenisseysk, Siberia, Russia, 3 March 1901**
***Died* Moscow, USSR, 5 February 1982**

Grigory Shneerson was a prominent Soviet musicologist who came into disfavor during the cultural crackdowns of the late 1940s but eventually reestablished his ideological credentials and became a spokesman for the aesthetic doctrines promulgated by the Composers Union.

The Siberian-born Shneerson studied piano and music theory at the Petrograd Conservatory from 1915 to 1918 and then went to Moscow to take private lessons with Nikolay Metner and Konstantin Igumnov while supporting himself as an accompanist in the Moscow Proletkult drama studio. During the

1920s he was music director at several theaters in Moscow. By 1933 he was general secretary of the International Music Bureau and was building a reputation as a musicologist specializing in contemporary music of the United States, China, France, Germany, and England. The increase in cultural exchanges between the USSR and the United States brought on by the establishment of diplomatic relations in 1933 gave Shneerson access to U.S. music periodicals, whose contents he summarized for Soviet readers with comments on the superiority of Soviet art.

In 1935 Shneerson was made chief of the foreign bureau of the powerful Composers Union. In this post, which he held until 1940, he supervised all contacts made by Soviet composers with outsiders, including the mailing of scores for performance abroad. From 1942 to 1948 he filled a similar role as head of the music department of VOKS, the All-Union Society for Cultural Relations with Foreign Countries.

In 1948, a few months after the 30th anniversary of the October Revolution, Soviet composers were subjected to an ideological purge that cost many their jobs and put an end to experimentation with formalism and other modernist trends current in the West. The following year, the attack was extended to historians, critics, and theorists of music. Shneerson and 31 other musicologists were accused of contaminating Soviet music with decadent Western influences and were censured and blacklisted by the Union. A number of recantations followed, and by 1950 the chastised musicologists were at work on a new set of textbooks that followed more closely the tenets of Socialist Realism. Shneerson, who had become editor of the overseas section of the influential journal *Sovetskaya Muzyka* in 1948, was allowed to continue in the job and held it until 1961. In 1968 he was named president of the Soviet committee for *RILM* abstracts and was elected a corresponding member of East Germany's Academy of Arts.

Between 1949 and 1974 Shneerson published 15 books on Chinese and Western music and on the Soviet composer Aram Khatchaturian. In *Music in the Service of Reaction* (1952) he denounced American jazz as "demoralizing" and took Igor Stravinsky to task for having abandoned his homeland to become a "stateless composer" prostituting himself in the "American market of decadent aesthetics." Several of his books were published in foreign-language editions. J.P.

Education Petrograd Conservatory 1915–18; private studies, Moscow 1918, 1921–23. **Career** Pianist, drama studio, Moscow Proletkult early 1920s; music dir., several theaters in Moscow ca. 1920s; gen. secty., Intl. Music Bureau, Moscow 1931–35; head, Foreign Bureau, Composers Union 1935–40; head, Music Dept., VOKS (USSR Soc. for Cultural Relations with Foreign Countries) 1942–48; ed., Overseas Sect., *Sovetskaya Muzyka* jrnl. 1948–61; blacklisted for antipatriotic activities ca. 1949; pres., Soviet Cttee. for *RILM* (Intl. Repertory of Music Literature) abstracts from 1968. **Member** (Corresp.) Acad. of Arts, East Germany 1968. **Author** *Sovremennaya angliyskaya muzyka* [*Contemporary English Music*], 1949; *Sovremennaya amerikanskaya muzyka* [*Contemporary American Music*], 1949; [*Music in the Service of Reaction*], 1952; *Muzykalnaya kultura kitaya* [*Chinese Musical Culture*], 1952; (ed.) *Pesni narodov mira* [*Folksongs of the World*], 1955–57; *Kompozitor Sin Sin-khay* [*The Composer Sin Sin-hai*], 1956; *Aram Khachaturian*, 1958 (English ed. 1959); *Muzyka frantsii* [*The Music of France*], 1958; (ed.) *Stati kitayskikh kompozitorov i muzykovedov* [*Articles by Chinese Composers and Musicologists*], 1958; (ed.) Leopold Stokowski, *Muzyka dlya vsekh* [*Music for All of Us*], 1959; *O muzyka zhivoy i mertvoy* [*Music Living and Dead*], 1960; *Ernst Bush* [*Ernst Busch*], 1962; (ed.) *Zarubezhnaya literatura o muzyke,* [*Foreign Literature on Music*], 1962; *Frantsuzskaya musyka XX veka* [*French Music of the Twentieth Century*], 1964; *Ernst Bush i evo vremya* [*Ernst Busch and His Time*], 1971; *Muzykalnaya kultura narodov; traditsii i sovremennost* [*Musical Cultures of Peoples: Traditions and the Present*], 1973; *Izbranniye stati* [*Selected Articles*], 1974.

Further reading Boris Schwarz, *Music and Musical Life in Soviet Russia, 1917–1970,* 1972.

BEN NICHOLSON
Painter
***Born* Denham, Buckinghamshire, England, 10 April 1894**
***Died* London, England, 6 February 1982**

Ben Nicholson, the most prominent British abstract painter and one of the foremost modernists of his generation, was born into a family of painters. His father, Sir William Nicholson, was a popular painter of still lifes and landscapes; his mother and uncle, Mabel and James Pryde, were also successful artists. Nicholson was encouraged to paint from an early age, and after a brief attendance at Gresham's, a private school, and a period of private tuition, he entered the Slade School of Art in London in 1910. From the first, however, he showed a strong stubbornness and independence of mind, choosing to shun both the established art world and the affluent social milieu of art patronage in which his father, an elegant and witty man, figured prominently. After completing only a few terms of formal training at the Slade School, Nicholson began an independent course of study, traveling in France, Italy, and the United States. He was exempted from military service during World War I on grounds of ill health.

Nicholson's personal style was slow to form, and critics of his work have conjectured that his parents' encouragement, far from being beneficial, was a hindrance to his early development. His earliest paintings, which reveal the influence of his father's style, are still lifes of bottles and pitchers and fragmentary landscape sketches. His first experience of pre-Cubist art, notably the paintings of Cézanne, accentuated his inclination to depict objects two-dimensionally, but even when, during the early 1920s, he began to work in a semi-abstract style, he continued to draw his inspiration from nature and domestic objects. The principal influence on his early career was the Cubist Georges Braque, whose still lifes, like Nicholson's, are a marriage of figurative and abstract qualities.

Courtesy of André Emmerich Gallery

The single most important event of Nicholson's artistic life was his meeting in 1933 with Piet Mondrian, the austere Dutch painter who sought to purge all figurative and objective elements from his work. "All art," said Mondrian, "expresses the rectangular relationship," a dictum that Nicholson took to heart and that inspired him to create a series of relief compositions. These hybrid works, which are both paintings and sculptures, consist of squares and circles incised in, or applied to, wooden rectangles. Many of the most successful examples were executed in white in an attempt to create an abstraction of absolute purity. John Russell wrote in *The New York Times* after Nicholson's death: "There was something of sculpture, something of architecture, and something of painting in the ordered limpidity of these simple-seeming statements. If there is such a thing as perfection in art, these reliefs laid claim to it." Other critics considered them dry and repetitive. After his meeting with Mondrian, Nicholson became an active member of the British avant-garde, joining a group of artists and architects called Unit One and participating in the Paris exhibitions of Abstraction-Création, a group of French abstract painters. In 1937 he joined with the Constructivist sculptor Naum Gabo and the architect J. L. Martin to edit *Circle,* a short-lived journal of Constructivist art.

During the 1930s Nicholson remained attracted to the aims of pure abstraction pursued by Mondrian and Gabo, and continued to make relief paintings that exploit delicate spatial relationships between planes of pale color. He attributed his interest in form to the work of his second wife, the abstract sculptor Barbara Hepworth, with whom he moved in

1940 to the small Cornish fishing town and artistic community of St. Ives. After the war, however, he returned to the depiction of natural objects and he began to use warmer, brighter colors. In the still lifes and landscapes of his later years—much of which he spent in Switzerland, Italy, and the Aegean—he reconciled his attraction to pure form with his impulse to record the natural world by developing a style that combines architectonic forms with the more random shapes of nature in linear patterns. "I think that so far from being a limited expression understood by a few," he wrote, "abstract art is a powerful, unlimited, and universal language."

"It is Nicholson's historic achievement," wrote Patrick Heron in an evaluation in the *Manchester Guardian,* "to have united within his personal idiom both cubism and constructivism; both an essentially English linearity and a plastic granularity of expansive blank surfaces which is classical and which carries us to the stone and marble surfaces of Greece and the Mediterranean."

It was not until after World War II, when abstract art began to win both academic and popular recognition, that Nicholson's work became widely admired. Thereafter he won many honors, of which the most notable were the first prize at the Carnegie International Art Exhibition in Pittsburgh in 1952, which first brought him to international attention; the 1954 Ulisse Prize at the Venice Biennale; and the 1956 Guggenheim International Award. His 1954 retrospective toured France, Belgium, Holland, and Italy. He received the Order of Merit, Britain's highest artistic award, in 1968, and mounted his second retrospective at the Tate Gallery in 1969.

After the breakup of his marriage to Hepworth in the 1950s, Nicholson remarried and settled in London, where he continued to work on large abstract reliefs and paintings until his death at the age of 87. H.B.

Parents Sir William N., painter, and Mabel (Pryde) N. **Married** (1) Winifred Dacre Roberts, painter and writer (div.): Jake; Kate; one other son. (2) Barbara Hepworth, sculptor, 1931 (div.): Simon; Sarah; one other daughter. (3) Felicitas Vogler, writer and photographer, 1957. **Education** Haddon Court, Cockfosters; Gresham Sch., London; Slade Sch. of Art, London 1910–11; studied art in Europe 1912–14, Pasadena, CA 1918. **Career** Artist since early 1910s; joined Assn. Abstraction-Création, Paris 1933; member, Unit One 1933–35; co-ed., *Circle: International Survey of Constructivist Art,* London 1937. **Honors** First prize for painting, 39th Pittsburgh Intl. Exhib. 1952; Ulisse Prize, Venice Biennale 1954; Gov. of Tokyo Award, 3rd Intl. Exhib., Tokyo 1955; Grand Prix, 4th Intl. Exhib., Lugano, Switzerland 1956; Major Painting Prize, Guggenheim Foundn., NYC 1956; Intl. Prize for Painting, 4th São Paulo Bienal 1957; O.M. 1968; Rembrandt Prize, Goethe Foundn. 1974. **Solo exhibitions** Adelphi Gall., London 1924; Lefevre Gall., London 1932, 1935, 1937, 1939, 1945, 1947, 1948, 1950, 1952, 1954; Durlacher Gall., NYC 1951, 1952, 1955, 1956; retrospective, Stedelijk Mus., Amsterdam 1954; retrospectives, Tate Gall., London 1955, 1969, 1970; Gimpel Fits Gall., London 1955, 1957, 1959, 1960; Galerie Charles Lienhardt, Zurich 1959, 1960, 1962; Kestner Gesellschaft, Hanover, touring show 1959, 1967; Emmerich Gall., NYC 1961, 1965, 1974; Kunsthalle, Berlin 1961; Kunstmuseum, St. Gallen, Switzerland 1963; Marlborough Fine Art Gall., London 1963, 1967, 1970, 1971, 1972; retrospective, Dallas Mus. of Fine Art 1964; Crane Kallman Gall., London 1964, 1968, 1974; Fischer Fine Art Gall., London 1974; Redfern Gall., London 1974; Galerie Andre Emmerich, Zurich 1975; Waddington Galls., London 1976, 1978, 1980; Kasahara Gall., Osaka 1977; galls. in London, Dusseldorf, Milan, Brussels, Rome, many others. **Group exhibitions** Patterson's Gall., London 1923; Lefevre Gall., 1928, 1933, 1946; MOMA 1936, 1947–48; 39th Pittsburgh Intl. Exhib., Carnegie Inst. 1952; Venice Biennale 1954; 3rd Intl. Exhib., Tokyo 1955; 4th São Paulo Bienal 1957; retrospective, Crane Kallman Gall., London 1966; Palais des Beaux-Arts, Brussels 1973; galls. in Basel, Paris, London, many others. **Collections** Art

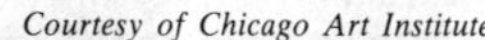
Courtesy of Chicago Art Institute

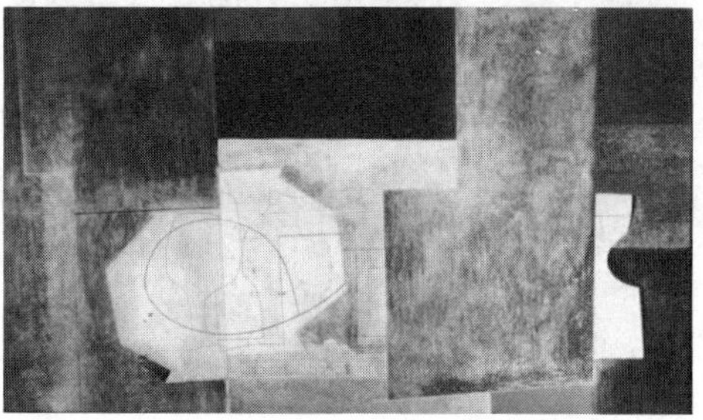

Gallery of Ontario, Toronto; Scottish Natl. Gall. of Modern Art, Edinburgh; Los Angeles County Mus. of Art; Neue Nationalgalerie, Berlin; MOMA; Stedelijk van Abbemuseum, Eindhoven, Netherlands; Kunsthaus, Zurich; Arts Council of Great Britain, British Council, and Tate Gall., London; Birmingham City Mus. and Art Gall., Leeds City Art Gall., Whitworth Art Gall. of Manchester, and Manchester City Art Gall., England; Albright-Knox Art Gall., Buffalo, NY; Carnegie Inst., Pittsburgh; Detroit Inst. of Arts; Walker Art Center, Minneapolis; Guggenheim Mus., NYC; others. **Author** of articles on abstract art in art jrnls.

Further reading James Throll Soby, *Contemporary Painters—Ben Nicholson,* 1949; J. P. Hodin, *Ben Nicholson, the Meaning of His Art,* 1957; John Russell, *Ben Nicholson: Drawings, Paintings and Reliefs 1911–1968,* 1969; J. Reichardt, "Ben Nicholson Now,"in *Art International,* Oct. 1971.

JOHN HAY WHITNEY

Diplomat, publisher, investor, and sportsman
***Born* Ellsworth, Maine, USA, 17 August 1904**
***Died* Manhasset, New York, USA, 8 February 1982**

John Hay Whitney, scion of one of the greatest American fortunes, made a prominent mark in many fields of endeavor. He was an investor and philanthropist, newspaper publisher and movie mogul, horse breeder and racing enthusiast, and served during Pres. Dwight Eisenhower's second term as ambassador to Britain, adroitly smoothing relations between the two allies following the Suez crisis.

Known as "Jock" from early childhood, Whitney was born in 1904 while his parents were vacationing in Maine. His maternal grandfather and namesake, John Hay, had been Pres. Lincoln's private secretary and biographer, and secretary of state in the William McKinley and Theodore Roosevelt administrations. Hay had also been ambassador to Britain. His paternal grandfather was William Collins Whitney, who had made millions in street railways and real estate, and had been Secretary of the Navy under Pres. Grover Cleveland. Following family tradition, Jock Whitney was sent to Groton and Yale, where he played polo and stroked for the crew. His postgraduate studies in literature at New College, Oxford University, were interrupted in 1927 by the death of his father, the philanthropist Payne Whitney, and young Whitney returned to the United States to take over the family fortune.

Like many young men of his class, Whitney held, for a short time, a menial job on Wall Street, but soon left to devote himself to more important affairs. In 1933 he set up Pioneer Pictures, which intended to make short subjects in Technicolor. He later greatly expanded his interest in movies by joining with David Selznick to form Selznick International Pictures, of which Whitney was the New York-based chairman. His greatest success was in buying the screen rights to the then-unpublished novel by Margaret Mitchell, *Gone with the Wind,* and in insisting that the company spend the enormous sum (for the time) of $4.25 million to make the film as authentic as possible. *Gone with the Wind* became one of the greatest hits in movie history, earning $74 million by 1976. Other Selznick International successes included *A Star Is Born, The Prisoner of Zenda,* and *Rebecca.* Whitney also made astute investments in the Broadway stage, most notably in *Life With Father,* one of the theater's longest-running shows, and *A Streetcar Named Desire.*

During the 1930s, Whitney's reputation was that of a millionaire sportsman with a knack for clever investments. He owned large strings of horses in America and England, and his many homes and lavish parties on both sides of the Atlantic cost gigantic sums of money. He was player-manager of a successful polo team which he funded himself; the team, called Greentree after his Long Island estate, won two successive U.S. championships before being disbanded in 1940.

The coming of World War II brought great changes to Whitney's life. He liquidated most of his Hollywood holdings, was divorced from his socialite wife of ten years, and entered national service in the Office of the Coordinator of Inter-American Affairs under Nelson Rockefeller, where he headed the motion-picture division. He left Washington two years later to attend officers candidate school, was commissioned a captain in the Air Corps, and served in Britain and the Mediterranean theater. In 1944 he was captured by the Germans in southern France but managed to escape and rejoin the advancing Allied armies. For his war service he received the Legion of Merit and the Bronze Star, and was named a commander of the Order of the British Empire and a chevalier in France's Legion of Honor. He had married a second time in 1942, to Betsey Cushing Roosevelt, the first wife of Pres. Franklin Roosevelt's eldest son, James, and later adopted their two daughters.

In 1946 he initiated three major enterprises. With one part of his fortune he founded a venture-capital investment house, J. H. Whitney & Co., which quickly began to make money in chemicals and frozen orange juice. A second part went to form the John Hay Whitney Foundation, a philanthropy that provided fellowships for educators and college students until 1972 and thereafter funded community development projects. A third part comprised his private holdings in investments and real estate.

Courtesy of Whitney Communications

A lifelong Republican of the moderate-to-liberal persuasion, Whitney was a substantial contributor to both of Pres. Eisenhower's campaigns, yet accepted only with reluctance the appointment to the Court of St. James. He served as ambassador from 1957 to 1961, each year spending at least $100,000 of his own funds in that most costly U.S. diplomatic post, and in the end was given much credit for the improvement in Anglo-American relations after the dangerous disagreements that arose over Suez in 1956.

While still ambassador, Whitney purchased a controlling interest in the *New York Herald Tribune,* and as editor in chief and publisher set out to make the long-ailing newspaper a financial success. This he was never able to do, despite the infusion of $40 million of his own money into the enterprise. The paper closed in 1966, although its Paris-based international edition, which Whitney also acquired, continues to be moderately successful. Other media investments by Whitney Communications were in the Sunday newspaper supplement *Parade,* in the magazines *Art in America* and *Interior Design,* in community newspapers, and in cable television.

His interest in horse breeding and racing never faltered. In 1944, upon the death of his mother, Helen Hay Whitney, who was called in her time the First Lady of the American Turf, Whitney and his sister, Joan Whitney Payson (who was later to become principal owner of the New York Mets baseball team), took over the management of their mother's Greentree Stud in Lexington, Kentucky, and Greentree Stable on Long Island. Their horses enjoyed regular successes at the track as Jock tried to follow advice his mother had given him—to learn to lose as if you like it, and to win as if you're used to it. "I have found myself on occasion, unfortunately, winning very vociferously," Whitney admitted. He was chairman of the American Thoroughbred Breeders Association, president of the Thoroughbred Racing Association, governor of the Turf and Field Club, and steward of the Jockey Club.

Whitney owned one of the world's largest private collections of Impressionist and post-Impressionist art, including Renoir's celebrated *Le moulin de la galette.* He served for several years as chairman of the Museum of Modern Art, New York, and vice president of the National Gallery in Washington. His treasures were divided among his many residences, which included his Long Island estate; several apartments and a town house in New

York; estates on Fishers Island in Long Island Sound, Saratoga Springs, New York, and Thomasville, Georgia; a cottage on the Augusta National golf course in Georgia; and a flat in London. His fortune was estimated shortly before his death to be in excess of $200 million. A.K.

Parents Payne W., philanthropist, and Helen (Hay) W., horse breeder. **Married** (1) Mary Elizabeth Altemus, socialite, 1930 (div. 1940). (2) Betsey Cushing Roosevelt 1942: Sara Wilford; Kate (stepdaughters). **Education** Miss Chapin's Sch.; Groton Sch. 1916–22; Yale Univ., B.A. 1926; New Coll., Oxford 1926–27. **Mil. service** Officers candidate sch. 1942; capt., 8th USAAC Combat Intelligence Div., U.K. 1942; col. and liaison officer, Comdr., Allied Air Forces, North Africa 1943; POW 1944 (escaped). **Career** Clerk, Lee Higginson & Co., NYC 1929; dir., Pan American Airways 1931–42; bd. chmn., Freeport Sulphur Co. 1932–42, 1948–57; cofounder, Pioneer Pictures 1933; bd. chmn., Selznick Intl. Pictures 1935–40; capt., Greentree polo team 1930s; founder, Wharton-Gabel Corp. theatrical investment firm 1940; dir., Motion Picture Div., Office of Coordinator of Inter-American Affairs 1940–42; co-owner, Greentree Stud, Lexington, KY, and Greentree Stable, L.I., NY, since 1944; special advisor and consultant on public affairs, U.S. State Dept. 1945; founding chmn., J. H. Whitney Foundn. since 1946; founding partner, J. H. Whitney & Co. since 1946; ambassador to U.K. 1957–61; bd. chmn., Whitney Communications Corp. since 1958; publisher 1958–66 and ed. in chief 1961–66, *New York Herald Tribune;* dir. and member of editorial cttee., *World Journal Tribune* 1966–67; chmn., *International Herald Tribune* since 1967; dir., Dun and Bradstreet Cos., Inc. 1971–75; partner, Whitcom Investment Co.; dir., Great Northern Paper Co. and Publications Research Corp. • Commn. member: New York Racing Commns. 1934–43; (vice chmn.) Secty. of State's Public Cttee. on Personnel (Wriston Cttee.) 1954–55; Randall Commn. on Foreign Economic Policy 1954; Pres.'s Commn. on Education Beyond High Sch. 1956; U.S. Natl. Commn. for UNESCO; New York State Youth Commn. **Officer** Dir.: Educational Broadcasting Corp. 1969–70; Corp. for Public Broadcasting 1970–72; Friends of the Whitney Mus. of American Art; Amer. Soc. of the French Legion of Honor; Saratoga Assn. for Improvement of Breeding of Horses. • Pres.: MOMA film library since 1935; MOMA 1941; Thoroughbred Racing Assn. • Trustee: MOMA 1930–76; North Shore Hosp., Manhasset, NY 1950–73; New York Racing Assn. 1955–81; Carnegie Endowment for Natl. Peace 1961–64; Natl. Gallery of Art, Wash. DC 1961–79; Saratoga Performing Arts Center 1963–77; Natl. Mus. of Racing; U.S. Trust Co.; Cttee. for Economic Development; Natl. Planning Assn. • V.P.: Saratoga Performing Arts Center 1963–72; Natl. Gall. of Art, Wash. DC 1963–79; Westchester Racing Assn.; Pilgrims of the United States. • Chmn.: MOMA 1946–56; finance cttee., Citizens for Eisenhower-Nixon 1952; United Republican Finance Cttee. 1954–57; natl. bd., English-Speaking Union 1961–63; bd., Amer. Thoroughbred Breeders Assn. • Gov.: New York Hosp. 1927–74; Turf and Field Club; Ditchley Foundn. Ltd.: Hundred Year Assn. of New York. • Other: steward, Jockey Club 1928–80; fellow 1955–70 and sr. fellow 1970–73, Yale Corp.; bd. member, *Scientific American.* **Member** Cttee. on Foreign Affairs, Carnegie Endowment for Natl. Peace 1962; Saratoga Springs Commn. 1971–74; Republican Party; New York State Banking Bd.; (grad. member) Business Council; Business Cttee. for the Arts; Helen Hay Whitney Foundn.; Univ. Council, Yale. • Clubs: Royal and Ancient; White's; Buck's; Scroll and Key; Augusta Natl. Golf; New York Yacht; Racquet and Tennis; Yale; Links; Knickerbocker; River; Meadow Brook. **Honors** Won two U.S. Open polo championships as capt. of Greentree team 1930s; Legion of Merit and Bronze Star 1945; CBE, U.K. 1948; gold medal, Hundred Year Assn. 1953; Yale Medal 1954; Tuition Plan Award, Yale Univ. 1955; hon. fellow, New Coll., Oxford 1957; Einstein Commemorative Award 1957; chevalier, Légion d'Honneur, France 1962; assoc. kt., Order of the Hosp. of St. John of Jerusalem, U.K. 1963; Franklin Medal, Royal Soc. of Arts, London 1963; Lovejoy Award, Colby Coll. 1964; St. Bernard's Associates Award 1974; John Hay Whitney Professorship in the

Humanities established in his name, Yale Univ. 1977; La Grande Médaille du Vermeil, Paris; hon. trustee, MOMA; hon. member, Jockey Club of U.K.; hon degrees from univs. of Yale, Colgate, Brown, Exeter, and Columbia, and from Kenyon and Colby colls.

Further reading E. J. Kahn, Jr., *Jock,* 1981.

MARTHE RICHARD

Allied secret agent and campaigner against houses of prostitution
***Born* Blamont, Meurthe-et-Moselle, France, 15 April 1889**
***Died* Paris, France, 9 February 1982**

Marthe Richard was a spy for French military intelligence during World War I and worked for the Resistance during World War II. In 1945, as a member of the Paris Municipal Council, she demanded that the state-licensed brothels in France be declared illegal; the act which outlawed them was popularly given her name.

Born Marthe Betenfeld in Lorraine, eastern France, the daughter of a military officer, she had a troubled youth and escaped from a reform school at the age of 17. She married an attorney, Henri Richer, and became one of the first woman parachutists and aviators, receiving her pilot's license at the age of 22 in 1912. She was familiar with firearms and an expert driver and spoke several languages fluently, including German. When her husband was killed in May 1916 at the Battle of Verdun, she was recruited by Capt. Ladoux, chief of military intelligence, to seduce Baron Hans von Krohn, the German naval attaché and espionage chief of Spain.

Once in San Sebastián, site of a large German enclave, Richard—the name she had adopted as her *nom de guerre*—quickly got to meet von Krohn, who fell deeply in love with her. The Germans, thinking they had ensnared her as their agent, sent her back to Paris with instructions to obtain figures on armament production; she returned to Spain with false information, then secured for the French true details of the German submarine U-52, which she had inspected at Cádiz in von Krohn's company. Von Krohn then sent her on a mission to Argentina, carrying instructions to German agents and several vials of a powerful chemical intended to contaminate Allied grain stores; but neither instructions nor poisons reached their targets.

Richard proposed a plan to kidnap von Krohn and intern him in France, but Capt. Ladoux preferred that she stay in Spain as a spy within the German colony. She remained there as von Krohn's mistress for two more years, admitting her duplicity to him before returning home. Much of her espionage work was done at her own expense because the intelligence service was pathetically short of funds.

After the war, Richard was awarded the Légion d'Honneur and became the subject of a series of best sellers describing her exploits. She published several books of her own, including *I Spied for France,* which came out in French and English editions in 1935. About the same time, a popular film, *Marthe Richard, Spy,* was released starring Edwige Feuillère in the title role and Erich von Stroheim as von Krohn. Her second husband, the Englishman Thomas Crompton, a director of the Rockefeller Foundation, died in 1928.

During the Nazi occupation, Richard helped set up a kind of underground railroad to facilitate the escape of Allied airmen who had been shot down over France. As an employee of the Vichy Air Ministry, she was able to forge documents for the flyers, whom she hid in her apartment under the noses of German officials.

Richard was elected to the Paris Municipal Council after the liberation, and immediately mounted a furious campaign against the city's 178 licensed and medically supervised houses of prostitution. Young women were encouraged to become prostitutes, she said, because it was the only well-paying employment open to them—a typical salesgirl earned less than 7,000 francs per month, a prostitute more than five times that amount—and they were kept in perpetual debt by the brothel owners. She demanded an end to discrimination against women in industrial hiring and a program of vocational training for ex-prostitutes. "I was not concerned about the pleasure given to men," she explained later, "only about the hurt given to women." The powerful brothel owners, organized into the Friendly Society of Furnished Hotel Keepers, fought her hard, even instigating a suit against her which claimed that she had accepted money for the release of a German prisoner after the liberation, but she was acquitted of the charge.

In 1946 all prostitution was declared illegal in France under the Richard Law; the following year Richard ran for reelection and was defeated. Her suggestions for economic rehabilitation projects were never enacted, and by 1970 there were 35,000 illegal prostitutes in Paris.

In 1952, Richard made new headlines when she declared herself in favor of *maisons de rendezvous*—government-sponsored apartments where prostitutes could entertain clients and lovers could meet in safety. "I'm not against sex, with or without love," she said. "But it should be free—not exploited as it was in the days of the officially recognized houses of tolerance. I am convinced that free love is the only solution." In 1973, when she was 84, she supported a plan to establish "Eros Centers" on the model of those in Germany. She died at the age of 92. A.K./J.P.

Born Marthe Betenfeld; code name L'alouette. **Father** a military officer. **Married** (1) Henri Richer, lawyer, ca. 1907 (d. 1916). (2) Thomas Crompton, dir. of Rockefeller Foundn. (d. 1928). **Career** Pilot and parachutist from 1912; founder, Patriotic Union of the Airwomen of France ca. 1915; spy for French military intelligence, Spain 1916–18; worked for Vichy Air Ministry and organized escape routes for the Resistance, WWII; member, Paris Municipal Council 1945–47. **Honors** Chevalier, Légion d'Honneur 1933. **Author** *Mon destin de femme* [*My Womanly Destiny*], 1924; *Ma vie d'espionne au service de la France,* 1935 (trans. as *I Spied for France,* 1935); *Espions de guerre et de la paix* [*Spies of War and Peacetime*], 1938; *Faire face* [*Confront*], 1947; *Mes dernières missions secrètes, 1936–39* [*My Last Secret Missions*].

ELEANOR (TORREY) POWELL

Dancer and actress

***Born* Springfield, Massachusetts, USA, 21 November 1912**

***Died* Beverly Hills, California, USA, 11 February 1982**

Courtesy of MGM Studios

Eleanor Powell, billed as "the world's greatest feminine tap dancer"—she once said "I'd rather dance than eat"—starred in a series of Metro-Goldwyn-Mayer musical extravaganzas of the 1930s and 1940s.

Powell began studying ballet at the age of six. When she was 13, revue producer Gus Edwards spotted her doing gymnastics on the beach at Atlantic City and hired her to perform classical dance routines in a local club. In 1928 she debuted with the Co-Optimists troupe in New York City and took up the study of tap dancing. After ten lessons she had learned to tap with machine-gun rapidity—up to five taps a second.

Powell was 17 when she appeared in her first Broadway show, *Follow Through* (1929). She was cast in *Fine and Dandy* (1929), Flo Ziegfeld's *Hot-Cha* (1932), *George White's Scandals* (1932), and had a guest spot in MGM's film version of *George White's Scandals of 1935.* The following year she was given the lead in MGM's *Broadway Melody of 1936,* was an instant success, and was signed to a seven-year contract with the studio.

Her first substantial movie role was in *Born to Dance* (1936), in which she tapped and sang her way through several elaborately staged numbers, including a finale atop a full-scale set of a battleship complete with sequined cannon fired by singing sailors. MGM followed up with a series of lavish productions, many under the direction of Roger Edens, that were little more than showcases for her tapping ability, among them *Broadway Melody of 1938, Rosalie,* and *Honolulu.* She reached the peak of her film career with *Broadway Melody of 1940,* in which her rapid-fire precision and sweeping style were matched with the elegance and sophistication of Fred Astaire.

After a string of lesser films in the early 1940s, Powell married actor Glenn Ford in 1943, and by 1946 had retired from show business to raise her son. Her last film, *The Duchess of Idaho,* was released in 1950. A devout Presbyterian, she taught Sunday school through the 1950s and from 1953 to 1956 starred in her own televised religion program, "Faith of Our Children," for which she won five Emmy Awards. Following her divorce from Ford in 1959, she embarked on a brief but well-received comeback, dancing in musical revues in Las Vegas and New York. She died of cancer. S.A.

Married Glenn Ford, actor, 1943 (div. 1959); Peter, b. 1946. **Religion** Presbyterian. **Education** High sch., Springfield, MA; ballet lessons; tap-dancing lessons, NYC late 1920s. **Career** Dancer and actress in nightclub revues 1925–35 and 1960–64, in Broadway musicals 1929–36, in films 1935–50; Sunday sch. teacher 1940s–50s; creator and actress 1953–56, "Faith of Our Children" TV series. **Honors** Emmy Award five times, for "Faith of Our Children," 1953–56; Brother Award, for "Faith of Our Children," Natl. Conference of Christians and Jews. **Revues** Ritz Grill, Atlantic City, NJ 1925; *Co-Optimists,* NYC 1928; *Follow Through,* NYC 1929; *Fine and Dandy,* NYC 1929; *Hot-Cha,* NYC 1932; *George White's Scandals,* 1932; *At Home Abroad,* NYC 1936; solo shows, Las Vegas and NYC 1961; others. **Films** *George White's Scandals of 1935; Broadway Melody of 1936,* 1935; *Born To Dance,* 1936; *Broadway Melody of 1938,* 1937; *Rosalie,* 1938; *Honolulu,* 1939; *Broadway Melody of 1940,* 1939; *Lady Be Good,* 1941; *Ship Ahoy,* 1942; *I Dood It!,* 1943; *Thousands Cheer,* 1943; *Sensations of 1945,* 1944; *The Duchess of Idaho,* 1950; *That's Entertainment,* 1974.

TAKASHI SHIMURA
Film actor
***Born* Hyogo prefecture, Japan, 1905**
***Died* Tokyo, Japan, 11 February 1982**

Takashi Shimura was known to millions of movie aficionados in Japan and the West as the formidable *ronin* who led a small band of warriors in a heroic battle to save a farming village from bandits in Akira Kurosawa's classic 1954 film *Shichinin no Samurai (Seven Samurai).* Long a member of Kurosawa's acting team, he appeared in most of the director's finest films, including *Rashomon* and *Ikiru.*

Born in Hyogo prefecture on the island of Honshu, Shimura began his career as a stage actor in the 1930s before joining the Toho film studios in 1941. His first film, *The Last Days of Edo* (1941), was undistinguished, but Kurosawa gave him a small part in his own first film, *Sanshiro Sugata,* a commercially successful judo epic, and later hired him to play the embittered, alcoholic doctor who nurses a gangster back to health in *Yoidore Tenshi* (1948; *Drunken Angel).* The deftness of Shimura's performance impressed Kurosawa, and he became part of a group of actors, also including Toshiro Mifune and Seiji Miyaguchi, whom Kurosawa used again and again, often casting them in a film before writing the script in order to fit the role to the talent. Shimura played the woodcutter in *Rashomon* (1950), the dying businessman who redeems his wasted life by an act of social

Courtesy of Japan Society

virtue in *Ikiru* (1952; *Living),* and the man driven mad by the specter of thermonuclear annihilation in *Ikimono no Kiroku* (1955; *Record of a Living Being).* His sensitivity, restraint, and physical control were especially well used in *Seven Samurai,* a film whose emotional impact depends to a large extent on his interpretation of the pivotal character of Kambei, the disciplined and courageous samurai leader.

Although Shimura worked for other directors—he appeared in several low-budget science-fiction films for the Honda studios, the best known of which was *Godzilla, King of the Monsters* (1954)—only Kurosawa seemed to know how to bring out his powers as an actor. Among Shimura's later films for Kurosawa were *Kumonosu-jo* (1957; *Throne of Blood), Warui Yatsu Hodo Yoku Nemuru* (1960; *The Bad Sleep Well), Yojimbo* (1961), *Tengoku to Jugoku* (1963; *High and Low),* and *Akahige* (1965; *Red Beard).* He was awarded Japan's Medal of Honor with Purple Ribbon in 1976 and the Order of the Rising Sun, Fourth Class, in 1980 for his contributions to the performing arts. When he made his last film for Kurosawa, *Kagemusha* (1979), he was already suffering from the pulmonary emphysema of which he died. S.A./J.P.

Married Masako. **Career** Stage actor 1930s; film actor, Toho studios from early 1940s, Honda studios from mid-1950. **Honors** Medal of Honor with Purple Ribbon 1976; Order of Rising Sun, 4th Class, 1980. **Films** [*The Last Days of Edo*], 1941; *Sanshiro Sugata,* 1943; [*The Most Beautiful*], 1944; [*They Who Step on the Tiger's Tail*], 1945; [*Those Who Make Tomorrow*], 1946; [*No Regrets for Our Youth*], 1946; [*Snow Trail*], 1947; *Yoidore Tenshi* (rel. as *Drunken Angel*), 1948; [*The Quiet Duel*], 1949; [*Stray Dog*], 1949; [*Scandal*], 1950; *Rashomon,* 1950; [*Sanshiro at Ginza*], 1950, *Hakuchi* (rel. as *The Idiot*), 1951; [*Stolen Love*], 1951; *Ikiru* (rel. as *Living*), 1952; [*Eagle of the Pacific*], 1953; *Geisha Konatsu,* 1954; [*Godzilla, King of the Monsters*], 1954; *Shichinin no Samurai* (rel. as *Seven Samurai*), 1954; [*Mother's First Love*], 1954; [*Last Embrace*], 1955; [*No Response from Car 33*], 1955; [*The Tears of the Geisha Konatsu*], 1955; *Ikimono no Kiroku* (rel. as *Record of a Living Being* and *I Live in Fear*), 1955; [*No Time for Tears*], 1955; [*The Grass Whistle*], 1955; [*Godzilla's Counterattack*], 1955; [*I Saw the Killer*], 1956; [*Musashi and Kojiro*], 1956; [*The Lord Takes a Bride*], 1957; *Kumonosu-jo* (rel. as *Throne of Blood*), 1957; [*The Mysterians*], 1957; [*The Dead End*], 1958; *Kakushi Toride no San-akunin* (rel. as *The Hidden Fortress*), 1958; [*The High Flying Bride*], 1959; *Tetsuwan Toshu Inao Monogatari,* 1959; [*Samurai Saga*], 1959; [*The Three Treasures*], 1959; *Shobushi to Sono Musume,* 1959; [*I Bombed Pearl Harbor*], 1960; [*Man Against Man*], 1960; *Warui Yatsu Hodo Yoku Nemuru* (rel. as *The Bad Sleep Well*), 1960; *Yojimbo,* 1961; [*Challenge to Live*], 1961; *Tsubaki Sanjuro* (rel. as *Sanjuro*), 1962; [*Gorath, Killer Whale*], 1962; *Chushingura* (rel. as *The Loyal 47 Ronin*), 1962; *Tengoku to Jugoku* (rel. as *High and Low*), 1963; *Kwaidan,* 1964; [*Ghidrah, the Three-Headed Monster*], 1965; *Akahige* (rel. as *Red Beard*), 1965; [*The Soundless Cry*], 1965; [*Night in Bangkok*], 1965; [*The Retreat from Kisha*], 1965; [*Frankenstein Conquers the World*], 1966; [*The Harbor of No Return*], 1966; [*The Emperor and a General*], 1967; [*Industrial Spy*], 1968; [*The Bride from Hades*], 1968; [*Zatoichi's Conspiracy*], 1974; *Kagemusha,* 1979; [*The Love and Faith of Ogin*], 1982; others.

Further reading Donald Richie, *The Films of Akira Kurosawa,* 1970.

FERNANDO VALERA (APARICIO)
Spanish Republican official
***Born* Spain, circa 1899**
***Died* Paris, France, 13 February 1982**

Fernando Valera Aparicio was a minister in the Republican government that ended shortly after the Spanish Civil War began in 1936. He became a leader and eventually the last president of the Republican government-in-exile during Francisco Franco's dictatorship (1939–75).

In the early 1930s, Valera was a founder of the Radical Socialist Republican Party, which was a participant in the Popular Front government. He served in that government in a succession of posts that included general director of agriculture (1932) and industry (1936) and undersecretary of justice (1934) and public works (1937). He was undersecretary for communications when the civil war broke out. Most of the surviving Republicans, Valera among them, fled Spain following Franco's ultimate triumph in 1939, and from foreign bases—principally Paris and Mexico City—steadfastly proclaimed their exiled government's legitimacy and condemned Franco as a usurper. Valera continued to be an effective Republican publicist, raised money to support the government, and held the ministries of finance and domestic and international relations. In 1971 he succeeded Claudio Sánchez Albornoz as president.

In the early 1970s, near the end of Franco's life, when all could see change coming in Spain, the aging Republicans realized their hour would not come again. "When Franco dies," Valera admitted in 1974, "the Republican government won't take over. We're getting old and we'll disappear soon. But our ideas will survive." Many of his colleagues returned to Spain following democratic elections in 1977, and his government-in-exile voted to return the archives of the Republic to the Spanish state. Valera, however, would not go back, believing that the monarchy had been illegally restored and that his government's legitimacy had not been weakened by events. "I can't live in a society without Republican laws and institutions," he said in a 1977 interview. "*I* would not be returning to Spain, only my body without my soul."

Valera was, since 1924, a dedicated member of the Freemasons. He was buried in Montparnasse Cemetery in Paris. A.K.

Religion Roman Catholic. **Career** Co-founder, and member of Natl. Exec. Cttee., Radical Socialist Republican Party early 1930s. • With Republican govt.: pres., Republican candidature, municipal elections 1931; constituent rep. and first secty. of Constitution Cttee. 1931; gen. dir. of agriculture 1932; undersecty. of justice ca. 1934; rep., Republican Union 1936; gen. dir. of industry 1936; undersecty. of communications 1936; undersecty. of public works 1937; member, Permanent Court Delegation. • With Republican govt.-in-exile, France and Mexico ca. 1939–77; gen. dir. of information; minister of finance; minister of domestic and intl. relations; v.p., council of ministers 1946–71; minister of the House 1949; pres. 1971–77. **Member** Mason, 33°. **Author** *Liberalismo* [*Liberalism*], 1930; *Introducción al estudio de la filosofía* [*Introduction to the Study of Philosophy*], 1930; *Tópicos revolucionarios* [*Revolutionary Topics*], 1931; *Alma republicana* [*Republican Soul*], 1935; *El sendero inmóvil* [*The Fixed Path*], 1944; (trans). N. J. Spykman, *Estados Unidos frente al mundo,* 1944; "Diálogo de las Españas," "Reivindicación de un pueblo calumniado," and "Evolución de España," nos. 3–5 in series *Documentas y estudios sobre la República española,* 1967–68.

NOAH DIETRICH
Chief aide to Howard Hughes
***Born* Batavia, Wisconsin, USA, 28 February 1889**
***Died* Palm Springs, California, USA, 15 February 1982**

Noah Dietrich was, for more than 32 years, the director of the financial empire owned by Howard Hughes, the bizarre, reclusive billionaire industrialist. His book about their association, *Howard, The Amazing Mr. Hughes* (1971), was very popular and generally accepted as being an insider's authentic account.

Dietrich, the son of a Methodist minister, was a self-taught accountant who left home in Wisconsin at 18 to take a job as a bank clerk in a frontier town in New Mexico. He moved to Los Angeles in 1911 to work as an auditor in a real-estate company. He became a certified public accountant in 1923 and met Hughes two years later. The 19-year-old millionaire had just inherited $1.3 million in the Hughes Tool Company, the principal manufacturer of oil drilling bits, and needed a financially astute assistant.

Dietrich's starting salary was $10,000 a year, very considerable for the 1920s. He supervised the Hughes investments, some of which were hugely successful, although Dietrich claimed that the real money was not made until after World War II. As an example, the large Hughes interest in Trans-World Airlines grew in value from $12.3 million to $560 million by the time it was sold. Extensive real estate speculation during the southern California land boom made even greater profits. The Hughes Aircraft Corporation became one of the most important defense contractors.

Hughes's failures attracted more publicity. He lost millions for RKO Pictures, though he improved his own investment by the time he left the company. His most famous disaster was the huge plywood seaplane, popularly called the Spruce Goose, which flew only once.

Although Dietrich was a gifted money manager, Hughes kept the spotlight all to himself. "Noah," he was reported to have said, "you stay in the background and let the public get the impression that I'm the big business figure." Dietrich did Hughes's bidding for more than three decades—including bribing the husbands and fathers of Hughes's paramours when necessary—yet had no respect for him as a man: "He never had any friends. He didn't want any friends. He never did a humane act to my knowledge, except with an ulterior motive." Yet Dietrich loved his job. "It was 24 hours a day, two vacations in 32 years, and he'd call me at three A.M. just as readily as he would at three in the afternoon. But it was a challenge, and it was exciting, a conflict between an orthodox businessman on one side and an unorthodox playboy on the other."

Dietrich split from the Hughes empire in 1957 in a bitter dispute over Hughes's management style and Dietrich's salary, which by then had grown to half a million dollars a year, plus expenses. He sued Hughes for $2.1 million in severance compensation and settled out of court for a substantial portion of that.

His book, in addition to being one of the few reliable accounts of Hughes's life—the subject of hundreds of books and articles—was also part of a literary controversy in the early 1970s when Clifford Irving, a professional writer, came forward with what he claimed to be Hughes's autobiography. It was thought that Irving, who was later jailed for extortion, had used Dietrich's first draft as the basis of his hoax.

Dietrich served as consultant to a number of businesses after leaving Hughes's employ. He suffered from myasthenia gravis and died of a heart ailment. A.K.

Parents John D., Methodist minister, and Sarah (Peters) D. **Married** (1) Gladys Thomas 1910 (div. 1935). (2) Carol Hoyt 1936 (div. 1955). (3) Mary Brever 1955. **Children** Elizabeth Dietrich Jewell; Katharine Dietrich O'Hara; John; Anthony; Susan. **Religion** Agnostic. **Education** Public schs. in Janesville, WI. **Career** Bank cashier, Maxwell, NM 1910–11; auditor, Los Angeles Suburban Land Co. 1911–17; asst. comptroller, E. L. Doheny, NYC 1917–20; sr. accountant, Haskins & Sells, L.A. 1920; comptroller, H. L. Arnold 1921–25; qualified as certified public accountant 1923. • Exec. asst. to Howard Hughes 1925–45; exec. v.p. 1945–57 and dir., Hughes Tool Co., Houston; chmn., RKO Pictures 1949–55; dir. and chmn. of finance cttee., Trans-World Airlines; dir., Gulf Brewing Co.; dir., Natl. Bank of Commerce, Houston. • Corporate consultant, Century City, L.A. since 1957; delegate to Pres. Truman's Labor-Management Conference. **Officer** Dir. and regional v.p., Natl. Assn. of Manufacturers 1941–50. **Member** Bd. of regents, Univ. of Houston; advisory council, Notre Dame Univ. **Honors** First prize for accounting, Natl. Automobile Dealers Assn. 1923. **Author** (Jtly.) *Howard, The Amazing Mr. Hughes,* 1971. **Contributor** to trade jrnls.

Further reading Howard Hughes, *My Life and Opinions,* 1972; Donald L. Bartlett, *Empire,* 1979.

KURT ENOCH
Book publisher
***Born* Hamburg, Germany, 22 November 1895**
***Died* Puerto Rico, 15 February 1982**

Kurt Enoch fled Germany during the Hitler years, leaving behind a successful publishing career, and eventually became an influential and innovative publisher in the United States. He was co-founder of New American Library (NAL), one of the earliest U.S. publishers of paperback books.

He was born into a publishing family; his father, Oscar, started the house which came to be known as Enoch Brothers in Hamburg. Kurt studied at Friedrich Wilhelm University in Berlin in 1914–15, then enlisted in the German Army and won a field commission late in World War I. He received a doctorate in political economy from the University of Hamburg in 1921 and the following year joined the family firm, a general house whose list included several British and U.S. authors. In 1932, he co-founded the Albatross Modern Continental Library, which aimed to reach the considerable English-language market on the Continent.

The Nazi laws proscribing Jewish-owned businesses forced Enoch from Germany in the mid-1930s, but he quickly set up operations in Paris and London. In 1940 he arrived in New York and two years later was named a vice president of Penguin Books, which was then just entering the U.S. market. He was Penguin's U.S. president from 1945 to 1947, when he left to start New American Library of World Literature, Inc.

His partner in NAL was Victor Weybright, whose editorial skills complemented Enoch's expertise in production and distribution. Under its major imprints, Signet, Mentor, and Key Books, NAL was, for a time, the largest and most successful paperback publisher in the country. Long before the term "quality paperbacks" became current, NAL, under the slogan "Good Reading for the Millions," was offering softcover books of literary value, with appropriate typography and cover design. Its lists combined popular and scholarly titles, and included works by Faulkner, Lawrence, Joyce, and Shaw as well as the thrillers of

Mickey Spillane, Ian Fleming, and James M. Cain; a large part of its sales were to college bookstores. When, in 1960, the company was acquired by the Los Angeles-based Times-Mirror Company, Enoch became a vice president and director of that company and the president of its book division. After retiring from Times-Mirror in 1967, he was a publishing consultant in New York.

Enoch was director of the American Book Publishers Council from 1961 to 1963, and from 1968 was a board member of the National Book Committee. He died while vacationing in Puerto Rico. A.K.

Parents Oscar E. and Rosa (Neumann) E. **Married** (1) Hertha Rehse Frischman 1921 (d. 1934): Ruth Enoch Gruenthal; Mirjam Enoch Stevens. (2) Margaret M. Heineman 1937. **Emigration** Left Germany 1936; emigrated to U.S. 1940; naturalized 1947. **Education** Friedrich Wilhelm Univ., Berlin 1914–15; Univ. of Hamburg, doctorate in political economy 1921. **Mil. service** Lt., artillery, German army, WWI; French Army 1940. **Career** Gen. mgr., then partner, Gebrueder Enoch Verlag and Oscar Enoch Verlag, Hamburg 1922–36; co-founder, Albatross Modern Continental Library, Hamburg 1932; founder and dir., Continental SRL Publishing Co., Paris; founding dir., Enoch Ltd. and Imperial Book Co., London 1936–40; book-publishing consultant, NYC 1940–42; v.p. 1942–45, and pres. and managing dir. 1945–47, Penguin Books, Inc.; co-founder 1947, and pres. and dir. 1947–60, New American Library of World Literature, Inc.; pres. of Book Div., v.p., and dir., Times-Mirror Co., L.A. 1960–67; book-publishing consultant since 1967. **Officer** Dir. 1960–65 and member since 1965, Franklin Book Programs, Inc.; dir., Amer. Book Publishers Council 1961–63. **Member** U.S. Book Industry delegation to USSR 1962; natl. bd., Natl. Book Cttee., Inc. since 1968; natl. advisory council, Hampshire Coll. since 1970; Amer. Inst. of Graphic Arts; Pen Club.

Further reading Victor Weybright, *The Making of a Publisher* 1967; John Tebbel, *A History of Book Publishing in the United States,* 1980.

RICHARD B(RANDON) KERSHNER

Developer of missiles and satellites

Born **Crestline, Ohio, USA, 11 October 1913**

Died **Silver Spring, Maryland, USA, 15 February 1982**

During his 32 years at the Applied Physics Laboratory (APL) of Johns Hopkins University, Richard B. Kershner played a major role in developing missiles and satellites for the U.S. government and was responsible for the success of the Transit navigational satellite system, now used by ships of almost all nations. At a time when skeptics were criticizing the high cost of the space effort, *Space World* magazine heralded Kershner's "lighthouses in space" as "the first application of space technology that will be of direct practical benefit to people on earth."

Kershner grew up in Baltimore, Maryland, where his father was headmaster of the Franklin Day School. He pursued an accelerated academic program at Johns Hopkins University and received his Ph.D. in mathematics at the age of 23. After teaching for five years, he began working on government-sponsored ballistics projects, first at the Carnegie Institution's Geophysical Laboratory in Washington, D.C., and then at the Allegheny Ballistics Laboratory in Cumberland, Maryland. In 1946 he joined the Johns Hopkins Applied Physics Laboratory, where he took on a major assignment—the planning and production of the U.S. Navy's first surface-to-air missile, the Terrier. Work began in 1949, and the 1,200-pound solid-fuel guided missile was operational by the mid-1950s. For his contributions, Kershner won the Distinguished Public Service Award, the Navy's highest civilian honor.

In 1957 the Navy began developing a submarine-launched ballistic missile, the Polaris. Kershner headed the APL team that evaluated the design of that missile. For this project, too, he received the Distinguished Public Service Award. He won it an unprecedented third time in 1967 for his work on the Transit navigational system.

The Transit project was an indirect result of Sputnik I, the Soviet satellite whose launching on October 1957 inaugurated the space race. Two APL scientists found that they were able to calculate Sputnik's position and orbit from the variations in frequency of its beeping radio signals. Like the whistle of a passing train, the beeps increased in frequency as Sputnik approached and dropped in frequency after it had flown by (the Doppler effect). The suggestion was made that the process could be reversed—that an observer could determine his own position on the earth's surface by measuring the Doppler effect on signals from a single satellite whose orbit was known. In 1958 Kershner was appointed head of the laboratory's space department and was charged with developing a practical system of satellite navigation.

The result of this project was the Transit system, which required three to five satellites in orbit simultaneously in order to serve ships anywhere on the globe. The first satellite was successfully launched from Cape Canaveral in April 1960, but failed launchings of subsequent satellites delayed the full implementation of the system for several years. One Transit booster rocket fell on Cuba, killing a cow and precipitating charges of "Yankee provocation." But Kershner and his group worked continually to perfect the satellites, reducing their weight by half and introducing innovative stabilization techniques. By 1964, Polaris submarines and other Navy ships were using Transit as a navigational aid, and in 1967 the system was released for worldwide commercial use. Today, any ship with computerized navigation equipment can use Transit to plot its position to within a tenth of a mile in any kind of weather. The Transit system is especially useful in less-traveled sea lanes, where land-based navigational beacons are lacking.

After his success with Transit, Kershner went on to supervise the development of several other satellites, including MAGSAT, which measures the magnetic field of the earth; GEOS, a series of geodetic satellites; and the SAS series of small astronomy satellites. In 1972 Kershner became the assistant director of the laboratory, and even after his retirement in 1978 he remained its principal advisor for space systems. In the fall of 1981 he was named one of the APL's first senior fellows. He died of respiratory failure following a long illness. P.D.

Parents James Alexander K., headmaster, and Eva Della (Shoemaker) K. **Married** Mary Amanda Brown 1935: Richard Brandon, Jr.; James Williamson. **Education** Johns Hopkins Univ., Baltimore, Ph.D. in mathematics 1937. **Career** Instr. in mathematics, Univ. of Wisconsin 1937–40; asst. prof. of mathematics, Johns Hopkins Univ. 1940–42; mathematician, Geophysics Lab., Carnegie Instn., Wash. DC 1942–44; mathematician, Allegany Ballistics Lab., Cumberland, MD 1944–46. • With Applied Physics Lab., Johns Hopkins Univ., Silver Spring, MD: joined 1946; head, space development dept. 1958–78; asst. dir. 1972–78; principal advisor since 1978; sr. fellow since 1981. **Fellow** Amer. Inst. of Aerospace and Astronautics. **Member** Amer. Assn. for Advancement of Science; Philosophical Soc. of Washington; Phi Beta Kappa; Sigma Xi. **Honors** Presidential Certificate of Merit 1948; Distinguished Public Service Award, Navy Dept. 1958, 1961, 1967; Hays Award 1969 and Navigation Satellite Div. Award 1981, Inst. of Navigation; Eisenhower Medal, Johns Hopkins Univ. 1981. **Inventor** Jet control by rotatable offset nozzle; radar antenna-positioning device. **Author** *The Anatomy of Mathematics,* 1950.

NICHOLAS ROOSEVELT
Diplomat and writer
Born **New York City, USA, 12 June 1893**
Died **Monterey, California, USA, 16 February 1982**

Nicholas Roosevelt was a second cousin of Pres. Theodore Roosevelt and a prominent member of that branch of the family. A lifelong Republican, he served in diplomatic posts under Pres. Herbert Hoover. For many years he was a New York-based newspaper writer, and he produced several books both during his journalistic career and after his retirement to Big Sur, California.

His father was J. West Roosevelt, a surgeon and the president's first cousin. Nicholas graduated from Harvard in 1914, but left graduate school the same year to enter the diplomatic service. He served as attaché in Paris until 1916, then briefly in Madrid. When the United States entered World War I, he quickly trained as a reserve officer, and returned to France as a captain in the infantry until the Armistice. He was appointed an aide to Woodrow Wilson when the president visited Paris late in 1918, then was asked by Arthur Coolidge, one of his professors at Harvard, to join the U.S. Commission to Negotiate Peace. He spent several months in Vienna and Budapest.

Returning home in 1919, Roosevelt soon became involved in Republican politics, backing Gen. Leonard Wood for the presidential nomination in 1920. He had no part in the Warren Harding admnistration, joining the editorial staff of the *New York Tribune* in 1921 as editorial writer and special correspondent. He moved to *The New York Times* in the same capacity two years later, and was sent on a tour of Indonesia and the Philippines in 1924–25. In 1926 he published a book, *The Philippines: A Treasure and a Problem,* sharply criticizing U.S. democratization efforts in the islands and the Filipino political establishment. When Pres. Hoover appointed Roosevelt vice governor of the Philippines in 1930, the objections in Manila were so strong that the appointment was withdrawn. Shortly thereafter he was named U.S. minister to Hungary, where he served until Pres. Franklin Roosevelt, a distant cousin, came into office. Before entering government service Roosevelt had written two other political studies, *The Restless Pacific* (1928) and *America and England?* (1930).

In 1933, Roosevelt rejoined the editorial staff of the *Herald Tribune,* where until 1942 he wrote many dispatches and editorials. He was a confirmed internationalist, and his wide travels in Europe and Asia convinced him that Germany and Japan were preparing for war. Each winter the paper granted him leave, and he lectured throughout the country on the dangers of fascist militarism.

Roosevelt had little regard for Franklin Roosevelt or his administration's New Deal, but when war came he joined the Office of War Information in 1942 as deputy director with special liaison responsibility to the Army and Navy. It was an especially frustrating job, and in 1944 he left government service to become assistant to the publisher of the *Times,* Arthur Sulzberger. He resigned in 1946 and went to live in Big Sur, where he continued to write and from 1962 served on the California Recreation Commission.

The best-known of Roosevelt's books is probably his autobiography, *A Front Row Seat,* which was published in 1953. He also wrote a memoir, *Theodore Roosevelt: The Man as I Knew Him* (1967), and two cookbooks, *Creative Cooking* (1956) and *Good Cooking* (1959). His last book, *Conservation, Now or Never* (1970), reflected his long-standing concern with environmental issues.

A.K.

Parents J. West R., surgeon, and Laura (d'Orémieulx) R. **Married** Tirzah Maris Gates 1936 (d. 1961). **Education** Harvard Univ., A.B. 1914. **Mil. service** Capt., 322nd Infantry Battalion, U.S. Army 1917–19; deputy dir., Office of War Information 1942–44. **Career** Joined diplomatic service 1914; attaché, U.S. Embassy, Paris 1914–16; secty., Amer. Intl. Corp. mission to Spain 1916–17; attached to Amer. Commn. to Negotiate Peace 1919; editorial writer, *New York Tribune* 1921–23; editorial writer and special corresp., *New York Times* 1923–30; vice gov., Philippine Islands 1930; minister to Hungary 1930–33; member of editorial staff, *New York Herald Tribune* 1933–42; asst. to publisher, *New York Times*

1944–46. **Member** California Recreation Commn. since 1962; Republican Party; Amer. Garlic Soc.; Century Club, NYC; Metropolitan Club, Wash. DC. **Author** *The Philippines: A Treasure and a Problem,* 1926; *The Restless Pacific,* 1928; *America and England?,* 1930; *The Townsend Plan,* 1936; *A New Birth of Freedom,* 1938; *A Front Row Seat* (autobiography), 1953; *Creative Cooking,* 1956; *Good Cooking,* 1959; *Theodore Roosevelt: The Man as I Knew Him,* 1967; *Conservation, Now or Never,* 1970.

THELONIOUS (SPHERE) MONK
Jazz musician
***Born* Rocky Mount, North Carolina, USA, 10 October 1917**
***Died* Englewood, New Jersey, USA, 17 February 1982**

Thelonious Sphere Monk was one of the giants of jazz, a startling pianistic innovator whose compositions, though deeply influential in rhythm and harmony, were extremely difficult for other musicians to duplicate faithfully. His rigid integrity and refusal to follow fashion in anything gave him a reputation for being enigmatic and even perverse, and during his long career he suffered years of critical misunderstanding and neglect. Yet most people who knew modern jazz were always aware of his greatness. To Randy Weston, a pianist who studied under him, Monk was "as complete an original as it is possible to be."

When he was four years old his mother moved him and two other children to New York while her husband, who was also named Thelonious, remained in North Carolina. The family found a small apartment at 243 West 63rd Street in the black neighborhood then known as San Juan Hill. This apartment was Monk's home until late in his life.

Young Thelonious began playing the piano by ear at the age of 6, and when he was 11 was sent for lessons at 75 cents an hour. He played the organ in a church for a while, and by age 13 had been in local bands that often played for rent parties in the early days of the Great Depression. He was a frequent winner of the amateur nights held each week at the Apollo Theater in Harlem—so frequent, in fact, that the management refused to allow him to compete further. At 16 he left Stuyvesant High School to tour with a band accompanying an evangelist. The jazz pianist Mary Lou Williams heard him when the troupe passed through Kansas City. Years later she said, "He was playing the same style then that he is now."

Back in New York, Monk became pianist in the house band of Minton's Playhouse in Harlem. During the late 1930s and early 1940s he played there in countless late-night jams with other young musicians: saxophonist Charlie "Bird" Parker, trumpeter Dizzy Gillespie, drummer Kenny Clarke, and guitarist Charlie Christian. Together they invented the music that became known as bebop, the origin and essence of modern jazz. "I was calling it bipbop," said Monk, "but the others must have heard me wrong." The others worked at the new musical form, broadened it, making it accessible to more people, and became stars in the process. Monk was not with them in this, however, for even early in his career he refused to compromise his music, which was difficult, dissonant, and definitely outside the mainstream. Ran Blake, writing in *The New Groves Dictionary of Music,* described his style as "involving a heavy attack and distinctive 'clanging' timbre, crushed notes and clusters, and left-hand chords made up of seconds and sixths instead of conventional triadic jazz harmonies. This economical approach emphasized his unique, often humorous sense of rhythmic anticipation and delay, tempo suspension and silence, and allowed him when improvising to explore different aspects of themes with unusual rigour."

The next 20 years were hard for Monk. Critics largely ignored him, and steady employment was rare. There were occasional successes: in 1944 "Round Midnight"—one of his earliest compositions—was recorded by Cootie Williams's band with Monk's pupil Bud Powell at the piano; the same year he made his first recordings with a group led by Coleman Hawkins, the great saxophonist of an earlier generation. He began to record in his own name for the Blue Note label in 1947, but his work failed to reach a wide audience. In 1951 he was arrested with Bud Powell and charged with possession of heroin. Although it was known by everyone that he was not a user, Monk refused to talk to the police and was jailed for 60 days, after which his cabaret card—a police license then required for all performers in New York—was taken away from him.

For the next six years, though he made a few records and appeared out of town, he was silent in New York. To the question "What is jazz?" Monk had once replied, "New York, man. You can feel it. It's around in the air." Referring later to those difficult years, he said, "I didn't get raggedy. They thought I'd become a bum, but I fooled 'em. I stayed on the scene." His inspiration never abandoned him, and he composed during this time some of the mainstays of his repertoire, including "Blue Monk," "Bemsha Swing," "Little Rootie Tootie," and "Pannonica." The last was named for Baroness Pannonica ("Nica") de Koenigswarter, a member of the English Rothschild family and the wealthy friend of several jazz musicians, including Bird Parker, whom she cared for in the last sad days of his life. The Baroness helped Monk regain his cabaret card, and his performing career quickly revived. He began playing regularly at the Five Spot Café on the Lower East Side, most notably in a quartet with saxophonist John Coltrane, and he often played in another with tenor saxophonist Charlie Rouse.

During the late 1950s and early 1960s, Monk began to receive the kind of popular and critical attention that had always passed him by. He had a triumphal tour of 20 European cities, made many successful appearances at jazz festivals, and performed with large orchestras at memorable concerts at Town Hall in 1959, Philharmonic Hall in 1963, and Carnegie Hall in 1964. He was the subject of a *Time* magazine cover story in February 1964. Good money from recording began to come his way after he signed with Columbia, a major label. The albums he recorded during these years were among his best, and included *Misterioso, Brilliant Corners, 5 by 5,* and *Thelonious in Action.*

Ill health limited his appearances during the 1970s, although he continued to perform in the New York City half of the Newport Jazz Festival. His last public performance was in 1976 at Carnegie Hall. When he had to abandon his 63rd Street apartment because the building was to be demolished, he moved to Nica de Koenigswarter's estate in Weehawken, New Jersey.

Monk married Nellie Smith, a childhood friend, in 1948, and later wrote for her "Crepuscule for Nellie." (Their two children, Thelonious Sphere, Jr., and Barbara, are members of the successful disco trio T. S. Monk.) Other memorable Monk compositions include "Straight No Chaser," "Epistrophy," "Ruby My Dear," "Nutty," "Off Minor," and "Well, You Needn't." Monk also wrote the score for the Roger Vadim film *Les liaisons dangereuses.*

With his large collection of unusual hats and his famous shuffling dance, rapt beside the piano, Monk was a figure antithetical to fashion in popular music, a field where fashion has always seemed as changeable as air. His enigmatic quality which so baffled the hipsters of the 1940s and 1950s—they called him the High Priest of Bebop—was really nothing more than honesty, the few spare words of a man who knew where he was going and would not be deflected from his goal. "Jazz is America musically," he said in 1961. "It's all jazz, everywhere. When I was a kid, I felt that something had to be done about all that jazz. So I've been doing it for 20 years. Maybe I've turned jazz another way. Maybe I'm a major influence. I don't know. Anyway, my music is my music, on my piano, too. That's a criterion of something. Jazz is my adventure. I'm after new chords, new ways of syncopating, new figurations, new runs. How to use notes differently. That's it. Just using notes differently."

Monk died two weeks after suffering a stroke. A.K.

Born Thelonious Junior Monk. **Parents** Thelonious M. and Barbara (Batts) M., civil service worker. **Married** Nellie Smith 1948:

Thelonious, drummer, b. 1950; Barbara, jazz musician, b. 1954. **Education** Stuyvesant High Sch., NYC until age 16. **Career** Jazz pianist and composer since early 1930s; pioneer of bebop style; played with various bands at Minton's Playhouse and other clubs, NYC early 1940s; associated with Kenny Clarke, Dizzy Gillespie, Charlie Christian; led small groups 1944–59; cabaret card revoked 1951–57; formed big band 1959; led quartet 1960s; played at jazz festivals and in major cities of U.S. and Europe; world tour with Giants of Jazz 1971–72. **Honors** Best jazz pianist, *Down Beat* intl. critics poll 1958, 1959, 1960; Guggenheim Fellowship 1975; honored at Pres. Carter's jazz party 1978; elected to Down Beat Magazine Hall of Fame. **Film soundtrack** *Les liaisons dangereuses,* 1959. **Albums** *At Town Hall; Brilliant Corners; 5 by 5; Misterioso; Thelonious in Action; Monk's Music; It's Monk's Time; Monk Plays Duke Ellington; Thelonious Himself; The Unique; Thelonious Alone in San Francisco; Monk, Vols. I & II; Quintets; Trios; Work!; Bird & Diz; Nica's Tempo; Complete Genius; Criss-Cross; Straight No Chaser; Underground; Who's Afraid of the Big Band Monk; Smithsonian Collection; Something in Blue; Monk's Dream; The Man I Love; Giants of Jazz;* others. **Compositions** "Round Midnight"; "Well, You Needn't"; "Straight No Chaser"; "Off Minor"; "Epistrophy"; "Pannonica"; "Crepuscule for Nellie"; "Bemsha Swing"; "Blue Monk"; "Little Rootie Tootie"; "Nutty"; "Ruby, My Dear"; "Hackensack"; "Friday the Thirteenth"; "Eronel"; "Criss-Cross"; "Evidence"; "Gallop's Gallop"; many others.

Further reading "The Loneliest Monk," in *Time,* 28 Feb. 1964; J. Goldberg, *Jazz Masters of the Fifties,* 1965; M. Williams, *The Jazz Tradition,* 1970; Mark C. Gridley, *Jazz Styles,* 1978.

LEE STRASBERG
Acting teacher, actor, and stage director
***Born* Budzanow, Galicia, Austria-Hungary, 17 November 1901**
***Died* New York City, USA, 17 February 1982**

Lee Strasberg, for 34 years the artistic director and guiding spirit of the Actors Studio in New York, did more to shape the character of modern American acting on the stage and in films than any other single figure. He exerted an enormous influence on the actors of his time, not by personal example, although late in life he appeared in several films, but through his teaching, which guided the careers of many of the most celebrated modern American actors, including Marlon Brando, Rod Steiger, Jane Fonda, Patricia Neal, James Dean, Robert De Niro, Jack Nicholson, Joanne Woodward, Paul Newman, Al Pacino, Dustin Hoffman, and Lee J. Cobb. Most of the actors he trained have not excelled in classical roles; the extreme form of naturalism that he practiced was best suited to the portrayal of ordinary people caught in situations of conflict or danger—the basic material of American drama. He created, as a writer in the *Times* of London put it, "an indigenously American style of acting and the body of doctrine needed to support it."

Strasberg's technique was derived largely from the ideas of Konstantin Stanislavsky, director of the Moscow Art Theatre at the turn of the century, who had sought to replace the conventional "theater of representation" with the "theater of living experience." In order to produce actors capable of this kind of realism, he had developed a system of training, known as "the Method," that based the outward expression of psychological states on a scientific (or pseudoscientific) understanding of human behavior, rather than on mere instinct or artifice. He also worked out a set of mental and physical exercises by which actors could organize their emotions for instant recollection when creating a character.

Before Strasberg had ever heard of Stanislavsky, however, he had absorbed the naturalism of the Yiddish theater, in which he received his first dramatic training. He was born in a small settlement in Galicia and was brought at the age of seven to Manhattan's

Lower East Side, where his father, formerly a stonecutter, worked in the garment industry and was active in a trade union that supported community theater. While he was still a schoolboy—and still known by his original name of Israel Strassberg—he joined the amateur Progressive Dramatic Club, whose leaders were well versed in Stanislavsky's theories. After leaving Townsend Harris Hall high school in 1918 to work as a clerk in a wig factory, he studied acting at the American Laboratory Theatre under Richard Boleslavski and Maria Ouspenskaya, both former students of Stanislavsky. He also became a member of an amateur group that gave performances in the Chrystie Street Settlement House, a social center in the Lower East Side, where he gained his first experience as a director. At the same time he embarked on a serious study of dramatic theory that gave him an immense range to supplement his practical skill.

Courtesy of John Springer Associates

His professional career in the theater began in 1924 when he joined the Theatre Guild as an actor and assistant stage manager. At the Guild he met Harold Clurman and Cheryl Crawford, who shared his ambition to break away from the commercial standards of the New York theater and create a company for the production of artistically notable plays. They established an informal workshop at which Strasberg expounded his ideas on technique. In 1931, 28 performers led by Strasberg, Clurman, and Crawford founded the Group Theatre and produced Paul Green's *The House of Connelly* on Broadway, making the first step toward what they hoped would become an indigenous American theater responsive to social conditions. Strasberg remained with the Group until 1937, achieving his most notable success as the director of *Men in White* (1933), for which the author, Sidney Kingsley, won the 1934 Pulitzer prize. In his account of the Group Theatre, *The Fervent Years* (1957), Harold Clurman described Strasberg as "one of the few artists among American theater directors. He is the director of introverted feeling, of strong emotion curbed by ascetic control. . . . The effect he produces is a classic hush, tense and tragic. . . . The roots are clearly in the intimate experience of a complex psychology, an acute awareness of human contradiction and suffering."

After resigning from the Group, Strasberg directed several Broadway successes, including Clifford Odets's *Clash by Night* (1941), but spent most of the 1940s in Hollywood. He returned to New York in 1948 to become director of the Actors Studio, a venture begun by Elia Kazan, Cheryl Crawford, and Robert Lewis. The purpose of the Studio was not to offer a formal curriculum, but to provide a workshop in which actors could experiment and find inspiration. From its inception the Studio has been supported entirely by charitable contributions—its members pay no fees. Although numerous productions were given privately at the Studio, the results of the workshops were rarely seen in the theater. In 1963 the Studio's only Broadway season received lukewarm reviews, and Strasberg's major directing venture, Chekhov's *Three Sisters,* which was given on Broadway in 1963 and again at the London World Theater Season of the following year, was not highly praised. By the 1970s, however, Strasberg's reputation as the finest American teacher of acting had spread throughout the world, and he was frequently invited to give lectures and seminars in Europe. At his 75th birthday it was estimated that actors trained by him had received 24 Academy Awards and 108 nominations.

Strasberg's effectiveness as a teacher derived from his interest in the psychology of dramatic interpretation, and from his emphasis on the actor's private personality as the raw material from which a performance should be created. Fusing the insights of Stanislavsky with some of the assumptions of modern psychology, he instructed his students to create previous and subsequent histories for the characters they played, and directed them to relive their personal experiences—everything from the mundane, such as taking a bath, to the tragic, such as losing a parent—in order to tap sources of unfeigned emotion. "No impulse, from the most spiritual to the most destructive, was unacceptable as long as it could be transmuted into the creative experience," wrote his daughter Susan, the actress, in her autobiography. The object of this training was to break down the artificiality of acting to a point at which the actor identified so thoroughly with the role that it virtually ceased to be distinct from his or her private self. In this way, the personality of the performer became a functional part of stage technique. He also taught relaxation and other exercises designed to maximize the actor's physical control. "The Method," Strasberg once said, "is really a summation of what actors have always done unconsciously whenever they have done well."

Given to intemperate rages and dogmatic pronouncements, Strasberg attracted or repelled people according to their valuation of his work. His detractors, who included his one-time colleague Stella Adler, criticized his approach as self-indulgent and pedestrian in its stress on behavioral motivation at the expense of imaginative interpretation; others accused him of practicing psychiatry without a license and of producing actors noteworthy for self-absorption, excessive mannerisms, and mumbling inarticulateness. But Tennessee Williams, many of whose plays were first performed by students of Strasberg, felt that the Method brought to his work an extraordinary intensity. The actors themselves tended to regard Strasberg as a combination of tyrant, saint, and father, and accepted his blistering attacks on their performances with the enthusiasm of zealous penitents glad to receive chastisement.

Strasberg retired as an actor in 1929 but made a remarkable comeback in 1974, playing the part of the Jewish gangster Hyman Roth in the film *The Godfather, Part II.* He was thereafter much in demand as a film actor, and played parts in *Going in Style* (1979), *And Justice for All* (1980), and the television film *Skokie* (1981). On the Sunday before his death from a heart attack he appeared in a chorus line during a benefit performance at Radio City Music Hall. *A Dream of Passion,* his book on directing, will be published posthumously.

H.B./J.P.

Born Israel Strassberg. **Parents** Baruch Meyer S. and Ida (Diner) S. **Married** (1) Nora Z. Krecaun 1926 (d. 1929). (2) Paula Miller, theatrical dir. and coach, 1934 (d. 1966): Susan, actress; John. (3) Anna Mizrahi, actress, 1968: Adam Lee Baruch; David Lee Isaac. **Religion** Jewish. **Emigration** Brought to U.S. 1909; naturalized 1936. **Education** Poale Zion Sch., NYC; public schs., NYC; Townsend Harris Hall, NYC, left 1918; Amer. Lab. Theatre, NYC early 1920s. **Career** Amateur actor with Progressive Dramatic Club, NYC 1911–17; worker in theatrical wig factory, NYC ca. 1918; asst. stage mgr., Theatre Guild, NYC 1924; dir. and actor, Students of Art and Drama, Chrystie Street Settlement House, NYC 1925; actor, Theatre Guild 1925–31; co-founder and dir., Group Theatre, NYC 1931–37; artistic dir. and acting teacher, Actors Studio, NYC since 1948; artistic dir., Actors Studio Theatre, Inc. 1962–66; film actor since 1974; founder, Lee Strasberg Inst. of Theatre, NYC and LA 1969. • Lectr.: Spoleto Festival 1962; Stanislavsky Centennial, Moscow 1963; Paris 1967; East Berlin 1979; also Germany, Argentina, Japan, and univs. of Harvard, Brown, Brandeis, Minnesota, Northwestern, and California at Los Angeles. **Member** AEA; AFTRA; SAG. **Honors** Kelcey Allen Award, NYC 1961; Centennial Gold Medal, Boston Coll. 1963; Academy Award nomination, for *The Godfather, Part II,* 1975; elected to Theatrical Hall of Fame 1982; bldg. named in his honor at Hebrew Univ.; hon. degree, Univ. of Florida. **Stage actor** (all NYC) *Processional,* 1925; *The Garrick Gaieties,* 1925; *Goat Song,* 1926; *The Chief Thing,* 1926; *Four Walls,* 1927; *Red Rust,* 1929; *The Garrick Gaieties,* 1930; *Green Grow the Lilacs,* 1931. **Director** (all NYC) *The House of Connelly,* 1931; *Night over Taos,* 1932; *Success Story,* 1932; *Hilda Cassidy,* 1933; *Men in White,* 1933; *Gentlewoman,* 1934; *Gold Eagle Guy,* 1934; *The Case of Clyde Griffiths,* 1936; *Johnny Johnson,* 1936; *Many Mansions,* 1937; *Roosty,* 1938; *All the Living,* 1938; *Dance Night,* 1938; *Summer Night,* 1939; *The Fifth Column,* 1940; *Clash by Night,* 1941; *RUR,* 1942; (also producer) *Apology,* 1943; *South Pacific,* 1943; *Skipper Next to God,* 1948; *The Big Knife,* 1949; *The Closing Door,* 1949; *The Country Girl,* 1950; *Peer Gynt,* 1951; *The Three Sisters,* 1963,

London 1964. **Film actor** *The Godfather, Part II,* 1974; *The Cassandra Crossing,* 1976; *Boardwalk,* 1979; *Going in Style,* 1979; *And Justice for All,* 1980; *The Last Tenant* (TV film), 1981; *Skokie* (TV film), 1981. **Author** (Ed.) *Famous American Plays of the 1950's,* 1963; *A Dream of Passion,* 1982; "Acting, Directing, and Production," in *Encyclopaedia Britannica;* also articles in *Encyclopedia Spettacolo* and in jrnls. and mags. **Personal papers** at Wisconsin Center for Theatre Research, Univ. of Wisconsin.

Further reading Harold Clurman, *The Fervent Years,* 1957; Robert H. Hethmon, ed., *Strasberg at the Actors Studio,* 1965; Cindy Adams, *Lee Strasberg,* 1980; David Garfield, *A Player's Place,* 1980; Susan Strasberg, *Bittersweet,* 1980.

RAYMOND M(ILNER) WHEELER

Physician and investigator of malnutrition
***Born* Farmville, North Carolina, USA, 30 September 1919**
***Died* Charlotte, North Carolina, USA, 17 February 1982**

Raymond M. Wheeler, a modest and dedicated North Carolina physician, documented during the 1960s the extensive hunger and malnutrition in the rural American South. His findings were given wide publicity by book and film and resulted in the marked improvement of federal public-aid programs.

Wheeler did premedical work at the University of North Carolina and received his M.D. from Washington University in St. Louis in 1943. He served as a medical officer in the army from 1944 to 1946, winning the Silver Star and Purple Heart. He returned to North Carolina in 1946 and began the private practice of internal medicine in Charlotte in 1948.

From 1956, Wheeler was a member of the North Carolina Council on Human Relations and the Southern Regional Council, both biracial civil-rights organizations. He served as president of the former from 1957 to 1961 and was chairman of the executive committee of the Southern Regional Council from 1964 to 1969 and its president from 1969 to 1974.

In 1967, working through the Southern Regional Council and the Field Foundation, Wheeler led a group of doctors on a tour of four rural counties in Mississippi, a state that was thought to be effectively reaching its poor with federally sponsored antipoverty and food programs. They met nearly 700 children and conducted extensive interviews with two dozen families. Later, before a U.S. Senate subcommittee, they described what they found as "pitiful," "alarming," "unbelievable," and "appalling": "In every county we visited," they said, there was "obvious evidence of severe malnutrition." Then going further, they added, "The boys and girls we saw were hungry—weak, in pain, sick; their lives are being shortened. . . . They are suffering from hunger and disease and directly or indirectly they are dying from them—which is exactly what 'starvation' means." Wheeler furthermore attested to an "absence of compassion and concern" among the professionals charged with poor people's health and welfare.

The outcry was immediate, and largely predictable. Orville Freeman, then secretary of agriculture, announced that he would drastically restructure federal food programs, especially the new food stamp program, to reach more of the poor. Mississippi's deeply conservative senators, John Stennis and James Eastland, denounced the doctors for "libel and slander." "I deny," said Eastland, "there is mass malnutrition in the Mississippi Delta." To which Dr. Wheeler evenly replied, "I invite Senator Eastland and Senator Stennis to come with me to the vast farmlands of the Delta. I will show them the children with their shriveled arms and swollen bellies, their hunger, and pain."

The Southern Regional Council report, *Hungry Children,* was largely based on the doctors' work, and Wheeler advised on the film *Hunger in America.* Both were released in 1968.

In 1970, Wheeler testified before the Senate Subcommittee on Migratory Labor on the results of a visit he and three other doctors had made to colonies of migrant workers in Florida, Texas, and Michigan. "How can you justify," he demanded of the senators, "the endless words and the devious political maneuvers which have delayed and withheld meaningful aid to children who don't have enough to eat? . . . The children we saw . . . have no future in our society. Malnutrition since birth has already impaired them, physically, mentally, and emotionally."

Wheeler subsequently served as president or chairman of other antipoverty civil-rights organizations, including the Children's Foundation, the National Sharecroppers' Fund, the North Carolina Hunger Foundation, the Voter Education Project, and Southerners for Economic Justice. He died of a heart attack.
A.K.

Parents George Raymond W. and Sallie Kate (Collins) W. **Married** (1) Mary Lou Browning 1942 (div. 1956): Linda Lou; Margaret Browning; David Stewart. (2) Julie Buckner Carr 1958. **Religion** Unitarian. **Education** Univ. of North Carolina, certificate in medicine 1941; Washington Univ., St. Louis, MO, M.D. 1943; intern, Barnes Hosp., St. Louis 1943–44; asst. resident in medicine, North Carolina Baptist Hosp., Winston-Salem, NC 1946–48; diplomate, Amer. Bd. of Internal Medicine. **Mil. service** Capt., Medical Corps, U.S. Army 1944–46. **Career** Private practice in internal medicine, Charlotte, NC since 1948; chmn., dept. of medicine, Charlotte Memorial Hosp. 1961–63; clinical assoc. prof. of medicine, Univ. of North Carolina Medical Sch. 1966–70. • Member, Field Foundn. Commn. on Hunger in Mississippi 1967; member, Citizens Bd. Inquiry into Hunger in U.S. 1968; consultant, *Hunger in America* documentary film 1968; member, Citizens Bd. Inquiry into Brookside Strike 1974. **Officer** Pres. 1957–61 and member since 1956, Council on Human Relations; exec. cttee. chmn. 1964–69, pres. 1969–74, and member since 1956, Southern Regional Council; member, bd. of dirs., Voter Education Project 1970–75; chmn., bd. of dirs., Children's Foundn. 1973–74; exec. cttee. chmn. 1976–78 and pres. since 1978, Natl. Sharecroppers' Fund; exec. cttee. chmn. 1975–77 and pres. 1977–79, North Carolina Hunger Coalition; member, bd. of dirs., Southerners for Economic Justice since 1977. **Fellow** Amer. Coll. of Physicians. **Member** Amer. Public Health Assn.; Mecklenburg County Medical Soc.; Democratic Party. **Honors** Silver Star and Purple Heart, WW II; Distinguished Service Award, Univ. of North Carolina Medical Sch. 1969; Graham Award, North Carolina Civil Liberties Union. **Contributor** to *Hungry Children,* 1968.

DAME (EDITH) NGAIO MARSH
Detective novelist and theatrical producer
***Born* Christchurch, New Zealand, 23 April 1899**
***Died* Christchurch, New Zealand, 18 February 1982**

The detective fiction of Dame Ngaio Marsh has been favorably compared with that of Agatha Christie and Dorothy Sayers. The critic Howard Haycraft said of her work: "It is doubtful if any other practitioner of the form to-day writes with so vivid a talent for picturization, so accurate a grasp of 'timing,' or so infallible a sense of dramatic situation." In Marsh's life, however, fiction writing took second place to the theater, in which she was passionately engaged as producer, director, actress, and writer. Her elevation to the rank of dame commander of the Order of the British Empire in 1966 was not for her literary work, as many of her devoted readers might have thought, but for her theatrical work, particularly her staging of the plays of Shakespeare.

Marsh was born on the outskirts of Christchurch in New Zealand's South Island to parents who were active in amateur theatricals (her mother was descended from Jamaican planters, her father from an English family that had engaged in piracy). She was educated at St. Margaret's College, a school run by an Anglo-Catholic religious order. Her English literature teacher had a strong impact on her and gave her "a present I value more than any other: an abiding passion for the plays and sonnets of Shakespeare."

With the help of scholarships, Marsh went to the School of Art at Canterbury University College, determined to become a serious painter. Her plans changed after she saw a performance by the Allan Wilkie Shakespeare Company. She submitted "a terrible romantic drama" to Wilkie; the play was rejected, but she was offered an acting contract and toured with the company for two years, after which she spent four years producing, directing, and writing for amateur theater groups. In 1928 she traveled to England to stay with friends, a family who were to appear as the Lampreys in her 1940 novel *Death of a Peer* (British title: *A Surfeit of Lampreys*), in which their unbelievable eccentricities almost overwhelm the plot. Marsh, with one of the Lamprey girls, began a small business in London that eventually encompassed an interior decorating service.

One rainy Sunday morning in 1932, inspired by a Dorothy Sayers novel, she began her first book, *A Man Lay Dead,* which sprang from the premise that a real corpse is discovered instead of a make-believe one at a party where the then-popular "Murder Game" is being played. She left the manuscript with an agent when she was summoned back to New Zealand because of her mother's fatal illness; shortly afterward she learned, to her surprise, it had been accepted for publication.

A Man Lay Dead proved to be the first of a series of mystery novels that eventually numbered more than 30. The hero of all of them is Roderick Alleyn (named after the Elizabethan actor Edward Alleyn), a tall, lean, suave diplomat turned detective, whose wife, the painter Agatha Troy, and colleagues, including his manservant Vassili, Inspector "Br'er" Fox, journalist Nigel Bathgate, and fingerprint expert Sgt. Bailey, also figure prominently in the plotting. Marsh's novels are straightforward whodunits that feature bizarre modes of death (in *Overture to Death,* for instance, the victim is shot by a gun hidden in the piano on which he is playing the opening chords of Rachmaninoff's Prelude in C Minor). The best of them—naturally enough, considering Marsh's love for the theater—have theatrical plots and particularly well-observed theatrical characters. Critics have noted that her novels are naturalistic and recreate in very convincing terms the social and physical circumstances around which the plots are built. A number of her books were later adapted for the stage and television.

Although she bowed to pressure from her American and English readers by adding a chapter on her detective fiction when she recently revised her autobiography, *Black Beech and Honeydew,* Marsh will be remembered in New Zealand mainly for her services to drama. In 1942, despite her wartime job as a hospital bus driver for the Red Cross, she found time to produce *Outward Bound* for the Canterbury University Drama Society. The following year she persuaded the students to stage *Hamlet*—the first production of a Shakespeare play in the country in 20 years. It was a tremendous success, and the group, under her tutelage, became the nucleus of a semiprofessional company that toured Australia and New Zealand. She produced and directed ten Shakespeare plays and wrote several books on play production. New Zealand acknowledged her work by naming the new theater on the Canterbury University campus after her.

Dame Ngaio (whose first name, pronounced *Ny*-o, is the Maori name for a flowering tree) was also a painter and the author of several books on her homeland. She died at the age of 82 after completing another novel scheduled to be published posthumously.
B.D./J.P.

Courtesy of Hughes Massie Ltd.

Parents Henry Esmond M. and Rose Elizabeth (Seager) M. **Education** St. Margaret's Coll., Christchurch 1910–14; Canterbury Univ. Coll. Sch. of Art, Christchurch (scholarship) 1915–20. **Mil. service** Driver for Red Cross transport unit, N.Z., WWII. **Career** Actress with Allan Wilkie Shakespeare Co., on tour in Australia and N.Z. 1920–23; theatrical producer, N.Z. 1923–27; interior decorator, London 1928–32; writer of detective novels since 1934; producer, D.C. O'Connor Theatre Management, N.Z. 1944–52; founder, British Commonwealth Theatre Co. 1949; dir. and producer of plays by Shakespeare, Shaw, and Pirandello, Canterbury Univ. and London. **Fellow** FRSA. **Member** Detection Club. **Honors** Third prize, for *I Can Find My Way Out, Ellery Queen's Mystery Magazine* contest 1946; hon. lectr. in drama, Canterbury Univ. 1948; OBE 1948; Ngaio Marsh Theatre founded at Canterbury Univ. 1962; DBE 1966; Grand Master Award, Mystery Writers of America 1977; hon. degree from Canterbury Univ. **Novels** *A Man Lay Dead,* 1934; *Enter a Murderer,* 1935; (jtly.) *The Nursing-Home Murder,* 1935; *Death in Ecstasy,* 1936; *Vintage Murder,* 1937; *Artists in Crime,* 1938; *Death in a White Tie,* 1938; *Overture to Death,* 1939; *Death at the Bar,* 1940; *Death of a Peer* (in U.K. as *Surfeit of Lampreys),* 1940; *Death and the Dancing Footman,* 1941; *Colour Scheme,* 1943; *Died in the Wool,* 1945; *I Can Find My Way Out* (novelette), 1946; *Final Curtain,* 1947; *A Wreath for Rivera* (in U.K. as *Swing, Brother, Swing),* 1949; *Night at the Vulcan* (in U.K. as *Opening Night),* 1951; *The Bride of Death* (in U.K. as *Spinsters in Jeopardy),* 1955; *Scales of Justice,* 1955; *Death of a Fool* (in U.K. as *Off with His Head),* 1956; *Singing in the Shrouds,* 1958; *False Scent,* 1960; *Hand in Glove,* 1962; *Dead Water,* 1963; *Killer Dolphin* (in U.K. as *Death at the Dolphin),* 1967; *Clutch of Constables,* 1969; *When in Rome,* 1970; *Tied Up in Tinsel,* 1972; *Black as He's Painted,* 1975; *Last Ditch,* 1977; *Grave Mistake,* 1978; *Photo Finish,* 1980; *Light Thickens,* 1982. **Short-story collections** *A Three-Act Special* (juvenile), 1960; *Another Three-Act Special* (juvenile), 1962. **Other books** (Jtly.) *New Zealand,* 1942; *A Play Toward: A Note on Play Production,* 1946; *Perspectives: The New Zealander and the Visual Arts,* 1960; *Play Production,* 1960; *New Zealand* (juvenile), 1964; *Black Beech and Honeydew: An Autobiography,* 1966. **Plays** (Jtly.) *The Nursing Home Murders,* 1935; (jtly.) *False Scent,* 1962; *The Christmas Tree* (juvenile), 1962; *A Unicorn for Christmas,* 1965; *Murder Sails at Midnight,* 1972; *Evil Liver* (television script), 1975. **Manuscript collections** in Boston Univ.'s Mugar Memorial Library and in Alexander Turnbull Library, Wellington, N.Z.

Further reading Howard Haycraft, *Murder for Pleasure,* 1968; A. E. Murch, *The Development of the Detective Novel,* 1968; Jacques Barzun and Wendell Hertig Taylor, *A Catalogue of Crime,* 1971; Julian Symons, *Mortal Consequences,* 1972; Earl F. Bargainnier, "Ngaio Marsh's 'Theatrical' Murders," in *Armchair Detective,* Apr. 1977.

DAME MARGERY (FREDA) PERHAM

Expert on British colonial affairs
***Born* Bury, Lancashire, England, 6 September 1895**
***Died* England, 19 February 1982**

Dame Margery Perham's was the major academic voice in British colonial administration during the years of the empire's decline. Her carefully thought-out projections for eventual self-rule by Africans were outpaced by events in the continent during the 1950s and 1960s, but she always held to "my old-fashioned view that, by any balanced historical judgment of the history of imperialism and the character of the Africa we annexed, our colonial rule was, on balance, an immense and essential service to Africa."

The daughter of a prosperous North Country businessman, Margery Freda Perham began her education at St. Stephen's College, Windsor, and St. Anne's School, Abbots Bromley, which led to her winning an open scholarship to St. Hugh's College, Oxford University. She did exceptionally well there, taking a first-class honors degree in modern history in 1917, and shortly thereafter was appointed assistant lecturer at Sheffield University. Overwork and parental opposition to a career eventually led to a breakdown, and to recover her health she was sent to Africa in 1922 to visit her sister, whose husband, Maj. Henry Rayne, was a district commissioner in Somaliland. The year in Africa was the turning point of her life: she came to love the land and the people and began to observe closely the way they were governed. A popular novel, *Major Dane's Garden* (1924), was the first result of her year away, but much more work was to follow.

On returning home, Perham was able to go to Oxford instead of back to Sheffield, for her old college offered her a teaching post. She was tutor in modern history from 1924 to 1929, when she won a Rhodes Travelling Fellowship for three years to study "the administration of colored races" in North America, Polynesia, Australia, and East and West Africa. This was extended in 1932 by a Rockefeller Travelling Fellowship to East Africa and the Sudan. By the end of her tour she had decided that African colonial administration was her major interest, and shortly afterward she began to publish her most influential books.

Chief among these was *Native Administration in Nigeria* (1937), which challenged the Colonial Office to understand that independence in Britain's African possessions should be planned for as an imminent rather than a long-term fact. She thoroughly explored the concept of indirect rule, first formulated by Frederick J. D. Lugard, later Lord Lugard (1858–1945), when he was administrator of Nigeria in the late 1890s and unifier of the country in 1912–14. She firmly supported the fostering of native African governmental institutions, and insisted that well-meaning steps toward the Africanization of the Colonial Service were misguided and would "create a vested interest which would make its demolition at the appropriate time very difficult." Her ideas were widely heeded in both East and West Africa, as well as London, to the certain betterment of the incipient colonial disengagement.

In 1939, Perham was appointed reader in colonial administration at Oxford and elected to the first official fellowship at Nuffield College, a new postgraduate institution specializing in social-science research. When she was not traveling extensively in Africa her formidable energies were concentrated in Oxford, where she was instrumental in setting up the Institute of Colonial (later Commonwealth) Studies, now a major teaching and research arm of the university. She was the institute's director from 1945 to 1948. Its considerable library was formed around a nucleus of books and manuscripts collected by Perham herself.

Her major academic contribution was undoubtedly her work on Lord Lugard, who in his later years was Britain's most important authority on colonial affairs. Her well-received authorized biography, *Lugard: The Years of Adventure* (1956) and *Lugard: The Years of Authority* (1960), was based on her close association with him during his very active retirement. She also edited, with Mary Bull, *The Diaries of Lord Lugard* in three volumes (1959). She was the first woman chosen, in 1961, to give the BBC's Reith Lectures, *The Colonial Reckoning,* which was widely appreciated as a condensation of her life's work.

The African "winds of change," in Harold Macmillan's phrase, blew rather too forcefully for Perham in her later years, as the accelerated pace of independence brought chronic instability to the continent. She attempted to intervene in the bloody Nigerian civil war in 1969, pleading with the secessionist Ibos in Biafra to lay down their arms, but was unsuccessful. Her numerous articles for and letters to the *Times,* written over several decades, were collected in the two-volume *The Colonial Sequence* (1967, 1970). She published the diaries of her travels in *African Apprenticeship* (1974) and *East African Journey* (1976). Perham's other influential works included *Africans and British Rule* (1941), *Race and Politics in Kenya* (1944), and *The Government of Ethiopia* (1948).

Perham was made a CBE (1948) and a DCMG (1965), and was elected a fellow of the British Academy in 1961. She held honorary doctorates from St. Andrews, Southampton, London, Birmingham, Cambridge, and Oxford Universities, and was an honorary fellow of St. Hugh's and Nuffield, of Makerere College, Uganda, and of London University's School of Oriental and African Studies.

A.K.

Parents Frederick P., businessman, and Marion (Needell) P. **Religion** Church of England. **Education** St. Stephen's Coll., Windsor; St. Anne's Sch., Abbots Bromley; St. Hugh's Coll., Oxford (scholarship), B.A. 1919, M.A. (1st Class) 1919; Rhodes Travelling Fellowship, North America, Polynesia, Australia, Africa 1929–32; Rockefeller Travelling Fellowship, Intl. Inst. of African Languages and Culture, East Africa and Sudan 1932. **Career** Asst. lectr. in history, Sheffield Univ. ca. 1919–20; in Somaliland 1922–23; tutor in modern history and fellow 1924–29, and research fellow 1930–39, St. Hugh's Coll., Oxford; research lectr. in colonial admin., Oxford Univ., 1935–39; vice chmn., Oxford Univ. Summer Sch. of Colonial Admin. 1937–38; reader in colonial admin., Oxford Univ. 1939–48; official fellow, Nuffield Coll., Oxford 1939–63; dir., Oxford Univ. Inst. of Colonial Studies 1945–48; Reith Lectr., BBC 1961; chmn., Oxford Univ. Colonial Records Project 1963–73. • Series ed: *Colonial and Comparative Studies* (formerly *Colonial Research Publications)* since 1946; *Studies in Colonial Legislatures* I–IV; *The Economics of a Tropical Dependency* I and II. **Officer** Pres.: Univs.' Mission to Central Africa 1963–64; African Studies Assn. of U.K. 1963–64. **Fellow** FBA since 1961; Amer. Acad. of Arts and Sciences since 1969. **Member** Advisory Cttee. on Education in the Colonies 1939–45; Higher Education Commn. 1944; West Indies Higher Education Cttee. 1944; exec. cttee., Inter-Univ. Council on Higher Education Overseas 1946–67; Colonial Social Science Research Council 1947–61; Royal Commonwealth Soc. **Honors** CBE 1948; DCMG 1965; Gold Wellcome Medal, Royal Africa Soc.; hon. fellow of Nuffield Coll. since 1963, St. Hugh's Coll., Makerere Coll., Uganda, and London Univ. Sch. of Oriental and African Studies; hon. degrees from univs. of St. Andrews, Oxford, Southampton, London, Birmingham, and Cambridge. **Author** *Major Dane's Garden* (novel), 1925; *Josie Vine,* 1927; (jtly.) *The Protectorates of South Africa,* 1935; (ed). *Ten Africans,* 1936; *Native Administration in Nigeria,* 1937; *Africans and British Rule,* 1941; (jtly.) *Race and Politics in Kenya,* 1944; (co-ed.) *African Discovery,* 1946; *The Government of Ethiopia,* 1948; *Lugard: The Years of Adventure, 1858–1898,* 1956; (co-ed.) *The Diaries of Lord Lugard,* vols. 1–3, 1959; *Lugard: The Years of Authority, 1898–1945,* 1960; *The Colonial Reckoning,* 1961; (co-ed.) *The Diaries of Lord Lugard,* vol. 4, 1963; *Colonial Sequence,* vol. 1, 1967, vol. 2, 1970; *African Apprenticeship* (autobiography), 1974; *East African Journey,* 1976. **Contributor** of numerous articles and essays to *Times* of London and professional jrnls.

Further reading K. Robinson and F. Madden, eds., *Essays in Imperial Government Presented to Margery Perham* (festschrift), 1963.

RENÉ (JULES) DUBOS
Microbiologist and environmentalist
Born **Saint-Brice-sous-Forêt, Île-de-France, France, 20 February 1901**
Died **New York City, USA, 20 February 1982**

From a distinguished career in bacteriology—during which he isolated the first antibiotic substance to be used in commercial preparations and helped develop a vaccine against tuberculosis—René Dubos became a leading spokesman for the environmental movement. In a series of books and lectures, he argued persuasively that the cause of disease in humans is to be sought in the stresses and strains imposed on them by their modes of living, which break down their internal defense mechanisms and render them vulnerable to the effects of the microorganisms they carry within. The idea that the state of the environment and the organization of society are directly connected to the preservation of health gained wide acceptance in the 1960s and 1970s largely as a result of Dubos's work. He also warned against a too ready trust in the ability of technologists and scientists to provide quick answers to social problems. His warnings, however, were tempered by a buoyant sense of optimism that people, once alerted to the interdependence of environment and health, would choose the sensible course and opt to protect both.

Dubos spent his early childhood in farming villages in the Île-de-France and moved with his family to Paris when he was 13. After his father was killed in World War I, he helped his mother run their butcher shop while he attended the Collège Chaptal. He obtained a scholarship to the Institut National Agronomique and received a B.S. in 1921.

Dubos's first job after graduation was as assistant editor of a journal published by the International Institute of Agriculture in Rome. An article on soil microbes by the Russian microbiologist Sergei Winogradsky stimulated his interest in bacteriology, and he decided to seek training in the United States. He raised money for the voyage by doing translations and showing the city's sights to tourists. When, in 1924, he finally embarked at Le Havre for New York, he discovered that one of his fellow passengers was Selman A. Waksman, head of the soil microbiology division of the New Jersey Experiment Station at Rutgers University, whom he had guided through the Borghese Gardens a few months earlier. Waksman invited him to Rutgers, and for the next three years Dubos worked there as a research assistant and instructor while conducting studies on the decomposition of cellulose by soil bacteria. In 1927, not long before he obtained his Ph.D., he met Oswald T. Avery, a bacteriologist at the Rockefeller Institute for Medical Research in New York, who was investigating pneumonia. Avery had discovered that the pneumococcus organism is surrounded by a cellulose-like polysaccharide capsule that protects it from attack by antibodies defending the host from infection. He was seeking an enzyme that could decompose this capsule. Dubos offered to try to find a soil microorganism that produces just such an enzyme.

Upon Waksman's recommendation, Dubos joined the staff of the Institute (now Rockefeller University), where he was to remain for more than 40 years. His first three years were occupied in solving Avery's problem. He treated a variety of soils with solutions rich in capsular polysaccharide, reasoning that only those soil microorganisms capable of adapting to this limited diet would continue to flourish. A sample of cranberry bog soil provided by Waksman finally yielded the bacterial culture that Dubos had been looking for—a bacillus which, in the poor nourishment of the bog soil, had been forced to produce an enzyme capable of breaking down the capsule in order to digest its contents. (The concept that an organism will react in new and sometimes unforeseen ways under adverse conditions in order to survive was to become a central theme of Dubos's later work.) The enzyme did not prove effective in treating human beings, but was proven to fight pneumococcal infections in a number of animal species.

For the next nine years, Dubos tested soil samples in the hope of finding a microbial by-product that would destroy different kinds of living pathogenic bacteria. In 1939 he was able to announce that he had isolated a substance called tyrothricin, which is capable of killing staphylococcus, pneumococcus, and streptococcus germs in animals and human beings. Tyrothricin—which was later broken down into two components, gramicidin and tyrocidine—is produced by the organism *Bacillus brevis*. Although too toxic for internal use, tyrothricin proved highly effective for treating such surface conditions as boils and ear infections. Industrial firms quickly began large-scale production of tyrothricin from vats of *Bacillus brevis* for use in human and veterinary medicine. It was the first commercial production of an antibiotic and the first domestication of a microorganism for medicinal purposes. Dubos's success prompted a reexamination of the antibiotic properties of penicillin and encouraged Waksman in his efforts to isolate streptomycin. The age of antibiotics had begun.

In 1944, after two years at Harvard Medical School doing war work in tropical medicine, Dubos returned to the Rockefeller Institute to investigate the causes of tuberculosis, of which his wife had died a few years earlier. (His second wife, who had been his laboratory assistant, also developed tuberculosis—the disease was common among bacteriologists—and recovered after nine months in a sanitarium.) Previous researchers had been hampered by the fact that laboratory strains of tuberculosis bacilli gradually metamorphose until they no longer resemble those found in vivo. Dubos found ways of cultivating these bacilli quickly enough so that they remained unchanged. As a result, experimenters were able to produce tuberculosis in mice and to develop the Bacillus Calmette-Guérin vaccine, which virtually eradicated the disease in the West. Dubos summarized this and other recent developments in his first two books, published in 1945 and 1948.

His first wife's experience of recurrent tuberculosis—she had survived an attack in childhood only to have the dormant germ revive during World War II, when she was worried about her family in France—helped confirm Dubos's suspicion that economic, emotional, and social disruptions in people's lives can render them susceptible to infection. Following the publication in 1950 of his well-received biography of the pioneering bacteriologist Louis Pasteur, Dubos collaborated with his second wife on *The White Plague—Tuberculosis, Man, and Society,* in which he adduced evidence to show that tuberculosis thrives in areas where people lack adequate protein nourishment. In *Mirage of Health* (1959) he discredited the belief, widespread in industrialized nations, that scientific research can achieve a disease-free utopia through ever more advanced drugs and operations, without ameliorating the socioeconomic conditions that give rise to disease in the first place. Here and in other writings he pointed out that each change in the way of life of a given population brings about changes in that population's level of resistance to infectious agents and in the variety of infectious agents to which it is vulnerable: leprosy, measles, and rheumatic fever, once prevalent in Europe, became markedly less severe and less widespread there without benefit of medical intervention; and bronchitis and poliomyelitis increased, largely because of changes in living and working conditions, washing habits, food and air quality, and other environmental factors. Dubos's research during the 1950s supported his view that many characteristics (including body size, organ size, growth rate, and resistance to infection) are influenced by the environment and are not simply the products of genetic endowment.

It was Dubos's contention that humans, like all organisms, must adapt to their environment in order to live, and that the degree of successful adaptation is expressed as a measure of their greater or lesser health. In a technologically advanced society, the rapid pace of change, existence in artificial rather than natural surroundings, and constant exposure to toxic chemicals, pollution, noise, and other by-products of industry combine to put an almost unbearable strain on the adaptability of the human organism, and make its responses to further innovations increasingly harder to predict. This was the subject of *Man Adapting* (1965) and of *So Human an Animal* (1968), which won the Pulitzer Prize for general nonfiction, and of which the naturalist Joseph Wood Krutch said, "I have read no other

Courtesy of Rockefeller University

book which so clearly explains why science is indispensable but not omnicompetent."

Dubos continued his challenge to the scientific establishment in *Reason Awake: Science for Man* (1970). "As the power of science increases," he wrote, "its uses become less sacred, more trivial, more brutal, and often more immoral. . . . As a community we [scientists] have betrayed our ideals by . . . promoting our wares through irresponsible promises to society of perfect health, economic prosperity, and military power." He criticized the common practice of introducing new substances and devices into the marketplace without adequate testing. He was particularly outraged at the introduction in the late 1960s of laundry detergents containing enzymes produced by a bacillus similar to the one from which he had extracted tyrothricin in the 1930s, and which could, he warned, cause allergic reactions, clumping of red blood cells, and kidney lesions.

During the early 1970s, Dubos, now recognized as a leading environmental thinker, was appointed by Pres. Nixon to the Citizens' Advisory Committee on Environmental Quality, and was the co-author, with economist Barbara Ward, of the landmark report *Only One Earth* for the U.N. Conference on the Human Environment. In 1971, after reaching mandatory retirement age at Rockefeller University, he became university professor and director of environmental studies at the State University of New York College at Purchase and advisor to Richmond College on Staten Island, meanwhile continuing to lecture and write. The theme of his work in the last decade was the hopeful expectation that ordinary people would recognize the dangers of living in an industrialized society and would take responsibility, on a local level, for improving the quality of life, resisting the power of the technocracy, protecting the earth from nuclear and chemical pollution, and slowing the pace of unnecessary change. He cited as reason for optimism such acts of creative reclamation by private citizens as the establishment of a bird sanctuary on three man-made islands of garbage in New York City's Jamaica Bay and the successful campaign to prevent Kennedy Airport from extending a runway into the bay. "Thinking globally and acting locally" became the motto of the René Dubos Center for Human Environments in the Bronx, which was founded in 1980 to promote just such activities.

Dubos was the recipient of numerous awards and of more than 30 honorary degrees. His last book, *Celebrations of Life,* was published in 1981. He died of heart failure on his 81st birthday. J.P./P.D.

Parents Georges Alexandre D., butcher, and Adeline Madeleine (de Bloedt) D. **Married** (1) Marie Louise Bonnet, teacher, 1934 (d. 1942). (2) Letha Jean Porter, bacteriologist, 1945. **Emigrated** to U.S. 1924; naturalized 1938. **Education** Primary schs., Henonville and Paris; Coll. Chaptal, Paris 1915–19; Inst. Natl. Agronomique, Paris, B.S. 1921; Rutgers Univ., New Brunswick, NJ, Ph.D. 1927. **Mil. service** French Army 1921–22. **Career** Asst. ed., *International Agriculture Intelligence,* Intl. Inst. of Agriculture, Rome 1922–24; research asst. in soil microbiology and instr. in bacteriology, New Jersey Experiment Sta., Rutgers Univ. 1924–27. • With Rockefeller Inst. of Medical Research (now Rockefeller Univ.), NYC: fellow 1927–28; asst. 1928–30; assoc. 1930–38; assoc. member 1938–41; member 1941–42, 1944–56; member and prof. 1957–71; prof. emeritus since 1971; founder, dept. of environmental biomedicine. • Fabyan Prof. of Comparative Pathology and Tropical Medicine, Harvard Medical Sch. 1942–44; ed., *Journal of Experimental Medicine* 1946–72; Baker Lectr., Sch. of Public Health, Univ. of Michigan 1961; univ. prof. and dir. of environmental studies, SUNY at Purchase since 1970; advisor, Richmond Coll., NYC since 1970; contributing ed. and columnist, *American Scholar* since 1970; member, Citizens' Advisory Cttee. on Environmental Quality 1970–75; founder 1980 and chmn., bd. of trustees, René Dubos Center for Human Environments, NYC. **Officer** Pres.: Harvey Soc. 1951; Soc. of Amer. Bacteriologists 1951. **Member** Amer. Acad. and Inst. of Arts and Letters since 1979; Natl. Acad. of Sciences; Amer. Philosophical Soc.; Natl. Research Council; Century Assn. **Honors** Phillips Memorial Award, Amer. Coll. of Physicians 1940; Johnson Award, Amer. Acad. of Pediatrics 1940; Wilson Medal, Amer. Clinical and Climatological Assn. 1946; Lasker Award, Amer. Public Health Assn. 1948; Trudeau Award, Natl. Tuberculosis Assn. 1951; Pharmaceutical Industries Award 1952; Triennial Prize Lecture Award, Massachusetts Gen. Hosp. 1953; Hitchcock Award, Univ. of California 1954; Ricketts Award, Univ. of Chicago 1958; Passano Award, AMA 1960; Koch Centennial Award, Robert Koch Inst., Berlin 1960; Modern Medicine Award 1961; Phi Beta Kappa Science Award 1963, for *The Unseen World,* and 1966, for *Man Adapting;* Science Achievement Award, AMA 1964; Arches of Science Award, Pacific Center 1966; Pulitzer Prize for nonfiction, for *So Human an Animal,* 1969; Clark Award 1970; Prix Intl., Inst. de la Vie 1972; Washburn Award, Boston Mus. of Science 1974; Forsythia Award, Brooklyn Botanic Garden 1974; Cullum Geographical Medal 1975; Tyler Ecology Award 1976; Penfield Award, Vanier Inst. of the Family 1979; elected to 75th Anniversary Living Hall of Fame, Amer. Lung Assn. 1980. • Hon. degrees from univs. of Rochester, Harvard, Liège, Rutgers, Paris, Rio de Janeiro, Alberta, Pennsylvania, California, St. John's, Wesleyan, Queen's (Canada), Sherbrooke, Loyola, Clark, Marquette, Catholic (Wash. DC), Fairfield, Jefferson, Calgary, Rockefeller, and Guelph (Canada), from Colby, Carleton, Beloit, Kalamazoo, Bard, Williams, University (Dublin), Kenyon, and Marietta colls., and from New Sch. for Social Research, Acad. de Lille, others. **Author** *The Bacterial Cell,* 1945; *Bacterial and Mycotic Infections of Man,* 1948; *Louis Pasteur,* 1950; *The White Plague—Tuberculosis, Man and*

Society, 1952; *Biochemical Determinants of Microbial Disease,* 1954; *Mirage of Health,* 1959; *Pasteur and Modern Science,* 1960; *Dreams of Reason,* 1961; *The Unseen World,* 1962; *The Torch of Life,* 1962; *Health and Disease,* 1965; *Man Adapting,* 1965; *Man, Medicine and Environment,* 1968; *So Human an Animal,* 1968; *Reason Awake: Science for Man,* 1970; *A God Within,* 1972; (jtly.) *Only One Earth,* 1972; *Beast or Angel?,* 1974; *Of Human Diversity,* 1974; *The Professor, the Institute and DNA,* 1976; *The Resilience of Ecosystems,* 1978; *The Wooing of the Earth,* 1980; (jtly.) *Quest: Reflections on Medicine, Science, and Humanity,* 1980; *Celebrations of Life,* 1981. **Contributor** of more than 200 papers to scientific jrnls.

Further reading Selman A. Waksman, "Dr. René J. Dubos—A Tribute," in *Journal of the American Medical Association,* vol. 174, no. 5, 1 Oct. 1960; C. H. Waddington, "A Matter of Life and Death," in *New York Review of Books,* 6 May 1969; John Cullane, *"En Garde,* Pessimists! Enter René Dubos," in *New York Times Magazine,* 17 Oct. 1971.

EDWARD C(LAUS) FRANKLIN
Immunologist
Born **Berlin, Germany, 14 April 1928**
Died **New York City, USA, 20 February 1982**

Edward C. Franklin's research into the body's production and metabolism of antibody proteins clarified the causes of the autoimmune reactions that occur in rheumatic diseases and in certain cancers and shed light on the process of aging.

A native of Germany, Franklin came to the United States with his family at the age of 11 as a refugee from the Nazis and settled in the New York City area. He graduated from Harvard in 1946, obtained his M.D. in 1950 from the New York University School of Medicine, and served in five army hospitals during the Korean War.

Franklin began his research career in 1955 at the Rockefeller Institute for Medical Research in New York City and within two years had made his first significant contribution to immunology. Under the direction of Henry G. Kunkel, he studied the proteins in the blood of patients suffering from rheumatoid arthritis and identified one such protein, called the rheumatoid factor, as an antibody. Antibodies are normally produced by the body in reaction to the presence of bacteria, viruses, and other foreign substances. Since no such invaders could be detected in the blood of Franklin's patients, his discovery raised the possibility that rheumatoid arthritis is an autoimmune disease—one in which the body mistakenly attacks its own tissues. This interpretation is now accepted by most medical researchers.

Courtesy of New York Medical Center

In 1958 Franklin joined the faculty of the New York University School of Medicine and the staff of Bellevue Hospital; in 1962 he also became an attending physician at University Hospital. He was named director of the NYU Medical Center's multidisciplinary Rheumatic Diseases Study Group in 1968, and from 1973 he headed the Irvington House Institute, a research center for the study of clinical and basic immunology. The two organizations were merged under his directorship in 1975.

During the 1960s, Franklin identified a rare disorder of the lymphoid system—since known as Franklin's disease—that is characterized by the production of abnormal immunoglobulins (antibodies formed in the lymphocytes). He subsequently discovered amyloid, a glycoprotein derived from immunoglobulins, which is deposited in fibrous lumps in the bodies of arthritis sufferers, and proved that the accumulation of amyloid in tissues is related to the aging process. On the basis of this and other work, some researchers now believe that aging itself may be a form of autoimmune reaction. Dr. Dorothea Zucker-Franklin, his wife since 1956, collaborated with him on much of this research.

Franklin was elected to the presidency of the American Society for Clinical Investigation in 1974 and to the National Academy of Sciences in 1979. He died at the age of 53 after a long illness. P.D.

Parents Ernest A. F. and Ilse (Joachim) F. **Married** Dorothea Zucker, medical researcher, 1956: Deborah Julie, b. 1964. **Emigrated** to U.S. 1939; naturalized 1944. **Religion** Jewish. **Education** Forest Hills High Sch., NY; Harvard Coll., B.S. 1946; New York Univ. Sch. of Medicine, M.D. 1950; intern, Beth Israel Hosp., NYC 1950–51; resident in medicine, Montefiore Hosp., NYC 1951–52, and Bronx Veterans Admin. Hosp., NYC 1954–55; diplomate, Amer. Bd. of Internal Medicine. **Mil. service** First lt., U.S. Army, Korea 1952–54. **Career** Asst. 1955–57, asst. physician 1955–58, and assoc. 1957–58, Rockefeller Inst., NYC; sr. investigator, Arthritis and Rheumatism Foundn. 1958–63; career scientist, New York City Health Research Council since 1963; advisor, NIH and Amer. Heart Assn. • With New York Univ. Medical Center: asst. prof. of medicine 1958–63, assoc. prof. of medicine 1963–68, prof. of medicine and dir. of Rheumatic Diseases Study Group since 1968, and dir. of Irvington House Inst. since 1973, New York Univ. Sch. of Medicine, NYC; asst. visiting physician 1958–63, assoc. visiting physician 1963–68, and visiting physician since 1968, Bellevue Hosp., NYC; asst. attending physician 1962–63, assoc. attending physician 1963–68, and attending physician since 1968, Univ. Hosp. **Officer** Pres. 1974 and council member, Amer. Soc. for Clinical Investigation. **Fellow** Macy Foundn.; Arthritis Foundn. **Member** Amer. Assn. of Physicians since 1969; Natl. Acad. of Sciences since 1979; Soc. of Experimental Biology and Medicine; Amer. Assn. of Immunologists; Amer. Rheumatism Assn.; Harvey Soc.; Amer. Assn. for Advancement of Science; Amer. Soc. of Biological Chemistry; Democratic Party. **Contributor** of over 250 papers to professional jrnls.

DEREK AINSLIE JACKSON

Spectroscopist

***Born* London, England, 23 June 1906**

***Died* Lausanne, Switzerland, 20 February 1982**

Derek Ainslie Jackson carried out groundbreaking research in high-resolution spectroscopy. Born into a wealthy family, he was educated at Rugby and Cambridge, where he obtained his M.A. with honors in 1927. While a student, he visited the Berlin laboratory of H. Schüler, where a new frontier in spectroscopy was opening up.

By that time, scientists had identified the spectral lines characteristic of various elements and had analyzed their fine structure; the explanation of these phenomena in quantum terms during the 1920s had cast new light on the nature and structure of the atom. The spectra of some elements had revealed hints of hyperfine structure, but so narrowly separated were some of these lines that the random thermal motion of atoms was enough to obscure them. By cooling his spectrographic equipment—a hollow cathode light source—Schüler was able to reduce this distortion, known as Doppler widening, and reveal the hyperfine structure.

Jackson, intrigued by the challenges posed

by this new field, performed some calculations based on a suggestion made a few years before by the physicist Wolfgang Pauli. Pauli thought that the hyperfine structure might be explained if nuclei, like electrons, had a spin and an associated strength—the nuclear magnetic moment. The interaction between the magnetic moment of the nucleus and the magnetic field produced by the motions of electrons would then account for the appearance of the subtle lines in the spectra. By measuring accurately the energy spacings in the hyperfine structure, Jackson was able to estimate, for the first time, the actual value of the nuclear magnetic moment.

In 1927 Jackson took a research post at Oxford University's Clarendon Laboratory. He was appointed a lecturer at the university in 1934. Between 1933 and 1938, he and his associate H. G. Kuhn worked on adapting the atomic beam for use in their research. The particles in this highly focused beam show very little sideways motion; by crossing it with a beam of light at right angles Jackson and Kuhn achieved even greater reductions in the Doppler distortion of spectral lines. The technique proved useful for studying such phenomena as isotope shift.

Courtesy of Marie Christine Jackson

During World War II, Jackson joined the Royal Air Force Volunteer Reserve and developed methods of countering enemy jamming of radar and communications. He also saw combat as an air gunner, served as a wing commander, and was decorated with the Air Force Cross and OBE. He returned to Oxford as a professor of spectroscopy in 1945 and was made a fellow of the Royal Society two years later.

Jackson spent his own money freely to further his scientific research and left England in 1951 to avoid the postwar tax laws. He spent 1950 as a visiting professor at Ohio State University, lived for two years in the Republic of Ireland, and in 1953 settled in Switzerland. He was then offered the facilities of the Laboratoire Aimé Cotton in Paris, part of the National Center for Scientific Research. The laboratory boasted an improved version of the Fabry-Pérot interferometer, a device used for the precise measurement of optical wavelengths and very narrow spectral lines, and Jackson was able to take advantage of its high resolving power to study hyperfine structures. In later years he spent most of his time in Switzerland. P.D.

Parents Sir Charles James J. and Ada (Williams) J. **Married** (1) Poppet John 1931. (2) Pamela Mitford 1936 (div. 1951). (3) Janetta Woolley Kee 1951 (div. 1956): Rose Janetta. (4) Consuelo Regina Maria Eyre (div. 1959). (5) Marie-Christine Reille 1968. **Emigrated** to Ireland 1951, France 1953. **Education** Rugby Sch.; Trinity Coll., Cambridge, M.A. (1st Class) 1927; Oxford Univ., D.Sc. 1936. **Mil. service** Observer, RAF Volunteer Reserve 1940–45; air gunner and wing comdr., RAF 1943. **Career** Researcher in spectroscopy 1927–39, univ. lectr. 1934, and prof. of spectroscopy 1945–48, Oxford Univ.; visiting prof., Ohio State Univ. 1950; research prof., Faculté des Sciences, Laboratoire Aimé Cotton, Centre Natl. de la Récherche Scientifique, Bellevue and Orsay, France since 1953. **Fellow** FRS 1947. **Honors** DFC; OBE; AFC; officer, Legion of Merit, U.S.; chevalier, Légion d'Honneur, France; hon. asst., Dunkirk Observatory 1952–53. **Contributor** of numerous articles to jrnls. of physics.

GERSHOM G(ERHARD) SCHOLEM

Scholar of Jewish mysticism

***Born* Berlin, Germany, 5 December 1897**

***Died* Jerusalem, Israel, 20 February 1982**

Judaism as a living religion, hard pressed to survive the ravages of the Nazis, has also had to face, in this century, the threat of internal collapse from the cancerous effects of secularism, assimilationism, rationalist skepticism, and Orthodox dogmatism. It would probably not have been able to withstand these still very real challenges if not for the work of the great German-born scholar Gershom Scholem, who broke open its petrifying outer shell to reveal a long-suppressed mystical tradition, still flowing with vitality after almost two millennia. By demonstrating the pluralistic, even protean, nature of Jewish belief and practice in the past, he disproved the claim of rabbinic (Orthodox) Judaism to sole authenticity and thereby opened the way for the rediscovery of religious identity by modern Jews disenfranchised by that claim.

Before Scholem, Jewish mysticism, known as Kabbalah ("received learning"), was a despised subject among historians of religion, debased by the Romantics and dismissed by apologists in the West as an occult aberration from the rational principles of monotheism which, they insisted, constitute normative Judaism (and which, not incidentally, made Judaism more acceptable in liberal Christian societies). Scholem's research forced the reevaluation of the subject by both Jewish and Christian scholars and was responsible for the establishment of a new and influential field of study. His rescue of the Kabbalah from oblivion, and his wholesale recasting of accepted ideas of Jewish history, is considered one of the greatest intellectual achievements of the age, comparable to Freud's, though hardly as well known. Among the writers and thinkers for whom it opened fruitful avenues of imagination are Jorge Luis Borges, the Argentine poet and fabulist, and Harold Bloom, professor of humanities at Yale University, who derived from it an elaborate theory of literary criticism.

Courtesy of American Friends of the Hebrew University

Mysticism, Scholem demonstrated, is a dialectical process by which certain tensions—between institutionalized religious custom and the individual's direct experience of God; between the claims of theology and the realities of history—produce new growth in the spiritual life of a people, transforming it from within while keeping its outward forms intact. Jewish mysticism, which began in the first century B.C. under gnostic influence, was, in particular, an attempt to recover the immediacy of revelation by treating language, especially the language of the sacred books, as an agent of divine creation. Its practitioners in medieval Spain and Palestine created a complex theory of God's inner life that was transmuted by their successors into a powerful doctrine motivating the messianic hysteria of Sabbateanism in the seventeenth century and the flowering of Chassidism in the eighteenth. Scholem's explication of these mystical movements demonstrated, so far without convincing critical challenge, that Judaism, far from being a unified tradition subject to steady historical development, is an oceanic flow encompassing ideas and practices of every extreme, the treasury of mythical, emotional, and instinctive forces beyond the limits and control of monotheism.

Scholem's achievement is the more remarkable considering the circumstances of his birth and upbringing. His family, which was in the printing business, was thoroughly assimilated into well-to-do Berlin society. Scholem, the youngest of four sons, was given a classical education and went on to the university with the intention of becoming a mathematician. Early in adolescence he was unexpectedly possessed by an intense curiosity about Judaism and its various manifestations, of which all knowledge had been denied him. He began to study Hebrew, in the conviction that an understanding of Jewish history is essential to a committed Jewish life, and became a Zionist, in the conviction that the renewal of Judaism would be accomplished only where Jews could encounter their tradition in freedom and assuredly not in the poisoned atmosphere of Europe, whose coming horrors he clearly foresaw (his brother, a Communist politician, was murdered in Buchenwald concentration camp). His anarchist views, especially his opposition to World War I, brought him expulsion from his secondary school and banishment from his parents' home; at the same time he began to acquire a reputation for academic brilliance and to associate with such leaders and gadflies of German Jewry as Martin Buber and Franz Rosenzweig. He took his doctorate in Semitics from the University of Munich in 1922 and the following year emigrated to Palestine, where he became a librarian in Hebraica and Judaica in what was soon to become the Hebrew University of Jerusalem. In 1925 he was appointed lecturer and in 1933 professor of Jewish mysticism.

His first 18 years there were occupied in basic technical studies, including the recovery, edition, and philological analysis of neglected kabbalistic texts and manuscripts. At the end of that time he published *Major Trends in Jewish Mysticism* (1941), an extraordinarily wide-ranging, impeccably documented, and massively detailed piece of historical synthesis. Most of his later studies—including his biography of the false messiah Sabbetai Tsevi (1957–58; English ed. 1973), *On the Kabbalah and Its Symbolism* (1960; English ed. 1965), *The Messianic Idea in Judaism* (1971), and his 150-page entry on Kabbalah in the *Encyclopaedia Judaica*—were built on the foundation of this work.

By the end of his life Scholem was an internationally renowned scholar and a legend in Jewish intellectual circles, as much for his vigorous and avowedly anarchistic individualism and playful defiance of every kind of authority as for his powers of insight and the dense, precise, lucid quality of his prose. Many of his readers tantalized themselves with the question of whether or not Scholem was himself a kabbalist. On this point Scholem remained enigmatic, but the novelist Mark Mirsky has correctly observed that his books, by their very brilliance, are a species of the magical arts. Robert Alter, in an article in *Commentary,* wrote, "Scholem has the kind of ironic intelligence that delights in contradictions, that can hold the multiple attributes of the subjects it scrutinizes in clear simultaneous view. . . . As a result, his account of the Jewish past can accommodate the full power of its most seemingly alien manifestations while seeing in overview the distinct limitations of their historical field of operation. Similarly, he can affirm the revolutionary significance of the Zionist fulfillment with an acute awareness of its looming ambiguities. . . . His involvement with the past is intellectually linked with a deep concern for the complexities of history unfolding in the present."

Scholem lived nearly all his adult life in Jerusalem, occasionally undertaking lectureships and visiting professorships at universities in Europe and the United States. He was a participant in the annual Eranos Conferences and a contributor to the Eranos yearbook, and the author of innumerable essays, articles, and reviews in scholarly and Jewish periodicals. In his later years he wrote a memoir of his friendship with the essayist and critic Walter Benjamin, who killed himself in 1940 during the Nazi persecutions. His final book was the autobiographical *From Berlin to Jerusalem.* J.P.

Born Gerhard Scholem. **Parents** Arthur S., printer, and Betty (Hirsch) S., businesswoman. **Married** (1) Elsa Burchhardt 1923 (div. 1936). (2) Fania Freud 1936. **Religion** Jewish. **Emigrated** to Palestine 1923; citizen of Israel since 1948. **Education** Luisenstadtisches Gymnasium, Berlin; Univ. of Berlin 1915–17; Univ. of Jena 1917–18; Univ. of Berne 1918–19; Univ. of Munich, Ph.D. in Semitics 1922. **Mil. service** Infantry, German Army, 1917, discharged after 2 months as unfit. **Career** Researcher and trans. of Kabbalah since 1919. • With Hebrew Univ. of Jerusalem: head of dept. of Hebraica and Judaica, Natl. and Univ. Library 1923–27; lectr. 1925–33; prof. of Jewish mysticism 1933–65; dean 1941–43; prof. emeritus since 1965. • Visiting prof.: Jewish Inst. of Religion, NYC 1938; Brown Univ., Providence, RI 1956–57; Hebrew Union Coll., Cincinnati 1966; Boston Univ. 1975. **Officer** V.P., Jewish Cultural Reconstruction, Inc., and Israeli rep. in salvation of Jewish cultural treasures 1946–50; v.p. 1962–68 and pres. 1968–74, Israel Natl. Acad.

of Sciences and Humanities. **Member** British Acad.; Royal Acad., the Netherlands; Amer. Acad. for Jewish Research; Amer. Acad. of Arts and Sciences; Westfäliche Akad. der Wissenschaften; Akad. der Künste, Berlin. **Honors** State Prize of Israel for Jewish Studies 1958; Rothschild Prize for Jewish Studies 1962; many other awards. **Author** *Bibliographia Kabbalistica,* 1927; *Khalomotav shel ha-Shabtai R. Mordecai Ashkenazi* [*The Dreams of R. Mordecai Ashkenazi, the Sabbatean*], 1938; *Perakim le-Toledot Sifrut ha-Kabbalah* [*Chapters toward a History of the Literature of the Kabbalah*], 1931; *Major Trends in Jewish Mysticism,* 1941, 3rd rev. ed. 1954; *Ha-Mistorin ha-Yehudi ve-ha-Kabbalah* [*The Jewish Mystery and the Kabbalah*], 1943; *Reshit ha-Kabbalah* [*The Origins of the Kabbalah*], 1948; *Shabtai Tsevi,* 2 vols. 1957–58 (trans. as *Sabbetai Sevi, the Mystical Messiah, 1626–1676,* 1973); *Jewish Gnosticism, Merkabah Mysticism, and Talmudic Tradition,* 1962, 2nd improved ed. 1965; *Zur Kabbala und ihrer Symbolik,* 1960 (trans. as *On the Kabbalah and Its Symbolism,* 1965); *Von der mystischen Gestalt der Gottheit: Studien zu Grundbegriffen der Kabbala* [*On the Mystical Character of the Divine: Studies on the Fundamental Idea of the Kabbalah*], 1962; *Ursprung und Anfänge der Kabbala* [*The Origins and Beginnings of the Kabbalah*], 1962; *Judaica,* I, 1963, II, 1970, III, 1973; *Ha-Kabbalah be-Provants* [*The Provençal Kabbalah*], 1963; *Ha-Kabbalah be-Geronah* [*The Geronese Kabbalah*], 1964; *Ha-Kabbalah shel Sefer ha-Temunah ve-shel Abraham Abulafia* [*The Kabbalah of the Book of the Picture and of Abraham Abulafia*], 1964; *Die Erforschung der Kabbala von Reuchlin bis zur Gegenwart* [*The Investigation of the Kabbalah from Reuchlin to the Present*], 1969; *Über einige Grundbegriffe des Judentums* [*On Some Fundamental Ideas of Judaism*], 1970; *The Messianic Idea in Judaism, and Other Essays on Jewish Spirituality,* 1971; *Mekharim u-Mekorot le-Toledot ha-Shabta'ut ve-Gilguleha* [*Researches and Texts on the History of Sabbateanism and Its Metamorphoses*], 1974; *Kabbalah,* 1974; *Devarim be-Go: Pirkei Morashah u-Tehia* [*Explications and Implications: Chapters of Inheritance and Renewal*], 2 vols., 1975; *Walter Benjamin: Die Geschichte einer Freundschaft,* 1975 (trans. as *Walter Benjamin: The Story of a Friendship,* 1971); Werner J. Dannhauser, ed., *On Jews and Judaism in Crisis,* 1976; *Von Berlin nach Jerusalem: Jugenderinnerungen,* 1977 (trans. as *From Berlin to Jerusalem: Memories of My Youth,* 1980). **Editor** (Also trans. and commentator) *Das Buch Bahir* [*The Book "Bahir"*], 1923, rev. 1970; (also trans.) Abu Aflah, *Sefer ha-Tamar* [*The Book of the Palm*], 1927; *Kabbalot R. Ya'akov u-R. Yitzhak Kohen,* 1927; *Kitvei ha-Yad ha-Ivriyim* [*Hebrew Manuscripts*], 1930–34; *Kitvei Yad be-Kabbalah ha-Nimtzaim be-Bet ha-Seferim ha-Le'umi ve-ha-Universitah bi-Rushalayim* [*Hebrew Manuscripts Found in the National and University Library in Jerusalem*], 1930; (also trans.) *Die Geheimnisse der Schöpfung: Ein Kapitel aus dem Sohar* [*The Mysteries of Creation: A Chapter from the Zohar*], 1935, rev. 1973; *Zohar—The Book of Splendor: Basic Readings from the Kabbalah,* 1949; Walter Benjamin, *Berliner Chronik* [*Berlin Chronicle*], 1971; (jtly.) Walter Benjamin, *Briefe* [*Letters*], 2 vols., 1966; *Walter Benjamin and Gershom Scholem: Briefwechsel* [*Correspondence*], 1980; many other translations and editions of kabbalistic texts. **Contributor** to *Encyclopaedia Judaica, Eranos Jahrbuch,* and many periodicals. **Recording** *The Religious Dimensions of Judaism,* 1976.

Further reading E. E. Urbach et al., eds. *Studies in Mysticism and Religion, Presented to Gershom G. Scholem on His Seventieth Birthday,* 1967; Herbert Weiner, *9½ Mystics: The Kabbala Today,* 1969; Robert Alter, "The Achievement of Gershom Scholem," in *Commentary,* Apr. 1973; Mark Jay Mirsky, *My Search for the Messiah,* 1977; David Biale, *Gershom Scholem: Kabbalah and Counter-History,* 1979.

MISCHEL CHERNIAVSKY
Cellist
***Born* Uman, Kiev province, Russia, 2 November 1893**
***Died* near Dieppe, France, 21 February 1982**

The cellist Mischel Cherniavsky was the youngest member of the Cherniavsky Trio, which enjoyed worldwide success in the first quarter of this century. After the trio disbanded in 1923, Cherniavsky, who had become a British subject, enjoyed a considerable solo career until his retirement in 1958.

Mischel was the sixth of nine children. He and his brothers Leo, a prodigy on the violin, and Jan, a pianist, studied music in early childhood with their father, a Ukrainian conductor and musical scholar. Soon after forming the trio in 1901 they made a sensational tour of Russia which ended with a performance before Czar Nicholas II in 1903, when Mischel was seven. The family left for Vienna in 1904, where—amid wildly popular tours of Western Europe—Mischel was able to study under David Popper while Leo was the pupil of the great violinst Leopold Auer. In 1908–09, from their new home in London, where Mischel studied with Herbert Walenn, the trio made their first international tour to South Africa, which they followed in 1912–14 with a tour of India, Australia, and New Zealand. Their first performance in the United States was in New York in 1917. They were well received everywhere, and frequently appeared with great singers of that era, including Clara Butt, Amelita Galli-Curci, and John McCormack.

During his solo career, Cherniavsky was frequently associated with the London Philharmonic Orchestra and its longtime conductor, Sir Thomas Beecham. In 1940 he was a leader in the successful appeal for funds to save the orchestra. During the early war years he played for troops throughout the United Kingdom and also for Mrs. Winston Churchill's Aid to Russia Fund.

Cherniavsky's last public performance occurred in 1958, when he appeared as soloist with Beecham and the Philharmonic in one of his best-received pieces, Saint-Saëns's Cello Concerto in A minor, which he had played for Camille Saint-Saëns himself as a boy of 12.

A.K.

Father Abraham Cherniavsky, conductor and music scholar. **Married** Mary Angus Rogers 1919 (d. 1980): Michael; David; John; Felix; Mark. **Religion** Of Jewish birth. **Emigration** British citizen since 1922. **Education** Studied violin with father; studied cello with David Popper and Herbert Walenn. **Career** Toured Europe, England, South Africa, India, N.Z., Australia, Canada, and U.S. as cellist with Cherniavsky Trio 1901–23; recitalist and soloist with major orchs. 1923–58; played concerts for soldiers in U.K., and organized concerts for Aid to Russia Fund in Canada, WWII.

Further reading Gdal Saleski, *Famous Musicians of Jewish Origin,* 1949.

MURRAY THE K
Disc jockey and rock entrepreneur
***Born* New York City, USA, 14 February 1922**
***Died* Los Angeles, California, USA, 21 February 1982**

The musical and cultural phenomenon that was 1960s rock 'n' roll—a potent combination of adolescent frustration and idealism, high-powered hype, corporate greed, and a fair amount of true artistry—owed some of its early success to the efforts of the New York disc jockey Murray the K. While tirelessly courting the rich and famous and hustling to keep his own face before the public, Murray the K managed for years to keep on the cut-

ting edge of new developments in rock, introducing obscure black and British acts that quickly became vast moneymakers, giving AM rock radio stations their frenetic pace, and revolutionizing FM radio with progressive rock programming.

Born in the Bronx, Murray Kaufman was the son of a leather dealer and a vaudeville pianist. He quit high school and by his mid-20s was working the Catskill resort circuit as an emcee. After a short stint as a catcher for the New York Yankees' farm team, he joined the New York radio station WMCA as an announcer and talk-show host. In 1958 he moved to WINS to play pop records for an all-night show called "Swingin' Soiree." It was switched to the evening hours the next year and immediately began to build a huge cult following among teenagers, who enjoyed the manic outpouring of screams, yowls, gasps, war cries, and slang chatter—"What's happenin' baby!"—with which Murray filled the airwaves between songs and commercials.

In 1959 he brought his act directly to his audience as the host of live shows at the Fox and Paramount theaters in Brooklyn, where he introduced Dion, Stevie Wonder, Little Anthony and the Imperials, the Temptations, Smokey Robinson, Dionne Warwick, Bobby Darin (with whom he co-authored "Splish Splash"), and innumerable other soon-to-be pop stars. He also helped the Who, the Cream, and other major groups of the British Invasion get their start in the United States, helped the young Jimi Hendrix find bookings in Greenwich Village clubs, and got the Rolling Stones, then fresh out of London and barely known, a concert at Carnegie Hall and a hit cover of Billy Womack's "It's All Over Now." His fame reached its peak in 1964, when he befriended the Beatles at their first U.S. press conference, got himself hired as master of ceremonies for their concerts in Shea Stadium and Carnegie Hall, and maneuvered his way into their entourage with such determination that he was dubbed "the fifth Beatle." In 1966 he opened a multimedia dance hall, Murray the K's World, in a converted hangar in Roosevelt Air Field on Long Island.

That same year, WINS changed to an all-news format and Murray the K, abandoning his AM hysteria, shifted to WOR on the FM dial to colonize airwaves that had hardly been touched by rock. He was the first to play album cuts rather than Top 40 singles and to build programs around a theme—antiwar songs or love songs, for example. He quit a year and a half later when the WOR management decided to institute a packaged playlist.

Although he subsequently worked for a number of other radio stations in New York and Toronto, his career rapidly declined. He was able to cash in on the recent nostalgia craze for the 1950s and 1960s, hosting a few concerts and TV specials and appearing in commercials for "oldies" record sets, but several attempts at comebacks failed and a syndicated radio show called "Soundtracks of the Sixties" was cancelled in 1981. He died at the age of 60 after a ten-year battle with cancer.

J.P.

Born Murray Kaufman. **Parents** Max K., leather merchant, and Jean Greene, vaudeville pianist. **Married** twice, both wives named Jackie, the second an actress; three sons. **Education** DeWitt Clinton High Sch., NYC. **Career** Child dancer in films; nightclub master of ceremonies and song and dance performer, Catskill resort circuit late 1940s; catcher, New York Yankees baseball farm team ca. 1950–51. • Radio disc jockey: WMCA, NYC early 1950s; "Swingin' Soiree," WINS, NYC 1958–66; (also program dir.) WOR-FM, NYC 1966–68; CHUM, Toronto late 1960s; WNBC, NYC 1970s; syndicated radio show "Soundtracks of the Sixties" late 1970s–81. • Co-author of pop song "Splish Splash" 1958; host, live rock shows, Fox and Paramount theaters, Brooklyn, NY and other locations 1958–ca. 64; recorder and publisher of pop music; producer, federally funded TV special to promote Job Corps 1965; founder and operator, Murray the K's World rock club, Roosevelt Field, L.I., NY 1966. **Honors** Numerous awards from rock music fan groups. **Member** President's Council on Drug Abuse late 1960s, 1972. **Recordings** *The Lone Twister; Out of the Bushes.*

Further reading Tom Wolfe, *The Kandy-Kolored Tangerine-Flake Streamline Baby,* 1965; Richard Price, "Going Down with Murray the K," in *Rolling Stone,* 15 Apr. 1982.

SIR ROBERT (HEATLIE) SCOTT

Civil servant and Japanese prisoner of war
Born **Peterhead, Scotland, 20 September 1905**
Died **26 February 1982**

Sir Robert Scott was a symbol of resistance during the Japanese occupation of Singapore. When the story of his imprisonment and defiance became known at the end of World War II, he became a hero in Britain and later served with distinction in a number of ministerial posts.

Robert Heatlie Scott was the son of T. H. Scott, a civil engineer, who moved his family to Trinidad just before World War I. The boy prepared for university entrance at Queen's Royal College in Trinidad and at 15 won a scholarship to New College, Oxford University, which made him wait two years before enrolling. He read law and was called to the bar at Gray's Inn in 1927, but decided to enter the Consular Service in preference to staying in London as a barrister. He was posted to the Far East and served in many places there, including Peking, Shanghai, Canton, Chungking, Hong Kong, and Manchuria. He mastered several languages, especially Chinese and Japanese. In 1940–41 he conducted the official British propaganda effort in Japan, which vainly aimed to dissuade the Japanese from entering the war on the Axis side. He was transferred to Singapore in 1941 to set up a branch of the Ministry of Information, but the Japanese net was closing on all of Southeast Asia, and the crown colony soon found itself gravely menaced.

Scott was appointed to the governor's war council, where he helped supervise the orderly evacuation of dependents and, as best he could, the defense of the city. He was on one of the last boats to leave (having sent his wife on before him to Australia), but it was stopped by Japanese warships several hours out of Singapore. After a long and tense wait, Scott and several others decided to row their ship's harbor dinghy to the nearest destroyer to try to negotiate with its captain for the release of the refugee boat. In the stormy night, amid much confusion, the Japanese opened fire and sank the refugee ship. When the news reached Australia, everyone assumed that Scott had lost his life along with all the others, but in fact his small boat reached the coast of Sumatra before he was captured by the Japanese and returned to Singapore.

His imprisonment was not especially arduous at first, although he spent seven months

Courtesy of British Ministry of Defence

in solitary confinement; but the Japanese had long suspected him of spying, and when in September 1943 a commando raid from Australia destroyed several Japanese tankers in Singapore harbor, Scott was assumed by his captors to have been behind the operation. He was found to have helped hide a radio in the Changi jail and thereupon was subjected to many months of intense torture to get him to confess. Despite the effects of prolonged beatings, lack of sleep, a starvation diet, and promises of execution, he was able to outwit and infuriate his interrogators. When he refused to make any statement he was court-martialed for anti-Japanese propaganda and sentenced in November 1944 to six years at hard labor in the infamous Outram Road prison. He suffered a total collapse, however, soon after his term began (during his ordeal he contracted dysentery, beriberi, and scabies and lost more than 100 pounds) and was in an enemy internment hospital at the time of the liberation of Singapore.

Scott testified against the invaders during the war-crimes trials held in Singapore—"reluctantly," he said, "because I did not hold with war crimes trials." He became famous for his calm demeanor at the trials and the coolness with which he confronted his captors. Then, reunited with his wife, he returned to Britain to convalesce. Although many doubted his ability to resume his former brilliant foreign-service career, he did so after several years' recuperation, and served with distinction as assistant undersecretary of state at the Foreign Office (1950–53) and minister at the British embassy in Washington (1953–55). He was knighted in 1954 and named U.K. commissioner general for Southeast Asia in Singapore (1955–59), where he was warmly welcomed back by many of his former fellow-prisoners. He closed his career with a stint as the first civilian commandant of the Imperial Defence College (1960–61), then was named permanent undersecretary, one of the top civil-service officers, in the Ministry of Defence (1961–63). He retired to Scotland where he was from 1968 lord lieutenant of Tweeddale and a justice of the peace. A.K.

Father T. H. Scott, civil engineer. **Married** Rosamond Dewar Durie 1933: one son, Royal Marine officer (d.); one daughter. **Education** Inverness; Queen's Royal Coll., Trinidad; New Coll., Oxford (scholarship); called to the bar, Gray's Inn, 1927. **Career** Joined H.M. Consular Service 1927; served in Peking, Shanghai, Canton, Chungking, Hong Kong, Manchuria; organized British propaganda campaign in Japan 1940–41; organizer of branch of Ministry of Information and member of Gov.'s War Council, Singapore 1941; imprisoned and tortured by Japanese in Singapore 1941–44, court-martialed and sentenced to six years at hard labor 1944, liberated 1945; asst. undersecty. of state, Foreign Office 1950–53; minister, British Embassy, Wash. DC 1953–55; commnr. gen. for U.K. in Southeast Asia 1955–59; commandant, Imperial Defence Coll. 1960–61; permanent undersecty., Ministry of Defence 1961–63. **Honors** CBE 1946; CMG 1950; KCMG 1954; GCMG 1958; J.P. 1968; lord lt. of Tweeddale (formerly of Peebleshire) since 1968; hon. degree, Univ. of Dundee. **Author** "Torture and Starvation in Singapore," *Times* of London, 15 Sept. 1945.

Further reading Noel Barber, *A Sinister Twilight: The Fall of Singapore,* 1942; Ian Morrison, *Malayan Postscript,* 1942.

MARCH

FRANK SARGESON
Short-story writer and novelist
***Born* Hamilton, Waikato, New Zealand, 23 March 1903**
***Died* Auckland, New Zealand, 1 March 1982**

The cultural life of New Zealand since the arrival of white settlers in the early part of the nineteenth century has been dominated by the classical traditions of Europe, particularly those of England. The efforts of contemporary writers to create a national literature received their greatest impetus from the work of Frank Sargeson, the first New Zealand fiction writer to gain an international reputation without becoming an expatriate. The theme of most of his books is the emancipation of the individual—usually an adolescent male of bisexual or homosexual leanings—from the stultifying conformism of New Zealand society, and if this did not endear him to New Zealanders in general, it made him something of a hero to many young writers and critics, for whom he served as a model and mentor.

Courtesy of Dominion and Sunday Times

Sargeson, whose real name was Norris Frank Davey, was born in a dairy-farming district in the North Island; his grandparents were immigrants from Belfast and London, his father a town clerk and strict follower of Noncomformist religious principles. At the age of 17 he left school to go to work. He studied, at home, a university course in law that enabled him to qualify as a solicitor of the Supreme Court in 1926. Unsettled, however, by the prospect of a monotonous middle-class existence, he went on a walking tour of Europe and began writing a novel along the lines of Joyce's *Portrait of the Artist as a Young Man*. Returning for good to New Zealand in 1928, he briefly held a job as a government estates clerk and then went to live on his uncle's sheep farm, where he began writing in earnest. His family, thinking him a hopeless failure, gave him a cottage on the beach at Takapuna, a few miles north of Auckland, which became his home for the rest of his life. Until 1965, when he published *Memoirs of a Peon*, he wrote short stories, sketches, and novellas, many of which appeared in *New Writing* in England and *New Directions* in the United States. His early and oversimplified treatment of leftist political themes gave way, beginning with *A Man and His Wife* (1940) and more fully in the novella *That Summer* (1946), to the complicated rendering of individual dilemmas and self-liberations on which his reputation was based.

Sargeson has been called both an "imaginative realist" who constructs complicated webs of allusion and symbol and a "documentary novelist" who has helped to define the nation's collective identity, usually by scourging its corrupt puritanism and bourgeois aspirations. He was gifted with a good ear for speech and was the first New Zealand writer to use the local vernacular in his dialogue. E. M. Forster mentioned his ability "to combine delicacy with frankness." He sought never to use the same style twice, experimenting with stream-of-consciousness techniques (*I Saw in My Dream*, 1949), epistolary form (*I for One*, 1954), elaborate social satire in the manner of the eighteenth-century picaresque novel (*Memoirs of a Peon*, 1965), ironic comedy (*Joy of the Worm*, 1969), and sexual grotesquerie (*A Game of Hide and Seek*, 1972).

Sargeson was one of the few New Zealand writers to be listed in *The Oxford Companion to English Literature*. He was offered the OBE in 1972, but declined it to protest the lack of a lending royalty for authors whose books circulate from public libraries. In the latter part of his life he was considered the dean of the growing New Zealand literary community. In addition to his novels, he was the author of two plays and three volumes of memoirs. J.P.

Born Norris Frank Davey. **Father** a storekeeper and town clerk. **Education** Hamilton High Sch., N.Z., left 1920; home law course, Univ. of New Zealand; admitted as solicitor, Supreme Court of New Zealand 1926. **Career** Traveled in England and Europe 1927–28; estates clerk, New Zealand Public Trust, Wellington 1928–29; writer since late 1920s; journalist. **Honors** Centennial City Competition Prize 1940; New Zealand Govt. Pension 1947–68; Church Prize 1952, 1966; Mansfield Award 1965; hon. degree from Univ. of Auckland. **Novels** *When the Wind Blows*, 1945; *I Saw in My Dream*, 1949; *I for One*, 1954; *Memoirs of a Peon*, 1965; *The Hangover*, 1967; *Joy of the Worm*, 1969; *Man of England Now*, 1972; *A Game of Hide and Seek*, 1972; *Sunset Village*, 1976. **Short-story collections** *Conversations with My Uncle and Other Sketches*, 1936; *A Man and His Wife*, 1940; *That Summer and Other Stories*, 1946; *Collected Stories, 1935–63*, 1964; *The Stories of Frank Sargeson*, 1973. **Plays** *Wrestling with the Angel; Two Plays; A Time for Sowing* and *The Cradle and the Egg*, 1964. **Memoirs** *Once Is Enough*, 1972; *More than Enough*, 1975; *Never Enough*, 1977. **Editor** *Speaking for Ourselves: A Collection of New Zealand Stories*, 1945. **Manuscript collection** in Alexander Turnbull Library, Wellington, N.Z.

Further reading Helen Shaw, ed., *The Puritan and the Wolf: A Symposium of Critical Essays on the Work of Frank Sargeson*, 1955; H. Winston Rhodes, *Frank Sargeson*, 1969.

PHILIP K(INDRED) DICK
Science-fiction writer
***Born* Chicago, Illinois, USA, 16 December 1928**
***Died* California, USA, 2 March 1982**

Philip K. Dick used the literary conventions of science fiction to put forward some unorthodox ideas about the nature of reality. Many critics and readers considered his darkly humorous novels and stories among the best in the genre. Wrote Brian Aldiss in his critical history of science fiction, *Billion Year Spree*: "In his novels things are never what they seem. Between life and death lie the many shadow lands of Dick, places of hallucination, artificial reality, dim half-life, paranoid states . . . full of disconcerting artifacts, scarecrow people, exiles, robots with ill consciences. . . . He is one of the masters of present-day discontents."

Born in Chicago, Dick moved with his family to California as a child and attended Berkeley High School. After dropping out of college to avoid compulsory ROTC service, he drifted from job to job, including radio announcer for a classical music station and manager of a record store, while writing in his spare time. In 1951 he sold his short story "Beyond Lies Wub" to the now-defunct magazine *Planet*. Over the next four years he published scores of short stories in the science-fiction pulps. His first novel, *Solar Lottery* (British title: *World of Chance*), appeared in 1955 and was followed by a steady stream of novels, most of them short—under 200 pages—and many of them printed only in paperback editions with lurid covers.

Dick's stories and novels are all thematically linked and can be considered facets of the same large work. Building on the standard clichés of science fiction—space travel, multiple universes, wise alien races, ESP, robots, androids, and the like—he constructed intricate worlds that often seemed to be satiric versions of California transplanted to Mars or another galaxy. In contrast to the cardboard heroes that populate the majority of science-fiction works, Dick's characters are ordinary people desperately trying to survive in and cope with a malicious or simply indifferent universe, and they are deftly and sympathetically drawn in a realistic style.

In a statement in *Contemporary Authors*, Dick explained: "My main occupation is the question, 'What's reality?' Many of my stories and novels deal with psychotic states or drug-induced states by which I can present the concept of a multiverse rather than a universe." He claimed to have derived some of his material from psychdelic hallucinations (and reportedly sustained damage to his pancreas from excessive drug use). *The Man in the High Castle*, which won the 1962 Hugo Award, presents an alternate universe in which Japan and Germany win World War II and jointly occupy the United States, while an American hiding in the Rocky Mountains writes a novel in which Hitler loses the war. *Martian Time-Slip* (1964) describes the psychological and social effects of a "temporal dislocation" on Mars from the distorted points of view of (among others) a schizophrenic, a suicide, and a Martian named Heliogabalus, whose perception is outside time itself. The protagonist of *A Scanner Darkly* (1977) is a drug addict hired by the police to inform on himself, and who, under the influence of the mysterious and deadly drug "Substance D," gradually splits into two personalities before losing his mind completely.

The political and philosophical dimensions of Dick's work won him a small but loyal readership outside the ranks of science fiction fandom and earned him comparison to such fabulists and visionaries as Jorge Luis Borges, Kafka, and Aldous Huxley. However, his work was largely ignored by mainstream critics and readers. His later novels, particularly *A Scanner Darkly*, *The Divine Invasion* (1981), and *Valis* (1981), display his increasing interest in theology. "I seek to contact some vein of cognition, some perceptual entity outside myself, outside our own race . . . where this entity would be, if anywhere at all, I can't say." *Blade Runner*, a film version of his novel *Do Androids Dream of Electric Sheep?*, was released in the summer of 1982.

Dick died of heart failure at the age of 53.

S.A.

Also wrote under pseudonym Richard Phillips. **Parents** Joseph Edgar D., federal govt. employee, and Dorothy (Kindred) D. **Married** (1) . . . (2) . . . (3) . . . : Laura. (4) . . . : Isolde. (5) Tessa Busby 1973: Christopher. **Religion** Episcopalian. **Education** Berkeley High Sch., CA, grad. 1945; Univ. of California, Berkeley ca. 1945–46. **Career** Hosted classical music program, KSMO-AM radio station, Berkeley 1947; operated record store, CA 1948–52; science-fiction writer since ca. 1951; radio scriptwriter, Mutual Broadcasting System; lectr. for antidrug and antiabortion orgs. **Member** Science Fiction Writers of America; Animal Protection Inst. **Honors** Hugo Award, for *The Man in the High Castle*, 1962; Campbell Memorial Award, for *Flow My Tears, the Policeman Said*, 1974. **Novels** *Solar Lottery* (in U.K. as *World of Chance*), 1955; *The World Jones Made*, 1956; *The Man Who Japed*, 1956; *Eye in the Sky*, 1956; *The Cosmic Puppets*, 1957; *Time Out of Joint*, 1959; *Dr. Futurity*, 1960; *Vulcan's Hammer*, 1960; *The Man in the High Castle*, 1962; *The Game-Players of Titan*, 1963; *Martian Time-Slip*, 1964; *The Simulacra*, 1964; *The Penultimate Truth*, 1964; *Clans of the Alphane Moon*, 1964; *The Three Stigmata of Palmer Eldritch*, 1965; *Dr. Bloodmoney; or, How We Got Along After the Bomb*, 1965; *The Crack in Space (Cantata 140)*, 1966; *Now Wait for Last Year*, 1966; *The Unteleported Man*, 1966; *Counter-Clock World*, 1967; *The Zap Gun*, 1967; (jtly.) *The Ganymede Takeover*, 1967; *Do Androids Dream of Electric Sheep?*, 1968; *Ubik*, 1969; *Galactic Pot-Healer*, 1969; *A Maze of Death*, 1970; *Our Friends from Frolix 8*, 1970; *The Philip K. Dick Omnibus*, 1970; *We Can Build You*, 1972; *Flow My Tears, the Policeman Said*, 1974; (jtly.) *Deus Irae*, 1976; *A Scanner Darkly*, 1977; *Confessions of a Crap Artist*, 1978; *The Divine Invasion*, 1981; *Valis*, 1981; *The Transmigration of Timothy Archer*, 1982; *Valis Regained* (unfinished).

Short-story collections *A Handful of Darkness,* 1955; *The Variable Man and Other Stories*, 1956; *The Preserving Machine and Other Stories*, 1969; *The Book of Philip K. Dick* (in U.K. as *The Turning Wheel and Other Stories),* 1973; *The Best of Philip K. Dick*, 1977; *The Golden Man*, 1980. **Contributor** of more than 100 short stories to science fiction mags.

Manuscript collection at California State Univ., Fullerton.

Further reading Brian Aldiss, *Billion Year Spree: A True History of Science Fiction*, 1973; Norman Spinrad, *Modern Science Fiction*, 1974; Bruce Gillespie, ed., *Philip K. Dick: Electric Shepherd*, 1975.

WILLIAM POLLOCK
Union leader
Born **Philadelphia, Pennsylvania, USA, 12 November 1899**
Died **Ocean City, New Jersey, USA, 3 March 1982**

William Pollock served for 16 years as president of the Textile Workers Union of America, leading the long, slow, but ultimately victorious fight to extend union protection to workers in the Southern textile industry.

He was one of nine children of Scottish immigrant parents who had come to Philadelphia in 1876. His father was a weaver. He left high school at 14 to work, and earned his diploma afterward by going to night school. Taking up his father's trade in Philadelphia in 1920, Pollock immediately joined Local 25 of the United Textile Workers of America and became business agent of the local in 1931. During the Great Depression he was the Pennsylvania labor representative on the National Recovery Administration and a member of the Philadelphia Labor Board.

In 1937, when the United Textile Workers agreed to join the CIO, Pollock joined the organizing committee and helped to form the Textile Joint Board in Philadelphia, on which he served as manager. Two years later the union decided to merge with other textile unions to form the Textile Workers Union of America (TWUA), and Pollock became the first secretary-treasurer of the general union, a post he held until 1953, when he was elected executive vice president.

The founder and longtime president of the TWUA was Emil Rieve, whose health prevented him from seeking reelection in 1956. Pollock was unanimously chosen to succeed him, and was reelected to the presidency seven times. His tenure was marked by the union's attempts to organize the South's giant textile manufacturers, chief among which was the J. P. Stevens Company. Stevens workers were grossly underpaid, even by the standards of an ill-paying industry, and in addition were threatened with reprisals and plant closings if they joined a union or demanded collective bargaining. The National Labor Relations Board, in a historic decision, sided with the union and in 1969 Stevens was forced to hold fair elections.

Until his retirement in 1972, Pollock held several offices in the national AFL-CIO organization, including membership on the executive committee from 1956 and on the executive council from 1967. He was the author of *Textiles: A National Crisis* (1956), *No Rights at All* (1957), and *An Industry That's Sick* (1958). A.K.

Courtesy of Bachrach Photo Service

Parents Louis P., weaver, and Agnes (Garner) P. **Married** Anne Mae Keen 1919: William Francis, Jr.; Kenneth William. **Religion**

Congregationalist. **Education** Left high sch. 1914; night high sch., grad. 1917. **Career** Office boy ca. 1914; shipyard worker 1914–20; textile weaver 1920–30. • With United Textile Workers of America: joined Local 25, Phila. 1920; Local 25 business agent 1931–37; gen. organizer, Textile Workers Organizing Cttee. 1937–39; mgr., Textile Jt. Bd. 1937–39. • With Textile Workers Union of America: gen. secty.-treas. 1939–53; exec. v.p. 1953–56; gen. pres. 1956–72. • With AFL-CIO: exec. cttee. member, Industrial Union Dept. since 1956; gen. bd. member 1956–68; v.p. and exec. council member since 1967. • Labor rep. for PA, Natl. Recovery Admin. 1933–35; member, Philadelphia Labor Bd. 1933–35; member, Federal Textile Commn., WWII; delegate, Inter-Amer. Conference of Free Trade Unions, Mexico City 1951; member, Labor Advisory Bd., Pres.'s Cttee. on Equal Employment Opportunity ca. 1965; treas., Inter-Amer. Textile and Garment Workers Fedn. 1967–70; exec. cttee. member, Intl. Fedn. of Textile, Garment and Leather Workers 1967–70. **Officer** Co-chmn., Natl. Labor Div., March of Dimes. **Member** Old Timers Assn.; Lighthouse Boys Club; Ocean City Fishing Club, NJ; Garden Civic Assn. **Author** *Textiles: A National Crisis*, 1956; *No Rights at All*, 1957; *An Industry That's Sick*, 1958.

DOROTHY (ENID) EDEN

Romantic novelist

***Born* Canterbury, New Zealand, 3 April 1912**

***Died* London, England, 4 March 1982**

Dorothy Eden was one of the most popular and prolific contemporary writers of romantic fiction. Born and raised on a sheep farm in New Zealand's Canterbury Plains, she left school at the age of 16 to work as a legal secretary, writing short stories for women's magazines in her spare time. Her first novel, *The Laughing Ghost*, was published in 1943; thereafter she produced an average of a book a year. In 1954 she moved to London, where she supported herself selling books at Harrods department store.

Sleep in the Woods (1960), a saga of New Zealand's pioneer days, was Eden's first international success. She entered the huge American market for Gothic fiction in 1969, when *The Vines of Yarrabee* made the best-seller lists on both sides of the Atlantic. Her subsequent books sold so well—some 5 million in a space of seven years—that by 1977 she was in Britain's 83 percent "supertax" bracket. Her books have been translated into 18 languages.

Eden's novels stuck firmly to the conventional subject matter of romantic fiction: passion, checked and unchecked, among the aristocratic and servant classes, especially of the eighteenth and nineteenth centuries. *The Vines of Yarrabee*, her best-known work, was the story of an adulterous love triangle involving an ambitious Australian wine grower, his cultured but cold wife, and his housekeeper, a wronged woman with rape and penal servitude in her past. Like many of Eden's books, it was well researched and full of historical detail, but predictable. Devotees of her writing liked her skilled storytelling and authentic backgrounds.

Courtesy of Jerry Bauer

Since the mid-1960s, Eden suffered from rheumatoid arthritis, a crippling disease that gradually cut her writing time down to two hours a day. She was the founder of a trust fund that financed the study of the disease by New Zealand physicians. Her death at the age of 69 was from cancer. J.P.

Also wrote under the pseudonym of Mary Paradise. **Parents** John E., farmer, and Eva Natalie E. **Emigrated** to England 1954. **Education** Public schs., N.Z. **Career** Short-story writer since ca. 1928, novelist since 1943; legal secty., N.Z. 1928–54; saleswoman, book dept., Harrods dept. store, London ca. 1954–60; founder, trust fund for study of rheumatoid arthritis. **Author** *The Laughing Ghost*, 1943; *We Are for the Dark*, 1944; *Summer Sunday*, 1946; *Walk into My Parlour*, 1947; *The Schoolmaster's Daughters*, 1948; *Crow Hollow*, 1950; *Voice of the Dolls*, 1950; *Cat's Prey*, 1952; *Lamb to the Slaughter*, 1953; *Bride by Candlelight*, 1954; *Darling Clementine*, 1955; *Death Is a Red Rose*, 1956; *The Pretty Ones*, 1957; *Listen to Danger*, 1958; *Deadly Travellers*, 1959; *The Sleeping Bride*, 1959; *Samantha*, 1960 (as *Lady of Mallow*, 1962), 1960; *Sleep in the Woods*, 1960; *Afternoon for Lizards*, 1961; *Whistle for the Crows*, 1962; *The Bird in the Chimney*, 1963; *Bella*, 1964; *Darkwater*, 1964; *The Marriage Chest*, 1965; *Ravenscroft*, 1965; *Never Call It Loving: A Biographical Novel of Katherine O'Shea and Charles Stewart Parnell*, 1966; *Siege in the Sun*, 1967; *Winterwood*, 1967; *The Shadow Wife*, 1968; *Yellow Is for Fear, and Other Stories*, 1968; *The Vines of Yarrabee*, 1969; *Melbury Square*, 1970; *Waiting for Willa*, 1970; *An Afternoon Walk*, 1971; *The Brooding Lake*, 1972; *Shadow of a Witch*, 1972; *Speak to Me of Love*, 1972; *The Millionaire's Daughter*, 1974; *The Time of the Dragon*, 1975; *Night of the Letter*, 1976; *The Daughters of Ardmore Hall*, 1976; *Face of an Angel*, 1976; *Bridge of Fear*, 1976; *The House on Hay Hill and Other Romantic Fiction*, 1976; *The Marriage Chest*, 1978; *The Storrington Papers*, 1978; *The Salamanca Drum*, 1979; *An Important Family*, 1982. **Contributor** of short stories to *Redbook*, *Good Housekeeping*, and other mags.

JOHN BELUSHI
Comedian and actor
***Born* Chicago, Illinois, USA, 24 January 1949**
***Died* Los Angeles, California, USA, 5 March 1982**

Within a year after he was first introduced to nationwide audiences as one of the Not Ready for Prime Time Players on NBC-TV's "Saturday Night Live," the satiric comedian John Belushi had become something approaching a folk hero—a master parodist whose cynical wit embodied the general disillusionment of people coming to maturity in the social wasteland of the late 1970s. Part of his appeal was the dual nature of his stage persona: he was both a maniac seething with rage at everything that is wrong with the world—government, mortality, the weather—and a stocky big brother protectively warning the kids at home to "wise up" before they got hurt. His impersonations of Henry Kissinger, Truman Capote, Marlon Brando, and other examples of public ego were perfect and merciless.

Some of Belushi's manic energy seems to

have derived from the suddenness of his conversion from middle-American straight arrow to cynic. He grew up in Wheaton, Illinois, a conservative town on the outskirts of Chicago. Both his parents were of Albanian descent; his father, a restaurant owner and bartender, had emigrated from the village of Qytetes in the 1930s, and he was raised partly by a grandmother who spoke no English. In high school he was captain of the football team, drummer in a rock band, a member of the drama club, choir, and debating team, and the 1967 Homecoming King; he also had a high-school sweetheart whom he later married. He spent the two years after his graduation enrolled at various colleges to avoid the Vietnam War draft and was downed by a blast of tear gas in the riots at the 1968 Democratic Convention.

The following year, Belushi and two friends took over a coffeehouse in the basement of a Chicago church, where they staged shows of improvised satire to audiences made up of passers-by whom Belushi corralled off the street. After a fight with a local gang forced them to close, Belushi won a job with the improvisation troupe Second City, which gave him the opportunity to practice his act eight times a week. "He always worked at the top of his intelligence," recalled Del Close, the group's director. "He knew that laughs were not the point, that the integrity of the character was the point and the laughs would follow."

In 1972 Belushi was hired for the cast of a rock-music revue written by the staff of *National Lampoon*, a magazine specializing in irreverent satire with a readership made up of mostly college students. *National Lampoon's Lemmings*, originally booked into a Greenwich Village club for six weeks, was greeted with enthusiasm by the critics and lasted ten months, with Belushi's painfully exact caricature of rock singer Joe Cocker the high point of the show. He was adopted by the *National Lampoon* group, worked as a writer, director, and performer on "The National Lampoon Radio Hour," and appeared in *The National Lampoon Show* Off Broadway in 1975.

In the spring of that year, NBC-TV decided to chance a live comedy show based on the *Lampoon*'s peculiar combination of sophisticated and sophomoric humor. Several of the writers and cast members were veterans of the magazine's productions and of Second City. By the end of its first season, "Saturday Night Live" commanded a vast audience, and its seven actors were celebrities.

The shows were built around a set of characters developed by the players. Belushi's included a samurai warrior incongruously at home behind a deli counter or on the dance floor of a disco club, a self-conscious killer bee, and the owner of a restaurant where the staff speaks nothing but Greek. Most inspired of all was his transformation into a rough-voiced, exuberant Chicago blues singer, backed by his "SNL" partner Dan Aykroyd and a first-rate band. The act produced a best-selling album, *Briefcase Full of Blues*, and a movie, *The Blues Brothers*.

In 1978, Belushi, his star on the rise, committed himself to three films in addition to his schedule of 20 live television shows. The first to be released was *National Lampoon's Animal House*, a low-budget frat-house comedy in which Belushi, as the wildly boorish Bluto Blutarsky, threw food, grunted, urinated, and smashed beer bottles against his forehead. It was the most profitable film comedy ever made. Universal Pictures immediately signed him to a three-year contract, and the following year he and Aykroyd left "Saturday Night Live" for Hollywood. None of his subsequent films, however, were as successful. After a bit part in *Goin' South* (1978), a bigger part in *Old Boyfriends* (1978), and a starring role in Steven Spielberg's spectacular failure *1941* (1979), he played a tough but love-stricken Chicago reporter in *Continental Divide* (1981) and a mild-mannered suburban man in a paranoid dream come true in the film adaptation of Thomas Berger's *Neighbors* (1981), neither of which did as well as expected at the box office.

Offscreen, Belushi was a vibrant and volatile personality who was famous for his ability to stay up three nights in a row touring rock clubs and drinking. His energies fed a wide circle of friends, to whom he was both gadfly and guardian. Several comedians and actors owe their jobs to him, and he was also responsible, through the Blues Brothers act, for reviving the careers of neglected blues and soul artists by introducing them to white audiences. His outrageous impositions were legendary: he was known to walk into the homes of complete strangers, make himself a sandwich, and take a nap on the couch. Nearly every article written on him since 1978 mentioned the possibility, even the probability, of his burning out. "I get nervous, and I am capable of doing something to blow it on purpose," he told a *Rolling Stone* interviewer in 1978. "A lot of actors have that problem."

He was found dead in a rented Los Angeles bungalow of an overdose of cocaine and heroin. His friends said that he had a horror of needles, and his doctor said that he was allergic to certain narcotics and knew it. A rock singer named Cathy Evelyn Smith later claimed to have injected him herself, and at the time of writing she was being sought by the police. J.P.

Parents Adam B., restaurant owner, and Agnes B. **Married** Judy Jacklin, book designer, 1976. **Religion** Baptized into Albanian Orthodox Church. **Education** Central High Sch., Wheaton, IL, grad. 1967; drama student, various midwestern colls. 1967–69. **Career** Actor, summer stock 1967; partner and comedian, Universal Life Church Coffeehouse, Chicago 1969; comedian, Second City improvisation troupe, Chicago ca. 1969–72; stage actor, NYC and on tour 1972–75; comedian, "Saturday Night Live," NBC-TV 1975–79; singer with Blues Brothers band since 1978; film actor since 1978. **Member** AFTRA. **Stage** *National Lampoon's Lemmings*, NYC 1973; (also co-writer and co-dir.) *National Lampoon Show*, NYC 1975. **Radio** (also co-writer and co-dir.) "National Lampoon Radio Hour" ca. 1974. **Television** "Saturday Night Live," 1975–79; guest appearances on Steve Martin and Richard Pryor specials and other shows. **Films** *National Lampoon's Animal House*, 1978; *Goin' South*, 1978; *Old Boyfriends*, 1979; (voice) *Shame of the Jungle*, 1979; *1941*, 1979; *The Blues Brothers*, 1980; *Continental Divide*, 1981; *Neighbors*, 1981. **Recordings** *Briefcase Full of Blues*, 1979; *Made in America*, 1980; *The Best of the Blues Brothers*, 1981; also *National Lampoon Radio Hour* albums.

Further reading Charles M. Young, "Son of Samurai," in *Rolling Stone*, 10 Aug. 1978; Tony Schwartz, "College Humor Comes Back," in *Newsweek*, 23 Oct. 1978; Mitchell Glazer and Timothy White, eds., "John Belushi: Made in America," in *Rolling Stone*, 29 Apr. 1982.

CLIFFORD P(HILIP) CASE
U.S. senator
***Born* Franklin Park, New Jersey, USA, 16 April 1904**
***Died* Washington, D.C., USA, 5 March 1982**

Clifford P. Case was a widely respected national politician, a moderate-liberal Republican who represented New Jersey in the U.S. Congress for 32 years, of which he spent 24 in the Senate. His first election as a senator came after a bitter campaign in which he ran against the right wing of his own party as well as his Democratic opponent. Four distinguished terms later, his party denied him renomination and supported instead an extreme conservative, who lost in the general election.

The son of a Dutch Reformed pastor, Clifford Philip Case spent much of his youth in Poughkeepsie, New York, where he attended high school. He graduated from Rutgers, New Jersey's state university, in 1925. In 1928 he received his law degree from Columbia University, was admitted to the New York bar, and began to work for the Wall Street firm of Simpson Thatcher & Bartlett, with which he remained associated for the next 25 years. The same year he also married Ruth Smith and settled in Rahway, a town in north-central New Jersey.

For a decade Case practiced corporate law, then entered politics in 1938, winning election to the Rahway Common Council, where he served until 1942. He was a member of the New Jersey House of Assembly in 1943 and 1944 and was elected to Congress in 1945 from his home district, the sixth.

His tenure as representative was marked by a prolabor stance and an attempt to forge a spirit of bipartisanship both in his district and in the Congress. He strongly supported Dwight Eisenhower for the presidency and ran 10,000 votes ahead of him in his own district in the 1952 election. In 1953, however, when the state party leaders refused to back him for governor, Case resigned from Congress and accepted the presidency of the Fund for the Republic, a civil-liberties organization.

His resignation so dismayed the Republican leaders—the party lost the sixth district in the ensuing special election—that they pleaded with Case to return to politics and run for the Senate in 1954. With the enthusiastic encouragement of the Eisenhower administration, he did so.

That campaign was one of the nastiest in the history of New Jersey's fractious politics. Early on, Case issued a 1,500-word statement condemning the Communist-hunting tactics of Sen. Joseph McCarthy. "As a member of the United States Senate," Case said, "I shall vote against continuing Sen. McCarthy as chairman, or as a member, of the Committee on Government Operations." It was an extraordinarily courageous stance for the candidate to take; only one Republican senator up to that time had spoken out against McCarthy. New Jersey's Republican right became violently incensed and vowed Case would not win. They assailed him as "a pro-Communist Republicrat," "Stalin's choice for senator," and "a socialist." There was even a charge, which some traced to McCarthy himself, that Case's sister had been a member of a Communist-front organization. National Republican figures came to campaign at his side, he received five separate endorsements from Eisenhower, and only three weeks before the election a favorable cover story appeared in *Time* magazine. In the end, in a strongly Democratic year, Case won the election by 3,500 votes among 1.8 million cast—a margin of one-fifth of one percent.

In the Senate, Case eventually became the ranking Republican on the Foreign Relations Committee and also served influentially on the committees of Appropriations, Atomic Energy, and Intelligence. He was identified with several pieces of landmark legislation, especially the Civil Rights Act of 1964 and the War Powers Act of 1973, the latter a clear reassertion of Congress's role in foreign policy. He was among the first senators to criticize U.S. involvement in the Vietnam War and was a strong supporter of labor and Israel. He was an early advocate of full financial disclosure by congressmen, and for many years, before such disclosure became mandatory, he would enter his income and assets in the *Congressional Record*. Always a maverick in his party, he frequently received a zero rating from Americans for Conservative Action, and in the John Kennedy administration was the only Republican senator to vote in favor of medical care for the elderly. "I am a Republican," Case said, defining his political

creed, "and I believe in the Republican Party. But I have my own convictions as to what the Republican Party should stand for, and I intend to fight for them as hard as I can. And I will not be driven away from my Republicanism simply because some Democrats happen to agree with me on certain issues—and some Republicans don't."

Liberal Republicans became an especially endangered group after 1976, as right-wing insurgents gradually captured control of the national party. Case, whose three reelections to the Senate were easy wins compared to his first try, was challenged in the 1978 primary by a Ronald Reagan protégé, Jeffrey Bell, who won by a narrow margin only to be soundly defeated by the Democrat, Bill Bradley.

In retirement, Case served as chairman of Freedom House, a libertarian philanthropic organization based in New York and Washington, and of a coalition of groups opposed to the U.S. plan to sell AWACS radar-equipped planes to Saudi Arabia. He was the recipient of many honorary doctorates and was a member, among many organizations, of the Council on Foreign Relations. Shortly before his death of lung cancer at the age of 77, he was mentioned as a possible interim replacement for New Jersey's Sen. Harrison Williams, who was forced to resign his seat as a result of his conviction in the Abscam scandal.

A.K.

Parents Clifford Philip C., Dutch Reformed minister, and Jeanette McAlpin (Benedict) C. **Married** Ruth Miriam Smith 1928: Mary Jane Weaver; Ann Holt; Clifford Philip III. **Religion** Dutch Reformed; later Presbyterian. **Education** Poughkeepsie High Sch., NY, grad. 1921; Rutgers Univ., New Brunswick, NJ, A.B. 1925; Columbia Law Sch., LL.B. 1928; admitted to New York bar 1928. **Career** Assoc. 1928–39 and partner 1939–53, Simpson Thatcher & Bartlett law firm, NYC; member, Common Council, Rahway, NJ 1938–42; member, House of Assembly, New Jersey Legislature 1943–44; Republican rep. to U.S. Congress from NJ 6th district 1945–53; pres., Ford Foundn. Fund for the Republic 1953–54; U.S. sen. from NJ 1955–79, served on Foreign Relations, Atomic Energy, Intelligence, and Appropriations cttees.; delegate, Republican Natl. Conventions 1956, 1964, 1968; counsel, Curtis Mallet Prevost Colt & Mosle law firm, NYC and Wash. DC since 1979; bd. chmn., Freedom House, NYC and Wash. DC since 1979; visiting prof., Rutgers Univ. 1979; chmn., coalition of citizens' groups opposed to AWACS sale 1980–81. **Officer** Dir.: Amer. Inst. for Retarded Children; NJ chapter, Arthritis and Rheumatism Foundn.; *Columbia Journal of Law and Social Problems.* • Trustee: Rutgers Univ. 1945–59; Amer. Red Cross, NJ. **Member** Bar Assns.: City of New York since 1928; New York County; New York State; Wash. DC; Amer. Bar Assn. • New Jersey Soc. for Crippled Children and Adults; Bd. of Foreign Missions, Reformed Church in America; Council on Foreign Relations; Republican Party; Phi Beta Kappa; Delta Upsilon; Phi Delta Phi; Assn. of Ex-Members of Squadron A, NYC. • Clubs: Ilderan Outing; Century Assn.; Elks; Essex, Newark; Downtown Assn., NYC; Metropolitan and Federal City, Wash. DC. **Honors** Award, *Liberty*, 1951; Medal of Merit, New Jersey Dept., Jewish War Veterans 1953; hon. degrees from univs. of Rutgers, Columbia, Princeton, Yeshiva, Fairleigh Dickinson, and Seton Hall, and from Middlebury, Rider, Rollins, Bloomfield, Upsala, Kean, and Ramapo colls.

EDWARD L. PATTON

Builder of Trans-Alaska oil pipeline
Born **Newport News, Virginia, USA, circa 1917**
Died **Bellevue, Washington, USA, 5 March 1982**

Edward L. Patton was president, chairman, and chief executive officer of the Alyeska Pipeline Service Company, formed in 1970 by a consortium of international oil companies to build the Trans-Alaska Pipeline System. He presided over the construction project from start to finish, watching helplessly as costs rose more than 300 percent over his initial estimates to $7.7 billion.

Courtesy of Alyeska Pipeline Service Co.

Patton was a chemical engineer by training, a Georgia Tech graduate of 1938 who spent his entire career—except for five years in the Navy during World War II—in the employ of the company known today as Exxon. He served in a series of management positions from 1946 to 1964, spent two years as an advisor in the Mediterranean, Mideast, and Far East, and in 1966 was put in charge of the construction and management of a refinery at Benicia, California, on San Francisco Bay.

In the late 1960s, after 18 months of searching, Exxon and Atlantic Richfield found recoverable petroleum reserves of some 9.7 billion barrels in the Prudhoe Bay Field on Alaska's North Slope. Of the field's 16 owners, three companies—Exxon, Arco, and British Petroleum—owned 93 percent and decided to set up Alyeska to build a pipeline stretching 800 miles across mountain ranges and frozen tundra to the port of Valdez. Patton, who had no previous pipeline experience, was appointed head of the new company largely on the strength of his past effectiveness as a negotiator.

After a quick course in the intricacies of pipeline technology, Patton began his first negotiating task, to win a settlement of the long-pending Alaskan native claims so that rights of way could be legally established for the pipeline. The oil companies Alyeska represented supported the $1 billion distributed to the natives under the Native Claims Settlement Act of 1972. Getting the actual rights of way was an even more demanding job, requiring another special act of Congress which became law in November 1973. The following spring Patton had crews in place ready to start construction.

Costs began to mount immediately. Patton himself had offered an estimate of $2 billion in 1971, but inflation, plus the extremely expensive no-strike labor contract that Patton had supported, proved too much for his projection. There was considerable theft of equipment and widespread featherbedding among the 22,000 workers, who were all receiving premium wages. The pipeline also had to solve some novel engineering problems, the most difficult of which was keeping the oil heated and hence fluid across the miles of permafrost. Problems with defective welding had to be overcome, as well as public dismay when it was learned, after a simulated attack by the U.S. Army Rangers, that it would be impossible to protect the pipeline from sabotage.

Finally, however, in June 1977, Patton saw the pipeline completed. The first cargo of North Slope oil left Valdez two months later. In an interview at the time, he offered little information about the enormous overruns, but acknowledged indirectly that he had been blamed: "I guess when costs escalate as fast as they did, everybody blamed everybody they could." He also expressed lingering exasperation with environmental interests, many of whom had strenuously fought the pipeline as a devastating threat to the fragile Arctic tundra, and said that some of the overrun money went to pay for needless environmental impact statements.

Patton retired in 1978 and went to live in the Pacific Northwest, where he died of brain cancer. A.K.

Married Dorothy: Judith Patton Leach; Laura Patton Ballard; Barbara Patton Tucker; Edward J. **Education** Georgia Inst. of Technology, B.S. 1938. **Mil. service** Comdr. of antisubmarine and escort vessels, U.S. Navy, Caribbean, North Atlantic, and Pacific 1941–46. **Career** With Exxon Corp. (formerly Standard Oil of New Jersey and Humble Oil Refining Co.) 1938–41 and 1946–78: chemical engineer, Baton Rouge, LA 1938–41; management positions in Baton Rouge, Norway, other locations 1946–64; advisor, refinery operations in Mediterranean, Mideast, and Far East 1964–66; head of construction and operation, refinery at Benicia, CA 1966–70; loaned to Alyeska Pipeline Service Co. as pres. 1970–78 and chmn. and chief exec. officer 1976–78.

AYN RAND
Novelist and lecturer
Born **St. Petersburg, Russia, 2 February 1905**
Found dead **New York City, USA, 6 March 1982**

Ayn Rand was the author of two best-selling novels, *The Fountainhead* (1943) and *Atlas Shrugged* (1957). In these and other books and in her newsletters and lectures she propounded a philosophy called objectivism, which holds that "rational selfishness" and unfettered capitalism are the only means to personal and societal salvation and that their opposite, "the primordial morality of altruism," can lead only to "slavery, brute force, stagnant terror, and sacrificial furnaces." "My philosophy, in essence," she said, "is the concept of man as a heroic being, with his own happiness as the moral purpose of his life, with productive achievement as his noblest activity, and reason as his only absolute." Her novels possess great scope and narrative drive, and her major characters are never merely fallible humans, but protean types who declaim their defiant individualism in lengthy, passionate speeches. To her many devoted followers Rand was the fierce and righteous prophet of a new order; to her rather more numerous critics she seemed either overwhelmingly silly or fanatically sinister.

Born in St. Petersburg, Russia, the daughter of a prosperous Jewish merchant, she showed great precocity in reading and writing, and earned a degree in history in 1924 from Leningrad University. Two years later she seized the opportunity to leave the Soviet Union, going to Chicago to live with an aunt. She soon moved to Hollywood and eventually found work as a film extra and wardrobe assistant at RKO pictures. On the set of Cecil B. DeMille's *King of Kings* she met another extra, Frank O'Connor (not the writer), whom she married in 1929. He died in 1979.

Rand began to write for the screen in 1931 and sold RKO a scenario, *Red Pawn*, about a wife's brave rescue of her husband from a Soviet slave-labor camp. It was never filmed, but the $1,500 she was paid for it allowed her to quit her job and begin working full-time on her own writing projects. One of the first of these, the play *Penthouse Legend* (1933), was a clever courtroom drama in which the audience is allowed to decide the beautiful defendant's guilt or innocence of murder. As *The Night of January 16th* it had a successful Broadway run in 1935–36 and has since frequently received amateur and student productions. The author disowned the play and the 1941 film made from it, claiming that her ideas had been removed by rewriters. In 1973 her original *Penthouse Legend* had a brief run Off Broadway.

Courtesy of Caxton Publishers

Her first novel, *We the Living* (1936), was a love story set in the Soviet Union of 1922. Its theme, in Rand's words, is "the supreme value of a human life and the evil of the totalitarian state that claims the right to sacrifice it." The savagery of collectivist society was the subject of her next work of fiction, the novella *Anthem* (1938), a defense of egoism in which the stubborn hero rediscovers the meaning of the word "I." By the mid-1930s Rand had begun work on a much larger novelistic treatment of the same principles, this one to be set in the United States. Because her hero was an architect, she worked without pay in 1937 as a typist in the New York offices of the noted architect Eli Jacques Kahn. The finished work, *The Fountainhead*, was rejected by a dozen publishers before Bobbs-Merrill bought it in 1943. It is the story of Howard Roark, a determined and powerful architectural genius who blows up his greatest project, a brilliantly innovative housing development, when he discovers that bureaucrats have tampered with his designs. The book had a natural commercial appeal which grew steadily, and Warner Brothers made a film of it in 1949 starring Gary Cooper and Patricia Neal. The movie, for which Rand wrote the screenplay, was almost universally condemned by the critics as vague and pretentious bluster, but has since become something of a camp classic.

In 1951 Rand and her husband moved to New York, where she continued work on another novel, one that was to dwarf the 750 pages of *The Fountainhead*, which she described as "only an overture." *Atlas Shrugged* appeared in 1957 to considerable critical derision, but immediately became a best seller. It is set in a grim collectivist future, a time when the rest of the world has already been fatally weakened by the perverted values of altruism and even the United States is gravely menaced. John Galt, a great physicist, is the leader of the "producers" who decide to withdraw their power from society and retreat to Colorado to watch the entire collectivist system collapse. As they reemerge to make over the world in their objectivist image, Galt "raised his hand and over the desolate earth he traced in space the sign of the dollar."

Rand's growing coterie of avid disciples received this book as the bible of their movement. Chief among them was Nathaniel Branden, an amateur psychologist who founded the Nathaniel Branden Institute in New York where he and Rand taught objectivism together until 1968, when he quarreled with her and left the movement. One of her most famous disciples was Alan Greenspan, who in 1974 was appointed by Richard Nixon as chairman of the President's Council of Economic Advisers and held that office through Gerald Ford's administration.

During the 1960s and 1970s Rand turned away from what she called "romantic fiction," preferring to teach through the essay in a more direct, polemical style. Her nonfiction works include *For the New Intellectual* (1961), *America's Persecuted Minority: Big Business* (1962), *The Virtue of Selfishness: A New Concept of Egoism* (1965), *Capitalism: The Unknown Ideal* (1966), *The Romantic Manifesto: A Philosophy of Literature* (1969), and *The New Left: The Anti-Industrial Revolution* (1971). Her last book, *Philosophy: Who Needs It?*, was published in October 1982. The Rand newsletter, first called *The Objectivist* and then *The Ayn Rand Letter* after Branden's departure, was published from 1962 to 1976.

Rand was never more controversial than when expressing her opinions of contemporary political figures or ideas. In addition to attacking the New Left as "blatantly irrational" young "hoodlums," she hated the "grotesque phenomenon" of Women's Liberation: "sloppy, bedraggled, unfocused females" who want only "to surpass the futile sordidness of a class war by instituting a sex war." It was perhaps not surprising that she opposed religion, Medicare, public housing, the income tax, any and all government aid, the consumer-protection movement, and the ecology movement; what is remarkable is that her ideology was so narrow as to exclude the extremely conservative likes of William F. Buckley, Jr. (for his belief in God), the Libertarian Party of the New Right ("anarchists . . . without philosophy or consistency"), and Ronald Reagan ("since he denies the right to abortion, he cannot be a defender of any rights"). But her rigidity and consistency, in the eyes of her disciples, were part of her irresistible attractiveness. She came to shun all interviews, convinced that the press were "looters," far too stupid and careless to present her ideas clearly. Her favorite audiences were composed of college students, and she frequently, especially in the 1960s, lectured on objectivism at universities throughout the country.

After Rand's death, her body was put on display in a funeral home in Manhattan. Next to it was propped a six-foot dollar sign, the very symbol and totem that she had made her own. A.K.

Born Alissa R. **Father** a businessman. **Married** Frank O'Connor, actor and artist, 1929 (d. 1979). **Religion** Of Jewish birth; atheist since ca. 1918. Emigrated to U.S. 1926; naturalized 1931. **Education** Private sch., St. Petersburg, Russia; Univ. of Leningrad, degree in history 1924. **Career** Mus. guide, Leningrad 1924. • In Hollywood: movie extra and jr. screenwriter, Cecil B. DeMille studio 1926–28; filing clerk, then office mgr., Wardrobe Dept., RKO 1929–32; screenwriter, Universal, Paramount, and MGM 1932–34 and Hal Wallis Productions 1944–49; free-lance reader, RKO and MGM 1934–35. • Volunteer typist, architectural firm of Eli Jacques Kahn, NYC 1937; script reader, Paramount, NYC 1941–43; also waitress, office clerk, other jobs. • Playwright since 1933, novelist since 1936, writer and lectr. on philosophy of objectivism since 1946; lectr., Nathaniel Branden Inst., NYC ca. 1958–68; visiting lectr. at Yale Univ., Princeton Univ., Columbia Univ., Univ. of Wisconsin, Johns Hopkins Univ., Harvard Univ., Massachusetts Inst. of Technology, U.S. Military Acad. at West Point, Ford Hall Forum in Boston, many other instns.; ed., *The Objectivist Newsletter* (later called *The Objectivist*) 1962–71 and *The Ayn Rand Letter* 1971–76. **Honors** Hon. degree from Lewis and Clark Univ. **Novels** *We the Living*, 1936; *Anthem*, 1938; *The Fountainhead*, 1943; *Atlas Shrugged*, 1957. **Plays** *Penthouse Legend* (produced as *The Night of January 16th* and disowned by Rand in that form; also known as *Woman on Trial*), 1933; *The Unconquered*, 1940. **Screenplays**

Courtesy of Phyllis Cerf

Red Pawn (not filmed), 1932; (jtly.) *You Came Along*, 1945; *Love Letters*, 1945; *The Fountainhead*, 1949; *Atlas Shrugged* (TV miniseries; unfinished). **Other** *Textbook of Americanism*, 1946; *Notes on the History of American Free Enterprise*, 1959; *Faith and Force: The Destroyers of the Modern World*, 1961; *For the New Intellectual*, 1961; *The Objectivist Ethics*, 1961; *America's Persecuted Minority: Big Business*, 1962; *Conservatism: An Obituary*, 1962; *The Fascist "New Frontier,"* 1963; *The Virtue of Selfishness: A New Concept of Egoism*, 1965; (jtly.) *Capitalism: The Unknown Ideal*, 1966; *Introduction to Objectivist Epistemology*, 1967; *The Romantic Manifesto: A Philosophy of Literature*, 1969; *The New Left: The Anti-Industrial Revolution*, 1971; *Philosophy: Who Needs It?*, 1982. **Interview** in *Playboy*, Mar. 1964. **Manuscript collection** in Library of Congress, Wash. DC.

Further reading Nathaniel and Barbara Branden, *Who Is Ayn Rand?*, 1962; William O'Neill, *With Charity Toward None: An Analysis of Ayn Rand's Philosophy*, 1971; Jerome Tuccille, *It Usually Begins with Ayn Rand: A Libertarian Odyssey*, 1972; Sidney Greenberg, *Ayn Rand and Alienation*, 1977; Barbara Grizzuti Harrison, "Psyching Out Ayn Rand," in *Ms.*, Sept. 1978.

VISCOUNT BLAKENHAM
John Hugh Hare
British Cabinet minister and chairman of the Conservative Party
***Born* 22 January 1911**
***Died* 6 March 1982**

John Hugh Hare, first Viscount Blakenham, headed several departments in Conservative governments during the 1950s, then held the crucial chairmanship of the party during the prime ministry of Sir Alec Douglas-Home, which he resigned following the Labour Party's victory of October 1964.

He was born an aristocrat, the third son of the fourth Earl of Listowel, and was educated at Eton. Instead of following his two elder brothers to Oxford, he was sent by his father to work in a brokerage house on Wall Street, arriving in New York shortly before the Crash of 1929. On returning home he worked for a few years in the City of London before entering politics in 1937, when he was elected alderman on the London County Council, a post he held until 1952. During World War II, Hare was at first a member of the Territorial Army, was embodied in the Suffolk and Norfolk Yeomanry, and was finally transferred to the First Army in North Africa. He then participated in the Allied landings at Salerno and Anzio, was mentioned in dispatches, and as a lieutenant colonel received an OBE in 1945, along with the U.S. Legion of Merit.

Hare left his unit early in order to run for Parliament in the 1945 general election, winning his district, a safe Conservative seat in rural Suffolk, by a comfortable margin. He retained the seat—known since 1950 as Sudbury and Woodbridge—with similar ease in every election he contested, building in the process a strong local organization. He served as a deputy to Lord Woolton, the party chairman, from 1951 to 1955.

Hare began his ministerial career as minister of state for colonial affairs, a post he held for less than a year before moving, on the eve of the Suez invasion, to become secretary of state for war (1956–58). As minister of agriculture, fisheries, and food (1958–60), he defended Britain's rights in a fishing dispute with Iceland and gave support to the country's many beleaguered small farmers, of whom he counted himself as one. In the role of minister of labour (1960–63), the one he liked the best, he was remembered by both union and management sides as a fair and amiable conciliator during the years of the Macmillan government's austere incomes policy.

Harold Macmillan's decision to resign in 1963 led to a great upheaval within the Tory ranks, and when Douglas-Home emerged as the party's choice to succeed him, the new prime minister appointed Hare, a close parliamentary ally, as party chairman. At the same time he was elevated to the House of Lords as Viscount Blakenham, one of the last hereditary peers to be created before the practice was abolished in 1965.

Blakenham's tenure at Conservative Central Office was short and troubled. The party was badly split by the bitter succession struggle, and the Labour Party was making spectacular gains in by-elections. The Labour victory in 1964 was not as overwhelming as had been feared, but Blakenham knew he had to resign, and within a few months did so. His successor was Edward du Cann.

Blakenham was an avid gardener and served from 1971 as treasurer of the Royal Horticultural Society, which awarded him its Victoria Medal of Honor in 1974. He was deputy lieutenant for Suffolk from 1968. A.K.

Father Fourth Earl of Listowel. **Married** Hon. Beryl Nancy Pearson 1934: Michael John, b. 1968; Mary Anne Sergison-Brooke, b. 1936; Joanna Freda Breyer, b. 1942. **Education** Eton Coll. **Mil. service** Joined Territorial Army ca. 1939, embodied in Suffolk and Norfolk Yeomanry; afterward lt. col, 55th Anti-Tank Regiment, 1st Army, North Africa, Sicily, and Italy, WWII. **Career** Employed in brokerage house, NYC 1929–32; employed in financial district, London ca. 1932–37; alderman, London Cty. Council 1937–52; farmer since ca. 1945; Conservative M.P. for Woodbridge div. of Suffolk 1945–50 and for Sudbury and Woodbridge div. of Suffolk 1950–63; vice-chmn. 1951–55 and chmn. 1963–65, Conservative Party Org.; minister of state for colonial affairs 1955–56; secty. of state for war 1956–58; minister of agriculture, fisheries, and food 1958–60; minister of labour 1960–63; chancellor of the Duchy of Lancaster and deputy leader of House of Lords 1963–64. **Officer** Chmn.: London Municipal Soc. 1947–52; council, Toynbee Hall since 1966; governing body, Peabody Trust since 1967. • Treas., Royal Horticultural Soc. since 1971. **Member** White's Club; Pratt's Club. **Honors** MBE 1943; mentioned in dispatches, WWII; Legion of Merit, U.S. 1945; OBE 1945; P.C. 1955; created 1st Viscount of Little Blakenham 1963; deputy lt., Suffolk since 1968; Victoria Medal of Honor, Royal Horticultural Soc. 1974.

Further reading J. W. M. Thompson, "'Doing a Truman'—Awfully Nicely," in *Spectator*, 15 May 1964.

LORD BUTLER OF SAFFRON WALDEN
Richard Austen Butler
British Conservative leader
***Born* Attock Serai, India, British Empire, 9 December 1902**
***Died* Great Yeldham, Essex, England, 8 March 1982**

Rab Butler was one of the ablest British politicians of the century. He held every important government office except the prime ministry, which he twice failed to persuade his party to give him. After the Conservative defeat of 1964 he retired from politics, accepted a life peerage, and for 13 years was master of Trinity College, Cambridge University.

He was the eldest son of Sir Montagu Butler, then an official in the Indian Civil Service who was shortly to become governor of India's Central Provinces and later master of Pembroke College, Cambridge. The Butler family had an illustrious history in both education and foreign service: two ancestors were headmasters of Harrow; two others were masters of Pembroke; his great uncle, H. M. Butler, was master of Trinity; his uncle Sir Harcourt was governor of Burma; and another uncle, Sir Geoffrey, was fellow of Pembroke, member of Parliament for Cambridge University, and a figure of considerable influence in the Conservative Party. Through his mother's family, Butler was a descendant of the economist Adam Smith.

Butler was sent to England for schooling along with his brother and two sisters. He attended Marlborough, where a fall from a horse permanently weakened one arm and where he had a generally undistinguished career. From there he was sent up to Pembroke, the family college, where he first displayed the brilliance which was always afterward to seem a natural attribute. He took firsts in both parts of the modern languages tripos, then a first in history, and in his third year, 1924, was president of the Cambridge Union. He immediately won a fellowship and tutorship in history at Corpus Christi College, which he held until 1929.

In 1926, Butler married Sydney Courtauld, the only child of the wealthy textile manufacturer Samuel Courtauld. The financial security that came from this marriage—the Butler family was neither landed nor wealthy—enabled him to enter politics on considerably easier terms than would have been his lot otherwise. He was selected to contest a safe Tory seat, Saffron Walden in Essex, which he won in 1929 and held in every election until he gave it up in 1965. Experience in government came his way very quickly. In 1931 he was appointed parliamentary private secretary to the secretary of state for India, Sir Samuel Hoare, who engineered his promotion to junior minister—undersecretary of state for India—the next year. Much of his five-year tenure at the India Office was spent in drafting and securing passage of the Government of India Act, which entailed the liberalization of colonial administration in the subcontinent. In this task he first found himself in opposition to Winston Churchill, then an influential Tory backbencher long out of power. Butler's adroitness in maneuvering the massive and complex bill through Parliament secured his reputation.

After a year (1937–38) in a junior role at the Ministry of Labour, he received another important assignment: undersecretary of state for foreign affairs. Neville Chamberlain had become prime minister in 1937 and upon Anthony Eden's resignation as foreign secretary in 1938 appointed Lord Halifax, former viceroy of India, to take his place. Because Halifax could not answer in the Commons, the job of defending the government's foreign policy fell to Butler as his deputy. Chamberlain's appeasement of Hitler's aggression was the policy in question; it was supported by a majority of Tory M.P.s, and Butler energetically defended "the construction of peace" in Parliament day after day against bitter attacks by Churchill, Eden, and their allies. Yet Churchill, when he took over the government following Chamberlain's resignation, retained his old Commons adversary in his post at the Foreign Office. Butler's tenacity as a debater kept him from joining Chamberlain's men in political oblivion.

Butler was never a close friend nor a great admirer of Churchill, and often told of the prime minister sending for him in 1941 and offering him the presidency of the Board of Education, which though a full ministry was no cabinet post and was widely considered a political backwater. "I could have the day to think it over," Butler recalled. "I replied that I needed no time for reflection, since this was the one job I would like to have more than any other. At which the Old Man growled, 'Just like you, Rab, but I offered it to you as an insult.'" Acting against Churchill's strict instructions to confine his energies to administration, Butler set out to change education in Britain, in his own words, "to harness to the educational system the wartime urge for social reform and greater equality." The Education Act of 1944—popularly called the Butler Act—was his brainchild and one of the most important reform laws of the age. It provided for the first time a coordinated national system of free public education for everyone, and has been the basis of all subsequent educational change in Britain.

With the end of the war the coalition government was disbanded, and in the 1945 general election the Conservatives were badly beaten. Butler, rather than take a post in the shadow cabinet, went to the Conservative Central Office, where he headed the newly created research department. He made the relatively obscure post one of the most important in the party during the years in opposition, and more than anyone else, was responsible for giving postwar Conservatism a progressive image, one committed to full employment and even to Labour's "welfare state," while still insisting on a prominent role for private enterprise and on the party's professional abhorrence of socialism. His department's policy papers appalled diehard backbenchers, but Butler's ideas, such as the 1947 "Industrial Charter," caught the temper of the time and enabled the Tories to return to power in 1951.

As chancellor of the Exchequer throughout Churchill's second ministry (1951–55), Butler had one of his greatest successes. His chancellorship coincided with Britain's longest period of postwar prosperity, and his budgets were able gradually to slacken the austere controls which the Labourites had been forced to impose. A particularly generous budget in 1955 certainly benefited his party in the following month's general election, but the harsher supplementary budget he presented in October brought outraged howls from the opposition and severe criticism from within Tory ranks as well. Exhausted by his efforts as chancellor, Butler relinquished the office during Eden's first cabinet shuffle in December 1955, taking the less demanding posts of lord privy seal and leader of the House of Commons.

In the Suez crisis of 1956, Butler was known to be against the abortive British, French, and Israeli invasion of the canal, though he said nothing in public. His opinions did little to increase his popularity in the party, however, and when Eden saw the necessity to resign in January 1957, the Tories turned away from Butler, widely regarded as the heir-apparent, and adopted Harold Macmillan, then rather less well known, as their leader. The story was circulated that Churchill had even advised the Queen against sending for Butler. Humiliated by the rejection, Butler nevertheless stayed in the government, remarking wryly, "It is not very often that one is nearly prime minister." Macmillan added the post of home secretary to Butler's two other portfolios, and in that office he was credited with liberalizing the betting and licensing laws and with passage of a widely praised act on prison reform. He remained lord privy seal until 1959, when he began two years of service as chairman of the party. He relinquished the leadership of the House in 1961 when he took over the British side in membership negotiations with the European Common Market. In 1962 he became head of the newly created Central Africa Office, where he had some initial success in the difficult negotiations with the secessionists of the Federation of Rhodesia and Nyasaland.

Butler left the Home Office in mid-1962 to

become first secretary of state and deputy prime minister, and he was again popularly perceived as being next in line of succession. Macmillan decided to resign in mid-1963, precipitating a furious struggle that came to a head at the party conference in October. Although Butler arrived at the conference as acting prime minister because of Macmillan's illness, the delegates nevertheless again turned away from him, finally acclaiming the foreign secretary, the Earl of Home, as the new party leader. "I ought to have pushed more and got it for myself," was Butler's reaction. Yet he refused to join two protégés from his research department days, the M.P.s Iain MacLeod and Enoch Powell, who quit the government rather than countenance the way their mentor had been treated. "It seemed to me," he reflected later, "that the most unselfish way of achieving unity was to serve with a friend rather than force the issue the other way."

He lasted barely a year as foreign secretary before new general elections drove the Tories from their 13 years of power. He had no stomach for another stint in opposition, however, and so a few months after the election Butler, who had refused an earldom the previous year, accepted a life peerage from Harold Wilson's government and with it the mastership of Trinity. The latter office, while one of the few university posts in the gift of the Crown, was necessarily subject to the government's acquiescence.

His years out of politics in Cambridge were happy enough, by all accounts, for he was not by nature a nurser of wounds. His memoirs,

The Art of the Possible (1971), were written with a sunny irony untinged by enmity or remorse. He was at Trinity during the Prince of Wales's three years as an undergraduate, and though he was too old to be vice chancellor of the university, he participated fully in the life of his college and was warmly remembered as an expert mediator and a kind host. He was prolonged in the mastership in 1973 by a strong majority of the fellows, and retired from the post to his Essex farm in 1978 with his second wife, Mollie Courtauld (the widow of his first wife's cousin), whom he had married in 1959.

Butler held honorary degrees from nearly 20 universities in Britain and abroad, and was for a long time a popular chancellor of both Essex and Sheffield universities. He had similarly long tenures as president of the Modern Language Association, the Royal Society of Literature, and the National Association of Mental Health. He was made a Companion of Honor in 1954 and a Knight of the Garter in 1971. A.K.

Parents Sir Montagu S. D. B., gov. of Central Provinces, India, and master of Pembroke Coll., Cambridge, and Ann Gertrude (Smith) B. **Married** (1) Sydney Courtauld 1926 (d. 1954): Adam Courtauld, politician; Richard Clive, farmer; Samuel James; Sarah Teresa Mary. (2) Mollie Montgomerie Courtauld 1959. **Religion** Church of England. **Education** Marlborough Sch., Wilts., grad. 1920; studied French and German literature, Abbeville, France 1920–21; Pembroke Coll., Cambridge, M.A. (double 1st Class in modern languages and history) 1925. **Career** Fellow, tutor, and lectr. on French history, Corpus Christi Coll., Cambridge 1925–29; Conservative M.P. for Saffron Walden div. of Essex 1929–65; parliamentary private secty. to Secty. of State for India 1931; member, Indian Franchise Cttee. 1932; undersecty. of state, India Office 1932–37; parliamentary secty., Ministry of Labour 1937–38; undersecty. of state for foreign affairs 1938–41; minister of education 1941–45; member, Cabinet Reconstruction Cttee. 1943–45; minister of labour 1945; chancellor of the Exchequer 1951–55; lord privy seal 1955–59; leader of House of Commons 1955–61; home secty. 1957–62; cabinet minister for Common Market negotiations 1961; head of Central Africa Office 1962–63; deputy prime minister and 1st secty. of state 1962–63; secty. of state for foreign affairs 1963–64. • With Conservative Party: chmn., Research Dept. 1945–64; chmn., Advisory Cttee. on Policy 1950–64; chmn. of party org. 1959–61. • Master of Trinity Coll., Cambridge 1965–78; Azad Memorial Lectr., Delhi 1970; Nehru Memorial Trust Lectr.; Churchill Memorial Lectr.; Romanes Lectr., Oxford Univ.; Leake Lectr. **Officer** Chmn.: council, Natl. Union of Conservative Assns. 1945–56; council, Royal India Soc. 1946; Home Office Cttee. on Mentally Abnormal Offenders 1972–75; council, Trinity Coll., Cambridge; Anglo-Netherlands Soc. • Pres.: Cambridge Union 1924; Natl. Assn. of Mental Health since 1946; Royal Soc. of Literature since 1951; Natl. Union of Conservative Assns. 1956; Modern Language Assn. • Other: dir., Courtaulds 1946–51 and 1965–69; rector, Glasgow Univ. 1956–59; high steward, Cambridge Univ. 1958–66; chancellor, Sheffield Univ. 1960–78; chancellor, Univ. of Essex since 1962; high steward, City of Cambridge since 1963; co-founder, Mental Health Trust. **Fellow** Royal Geographical Soc. **Member** British Cttee. for UNESCO 1947; Fitzwilliam Mus. Syndicate, Cambridge Univ. • Clubs: Athenaeum; Carlton; Farmers'; Beefsteak; Grillions. **Honors** P.C. 1939; C.H. 1954; freedom of Saffron Walden 1954; created Lord Butler of Saffron Walden, life peer, 1965; K.G. 1971; hon. fellow of Pembroke Coll., Cambridge, 1941, Corpus Christi Coll., Cambridge, 1952, and St. Anthony's Coll., Oxford, 1957; hon. degrees from univs. of Leeds, Oxford, Cambridge, Nottingham, Bristol, Sheffield, St. Andrews, Glasgow, Reading, Durham, Calgary, Liverpool, and Witwatersrand. **Author** *The Art of the Possible* (autobiography), 1971; (ed). *The Conservatives: A History from Their Origins to 1965*, 1977.

Further reading Francis Boyd, *Richard Austen Butler*, 1956; Gerald Sparrow, *R.A.B.: Study of a Statesman*, 1965; Patrick Cosgrave, *R. A. Butler: An English Life*, 1981.

KENNETH H(AY) KINGDON
Atomic physicist
***Born* Montego Bay, Jamaica, British West Indies, 13 May 1894**
***Died* Schenectady, New York, USA, 9 March 1982**

The discovery in 1939 that uranium can undergo fission raised questions about how the various isotopes of uranium differ in their susceptibility to splitting. With world war imminent, several researchers, including Kenneth H. Kingdon, worked under great pressure to isolate the minute samples of fissionable material that would later yield the information necessary to build the first atomic bomb.

Kingdon was born to Canadian missionary parents in Jamaica and received a B.A. from McMaster University in Ontario in 1914. During World War I he served with the Canadian Army in England, where he conducted antisubmarine research. He obtained a Ph.D. in physics from the University of Toronto in 1920 and joined the staff of the General Electric Research Laboratory (now part of G.E.'s Research and Development Center) in Schenectady, New York.

In 1924, Kingdon and the Nobel Prize-winning chemist Irving Langmuir discovered that a film of cesium vapor deposited on hot tungsten filaments greatly increased their emission of electrons; they patented improved filaments for radio receiving-tubes and other devices. Kingdon also worked on developing photoelectric cells, and his study of sparking in gaseous discharge tubes led to improvements in the design of rectifiers and other equipment used to control high-powered alternating currents.

In 1939, Kingdon and Herbert C. Pollock turned to the task of separating the three natural isotopes of uranium, U-234, U-235, and U-238. More than 99 percent of natural uranium is composed of U-238, but theoretical physicists, including Niels Bohr, suspected that U-235 was the essential ingredient for a nuclear reaction. U-235 nuclei, they believed, would split under a slow neutron bombardment, releasing more neutrons and starting a chain reaction that would liberate vast amounts of energy. To verify this theory, however, the physicists needed to test each isotope individually.

Kingdon and Pollock separated U-235 from U-238 by taking advantage of the atoms' differences in weight. Using a large mass spectrometer, they stripped electrons from uranium atoms and then drove the positively-charged ions through a strong magnetic field. The lighter U-235 ions were deflected more readily than those of U-238, and when the speeding particles hit a platinum collecting plate, the microscopic deposits landed a short distance apart. A similar experiment was performed by Albert Neir of the University of Minnesota. Physicists at Columbia University tested both the Schenectady and the Minnesota samples in March 1940 using their 150-ton cyclotron. The prediction concerning U-235 held true, and the path was clear for the development of the first atomic pile in 1942 and the first uranium bomb in 1945.

During World War II, Kingdon developed advanced antisubmarine training devices and attack plotters and a sophisticated acoustic torpedo for the U.S. Navy. He spent the last year of the war with Ernest Lawrence's Manhattan Project support team at Berkeley, California. After the war he returned to the G.E. Laboratory as assistant director. When the Atomic Energy Commission and G.E. set up the Knolls Atomic Power Laboratory in Schenectady in 1946, Kingdon was appointed tech-

Courtesy of General Electric Inc.

nical manager in charge of a multidisciplinary group of scientists conducting research on reactor design. The keystone of this effort, the laboratory's experimental reactor, came on line in April 1948.

Kingdon left Knolls in 1954 and retired from G.E. in 1959. In the 1960s he was a consultant for Bethlehem Steel and other firms. He died at the age of 88. P.D.

Parents Missionaries. **Married** Leah Mae Zeh 1924: Elizabeth Kingdon Grünwald, opera singer. **Emigrated** to U.S. 1920. **Education** McMaster Univ., Hamilton, Ontario, B.A. 1914; Univ. of Toronto, Ph.D. in physics 1920. **Mil. service** Antisubmarine research, Canadian Army, England, WWI; munitions and antisubmarine research, U.S. Navy 1940–44; atomic bomb research, Univ. of California Radiation Lab., Berkeley 1944–45. **Career** With General Electric Research Lab. (now G.E. Research and Development Center), Schenectady, NY: research physicist 1920–59; asst. dir. in charge of atomic power research 1946; co-founder 1946 and technical mgr. 1946–54, Knolls Atomic Power Lab; sector mgr. in charge of project analysis 1954–59. • Consultant 1960s: Bethlehem Steel Corp.; Allmanna Svenska Electriska Atiebalaget; other corps. • **Patents** X-ray machine; photoelectric cell; other electronic devices. **Fellow** Amer. Physical Soc. **Honors** Jt. certificate of appreciation, U.S. War Dept. and Navy Dept., WWII; certificates of commendation, Bureaus of Ships and Ordnance, U.S. Navy, WWII; hon. degree from Union Coll. **Author** of articles and papers on atomic and electronic research in scientific jrnls.

Further reading William L. Laurence, *Dawn over Zero*, 1946; Samuel Glasstone, *Source Book on Atomic Energy*, 1950.

ZVI YEHUDA (BEN AVRAHAM HaKOHEN) KOOK

Spiritual leader of the Israeli ultranationalist movement
Born **Zimel, Kovno province, Lithuania, Russian Empire, 1891**
Died **Jerusalem, Israel, 9 March 1982**

Zvi Yehuda Kook was the spiritual mentor of thousands of religious Zionists and of the movement to which many of them belong, the ultranationalist Gush Emunim (Bloc of the Faithful). In his writings and lectures he called for the Jews as a nation to practice *teshuvah*, the return to the strict observance of religious law, which he considered a prerequisite to their divinely ordained union with the Land of Israel.

Kook's father was Rabbi Avraham Yitzhak Kook (known as Rav Kook), the first Chief Rabbi of Palestine (1921–35) and one of the most respected and influential figures in modern Jewish Orthodoxy. Unlike most other Orthodox leaders in the early part of this century, Rav Kook supported the efforts of the secular Zionist movement to rebuild the Jewish nation in its original homeland; he taught that the Jews and the biblical land of Israel were given to each other by God in order to fulfill each others' inherent holiness, and announced the beginning of a new messianic era in which the Temple would be restored. He was the founder of the Merkaz ha-Rav Yeshiva in Jerusalem for the study of Torah and its application to contemporary problems of nation building.

Zvi Yehuda Kook was 13 when the family moved to Palestine from Lithuania in 1904. He studied at the Etz Chaim Yeshiva in Jerusalem, was ordained to the rabbinate, and became a proselytizer for his father's program of national renewal. As a young man he traveled to Poland on a fund-raising mission. He served as an administrator and teacher at Merkaz ha-Rav and took over as head of the yeshiva after Rav Kook's death in 1935. The rest of his life was devoted to spreading his father's teachings and editing his writings.

The political implications of Rav Kook's teachings began to be felt after the Six-Day War of 1967, when the Israeli armed forces regained control of the Old City of Jerusalem and captured territory on the West Bank of the Jordan River that had been part of the nation in biblical times. These events were interpreted by many Israelis as evidence of the national restoration that Kook had prophesied. A movement known as Greater Israel began to coalesce around Zvi Yehuda Kook, who encouraged his followers to found new communities throughout the boundaries of the biblical homeland. Early in 1974, a number of its members formed the Gush Emunim, whose purpose was to restore the country's dedication to its spiritual and historical mission after the demoralization of the Yom Kippur War and to fight all attempts by the government to give away biblical territory as part of a peace settlement with the Arabs.

Over the next few years, the Gush Emunim, with Kook as its spiritual leader, became a key element in the right-wing National Religious Party and was instrumental in the election to the prime ministry in 1977 of Menachem Begin, whom Kook served as an advisor. He withdrew his support from both Begin and the NRP after they acquiesced in the territorial concessions of the Camp David agreement. In an interview, Kook said: "We are not a nation of conquerors. We are returning to the land of our fathers. No one, no prime minister, has the authority to renounce any part of the country. It belongs to the entire people of Israel, to the Jews of Pakistan, the United States and the Soviet Union." Arabs were welcome to live in Israel, he added, but as individual citizens rather than as a nation.

Kook's death, after an illness of several years, occurred while members of the Gush Emunim were being forcibly evicted from settlements in the Sinai by the Israeli army in preparation for the return of the Sinai to Egypt. J.P.

Father Avraham Yitzhak HaKohen Kook, Chief Rabbi of Palestine. **Married** Hava Leah Hutner 1922 (d.). **Religion** Orthodox Jewish. **Emigrated** to Palestine 1904; Israeli citizen since 1948. **Education** Etz Chaim Yeshiva, Jerusalem; ordained to the rabbinate. **Career** Admin. since 1920s and head since 1935, Merkaz ha-Rav Yeshiva, Jerusalem; spiritual leader since 1967, Greater Israel movement; spiritual leader since 1974, Gush Emunim (Bloc of the Faithful); active in Natl. Religious Party 1970s; advisor to Prime Minister Menachem Begin 1977–ca. 79; ed. of his father's writings. **Author** *Li-Netivot Israel* [*On the Paths of Israel*], 1967; numerous articles in Israeli publications.

Further reading Herbert Weiner, *9½ Mystics: The Kabbala Today*, 1969; Rael J. Isaac, *Israel Divided: Ideological Politics in the Jewish State*, 1976; David J. Schnall, *Radical Dissent in Contemporary Israeli Politics*, 1979.

HARRY (GRAHAM) CARTER
Typographer and archivist of the Oxford University Press
Born **Croydon, London, England, 27 March 1901**
Died **England, 10 March 1982**

Courtesy of Oxford University Press

Harry Carter was one of the most knowledgeable and experienced typographers in Britain and wrote on the subject with unusual lucidity. As head of design at Her Majesty's Stationery Office in the postwar years, he was responsible for the adoption of a neat, readable typeface for government publications. For 26 years he was the archivist of the Oxford University Press, of which he published a learned history in 1975.

Carter was born in a suburb of London, attended Bedales School, earned a master's degree from Queen's College, Oxford, and was called to the bar by Lincoln's Inn in 1935. During the 1920s he began studying metal and wood engraving and type punch cutting at London's Central School of Art and Design, where he met many of the major figures involved in the contemporary renaissance of typography and fine book design in Britain. From 1928 to 1929 he studied typography at the Monotype Corporation Works, the first engravers to introduce mass-production typefaces based on Garamond, Baskerville, and other classic designs. He spent eight years as an assistant at the Kynoch Press, and was the author, with its manager Herbert Simon, of the manual *Printing Explained* (1931). In 1930 he published *Fournier on Typefounding*, a translation of *Manuel typographique* by the eighteenth-century engraver Pierre-Simon Fournier. Francis Meynell, head of the Nonesuch Press, hired him as production manager in 1937, and he had an important role in the design of the firm's handsome editions of the works of Dickens, Milton's *Comus*, and Gilbert White's *The Natural History and Antiquities of Selborne*.

During World War II, Carter's facility with languages—he knew Russian, Arabic, and Hebrew, among others—earned him assignments as a postal censor in Palestine and as a consular official in Rumania and Egypt. After the war, Meynell, now typographical advisor to Her Majesty's Stationery Office, asked him to head the bureau's design and layout section. According to Ruari McLean, author of *Modern Book Design*, the two almost single-handedly redesigned government publications to make them look "as if they had been written by and for human beings." Carter was made OBE in 1951 for his Stationery Office service.

As archivist of the Oxford University Press from 1954 to 1980, Carter edited Joseph Moxon's *Mechanick Exercises on the Whole Art of Printing* (1962) and Stanley Morison's massive treatise *John Fell, the University Press, and the "Fell" Types* (1969). In 1975 he published the first volume of the projected multivolume *History of the Oxford University Press*, an exhaustive study of England's first press from the Middle Ages to the late eighteenth century. Richard Ollard observed in the *Times Literary Supplement*: "The author's account of the typographical history of his subject is a model of lucid expression. . . . But what gives his book its special fascination—like that of publishing itself—is its peculiar combination of the commercial, the industrial, the learned, and the aesthetic."

Carter was the designer and engraver of typefaces in Hebrew, Russian, and English. His Lyell Lectures, delivered in 1968, were published as *A View of Early Typography*. He died at the age of 80, two years after his retirement from Oxford University Press. S.A.

Parents Henry C. and Sarah (Addison) C. **Married** Ella Mary Garratt 1934 (d. 1977): two sons. **Education** Bedales Sch.; Queen's Coll., Oxford, M.A.; Central Sch. of Art and Design, London 1920s; called to the bar by Lincoln's Inn 1935. **Mil. service** Postal censor, England and Palestine 1939–45; consular official, Rumania and Egypt, WWII. **Career** Trainee in type design, Monotype Corp. Works 1928–29; asst. to mgr., Kynoch Press 1929–37; production mgr., Nonesuch Press 1937–38; head, design and layout sect., H.M. Stationery Office 1946–53; archivist, Oxford University Press 1954–80; Lyell Lectr., Oxford Univ. 1968; designer of Hebrew, Russian, and English typefaces. **Honors** OBE 1951. **Author** (Trans.) Pierre-Simon Fournier, *Fournier on Typefounding*, 1930; (jtly.) *Printing Explained*, 1931; *Wolvercote Mill*, 1957; (co-ed.) Joseph Moxon, *Mechanick Exercises on the Whole Art of Printing*, 1962; (ed.) Stanley Morison, *John Fell, the University Press, and the "Fell" Types*, 1969; *A View of Early Typography*, 1969; *A History of the Oxford University Press*, vol. 1, 1975; (trans. and ed.) C. Enschede, *Typefoundries in the Netherlands*, 1978. **Contributor** of articles on typography and type to bibliographical jrnls.

Further reading Francis Meynell, *My Lives*, 1971.

HORACE (VICTOR) GREGORY
Poet, translator, editor
***Born* Milwaukee, Wisconsin, USA, 10 April 1898**
***Died* Shelburne Falls, Massachusetts, USA, 11 March 1982**

Horace Gregory was one of the foremost poets of the American left, whose large published output included classical translations, editions and anthologies of others' work, biographies, literary criticism, and a memoir, besides several books of poetry. His wife, with whom he often collaborated, was the poet Marya Zaturenska; they married in 1925 and she predeceased him by only seven weeks.

Gregory was brought up in Milwaukee, attended the German-English Academy, and, during the summers, studied painting at the Milwaukee School of Fine Arts. He studied classics at the University of Wisconsin, graduated in 1923, then began a career as a free-lance poet and writer for such magazines as *New Republic, New Masses,* and the *Nation.*

He achieved a remarkable success with his first book of poems, *Chelsea Rooming House* (1930). Though some had been written as many as five years before 1930, they were taken together as poems for the Great Depression, hard and bitter pictures of the wasted, downtrodden poor who drift through the cold and remorseless city. The dreams, fears, and frustrations of these people are described by Gregory without condescension, in their own language, at the same time that his narrative voice condemns the implacable greed of capitalism as the source of America's deadly blight. Gregory's other poems of the 1930s, somewhat less desperate and strident in tone and often less powerful in effect, were collected in *No Retreat* (1933), *Chorus for Survival* (1935), and, retrospectively, in *Poems 1930–1940* (1941).

Many critics hold that Gregory's most considerable accomplishment was his translation of the love poems of Catullus (1931, revised 1956) and Ovid (1964) and of the latter's *Metamorphoses* (1958). Although their linguistic and formal fidelity to their originals is of a high order, the translations successfully employ modern verse rhythms, idiomatic language, and Gregory's sure narrative command.

Gregory's teaching career began in 1934 when he joined the English department at Sarah Lawrence College in Bronxville, New York. He remained there until 1960, when he was named professor emeritus. Shortly after becoming an academic, he began to produce anthologies of poetry and prose, among them *Critical Remarks on the Metaphysical Poets* and *The Triumph of Life: Poems of Consolation for the English-Speaking World* (both 1943). He also published collections of the works of Sherwood Anderson (1949), Robert Browning (1956), Longfellow (1964), Cummings (1965), and Byron (1969). With Zaturenska, who received the Pulitzer Prize for poetry in 1938, he published *A History of American Poetry 1900–1940* (1946) and the anthologies *The Mentor Book of Religious Verse* (1957), *The Crystal Cabinet: An Invitation to Poetry* (1962), and *The Silver Swan: Poems of Romance and Mystery* (1966).

Gregory's literary biographies were numerous and wide-ranging. They include a collaboration with James T. Farrell on the Hoosier poet James Whitcomb Riley (1951), plus studies of Amy Lowell (1958), James McNeill Whistler (1959), and Dorothy Richardson (1967). He published his autobiography, *The House on Jefferson Street,* in 1971; his collected essays, *Spirit of Time and Place,* in 1973; and his last book of poems, *Another Look,* in 1976.

In 1965, Gregory won American poetry's most coveted award, the Bollingen Prize. This was given in recognition of the retrospective collection, *Collected Poems,* which had appeared the previous year. A.K.

Parents Henry Bolton G., businessman and newspaper ed., and Anna Catherine (Henkel) G. **Married** Marya Zaturenska, poet, 1925 (d. 1982): Joanna Elizabeth Zeigler; Patrick Bolton. **Religion** Episcopalian. **Education** Milwaukee Sch. of Fine Arts, summers 1913–16; German-English Acad., Milwaukee 1914–19; Univ. of Wisconsin, Madison, B.A. 1923. **Career** Free-lance writer, NYC and London 1923–34; lectr. on poetry, writing, and critical theory 1934–60, and prof. emeritus since 1960, Sarah Lawrence Coll., Bronxville, NY;

lectr., New Sch. for Social Research, NYC 1955–56; ed., *The Tiger's Eye* mag. **Member** Natl. Inst. of Arts and Letters since 1964. **Honors** Lyric Prize 1928 and Levinson Prize 1934, *Poetry,* Chicago; Loines Award, Natl. Inst. of Arts and Letters 1942; Union League Civic and Arts Foundn. Award 1951; Guggenheim Fellowship 1951; Fellowship Award, Acad. of American Poets 1961; Bollingen Prize, for *Collected Poems,* Yale Univ. 1965; Horace Gregory Award established in his name 1969, and writing program named after him, Sarah Lawrence Coll.; Merrill Foundn. Award 1978; hon. degree from Univ. of Wisconsin. **Poetry** *Chelsea Rooming House: Poems* (in U.K. as *Rooming House*), 1930; *No Retreat: Poems,* 1933; *Wreath for Margery,* 1933; *Chorus for Survival,* 1935; *Poems 1930–1940,* 1941; *Fortune for Mirabel,* 1941; *Selected Poems,* 1951; *The Door in the Desert,* 1951; *Medusa in Gramercy Park,* 1961; *Alphabet for Joanna: A Poem* (juvenile), 1963; *Collected Poems,* 1964; *Another Look,* 1976. **Criticism and biography** *Pilgrim of the Apocalypse: A Critical Study of D. H. Lawrence,* 1933; *The Shield of Achilles: Essays on Beliefs in Poetry,* 1944; (with Marya Zaturenska) *A History of American Poetry 1900–1940,* 1946; (jtly.) *Poet of the People: An Evaluation of James Whitcombe Riley,* 1951; *Amy Lowell: Portrait of the Poet in Her Time,* 1958; *The World of James McNeill Whistler,* 1959; *The Dying Gladiators and Other Essays,* 1961; *Dorothy Richardson: An Adventure in Self-Discovery,* 1967; *The House on Jefferson Street: A Cycle of Memories* (autobiography), 1971; *Spirit of Time and Place: The Collected Essays of Horace Gregory,* 1973. **Editor** (Jtly.) *New Letters in America,* 1937; *Critical Remarks on the Metaphysical Poets,* 1943; *The Triumph of Life: Poems of Consolation for the English-Speaking World,* 1943; *The Portable Sherwood Anderson,* 1949; Violet Paget, *Snake Lady,* 1954; Robert Browning, *Selected Poetry,* 1956; (with M. Z.) *The Mentor Book of Religious Verse,* 1957; (with M. Z.) *The Crystal Cabinet: An Invitation to Poetry,* 1962; (jtly.) *Riverside Poetry 4: An Anthology of Student Verse,* 1962; *Evangeline and Selected Tales and Poems of Longfellow,* 1964; E.E. Cummings, *Selected Poems,* 1965; (with M. Z.) *The Silver Swan: Poems of Romance and Mystery,* 1966; *Selected Poems of George Gordon, Lord Byron,* 1969. **Translator** Catullus, *Poems,* 1931, rev. as *Poems, Translated* (in U.K. as *The Poems of Catullus*), 1956; Ovid, *The Metamorphoses,* 1958; *The Love Poems of Ovid,* 1964. **Contributor** to *New Republic, Nation, Vanity Fair, Atlantic Monthly, New Verse, Poetry, New Masses, Saturday Review of Literature, Partisan Review, Commonweal,* and other mags. and jrnls. **Recording** *Selected Poems of Catullus,* 1979.

Further reading M. L. Rosenthal, *The Modern Poets,* 1965; Horace Gregory Issue, *Modern Poetry Studies,* May 1973.

LEONID (OSIPOVICH) UTYOSOV
Soviet jazz musician
***Born* Odessa, Russia, 9 March 1895**
***Death announced* Moscow, USSR, 12 March 1982**

Leonid Utyosov was an actor, singer, and bandleader, and one of the foremost originators and purveyors of jazz in the Soviet Union. He was banned from performing late in Stalin's reign, when many divergent cultural forms were forbidden, but came back after the dictator's death to renewed national popularity.

Utyosov learned to play the violin as a child, and from 1911 was working in plays and revues in theaters around the Odessa region. He was talented enough to make the transition to Moscow and Petrograd by 1921, appearing in operettas by Offenbach and Lehár. Soon afterward he gave a kind of one-man show, *From Tragedy to Tragedy,* in which he acted comic and dramatic roles, did acrobatics, played the guitar and the violin, and led the orchestra and chorus.

American jazz swept Europe during the 1920s and won many Soviet adherents. Sidney Bechet's tour of the country with his group in 1925 was sensationally popular. In 1929, Utyosov set up the first theatrical band, which he called Tea Jazz, and was its soloist, conductor, and master of ceremonies. The group was later officially organized as the State Variety Orchestra of the Russian Republic. Utyosov wrote and appeared in two musical comedies featuring jazz, *Jazz at the Crossroads* (1930) and *Musical Magazine* (1932), and starred in the first Soviet musical film, *Vesyoliye rebata* (1932; *Moscow Laughs*).

In some official circles, there was always a sense of jazz as decadent and bourgeois. Even a writer as eminent as Maxim Gorky, in his *Music of the Fat Ones* (1931), inveighed against its connections with capitalism. Yet it was tacitly tolerated until World War II put an end to all forms of noncommunist expression. The Cold War and its accompanying anti-Americanism seemed to seal its doom, but soon after Stalin's death jazz was again performed to large audiences.

Utyosov kept up his career as a popular singer even during the war, when several patriotic songs of his own composition became well known. He also frequently performed songs by other popular Soviet composers, including those by Matvei Blanter, Aleksander Tsfasman, and T. N. Khrennikov. In 1961, Utyosov argued in an article written for the Ministry of Culture's journal *Sovetskaya Kultura* that jazz was much needed in the Soviet Union, even asserting that it was a native art form that originated at weddings and festivals in Odessa long before it was ever heard in New Orleans.

Utyosov was named a National Artist of the Soviet Union on his 70th birthday in 1965. He was the author of three books, *Notes of an Actor* (1939), *With Song Through Life* (1961), and *Thank You, My Heart* (1976). A.K.

Education Violin lessons. **Career** Singer and musician, small theaters and variety shows, Kremenchug, Odessa, Kherson, and Zaparozhye 1911–20s; actor, singer, musician, and writer, revues and operettas in Moscow and Petrograd 1921–late 1920s; founder 1929, conductor, and soloist, Tea Jazz group, Leningrad, later reorganized as Gosudarstvennyi Estradnyi Orkestr (State Variety Orch. of the Russian Republic); film actor 1930s; solo singing career. **Honors** Natl. Artist of the Soviet Union 1965. **Operetta performer** [*Silva*], [*Beautiful Elena*], and [*Count Luxembourg*], Moscow and Leningrad 1920s; *Shelmenko,* Moscow 1955. **Revue performer and writer** [*From Tragedy to Tragedy*], ca. 1922; [*Jazz at the Crossroads*], 1930; [*Musical Magazine*], 1932. **Film** *Vesyoliye rebata* (rel. in U.S. as *Moscow Laughs*), 1932. **Author** *Zapiski Aktera* [*Notes of an Actor*], 1939; *S pesnei po zhizni* [*With Song Through Life*], 1961; *Spasibo, serdce* [*Thank You, My Heart*], 1976.

Further reading Clifton Daniel, "Muscovite Ramblers," in *New York Times Magazine,* 17 Apr. 1955.

AURÉL BERNÁTH

Painter

***Born* Marcali, Somogy county, Hungary, 13 November 1895**

***Died* Budapest, Hungary, 13 March 1982**

As one of a small number of Hungarian painters who tried to forge a progressive national style between the two world wars, Aurél Bernáth applied the methods of the French post-Impressionists to the depiction of scenes of everyday life in Hungary. A survivor of the political and cultural upheaval that followed the abortive anti-Soviet uprising of 1956, he adapted his art to the requirements of Socialist Realism, exerting a strong influence on the next generation of Hungarian painters.

Born in the southwest of the country, Bernáth attended grammar school in Budapest and then studied art at the city's Free School of Nagybánya. The Nagybányan painters, who took their name from the small village in Rumania where they spent their summers, were committed to developing a Hungarian national art based on the naturalism of the French painters Gustave Courbet and Jules Bastien-Lepage and on the *plein air* (outdoor) techniques of the Impressionists. During the turbulent period in Hungary just after World War I, Bernáth studied and painted in Berlin, where he first exhibited his work in 1923, and in Vienna, Italy, and Paris, where he discovered the post-Impressionists Gauguin and Cézanne. After experimenting briefly with abstract art, he developed a lyrical, contemplative style in which natural forms were made to convey mood and emotion. He returned to Budapest in 1926 and became one of a number of artists dedicated to forwarding the vision of the Nagybánya group.

Bernáth's paintings of the late 1920s and early 1930s are notable for their bright, jewel-like colors, their simplicity of detail, and the glimmering light that washes across the landscapes and figures. "It is not the subject of the picture that is important," he said, "but the spiritual reality that is realized by it." *Riviera* (1926), a landscape of glowing colors embedded in a somber blue ground, is widely considered his masterpiece. Other well-known works include *Hegedümüvésznö* [*Violinist*], *Venus,* and several self-portraits in glazed oils. By the late 1930s his influence was visible in the work of other artists, particularly István Szönyi, Róbert Berény, and Jeno Barcsay.

Courtesy of Hungarian National Gallery

With the creation of the Hungarian People's Republic after World War II, a group of artists began to coalesce around Bernáth, meeting regularly in Budapest's Gresham Café, an artist's haunt since the 1920s. This group carried forward the representational and nationalistic traditions of the Nagybánya School while feuding with the Surrealist and Constructivist ideologues of the so-called European School. The invasion of Hungary by the Soviet Union in 1956 and the installation of a Kremlin-controlled government put an end to most of the abstract experiments in art. However, Bernáth, whose paintings were apolitical, naturalistic, and visually appealing, remained in favor and was allowed to teach at the Budapest College of Fine Arts. While continuing to paint folk scenes and local landscapes, he also painted murals on the history of labor for public buildings and the Budapest subway.

A retrospective of Bernáth's work, first shown in Budapest in 1956, was sent to London and the Venice Biennale in 1962 and was well received by the critics. In 1956 he won a gold medal for his large canvas *Panorama of Budapest,* and in 1964 was made an Eminent Artist of the Hungarian People's Republic. He was also the author of several volumes of art criticism, essays, and biographies of artists. S.A.

Parents Béla B., lawyer, and Attala (Roboz) B. **Married** Alice Pártos, physician, 1927 (d. 1966): Mária, art historian, b. 1935. **Religion** Roman Catholic. **Education** High sch., Budapest, grad. 1913; Free Sch. of Nagybánya, Budapest 1915–16; studied art in Berlin, Vienna, Italy, France, and U.K. ca. 1921–26. **Mil. service** Austro-Hungarian Army 1916–18. **Career** Artist since mid-1910s; prof., Coll. of Fine Arts, Budapest 1945–73; chief ed., *Magyar Müvézet* [*Hungarian Art*] mag., and member of secretariat, Hungarian Patriotic People's Front, Budapest 1945–49; designer of murals for Budapest bldgs. and subways 1950s; editorial bd. member, *Information Hungary* book 1968. **Officer** Pres., Assn. of Hungarian Artists, Budapest. **Member** PEN Club, Budapest; Szinyei Merse Soc. **Honors** Prize for painting *Riviera,* Hungarian Natl. Art Gall., Budapest ca. 1926; Kossuth Prize, Presidential Council of the Hungarian People's Republic 1948, 1970; Munkácsy Prize 1950; gold medal, for painting *Panorama of Budapest,* Brussels World's Fair 1958; Eminent Artist of the Hungarian People's Republic 1964; Banner, Order of the Hungarian People's Republic 1975. **Exhibitions** Sturm Gall., Berlin 1923; Hungarian Natl. Art Gall. 1926; retrospective, Budapest 1956, London and Venice Biennale 1962. **Collections** Hungarian Natl. Gall.; other public and private collections in Europe and U.S. **Author** *Irások a müvészetrol* [*Essays on Art*], 1947; *Igy éltünk Pannoniában* [*So We Lived in Pannonia*], 1956; *Kor es pálya* (autobiography), 3 vols., 1958–62; *Utak Pannoniából* [*Ways from Pannonia*], 1960; *A Muzsa körül* [*Around the Muse*] (art criticism), 1962; *A Muzsa udvarában,* 1967; *Gólyáról, Helgáról, halálról* [*Stork, Helga, and Death*], 1971; *Lássuk, mire megyünk,* 1973; *Kisebb világok: napló* (art criticism), 1974; *Feljegyzések éjfél köröll: napló* (biography), 1976; *Egy festö feljegyzései* (biography), 1978.

Further reading Anatal Kampis, *The History of Art in Hungary,* 1966.

FELIX (MUSKETT) MORLEY
Newspaper editor and college president
Born **Haverford, Pennsylvania, USA, 6 January 1894**
Died **Baltimore, Maryland, USA, 13 March 1982**

Felix Morley followed a brilliant academic career with equally distinguished ones in journalism and education. He won a Pulitzer Prize for his editorial writing in the *Washington Post* and served during World War II as president of Haverford College near Philadelphia.

Morley was born into a Quaker family. His father was a professor of mathematics at Haverford who moved his family to Baltimore in 1900 to accept a similar position at Johns Hopkins University. Morley returned to Haverford for his university degree, which he received in 1915, then served for a time in a British ambulance unit during World War I. After spending two years as a reporter, he won a Rhodes scholarship and from 1919 to 1921 read modern history at New College, Oxford University. He spent the following year at the London School of Economics on a Hutchinson Fellowship. (Morley's was the only family to produce three Rhodes scholars. His elder brother, Christopher, was a well-known novelist, poet, and essayist; his younger brother, Frank, was a London-based novelist and editor.)

Morley began to write editorials for the

Baltimore Sun in 1922 and continued with that paper until 1929, traveling to the Far East as a special correspondent in 1925–26 and to Geneva in 1928–29 as a Guggenheim Fellow reporting on the League of Nations. A committed internationalist who believed in the organization's potential to prevent war, he held the post of director of the Geneva office of the U.S. League of Nations Association in 1929–31. He returned home to join the staff of the Brookings Institution in Washington, which awarded him his Ph.D. in 1936.

When Eugene Meyer bought the *Washington Post* in 1933, it was a moribund paper in desperate need of editorial vigor. The distinction which Morley brought to the editorial page earned him his Pulitzer in 1936, the first such prize ever awarded a *Post* writer. He was often critical of the Franklin Roosevelt administration's economic policies and especially of its clashes with the Supreme Court, yet one of his editorials—on the necessity of making plain the determination of the United States to join forces with the democratic nations of Europe, in order to discourage further aggression by Germany and Italy—was praised by Roosevelt as the accurate expression of his own views. Concerning the function of newspapers in a democracy, Morley said: "The problem is not so much to develop an informed public opinion as it is to build a critical public opinion. None of us . . . can any longer hope to have more than a fragmentary understanding of the infinitely complicated world in which we live. But we can, and we definitely should, develop a critical faculty which shall be instinctively hostile to every dogmatic statement [and] instinctively insistent on the importance of proof for every flat assertion."

Courtesy of Isabel M. Morley

In 1940 Morley left the *Post* to take the Haverford presidency, saying he did not believe that it would be possible to run an objective editorial page from Washington in wartime. He returned to journalism after the war as co-founder of the magazine *Human Events,* Washington correspondent for *Barron's Weekly,* and frequent contributor to *Nation's Business.* He also published several books in which he warned against the threat posed to the republic by the centralization of power in the federal government, by the capitulation of Congress to special-interest groups, and by constant foreign intervention and military spending. His memoirs, *For the Record,* appeared in 1979. He received numerous awards and honorary degrees.

After his retirement, Morley lived with his wife on Gibson Island, off the coast of Maryland. He died of cancer at the age of 88.

A.K.

Parents Frank M., mathematics prof., and Lilian Janet (Bird) M. **Married** Isabel Middleton 1917: Lorna Janet; Christina Bird Borden; Anthony Jefferson; Felix Woodbridge (d.). **Religion** Quaker, then Episcopalian. **Education** Friends Sch., Baltimore, grad. 1911; Haverford Coll., PA, A.B. 1915; Honor Sch. of Modern History, New Coll., Oxford (Rhodes scholarship), A.B. 1921; Hutchinson Research Fellow, London Sch. of Economics 1921–22; Guggenheim Fellow in political science, Univ. of Geneva 1928–30; Brookings Instn., Wash. DC, Ph.D. 1936. **Mil. service** Ambulance driver, British Red Cross, Flanders 1915–16; ROTC, U.S. Army 1917; Wartime Emergency Employment Service, U.S. Dept. of Labor 1917–18; consultant, War Manpower Commn. 1942–45; advisor and consultant, Amer. Specialized Training Program, WWII. **Career** Reporter, *Philadelphia Public Ledger* 1916–17; staff writer, Wash. DC bureau, UPI 1917 and *Philadelphia North American* 1919; editorial staff writer 1922–29, Far East corresp. 1925–26, and Geneva corresp. 1928–29, *Baltimore Sun;* lectr. on politics, St. John's Coll., Annapolis, MD 1924–25; dir., Geneva office, League of Nations Assn. 1929–31; staff member, Brookings Instn., Wash. DC 1931–33; ed., *Washington Post* 1933–40; pres., Haverford Coll., PA

1940–45; Cutler Memorial Lectr., Univ. of Rochester 1941; co-founder, pres., and ed., *Human Events* mag. 1945–50; editorial writer, *Nation's Business* jrnl. 1946–70; Wash. DC corresp., *Barron's Weekly* 1950–54; foreign affairs commentator, NBC radio. **Officer** Trustee: Sidwell Friends Sch., Wash. DC 1936–40; St. John's Coll. 1937–38; Bliss Sch. 1948–50; Presidential Library Assn.; Herbert Clark Hoover Memorial Foundn. • Other: Member, bd. of dirs., Washington Coll., MD 1953–67; vestryman, Episcopal Church 1968–70; chmn., Inst. of Social Science Research. **Fellow** Royal Economics Soc., U.K. **Member** Advisory bd., Amer. Enterprise Assn. 1949–72; lay advisory bd., Anne Arundel Community Coll. 1961–70; exec. cttee., Key Sch., MD 1962–70; Human Relations Commn., Anne Arundel Cty., MD 1966–68; Council on Foreign Relations; Federal Advisory Council; U.S. Employment Service; Phi Beta Kappa; Gibson Island Club; (charter member) Mont Pelerin Soc. **Honors** Hart, Schaffner and Marx Prize, for *Unemployment Relief in Great Britain,* 1924; Pulitzer Prize for editorial writing, for *Washington Post* editorials, 1936; Volker Distinguished Service Award 1961; Outstanding Alumnus Award, Friends Sch. 1977; hon. degrees from univs. of George Washington, Towson State, and Pennsylvania, and from Lebanon Valley, Hamilton, Bethany, and Western Maryland colls. **Author** *Unemployment Relief in Great Britain,* 1924; *Our Far Eastern Assignment,* 1926; *The Society of Nations,* 1932; *The Power in the People,* 1949; *The Foreign Policy of the United States,* 1951; *Gumption Island* (novel), 1956; *Essays on Individuality,* 1958; *Freedom and Federalism,* 1959; *For the Record,* 1979; *The Message* (unpublished). **Contributor** of articles on politics, economics, and social issues to newspapers, jrnls., and mags.

NIKOLAI P(ETROVICH) KAMANIN
Director of cosmonaut training in the USSR
***Born* Melenki, Vladimir province, Russia, 18 October 1908**
***Death announced* Moscow, USSR, 14 March 1982**

Once they had successfully launched Sputnik I, the leaders of the Soviet space effort began planning another historic first: placing a human being in earth orbit. In 1960, Air Force Gen. Nikolai P. Kamanin was charged with selecting and training the first group of 20 cosmonauts. For more than a decade Kamanin played an important role in the manned space flight program, with its early triumphs and later tragedies; his retirement followed soon after the deaths of three cosmonauts in the spaceship Soyuz 11 in 1971.

Kamanin, the son of a shoemaker, was born in Melenki, northeast of Moscow. He attended military flight school in Leningrad, volunteered for the Red Army in 1928, and joined the Communist Party in 1932, a year after he became senior pilot and flight commander. In 1934 he was named a Hero of the Soviet Union for leading the rescue of the crewmen and scientists aboard the icebreaker *Chelyuskin* when it sank in the Arctic Ocean.

After graduating from the Zhukovsky Air Force Academy in 1938, Kamanin headed an air brigade that saw action in the Russo-Finnish War of 1939–40. From May 1942 until the end of World War II he commanded the 5th Assault Air Corps. During the postwar years, as a member of the Air Force general staff, he headed DOSAAF, the largely civilian organization that promotes cooperation with the armed services.

Kamanin was appointed to head the space program's training section in 1960 and picked 20 jet pilots as candidates for the cosmonaut corps. On 12 April 1961, Yuri Gagarin became the first of the group to circle the earth in the spaceship Vostok. Kamanin played an important part in organizing the longer and more elaborate flights that followed, including the launching of the first female cosmonaut in 1963 and the first spacewalk in 1965; he was also responsible for training three more groups of cosmonauts, raising the size of the corps to 50 by the end of the decade.

Kamanin occasionally served as a spokesman for the government on space matters, responding favorably to Pres. John Kennedy's

1963 proposal for a joint U.S.-Soviet space flight and asserting, when necessary, the superiority of the Soviet space program. He attributed the deaths of three American astronauts in a launch-pad fire in January 1967 to excessive haste on the part of the United States, adding, "We are not chasing any space records." Before the month was out, a Soviet cosmonaut died in a crash-landing in the Ural Mountains.

Kamanin's last promotion, from lieutenant general to colonel general, came in 1967. In the ensuing years the Americans took the lead in space. The Soviets were still capable of space spectaculars, notably the "troika flight" of three Soyuz capsules and seven cosmonauts in October 1969, but this achievement was overshadowed by the American moon landing a few months before. The Soviet manned-space effort showed signs of slowing in 1970, and it came to a disastrous halt in 1971 when three cosmonauts were asphyxiated during the landing of Soyuz 11. Kamanin, by now a familiar figure with the Russian public—he had even played long-distance chess with orbiting cosmonauts—was dismissed, reportedly for having ordered the crew to land despite an air leak in the pressurized cabin, and his place was taken by the popular cosmonaut Vladimir Shatalov.

Little was heard of Kamanin in the West after his forced retirement, and the government's obituary announcement gave no details of his death. P.D.

Father a shoemaker. **Education** Military-Theoretical Flight Sch., Leningrad, grad. 1928; Zhukovsky Air Force Acad., grad. 1938; Gen. Staff Acad., grad. 1950. **Career** Joined Red Army 1928; sr. pilot, flight comdr., and comdr. of flight detachment, USSR Air Force 1931–34; member, CPSU since 1932; comdr., air brigade 1938–41; served in Russo-Finnish War 1939–40; comdr., 5th Assault Air Corps, 2nd Air Army, Eastern Europe 1942–45; dir. late 1940s–53 and first deputy chmn. 1953–58, DOSAAF (Voluntary Soc. for Cooperation with Army, Air Force, and Navy); joined USSR space program ca. 1958; dir. of cosmonaut training 1960–71; promoted from lt. gen. to col. gen. 1967. **Honors** Hero of Soviet Union 1934; Order of Lenin three times; Order of Red Banner; Order of Suvorov, 2nd Class; Order of Kutuzov, 2nd Class; Order of Red Star; other honors and awards. **Author** *Pervyi grazhdanin vselennoi* [*First Citizen of Space*], 1962; (jtly.) *Experimentalnaya kosmicheskaya stantsiya na orbite* [*Experimental Space Station in Orbit*], 1969; (jtly.) *Semero na orbite* [*Seven in Orbit*], 1969; (ed.) *Pochta kosmonavtov* [*The Mail of the Cosmonauts*], 1970; *Letchiki i kosmonavty* [*Aviators and Cosmonauts*], 1971; (jtly.) *Krylya: ocherki o peredovykh aviatorakh* [*Wings: Sketches of Prominent Aviators*], 1971; *Starty v nebo* [*Launchings into the Sky*], 1976.

Further reading James E. Oberg, *Red Star in Orbit,* 1981.

(JOHN) EDGELL RICKWORD
Writer, literary critic, and editor
***Born* Colchester, Essex, England, 22 October 1898**
***Died* England, 15 March 1982**

Edgell Rickword, though little remembered today, distinguished himself during the period between the world wars as poet, critic, and editor. A committed Marxist, he was a founder and editor of *Left Review,* one of the most memorable little magazines of the 1930s.

Born into an impoverished middle-class family in Colchester—his father was borough librarian in that part of Essex—Rickword recalled that he "felt himself a socialist since about 1911" when he witnessed a lockout of striking engineers. He attended the local grammar school on scholarship and enlisted in the army immediately on leaving school in October 1916. A year later he received a commission in the Royal Berkshire Regiment, was posted to the 5th Battalion in France, and was twice wounded—first in the Battle of the Somme and then during the German retreat shortly before the Armistice, when he was permanently blinded in one eye. He was awarded the Military Cross for distinguished service.

Rickword went up to Pembroke College, Oxford University, on a service scholarship just after the war, but lack of money forced him to quit after four terms. He began to eke out a precarious living from writing to support his new wife and family. Fortunately, his taste in literature was advanced and assured: by 1918 he had already read Joyce's *Portrait of the Artist as a Young Man* and Siegfried Sassoon's *Counterattack and Other Poems*. His first book of poetry, *Behind the Eyes* (1921), was considered promising. By 1924 he had produced several widely praised essays on poets then not widely appreciated: Charles Baudelaire, Stéphane Mallarmé, John Donne, Christopher Marlowe, and T. S. Eliot. This precocious mastery of the modernist sensibility was confirmed by his critical work *Rimbaud: The Boy and the Poet* (1924), the first critique in English of the great precursor of symbolism.

Rickword and his friend Douglas Garman were the founders and editors of the *Calendar of Modern Letters,* a journal with uncompromisingly high standards of literary creativity and criticism. Running from March 1925 until July 1927, it published, among much other work of merit, a series of lengthy critical essays called "Scrutinies," which the Cambridge critic F. R. Leavis acknowledged as a direct influence on both his critical attitudes and his own journal, *Scrutiny,* which first appeared five years later. The *Calendar* counted D. H. Lawrence, Hart Crane, and Robert Graves among its regular contributors.

Rickword's zenith as a poet was *Invocations to Angels* (1928), in which his debt to Donne, evident in the title, was widely remarked. The collection contains his best-known war poems, including "The Soldier Addresses His Body," "Winter Warfare," and "Trench Poets," with its poignant opening, "I knew a man, he was my chum,/but he grew darker day by day,/and would not brush the flies away,/nor blanch however fierce the hum/of passing shells." His poetry at its best is eloquent, urbane, and grave, yet simultaneously exact and carefully controlled. He looked to Donne as his greatest influence; much of his poetry has a distinctly Metaphysical feeling in almost every respect.

His inspiration, however, soon failed him: the stories he collected in *Love One Another* (1929) and the verse satires in *Twittingpan* (1931) marked the virtual end of his literary creativity. During the 1930s he became deeply involved in leftist politics. While others of his generation and political bent, notably W. H. Auden and Cecil Day Lewis, were able to make effective poetry out of the turbulent historical moment, Rickword said he found "*too much* emotional stimulus" in "the actual social struggle," and he turned all his energies to editing. He began working for Lawrence and Wishart, a leftist publishing house in London, and was closely involved in their decision to launch *Left Review,* the first issue of which appeared in October 1934. It was an attempt to reach the working people of Britain and involve them in the reality of the anti-Fascist struggle, especially in the Spanish Civil War. Not all the contributors were Communists; in addition to the poets Day Lewis, Stephen Spender, and Hugh MacDiarmid, they included J. D. Bernal, Storm Jameson, and Nancy Cunard. Rickword served as editor from January 1936 to July 1937. By the time *Left Review* ceased publication in May 1938 it had become increasingly doctrinaire in its Stalinism, yet retained an extraordinarily faithful readership who kept it going for some months before the end by means of a "fighting-fund."

Rickword edited another Marxist journal, *Our Time,* from 1944 to 1947. His research yielded several works on English radicalism, including *Milton, the Revolutionary Intellectual* (1940) and *Radical Squibs and Loyal Ripostes* (1971), a study of Regency satirical pamphlets. His *Collected Poems* did not do well when published in 1947, but were warmly received when reissued 20 years later. By that time there was considerable interest in the history of British leftism: all three of the journals Rickword edited were integrally reprinted during the 1960s. A.K.

Father a librarian. **Married** . . . ca. 1920: two children. **Education** Dame's sch.; Colchester Grammar Sch. (Foundation Scholarship) through 1916; Pembroke Coll., Oxford (service scholarship) 1919–ca. 1921. **Mil. service** Joined Artists' Rifles 1916; lt., 5 Battalion, Royal Berkshire Regiment, France 1917–18 (wounded). **Career** Poet, essayist, and jrnl. ed. since late 1910s; co-founder 1925 and co-ed. 1925–27, *Calendar of Modern Letters* literary jrnl.; ed., Wishart (later Lawrence and Wishart) publishing house ca. 1927–34; assoc. ed. 1934–38 and ed. 1936–37, *Left Review;* ed., *Our Time* jrnl. 1944–47. **Honors**

M.C., WWI; Arts Council Prize 1966; hon. degree from Univ. of Essex. **Poetry** *Behind the Eyes,* 1921; *Invocations to Angels, and the Happy New Year,* 1928; *Twittingpan and Some Others,* 1931; *Collected Poems,* 1947; *Fifty Poems,* 1970; *Behind the Eyes: Selected Poems and Translations,* 1976. **Short-story collection** *Love One Another: Seven Tales,* 1929. **Literary criticism and biography** *Rimbaud: The Boy and the Poet,* 1924; *Milton, the Revolutionary Intellectual,* 1940; *William Wordsworth 1770–1850,* 1950; (jtly.) *Gillray and Cruikshank: An Illustrated Life of James Gillray (1756–1815) and of George Cruikshank (1792–1878),* 1973; *Essays and Opinions 1921–1931,* 1974; *Literature in Society 1931–78,* 1978. **Editor** *Scrutinies of Various Writers,* vol. 1, 1928, vol. 2, 1931; (jtly.) *A Handbook of Freedom: A Record of English Democracy Through Twelve Centuries,* 1939; *Soviet Writers Reply to English Writers' Questions,* 1948; Christopher Caudwell, *Further Studies in a Dying Culture,* 1949; *Radical Squibs and Loyal Ripostes: Satirical Pamphlets of the Regency Period 1819–1821,* 1971. **Translator** (Jtly., as John Mavin) François Porché, *Charles Baudelaire: A Biography,* 1928; Marcel Coulin, *Poet Under Saturn: The Tragedy of Verlaine,* 1932; Ronald Firbank, *La princesse aux soleils, and Harmonie,* 1973. **Manuscript collection** in British Library, London.

Further reading David Holbrook, "The Poetic Mind of Rickword," in *Essays in Criticism,* July 1962; H.D. Ford, *A Poet's War: British Poets and the Spanish Civil War,* 1965; C. H. Sisson, *English Poetry, 1900–1950,* 1971.

VASILY (IVANOVICH) CHUIKOV
Marshal of the Red Army, defender of Stalingrad
Born **Serebriany Prudy, near Moscow, Russia, 12 February 1900**
Died **Moscow, USSR, 18 March 1982**

One of the most renowned Soviet heroes of World War II, Vasily Chuikov was the tough general charged with the defense of Stalingrad against the Nazis. With grim determination and a fearful loss of life, the Red Army held the city, thereby stopping the German advance into the Soviet Union. His army's victory represented the political and psychological turning point of the war on the eastern front.

One of 12 children born to a peasant family in the Tula region, Chuikov was with several of his brothers at the naval base of Kronstadt when the Bolshevik Revolution broke out. He joined the Red Army as soon as it was formed early in 1918, and during the civil war fought against the White Army and its foreign allies on both the Siberian and Polish fronts. He was a very early member of the Communist Party of the Soviet Union, joining in 1919.

After graduating from Frunze Military Academy in 1925, Chuikov was sent to China, where he served as military counselor to Chiang Kai-shek from 1926 until 1937. He returned home to a tour of command on the Karelian Isthmus in the Russo-Finnish War, then went back to China as Soviet military attaché. In the spring of 1942, in Moscow, he received command of the 64th Army, and in July and August of that year won great credit leading the difficult retreat across the Don steppes, a desolate region that had been completely burned over by the Nazis. In September 1942 he was given command of the 62nd Army, charged by Stalin himself with holding, at all costs, the industrial city on the Volga, formerly called Tsaritsyn, which had been renamed in Stalin's honor. It was Chuikov's finest hour, and the Red Army's as well; their courage and fortitude became celebrated throughout the world.

Up to 22 German divisions had the city surrounded by mid-September, following two months of steady pressure on a withdrawing Soviet force. The defenders had their backs to the Volga, with their artillery mounted on the river's other, eastern bank. The Nazis launched wave after wave of heavy attacks, using bombers, tanks, and sheer numbers of men. For three months the outside world, though aware of the ongoing battle, had no news whatsoever, for the Soviets refused to admit a single foreign correspondent into the city. Finally, on December 22, the American reporter Henry Shapiro of the United States won an exclusive telephone interview from front headquarters with Chuikov, who was in the city itself. "Hitler put the best he had against Stalingrad," said the general, who estimated that the worst of the five-month battle was by then over. "He did not spare quantity or quality. . . . Our forces were not equal. The enemy had superiority at all points all the time."

He spoke of the uniqueness of the encounter in his experience, of the constant, bloody, "close-distance fighting, and I don't mean the kind of fight we study at the military academies. . . . Here we hold each other in a deadly grip. The distance between trenches is 20 to 100 meters." The heroism of the defenders often "took the form of mass self-sacrifice. When an enemy group ten to fifteen times larger than one of our units attacked us our soldiers would send a signal to our batteries, ordering them to fire. . . . While they would be killed by their own guns, they would take ten to fifteen times their number of Germans with them. . . . I believe that if the military machines used against us had been used against any army in the world, including the Germans, they could not have endured one-tenth what we endured." Soviet losses, never officially acknowledged, amounted to over 400,000 men, 100,000 more than the Germans. Yet the Nazi advance was stopped, and when Chuikov finally reviewed his remaining troops at a victory celebration on 1 February 1943 he had the special satisfaction of knowing that the German commander, Gen. Friedrich von Paulus, was his prisoner.

"General Stubbornness," as Chuikov was nicknamed by his troops at Stalingrad, ended World War II as commander of the 8th Army, which in the spring of 1945 engaged the nearly crushed remnants of the German military machine in the Battle of Berlin. On 1 May 1945 he accepted the surrender of Gen. Hans Krebs, chief of the Army General Staff. "Today is the first of May," Krebs began, "a great holiday for our two nations." But Chuikov cut him short. "*We* have a great holiday today," he said curtly. "How things are with you over there it is less easy to say." He remained in occupied Germany after the war as commander of Soviet forces. From 1949 to 1954 he was the chairman of the Allied Control Commission; his fellow commanders found him notoriously difficult to deal with.

The Red Army's political commissar for the Stalingrad defense was none other than Nikita Khrushchev, who a few years after Stalin's death in 1953 became the most powerful man in the Soviet Union. Chuikov was one of his protégés and began receiving rapid promotions. In 1955 he was advanced to marshal's rank, in 1960 was made commander in chief of all Soviet land forces, and in 1963 became first deputy minister of defense and simultaneously head of the Soviet civil-defense effort. He was also a member of the Central Committee of the CPSU from 1961.

Khrushchev's fall, however, marked the virtual end of Chuikov's career. In the reaction against the former dictator there were once again attempts to rewrite Soviet history, assertions that Marshal Georgi Zhukov, not Chuikov, had been the hero of Stalingrad and had received the German surrender in Berlin. This denigration of the great soldier's role continued until the end of his life: news of his death, which occurred after a long illness, was relegated to the third page of the Soviet Army's newspaper, *Red Star*.

Chuikov was a physically powerful, belligerent man who had been wounded in action many times; his two rows of gold teeth testified to one such occasion. "His hands were the size of hams," an American officer reported. "You felt he would shoot you without any qualms, if someone gave the order." He was heavily decorated, winning (in addition to many foreign awards, including the Distinguished Service Cross of the United States) the Order of Lenin five times, the Order of the Red Banner four times, the Order of Suvorov, First Class, three times, the Hero of the USSR twice, and the Order of the October Revolution. In 1969 he was an official Soviet representative at the funeral of Pres. Dwight Eisenhower. A.K.

Parents peasants. **Education** Apprenticed to mechanic in weapons factory, Tula ca. 1912; attended military sch.; Frunze Military Acad., grad. 1925. **Career** Joined Red Army 1918; regiment comdr., Siberian front 1919, Polish front 1920; joined CPSU 1919; military advisor to Chiang Kai-shek, China 1926–37; comdr., Rifle Corps 1938; army comdr., Karelian Isthmus, Russo-Finnish War 1939–40; chief, military mission to China 1941–42; comdr., 64th Army 1942; comdr., 62nd Army, Stalingrad 1942–43; comdr., 8th Army, Germany 1944–45; comdr. of Soviet forces 1946–49 and chmn. of Allied Control Commn. 1949–54, occupied Germany; deputy since 1946 and member 1952–61, USSR Supreme Soviet; candidate member 1952–61 and member since 1961, CPSU Central Cttee.; comdr., Kiev Mil. District 1953–60; candidate member, Central Cttee. Presidium, Ukrainian C.P. 1954–60; appointed marshal 1955; comdr. in chief, Soviet land forces 1960–64; appointed 1st deputy minister of defense 1963; head of civil defense 1963–72; member, Inspector Gen.'s Group, Ministry of Defense since 1972. **Honors** Order of Lenin 5 times; Order of Red Banner 4 times; Order of Suvorov, 1st Class, 3 times; Order of October Revolution; Hero of USSR twice; DSC, U.S.; other orders and medals. **Author** [*The Beginning of the Road*]; one other book; articles on military strategy.

Further reading Walter Kerr, *The Russian Army,* 1944.

ALAN F(ERNAND) BADEL

Actor and producer

***Born* Rusholme, Manchester, England, 11 September 1923**

***Died* 19 March 1982**

Alan Badel, one of the leading British actors of his generation, was admired as much for his striking appearance as for his robust but lyrical style of performance. His good looks, resonant voice, and energetic manner made him the very epitome of a stage actor, and made him ideally suited to the roles of Romeo, Hamlet, and Othello, which he played in a full-blooded romantic fashion. Unlike many popular romantic leading players, however, he was extremely versatile, and won great praise for his portrayals of Ariel in *The Tempest* and the Fool in *King Lear.* To American audiences he was well known for his only Broadway appearance—as Hero, the sinister seducer in Jean Anouilh's play *The Rehearsal.*

Badel was an outspoken champion of the traditional arts of stage acting. "Television," he once said, "is for making oneself famous. Films are for making money. And the actor's proper place is in the theater." It is therefore fitting that he will be remembered in Britain chiefly for two outstanding performances in roles that demand a high degree of histrionic display: Richard III, and Edmund Kean in Jean-Paul Sartre's dramatization of the life of the great nineteenth-century English actor. Badel was an apt choice for the part of Kean; both actors had made their mark in *Richard III* and *Othello,* and both relied on their emotional and physical vitality to engage their audiences. To watch Kean, said Samuel Coleridge, was like "reading Shakespeare by flashes of lightning," and Badel at his very best was also capable of bringing extraordinary insight to a part. Clive Barnes, reviewing the play in *The New York Times,* said: "This is a virtuoso performance by a virtuoso actor, funny, happy, and brilliant. Mr. Badel preens his way through the play, devilishly pleased with himself, and yet always with that hint, that tiny self-doubt of a suggestion, that he is also able to laugh at himself. Also Mr. Badel manages to convince one that Kean was really a great actor—which is no small achievement."

Badel was born in a suburb of the industrial city of Manchester, the son of a French businessman who had emigrated after World War I and his English wife. His childhood was enlivened by long visits with his French relatives, who kept a small shop near Lyons. After attending a local high school, he entered the Royal Academy of Dramatic Art in London, where he won the school's highest award, the Bancroft Gold Medal, at his graduation in 1941. He married a fellow student, Yvonne Owen, in 1942. Their daughter, the actress Sarah Badel, was born in 1943. He made his professional debut as Pierrot in *L'enfant prodigue* at the Mercury Theater, London, in August 1941 and the following year had small parts in *Macbeth* (with John Gielgud in the title role) and in *The Young Mr. Pitt,* his first film.

This promising beginning was interrupted by military service. Badel joined the 6th Airborne Division's Parachute Regiment in 1942, and rose to the rank of platoon sergeant. During the Battle of the Bulge he was made partly deaf by an exploding shell. He remained in the army until 1947 as a member of the Army Play Unit, entertaining troops in the Middle East and in Germany. In 1947 he joined a small repertory company in the provincial town of Farnham before becoming a member of the Birmingham Repertory Theatre, where he first attracted notice for his performance as Richard III. Between 1949 and 1956, he acquired a national reputation at the Shakespeare Memorial Theater in Stratford-on-Avon, where, after an initial appearance as Ratty in *Toad of Toad Hall* (1949), he played a succession of Shakespearean parts, including Claudio in *Measure for Measure* (1950), and Fool in *King Lear* (1950), Justice Shallow in *Henry IV, Part 2* (1951), and the title role in *Hamlet* (1956).

Badel was equally successful on the London stage, where he appeared in Shakespeare (*Romeo and Juliet,* 1952), in Ibsen (*Hedda Gabler,* 1954), and in modern works such as Hochwalder's *The Public Prosecutor* (1957), which he also directed. In 1958 he formed, with Viscount Furness, Furndel Productions, a company whose brief existence was notable for two excellent and popular plays: *Ulysses in Nighttown* (1959), an adaptation of Joyce's novel in which Badel played Stephen Dedalus, and Gore Vidal's *Visit to a Small Planet* (1960), in which he took the part of Kreton. Badel also worked in films during the 1950s, and by the early 1960s had acquired a television following for his performances of romantic roles such as Darcy in *Pride and Prejudice* (1957) and Don Juan in Shaw's *Don Juan in Hell* (1962). He was twice named British Television Actor of the Year. Neither of his visits to the United States during the 1950s added to his reputation. In 1951 he played John the Baptist in William Dieterle's film *Salome* (released 1953), an especially turgid biblical epic starring Rita Hayworth and Charles Laughton, and in 1953 he played the Fool in Orson Welles's television adaptation of *King Lear.* He received appreciative notices, however, for his Broadway appearance in Anouilh's *The Rehearsal* (1963), in which he repeated a London triumph of the previous year.

Given Badel's low opinion of the film industry, it is not surprising that he never excelled in that medium. Of his 20 film appearances, which include *Day of the Jackal* (1973) and *Nijinsky* (1979), the best was perhaps his relatively small part in Lindsay Anderson's version of David Storey's novel *This Sporting Life* (1963). The culmination of his career was *Kean* (1970), a bravura performance in which he held the stage for two hours, evoking an actor's attempts to submerge his private troubles in his theatrical personality. His last appearance in the United States was in *Shōgun* (1980). H.B.

Parents Auguste Firman B., city office mgr., and Elizabeth Olive (Durose) B. **Married** Marie Yvonne Owen, actress, 1942: Sarah, actress, b. 1943. **Education** Burnage High Sch., Manchester, GCE 1939; RADA, London (scholarship), grad. 1941. **Mil. service** Platoon sgt., Parachute Regiment, 6th Airborne Div., and Army Play Unit, Mideast and Germany 1942–47. **Career** Actor, on stage since 1938, in films since 1942, on TV since 1953; appeared with Farnham Repertory Co. 1947, Birmingham Repertory Theatre 1949, and Shakespeare Memorial Theatre, Stratford-on-Avon 1950, 1951, 1956; co-founder, Furndel Productions Ltd. 1958. **Member** RADA; AEA, U.S. and U.K. **Honors** Bancroft Gold Medal, RADA 1941; Star and Defence Medal, WWII; twice TV Actor of the Year, including 1963 for *The Lover;* (jtly.) best male performer, *Variety* poll of London theater critics, for *Kean,* 1971. **Stage** (all London, except as noted) *The Black Eye,* Oxford 1940; *L'enfant prodigue,* London and tour 1941; *Macbeth,* London and tour 1942; *Othello,* Mideast, WWII; *Exercise Bowler,* Germany, WWII; *The Corn is Green,* Farnham 1947; *Peace in Our Time,* 1947; *Frenzy,* 1948; *Toad of Toad Hall,* Stratford 1949; *Beauty and the Beast,* 1950; *A Midsummer Night's Dream,* 1951; *The Other Heart,* 1952; *Romeo and Juliet,* 1952; *Hedda Gabler,* 1954; (also dir.) *The Public Prosecutor,* 1957; (also co-producer) *Ulysses in Nighttown,* London, Paris, and the Netherlands 1959; (co-producer only) *The Ark,* 1959; (also co-producer) *Visit to a Small Planet,* 1960; (co-producer only) *Roger the Sixth,* 1960; *The Life of the Party,* 1960; *The Rehearsal,* London 1961 and NYC 1963; *Man and Superman,* 1966; *Kean,* Oxford 1970 and London 1971; *Othello,* Oxford 1970 and London 1971; *Richard III,* 1976. • With Birmingham Repertory Theatre, 1949: *The Modern Everyman; Richard III; The Mar-*

vellous History of St. Bernard; Diary of a Scoundrel. • With Stratford Festival Season, 1950: *Much Ado About Nothing; Measure for Measure; Henry VIII; Julius Caesar; King Lear.* 1951: *Henry IV, Part 2; The Tempest; Henry V.* 1956: *Hamlet; Love's Labour's Lost; Measure for Measure.* **Films** *The Young Mr. Pitt,* 1942; *The Stranger Left No Card,* 1953; *Salome,* 1953; *Will Any Gentleman,* 1953; *Three Cases of Murder,* 1954; *Magic Fire,* 1956; *This Sporting Life,* 1963; *Bitter Harvest,* 1963; *Children of the Damned,* 1964; *Arabesque,* 1966; *Otley,* 1968; *Where's Jack?,* 1969; *The Adventurers,* 1970; *Day of the Jackal,* 1973; *Luther,* 1974; *Telefon,* 1977; *The Medusa Touch,* 1978; *Force Ten from Navarone,* 1978; *Nijinsky,* 1979. **Television** *King Lear,* 1953; *Pride and Prejudice,* 1957; *The Complaisant Lover,* 1961; *Don Juan in Hell,* 1962; *The Prisoner,* 1963; *The Lover,* 1963; *A Couple of Dry Martinis,* 1965; *Gordon of Khartoum,* 1966; *A King and His Keeper,* 1970; *Shōgun,* 1980; *Vanity Fair; The Count of Monte Cristo; The Raging Calm.*

J(IWATRAM) B(HAGWANDAS) KRIPALANI

Indian patriot and associate of Mahatma Gandhi
Born **Hyderabad, India, British Empire, 1888**
Died **Ahmedabad, India, 19 March 1982**

The acharya ("revered teacher") J. B. Kripalani was one of Mohandas K. Gandhi's earliest disciples and among the last surviving leaders of the long struggle against British colonialism, which culminated in Indian independence in 1947. After the Mahatma's murder in 1948, Kripalani fell out with Gandhi's political successors and began a long career as a political gadfly, becoming a source of intense irritation to his former allies.

Kripalani's politically rebellious nature was evident even in his youth, when he was successively expelled from Wilson College, Bombay, and Sind College, Karachi, for his radical views and actions. In 1912 he finally obtained a degree from Fergusson College, Poona, but was soon suspended from teaching in the Bombay area for interesting his pupils in politics. That same year he moved to Bihar, far to the east, where he began to teach in a college in Muzaffarpur affiliated with Calcutta University, and became deeply concerned with the extreme poverty and misery of the Biharis.

He had come under the influence of Aurobindo Ghosh (later Sri Aurobindo), who was then preaching the violent overthrow of British rule, but the gentler methods espoused by Gandhi eventually won his complete loyalty. He first met Gandhi in 1914 and in Champaran in 1917 participated in the first large-scale satyagraha (Gandhi's method of organized nonviolent resistance), directed against British control of the indigo trade. He was among those arrested, and served the first of many jail sentences. In 1918 he accepted the post of private secretary to Madan Mohan Malaviya, a moderate political reformer and a founder of Benares Hindu University, where Kripalani became professor of politics in 1919. The following year he resigned to follow Gandhi full time.

He joined the Mahatma in the salt satyagraha in 1920, and was arrested and jailed for a year. On his release he went to Gujarat, a province in the west of the country near his home region of Sind, and from 1922 until 1927 was the principal (acharya) of Gujarat Vidyapith, a Gandhian project to educate and emancipate the people of that particularly backward area. The title he held there stuck with him all his life. After another stretch of imprisonment in the early 1930s during the civil-disobedience campaign, Kripalani was elected in 1934 to the working committee of the clandestine Congress Party and to the general secretaryship of the party organization, remaining in the latter post until 1946. He was interned with other members of the working committee from August 1942 until June 1945, and the year after his release, on the eve of independence, was elected president of the Congress Party.

Kripalani was never known as a conciliator, and his frequent and intemperate use of mordant sarcasm led him into constant conflict with other leading disciples, especially Jawaharlal Nehru, Sardar Patel, and Vinobha Bhave, who became important figures in the new government. They tried to exclude Kripalani from all decision making, and in disgust he resigned as president late in 1947. In 1951 he formed, with others on the left of the party, the Congress Democratic Front, only to break altogether with the Congress later in the same year. He took several parliamentary allies with him into a new party of his foundation, the Kizan Mazdoor Praja, which allied itself three years later with the Socialist Party to form the Praja Socialist Party, of which he was chairman for three years.

As a deputy on the opposition front bench, Kripalani was vehement in his denunciation of the government's handling of many crises, especially the 1962 border dispute with China and the Assamese atrocities against Bengalis. He never tired of accusing the Congress leaders of breaking faith with Gandhi's precepts, which was certainly his most stinging rebuke. In 1973 he called a meeting of opposition parties to protest Indira Gandhi's government's encroachment on civil liberties, and though no longer in the Lok Sabha (he had resigned in 1970), was instrumental in the emergence of the Janata Party coalition and the selection of Morarji Desai from among many opposition figures to be prime minister. He led the rejoicing at Mrs. Gandhi's defeat in 1977 and the installation of India's first non-Congress government. He withdrew from public life altogether in 1978 and lived for several years in ascetic contemplation at the Gandhi Ashram in Lucknow.

Kripalani was the author of several books on the methods of nonviolent revolution and two memoirs of the Mahatma, *Gandhi the Statesman* (1951) and *Gandhi, His Life and Thought* (1970). In the former book he wrote of Gandhi as "not merely a spiritual reformer, but a statesman who judged the political and economic situation in India correctly and devised well-conceived measures to meet it. . . . If he had not been a wise and shrewd politician, all his spiritual and moral fervor could not have achieved the country's freedom."

Kripalani was 94 when he died of respiratory and cardiac failure. A.K.

Father Bhagwandas K. **Married** Sucheta Mazumder 1936 (d. 1974). **Education** Wilson Coll., Bombay; Sind Coll., Karachi; Fergusson Coll., Poona, B.A., M.A. 1912. **Career** Teacher, Sukkur sch. ca. 1912; prof., Bihar Bhumihar Coll., Muzaffarpur 1912–17; asst. to Mohandas Gandhi, indigo satyagraha, Champaran 1917–18; imprisoned ca. 1918; private secty. to Pandit Madan Mohan Malaviya 1918; prof. of politics, Benares Hindu Univ. 1919–20; village political organizer for Gandhi, Uttar Pradesh early 1920s; founder and dir., Shri Gandhi Ashram, Varanasi, Uttar Pradesh ca. 1920; joined salt satyagraha 1920; imprisoned 1920–21; co-founder 1922 and principal 1922–27, Gujarat Vidyapith education project; imprisoned 1932, 1933. • With Congress Party: member, working cttee. 1934–40s; gen. secty. 1934–46; pres. 1946–47; co-founder, Congress Democratic Front 1951; resigned 1951. • Imprisoned 1942–45; member, Constituent Assembly 1946–51; founder, *Vigil* political jrnl. 1950; member, provisional parliament 1950–52; co-founder 1951 and chmn. 1951–54, Kisan Mazdoor Praja Party; member, Lok Sabha (lower house of parliament) 1952–57, 1957–62, 1963–70; co-founder 1954 and chmn. 1954–57, Praja Socialist Party; co-founder and leader, Natl. Sangharsh Samiti 1973; co-founder and member, Janata Party ca. 1974–78. **Author** *The Gandhian Way,* 1938, 3rd rev. ed. 1945; *Fateful Year,* 1948; *Gandhi the Statesman,* 1951; *Voice of Vigilance: Speeches,* 1959; *Gandhian Thought,* 1961; *Gandhi, His Life and Thought,* 1970; *Freedom in Peril,* 1977; many pamphlets and published speeches.

Further reading Mohandas K. Gandhi, *Autobiography,* 1948; Michael Brecher, *Nehru: A Political Biography,* 1959; Robert Payne, *The Life and Death of Mahatma Gandhi,* 1969.

HARRY H. CORBETT
Actor
***Born* Rangoon, Burma, 28 February 1925**
***Died* Hastings, England, 21 March 1982**

Harry Corbett's successful but relatively undistinguished early career as a player of supporting roles in British theater and films gave no indication that he would become, during the 1960s, one of the most popular television actors in the United Kingdom. At the height of their fame, Corbett and Wilfrid Brambell, the stars of "Steptoe and Son," drew an audience of 27 million—more than half the population of Britain. The success of the series, which ran from 1962 through 1965 and was revived in 1970, was just as unpredictable. Corbett, as the younger Steptoe, and Brambell, as his sly, contankerous father, played the owners of a junkyard in the East End of London. The two rag-and-bone men (as they are known in British parlance) scour their neighborhood on a cart drawn by an aging horse, Hercules, searching for refuse to sell as scrap. From this unprepossessing material the scriptwriters, Alan Simpson and Ray Galton, evolved a poignant comedy that the *Times* of London described as "a profound statement about human relationships." The action is entirely confined to a small, dirty room cluttered with bric-a-brac that the Steptoes glean from the streets. The comedy, and sometimes tragicomedy, derives from the antagonism between father and son. Harold, Corbett's character, is a melancholy but eternally hopeful dreamer who cherishes aspirations to culture and elegance. He wears a tie salvaged from a trash can, brings home cheap reproductions that he imagines to be fine art, and tries to reform his father's table manners. Albert Steptoe, who cheats and steals from his son, undermines these pretensions with coarse sneers and refuses to change his filthy habits. He is, as Harold laments in episode after episode, "a dirty ol' man." Their bickering, however, usually ends in a pathetic reconciliation that reaffirms their mutual dependence and affection.

In its reliance on timing and character portrayal, and the absence of farce or slapstick, the series was extremely original, but the episodes weakened as Simpson and Galton stretched their original conception to the point of embarrassing sentimentality. An American attempt to repeat the formula, entitled "Sanford and Son" (1972), with comedian Redd Foxx as the father, was a pallid imitation of the original and tried unsuccessfully to substitute black American mannerisms for Corbett and Brambell's Cockney.

Corbett, although he played a Cockney successfully, was born in Burma, the son of an army officer, and was brought up by an aunt in Manchester after the death of his mother in 1928. He served in the Royal Marines during World War II and trained as a medical technician before joining a small theater repertory company as an understudy. He began his professional career in 1951 as a member of Joan Littlewood's Theatre Workshop Company, which was celebrated for its avant-garde productions of classics at the Theatre Royal in the London district of Stratford East. For the next ten years Corbett played in classical and contemporary dramas and comedies, both in London and in the provinces, and also took supporting parts in films, of which he made more than 30 during his entire career.

After his appearance in "Steptoe and Son," which grew out of a brief comedy sketch first seen on British television in 1962, Corbett became nationally known. His association with the series both advanced his career and made it difficult for him to shed his own reputation and undertake different roles. Attempts to make the series into feature films (*Steptoe and Son,* 1972; *Steptoe and Son Ride Again,* 1973) were not notably successful; he won more acclaim for his portrayal of *Macbeth* in a London production of 1973. Thereafter he made numerous appearances in pantomime, variety shows, and television situation comedies. He was awarded the OBE in 1976. He died of a heart attack at the age of 57. H.B.

Father an army officer. **Married** (1) Sheila Steafel, actress (div.). (2) Maureen Blott 1969: Two children. **Mil. service** Royal Marines, WWII. **Education** Trained as a radiographer late 1940s. **Career** Understudy, Chorlton Repertory Co. ca. 1950; actor, Theatre Workshop Co., Stratford East, London 1951–61; film actor since ca. 1954; TV actor since ca. 1961. **Honors** OBE 1976. **Stage** (All London except as noted) *The Dutch Courtesan,* 1954; *An Enemy of the People,* 1954; *The Flying Doctor,* 1954; *Johnny Noble,* 1954; *Arden of Faversham,* 1954; *The Cruel Daughters,* 1954; *The Good Soldier Schweik,* 1954; *The Prince and the Pauper,* 1954; *Richard II,* 1955; *The Other Animals,* 1955; *Volpone,* 1955; *The Midwife,* 1955; *The Legend of Pepito,* 1955; *Mother Courage and Her Children,* Devon Festival 1955; *Hamlet,* U.K. tour and Moscow 1955; *The Power and the Glory,* 1956; *The Family Reunion,* 1956; *The Way of the World,* 1956; *Nekrassov,* 1957; *Kookaburra,* 1959; *Progress to the Park,* 1959 (dir. 1960); *Ned Kelly,* 1960; *Macbeth,* Bristol 1960; *Period of Adjustment,* Bristol 1961; *The Flanders Mare,* Bristol 1961; *The Big Client,* Bristol 1961; *What a Crazy World,* 1962; *Who'll Save the Plowboy?,* 1963; *Travelling Light,* 1965; *Fill the Stage with Happy Hours,* 1967; *Little Jack,* 1969; *Last of the Red Hot Lovers,* Australian tour 1972; *Macbeth,* 1973; *Cinderella,* 1974. **Film** *The Passing Stranger,* 1954; *Floods of Fear,* 1958; *Nowhere To Go,* 1958; *In the Wake of a Stranger,* 1959; *Shake Hands with the Devil,* 1959; *Shakedown,* 1960; *Cover Girl Killer,* 1960; *The Big Day,* 1960; *The Unstoppable Man,* 1960; *Marriage of Convenience,* 1960; *Wings of Death,* 1961; *Time To Remember,* 1962; *Some People,* 1962; *Sparrows Can't Sing,* 1963; *Sammy Going South* (in U.S. as *A Boy Ten Feet Tall*), 1963; *Ladies Who Do,* 1963; *What a Crazy World,* 1963; *The Bargee,* 1964; *Rattle of a Simple Man,* 1964; *Joey Boy,* 1965; *Carry On Screaming,* 1966; *The Sandwich Man,* 1966; *Crooks and Coronets* (in U.S. as *Sophie's Place*), 1969; *The Magnificent Seven Deadly Sins,* 1971; *Steptoe and Son,* 1972; *Steptoe and Son Ride Again,* 1973; *Percy's Progress,* 1974; *Hardcore,* 1976; *Adventures of a Private Eye,* 1977; *Jabberwocky,* 1977. **Television** "Steptoe and Son," 1962–65, 1970–74; *Grundy and Potter; Tales of the Unexpected;* many appearances on comedy and variety series.

BENJAMIN (FRANKLIN) FEINGOLD

Pediatric allergist and creator of the Feingold diet for hyperactive children
Born **Pittsburgh, Pennsylvania, USA, 15 June 1900**
Died **San Francisco, California, USA, 23 March 1982**

In 1973, Benjamin Feingold, a pediatrician and clinical allergist, told a convention of the American Medical Association that many cases of hyperactivity in children are caused by an allergy to synthetic additives in processed foods and to salicylate, a natural substance found in certain vegetables and fruits. He claimed further that the condition of such children can be improved without the use of medication by placing them on a diet free of all salicylates, preservatives, and artificial colorings and flavorings. Scientific tests of the diet have come up with widely differing results, but it has been adopted by some 200,000 children and has the enthusiastic support of many parents and teachers.

Feingold, who received his medical training at the universities of Pittsburgh and Göttingen, did his first work in allergy under the supervision of Clement von Pirquet, the founder of allergy as a medical specialty, at the Children's Clinic of the University of Vienna, where he was house officer in 1928–29. With the exception of the war years, which he spent as an officer in the U.S. Naval Reserve, he practiced pediatrics and allergy in Los Angeles from 1932 until 1951, when he was appointed the head of the newly formed Department of Allergy at the Kaiser Foundation Hospital and Permanente Medical Group in San Francisco. Feingold established allergy clinics in affiliate hospitals throughout northern California and set up a central laboratory for the preparation of allergens for use in diagnosis and treatment. He became director of the medical entomology laboratory in 1957 and in 1961 received a grant from the National Institutes of Health to look into the problem of the common flea, which thrived in the Bay area and whose itchy bites drove residents to distraction. The findings of his research group showed that a quasi-allergic reaction occurs in

Courtesy of Kaiser Permanente Hospitals

genetically predisposed people when hapten (a chemical of low molecular weight) in flea saliva combines with the protein of the skin. This prompted Feingold to extend his research to drugs and food additives, which are also low-molecular-weight compounds, to find out how they act on the immune system of the body.

Working with patients at the allergy clinic, he first studied aspirin (acetylsalicylic acid), a little-understood drug capable of both beneficial and destructive effects. From researcher W. B. Shelley the group learned that some foods contain a natural salicylate radical that can induce the same type of adverse reaction caused by aspirin. A list of foods that contain natural salicylates—including apricots, peaches, oranges, raspberries, cucumbers, tomatoes, and raisins—was drawn up, and patients were asked to exclude these items from their meals. It was discovered that those patients still showing signs of salicylate sensitivity in spite of the diet were reacting to tartrazine, also known as Yellow No. 5, a dye used in drugs as well as food. The K-P (for Kaiser-Permanente) diet was revised to exclude all artificially flavored or colored foods, drugs, and vitamins, as well as those that contain natural salicylates.

An unexpected side effect was discovered in 1965 when a young woman came to Feingold's office suffering from giant hives, which disappeared 72 hours after she went on the diet. Feingold received an inquiry about her treatment from the center's chief of psychiatry. Further conversation revealed that the patient had been in psychotherapy for two years for hostility and aggressiveness and that in less than two weeks on the diet her behavior had completely changed.

Feingold retired as chief of allergy at Kaiser-Permanente in 1970 but continued to work on the diet as chief emeritus. His announcement in 1973 that the diet had been successfully applied to hyperactive children placed him in the center of a furor over the treatment of these children and over the use of additives by the food-processing industry. Hyperactive children (who are also referred to as hyperkinetic or attention-deficit-disorder children) are subject to behavioral disturbances—including bursts of activity, tantrums, and nonstop talking—that make learning and day-to-day living difficult. Current medical management of the disorder usually calls for treatment with the amphetamine Ritalin and sometimes with tranquilizers.

Feingold claimed that of the several hundred children whom he had placed on an additive- and salicylate-free diet, about half had experienced a significant reduction of symptoms and were able to stop using medication. He described the diet in his 1975 book *Why Your Child Is Hyperactive,* which sold 180,000 copies, and collaborated with his wife on a cookbook for followers of the diet that was published in 1979. "My basic hypothesis," he told *Good Housekeeping* magazine in 1978, "states that any compound, whether natural or synthetic, has the capacity to cause adverse reactions in an individual with the appropriate genetic profile. . . . We have always experienced adverse reactions to foods even before the days of synthetic additives, but now we are experiencing an epidemic which can in great measure be attributed to the changes in our food supply, especially over the past 50 years." He appealed in vain to the U.S. Food and Drug Administration to require clear labeling of foods containing additives and to encourage the marketing of foods free from artificial colors and flavors.

Several research studies have been conducted on Feingold's hypothesis. One report issued in 1980 by the Nutrition Foundation, an organization largely financed by the processed-food industry, showed no link at all between diet and hyperactivity, but other researchers criticized the investigators for using too small a dosage in their experiments and for excluding some additives but not others. Another study published in 1980 confirmed that artificial food dyes—most of which are coal-tar derivatives and which are widely used in processed cereals, cheeses, margarine, luncheon meats, soft drinks, baked goods, and candy (all banned from the K-P diet)—do impair the behavior of certain hyperactive children. However, many physicians are still cautious about prescribing the diet for their patients. A group of parents who voluntarily put their hyperactive children, and in some cases their whole families, on the diet have formed the Feingold Association, which now has a membership of 30,000 families.

Feingold continued to promote the diet until his death of cancer at the age of 81.

B.D./J.P.

Parents Mayer Jacob F. and Ray Libbie (Robins) F. **Married** Helene Samuels 1951: Richard; Fred; Ray; Judith; Marshall Mayer (stepson). **Religion** Jewish. **Mil. service** Comdr., USNR, South Pacific 1941–45. **Education** Univ. of Pittsburgh, PA, B.S. 1921, M.D. 1924; intern, Passavant Hosp., Pittsburgh 1924–45; fellow in pathology, Univ. of Göttingen, Germany 1927. **Career** House officer, Children's Clinic, Univ. of Vienna 1928–29; clinical instr. of pediatrics, Northwestern Univ. Sch. of Medicine 1929–32; attending physician in pediatrics and infectious diseases, Los Angeles County Gen. Hosp. 1932–38; attending physician in pediatrics 1932–41 and chief of pediatrics 1945–51, Cedars of Lebanon Hosp., L.A.; attending physician in pediatrics 1932–51 and assoc. physician in allergy, 1945–51 Los Angeles Children's Hosp. • With Kaiser Foundn. Hosp. and Permanente Medical Group, S.F.: chief, Dept. of Allergy 1951–69; chmn. of central research cttee. 1952–70, and founder of all Depts. of Allergy, Kaiser Foundn. Hosps. of Northern CA; dir., Lab. of Medical Entomology 1957–70; chief emeritus, Dept. of Allergy since 1969. • Writer and lectr. on diet and hyperactivity since 1973. **Fellow** Amer. Coll. of Allergy; Amer. Acad. of Pediatrics; Amer. Acad. of Allergy. **Author** *Introduction to Clinical Allergy,* 1973; *Why Your Child Is Hyperactive,* 1975; (jtly.) *The Feingold Cookbook for Hyperactive Children,* 1979; numerous articles in professional jrnls.

Further reading Joseph R. Hixson, "New Hope for Hyperactive Children," in *New York Times Magazine,* 24 Aug. 1980.

MARIO PRAZ
Literary critic, essayist, and art collector
***Born* Rome, Italy, 6 September 1896**
***Died* Rome, Italy, 23 March 1982**

Mario Praz, the foremost Italian critic of English literature and one of the most notable men of letters of his time, belonged to no school of critical thought and created no method that could be borrowed or emulated. In his last collection of essays, *Voices Backstage* (1980), he described himself self-effacingly as a man "gifted with imperfect intelligence," who followed no philosophical system, but occupied himself with "relics cast up on the far side of the grand sea of being." His avowed fascination with the bizarre and neglected gave rise to his widely appreciated early book, *La carne, la morte e il diavolo nella letteratura romantica* (1930), which an anonymous *Times Literary Supplement* reviewer praised as a major contribution to "the pathology of literature." The complex subject of this enduringly famous book was the erotic sensibilities of British, French, and Italian Romantic writers, and the pervasive role played in their work by a morbid fascination with certain character types: the lustful, Byronic rake; the female victim of a devil-seducer; and the femme fatale who, like Oscar Wilde's Salome, lures men with her cold, unresponsive beauty. Growing interest in psychoanalysis during Praz's lifetime brought his inquiry out of the realm of pathology into that of common critical discourse, but did not reduce the value of his analysis of such writers as Byron, the Marquis de Sade, Keats, Huysman, and Wilde.

The book remains a seminal study of what is now called "decadence," and the title of its English translation, *The Romantic Agony* (1953), now serves as a catchword for a range of feelings associated with late Victorian and *fin de siècle* art and literature. In works as disparate as Gothic novels and the drawings of Aubrey Beardsley, Praz traced sensual and sadistic impulses to possess and defile the virginal and mystical, showing that such longings, when satisfied, become nihilistic and suicidal.

The hallmarks of Praz's criticism were his interest in literature as a reflection of human custom and peculiarity, and his mannered, belletristic style, which was better suited to elegant generality in the essay form than to the treatise. Both these characteristics made him a distinctive, if not unique, writer at a time when criticism in English was becoming increasingly formal, systematic, and removed from ordinary language. Praz did not confine himself to a narrow scholarly specialty, but commented with fluent assurance on literature of all European languages. In his series of essays collected under the misleading title *Anglo-Saxon Literary Chronicles* (4 vols., 1951, 1966), he ranged over the whole field of English literature, from Chaucer to Virginia Woolf, while in more extensive studies he wrote on the history of furniture, Machiavelli's influence in England, Victorian fiction, and a host of other subjects. Reviewing his work *On Neoclassicism* (1940; English ed. 1968), Robert Rosenblum admired the "rich solution of history, biography, and letters," and in general, Praz's work was well received in Britain and the United States. There were some, however, who complained that in his fondness for generalization and cross-cultural synthesis he did insufficient justice to individual works. It might be said in his defense that he left thorough accounts to less able writers.

Having begun as a collector of literary impressions, Praz became an assiduous collector of objects, filling his apartment in Rome with furniture, painting, and sculpture of the Empire and Regency periods. It is clear from his volume of autobiographical essays, *The House of Life* (1958; English ed. 1964), that these objects eventually displaced people in Praz's affections. Frank Kermode, reviewing this book in the *New Statesman* in 1964, was perhaps the first to perceive that his passion for scholarship was the corollary of his "habitual detachment from persons." Praz himself, writing in the series *World Authors,* acknowledged that his devotion to neoclassical artifacts had been the cause of his divorce in 1945 from his English wife Vivyan Eyles, whom he married in 1934 while a professor of Italian studies at Manchester University.

Praz was descended, on his father's side, from Swiss ancestors who had settled in northern Italy during the sixteenth century. His maternal forebears were the noble family of Di Marsciano, whose fortunes had declined and whose property in Orvieto had long since passed into other hands. He spent the first four years of his life in Switzerland, but was educated in Florence and described himself, in *World Authors,* as "a Tuscan by election." In *The House of Life* he recounted his early studies of law and Greek, which he abandoned in favor of art and literature before 1920. His interest in England was fostered by "Vernon Lee" (Violet Paget), an expatriate English writer who offered him not only literary counsel, but also advice on English customs. His vocation was confirmed when, in 1923, he obtained a scholarship to study in London, and began work on the poets John Donne and Richard Crashaw. In 1924 he became a lecturer in Italian at Liverpool University, where he remained for eight years before taking up the post of professor of Italian studies at Manchester University. From 1934 until his retirement he was professor of English at the University of Rome.

The extraordinary breadth of Praz's erudition was displayed in a succession of lectures, scholarly articles, essays, and books. In Great Britain, where he was better known than in his native country, he made important contributions to English studies with *The Romantic Agony, Studies in Seventeenth-Century Imagery* (1934; English ed., 2 vols., 1939, 1947), *The Hero in Eclipse in Victorian Fiction* (1952; English ed. 1956), *The Flaming Heart* (1958), and *Mnemosyne: The Parallel Between Literature and the Visual Arts* (1970). Although he had an absolute command of both languages, he generally wrote in Italian and did not translate his own work. He did, however, make several translations of English works, including two Shakespeare plays, into Italian. His many honors included degrees from the universities of Cambridge, the Sorbonne, and Uppsala, and the honorary title of KBE, awarded by the British government in 1962 in recognition of his services to English letters.

H.B.

Parents Luciano P., bank clerk, and Giulia Testa (Di Marsciano) P. **Married** Vivyan

Eyles 1934 (div. 1945): Lucia Praz Shakir. **Education** Ginnasio-Liceo Galileo, Florence, grad. 1914; Univ. of Bologna 1914–15; Univ. of Rome, J.D. 1918; Univ. of Florence, Ph.D. 1920; studied in British Mus., London, on govt. scholarship 1923–25; qualified for title of libero docente in English literature 1925. **Career** Sr. lectr. in Italian, Liverpool Univ. 1924–32; prof. of Italian studies, Manchester Univ. 1932–34; prof. of English language and literature 1934–66 and prof. emeritus since 1966, Univ. of Rome. • Annual Italian Lectr., British Acad. 1928; Mellon Lectr., Natl. Gall. of Art, Wash. DC 1967; ed., *English Miscellany,* Rome; co-ed., *La Cultura.* **Officer** Pres. 1962–65 and member of standing cttee., Intl. Assn. of Univ. Professors of English. **Member** (Natl. member) Accademia dei Lincei since 1952; Amer. Acad. of Arts and Sciences since 1969; PEN. **Honors** Gold medal, British Acad. 1935; hon. member, Modern Language Assn., U.S. 1954; gold medal, Italy 1958; Feltrinelli Prize, Accademia dei Lincei 1960; KBE, U.K. 1962; gran'ufficiale della Repubblica Italiana 1972; Golden Pen Award, Italy 1982; hon. degrees from univs. of Cambridge, Paris, Uppsala, and Aix-Marseilles. **Author** *La fortuna di Byron in Inghilterra* [*The Fortunes of Byron in England*], 1925; *Secentismo e marinismo in Inghilterra* [*Seventeenth-Century Literary Affectations in England*], 1925; *Machiavelli and the Elizabethans,* 1928; *Penisola pentagonale,* 1928 (trans. as *Unromantic Spain,* 1929); *The Italian Element in English,* 1929; *La carne, la morte e il diavolo nella letteratura romantica,* 1930 (trans. as *The Romantic Agony,* 1933); *Study sul concettismo,* 1934 (trans. as *Studies in Seventeenth-Century Imagery,* vol. 1, 1939, vol. 2, 1947, rev. ed. 1964; *Storia della letteratura inglese* [*History of English Literature*], 1937, rev. ed. 1960; *Studi e svaghi inglesi* [*English Studies and Miscellanies*], 1937; *Gusto neoclassico,* 1940 (trans. as *On Neoclassicism,* 1968); *Machiavelli in Inghilterra ed altri saggi* [*Machiavelli in England and Other Essays*], 1942, rev. ed. 1962; *Viaggio in Grecia* [*Voyage in Greece*], 1943; *Fiori freschi* [*Fresh Flowers*], 1943; *Outline of English Literature,* 1943; *Ricerche anglo-italiane* [*Anglo-Italian Researches*], 1944; *Richard Crashaw,* 1945; *La filosofia dell'arredamento,* 1945 (trans. as *An Illustrated History of Interior Decoration from Pompeii to Art Nouveau,* 1964); *Motivi e figure* [*Motifs and Imagery*], 1945; *La poesia metafisica inglese del seicento, John Donne* [*English Metaphysical Poetry of the Seventeenth Century*], 1945; *Il dramma elisabettiano* [*Elizabethan Drama*], 1946; *Geoffrey Chaucer e i racconti di Canterbury* [*Geoffrey Chaucer and the Canterbury Tales*], 1947; *Prospettiva della letteratura inglese da Chaucer a V. Woolf* [*Views of English Literature from Chaucer to Woolf*], 1947; *La poesia di Pope e le sue origini* [*The Poetry of Pope and Its Origins*], 1948; *Cronache letterarie anglosassoni* [*Anglo-Saxon Literary Chronicles*], vols. 1–2, 1951, vols. 3–4, 1966; *Il libro della poesia inglese* [*The Book of English Poetry*], 1951; *La casa della fama, saggi di letteratura e d'arte* [*The House of Fame, Essays on Literature and Art*], 1952; *Lettrice notturna* [*Night Reader*], 1952; *La crisi dell'eroe nel romanzo vittoriano,* 1952 (trans. as *The Hero in Eclipse in Victorian Fiction,* 1956); *Il mondo che ho visto: Viaggi in Occidente* [*The World I Have Seen: Voyages in the West*], 1955; *The Flaming Heart, Essays on Crashaw, Machiavelli, and Other Studies of the Relations Between Italian and English Literature from Chaucer to T. S. Eliot,* 1958; *La casa della vita* (autobiography), 1958 (trans. as *The House of Life,* 1964); *Bellezza e bizzarria* [*The Beautiful and the Bizarre*], 1960; *I volti del tempo* [*Aspects of the Time*], 1964; *Panopticon romano* [*Roman Panopticon*], 1967; *Caleidoscopio shakespeariano* [*Shakespearean Kaleidoscope*], 1969; *Mnemosyne: The Parallel Between Literature and the Visual Arts,* 1970; *Scene di conversazione,* 1970 (trans. as *Conversation Pieces: A Survey of the Intimate Group Portrait in Europe and America,* 1971); *Il patto col serpente* [*The Pact with the Serpent*], 1972; *Il giardino dei sensi, studi sul manierismo e il barocco* [*The Garden of the Senses, Studies on Mannerism and the Baroque*], 1975; *Panopticon romano secondo,* 1978; *Perseo e la Medusa, dal romanticismo all'avanguardia* [*Perseus and Medusa, from Romanticism to the Avant-Garde*], 1979; *Voce dietro la scene, un'antologia personale* [*Voices Backstage, A Personal Anthology*], 1980. **Translator** Charles Lamb, *I saggi di Elia,* 1924; *Poeti inglesi dell'ottocento* [*English Poetry of the Nineteenth Century*], 1925; William Shakespeare, *Measure for Measure* and *Troilus and Cressida,* 1939; works by Walter

Pater, Jane Austen, Joseph Addison, George Moore, T. S. Eliot, many others. **Editor** *Antologia della letteratura inglese* [*Anthology of English Literature*], 1936; Shakespeare, *Teatro* [*Drama*], 1943–47; *Antologia della letteratura straniere* [*Anthology of Foreign Literature*], 1947; (gen. ed.) *Teatro elisabettiano* [*Elizabethan Drama*], 1948; *Tre drammi elisabettiani* [*Three Elizabethan Dramas*], 1958; *Shakespeare, Tutte le opere* [*Shakespeare Complete Works*], 1964; selected works of Gabriele D'Annunzio, Lorenzo Magalotti, others. **Contributor** of several thousand essays and reviews to literary and philological periodicals in Italian and English.

Further reading V. and M. Gabrieli, eds., *Friendship's Garland: Essays Presented to Mario Praz on His Seventieth Birthday* (festschrift), 1966.

MARIETTA (SERGEYEVNA) SHAGINYAN
Writer
Born **Moscow, Russia, 21 March 1888**
Death announced **Moscow, USSR, 23 March 1982**

Marietta Shaginyan was the doyenne of Soviet letters, who after the Bolshevik Revolution abandoned a promising career as a Symbolist poet to write revolutionary prose. She was the officially approved and much-decorated author of some 80 works of fiction, criticism, biography, and history.

She was born in Moscow, the daughter of a doctor of Armenian descent, and was educated in philology and history at the Moscow Higher Women's Courses. During her student years she made a pilgrimage—the first trip of what was to be a lifetime of traveling—to Weimar, Jena, and Frankfurt-am-Main in Germany to visit sites associated with Goethe. She remained devoted to the great German's works and life, publishing the critique *Goethe* in 1950.

Among Shaginyan's earliest poems was the romantic and idealistic "Song of the Worker," which appeared in the 20 May 1906 issue of *Artisan Voice,* a new weekly which for a time, during the brief cultural thaw after the Revolution of 1905, was permitted to discuss proletarian ideas. Her first book of poems, *First Meetings* (1909), reflected a young woman's confidence in humanity; her second, *Orientalia* (1913), was widely praised, the critics acclaiming her as a promising Symbolist of the younger generation. Her novel *One's Own Fate* (1916) castigated the Russian intelligentsia for its dreamy inertia.

She wrote very little poetry after the Bolshevik Revolution of 1917, finding prose a more appropriate vehicle for celebrating the new order. Her short novels *Change* (1922) and *The Adventure of a Society Lady* (1923) were among the first to employ Bolsheviks as heroes and to contain an ideological message as a central theme. Her next books took a standard Western genre, detective fiction, and infused it with revolutionary ideology to produce proletarian adventure novels: *Mess-Mend: Or, The Yankees in Petrograd* (1924) and *Laurie Lane, Metalworker* (1925) were anticapitalist in tone, supposedly written by a U.S. worker in Russia named Jimmy Dollar. *Kik* (1929) was similar in style, another attack on the indifference of the country's intelligentsia.

Shaginyan took to heart Stalin's first Five-Year Plan (1928–33), with its exhortation to artists to develop Socialist Realism. She traveled to Armenia, where she lived for nearly four years on the building site of a hydroelectric power station on the Dzoraget River. From this experience came the massive *Hydrocentral* (1931), one of the first truly proletarian novels. "The characters in the novel," she later recalled, "were based on real people whom I loved and got to know really well. In this book, to which I wholly devoted myself, I strove toward socialist realism for the first time in my life with a supreme effort and to the best of my ability." *Hydrocentral,* which was reprinted many times (even as recently as 1979), apparently established her reputation as a reliable Communist, for she completely escaped the Stalinist terror of the 1930s that annihilated, among millions of others, so many of the best talents of Russian literature. She was awarded a doctorate of philology in 1944 for a dissertation on the Ukrainian poet Taras Shevchenko.

Shaginyan began to study the life of V. I. Lenin, the father of the country, in the 1930s. She had never met him, but became friendly with his widow, Nadezhda Krupskaya, and his sister, Maria Ulyanova. With their advice, she began a series of essays on Lenin ("Lenin's University," 1933; "The Lenin Museum," 1936; "Lenin's Ancestors on His Father's Side," 1937; "Lenin's Lifelong Friend and Companion," 1939—the last a portrait of Krupskaya). This was the beginning of what was to be her best-received work, *The Ulyanov Family,* a fiction-nonfiction tetralogy first published in 1938, then revised and republished in 1958 after de-Stalinization. She won the Lenin Prize for this work in 1972. The last volume of the tetralogy was published in English in 1974 as *Retracing Lenin's Steps.*

Among her many other books were *Journey Through Soviet Armenia* (1950; English ed. 1954), which gained her the Stalin Prize in 1951; *Recollections of Rachmaninoff* (1957); critical biographies of Goethe, Shevchenko, the twelfth-century poet Nizami Ganjavi, and the Russo-Czech musician Josef Mysliveček. Her memoirs *Man and Time* appeared in 1979, as did her *Literary Diary.* With her husband, Y. S. Khachatryants, she published several works on Armenian folklore.

Shaginyan's awards included three Orders of Lenin, two Orders of the Red Banner, the Order of the Red Star, and the Badge of Honor. In 1978, on her 90th birthday, she was awarded her country's highest civilian decoration, the Hero of Socialist Labor. A.K.

Father a doctor. **Married** Y. S. Khachatryants, writer and folklorist (d.). **Education** Moscow Higher Women's Courses; doctorate in philology 1944. **Career** Writer since early 1900s; member, CPSU since 1942; bd. member, Writers Union. **Member** (Corresp.) Armenian Acad. of Sciences. **Honors** Stalin Prize, for *Journey Through Soviet Armenia,* 1951; Lenin Prize, for tetralogy *The Ulyanov Family,* 1972; Hero of Socialist Labor 1978; Order of Red Banner twice; Order of Lenin three times; Order of Red Star; Badge of Honor. **Poetry** [*First Meetings*], 1909; [*Orientalia*], 1913. **Fiction** *Svoya Sudba* [*One's Own Fate*], 1916; *Peremena* [*Change*], 1922; [*The Adventure of a Society Lady*], 1923; (as Jimmy Dollar) *Mess-Mend: ili ianke v Petrograde* [*Mess-Mend: or The Yankees in Petrograd*], 1924; (as Jimmy Dollar) [*Laurie Lane, Metalworker*], 1925; [*The Thornton Factory*], 1925; *Izbrannye rasskazy* [*Selected Stories*], 1927; *Vostochnye rasskazy* [*Oriental Stories*], 1928; *Kik,* 1929; *Gidrotsentral* [*Hydrocentral*], 1931; *Povesti i rasskazy* [*Tales and Stories,*], 1933; *Sobranie sochinenii* [*Collected Works*], 4 vols., 1933; [*Diary of a Deputy to the Moscow Soviet*], 1935. **Historical fiction and biography of Lenin and his family** Under gen. title *Semya Ulyanovykh* [*The Ulyanov Family*]: *Bilet po istorii* [*Ticket to History*], 1930; *Semya Ulyanovykh* [*The Ulyanov Family*], 1935, rev. ed. 1958; *Pervaya Vserossilskaya* [*The First All-Russian Exhibition*], 1965; *Chetyre uroka u Lenina* [*Four Lessons from Lenin*], 1970 (trans. as *Retracing Lenin's Steps,* 1974). Related works: *Leniniana* [contains *The Ulyanov Family,* sketches, and essays], 1977; others. **Biography, memoirs, essays, travel, and social commentary** *Istoria iskusstva* [*History of Art*], 1922; *Dnevniki 1917–1931* [*Journals*], 1932; *Kak ya rabotala nad "Gidrotsentralyu"* [*How I Worked on "Hydrocentral"*], 1933; *Literatura i plan* [*Literature and State Planning*], 1934; *Dnevnik moskvicha* [*Diary of a Muscovite*], 1942; *Sovetskoe zakavkaze* [*The Soviet Transcaucasus*], 1946; *Taras Shevchenko,* 1946; *Po dorogam pyatiletki* [*On the Roads of the Five-Year Plan*], 1947; *Göte*[*Goethe*], 1950; *Izbrannoe 1911–1948* [*Selected Works*], 1948; *Puteshestvye po Sovetskoy Armenii,* 1950 (trans. as *Journey Through Soviet Armenia,* 1954); *Dnevnik pisatelya* [*Diary of a Writer*], 1953; *Creative Freedom in the Soviet Union,* 1953; *Etiudy o Nizami* [*Studies on Nizami Ganjavi*], 1955; [*Recollections of Rachmaninoff*], 1957; *Ob iskusstve i literature* [*On Art and Literature*], 1958; *Povest o dvukh sestrakh i o volshebnoy strane mertse* [*The Tale of Two Sisters and the Magic Country Mertz*], 1959; *Zarubezhnye pisma* [*Letters from Abroad*], 1959; *Ob armyanskoy literature i iskusstve* [*On Armenian Literature and Art*], 1961; *Voskresenye iz mertvykh* [*Resurrection from the Dead*], 1964, issued as *Josef Myslivechek,* 1968; *Ocherki raznykh let* [*Sketches of Different Years*], 1977; *Isbrannye proizvedeniya*

[*Selected Works*], 1978; [*Literary Diary*], 1979; *Chelovek i vremya* [*Man and Time*], 1980; others. **Contributor** to Soviet periodicals.

Further reading Konstantin Srebrakov, "Doyenne Authoress," in *Soviet Literature,* no. 9, 1977; Alexei Surkov, "A Many-Sided Talent," in *Soviet Literature,* no. 4, 1978.

HARRIET S(TRATEMEYER) ADAMS

Writer of mystery novels for children

***Born* Newark, New Jersey, USA, 11 December 1892**

***Died* Maplewood, New Jersey, USA, 27 March 1982**

The series of children's mystery books put out by the Stratemeyer Syndicate—*Nancy Drew, The Hardy Boys, The Bobbsey Twins, Tom Swift, Jr.,* and *The Dana Girls*—have entranced several generations of American children, many of whom formed, as a result, the lifelong habit of reading for pleasure. The books feature suspenseful plots, happy endings, and heroes and heroines of reassuring competence and friendliness. Since 1930, they have all been, to varying degrees, the work of one author, Harriet Stratemeyer Adams. Using four different pseudonyms, she wrote 200 novels herself and supervised the plotting and editing of some 1,000 others which were completed by hired writers.

The Stratemeyer Syndicate was founded in 1906 by Edward Stratemeyer, who invented the main characters for these and 100 other series. His daughter came to work for the firm as an editor in 1915 after graduating from Wellesley College in Massachusetts, where she had been a student reporter for the *Boston Globe.* In 1930 Stratemeyer died, and Adams, the wife of an investment broker and the mother of four children, took over the enterprise as senior partner. In addition to writing and editing, she made sure that the characters maintained the proper public image, checking the cover art for each book, for example, to see that the protagonists were depicted with neat hair and clothes. In later years she oversaw the revision of earlier books to eliminate ethnic stereotypes.

The formula for writing the mysteries was laid down by Stratemeyer and is still followed by syndicate writers. The first page grabs the reader's attention; each chapter presents a combination of action, humor, and suspense, and builds up to a cliff-hanger ending; although the characters are often in physical danger, no one is hurt much beyond a bruise

Courtesy of Stratemeyer Syndicate

or two; educational passages are worked into the narrative; and justice is always allowed to triumph.

Though the novels are exciting, they conspicuously lack that subtlety of characterization and imaginative language that make for the best literature, and children's librarians have frequently tried to discourage children from reading them. Defenders of the series point out that Adams' teenage detectives provide role models for children, especially girls, in a way that few other juvenile books can match. Nancy Drew, for example, is intelligent, resourceful, altruistic, courageous, and an expert driver, and though she has a boyfriend she does not depend on him for initiative or rescues. "If I made Nancy liberated, I was unconscious of the fact," Adams said in

1980, the 50th anniversary of the series. "She's like me . . . she's the best of the modern young women."

The series, now numbering over 60 volumes, has sold more than 70 million copies in the United States and has appeared in at least a dozen languages, including Icelandic and Malay. It was the basis for a number of feature films made by Warners in 1939. Television adaptations of *Nancy Drew* and *The Hardy Boys* began running in 1977.

Adams died of a heart attack while watching *The Wizard of Oz* on television. J.P.

Born Harriet Stratemeyer. Wrote under pseudonyms Caroline Keene, Laura Lee Hope, Franklin W. Dixon, and Victor W. Appleton 2d. **Parents** Edward S., writer and businessman, and Magdalene (Van Camp) S. **Married** Russell Vroom Adams, investment broker, 1915 (d. 1965): Russell Vroom, Jr., pilot, 1916 (d. 1942); Patricia Stratton Adams Harr, b. 1921; Camilla Anne Adams McClave, coll. admin., b. 1923; Edward Stratemeyer, production mgr., b. 1925. **Religion** Presbyterian. **Education** Wellesley Coll., MA, B.A. 1914. **Career** Reporter, *Boston Globe,* coll. years; ed. 1915–30 and sr. partner since 1930, Stratemeyer Syndicate, Maplewood, NJ. **Officer** Founder, Maplewood Women's Club 1916; founder and pres., New Jersey Wellesley Club; publicity chmn., Amer. Red Cross; county committeewoman, Republican Party. **Member** Horatio Alger Soc.; League of American Pen Women; New Jersey Women's Press Club; New York Wellesley Club; Zonta; Business and Professional Women's Club; Girl Scouts USA. **Honors** Alumnae Achievement Award, Wellesley Coll. 1978; Literary Outstanding Mother of the Year, Natl. Mother's Day Commn. 1979; Edgar Award, Mystery Writers of America 1980; hon. degrees from Upsala and Kean colls. **Author** *The Nancy Drew Cookbook: Clues to Good Cooking,* 1973; *The Nancy Drew Sleuth Book: Clues to Good Sleuthing,* 1979; *Nancy Drew and the Hardy Boys: Super Sleuths!,* 1981; more than 200 titles in the *Nancy Drew, Hardy Boys, Dana Girls, Bobbsey Twins,* and *Tom Swift, Jr.,* series.

Further reading Frances Fitzgerald, "Women, Success, and Nancy Drew," in *Vogue,* May 1980.

FAZLUR R(AHMAN) KHAN

Architectural engineer

***Born* Dacca, India, British Empire, 3 April 1929**

***Died* Saudi Arabia, 27 March 1982**

Fazlur Khan, an engineer with the prominent architectural firm of Skidmore, Owings & Merrill, was responsible for the design of numerous corporate headquarters, office complexes, and other buildings, including the Sears Tower in Chicago, nearly a quarter of a mile high and the tallest building in the world.

Born in Dacca, India (now Bangladesh), Khan graduated from the University of Dacca with a bachelor's degree and came to the United States on a Fulbright Scholarship in 1952. After receiving two master's degrees and a doctorate in structural engineering from the University of Illinois, he joined the Chicago office of Skidmore, Owings & Merrill as a project engineer. In 1970 he became a general partner. Not an architect himself, he worked in close collaboration with the firm's architects to develop the sophisticated designs required for today's superskyscrapers and large-span structures. He was the recipient of many awards.

Among Khan's major projects were the 60-inch solar-telescope mount for the Kitt Peak Observatory in Arizona (1962, with Myron Goldsmith), the Spectrum Arena in Philadelphia (1967), and the John Hancock Center in Chicago, a 95-story tower notable for its dramatic exterior trusses (1970, with Bruce Graham). His large-span designs for the headquarters of Baxter Travenol Laboratories in Deerfield, Illinois (1975) and for the Haj Terminal at King Abdul Aziz International Airport in Saudi Arabia (1980) both featured roofs suspended by cables.

Khan was best known for the $150-million Sears Tower (1974, designed in collaboration with Graham and William E. Dunlap), for which he devised the "bundled tube" structural system. Instead of the usual steel skeleton, the building was constructed of nine giant aluminum towers bound together by diagonal trusses into a single 225-foot-square "megatube." Two tubes terminated at the 50th floor, two at the 66th, and three at the 89th, with the last two extending the full 110 stories. Khan's efficient design saved Sears, Roebuck and Co. more than $10 million in structural steel costs. The tower won the admiration of most architects and engineers, but was criticized by some on aesthetic grounds. "It hits the ground with a clank and 2,000 pounds of aluminum," said William Marlin in *Architectural Forum.* Others complained that it adds to the already severe congestion of Chicago's Loop area.

Courtesy of Skidmore Owings and Merrill

In the late 1970s and early 1980s, Khan worked on projects in the United States, Canada, Iran, Saudi Arabia, and Malaysia. His Hubert H. Humphrey Metrodome in Minneapolis, a sports stadium sunk nine stories into the ground and covered with a floating plastic dome supported by air pressure from a battery of electric fans, opened in the spring of 1982. He died of a heart attack while traveling in Saudi Arabia. S.A.

Parents Abdur Rahman K. and Khadija (Khanum) K. **Married** Liselotte A. Turba 1959: Yasmin Sabina; Martin (stepson). **Emigrated** to U.S. 1952; naturalized 1967. **Education** Univ. of Dacca, Pakistan, B.S. 1950; Univ. of Illinois, Champaign-Urbana (Fulbright Scholarship), M.S. 1953, M.S. 1955, Ph.D. in structural engineering 1955; registered structural engineer, IL, Hong Kong; registered professional engineer, LA, MA, NY, OH, TX, WI, Wash. DC. **Career** With Skidmore, Owings & Merrill architectural firm, Chicago; project engineer 1955–57; sr. project engineer 1960–65; assoc. partner 1966–70; gen. partner since 1970. • Lectr., Univ. of Dacca 1950–52; exec. engineer, Karachi Development Authority, Pakistan 1958–60; adjunct prof. of architectural engineering, Illinois Inst. of Technology since 1966. **Officer** Chmn., and member of steering cttee., Intl. Council on Tall Buildings and Urban Habitat; founding chmn., Chicago Cttee. on High-Rise Buildings. **Fellow** Amer. Concrete Inst.; Amer. Soc. of Civil Engineers. **Member** Advisory cttee., Aga Khan Program on Islamic Architecture, Harvard Univ./Massachusetts Inst. of Technology; Amer. Inst. of Steel Construction; Amer. Welding Soc.; Chicago Architectural Club; Intl. Assn. for Bridges and Structural Engineering; Mayor's Advisory

Courtesy of Ezra Stoller © ESTO

Commn. on Building Code Amendments, Chicago; Natl. Acad. of Engineering; Prestressed Concrete Inst. **Honors** From Amer. Soc. of Civil Engineers: award for meritorious technical paper, TX sect. 1968; Civil Engineer of the Year and Life Membership Award, IL sect. 1972; Chicago Civil Engineer of the Year 1972; Middlebrooks Award 1972; Howard Award 1977; Earnest Award, Cleveland sect. 1979. • Construction Man of the Year 1966, 1969, 1971, and Man of the Year 1972, *Engineering News-Record;* Chicagoan of the Year in Architecture and Engineering 1970; Wason Medal 1970 and Lindau Award 1973, Amer. Concrete Inst.; special citation 1971 and Kimbrough Medal 1973, Amer. Inst. of Steel Construction; Alumni Honor Award, Univ. of Illinois 1972; Faber Medal, Instn. of Structural Engineers, London 1973; award, Natl. Acad. of Engineering 1973; State Service Award, Illinois Council, Amer. Inst. of Architects 1977; award for Haj Terminal, King Abdul Aziz Intl. Airport, *Progressive Architecture* 1981; hon. degrees from univs. of Lehigh and Northwestern and from Eidgenossische Technische Hochschule, Zurich. **Structural designer** Hartford Fire Insurance Co., Chicago, Office Bldg. I, 1961, and II, 1971; 60-inch solar-telescope mount, Kitt Peak Observatory, AZ 1962; U.S. Air Force Acad., Colorado Springs, CO 1962; Circle Campus, Univ. of Illinois 1965; Spectrum Arena, Phila. 1967; John Hancock Center, Chicago 1970; Control Data Center, Houston 1971; One Shell Plaza, Houston 1971; W. D. & H. O. Wills Corporate Headquarters and Tobacco Processing Facility, Bristol 1974; Bu Ali Sina Univ., Hamadan, Iran 1974; Sears Tower, Chicago 1974; Bandar Shahpur New Town, Iran 1975; Baxter Travenol Labs., Inc., Deerfield, IL 1975; Hyatt Intl. Hotel, Kuwait City, Kuwait 1978; King Abdul Aziz Univ., Makkah, Saudi Arabia 1978; Edmonton Center, Alta., Canada 1980; Haj Terminal, King Abdul Aziz Intl. Airport, Jiddah, Saudi Arabia 1980; Univ. Kebangsaan Sabah Kampus, Kota Kinabalu, East Malaysia 1981; Hubert H. Humphrey Metrodome, Minneapolis 1982; 780 Third Ave., NYC; One Magnificent Mile, Chicago; many other engineering designs for corporate, institutional, and public bldgs. **Contributor** of papers on architectural and structural engineering to professional jrnls.

Further reading William Marlin, "Sears Tower: The Mail-Order Approach to Urban Form," in *Architectural Forum,* Jan.-Feb. 1974.

WILLIAM F(RANCIS) GIAUQUE
Chemist
Born **Niagara Falls, Ontario, Canada, 12 May 1895**
Died **Oakland, California, USA, 28 March 1982**

Nobel laureate William Giauque dedicated more than 60 years to cryogenics, the study of the properties of matter at very low temperatures. Among his accomplishments were the discovery of two previously unrecognized isotopes of oxygen, the development of an innovative technique for reaching temperatures near absolute zero, and the first demonstration of the validity of the third law of thermodynamics. Giauque often spent days without food or sleep while managing a delicate experiment; according to Prof. David Lyon, one of his former students, "Watching him work was like watching a bulldog. He'd tear a problem apart until he could reduce it to its very simplest parts."

Born in Canada to American parents, Giauque attended grammar schools in Michigan. After completing high school, he worked for two years in the laboratory of a chemical company, then enrolled in the College of Chemistry at the University of California at Berkeley, where he began low-temperature research under G. E. Gibson and Gilbert Lewis. He earned his Ph.D. in 1922, joined the chemistry faculty the same year, and was made a full professor in 1934. He spent his entire academic career at Berkeley, retiring as director of chemical research in 1981, when he was 86.

During the 1920s and 1930s, Giauque's research focused on measuring entropy, the degree of disorder in matter, in substances near zero on the absolute (Kelvin) scale (−459.69° F or −273.16° C). At such temperatures, the usual thermal chaos of molecules and atoms is considerably reduced, and natural phenomena become simpler to observe. By carefully applying small amounts of heat, Giauque was able to calculate the entropy and other thermodynamic properties of supercold substances with ten times more accuracy than any previous researcher. The chemical industry was quick to seize on his results and apply them to the faster and cheaper development of new steel, glass, rubber, and other products. Giauque's painstaking measurements of entropy also confirmed the recently postulated third law of thermodynamics, which states that, at zero degrees absolute, perfectly ordered (crystalline) substances show zero entropy.

Giauque verified his laboratory results using spectroscopy, since the spectra produced by gases are indicative of their thermodynamic properties. In 1929, while studying the entropy of oxygen, Giauque and his student Herrick L. Johnson became puzzled by certain unexplained faint lines in its spectrum. After months of work, Giauque realized that the lines must represent small amounts of two unknown isotopes, oxygen-17 and oxygen-18. This discovery also revealed that chemists and physicists had unwittingly been using slightly different atomic-weight values; the result was the calibration of separate scales. A revised unified scale was adopted in 1961.

Between 1927 and 1933, Giauque developed the adiabatic magnetic cooling technique. Until then, researchers had relied on nineteenth-century methods of liquefying gases using a variation of the common air pump. As anyone who has used a bicycle pump knows, a gas becomes hotter when it is compressed and cooler when it expands. If the process is repeated often enough, and the heat generated by compression is carried off, the gas will condense. While studying the work of the Dutch scientist Heike Kammerlingh Onnes, who had attained temperatures as low as 0.8° absolute with liquid helium using the pump method, Giauque conceived of a method of lowering temperature still further. Every atom has north and south magnetic poles, like a bar magnet, and in any given substance the polar axes of the atoms point randomly in all directions. When a powerful magnetic field is applied to certain so-called paramagnetic substances, the atomic polar axes align themselves with the field's lines of force, generating heat in the process. It should be possible, Giauque reasoned, to set up a cooling cycle by carrying off this heat, removing the magnetic field to disorder the atoms again, and repeating the process several times. Such a cycle would cool the paramagnetic substance down to temperatures impossible to achieve by gaseous expansion alone.

The paper describing his idea appeared in 1927, a few months after a similar suggestion was published in Europe. The problems of obtaining funding and constructing equipment, including a sufficiently powerful magnet, delayed actual tests until 1933, when Giauque and Duncan MacDougall obtained a temperature of 0.1° absolute in previously cooled gadolinium sulphate using a magnet of about 8,000 gauss. Later experiments with a magnet of over 100,000 gauss achieved temperatures as low as one-thousandth of a degree absolute. Traditional thermometers were useless in this temperature range, and Giauque found it necessary to develop substitutes.

During World War II, Giauque organized a Berkeley group that designed a mobile liquid-oxygen production unit for the U.S. government. In 1949 he was awarded the Nobel Prize in chemistry for his work in low temperatures. He was named professor emeritus at Berkeley in 1962, but was promptly recalled in order to direct the low-temperature research program; his own research focused on magnetothermodynamic measurement and magnetic design. A cryogenics laboratory bearing his name opened on the Berkeley campus in 1966. He died after a short illness at the age of 87. P.D.

Parents William Tecumseh Sherman G. and Isabella Jane (Duncan) G. **Married** Muriel Frances Ashley, spectroscopist and botanist, 1932 (d. 1981): William Francis Ashley; Robert David Ashley. **Education** Public schs., MI; Collegiate Inst., Niagara Falls, Ontario; Univ. of California, Berkeley, B.S. 1920, Univ. Fellow 1920–21, Goewey Fellow 1921–22, Ph.D. in chemistry with minor in physics 1922. **Mil. service** Designed mobile liquid-oxygen production units and other classified research for U.S. Govt. 1939–44. **Career** With Hooker Electromechanical Co., Niagara Falls, NY ca. 1918–20. • With chemistry dept., Univ. of California, Berkeley: instr. 1922–27;

Courtesy of University of California

asst. prof. 1927–30; assoc. prof. 1930–34; prof. of chemistry 1934–77; faculty research lectr. 1947–48; dir. of research program 1962–81; prof. emeritus since 1962. **Fellow** Amer. Physical Soc.; Amer. Acad. of Arts and Sciences. **Member** Cttee. on Low Temperature Scales, Natl. Research Council 1936–38; Natl. Acad. of Sciences since 1936; Amer. Chemical Soc.; Amer. Assn. of Univ. Professors; Amer. Philosophical Soc.; Sigma Xi; Phi Lambda Upsilon; Inst. Intl. du Froid; Berkeley Faculty Club. **Honors** (Jtly.) Discovery Prize, Pacific Div., Amer. Assn. for Advancement of Science 1929; Chandler Medal and Lectr., Columbia Univ. 1936; Cresson Medal, Franklin Inst. 1937; Nobel Prize in chemistry 1949; Gibbs Medal, Amer. Chemical Soc. 1951; Lewis Medal 1956; low-temperature lab. founded in his name 1966, and hon. fellow, Univ. of California, Berkeley; hon. degrees from univs. of Columbia and California. **Author** of over 200 papers on chemistry, physics, and cryogenics in scientific jrnls.

Further reading A. Tiselius, "The 1949 Nobel Prize for Chemistry," in *Les Prix Nobel en 1949,* 1950; Eduard Farber, *Nobel Prize Winners in Chemistry: 1901–61,* 1963; K. Mendelssohn, *The Quest for Absolute Zero,* 1977.

HELENE DEUTSCH
Psychoanalyst
Born **Przemyśl, Galicia, Austria-Hungary, 9 October 1884**
Died **Cambridge, Massachusetts, USA, 29 March 1982**

One of the foremost teachers among the second generation of psychoanalysts, the immediate followers of Sigmund Freud, Helene Deutsch was the first female pupil to be analyzed by Freud himself. Although an early socialist and a campaigner for the rights of women to education and employment, she was sharply attacked in her later years by feminists who believed that her well-known Freudian exposition of female psychology was incorrect and demeaning to women.

She was born Helene Rosenbach, the youngest of four children of a respected attorney and legal scholar. After studying at a boarding school, she was tutored as a debutante by her mother, whom she considered "very reactionary . . . a mean woman, and I did not want to be like her." She ran away from home at the age of 12 after her mother forbade her to study further for eventual university entrance. When the police returned her to her parents, she vowed to continue to escape until her father signed an agreement guaranteeing her an education.

Still incorrigible at 16, she met and fell in love with Herman Lieberman, the leader of the Polish Social Democratic Party. He was a public man in his thirties, married with two children, and the scandal touched both their families. In the course of a long and difficult affair, she became a committed political activist, smuggling propaganda to the Russian frontier, organizing strikes among working women, and even throwing herself in front of the militia's horses. "I was always burning to be arrested," she recalled, yet she never was.

She followed Lieberman to Vienna in 1907, when he was elected to parliament, and became a medical student, one of only three women then enrolled. Her growing interest in medical science accompanied a decline in her active radicalism, and she soon broke with Lieberman. In 1912, just before becoming a doctor, she married Dr. Felix Deutsch, a practicing internist. The departure of most male psychiatrists to the army during World War I enabled her to take a position at the renowned Wagner-Jauregg Clinic, the focus of official Viennese psychiatry, where she gained considerable clinical psychiatric expertise; but she lost her standing when the men returned and was forced to withdraw from the staff once she decided to follow Freud.

Deutsch's psychoanalysis by Freud began in late 1928, only a short while after she became his pupil, and lasted just short of a year. She reluctantly gave up her hour with the master when he told her he needed it for an old patient, the famous Wolf-Man, who required treatment again. In any case, he told her, "You do not need any more; you are not neurotic." Over the next few years Deutsch assumed an important role in Freud's circle of friends and colleagues—her husband was for a time his personal physician. Her academic-clinical background was greatly respected; even more so was her extraordinary teaching ability. In particular, her gift for astute diagnosis of complex cases was remarked by all who studied with her. During another year of analysis in 1923 with Karl Abraham in Berlin, she had a chance to observe the workings of the Berlin Psychoanalytic Institute, and after returning to Vienna the following year founded the Vienna Psychoanalytic Institute along the same lines. She remained its director for nine years, responsible for the training of a whole generation of Freudian psychoanalysts. Her Saturday evening salon, the Black Cat Card Club, was widely attended and influential. In 1934, before the Nazi Anschluss and against Freud's wishes, the Deutsches left Vienna for Boston, Massachusetts, where another institute was soon in operation, which she served as director for several years.

Deutsch's best-known and most controversial book was *The Psychology of Women* (1944, 1945), which covered, in two volumes, the growth and maturation of the female psyche from girlhood to motherhood. She saw satisfactory maturity in women attained only in the abandonment of certain so-called masculine-active tendencies in favor of feminine-passive ones. Mentally healthy women, she wrote, subordinate their identities to those of the males in their lives, and are "always willing to renounce their own achievements without feeling that they are sacrificing something." The female urge to nurturing and passivity arises, in her view, from a "genital trauma" involving the transference of sexual pleasure from the "phallic" clitoris to the "masochistic" vagina, rather than from penis envy, as in the traditional Freudian view; and a woman's successful accomplishment of coitus, pregnancy, and childbirth rests upon the proper combination of narcissistic and masochistic elements in the female nature.

Yet however many or reformative were her differences with Freud's own old-fashioned and illiberal views regarding women, Deutsch's ideas have, understandably, come under relentless attack by feminists since the 1960s. To them, her analysis strongly reinforces the patriarchal attitudes that have kept women oppressed for centuries; some even called her "a traitor to her sex." Deutsch typically brushed aside her detractors' objections and insisted on the basic human truth of her analysis.

Many of her fellow psychiatrists, however, believe Deutsch's most important contribution to her field lies in the diagnostic works she regularly published in learned journals, extending all the way back to 1918. Among these, her book *Psychoanalysis of the Neuroses* (1930, revised in 1965 as *Neuroses and Character Types*) is still regarded as a classic of descriptive exposition. Her last book was a well-received memoir, *Confrontations with Myself* (1973). Healthy and vigorous almost until the end of her life, she continued to reside in the Boston area after her husband's death in 1964. In 1962 she received the Menninger Award "for epochal contributions to psychoanalysis." She died at the age of 97.
A.K./J.P.

Born Helene Rosenbach. **Parents** Wilhelm R., lawyer and jurist, and Regina R. **Married** Felix Deutsch, internist and psychoanalyst, 1912 (d. 1964): Martin, physicist, b. 1917. **Religion** Jewish. **Emigrated** to U.S. 1934; naturalized. **Education** Boarding sch.; studied in Lvov and Zurich for univ. entrance examination ca. 1907; Univ. of Vienna Medical Sch., M.D. 1912; didactic analysis with Sigmund Freud, Vienna 1918–19; didactic analysis with Karl Abraham, Berlin Psychoanalytic Inst. 1923–24. **Career** Journalist and social activist 1900s; asst. 1912–19 and civilian war dr. WWI, Wagner-Jauregg Clinic, Univ. of

Vienna; psychoanalyst since 1918; member 1918–34 and dir. of Training Inst. 1925–34, Vienna Psychoanalytic Soc.; organizer, Ambulatory Clinic, Vienna 1922; seminar teacher, Berlin Psychoanalytic Inst. 1923–24; member, Intl. Training Commn., Intl. Psychoanalytic Congress 1927; founder and leader, Black Cat Card Club salon, Vienna 1920–early 30s.; in private practice, Cambridge, MA since 1934; member since 1937, training analyst ca. 1937–ca. 1962, and pres. of Inst. 1939–41, Boston Psychoanalytic Soc.; assoc. psychiatrist, Massachusetts Gen. Hosp., Boston 1937–46. • Guest lectr., Intl. Congress of Psychic Hygiene, U.S. 1930; Brill Lectr., New York Psychoanalytic Inst. 1955. **Member** Acad. of Arts and Sciences, Cambridge, MA. **Honors** Hon. psychiatrist, Massachusetts Gen. Hosp. since 1957; Menninger Award, Amer. Psychoanalytic Assn. 1962; hon. prof., Boston Univ. **Author** *Psychoanalyse der Neurosen,* 1930 (trans. as *The Psychoanalysis of the Neuroses,* 1932), rev. as *Neuroses and Character Types: Clinical Psychoanalytic Studies,* 1965; *The Psychology of Women: A Psychoanalytic Interpretation,* vol. 1, 1944, vol. 2, 1945; *Selected Problems of Adolescence,* 1967; *Confrontations with Myself* (autobiography), 1973. **Contributor** of more than 50 papers to psychoanalytic jrnls.

Further reading Franz Alexander et al., *Psychoanalytic Pioneers,* 1966; Paul Roazen, *Freud and His Followers,* 1975; Suzanne Gordon, "Helene Deutsch and the Legacy of Freud," in *New York Times Magazine,* 30 July 1978.

WALTER HALLSTEIN

Founder of the European Economic Community
***Born* Mainz, Germany, 17 November 1901**
***Died* Stuttgart, West Germany, 29 March 1982**

Courtesy of German Information Center

Walter Hallstein, a jurist by training, became during the 1950s a close foreign-policy aide to Konrad Adenauer, the West German chancellor, then was named the first president of the European Economic Community's executive commission. He served for eight years in that post with great distinction, but was finally forced to resign because he had incurred the enmity of Pres. Charles de Gaulle of France.

Hallstein found his vocation in the law at an early age and studied the subject at the universities of Bonn, Munich, and Berlin, the last of which awarded him its doctorate of law. He was appointed professor of Rostock University at the age of 28, an honor almost unheard-of in Germany for one so young. In 1941 he moved to Frankfurt-am-Main as professor of comparative law and director of the university's Institute for Comparative Law, but was soon drafted for service in World War II. As an artillery first lieutenant in the Wehrmacht, Hallstein was sent to France. In Cherbourg, in 1944, he was captured by Allied soldiers and interned in prisoner-of-war camps, first in Scotland and then in Camp Como, Mississippi, where he set up university courses for his fellow prisoners in law, social sciences, and languages.

Repatriated soon after the war ended in Europe, Hallstein returned to Frankfurt, where his first task was to get the university running again under the Allied occupation. He was elected rector in 1946, and in 1948–49 was visiting professor at Georgetown University in Washington, D.C., the first German academic to be invited to the United States since the 1930s.

In 1948, at a conference on European unity in The Hague, Hallstein first met Adenauer. He created such a favorable impression that two years later he was named head of the German delegation to the Paris conference to discuss the plan of Robert Schuman, France's foreign minister, to set up an international entity for regulating Europe's production and sale of coal and steel. Hallstein's French opposite number was Jean Monnet, like himself a committed European supranationalist. The European Coal and Steel Community was a success virtually from its inception. Hallstein became secretary of state for foreign affairs of the German Federal Republic in 1951, second in rank to the foreign minister, Heinrich von Brentano. He gave his name to the Hallstein Doctrine, a tenet which aimed to reunify Germany by having Bonn break diplomatic relations with all states, except the Soviet Union and its satellites, that recognized the East German regime. The doctrine was never especially successful and was abandoned as West German policy a few years later when Chancellor Willy Brandt began his *Ostpolitik,* the rapprochement with the Soviet bloc. Hallstein was also largely responsible for solidifying Germany's relations with France, the essential foundation of any plan for European unity. In 1955 he led the German delegation to a conference in Messina, Sicily, that resulted in the establishment in 1958 of the European Atomic Energy Commission (Euratom) and the European Economic Community. The 248 articles of the Treaty of Rome, signed in 1957, represent the constitution of the Common Market.

Hallstein's presidency of the EEC's executive commission was marked by a cool and analytical approach to the competing interests of the member nations and complete dedication to his work, which became an endless string of 12-hour days. The favorable economic climate prevailing in Europe in the late 1950s and early 1960s—notably the West German boom—was exceptionally good news for the fledgling organization. Hallstein counted its first years a great success and planned for further integration. He did not count on Gen. de Gaulle as an adversary.

De Gaulle returned to power in France in 1958, only months after the EEC's inception. He had been on record as opposing the organization, but decided instead to use it for France's ends, though he had great contempt for the supranationalists in the EEC's Brussels headquarters—"a band of technocrats," he called them, "*les apatrides*" (stateless men). He and Hallstein clashed repeatedly (though never face to face) over several issues: Great Britain's application for membership, which de Gaulle finally vetoed; various plans to expand EEC authority in the member nations; and the deference regularly shown Hallstein on his travels around the world. In the United States, in particular, Hallstein was frequently called "the President of Europe," much to de Gaulle's outrage. Finally, when Hallstein tried to win French support for greater political integration by means of a financially attractive farm package, de Gaulle decided he had had enough. He recalled his ambassador from the EEC in June 1965, and for the next seven months there was a real question of whether the organization could survive. Hallstein reacted with uncharacteristic imprudence, saying that if de Gaulle succeeded in preventing European unity it would be "the greatest destructive act in the history of Europe . . . since the days of Hitler." Reaction in Paris to this assertion by the former Wehrmacht lieutenant was practically apoplectic.

From then on, all could see that Hallstein's days as president were numbered. In the compromise by which France agreed to return to the EEC in January 1966, the Coal and Steel Community, Euratom, and the EEC were merged into one organization, with one secretariat and one president—but that president was not to be Hallstein. He tendered his resignation in June 1967, just before the new commission came into being, and returned to Germany. He was a Christian Democratic member of the Bundestag from 1969 to 1972, but party politics held no great interest for him, and he declined to seek reelection.

Hallstein was the recipient of 20 honorary doctorates and nearly 30 foreign orders and decorations, of which he was proudest of the International Charlemagne Prize of the city of Aix-la-Chapelle/Aachen (1961) and the Robert Schuman Prize (1969). In addition to several law texts, he wrote books on European unity, notably *United Europe: Challenge and Opportunity* (1962) and *Europe in the Making* (1972). A.K.

Parents Jakob H., govt. surveyor, and Anna (Geibel) H. **Religion** Protestant. **Education** Humanistische Gymnasium, Mainz, grad. 1920; Univs. of Bonn and Munich; Univ. of Berlin, Dr. Jur. 1925. **Mil. service** First lt., artillery, Wehrmacht, France 1943–44; captured by U.S. 1944; POW, Scotland and MS 1944–45, organized camp univ. **Career** Asst. 1925, asst. teacher 1927, and privatdozent 1929–30, law faculty, Univ. of Berlin; research fellow, Kaiser Wilhelm Inst. of Foreign and Intl. Civil Law, Berlin 1927–30; prof., Univ. of Rostock 1930–41; prof. of comparative law since 1941, dir. of Inst. for Comparative Law 1941–44, and rector 1946–48, Univ. of Frankfurt-am-Main; co-ed., *Deutsche Juristen-Zeitung* lawyers' jrnl. since 1946; visiting prof., Georgetown Univ., Wash. DC 1948–49 and Princeton Univ. 1968. • Chmn., German Cttee., UNESCO 1949–50; leader, German delegation to Schuman Plan conference, and co-founder, European Coal and Steel Community, Paris 1950; secty. of state, West German Federal Chancellery 1950; secty. of state for foreign affairs, West Germany 1951–58; leader, German delegation, organizational conference for European Atomic Energy Commn. and EEC, Sicily 1955; pres., Commn. of European Economic Community, Brussels 1958–67; pres., European Movement 1968–74; advisor, Action Cttee. for the United States of Europe 1969; Christian Democratic member, Bundestag 1969–72. **Officer** Bd. chmn., Max Planck Inst. **Member** (Corresp.) Hellenic Inst. of Intl. and Foreign Law, Athens 1954; Science Advisory Council, German Ministry of Economics; Deutschen Gesellschaft für Rechtsvergleichung; Deutschen Vereinigung für Internationales Recht, Deutschen Juristentages. **Honors** Grand Cross of Merit with Star and Sash 1954; Charlemagne Prize, City of Aix-la-Chappelle/Aachen 1961; Medal of Merit, Bavaria 1965; Robert Schuman Prize 1969; hon. citizen, Brussels 1971; medal, City of Athens; Grand Cross of Merit, Kts. of Jerusalem; decorations from the Vatican, Italy, Greece, Argentina, Brazil, Iceland, Thailand, Iran, Austria, Peru, Mexico, Sweden, Chile, Belgium, Liberia, Bolivia, Luxembourg, Cuba, Venezuela, Togo, Nigeria, other nations; hon. degrees from univs. of Georgetown, Padua, Tufts, Maine, Adelphi, New York, Harvard, Nebraska Wesleyan, Columbia, Johns Hopkins, Creighton, Liège, Bradford, Sussex, Nancy, Louvain, Oviedo, Hamburg, and Tübingen, and from Colby Coll. **Author** *Der Lebensversicherungsvertrag im Versailler Vertrag* [*The Life-Insurance Contract in the Versailles Treaty*], 1926; *Die Aktienrechte der Gegenwart* [*The Right To Share in the Present*], 1931; *Die Berichtigung des Gesellschaftskapitals* [*The Adjustment of Corporate Capital*], 1942; *Die Wiederherstellung des Privatrechts* [*The Restoration of Civil Law*], 1946; *Wissenschaft und Politik* [*Science and Politics*], 1949; *Der Schumann-Plan* [*The Schuman Plan*], 1951; *Probleme des Schumann-Planes* [*Problems of the Schuman Plan*], 1951; (ed.) *Europäisches Recht* [*European Law*], 1953; *Gross- und Klein-Europa* [*Greater and Smaller Europe*], 1959; *United Europe: Challenge and Opportunity,* 1962; (jt. ed.) *Zur Integration Europas* [*On European Integration*], 1965; *Wege nach Europa* [*Roads to Europe*], 1967; *Europa 1980,* 1968; *Der unvollendete Bundesstaat,* 1969 (trans. as *Europe in the Making,* 1972); *Die Europäische Gemeinschaft* [*The European Community*], 1973; *Europäische Reden* [*European Speeches*], 1979.

Further reading Edwin Dale, Jr., "Hallstein Runs an Uncommon Experiment," in *New York Times Magazine,* 15 July 1962; Richard Mayne, *The Recovery of Europe,* 1970.

F(REDERICK) G(EORGE) MANN
Chemist
***Born* London, England, 29 June 1897**
***Died* Cambridge, England, 29 March 1982**

F. G. Mann, a Cambridge University researcher for more than four decades, pioneered in the synthesis of complex metallic chemical compounds and helped elucidate their three-dimensional structure. His textbooks on organic chemistry and metallic compounds are standard references.

Mann was the son of a civil servant in the British Admiralty and studied at Battersea Polytechnic Boys Secondary School and the University of London. In 1917, he joined the Special Brigade of the Royal Engineers and was sent to France to work on the development of chemical weapons. He obtained his B.Sc. from the University of London in 1919 and the following year became a research student at Downing College, Cambridge University, which awarded him the doctorate in 1923.

From 1922 to 1930, Mann assisted the noted chemist Sir William Jackson Pope, who was studying coordination compounds (molecules consisting of a central metal atom surrounded by groups of nonmetallic atoms). Some of the most important biological substances, including chlorophyll and hemoglobin, are coordination compounds. Pope and Mann synthesized these compounds by treating simpler metallic substances with polyamines, organic molecules that contain nitrogen, and then worked out the new molecules' spatial configurations.

Mann became a fellow of the Royal Institute of Chemistry in 1929 and a lecturer at Cambridge in 1930. In 1932 he became only the second chemist to synthesize a purely inorganic (carbon-free) coordination compound. Turning from polyamines, he prepared new compounds of phosphorus and arsenic—the tertiary phosphines and arsines—and used these to derive coordination compounds. His work on phosphines laid the basis for their widespread use in industrial catalytic processes such as the production of polyethylene.

Courtesy of Barbara Mann

Mann spent years investigating the composition and structure of compounds formed by the elements of Group V of the periodic table. The detailed and highly technical treatise that resulted, *The Heterocyclic Derivatives of Phosphorus, Arsenic, Antimony, Bismuth, and Silicon* (1950), is still used by specialists. He also contributed to the improvement of the quality of black and white photographic films by developing new kinds of photosensitive cyanine dyes. These dyes, added in small amounts to photographic emulsions, increase the films' sensitivity to light.

Mann was elected a fellow of the Royal Society in 1947. He retired from Cambridge in 1964 as emeritus reader in organic chemistry. In 1966 he wrote a history of the development of coordination chemistry at Cambridge for the *Advances in Chemistry* series. He had a lifelong passion for golf and was the author of *Lord Rutherford on the Golf Course* (1976), a wryly humorous memoir of the great Cambridge physicist. P.D.

Parents William Clarence Herbert M., civil servant, and Elizabeth Ann (Casswell) M. **Married** (1) Margaret Reid Shackleton, lectr., 1930 (d. 1950): Shirley Margaret Shackleton Bourke, teacher, b. 1932; Carola Mary Shackleton Carr-Brion, teacher, b. 1934. (2) Barbara Thornber, secty., 1951: Elizabeth Hilary Frances, librarian, b. 1954. **Religion** Agnostic. **Education** Battersea Polytechnic Boys Secondary Sch., London 1909–14; Univ. of London, B.Sc. (honors) 1919; Downing Coll., Cambridge, Ph.D. in chemistry 1923. **Mil. service** Second lt., Special Brigade, Royal Engineers, British Expeditionary Force, France 1917–19. **Career** With Cambridge Univ.: research asst., Downing Coll. 1922–30; lectr. in chemistry 1930–46; fellow and lectr. 1931–64, praelector in chemistry 1960–64, and reader emeritus in organic chemistry since 1964, Trinity Coll.; reader in organic chemistry 1946–64. • Tilden Lectr., Chemical Soc. 1943; visiting sr. prof. of chemistry, Univ. of Hawaii 1946–47. **Officer** Examiner 1955–60 and council member 1942–45 and 1948–51, Royal Inst. of Chemistry, London; v.p. 1958–61 and council member 1935–38, 1940–43, and 1946–49, Chemical Soc., London. **Fellow** Royal Inst. of Chemistry 1929; FRS 1947. **Member** (Life member) Wildfowl Trust, Slimbridge; (life member) Jersey Wildlife Preservation Trust; Cambridge Bird Club; Gog Magog Golf Club, Cambridge. **Honors** Transition Metal Chemistry Award, Chemical Soc. 1977; hon. degrees from univs. of London and Cambridge. **Author** (Jtly.) *Practical Organic Chemistry,* 1936; (jtly.) *Introduction to Practical Organic Chemistry,* 1939; *The Heterocyclic Derivatives of Phosphorus, Arsenic, Antimony, Bismuth, and Silicon* 1950; "The Development of Coordination Chemistry at the University of Cambridge, 1925–1965," in *Advances in Chemistry,* no. 62, 1966; *Lord Rutherford on the Golf Course,* 1976. **Contributor** to *Proceedings of the Royal Society, Journal of the Chemical Society, Journal of the Society of Chemical Industry,* other scientific jrnls.

CARL ORFF
Composer and music educator
***Born* Munich, Germany, 10 July 1895**
***Died* Munich, West Germany, 29 March 1982**

Carl Orff was the composer of *Carmina burana,* a stage spectacle of remarkable hedonistic energy that brought to life the drunken world of the wandering minstrels and monks of medieval Europe. In this and later works he sought to reunify the arts of theater, music, language and movement in order to tap the metaphysical sources of Western culture. "I have never been concerned with music as such," he once said, "but rather with music as spiritual discussion." He was also the founder of a famous method for teaching music creativity to children and the originator of the Orff Instrumentarium, a collection of percussion instruments used in the teaching program.

Orff was born into an aristocratic Bavarian family and began studying piano, organ, and cello at the age of five. His earliest compositions, written down with his mother's help, were orchestrations for piano, zither, violin, and glockenspiel of his own puppet-theater librettos. Some of his pieces were first tried out at the court of Prince Luitpold, regent of Bavaria, by the band of the elite army regiment commanded by Orff's father. By the age of 15 Orff had published over 50 songs; the following year he completed *Also sprach Zarathustra,* a large-scale choral setting of Nietzsche's text. After his graduation in 1914 from the Munich Academy of Music, he worked for some years as a conductor—first at the Munich Kammerspiele, then, following a brief tour in the army, at the Mannheim and Darmstadt opera houses—before returning to Munich in 1919 to concentrate on composing. From Heinrich Kaminski, with whom he took private lessons in 1921 and 1922, he derived an interest in the work of the sixteenth-century Mantuan composer Claudio Monteverdi, several of whose works he arranged in modern style.

In 1924 Orff began his lifetime preoccupation with musical education by founding, together with Dorothy Günther, a school for the training of eurhythmics teachers through a program of improvisation exercises, gymnastics, and dance. To encourage his pupils' experimentation with music, he developed, in collaboration with the piano maker Karl Maendler, a set of easy-to-play percussion instruments, some modeled on those of the Indonesian gamelan ensemble. The object of his teaching was to draw children into the enjoyment of group improvisation by introducing them to the most accessible elements of folk music, especially those connected with dramatic performance. The Ministry of Culture asked Orff to create a nationwide program for the elementary schools, but further action was delayed until after World War II, when he began a five-year series of radio broadcasts that resulted in the publication of a multivolume and multirecord collection of exercises entitled *Orff-Schulwerk—Musik für Kinder.* These exercises, translated into many languages, including English, Japanese, and Welsh, were soon to revolutionize music education worldwide. In 1951, Orff's student Gunild Keetman was appointed to teach his methods at the Mozarteum Academy for Music and Dramatic Arts in Salzburg. Ten years later Orff left a position as professor at the Hochschule für Musik in Munich to become director of the Mozarteum's new Carl Orff Institute, which became a gathering place for music educators from around the world.

By that time, Orff had achieved international fame as the composer of the dramatic cantata *Carmina burana* and other works that combined music and drama in a manner consciously imitative of folk ritual. Published in 1937, when Orff was 42, *Carmina burana,* with its physically compelling rhythms and bawdy texts, was as offensive to some as it was fascinating to others. It was based on a thirteenth-century manuscript discovered in 1803 in the ancient Benedictine monastery at Beuron, 30 miles south of Munich (the Latin title means "songs of Beuron"), containing 200 goliard songs in Vulgar Latin, Old French, and Middle High German. Orff selected 24 of the songs—including one to be sung by a swan roasting on a spit—and arranged them into three sections for chorus and orchestra, to be performed with a pantomime accompaniment. When the work was completed, Orff instructed his publisher to destroy his previous compositions: "With *Carmina burana* my collected works begin." The cantata was the first part of a trilogy completed by *Catulli carmina* (1943), a revision of a pre-1937 work, and by *Trionfo di Afrodite* (1953), based on poems by Catullus, Sappho, and Euripides. A 62-minute film version of *Carmina burana* was produced in 1975 to honor Orff's 80th birthday.

In his search for the wellsprings of Western spiritual tradition—which, in his opinion, were also the sources of authentic music and drama—Orff delved further and further back into history for the inspiration for his subsequent works. *Der Mond* (1939) and *Die Kluge* (1943) were adapted from Bavarian folk tunes, *Die Bernauerin* (1947) and *Astutuli* (1953) from folk legends in Bavarian dialect; *Comoedia di Christi resurrectione* (1957) and *Ludus de nato infante mirificus* (1961) were settings of medieval mystery plays for Easter and Christmas. During the 1940s he also revised his repudiated arrangements of works by Monteverdi. The finest achievement of his later career is held by most critics to be the trilogy based on classical dramas: *Antigonae* (1949), *Ödipus, der Tyrann* (1959), and *Prometheus* (1966), which alone employed more than 70 percussion instruments, including gongs, harps, xylophones, and six pianos, and a startling variety of sighs, screams, and moans. ("The simpler and more reduced to essentials an utterance," Orff said, "the more immediate and profound its effect.") Among his last pieces were *De temporum fine comoedia,* based on Sybilline prophecies about the doom of the world, and *Rota,* which was used to accompany the opening of 1972 Olympic Games in Munich.

Courtesy of German Information Center

Musically, Orff's later pieces were elaborations of the style he first developed for *Carmina burana,* a style that relied heavily on rhythm and percussion—indeed, that used even strings and winds in a percussive manner—with melody no more than an outgrowth of the text. Most of his works are constructed of blocklike chunks of sound driven forward by endlessly repeated ostinati. His vocal and choral writing ranges from free recitative and Sprechstimme to melismatic passages such as are found in Oriental music and chanting techniques influenced by Gregorian chant and plainsong.

The brutish, forceful nature of Orff's music and the effectiveness of his musical and visual spectacles earned him a wide international following, though many critics deplored his rejection of sophisticated compositional techniques in favor of simple physical appeal. Wrote Hanspeter Krellman in *The New Groves Dictionary of Music,* "Orff's success has been in proving the potency of barbarism, and its limitations."

Orff was a fiercely private man who refused to reveal much about his personal life. He did authorize a "musical biography" by Andreas Liess which has been translated into English. He was the recipient of numerous prizes and awards, including West Germany's Order "Pour le mérite" and the Grand Federal Cross of Merit, and was a member of the Bavarian Academy of Fine Arts. He died of cancer at the age of 86. J.P./B.D.

Parents Heinrich O., army officer, and Paula (Köstler) O. **Married** (1) . . . : Godela, actress. (2) Liselotte. **Education** Private music lessons; Akad. der Tonkunst, Munich, grad. 1914; studied with Heinrich Kaminski 1921–22. **Mil. service** German Army 1917–18. **Career** Composer since childhood; coach and conductor, Kammerspiele, Munich 1915–17; asst. conductor, Nationaltheater, Mannheim, and Landestheater, Darmstadt, 1918–19; co-founder 1924 and instr. 1925–30, Güntherschule for gymnastics, dance, and music, Munich; dir. and conductor, Munich Bach Soc. 1930–ca. 1935; broadcaster, "Schulwerk," Bavarian Radio 1948–53, TV series 1957–58; prof. and head of master class in composition, Staatliche Hochschule für Musik, Munich 1950–60; dir., Carl Orff Inst., Mozarteum Acad. for Music and Dramatic Art, Salzburg since 1961. **Member** Bavarian Acad. of Fine Arts 1961; Swedish Acad.; Acad. di Santa Cecilia, Rome. **Honors** Munich Music Prize 1947; New York Music Critics Prize, for *Carmina burana,* 1954; kt., Order "Pour le mérite" for Art and Science, West Germany 1956; Bremen Music Prize 1956; Grand Federal Cross of Merit 1959, with Star 1965, with Sash 1972; Mozart Prize, Goethe-Stiftung, Basel 1969; Carl-Orff-Schule named in his honor, Berlin 1966, and Carl Orff Street, Burghausen 1967; Humboldt gold medal, Humboldt Gesellschaft für Wissenschaft, Kunst, und Bildung 1971; Romano-Guardini Prize 1974; hon. citizen of Munich and Salzburg 1975; hon. member of Mozarteum 1960, Münster State Theater 1965, European Bildungsgemeinschaft 1973; Frankfurther Goethe-Plakette; Grand Silver Medal, Salzburg; hon. degrees from univs. of Tübingen and Munich. **Stage works** *Carmina burana,* 1937; *Der Mond,* 1939; *Die Kluge,* 1943; *Catulli carmina,* 1943; *Die Bernauerin,* 1947; *Antigonae,* 1949; *Astutuli,* 1953; *Trionfo di Afrodite,* 1953; *Comoedia di Christi resurrectione,* 1957; *Ödipus, der Tyrann,* 1959; *Ludus de nato infante mirificus,* 1961; *Ein Sommernachtstraum,* 1964; *Prometheus,* 1966; *De temporum fine comoedia,* 1973. **Adaptations of stage works by Claudio Monteverdi** *Orfeo,* 1925; *Tanz der Spröden,* 1925; *Klage der Ariadne,* 1925; *Ballo dell'Ingrate; L'incoronazione di Poppea.* **Instrumental works** *Leonce und Lena,* 1918; *Kleines Konzert,* 1927; *Entrata,* 1927. **Choral works** Lieder to texts by Werfel, Trakl, Klabund, Nietzsche, others, ca. 1920; *Des Turmes Auferstehung,* 1920; *Cantus-firmus-Sätze,* 1929; *Werkbuch I* (cantatas), 1929–30; *Werkbuch II; Catulli carmina I,* 1930; *Catulli carmina II,* 1931; *Concènto di voci,* 1930, 1956; *Die Sänger der Vorwelt,* 1955; *Nänie und Dithyrambe,* 1956; *Stücke,* 1969; *Rota,* 1972. **Exercises for children's musical education** *Orff-Schulwerk—Musik für Kinder,* 5 vols. 1930–35, rev. 1950–54 (made into film *Musik für Kinder,* 1954); *Jugendmusik,* 1948, 1952, 1954. **Author** *Carl Orff und sein Werk* (autobiography), 8 vols. from 1975.

Further reading Andreas Liess, *Carl Orff: His Life and Music,* 1966; K. Simpson, ed., *Some Great Music Educators,* 1976; Hans Schneider, *The Schulwerk,* 1978.

CHARLES ALLEN THOMAS
Chemist and president of Monsanto Chemical Company
***Born* Scott County, Kentucky, USA, 15 February 1900**
***Died* Albany, Georgia, USA, 29 March 1982**

As a research chemist, Charles Allen Thomas developed a variety of products, including a widely used antiknock gasoline additive, and headed the plutonium-refining project for the first atomic bomb. He later made a successful transition from scientist to business executive, serving as president of the giant Monsanto Chemical Company for nine years.

The son of a farmer and minister, Thomas earned his A.B. from Transylvania College in Kentucky and joined the General Motors Research Corporation in 1923 while studying for his M.S. at the Massachusetts Institute of Technology. Under the direction of Charles Kettering, Thomas and a team of G.M. researchers discovered a compound, tetraethyl lead, that increased the efficiency of gasoline and eliminated the "knocking" problem common to lower-grade gasolines. It left a lead residue in motors, but Thomas found that he could prevent the problem by adding bromine; he then devised a cheap method of extracting bromine from sea water. In 1924 he transferred to G.M.'s newly established Ethyl Gasoline Corporation. Two years later he left the firm and with another G.M. chemist, Carroll Hochwalt, founded an independent research laboratory that made fire extinguisher formulas, synthetic rubber, and products for the automobile, liquor, and meat industries.

In 1936, Thomas & Hochwalt Laboratories was acquired by Monsanto, which was growing rapidly by engulfing smaller firms. Thomas, who netted a large share of Monsanto stock in the transaction, became the company's central research director and concentrated on developing new olefins, aromatics, and synthetic resins from petroleum hydrocarbons for the burgeoning plastics market.

During World War II Thomas worked on explosives, rocket fuels, and a gasoline contaminant for use by the British government in the event of a German invasion. In 1942 he was put in charge of the final stages of the Manhattan Project's plutonium-239 refining program; the fuel he helped produce was used in the first atomic-bomb test (which Thomas attended) at Alamogordo, New Mexico, on 16 July 1945, and in the bomb that was dropped on Nagasaki three weeks later. He ran the Clinton Laboratories at Oak Ridge, Tennessee, for Monsanto and the government in 1945, and the following year was one of the authors of *A Report on the International Control of Atomic Energy,* popularly known as the Acheson-Lilienthal Report, for the U.N. Atomic Energy Commission. The report was widely praised, but its plan for the peaceful use of atomic energy under the supervision of an international body was never implemented.

Thomas joined the board of Monsanto in 1942, was made a vice president in 1945, and was promoted to president in 1951. This was a period of growth for the company: it climbed to fifth place among U.S. chemical producers in the early 1950s and became the world's largest producer of elemental phosphorus, a key ingredient in artificial fertilizers. In 1951 Monsanto competed for a government contract to construct a prototype commercial nuclear reactor under the AEC's industrial participation plan, which Thomas had helped formulate, but the company eventually abandoned the project. He stepped down as president in 1960, served as board chairman until 1965, and resigned from the board in 1970.

The holder of 14 honorary degrees and numerous honors from science and industry, Thomas never lost his fascination with unusual chemical phenomena and even devised special tricks for professional magicians. He died at the age of 82. S.A.

Parents Charles Allen T., minister of Disciples of Christ, and Francis (Carrick) T. **Married** (1) Margaret Stoddard Talbott 1926 (d.): Charles Allen, molecular biologist, b. 1927; Margaret Talbott Tenge Walsh; Frances Carrick Martin; Katharine Tudor O'Neil. (2) Margaret Porter 1980. **Religion** Disciples of Christ. **Education** Public schs., Lexington, KY; Transylvania Coll., Lexington, KY, A.B. 1920; Massachusetts Inst. of Technology, M.S. 1924. **Career** Research chemist, General

Courtesy of Monsanto Company

Motors Research Corp. 1923–24 and G.M.'s Ethyl Gasoline Corp. 1924–25; co-founder and pres., Thomas & Hochwalt Labs., Dayton, OH 1926–36. • With Monsanto Chemical Co.: central research dir. 1936–45; bd. member 1942–70; v.p. and technical dir. 1945–47; member 1945–47, vice chmn. 1948, and chmn. 1949, exec. cttee.; exec. v.p. 1947–51; pres. 1951–60; bd. chmn. 1960–65; chmn., finance cttee. • Deputy chief and head of plutonium-refining project 1942–43, and sect. member 1943–46, Natl. Defense Research Council; dir., Clinton Labs., Oak Ridge, TN 1945, and ed., *Chemistry and Metallurgy of Plutonium* (jrnl.) 1945–46, Manhattan Engineering District; member, scientific panel, U.N. Atomic Energy Commn. 1946; chmn., science manpower advisory cttee., Natl. Security Resources Bd. 1950; member, science advisory cttee., Office of Defense Mobilization 1951; consultant, Natl. Security Council 1953. **Officer** With Amer. Chemical Soc.: dir., and member of editorial bd., 1937–38; pres. 1948; bd. chmn. 1950–53. • Dir.: Metropolitan Life Insurance Corp.; RAND Corp.; Southwestern Bell Telephone Co.; First Natl. Bank of St. Louis; St. Louis Union Trust Co.; Chemstrand Corp. • Other: chmn., bd. of trustees, Washington Univ.; chmn., visiting cttee., dept. of physics, Massachusetts Inst. of Technology; vice chmn. and bd. member, St. Louis Research Council; curator, Transylvania Univ.; trustee, John and Olga Queeny Educational Foundn. and Carnegie Corp. **Fellow** Amer. Acad. for Advancement of Science; Amer. Acad. of Arts and Sciences. **Member** Business Council, U.S. Dept. of Commerce since 1955; (founding member) Amer. Acad. of Engineering; Natl. Acad. of Sciences; Natl. Acad. of Engineering; Amer. Philosophical Soc.; Amer. Inst. of Chemical Engineers; Amer. Inst. of Chemists; Chemical Soc. of London; Electrochemical Soc., Inc.; Franklin Inst.; Faraday Soc.; Soc. of Chemical Industry; Republican Party; (life member), Massachusetts Inst. of Technology Corp.; advisory bd., St. Louis Council, Boy Scouts of Amer.; bd., St. Louis Crime Commn.; Phi Beta Kappa; Sigma Xi; Alpha Chi Sigma. • Clubs: Chemists, NYC; Links, NYC and Wash. DC; Cosmos, Wash. DC; Log Cabin, Noonday, Racquet, and St. Louis Country, St. Louis. **Honors** Medal for Merit 1946; gold medal, Amer. Inst. of Chemists 1948; Missouri Honor Award 1952; Perkin Medal, Amer. sect., Soc. of Chemical Industry 1953; Priestly Medal, Amer. Chemical Soc. 1955; Order of Leopold 1962; Palladium Medal, Amer. sect., Soc. de Chimie Industrielle 1963; Man of the Year, *Globe Democrat* 1966; hon. degrees from univs. of Washington, St. Louis, Princeton, Ohio, Wesleyan, Brown, Alabama, Missouri, and Lehigh, from Transylvania, Hobart, Kenyon, Simpson, and Westminster colls., and from Brooklyn Polytechnic Inst. **Patents** Eighty-six U.S. and foreign patents for chemical products. **Author** *Anhydrous Aluminum Chloride in Organic Chemistry,* 1941; (jtly.) *A Report on the International Control of Atomic Energy,* 1946. **Contributor** of papers on chemistry to scientific jrnls.

Further reading David E. Lilienthal, *The Journals of David E. Lilienthal: The Atomic Energy Years 1945–1950,* 1964.

NATHAN F(ARRAGUT) TWINING
Chairman, Joint Chiefs of Staff
***Born* Monroe, Wisconsin, USA, 11 October 1897**
***Died* Lackland Air Force Base, Texas, USA, 29 March 1982**

Nathan F. Twining, a military airman from 1923, was the first Air Force general to head the Joint Chiefs of Staff. He brought a voice of affability and relative calm to the highest U.S. military circles at a time of particularly intense interservice rivalry. He was a consistent and strong advocate of the worldwide projection of U.S. power and even counseled the use of nuclear weapons during several crises.

Twining's father was a banker, but the family, whose roots in America date from 1635, had become distinguished in military service. His uncle, Nathan C. Twining, was a rear admiral during World War I, and two of his brothers went to Annapolis. After service on the Mexican border as a corporal in the Oregon National Guard in 1916–17, he failed the Annapolis entrance examination, then took the one for West Point and passed. He became a member of the accelerated class of 1918, whose course of study was completed in 16 months. He graduated near the middle of his class and received an infantry commission on 1 November 1918, too late for service in the war.

Twining switched to air training in 1923, flying his first solo in a Jenny of World War I vintage. He joined the newly formed Army Air Corps in 1926 and began to rise through the ranks. He attended the Air Corps Tactical School (1935–36) and the Army's Command and General Staff School (1936–37). Entering World War II as a major, in 1943 he was named commanding general of the 13th Air Force, a new unit assigned to cover the campaign in the Solomon Islands. On 26 January 1943 he was on a B-17 heavy bomber which a severe tropical storm forced down in the Coral Sea near the New Hebrides Islands. Along with the 14 crew members, Twining took to the life rafts as the plane quickly sank. With no water but collected rain and no food but the raw meat of an albatross shot by Twining, the crew drifted for six days before being spotted by a Navy rescue plane. Twining immediately returned to duty as commander of all air support for the invasion and occupation of the Treasury Islands and Bougainville. On the

Courtesy of U.S. Air Force News and Info. Center

latter island his bombers destroyed some 700 Japanese planes from August to November of 1943.

Twining was transferred to the Mediterranean theater as commanding general of the 15th Air Force, taking over from Maj. Gen. James Doolittle. From bases in southern Italy he directed bombing raids on Bologna, Vienna, Budapest, and Regensburg, Bavaria. His most important task, however, was planning the two months of strikes (April–May 1944) that completely devastated the 11 Axis oil fields and refineries in Ploesti, Rumania, thereby denying the Germans their only European petroleum resource.

As soon as the war was over in Europe, Twining was named to succeed Curtis LeMay as commanding general of the 20th Air Force, based on the Mariana Islands. From there, incendiary raids were launched against the Japanese home islands, and in August 1945 B-29 Superfortresses from his command flew the fateful missions that dropped the atomic bombs on Hiroshima and Nagasaki.

After several postwar assignments, principally that of commanding general of the

Alaskan Command (1947–50), Maj. Gen. Twining returned to Washington. In May 1950 he became deputy chief of staff for personnel and the following October received temporary four-star rank as vice chief of staff. His varied background in command marked him out for further promotion, and after standing in as chief of staff during the long illness of Gen. Hoyt Vandenberg, he was named chief of staff of the Air Force in May 1953 by Pres. Dwight Eisenhower. He was advanced to chairman of the Joint Chiefs of Staff in 1957, reappointed to a second term in 1959, and retired after undergoing a lung-cancer operation in 1960.

During Twining's tenure on the Joint Chiefs, his service experienced a large buildup, costing many billions of dollars, and completed the transition from propeller aircraft to jets. Twining believed that any future world wars would be short, and the U.S. ability to project air power, decisive. He continually stressed the importance of the Strategic Air Command, with some of its bombers always in the air and ready to fly off and annihilate Moscow at a moment's notice. He also pressed for the quick development and deployment of intercontinental ballistic missiles.

He spoke often in favor of U.S. intervention in foreign military crises: he advocated using tactical nuclear weapons in 1954 against the Vietnamese at Dien Bien Phu and bombing the Chinese mainland during the dispute over the islands of Quemoy and Matsu. He also successfully urged the U.S. invasion of Lebanon in 1958 to put down a pro-Nasser rebellion.

After retiring, Twining served for seven years (1960–67) as vice chairman of the publishing house of Holt, Rinehart & Winston. In 1964 he was an advisor to Barry Goldwater during the latter's ill-fated campaign for the presidency. Goldwater's single greatest mistake was to advocate the use of nuclear weapons in Vietnam, where the United States had just become an active belligerent. Everything in Twining's background suggests he would have been likely to offer such advice. In 1966, Twining ran unsuccessfully as a Republican for the U.S. Senate from New Hampshire. In his last years he lived at the Air Force Village in San Antonio, Texas. He was elected to the Aviation Hall of Fame in 1978.

Twining was decorated by seven foreign countries with their highest military awards. His U.S. decorations included two Distinguished Service Medals, the Legion of Merit, the Distinguished Flying Cross, the Bronze Star, and the Air Medal. A.K.

Parents Clarence Walter T., banker, and Maize (Barber) T. **Married** Maude McKeever 1932: Richard Grant, USAF officer; Nathan Alexander; Olivia Barber Twining Hansell. **Education** U.S. Military Acad., West Point, NY, grad. 1918, officer cadet 1919; Infantry Sch., Ft. Benning, GA 1919–20; Primary Flying Sch., Brooks Field, TX 1923; Advanced Flying Sch., Kelly Field, TX 1924; Air Corps Tactical Sch., AL 1935–36; Command and Gen. Staff Coll., Ft. Leavenworth, KS 1936–37. **Career** Promotions: corp. 1916; sgt. 1917; commissioned 2nd lt. 1918; 1st lt., temporary 1920, permanent 1923; capt. 1935; maj., temporary 1938, permanent 1940; lt. col., temporary 1941, permanent 1942; col., temporary 1942; brig. gen., temporary 1942, permanent 1946; maj. gen., temporary 1943, permanent 1948; lt. gen., temporary 1945; gen., temporary 1950. • Assignments: Co. H, 3rd Oregon Infantry, Natl. Guard, Mexican border 1916–17; ground observer, U.S. Army, Germany, Belgium, France, Italy 1919; with 29th Infantry Regiment, Ft. Benning, GA 1920; aide to Brig. Gen. B.A. Poore, Camp Travis, TX, Ft. Logan, CO, Ft. Sam Houston, TX 1922–23; flying instr., Brooks Field, TX 1924–25; transferred to USAAC 1926; flying instr., March Field, CA 1927–29; adjutant, personnel officer, HQ detachment comdr., and comdg. officer of 26th Attack Squadron, 18th Pursuit Group, HA 1929–30; squad comdr., 3rd Attack Group, 90th Attack Squadron, 60th Service Squadron, Ft. Crockett, TX 1932–34; adjutant, 3rd Air Group, Ft. Crockett, TX 1934–35; engineering officer, U.S. Army Air Mail Service, Chicago 1934; asst. operations officer, 3rd Wing, LA ca. 1935–36; Air Corps technical supervisor, San Antonio Air Depot, TX 1937–40; asst. chief, then chief, Inspection Div. 1940, and asst. exec. and dir. of war org. and movements 1942, Office of Chief of Air Corps; joined Air Corps Operations Div. 1941; chief of staff to Maj. Gen. M. F. Harmon 1942; comdg. gen., 13th Air Force, and comdr., Aircraft, Solomon Islands 1943; comdr., 15th Air Force, Italy 1943–45; comdr., Mediterranean Allied Strategic Air Forces 1944; comdr., 20th Air Force, Pacific theater 1945; assigned to Continental Air Force HQ, Wash. DC 1945; comdg. gen., Air Matériel Command, OH 1945–47; transferred to USAF 1947; comdg. gen., Alaskan Depot, and comdr. in chief, Alaskan Command, 1947–50; deputy chief of staff for personnel, Wash. DC 1950; vice chief of staff, USAF 1950–53; chief of staff, USAF 1953–57; chmn., Jt. Chiefs of Staff 1957–60. • Vice chmn., Holt, Rinehart & Winston, Inc. 1960–67; advisor, Barry Goldwater presidential campaign 1964; Republican candidate for U.S. Senate from NH 1966; dir., United Technology Labs., Inc.; consultant, Martin-Marietta, Inc., and Daisy Manufacturing Co. **Member** Natl. advisory bd., Amer. Security Council. **Honors** Forrestal Memorial Award, Natl. Security Industrial Assn. 1961; named to Aviation Hall of Fame 1978; Distinguished Service Medal, Army and Navy; Legion of Merit with Oak Leaf Cluster; Croix de Guerre with two Palms, and comdr., Légion d'Honneur, France; hon. KBE, U.K.; Medal of Merit with Swords, Poland; Order of the Sphinx, Greece; Aviation Cross, 1st Class, Peru; Order of White Elephant, Thailand; Medal of Merit, Egypt; many other military honors and awards.

APRIL

GOBIND BEHARI LAL

Reporter and science writer

***Born* Delhi, India, British Empire, 9 October 1889**

***Died* San Francisco, California, USA, 1 April 1982**

Gobind Behari Lal, winner of the Pulitzer Prize for distinguished reporting in 1937, was one of the first journalists to specialize in science writing. The son of the governor of the Indian state of Bikaner, he received bachelor's and master's degrees from the University of the Punjab and began his career as a journalist with the Delhi newspapers. In 1912 he came to the United States to do postgraduate research in Indian history at the University of California; he continued to do free-lance writing for magazines and newspapers, and in 1925 was hired by the Hearst Syndicate as a feature writer for the *San Francisco Examiner.* He worked for Hearst papers in San Francisco, New York, and Los Angeles for the rest of his career.

Lal interviewed many of the great scientists, writers, and statesmen of his time, including Albert Einstein, Enrico Fermi, Sinclair Lewis, Somerset Maugham, and Mohandas Gandhi. But his greatest interest was in science reporting: he sought "to create among the readers a lust for the knowledge of science, which destroys superstition and all kinds of false assumption and raises the power of the human brain." He was the first reporter to cover cancer research, and he regularly wrote on topics in science and medicine for several news services from the 1930s to the 1950s. In addition to the Pulitzer Prize, which was awarded jointly to Lal and four other journalists, he was the recipient of a Guggenheim Fellowship and awards from the American Medical Association and the American Association for the Advancement of Science. The government of India honored him in 1969 and 1973 for his work on behalf of the national independence movement. He died of cancer at the age of 92.

S.A.

Parents Bishan L., gov. of state of Bikaner, and Jagge (Devi) L. **Emigrated** to U.S. 1912. **Education** St. Stephen's High Sch., Delhi 1900–03; St. Stephen's Coll., Univ. of Punjab, B.Sc. 1907, M.A. 1908; research fellow in social sciences, Univ. of California 1912–17; Watumull Foundn. Research Fellow, Columbia Univ. 1946–48; postgrad. work at British univs. **Career** Asst. prof. of gen. science, Hindu Coll., Univ. of Punjab 1909–12; journalist and science writer since late 1900s; writer for Delhi newspapers ca. 1909–12; freelance science writer and lectr., U.S. since 1912; science ed., Universal Service, Intl. News Service, and American Weekly news service 1930s–50s; active in Indian independence movement. • Hearst newspaper chain: feature writer, *San Francisco Examiner* 1925–30; reporter for newspapers in NYC and L.A.; sr. ed. emeritus since 1954. **Officer** Pres., Natl. Assn. of Science Writers 1940–41. **Honors** Pulitzer Prize for distinguished reporting 1937; Westinghouse Distinguished Science Writers Award, Amer. Assn. for Advancement of Science 1946; Guggenheim Fellowship 1956; citation, AMA 1958; Taraknath Das Foundn. Prize, Columbia Univ. 1958; Padma Bushar 1969 and Tamra Patra 1973, India; hon. life member, Natl. Assn. of Science. **Author** *Joseph Mazzini as a Social Reformer,* 1915; *Politics and Science in India,* 1920; *The Chemistry of Personality,* 1932. **Contributor** Articles on science and social issues to newspapers and magazines.

JUNIUS B(OUTON) BIRD
Archeologist
***Born* Rye, New York, USA, 21 September 1907**
***Died* New York City, USA, 2 April 1982**

Archeologist Junius Bird was a seasoned field excavator who traveled from Greenland to Tierra del Fuego on expeditions for the American Museum of Natural History. He was an authority on pre-Columbian cultures and the world's leading expert on New World textiles.

The son of an entomologist and the younger brother of a paleontologist, Bird attended Columbia University for two years before going on his first archeological expedition, to Baffin Island, in 1927. Soon after, he joined the staff of the American Museum of Natural History, headquartered in New York City, for which he conducted archeological digs throughout the Americas, first as a field assistant (1931–39), then as assistant curator (1939–46) and associate curator (1946–57). In 1930 he searched for ancient Eskimo dwellings with the Bartlett Expedition to East Greenland, and in June of 1934 returned to the Arctic Circle to survey Eskimo sites with his bride of two weeks.

Bird made his first major archeological find in the mid-1930s during an expedition to Fell's Cave and Palli Aike Cave in southern Chile. There he found evidence of ancient human remains dating from circa 9000 B.C., the earliest then known in South America, intermingled with skeletons of extinct horses and the giant sloths called *Megatheria.* This gave rise to speculation that the now-extinct *Megatheria* may have been domesticated by these early Indians. Between 1946 and 1947 Bird supervised the excavation of a huge midden at Huaca Prieta in northern Peru, where thousands of textile fragments, dating from circa 3000 B.C., were unearthed. His analysis of the fabrics and patterns revealed that the Peruvian fishing-farming cultures of that period were much more sophisticated than had been assumed. He also conducted excavations closer to home, including sites in South Dakota, Louisiana, and Bear Mountain State Park in New York State, where a troop of Girl Scouts had accidentally uncovered an Iroquois camp four centuries old.

Courtesy of American Museum of Natural History

As curator of the museum's archeology department from 1957 to 1973, Bird organized several popular exhibitions, notably "Art and Life in Old Peru" (1962) and the permanent exhibition of pre-Columbian gold artifacts that opened in 1971. In 1957 he received the Viking Fund Award, a joint honor of the Society for American Archeology, the American Anthropological Society, and the American Association of Physical Anthropology. Upon his retirement he was named curator emeritus of South American archeology. He died after a long illness at the age of 74.

S.A.

Parents Henry B., entomologist, and Harriet B. **Married** Margaret McKelvy, archeologist, 1934: Robert McKelvy; Harry Bouton; Thomas Lee. **Education** Columbia Univ. 1925–27. **Career** With Amer. Mus. of Natural History, NYC: field asst. 1931–39; asst. curator of South American archeology 1939–46; assoc. curator 1946–57; curator of archeology 1957–73; organized exhibitions "Art and Life in Old Peru" 1962 and "Gold of the Americas" 1971; curator emeritus of South American archeology since 1973. • Archeologist, State Mus., PA 1929; consultant, Mus. of Primitive Art, NYC since 1956; instr., U.S. univs. **Field expeditions** Baffin Island 1927; Bering Straits 1928; Susquehanna and Juniata river valleys, PA 1929; Bartlett Expedition, East Greenland 1930; Yucatán and Honduras 1931; Cape York, Greenland 1932; Tierra del Fuego 1932–33; Southampton Island and Melville Peninsula, Canada 1933; Labrador 1934; Fell's Cave and Palli Aike Cave, southern Chile 1934–37; Alta. and Sask. 1936; South Dakota badlands 1940; northern Chile 1941–42; Bear Mt., NY 1943; Huaca Prieta, northern Peru 1946–47; Poverty Point, LA 1950. **Officer** Corresp. secty., New York Acad. of Sciences 1951–55; trustee, Textile Mus., Wash. DC since 1957; pres., Amer. Soc. of Archeologists 1961–62. **Honors** Viking Fund Award 1957; awards from govt. of Peru, Explorers Club, and the Wenner-Gren Foundn. for Anthropological Research; Junius Bird Expedition named for him, Amer. Mus. of Natural History; hon. degree from Wesleyan Univ. **Author** of numerous papers on the archeology of the Americas.

ANDREW J(OHN) BIEMILLER

Chief lobbyist, AFL-CIO

***Born* Sandusky, Ohio, USA, 23 July 1906**

***Died* Bethesda, Maryland, USA, 3 April 1982**

For a quarter of a century one of the most powerful and effective lobbyists in the U.S. Congress, Andy Biemiller was often called the voice of organized labor in America. He is credited with having influenced, in one capacity or another, every piece of liberal legislation passed since the 1950s, especially the civil-rights acts.

Born to Quaker parents, Biemiller was raised in Ohio by his widowed mother, who took in boarders to put her children through school. He received an A.B. from Cornell University before his 20th birthday. He was an instructor in history at Syracuse University from 1926 to 1928, then from 1929 to 1932 at the University of Pennsylvania, where he did graduate work on the history of the British trade-union movement. His growing political commitment to socialism led him to move to Wisconsin in 1932 to write for the *Milwaukee Leader,* a socialist newspaper. He was elected on the Progressive Party ticket to the Wisconsin legislature in 1936, and in 1939 became the party's floor leader. He served in the legislature until the war called him in 1941 to Washington, where he was for three years a deputy to Joseph Keenan, vice chairman for labor production on the War Production Board.

In 1944, Biemiller was elected to the U.S. Congress from a marginal district in Milwaukee. Defeated for reelection in the Republican landslide of 1946, he was elected again in 1948 and defeated twice more, in

1950 and 1952. In 1948, though out of office, he had the crucial role on the platform committee at the Democratic National Convention of drafting the minority civil-rights plank. Introduced at the convention by Hubert Humphrey, then adopted, the plank caused the Dixiecrats to bolt the party.

After a brief spell (1951–52) as special assistant to the secretary of the interior, Biemiller was hired by George Meany as legislative liaison for the AFL. When the AFL and CIO merged in 1956, he became legislative director of the new organization. Meany's advice, which Biemiller often repeated, was "Don't beg, don't threaten, and don't think you are always 100 percent right."

His first notable success came with the passage of the landmark Civil Rights Act of 1964. Labor was able to include in the bill, over Pres. Kennedy's objection, provision for a fair employment practices commission, a longtime labor goal. Title VII of the act established the Equal Employment Opportunity Commission, which became an increasingly effective force for equality in the workplace. Biemiller's relations with the Kennedy and Johnson administrations were always close and mutually supportive. "We were in agreement with the White House on almost every piece of legislation," he later recalled. These included bills on manpower training, education, and welfare, in addition to civil rights. He engineered labor's triumph over the American Medical Association in 1965 when the Medicare bill passed Congress. Biemiller remained with Meany and other conservative labor leaders firmly in Johnson's corner in support of the Vietnam War.

He worked actively for Humphrey's election in 1968, then returned to opposition during the Nixon administration. He later said he got the most satisfaction of his career out of leading the fight against Nixon's nominees to the Supreme Court, two of whom, Clement R. Haynsworth and G. Harrold Carswell, were rejected by the Senate. "Labor carried the load on that fight," he said. "We started out from scratch and nobody gave us a chance. But neither of those guys were fit to serve on the Court and it was the simplest kind of lobbying. It was a good battle." His campaign against William H. Rehnquist, a later Nixon nominee to the Court, was unsuccessful.

Biemiller's figure was every inch a pol's—large, amiable, slightly rumpled. His lobbying style was the old-fashioned one of buttonholing his favorite legislators—mainly powerful committee chairmen—in their offices, drinking their whiskey, coordinating their staffs on upcoming issues, and trying to purvey complete information, reliable gossip, sage advice, and appropriate campaign contributions. The thoroughgoing changes in Congress's rules during the 1970s had the effect of diminishing party discipline and hence the effectiveness of his lobbying. "It's been a lot of fun," he said on stepping down in 1978, "but Congress has changed tremendously and there isn't much fun left anymore."

He continued to reside near Washington after his retirement. He died of congestive heart failure at the age of 75. A.K.

Parents Andrew Frederick B., salesman, and Pearl (Weber) B. **Married** Hannah Perot Morris 1929: Andrew John, Jr., physician; Nancy Barbara Boerup. **Religion** Quaker. **Education** Sandusky High Sch., OH, grad. 1922; Cornell Univ., Ithaca, NY, A.B. 1926; Univ. of Pennsylvania 1928–32. **Career** History instr., Syracuse Univ. 1926–28; history instr., Univ. of Pennsylvania 1929–31; instr., summer sch. for workers, Bryn Mawr Coll., PA 1930–31; reporter, *Milwaukee Leader* 1932. • With labor orgs.: delegate, Philadelphia Central Labor Union 1929–31; member, Amer. Fedn. of Teachers since 1929; delegate 1934–37 and exec. bd. member 1935–36, Milwaukee Federated Trades Council, WI; special organizer, Wisconsin State Fedn. of Labor 1937–41; dir. of political education, Upholsterers' Intl. Union of North America 1947–48; legislative rep., Amer. Fedn. of Labor 1953–56. • With AFL-CIO: legislative rep. 1955; dir., Dept. of Legislation 1956–78; chief lobbyist 1956–78; chmn., staff cttee. on atomic energy. • Politics and govt.: education dir., Socialist Party, Milwaukee 1933–36; joined Democratic Party 1936; Democratic member 1937–41 and floor leader 1939–41, WI legislature; special asst. to vice chmn. for labor production, War Production Bd. 1941–44; Democratic rep. to U.S. Congress from WI 5th district 1945–47, 1949–51, served on Naval Affairs Cttee.; member, platform cttee., Democratic Natl. Convention 1948; special asst. to secty. of the interior 1951–52; public relations counselor, Wash. DC 1952–78; member, labor-management advisory cttee., Atomic Energy Commn. 1957; labor advisor, U.S. delegation to GATT Conference 1957, 1961; member, citizens' advisory cttee., Outdoor Recreation Resources Review Commn. 1960–61; management-labor textile advisory cttee., Dept. of Commerce 1961–78; member, Presidential Task Force on Career Advancement 1966–67; active in Hubert Humphrey's presidential campaign 1968; member, consumer cttee. on automobile insurance and compensation, Dept. of Transportation. **Member** Natl. Petroleum

Council 1975; Democratic Party; Delta Kappa Epsilon; Newspaper Guild; Natl. Press Club; Kenwood Golf and Country Club. **Honors** Dewey Award, United Fedn. of Teachers, Amer. Fedn. of Teachers 1972; award for outstanding leadership on civil-rights issues, League for Individual Democracy. **Contributor** of articles on politics and labor to *American Federationist, Yale Law Review, Industrial Labor Quarterly,* other jrnls.

Further reading Joseph C. Goulden, *Meany,* 1972.

WARREN OATES
Film and television actor
Born **Depoy, Kentucky, USA, 5 July 1930**
Died **Los Angeles, California, USA, 3 April 1982**

During the 1950s and 1960s, few film or television westerns could achieve the proper degree of gritty authenticity without an appearance by Warren Oates doing one of his expert turns as a seedy redneck or quick-fisted tough. Oates's mature work for adventurous directors such as Sam Peckinpah and Monte Hellman earned him a reputation as one of Hollywood's most versatile and talented character actors, and proved, according to critic David Thomson, that "a plain, balding man with a toothy grin could carry a movie." He invariably played small men harshly used by life and always on the edge of crime, violence, or insanity, but he brought to these roles a penetrating honesty and moral perception that lifted them above the stereotypical.

Oates was born in the coal-mining region of western Kentucky, where his father ran a general store, and spent a good part of his childhood picking fruit, loading sand, and getting into fights. After a hitch in the Marines as an aircraft mechanic, he studied acting at the University of Louisville for three years and then headed for New York City, where he survived on odd jobs while playing minor roles in television dramas. He followed the industry when it moved to Hollywood in the mid-1950s and established himself as a dependable bit player in such western series as "Have Gun, Will Travel," "Gunsmoke," "Trackdown," and "Wanted, Dead or Alive." "I was the fourth heavy," he explained, "the nutty son who was quiet and would suddenly explode. If you exploded convincingly, maybe next time you got the chance to play the third heavy, and if you did that well, you got to be second heavy."

Oates began working in films in 1958 and was hired by Peckinpah for three influential westerns: *Ride the High Country* (1962), *Major Dundee* (1965), and *The Wild Bunch* (1969). By the early 1970s he was getting lead roles and resoundingly favorable reviews. He played a pair of twin brothers with converging identities in Monte Hellman's *The Shooting* (1966), a malevolent Southerner in *In the Heat of the Night* (Norman Jewison, 1969), a schizophrenic car driver in *Two-Lane Blacktop* (1971, also by Hellman), the lead in John Milius's *Dillinger* (1974), and a doomed whaler in Peckinpah's *The White Dawn* (1974). In *Bring Me the Head of Alfredo Garcia* (Peckinpah, 1974), he made the most of a

juicy part as a down-at-heels American tracking a bandit through Mexico for a million-dollar reward. He excelled in putting across the kind of rough morality, bloody but sincere, on which most westerns are based. Many of his movies appealed to a specialized audience, went into limited release, and are rarely shown, but he still managed to build up something of a cult following.

After weathering a succession of crises, marital and physical, in the early 1970s, Oates settled down in Hollywood with his second wife and two children. His last films were *Stripes* (1980), a service comedy, and *The Border* (1981), with his close friend Jack Nicholson. He died of a heart attack at the age of 51. S.A.

Father a storekeeper and itinerant laborer. **Married** (1) . . . (div. ca. 1971). (2) Vickery. **Children** Two. **Religion** Raised a Baptist. **Education** Public schs., Louisville, KY; Univ. of Louisville 1950–53; studied acting, NYC mid-1950s. **Mil. service** Airplane mechanic, U.S. Marines 1948–50. **Career** Dishwasher, hat checker, stunt tester, other odd jobs NYC early 1950s; TV actor since 1953; film actor since 1958. **Films** *Up Periscope,* 1958; *Yellowstone Kelly,* 1959; *The Rise and Fall of Legs Diamond,* 1960; *Private Property,* 1960; *Ride the High Country,* 1962; *Hero's Island,* 1962; *Mail Order Bride,* 1963; *The Rounders,* 1965; *Major Dundee,* 1965; *Return of the Seven,* 1966; *The Shooting,* 1966; *Welcome to Hard Times,* 1967; *In the Heat of the Night,* 1967; *The Split,* 1968; *Crooks and Coronets,* 1969; *The Wild Bunch,* 1969; *Easy Rider,* 1969; *Smith,* 1969; *Barquero,* 1970; *There Was a Crooked Man,* 1970; *Two-Lane Blacktop,* 1971; *The Hired Hand,* 1971; *Chandler,* 1972; *The Thief Who Came to Dinner,* 1973; *Tom Sawyer,* 1973; *Kid Blue,* 1973; *Dillinger,* 1974; *Cockfighter,* 1974; *Badlands,* 1974; *Bring Me the Head of Alfredo Garcia,* 1974; *The White Dawn,* 1974; *Race with the Devil,* 1975; *92 in the Shade,* 1976; *Drum,* 1976; *Dixie Dynamite,* 1976; *China 9, Liberty 37,* 1978; *The Brink's Job,* 1978; *Sleeping Dogs,* 1978; *1941,* 1979; *Stripes,* 1981; *The Border,* 1982; many others. **Television series** "Have Gun, Will Travel"; "Gunsmoke"; "Wanted, Dead or Alive"; "Playhouse 90"; "Rifleman"; "Lawman"; "Laramie"; "Bat Masterson"; "Bonanza"; "Stoney Burke"; "Twilight Zone"; "Outer Limits"; "Big Valley"; many others. **Television movies** *My Old Man,* 1980; *Baby Makes Six; East of Eden.* **Interview** F. Albert Bomar and Alan J. Warren, "Warren Oates," in *Film Comment,* Feb. 1981.

ABE FORTAS
Associate justice of the U.S. Supreme Court
***Born* Memphis, Tennessee, USA, 19 June 1910**
***Died* Washington, D.C., USA, 5 April 1982**

Abe Fortas had been for years one of Washington's most influential attorneys when in 1965 his old friend and client Lyndon Johnson named him to the U.S. Supreme Court. Three years later the president failed to secure Fortas's confirmation as chief justice, and in 1969 a scandal forced his resignation. His withdrawal from the Court marked the beginning of the end of its long period of liberal activism in constitutional interpretation.

Fortas was the youngest of five children of an Orthodox Jewish cabinetmaker who had emigrated to the United States from England early in the first decade of the century. The young man attended public schools while supplementing his family's modest income by playing the violin at dances. He attended Southwestern College in Memphis, graduating in 1930, and was accepted at Yale Law School. At Yale he did astonishingly well, graduating Phi Beta Kappa and first in his class; he was editor in chief of the *Yale Law Journal* and became a special favorite of William O. Douglas, a professor at the law school, who managed to get his protégé hired as an assistant professor. Fortas remained in New Haven until 1937, much of the time commuting to Washington on weekends and holidays to work part-time for the Franklin Roosevelt administration. He was assistant chief of the legal division of the Agricultural Adjustment Administration in 1933–34, then from 1934 until 1937 served as assistant director of a corporate-reorganization plan for the Securities and Exchange Commission (SEC), of which Douglas had been appointed chairman.

In 1937, Fortas left Yale for a full-time appointment as legal consultant to the SEC, and the following year was named assistant director of the commission's public utilities section. From 1939 to 1940 he was general counsel to the Public Works Administration, then became director of the power division in the Interior Department, which was headed by Harold Ickes, one of the most astute and powerful politicians of the New Deal era. He rose quickly under Ickes's tutelage, was appointed undersecretary of the interior in 1942, and served ably as Ickes's chief aide until 1945, when he left briefly to join the service. Discharged after only a month because of an old vision disorder, he was appointed by Pres. Harry Truman to serve as legal advisor on the U.S. delegation to the 1945 San Francisco organizational meeting of the United Nations and to the 1946 London meeting of the General Assembly. Yet he found he was no longer satisfied with government service, and in common with many New Deal lawyers decided to go into private practice.

Fortas's initial partner was Thurman Arnold, a former federal judge who had headed the antitrust division in the Justice Department. Later they took on as a founding partner Paul Porter, another New Dealer who had directed the Office of Price Administration and the Federal Communications Commission. Arnold, Fortas & Porter became, in short order, one of the capital's most successful firms, with Fortas by all accounts its organizing genius. His work during two decades as senior partner involved several distinct areas: representing the firm's large corporate clients, which included Pan American, Lever Brothers, Coca-Cola, and Philip Morris; defending the victims of the McCarthyite persecution of the 1950s, among whom Owen Lattimore was his best-known client; and defending indigents in criminal cases, a practice that sometimes led to landmark court decisions. Of these, the most famous was *Gideon* v. *Wainwright* (1963), in which Fortas persuaded the Supreme Court to rule unanimously requiring the states to provide free legal counsel for every poor defendant charged with more than a trivial crime. His last and best-known area of involvement was in the personal and political affairs of Lyndon Johnson.

The two met in the mid-1930s, when Johnson was an ambitious young aide to a Texas congressman, and their relationship flourished as both moved up the ladder of power in Washington. In 1948, Rep. Johnson, having been declared the winner of the Texas Democratic primary for the U.S. Senate by 87 disputed votes, had his name struck from the ballot by a federal judge in Texas. In desperation he turned for help to Fortas, who promptly appealed to Justice Hugo Black and won a reversal of the order as improper federal interference in state election procedures. By his timely intervention, Fortas probably saved Johnson's career, and the new senator never forgot it. Fortas was later to draw up a trust to separate Vice Pres. Johnson from control over the family television holdings. When Pres. John Kennedy was assassinated on 22 November 1963, Fortas was one of the first people Johnson called from Dallas, and he was waiting by the steps of Air Force One when the new president reached Washington. He took on the organization of the Warren Commission that investigated Pres. Kennedy's assassination, was chief troubleshooter during the Walter Jenkins affair (just as he had effectively doused many of the fires around the Bobby Baker scandal several years before), and provided advice to the president on such matters as the U.S. invasion of the Dominican Republic and the conduct of the

Vietnam War. On the last subject he was by most accounts an extreme hawk. He was offered the post of attorney general when Robert Kennedy resigned in 1964, but turned it down: he knew how mercilessly demanding Johnson was to work for, had no desire to return to government service, and greatly valued the independence and financial rewards offered by private practice.

Yet when Justice Arthur Goldberg resigned from the Court to become ambassador to the United Nations, Johnson persuaded Fortas to take his place, naming him on 28 July 1965. "This is a case," said the president in announcing the nomination, "of the job seeking out the man." The appointment received wide approval. Although he was the first man named to the Court straight from the private practice of law since 1931, and although he had to answer to charges of cronyism before the Senate Judiciary Committee, Fortas easily won confirmation and took office on 4 October. His was the so-called Jewish seat on the Court, a tradition that had begun in 1916 with the appointment of Justice Louis Brandeis and that has been inoperative since the beginning of Richard Nixon's presidency.

Fortas's tenure on the Court was marked by a number of important decisions in which he often, as Goldberg had, cast the decisive vote. It was this swing vote that made possible the landmark ruling in *Miranda* v. *Arizona* (1966), which extended many of the principles enunciated in the *Gideon* decision, placing limits on the freedom of the police to interrogate criminal suspects. His vote was crucial in two decisions that declared state-required loyalty oaths for public employees unconstitutional. His most famous opinion, *In re Gault* (1967), was an important milestone in juvenile justice, establishing due process and fair treatment for young offenders caught up in the often haphazard and semijudicial procedures of the U.S. juvenile court system. "Under our Constitution," read his most memorable line from *Gault,* "the condition of being a boy does not justify a kangaroo court." Though most of his votes and concurring opinions were firmly within the liberal traditions of the Warren Court, others dismayed his supporters. Having been a corporate lawyer, he was generally antagonistic to federal regulatory law and sympathetic to corporate defendants in antitrust cases; and he was far less liberal than the majority in cases involving freedom of the press. In *Ginzburg* v. *United States* his vote allowed a five-to-four decision that sent publisher Ralph Ginzburg to prison for "pandering" and obscenity.

Johnson named Fortas chief justice in June 1968, two months after withdrawing from the presidential race. As a lame-duck president, Johnson had only limited power to influence the Senate confirmation process, and the opinion was widely expressed that the new president, to be elected that November, should not be denied the right to nominate the next chief justice. The issue of cronyism was raised again, for it was well known that Fortas had never ceased giving political counsel to Johnson. Fortas took the unprecedented step (for a nominee to the chief justiceship) of appearing before the Judiciary Committee to answer the charge. "The president," he allowed, "does me the honor of having confidence in my ability, apparently, to analyze a situation and to state the pros and cons." Then he read a carefully annotated list of past justices who had served past presidents. It was a performance that satisfied few. A minority coalition of Republicans and Southern Democrats, powerful and antiliberal, decided to filibuster the nomination. They succeeded in preventing a vote, and on 3 October Johnson withdrew the nomination, calling the decision "historically and constitutionally tragic." He sent up no other nomination. Fortas returned to the Court as associate justice, and Earl Warren, though in poor health, remained as chief justice, determined, some said, not to allow his old enemy Nixon to have the chance of replacing him.

Fortas's downfall came in May 1969, when *Life* magazine reported that in 1966, while on the Court, he had accepted $20,000 from Louis E. Wolfson, who by mid-1969 was in federal prison for stock manipulation. Fortas had returned the money a year later, once Wolfson was indicted, and in a carefully crafted statement issued the day the *Life* article appeared he completely denied wrongdoing. Yet he never addressed himself to the obvious impropriety of his actions, to his seeming inability, ever since he joined the Court, to stop behaving like a Washington lawyer. His old enemies in Congress immediately demanded his impeachment. After Attorney Gen. John Mitchell intervened with Chief Justice Warren, claiming (falsely, as it later turned out) that the government had "far more serious" information than had been made public, Fortas saw he had to resign. He did so on 16 May, the first justice in history to leave the Court under the pressure of public criticism.

By the spring of 1970, he had started a new law firm, Fortas & Koven, and had returned, only slightly chastened, to the comfortable Washington life he had enjoyed before 1965. His wife, Carolyn Agger Fortas, whom he had married in 1935, remained a senior partner and top tax expert in his old firm, now known as Arnold & Porter. He never published the memoirs he reportedly wrote during the 1970s, always publicly claiming that he had taken a vow of perpetual silence in the matter of his past associations. He remained throughout his life a passionately engaged amateur violinist. Shortly before his death he appeared in a case before the Court for the first time since his resignation. He said in an interview at the time that he aimed to continue in the law "until my clients retire me or the Lord retires me." He died two weeks later in his home of a ruptured aorta. A.K.

Parents William F., cabinetmaker, and Ray (Berson) F. **Married** Carolyn Eugenia Agger, economist and lawyer, 1935. **Religion** Jewish. **Education** South Side High Sch., Memphis, TN; Southwestern Coll., Memphis, A.B. 1930; Yale Law Sch., LL.B. 1933. **Mil. service** Joined U.S. Navy 1945; received medical discharge. **Career** Ed. in chief, *Yale Law Journal* 1932–33; asst. prof. of law 1933–37 and visiting prof. of law 1946–47, Yale Univ.; partner, Arnold, Fortas & Porter law firm, Wash. DC 1946–65; partner, Fortas & Koven law firm, Wash. DC since 1969. • With U.S. Govt.: asst. chief, Legal Div., Agricultural Adjustment Admin. 1933–34; asst. dir. of corporate-reorganization study 1934–37, legal consultant 1937–38, and asst. dir. of Public Utilities Div. 1938–39, Securities Exchange Commn.; gen. counsel, Public Works Admin. 1939–40; dir., Div. of Power 1941–42, and undersecty. 1942–46, Dept. of Interior; member, Bd. of Legal Examiners, Civil Service Commn. 1941–43; member, Pres.'s Cttee. to Study Changes in Organic Law of Puerto Rico 1943; advisor, U.S. delegation to U.N. organizational conferences, S.F. 1945, London 1946; assoc. justice, U.S. Supreme Court 1965–69; member, Pres.'s Cttee. on Equal Opportunity in Armed Forces; member, Cttee. on Rules of Practice and Procedure. • Member, Judicial Conference of U.S. and District of Columbia Circuit; member, Natl. Citizens' Cttee. for Community Relations; member, advisory cttee. on free press—fair trial, Amer. Bar Assn. **Officer** Dir.: (also v.p. and gen. counsel) Greatamerica Corp.; (also v.p.) Federated Dept. Stores; SuCrest Corp.; Madison Natl. Bank; Franklin Life Insurance Co.; Braniff Airlines. • Trustee: Carnegie Hall Corp.; Carnegie Hall Intl.; Washington Gall. of Modern Art; White Psychiatric Foundn.; Kennedy Center for Performing Arts; Festival Casals, Inc.; Russell Sage Foundn.; Marlborough Sch. of Music; Amer. Judicature Soc.; (also chmn., bd. of dirs.) Kennedy Center Productions Inc. • Overseer, Coll. of the Virgin Islands. **Member** Visiting cttee., Univ. of Chicago Law Sch.; advisory council, Sch. of Advanced Intl. Studies, Johns Hopkins Univ.; Federal Bar Assn.; Amer. Bar Assn.; Order of Coif; Phi Beta Kappa; Omicron Delta Kappa. **Contributor** to legal and other periodicals.

Further reading Fred Rodell, "The Complexities of Mr. Justice Fortas," in *New York Times Magazine,* 28 July 1968; Victor S. Navasky, "In Washington, You Just Don't Not Return a Call from Abe Fortas," in *New York Times Magazine,* 1 Aug. 1971; Catherine A. Barnes, *Men of the Supreme Court,* 1978.

HELEN LAWRENSON
Writer and magazine editor
***Born* LaFargeville, New York, USA, 1 October 1907**
***Died* New York City, New York, USA, 5 April 1982**

Helen Lawrenson was a witty, engaging writer and woman-about-town who for four years during the early 1930s was an editor of *Vanity Fair* magazine, one of the most distinguished and influential American publications of its time. She began to write for *Esquire* in 1936, and her first article for that magazine, "Latins Are Lousy Lovers," has always been regarded by *Esquire* editors as "the most notorious piece" in the magazine's history. It was also the first piece contributed by a woman.

She was born Helen Brown in upstate New York to a family of moderate means, attended Vassar College for two years, and found her first job on the *Syracuse Herald,* "working," she recalled later, "with hard-boiled *Front Page* types (at least, that's the way we all tried to act)." She moved to New York in 1930 and, after a stint working in a Womrath bookstore, was hired in late 1931 by Condé Nast, owner and publisher of *Vogue* and *Vanity Fair,* to join the staff of the latter magazine, whose editor was Frank Crowninshield and whose staff included Clare Boothe Brokaw, later Clare Boothe Luce.

Courtesy of Random House

She began to frequent the smart café society enjoyed by her colleagues, and honed her naturally acute writing style to rapier sharpness by doing captions, film criticism, and a column, "The Doe at Eve," which contained tart descriptions of all the famous nightclubs and former speakeasies of New York. In 1933 she succeeded Luce as managing editor. She also became the lover of Condé Nast, by most accounts a rather stiff man of grim demeanor who had the entrepreneur's intuition of surrounding himself with brilliant people, both on his magazines and, by and large, at his frequent and extraordinarily lavish parties. Yet though she professed to find him a "kind, gentle, tolerant man," she grew weary of his anti-New Deal politics and the selfish ignorance—or even open fascism—of much of high society. "I certainly never felt as if I belonged and, if the others could have read my thoughts, they would have shrunk from me, aghast."

She left *Vanity Fair* in 1936 and began to write for *Esquire,* though her affair with Nast continued for some time longer. She had several other lovers, including the financier Bernard Baruch and the gangster Bumpy Johnson, and she was unhappily married twice. "Latins Are Lousy Lovers" caused a considerable sensation, and though it was written under a pseudonym, her authorship was quickly discovered. Its opinions and revelations, however unheard-of at the time, would raise few eyebrows today.

In 1939 she met and married her third husband, Jack Lawrenson, a charismatic Irish-born leftist who was a co-founder of the National Maritime Union, and she lived for many years with him in Greenwich Village, shunning the glamorous life she had led. She continued to write for *Esquire,* and over the years her by-line appeared there more often than that of any other writer; she also wrote for an assortment of periodicals ranging from *Rolling Stone* to *Reader's Digest.* She was at her husband's side as he attempted unsuccessfully to reform the violent and crime-ridden longshoremen's organization. After a long and dangerous struggle against Joseph

Courtesy of Harry Benson

Curran, the head of the union, and his goons and police backers, Jack Lawrenson was forced to resign from the union's vice presidency in 1950. Together they managed a moving and storage business in the Village until he died in 1957, a broken man, and she went to live abroad. Their daughter Johanna is married to political activist Abbie Hoffman.

Lawrenson, who always claimed she never liked to write, finally completed her memoirs of the 1930s and later decades, which she published as *Stranger at the Party* (1975) and *Whistling Girl* (1978). Her only novel, *Dance of Scorpions,* a treatment of life in the 1960s, was to appear a few months after her death. She bristled when some reviewers suggested that *Stranger at the Party* might not contain the whole truth. "I wouldn't deign to make up stories, especially about well-known people. I'm noted for being accurate. I never lie, but I sometimes tell too much. I'm not a celebrity. I'm not a film star. Nobody was waiting for my autobiography, so I *had* to tell the truth."

Lawrenson died at the age of 74 of coronary artery disease and diabetes. A.K.

Born Helen Strough Brown; also wrote as Helen Brown Norden. **Father** Lloyd E. Brown. **Married** (1) . . . (div.). (2) . . . (div.). (3) Jack Lawrenson, co-founder of Natl. Maritime Union, 1939 (d. 1957): Johanna Hoffman, model, b. 1941; Kevin, photographer, b. 1946 (d. 1979). **Religion** Episcopalian. **Education** Goodyear-Burlingame Sch., Syracuse, NY 1915–22; Bradford Acad., MA, grad. 1924; Vassar Coll., Poughkeepsie, NY, 1924–26. **Career** Reporter, *Syracuse Herald,* NY 1926–30; worked in Womrath bookstore, NYC 1930; staff writer 1931–33 and managing ed. 1933–36, *Vanity Fair* mag., NYC; writer for *Esquire* and other mags. since 1936; co-mgr. of moving and storage business, NYC through 1957. **Member** Democratic Party. **Author** *Stranger at the Party* (memoirs), 1975; *Whistling Girl* (memoirs), 1978; *Dance of Scorpions* (novel), 1982. **Contributor** of articles to *Vogue, Glamour, House and Garden, Town and Country, Collier's, Coronet, Harper's Bazaar,* many other mags.

Further reading Caroline Seebohm, *The Man Who Was Vogue,* 1982.

PAVEL (ALEKSEYEVICH) ROTMISTROV
Chief of Soviet Army armored units
Born **Skovorovo (now Kalinin region), Russia, 23 June 1901**
Death announced **Moscow, USSR, 7 April 1982**

Pavel Rotmistrov was one of the most brilliant and daring Allied tank commanders of World War II. He was responsible for a major victory, the biggest armored engagement of the war, during the battles of Kursk and Orel in 1943. He later rose to the top of the ranks to become, in 1962, the chief marshal of all Soviet armored forces.

Rotmistrov, the son of a blacksmith, joined the Communist Party and the Red Army in 1919 and fought in the civil war, notably in the suppression of the naval revolt against the

Bolsheviks at Kronstadt. He spent much of the 1920s studying military science, and graduated from the Frunze Military Academy in 1931 at the head of his class. He had decided at the academy that he was most interested in tank warfare, and mastered that specialty during the 1930s. He was a colonel and commander of a tank brigade in the Russo-Finnish War of 1939–40, and again during the Nazi invasion of the Soviet Union in 1941. His first distinction in battle was gained in the winter of 1941–42 when the Red Army prevented the German juggernaut from taking Moscow, and unusually rapid promotions followed. He saw action in most of the important armored contests of the Eastern theater: he commanded the 3rd Guards Tank Corps in the defense of Stalingrad, and from February 1943 was a lieutenant general commanding the 5th Guards Tank Army on the Steppe front in the Ukraine under Marshal Ivan Konev.

On 12 July 1943, near the village of Prokhorovka, south of Kursk, more than 1,500 German and Soviet tanks fought what is still the largest armored battle on record. Rotmistrov sent his tank army through the German armored line, and for an entire day, amid utter chaos, the two equally matched forces tried to destroy each other. The strategy of battle often seemed to be forgotten as both sides resorted to suicide charges, roaring up to an enemy vehicle and firing at point-blank range. When the smoke cleared the Soviets were the clear winners, as the Germans had lost more than 300 tanks and 10,000 men. Soviet tank superiority was demonstrated, and the Nazi advance into the Ukraine was definitively checked.

Rotmistrov continued to serve under Marshal Konev, a close friend, for another year. In February 1944 he was promoted to tank marshal, and the following July, in a lightning-swift drive against the routed German armies, his armored units recaptured the city of Minsk, having covered 80 miles in two days. In August he was named deputy commander of the Red Army's armored and mechanized troops, and held that command until the fall of Berlin.

After the war, Rotmistrov remained in East Germany for a short time to command the armored wing of the army of occupation, then held a similar command in the Far East from 1945 until 1947. Beginning in 1948, however, he turned his attention to military instruction. He was successively head of the department of armored warfare (1948–56) and deputy head of the department of strategy and tactics (1956–58) at the Voroshilov Higher Military Academy. He then headed the Military Academy of Armored Troops (1958–64), was assistant defense minister for military education (1964–68), and in 1968 was named inspector general of the ministry's group of inspectors general. His promotion to chief marshal of armored troops occurred in 1962.

He received many decorations, chief among which were five Orders of Lenin, four Orders of the Red Banner, and the Order of the October Revolution. He earned a doctorate in military science in 1956, and was the author of several articles on the theory and history of armored warfare and a book on the subject, *Time and Tanks* (1972). A.K.

Father a blacksmith. **Education** Frunze Military Acad., grad. 1931; doctorate in military science 1956. **Career** Joined CPSU and Red Army 1919; served in civil war; col. and comdr. of tank brigade, Russo-Finnish War 1939–40; chief of staff, 3rd Mechanized Corps 1941; comdr., 8th Tank Brigade 1941–42; comdr., 3rd Guards Tank Brigade, then 7th Guards Tank Corps, 1942; comdr., 3rd Guards Tank Corps, Stalingrad 1942–43; lt. gen. and comdr., 5th Guards Tank Army, Ukraine 1943–44; appointed tank marshal 1944; deputy comdr. of tank and mechanized troops 1944–45; comdr. of tank and mechanized troops, Soviet Forces Group, Germany 1945 and Far East 1945–47; head of dept. of armored warfare 1948–56 and deputy head of dept. of strategy and tactics 1956–58, Voroshilov Higher Military Acad.; head of Military Acad. of Armored Troops 1958–64; appointed chief marshal of armored troops 1962; asst. minister of defense for higher military education 1964–68; appointed inspector gen., Group of Inspectors Gen., Ministry of Defense 1968. **Honors** Hero of Soviet Union 1965; Order of Lenin five times; Order of October Revolution; Order of Red Banner four times; Order of Suvorov, 1st and 2nd Class; Order of Kutuzov, 1st Class; Order of Red Star; various medals; five foreign orders and medals. **Author** *Vremya i tanki* [*Time and Tanks*], 1972.

LOWELL EDWARDS
Inventor
***Born* Oregon, USA, 1898**
***Died* Oregon, USA, 8 April 1982**

Although medical researchers are still seeking to create a satisfactory artificial heart, mechanical heart valves have been widely used since the early 1960s. The most successful of these, the Starr-Edwards mitral valve, was the creation of a retired inventor, Lowell Edwards, who built the first prototype in a backyard toolshed.

Edwards had previously had a long career with the airline, paper, and pulp industries. Among his earlier inventions were a fuel-booster pump, still used by major aircraft manufacturers, and a hydraulic tree-bark remover. After his first retirement in the mid-1950s, he became interested in biomechanical engineering, particularly in the problem of designing an artificial heart.

In discussions with surgeons at the University of Oregon Medical School, Edwards learned that artificial replacements for the mitral valve—the left ventricular valve that controls the flow of oxygenated blood from the left auricle of the heart—had been implanted in several patients, but with poor results. The valves tended to stick, and their loud popping noise had driven some patients to commit suicide. Abandoning attempts to build a complete mechanical heart, he designed, in collaboration with cardiac surgeon Albert Starr, a new and virtually silent mitral valve, doing much of the work in a tiny laboratory behind his Oregon home. Called a caged-ball valve, it consists of a silastic rubber ball that moves back and forth within a stainless-steel cage. The valve is attached to the ventricular wall by a knitted Teflon sewing ring. As the left auricle contracts in a normal heartbeat, pressure in the chamber pushes the ball to the end of the cage and opens the valve. When the left ventricle contracts, in turn, to push blood through the aorta, the occluding ball is forced upward, seating in the Teflon ring and closing the valve.

The Starr-Edwards mitral valve was successfully implanted by Starr for the first time in a 52-year-old man in September 1960. In 1961 Edwards founded Lowell Edwards Laboratories in Santa Ana, California, to handle production of the valve, which climbed to over 24,000 units within four years. In 1966 the firm was purchased by the American Hospital Supply Corp. By the early 1980s, some 160,000 improved valves in the mitral, aortic, and tricuspid positions were in use, with a high survival rate for patients.

Edwards, who was awarded the Layman's Citation of the American Medical Association for his heart valve in 1963, continued his research into biomechanical devices until the late 1970s. He died of complications following abdominal surgery at the age of 84. S.A.

Married Margaret. **Career** Inventor for aircraft, pulp, and paper industries ca. 1920s–ca. 1957; founder 1961 and pres. 1961–66, Edwards Labs., Santa Ana, CA. **Honors** Layman's Citation, AMA 1963. **Patents** Hydraulic tree debarker; airline fuel booster pump; Starr-Edwards heart valve; many others.

Further reading Douglas Behrendt and W. Gerald Austen, "Current Status of Prosthetic Valves for Heart Valve Replacement," in *Valvular Heart Disease,* 1974.

ROBERT (HANS GUNTHER) HAVEMANN
Writer, chemist, and East German political dissident
***Born* Munich, Germany, 11 March 1910**
***Died* Grünheide, near East Berlin, East Germany, 8 April 1982**

Robert Havemann was a physical chemist by training and a professor of chemistry who became one of East Germany's leading dissidents. A committed Marxist since the 1930s, his critiques of the German Democratic Republic were at first tolerated, then banned. Ousted from his teaching position and the party since 1964, he nevertheless steadfastly refused to be exiled and continued to insist on the correctness of his Marxism.

The son of a teacher and an artist, he joined the German Communist Party (Kommunistische Partei Deutschlands; KPD) in 1932 while studying chemistry in Berlin. The following year, with the Nazis in power and Havemann in the antifascist underground, he was appointed lecturer at the Kaiser Wilhelm Institute of Chemistry and Electrochemistry. In 1938 he helped found the underground group called European Union, which was able to organize the rescue of Jews and political prisoners. The Gestapo arrested him and other European Union leaders in 1943 and hanged all but Havemann in May of the following year. His expertise in physical chemistry and the work he had done for the war effort undoubtedly saved his life. He was imprisoned for several months in the Brandenburg fortress, where he contracted tuberculosis and typhus, and where he continued to participate in underground activities with fellow KPD members, among whom was Erich Honecker, now head of the East German Communist Party (Sozialistische Einheitspartei Deutschlands; SED).

Havemann returned to the Kaiser Wilhelm Institute in 1945, and in 1950 was made professor at Humboldt University in Berlin. He welcomed the arrival of communism in Germany, though not the country's partition. He joined the SED on its foundation in 1949 and later that year was among the founders of the Volkskammer, the East German parliament. During the 1950s he probably worked for the Soviet Union's nuclear-research program; he was awarded East Germany's National Prize in 1959.

Havemann first came into official disfavor in 1964, after delivering a series of lectures at Humboldt University called "Scientific Aspects of Philosophical Problems." In these he criticized the philosophical proponents of dialectical materialism for their dogmatic unwillingness to adapt their political reality to scientific change. Though he was far from criticizing basic Communist precepts, he ridiculed institutionalized dogmatism as the "Main Administration of Eternal Truths." The lectures were published in West Germany the same year under the title *Dialectics Without Dogma.* He quickly lost his university post and was expelled from the party. In 1966 his membership in the Academy of Sciences was annulled.

Havemann always believed in the inherent superiority of Socialistic Eastern Europe over the West. "Bourgeois society," he wrote in 1980, "is still capitalistic but hardly democratic; and real socialism is no longer capitalistic, but not yet socialist and not yet democratic." This "real" socialism, he believed, had not yet come into being anywhere in the world and was greatly hindered in the Eastern bloc by the persistence of dogmatic Stalinism; he considered communism a "productive utopia" that could never be arrived at, only striven for. This was the grossest heresy in the rigidly dogmatic state of East Germany, yet Havemann was never imprisoned, possibly because he still had some friends—like Honecker—in the political hierarchy. His political writings, however, were never allowed to be published in his own country: West German houses brought out his books, and he was harassed during the 1970s for receiving royalty income from the West.

He strongly supported both the Prague Spring of 1968, which was quickly annihilated by troops of the Warsaw Pact, and the Solidarity movement in Poland, which was crushed in late 1981 by the imposition of martial law. He treated the former phenomenon in his best-known book, *Questions, Answers, Questions,* which was published throughout the West in 1971–72. Following the end of the Polish experiment, he wrote a somewhat optimistic letter to *L'Unità,* the newspaper of the Italian Communist Party, in which he said that

Solidarity would remain a central force in Polish society and might even become allied with a "renewed" Polish Communist Party. *Questions, Answers, Questions* also describes the grim similarities between his interrogations at the hands of the Gestapo in 1943 and the Bureau of State Security in 1966.

Havemann risked grave official displeasure in 1976 when he organized resistance to the decision to deport his friend Wolf Biermann, a well-known East German dissident, poet, and musician. He ran an even greater risk in making public a letter he wrote to Leonid Brezhnev in late 1981, just before the Soviet president's visit to West Germany, in which he demanded that all "occupation troops" be withdrawn from the two German states, which could then become a nuclear-free zone, reunited and free to choose a common destiny. In his last years, in fact, Havemann was one of the most revered leaders of the East German antinuclear peace movement, which was strictly discouraged if not absolutely outlawed. One of his last public statements was a letter to the leftist newspaper *Frankfurter Rundschau,* claiming that the East German peace movement was in full swing and would eventually, allied with similar movements in other countries, lead to a complete transformation of Europe's postwar political stagnation.

Although no East German news organ reported his death, and there was reportedly a heavy police presence at his funeral, several hundred people turned out to pay their respects to Havemann in East Berlin on 18 April. A.K.

Parents Father a teacher, mother an artist. **Married** (1) . . .: Florian; Frank; Sybille. (2) Katja: Franziska. **Education** Gymnasiums, Hannover and Bielefeld; univs. of Munich and Berlin 1929–33; studied at Robert Koch Hosp., Berlin (German Research Council scholarship) ca. 1933; Univ. of Berlin, Dr. Phil. 1935; qualified as univ. lectr. 1943. **Career** Joined German Communist Party (KPD) 1932; member of scientific staff, dept. of physical chemistry, Kaiser Wilhelm Inst., Berlin 1932–33; research asst., Inst. of Pharmacology, Univ. of Berlin 1937–43; co-founder of European Union resistance movement; arrested by the Nazis and condemned to death for high treason 1943, execution twice postponed; imprisoned 1943–45, freed by Soviet Army 1945. • Acting head, Kaiser Wilhelm Soc. for Advancement of Science 1945; staff member 1945–48 and admin. head 1945–50, Kaiser Wilhelm Inst.; prof. of physical chemistry 1946–64 and head of Inst. of Physical Chemistry 1950–64 (expelled for political activities), Humboldt Univ., East Berlin; head, Center for Photochemistry, East German Acad. of Sciences, Berlin-Adlershof 1965. • Co-founder, Volkskammer (People's Chamber); co-founder ca. 1945, and member of presidium 1945–48, League of Culture parliamentary party; joined East German Communist Party (SED) 1949; member, Presidium, German Peace Council 1949; deputy to Volkskammer 1950–64; expelled from SED 1964 for political activities. • Writer on political subjects since mid-1960s; active in underground peace movement since 1970s; placed under house arrest and 24-hour surveillance 1976; convicted on charges of currency and customs violations 1979. **Member** East German Acad. of Sciences, expelled 1966; (founding member) Cttee. of Members of the

Courtesy of German Information Center

Antifascist Resistance, expelled 1975. **Honors** Order of Merit in Silver 1954; Medal for Fighters of Fascism 1933–45, 1958; Natl. Prize, 2nd Class, 1959. **Author** *Einführung in die chemische Thermodynamik* [*Introduction to Chemical Thermodynamics*], 1957; *Dialektik ohne Dogma?* [*Dialectics Without Dogma?*], 1964; *Fragen Antworten Fragen: aus der Biographie eines deutschen Marxisten,* 1970 (trans. as *Questions, Answers, Questions: From the Biography of a German Marxist,* 1972, and as *An Alienated Man,* 1973); *Rückantworten an die Hauptverwaltung "Ewige Wahrheiten"* [*Replies to the Main Administration of "Eternal Truths"*], 1971; *Berliner Schriften* [*Berlin Writings*], 1976; *Morgen: Die Weltsysteme am Scheideweg* [*Morning: The World Systems at the Crossroads*], 1980.

Further reading Karl H. Kahrs, "The Theoretical Position of the Intra-Marxist Opposition in the GDR," in *East Central Europe,* vol. 6, part 2, 1979.

MAX(IMILLIAN JAKOB) HERZBERGER
Optical researcher and theoretical physicist
***Born* Charlottenburg, Germany, 7 March 1899**
***Died* New Orleans, Louisiana, USA, 9 April 1982**

Max Herzberger's most important achievement, the development of lenses that are completely free from color distortion, solved a 300-year-old problem in optics. A student of Albert Einstein in the 1920s, Herzberger spent four decades working with such leading optical companies as Zeiss and Kodak, then turned to the development of a general field theory as a professor of theoretical physics at universities in Switzerland and the United States.

The German-born Herzberger showed an early aptitude for mathematics, and by the age of ten had progressed so far that he was no longer required to attend mathematics classes. At the University of Berlin, where he was befriended by Einstein, he earned a doctorate in mathematics with a dissertation on hypercomplex numbers. He entered the field of geometrical optics in 1923 as a lens designer, and in 1927 joined the Zeiss optical works as assistant to the director. In 1931 he published a book on the neglected techniques of William Rowan Hamilton, who a century earlier had used variational calculus to simplify complex problems in optics.

Soon after the Nazis came to power, Herzberger, who was Jewish, was dismissed from his job, and his teaching qualifications, which had been accepted by the University of Jena, were revoked. In 1934 he and his wife and three young children escaped from Germany to the Netherlands. He taught for a year at the University of Delft, but Einstein, who was now at the Institute for Advanced Study in Princeton, advised him to emigrate to the United States. Einstein's letter of recommendation helped him get a job in 1935 as research associate with the Eastman Kodak Company in Rochester, New York, where he remained until 1965.

Two years after joining Kodak, Herzberger became interested in chromatic aberration, a distortion in photographic and telescopic images caused by the unequal refraction of the various wavelengths of light as it passes through a glass lens. Most lenses can focus clearly only one color at a time. The out-of-focus colors make telescope observations difficult, especially at high magnifications where color and edge definition are critical. Isaac Newton first tackled the problem in 1666, but was unable to solve it. Eighteenth-century scientists experimenting with compound lenses found that they could focus two colors at the same time using certain combinations of two kinds of glass. But even with these achromat lenses, the other colors were still blurred.

Herzberger, whose approach to optics was mathematical rather than empirical, worked out a formula in 1942 by which he could calculate the refractive properties of any kind of glass for any wavelength of visible light. He demonstrated that it should be possible to construct a color-perfect triplet lens given three kinds of glass with the right qualities. Using his formula, Kodak succeeded in producing a superachromat microscope. But no camera lens followed, despite the potential contributions of such a lens to aerial reconnaissance in wartime, because of practical problems of mass-production: a billion combinations of glass lenses might have to be analyzed before the right combination was found.

The color-perfect camera lens remained a mere possibility for three decades. In that time, Herzberger made other contributions to optical research, including a simple method for describing optical errors in images, and wrote *Modern Geometrical Optics* (1958), still a standard reference in the field. Upon his retirement from Kodak in 1965, he moved to Zurich, where he taught at the Eidgenossische Technische Hochschule and began to pursue an interest in theoretical physics. He sought to develop a general field theory that would correlate the tenets of classical physics with those of relativity and quantum mechanics, a task Einstein had also set himself in his later years. From 1969 he was a consulting professor at Louisiana State University at New Orleans.

Courtesy of University of New Orleans

It was here that Herzberger finally completed his work on the superachromat lens. Together with assistant professor George Ioup, he devised a computer program to match different types of glass. Of the billion or more possibilities, 400 combinations were found that could produce the desired effect. Zeiss soon began production of a superachromat telephoto lens that is now much used in aerial photography.

Herzberger was an expert chess player and a member of numerous scientific societies in the United States and Europe. He died at the age of 83. P.D.

Parents Leopold H. and Sonja (Behrendt) H. **Married** Edith Kaufmann 1925: Ruth Rosenberg; Ursula Bellugi-Klima; Hans George. **Religion** Reform Jewish. **Emigrated** to the U.S. 1935; naturalized 1940. **Education** Schiller Real Gymnasium 1917; Univ. of Berlin, M.S., Ph.D. in mathematics 1923; Univ. of Jena 1923–24. **Mil. service** German Army 1917–19. **Career** Lens designer, Emil Bosch, Bathenow, Germany 1923–25; head, calculation bureau, E. Leitz Co., Wetzlar, Germany 1925–27; mathematician and personal asst. to dir., C. Zeiss Co., Jena, Germany 1927–34; docent of optics, Univ. of Delft, The Netherlands 1934; lectr. in optics, Scophony Television Co., London 1935. • Sr. research assoc. and dir. of geometric optics research sect., Eastman Kodak Co., Rochester, NY 1935–65; member, Inst. for Advanced Study, Princeton 1946; lectr., Optical Soc. of Amer. 1962–63; prof. of physics, Eidgenossische Technische Hochschule, Zurich 1965–69; consulting prof. of physics, Louisiana State Univ., New Orleans 1969–77. • Ed., *Journal of the Optical Society* 1947–59; member, advisory bd., *Optical Spectrum* jrnl. since 1971. **Officer** Member, bd. of dirs., Jewish Welfare Council 1942, 1953–57, 1960–64; pres. 1949, v.p. 1949–69, and member since 1949, New York State Chess Assn.; chapter pres., Sigma Xi 1964–65; chmn., Rochester Optical Soc. **Fellow** Amer. Assn. for the Advancement of Science since 1955; Louisiana Acad. of Sciences since 1980; Optical Soc. of Amer. **Member** (Corresp.) Bavarian Acad. of Sciences 1957; Amer. Mathematics Soc.; German Mathematical Soc.; Swiss Optical Soc.; Swiss Physical Soc.; New York Acad. of Sciences; Amer. Chess Assn. **Honors** Cressy Morrison Prize, New York Acad. of Sciences 1945; Ives Medal, Optical Soc. of Amer. 1962. • Hon. member: Deutsche Optische Gesellschaft 1969; Omicron Delta Kappa, New Orleans 1971; Rochester Optical Soc. 1977; Sigma Xi.

Patents on lenses and optical instruments. **Author** *Strahlenoptik* [*Ray Optics*], 1931; *Modern Geometrical Optics,* 1958; (jtly.) *Handbook of Physics,* 1958. **Contributor** to *McGraw-Hill Encyclopedia of Science and Technology;* author of more than 200 articles on optics, mathematics, and physics in scientific and technical jrnls.

WILFRID PELLETIER

Conductor and music educator

***Born* Montreal, Canada, 20 June 1896**

***Died* New York City, USA, 9 April 1982**

The Canadian-born conductor Wilfrid Pelletier spent 33 years at the Metropolitan Opera House in New York, where, in addition to serving as director of French repertoire, he conducted the Sunday Concerts and founded "The Metropolitan Opera Auditions of the Air" radio program. He was also active in his native Montreal as the founder and director of a symphony orchestra, a conservatory, a music festival, and two series of children's concerts, and in Quebec province as director general of music education. He was known as "the grandfather of music in Quebec."

Pelletier received his first musical training from his father, a baker by trade and a musician by avocation, who conducted a concert band that included several members of his own family. He got his first job as a drummer with the local parish temperance band at the age of 12 and studied to become a pianist. In 1915 he was awarded the coveted Prix d'Europe, a government scholarship, on the second attempt, and traveled to Paris to study piano, harmony, composition, and opera repertoire with Camille Bellaigue, Isidor Philippe, Charles Widor, and Marcel Rousseau. He returned to the United States two years later as piano soloist with a French orchestra. After the orchestra's tour was abruptly canceled, he found a job as accompanist to the soprano Marie Sundelius. Pierre Monteux went backstage after their recital and not only engaged him as an assistant conductor for the French National Orchestra but gave him an introduction to Giulio Gatti-Casazza, general manager of the Metropolitan Opera. As a rehearsal pianist at the Met, he coached such famous singers as Caruso, Gigli, Lily Pons, and the soprano Rose Bampton, who became his third wife, and proved so versatile and dependable that he was soon promoted to assistant conductor. Chicago's Ravinia Opera Company engaged him as assistant conductor for its summer seasons, and he was also in demand by the San Francisco Opera Company. His first major assignment came in 1922, when he conducted one of the Sunday Concerts at the Metropolitan, and two years later he was appointed artistic director of the series. In 1929 he became director and conductor of French repertoire, a position he held for 21 years.

Pelletier will probably be best remembered in the United States as the founder and director of "The Metropolitan Opera Auditions of the Air," which discovered many talented young singers, among them Eleanor Steber, Leonard Warren, and Robert Merrill. Since

Courtesy of Andre Larose

the 1930s he was a frequent conductor on radio programs, and in 1951 he succeeded his friend Arturo Toscanini as conductor of the NBC Symphony.

While still active at the Met, Pelletier threw his energies behind a plan to found a symphony orchestra in his native city. The venture was successful, and the Montreal Symphony Orchestra gave its first concert in 1935. The same year, Pelletier inaugurated the Matinées Symphoniques pour la Jeunesse. Similar concerts for English-speaking children began in 1947. The overwhelming interest aroused by these musical activities led to the founding in 1936 of the Montreal Festivals, over which Pelletier presided until the final program in 1965.

The dearth of first-rate Canadian musicians prompted Pelletier to establish a music conservatory in Canada, in the European tradition. With the support of Hector Perrier, provincial secretary of Quebec, courses were begun in 1943 with Pelletier as director. He continued in that post until 1961, when he was appointed director general of music education by the Quebec Ministry of Cultural Affairs.

Though Pelletier lived in Manhattan, he made weekly visits during the season to his offices in Montreal and Quebec. Montreal honored him by naming a music school, a grammar school, and a concert hall after him, and his name was also given to a lake in a national park in Quebec. He retired in 1970. He died of pneumonia at the age of 85.

B.D.

Courtesy of NFB Phototeque

Parents Elzéar P., baker and bandleader, and Zélire Sévigny P. **Married** (1) Berthe Jeannotte 1915 (div. 1922): Camille, b. 1916; François, b. 1918 (d. 1972). (2) Queena Mario, opera singer, 1925 (div. 1935). (3) Rose Bampton, opera singer, 1937. **Religion** Roman Catholic; later Protestant. **Emigrated** to U.S. 1917; naturalized 1935. **Education** Parochial schs., Montreal; Prix d'Europe scholarship for study in Paris 1915–17, Govt. of Quebec. **Career** Drummer with St. Peter's Parish Temperance Band, 65th Regimental Band, and other groups during sch. years, Montreal; pianist, Natl. Theater Orch., Montreal 1910; rehearsal pianist, Montreal Opera Co. 1911–13; orderly, Paris hosp., WWI; asst. conductor and soloist, French Natl. Orch. 1917; accompanist, NYC 1917. • With Metropolitan Opera Co. and Assn., NYC: music coach and rehearsal pianist 1917–19; asst. conductor 1922–32; conductor 1922–50 and artistic dir. 1924–50, Sunday Concerts; conductor and dir. of French repertoire 1929–50; founder 1934 and dir. 1934–46, "Metropolitan Opera Auditions of the Air" radio program. • Conductor and/or music dir.: (asst.) Antonio Scotti touring co. ca. 1918–22; Ravinia Opera Co., Chicago 1923–33; San Francisco Opera Co. 1923–33; (founder 1935) Montreal Symphony Orch.; (founder 1935) Montreal Symphony Orch. Matinées Symphoniques pour la Jeunesse; (founder 1947) Montreal Symphony Orch. Young People's Concerts; (founder 1936) Montreal Festival 1936–65; (also artistic dir.) Quebec Symphony Orch. 1942–47; NBC Symphony Orch. 1951; New York Philharmonic Orch. Children's Concerts 1953–57; New York Opera 1960–61; Los Angeles Opera Co.; Los Angeles Philharmonic Orch.; radio programs in U.S. and Canada • Founder 1942 and dir. gen. 1942–67, Conservatoire de Musique et d'Art Dramatique, Montreal; conducted survey of European conservatories for Canadian govt. 1957; dir. gen. of music education, Ministry of Cultural Affairs, Quebec 1961–70; appointed bd. chmn., Place des Artes, Montreal 1964; founding member, Soc. of Contemporary Music, Quebec 1966; bd. head, *Vie Musicale* mag. 1965–71; artistic consultant, Canadian Ministry of Culture since 1968; natl. pres., Jeunesses Musicales du Canada since 1968. • Composer of music for opera and film; conducted numerous recordings of symphonies and operatic excerpts and abridgments; conducted operatic sequences in film *Big Broadcast of 1938;* radio broadcasts include "Talent Festival" on CBC 1966–67, "Simmons Hour," "Packard Hour," "Firestone Program." **Honors** CMG 1946; kt., Order of King of Denmark 1946; chevalier, Légion d'Honneur 1947; Canada Council Medal 1962; C.C. 1968; prize, Concert Soc. of the Jewish People's Sch. and Peretz Schs. 1971; Canadian Music Council Medal 1975; Christian den Tiendes Frihedsmedalje, Denmark; hon. degrees from univs. of Montreal, Alberta, McGill, Ottawa, Laval, and Quebec, and from Banff Sch. of Fine Arts, Hobart and William Smith Coll., and New York Coll. of Music; concert hall, grammar sch., music sch. of Sisters of St. Anne, and city street named after him, Montreal; lake in natl. park named after him, Quebec province. **Author** *Une symphonie inachevée* [*An Unfinished Symphony*] (autobiography), 1972; (contributor) E. MacMillan, ed., *Music in Canada,* 1955. **Biographical documentary film** by Natl. Film Bd. of Canada 1960. **Manuscripts and papers** in Archives Nationales du Quebec.

Further reading Louise G. McCready, *Famous Musicians: MacMillan, Johnson, Pelletier, Willan,* 1957; John W. Freeman, "Pelly," in *Opera News,* 13 May 1967.

BARON GREENWOOD OF ROSSENDALE
(Arthur William James) "Anthony" Greenwood
Labour cabinet minister
***Born* Leeds, England, 14 September 1911**
***Died* London, England, 12 April 1982**

Baron Greenwood of Rossendale was, as Anthony Greenwood, an attractive, energetic, and respected cabinet member in Harold Wilson's first and second governments. Usually identified with the left wing of the Labour Party, he was notably unsuccessful in intraparty power struggles. After Labour's defeat in 1970 he was sent to the House of Lords and had no further role in national government.

He was christened Arthur William James Greenwood, son of the powerful Labour politician Arthur Greenwood, M.P., sometime minister and deputy leader of the party. He attended Merchant Taylors' School and Balliol College at Oxford University, where he was president of the Union in 1933, his final year. After a series of international debating tours and a visit to Germany soon after the Nazi accession to power, he took a position with the National Fitness Council in 1938–39.

Greenwood began his government service with the coming of war, serving with the Ministry of Information in London, Moscow, and Cairo. Later in the war he was an intelligence officer with the Royal Air Force, and just after the end of hostilities was named to the Allied Reparations Commission in Moscow, attended the Potsdam Conference, and was a member of the organizing committee of the Inter-Allied Reparations Agency.

He stood for Parliament in the constituency of Heywood and Radcliffe (Lancashire) in a by-election in 1946, holding the seat, which was renamed Rossendale in 1950, until he left the Commons in 1970. He was vice chairman of the Parliamentary Labour Party in the early 1950s, and from 1955 was a member of the shadow cabinet. In 1960, however, when the leader of the party, Hugh Gaitskell, refused to accept the party conference's decision in favor of unilateral nuclear disarmament, Greenwood resigned from the shadow cabinet in protest and offered to challenge Gaitskell for the leadership if no one else came forward. Harold Wilson, Greenwood's more centrist parliamentary ally, eventually made the challenge, but Gaitskell overwhelmingly defeated him. Greenwood made another challenge himself in 1961, with an even more one-sided result.

He was elected vice chairman of the party in 1962, succeeded to the chairmanship on Gaitskell's death in 1963, and held that office during the general election campaign and Labour victory of 1964. Prime Minister Wilson included him in the cabinet as secretary of state for colonial affairs, where he initiated an accelerated program of decolonialization and oversaw the independence of Aden, Guyana, Mauritius, and several islands in the West Indies. In late 1965, in one of the numerous cabinet reshuffles of the Wilson years, he was named minister for overseas development, in charge of aid to countries that were formerly dependent territories. He held that ministry only eight months before being shifted to the ministry of housing and local government. This was a logical move, for in 1956 Greenwood had led the working party which forged Labour's famous housing-policy document, *Homes for the Future,* committing the party, when in government, to a large increase in public-housing construction. He proceeded to put these recommendations into practice while minister, and saw 400,000 new homes built in 1967. Unfortunately, national economic difficulties forced him to accede to a cutback in the program in succeeding years, which brought sharp attacks on him from his colleagues on the Labour left. In 1969, in yet another of Wilson's shakeups, his department was placed under Anthony Crosland, secretary of state for local government and regional planning, and Greenwood, though still minister of housing, was dropped from the cabinet.

The nadir of Greenwood's political career had come in mid-1968, when, as Wilson's candidate for the new post of secretary general of the party, he was soundly defeated by Harry Nicholas, a veteran trade-union organizer. It is typical of the unpredictable fractiousness of Labour politics that Greenwood's election was considered a foregone conclusion until the very day of the meeting of the party's National Executive. Although Greenwood was generally considered the most leftist member of the government, he was held in suspicion by the rank and file, who believed that power had compromised his principles. He decided not to contest the 1970 election, and in Wilson's honors list for the dissolution of Parliament, he was created a life peer.

Lord Greenwood's duties in the House of Lords were comparatively limited. From 1970 to 1978 he was a member of the board of the Commonwealth Development Corporation, though Edward Heath's government rescinded his appointment as chairman. He was also, from 1977 to 1979, chairman of the Lords' Select Committee on Europe. It was his numerous extraparliamentary offices which filled up most of his time during the 1970s. Among these he was chairman of the Housing Association from 1972, president of the Housing Centre from 1975, chairman of the Local Government Training Board from 1975, and president of the Association of Metropolitan Authorities from 1974. He was an officer of such diverse groups as the National Marriage Guidance Council, the National Society for the Abolition of Cruel Sports, the Pure Rivers Society, the Christian Socialist Movement, and the Cremation Society. He was also prochancellor of the University of Lancaster (1972–78), a justice of the peace from 1950, and deputy lieutenant for Essex from 1974. He died at the age of 70 of a heart attack. A.K.

Father Arthur Greenwood, Labour M.P. **Married** Gillian Crawshay Williams 1940: Susanna Catherine Crawshay Gardiner, b. 1943; Dinah Karen Crawshay Murray, b. 1946. **Education** Kingston Grammar Sch.; Merchant Taylors' Sch.; Balliol Coll., Oxford, M.A. ca. 1933. **Mil. service** Flight lt. and intelligence officer, RAF 1942–46. **Career** On lecture and debating tours mid-1930s; with Natl. Fitness Council 1938–39; with Ministry of Information, London, Moscow, and Cairo 1939–42; with Allied Reparations Commn., Moscow 1945; attended Allied Reparations Conference in Paris and Potsdam Conference 1945; member, Organizational Cttee., Inter-Allied Reparations Agency 1945–46. • Member, Hampstead Borough Council 1945–49; Labour M.P. for Heywood and Radcliffe div. of Lancs. 1946–50 and for Rossendale div. of Lancs. 1950–70. • Parliamentary private secty. to Postmaster Gen. 1949–50; vice chmn., Parliamentary Labour Party 1950–51; vice chmn., Parliamentary Cttee. of Labour Party 1951–52, 1955–60; member 1954–70, vice chmn. 1962–63, and chmn. 1963–64, Natl. Exec. Cttee., Labour Party; chmn., Labour Parliamentary Assn. 1960–71. • Opposition spokesman on works 1955–59, home affairs 1956–59, education 1959–60; cabinet member 1964–69; secty. of state for colonial affairs 1964–65; minister of overseas development 1965–66; minister of housing and local govt. 1966–70. • In House of Lords since 1970: chmn. designate 1970 and bd. member 1970–78, Commonwealth Development Corp.; chmn. of Select Cttee. on Europe and deputy speaker 1977–79; principal deputy chmn. of cttees. 1977–80. **Officer** Chmn.: U.K. Housing Assn. since 1972; Local Govt. Staff

Commn. 1972–76; Local Govt. Training Bd. since 1975; Integrated Professional Development Service since 1975; Isle of Man Parliamentary Group since 1975; British Council for Rehabilitation of Disabled 1975–77. • Vice chmn.: (deputy chmn.) Housing Corp. 1974–77; Parliamentary Group on Civil Liberties; Parliamentary Christian Socialist Group. • Pres.: Oxford Union 1933; Socialist Educational Assn. 1963–72; Cremation Soc. since 1970; Urban District Councils Assn. 1971–72; Pure Rivers Soc. 1971–76; Josephine Butler Soc. 1971–76; London Soc. 1971–76, 1979; River Thames Soc. 1971–78; Assn. of Metropolitan Authorities since 1974; British Trust for Conservation Volunteers 1974–79; Nehru Memorial Trust 1975; Housing Centre since 1975; Essex Assn. of Local Councils since 1977; River Stour Trust since 1977; Hampstead Heath Labour Party. • V.P.: Bldg. Societies Assn. since 1971; Assn. of District Councils since 1974; Advisory Bd. on Redundant Churches since 1975; Natl. Marriage Guidance Council; Commonwealth Parliamentary Assn.; Natl. Soc. for Abolition of Cruel Sports; Royal Soc. for Prevention of Cruelty to Animals; British Rheumatic Assn.; Central Council for Rehabilitation. • Other: member, Cttee. of Inquiry on Rehabilitation of Disabled Persons 1953; member of bureau, Socialist Intl. 1960–70; bd. member, Central Lancashire New Town Development Corp. 1971–76; prochancellor, Univ. of Lancaster 1972–78; dir. since 1972 and chmn. 1974–76, Britannica Bldg. Soc. (formerly Leek, Westbourne and Eastern Counties Bldg. Soc.); conciliator, Intl. Centre for Settlement of Investment Disputes 1975. **Member** Transport and General Workers' Union; Savile Club; Royal Automobile Club. **Honors** J.P., London 1950; created Baron Greenwood of Rossendale, life peer, 1970; deputy lt., Essex 1974; P.C. 1974; hon. degree from Univ. of Lancaster 1979.

Further reading Sir Harold Wilson, *The Labour Government, 1964–70,* 1971.

SIR WILLIE MORRIS
Diplomat
***Born* Yorkshire, England, 3 December 1919**
***Died* England, 13 April 1982**

The British diplomat and Arabist Sir Willie Morris served in ambassadorial posts throughout the Mideast from 1968 to 1979. Noted for his blunt honesty, common sense, and lack of personal ambition, Morris did much to maintain Britain's credibility with the Arabs during the turbulent 1960s and 1970s.

The son of a Yorkshire millworker, Morris read history at St. John's College, Oxford, and took a first in jurisprudence in 1947. He served with the Royal Navy during World War II in French West Equatorial Africa and Germany, then entered the Foreign Service in 1947 as third secretary at the Middle East Centre for Arab Studies. From 1948 to 1952 he was posted to Cairo.

After a return to the Foreign Office as first secretary of the African department (1952–54) and a tour as first secretary in Washington (1955–59), he went to Jordan (1960–63) as counselor and chargé d'affaires. During the 1967 Arab-Israeli War he was head of the Foreign Office's Eastern department and a fellow in international affairs at Harvard.

In 1968 Morris was made ambassador to Saudi Arabia during the difficult period of British withdrawal from the Gulf region. He served as ambassador to Ethiopia just before the overthrow of the monarchy and the Eritrean revolt, and was finally ambassador to Egypt (1975–79), the top Mideast position in the service. He was created KCMG in 1977. Declining health forced him to retire early, and from 1979 he was a director of Lloyd's Bank International. He died at the age of 62.

C.M.

Father a millworker. **Married** Ghislaine Margaret Trammell 1959: Peter; David; Stephen. **Education** Batley Grammar Sch., Yorks.; St.

John's Coll., Oxford, M.A. (1st Class) 1947; Canadian Natl. Defence Coll. 1954. **Mil. service** Seaman in French West Equatorial Africa, trawler exec. officer, and operations officer in Kiel, Germany, Royal Navy 1940–45. **Career** With Foreign Service: Third secty., Middle East Centre for Arab Studies 1947; 2nd secty., British Embassy, Cairo 1948–52; 1st secty. 1951; 1st secty., African Dept., Foreign Office, London 1952–54; 1st secty.. British Embassy, Wash. DC 1955–59; counselor 1960–63 and chargé d'affaires 1960–62, British Embassy, Amman, Jordan; head of Eastern dept., Foreign Office 1963–67. • Ambassador: Saudi Arabia 1968–72; Yemen (nonresident) 1971; Ethiopia 1972–75; Egypt 1975–79. • Dir., Lloyd's Bank Intl. since 1979. **Fellow** Center for Intl. Affairs, Harvard Univ. 1966–67. **Member** Clubs: Travellers'; Pall Mall. **Honors** CMG 1963; KCMG 1977.

LOUIS de GUIRINGAUD
Foreign minister of France
***Born* Limoges, France, 12 October 1911**
***Died* Paris, France, 15 April 1982**

Louis de Guiringaud was a career diplomat who served as foreign minister from 1976 to 1978 in the government of Raymond Barre during the presidency of Valéry Giscard d'Estaing. His tenure at the Quai d'Orsay was marked by an exceptional attention and sensitivity to third-world issues, which carried over into the succeeding Socialist administration of François Mitterrand.

De Guiringaud was born into a military family of the provincial aristocracy—his father was a cavalry officer—and was educated at the Lycée Saint-Louis in Paris and at the Sorbonne. He won admission to the prestigious École des Sciences Politiques, and ended with degrees and diplomas in law, letters, and political science.

He joined the foreign minister's staff in 1936 and the diplomatic service in 1938. His first foreign assignments were in Ankara, Turkey (1938–39) and Damascus (1940), after which he returned to the central administration in what had become the Axis-supported Vichy government. He quickly came to realize he had made an error in not joining the Free French side in 1940, and when his friend René Massigli, Free French commissioner for foreign affairs, asked him to come to Algiers, he left Vichy for good. Although his expertise was needed, the Consultative Assembly in Algiers was unwilling to accept him as a new colleague, and he immediately resigned from the diplomatic corps to join the armed forces. He became regimental captain in North Africa, fought alongside the Allies in Italy and during the recapture of France, and was several times seriously wounded.

De Guiringaud rejoined the foreign service in 1945 and was posted to London as first secretary, where he served until 1949. He was then assigned as political director to the French High Commission in occupied Germany (1949–52). From there he went to the

Courtesy of French Embassy

United States, where he served as consul general in San Francisco (1952–55) and then as deputy (1955–57) to Hervé Alphand, the French permanent representative to the United Nations. When Alphand's successor, Bernard Cornu-Gentille, became ill in late 1956, it fell to de Guiringaud to serve as president of the Security Council during the invasion of Egypt by France, Britain, and Israel.

His first ambassadorship (1957–60) was to Ghana, a newly independent country formerly under British administration. Throughout his career he was interested in projecting French concern and influence into third-world areas where French colonial power had been weak or nonexistent. In the central administration from 1960 to 1962, he headed the section on Moroccan and Tunisian affairs, then for a year was deputy high representative to Algiers. He was inspector general of French diplomatic posts (1963–66), then served a lengthy tour (1966–72) as ambassador to Japan. Finally, he returned to the United Nations as France's permanent representative (1972–76).

De Guiringaud was preparing to retire when he was called to head the Quai d'Orsay; the weight of his experience in third-world affairs was not equaled in any other senior diplomat, and Pres. Giscard d'Estaing needed an advisor with precisely that expertise. In addition to securing North-South relations, as they have come to be called, a very high place on the French diplomatic agenda, he had to contend with several acute problems: the painful ordeal of the French hostages held by the Polisario Liberation Front in Chad, the subsequent French invasion of Chad, and the damage to the national reputation incurred in backing Jean Bedel Bokassa (later Emperor Bokassa I) in Central Africa. In the summer of 1977, de Guiringaud was forced to cut short an important diplomatic initiative in English-speaking Africa when he was threatened by anti-French rioting in Tanzania. Shortly before his retirement, he issued a strongly worded criticism of the rightist Christian militias in Lebanon that elicited a violent storm of anti-French sentiment in Beirut.

In addition to winning the Croix de Guerre for his valiant war service, de Guiringaud was made in 1976 a grand officer of the Légion d'Honneur. His death, in his apartment in Paris, was a suicide; he shot himself in the heart with a hunting rifle. The French newspapers reported that he had been depressed for several weeks. A.K.

Parents Pierre de G., cavalry officer, and Madeleine (de Catheu) de G. **Married** Claude Mony 1955: one son. **Education** Lycée Buffon; Lycée Saint-Louis, Paris; law faculty, Univ. of Paris, licencié en droit; Sorbonne, licencié ès lettres; École des Sciences Politiques, Paris, diplôme. **Mil. service** Capt., 4th regiment, Moroccan Spahis, North Africa, Italy, France, and Germany 1944–45 (wounded). **Career** Joined staff of Minister for Foreign Affairs 1936; joined Diplomatic Service 1938; attaché, French Embassy, Ankara 1938–39; with staff of French High Commnr., Damascus 1940; with central admin., Foreign Office 1942–43; dismissed by Vichy govt. 1943; special asst. to Commnr. for Foreign Affairs, Free French provisional govt., Algiers 1943–44; reinstated in Diplomatic Service 1945; 1st secty., French Embassy, London 1946–49; dir. gen. of political affairs, Office of French High Commnr., Occupied Germany 1949–52; consul gen., S.F. 1952–55; minister plenipotentiary 1954; deputy permanent rep. to U.N. 1955–57; ambassador to Ghana 1957; head of Moroccan and Tunisian affairs, Foreign Office 1960; deputy high rep. to Algeria 1962; inspector gen. of diplomatic and consular posts 1963–66; ambassador to Japan 1966–72; permanent rep. to U.N. Security Council and chief of French mission to U.N. 1972–76; technical chmn., Conference on Intl. Economic Cooperation, Paris 1975; minister of foreign affairs 1976–78; pres. of French delegation to U.N. Org. 1978; consultant, Lazard Frères, Paris since 1979; member, European Advisory Bd., IBM since 1979. **Officer** Pres.: Soc. Centrale d'Étude et de Conseil since 1979; (also member since 1979) bd., U.N. Inst. of Training and Research 1980. **Member** Clubs: Jockey, Golf de Morfontaine, and Union Interalliée, all Paris. **Honors** Chevalier, WWII, and grand officier 1976, Légion d'Honneur; Croix de Guerre 1945; hon. ambassador of France 1975; Grand Cross of Rising Sun, Japan; other foreign decorations; hon. municipal councilor, Castelsarassin.

C. Y. TUNG
Tung Chao-Yung
Maritime magnate
Born Shanghai, China, 1911
Died Hong Kong, 15 April 1982

C. Y. Tung was one of the world's most successful shipowners, a man of genial and somewhat retiring manner who was nevertheless daring and flamboyant in his business affairs. He managed to prosper and to keep virtually his entire fleet at sea even during the world economic downturn that began with the oil embargo of 1974.

He was born into a moderately prosperous family in the metals business. His first experience with shipping came in adolescence, when he was sent to learn chandlering, the provisioning and outfitting of ships. He soon became assistant manager of the Tianjin Navigation Company, a principal carrier of railroad materials, and by the age of 24 was vice president of the Tianjin Shipowners Association. His wife, Koo Lee Ching, whom he married about that time, was from a family prominent in Chinese coastal shipping.

At the beginning of hostilities between China and Japan in 1937, C. Y. (as he was everywhere known) moved his headquarters to Hong Kong, where they remained after the end of World War II. A partisan of the Chinese Nationalist cause, he withdrew from all contact with mainland China after the Communist accession to power in 1949. His business grew in the postwar period by providing badly needed cargo capacity for concerns in North and South America.

At the time of his death his highly diversified merchant-marine empire comprised a fleet of over 150 vessels with an aggregate deadweight tonnage of 11 million tons and with an insured value of nearly $2 billion. Although most of his ships were oil tankers, he also made profits from dry cargo vessels (containerships), bulk carriers, liquefied gas carriers, and passenger liners. For years his largest oil carrier was the 386,000-ton *Brazilian Hope,* which is on a long lease to Petrobras, the Brazilian national oil company. Among the passenger vessels, certainly his most spectacular purchase came in 1970, when for $3.2 million he bought the Cunard Line's *Queen Elizabeth,* which he intended to convert into a floating educational institution, the *Seawise University* (the pun on his name was quite intentional). He watched in horror in 1972 as the ship caught fire during refitting and sank in Hong Kong harbor, but soon provided another ship, renamed the *Universe Campus,* to carry on the idea.

His rapid ascent continued apace even during the late 1970s, a time when at least 100 million tons of excess shipping capacity was available in the world. Undaunted by his competitors' unused tankers, he proceeded with an ambitious shipbuilding program in Europe and Asia. In 1980 the launch of the 564,763-ton *Seawise Giant* was testimony to his abiding confidence in supertankers. His launchings were always lavish and gala affairs, held wherever in the world one of his ships was being built. His death of a heart attack occurred only hours after he welcomed Prince Rainier and Princess Grace of Monaco to Hong Kong for another of his famous three-day launching parties.

Unlike most shipping tycoons, who merely provide financing for their vessels' construction and then lease them out for service, C. Y.'s group provided all services for his ships, exclusive of construction—financing, running, insuring, and maintaining. "That's the whole fun," he often said. By this criterion, he ranked among the very biggest of the world's shipowners, along with the American Daniel K. Ludwig and the Greek C. M. Lemos.

A man of ascetic habits as well as a frequent world traveler, C. Y. stepped down in 1978 as chief of his group of companies in favor of his two sons, C. H. Tung, head of the Hong Kong office, and C. C. Tung, who directs Western operations from an elegant skyscraper on Wall Street designed by I. M. Pei, an old friend of C. Y.'s. A.K.

Parents in metals business. **Married** Koo Lee Ching: Chee-Hwa, head of Tung Group's cargo operations, Hong Kong; Chee-Chen, head of Tung Group's North and South

America operations; Shirley Peng; two other daughters. **Career** Trained in ship-provisioning firm; asst. mgr., Tianjin Navigation Co.; founder, Chinese Maritime Co., Shanghai 1930s, moved base of operations to Hong Kong 1937; elected v.p., Shipowners Assn., Tianjin (Tientsin) 1937; rep. of Allied Forces to Chiang Kai-shek in matters of shipping, Chongqing (Chungking) 1945; chmn. until 1978 and hon. chmn. since 1978, Tung Group. • Shareholder: Orient Overseas Container (Holdings) Ltd. since 1973; Furness Whity, U.K. since 1980; Amer. Asian Bank, S.F.; Island Navigation; many other firms. **Honors** Chevalier, Légion d'Honneur, France 1977.

RAY WINFIELD SMITH

Businessman, archeologist, and collector of ancient glass
***Born* Marlboro, New Hampshire, USA, 4 June 1897**
***Died* Houston, Texas, USA, 17 April 1982**

Ray Winfield Smith pursued careers as an oilman, government official, and international businessman, but he was best known as an Egyptologist and as the owner of what was widely considered the world's largest and finest privately owned collection of ancient glass.

Smith earned a B.S. degree from Dartmouth College in 1918. He first became interested in archeology while working for the Sinclair Oil Co. in Europe during the 1920s and 1930s. Fascinated by the beauty of the ancient glass that he saw in Europe's great museums and churches—glass fabricated before the twelfth century, the start of the modern era in glassmaking—he began to accumulate fragments and whole pieces on his travels. He founded his own import-export firm in 1936 and served with the Army Air Corps during World War II and with the U.S. government in occupied Germany. In 1955 he initiated a research program, in collaboration with Edward Sayre of the Brookhaven National Laboratory on Long Island, into the chemical composition and origins of ancient glass artifacts. Smith furnished minute samples from more than 450 objects from the world's great collections, and Sayre subjected the samples to spectroscopic, x-ray, and neutron-activation analysis using the Brookhaven equipment.

On the basis of their results, Smith and Sayre divided ancient glassmaking into several distinct periods and geographical areas, each producing glass of a unique chemical composition. They showed that trade in glassware was widespread throughout the Mediterranean and Middle East, and even disproved some cherished myths about famous individual pieces. A magnificent green cut-glass bowl in the Cathedral of San Lorenzo in Genoa, believed by generations of Italian Christians to be the cup that Jesus used at the Last Supper, was shown by their methods to have been made from the glass formula characteristic of Islamic artisans of the seventh to ninth centuries. Smith sold his multimillion dollar collection at auction to various museums and individuals in 1975.

His career as an Egyptologist also resulted in the reevaluation by historians of some longstanding ideas about Egypt's past. In 1965, under the auspices of the University of Pennsylvania, he organized the Akhenaten Temple Project, whose goal was the study, cataloguing, and reassembly of some 40,000 building blocks (called *talalat)* from the site of a destroyed temple at Karnak, in Thebes, built during the reign of the pharaoh Akhenaten. After a decade of work, Smith and archeologist Donald Redford, with the help of scores of assistants and a computer, pieced together surprising new information about Akhenaten (also spelled Ikhnaton) from carvings on the blocks. Their evidence suggested that the religious, social, and artistic reforms previously thought to have been introduced by the pharaoh, including monotheistic sun-worship and a more naturalistic representational style, were actually the work of his queen Nefertiti, whose image appears twice as often as his on the *talalat.* They also deduced that Akhenaten suffered from a glandular disorder.

Smith was a founder and chairman of the International Committee on Ancient Glass and the author of *Glass from the Ancient World* (1957) and the first volume of the Akhenaten Temple Project report (1976).

Since 1974 he taught at Dartmouth College and supported a lecture series there. He was a staunch Republican and contributed to the presidential campaigns of Dwight Eisenhower and Richard Nixon. He was also the inventor of drilling and elevator safety devices. He died at the age of 84. S.A.

Parents John Henry S. and Ellen Maria (Stone) S. **Married** Bonnie D. Jones 1923: Michael Frans; Champney Fowlis. **Education** Dartmouth Coll., NH, B.S. 1918. **Mil. service** Second lt., Ordnance Dept., AEF 1918–19; lt. col., USAAC 1944–45. **Career** With Sinclair Oil Co., Belgium, the Netherlands, Germany 1922–36; founder and dir., import-export firm, Houston 1936–42. • With U.S. govt.: U.S. attaché, Olympic Games, Amsterdam 1928; official 1946–55; economic advisor to U.S. comdr., Berlin 1951–52; U.S. commnr., Military Security Bd., Germany 1952–55. • Expert on ancient glassmaking; pres., Ray W. Smith Foundn. 1955–73; consultant, Brookhaven Natl. Labs., L.I., NY 1950–60s; founder, project dir., and sr. report ed., Akhenaten Temple Project, Egypt 1965–72; faculty member and member of supervising cttee. for Ray W. Smith Lectures, Dartmouth Coll. since 1974; dir., research project on the City of Isfahan, Iran; member, bd. of editorial review, *Journal of Glass Studies.* **Officer** Chmn. 1946–68 and co-founder, Intl. Cttee. on Ancient Glass; chmn., cttee. on ancient glass 1955–68 and trustee 1957–66, Archeological Inst. of Amer.; v.p. and exec. dir., Eisenhower-Nixon Club, Wash. DC 1956; officer of Republican inaugurating cttee., Wash. DC 1957; gen. chmn., New Hampshire Volunteers for Nixon-Lodge 1960; dir., Amer. Research Center Egypt, Cairo 1963–65. **Fellow** German Archeological Inst.; (also council member) Amer. Assn. for Advancement of Science. **Member** Bd. of visitors, Boston Mus. of Fine Arts 1956–62; Republican Party; Sigma Alpha Epsilon; Army and Navy Club, Wash. DC. **Honors** Purple Heart; Legion of Merit; award, Amer. Inst. of Archeology; hon. degree from Dartmouth Coll. **Author** *Glass from the Ancient World,* 1957; (jtly.) *The Akhenaten Temple Project,* vol. 1, 1976. **Contributor** of numerous articles on archeology and ancient glass to *National Geographic* and other mags. **Patents** for directional drilling and elevator safety devices. **Other** Exhibition of ancient glass collection, Sotheby Parke-Bernet, NYC 1975; interview in "Mystery of Nefertiti," TV program, 1977.

J(ACOB) GEORGE HARRAR

Botanist and president of the Rockefeller Foundation

***Born* Painesville, Ohio, USA, 2 December 1906**

***Died* Scarsdale, New York, USA, 18 April 1982**

The plant pathologist and agricultural researcher J. George Harrar was one of the masterminds of the so-called "Green Revolution," by which crop production in the third world during the 1950s and 1960s was greatly increased by the application of modern agricultural methods and the development of new crop varieties. He believed that private philanthropies could successfully tackle many international problems, such as world hunger, too complex or too politically controversial for national governments. For nearly three decades he was associated with the Rockefeller Foundation, first as the organizer of model agricultural assistance programs in Mexico, South America, and Asia, and later as an officer. During his tenure as president of the foundation from 1961 to 1972, almost $400 million was distributed to underdeveloped countries to establish agricultural education programs and research stations and within the United States to support a wide range of activities.

Harrar, the son of an engineer, earned degrees in biology and botany from Oberlin College in Ohio and from Iowa State College. In 1929 he joined the biology faculty of the College of Agriculture of the University of Puerto Rico, and within a year was promoted to chairman of the department. After earning his Ph.D. from the University of Minnesota, he taught biology at the Virginia Polytechnic In-

Courtesy of Fabian Bachrach

stitute and from 1941 to 1943 was on the staff of Washington State College, where he headed the plant pathology department and the phytopathology division of the agricultural research station.

The Rockefeller Foundation of New York had recently established, in cooperation with the Mexican Ministry of Agriculture, a program providing technical assistance and training to farmers. Harrar was asked to direct the program in 1943. Together with other American specialists, including Sterling Wortman and Norman Borlaug, he scoured the Mexican countryside for native varieties of corn and wheat, and instituted a hybridization program to develop disease-resistant strains. By 1959, Mexico, which formerly had been forced to import hundreds of thousands of tons of grain annually to feed its population, was self-sufficient in corn and wheat and was increasing its potato, legume, and other vegetable crops. Similar programs were founded by Harrar in Colombia, Chile, and India.

Harrar administered the Rockefeller Foundation's Division of Natural Sciences and Agriculture from 1952 to 1955, when he was elected a foundation vice president. He succeeded Dean Rusk as president in 1961. The Rockefeller Foundation was then in the process of establishing, in partnership with the Ford Foundation, a multinational network of tropical agricultural research centers, including the International Rice Research Institute in the Philippines, the International Center for Maize and Wheat Improvement in Mexico, and centers in Colombia and Nigeria. Harrar also oversaw the disbursement of foundation funds for equal opportunity programs, environmental action groups, and arts organizations in the United States. He retired in 1972.

Harrar was a member of several governmental and international scientific bodies and the holder of dozens of honors from the United States and countries in Asia and Latin America. He co-authored *Guide to Southern Trees* (1946) and *Principles of Plant Pathology* (1957). His papers and articles on international cooperative-assistance programs were collected in *Strategy for the Conquest of Hunger* (1967). S.A.

Parents Ellwood Scott H., engineer, and Lucetta Elsie (Sterner) H. **Married** Georgetta Steese 1930: Cynthia Ann Wilson; Georgetta Louise Denhardt. **Religion** Congregationalist. **Education** South High Sch., Youngstown, OH; Oberlin Coll., OH, A.B. 1928; Iowa State Coll., teaching fellow 1928–29, M.Sc. 1929; Univ. of Minnesota (Firestone Fellow), Ph.D. in plant pathology 1935. **Career** Asst. prof. of botany 1929–30, and chmn., dept. of biology, 1930–33, Coll. of Agriculture, Univ. of Puerto Rico, Rio Piedras; instr. of plant pathology, Univ. of Minnesota 1934–35; asst. prof. 1935–37, assoc. prof. 1937–41, and prof. of biology 1941, Virginia Polytechnic Inst., Blacksburg, VA: chmn., plant pathology dept., and div. head, Experimental Research Station, Washington State Coll., Pullman, WA 1941–43. • With Rockefeller Foundn., NYC: dir., Mexican Agricultural Program 1943–51; deputy dir., Div. of Natural Sciences and Agriculture 1952–55; dir. for agriculture 1955–59; v.p. 1959–61; pres. and trustee 1961–72; pres. emeritus and life fellow since 1972; co-founder, Intl. Agricultural Research Center. • Co-founder, Consultative Corp. on Intl. Agricultural Research 1971; White Prof. at Large, Cornell Univ. 1971–77. **Officer** Chmn.: advisory cttee. for science development in Latin America, Natl. Acad. of Sciences/Natl. Research Council 1960–62; presidential mission on aphthous fever,

Argentina 1962; natl. advisory council, Monell Chemical Senses Center, Univ. of Pennsylvania since 1968; governing council, Rockefeller Archives Center 1973–79; Intl. Agricultural Development Service since 1975; Overseas Development Council. • Trustee: Pan American Sch. of Agriculture, Honduras since 1954; (also pres. 1961–72 and bd. chmn. since 1971) Gen. Education Bd. 1960–61; Oberlin Coll. 1962–73; (also chmn. 1972) Nutrition Foundn., NYC 1964–77; (also v.p.) The Foundation Center 1969–75; Near East Foundn.; Acad. of Natural Sciences. • Dir.: survey of science and technology and sub-Saharan Africa program, Natl. Acad. of Sciences; Campbell Soup Co. since 1962; Pres.'s Gen. Advisory Cttee. for Assistance Programs 1965–69; Dreyfus 3rd Century Fund; Intl. Flavors and Fragrances; Merck and Co., Inc.; Viacom Intl. **Fellow** Amer. Assn. for Advancement of Science; Amer. Phytopathological Soc.; Royal Soc. of Arts. **Member** Visiting cttee., biology dept., Harvard Univ. 1957–63; U.S. Natl. Cttee., Intl. Union of Biological Sciences 1959; various panels, Pres.'s Science Advisory Cttees. since 1960; advisory cttee., Natl. Acad. of Sciences 1960–62; advisory bd., Inter-Amer. Inst. of Agricultural Sciences, Costa Rica 1960s; advisory bd., Natl. Research Council 1960s; cttee. on intl. centers of medical research and training, NIH 1961–62; advisory bd., Intl. Nutrition Sch., Columbia Univ. 1964–68; cttee. on science and public policy, Natl. Acad. of Sciences 1967–71; Commn. on U.S.–Latin American Relations; Amer. Acad. of Arts and Sciences; Amer. Philosophical Soc.; Natl. Acad. of Agriculture, Italy; Mycological Soc. of Amer.; (corresp.) Acad. of Arts and Sciences, Puerto Rico; Amer. Soc. of Naturalists; Rockefeller Univ. Council; Council on Foreign Relations, Inc.; Phi Delta Theta; Sigma Xi; Sigma Delta Psi; Gamma Delta Sigma; Gamma Alpha. **Member** Clubs: Century Assn.; Cosmos, Wash. DC; University, Hemisphere, and Rockefeller Center Luncheon, NYC. **Honors** Certificate of Merit, Univ. of Florida 1950; Medal of Agricultural Merit, Coll. of Agriculture, Saltillo, Mexico 1952; outstanding achievement award, Univ. of Minnesota 1953; Cruz de Boyaca, Colombia 1954; officer 1958 and grand officer 1962, O'Higgins Order of Merit, Chile; citation of merit, Univ. of Arizona 1960; Presidential Award, Amer. Public Health Assn. 1962; Public Welfare Medal, Natl. Acad. of Sciences 1963; Order of the Golden Heart, Philippines 1964; Stakman Award 1969; distinguished achievement citation, Iowa State Univ. 1970; Browning Award, Amer. Soc. of Agronomy 1971; kt. comdr., Order of the Crown of Thailand 1971; Uribe Order of Merit in Agriculture, Colombia 1973; Atwater Medal 1974; Americas Award 1974; Underwood-Prescott Memorial Award 1975; hon. chmn., Population Crisis Cttee.; hon. member of Ecuadorian Assn. of Agricultural Engineers and Brazilian Soc. of Geneticists; hon. degrees from univs. of California, Nebraska, Florida, West Virginia, Ohio State, Emory, Clemson, Illinois, Arizona, Utah State, Columbia, Rockefeller, Washington, Central (Quito), Andes, and Colombia, and from Oberlin and Ripon colls. **Author** (Jtly.) *Guide to Southern Trees,* 1945; (jtly.) *Principles of Plant Pathology,* 1957; *Strategy for the Conquest of Hunger,* 1967. **Contributor** of more than 60 papers on phytopathology and mycology to scientific jrnls. and 50 articles on world agriculture, population, nutrition, environmental quality, education, and other subjects to gen. mags.

ARCHIBALD MacLEISH

Poet, playwright, and statesman

Born **Glencoe, Illinois, USA, 7 May 1892**

Died **Boston, Massachusetts, USA, 20 April 1982**

Archibald MacLeish was one of the best known of American poets, whose principal theme was undoubtedly democracy in all its challenges, triumphs, and complexity. For his poetry and drama he won the Pulitzer Prize three times, and as a public man he was at least equally honored: he was perhaps the most influential and distinguished of all Librarians of Congress, and for more than a decade held the prestigious Boylston Professorship of Rhetoric and Oratory at Harvard University.

He was born into an extraordinary family. His father, Andrew, had emigrated from Scotland in 1856 and had become a rich and successful department-store magnate and a founder of the University of Chicago. His mother, Martha Hillard, was a Vassar graduate who had been president of Rockford College in Illinois before her marriage. Young MacLeish was sent East to Hotchkiss in Connecticut for preparatory school, then entered Yale in 1911. He did well there, edited the literary magazine, played football, and graduated Phi Beta Kappa in 1915.

The following year he married and entered Harvard Law School. As soon as the United States became involved in World War I, however, MacLeish joined the Army, serving in France with the artillery, and rising from private to captain before his discharge. His brother Kenneth was killed in action. He returned to Harvard, from which he took his law degree in 1919, placing near the top of his class, and was also an editor of the *Harvard Law Review.* He taught government at Harvard until 1921, simultaneously joining the Boston law firm of Choate, Hall & Stewart, where he gained considerable experience in trial work.

Poetry, however, was even then the most central of his interests. In 1923 he quit the firm and left for Paris with his wife and two small children. Living on the Left Bank, he came to know Ernest Hemingway, John Dos Passos, and other members of the American literary group called by Gertrude Stein the "Lost Generation." They had come to Europe to find the creative freedom they believed America could not offer. In later life, MacLeish balked at the label "expatriate," saying he had never for a moment intended to stay in Europe. He found inspiration there, nevertheless, and his prolific published output began with the verse collections *The Happy Marriage* (1924), *The Pot of Earth* (1925), *Nobodaddy* (1925, a verse play), *Streets in the Moon* (1926), *The Hamlet of A. MacLeish* (1928), and *New Found Land* (1930), the last comprising poems he had written before returning home in 1929.

He left for Mexico almost as soon as he got back, traveling by burro and on foot to retrace the route of Hernando Cortés in the sixteenth century. What came from this adventure was a long narrative poem, *Conquistador* (1932), much of which was a verse paraphrase of Bernal Díaz del Castillo's *Conquest of New Spain* (1568). It won MacLeish the Pulitzer Prize for poetry in 1932.

MacLeish and his family moved permanently to a farm in Conway, in western Massachusetts, which he had bought in 1920 and which remained his home all his life. Early in the Great Depression he was hired by his friend Henry Luce to write articles on a wide variety of political and cultural subjects for Luce's new business magazine, *Fortune,* which had first appeared just before the Crash of 1929. As the Depression grew more severe, MacLeish's poetry became more overtly political, passionately engaged in the struggle to improve the lot of the common man and to awaken the social conscience of the wealthy. This was an important motif of such collections as *Frescoes for Mr. Rockefeller's City* (1933), *Public Speech* (1936), *Land of the Free—U.S.A.* (1938), and *America Was Promises* (1939). In the title poem of the last book he attacked native greed, rampant and insatiable:

The Aristocracy of Wealth and Talents
Turned its talents into wealth and lost them.
Turned enlightened selfishness to wealth.
Turned self-interest into bankbooks: balanced them.
Bred out: bred to fools.

On the other side were the people, long-suffering and noble:

The people had promises: they'd keep them.
They waited their time in the world: they had wise sayings.
They counted out their time by day to day.
They counted it out day after day into history.

President Franklin Roosevelt, whom MacLeish greatly admired, finally prevailed on the poet in 1939 after a lengthy campaign of persuasion to accept the Librarianship of Congress. MacLeish did not at all want the job, fearing that its constant public demands would kill the poetry in him. "I should . . . feel, in taking it, that I have given up my own work pretty much for the rest of my life," he wrote to the president, who as usual would not be denied. He was easily confirmed by the Senate despite sharp opposition from rightists in Congress and the American Library Association,

Courtesy of Harvard University

whose president said he would "no more think of him as Librarian of Congress than as chief engineer of a new Brooklyn Bridge." Yet MacLeish was successful in the job, especially in two areas: he reorganized and simplified the administration, which had grown sluggish and cumbersome during the 40-year tenure of his predecessor, Herbert Putnam; and by his eminence he attracted the public's attention to the library as a major national resource.

Roosevelt appointed him in October 1941 to hold the simultaneous job of director of the new Office of Facts and Figures, a kind of clearinghouse to coordinate government information in wartime. He received considerable Congressional criticism for departing from his mandate when the office published in 1942 a pamphlet countering Nazi propaganda. When the office was merged in mid-1942 with other agencies to form the Office of War Information, MacLeish served as assistant director for policy until February 1943, when he returned full-time to the library. He resigned in 1944, only to accept Roosevelt's offer of another new post, that of assistant secretary of state for public and cultural affairs. In this role he assisted in the drafting of the United Nations charter in San Francisco in April 1945 and the same year headed the U.S. delegation to the London conference that founded UNESCO. He left the State Department, however, shortly after Roosevelt's death.

His tenure of the Boylston professorship at Harvard coincided with the most productive and rewarding period of his life. His *Collected Poems* (1952) won him another Pulitzer Prize, as well as the Bollingen Prize and the National Book Award. And *J.B.* (1958), his paraphrase of the Book of Job, had the almost unprecedented good fortune (for a verse play) to become a Broadway hit, winning for him in 1959 his third Pulitzer Prize and a Tony Award. None of his other dramatic efforts enjoyed anything like this success. In addition to *Panic* (1935), *The Fall of the City* (1937), and *Air Raid* (1938), these included *This Music Crept by Me upon the Waters* (1953), *Herakles* (1967), and *The Great American Fourth of July Parade* (1975). *Six Plays* (1980) was a retrospective collection.

Courtesy of Library of Congress

MacLeish was outspokenly opposed to Sen. Joseph McCarthy and his followers, inveighing against the new spirit of persecution in America in both his poems and public speeches. He was perhaps the most influential among the U.S. literary figures who successfully pleaded for Ezra Pound's release after 12 years from St. Elizabeths Hospital in Washington. Pound had been accused of wartime treason and then incarcerated in the mental hospital; he was an old friend from MacLeish's Paris years, though MacLeish made it clear that he disapproved of Pound's politics.

After retiring from Harvard in 1962, MacLeish continued his writing in Conway. He collaborated on *The Eleanor Roosevelt Story* (1965), a book whose film version won an Academy Award in 1966. His poems became somewhat more personal in tone, less didactic and politically involved. His later poetry comprises *The Wild Old Wicked Man* (1968), *The Human Season* (1972), *New and Collected Poems 1917–1976* (1976), and *On the Beaches of the Moon* (1978).

In addition to honorary degrees from many of the most eminent universities in the United States and Canada, MacLeish received the National Medal for Literature (1978) and the Presidential Medal of Freedom (1977). He was a longtime member and sometime president (1953–56) of the American Academy of Arts and Letters, and won its gold medal for poetry in 1979. He died at the age of 89, two weeks after undergoing exploratory surgery.

A.K.

Parents Andrew M., businessman, and Martha (Hillard) M., educator. **Married** Ada Taylor Hitchcock, singer, 1916: William Hitchcock; Mary Hillard Grimm; Kenneth (d.); Brewster Hitchcock (d.). **Education** Hotchkiss Sch., Lakeville, CT; Yale Univ., A.B. (Phi Beta Kappa) 1915; Harvard Univ., LL.B. (Fay Diploma) 1919. **Mil. service** Capt. field artillery, U.S. Army, France 1917–19. **Career** Poet since mid-1910s; playwright since mid-1920s; essayist and nonfiction writer since late 1920s. • Lectr. in govt., Harvard Univ. 1919–21; lawyer, Choate, Hall & Stewart, Boston 1920–23; traveler and poet, Europe 1923–29; writer and ed., *Fortune* mag., NYC 1929–38; lectr., Princeton Univ. 1937; curator of Nieman Foundn. in Journalism 1938 and Boylston Prof. of Rhetoric and Oratory 1949–62, Harvard Univ.; Rede Lectr., Cambridge Univ. 1942; Simpson Lectr., Amherst Coll., MA 1963–67. • U.S. govt., Wash. DC: librarian of Congress 1939–44; dir., Office of Facts and Figures 1941–42; asst. dir. for policy, Office of War Information 1942–43; asst. secty. of state for public and cultural affairs 1944–45; fellow in Amer. letters, Library of Congress 1949–56. • Member, U.S. delegation to Conference of Allied Ministers of Education 1944; member of conference to draft U.N. charter, S.F. 1945; chmn., U.S. delegation to UNESCO chartering conference, London 1945; deputy chmn., U.S. delegation to UNESCO organizational meeting, Geneva 1946; exec. bd. member, UNESCO 1946. **Officer** Pres., Amer. Acad. of Arts and Letters 1953–56. **Member** Clubs: Century Assn., NYC; Tavern Club, Boston. **Honors** Shelley Memorial Award 1932; Pulitzer Prizes, 1932, for epic poem *Conquistador,* 1953, for *Collected Poems,* and 1959, for play *J.B.;* Golden Rose, New England Poetry Club 1934; Levinson Prize, *Poetry* 1941; Légion d'Honneur, France, WWII; Bollingen Prize, for *Collected Poems,* 1953; Natl. Book Award, for *Collected Poems,* 1953; Sara Josepha Hale Award 1958; Tony Award, for *J.B.,* 1959; award, Natl. Assn. of Independent Schs. 1959; fellowship, Acad. of Amer. Poets 1965; Presidential Medal of Freedom 1977; Natl. Medal for Literature 1978; gold medal for poetry, Amer. Acad. and Inst. 1979; comdr., Order El Sol del Peru; hon. degrees from univs. of Wesleyan, Yale, Pennsylvania, Illinois at Urbana-Champaign, Columbia, Harvard, Princeton, Massachusetts, York (Toronto), Johns Hopkins, California at Berkeley, Queen's (Ontario), Puerto Rico, Brandeis, and Washington at Seattle, and from Colby, Rockford, Carleton, Dartmouth, Amherst, Union, and Williams colls. **Poetry** *Songs for a Summer's Day (A Sonnet-Cycle),* 1915; *Tower of Ivory,* 1917; *The Happy Marriage and Other Poems,* 1924; *The Pot of Earth,* 1925; *Streets in the Moon,* 1926; *The Hamlet of A. MacLeish,* 1928; *Einstein,* 1929; *New Found Land: Fourteen Poems,* 1930; *Before March,* 1932; *Conquistador,* 1932; *Frescoes for Mr. Rockefeller's City,* 1933; *Poems, 1924–1933,* 1933 (in U.K. as *Poems,* 1935); *Public Speech: Poems,* 1936; *Land of the Free—U.S.A.,* 1938; *America Was Promises,* 1939; *Actfive and Other Poems,* 1948; *Collected Poems, 1917–1952,* 1952; *Songs for Eve,* 1954; *Collected Poems,* 1963; *The Wild Old Wicked Man and Other Poems,* 1968; *The Human Season: Selected Poems 1962–1972,* 1972; *New and Collected Poems 1917–1976,* 1976; *On the Beaches of the Moon,* 1978. **Stage plays** *Nobodaddy,* 1926; *Union Pacific* (ballet scenario), 1934; *Panic: A Play in Verse,* 1935; *J.B.: A Play in Verse,* 1958; *Three Short Plays,* 1961; *Our Lives, Our Fortunes, and Our Sacred Honor* (produced as *The American Bell),* 1962; *Herakles: A Play in Verse,* 1965; *Magic Prison* (libretto), 1967; *An Evening's Journey to Conway, Massachusetts: An Outdoor Play,* 1967; *Scratch,* 1971; *The Great American Fourth of July Parade,* 1975; *Six Plays,* 1980. **Screenplays** *Grandma Moses,* 1950; *The Eleanor Roosevelt Story,* 1965. **Radio plays** *The Fall of the City: A Verse Play for*

Radio, 1938; *Air Raid: A Verse Play for Radio,* 1938; *The States Talking,* 1941; *The American Story: Ten Radio Scripts,* 1944; *The Trojan Horse,* 1952; *This Music Crept by Me upon the Waters,* 1953. **Television play** *The Secret of Freedom,* 1959. **Other** (Jtly.) *Housing America,* 1932; (jtly.) *Jews in America,* 1936; (jtly.) *Background of War,* 1937; *The Irresponsibles: A Declaration,* 1940; *The Next Harvard, As Seen by Archibald MacLeish,* 1941; *A Time to Speak: The Selected Prose of Archibald MacLeish,* 1941; *The American Cause,* 1941; *American Opinion and the War: The Rede Lecture,* 1943; *A Time To Act: Selected Addresses,* 1943; *Poetry and Opinion: The Pisan Cantos of Ezra Pound: A Dialogue on the Role of Poetry,* 1950; *Freedom is the Right to Choose: An Inquiry into the Battle for the American Future,* 1951; *Poetry and Journalism,* 1958; *Emily Dickinson: Papers Delivered at Amherst College,* 1960; *Poetry and Experience,* 1961; (ed.) Felix Frankfurter, *Law and Politics,* 1962; *The Dialogues of Archibald MacLeish and Mark Van Doren,* 1964; *The Eleanor Roosevelt Story,* 1965; *Remarks at the Dedication of the Wallace Library, Fitchburg, Massachusetts,* 1967; *A Continuing Journey,* 1968; *The Great American Frustration,* 1968; (jtly.) *The University—The Library: Papers . . . ,* 1972; *Riders on the Earth,* 1978; R. H. Winnick, ed., *Letters of Archibald MacLeish 1907–1982,* 1983. **Recording** *Archibald MacLeish Reads His Own Poetry.* **Manuscript collections** in Library of Congress, Yale Univ., and Harvard Univ. **Interview** George Plimpton, ed., *Writers at Work: The Paris Review Interviews,* 5th series, 1981.

Further reading Arthur Mizener, *A Catalogue of the First Editions of Archibald MacLeish,* 1938; Signi Lenea Falk, *Archibald MacLeish,* 1965; Grover Smith, *Archibald MacLeish,* 1971; Edward J. Mullahy, *Archibald MacLeish: A Checklist,* 1973.

MARÍA LUISA PACHECO
Painter
***Born* La Paz, Bolivia, 22 September 1919**
***Died* New York City, USA, 21 April 1982**

Pacheco, Maria: Courtesy of Ralph Llenera

María Pacheco, whose abstract canvases evoke the landscapes of her native Bolivia, began her career in middle age, while raising a family. She studied art in La Paz in the 1940s, painting traditional Bolivian themes in a representational style, then traveled to Madrid in the early 1950s. There, she became familiar with the work of progressive Spanish artists such as Antonio Tapies, and her own work became more abstract. In 1956, she moved to the United States and settled in New York, where she came under the influence of the abstract expressionists, particularly Willem de Kooning and Jackson Pollock.

By the mid-1960s, Pacheco had found her own style. On a base of painted plywood and collaged materials, including sand, she applied broad slashes of heavily impasted paint in earth colors, grays, turquoise blues, and glowing reds. Her paintings of this period are mainly abstractions of massive totemic figures based on the hieratic art of Bolivia's pre-Columbian Tiahuanaco empire. In the 1970s, she painted in a looser, more abstract style, using vertical slabs of impasto to suggest the mountain ranges of the Andes.

Pacheco first showed her work in the United States in 1957 at the Pan American Union in Washington, D.C. She exhibited regularly thereafter in the United States and in Bolivia and other Latin American countries, and mounted a retrospective at the Museo Nacional de Arte in La Paz in 1976. Her paintings are held in numerous collections, including the Guggenheim Museum in New York City, the Pan American Union, and the Museums of Modern Art in São Paulo, La Paz, and Rio de Janeiro. She was awarded three Guggenheim Fellowships, in 1958, 1959, and 1960.

Pacheco died of a brain tumor at the age of 62. S.A.

Married (1) . . . : María Eugenia Azcarrunz; Julio. **Religion** Roman Catholic. **Emigrated** to U.S. 1956; naturalized. **Education** Acad. de Bellas Artes, La Paz, Bolivia; Real Acad. San Fernando, Madrid; studied painting with Daniel Vazquéz Diaz, Madrid. **Career** Homemaker to 1952, then painter. **Member** MOMA. **Honors** Fellowship, govt. of Spain 1951; first prize, Salon Nacional Pedro D. Murillo, La Paz 1953; first prize, National Contest, La Paz 1954; prize for painting, 2nd Biennial of Spanish-American Art, Havana 1954; Guggenheim Fellowships 1958, 1959, 1960; award, 5th Bienal, São Paulo 1959; 2nd prize, Latin American Exhib. of Paintings, Barranquilla, Colombia 1959; acquisition prize, Pan American Union, Wash. DC 1959; Tredicesimo Premio, Lissone, Italy 1963; acquisition prize, Dallas Mus. of Art, TX 1969. **Solo exhibitions** Galeria Municipal, La Paz 1953; Pan American Union, Wash. DC 1957; Inst. of Contemporary Arts, Lima, Peru 1960 and 1966; Lee Ault & Co., NYC 1971, 1974, 1977; Instituto Cultural Alemán, Santa Cruz, Bolivia 1972; retrospective, Museo Nacional de Arte, La Paz 1976; Signs Gall., NYC 1982; other galls. in Buenos Aires, Santiago, La Paz, Caracas, and NYC. **Group exhibitions** São Paulo Bienal, 1953, 1955, 1957; Contemporary Painting and Sculpture, Urbana, IL 1963; others. **Collections** Guggenheim Mus., NYC; Mus. of Univ. of Texas at Austin; Mus. of Art, Dallas; Museos de Bellas Artes of Caracas and Buenos Aires; Museums of Modern Art of Rio de Janeiro, São Paulo, La Paz, Barranquilla, and Santiago; Gibbes Art Gall., Charleston, SC; Casa de la Cultura, Santa Cruz; Pan American Union, Wash. DC; numerous corps. in U.S. and South America.

Further reading Leopoldo Castedo, *A History of Latin American Art and Architecture,* 1969; Jacqueline Barnitz, *Review 75: Five Women Artists,* 1975.

MELVILLE BELL GROSVENOR
Chairman of the National Geographic Society
***Born* Washington, D.C., USA, 26 November 1901**
***Died* Miami, Florida, USA, 22 April 1982**

In 1957, Melville Bell Grosvenor became the fourth member of his family to serve as president of the National Geographic Society, the world's largest nonprofit scientific and educational organization, and the second to edit its magazine, *National Geographic.* Under his direction, the magazine assumed its present format and the society more than doubled in size, from slightly over 2 million to 5.5 million members.

The National Geographic Society, originally an association of geographers, cartographers, and laymen dedicated to geographical research, was founded in 1888 by Grosvenor's great-grandfather, Gardiner Greene Hubbard. Hubbard's son-in-law, Alexander Graham Bell, the inventor of the telephone, took over the presidency after Hubbard retired, and Bell's son-in-law, Gilbert Hovey Grosvenor, Melville's father, edited the magazine from 1899 to 1954.

Young Grosvenor attended private schools and was tutored by his grandfather and father in photography and writing. He graduated from the U.S. Naval Academy, where he acquired a lifelong love of sailing, in 1923, and rose to the rank of ensign during a year of service on the U.S.S. *Delaware* and the U.S.S. *West Virginia.*

Grosvenor joined the staff of the society's magazine in 1924 as assistant chief of illustrations. *National Geographic,* which had evolved from a technical publication into a profusely illustrated popular magazine, was then introducing high-quality color photography. The first natural-color aerial photographs ever published appeared in its pages and were taken in 1930 by Grosvenor from a dirigible over New York City and Washington. As an assistant editor (1935–51) he contributed numerous articles, accompanied by his own photographs, on his travels in Europe, the Middle East, and North America. In 1954, the year his father stepped down as editor of the magazine, Grosvenor was named associate editor and a vice president of the society.

As president and editor from 1957 to 1967, Grosvenor inaugurated several major projects for the society, including the publication of its first atlas and globe, the modernization of its printing plant, the production of color television programs for network distribution, and the updating of the magazine's cover format to incorporate color photographs as well as text. He did not tamper with the magazine's detached, educative tone and its presentation of articles on exotic locales and wildlife. The romance of scientific discovery was emphasized in *National Geographic*'s reports on the work of anthropologist L. S. B. Leakey and its continuing series on oceanographer Jacques Yves Cousteau, whose research was funded, in part, by the society's expanding grants program. Grosvenor also edited or oversaw the production of dozens of the society's books. He was active in the environmental and conservation movements, including the effort to save the California redwood forests from destruction by real-estate developers.

In 1967 Grosvenor became editor in chief of the magazine and chairman of the society's board of trustees, leaving the day-to-day administration to his son Gilbert Melville Grosvenor, now president. He was elected chairman emeritus in 1976 and editor emeritus in 1977. He died of cardiac arrest at his home in Miami at the age of 80. S.A.

Parents Gilbert Hovey G., ed., *National Geographic Magazine,* and Elsie May (Bell) G. **Married** (1) Helen North Rowland 1924 (div.): Helen Rowland Lemmerman; Alexander Graham Bell, capt., U.S. Navy (d.); Gilbert Melville, pres., Natl. Geographic Soc. (2) Anne Elizabeth Revis 1950: Edwin Stuart, ed.; Sara Anne. **Religion** Presbyterian. **Education** Private schs.; U.S. Naval Acad., Annapolis, MD, B.S. 1923. **Mil. service** Ensign, U.S. Navy 1923–24. **Career** With *National Geographic Magazine,* Wash. DC: asst. chief of illustrations div. 1924–35; asst. ed. 1935–51; sr. asst. ed. 1951–54; assoc. ed. 1954–57; ed. 1957–67; ed. in chief 1967–77; ed. emeritus since 1977. • Natl. Geographic Soc., Wash. DC: v.p. 1954–57; pres. 1957–67; chmn., bd. of trustees 1967–76; chmn. emeritus since 1976. • Founding ed., *Wild Acres Weekly* mag. **Officer** Trustee: George Washington Univ.; Univ. of Miami; Jackson Hole Preserve, Inc.; White House Historical Assn.; Mus. of Science, Miami. • Other: advisory dir., Riggs Natl. Bank; dir., Chesapeake and Potomac Telephone Co.; assoc., Woods Hole Oceanographic Inst. **Fellow** Royal Geographical Soc., U.K. **Member** Natl. Parks, Historic Sites, Bldgs. and Monuments Advisory Council, U.S. Secty. of the Interior; Assn. of

Courtesy of National Geographic

Amer. Geographers; Amer. Geographical Soc.; Natl. Audubon Soc.; New York Zoological Soc.; Amer. Mus. of Natural History; Robert Coll., Istanbul. • Clubs: Cruising; Natl. Press; Overseas Writers; Cosmos; Chevy Chase; Metropolitan, NYC; Explorers; Alfalfa; Literary; Gibson Island; Bath, Miami. **Honors** Gold medal, Washburn Award 1964, and scholarship named after him, Mus. of Sciences, Boston; distinguished service award 1969 and hon. v.p. 1970, Amer. Forestry Assn.; Eisenhower Award, People to People, Inc. 1970; Intl. Oceanographic Foundn. Medal, Rosensteil Sch., Univ. of Miami 1975; Natl. Heritage Award, Parks Canada 1980; hon. pioneer, Alexander Graham Bell chapter, Telephone Pioneers of America; member, Photo Marketing Hall of Fame; Military Order of Christ, Portugal; Order of Merit, Italy; Conservation Award, Natl. Park Service; Albright Conservation Award; hon. degrees from univs. of Miami, New Brunswick, George Washington, and Brown. **Editor in chief** Rhys Carpenter et al., *Everyday Life in Ancient Times; Highlights of the Beginnings of Western Civilization in Mesopotamia, Egypt, and Rome,* 1961; James M. Daley et al., *National Geographic Atlas of the World,* 1963; *Wondrous World of Fishes,* 1965; Merle Severy, ed., *Wild Animals of North America,* rev. ed. 1967; many other *National Geographic* books. **Editor** *Australia and New Zealand: A Selection of Descriptive Articles Which Have Appeared in Recent Years in the Pages of the National Geographic Magazine,* 1943; *National Geographic Index 1947–63 Inclusive,* 1964. **Contributor** *The National Geographic Book of Dogs,* 1958, rev. as *Man's Best Friend: National Geographic Book of Dogs,* 1971; *John Fitzgerald Kennedy: The Last Full Measure,* 1964; *America's Historylands: Touring Our Landmarks of Liberty,* 1967; articles and photographs in *National Geographic Magazine.*

FRED(ERICK RONALD) WILLIAMS
Painter and printmaker
***Born* near Melbourne, Australia, 23 January 1927**
***Died* Melbourne, Australia, 22 April 1982**

Since the mid-1960s, Fred Williams was widely regarded as Australia's premier landscape painter. In his studies of the bush country, he balanced the directness and sensitivity of a master watercolorist with the formal discipline of a minimalist and color-field painter. In the opinion of many critics, he completely changed the way Australians viewed their own land.

Born outside Melbourne in 1927, Williams attended the art school of the National Gallery of Victoria from 1943 to 1948. After working as an assistant plumber to pay for his studio, supplies, and classes in life drawing, he traveled to London in 1951 to study at the Chelsea Art School and the Central School of Art and Design. During his years in England he worked mostly on portraits and nudes, mastered the various intaglio printmaking techniques, and studied the paintings of Matisse, Cézanne, and Daumier, his main influences. He returned to Australia in 1957.

Shortly thereafter he began to paint his first landscapes around Sherbrooke Forest in Victoria and Mittagong in New South Wales, and his distinctive, loosely representational style quickly emerged. Using the characteristic Australian palette—pale green, ochre, brick red, and sky blue—he explored in each painting the formal geometry of the bush, focusing on details of trees and rocks rather than on the identity of any particular locale. He often elevated or eliminated the horizon line and employed a wide variety of animated, almost alphabetic brushstrokes. "There is much about his compositions that is reminiscent of music," wrote Bernard Smith in *Australian Painting* (1971). "Trees spread themselves across scoriated surfaces like notes on a musical score; the lower and heavier rhythms are in the lower parts of the painting, the more rapid and scintillating dance above the horizon line like a descant." Starting with a gouache or oil sketch on the site, Williams would return to his studio and distill the image, usually through the intermediate stage of an etching, into the final painting. He worked on as many as 20 paintings at a time.

Williams's work received unfavorable criticism when it was first shown around Melbourne in the late 1950s. Robert Hughes called his landscapes "stale exercises in the manner of Matisse," while others found them insipid, saccharine, and provincial. He was not invited to show in the famous "antipodean" exhibition of 1959, which included Melbourne's most respected representational painters. But by 1966 his expertise had increased, tastes had changed, and such critics as Wallace Thornton were proclaiming him Australia's greatest landscape painter.

Williams's best-known works are his late-1960s landscapes of Upwey (where he lived), Lysterfield, the aboriginal graves at Tiboo-burra, and the You Yangs hills, all near Melbourne. Under the influence of American minimalism and color-field painting, he gradually purged all detail from his landscapes until, by the early 1970s, they were little more than flat fields of subdued color divided by white lines and random flecks. He returned to a more representational style and a freer technique in the mid-1970s for his Gorge series and his seascapes of Erith Island, Sorrento, and Walkerville, on the south coast near Melbourne.

Williams, who is represented in every Australian national collection as well as collections in Europe and the United States, was awarded several major Australian art prizes and was made OBE in 1976. He died of cancer at the age of 55. S.A.

Father A. A. W. **Married** Lyn Watson 1961: Isobel; Louise; Kate. **Education** Sch. of the Natl. Gall. of Victoria, Melbourne 1943–48; Chelsea Art Sch. and Central Sch. of Art and Design, London 1951–56; Rubinstein and Dyason Travelling Scholarships 1963. **Career** Asst. plumber 1940s; painter and printmaker since ca. 1945. **Officer** Founder and pres., Print Council of Australia. **Member** Commonwealth Art Advisory Bd. 1972–73; acquisitions cttee. 1973–74 and council since 1975, Australian Natl. Gall.; Visual Arts Bd., Australian Council 1973–75. **Honors** Transfield Prize 1964; Georges Prize 1966; Wills Prize 1966; McCaughey Prize 1966; Trustees Watercolour Prize 1966; Wynne Prize 1966, 1977; OBE 1976; hon. degree from Monash Univ. **Solo exhibitions** Australian Galls., Melbourne 1956; Gall. of Contemporary Art, Melbourne 1957; MOMA 1977; retrospective, Natl. Gall. of Victoria, Melbourne 1980; Fischer Fine Art Gall., London 1980; many others. **Group exhibitions** Contemporary Art Soc., Royal Tour 1954; Four Arts in Australia, Southeast Asian tour 1962; Tate Gall., London 1963; Intl. Exhib. of Drawing and Painting, Lugarno, Switzerland 1964; Intl. Exhib. of Printmaking, Cracow 1966; many others. **Collections** All Australian state collections; MOMA; Victoria and Albert Mus., London; Mertz Coll., USA; Adelaide Festival Theatre; many other public and private collections. **Author** *Fred Williams, Etchings*.

Further reading Bernard Smith, *Australian Painting,* 1971; Patrick McCaughey, *Fred Williams,* 1981.

VILLE RITOLA
Long-distance runner
***Born* Finland, 1896**
***Died* Helsinki, Finland, 24 April 1982**

The chief rival to Paavo Nurmi at the 1924 Olympic Games was his countryman Ville Ritola, one of the great long-distance runners produced by Finland in the early part of the century. He won a total of eight Olympic medals: four gold and one silver in Paris in 1924, and one gold and two silver in Amsterdam in 1928.

Ritola came to New York City at the age of 17 to work in the construction industry and began running under the guidance of Finnish-born coaches when he was 23. He built up his stamina by training in weighted rubber boots and competed in numerous U.S. track meets before qualifying in 1924 for the Finnish Olympic team.

In Paris he was presented with a difficult schedule, with either a race or a heat slated for each of the seven days between 6 July and 12 July. On the first day he broke the world record for the 10,000-meter run with a time of 30:23.2. On 9 July he broke the Olympic record in the 3,000-meter steeplechase with a time of 9:33.6, half a lap in front of the next runner.

He and Nurmi met in competition for the first time on 10 July in the 5,000-meter run. Nurmi, who had set an Olympic record in the 1,500-meter run earlier in the day, finished two-tenths of a second ahead of him. He came in second to Nurmi again the following day in the 3,000-meter team run—though the team won the gold—and once more in the 10,000-meter cross-country on 12 July, when he took both a team gold and an individual silver.

Their contest was resumed in Amsterdam in 1928. In the 10,000-meter run they raced together stride for stride; then, in the final lap, Nurmi shot ahead and won by six-tenths of a second. A few days later they matched strides again in the 5,000-meter run, but this time Ritola crossed the tape two seconds ahead of Nurmi—the first and only time he defeated him. At least one observer suggested that Nurmi had let Ritola win. In their last meeting, in the 3,000-meter steeplechase, Ritola took a spill at the water jump and withdrew from the race without finishing, and Nurmi came in second to another Finnish runner.

By 1932 both Nurmi and Ritola had turned professional. Ritola eventually held a total of 18 U.S. championships. He died in Finland at the age of 86. J.P.

Emigrated to the U.S. 1913 but retained Finnish citizenship. **Career** Bridge construction worker, NYC; long-distance runner from 1919. **Honors** Olympic Games, Paris 1924: gold medal and world record, 10,000-meter run; gold medal and Olympic record, 3,000-meter steeplechase; silver medal, 5,000-meter run; team gold medal, 3,000-meter run; team gold medal and individual silver medal, 10,000-meter cross-country. • Olympic Games, Amsterdam 1928: gold medal, 5,000-meter run; silver medal, 10,000-meter run. • Holder of 18 U.S. titles.

Further reading Dick Schaap, *An Illustrated History of the Olympics,* 1975.

W(ILLIAM) R(ILEY) BURNETT
Novelist and screenwriter
Born **Springfield, Ohio, USA, 25 November 1899**
Died **Santa Monica, California, USA, 25 April 1982**

W. R. Burnett's first published novel, the best-selling *Little Caesar,* became one of the earliest and best gangster films and catapulted to stardom Edward G. Robinson in the role of Rico, a violent gang leader. Over a long and productive Hollywood career, Burnett wrote some 35 novels and was associated with the writing of 60 motion pictures.

He graduated from the Miami Military Institute in Germantown, Ohio, then for one semester attended the College of Journalism at Ohio State University (1919–20). From 1921 until 1927 he worked as a statistician for the Ohio Bureau of Labor Statistics, writing unsold short stories and novels in his spare time. Moving to Chicago in 1927, he watched "as a rather appalled observer" while underworld forces fought it out over the city they largely controlled. From this firsthand observation came *Little Caesar* (1929), a story of corruption and betrayal told from a gangster's point of view and in his own language. It was a huge success, became a selection of the Literary Guild, and received newspaper serialization. The film rights were acquired by Warner Brothers, who brought Burnett to Hollywood as a consultant at a salary of $1,000 a week.

He later claimed he "had no desire to write for the pictures," believing film to be "a mass medium, and if you're going to appeal to the masses, forget it." He nevertheless remained in southern California for the rest of his life, and during the 1930s and 1940s "worked for every major studio—even Republic, which was known then as Repulsive." His next novel, *The Iron Man* (1930), set in the world of prize fighting, was also a hit movie starring Lew Ayres, as was his screenplay for *Scarface,* starring Paul Muni.

Burnett was an inveterate gambler, and despite a salary enormous for the times—$3,500 a week by the mid-1930s—he went broke in 1938. "My problem was never making money. It was keeping it. . . . Luckily, I wrote *High Sierra* in 1938 and made it all over." The fast-moving story of the final days of Roy Earle, the last surviving member of the Dillinger Gang, it became a screenplay with John Huston's collaboration and then was made into a highly successful movie in 1941 starring Humphrey Bogart. His other triumphs of the 1940s were his screenplay for *This Gun for Hire,* which made a star of Alan Ladd, and his novel and screenplay for *The Asphalt Jungle.*

During the late 1950s and 1960s, Burnett continued to produce novels at the rate of about one a year, but *The Cool Man* (1968) was the last until *Goodbye, Chicago* appeared in 1980, the year he won the Grand Master Award of the Mystery Writers of America. His screenplays were still sought by the studios, despite his reputation as being an extremely demanding colleague. His final screen successes were *Sergeants Three,* starring Frank Sinatra and Dean Martin, and *The Great Escape,* starring Steve McQueen and James Garner. The last film he worked on was *Ice Station Zebra* in 1968. He also did some writing for television, contributing to such series as "Naked City," "The Untouchables," "77 Sunset Strip," and "Bonanza."

Burnett won the Writers Guild of America award in 1949 for *Yellow Sky,* and was nominated in 1942 for an Academy Award for his screenplay for *Wake Island.* He died at the age of 82. A.K.

Also wrote under pseudonyms John Monahan and James Updyke. **Parents** Theodore Addison B. and Emily Updyke Colwell (Morgan) B. **Married** (1) Marjorie Louise Bartow 1921. (2) Whitney Forbes Johnstone 1943: William Riley III; James Addison. **Religion** Episcopalian. **Education** East High Sch., Columbus, OH; Miami Military Inst., Germantown, OH, grad. 1919; Coll. of Journalism, Ohio State Univ., Columbus 1919–20. **Career** Professional boxer ca. 1920; statistician, Ohio Bureau of Labor Statistics 1921–27; writer since 1928; consultant to Warner Bros. since 1929; screenwriter since 1931. **Member** Acad. of Motion Picture Arts and Sciences; Democratic Party; Writers Club, Hollywood; Players Club, NYC. **Honors** O. Henry Memorial Prize, for story "Dressing Up," *Harper's* 1930; Acad. Award nomination for best original screenplay, for *Wake Island,* 1942; (jtly.) Writers Guild of America award, for *Yellow Sky,* 1949; Poe Award 1951 and Grand Master Award 1980, Mystery Writers of America. **Novels** *Little Caesar,* 1929; *Iron Man,* 1930; *Saint Johnson,* 1930; *The Silver Eagle,* 1932; *The Giant Swing,* 1932; *Dark Hazard,* 1933; *The Goodhues of Sinking Creek,* 1934; *Good-*

Courtesy of Joseph Haworth

bye to the Past, 1934; *King Cole* (in U.K. as *Six Days' Grace*), 1936; *The Dark Command: A Kansas Iliad,* 1938; *High Sierra,* 1940; *The Quick Brown Fox,* 1942; *Nobody Lives Forever,* 1943; *Tomorrow's Another Day,* 1945; *Romelle,* 1946; *The Asphalt Jungle,* 1949; *Stretch Dawson,* 1951; *Little Man, Big World,* 1951; *Vanity Row,* 1952; (as John Monahan) *Big Stan,* 1954; *Captain Lightfoot,* 1955; *Pale Moon,* 1956; (as James Updyke) *It's Always Four O'Clock,* 1956; *Underdog,* 1957; *Bitter Ground,* 1958; *Mi Amigo,* 1963; *Conant,* 1961; *Round the Clock at Volari's,* 1961; *The Goldseekers,* 1962; *The Widow Barony,* 1962; *The Abilene Samson,* 1963; *The Winning of Mickey Free,* 1965; *The Cool Man,* 1968; *Goodbye Chicago,* 1981. **Other books** *Adobe Walls: A Story of the Last Apache Rising,* 1953; *The Roar of the Crowd: Conversations with an Ex-Big Leaguer,* 1964. **Screenplays** (most jtly.) *The Finger Points,* 1931; *The Beast of the City,* 1932; *Scarface,* 1932; *The Whole Town's Talking,* 1935; *36 Hours To Kill,* 1936; *Some Blondes Are Dangerous,* 1937; *King of the Underworld,* 1938; *High Sierra,* 1941; *The Get-Away,* 1941; *This Gun for Hire,* 1942; *Wake Island,* 1942; *Background to Danger,* 1943; *Crash Dive,* 1943; *Action in the North Atlantic,* 1943; *San Antonio,* 1945; *Nobody Lives Forever,* 1946; *Belle Starr's Daughter,* 1948; *Yellow Sky,* 1948; *The Asphalt Jungle,* 1950; *Vendetta,* 1950; *The Racket,* 1951; *Dangerous Mission,* 1954; *Captain Lightfoot,* 1955; *Illegal,* 1955; *I Died a Thousand Times,* 1955; *Accused of Murder,* 1956; *September Storm,* 1960; *Sergeants Three,* 1962; *The Great Escape,* 1963; *Ice Station Zebra,* 1968. **Television scripts** "Bonanza," "Naked City," other adventure series.

LYMAN H(ENRY) BUTTERFIELD

Historian and editor of the Adams Papers
***Born* Lyndonville, New York, USA, 8 August 1909**
***Died* Boston, Massachusetts, USA, 25 April 1982**

Lyman H. Butterfield was chief editor of the Adams Papers, a massive record of the diaries, letters, and notes of the prominent Massachusetts patriot family. His meticulous research set a standard for historical scholarship and made available to the public an invaluable fund of source material on the development of the nation.

The son of a high-school principal, Butterfield attended Harvard University, graduating summa cum laude in 1930. He recalled that in the fall of his senior year he had as a tutor Bernard DeVoto, a new instructor in the English department, who was amazed at his brilliant pupil's ignorance of American literature and set him a heavy program of reading, "a blueprint that was to refashion my world." Butterfield taught English at Harvard himself for seven years after his graduation (he took his A.M. in 1934) and then at Franklin and Marshall College (1937–46). In 1946 he left full-time teaching for good, having been hired as assistant (later associate) editor to Julian P. Boyd, librarian of Princeton University, on the papers of Thomas Jefferson. Just as the first five volumes were appearing (1950–52), Butterfield published his first major work, the two-volume *Letters of Benjamin Rush* (1951), the correspondence of the surgeon general of the Continental Army and close friend of Adams and Jefferson.

From 1951 to 1954, Butterfield was director of the Institute of Early American History and Culture in Williamsburg, Virginia, from which he was called by the Massachusetts Historical Society, the trustee and repository of the Adams Papers, to direct the Herculean effort required to edit them, financing and publication details having been arranged before the project began.

Aided by only a small staff and working in extremely cramped quarters, Butterfield began the task in 1954, with more than 300,000 basically uncatalogued manuscript pages before him. They comprised the personal writings of John Adams (1735–1826), second president of the United States; his wife Abigail (1744–1818); their son John Quincy Adams (1767–1848), sixth president; his son Charles Francis Adams (1807–1886), Lincoln's minister to Britain during the Civil War; and his sons, the industrialist Charles Francis Adams (1835–1915), the politician John Quincy Adams (1833–94), the historian Brooks Adams (1848–1927), and Henry Adams (1838–1918), author of *Mont St. Michel and Chartres*, *The Education of Henry Adams*, and *Democracy*. The papers were so numerous because they had been kept intact by the family—whose members rarely threw away anything they had written—until 1905, when they were taken over by the Massachusetts Historical Society. Butterfield's initial task was to establish the principles of selection which would separate gold from dross: "We can't possibly publish every scratch from an Adams pen," he said in 1954. By the spring of 1955 he had completed the first inventory ever done of the collection, and publication of the first volumes, by the Belknap Press at Harvard, followed in 1961. They were extremely well received by historians, and the project and its editors were praised by Pres. John Kennedy. Twenty volumes had been published by the time Butterfield retired in 1975; six more have been completed by his successor, Robert J. Taylor; and the entire work is expected to fill more than a hundred volumes.

Butterfield's favorite among the Adamses came to be the first John Quincy Adams. "People have the fixed idea he was dull," he said. "Not at all. To be sure, he must have been something to live with, but as a public servant he never has been outdone." He added later, "No one likes the Adamses—until you study them." "What makes them so interesting was their total independence of the mood of the crowd. They're all different and yet they are alike."

He lectured in history at William and Mary College from 1951 to 1954 and at Harvard from 1955 to 1964. In addition to being a member of numerous state and national historical societies, he was a fellow of the American Academy of Arts and Sciences and received honorary doctorates from several universities.

His wife Elizabeth, whom he married in 1935, was the daughter of Cyrus Eaton, the Cleveland industrialist. Their son Fox is a Chinese scholar and newspaper reporter who was for several years chief of the *New York Times*'s bureau in Peking. Lyman Butterfield died at the age of 72 after a long illness.

A.K.

Parents Roy Lyman B., high-sch. principal, and Ethel (Place) B. **Married** Elizabeth Anne Eaton 1935 (d. 1978): Fox, journalist; Hester Butterfield McKelvey. **Education** Charlotte High Sch., Rochester, NY: Harvard Univ., A.B. (summa cum laude) 1930, A.M. 1934. **Career** Instr. and tutor in English, Harvard Univ. 1930–37; asst. prof. of English, then assoc. prof., Franklin and Marshall Coll., Lancaster, PA 1937–46; asst. ed., then assoc. ed., Papers of Thomas Jefferson project, Princeton Univ. 1946–51; library research assoc., Amer. Philosophical Soc. 1946–51; dir., Inst. of Early Amer. History and Culture, Williamsburg, VA 1951–54; lectr. in history and ed. of quarterly, Coll. of William and Mary, Williamsburg, VA 1951–54; ed. in chief 1954–75 and ed. emeritus since 1975, Adams Papers project, Massachusetts Historical Soc.; lectr. in history, Harvard Univ. 1955–64; consulting ed., Harvard Univ. Press 1965–75; consultant, "The Adams Chronicles" TV series. **Officer** Member, bd. of dirs.: *New England Quarterly* since 1956; Council on Library Resources, Inc. 1956–75; Harry S. Truman Library Inst. 1957–75. • Pres., Harvard chapter, Phi Beta Kappa. **Fellow** Amer. Acad. of Arts and Sciences; Soc. of Amer. Archivists. **Member** White House Fine Arts Cttee. ca. 1960–63; Natl. History Publishing Commn. 1964–75; Amer. History Assn.; New York State, Massachusetts, Mississippi Valley, and Pennsylvania historical socs.; Org. of Amer. Historians; Natl. Parks Assn.; ACLU; Amer. Philosophical Soc.; Amer. Antiquarian Soc.; Colonial Soc., MA; Old South Church Corp., Boston. **Honors** Welch Medal, Amer. Assn. for the History of Medicine 1956; Guggenheim Fellowship 1958–59; hon. consultant in American history, Library of Congress 1974–77; hon. consulting ed., Harvard Univ. Press since 1975; hon. degrees from Bucknell and Southeastern Massachusetts univs. and from Franklin and Marshall, Washington, and Monmouth colls. **Author** *John Witherspoon Comes to America*, 1953. **Editor** Richard Tickell, *Anticipation*, 1941; (jtly.) *The Papers of Thomas Jefferson*, vols. 1–5, 1950–52; *The Letters of Benjamin Rush*, 2 vols., 1951; (jtly.) *The Adams Papers*, vols. 1–20, 1961–75; (jtly.) *The Book of Abigail and John*, 1975.

JOHN PATRICK CARDINAL CODY

Roman Catholic archbishop of Chicago
Born **St. Louis, Missouri, USA, 24 December 1907**
Died **Chicago, Illinois, USA, 25 April 1982**

John Patrick Cardinal Cody was from 1965 until his death the archbishop of Chicago, the largest Roman Catholic see in the United States. Extremely authoritarian in administration and equally conservative in matters of faith and morals, he enjoyed solid majority support in the 2.5-million-member archdiocese until 1981, when he was accused of systematically diverting, over a lengthy period of time, tax-exempt church funds under his control to enrich a female friend of many years' standing. The federal investigation was incomplete at the time of his death.

The son of Irish immigrants, Cody entered the minor seminary in St. Louis, where his father was deputy fire chief, at the age of 12. Graduating in 1926, he was sent to the North American College in Rome. He proceeded to earn three doctorates, in philosophy (1928), sacred theology (1932), and canon law (1938), and was ordained a priest in 1931. In 1933 he began work in the Vatican Secretariat of State, the essential training ground for future prelates, where he remained until 1938 and where his superiors included Eugenio Cardinal Pacelli, the secretary of state, later Pope Pius XII, and Msgr. Giovanni Battista Montini, later Pope Paul VI.

Courtesy of Peggy Zarnek

In 1938 Cody was named secretary to John Cardinal Glennon of St. Louis and returned to America. During World War II he concentrated on archdiocesan administration and directed Catholic service clubs and relief work for prisoners of war. In 1947 he began his rise in the hierarchy when he was appointed auxiliary to the archbishop of St. Louis (1947–54). He was co-adjutor bishop and bishop of St. Joseph, Missouri (1954–56) and then of the combined sees of Kansas City–St. Joseph (1956–61), where he raised $6 million and built more than 30 new schools, convents, churches, and rectories. From 1961 to 1964 he was co-adjutor bishop with the right of succession at New Orleans. In that traditional Southern city he attained national renown as a strong supporter of school desegregation, at a time when the U.S. Catholic hierarchy was not notably supportive of civil rights. He even excommunicated three unregenerate segregationists, of whom the best known was Leander Perez, the boss of Plaquemines Parish. He began his tenure as archbishop of New Orleans only in 1964, so it was a surprise when the following year his old mentor, Paul VI, named him to succeed Albert Cardinal Meyer in Chicago. In 1967, at the pope's first consistory, Cody was elevated to the College of Cardinals.

Those Catholics in Chicago who expected that Cody would be an easygoing, vaguely liberal leader in the mold of Meyer or his predecessor, Samuel Cardinal Stritch, discovered otherwise. Cody was an iron-handed administrator who demanded unquestioning obedience and replaced those who would not give it. "I have the job and I'm responsible for it, nobody else," he said. He strongly opposed the rules on episcopal collegiality, or power sharing, promulgated by the Second Vatican Council, and on one occasion was censured by an association of dissident priests. Even his reputation as a defender of equal educational opportunity for blacks was called into question when he closed five inner-city parochial schools, citing budgetary constraints, at the same time that he was installing a $4-million closed-circuit television system throughout the archdiocese. He was, however, an expert businessman who ably managed the archdiocese's huge financial superstructure (in 1981 it had revenues of $285 million) and who helped make the Chicago see a model for others in the United States by instituting a parish fund-sharing plan, an insurance program for archdiocesan employees, a pension plan for priests and nuns, and the largest private school-lunch program in the country. He also established archdiocesan offices to counsel separated, divorced, widowed, ethnic, elderly, and handicapped Catholics, and to support the campus and pastoral ministry, the charismatic renewal movement, the permanent diaconate, the Hispanic apostolate, and antiabortion activities.

Despite his popularity with many of Chicago's Catholics, Cody's apparent high-handedness made him many enemies, of whom the most powerful were the *Chicago Sun-Times* and the Rev. Andrew Greeley, a Chicago priest, sociologist, journalist, and novelist well known for his contentious writing on the Church. In September 1981, after 18 months of investigation, the *Sun-Times* ran a six-page exposé of Cody's finances, charging that some $1 million had been taken from archdiocesan accounts under his sole control and given to Mrs. Helen Dolan Wilson of St. Louis, a former archdiocesan employee. Mrs. Wilson was a friend of Cody's from his youth, and they referred to themselves as cousins, although the relationship was by marriage (Mrs. Wilson's widowed father had married Cody's aunt) rather than by blood. She allegedly spent the money on investments, expensive clothes, and a luxurious home in Florida. A sexual liaison between them was nowhere asserted, but widely inferred.

The exposé had been bizarrely prefigured a few months before when Father Greeley, long a critic of Cody—he had called the cardinal a "madcap tyrant"—published his best-selling novel, *The Cardinal Sins*. In this tale of obsession, power, and greed within the hierarchy, a prelate is shown engaging in conduct similar to that with which Cody was charged. Greeley refused to comment on the apparent parallels or on whether he had contributed to the newspaper's investigation.

Cody adopted a wounded stance, refusing to reply directly to the charges (he called them a "vicious joke"), and claiming that it was the church and not he that was being attacked. The stress of facing a grand jury investigation into the alleged diversion of tax-exempt church funds may have worsened his heart condition. He died eight months before his scheduled retirement and four months after his last public appearance at a Christmas mass in Holy Name Cathedral. In a letter left to be read after his death, he forgave all his detractors, though he added that he was not sure that God would do so. Mrs. Wilson was not mentioned in his will (dated 6 January 1982, and bequeathing a modest estate to the archdiocese for the care of infirm and elderly priests), though she was the sole beneficiary of his $100,000 life-insurance policy. In July 1982 the U.S. district attorney for Northern Illinois announced that he had closed his investigation following Cody's death and would seek no indictments against anyone connected with the case. A.K.

Parents Thomas Joseph C., deputy fire chief, and Mary (Begley) C. **Religion** Roman Catholic. **Education** Holy Rosary Grammar Sch., St. Louis, MO; St. Louis Preparatory Seminary, grad. 1926; North Amer. Coll. in Rome 1926–32, ordained to the priesthood 1931; Propaganda Coll., Rome, Ph.D. 1928 and S.T.D. (summa cum laude) 1932; Apollinaris, Rome, J.C.D. 1938. **Career** Asst. to rector, North Amer. Coll. in Rome 1932–34; staff member, Vatican Secretariat of State 1933–38; teacher, North Amer. Coll. in Rome and Sacred Consistorial Congregation 1938; secty. to Archbishop of St. Louis 1938–40; chancellor and vice officialis, Metropolitan Tribunal of St. Louis 1940–50; dir. of Vatican relief work for Italian and German POWs, and dir. of three Natl. Catholic Community Service Clubs, St. Louis, WWII; appointed papal chamberlain with title of very rev. msgr. 1943; founder, Immaculata Parish, Richmond Heights, MO 1945; appointed domestic prelate with title of right rev. msgr. 1946; consecrecated a bishop and appointed titular bishop of Apollonia 1947; auxiliary to archbishop of St. Louis 1947–54; co-adjutor bishop with right of succession 1954–55, and bishop and apostolic admin. 1955–56, St. Joseph, MO; co-adjutor bishop with right of succession 1956 and bishop 1956–61, Kansas City–St. Joseph, MO; served on Commn. on

Seminaries and Studies, Vatican Council II, 1960; appointed titular archbishop of Bostra, Arabia, 1961; co-adjutor archbishop 1961–64, apostolic admin. 1962–65, and archbishop 1964–65, New Orleans, LA; archbishop of Chicago since 1965; elevated to cardinal 1967. • Curia appointments: Sacred Congregation for Evangelization of Peoples; Sacred Congregation for Divine Worship; Sacred Congregation for Clergy; Prefecture for Economic Affairs of Holy See. **Officer** Pres. gen., Natl. Catholic Educational Assn. 1962–65; chmn., Youth Dept., Natl. Catholic Welfare Conference 1963–68; trustee 1964–71 and member of bd. of trustees exec. cttee., Catholic Univ. of America; grand chancellor, DePaul Univ.; trustee and member of Pontifical Cttee., North Amer. Coll. in Rome; treas., Natl. Conference of Catholic Bishops; treas., U.S. Catholic Conference; 1st chmn., Bishop's Cttee. for Pro-Life Activities; natl. chaplain, Natl. Catholic Soc. of Foresters; high spiritual dir., Catholic Order of Foresters. **Member** Episcopal Cttee. on Priestly Formation, Natl. Conference of Catholic Bishops of United States; North Amer. Coll. Alumni Assn.; governing bd., Boy Scouts of America. **Honors** Benemeriti Medal, Vatican 1938; citations for wartime direction of community service clubs, U.S.; citation for wartime POW relief work, Italy; kt. of Holy Sepulchre 1957.

Further reading Gary McEoin, *The Inner Elite*, 1978; Rev. Charles Dahm, *Power and Authority of the Catholic Church: Cardinal Cody of Chicago*, 1981.

DAME CELIA JOHNSON
Actress
Born **Richmond, Surrey, England, 18 December 1908**
Died **Nettlebed, Oxfordshire, England, 25 April 1982**

Night. A suburban English railway station. As a train approaches at speed, a neatly dressed woman, bleak despair in her eyes, steps toward the edge of the platform—and, at the last second, hesitates. Rachmaninoff thunders on the soundtrack; the lights of the rushing train slap across the woman's face as she stands horrified by the nearness of death.

This, the dramatic climax of the film *Brief Encounter* (1945), was also the climax of Celia Johnson's acting career. It was a long career, if sporadic; over 50 years' work on the stage, in films, and on television. Yet that one screen performance overshadowed every other role she played. No matter what else she did, *Brief Encounter* was what she was remembered for.

Johnson was born into a doctor's family in Richmond, Surrey. After being privately educated in London and abroad, she studied at the Royal Academy of Dramatic Art, and made her debut in Huddersfield in 1928 in Shaw's *Major Barbara*. Her first London appearance came a year later, at the Lyric Theatre, Hammersmith, in a Spanish comedy, *A Hundred Years Old*. Success came readily; she got good notices in some fairly mediocre West End plays before landing a substantial role in *Cynara* (1930), with Gerald du Maurier and Gladys Cooper.

In 1931 she made her New York debut, playing Ophelia to Raymond Massey's Hamlet. During the 1930s she consolidated her position on the West End stage in a number of roles, and in two long-running plays in particular: *The Wind and the Rain* (1933) and Helen Jerome's version of *Pride and Prejudice* (1936), in which she was perfectly cast as Elizabeth Bennet. In 1935 she married Peter Fleming, the writer and traveler. By all accounts, it was an exceptionally happy marriage, and lasted until Fleming's death in 1971.

By now, Celia Johnson had established her range—a narrow one, but cut deep and true. Her acting depended on subtlety of inflection, on the effect of understatement; she was never even remotely histrionic.

After playing the heroine in the stage version of *Rebecca* (1940), she made a cautious entry into film with two propaganda shorts directed by Carol Reed, *A Letter from Home* (1941) and *We Serve* (1941). Her first feature film was another propaganda exercise, *In Which We Serve* (1942), a morale-boosting naval drama scripted and co-directed (with David Lean) by Noel Coward. Coward also starred, as the naval captain, and Johnson was excellent as his wife. The same Coward/Lean combination provided her with two more films. In *This Happy Breed* (1944) she was cast, less than ideally, as a working-class wife; and then came *Brief Encounter*.

A woman, happily married—though slightly bored—meets a young doctor, and finds herself, for the first time in her life, passionately in love. Eventually they agree to part; she contemplates suicide, then returns to her husband. It was a banal enough plot, but told with an honesty and lack of forced glamor which have made it a classic. Trevor Howard was good as the doctor, but Celia Johnson outshone him. The warmth and sympathy of her performance now seem to epitomize, not only its period, but a certain, very British style of acting. It can be (and often has been) parodied, but it is hard to imagine it done better.

It was five years before Johnson made another film; at this period her private life took precedence. On stage she was Shaw's *St. Joan* (1947) at the Old Vic, toured with the company in Italy as Viola in *Twelfth Night* (1950), and back in London was a superb Olga in *Three Sisters* (1951). Her fourth and last Coward film was the disappointing *The Astonished Heart* (1949); but *The Captain's Paradise* (1953), with Alec Guinness, gave her a rare chance to demonstrate her comic talent on screen. This was more often displayed on stage, as in *The Reluctant Debutante* (1955). Other notable West End roles included Robert Bolt's *Flowering Cherry* (1957); *The Grass Is Greener* (1958); *Out of the Crocodile* (1963); Ibsen's *The Master Builder* (1964) and Coward's *Hay Fever* (1965), both for the National Theatre; and Ayckbourn's *Relatively Speaking* (1967). At Chichester she was outstanding as Madame Ranevsky in *The Cherry Orchard* (1966).

Courtesy of Ballet Rambert

Her last film was *The Prime of Miss Jean Brodie* (1969), in which her acidulous Scots headmistress almost stole the picture from Maggie Smith. Thereafter she limited herself to the stage—playing Gertrude to Alan Bates's Hamlet (1970), and in *Kingfisher* (1977) with Ralph Richardson—and television, where in 1980 she was reunited with Trevor Howard in "Staying On," adapted from Paul Scott's novel. In 1981 she was made a Dame. She was in previews for *The Understanding*, with Ralph Richardson, when she died of a stroke, two days before the official first night. P.K.

Parents John Robert J., physician, and Ethel (Griffiths) J. **Married** Peter Fleming, journalist and critic, 1935 (d. 1971): one son; two daughters, one, Lucy, an actress. **Education** St. Paul's Girls' Sch., London, and abroad; RADA, London. **Career** Actress, on stage since 1928, in films since 1942. **Honors** New York Critics Award, for *Brief Encounter*, 1946; best supporting actress 1970 and best actress 1974, Soc. of Film and Television Arts; CBE 1978; DBE 1981. **Stage** (all London except as noted) *Major Barbara*, Huddersfield 1928; *A Hundred Years Old*, 1929; *Typhoon*, 1929; *The Artist and the Shadow*, 1930; *Debonair*, 1930; *Cynara*, 1930; *L'occasion*, 1930; *The Circle*, 1931; *Death Takes a Holiday*, 1931; *After All*, 1931; *Hamlet*, NYC 1931; *Punchinello*, 1932; *The Man I Killed*, 1932; *The Vinegar Tree*, 1932; *As It Was in the Beginning*, 1932; *To-Morrow Will Be Friday*, 1932; *Ten Minute Alibi*, 1933; *Another Language*, 1933; *These Two*, 1933; *Sometimes Even Now*, 1933; *The Key*, 1933; *The Wind and the Rain*, 1933; *Pride and Prejudice*, 1936;

Old Music, 1937; *Sixth Floor*, 1939; *Rebecca*, 1940; *The Doctor's Dilemma*, 1942; *St. Joan*, 1947; *Twelfth Night*, Italian tour 1950; *Three Sisters*, 1951; *It's Never Too Late*, 1954; *The Reluctant Debutante*, 1955; *Flowering Cherry*, 1957; *The Grass Is Greener*, 1958; (dir.) *Special Providence*, on double bill *Double Yolk*, 1960; *Chin-Chin*, 1960; *The Tulip Tree*, 1962; *Out of the Crocodile*, 1963; *The Master Builder*, 1964; *Hay Fever*, 1965, 1968, Toronto 1968; *The Cherry Orchard*, Chichester Festival 1966; *Relatively Speaking*, 1967; *Hamlet*, Nottingham 1970, London 1971; *Lloyd George Knew My Father*, 1972; *The Dame of Sark*, Oxford Festival and London 1974; *The Kingfisher*, 1977; *The Understanding*, 1982. **Films** *A Letter from Home* (short), 1941; *We Serve* (short), 1941; *In Which We Serve*, 1942; *Dear Octopus*, 1942; *This Happy Breed*, 1944; *Brief Encounter*, 1945; *The Astonished Heart*, 1949; *I Believe in You*, 1952; *The Captain's Paradise*, 1953; *The Holly and the Ivy*, 1954; *A Kid for Two Farthings*, 1956; *The Good Companions*, 1957; *The Prime of Miss Jean Brodie*, 1969. **Television** "The Distaff Side," 1952; "Staying On," 1981; "Ghosts"; "The Cellar and the Almond Tree"; "Mrs. Palfrey at the Claremont"; "Les Misérables"; "Romeo and Juliet"; "All's Well That Ends Well"; "Tales of Beatrix Potter"; "The Hostage Tower"; "The Potting Shed"; "Nanny"; "Number 10."

FRANK COPPOLA

Mafia leader

***Born* Partinico, Sicily, Italy, 1899**

***Died* Aprilia, near Rome, Italy, 26 April 1982**

Frank (Three Fingers) Coppola was one of the last of the old-style Mafia godfathers, a man whose unquestioned power reached from the lowest Sicilian peasant to important officers of the Italian government and judiciary. He was for decades, before his deportation in 1948, a key figure in the U.S. underworld, heavily involved in illegal currency scams and especially narcotics smuggling.

He left his wife and daughter behind in Sicily in 1926 when he illegally entered the United States, probably in order to escape one of the few effective anti-Mafia prosecutions ever mounted by the Italian government—by Mussolini's Fascists, directed by Cesare Mori. Under various assumed names, he ran several businesses in Louisiana, Michigan, and New York, rising to a position of considerable authority in the underworld, many of whose leaders were Sicilians like himself. In 1942, in Detroit, he attempted to gain legal-immigrant status, but was rebuffed. The U.S. government was determined to deport him, finally succeeding in January 1948.

Coppola arrived back in Italy a much feared and even envied man. He had clearly made millions in America, and his case—like that of his fellow deportees Lucky Luciano, Nicola Gentile, Joseph De Luca, and others—attracted national attention. The Italian authorities, however, considered him an "undesirable," and he was often sent into domestic exile to remote northern villages. By 1950, nevertheless, after he had masterminded the murder of the rebellious mafioso Salvatore Giuliano, he had established control over much of the Italian Mafia, and especially over one of its most lucrative sections, international drug trafficking. From his villa near Rome he oversaw an operation that processed raw opium from Turkey and Syria into heroin in Sicily, then shipped it to the United States in dummy Sicilian oranges.

In 1952, Coppola and Giuseppe Genco Russo were arrested in a nationwide sweep and named as the principal operatives in a Mafia drug-smuggling ring, an allegation corroborated by U.S. federal narcotics investigators. Another raid, in 1965, again implicated Coppola as head of the same drug ring. A large-scale Italian inquiry into international drug trafficking in 1971 reached the same conclusions. Yet Coppola spent almost no time in jail, always managing—by whatever means possible—to remain at liberty and in business.

He was briefly jailed in 1973, during a complex case concerning illegal police wiretapping, for the attempted murder of Angelo Mangano, a *questore* (police chief) in Rome. From his bed in the hospital ward of Rome's Queen of Heaven prison, Coppola accused Mangano of extorting money from him in exchange for erasing incriminating items from the tape recordings of his phone conversations. He was freed shortly thereafter.

His direct political power came from his control over all elections in his native city of Partinico, for both national and local offices. Danilo Dolci, the northerner who became one of the sharpest and most constructive critics of Sicilian society, has described in *The Man Who Plays Alone* (1969) the subtle pervasiveness of Coppola's power in preventing during the 1950s the construction of a badly needed dam on the Iato River. Although the dam would have created jobs, vastly increased cultivated acreage, and been a general boon to the populace in a water-poor area, the Mafia boss sided firmly against any change and in favor of the landlords, whose ancient and profitable rights to sell water to their tenants were threatened by the dam.

Coppola died of a lung disease at the age of 83. A.K.

Born Francesco Paolo Coppola. **Married**; one daughter. **Religion** Roman Catholic. **Emigration** Entered U.S. illegally 1926; applied for immigrant status 1942; deported to Sicily 1948. **Career** Gangster, Sicily and Italy, also U.S. 1926–48; convicted on charges of murder, criminal association, drug trafficking, extortion, and armed robbery; influential in Italian politics.

Further reading Michele Pantaleone, *The Mafia and Politics*, 1966; Danilo Dolci, *The Man Who Plays Alone*, 1969; Gaio Servadio, *Mafioso*, 1976.

MAY

WILLIAM PRIMROSE
Violist and teacher
***Born* Glasgow, Scotland, 23 August 1904**
***Died* Provo, Utah, USA, 1 May 1982**

The Scottish virtuoso William Primrose was responsible for restoring the reputation of the viola as a worthy instrument for a solo career. "If [Lionel] Tertis was the first protagonist," wrote Yehudi Menuhin, "Bill Primrose was certainly the first star of the viola."

Primrose was born to a musical family in Glasgow. His father was John Primrose, a teacher of violin and a violist with the Scottish Symphony Orchestra. At the age of four he began formal studies on a quarter-size violin with the Austrian teacher Camillo Ritter. He showed early signs of becoming a fine musician, often played at church concerts and at the Palette Club, a local meeting place for artists. He gave his first major performance—of the Mendelssohn Violin Concerto—at Glasgow's St. Andrew's Hall when he was 12 years old.

Landon Ronald, conductor of the Scottish Orchestra, heard him play in 1919 and persuaded the City of London to award him a scholarship to the Guildhall School of Music. For his 1923 debut at Queen's Hall, London, Primrose played Lalo's *Symphonie espagnole* and Elgar's Concerto in B Minor on the Betts Stradivarius, lent him by a friend. He graduated the following year from the Guildhall with the highest honors.

Though John Primrose owned a rare Amati viola, he refused to allow his son to touch it; the viola was still widely considered a secondary instrument, fit only for those who could not succeed with the violin. Since early childhood, however, his son had been fascinated with this forbidden treasure and frequently played it in secret. "When I am playing the viola," he once said, "I feel a sense of oneness with the instrument that I never felt when playing the violin." He also suspected that, quite apart from the pleasure he took in its deep rich tone, the scarcity of violists would greatly enhance his chances of joining a prestigious quartet or becoming first chair in a good orchestra if he switched to the larger instrument. The Belgian violin virtuoso Eugène Ysaÿe, with whom Primrose occasionally studied in the late 1920s, approved his decision and was later to tell friends of "a young man from Scotland who will blaze new paths in the years to come."

In 1930 the London String Quartet, who were touring North and South America, cabled Primrose with an invitation to join them. He was to remain with the group until it disbanded during the Depression five years later. During those years he also took every opportunity to appear as a soloist; after his first recital in Rio de Janeiro, a critic wrote that "there has never existed a viola player with such a phenomenal technique." But Primrose endured two lean years between the quartet's demise and an invitation to join the NBC Symphony under Toscanini in 1937. The following year he launched a radio program featuring viola music and organized the Primrose Quartet, which made its debut in 1939 to critical acclaim for the mature perfection of its playing.

Rumors of Toscanini's impending resignation prompted Primrose to launch out as a soloist. For four years he traveled with the tenor Richard Crooks, sharing the stage and

Courtesy of Brigham Young University

readily building up his repertory. During the many years of recitals that followed, the violist's constant accompanist was David Stimer, who was not only an excellent pianist but a worthy opponent in chess games during the long hours of travel.

In 1954 Primrose purchased the "Lord Harrington" Andrea Guarneri viola to replace his father's Amati and the two modern instruments he had played until then. By this time many composers, inspired by the quality of his playing, had written works for him. Notable among these were concertos by Béla Bartók and Darius Milhaud, but opportunities for performing them in America were few and far between; major U.S. orchestras were surprisingly hesitant to engage him as a soloist, apparently afraid of upsetting their own principal violas. Luckily for him the situation in Europe was very different.

From 1943 onward, Primrose battled increasing deafness, but he could still hear accurately on occasion, as his pupils at the Curtis Institute of Music in Philadelphia and the University of California at Los Angeles could attest. "Sometimes they think they could fool me," he commented, "but alas for them, they can't." He suffered a severe heart attack in 1963 while at Aspen, Colorado, but after his recovery he was able to join the faculty of Indiana University. He served as a judge in the BBC Viola Competition held in Glasgow in 1968. In 1970 he traveled to Japan to teach at the Tokyo University of Fine Arts.

His last years were spent at Brigham Young University in Provo, Utah, and it was to this school that he donated his extensive collection of music, books, recordings, and manuscripts. He was a U.S. citizen since 1955 and was made CBE in 1953. He died of cancer.

B.D.

Parents John P., violist and violinist, and Margaret (Whiteside) P. **Married** (1) Dorothy Friend 1928 (d. 1951): two daughters. (2) Alice Virginia French 1952 (div. 1969). (3) Hiroko Sawa 1970: Eiji; Susan; Mana. **Religion** Protestant. **Emigrated** to U.S. in 1935; naturalized 1955. **Education** Private studies with Camillo Ritter; Guildhall Sch. of Music, London (City of London Scholarship), grad. 1924; private lessons with Eugéne Ysaÿe, Brussels 1925–27. **Career** Violinist from childhood through 1927, solo debut 1923. • Violist since 1927: with London String Quartet 1930–35; toured Europe as soloist and with orchs. 1935–37; with NBC Symphony, NYC 1937–42; soloist since 1938; toured extensively in U.S., Canada, Latin America, Europe, Asia. • Founder, Primrose Quartet 1938; originator of radio program of viola music, NYC 1938; co-founding member, Edinburgh Festival Quartet 1952; co-founding member, Festival Quartet, Aspen Music Festival, CO 1955–62; co-founding member, Heifetz-Primrose-Piatigorsky Trio 1955–65. • Faculty member: Curtis Inst., Phila. 1940–50; Univ. of California at Los Angeles 1962–63; Indiana University 1965–70; Tokyo Univ. of Fine Arts and Music and Talent Education Inst., Matsumoto, Japan 1970–74; Brigham Young Univ., Provo, Utah since 1979; also Juilliard Sch., NYC, Univ. of Southern California, L.A., and Banff Centre of Fine Arts, London. **Member** Amer. Fedn. of Musicians; Savage Club, London; Lotos Club, NYC. **Honors** CBE 1953; hon. fellow, Guildhall Sch. of Music; hon. member of Middlesex, Surrey, and Yorkshire cricket clubs. **Recordings** of works by Aguirre, C. P. E. Bach, J. S. Bach, Bartók, Beethoven, Berlioz, Bloch, Boccherini, Brahms, Chopin, Dvořák, Handel, Roy Harris, Hindemith, Kreisler, Mozart, Paganini, Rameau, Schubert, Vaughan Williams, other composers. **Author** *The Art and Practice of Scale Playing on the Viola*, 1954; *Technique Is Memory*, 1960; *Walk on the North Side* (autobiography), 1978. **Private papers** and collection of viola materials in Harold B. Lee Library, Brigham Young Univ.

MUHAMMAD SEDDIQ BEN YAHYA

Algerian minister of foreign affairs
Born **Djidjelli (Jijel), Algeria, 30 January 1932**
Died **near the Irano-Turkish frontier, 3 May 1982**

Muhammad Ben Yahya, a resourceful and intelligent diplomat, served from March 1979 as Algeria's foreign minister. His moment of greatest distinction, in Western eyes, occurred during 1980–81, when he used Algeria's good offices to effect the repatriation of the U.S. hostages held in Iran. His death in a plane crash happened under mysterious circumstances as he was attempting to negotiate an end to the war between Iran and Iraq.

Born in a city in the east of Algeria, Ben Yahya received a law degree from the University of Algiers. He was active from his youth in his country's revolutionary politics, and in 1955 was elected president of the Algerian Islamic Students Association and ably represented that organization at the Bandung Conference in Indonesia in 1956. About that time he joined the National Liberation Front (FLN) and by 1959 was cabinet secretary in the provisional government of Ferhat Abbas in addition to holding the post of secretary in the National Council of the Algerian Revolution. He was a member of the FLN delegation to peace talks with the French in Évian (May 1961) and Lugrin (July 1961) and in August 1961 was retained as cabinet secretary when Yusuf Ben Kheddha succeeded Ferhat Abbas.

Algeria gained independence in mid-1962, and the following February Ben Yahya was appointed by Pres. Ahmed Ben Bella as ambassador to the Soviet Union, where he was the youngest ambassador in the diplomatic corps. He supported the coup d'état of Houari Boumedienne against Ben Bella in June 1965, and shortly thereafter was named ambassador to London, but he never took up that post. First he was sent back to Moscow for a short visit of reassurance, and by the time of his return, Algeria, conforming to a resolution of the Organization of African Unity, had broken diplomatic relations with Britain over its failure to put down the white rebellion in Southern Rhodesia.

An intellectual and an expert bureaucratic administrator with no local power base, Ben Yahya was greatly valued by Pres. Boumedienne, who named him in October 1966 to the first of several cabinet posts. He served as minister of information (1966–70), of higher education and scientific research (1970–77), and of finance (1977–79). Upon succeeding to the presidency after Boumedienne's death, Chadli Bendjedid named Ben Yahya in April 1979 to head the foreign ministry and diplomatic service. He took the place of Abdulaziz Bouteflika, a well-known and popular third-world diplomat who had opposed Bendjedid during the succession crisis.

Ben Yahya's talents as a negotiator and conciliator were called upon soon after he took office. Relations with France, the former colonial power, were at last put on a solid and cooperative footing, and he saw to it that Algeria handled Iranian interests in Washington after the United States broke diplomatic relations with Iran in April 1980. In the final months of the hostage crisis, he worked day after day in Algiers with U.S. Deputy Secretary of State Warren Christopher, and was perhaps the individual most responsible for persuading the Iranian captors to let the 52 American citizens go free. His thanks from Washington came several months later when the Reagan administration openly sided with Morocco against Algeria in the long-standing dispute over Western Sahara.

The plane crash that killed him and eight other high Algerian government officials happened after his Grumman G-2 left Teheran bound for a destination that was never announced, but was probably Baghdad. It had been Ben Yahya's first official visit to Teheran, where he was considered a trusted friend and honest go-between. The most convincing explanation that was offered for the crash—which is still officially unsolved—was that Ba'athist ultranationalists within the Iraqi military shot down the plane to prevent any negotiations with the enemy from taking place.

Less than a year earlier, on 30 May 1981, Ben Yahya had been gravely injured when his plane crashed near Bamako, Mali. By the time rescuers reached the crash a day later, his government had presumed him dead and all flags in Algeria were at half staff. Following months of recuperation in a French clinic, he was able once again to take up his post. After his death was announced for a second time in May 1982, tens of thousands of people paid tribute to him in the streets of Algiers.

A.K.

Father Seddiq B. **Religion** Muslim. **Education** Univ. of Algiers, lic. en droit. **Career** Pres., Algerian Islamic Students Assn. 1955. • With Natl. Liberation Front (Front Natl. pour Libération; FLN): joined 1956; corresp., Jakarta 1956; member, delegations to negotiations with France 1960–62; member, drafting cttee., Tripoli Charter 1962. • Member 1956–62 and secty., Natl. Council of Algerian Revolution; appointed chief of cabinet and secty. gen. of Algerian provisional govt. 1959; chief of cabinet, provisional govt. 1961; ambassador to USSR 1963–65; special envoy to USSR 1965; member, Algerian delegation to U.N. 1965–66; minister of information 1966–70; minister of higher education and scientific research 1970–77; minister of finance 1977–79; minister of foreign affairs since 1979.

BARON JANNER OF THE CITY OF LEICESTER
Barnett Janner
British politician and Zionist
***Born* Barry, Glamorgan, Wales, 20 June 1892**
***Died* United Kingdom, 4 May 1982**

Barnett Janner was for more than half a century a passionately committed leader of Great Britain's Jewish community. Trained as a lawyer, he served as first a Liberal, then a Labour member of Parliament, and in addition to interesting himself in all issues involving the Middle East and the State of Israel, was an effective force for equitable change in the politically sensitive areas of real-estate leases and rents.

Born in Wales to Lithuanian immigrants, Janner attended the county school and won a scholarship to University College, Cardiff, where after a distinguished career he graduated with a B.A. in law. He was articled to a solicitor in the City of London, then served during World War I with the Royal Garrison Artillery in France and Belgium, where his health was permanently impaired by German gas attacks. He was admitted as a solicitor after his return home in 1919.

Practicing law in Cardiff, Janner soon became involved in the Zionist movement. He was elected president of the South Wales

Zionist Council, and in 1925 joined the Board of Deputies of British Jews. He remained a faithful member of both organizations for the rest of his life, serving as president of the Board of Deputies from 1955 to 1964 and chairman (from 1940) and president (from 1950) of the Zionist Federation of Great Britain and Ireland.

His rise in politics was slow but assured. As a Liberal, he unsuccessfully contested the general election of 1929 for Cardiff Central, then moved to London, where in 1930 he lost a by-election in the Whitechapel and St. George's division of Stepney, in the East End. He won the seat the following year after a hard-fought campaign in which he challenged the Labour government's decision to restrict immigration to Palestine. The constituency had a large Jewish population and was heavily working-class, and Janner was a popular M.P., establishing friendships with people from all walks of life that endured despite his later change of constituencies. He is particularly remembered for his forthright defiance of the violent and public anti-Semitism brought to the East End during the 1930s by such groups as Oswald Mosley's Blackshirts. In 1931 he formed the Parliamentary Palestine Committee, and maintained a close association with those M.P.'s who were friendly to Zionist aspirations even after he narrowly lost his seat in 1935.

Shortly after his defeat he joined the Labour Party and was adopted as prospective parliamentary candidate for Leicester West, a seat then held by the diplomat Harold Nicolson. It took Janner until the general election of 1945—the year of the Labour landslide—to win the seat, but he continued to represent Leicester (after 1950 the North-West division) in every parliament until his elevation to the House of Lords in 1970. In that year his son, Greville Janner, a barrister and now the president of the Board of Deputies, was elected to his father's seat, switching in 1974 to his father's previous seat at Leicester West. Both constituencies have very small Jewish populations.

As independent and outspoken in the House of Lords as he was in the Commons, Janner was a loyal party man but never joined a Labour government, preferring the influential role of a backbencher able to disagree with any policy at any time. He was famous for his perseverance; he fought nearly 50 years to see Israel founded and secure; campaigned relentlessly for 17 years before Parliament finally ratified the Genocide Convention in 1969; and hung on tenaciously for more than a decade until he was finally able to shame Parliament into passing the Zoo Licensing Act of 1981, which imposed legal standards and controls on all of Britain's private zoos. He was also active in persuading the West German government to suspend the statute of limitations for war criminals. As a tribute to his years of steadfast support, Israel established the Janner Forest near Jerusalem in 1962. He was knighted in 1961.

Among his many offices, Janner served as chairman of the joint Lords-Commons Solicitors' Group, the Parliamentary Anglo-Benelux Group, and the Anglo-Israel Parliamentary Group, president of the Leaseholders Association, and vice president of the Monash branch of the British Legion, the Association of Municipal Corporations, and the Association of Jewish ex-Servicemen and Women. He was a notable collector of fine furniture, and was elected a fellow of the Royal Society of Arts.

Lord Janner made one of his last public appearances in July 1981 at an anti-PLO rally in Trafalgar Square. He died at the age of 89.
A.K.

Parents Joseph J. and Gertrude J. **Married** Elsie Sybil Cohen, social worker and J.P., 1927: Greville Ewan, barrister and politician, b. 1928; Ruth Joan Gertrude Rahle, Lady Morris of Kenwood. **Religion** Jewish. **Education** Barry County Sch., Wales; University Coll. of South Wales and Monmouthshire, Cardiff (County Scholarship), B.A.; articled to solicitor, City of London; admitted as solicitor 1919. **Mil. service** Royal Garrison Artillery, British Army, Belgium and France, WWI (wounded); air-raid warden, London 1940–45. **Career** Solicitor, Cardiff and London 1919–30s; in furniture industry 1920s–30s; Liberal M.P. for Whitechapel and St. George's Div. of Stepney, London 1931–35; joined Labour Party 1936; Labour M.P. for West Leicester 1945–50; Labour M.P. for North-West Div. of Leicester 1950–70. **Officer** With Bd. of Deputies of British Jews: member since 1925; chmn. of foreign affairs cttee. 1947–73; v.p.; pres. 1955–64; chmn., Israel cttee. • With Zionist Fedn. of Great Britain and Ireland: pres., South Wales Zionist Council 1920s; v.p. 1931–40; chmn. 1940–50; pres. since 1950. •

Pres.: Students' Representative Council, University Coll., Cardiff 1920s; Univ. of Wales Jewish Students' Union 1920s; (also founder) Parliamentary Palestine Cttee. 1931–48; Leicester Civil Soc.; Leaseholders Assn. of Great Britain; Assn. of Jewish Friendly Socs.; British ORT; European Council, World Confedn. of Gen. Zionists; others. • Chmn.: Interparliamentary Union; Anglo-Israel Parliamentary Group; Parliamentary Anglo-Benelux Group; Parliamentary Water Safety Group; (also vice chmn.) Lords and Common Solicitors Group; others. • V.P.: (also exec. member) Conference on Jewish Material Claims Against Germany, Inc. 1952; Assn. of Municipal Corps.; Assn. of Metropolitan Authorities; Assn. of Jewish ex-Servicemen and Women; Monash branch, British Legion; Leasehold Reform Assn.; British Maccabis; Maccabi World Union; others. • Patron, INTAKE; life gov., University Coll., Cardiff; gov., Ben-Gurion Univ. of the Negev, Israel. **Fellow** Royal Soc. of Arts; Inst. of Personnel Management. **Member** Cardiff Zionist Union 1920s; Welsh Univ. Students' Union 1920s; exec. cttee., Jewish Material Claims Against Austria 1953; exec., World Zionist Org.; exec., Franco-British Parliamentary Relations Cttee.; House of Commons Panel of Chmn.; Soc. of Labour Lawyers; Commonwealth Parliamentary Assn.; Wage Earning Children Cttee.; World Jewish Congress; exec., World Jewish Relief; council, Jewish Trust Corp.; Natl. Council for Soviet Jewry; British Friends of Magen David Adom; others. **Honors** Hon. secty., Parliamentary Palestine Cttee. 1930s; kt. 1961; forest in Israel named for him 1962; comdr., Order of Leopold II, Belgium 1963; comdr., Order of Orange-Nassau, Netherlands 1970; created Baron Janner of the City of Leicester, life peer, 1970; Freedom of the City of Leicester 1971; Freedom of the City of London; hon. pres., North-West Leicester Labour Party; hon. v.p., British Friends of Israeli War Disabled; hon. rents advisor, Labour Party; hon. degree from Univ. of Leeds. **Contributor** of articles to *Hansard* and other mags.

SIR (JOHN) DENIS (NELSON) HILL

Psychiatrist

***Born* Orleton, Herefordshire, England, 5 October 1913**

***Died* London, England, 5 May 1982**

The psychiatrist Sir Denis Hill was best known for his work in improving psychiatric services in the United Kingdom and for advocating the wider application of psychiatry to the social problems of the aged, the indigent, and the handicapped. His 40-year career in a succession of London hospitals encompassed clinical research, teaching, and health care administration.

The son of a lieutenant colonel in the British Army, Hill took his M.B. and B.S. degrees from St. Thomas's Hospital in London in 1937 and earned a diploma in psychological medicine in 1940. His first clinical experience was as a house physician and clinical researcher under Russell Brain and Grey Walter at Maida Vale Hospital in London. Walter, a physiologist, introduced him to the electroencephalograph (EEG), a newly invented device to measure the electrical impulses of the brain. Hill was the first to put the EEG to clinical use in investigating the physiological basis of epilepsy and other mental disorders as the chief assistant at the Department of Psychological Medicine of St. Thomas's Hospital and as an Emergency Medical Service physician at Belmont and Maudsley hospitals, London, during World War II.

After the war, Hill continued his clinical research in encephalography and forensic psychiatry. His EEG studies of a youth on trial for murder, which proved that the accused was in an abnormal state of mind at the time the crime was committed, were the first such studies to be accepted as evidence in a court of law. He taught at King's College Hospital and at Maudsley Hospital's Institute of Psychiatry. As a member of the Medical Research Council, the General Medical Council, and the Central Health Service Council in the late 1950s and early 1960s, he fought for greater recognition of psychiatry as a medical disci-

Courtesy of London Institute of Psychiatry

pline and for improving psychiatric teaching and research facilities. In his articles and papers, he addressed current deficiencies in medical education, the role of the psychiatrist in health-care institutions, and the economic and ethical ramifications of medical care for children with severe birth defects and the very old. In a 1978 article, "The Qualities of a Good Psychiatrist," he cited the depersonalization of psychiatric practice, caused by a shortage of adequately trained personnel and encouraged by medical and social bureaucracies, as one of the most pressing problems within the profession.

In 1961 Hill was appointed professor of psychiatry at Middlesex Hospital, a chair he had helped to create. By the mid-1960s he was the leading spokesman for the field in the United Kingdom. He joined the University of London's Institute of Psychiatry in 1966, the year in which he was knighted, and for the next 13 years oversaw its rapid diversification and growth. He was made an emeritus professor there in 1979. Hill was a fellow of the Royal College of Physicians since 1949 and of the Royal College of Psychiatrists since 1971.
S.A.

Father John Arthur H., military officer. **Married** (1) Phoebe Elizabeth Herschel Wade 1938 (div.): Anthony; Caroline. (2) Lorna Wheelan, child psychiatrist, 1962: Richard; Annabelle. **Education** Shrewsbury Sch., Shropshire; St. Thomas's Hosp., London, MRCS, LRCP 1935, M.B., B.S. 1937, MRCP, diploma in psychological medicine 1940. **Mil. service** Psychiatric specialist, Emergency Medical Service, Belmont and Maudsley Hosps., London 1939–46. **Career** Psychiatric house physician, Bethlem Royal Hosp., London 1936–37; neurological house physician, Maida Vale Hosp., London 1937–38; chief asst., Dept. of Psychological Medicine, St. Thomas's Hosp. 1938–44; physician and lectr. in psychological medicine, King's Coll. Hosp., London 1947–60; sr. lectr., Inst. of Psychiatry, Maudsley Hosp. 1947–60; prof. of psychiatry, Middlesex Hosp. Medical Sch., London 1961–66; prof. of psychiatry 1966–79 and prof. emeritus since 1979, Inst. of Psychiatry, Univ. of London. • Meyer Lectr., Amer. Psychiatric Assn. 1968; Goldman Lectr., New York Medical Coll. 1968; Jones Lectr., British Psychoanalytic Soc. 1970; Vickers Lectr., Mental Health Research Fund 1972; Maudsley Lectr., Royal Coll. of Psychiatrists 1972; Curran Lectr., St. George's Hosp., London 1980; Litchfield Lectr., Merton Coll., Oxford 1981; Lewis Lectr., Inst. of Psychiatry, London 1981. • Consultant: Postgrad. Medical Sch. 1946–47; Electroencephalogram Dept., Natl. Hosp. 1947–58; Queen Charlotte Hosp. 1952–56; Medical Dept., Civil Service since 1968; (corresp.) WHO 1975–79; Dept. of Health and Social Services since 1976; Medical Advisory Cttee. **Officer** With Gen. Medical Council: crown rep. since 1961; treas. 1977–78; acting pres. 1981; chmn., Penal Cases Cttee. and Special Cttee. on Mental Health; member of Exec., Penal Cases, Education, Public Health, Disciplinary, Special Conduct, and Overseas Cttees. • Chmn.: Mental Health Advisory Cttee. 1963–66; Jt. Subcttee. on Treatment of Acute Poisoning in Hosp., Ministry of Health 1966–67; Assn. of Univ. Teachers of Psychiatry 1966–73; Fedn. of Assns. of Clinical Profs. of the United Kingdom 1975–78; (also council member 1963) Cttee. on Psychological Medicine, Royal Coll. of Physicians. • Other: pres., psychiatry sect., Royal Soc. of Medicine 1964–65; member, bd. of govs., Jt. Hosp. 1966–79; trustee, Mental Health Foundn. **Fellow** FRCP 1949; Rock Carling Fellow, Nuffield Provincial Hosps. Trust 1969; Royal Coll. of Psychiatrists 1971. **Member** Medical Research Council 1956–60; Working Party on Special Hosps. 1959–61; Central Health Service Council 1961–67; hon. medical advisory panel, Dept. of Transport 1966–78; advisory council, Inst. of Criminology, Univ. of Cambridge since 1968; council, Court of Electors, Royal Coll. of Psychiatrists 1971–73; Working Party on Org. of Prison Medical Service 1964; Aarvold Cttee. 1972; Council for Science and Soc. since 1972; Butler Cttee. on Mentally Abnormal Offenders 1972–75; Forensic Research Liaison Group since 1975; South East Thames Regional Health Authority since 1976; Eugenics Soc. **Honors** Gaskell Gold Medal, Royal Medical-Psychiatric Assn. 1941; kt. 1966; hon. physician, Maudsley Hosp. 1948–60 and Bethlem Royal Hosp. **Editor** *Electroencephalography: A Symposium*, 1950. **Contributor** of numerous articles and chapters on psychiatry and social problems to medical jrnls. and textbooks.

HOWARD F(RANKLIN) FEHR
Mathematics educator
Born **Bethlehem, Pennsylvania, USA, 4 December 1901**
Died **New York City, USA, 6 May 1982**

America's public schools underwent a revolution in mathematics education during the 1960s. The controversial "new math," which replaced old-fashioned rote methods of teaching arithmetic with an integrated curriculum of fundamental mathematical concepts, was to a great extent the work of Howard F. Fehr, a specialist in math education at Columbia's Teachers College.

Courtesy of Columbia University

Born in Bethlehem, Pennsylvania, Fehr worked in the steel mills there while earning a B.A. in mathematics from Lehigh University (1923). He taught mathematics at a succession of high schools in Pennsylvania, then joined the faculty of the State Teachers College in Montclair, New Jersey, where he became a professor in 1946. From 1949 to 1967 he headed the mathematics teaching department of Teachers College at Columbia.

During the 1950s, there was a growing recognition among educators that current methods of primary and secondary mathematics instruction, based largely on rote memorization of the rules of arithmetic and Euclidean geometry, were inadequate to prepare children for life in a highly technical society. Moreover, secondary school curricula had failed to keep up with the major revisions undergone by mathematics since the 1920s and the explosive growth of new fields such as set theory, symbolic logic, and topology. The launching of the satellite Sputnik I by the Soviet Union in 1957 seemed to justify fears of American technical inferiority and impelled the government to give top priority to improving math and science instruction in public schools.

In 1961, Fehr published a highly influential report, *New Thinking in School Mathematics*, in which he advocated a thorough revision of current math curricula. He proposed that algebra, geometry, trigonometry, and analysis should be taught not as discrete subjects, but as aspects of a more general mathematics. What before were considered advanced concepts—functions, variables, sets, symbolic logic—were to be introduced in the primary grades to provide a basis for the sophisticated material—diophantine (multiple variable) equations, linear programming, and the like—to be taught in the high schools. At graduation, the average student would be equipped for a career in engineering, social science, physical science, or business and economic planning.

Textbooks on the new math, by Fehr and others, were in wide use by 1962, replacing in many cases texts from the 1920s or 1930s and creating an instant boom in the textbook-publishing industry. The change was not without controversy: parents found themselves completely unable to understand their children's homework, while many teachers were inadequately trained in new math themselves or resented having to relearn long-forgotten material. Most professional mathematicians praised the new math, but not all: Morris Kline, a mathematician with New York University, noted that "the new math fails, as did the old math, to tie math and science together."

In the mid-1960s, Fehr was a consultant for the Organization for Economic Development and Cooperation, the National Science Foundation, and UNESCO, devising new math curricula for India and the Arab states. From 1965 to 1973 he directed the Secondary School Mathematics Curriculum Improvement Study, which produced a unified mathematics program used in Canada, Europe, and the United States. Fehr was the author of more than 20 books, including several popular texts on algebra and geometry, and some 200 professional papers. He died after a long illness at his home in Manhattan. S.A.

Parents Quincy Howard F. and Minnie (Patterson) F. **Married** (1) Gladys Thomas 1924: Patricia Swanson; Barbara Savage. (2) Gisela Henle 1966: Gunter (stepson). **Education** Bethlehem High Sch., PA, grad. 1919; Lehigh Univ., Bethlehem, B.A. 1923, M.A. 1928; Columbia Univ., Ph.D. 1940; licensed to teach secondary sch. in PA and NJ. **Career** Steelworker, Bethlehem, PA 1920s. • Mathematics teacher: Bethlehem High Sch. 1923–25; High Sch. for Boys, Reading, PA 1925–27; South Side High Sch., Newark, NJ 1927–34. • With State Teachers Coll., Montclair, NJ: instr. 1934–36; asst. prof. 1936–40; assoc. prof. 1940–46; prof. of mathematics 1946–48. • Part-time mathematics instr., Newark Coll. of Engineering 1930–45 and Rutgers Univ. 1943–45; instr. 1946–48, prof. of mathematics 1948–49, and head of dept. of mathematics teaching 1949–67, Teachers Coll., Columbia Univ.; consultant in mathematical education, Org. for Economic Development and Cooperation 1959–65; Natl. Science Foundn. consultant to Org. of India Insts. 1964–66; ed., intl. sect., *Mathematics Teacher* jrnl. since 1965; consultant on improvement of mathematics education in the Arab states, UNESCO since 1967. **Officer** Pres., Assn. of Teachers Colls. of New Jersey 1940–41, 1944–45; pres., Assn. of Mathematics Teachers of New Jersey 1940–41; member, bd. of dirs. 1953–56 and pres. 1956–58, Natl. Council of Teachers of Mathematics; dir., Secondary Sch. Mathematics Curriculum Improvement Study, Columbia Univ. since 1965; co-chmn., mathematics curriculum seminar, UNESCO, France 1971. **Fellow** Amer. Assn. for Advancement of Science. **Member** Commn. on mathematics, College Entrance Examination Bd. 1955–60; U.S. Cttee. on Mathematics Instruction 1957–63; Intl. Commn. on Mathematics Instruction 1959–62; Mathematical Assn. of America; Amer. Mathematical Soc.; Natl. Council of Teachers of Mathematics; Central Assn. of Mathematics and Science Teachers; Natl. Education Assn.; Amer. Educational Research Assn.; Amer. Assn. of Univ. Professors; numerous foreign assns. of mathematics profs.; Phi Beta Kappa; Phi Delta Kappa; Republican Party. **Author** (Jtly.) *Senior Mathematics for High Schools*, 1940, rev. ed. 1956; *Secondary Mathematics—A Functional Approach for Teachers,* 1950, rev. ed. 1956; (jtly.) *Algebra, Course I*, 1955, rev. ed. 1962; (jtly.) *Algebra, Course II*, 1955, rev. ed. 1963; (jtly.) *Arithmetic at Work*, 1955; *What Research Says to the Teacher About Teaching High School Mathematics*, 1955; (jtly.) *Arithmetic in Life*, 1955; (trans.) *Introduction to the Theory of Sets*, 1958; (jtly.) *Geometry*, 1961; (jtly.) *Mathematics at Work*, 1962; (jtly.) *Mathematics in Life*, 1962; (jtly.) *Contemporary Mathematics for Elementary Teachers*, 1966; (jtly.) *Teach-*

ing Modern Mathematics in the Elementary School, 1967; *Unified Mathematics*, levels 1–4, 1972; *Introduction to Sets, Probability, and Hypothesis Testing*. **Editor** (Also contributor) *The Learning of Mathematics*, 1953; *New Thinking in School Mathematics*, 1960; *Synopses for Modern Secondary School Mathematics*, 1961; *Mathematical Education in the Americas*, 1962; *Mathematics Today: A Guide for Teachers*, 1964; *Mathematical Education in the Americas II*, 1967; *Trends III in Mathematical Education*, 1971. **Contributor** of more than 200 articles on mathematical education to professional jrnls.

NEIL BOGART
Pop-music record producer
***Born* New York City, USA, 3 February 1943**
***Died* Los Angeles, California, USA, 8 May 1982**

The American pop-music industry owes two of its biggest money-making phenomena, bubblegum and disco, to record entrepreneur Neil Bogart, whose nose for market trends was exceptionally sharp. An energetic promoter with a flashy style and a reputation for taking risks, he managed to make, lose, and regain a fortune before his death of cancer at the age of 39.

He was born Neil Bogatz in Brooklyn, the son of a postal credit-union clerk. After graduating from New York's High School for the Performing Arts, he tried a series of entertainment jobs under assumed names, including mambo dancing on the Catskill hotel circuit and a bit part (clothed) in a soft-core pornographic movie. He did some pop singing with Dick Clark's "American Bandstand" and had a hit record with "Bobby" in 1961, then entered the music business as an ad salesman and publicity man. Within three years he was running the Kama Sutra/Buddah label, which he turned into the successful purveyor of a bouncy, insipid derivative of rock music called bubblegum, very popular with preteenagers. (One of its biggest hits was entitled "Yummy, Yummy, Yummy, I've Got Love in My Tummy.") Buddah also did well with soul and R&B acts such as Gladys Knight and the Pips, Curtis Mayfield, and the Isley Brothers.

In 1973 Bogart left Buddah to found a new label, Casablanca. His first major release, a comedy album of excerpts from "The Tonight Show," sold so poorly that the company was nearly forced into bankruptcy. With borrowed money, Bogart gambled on recordings of unknown and untried acts. One, by the theatrical rock group Kiss, sold 2.5 million copies. Another, the single "Love To Love You Baby" by Donna Summer, shot up the charts and launched the disco craze. Eventually both acts were managed by Bogart's wife. Casablanca's roster soon included other eccentric but vastly successful groups, including the Village People and Parliament. By 1978 it was grossing $100 million and had gone into production of mass-entertainment films (*The Deep*, *Thank God It's Friday*, *Midnight Express*, and *Foxes*.)

Bogart's share in the business was bought out in 1980 by his co-owner, the Dutch-German conglomerate PolyGram. According to some reports, Bogart had failed to recognize that disco was on the way out and had sunk too much money into extravagant campaigns. His next project was Boardwalk, a multimedia

Courtesy of Harry Langdon

entertainment corporation that aimed to sell videodiscs, books, and films as well as records. The firm was rapidly growing at the time of Bogart's death. J.P.

Born Neil Bogatz. **Parents** Al M. B., postal credit-union clerk, and Ruth (Markoff) B. **Married** (1) Elizabeth Weiss 1965 (div. 1974): Jill; Timothy; Bradley. (2) Joyce, pop-music mgr., 1976: Evan. **Religion** Jewish. **Education** High Sch. for the Performing Arts, NYC; Brooklyn Coll. 1963–64. **Mil. service** U.S. Army 1961. **Career** Mambo dancer and model; (as Wayne Roberts) actor; (as Neil Scott) pop singer; (as Neil Stewart) employment agent; ad salesman, later 1st account exec., *Cashbox* mag.; asst. to natl. promotions dir., MGM Records; natl. promotions dir., v.p., and gen. mgr., Cameo-Parkway Records; gen. mgr., Kama Sutra/Buddah records 1967–73; co-founder and exec. pres., Casablanca Records (now Casablanca Records and FilmWorks), L.A. 1973–80; founder and bd. chmn., Boardwalk Entertainment Co. since 1980. **Officer** Member, bd. of govs., Cedar-Sinai Medical Center, L.A.; exec. v.p., Betty Ford Cancer Center, L.A.; co-chmn., entertainment cttee., Los Angeles Music Center; commnr., California Mus. of Science and Industry and Los Angeles Memorial Coliseum; founder and dir., First Natl. Bank of Beverly Hills; official of Jewish Foster Child Care, NY; coach, Little League, L.A. **Honors** Presidential Award, Natl. Assn. of Record Merchandisers 1977; Man of the Year, United Jewish Appeal–Fedn. of Jewish Philanthropies 1978.

GILLES VILLENEUVE
Racing-car driver
***Born* Berthierville, Quebec, Canada, 18 January 1950**
***Died* Louvain, Belgium, 8 May 1982**

Gilles Villeneuve, leader of the Ferrari motor-racing team, had a brief but remarkable career before his death in a crash at the age of 32. In four years on the elite Formula One circuit, he won six races and came within a few points of the world championship.

From boyhood, Villeneuve was thrilled with the sensation of speeding. He began racing snowmobiles at the age of 13 and took the national snowmobile championship in 1973, when he was 23. The following year he won seven out of ten races on the Formula Ford car circuit. On Formula Atlantic he won two successive championships, in 1976 and 1977, the second time beating Grand Prix world champion James Hunt. At Hunt's urging, the McLaren Racing Team offered Villeneuve a chance to drive a Grand Prix race at Silverstone, England. He did well enough to attract the attention of Italian racing-car manufacturer Enzo Ferrari, who signed Villeneuve to his team, widely considered to be the best in the world.

Villeneuve moved his wife and two small children to Monaco, from which he commuted to the Ferrari test track near Modena, Italy. With his first victory, at Montreal in 1978, he became the first Canadian to win a Grand Prix contest and to accrue points toward the world championship. He took three more victories (in South Africa, California, and New York) in 1979, finishing a close second to his teammate Jody Scheckter in the competition for the world title, and won major races in Monaco and Spain. In 1982 he was expected to gross some $3 million, more than any other Canadian athlete. Possibly because of his aggressive driving and insistence on taking bold chances—the very qualities that endeared him to racing enthusiasts—he was involved in numerous accidents and was nicknamed "Air Canada" for the frequency with which his car left the track. In October 1977, in Gotemba, Japan, his car hit another and jumped the guardrail, killing two spectators.

Villeneuve was nearing the end of a qualifying run at a racetrack in Zomber, Belgium, when he steered into a dangerous turn and bumped the rear tire of a slower car at 170 miles per hour. His Ferrari hit the curb and crashed into an embankment, throwing him across the track and into a steel fence. He was declared clinically dead at the scene and died in a hospital seven hours later of a broken neck and a severed spine. His funeral was attended by the prime ministers of Quebec and Canada. The Montreal racetrack was renamed in his honor. J.P.

Parents Seville V. and Georgette V. **Married** Joanne: Jacques; Melanie. **Religion** Roman Catholic. **Education** Studied trumpet. **Career** Snowmobile and car racer from his teens; on Formula Ford circuit 1974; on Formula Atlantic circuit 1975–77; on Formula One circuit with Ferrari racing team since 1977; owner of car dealership. **Championships** Canadian snowmobile champion 1973; Canadian driving champion 1976; Canadian Grand Prix 1978; South African Grand Prix 1978; U.S. Grand Prix West, Long Beach, CA 1979; U.S. Grand Prix East, Watkins Glen, NY 1979; Monaco Grand Prix 1981; Spanish Grand Prix 1981. **Honors** Male Athlete of the Year, Canada 1979; Montreal racetrack named in his honor 1982.

WILLIAM BEVERLY CARTER, JR.
Diplomat and journalist
Born **Coatesville, Pennsylvania, USA, 1 February 1921**
Died **Bethesda, Maryland, USA, 9 May 1982**

Although his was a relatively obscure name to the American public, W. Beverly Carter, Jr., a former journalist and an expert on Africa, was one of the highest-ranking black Americans in the nation's diplomatic corps. He caused a furor within the State Department in 1975 as a result of his controversial role in a hostage crisis involving Zairean terrorists, and another in 1979 when he joined fellow members of a U.N. subcommission in criticizing Israeli policy toward the Palestinians and the PLO.

Carter was born in southern Pennsylvania. After receiving his A.B. degree from Lincoln University in 1944, he worked as a reporter for the *Philadelphia Tribune* and the following year became city editor of the *Philadelphia Afro-American*, meantime studying law at Temple University. From 1948 to 1955 he served as an executive of the organization Journalists Associates. Following an unsuccessful campaign for Pennsylvania's Fourth Congressional District seat in 1954, he became publisher of the *Pittsburgh Courier* newspaper chain.

Carter joined the U.S. Foreign Service in 1965 and was appointed press attaché at the U.S. embassy in Nairobi, Kenya. He headed the U.S. Information Service in Lagos, Nigeria, from 1966 to 1969, when he became deputy assistant secretary of state for African affairs. He received his first appointment as an ambassador in 1972, when he was named U.S. envoy to Tanzania by Pres. Richard Nixon. One of only five blacks out of a total of 120 ambassadors in the diplomatic corps, he had excellent prospects for a long career and was slated for an appointment as ambassador to Denmark.

These prospects came to an end as a result of Carter's participation in negotiations to free three students, two American and one Dutch, who had been kidnapped from an animal-research station by Marxist rebels from neighboring Zaire. The rejection of the kidnappers' $460,000 ransom demand by the governments of Tanzania and Zaire brought the students under threat of execution. When two of the rebels appeared at the U.S. embassy in Dar-es-Salaam, Carter granted them temporary diplomatic immunity, opened negotiations between them and the hostages' parents using the services of an embassy translator, and arranged for the ransom money to be carried to Tanzania via diplomatic pouch. With the release of the last hostage on 24 July, Carter appeared to have achieved a diplomatic triumph.

His actions, however, were in violation of State Department rules laid down by Secretary of State Henry Kissinger, forbidding negotiations between envoys and terrorists. "If terrorist groups get the impression that they can force a negotiation with the U.S.," Kissinger explained, "then we may save lives in one place at the risk of hundreds of lives everywhere else." Carter had also antagonized the Zaire government of Mobutu Sese Seko, which did not want to see the rebel group legitimized by negotiations. Furious at Carter for engaging in what he called "an independent publicity campaign," Kissinger recalled him to Washington and blocked his upcoming appointment to the Danish post.

Courtesy of US State Department

The secretary of state's actions set off a fierce reaction from black leaders, the press, and the former hostages. The *New York Times*, in an editorial, approvingly cited Carter as an example to "those who would allow the exercise of governmental power to overshadow the fate of individuals." Columnist Carl Rowan, himself a former diplomat, wrote that Carter's mistake was upholding "the sanctity of human life." Kissinger backed down somewhat, telling representatives from the congressional Black Caucus that "nothing will be done to impede" Carter's career in the Foreign Service. Carter was subsequently named ambassador to Liberia, and in 1979 became the first black ever appointed to the post of ambassador-at-large.

Carter's second brush with controversy came in connection with his representation of the United States on the antidiscrimination subcommission of the U.N. Human Rights Commission. At a hearing in Geneva in September 1979, he voted in favor of two anti-Israeli resolutions, one urging that Israel restore the right of the Palestinians to self-determination by negotiating with the PLO, the other demanding an end to Israeli bombardment of PLO emplacements in southern Lebanon and deploring "the violation of the fundamental rights of the Arab population in Palestine." The vote was a breach of U.S. policy and was quickly repudiated by the State Department, which explained that Carter's membership on the commission was in a "personal and expert" rather than an official capacity.

Carter retired from the Foreign Service in January 1981 to become director of development and international affairs for the Geneva-based Inter-Maritime Group. He died a year later of a heart attack. M.T./J.P.

Parents William Beverly C. and Maria (Green) C. **Married** Carly Brown Pogue 1971: William Beverly III; Dion Pogue and Ann V. Pogue (stepchildren). **Education** Public schs., Phila.; Lincoln Univ., PA, A.B. 1944; Temple Univ. Law Sch., Phila. 1946–47; New Sch. for Social Research, NYC 1950–51. **Career** Reporter, *Philadelphia Tribune* 1943–45; city ed., *Philadelphia Afro-American* 1945–48; dir. and partner, Journalists Associates, Phila. 1948–55; publisher, *Pittsburgh Courier* 1955–64. • Joined Foreign Service 1965; press attaché, U.S. Embassy, Nairobi 1965–66; head of U.S. Information Service and embassy counselor for public affairs, Lagos 1966–69; deputy asst. secty. of state for African affairs, State Dept., Wash. DC 1969–72; ambassador to Tanzania 1972–75; ambassador to Liberia, 1976–79; ambassador-at-large and head of Office for Liaison with State and Local Govts., State Dept. 1979–81. • U.S. rep. to Subcommn. on Prevention of Discrimination and Protection of Minorities, U.N. Human Rights Commn. since 1972; dir. of development and intl. affairs, Inter-Maritime Group, Geneva since 1981. **Officer** Exec. secty., Lincoln Univ. Alumni Assn. 1952–55; pres., Natl. Newspaper Publishers Assn. 1958; secty., Pennsylvania Commn. on Civil Rights 1957–60; acting chmn., Bd. of Higher Education, Wash. DC 1972. **Member** NAACP; Natl. Urban League; Amer. Foreign Service Assn.; Alpha Boule; Sigma Pi Phi; Kappa Alpha Psi.

DENNIS SLONE
Epidemiologist
Born **Pretoria, South Africa, 9 January 1930**
Died **Lexington, Massachusetts, USA, 10 May 1982**

Dennis Slone played a major role in developing the field of drug epidemiology, the systematic study of the incidence and distribution of drug-related diseases. His report, *Birth Defects and Drugs in Pregnancy* (1977), is the most comprehensive review of the subject yet undertaken.

Born in South Africa, Slone was educated at the University of Pretoria and at the University of Witwatersrand Medical School. After completing his internship and residency in pediatrics, he emigrated in 1961 to the United States for further study at Harvard Medical School. His interest in drug epidemiology was stimulated by the recent tragedy in which thousands of children with severe birth defects had been born to women treated during pregnancy with thalidomide, a sedative and antiemetic drug approved for clinical use in Britain and West Germany. Slone's research on the subject of birth defects eventually resulted in almost 140 publications. Epidemiology is necessarily an inexact science because of the many environmental and genetic factors that bear on health, and Slone was known for the care he took to avoid compounding this inexactness in the design and execution of his experiments.

Starting in 1964, Slone taught at several medical schools in the Boston area while pursuing research at the clinical pharmacology unit of Lemuel Shattuck Hospital, the Boston Collaborative Drug Surveillance Program, and Boston University School of Medicine's drug epidemiology unit, which he co-founded in 1975. His work was funded by the U.S. Food and Drug Administration, the National Institutes of Health, and the pharmaceuticals industry.

The substances Slone investigated ranged from such common ingestants as caffeine, aspirin, and alcohol to thyroid supplements, spermicides, anticonvulsants, and CAT-scan premedication. He was one of the first researchers to monitor the effects of newly mar-

Courtesy of his family

keted drugs in order to spot unexpected reactions. With Samuel Shapiro, co-director of the Boston University drug epidemiology unit and a longtime friend, he pioneered in the simultaneous study of numerous medical variables. His *Birth Defects and Drugs in Pregnancy*, which was based on a sample of more than 50,000 pregnancies, gauged the possible links between several hundred different drugs and 600 kinds of fetal malformations. He found little risk associated with maternal use of aspirin, antiobiotics, sulfa drugs, tranquilizers, and drugs used to suppress nausea in early pregnancy. However, the low incidence of defects connected with these substances was, he noted, "more a matter of good fortune than anything else. Drug use [by pregnant women] over the [study's] recruitment period increased. We doubt whether the quality of the pregnancies was thereby improved. . . . To the extent that drugs may be *potentially* teratogenic, the women were taking greater and greater risks."

Despite the precision of Slone's methodology, several of his studies raised controversies, particularly his finding that heavy smoking is associated with heart attacks in women using birth-control pills. In 1981 he reported that women who use the pill for long periods of time remain unusually vulnerable to heart attacks for as many as nine years after stopping. These studies were contested by the tobacco and drug industries.

Slone developed a brain tumor in late 1981 and died seven months later at the age of 52.

P.D.

Parents Simon S. and Jane (Gerber) S. **Married** Anetta Roman Korsunski 1956: Gregory; Alan; Mark. **Religion** Jewish. **Emigrated** to U.S. 1961; naturalized 1967. **Education** Univ. of Pretoria 1948–49; Univ. of Witwatersrand Medical Sch., Johannesburg, M.B. and B.Ch. 1956; intern in medicine 1956 and intern in surgery 1957, Johannesburg Gen. Hosp.; intern in pediatrics 1958 and sr. resident in pediatrics 1959–61, Baragwanath Hosp., South Africa; clinical and research fellow in pediatric endocrinology, Children's Hosp. Medical Center and Harvard Medical Sch., Cambridge, MA 1961–63; diplomate, Amer. Bd. of Pediatrics 1963; research fellow, Baker Research Labs. and Harvard Medical Sch. 1963–64. **Career** Instr. in medicine 1964–66, sr. instr. in medicine 1966–68, and asst. prof. of medicine 1968–71, Tufts Univ. Sch. of Medicine, Boston; sr. physician 1964–66 and assoc. dir. of Clinical Pharmacology Unit 1964–69, Lemuel Shattuck Hosp., Boston; co-dir., Boston Collaborative Drug Surveillance Program, Boston Univ. Medical Center 1969–75; asst. prof. of medicine 1971–80; founder and co-dir. of Drug Epidemiology Unit since 1975, and research prof. in epidemiology since 1980, Boston Univ. Sch. of Medicine. • Consultant: Bureau of Drugs Advisory Panel System, U.S. Food and Drug Admin. 1970–71; Office of Technology Assessment, U.S. Congress since 1976; IMS America Ltd. 1978–80. **Member** Amer. Diabetes Assn.; Amer. Public Health Assn.; Soc. for Epidemiological Research; Drug Information Assn.; Amer. Soc. for Clinical Pharmacology and Therapeutics; Lawson Wilkins Pediatric Endocrine Soc.; Intl. Epidemiologic Assn.; Amer. Coll. of Preventive Medicine. **Author** (Contributor) Sally Kelly, ed., *Birth Defects: Risks and Consequences*, 1976; (jtly.) *Birth Defects and Drugs in Pregnancy*, 1977; (co-ed.) *The Epidemiological Evaluation of Drugs,* 1977; (jtly.) "Strategies for Studying the Effects of the Antenatal Chemical Environment on the Fetus," in *Drug and Chemical Risks to the Newborn*, 1980. **Contributor** of more than 130 articles on drug epidemiology to medical jrnls.

PETER (ULRICH) WEISS
Playwright
Born **Nowawes, near Berlin, Germany, 8 November 1916**
Died **Stockholm, Sweden, 10 May 1982**

Peter Weiss, author of *The Persecution and Assassination of Jean-Paul Marat as Performed by the Inmates of the Asylum of Charenton under the Direction of the Marquis de Sade* (1964), received international acclaim in the mid-1960s as the strongest, most exuberant force in the German theater since Bertolt Brecht. His later works, prose as well as plays, were generally less allegorical and more polemical than *Marat/Sade*, and consequently appealed to a smaller audience. "My plays do not have conventional lead roles," he said. "The lead roles are played by history and ideas."

Weiss bore a lifelong sense of horror at the narrowness of his escape from being either a victim of the Holocaust, or one of its perpetrators—he had friends on both sides of the line. He was born in a fashionable suburb of Berlin during World War I. His father was a well-to-do textile manufacturer from Czechoslovakia who had converted from Judaism to Lutheranism; his mother, a former actress, was a Swiss Lutheran. The family's exile from Germany began with the arrival in power of the Nazis. They spent two years (1934–36) in England, then moved to Prague, where young Weiss studied painting at the Art Academy (1936–38). After a short stay in Switzerland they finally, in 1939, settled in Göteborg, in neutral Sweden.

Weiss said later that in Sweden he found "the courage to starve or to write or do both." He set about learning Swedish, and became so proficient in that difficult language that he used it for his first published works, the poems in *Off and On* and *The Conquered* (both 1950) and the radio play *The Tower* (1948), about a circus aerialist. In 1952 he began work on a somewhat premature autobiographical work in German, *The Shadow of the Coachman's Body*, which was published in 1960. It was stylistically original, and spoke eloquently of the nightmarish experience he and his generation had lived through and of his guilt at having survived it; he followed this book with two sequels, *The Leavetaking* (1961) and *Vanishing Point* (1962), which won the Charles Veillon Prize for Literature in 1963. Throughout his life he was continually haunted by his lack of roots, by his sense of exile. "Perhaps I am the perpetual refugee," he said in an interview in 1966.

In 1964 his *Marat/Sade* received its first production at the Schiller Theater in West Berlin, where his earlier play *Night with Guests* had been staged the year before. A strange blending of Brechtian alienation techniques with Artaudian theater of cruelty, *Marat/Sade* used music, mime, and formal debate to unfold the conflict between the proto-Marxist Marat and the absolute individualist de Sade. Part of its effect came from the directness, as challenging as a slap in the face, with which it confronted the audience. It was staged as if it were, in fact, a play being performed by the inmates of an eighteenth-century madhouse, with the audience in the role of the bourgeois spectators for whose entertainment it was ordered. The tumultuous reception accorded the play by the German critics surprised Weiss. It had an extremely successful run, in a staging by Peter Brook for the Royal Shakespeare Company, both in London (1964) and New York (1965). In New York it won the Tony and Drama Critics Circle awards for best play.

Weiss's next play was *The Investigation* (1965), an "oratorio in eleven songs" that describes in documentary style, using the actual words of the testimony, the West German investigation into the Auschwitz concentration camp. Here again Weiss drew the audience bodily into the play, this time as the spectators of the trial, forced to absorb a sickening load of facts and details—everything from the color of the gas used in the death chambers to the dimensions of the ovens—and at the same time to question the self-righteousness of their own attitudes. In keeping with Weiss's inability to view the victims of Auschwitz as anything other than the representatives of suffering humanity, the word "Jew" was not mentioned even once. In Stockholm, Ingmar Bergman directed an uncut Swedish version that ran for five hours. Ulu Grosbard staged a two-hour version in New York in 1966. Next came *Song of the Lusitanian Bogey* (1967), a strong indictment of Portuguese colonial policies in Mozambique, Angola, and Portuguese Guinea. In 1968 it was the first play produced by the new Negro Ensemble Company in New York.

Weiss was a committed Marxist by the end of the 1960s, though hardly a rigid Communist, always speaking up for freedom of speech and against all repression. His Marxism informed his next two plays: *Vietnam Discourse* (1968; the full title in German runs to 42 words), an impassioned condemnation of U.S. imperialism in Vietnam—he considered Lyndon Johnson and his military commanders no better than the Nazis—and *Trotsky in Exile* (1971), which showed his sympathy for Trotsky's leftist Marxism and which lost him many Soviet admirers. Both were criticized as being little more than dramatized lectures, and Weiss agreed that they were better suited to stagings in factories and union halls than to commercial theater productions. His most recent play, *The Process*, loosely based on Kafka's *The Trial*, was in mid-1982 only beginning a run at the Royal Dramatic Theater in Stockholm, and has not yet received an English translation. He also spent several years writing a long, three-part "antifascist historical" novel, *The Aesthetics of Resistance* (1976).

Weiss painted regularly from the 1950s, and had a major retrospective exhibit in Zurich in 1979. He had become a Swedish citizen in 1948 and married in 1964 the Swedish artist Gunilla Palmstierna, who assisted him, usually as set designer, on most of his productions. He had one child from a previous marriage. Weiss died in Stockholm of a heart attack. A.K.

Courtesy of German Information Center

Parents Eugene W., textile manufacturer, and Frieda (Hummel) W., actress. **Married** (1) . . . : one daughter. (2) Gunilla Palmstierna, ceramist and set designer, 1964: two stepchildren. **Religion** Raised a Lutheran. **Emigration** Brought out of Germany 1934 to live in England, Czechoslovakia, and Switzerland; Czech citizen through his father; emigrated to Sweden 1939, naturalized 1948. **Education** Art Acad., Prague 1936–38. **Career** Painter and filmmaker since late 1930s, also illustrator and set designer; playwright, novelist, translator, and editor since 1940s. **Member** Swedish C.P.; German Acad. of Art; PEN Center, West Germany. **Honors** Charles Veillon Prize for literature, for *Vanishing Point*, Switzerland 1963; Lessing Prize, for *Marat/Sade*, Hamburg 1966; Heinrich Mann Prize, Acad. of Art, East Berlin, for *The Investigation*, 1966; Carl Albert Anderson Prize 1967; Thomas Dehler Prize 1977. **Plays** *Der Turm* [*The Tower*] (radio play), 1948; *Die Versicherung* [*Insurance*], 1952; *Die Verfolgung und Ermordung Jean-Paul Marats, dargestellt durch die Schauspiel gruppe des Hospizes zu Charenton unter Anleitung des Herrn de Sade: Drama in Zwei Akten*, 1964 (trans. as *The Persecution and Assassination of Marat as Performed by the Inmates of the Asylum of Charenton under the Direction of the Marquis de Sade: A Play*, 1965, and as *The Persecution and Assassination of Jean-Paul Marat as Performed by the Inmates of the Asylum of Charenton under the Direction of the Marquis de Sade: A Play*, 1966); *Die Ermittlung: Oratorium in 11 Gesängen*, 1965 (trans. as *The Investigation: A Play*, 1966, and as *The Investigation: Oratorio in 11 Cantos*, 1966); *Nacht mit Gästen* [*Night with Guests*], 1966; *Gesang vom Lusitanischen Popanz*, 1967 (trans. as *Song of the Lusitanian Bogey*, 1968); *Diskurs über die Vorgeschichte und den Verlauf des lang andauernden Befreiungskrieges in Viet Nam als Beispiel für die Notwendigkeit des bewaffneten Kampfes der*

Unterdrückten gegen ihre Unterdrücker, sowie über die Versuche der Vereinigten Staaten von Amerika die Grundlagen der Revolution zu vernichten, 1967 (trans. as *Discourse on the Progess of the Prolonged War of Liberation in Viet Nam and the Events Leading Up to It as Illustration of the Necessity for Armed Resistance Against Oppression and on the Attempts of the U.S.A. to Destroy the Foundations of Revolution*, 1970, and as *Discourse on Vietnam*, 1970); *Wie dem Herrn Mockinpott das Leiden ausgetrieben wird*, 1968 (trans. as *How Mr. Mockinpott Was Cured of His Sufferings*, 1973); *Trotzki im Exil: Stück in 2 Akten*, 1970 (trans. as *Trotsky in Exile*, 1971, and as *Trotsky in Exile: A Play*, 1972); *Hölderlin: Stück in Zwei Akten* [*Hölderlin: A Play in Two Acts*], 1971; *Der Prozess* [*The Process*], 1975. **Play collections** *Dramen* [*Plays*], 2 vols., 1968; *Stücke* [*Plays*], 1976–77. **Poetry** *Fran O Till O* [*Off and On*], 1950; *De Besegrade* [*The Conquered*], 1950. **Autobiographical novels** *Der Schatten des Körpers des Kutschers*, 1960 (trans. as *The Shadow of the Coachman's Body* in *Bodies and Shadows: Two Short Novels*, 1969, new trans. 1972); *Abschied von den Eltern*, 1961 (trans. as *The Leavetaking*, 1962, and as first part of *Exile: A Novel*, 1968); *Fluchtpunkt: Roman*, 1962 (trans. as *Vanishing Point*, 1966, and as second part of *Exile: A Novel*, 1968). **Other literary works** *Dokument I*, 1949; (trans.) J. C. Görsch, *Das Duell* [*The Duel*], 1953; *Avantgardefilm*, 1956; (trans.) August Strindberg, *Ein Traumspiel* [*A Dream Play*], and *Miss Julie*, 1963; *Das Gespräch der drei Gehenden*, 1963 (trans. as *The Conversation of the Three Wayfarers*, in *Bodies and Shadows: Two Short Novels*, 1969, and as *The Conversation of Three Walkers*, 1972); (jt. ed.) *Proceedings of the International War Crimes Tribunal*, 1967; (with Gunilla Palmstierna-Weiss) *Rapport on Forenta Staternas forstarkta angrepp mot Nordvietnam efter den 31 mars 1968*, 1968 (trans. as *"Limited Bombing" in Vietnam: Report on the Attacks Against the Democratic Republic of Vietnam by the United States Air Force and the Seventh Fleet After the Declaration of "Limited Bombing" by President Lyndon Baines Johnson on March 31, 1968*, 1969); *Notizen zum kulturellen Leben in der Demokratischen Republik Viet Nam*, 1968 (trans. as. *Notes on the Cultural Life of the Democratic Republic of Vietnam*, 1970); *Rapporte* [*Reports*], 1968–71; (contributor) Malcolm Caldwell, ed., *American Presence in South East Asia*, 1971; *Die Ästhetik des Widerstands* [*The Aesthetics of Resistance*], 1975; *Aufsätze, Journale, Arbeitspunkte: Schriften zu Kunst und Literatur* [*Essays, Journals, and Articles: Writings on Art and Literature*], 1979. **Illustrator** *Tusen o en Natt* [*1,001 Nights*], 1957; Hermann Hesse, *Kindheit des Zauberers: ein Autobiograph* [*The Magician's Childhood: An Autobiography*], 1974; Hermann Hesse, *Der verbannte Ehemann* [*The Exiled Husband*], 1977. **Films** [*Hallucinations*], 1953; [*Faces in Shadows*], 1956; [*The Mirage*], 1958; [*Interplay*]; [*The Studio of Doctor Faust*]; others. **Exhibitions** Retrospective, Zurich, 1979. **Interview** with Michael Roloff in *Partisan Review*, Spring 1965.

Further reading Walter Wager, *The Playwrights Speak*, 1967; Robert Brustein, *The Third Theatre*, 1968; Martin Esslin, *Reflections: Essays on Modern Theatre*, 1969; Ian Hilton, *Peter Weiss: A Search for Affinities*, 1970; O. Best, *Peter Weiss*, 1976.

MA YINCHU
Economist and educator
***Born* Cheng county, Zhejiang province, China, June 1882**
***Died* Peking, China, 10 May 1982**

Ma Yinchu, nearly a centenarian when he died, was a respected economist and president of Peking University when, in 1957, he came into conflict with Mao Zedong over his published recommendation that China's population growth be curbed. Ousted from his post three years later after a vituperative campaign against him in the official press, he lived in obscurity—even disappearing for a while during the Cultural Revolution—until formally rehabilitated by the Communist Party in 1979.

He was born Ma Yuan-shan, the son of a wealthy wine merchant. He began his studies in Shanghai, then completed a course in mineralogy at Beiyang University in Tianjin. He went to study in the United States in 1907 and received a B.A. from Yale in 1910 and a Ph.D. in economics from Columbia in 1914 with a dissertation entitled *Finances of the City of New York*. Returning to China in 1915, he quickly became one of the country's most respected economists, lecturing on the subject at Peking, Jiatong, Zhejiang, and Chongqing universities.

Ma was attracted to Marxist economics and was among the founders in 1918 of the Society for the Study of Marxism, yet he always refused to join the party, even resigning from the society just as it was becoming the embryonic Communist Party of China. From 1928 to 1947 he was a member of the Legislative Yuan, which was dominated by the Nationalists under Chiang Kai-shek, and was several times, during the war against Japan (1937–45), imprisoned or kept under house arrest for suspected Marxism and for criticizing Nationalist economic policies. After he fled to Hong Kong shortly before the Nationalists' fall in 1949, he received a telegram from Jou En-lai—an old friend and Ma's former pupil—inviting him to join the new Communist government in Peking. He was named president of Zhejiang University early in 1950 and president of Peking University—probably the top academic post in China—in August 1951.

There was absolute agreement among Chinese economists in the early 1950s that extraordinary rates of progress and modernization were vital to the country, and that action was needed immediately. Beyond that, practically every facet of economic planning was open to often intense dispute. Most orthodox Marxists insisted on a determined acceleration of growth in only a few sectors—heavy industry and machine tools were their favorites; Ma and his supporters (many of whom, like him, were educated in the West) consistently advocated a more diffuse, flexible, and people-oriented development, giving agriculture and consumer goods a fair share of government incentives.

When Mao and chairman Liu Shaoqi, then his second in command, finally came down on the side of heavy industrial development, Ma and his followers—the most powerful of whom was Prime Minister Jou—were left in a dangerously exposed position. Attacks against Ma in 1958–59 numbered in the hundreds, many of them grounded in personalities and politics rather than in economics; he was called "China's Malthus" and "a representative of the bourgeoisie." "I will never capitulate," he said, "to those critics who are bent on bringing others to submission by force and not by reasoning."

The controversy over population growth was mainly an extension of the wider economic debate. To Ma, as he explained in *New Principles on Chinese Population* (1957), it was axiomatic that the quality of the population and the productivity of the labor force had to be enhanced while unrestricted growth must be strictly discouraged. Mao sternly dismissed such contentions. "The solution is production," said the supreme leader. "Where you see a million mouths to feed, I see two million hands to work."

Ma endured two decades of enforced silence and even oblivion after his dismissal from the university in 1960. It was not until mid-1979 that the Communist Party ordered his rehabilitation: in September of that year he was appointed honorary president of Peking University and in December was elected a deputy from Peking to the 5th National Party Congress. All of his main economic recommendations had long since become a part of Chinese economic orthodoxy; most families are now limited to one child only, and a system of incentives and punishments has been instituted to enforce this policy. A.K.

Born Ma Yuan-shan. **Parents** Ma Ching Ch'ang, wine merchant, and Ma (Wang) Chiu Mien. **Married** (1) Mary Chang. (2) Wang Zhongzhen. **Education** Christian Middle Sch., Shanghai; Beiyang Univ., Tianjin; Yale Univ., B.A. 1910; Columbia Univ., Ph.D. in economics 1914. **Career** Lectr. and prof. of economics, Peking Univ. 1915–27; member of research dept. and dir. of Dept. of Note Issue, Bank of China ca. 1916–20; co-founder and prof. 1920 and dean ca. 1928–30s, Shanghai Coll. of Commerce; advisor, Natl. Commercial Bank 1920s; prof. of economics, Chekiang Univ. 1927–28; prof. of economics and dir. of research inst., Chiaotung Univ. 1928; lectr. in economics, Chinese War Coll. 1930s; prof. of economics and dean, Coll. of Commerce, Chongqing Univ. 1938–40; research fellow,

Academia Sinica 1947; prof., Hsing-li Sch. of Accounting, Shanghai 1947; prof., Chung-hua Industrial and Commercial Sch., Shanghai 1947. • Member, Legislative Yuan 1928–47; attended Kuomintung conference, Lushan 1930s; under Kuomintang house arrest, Hsifeng, Kweichow 1940–42; participated in antigovt. demonstrations, Hangzhou and Shanghai 1947–49; joined Communists 1949. • With Central People's Govt., People's Republic of China: delegate and natl. cttee. member 1949, standing cttee. member 1964 and 1978, and vice chmn. 1974–78, Chinese People's Political Consultative Conference; vice chmn., Financial and Economic Cttee., and member, Govt. Admin. Council 1949; pres., Zhejiang Univ. 1950–51; vice chmn., East China Military and Admin. Commn. 1950; council member 1950–59 and vice chmn. 1954–59, Sino-Soviet Friendship Assn.; pres., Peking Univ. 1951–60; standing cttee. member 1954 and 1959, deputy for Zhejiang province 1954–64, and deputy for Peking municipality 1979, Natl. People's Congress; exec. dir., People's Bank of China 1954–59; purged 1960; rehabilitated 1979. **Officer** Co-founder 1918 and member until ca. 1948; Soc. for the Study of Marxism; founder and 1st pres., Chinese Economics Soc. 1923; vice chmn., China Peace Cttee. 1949; vice chmn., China Cttee. for Promoting Foreign Trade 1952; dir., World Peace Council 1952. **Member** Preparatory cttee., Intl. Economic Conference 1952; Inst. of Philosophy and Social Sciences, Acad. of Sciences 1955–60s. **Honors** Hon. pres., Peking Univ. since 1979; hon. pres., Chinese Population Science Soc. **Author** *The Finances of the City of New York*, 1914; [*Economic Lectures*], 4 vols., 1924–28; *Chung-kuo kuan-shui wen-ti* [*China's Tariff Problems*], 1926; *Chung-hua yin-hang Lun* [*On Chinese Banks*], 1929; [*Essays on the Problems of the Economy*], 1932; *Chung-kuo ching-chi kai-tsao* [*China's Economic Reform*], 1935; [*Essays During the War Period*], 1945; *Ts'ai-cheng hsueh yü Chung-kuo ts'ai cheng: Li-lun yü hsien-shih* [*The Study of Finance and Chinese Financial Affairs: Theory and Reality*], 2 vols., 1948; [*New Principles of Chinese Population*], 1957; [*My Economic Theories, Philosophical Thoughts, and Political Convictions*], 1958. **Contributor** to Chinese newspapers and economic jrnls.

Further reading Yuan-Li Wu, *The Economy of Communist China: An Introduction*, 1965; Nai Ruenn Chen, *The Chinese Economy Under Communism*, 1969.

SIR RONALD BODLEY SCOTT

Hematologist and physician to King George VI and Queen Elizabeth II
Born **Bournemouth, Dorset, England, 10 September 1906**
Died **Parma, Italy, 12 May 1982**

Sir Ronald Bodley Scott was a world authority on diseases of the blood, particularly leukemia, and served as physician to King George VI from 1949 to 1952 and to Queen Elizabeth II from 1952 to 1973. In 1964 he attended the delivery of the Queen's youngest son, Prince Edward.

The son of a physician, Bodley Scott went to Marlborough College and took an honors degree in natural sciences from Brasenose College, Oxford, in 1928. He received his B.M., B.Ch., and M.A. degrees (Oxon.) from St. Bartholomew's Hospital Medical College in 1931, became a member of the Royal College of Physicians two years later, and in 1937 earned his doctorate in medicine from Oxford University with a thesis on the aspiration of bone marrow, a technique used in the diagnosis and treatment of leukemia and other blood disorders. During World War II he had charge of general hospitals in the Middle East and rose to the rank of lieutenant colonel in the RAMC. Afterward he rejoined the Woolwich Memorial Hospital, where he had been a physician since 1939, and joined the medical staff of St. Bartholomew's. He was a consulting physician to British Railways (from 1957), the British Army (1957–71), the Florence Nightingale Hospital (from 1958), the Royal Navy (from 1963), the King Edward

VII Hospital for Officers (from 1963), and the Ministry of Defense (from 1965).

In addition to being one of the most respected clinicians in the country, Bodley Scott was a skillful explicator and writer, and was the editor of the enormous 12th edition of *Price's Textbook of The Practice of Medicine* (1978). He was also the editor, since 1959, of the *Medical Annual*, and wrote *Cancer—The Facts* (1979), a reference source for nurses and physicians. In 1962 he was part of a nine-member team from the Royal College of Physicians that issued a report on the connection between tobacco smoking and cancer. He served as president of the Medical Society of London (1965–66), of the section on medicine of the Royal Society of Medicine (1967–78), and of the British Society for Haematology (1966–67). After his retirement in 1971 he continued to be active in numerous organizations, including the Society of Apothecaries of London, the British Heart Foundation, and the Imperial Cancer Research fund.

Bodley Scott was knighted KCVO in 1964 and was made GCVO in 1973, the year in which he left the service of the Royal Family. He was a fellow of the Royal College of Physicians since 1943. He died of injuries suffered in a road accident in Italy. C.M.

Parents Maitland B. S., physician, and Alice Hilda Durance George B. S. **Married** (1) Edith Daphne McCarthy 1931 (d. 1977): two daughters. (2) Jessie Gaston 1980. **Education** Marlborough Sch., Wilts.; Honours Sch. in Natural Sciences, Brasenose Coll., Oxford, B.A. 1928; St. Bartholomew's Hosp. Medical Coll., London, B.M., B.Ch., M.A. (Oxon.) 1931; MRCP 1933; Oxford Univ., D.M. 1937. **Mil. service** Lt. col., RAMC, and officer in charge, Medical Divs. of 63rd and 43rd Gen. Hosps., Mideast 1941–45. **Career** With St. Bartholomew's Hosp., London: chief asst. to medical unit 1934; physician 1946–65; sr. physician 1965–71; member, bd. of govs. 1966–71; consulting physician since 1971. • Physician 1936–71 and consulting physician since 1971, Woolwich Memorial Hosp., London; physician, Surbiton Gen. Hosp. 1946–64; principal medical officer, Equity and Law Life Assurance Soc. since 1952; physician, Florence Nightingale Hosp. since 1958; ed., *Medical Annual* since 1959; physician, King Edward VII Hosp. for Officers since 1963 and King Edward VII Hosp., Midhurst, since 1965; sr. medical advisor, Cavendish Medical Centre since 1975. • Physician to Household of King George VI 1949–52; physician to Queen Elizabeth II 1952–73; physician to the Royal Family 1964–73. • Consulting physician: British Railways, Eastern Region, since 1957; Royal Navy since 1963; British Army at home 1965–71. • Lectr.: Langdon Brown Lectr. 1957, Croonian Lectr. 1970, and Harveian Oratory 1976, Royal Coll. of Physicians; Lettsomian Lectr., Medical Soc. of London 1957; Thom Bequest Lectr., Edinburgh Royal Coll. of Physicians 1957. • Examiner in medicine: univs. of Oxford, London, Edinburgh, Glasgow, Cairo, Singapore; Royal Coll. of Physicians, London and Edinburgh; Conjoint Bd. **Officer** Council member 1963–66, censor 1970–72, and sr. censor and v.p. 1972, Royal Coll. of Physicians; pres. 1965–66 and trustee since 1972, Medical Soc. of London; pres., British Soc. for Haematology 1966–67; pres. of medical sect. 1967–68 and treas. since 1973, Royal Soc. of Medicine. • Chmn., bd. of trustees, Migraine Trust 1971–73; chmn., Medicines Commn. 1973–75; chmn. of Research Grants Cttee. 1970–75 and chmn. of council since 1975, British Heart Foundn. • Member of Court of Assts. since 1964, and master 1974, Soc. of Apothecaries of London; v.p., Coll. of Speech Therapists 1979; trustee, Nuffield Medical Benefaction. **Fellow** FRCP 1943. **Member** Council, Imperial Cancer Research Fund since 1968; Temporary Registration Assessment Bd., Gen. Medical Council 1973–76. **Honors** Hon. consultant in hematology, British Army at home 1957–65; hon. consultant in hematology, Ministry of Defence since 1965; KCVO 1964; Order of the Crown of Brunei and Order of the Family, Brunei, 1970; GCVO 1973; hon. member of British Haematology Soc., 1977, and member of Medical Soc. of London. **Author** (Ed.) *Price's Textbook of the Practice of Medicine*, 12th ed., 1978; *Cancer—The Facts*, 1979; papers in medical jrnls.

HUMPHREY SEARLE
Composer
Born **Oxford, England, 26 August 1915**
Died **London, England, 12 May 1982**

Humphrey Searle, a disciple of Anton Webern and Arnold Schoenberg, was one of the major contemporary British composers of serial music. The son of a civil servant, Searle was a classics scholar at New College, Oxford, before entering the Royal College of Music in 1937 to study composition under John Ireland. He spent the winter of that year in Vienna, where he attended the New Vienna Conservatorium and took private lessons with Webern. During World War II he was an intelligence officer and trained paratroopers for the RAF, and while in Germany helped research Hugh Trevor-Roper's book *The Last Days of Hitler*. He was a producer for the BBC from 1938 to 1940 and from 1946 to 1948, and an advisor to the Sadler's Wells Ballet from 1951 to 1957. After 1965 he spent much of his time teaching at the Royal College of Music and in Karlsruhe, Aspen, and California.

Searle's first published work was his *Suite No. 1* for string orchestra (1942). In his early works he began to move away from tonality toward the new musical grammar laid down by Webern, developing his senses of phrasing and logic under the influence of Schoenberg and exploring the possibilities of counterpoint, for which he showed a natural gift. After 1946 he relied almost exclusively on 12-tone technique. His solution to the problem of maintaining structural coherence and momentum in the absence of tonality was to base his music on literary works and to let the text supply both: his best-known compositions are a choral trilogy and three operas.

Two parts of the trilogy, *Gold Coast Customs* (1949) and *The Shadow of Cain* (1952), are settings of poems by Edith Sitwell, the other, *The Riverrun*, (1951), a setting of the final section of Joyce's *Finnegans Wake*. His operas, all written to librettos of his own devising, were the one-act *Diary of a Madman* (1958), from a story by Gogol; *The Photo of the Colonel*, 1964, after Ionesco; and an adaptation of *Hamlet* (1968). All three explored themes of insanity and fantasy, for which Searle obtained eerie musical effects through the use of electronic and taped music. He was also the author of five symphonies and much chamber music, which displayed his talent for the euphonious interweaving of instrumental voices.

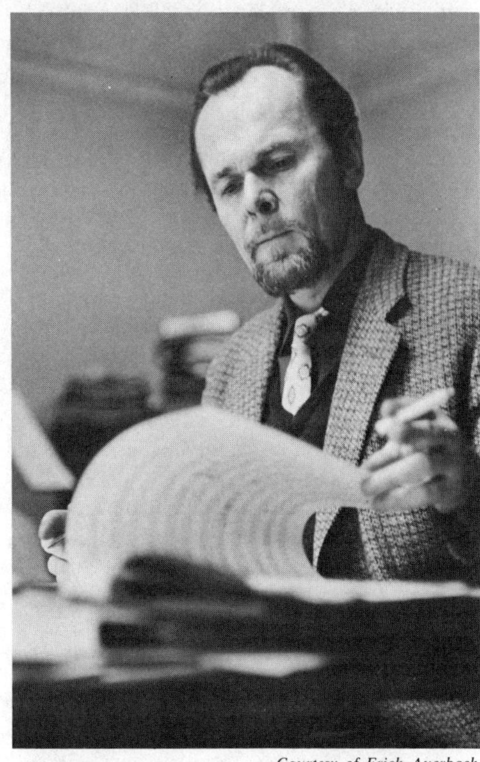
Courtesy of Erich Auerbach

Searle's books include *The Music of Liszt* (1954), on whom he was an authority, and *Twentieth-Century Composers* (1954). He translated biographies of Webern and Schoenberg and two volumes of Hector Berlioz's correspondence and edited Schoenberg's *Structural Functions of Harmony*. He was made CBE in 1968. C.M.

Parents Humphrey Frederic S., civil servant, and Charlotte Mathilde Mary (Schlich) S. **Married** (1) Margaret Lesley Gillen Gray 1949 (d. 1957). (2) Fiona Elizabeth Anne Nicholson, actress, 1960. **Education** Winchester Coll., Hants., grad. 1933; New Coll., Oxford, M.A. (honors) 1937; Royal Coll. of

Music, London 1937; New Vienna Conservatorium 1937–38; private studies in composition with Anton Webern, Vienna 1937–38. **Mil. service** Capt., Gloucestershire Regiment, Intelligence Corps and Paratroopers 1940–46. **Career** Composer since mid-1930s; program producer, BBC Music Dept. 1938–40 and 1946–48; free-lance 1948–51; advisor, Sadler's Wells Ballet 1951–57; prof. of composition, Royal Coll. of Music since 1965. • Resident composer, Stanford Univ., CA 1964–65; guest composer, Aspen Musical Festival, CO 1967; guest prof., Staatliche Hochschule für Musik, Karlsruhe 1968–72; visiting prof., Univ. of Southern California, L.A. 1976–77. **Officer** Gen. secty., Intl. Soc. for Contemporary Music 1947–49. **Fellow** FRCM 1966. **Member** Council, Composers Guild of Great Britain; council, Soc. for Promotion of New Music; Royal Musical Assn.; London Contemporary Music Centre; Savage Club, London. **Honors** Hon. secty., Liszt Soc. 1950–62; UNESCO Radio Critics' Prize, for opera *The Diary of a Madman*, 1960; Italia Prize 1965; hon. assoc., Royal Coll. of Music 1966; CBE 1968; hon. professorial fellow, University Coll. of Wales, Aberystwyth 1977. **Operas** *The Diary of a Madman*, 1958; *The Photo of the Colonel*, 1964; *Hamlet*, 1968. **Ballets** *Noctambules*, 1956; *The Great Peacock,* 1956; *Dualities*, 1963. **Symphonies** *No. 1*, 1953; *No. 2*, 1958; *No. 3*, 1960; *No. 4*, 1962; *No. 5*, 1964. **Orchestral music** *Suite No. 1*, 1942; *Night Music*, 1943; *Suite No. 2*, 1944; *Piano Concerto No. 1*, 1944; *Highland Reel*, 1946; *Second Nocturne*, 1946; *Fuga giocosa*, 1948; *Overture to a Drama*, 1949; *Poem*, 1950; *Concertante*, 1954; *Divertimento*, 1954; *Piano Concerto No. 2*, 1955; *Aubade*, 1955; *Scherzi*, 1964; *Zodiac Variations*, 1970; *Labyrinth*, 1971; *Fantasia on British Airs*, 1976; *Tamesis*, 1979; many incidental scores for radio. **Chamber and instrumental music** *Vigil*, 1944; *Intermezzo*, 1946; *Ballade*, 1947; *Quartet*, 1948; *Threnos and Toccata*, 1948; *Passacaglietta in nomine Arnold Schoenberg*, 1949; *Gondoliera*, 1950; *Piano Sonata*, 1951; *Suite*, 1955; *Toccata alla passacaglia*, 1957; *Suite*, 1957; *Variations and Finale*, 1958; *Three Movements*, 1960; *Prelude on a Theme of Alan Rawsthorne*, 1965; *Sinfonietta*, 1969; *Divertimento*, 1970; *Fantasia*, 1971; *Cat Variations*, 1971; *A Little Waltz*, 1972; *Fantasy and Toccata*, 1973; *Five*, 1974; *Il penseroso e L'allegro*, 1975. **Vocal music** *Two Songs*, 1946; *Put Away the Flutes*, 1947; *The Owl and the Pussycat*, 1951; *Three Songs*, 1954; *Burn-up*, 1962; *Counting the Beats*, 1963; *Oxus*, 1967; *Ophelia*, 1969; *The Donkey*, 1971; *Les fleurs du mal*, 1972; *A Nocturnall upon St. Lucie's Day*, 1974; *Contemplations*, 1975. **Choral music** *Song of the Birds*, 1936; *Song of the Sun*, 1964; *The Canticle of the Rose*, 1965; *A Little Hymn to Mary*, 1967; *I Have a New Garden*, 1969; *From "The Divine Narcissus,"* 1969; *Jerusalem*, 1970; *Kubla Khan*, 1973; *Rhyme Rude to My Pride*, 1974; *Skimbleshanks, the Railway Cat*, 1975; *My Beloved Spake*, 1976; *Dr. Faustus*, 1977. • Trilogy: *Gold Coast Customs*, 1949; *The Riverrun*, 1951; *The Shadow of Cain*, 1951. **Author** *The Music of Liszt*, 1954, rev. ed. 1966; *Twentieth Century Counterpoint*, 1954; (ed.) Arnold Schoenberg, *Structural Functions of Harmony*, 1954; *Ballet Music: An Introduction*, 1958, rev. ed. 1973; (ed.) *Hector Berlioz: Selected Letters*, 1966; (jtly.) *Twentieth-Century Composers 3: Britain, Scandinavia and the Netherlands*, 1972. **Translator** Josef Rufer, *Composition with Twelve Notes*, 1954; H. H. Stuckenschmidt, *Arnold Schoenberg*, 1959; Friedrich Wildgans, *Anton Webern*, 1966; Walter Kolneder, *Anton Webern*, 1967; (also ed.) *Hector Berlioz: A Selection from his Letters*, 1973; H. H. Stuckenschmidt, *Arnold Schoenberg: His Life, World, and Work*, 1977. **Contributor** to *Encyclopaedia Britanica, Dictionary of National Biography, Grove's Dictionary of Music and Musicians, Chambers's Encyclopedia, Proceedings of the Royal Musical Association*, and musical periodicals.

Further reading M. Schafer, *British Composers in Interview*, 1963; E. Routh, *Contemporary British Music*, 1972.

RENZO ROSSELLINI

Composer, conductor, and critic
***Born* Rome, Italy, 2 February 1908**
***Died* Monte Carlo, Monaco, 13 May 1982**

"I believe in tonality because I believe in God: tonality is a law of nature and therefore a creation of God." Thus Renzo Rossellini described his conservative musical aesthetic to *Opera News* in 1967, shortly before the American premiere of his opera *Uno Sguardo dal Ponte* (1961), based on Arthur Miller's play *A View from the Bridge* (1955). Rossellini believed that tonality is an essential element of the popular musical theater "that reflects life like a mirror, that is animated by human values." "I remain faithful to tradition," he added.

The tradition to which Rossellini belonged, and the tonal practices he observed, were those established by Mascagni, Leoncavallo, and Puccini during the 1890s, when realistic, or *verismo*, operas set a vogue for violent melodrama allied to music derived from the operas that Verdi wrote in midcareer. *La Traviata* and *Rigoletto*, for example, richly melodic, orchestrally complex, and irresistibly moving, provided the inspiration for Puccini's exploitation of sentiment and violence in *La Bohème* and *Tosca*. In following Puccini's example, however, Rossellini was trying to exploit an overworked vein to which he brought no fresh equipment. To the rather conservative critic Winthrop Sargeant, writing of *La Guerra* in the *New Yorker* in 1971, Rossellini seemed to be "Puccini's logical successor," but, he added, the tradition had degenerated. It became, in fact, the stock-in-trade of the movie-score composer, and it continues to flourish to this day in that medium: a thoroughly tonal, lyrically and dramatically limited means of musical expression that is capable of augmenting, but never supporting, a drama.

It was as a composer of scores for movies, particularly those of his younger brother, the producer and director Roberto Rossellini, that Renzo won his greatest success. Working in this medium, Rossellini was able to support himself as a composer while finding additional work as a conductor, teacher, and music critic of the Rome newspaper *Il Messaggero*. The son of a sculptor and architect, he received his musical education at the Conservatorio di Musica di Santa Cecilia in Rome, where he studied conducting with Bernardino Molinari, whose work as a teacher and conductor coincided with a period of renewed Italian interest in symphonic music. Rossellini was himself a teacher at conservatories and musical academies in Florence, Rome, Bologna, Varese, and Pesaro. He was married to Anita Limongelli and had one son, Franco, who became a producer of operas and films and was the stage director of his father's opera, *Uno Sguardo dal Ponte*, at its first production in the United States.

Rossellini wrote ten operas, including *Le Campagne* (1959), which was made expressly for television, a considerable amount of orchestral and chamber music, and scores for approximately 130 films, including Roberto Rossellini's classics of the realist cinema, *Open City* (1945) and *Paisan* (1946). An active conductor of opera, he directed many Italian performances of works from the standard repertory, favoring especially operas by Bellini, Donizetti, and Verdi. He spent the last nine years of his life as artistic director of the Monte Carlo Opera. H.B.

Father a sculptor and architect. **Married** Anita Limongelli: Franco, producer and dir. of films and operas. **Education** Conservatorio di Musica di Santa Cecilia, Rome. **Career** Dir., Pergolesi Musical Inst., Varese 1933–40; vice dir. and prof. of composition, Rossini Conservatory, Pesaro 1940–42; music critic, *Il Messaggero*, Rome ca. 1942–71; member of management cttee. since 1965, pres. since 1970, and artistic dir. since 1973, Natl. Opera and Orch. of Monte Carlo, Monaco; composer, chiefly of film scores and operas. **Member** Natl. Council, UNESCO since 1958; admin. council, Italian Soc. of Authors and Writers since 1966; Accademia Nationale di Santa Cecilia, Rome; Accademia Cherubini, Florence; Accademia Filarmonica, Bologna. **Honors** Cavalier, Grand Cross of Merit, Italy; comdr., Order of St. Charles. **Film scores** More than 90, including *White Ship*, 1941; *Open City*, 1945; *Paisan*, 1946; *Germany,*

Year Zero, 1947; *Stromboli*, 1949; *The Flowers of St. Francis*, 1950; *Europa*, 1951; *Journey in Italy*, 1952; *General Della Rovere*, 1959; *Long Live Italy*, 1960. **Operas** *Alcassino e Nicoletta*, 1930; *La Guerra*, 1956; *Il Vortice*, 1958; *La Piovre*, 1958; *Le Campagne*, 1959; *Uno Sguardo dal Ponte*, 1961; *Il Linguaggio dei Fiori*, 1963; *La Leggenda del Ritorno*, 1966; *L'Avventuriero*, 1968; *L'Annonce faite à Marie*, 1970; *La Reine Morte*, 1973. **Ballets** *La danza di Dassine*, 1935; *Racconto d'inverno*, 1947; *Canti del golfo di Napoli*, 1954; *Poemetti pagani*, 1960; *Il ragazzo e la sua ombra*, 1966. **Choral works** *Roma cristiana*, 1940; *La suora degli emigranti*, 1947; *Santa Caterina di Siena*, 1947. **Orchestral works** *Suite in tre tempi*, 1931; *Hoggar*, 1931; *Canti di Marzo*, 1935; *Stornelli della Roma bassa*, 1946; *Ut unum sint*, 1963; others. • Also composer of songs and instrumental works. **Author** *Polemica musicale* [*Musical Polemics*], 1962; *Pagine di un musicista* [*Pages of a Musician's Life*], 1964; *Addio del passato* [*Farewell to the Past*], 1968.

PETER BOARDMAN

Mountain climber
Born **Bramhall, Cheshire, England, 25 December 1950**
Disappeared **near the summit of Mount Everest, on the border between Nepal and Tibet, 17 May 1982**

JOE TASKER

Mountain climber
Born **Hull, Yorkshire, 1948**
Disappeared **near the summit of Mount Everest, on the border between Nepal and Tibet, 17 May 1982**

Peter Boardman and Joe Tasker, two of Britain's most daring and experienced young mountain climbers, were killed in a fall down the 10,000-foot Kangshung face of Mount Everest during an expedition up the unclimbed east-northeast ridge.

The two had been partners since 1976, when they undertook a first ascent of one of the most difficult climbs in the Himalayas, the west wall of Changabang, a 22,500-foot granite peak near the India-Tibet border. They climbed in the alpine style, without oxygen or a support team, in order to keep their ascent light and quick and their encounter with the forces of nature as direct as possible. (Siege expeditions, by contrast, involve masses of climbers and Sherpa porters, tons of equipment, including bottled oxygen, and a long and complicated plan of attack.) Because climbing without oxygen in very high altitudes entails a greater risk of hypothermia, frostbite, and brain damage, and because small expeditions have less chance of summoning help in a crisis, alpine-style mountaineering is considered by many too dangerous to try on the giant Himalayan peaks, where temperatures drop below −40°F, storms and avalanches strike without warning, and the climber is confronted with sheer walls of ice and rock. Boardman and Tasker were among the few who preferred lightweight climbing in the Himalayas, and their deaths may well provoke a backlash against it.

Boardman, a native of Cheshire, began climbing in his boyhood. As an English-literature student at the University of Nottingham, he made five British first ascents in the western Alps and led the first ascents of Koh-i-Mondi and Koh-i-Khaaik in the Hindu Kush. On the latter expedition, his three-member group seriously underestimated the mountain's difficulties and brought only enough food for a day's outing. The climb took five days. In a broadcast for the BBC, Boardman described his euphoria as they arrived, in a state of near collapse, at an Afghan village: "I had the most extraordinary feeling that there was never going to be anything to worry about again. . . . It was as if I had just recovered from a near-fatal illness and, on recovery, found every last bodily molecule subtly shifted. . . . I had shared kinship with people whose lives were a constant struggle for survival. I felt totally on top of Western life."

Peter Boardman *Courtesy of Hodder & Stoughton*

Boardman taught mountaineering in Scotland for two years beginning in 1973, and in 1975 became an official of the British Mountaineering Council. He quickly became known as an expert technical climber, and after his successful first ascent of the south face of Mount Dan Beard in the Central Alaskan Range was invited by Chris Bonington to join the large (100-member) British siege of the southwest face of Everest in the fall of 1975. He was, at 24, the youngest member of the group, and one of the few to reach the summit. The following year he accepted Joe Tasker's proposal for an alpine-style attack on Changabang, the third highest mountain in the world.

The Yorkshire-born Tasker, one of 11 children, was a former seminarian and had read sociology at Manchester University. He was a rock climber from his teens, and from 1971 to 1975 completed many climbs in the Alps, culminating in the first British winter ascent (and the first two-man winter ascent) of the north face of the Eiger in 1975. He and his partner, Dick Renshaw, then made a historic alpine-style climb up the southeast ridge of the Himalayan mountain Dunagiri, reaching the bottom in delirium after four days without food and water in subfreezing temperatures. His and Boardman's Changabang ascent, described by Boardman in *The Shining Mountain* (1978), was "the most advanced lightweight Himalayan climb so far achieved," according to *Mountain* magazine. Other mountaineers, spurred by their success, began trying alpine tactics on other Himalayan mountains.

During the next few years, Boardman took over the directorship of the International School of Mountaineering in Leysin, Switzerland, after its two previous directors were killed in climbing accidents, and in 1979 led a four-man group to the summit of Gauri Sankar in Nepal, while Tasker joined the winter expedition that came within 5,000 feet of the summit of Everest. They both took part in the two unsuccessful assaults on the west ridge of K2, the second highest mountain in the world, in 1978 and 1980, in the first ascent of Mount Kongur in the Chinese Pamirs in 1981, and in the first ascent of the north ridge of Kanchenjunga by a four-member team in 1982.

They died attempting to open a new route up Mount Everest as the lead climbers in a six-man alpine-style expedition led by Chris Bonington. Bonington's last glimpse of them, through binoculars, showed them about 2,000 feet below the summit, preparing to climb a rock-and-ice pinnacle on the sheer Kangshung snow wall. After radio contact was lost, the rest of the team waited for several days and in the end was forced to turn back without them.

Boardman's second book, *Sacred Summits*, was published late in 1982. Tasker was the

Joe Tasker *Courtesy of Hodder & Stoughton*

author of *Everest the Cruel Way* (1981) and *Savage Arena* (1982), an autobiography.

J.P.

Peter Boardman

Parents Alan Howe B. and Dorothy (Griffiths) B., lectr. **Married** Hilary Collins 1980. **Education** Stockport Grammar Sch., Cheshire; Univ. of Nottingham, B.A. 1972; University Coll. of North Wales, certificate in education 1973. **Career** Mountain climber since boyhood; instr. in mountaineering, Glenmore Lodge, Aviemore, Scotland 1973–75; natl. officer 1975–78 and v.p. since 1979, British Mountaineering Council, Manchester; dir., Intl. Sch. of Mountaineering, Leysin, Switzerland since 1978. **Expeditions** Five British first ascents in Alps, including north faces of Olan, Nesthorn, and Lauterbrunnen Breithorn, Europe 1970–71; leader, Univ. of Nottingham expeditions to Hindu Kush, Afghanistan, including first ascents of north faces of Koh-i-Mondi and Koh-i-Khaaik, 1972; first ascent of south face of Mt. Dan Beard, Central Alaskan Range 1974; expedition to Caucasus 1975; British expedition up southwest face of Mt. Everest, Himalayas, Nepal-Tibet 1975; winter traverse, High Tatras, Poland 1976; (with Joe Tasker) first ascent of west wall of Changabang, Garhwal Himalayas, India-Tibet 1976; Mt. Kenya, Kenya, and Mt. Kilimanjaro, Tanzania, 1977; west ridge of K2, Karakoram Range, Pakistan-China 1978 and 1980; Carstensz Pyramid, Snow Mts., New Guinea 1979; leader, expedition to south summit of Gauri Sankar, Himalayas, Nepal 1979; first ascent of north ridge of Kanchenjunga, Himalayas, Nepal-India 1979; first ascent of Mt. Kongur, Pamirs, China 1981; east-northeast ridge, Everest 1982. **Officer** Pres., Assn. of British Mountain Guides since 1979. **Member** Stockport Climbing Club, Cheshire; Alpine Club; Mynydd Climbing Club. **Honors** Rhys Memorial Prize, for *The Shining Mountain*, Soc. of Authors and Natl. Book League 1979. **Author** *The Shining Mountain: Two Men on Changabang's West Wall*, 1978; (contributor) Chris Bonington, ed., *Everest the Hard Way*, 1976; *Sacred Summits, A Climber's Year*, 1982.

Joe Tasker

Father a caretaker. **Education** St. Joseph's Seminary, Newcastle ca. 1961–69; Ushaw Coll., Durham; Manchester Univ. early 1970s. **Religion** Roman Catholic. **Career** Mountaineer since youth; teacher; proprietor of Magic Mountain mountaineering-equipment store; technical adviser and sales mgr., climbing-boot manufacturer; writer since 1981. **Expeditions** Numerous climbs in Alps 1971–75, including east face of Grandes Jorasses 1974 and first British winter ascent (also first winter ascent by two-member team) of north face of Eiger, Switzerland 1975; first two-man ascent of southeast ridge of Dunagiri, Garhwal Himalayas, India-Tibet 1975; (with Peter Boardman) first ascent of west wall of Changabang, Garhwal Himalayas, India-Tibet 1976; west ridge of K2, Karakoram Range, Pakistan-China 1978 and 1980; first ascent of north ridge of Kanchenjunga, Himalayas, Nepal-India 1979; British winter expedition, Mt. Everest, Himalayas, Nepal-Tibet 1980–81; first ascent of Mt. Kongur, Pamirs, China 1981; east-northeast ridge, Everest 1982. **Author** *Everest the Cruel Way*, 1981; *Savage Arena* (autobiography), 1982.

MERLE A(NTONY) TUVE

Physicist

Born **Canton, South Dakota, USA, 27 June 1901**

Died **Bethesda, Maryland, USA, 20 May 1982**

During a career that spanned half a century, Merle A. Tuve measured the force that holds the atomic nucleus together, probed the earth's atmosphere and crust, and mapped the reaches of the galaxy. His investigation into the effects of the earth's ionosphere on pulsed radio waves led directly to the development of radar. During World War II, he was in charge of the secret effort to develop the promixity fuse.

Tuve's interest in science and technology developed early. He and his childhood friend Ernest Lawrence, the future Nobel laureate in physics, built a telegraph between their houses; when the Lawrence family moved away, the two stayed in touch by ham radio. In 1918 Tuve entered the University of Minnesota, where he studied electrical engineering. He made his first major contribution to science as a doctoral student in physics at Johns Hopkins University in the mid-1920s.

Current scientific theory held that the transmission of radio signals over long distances is made possible by a layer of charged particles in the atmosphere that, it was hypothesized, reflects radio waves. In collaboration with Gregory Breit, a physicist at the department of terrestrial magnetism at the Carnegie Institution in Washington, D.C., Tuve set about verifying the existence of this layer. They modified a radio transmitter at the Naval Research Laboratory in Washington so that it would emit high-frequency radio pulses, and monitored the transmissions from a receiver at the Carnegie Institution a few miles away. The radio waves traveling directly from transmitter to receiver were picked up almost instantly, but each of these bursts was followed at a short interval by a fainter pulse, which was indeed reflected from the upper atmosphere. By measuring the delay, Tuve and Breit calculated the height of the reflecting layer, now called the ionosphere. Their work, published in 1925, earned Tuve his Ph.D. the following year. In Britain, the radio pulse method gave rise to radar, one of the vital air defense weapons of World War II. Radio pulses, emitted by a global network of hundreds of automatic ionosondes, are used to this day to study the ionosphere.

In 1926 Tuve joined Breit at the Carnegie Institution, where they soon began work on a particle accelerator for use in studying the atomic nucleus. Their goal was to direct a high-energy beam of protons into a chamber filled with hydrogen gas and to record the collisions between the beam's protons and the protons forming the hydrogen nuclei. The result would be a direct measure of the forces active in the nucleus.

Progress was slow, largely because their source of high voltage, a Tesla coil, worked poorly. After Breit left Carnegie in 1929, Tuve continued to work with Lawrence Hafstad, Otto Dahl, and others, perfecting a multistage tube that focuses and accelerates the protons. The Tesla coil was eventually replaced by a Van de Graaf electrostatic generator, which Tuve developed into a stable high-voltage source.

Now in possession of a precision instrument, in 1936 Tuve and his colleagues were finally able to carry out the study of the proton-proton interaction. The results of their experiments, analyzed by Breit, showed that a previously undetected force operated at short ranges within the nucleus, overcoming the electrical repulsion between the positively charged protons and binding them together. This force, called the strong nuclear force, is the most powerful of the four fundamental interactions (the others are gravity, electromagnetism, and the weak nuclear force). Louis Brown, a nuclear physicist at Carnegie, called Tuve's experiment "the most fundamental measurement in nuclear physics."

During World War II Tuve turned to military research. In 1940 he became chairman of Section T, the committee of the wartime Office of Scientific Research and Development, charged with improving antiaircraft defense. The antiaircraft guns of the time used shells whose fuses could be set to detonate a given number of seconds after firing. Though an improvement over fuses that detonated only on contact, these time fuses were inefficient against rapidly moving targets. Tuve set out to develop a fuse that would detonate whenever it neared its target—a "proximity" or "variable-time" fuse.

Section T quickly outgrew its quarters at the department of terrestrial magnetism and was moved to nearby Johns Hopkins University, where it became the Applied Physics Laboratory. By 1942, its staff had succeeded in developing a proximity fuse based on Tuve's prewar radio research. The key component was a radio set housed within the shell; its radio transmissions were reflected by the target as the shell approached, and at a given distance the reflected radio wave tripped a switch in the fuse, detonating the shell. The design required a number of small vacuum tubes of rugged construction and a battery that used a liquid electrolyte in a glass ampule. The mass manufacture of ampules required the conversion of production lines previously used to make Christmas tree lights, causing a shortage that went unexplained at the time.

The proximity fuse was introduced to the Pacific theater early in 1943, during the campaign of the Solomon Islands. Navy action reports for that year revealed a tripling in the effectiveness of antiaircraft fire using the new fuse. The devastation this caused the Japanese air force accounted in large part for its adoption of suicidal *kamikaze* tactics in 1944. In Britain the fuse saw widespread use in countering the first German *Vergeltungswaffe* (revenge weapon), the V-1 rocket; antiaircraft guns using proximity fuse shells brought down half of all V-1s destroyed. The fuse proved deadly against infantry as well during the Battle of the Bulge. In December 1944 Gen. George Patton described the fuse as "a wonderful achievement." Tuve received the Presidential Medal for Merit, and was made Commander, Order of the British Empire, for his role in its development.

After the war Tuve returned to the Carnegie Institution's department of terrestrial magnetism as its director (1946–66), and embarked on a series of investigations of the earth's crust. Using war-surplus land mines and depth charges, he studied the shock waves created in the solid earth by explosions in order to determine structural properties at depths up to 200 kilometers below the surface. Tuve and geophysicist H. E. Tatel carried out these tests at sites across the United States, comparing continental margins, ancient shield regions, and recently formed high plateaus. In 1957 the two led an expedition to the Andes, where, in collaboration with South American scientists, they established a network of seismographic stations to monitor the area's frequent earthquakes.

Courtesy of Carnegie Institution

Astronomy also drew Tuve's attention. In the mid-1950s he noted that the work of optical astronomers was hindered by inefficient photographic emulsions that could not register faint stellar images. By 1964, a joint scientific and industrial team organized by Tuve had developed a photoelectric image-intensifying device that tripled the effectiveness of telescopes. Soon after the war, Tuve and Tatel converted a captured German radar dish into a radio telescope and conducted the first U.S. survey of the northern Milky Way, looking for radio emissions from interstellar hydrogen clouds. Tuve later helped organize a radioastronomy institute at La Plata, Argentina, where observations could be made of the southern Milky Way and the Magellanic Clouds. After his retirement from the Carnegie Institution in 1966, he conducted an all-sky survey of the velocities of radio hydrogen, publishing his results in book form in 1973. He died of a heart ailment at the age of 80.

P.D.

Parents Anthony G. T. and Ida Marie (Larsen) T. **Married** Winifred Gray Whitman, physician, 1927: Trygve Whitman, health care admin. (d. 1972); Lucy Winifred T. Comly, cell biologist. **Religion** Episcopalian. **Education** Augustana Acad., Canton, SD 1915–18; Univ. of Minnesota, B.S. 1922, A.M. 1923; Johns Hopkins Univ., Baltimore, Ph.D. in physics 1926. **Mil. service** Developed proximity fuse for Natl. Defense Cttee. and U.S. Navy, WWII; chmn., Sect. T, Office of Scientific Research and Development 1940–45. **Career** Teaching fellow, Univ. of Minnesota 1922–23; instr. in physics, Princeton Univ. 1923–24; instr. in physics 1924–26 and dir. of Applied Physics Lab. 1942–46, Johns Hopkins Univ.; staff member 1926–46, dir. 1946–66, and distinguished service member since 1966, dept. of terrestrial magnetism, Carnegie Instn., Wash. DC. • Advisor, Sloan-Kettering Inst., 1948–53; ed., *Journal of Geophysical Research* 1949–58; co-founder, World Data Center; co-founder, Instituto Argentino de Radioastronomia, La Plata. **Officer** V.P., Amer. Assn. for the Advancement of Science 1947; chmn. of advisory panel on radio astronomy, Natl. Science Foundn. since 1953; trustee, Johns Hopkins Univ. since 1955; home secty., Natl. Acad. of Sciences 1966–72; chmn., geophysics research bd.,

Natl. Research Council/Natl. Acad. of Sciences 1966–72. **Fellow** Amer. Physical Soc.; Amer. Assn. for the Advancement of Science; Inst. of Electrical and Electronic Engineers; Amer. Acad. of Arts and Sciences; Inst. of Radio Engineers. **Member** Cttee. on growth, Natl. Research Council 1945–50; U.S. Natl. Commn. for UNESCO 1946–50; U.S. exec. cttee., Natl. Cttee. of Intl. Geophysical Year 1954–59; desalination research study cttee., Natl. Research Council/Natl. Acad. of Sciences; advisory cttee. on intl. science, Natl. Science Foundn.; cttee. on Latin American affairs, Natl. Acad. of Sciences; presidential science advisory cttee., Intl. Science Panel; Amer. Geophysical Union; Amer. Philosophical Soc.; Washington Acad. of Sciences; Philosophical Soc. of Washington; Tau Beta Pi; Phi Beta Kappa; Sigma Xi; Gamma Alpha; Cosmos Club. **Honors** Presidential Medal for Merit 1946; Research Corp. Award 1947; CBE 1948; Scott Award 1948; Comstock Prize, Natl. Acad. of Sciences 1949; Potts Medal, Franklin Inst. 1950; achievement medal, Univ. of Minnesota 1950; Barnard Medal, Columbia Univ. 1955; medal, Condor de los Andes, Bolivia 1955; Bowie Medal, Amer. Geophysical Union; Cosmos Club Award 1963; hon. degrees from Case, Carleton, Kenyon, Williams, and Augustana colls. and from univs. of Alaska and Johns Hopkins. **Author** of book on velocities of interstellar hydrogen, 1973. **Contributor** of articles on physics, geophysics, biophysics, and electrical engineering to scientific and technical jrnls.

Further reading John S. Steinhart, ed., *The Earth Beneath the Continents: A Volume of Geophysical Studies in Honor of Merle A. Tuve*, 1966; Ralph Baldwin, *The Deadly Fuze: The Secret Weapon of World War II*, 1980.

NIGEL GOSLING
Dance and art critic
***Born* London, England, 29 January 1909**
***Died* London, England, 21 May 1982**

Nigel Gosling was an influential critic for the *Observer* for 27 years, during which he helped promote modern trends in ballet and art.

Gosling, whose family was from East Anglia, was educated at Eton and Cambridge, then spent a year in Berlin with the diplomatic service. During the 1930s he dabbled in the arts, writing experimental fiction, studying painting with Roy de Maistre, and taking ballet classes. He was a conscientious objector on grounds of pacifism during World War II, and did alternate service with the Red Cross. In 1948, at the invitation of Richard Buckle, editor of *Ballet* magazine, he began to write dance criticism in collaboration with his wife Maude Lloyd, formerly a leading dancer with the Ballet Rambert. Their pen name, Alexander Bland, was taken from a Beatrix Potter storybook. The combination of her technical expertise and his flair for writing made Alexander Bland a respected authority in the world of English ballet, particularly after 1955, when the pair became the resident dance critics at the *Observer*. In 1962 Gosling also began writing art criticism for the *Observer* under his own name.

Gosling/Bland's reviewing style was gently ruminative, as if he were a knowledgeable friend confiding his thoughts to the reader; it was not intended to break new ground in aesthetic theory but to encourage higher standards of achievement among dancers and artists and of understanding among audiences. As Gosling, he wrote monographs on Gustav Doré, the photographer Félix Nadar, and the *Belle Époque* of pre-World War I Paris. As Bland, he co-authored *The Dancer's World* (1963) and *A History of Ballet and Dance in the Western World* (1976). He and his wife were close friends of Rudolf Nureyev since the early 1960s, edited his autobiography (1962), and wrote the text for two books of photographs, *The Nureyev Image* (1976) and *Fonteyn and Nureyev* (1979).

Gosling stopped writing on art for the *Observer* in 1975, but continued to serve as dance critic and general culture writer until his death of cancer at the age of 73. J.P.

Married Maude Lloyd, ballet dancer, 1939: Nicholas. **Education** Eton Coll.; King's Coll., Cambridge; studied painting with Roy de Maistre; ballet classes at Rambert Sch., London mid-1930s. **Mil. service** Conscientious objector service with Red Cross, WWII. **Career** With Foreign Service, Berlin, then painter and writer of experimental fiction, 1930s; ballet critic for various periodicals, in collaboration with wife, under pseudonym Alexander Bland since 1948; features ed. and gen. arts writer since 1950, dance critic (as Alexander Bland) since 1955, and art critic 1962–75, *Observer,* London. **Author** As Alexander Bland: (ed.) Rudolf Nureyev, *Nureyev,* 1962; *The Dancer's World,* 1963; *The Nureyev Image,* 1976; *A History of Ballet and Dance in the Western World,* 1976; *Fonteyn and Nureyev,* 1979; *The Royal Ballet: The First 50 Years.* • As Nigel Gosling: *Gustav Doré,* 1974; *Nadar,* 1977; *The Adventurous World of Paris 1900–14,* 1978; *Leningrad.*

CEVDET SUNAY

President of Turkey
***Born* Trabzon, Ottoman Empire, 10 February 1900**
***Died* Istanbul, Turkey, 22 May 1982**

Cevdet Sunay served as president of Turkey from 1966 to 1973, a period of growing tension in the country's politics between left and right and between professional politicians and the highly politicized military elite. After supervising a system of "guided democracy" mandated by the military, he left office in 1973 as Turkey began yet another ill-fated experiment with civilian rule.

Sunay was born in the ancient port city of Trabzon on the Black Sea, the son of Sabri Bey, a regimental mufti, or chaplain, in the Imperial Ottoman Army. He attended Istanbul Military High School, graduating as a second lieutenant at the age of 17. Sent immediately to the Palestine front, he was captured in 1918 by the British and was interned in the prison camp of Hejaz, near Cairo, where his father was also a prisoner.

On his return to Turkey he joined the nationalist forces led by Mustafa Kemal Atatürk and saw action against the French in the south and especially against the Greeks when they were defeated at the Sakarya River. He remained in the Army after the proclamation of the republic in 1923 and for the next 35 years rose steadily through the ranks, becoming a full general in 1959.

Sunay was not involved in the Army's coup d'état of May 1960 that deposed the government of Adnan Menderes. He was immediately made commander of all land forces and three months later chief of staff, both offices formerly held by the new president, Gen. Cemal Gürsel. The military government had his total support, even when it executed Menderes, the former prime minister, after a show trial. He remained close to Gürsel throughout his presidency, and grew friendly with Ismet Inönü, a veteran politician who took over as prime minister under army guidance in late 1961. In 1966, because of Gürsel's steadily deteriorating health, Sunay acceded to the requests of senior military leaders that he resign his commission and accept appointment as a senator, a preparatory step to succeeding to the presidency. Two weeks later he was elected to a seven-year term as Turkey's fifth president by both houses of parliament.

The prime minister since 1965 had been Suleyman Demirel, whose conservative Justice Party counted as adherents many former members of Menderes's discredited Democratic Party and was therefore distrusted by the military. Sunay managed to achieve a precarious modus vivendi with Demirel, always insisting on full Army participation in important government decisions. As politically based violence continued unabated throughout the country, however, Demirel made the mistake of blaming it on his leftist opposition in the Grand National Assembly. This was too much for the Army, and with Sunay's acquiescence they dismissed Demirel's government in March 1971. For the remainder of his term, although violence abated but little, Sunay had the advantage of working with a cooperative, nonpartisan government from which politicians, with their "bad habits and obstructionism," in the president's phrase, were excluded. He declined to seek a second term and handed over the presidency to Adm. Fahri Korutürk in October 1973, after which he spent a quiet retirement. He died after a long illness. A.K.

Parents Sabri Bey, regimental mufti (Muslim army chaplain), and Hatice Muhammedoglu. **Married** Atifet Bakirdağ 1929: Attila, physician; Argun, naval officer; Aysel Onel. **Religion** Muslim. **Education** Kuleli Military High Sch., Istanbul, grad. 1917; War Coll., Istanbul ca. 1923–27; Military Staff Acad., Istanbul 1927–30. **Career** With Turkish Army: 2nd lt., then 1st lt., Palestine front (wounded twice) 1917; POW, Hejaz 1918; fought in Turkish War of Independence under Mustafa Kemal Atatürk ca. 1919–1923; staff capt. 1930; comdr., 3rd Battery, 4th Artillery Div., Edremit 1930–34; maj., Operations Sect., 4th Corps 1934 and 1939–ca. 42; chief of staff, 1st Cavalry Div., Karaköse ca. 1935–38; comdr., 3rd Battalion, 5th Artillery Regiment 1938–39; lt. col. 1940; asst. instr. of tactics 1942 and instr. of tactics 1943, Military Staff Acad.; comdr., 72nd Artillery Regiment 1943–ca. 47; col. 1943; comdr., armored artillery regiment 1947; comdr., 1st Armored Brigade 1948; brig. gen. 1949; dir. of operations 1950 and 1957, deputy chief 1958–60, and chief of staff 1960–66, Gen. Staff Office; maj. gen. 1952; comdr., 33rd Div. 1952; comdr., 9th Div., Erzurum 1955; lt. gen. 1955; gen. of Army 1959; chief of land forces 1960. • Sen. 1966 and since 1973; pres. of Turkey 1966–73. **Honors** Decorations for valor, Germany and Turkey, WWI; citation for bravery 1922; Medal of Independence ca. 1923; KCB 1967; comdr., Legion of Merit, U.S.; other medals and decorations; hon. degrees from univs. of New York, Michigan, and Peshawar. **Author** of books on military strategy and tactics.

Further reading Metiu Tamkoc, *The Warrior Diplomats,* 1976.

SIR THOMAS DALLING
Veterinarian
Born **Liberton, near Edinburgh, Scotland, 23 April 1892**
Died **23 May 1982**

Sir Thomas Dalling's career spanned half a century and involved him in practically every aspect of veterinary medicine: general practice, research, teaching, administration, and international consulting work. He made important breakthroughs in the field of animal immunology, contributed to the control of foot and mouth disease in Europe, and fostered the development of veterinary education programs in many nations of the third world.

The son of a blacksmith, Dalling was born near Edinburgh and entered the Royal (Dick) Veterinary College in 1910, qualifying in 1914. During World War I he saw service with the Army Veterinary Corps in France, where he studied equine diseases. In 1919 he joined the staff of the Glasgow Veterinary College and served as the chief investigator at the Animal Diseases Research Association in Moredun, specializing in the study of clostridial bacteria, which cause dysentery in lambs. He became veterinary superintendent at the Wellcome Physiological Research Laboratories at Beckenham, Kent, in 1923. His innovative approach to developing vaccines against clostridial diseases was based on the transfer of passive immunity to the offspring through antibodies in the mother's milk. He also perfected the first vaccine against canine distemper, a widespread and often fatal viral disease.

Beginning in 1937, Dalling taught animal pathology at Cambridge University. In 1942 he was chosen to direct the Ministry of Agriculture's veterinary research laboratory in Weybridge, and in 1948 was promoted to chief veterinary officer. At the ministry, he worked on the problem of animal infertility, promoted artificial breeding in cattle, developed diagnostic tuberculins, encouraged the campaign to eradicate bovine tuberculosis, and advised many European countries on the control of animal diseases. He was knighted in 1951. In 1952 he became chief veterinary officer for the United Nations Food and Agriculture Organization. He traveled throughout the world for the FAO for 15 years, guiding the establishment of adequate veterinary education programs in tropical countries, and assisted the European Economic Community's effort to control foot and mouth disease in livestock.

Dalling was a member of the Royal Society of Medicine and the Royal Society of Edinburgh and presided over the Royal College of Veterinary Surgeons for three years. He died at the age of 90. P.D.

Father a blacksmith. **Education** George Heriot's Sch., Edinburgh; Royal (Dick) Veterinary Coll., Edinburgh; qualified MRCVS 1914; Cambridge Univ., M.A. ca. 1937. **Mil. service** Maj., Royal Army Veterinary Corps, France 1916–18. **Career** Gen. practitioner ca. 1914–16, 1919; staff member and researcher in biology, Glasgow Veterinary Coll. ca. 1919–23; chief investigator, Animal Diseases Research Assn., Moredun, Scotland early 1920s; veterinary supt., Wellcome Physiological Research Labs., Beckenham, Kent 1923–37; prof. of animal pathology, Cambridge Univ. 1937; dir. 1942–48 and chief veterinary officer 1948–52, Central Veterinary Lab., Ministry of Agriculture and Fisheries; veterinary consultant, U.N. Food and Agriculture Org. 1952–67. **Officer** Council member 1938–57, pres. 1948–51, and v.p. 1951–53, Royal Coll. of Veterinary Surgeons. **Fellow** FRSM; FRSE. **Member** Agriculture Research Council. **Honors** Fitzwygram and Williams Memorial Prizes 1914; Dalrymple-Champneys Cup and Medal 1935; Steele Memorial Gold Medal 1950; Baxter Prize 1951; kt. 1951; hon. fellow since 1951 and hon. assoc., Royal Coll. of Veterinary Surgeons; hon. degrees from univs. of Belfast, Glasgow, Bristol, and Edinburgh. **Contributor** of articles on veterinary medicine to professional jrnls.

HARRY (CAESAR) SOLOMON
Neuropsychiatrist
***Born* Hastings, Nebraska, USA, 25 October 1889**
***Died* Boston, Massachusetts, USA, 23 May 1982**

When Harry Solomon entered psychiatry, before World War I, the mentally ill were generally shut away in large, understaffed, and underequipped institutions with little hope of cure or rehabilitation. As a Harvard professor and president of the American Psychiatric Association, and as a pioneering director of the Massachusetts Mental Health Center, Solomon led the fight for more humane and effective treatment of mental patients.

Solomon, the son of a doctor (both parents had emigrated from Germany), grew up in Los Angeles and received his B.S. degree from the University of California at Berkeley in 1910. In 1914 he graduated from Harvard

Medical School, where he had specialized in the study of nervous and mental diseases, and joined the recently founded Psychopathic Hospital as an intern. He was greatly influenced by the neuropathologist Elmer E. Southard, who had been active in developing the hospital, and collaborated with him on the textbook *Neuro-Syphilis* (1917). Five years later, he and his wife Maida, a professor of social economics at Simmons College and a psychiatric social worker, published a book on the congenital form of the disease, *Syphilis of the Innocent.* From 1915 he was also on the faculty of the Harvard Medical School.

During World War I, Solomon served as a neuropsychiatrist with the Medical Corps in France. After his return to civilian life in 1919 he became increasingly concerned by the sorry state of mental-health care. Many large institutions were run like prisons: patients were deprived of their possessions, isolated, often drugged or tied down even if they showed no signs of violence. His opportunity to make drastic changes finally came in 1943 when he was appointed superintendent of the Massachusetts Mental Health Center, as the Boston Psychopathic Hospital was now called. Patients at MMHC were encouraged to regain a sense of identity, to work at a trade in preparation for their return to everyday life, to form self-help groups, and to regard the center as their home, always available should they need help. Solomon also introduced psychoanalysis in the treatment of severe mental disorders such as schizophrenia. The discharge rate rose from 35 percent to 90 percent during his 15-year administration.

At Harvard, where he became a full professor in 1940, Solomon urged that all medical students receive instruction in psychiatry. As chairman of the department of psychiatry from 1943 to 1956, he saw psychiatric training increase from 56 hours of classes to several hundred, almost equaling surgery in importance. He also worked to improve the medical school's facilities for instruction in forensic and child psychiatry.

In a presidential address to the American Psychiatric Association in 1958, Solomon deplored the incarceration of the mentally ill in enormous state-run hospitals—the notorious "snake pits" of novels and films—and called for smaller, better equipped institutions and the setting up of "halfway houses" to facilitate patient rehabilitation, all radical ideas at the time. Though his plan faced considerable opposition from state authorities across the nation, in his new post as commissioner of

Courtesy of Harvard Medical School

mental health for Massachusetts (1959–68) he pushed forward with plans for the construction of the kind of units he believed ideal. Versions of his program have since been adopted by most state mental health commissions.

Solomon served as president of the American Psychiatric Association, the American Neurological Association, and the Greater Boston Medical Society, and was a medical advisor to the National Research Council, the Veterans Administration, and the U.S. Public Health Service. He died at the age of 92.

B.D.

Parents Jacob S., physician, and Lena (Fist) S. **Married** Maida Herman, social worker and prof. of social economics, 1916: Peter Herman; Joseph Herman; H. Eric; Babette S. Rader. **Religion** Jewish. **Education** Los Angeles High Sch., grad. 1906; Univ. of California, B.S. 1910; Danvers State Hosp., MA; Harvard Univ., M.D. 1914; intern, Boston Psychopathic Hosp. 1914–15. **Mil. service** First lt., U.S. Medical Corps, France 1918–19; chief neuropsychiatric examiner, Boston Induction Center 1942–45; special consultant to Secty. of War 1944; with U.S. Office of Research and Development, WWII. **Career** With Harvard Medical Sch.: instr. in psychiatry and neuropathology 1915–25; asst. prof. of psychiatry 1925–36; assoc. prof. 1936–40; clinical prof. 1940–43; prof. and dept. chmn. 1943–56; emeritus prof. since 1956; chmn., dean's subcttee. on neuropsychiatry for the Veterans Admin., Boston district. • With Boston Psychopathic Hosp. (later Massachusetts Mental Health Center), Boston: asst. physician 1915–16; chief of staff 1916–17; chief of therapeutics 1917–43; supt. 1943–59. • Investigator 1915–58, interim commnr. 1959–62, and commnr. 1962–68, Massachusetts Dept. of Mental Health; neurologist and psychiatrist, Beth Israel Hosp., Boston since 1916; asst. neurologist, Massachusetts Gen. Hosp. since 1923; special instr. in clinical psychiatry, Simmons Coll. Sch. of Social Work; consultant to Veterans Admin., U.S. Public Health Service, other orgs. and instns. **Officer** With Amer. Psychiatric Assn.: member since early 1920s; chmn., program cttee. 1922–28; council member 1938; chmn., arrangements cttee.; pres. 1957–58. • Pres.: Boston Soc. of Neurology and Psychiatry 1928–29; New England Soc. of Psychiatry 1938–39; Amer. Neurological Assn. 1941; Assn. of Biological Psychiatry 1950; Assn. for Research in Nervous and Mental Diseases 1957; Amer. Psychopathic Assn. 1959; Greater Boston Medical Soc.; Massachusetts Psychiatric Soc. **Fellow** AMA. **Member** Subcttee. on neurology and personnel training, Natl. Research Council 1940; Alpha Omega Alpha since 1954; advisory cttee., Massachusetts Dept. of Public Welfare; advisory cttee., Massachusetts Bd. of Corrections; New England Soc. of Psychiatry; Amer. Acad. of Arts and Sciences; Sigma Xi; Phi Delta Epsilon; medical council, Veterans Admin.; bd. of consultants of Massachusetts Gen. Hosp., Massachusetts Charitable Eye and Ear Infirmary, Faulkner Hosp., other hosps. **Honors** Selective Service Medal, WWII; mental health center named for him, Lowell, MA; other awards. **Author** (Jtly.) *Neuro-syphilis,* 1917; (with Maida Solomon) *Syphilis of the Innocent,* 1922; (co-ed.) *Manual of Military Neuro-Psychiatry,* 1945; (jtly.) *Neuro-Syphilis,* 1946; (co-ed.) *Studies in Lobotomy,* 1950; (jtly.) *Frontal Lobes and Schizophrenia,* 1953. **Contributor** of articles to medical jrnls.

Further reading Entire issue, *Psychiatric Health,* Sept.–Oct. 1977.

NIKOLAI A(LEKSANDROVICH) MIKHAILOV
Soviet government official
Born **Moscow, Russia, 27 September 1906**
Died **USSR, 25 May 1982**

Nikolai Mikhailov was a former steelworker and journalist who rose to occupy several positions of power in the Soviet state. He was for many years the leader of the Komsomol, the CPSU's youth organization, later served as minister of culture during a period of important cultural exchanges, and was finally, as chairman of the State Committee for Publishing, the country's chief censor.

The son of a craftsman in Moscow, he began training as a metallurgist at the age of 18 in the Hammer and Sickle steel mill, and received an education while continuing to work. He joined the Communist Party in 1930 and from 1931 worked as a journalist, representing the party on the editorial board of his own plant's newspaper, then on the paper of the Dynamo electrical plant. In 1937 he became an editor of *Pravda,* the party's national newspaper, and at the same time executive editor of *Komsomolskaya Pravda,* the national paper of the Soviet youth organization. The next year he was named first secretary of the Komsomol's central committee and was elected deputy to the Supreme Soviet. In 1939, at the 18th Congress of the CPSU, he was elected to the Central Committee.

The Komsomol, while no backwater, was a fairly safe haven in a turbulent time for an ambitious young apparatchik, and Mikhailov did a good, quiet job there, taking credit in a speech before the 19th Congress of the CPSU in 1952 for the 100 percent increase in Komsomol membership—to 16 million, of whom 4 million eventually went on to full party membership. He was nevertheless promoted out of his job when he was elected to the Presidium and also to a secretaryship on the Central Committee. He was chosen to give the main speech—a fierce attack on U.S. imperialism—at the Lenin's Birthday celebrations in January 1953, one of Stalin's last public appearances.

In the rapid changes immediately following Stalin's death in March 1953, Mikhailov was dropped from the Presidium and as secretary of the Central Committee and was named to the job of first secretary of the Moscow regional party committee, whose previous occupant had been Nikita Khrushchev, the new national first secretary. In December 1953 he was one of a special three-judge court which conducted the treason trial of Lavrenti Beria, Stalin's secret-police chief, and his associates, of whom most, including Beria, were found guilty and executed. Three months later Mikhailov was posted as ambassador to Poland.

Generally regarded as a protégé of Khrushchev and Premier Nikolai Bulganin rather than of Georgi Malenkov, Stalin's immediate successor, Mikhailov was recalled from Warsaw in March 1955 to be minister of culture, replacing Malenkov's man, Georgi Aleksandrov, whom Stalin had purged from his job as head of Agitprop in 1947 for exhibiting Westernist tendencies. Observers feared that the Ministry of Culture, which had been formed from several different agencies only after Stalin's death, was being jerked back into Stalinist rigidity, but Mikhailov was to preside over the beginnings of the only cultural thaw the Soviet Union has experienced since the Stalinist terror began in the 1920s. He inaugurated a cultural-exchange program with the United States in September 1955, and expanded similar programs with most other Western countries. Considerable incentive was given to creative artists in the fields of cinema, music, drama, and the museum arts. The main rationale for the relaxation was offered in Khrushchev's famous de-Stalinization speech to the 20th Congress of the CPSU in February 1956, in which he called for more freedom for Soviet artists. Mikhailov finally, however, was apparently found not to be a bureaucratic innovator but only a follower of orders, and he was replaced in 1960 by Yekaterina Furtseva, during whose ministry Soviet artists undertook the most daring and interesting of the modernization experiments.

Mikhailov served as ambassador to Indonesia from 1960 to 1965. After the fall of Khrushchev, at the beginning of a new cultural freeze, he was recalled to Moscow to be chairman of the publishing committee of the Soviet Union's Council of Ministers. In a position very much subordinate to the intellectual overlordship of Mikhail Suslov, the party's chief ideologist, Mikhailov was responsible for the ideological purity of everything printed or shown in the USSR. He retired after 1970 on a special pension. Among his awards were three Orders of Lenin and the Order of the Patriotic War, First Class. A.K.

Father a handicraftsman. **Education** Plant sch., Hammer and Sickle steel plant, Moscow ca. 1924–32. **Career** Worker 1924–ca. 31 and ed. of plant newspaper 1931, Hammer and Sickle steel plant; ed., plant newspaper, Dynamo electrical plant, Moscow mid-1930s. • With CPSU: member since 1930; member 1939–66, secty. 1952–53, and member of Presidium 1952–53, Central Cttee.; first secty., Moscow cttee. 1953. • Dir., party sector press, Proletarskii ward, Moscow 1931; journalist and editorial staff member, *Pravda* 1937; exec. ed., *Komsomolskaya Pravda* 1937–38, and first secty. of Central Cttee. 1938–52, Komsomol (All-Union Communist Youth League); delegate to 18th–21st and 23rd party congresses. • Deputy, USSR Supreme Soviet 1938; organizer and vice chmn., World Fedn. of Democratic Youth 1945; ambassador to Poland 1954–55; minister of culture 1955–60; delegate and exec. cttee. member, Interparliamentary Union, Helsinki 1955; ambassador to Indonesia 1960–65; chmn., State

Cttee. for Publishing, Council of Ministers 1965–70; deputy, Moscow City Soviet; deputy to 2nd–5th and 7th convocations of USSR Supreme Soviet. **Honors** Order of Lenin, three times; Order of the Great Patriotic War, 1st Class; other medals and honors.

Further reading Ralph Talcott Fisher, Jr., *Pattern for Soviet Youth; A Study of the Congresses of the Komsomol, 1918–1954,* 1959.

ROMY SCHNEIDER
Actress
Born **Vienna, Austria, 23 September 1938**
Died **Paris, France, 29 May 1982**

Romy Schneider was considered by many to be one of the greatest European film stars of her generation, a highly intelligent actress whose performances in more than 60 films were rarely less than interesting and often quite compelling. She worked for many of the best and most innovative directors, and a remarkably high proportion of the films of her maturity are of lasting artistic merit.

She was born to a famous theatrical couple: her father was the Austrian stage actor Wolf Albach-Retty, and her mother, Magda Schneider, was the German star of scores of lavish musical films of the 1930s. She spent much of World War II near Berchtesgaden in the Bavarian Alps, and afterward was sent to a convent school near Salzburg. At the age of 14 she left school, never to return, in order to work in her first film, *Wenn der weisse Flieder wieder blüht* (1953; *White Lilies),* starring her mother, who had come out of retirement for the occasion. Other historical romances followed, notably the three "Sissi" films she made for Ernst Marischka, sentimental costume dramas in which she played the young Empress Elizabeth of Austria. They were extremely popular in Europe, and are, even today, often seen there on television, but they seemed to imprison her in the type of a rather saccharine ingenue, a type she did not dispel by her success in remakes of German prewar hits, of which the best known was *Mädchen in Uniform* (1958). Near the end of her life, she recalled her childhood career: "To start in this business very young is all very well. But some day or other you have to pay the price for it, and it can be very heavy."

In 1958, while making *Christine* for Pierre Gaspard-Huit, she met and began a five-year love affair with the French actor Alain Delon. He introduced her around Paris, where she met the Italian director Luchino Visconti. Her first great success in France came in 1961, when Visconti directed her and Delon in a Paris stage version of John Ford's Jacobean drama, *'Tis Pity She's a Whore.* The following year she starred for Visconti in his segment of the multidirector film, *Boccaccio '70,* as a young wife who allows her husband to pay her for sex in order to save her marriage. The role was one of the best in the film, and it brought her international fame.

Her repertory began to expand over the next several years along with her exposure to diverse directorial methods. She played the part of the bizarre, fantasy-ridden nurse Leni in Orson Welles's version of Kafka's *The Trial* (1962), and the next year appeared in two

Courtesy of German Information Center

Hollywood films, as a violinist forced into prostitution in Carl Foreman's *The Victors* and as an Austrian woman in love with a priest in Otto Preminger's *The Cardinal.* She next established her eminence in the genre of light comedy, appearing opposite Jack Lemmon in David Swift's *Good Neighbor Sam* (1964) and as the language-teacher heroine amid an international cast in Clive Donner's *What's New, Pussycat?* (1965), which starred Peter Sellers.

From the mid-1960s, Schneider's career was primarily devoted to films by French directors. She worked extensively for Claude Sautet, making *Les choses de la vie* (1970; *The Things of Life*); *Max et les ferrailleurs* (1971); *César et Rosalie* (1972), a warm comedy with Yves Montand; *Mado* (1976); and *Une histoire simple* (1978; *A Simple Story*), for which she won a César, the French equivalent of an Oscar. She won another in 1976 for *L'important c'est d'aimer* (1975; *The Important Thing Is Love),* by the Franco-Polish director Andrzej Zulawski. Her other notable roles were as the assassin's girlfriend in Joseph Losey's *The Assassination of Trotsky* (1972), and a more mature Elizabeth of Austria in Visconti's *Ludwig* (1973). She also played in Robert Enrico's *Le vieux fusil* (1975; *The Old Gun*), Costa-Gavras's *Claire de femme* (1979), and Bertrand Tavernier's *La mort en direct* (1979; *Deathwatch*). Her last film was Jacques Rouffio's *La passante du Sans-Souci* (1982).

In 1966, Schneider married the German actor-director Harry Meyen-Haubenstock, once an inmate in a Nazi concentration camp, who used the stage name Harry Meyen. He committed suicide in 1979, several years after their divorce. A second marriage to Daniel Biasini, a photographer, was of short duration.

Her death occurred in a friend's apartment in Paris, just ten months after the accidental death of her 14-year-old son, David Haubenstock, who was impaled on a fence he was climbing at his father's parents' house. Schneider was at the time just recovering from a serious kidney operation, and the ferocious intrusions of the press, along with the horrifying nature of her son's death when she was absent from him, kept her gravely depressed for some time thereafter. On the day of her death, initial police reports suggested a suicide, but the public prosecutor later announced that she had suffered a cardiac arrest. She was buried in the little village of Boissy-sans-Avoir, west of Paris, where she had just the month before purchased a farm and cemetery plot. Magda Schneider, her mother, took custody of her five-year-old daughter. A.K.

Born Rosemarie Magdalena Albach-Retty. **Parents** Wolf Albach-Retty, actor, and Magda Schneider, singer and actress. **Married** (1) Harry Meyen-Haubenstock, actor and dir., 1966 (div. 1975): David Christophe 1967 (d. 1981). (2) Daniel Biasini, photographer, 1975 (separated): Sarah Magdalena 1977. **Emigrated** Lived in France since 1960s. **Education** Convent sch., Salzburg, left at age 14. **Career** Film actress since childhood; occasional stage and TV roles. **Honors** Prize, for *The Trial,* French Film Acad. 1962; César, 1976, for *L'important c'est d'aimer*, and 1979, for *Une histoire simple*; best actress, Taormina Film Festival, for *L'important c'est d'aimer*, 1976; Federal Film Prize and Gold Filmband, for *Gruppenbild mit Dame*, West Germany 1977; David di Donatello Prize, Italy 1979. **Films** *Wenn der weisse Flieder wieder blüht* (rel. as *White Lilies*), 1953; *Feuerwerk*, 1954; *Mädchenjahre einer Königin* (rel. as *The Story of Vickie*), 1954; *Der letzte Mann*, 1955; *Die Deutschmeister* [*Mam'zelle Cricri*], 1956; *Sissi*, 1956; *Kitty und die grosse Welt*, 1956; *Sissi—die junge Kaiserin*, 1957; *Robinson soll nicht sterben* (rel. as *The Girl and the Legend*), 1957; *Monpti*, 1957; *Sissi, Schicksaljahre einer Kaiserin*, 1958; *Scampolo*, 1958; *Mädchen in Uniform*, 1958; *Die schöne Lügnerin*, 1959; *Die Halbzarte*, 1959; *Christine*, 1959; *Ein Engel auf Erden* (rel. as *Angel on Earth*), 1959; *Katia* (rel. as *Magnificent Sinner*), 1960; *Le combat dans l'île*, 1961; *Forever My Love* (combination of three Sissi films), 1962; *Boccaccio '70*, 1962; *The Trial*, 1962; *The Victors*, 1962; *The Cardinal*, 1963; *Good Neighbor Sam*, 1964; *What's New, Pussycat*?, 1965; *10:30 P.M. Summer*, 1966; *Triple Cross*, 1966; *La Voleuse* (rel. as *Schornstein No. 4*), 1966; *Otley*, 1968; *La piscine* (rel. as *The Swimming Pool*), 1969; *My Lover, My Son*, 1969; *Qui*? (rel. as *The Sensuous Assassin*), 1970; *Les choses de la vie* (rel. as *The Things of Life*), 1970; *La califfa*, 1970; *Bloomfield* (rel. as *The Hero*), 1971; *Max et les ferrailleurs*, 1971; *César et Rosalie*, 1972; *The Assassination of Trotsky*, 1972; *Ludwig ou le crépuscule des dieux (rel. as Ludwig, or Twilight of the Gods*), 1973; *Le train*, 1973; *Le trio infernal*,

1974; *Un amour de pluie* (rel. as *Loving in the Rain*), 1974; *Le mouton enragé* (rel. as *Love at the Top*), 1974; *L'important c'est d'aimer* (rel. as *The Important Thing Is Love*), 1975; *Les innocents aux mains sales* (rel. as *Dirty Hands*), 1975; *Le vieux fusil* (rel. as *The Old Gun*), 1975; *Une femme à sa fenêtre* (rel. as *A Woman at Her Window*), 1976; *Mado*, 1976; *Gruppenbild mit Dame* (rel. as *Group Picture with Lady*), 1977; *Une histoire simple*, (rel. as *A Simple Story*), 1978; *Last Embrace*, 1979; *Bloodline*, 1979; *Clair de femme*, 1979; *Lo sconosciuto*, 1979; *La mort en direct* (rel. as *Deathwatch*), 1979; *Garde à vue*, 1982; *La passante du Sans-Souci*, 1982; others. **Stage** *'Tis Pity She's a Whore*, Paris 1961; others.

ALBERT NORDEN

Journalist and chief East German propagandist
Born **Myslowitz, Upper Silesia, Austria-Hungary, 4 December 1904**
Died **East Berlin, East Germany, 30 May 1982**

By the time of his death at the age of 77, Albert Norden was the oldest member of East Germany's Politburo. Reportedly an extreme hard-liner, he was for many years in charge of propaganda and was responsible, along with the rest of the Communist leadership, for making East Germany one of the most rigidly controlled states of the Soviet bloc.

Norden was born in Silesia, the son of a rabbi, and attended school in Elberfeld. At 13 he joined the Free Socialist Youth and at 15, in 1920, joined both the Communist Youth Union and the German Communist Party (Kommunistische Partei Deutschlands; KPD). He served an apprenticeship to a carpenter but left the craft in 1924 to train as a journalist on *Freiheit,* a Communist newspaper in Düsseldorf. During the following years of the Weimar Republic, when he was often arrested for illegal political activity, he worked as an editor for all the principal German Communist dailies: the *Halle/Saale Klassenkampf* (1924), the *Hamburger Volkszeitung* (1925), the *Essen Ruhr-Echo* (1930), as well as the KPD newspaper *Rote Fahne* (1929; 1930–33).

As a Communist, a Jew, and a writer, Norden was in increasing danger of assassination as the Nazis grew stronger, and in 1933 he left Germany. His exile was long; he lived in Czechoslovakia, Denmark, and France, where he was arrested and interned in 1939 after the war with Germany began. He secured his release and left for the United States, where beginning in 1941 he worked for the formation of the Council for a Democratic Germany and edited the anti-Nazi bulletin *Germany Today*. After the war he learned that his father had been killed in the Nazi extermination camp at Theresienstadt in Bohemia.

Norden returned to Berlin in 1946 and immediately began to help build Communism in occupied Germany. In 1948–49 he was chief editor of *Deutschlands Stimme,* then from 1949 to 1952 served the new East German state as director of the press section in the Information Office. He held several positions where his considerable public-speaking ability was called into play, including secretary of the Committee for German Unity (1954) and as a spokesman for the National Front (from 1954). He was first named to the Central Committee of the SED (Sozialistische Einheitspartei Deutschlands, the East German party) in 1955 and from 1958 was a full member of the Politburo, the country's pinnacle of power.

In addition to his official task of supervising East Germany's propaganda effort, Norden was a voluminous writer of books, pamphlets, and articles which seemed to grow more dogmatic and intemperate as his power increased. He was never much in favor of cooperation with West Germany, which he often referred to as "a monopoly capitalist NATO state" in contrast with "the German socialist nation" that was East Germany. He praised the Berlin Wall as an "anti-Fascist" construction, and was scathingly critical of West Germany's *Ostpolitik* of friendly relations with Soviet bloc countries.

That he was able to retain power for so long is perhaps a testimony to the popularity, at

Courtesy of German Information Center

least among the elite, of his undeviatingly hard-line political attitudes. He was reportedly not supportive of either First Secretary Walter Ulbricht or his successor, Erich Honecker. He managed to avoid being ousted even during the periods of especially severe anti-Semitism in 1952–53 and 1967–68. (Before the Warsaw Pact invasion of Czechoslovakia, *Neues Deutschland,* the SED daily, editorialized that "Zionism is in control in Prague.") He retired from most of his positions only in 1981.

Norden's best-known books were *On the Nation* (1952), *Between Berlin and Moscow* (1954), and *Forgers* (1959). In 1953 he was appointed to the largely honorary post of professor of modern history at the Humboldt University in Berlin. His decorations include most of those given by his country, especially its highest award, the Karl Marx Order, which he received twice, in 1969 and 1981. A.K.

Father a rabbi. **Married;** one child. **Religion** Of Jewish birth; later atheist. **Emigration** Left Germany 1933; deprived of German citizenship 1938; interned in France 1939–41; returned to Germany from U.S. 1946. **Education** Gymnasium, Elberfeld. **Career** Joined Free Socialist Youth 1918, Communist Youth Union 1920, German Communist Party (KPD) 1920; apprenticed to carpenter, Elberfeld 1921–23, and joined German Wood Workers Assn. 1921; trainee, *Freiheit* Communist newspaper, Düsseldorf 1924; deputy chief ed., *Klassenkampf* newspaper, Halle-Saale 1924; deputy chief ed., *Hamburger Volkszeitung* newspaper 1925; ed. 1929 and deputy chief ed. 1930–33, *Rote Fahne* KPD newspaper; chief ed., *Ruhr-Echo,* Essen 1930; arrested 1923, 1924, 1926; forced to leave Germany 1933. • Writer for KPD press, Czechoslovakia, Denmark, and France 1933–37; secty., action cttee., German anti-Nazi movement, France 1937–39; interned as enemy alien, France 1939–41; in U.S. 1941–46; ed., *Germany Today* anti-Nazi bulletin, U.S., WWII years, and co-founder, Council for a Democratic Germany 1946; returned to East Germany 1946. • Press chief, German Economic Commn. ca. 1947; chief ed., *Deutschlands Stimme* newspaper, Berlin 1948–49; deputy, People's Council, Provisional People's Chamber 1947–50; chief, press sect., East German Office of Information 1949–52; prof. of modern history, Humboldt Univ., Berlin since 1953; chief, Office of Standing Delegation for the Peaceful Resolution of the German Question 1953; secty. of state, Cttee. for German Unity 1954; spokesman 1954 and member of Presidium of Natl. Council since 1954, Natl. Front; member of Presidium, German Peace Council since 1958; member of Bureau since 1958 and v.p. 1977, World Peace Council; deputy 1958–81 and member of Cttee. for Foreign Affairs 1967–76, Volkskammer (People's Chamber). • With Central Cttee. of East German Communist Party (SED): member since 1955; secty. 1955–81; full member of Politburo 1958–81; secty. and chief of Agitation Commn., Politburo 1963–81. **Honors** Natl. Prize, 2nd Class, 1951; Order of Merit of the Fatherland, in Silver 1958 and in Gold 1964; Karl Marx Order 1969 and 1981; Hero of Labor; Medal of Merit, with Gold Star of Intl. Friendship and with Grand Star of Intl. Friendship; Medal for Participation in Armed Struggle of German Working Class; Medal for Struggle Against Fascism; Order of Intl. Friendship, USSR. **Author** (As Hans Behrend) *Die wahren Her-*

ren Deutschlands, 1939 (trans. as *The Real Rulers of Germany*, 1939); *The Thugs of Europe*, 1942; (jtly.) *The Lessons of Germany*, 1945; *Lehren deutscher Geschichte* [*Teaching German History*], 1947; *So werden Kriege gemacht!*, 1950 (trans. as *Thus Wars Are Made*, 1970); *Um die Nation* [*On the Nation*], 1952; *Zwischen Berlin und Moskau* [*Between Berlin and Moscow*], 1954; *Die spanische Tragödie*, 1956, rev. as *Das spanische Drama*, 1961; *Fälscher: Zur Geschichte der deutsche-sowjetischen Beziehungen [Forgers: On the History of German-Soviet Relations*], 1959; [*Selected Speeches and Essays*], 4 vols., 1964–74; *Die Nation und Wir* [*The Nation and Us*], 1965; *Herrscher ohne Krone* [*Monarchs Without Crowns*], 1973; *Fünf Jahrzehnte im Dienst seiner Klasse* [*Five Decades in the Service of His Class*], 1974; *In Aktion für das sozialistische Vaterland* [*In Action for the Socialist Fatherland*], 1969; *Vergiftete Waffe gegen Frieden und Sozialismus* [*Poisoned Weapons Against Peace and Socialism*], 1978; *Der Mensch im Mittelpunkt* [*The Man in the Center*], 1979.

KARA (ABULFAZ-OGLY) KARAYEV
Azerbaijani composer
Born **Baku, Azerbaijan, 5 February 1918**
Died **Baku, Azerbaijan, USSR, May 1982**

Kara Karayev was one of the foremost proponents and practitioners of Azerbaijani music, a skilled composer of ballets, symphonies, operas, and scores for stage and screen. Much of his best-received work is strongly propagandistic in nature, reflecting his training and belief in the tenets of Socialist Realism, the Soviet Union's official artistic doctrine.

He began his studies in piano at the conservatory in his native city of Baku (1930–35), then attended the Azerbaijan State Conservatory, where he first began to explore in depth the folk music of his people. In 1937 he led an expedition that studied Azerbaijani folklore, and transcribed many native songs and dances. He went to the Moscow Conservatory in 1938, studying composition first with Georgi Aleksandrov and then, from 1942 to 1946, with Dmitri Shostakovich. Shostakovich's influence was apparent in Karayev's prizewinning verse opera, *Fatherland* (1945), written jointly with his countryman Akhmet Jevdet Hajiyev, which won the State Prize in 1946. About the same time, his first symphony *(Great Patriotic War,* 1944) received its first performance. He was also awarded a medal for heroic work during World War II.

During the late 1940s and early 1950s, Karayev's music owed much to the inspiration of the twelfth-century Azerbaijani-Iranian poet Nizami Ganjevi, particularly the choral piece *Autumn,* the symphonic poem *Leili and Mejnun* (which won him another State Prize in 1948), and the symphonic suite *Seven Beauties,* which he reworked as a full-length ballet of the same name. Adapted from Nizami's epic poem *Khamse, Seven Beauties* blends several national dances with a symphonic development in the style of Prokofiev to tell the story of a cruel shah outwitted by the bravery and resourcefulness of his people.

The composer's commitment to social justice is even more evident in *Path of Thunder,* his second ballet, based on the antiapartheid novel of the South African writer Peter Abrahams. The tragic story of the love of a black man and a white woman, it is underlined by Karayev's adaptation of black southern African music in the highly symphonic score. It was first performed by the Kirov Ballet in 1957 and won the Lenin Prize in 1967. His other works based on non-Soviet sources were the symphonic poem *Don Quixote* (1960), with its Spanish overtones; *Tenderness* (1972), an operatic monodrama for a female voice which was based on a story by Henri Barbusse; the musical comedy *Cyrano de Bergerac* (1973), adapted from the play by Edmond Rostand; and the *Vietnam Suite* (1967).

In 1959, Karayev wrote the score for the highly praised production at the Pushkin Theater, Leningrad, of Vishnevsky's *An Optimistic Tragedy,* which was performed the same year in Paris at the Théâtre des Nations. His other incidental music accompanied some 20 plays and 20 films.

Karayev was long active in the musical life

of Azerbaijan. He served as artistic director of the Baku Philharmonic Orchestra (1941–42); was a teacher (1946–49), rector (1949–52), and professor (from 1959) at the Azerbaijan State Conservatory; and president (from 1953) and secretary (from 1956) of the Azerbaijani Composers Union. He was a member of the Communist Party from 1946, a delegate to the 22nd through the 25th Party Congresses, and a deputy to the 5th through 10th Supreme Soviets. In 1959 he was named National Artist of the USSR and to the Azerbaijani Academy of Sciences. He was also made a Hero of Socialist Labor and was awarded two Orders of Lenin, the Order of the October Revolution, and the Order of the Red Banner of Labor. The Soviet Union's minister of culture, P. N. Demichev, formed part of the honor guard at Karayev's memorial service in Moscow on 17 May. A.K.

Education Baku Musical Technical Sch. 1930–35; Azerbaijan State Conservatory 1935–38; Moscow Conservatory 1938–46. **Career** Composer and conductor since mid-1930s; led expedition to study Azerbaijani folklore and music 1937; artistic dir., Baku Philharmonic Orch., Azerbaijan 1941–42; instr. 1946–49, rector 1949–52, and prof. of composition since 1960, Azerbaijan State Conservatory; dir., musical sect., Inst. of Azerbaijani Art, Azerbaijan SSR Acad. of Sciences 1949–50. • Bd. member since 1948, chmn. since 1952, and 1st secty. since 1956, Union of Soviet Azerbaijani Composers; member, Union of Creative Cinematic Workers since 1957. • Member, CPSU since 1946; delegate to 22nd through 25th CPSU Party Congresses; member of Central Cttee., Azerbaijan C.P.; deputy, 5th through 10th USSR Supreme Soviets; deputy, Supreme Soviet of Azerbaijan SSR. **Member** Azerbaijan Acad. of Sciences since 1959. **Honors** Medal for heroism, WWII; medal for defense of Caucasus; State Prize 1946, for opera *Fatherland,* and 1948, for symphonic poem *Leili and Mejnun;* Natl. Artist of Soviet Union 1959; Lenin Prize, for ballet *In the Path of Thunder,* 1967; Stalin Prize twice; Order of Lenin twice; Hero of Socialist Labor; Order of Red Banner of Labor; Order of October Revolution. **Operas** *Aina*, 1941; (jtly.) *Veten* [*Fatherland*], 1945; *Nezhnost* [*Tenderness*], 1972; (jtly.) *Rodina* [*The Homeland*]. **Ballets** *Sem krasavits* [*Seven Beauties*], 1952; *Tropoyu groma* [*In the Path of Thunder*], 1957. **Musical comedy** *Cirano de Berzherak*, 1973. **Vocal orchestrations** *Pesnya serdtsa* [*Song of the Heart*], 1938; *Pesnya schastya* [*Song of Happiness*], 1947; *Partiya nasha* [*Our Party*], 1959; *Gimn druzhbe* [*Hymn to Friendship*], 1972. **Choral works** *Kolibelnaya* [*Lullaby*], 1939; *Osen* [*Autumn*], 1947; *Pesnya neftyanikov morya* [*Song of the Marine Oil Workers*], 1954. **Song collections** *6 rubayi* [*Six Songs from the Rubaiyat of Omar Khayyam*], 1946; *Na kholmakh Gruzii* [*On the Hills of Georgia*], 1949; *Ya vas lyubil* [*I Loved You*], 1949. **Orchestral works** *Azerbaijanskaya syuita* [*Azerbaijan Suite*], 1939; *Symphonies, No. 1* [*Great Patriotic War*], 1943, *No. 2,* 1946, and *No. 3*, 1965; *Leili i Mejnun*, 1947; *Sem krasavits* [*Seven Beauties*], 1949; *Albanskaya rapsodiya*, 1952; *Don Kikhot*, 1960; *Klassicheskaya syuita*, 1966; *Vetnamskaya Syuita* [*Vietnam Suite*], 1967; *Violin Concerto*, 1967. **Chamber music** *Quartettino*, 1942; *String Quartets, No. 1*, 1942, and *No. 2*, 1946; *Sonata*, 1960. **Piano works** *Sonatinas*, 1940 and 1943; *24 Preludes*, 1951. **Incidental music** [*An Optimistic Tragedy*], 1957; *Neistovy gaskonets* [*The Mad Gascon*]; 18 other stage works; 20 films. **Contributor** of articles and reviews on Azerbaijani music and composers to music jrnls.

JUNE

RONALD (FREDERICK HENRY) DUNCAN

Dramatist, poet, essayist, and journalist
Born **Salisbury, Rhodesia, 6 August 1914**
Died **Devon, England, 3 June 1982**

Ronald Duncan was a fierce individualist who produced a prodigious number of literary works during a long career, most of which were greeted by neither publicity nor popularity. He was an unorthodox Christian and a born controversialist, and his iconoclastic opinions—particularly about his contemporaries in the drama—were often widely reported.

He was born in Africa and spent much of his childhood in London. He claimed that his father (Reginald John Dunkelsbuhler, who changed his name to Duncan) was the illegitimate son of the crown prince of Bavaria. "I was born," he said later, "with a silver spoon in my mouth. I have learned not to regret this." Expelled from his public school, he was sent for a time to a school in Switzerland, then was admitted to read English under F. R. Leavis at Downing College, Cambridge. He was a socialist by the time he left university in 1936, the height of the Great Depression. He wrote and printed at his own expense a pacifist pamphlet and sent a copy to Mahatma Gandhi, who replied by inviting Duncan to stay with him in his ashram in India. He remained a staunch admirer of Gandhi all his life, and published *Selected Writings of Mahatma Gandhi* in 1951.

Duncan founded a literary magazine, *The Townsman,* in 1938 and edited it until 1946 "from a remote water mill in North Devon." A pacifist commune which he began during the war foundered: "lacking a religious discipline," he recalled, "there was chaos." He began to produce volumes of poems and verse plays regularly. Among the first of the latter, *This Way to the Tomb: A Masque and Anti-Masque,* with music by his friend Benjamin Britten, was given an important production during a revival of modern verse drama in 1945 at the Mercury Theatre, London. The masque concerns the temptations of St. Anthony, ending with his triumph over Pride and his assumption into heaven. The antimasque treats themes of temptation in a modern setting. The play strongly evokes T. S. Eliot's dramatic style, and to Duncan, "it did seem that we had the theatre of 'realism' on the run." The numerous exceptions taken to this and his other plays by the critics began his long-running feud with the critical establishment—"glib phoneys," he called them, "with a gift for writing slick phrases that are insulting without being libellous." Among his other dramas were *Nothing Up My Sleeve* (1950, republished as *St. Spiv* in 1971), about redemption in cockney London; *Don Juan* (1953) and *The Death of Satan* (1954), both given their premieres at the Devon Festival of the Arts, which Duncan founded; *The Catalyst* (1958), a morality play about a ménage à trois, which was at first banned by the Lord Chamberlain; *Abelard and Heloise* (1960), an epistolary drama; and *The Seven Deadly Virtues: A Contemporary Immorality Play* (1968). He wrote the libretti for Benjamin Britten's opera *The Rape of Lucretia* (1946) and for *Christopher Sly* (1960), an opera by Thomas Eastwood, and translated and adapted several plays by Continental dramatists, including Jean Cocteau's *The Eagle Has Two Heads* (1948) and *The Typewriter* (1948), Jean Giraudoux's *The Apollo de Bellac* (1957), and Jean-Paul Sartre's own adaptation of Euripedes' *The Trojan Women* (1967). His *Collected Plays* appeared in 1971.

In 1955, Duncan was among the founders of the English Stage Company, whose home is the Royal Court Theatre in Chelsea, London. A few of his plays were produced there, but he came to disagree completely with the principles of selection for the works the company produced. Realistic or naturalistic plays such as those by John Osborne—one of Duncan's many bêtes noires—were anathema to him, yet they comprised the great majority of the Royal Court's successful repertory. He severed all connections with the company in 1966.

Duncan counted among his friends many of Britain's most eminent figures, among them Britten (his last book was *A Memoir of Benjamin Britten,* 1981), Eliot (whose firm, Faber & Faber, were Duncan's publishers for many years), and even Queen Mary, who was said to admire greatly his plays' high moral standards. His enemies were perhaps more numerous, and he never forgave or forgot: in 1980 he wrote a notably vitriolic obituary in the *Spectator* on his old nemesis Kenneth Tynan.

The proprietor of a working farm in Welcombe, Devon, since the late 1930s, Duncan wrote "Jan's Journal," a weekly country-life column, for Lord Beaverbrook's *Evening Standard* from 1946 until 1956. These columns were published in several collections. His autobiography in three volumes, *All Men Are Islands* (1964), *How to Make Enemies* (1968), and *Obsessed* (1975), was characteristically outspoken and extremely hard on the opposition. A.K.

Parents Reginald John Dunkelsbuhler (changed name to Duncan) and Ethel (Cannon) Dunkelsbuhler. **Married** Rose Marie Theresa Hansom 1941: Briony; Roger Jeremy. **Religion** Christian. **Education** Public sch., London; private sch., Switzerland; Downing Coll., Cambridge, M.A. 1936. **Career** Poet, playwright, novelist, and essayist since mid-1930s; founder 1938 and ed. 1938–46, *The Townsman* mag., London; columnist, *Evening Standard,* London 1946–56; founder, Devon Festival of the Arts, Bideford 1953; co-founder 1955 and member 1955–65, English Stage Co., Royal Court Theatre, London. • Farmer, Bideford, Devon since 1939. **Member** Socialist Party since 1930s; Garrick Club. **Plays and libretti** *Birth,* 1937; *The Dull Ass's Hoof,* 1940; *This Way to the Tomb: A Masque and Anti-Masque,* 1945; *Amo Ergo Sum* (cantata), 1948; *Stratton,* 1949; *Nothing Up My Sleeve,* 1950, rev. as *St. 'Orace,* 1964, as *St. Spiv,* 1971; *St. Peter,* 1951; *Our Lady's Tumbler,* 1951; *Don Juan,* 1953; *The Death of Satan,* 1954; *The Catalyst,* 1958, rev. as *Ménage à Trois,* 1963; *Christopher Sly,* 1960; (also dir., London 1973) *Abelard and Heloise: A Correspondence for the Stage,* 1960; *The Rabbit Race,* 1963; *O-B-A-F-G: A Play in One Act in Stereophonic Sound,* 1964; *The Seven Deadly Virtues: A Contemporary Immorality Play,* 1968; *The Gift,* 1968; *Torquemada,* 1969; *The Rehearsal,* 1971; *Collected Plays,* 1971; *Sloshed,* 1974. **Translations and adaptations of plays and libretti** Jean Cocteau, *The Eagle Has Two Heads* and *The Typewriter,* 1948; André Obey, *The Rape of Lucretia,* 1948; C. A. Puget and Pierre Bost, *A Man Named Judas,* 1956; (jtly.) Harold Brett, *The Cardinal,* 1957; Jean Giraudoux, *The Apollo de Bellac,* 1958; Martin Walser, *The Rabbit Race,* 1963; Euripides/Sartre, *The Trojan Women,* 1967. **Television plays** *The Portrait,* 1954; *The Janitor,* 1955; *Preface to America,* 1959; *Not All the Dead Are Buried,* 1960; *The Rebel,* 1969; *Still Life,* 1970; *Mandala,* 1972. **Screenplay** *Girl on a Motorcycle,* 1968. **Novels** *The Last Adam,* 1952; *St. Spiv,* 1961. **Short-story collections** *The Perfect Mistress and Other Stories,* 1969; *A Kettle of Fish,* 1971; *The Tale of Tails,* 1975; *The Uninvited Guest,* 1981. **Poetry** *Postcards to Pulcinella,* 1941; *The Mongrel and Other Poems,* 1950; *The Solitudes,* 1960; *Judas,* 1960; *Unpopular Poems,* 1969; *Man, Part 1,* 1970; *Man, Part 2,* 1972; *Man, Part 3,* 1972; *Man, Parts 4 and 5,* 1974; *For the Few,* 1977; (jtly.) *The Ward,* 1978; *Selected Poems,* 1978; *Auschwitz,* 1979; *Collected Poems,* 1981. **Other** *The Complete Pacifist,* 1937; (as the Bishop of Marsland) *The Rexist Party Manifesto,* 1937; (as Maj. Gen. Marsland) *Strategy in War,* 1937; *Journal of a Husbandman,* 1944; *Home-made Home,* 1947; *Jan's Journal 1,* 1949; *Tobacco Growing in England,* 1950; *The Blue Fox,* 1951; *Jan at the Blue Fox,* 1952; *Where I Live,* 1953; *Jan's Journal 2,* 1954; *All Men Are Islands: An Autobiography,* 1964; *Devon and Cornwall,* 1966; *How To Make Enemies* (autobiography), 1968; *Dante's "De Vulgaria eloquentia,"* 1973; *Obsessed* (autobiography), 1975; *Mr. and Mrs. Mouse,* 1977; *The Encyclopaedia of Ignorance,* 2 vols., 1977; *A Memoir of Benjamin Britten,* 1981. **Editor** *Songs and Satires of John Wilmot, 2nd Earl of Rochester,* 1948; Ben Johnson, *Selected Poems,* 1949; *Selected Writings of Mahatma Gandhi,* 1951; (jtly.) *Classical Songs for Children,* 1965; (jtly.) *The Penguin Book of Accompanied Songs,* 1973; (jtly.) *Lying*

Truths, 1979. **Translator** Jean Cocteau, *Diary of a Film: La Belle et le Bête,* 1950. **Interview** William B. Wahl, *Ronald Duncan: Verse Dramatist and Poet,* 1973. **Manuscript collection** at Univ. of Texas, Austin.

Further reading Max Walter Haueter, *Ronald Duncan: The Metaphysical Content of His Plays,* 1969; William B. Wahl, *A Lone Wolf Howling,* 1973; Harold Lockyear et al., eds., *A Tribute to Ronald Duncan,* 1974.

JUNZABURŌ NISHIWAKI
Poet and scholar
***Born* Ojiya, Niigata Prefecture, Japan, 20 January 1894**
***Died* Ojiya, Niigata Prefecture, Japan, 5 June 1982**

Junzaburō Nishiwaki, one of Japan's most prominent literary modernists and scholars of English literature, did much to break the insularity of the Japanese literary tradition and introduce his contemporaries to European and American writing of the 1920s and 1930s. As professor of English at Keiō University, and translator of William Langland and Geoffrey Chaucer, he was also instrumental in awakening Japanese interest in Middle English literature.

Although interested in English from an early age, Nishiwaki's earliest ambition was to become a painter. In 1911 he went to Tokyo to study with Kuroda Seiki, leader of the "White Horse" school of painting, which attempted to fuse styles of European and Japanese art. He abandoned art, however, to become a student of economics at Keiō University, from which he graduated in 1917. He then worked for the English-language *Japan Times,* for the Japanese Foreign Office, and as a teacher in the preparatory course at Keiō University, but having retained an interest in English, decided to study English literature at Oxford University. He arrived in England in 1922, and spent a year in London before enrolling at Oxford as a student of Old and Middle English literature. In London, and at Oxford, where he became a friend of the poet and satirical novelist John Collier, he developed an enthusiasm for the writing and aesthetic theories of Ezra Pound, T. S. Eliot, Wyndham Lewis, James Joyce, and the French surrealist poet André Breton. Nishiwaki's first book of poems, *Spectrum* (1925), written in English and published in London, was profoundly influenced by the disjointed, allusive style of T. S. Eliot's earlier poems.

After his return to Japan in 1925, Nishiwaki became professor of English at Keiō University and a regular contributor to *Shi to Shiron* [*Poetry and Poetics*], a journal that promulgated avant-garde literary theory and exerted a strong influence on modern Japanese literature. It was partly due to Nishiwaki's efforts as both critic and poet that Japanese writers of the period looked beyond their own country for stylistic models. Nishiwaki, according to a writer in the *Times* of London, "was the first Japanese to achieve a successful marriage between the western and the eastern worlds using the language of surrealism." While winning a reputation as one of Japan's leading poets for his first major volume of poems, *Ambarvalia* (1933), Nishiwaki also, through his teaching, established Keiō University as an important center of English studies in Japan. He published several books on English literature, including a three-volume history of modern literature (1948), an introduction to Old English literature (1948), a study of William Langland (1933), and several translations, including Japanese renderings of Chaucer's *Canterbury Tales* and T. S. Eliot's *Waste Land.* His liberal political beliefs, and his broad acquaintance with European culture, caused him to take a stand against Japanese fascism. During World War II he refused to write as a protest against the actions of the military government.

After World War II Nishiwaki began to write longer narrative poems in which his interest turned to the culture of his native country and oriental philosophy in general. These included *The Traveler Does Not Return* (1947). His *Collected Poems* were published in 1963, and were followed by his last works, *Record of the Rites* (1967), *Joka* (1969), and *Mankind* (1979). He was an honorary member of the American Academy of Arts and Sciences, and several times a nominee for the Nobel Prize. H.B.

Father a banker. **Married** (1) Marjorie Bittle, painter (div.). (2) Saeko (d. 1975): one son. **Education** Middle sch., grad. 1911; studied painting with Kuroda Seiki, Tokyo ca. 1911–13; studied economics, Keiō Univ., Tokyo, grad. 1917; studied Old and Middle English, New Coll., Oxford 1923–25. **Career** Staff writer, *Japan Times,* and employee of Japanese Foreign Office late 1910s. • With Keiō Univ.: instr. in English 1920–22; prof. of English literature since 1926; dean of dept. of English literature; prof. emeritus. • Poet and critic, in Japanese and English, since 1920s; contributor to *Shi to Shiron* mag. 1928–31. **Member** Japan Acad. of Arts. **Honors** Person of Cultural Merit, Japan 1971; foreign hon. member, Amer. Acad. of Arts and Sciences. **Poetry** *Spectrum* (in English), 1925; *Poems Barbarous* (in English), 1930; *Anbaruwaria* [*Ambarvalia*], 1933; *Tabibito Kaerazu* [*The Traveler Does Not Return*], 1947; [*January in Kyoto*], 1956; [*Remembering the Things in the Past*], 1960; [*Fertile Goddess*], 1962; [*Aeternitas*], 1962; *Reiki* [*Record of the Rites*], 1967; *Joka,* 1969; *Shishū*, 1975; [*Mankind*], 1979; others. **Essays and criticism** [*European Literature*], 1933; [*William Langland*], 1933; *Beiei shisōshi* [*A History of Thought in America and England*], 1941; *Koeinbungaku kenkyū josetsu* [*Introduction to Old English Literature*], 1947; [*A History of Modern English Literature*], 3 vols., 1948; *Kindai no gūwa,* 1953; *Wa no aru sekai*, 1958; *Shigaku* (on Baudelaire), 1968; *Taidan shū*, 1972; *Nohara o yuku,* 1972; (ed.) *Rōdoku no shishū*, 1967; (ed.) *Shi no hon,* 1974; *Shi to shiron*, 1975; many others. **Collections** [*Complete Poetical Works*], 1963; *Zenshū* [*Collected Works*], 1971–73; [*Selected Works*], 1979. **Translations** Geoffrey Chaucer, *The Canterbury Tales*, 1949; T. S. Eliot, *The Waste Land*, 1952; others.

Further reading A. R. Davis, *Modern Japanese Poetry,* 1979.

SIR GEORGE SCHUSTER
Government financial advisor and public servant
Born 25 April 1881
Died Middle Barton, Oxfordshire, England, 5 June 1982

Sir George Schuster, an authority on finances and economics who served as advisor and planner in a succession of British governments, began his career in Queen Victoria's reign. He was a finance minister in colonial Africa and India and sat in Parliament as a National Liberal during World War II. In his later years he was active in public service as an official of Atlantic College in Wales and as a member of the Oxford County Council.

Schuster was a scholar at Charterhouse and took a first in Greats from New College, Oxford, where he was an Exhibitioner. He was called to the bar in 1905 but never practiced, instead joining his family's firm in the City. He was about to enter politics in 1914 but when World War I broke out went to France with the Oxfordshire Hussars and then to North Russia with the Murmansk Force. He received the Military Cross, and was made CBE in 1918.

Beginning in 1922, Schuster was, for five years, financial secretary in the Sudan. From 1928 to 1934 he was finance minister on the executive council of the Viceroy of India and succeeded in establishing for the first time a unified system of economic planning involving all of India's regions. On one occasion he was wounded by a bomb attack in the Assembly.

On returning to England, Schuster, who had been knighted KCMG in 1926 and KCSI in 1931, spent several years on government committees concerned with food supply, industry, and colonial development. From 1938 to 1945 he represented Walsall, Staffordshire, in Parliament for the National Liberals, and contributed to war production and postwar economic planning as a member of the Select

Committee on National Expenditure and the Government Committee on Industrial Productivity.

After his retirement from government service in the 1950s, Schuster chaired the board of the Oxford Regional Hospital and served eight terms on the Oxford County Council, where he retained an elected seat until the age of 93. He was a founder of Voluntary Service Overseas and chairman of the governing board of the United World College of the Atlantic, an international school in Wales for which he raised £1.5 million. His memoirs, *Private Work and Public Causes,* were published in 1979. He died at the age of 101, the oldest member of Lincoln's Inn and one of only four members of Parliament to become a centenarian. C.M.

Father Ernest S., financier. **Married** Hon. Gwendolen Parker 1908 (d. 1981): John; another son (d. 1941). **Religion** Christian. **Education** Charterhouse Sch. (scholar), Godalming, Surrey; New Coll., Oxford (Classical Exhibitioner), 1st Class in Greats 1903; called to the bar by Lincoln's Inn 1905. **Mil. service** Queen's Own Oxfordshire Hussars and on staff, France 1914–18; antiaircraft and quartermaster-gen., Murmansk Force, North Russia, and lt. col., Territorial Force Reserve, 1919. **Career** Partner, Schuster, Son & Co., London, and dir. of numerous cos., 1908–14; reported on economic conditions in Central Europe for Anglo-Danubian Assn. Ltd. 1920; chief asst., Org. of Intl. Credits, League of Nations 1921; member, advisory cttee. to Treasury under Trade Facilities Act 1921–22; financial secty., Sudan 1922–27; chmn., advisory cttee., Colonial Secty. on East African Loans 1926–28; economic and financial advisor, Colonial Office 1927–28; member, East African Commn. on Closer Union 1928; financial minister, Exec. Council, Viceroy of India 1928–34; chmn., Jt. Cttee. of Inquiry into Anglo-Argentine Meat Trade 1935–38; member, Colonial Development Advisory Cttee. 1936–38; chmn., Home and Colonial Stores 1936–46; bd. member, Westminster Bank 1936–70; Natl. Liberal M.P. for Walsall, Staffs. 1938–45; member, Select Cttee. on Natl. Expenditure 1939–45; chmn., Cotton Industry Working Party 1945–46; member, Govt. Cttee. on Industrial Productivity, and chmn. of its Panel on Human Relations, 1947–51; member and treas., Medical Research Council 1947–51; advisor on economic and financial policies, Malta 1950, 1956–57; chmn., Oxford Regional Hosp. Bd. 1951–63; member, Oxford County Council 1952–74; chmn., Acton Soc. Trust 1959; dir. of eight cos. from 1962; chmn., bd. of govs., United World Coll. of Atlantic, Wales 1963–73; v.p., Intl. Council, United World Colls.; member of governing bd., Charterhouse. **Member** Athenaeum Club; Brooks's Club; Heythrop Hunt, Oxon. **Honors** Mentioned four times in dispatches, and M.C., WWI; CBE 1918; KCMG 1926; KCSI 1931; hon. treas., Voluntary Service Overseas; Order of St. Vladimir; hon. degree, Oxford Univ. **Author** *India and Democracy,* 1941; *Christianity and Human Relations in Industry,* 1951; *Private Work and Public Causes* (memoirs), 1979.

KENNETH REXROTH

Poet, critic, painter, translator, columnist

***Born* South Bend, Indiana, USA, 22 December 1905**

***Died* Montecito, California, USA, 6 June 1982**

Kenneth Rexroth was an American original, among the most politically engaged of modern poets, who diligently practiced several artistic careers during the course of an eventful and influential life. He participated in the so-called second Chicago renaissance after World War I and was a leading figure in the cultural life of San Francisco from the late 1920s to the mid-1960s, nurturing both the Beat and the cosmic-consciousness movements.

He was born in Indiana but was orphaned at the age of 13 and moved to the South Side of Chicago to live with an aunt. He never had time for high school, but drifted into a wide variety of odd jobs: labor organizer for the Wobblies, horse wrangler, harvest hand, soda jerk, factory worker, mental-hospital orderly. During this period of wandering, he usually spent his winters in Chicago (he had moved to the Near North Side, the Bohemian district), and got to know many of the most important figures of the day, such as Clarence Darrow, Carl Sandburg, Vachel Lindsay, Eugene V. Debs, Ben Hecht, Charles MacArthur, and Frank Lloyd Wright. James T. Farrell included him in *Studs Lonigan* as Kenny, the "blue-eyed, dizzy-faced" drugstore clerk with the "nervous, original walk."

In 1927 Rexroth married the first of his four wives and moved to San Francisco. There he joined the John Reed Club and other organizations composed of ex-Wobblies; he saw himself as "consistently antipolitical—an anarchist and war resister." His membership application was rejected by the Communist Party in 1930 because they doubted he could be a loyal follower. Although too old to serve, he registered as a conscientious objector in World War II and worked again as an aide in a mental hospital.

His early poems were influenced by the Imagist movement of the first two decades of the century and by the more recent Surrealism, although Rexroth once classified himself as a "literary cubist." The poems appeared in several of the little magazines of the period, including *Blues, Poetry,* and *New Masses,* but they were not collected together until he published *The Art of Worldly Wisdom* in 1949. He admired William Carlos Williams most among twentieth-century poets, and always strove for language of simple directness, the inherent vitality of American speech. His published poetry ranges from the poems on Sacco and Vanzetti and the Spanish civil war of *In What Hour* (1941) through *The Dragon and the Unicorn* (1952), a lengthy verse account of a year's travel, filled with denunciations of capitalist excess, to the poems of his maturity, such as the well-received *The Heart's Garden, The Garden's Heart* (1968), concerned with the quest for enlightenment and the need to transcend "the web of cause and effect." Rexroth belonged to many religions during his life, including Roman and Anglo-Catholicism and Buddhism, but in the end left them all behind.

During the 1950s, San Francisco became a center for the Beat Generation, and Rexroth, because of his colloquial, enjambed verse and unorthodox life-style, served for a time as a

Courtesy of New Directions Pub. Inc.

kind of godfather to the movement. He was master of ceremonies at a famous gathering at the Six Gallery in 1955 when Philip Lamantia, Gary Snyder, Allen Ginsberg, and others read their poems. Somewhat later, with Ginsberg and Lawrence Ferlinghetti, he founded the Poetry Center at San Francisco State University. He often gave jazz-accompanied readings himself during this period, both in California and in Greenwich Village, New York City. He did not, however, stay long with the Beats, whom he professed to find unrigorous, and often in later years spoke disparagingly of them and of his association with them. He was the model for Reinhold Cacoethes, the leading San Francisco anarchist, in Jack Kerouac's *The Dharma Bums* (1958).

Rexroth was producing translations from the age of 15; he called them "poetic exercises in contact with the noblest minds." They are among the most admired of his poems, and were published in collections from each language—Japanese, Chinese, Greek and Latin, Spanish, and French—from 1952 to 1979. He also occasionally edited the poems of others, and was among the first to appreciate the poetry of D. H. Lawrence and Czesław Miłosz, publishing selections from their work in 1948 and 1973, respectively. Rexroth's prose, mostly in essay form, was popular for its iconoclastic force and curmudgeonly tone, and included *Bird in the Bush* (1959), *Assays* (1961), *The Elastic Retort* (1973), and especially *An*

Autobiographical Novel (1966), which told the story of his wandering youth and beginnings as a poet.

Rexroth painted seriously from the 1920s, primarily in an abstract style, and had solo shows in California, New York, Chicago, and Paris. He was also a journalist: San Francisco correspondent for the *Nation* magazine from 1953 and columnist for the *San Francisco Examiner* from 1958 to 1968. In the latter year he moved to Santa Barbara to lecture at the university, and except for extensive traveling—particularly to Japan, his favorite place to visit—lived there for the rest of his life. Over the years he received several poetry awards, including those commemorating William Carlos Williams, Eunice Tietjens, Shelley, and Amy Lowell. In 1969 he was elected to the National Institute of Arts and Letters. A.K.

Parents Charles Marion R., wholesale druggist, and Delia (Reed) R. **Married** (1) Myrtle Schaefer (Andrée Dutcher), painter, 1927 (d. 1940). (2) Marie Kass 1940 (div. 1948). (3) Martha Larsen 1949 (div. 1961): Marianna, b. 1950; Katherine. (4) Carol Tinker, painter and poet. **Religion** Tried many; at various times Roman Catholic, Buddhist, other faiths. **Education** Englewood High Sch., Chicago; Art Inst. of Chicago; Art Students League, NYC; New Sch. for Social Research, NYC. **Mil. service** Conscientious objector, WWII: worked as hosp. attendant. **Career** Farmhand, factory worker, soda jerk, other odd jobs early 1920s; lobbyist, Industrial Workers of the World 1920s; painter, writer, critic, and poet since 1920s; writer, WPA 1930s; San Francisco corresp., *Nation* mag. 1953; columnist, *San Francisco Examiner* 1958–68; cofounder, Poetry Center, San Francisco State Univ. late 1950s; columnist, *San Francisco Magazine* and *San Francisco Bay Guardian* 1968–70s; lectr., Univ. of California, Santa Barbara 1968–74; host, literary radio show, Pacifica Radio, S.F. late 1960s–70s. **Member** John Reed Club, S.F. 1930s; Natl. Inst. of Arts and Letters since 1969. **Honors** California Literary Silver Medal for Poetry 1941, for *In What Hour,* and 1945, for *The Phoenix and the Tortoise;* Guggenheim Fellowship, U.K., France, and Italy, 1948–49; Tietjens Award, *Poetry,* Chicago 1957; Shelley Memorial Award, Poetry Soc. of America 1958; Amy Lowell Fellowship 1958; Natl. Inst. of Arts and Letters grant 1964; Copernicus Award, Acad. of Amer. Poets, for *New Poems,* 1975; sr. Fulbright Fellowship 1975; Rockefeller Foundn. grant; Longview Award; William Carlos Williams Award, *Contact Magazine;* Chapelbrook Award; Commonwealth Medal, twice; Akademische Austauschdienst Award, Germany. **Poetry** *In What Hour,* 1941; *The Phoenix and the Tortoise,* 1944; *The Art of Worldly Wisdom,* 1949; *The Signature of All Things: Poems, Songs, Elegies, Translations, and Epigrams,* 1950; *The Dragon and the Unicorn,* 1952; *In Defense of the Earth,* 1956; *The Homestead Called Damascus,* 1963; *Natural Numbers: New and Selected Poems,* 1963; *The Complete Collected Shorter Poems of Kenneth Rexroth,* 1968; (contributor) *Penguin Modern Poets 9,* 1967; *The Heart's Garden, The Garden's Heart,* 1967; *The Collected Longer Poems of Kenneth Rexroth,* 1968; *The Spark in the Tinder of Knowing,* 1968; *Sky Sea Birds Trees Earth House Beasts Flowers,* 1970; *New Poems,* 1974; *On Flower Wreath Hill,* 1976; *The Silver Swan: Poems Written in Kyoto 1974–1975,* 1976; *The Morning Star: Poems and Translations,* 1979. **Plays** *Beyond the Mountains,* 1951. **Essays and criticism** *Bird in the Bush: Obvious Essays,* 1959; *Assays,* 1961; *An Autobiographical Novel* (autobiography), 1966; *Classics Revisited,* 1968; *The Alternative Society: Essays from the Other World,* 1970; *With Eye and Ear,* 1970; *American Poetry: In the Twentieth Century,* 1971; Eric Mottram, ed., *The Rexroth Reader,* 1972; *The Elastic Retort: Essays in Literature and Ideas,* 1973; *Communalism: From Its Origins to the Twentieth Century,* 1974. **Editor** D. H. Lawrence, *Selected Poems,* 1948; *The New British Poets: An Anthology,* 1949; *Four Young Women: Poems,* 1973; David Meltzer, *Tens: Selected Poems 1961–1971,* 1973; *The Selected Poems of Czesław Miłosz,* 1973; *The Buddhist Writings of Lafcadio Hearn,* 1977. **Translator** O. V. de L.-Miłosz, *Fourteen Poems,* 1952; *100 Poems from the Japanese,* 1955; *100 Poems from the Chinese,* 1956; *30 Spanish Poems of Love and Exile,* 1956; *100 Poems from the Greek and Latin,* 1962; *Poems from the Greek Anthology,* 1962; Pierre Reverdy, *Selected Poems,* 1969; *Love and the Turning Earth: 100 More Classical Poems,* 1970; *Love and the Turning Year: 100 More Chinese Poems,* 1970; *100 Poems from the French,*

1970; (jtly.) *The Orchid Boat: Women Poets of China,* 1972; *100 More Poems from the Japanese,* 1976; (jtly.) *The Burning Heart: Women Poets from Japan,* 1977; Shiraishi Kazuko, *Seasons of Sacred Lust,* 1978; (jtly.) Li-Ching-Chao, *Complete Poems,* 1979. **Libretto** *Original Sin.* **Recording** (Jtly.) *In the Cellar.* **Exhibitions** of paintings in galleries in NYC, S.F., L.A., Paris, Santa Barbara, others. **Contributor** to *Poetry, New Masses, Esquire, Atlantic, Harper's, Saturday Review,* other mags.

Further reading Morgan Gibson, *Kenneth Rexroth,* 1972; Geoffrey Gardner, ed., *For Rexroth,* 1980.

WOLF SZMUNESS

Epidemiologist

***Born* Warsaw, Poland, 12 March 1919**

***Died* New York City, USA, 6 June 1982**

One of the world's major public health problems is viral hepatitis B, a highly infectious, sometimes fatal inflammation of the liver. An estimated half million people contract the disease annually, and the number of chronic carriers is probably 200 million worldwide. Hepatitis B is also believed to lead to chronic cirrhosis of the liver, and, in some cases, to primary hepatocellular carcinoma of the liver, the world's third most common cancer. A vaccine against hepatitis B was developed in the late 1970s and was proved 96 percent effective in a complicated field test designed by Wolf Szmuness, a senior investigator with the New York Blood Center.

Szmuness arrived at his career in epidemiology after surviving the Nazi assault on Poland and incarceration in a Soviet forced-labor camp. A native of Warsaw, he studied medicine at the University of Pisa, Italy, from 1937 to 1939, and was back in Warsaw in September 1939 when the Germans invaded. He was trapped in the home of some friends whom he happened to be visiting and was unable to rejoin his family; he never saw them again. He escaped to the Soviet Union, but was arrested and sent to a labor camp outside the city of Prokopjevsk, in western Siberia. Eventually the authorities discovered that he had been a medical student and assigned him to supervise sanitary conditions in the camp. He was later placed in charge of epidemiology for the entire region.

Released in 1946, Szmuness enrolled in classes at the Institute of Medicine in Tomsk, 200 miles northwest of Prokopjevsk. An epidemic of typhoid fever broke out, and Szmuness was called in as a consultant to the doctor in charge. He was introduced to the doctor's daughter Maya, also a medical student, and within a week they were married. In 1950 he received his physician's diploma and the following year moved his family to Kiev, where he served as city and provincial epidemiologist and earned his doctorate from the Kharkov Medical Institute. From 1955 to 1959 he headed the department of epidemiology at the Odessa State Institute for Postgraduate Training of Physicians in Zaporozhye. His wife nearly died there of hepatitis B contracted from an infected blood transfusion during a gallbladder operation.

In 1959 Szmuness finally obtained permission to return to Poland and settled in Lublin, where he taught epidemiology at the State Institute of Rural Medicine and Hygiene and the Academy of Medicine. He was dismissed for refusing an order to all state employees to attend an anti-Israel rally during the 1967 Mideast War. With the help of the U.S. Embassy he was given an exit visa as a religious and political refugee and left the country with his wife and daughter. He arrived in New York in 1969 and found a job at the New York Blood Center as a medical technician. He was soon conducting his own experiments on hepatitis, and by 1973 was head of the epidemiology laboratory.

In 1978 Szmuness began the trial of the new hepatitis B vaccine, which had been developed by the American pharmaceutical firm of Merck, Sharp, and Dohme from the purified extract of the virus's surface antigen (the protein coating that provokes the human immune response). The test, one of the best-planned and executed of its kind, was conducted among 1,083 homosexual males, whose chances of getting hepatitis are 10 to 15 times

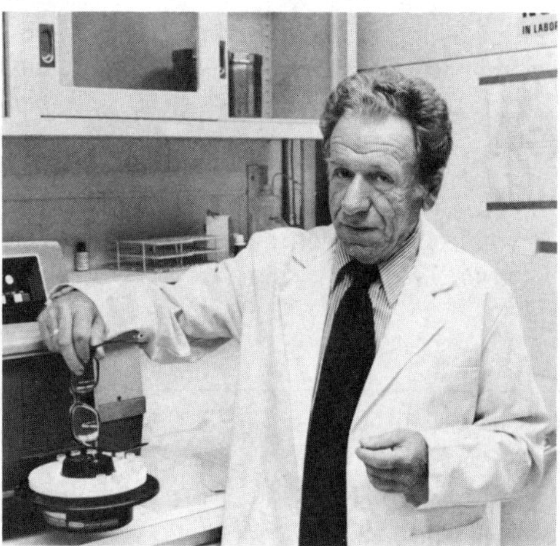

Courtesy of New York Blood Center

higher than the rest of the population. Half the volunteer subjects received the vaccine and half received a placebo; neither they nor their doctors knew which was which. The results, made public in 1980, were unambiguously positive. Only 3.4 percent of those vaccinated contracted hepatitis during the course of the experiment, and most of those did so early in the treatment, before the vaccine had taken hold. Among those who received the placebo, by contrast, 27 percent caught hepatitis. Enthusiastic press reports claimed that the vaccine would also prevent hepatocellular carcinoma, but Szmuness called the reports premature: since this form of liver cancer develops long after a person has contracted hepatitis B, 20 or 30 years would have to elapse before a mass vaccination program could show results.

Szmuness's experiments among other high-risk groups included a study of the patients and staff members of kidney dialysis centers, who risk infection from contaminated blood, and of tribes in South Africa, where hepatitis B is widespread and where newborn babies frequently catch the disease from their mothers. The results of these studies had not been published at the time of Szmuness's death, which came after a long illness.

P.D./J.P.

Married Maya 1946: Helena. **Emigrated** to USSR 1939; returned to Poland 1959; emigrated to U.S. 1969, naturalized 1974. **Education** Gymnasium, Warsaw, grad. 1937; faculty of medicine, Univ. of Pisa, Italy 1937–39; Inst. of Medicine, Tomsk, Siberia, USSR, physician's diploma 1950; Central Postgrad. Medical Inst., Moscow 1952, 1957; Kharkov Medical Inst., Ukrainian USSR, Ph.D. 1955; course in rural medicine and hygiene, WHO, Helsinki 1961; Acad. of Medicine, Lublin, Poland, doctorate in medical science 1964. **Career** Imprisoned in labor camp, Prokopjevsk, Siberia, USSR ca. 1939–46; city and provincial epidemiologist, Kiev-Voroshilovgrad region, Ukrainian SSR 1951–55; chief, dept. of epidemiology, Odessa State Inst. for Postgrad. Training of Physicians, Zaporozhye, Ukrainian SSR 1955–59; chief, dept. of epidemiology, State Inst. of Rural Medicine and Hygiene, Lublin, Poland 1959–63; assoc. prof. of medicine, Acad. of Medicine, Lublin 1964–67; on research grant, Microbiological Labs., Inst. Superiore di Sanità, Rome 1968–69. • With New York Blood Center, NYC: medical technician and research assoc. 1969–70 and assoc. investigator 1970–73; Lab. of Virology; head, Lab. of Epidemiology since 1973; investigator 1975–76; sr. investigator since 1976. • Asst. prof. of epidemiology 1973–75 and prof. of epidemiology since 1975, Sch. of Public Health, Columbia Univ.; assoc. ed., *American Journal of Epidemiology* since 1978; consultant, Amer. Red Cross. **Officer** Chmn., Intl. Symposium on Viral Hepatitis 1981. **Member** U.S.-Japan Scientific Cttee., Natl. Inst. of Allergy and Infectious Diseases, NIH since 1978; Blood Diseases and Resources Advisory Cttee., Natl. Heart, Lung and Blood Inst., NIH since 1979; Soc. for Epidemiologic Research; Intl. Epidemiologic Assn.; Amer. Epidemiological Soc. **Contributor** of more than 120 papers on epidemiology and public health to scientific and medical jrnls.

FERDINAND (WALDO) DEMARA
Impostor
***Born* Lawrence, Massachusetts, USA, 12 December 1921**
***Died* West Anaheim, California, USA, 7 June 1982**

A skilled impostor, forger, and liar, Ferdinand Demara spent most of his life assuming the identities of other people. With sheer nerve, a talent for bluster, and an ability to learn quickly the rudiments of any field, he successfully posed as a professor of psychology, a college dean, a naval surgeon, a prison warden, a cancer researcher, a Sunday-school teacher, and several other things. Unlike the average con man, Demara was intent on doing good, and more often than not, when he was discovered, those he had fooled forgave him and even wanted him back. His life story was made into a best-selling book and a Hollywood movie.

Demara was born in the small mill town of Lawrence, Massachusetts, to a well-to-do family. When he was 11, his father's movie-theater business went bankrupt, and the family was forced to move to a small house in the poor section of town. A large, awkward child, Demara was uncomfortable in school, and gravitated to religion. At the age of 16, already almost six feet tall and weighing 200 pounds, he ran away from home to join a Trappist monastery in Rhode Island. Two years later, finding the strict Trappist life too confining, he headed for Boston. He enlisted in the Army, but deserted before finishing boot camp; next he enlisted in the Navy and was assigned to a destroyer in the North Atlantic, then to the Navy Hospital School.

After being rejected for advanced medical training because of his lack of education, Demara deserted the Navy as well and began his career as an impostor by copying from a college catalogue the credentials of Dr. Robert Linton French, a psychologist, under whose name he entered first a Trappist monastery in Kentucky and then another monastery in Chicago. The Navy caught up with him in Olympia, Washington, in 1947, where, still posing as French, he was teaching psychology in a small Benedictine school. He conducted his own defense at his court-martial for desertion in time of war and spent 18 months in the U.S. Disciplinary Barracks at San Pedro, California. The Army located him there and gave him a dishonorable discharge.

On his release from prison, Demara assumed the identity of Dr. Cecil Hamann, a zoologist and cancer researcher. He studied law briefly at Northwestern University, then presented himself as a teacher to yet another monastic order in Maine. While serving his novitiate, he befriended Dr. Joseph Cyr, a Canadian physician. Offering to help the doctor obtain a license to practice in the United States, Demara took his papers and in 1951 applied, as Cyr, for a medical commission in the Royal Canadian Navy. He was assigned to the H.M.S. *Cayuga,* on duty off the coast of Korea during the war. Amazingly, Demara, using knowledge gleaned from medical textbooks, was quite successful as a ship's surgeon, pulling teeth, sewing up wounds, and even extracting bullets and resectioning the lung of a Korean soldier. He was so successful, in fact, that a newspaper story about the

heroic doctor was published in the Canadian press. The article attracted the attention of the real Dr. Cyr, who alerted the Royal Navy. Demara was discharged and sent back to the United States. In 1952, an article about his exploits, with photographs, was published in *Life* magazine.

Over the next few years Demara posed as a lieutenant warden in a Texas prison, a teacher of Eskimos in Alaska, a civil engineer in Yucatán, a Latin teacher in Maine, and a host of other people. He was brought to trial on charges ranging from vagrancy to embezzlement and, acting as his own lawyer, managed to get himself acquitted more than once. In 1959, author Robert Crichton published his biography, *The Great Impostor*. The book was an immediate success—Tony Curtis starred in a film version the following year—but the publicity put an end to Demara's career as a fake. He later disavowed both the book and the movie, calling them inaccurate.

Little is known of his motivation to live other people's lives. He never underwent psychoanalysis, even while in prison, and he delighted in giving out false information on himself. "I am a superior sort of liar," he told Crichton. "I don't tell any truth at all, so then my story has a unity of parts, a structural integrity, and this way sounds more like the truth than truth itself." Psychiatrists labeled him a borderline schizophrenic and a manic depressive of extremely high intelligence. "Every time I take a new identity," he said, "some part of me dies."

Demara lived under his own name—by all reports, unhappily—after 1959, working as a Baptist minister and as a visiting counselor at Good Samaritan Hospital in Anaheim, California. He became ill in 1980 and died of a heart attack at the age of 60. S.A.

Father a movie-theater owner and film projectionist. **Religion** Roman Catholic; Baptist minister from 1960s. **Education** Central Catholic High Sch., Lawrence, MA, left ca. 1937; (under alias) U.S. Navy Hosp. Sch. 1942, also studied philosophy, law, theology, ethics, and other subjects at various colls. and univs. **Mil. service** Enlisted in U.S. Army 1941, deserted 1941, dishonorable discharge ca. 1948; medical corpsman in U.S. Navy 1942, deserted 1942, court-martialed 1947, imprisoned in U.S. Disciplinary Barracks, San Pedro, CA ca. 1947–48; (under aliases) surgeon lt. at naval hosp. in Halifax, Nova Scotia, and on H.M.S. *Cayuga* off Korea, Royal Canadian Navy 1951. **Career** Impostor under various aliases: Cistercian and Trappist monk ca. 1938–44; dean of philosophy, Gannon Coll., Erie, PA 1945–46; psychology teacher late 1940s; hospital orderly late 1940s; military surgeon, Royal Canadian Navy 1951; asst. prison warden, TX ca. 1955; civil engineer, Yucatán ca. 1956; teacher, Eskimos, Alaska ca. 1956; Sunday-sch. teacher, Maine 1956–57; imprisoned 1957; English, French, and Latin teacher, MA ca. 1958–59; also coll. dean, cancer researcher, other jobs. • Under own name, Baptist minister and hosp. counselor 1959–ca. 1980.

Further reading Robert Crichton, *The Great Impostor,* 1959.

SATCHEL PAIGE

Baseball pitcher

***Born* Mobile, Alabama, USA, 7 July 1906**

***Died* Kansas City, Missouri, USA, 8 June 1982**

Satchel Paige was a masterful pitcher and colorful showman whose endurance and longevity made him a permanent part of baseball legend.

Paige spent over 20 years in the Negro Leagues, finally reaching the major leagues with the Cleveland Indians in 1948, at the age of 42. He pitched in the 1948 World Series, made the 1952 American League All-Star Team, and in 1971 became a member of the Baseball Hall of Fame. His last stint in the majors was three scoreless innings in 1965 when he was 59. During his seemingly endless career, the tall, thin righthander compiled incredible (though largely unverifiable) statistics, including pitching in over 2,500 games and throwing over 100 no-hitters.

Leroy Paige was born in 1906 in a poor black section of Mobile, Alabama. Until the 1950s, when his birth certificate was found, he kept his exact age a mystery, claiming that the certificate had been eaten by a goat along with the family bible. He was the seventh of 11 children born to John Paige, a gardener, and Lula Paige, a washerwoman. By the age of seven, he was working in a railway depot carrying bags. He picked up the nickname Satchel after he rigged a device that enabled him to carry several satchels at once.

Paige first pitched in grammar school, but received his earliest formal coaching at reform school, where he spent more than five years for shoplifting. By 1924, he had returned to Mobile and needed work. He tried out for the Mobile Tigers, a semi-pro ballclub on which his older brother Wilson played. After throwing ten swinging strikes past the manager, Paige had a job. His record for the 1924 season was about 30 wins and one loss. He received a dollar a game and was often paid in kegs of lemonade.

After a long winning streak that lasted a few seasons, Paige attracted the attention of the Chattanooga Black Lookouts of the Negro Southern League, and signed with them for $50 a month. In 1928 he signed with the Birmingham Black Barons, but was traded to the Nashville Elite Giants near the end of the 1929 season. During the winter of 1929 he pitched in Cuba, starting a string of 29 years in which he pitched all year long—a grueling schedule that would quickly wear out most pitchers. The Baltimore Black Sox soon recruited him to pitch against a barnstorming team led by Babe Ruth. Though he never got the chance to pitch against Ruth during the tour, Paige greatly impressed the major leaguers, especially when he pitched a 22-strikeout game that easily eclipsed the major-league strikeout record.

Courtesy of National Baseball Hall of Fame

In 1931, the Elite Giants disbanded and Paige joined the Pittsburgh Crawfords, one of the greatest teams ever assembled. Its star attraction, in addition to Paige, was Josh Gibson, an awesome power hitter and an outstanding catcher. The club's promoters guaranteed that Paige would strike out the first nine men he faced and that Gibson would hit two home runs. Paige filled ballparks throughout the Negro Leagues and opened up the major-league ballparks to black teams. In 1933 he won 21 games in a row, compiled a season total of 31 wins, and threw 62 consecutive shutout innings. The following year he played winter ball on the West Coast against major leaguers led by the fireballing righthander Dizzy Dean.

After playing with a team from Bismarck, North Dakota, for two years and leading them to a victory in a national tournament, Paige rejoined Pittsburgh in 1936, but soon jumped his contract and went to Mexico. While pitching there, he developed severe arm trouble and was told by a specialist that he would never pitch again. Extremely depressed, he returned to the United States and was signed by the Kansas City Monarchs as a first baseman, for although he could not pitch, his name alone was still a draw. One day during the 1938 season the pain disappeared, and he never had any arm trouble again. Carried by Paige's pitching, the Monarchs won the Negro American League Championship from 1939 through 1942. In 1943, he received the most votes in the balloting for the Negro League's East-West All-Star Game and got the victory for the West team, thus becoming the first pitcher to win for both sides.

After visiting soldiers wounded on World War II battlefronts, Paige suggested that $10,000 of the receipts of the 1944 East-West Game be donated to help them. The teams' owners balked, though Paige said he would not participate if the game were not played for charity. The owners refused and Paige missed the game.

When Jackie Robinson broke baseball's color barrier in 1947, the majors were finally opened to Paige, who had been pitching successfully against major-league players in exhibition games for well over a decade. Cleveland Indians owner Bill Veeck, looking to bolster his pitching staff for the pennant drive, sent Abe Saperstein, owner of the Harlem Globetrotters basketball team, to find quality pitchers. Saperstein recommended Paige. On 7 July 1948, Paige's 42nd birthday, he signed with the Indians as baseball's oldest rookie and the first black pitcher in the American League. During his first appearance, on 9 July, he threw his hesitation pitch, a trick pitch that fooled the batter into swinging at the air while the ball remained in Paige's hand. Will Harridge, president of the American League, banned the pitch after the first game. Paige drew huge crowds in his 21 appearances that season and helped Cleveland to the pennant with a 6–1 record. He made only a brief appearance in the World Series, which Cleveland won, four games to two.

It was after the 1948 series that Paige told the public his now-famous rules for longevity: "Avoid fried meats which angry up the blood. If your stomach disputes you, lie down and pacify it with cool thoughts. Keep the juices flowing by jangling around gently as you move. Go very light on the vices, such as carrying on in society—the social ramble ain't restful. Avoid running at all times. And don't look back. Something might be gaining on you."

When Veeck left the Indians in 1949, the management decided not to keep Paige. He barnstormed for a while and turned down two offers from major-league clubs, waiting for Veeck's return to baseball. Veeck purchased the St. Louis Browns in 1951, and Paige, now 45 years old, was back in the majors. He only managed a 3–4 record in the 1951 season with the lowly Browns, but in 1952 won 12 games and was named to the American League All-Star team. The following year Veeck sold the club, and Paige was released by the new owners. He joined a barnstorming club run by Saperstein in 1954 and pitched in almost 150 games. In 1955, he rejoined the Monarchs, but interest in the Negro Leagues was waning and the Monarchs had become a traveling team, with no home stadium.

When Veeck got a job with the Miami Marlins of the International League, in the minors, Paige joined the team and recorded 11 wins against four losses; his 1.86 earned-run average was the best in the league for the 1956 season. Veeck left the team before the next season began. Paige stayed on for two more years, and in the 1958 offseason played a cavalry sergeant in a Robert Mitchum western, *The Wonderful Country,* after which he returned to barnstorming. His 1962 autobiography was entitled *Maybe I'll Pitch Forever.*

In 1965, he was signed by Charlie Finley, the owner of the Kansas City Athletics, who was always looking to boost attendance. At the age of 59, Satchel Paige, the oldest man to ever play in the major leagues—he had a rocking chair set up in the dugout and a nurse to massage his pitching arm—held the Boston Red Sox scoreless over three innings, allowing just one base hit. His last job in the major leagues was as a coach for the Atlanta Braves in 1968.

In 1971, Paige became the first man named to the Hall of Fame by the Committee of Negro Baseball Leagues, a special group formed to nominate black players who had been banned from the major leagues. Other players later named by this committee included Gibson and Oscar Charleston, teammates of Paige's on the 1931 Crawfords.

Paige appeared in public for the last time at the dedication ceremony for a Kansas City ballpark named in his honor. He suffered from heart trouble and emphysema and was in a wheelchair. A few days later he died of a heart attack at the age of 75. J.R.

Born Leroy Robert Page; family name changed to Paige. **Parents** John Paige, gardener, and Lula Paige, washerwoman. **Married** (1) Janet Howard 1934 (div. 1943). (2) Lahoma Brown 1947: six children. **Education** W.H. Council School, AL; Industrial School for Negro Children, Mount Megis, AL; Alabama Reform Sch. for Boys. **Career** Baseball pitcher, Negro Southern Assn. and Negro Natl. Assn.: Mobile Tigers 1924–27; Chattanooga Black Lookouts 1927; Birmingham Black Barons 1928–29; Nashville Elite Giants 1929; Baltimore Black Sox 1930s; Pittsburgh Crawfords 1931–34, 1936–37; Bismarck, ND team 1934–36; in Mexico ca. 1936; Kansas City Monarchs ca. 1937–47, 1955; offseason exhibition games 1929–65. • With major leagues: Cleveland Indians 1948–49; St. Louis Browns 1951–53; Kansas City Athletics 1965;

pitching coach, Atlanta Braves 1968. **Honors** Named to American League All-Star Team 1952; elected to Baseball Hall of Fame, Cooperstown, NY 1971; baseball park named after him, Kansas City 1982; day named after him, Springfield, IL. **Film actor** *The Wonderful Country,* 1958. **Author** (Jtly.) *Maybe I'll Pitch Forever* (autobiography), 1962.

Further reading Robert Rubin, *Satchel Paige,* 1974; Art Rust, Jr., *Get That Nigger Off the Field!,* 1976; William Brashler, *Josh Gibson: A Life in the Negro Leagues,* 1978.

RICHARD ST. BARBE BAKER

Silviculturist

***Born* West End, near Southampton, England, 9 October 1889**

***Died* Saskatoon, Saskatchewan, Canada, 9 June 1982**

Richard St. Barbe Baker devoted his life to the planting of trees and the reclamation of deserts. A widely traveled ecologist who surveyed millions of acres of land for the international society he founded, The Men of the Trees, he was convinced that the preservation and reclamation of the world's rapidly diminishing forests are vital to human survival. "Whenever a nation has neglected its trees," he wrote, "its civilization has suffered or vanished."

Baker's father, a horticulturist and a devout Evangelical, instructed his son in botany and instilled in him a reverence for life. After secondary studies at Cheltenham, he prepared for the ministry at Saskatchewan University, then read divinity at Cambridge. A skilled horseman, he joined King Edward's Horse at the outbreak of war in 1914 and served in France, where he was twice wounded.

In 1919 Baker returned to Cambridge, this time to study forestry. He obtained his diploma in 1920, and shipped out to Kenya to take a post as assistant forest conservator with the colonial Forest Service. He soon became concerned about the widespread destruction of Kenya's mahogany forests by nomadic farmers using slash-and-burn agricultural techniques. In 1922, the year of his conversion to the Baha'i faith, Baker persuaded the members of a local tribe to begin replanting barren areas in order to provide future sources of fuel; millions of trees were planted in the following years. This venture marked the birth of his organization. He initiated a similar venture in Nigeria, where he was stationed from 1924 to 1929. Within a few years he had recruited hundreds of members in several countries. "The Men of the Trees," he wrote in 1934, "believe that the act of planting a tree, which in itself is a practical deed, is also a symbol of a far-reaching ideal. . . . It will develop physical, moral, and spiritual qualities which are essential to the well-being of man."

Baker left the Forestry Service in 1929 to work full-time as head of his society. During the next few years he undertook a series of international lecture tours, bringing his conservationist message to the public and meeting with politicians and heads of state. He traveled 17,000 miles through North America in the mid-1930s to prepare a forestry plan, surveyed the forests of South America in 1936, and met with Pres. Franklin Roosevelt to discuss the necessity of reforestation. Roosevelt later made the planting of trees one of the main activities of the Civilian Conservation Corps.

From 1952 to 1953 Baker conducted a 9,000-mile ecological survey of the Sahara. His 1954 report, *Sahara Challenge,* attributed the existence of the desert to overgrazing in past centuries and its recent rapid advance to extensive cotton growing. He dedicated himself to halting the further spread of the desert through reforestation as a director of the Sahara Reclamation Co., founded in 1954 and based in Tangiers. In the decades that followed, Baker periodically convened or attended international conferences on the Sahara situation, and toward the end of his life saw modest success at Bon Saada in Algeria. He was also one of the first to call attention to the effects of massive deforestation on the earth's climate and oxygen supply, now a major concern of ecologists. Baker's books numbered more than 40, including three volumes of autobiography. His book *The Redwoods* (1943) preceded his successful campaign to save California's redwood and sequoia forests.

Baker settled in New Zealand in 1959. Three years later, at the age of 73, he made a 1,200-mile tour of the country on horseback, lecturing on trees to tens of thousands of schoolchildren. He continued to make inspection tours and attend conferences in a dozen countries over the next two decades. He died at the age of 92 while visiting Saskatoon.

P.D.

Parents John R. St. Barbe B., horticulturist, and Charlotte (Purrott) B. **Married** (1) Doreen Whitworth Long 1946 (div. 1958): Angela; Paul. (2) Catriona Burnett 1959. **Religion** Raised in the Evangelical Church; Baha'i since 1922. **Emigrated** to N.Z. 1959. **Education** Dean Close Sch., Cheltenham, England; Univ. of Saskatchewan, Canada ca. 1909–13; studied divinity 1913–14, then forestry 1919–20, Gonville and Caius Coll., Cambridge, forestry diploma 1920; Army Sch. of Education 1919. **Mil. service** King Edward's Horse, Royal Field Artillery and Remounts, British Army, France 1914–18 (wounded twice). **Career** Asst. forest conservator, Forest Service, Kenya 1920–23 and Nigeria 1924–29; founder 1922 and full-time dir. since 1929, The Men of the Trees; silviculturist, environmentalist, lectr., and govt. consultant on forestry and desert reclamation, U.K., U.S., Canada, Africa, Europe, South America, Australia, N.Z. since 1929; ed., *Tree Lover's Calendar* since 1929; organizer, forestry sch., Oxford Univ. 1938, also other schs.; founder 1940 and ed. since 1940, *Trees and Life* jrnl.; founder 1945 and dir. 1945–56, World Forestry Charter Gatherings; dir., Sahara Reclamation Co., Tangiers since 1954; founder, Jr. Men of the Trees 1956; convened first Redwood Reunion, Mill Creek, USA 1960; convened first Sahara Reclamation Conference, Rabat, Morocco 1964; sr. advisor, Baha'i delegation, U.N. conference, Nairobi 1976; co-founder, Ecoworld, Victoria, B.C.; delegate, World Forestry Congresses, Wilderness Conferences, and other conservationist conferences. **Officer** Pres., Intl. Tree Crops Inst. 1977. **Fellow** Intl. Inst. of Arts and Letters. **Member** Naval and Military Club. **Honors** OBE 1978; hon. degree from Univ. of Saskatchewan. **Author** *The Brotherhood of the Trees,* 1930; *Men of the Trees: In the Mahogany Forests of Kenya and Nigeria,* 1931; *Among the Trees,* 2 vols., 1935; *Arbor Day Planting,* 1935; *Trees: A Book of the Seasons,* 1940; *Africa Drums,* 1942, rev. ed. 1959; *The Redwoods,* 1943; *I Planted Trees* (autobiography), 1944; *Green Glory: The Story of the Forests of the World,* 1947, as *Green Glory: Forests of the World,* 1949; (jtly.) *The Lasting Victories,* 1948; *Trees: A Reader's Guide,* 1948; *New Earth Charter,* 1949; *Famous Trees,* 1953; *Sahara Challenge,* 1954; *Kabongo: The Story of a Kikuyu Chief,* 1955; *Land of Tané: The Threat of Erosion,* 1956; *Dance of the Trees: The Adventures of a Forester* (autobiography), 1956; *My Life—My Trees* (autobiography), 1956; *Kamiti: A Forester's Dream,* 1958; *Horse Sense: Story of My Horses in War and Peace,* 1962; *Trees of the World,* 1962; *Trees of the Bible Lands,* 1963; *The True Book About Trees,* 1963; *Famous Trees of New Zealand,* 1963; *Sahara Conquest: Reforestation,* 1966; *Caravan Story and Country Notes,* 1969; *Famous Trees of Bible Lands,* 1974; *The Tree of Life,* 1977; *Tall Timber,* 1978; several other books and numerous pamphlets. **Contributor** of articles on forestry and desert reclamation to mags. and jrnls.

GALA DALI

Wife, muse, and manager to Salvador Dali
***Born* Kazan, Russia, 1893**
***Died* Pubol, Catalonia, Spain, 10 June 1982**

"It was for her that I had just smeared myself with goat dung and aspic, for her that I had torn my best silk shirt to shreds, and for her that I had bloodied my armpits." So, in *The Secret Life of Salvador Dali,* the Surrealist painter described the outlandish and sinister antics that he performed to attract the attention of Gala Éluard, then the wife of the poet Paul Éluard and later Dali's Venus, Winged Victory, Beatrice, or Gioconda, according to the particular character of his fantasies. Their first meeting, evidently an instance of mutual love at first sight, took place in 1929 at Cadaques on the Costa Brava, where she and Éluard were visiting Dali with a small group of Surrealist artists, including Luis Buñuel. Although at first she found Dali's "Argentine tango slickness" distasteful, her reaction evidently concealed a deeper fascination. Seeking, according to Dali, "the fulfillment of her own myth," she met him on the beach several days later in order to avoid the distractions that caused Dali's fits of uncontrollable laughter and to question him as to whether his marked coprophilia was a Surrealist strategy designed to shock, or a psychopathological condition. During this meeting their peculiar bond was made. Éluard returned to Paris alone several days later.

"She was destined to be . . . my victory, my wife." But, Dali continues, "the beginnings of my sentimental relationship with Gala were marked by permanent character of diseased abnormality." Dali's profoundly exhibitionist nature makes it impossible to separate truth from self-advertisement in his confessions, but his famous pronouncement in his Sorbonne address of 1955, that Gala saved him "from becoming an authentic madman," has a ring of truth. Capable of enduring his infantile delusions and demands for attention, and having an indomitable will of her own, she channeled his energies into lucrative work, serving both as his model and his business manager. Dali paid tribute to her role in bringing a "classic" element to his work, in reconciling the fashion for Surrealism with tradition. He achieved this synthesis, however, in a merely parodic way. Those canvases in which Gala figures as Venus, St. Theresa, or an antique nude are pastiche recollections of the past, not creative assimilations. Nor did Gala succeed in restraining Dali's famous scatological predilections. It seems, rather, that she learned how to put her husband's notoriety to practical use, and won them a fortune by negotiating commissions. She lost this skill only in her final years when, in declining health, she relinquished their financial affairs to the shady ex-football player Enrique Sabater.

Despite her prominence as a model for numerous paintings, and her reputation for intelligence and strong character, Gala's nature remains elusive. Unlike her husband, she was not given to public displays, and many of the basic facts of her biography remain obscure. She was born Elena Deluvina Diakanoff in Kazan, a town on the Volga river. She was a student when she met the poet Éluard in 1913 in a sanatorium near Davos, Switzerland, where he was convalescing; they married, after a long separation, in February 1917, and lived in Paris. Éluard alludes to her, although not by the nickname that he gave her, in many of his lyrical poems, but by 1922, when she is said to have had an affair with Max Ernst, their marriage was probably failing. What became of their child, a daughter, is not recorded. She married Dali in 1935, six years after they first became a couple. In her later years she was Dali's nurse, and, according to some accounts, tyrant. She died at Pubol, Spain, in the twelfth-century castle given to her by her husband. H.B.

Born Elena Deluvina Diakanoff. **Married** (1) Paul Éluard, surrealist poet, 1917 (div.): one daughter. (2) Salvador Dali, surrealist artist, 1935 (church ceremony 1958). **Career** Artist's model to Dali from 1929, later his mgr. as well; appears in many of his paintings.

Further reading Salvador Dali, *The Secret Life of Salvador Dali,* 1961; Robert Decharnes, *The World of Salvador Dali,* 1962.

RAINER WERNER FASSBINDER

Film and play director and producer, scenarist, dramatist, and actor
***Born* Bad Wörishofen, Bavaria, Occupied Germany, 13 February 1946**
(other sources 31 May 1946)
***Died* Munich, West Germany, 10 June 1982**

In the late 1960s, after nearly four decades of decline and mediocrity, the German cinema experienced an unexpected resurgence. This was due largely to a handful of young directors who were promptly designated the German New Wave—although they had little in common, apart from being German. The youngest, most iconoclastic, and most energetically prolific of this group was Rainer Werner Fassbinder.

In his short life, Fassbinder directed over 40 full-length features, most of which he also scripted. He also produced, scripted, and acted in other people's films; produced plays for theater, television, and radio; and composed music and songs. The range of his work was as remarkable as its profusion; he readily adopted any genre or style that suited his purpose, and a highly wrought, intricate, and polished film might be followed by an impulsive sketch of a movie, seemingly dashed off impromptu. Throughout his work, though, certain themes remain constant: personal isolation, the destructiveness of intimate relationships, the social and moral exploitation of one person or class by another. The world he portrays is a cold one, obsessed with power.

Rainer Fassbinder was born in Bad Wörishofen, Bavaria, the only child of middle-class parents, and grew up in Munich, where his father, a doctor, had a practice. His parents' marriage was stormy and unhappy, ending in divorce when Fassbinder was six; the boy went to live with his mother, who took up translating as a profession. In order to work in peace, she generally sent her young son off to the cinema. Fassbinder grew up on a concentrated diet of movies, mainly American.

His more formal education was at the Rudolph Steiner school, followed by various secondary schools in Munich and Augsburg. He disliked them all, and left school with relief at 16, taking a succession of jobs—including decorating and journalism—and applying, unsuccessfully, for admission to the West Berlin Film and Television Academy. The same year, 1965, he shot his first film, a ten-minute short entitled *Der Stadtstreicher,*

Courtesy of German Information Center

followed the next year by another, *Das kleine Chaos.*

After attending a private drama school in Munich (a fellow student was the actress Hanna Schygulla), in 1967 Fassbinder joined one of the city's fringe theatre groups, the Action-Theater, where he acted in, directed, and adapted a number of plays. His first original play, *Katzelmacher,* was premiered there in 1968. Two months later the theater was closed by the city authorities, who were alarmed by its politically subversive tone. Ten members of the group, headed by Fassbinder, promptly formed the Antiteater, and among other works performed his second play, *Preparadise sorry now* (1968). The group lived communally, performing wherever space offered, in bars and disused cinemas.

Besides Fassbinder's plays, the Antiteater performed adaptations of works by Goethe, Jarry, Goldoni, and Sophocles, all radically (in both senses) rewritten. In 1969, they also produced Fassbinder's first full-length films: *Liebe ist kälter als der Tod (Love is Colder than Death), Katzelmacher,* and *Götter der Pest (Gods of the Plague).* All three were bleak, downbeat films, shot through with parody and quirky humor, and showing the diverse influence of Godard, Hollywood gangster B-movies, and the German minimalist director Jean-Marie Straub; all three displayed a thoroughly uncomplimentary view of modern German society. This was particularly true of *Katzelmacher,* based on his earlier play, in which Fassbinder himself played the Greek *Gastarbeiter* whose supposed sexual vigor arouses the violent hatred of his German hosts. Filmed in nine days, the picture won two major German film prizes.

Late in 1969, Fassbinder directed his first color film, *Warum läuft Herr R. Amok? (Why Does Herr R. Run Amok?),* in which a quiet, respectable petit-bourgeois suddenly goes berserk and slaughters his family. This macabre, often very funny satire won him his second Federal Film Prize.

During 1970 Fassbinder made six full-length films. They were a mixed bunch, including a historical allegory, *Die Niklashauser Fahrt;* a racial melodrama set in the American South, *Whity;* and another pastiche of B-movies, *Der Amerikanische Soldat (The American Soldier).* He also made a film about the filming of *Whity, Warnung vor einer heiligen Nutte (Beware of a Holy Whore),* in which he candidly exposed the tensions and intrigues that had threatened to break up his team. That same year he married Ingrid Caven, an Antiteater actress. They were divorced in 1971.

With the winding-up of the Antiteater collective, Fassbinder formed his own production company, Tango-Film, for which, with his stock company of actors, he made most of his subsequent films. *Der Händler der vier Jahreszeiten* (1971; *The Merchant of the Four Seasons)* was shot in 11 days, and was released simultaneously in cinemas and on television, bringing him for the first time to the attention of the general public. The story concerned a recurrent figure in Fassbinder's work: the inarticulate loser, vainly seeking the love he is incapable of inspiring. ("Most people suffer," Fassbinder once commented, "because they are incapable of really expressing their grief.") There followed one of his most stylized, histrionic, and verbose films, *Die bitteren Tränen der Petra von Kant* (1972; *The Bitter Tears of Petra von Kant),* a claustrophobic lesbian melodrama played by an all-female cast on a single elaborate set.

Thanks to the success of *Der Händler,* Fassbinder was commissioned by Westdeutscher Rundfunk to make an eight-episode "popular series" for television about a working-class family in Cologne. *Acht Stunden sind kein Tag* began transmission in mid-1972, and soon aroused controversy over the politically radical messages which Fassbinder skillfully wove into his soap-opera situations. After five 90-minute episodes, the series was dropped.

With *Angst essen Seele auf* (1973; *Ali—Fear Eats the Soul)* Fassbinder achieved international recognition, winning the Critics Prizes at Cannes and Venice, and gaining showings in several countries outside Germany. The film borrowed its plot from the 1955 Hollywood melodrama of cross-class marriage, *All That Heaven Allows,* directed by another major influence on Fassbinder, Douglas Sirk. Fassbinder's reworking introduces a racial twist: his heroine, a dumpy elderly charwoman, marries a handsome young Moroccan *Gastarbeiter.* Uncharacteristically, though, the film has a (relatively) happy ending.

In 1974 he was appointed director of the Theater am Turm in Frankfurt, where he directed some notable productions, while continuing to make films at the rate of three or four a year. *Effi Briest* (1974) proved a surprisingly respectful version of Fontane's classic novel, shot on the generous schedule of 58 days. *Faustrecht der Freiheit* (1974; *Fox and his Friends)* took up the recurrent theme of trust betrayed. Fassbinder himself starred as Fox, the working-class homosexual who wins a lottery and is adopted by the wealthy gay world of Munich, fleeced, and rejected.

Fassbinder's openly declared homosexuality, and his outspokenly left-wing politics, ensured him regular (and frequently hostile) attention from the media. One scandal broke over *Mutter Küsters Fahrt zum Himmel* (1975; *Mother Kusters Goes to Heaven),* turned down by the Berlin Film Festival for fear of political repercussions. A month later, Fassbinder resigned from the Theater am Turm when a play he had written was forbidden production on the grounds of alleged anti-Semitism. He then turned the play into a film script (written "in a state of trance" on a flight from Frankfurt to Los Angeles), which was filmed by the Swiss director Daniel Schmid as *Schatten der Engel* (1976) and shown at the Cannes Festival, causing the Israeli delegation to walk out. And for the second year running, Fassbinder had a film turned down by the Berlin Festival. This time it was *Satansbraten* (1976; *Satan's Brew),* a manic black comedy which the Festival organizers found in excessively bad taste. The enfant terrible himself commented that his films were "not so much provocative, as intended to activate thought processes."

Gradually, the improvisatory air of Fassbinder's earlier output was giving way to a more polished look, with intricate camera movements, and elaborate sets full of glass and mirrors. *Chinesisches Roulette* (1976; *Chinese Roulette)* returned to the hermetic world of *Petra von Kant,* with couples playing lethal power games in a country mansion. For *Despair* (1977) he filmed for the first time in English, and to a script not his own; it was written by the playwright Tom Stoppard, from a novel by Nabokov. Despite a striking performance by Dirk Bogarde, the film was found mannered and empty.

Far more successful, both artistically and financially, was *Die Ehe der Maria Braun* (1978; *The Marriage of Maria Braun),* which borrowed the conventions of a Joan Crawford movie to comment on the postwar history of Germany. It won first prize at the Berlin Festival, was shown widely abroad, and made Hanna Schygulla an international star. *In einem Jahr mit 13 Monden* (1978; *In a Year with 13 Moons)* was a more personal work, inspired by the suicide of Armin Meier, Fassbinder's lover, and expressing a mood of unrelieved desolation. Equally pessimistic, but in a more satirical vein, *Die dritte Generation* (1979; *The Third Generation)* tackled the taboo subject of terrorism.

Following the success of *Maria Braun,* Fassbinder planned a series of films using female protagonists to illuminate recent German history, and completed three: *Lili Marleen* (1980); *Lola* (1981); and *Veronika Voss* (1982), which won the Golden Bear at the Berlin Festival. With increasing budgets, something of his former astringency seemed to be lost; stylization showed signs of becoming kitsch. Fassbinder had also completed *Querelle of Brest,* a treatment of Genet's novel, with Jeanne Moreau, and was working on a new film at the time of his death, which was the result of a lethal combination of cocaine and sleeping pills. It could not be determined whether his death was accidental or deliberate.

In quality, Fassbinder's work was uneven; it could hardly be otherwise. His films could endear and repel, fascinate and bore, often almost simultaneously. The main object, for him, was to provoke a reaction, no matter what. "Art is not so important, anyway," he once said. "The only actuality that matters is in the viewer's head." P.K.

Parents Father a doctor; mother, Liselotte, trans. and sometime actress in Fassbinder's films under names Lilo Pempeit and Liselotte Eder. **Married** Ingrid Caven, actress, 1970 (div. 1971). **Education** Rudolph Steiner Sch., Munich; secondary schs. in Munich and Augsburg, left at age 16; Fridl-Leonhard Drama Studio, Munich ca. 1965–66. **Career** Various jobs as house painter, office worker, journalist 1962–65; actor, Action-Theater, Munich 1967; founding member, actor, dir., and playwright, Antiteater, Munich 1967–70; dir., Theater am Turm, Frankfurt 1974–75. • Film dir. since 1965; founding member, Filmverlag der Autoren film distribution org. 1970; founder, Tango-Film production co. 1971; film actor. **Honors** West German Critics Prize and Federal Film Prize, for *Katzelmacher,* 1969; Federal Film Prize for *Warum läuft Herr R. Amok?,* 1970; Critics Prizes, Cannes and Venice Film Festivals, for *Angst essen Seele auf,* 1974; Silver Bear of the Berlin Film Festival, Federal Film Prize, and David di Donatello Luchino Visconti Award, all for *Die Ehe der Maria Braun,* 1979; Golden Bear, for *Veronika Voss,* Berlin Film Festival 1982. **Film and television director** (also scenarist except as noted) *Der Stadtstreicher* (short), 1965; *Das kleine Chaos* (short), 1966; *Liebe ist kälter als der Tod* (rel. as *Love Is Colder than Death),* 1969; *Katzelmacher,* 1969; *Götter der pest* (rel. as *Gods of the Plague),* 1969; *Warum läuft Herr R. Amok?* (rel. as *Why Does Herr R. Run Amok?),* 1969; *Rio das Mortes,* 1970; *Whity,* 1970; *Die Niklashauser Fahrt,* 1970; *Der Amerikanische Soldat* (rel. as *The American Soldier),* 1970; *Warnung vor einer heiligen Nutte* (rel. as *Beware of a Holy Whore),* 1970; *Das Kaffeehaus,* 1970; *Pioniere in Ingolstadt* (rel. as *Recruits in Ingolstadt),* 1970; *Händler der vier Jahreszeiten* (rel. as *The Merchant of Four Seasons),* 1971; *Die bitteren Tränen der Petra von Kant* (rel. as *The Bitter Tears of Petra von Kant),* 1972; *Wildwechsel* (rel. as *Jail Bait*), 1972; *Acht Stunden sind kein Tag,* 1972; *Bremer Freiheit* (rel. as *Bremen Coffee),* 1972; *Welt am Draht,* 1973; *Angst essen Seele auf* (rel. as *Ali—Fear Eats the Soul),* 1973; *Martha,* 1973; *Nora Helmer,* 1973; *Fontane Effi Briest* (rel. as *Effi Briest),* 1974; *Wie ein Vogel auf dem Draht,* 1975; *Ich will doch nur, dass ihr mich liebt,* 1975; *Faustrecht der Freiheit* (rel. as *Fist-Right of Freedom* and as *Fox and his Friends),* 1975; *Mutter Küsters Fahrt zum Himmel* (rel. as

Mother Kusters Goes to Heaven), 1975; *Angst vor der Angst* (rel. as *Fear of Fear),* 1975; *Satansbraten* (rel. as *Satan's Brew),* 1976; *Chinesisches Roulette* (rel. as *Chinese Roulette),* 1976; *Die Frauen in New York,* 1977; *Bolweiser* (rel. as *The Stationmaster's Wife),* 1977; (dir. only) *Despair,* 1978; (dir. only) *Die Ehe der Maria Braun* (rel. as *The Marriage of Maria Braun),* 1978; *In einem Jahr mit 13 Monden* (rel. as *In a Year with 13 Moons),* 1978; (contributor) *Deutschland im Herbst,* 1978; (dir. only) *Die dritte Generation* (rel. as *The Third Generation),* 1979; (dir. only) *Berlin Alexanderplatz,* 1979; *Lili Marleen,* 1980; *Lola,* 1981; *Veronika Voss,* 1982; *Querelle of Brest,* 1982. **Scriptwriter** *Fernes Jamaica,* 1969; *Schatten der Engel,* 1976. **Film actor** *Tony Freunde,* 1967; *Der Bräutigam, die Komödiantin und der Zuhalter,* 1968; *Alarm,* 1969; *Al Capone im deutschen Wald,* 1969; *Baal,* 1969; *Frei bis zum nächsten Mal,* 1969; *Matthias Kneissl,* 1970; *Der plötzliche Reichtum der armen Leute von Kombach,* 1970; *Supergirl,* 1970; *Zärlichkeit der Wölfe,* 1973; *1 Berlin Harlem,* 1974; *Schatten der Engel,* 1976; *Kamikaze* (to be released); also appeared in many of his own films. **Dramatist** *Katzelmacher,* 1968; *Preparadise Sorry Now,* 1969; *Anarchie in Bayern,* 1969; *Werwolf,* 1969; *Blut am Hals der Katze,* 1971; *Die bitteren Tränen der Petra von Kant,* 1971; *Der Müll, die Stadt und der Tod,* 1974; adaptations of classic plays for avant-garde productions.

Further reading Tony Rayns, ed., *Fassbinder,* 1980; John Sandford, *The New German Cinema,* 1980; Peter Iden, ed., *Fassbinder,* 1981.

KARL (RITTER) von FRISCH
Ethologist
Born **Vienna, Austria-Hungary, 20 November 1886**
Died **Munich, West Germany, 12 June 1982**

Karl von Frisch, the 1973 Nobel laureate in physiology or medicine, devoted his scientific career to the study of animal behavior—the field now known as ethology. His painstaking investigations into the physiological bases of worm, insect, and fish behavior earned him a reputation as possibly the greatest experimental zoologist of his time. He is best known for his discovery of the complex dance language of bees and his thorough elucidation of their social behavior. "The life of bees is like a magic well," he said. "The more you draw from it, the more there is to draw."

Von Frisch was the son of a Viennese urologist. Medicine and scholarship were family traditions. He was tutored at home for a time and received a classical education at Catholic schools, but from his earliest years his main interest was in observing animals. By the time he was in his teens, his room in Vienna was crammed with 125 species of animals, and he had begun a collection of the local fauna near the family's summer home at Brunnwinkl that would later number over 5,000 specimens.

In 1905, at the urging of his father, von Frisch entered the University of Vienna to study medicine. Although he did well, his consuming passion remained zoology, and in 1908 he enrolled in Munich's Zoological Institute, headed by Richard Hertwig, who set him to work observing the behavior of solitary bees. From this sprang his lifelong fascination with bees and bee societies. For his doctoral thesis von Frisch investigated the ability of minnows to mimic the color of their surroundings. He received his degree in 1910 and was hired as a laboratory and teaching assistant.

Von Frisch soon became involved in his first scientific controversy. His opponent was Carl von Hess, director of the Munich Eye Clinic, who had concluded that fish and all invertebrates are color-blind. Von Frisch, using Pavlovian methods, trained fish to respond to colored objects, proving that they do see color as well as brightness. The work earned him a post as privatdozent, the first rung on the German academic ladder. Von Hess's refusal to admit defeat provoked von Frisch to conduct his first experiments on the visual abilities of honeybees, which he carried out at Brunnwinkl in the summer of 1912. Reasoning that the bright colors of flowers attract pollinating insects, he conditioned the bees to feed from dishes of sugar water placed on cardboard squares of a particular color. The bees soon responded to squares of that color and no other, even if the dishes contained no food. In 1914 he gave a public demonstration of this at a meeting of the German Zoological Society, conclusively proving his point.

Von Frisch was invalided out of the German Army because of his weak eyes in 1914. During World War I he worked at a military hospital in Vienna, where his brother Otto was superintendent, taking x-rays, administering anesthesia, and setting up a bacteriological laboratory. In 1917 he married and spent most of his honeymoon conducting experiments on bees.

Back in Munich after the war, von Frisch studied honeybees' sense of smell and found that their olfactory receptors are located on their antennae. In the course of his research, he noted how quickly the hive would congregate around a new food source after its discovery by a bee, and began to suspect that bees could communicate with each other. Closely observing the return of one bee to the hive from a nearby food dish, he made what he later called "the most far-reaching observation of my life." The bee performed a "round dance" on the honeycomb, at which the bees nearby became excited and flew out directly to the source of food. Von Frisch later proved that the scent of a visited flower clings to the body of a dancing bee, indicating to the audience what kind of flower to seek, and that the sweeter the food source, the more vigorous the bee's dance. His 1924 report on the subject before a German professional society was one of the first such lectures to make use of a film for documentation.

After teaching at Rostock and Breslau universities, von Frisch returned to Munich in 1925 to replace Richard Hertwig at the Zoological Institute. The zoology students were soon busy studying the vision and hearing of fish, while von Frisch embarked on a long and tedious investigation of bees' sense of taste. In 1927 he published *On the Life of Bees,* the first of his popular-science books. An English translation, *The Dancing Bees,* appeared in 1954.

As director of the institute from 1925 to 1946, von Frisch entered into negotiations with the Rockefeller Foundation of New York to obtain funding for more spacious quarters. While on a lecture tour of the United States in 1930 he learned that his application had been accepted. In the fall of 1932 he opened the new Munich Zoological Institute, the most advanced research facility of its kind in Europe. But the climate for scientific research had deteriorated. Many of the best scientists were being hounded out of Germany by the Nazis, and their jobs awarded to paid informers and political appointees. Those qualified scientists who remained carried out their research in growing isolation from their colleagues abroad and under the constant scrutiny of Nazi ideologues.

Von Frisch's *You and Life* (1936), a popular natural history and comparative physiology text for the general reader, reflects to some extent the racist attitudes of the time and place. In the book's concluding section, he expressed concern at the dangers posed to the genetic future of the human species by such problems as miscegenation and the survival and breeding of the mentally deficient. The solution he offered was a program of state-controlled human breeding. However, unlike many of his contemporaries, such as Konrad Lorenz, von Frisch raised the issue of human rights in his discussion of sterilization. So balanced was his treatment that relatively few revisions were required in postwar editions of the book. (An English translation, *About Biology,* appeared in 1962.)

In 1941 the authorities threatened von Frisch with dismissal after it was discovered that his mother's mother, though baptized, was of Jewish descent. (Von Frisch remarks in his autobiography that "the mixture was a good one.") He was able to keep his job through string-pulling by influential friends and because his services were needed to combat an epidemic disease then raging among honey-producing bees. His house and the institute were severely damaged in 1944 when Munich came under heavy bombardment by the Allies, and he removed to Brunnwinkl, taking half his staff.

At Brunnwinkl, von Frisch deduced the meaning of the bees' tail-wagging dance, which he had previously misinterpreted. Whereas the round dance informs a bee's hivemates that there is food somewhere nearby, the tail-wagging dance indicates the precise location of a faraway food source. The tempo of the dance gives the flight distance to the food. The bees revealed a number of unexpected abilities in their method of indicating the food's direction. Bees, von Frisch demonstrated, steer by the sun: in the course of flying to a food source, a bee "memorizes" the angle between her line of flight and the sun's position in the sky. On returning to the hive, the communicating bee, dancing on a vertical surface, reports the angular direction of the food source to her hivemates by referring to the direction of gravity: if the source is 45° to the left of the sun, the bee dances at a 45° angle to the left of vertical. The other bees then fly without hesitation to the waiting flowers or food dish.

Von Frisch reported these findings in 1946, soon after taking a post as professor of zoology in Graz, Austria. The scientific community, unwilling to believe that bees could communicate symbolically, greeted his results with skepticism. In 1948, W. H. Thorpe of Cambridge University visited Brunnwinkl to repeat the experiments and concluded that they were sound and that the astonishing results were correct. A year later, von Frisch demonstrated that bees can orient themselves correctly by observing the polarized light of the blue sky, even when the sun is hidden from view. That year he went on his second tour of the United States. His English-language lectures were published in 1950 under the title *Bees: Their Vision, Chemical Sense, and Language.*

Von Frisch returned to the University of Munich in 1950; he was made emeritus professor of zoology in 1958. In 1965, he published *The Dance Language and Orientation of Bees,* an encyclopedic summary of his research, detailing the social behavior and communication of bees with instructive comparisons to other social insects. Reviewing the book, sociobiologist Edward O. Wilson wrote that it would "surely take its place in the tiny group of genuine classics of scientific literature." Von Frisch's many students, including Martin Lindauer and others, carried on his experiments, making Germany the leading postwar center for the study of sensory physiology and behavior in insects.

Courtesy of German Information Center

In 1973, von Frisch, together with fellow ethologists Konrad Lorenz and Nikolaas Tinbergen, received the Nobel Prize in physiology or medicine, the first time that the award was given to behavioral scientists. At 86, von Frisch was the second oldest person to receive the prize. He was also the recipient of the prestigious Magellan Prize of the American Philosophical Society, the Orden "Pour le Mérite" of Germany, and the Balzan Prize in Biology. He continued to live in retirement in Munich, revising his previous books and coauthoring *Animal Architecture* with his son Otto. He died there at the age of 95. P.D.

Parents Anton Ritter von F., surgeon and urologist, and Marie (Exner) von F. **Married** Margarethe Mohr, nurse and artist, 1917: Johanna Schreiner; Maria; Helen Pflueger; Otto, biologist. **Religion** Roman Catholic by birth; later agnostic. **Education** Private tutoring; Piarist convent sch., Schottengymnasium, Vienna; medical sch., Univ. of Venice ca. 1905–07; Univ. of Munich, Ph.D. 1910; Biological Inst. for Marine Research, Trieste. **Mil. service** Medical researcher and asst., Army hosp., WWI. **Career** With Univ. of Munich: asst., Zoological Inst. 1910–12; privatdozent 1912–14; asst. prof. 1919–21; dir. of Zoological Inst. 1925–46; prof. of zoology 1925–46 and 1950–58; prof. emeritus since 1958. • Prof. of zoology and dir. of Zoological Inst., Univ. of Rostock 1921–23; prof. of zoology, Univ. of Breslau 1923–25; prof. of zoology, Univ. of Graz, Austria 1946–50. **Member** (Foreign member) Royal Soc., London; Linnaean Soc.; acads. of science of Washington, Boston, Munich, Vienna, Göttingen, Uppsala, and Stockholm. **Honors** Magellan Prize, Amer. Philosophical Soc. 1956; Kalinga Prize, UNESCO 1959; (jtly.) Nobel Prize in physiology or medicine 1973;

Orden "Pour le Mérite," Germany; Balzan Prize for Biology; hon. member, Royal Entomological Soc.; hon. member, Amer. Physiological Soc.; hon. degrees from univs. of Bern, Graz, Rostock, Harvard, and from Technische Hochschule, Zurich. **Author** *Sechs Vorträge über Bakteriologie für Krankenschwestern* [*Six Lectures on Bacteriology for Nurses*], 1918; *Aus dem Leben der Bienen,* 1927 (trans. as *The Dancing Bees,* 1954); *Du und das Leben: Eine Moderne Biologie für Jedermann,* 1936 (trans. as *About Biology,* 1962, and as *Man and the Living World,* 1963); *Duftgelenkte Bienen im Dienst der Landwirtschaft un Imkerei* [*Use of the Bee's Sense of Smell in Agriculture and Beekeeping*], 1947; *Zehn kleine Hausgenossen,* 1940 (trans. as *Ten Little Housemates,* 1960); *Bees: Their Vision, Chemical Senses, and Language,* 1950, rev. ed. 1971; *Biologie* (juvenile), 1953 (trans. as *Biology,* 1964); *Bienenfibel* [*A Guide to Bees*], 1954; *Sprach und Orientierung der Bienen* [*Language and Orientation of Bees*], 1961; *Das kleine Insektenbuch* [*The Little Insect Book*], 1961; *Erinnerungen eines Biologen,* 1962 (trans. as *A Biologist Remembers,* 1967); *Tanzsprach und Orientierung der Bienen,* 1965 (trans. as *The Dance Language and Orientation of Bees,* 1967); (jtly.) *Tiere als Baumeister,* 1974 (trans. as *Animal Architecture,* 1974); *Zwölf kleine Hausgenossen,* 1976 (trans. as *Twelve Little Housemates,* 1978). **Contributor** of more than 100 papers on animal behavior and physiology to scientific jrnls.

Further reading E. O. Wilson, "Karl von Frisch and the Magic Well," in *Science,* 23 Feb. 1968; W. H. Thorpe, "The Nesting Instinct," in *Times Literary Supplement,* 3 Oct. 1975.

MARIE RAMBERT

Founder and director of Ballet Rambert

***Born* Warsaw, Poland, 20 February 1888**

***Died* London, England, 12 June 1982**

The establishment of the art of ballet in Britain was principally the work of two women: Dame Ninette de Valois, the founder of the Royal Ballet, and Dame Marie Rambert, the founder of the less well-known but more influential Ballet Rambert. This small but dynamic company produced virtually all the best choreographers, dancers, and designers in the country, and is now the oldest ballet troupe performing there.

Rambert was the daughter of a Warsaw bookseller; the family name of Rambam was later changed to Ramberg, with Rambert a modification for the stage. As a young woman she was involved in the anticzarist revolutionary movement and was sent off to Paris to keep her out of trouble. She enrolled as a literature student at the Sorbonne, and, inspired by the dancing of Isadora Duncan, began to take dance lessons as well. In 1910 she entered Émile Jaques-Dalcroze's famous Institute for Applied Rhythm in Geneva, and the following year was asked to join the faculty.

When, in 1912, Vaslav Nijinsky was encountering difficulties in choreographing Igor Stravinsky's *The Rite of Spring* for the Ballets Russes in Paris, Rambert was recommended to him as an assistant. She trained the dancers in the Dalcroze method for six months, meanwhile studying with the ballet master Enrico Cecchetti, and danced in the corps de ballet herself on opening night in 1913, when the audience rioted. From 1914 to 1920 she was a dance student, eurhythmics teacher, and occasional performer and choreographer in London, where in 1918 she married the playwright and critic Ashley Dukes.

Rambert was a skilled dancer with good technique, but she had taken up the study of dance too late in life—her twenties—to achieve real excellence, and decided instead to open a school. In 1920 she accepted the first pupils of the Rambert School of Ballet, which offered a strictly classical course of training. By 1926 she had developed a company, the Marie Rambert Dancers. Both organizations moved in 1930 to a permanent home in the

Mercury Theatre, a converted church hall in the Notting Hill Gate neighborhood, and were jointly named the Ballet Club.

The death in 1929 of Serge Diaghilev, who had introduced the Russian ballet to England, left the fledgling dance world there in confusion. The Rambert company quickly emerged, in the description of the critic Alexander Bland, as a kind of hothouse dance nursery where fresh talent was forced into full bloom. Rambert, exercising her intuition for potential greatness, supervised the early attempts at choreography of Antony Tudor, Frederick Ashton, Andrée Howard, Walter Gore, and Frank Staff. Harold Turner and Sally Gilmour were among the many outstanding dancers she trained, and Sophie Fedorovich among the designers.

The company had practically no money, and all its members doubled as secretaries, prop makers, and costumers, as necessary; many had to take outside jobs in order to live. They were nonetheless kept at a fever pitch of creativity by the ferociously energetic Rambert, who, though barely five feet tall, could tyrannize in any one of six languages. Given the limitations of budget and space—the stage of the Mercury Theatre was a mere 18 feet square, its auditorium seated only 150—Ballet Rambert (as it was renamed in 1934) specialized in the production of "chamber ballets" that were finely polished gems of ensemble dancing.

The golden age of Ballet Rambert came to an end with World War II. The group finally outgrew its quarters and had to disband temporarily; it was revived by a grant from the Council for the Encouragement of Music and the Arts, predecessor of the Arts Council. Although it performed in military camps and the provinces with CEMA support, undertook full-length versions of *Giselle* and other classical ballets in order to attract new audiences, and went on a triumphant tour of Australia and New Zealand in 1948–49, it could not compete with the larger and more heavily subsidized companies, and suffered the defections of some of its best dancers and choreographers. In 1966, Rambert, with the help of choreographer Norman Morrice, reorganized Ballet Rambert into something resembling what it had been in the beginning, a small troupe dedicated to creating new and adventurous works, though now with the added influence of modern dance.

Rambert turned over the administration of Ballet Rambert to a team of directors in the mid-1970s, but remained its guiding spirit and chief fund raiser. In her old age, when she was respectfully admired as the grande dame of the British ballet, she continued to take dance classes and to practice at the barre. She was made Dame Commander of the British Empire in 1962 and published her autobiography, *Quicksilver,* in 1972. Both her daughters became dancers. She outlived her husband by 23 years, dying at the age of 94 of a stroke.

Courtesy of Ballet Rambert

J.P.

Born Cyvia Rambam; known as Myriam Ramberg (also spelled Rambach) in childhood; took professional name Marie Rambert 1913. **Parents** Yakov Ramberg (formerly Rambam), bookseller, and Yevguenia Alapina R. **Married** Ashley Dukes, playwright, 1918 (d. 1959): Angela Ellis, dancer, b. 1920; Helen, dancer, b. 1923. **Emigrated** to U.K.; naturalized 1918. **Education** Russian State Sch., Warsaw, grad. 1904; Sorbonne, Paris 1905–ca. 1910; Paris Opéra Ballet Sch.; with Émile Jaques-Dalcroze's Inst. for Applied Rhythm, Geneva 1910–13; with ballet instrs. Enrico Cecchetti in Paris 1912–13 and London late 1910s, Margaret Craske in London late 1910s, and Serafina Astafieva ca. 1915–17. **Career** Teacher of Dalcroze Eurhythmics at Dalcroze schs. in Geneva and Dresden ca. 1912 and with Serge Diaghilev's Ballet Russes, Paris 1912–13; asst. to Vaslav Nijinsky and member of corps de ballet, Ballets Russes 1912–13; solo dancer and choreographer 1913–20; teacher, London Sch. of Eurhythmics, and private dancing teacher, London ca. 1914–20. • Founder 1920 and dir., Rambert Sch. of Ballet, London; founder 1926 and dir., Marie Rambert Dancers, London; founder, Ballet Club, encompassing both sch. and dance co., 1931, group renamed Ballet Rambert 1934; dir. of Ballet Rambert 1934–41 and 1943–mid-1970s; dir., Mercury Theatre Trust Ltd. • Co-founder, Camargo Soc., London 1930; radio and TV personality. **Fellow** Royal Soc. of Arts 1963; (also v.p. 1962) Royal Acad. of Dancing. **Member** Grand council, Imperial Soc. of Teachers of Dancing. **Honors** CBE 1953; Queen Elizabeth II Coronation Award, Royal Acad. of Dancing 1956; chevalier, Légion d'Honneur, France 1957; diploma of associateship, Coll. of Art, Manchester 1960; DBE 1962; Jubilee Medal 1977; award, Composers Guild of Great Britain 1978; gold medal, Order of Merit, Poland 1979; hon. degree from Univ. of Sussex. **Author** (Trans.) M. I. Sizova, *Ulanova: Her Childhood and Schooldays,* 1962; *Quicksilver: An Autobiography,* 1972.

Further reading Lionel Bradley, *Sixteen Years of Ballet Rambert,* 1946; Mary Clarke, *Dancers of Mercury: The Story of Ballet Rambert,* 1962; Anya Sainsburg et al., eds., *Fifty Years of Ballet Rambert, 1926–76,* 1976.

KHALID IBN ABDUL AZIZ AL-SAUD
King of Saudi Arabia
Born **Riyadh, Arabia, 1914**
Died **Taif, Saudi Arabia, 13 June 1982**

Khalid, the fourth member of the House of Saud to be king of Saudi Arabia, died suddenly of a heart attack one day after arriving at his summer palace in Taif, in the mountains east of Mecca. He was a conservative member

of a generally conservative dynasty, yet few from outside the family were able to identify him with any particular policies, so unified a front did the rulers of the kingdom present to the outside world. He was immediately succeeded by his half brother, Crown Prince Fahd, and in accordance with custom was buried the same day.

Khalid was the son of Abdul Aziz, who later took the name Ibn Saud. The territory around Riyadh, his birthplace, had just been conquered by his father in his drive to unify the poor and desolate country, which for centuries had been inhabited by many mutually hostile tribes. Ibn Saud succeeded in his goal by the mid-1920s; by means of a carefully arranged series of perhaps as many as 300 dynastic marriages, which resulted in about 40 sons to carry on his rule, he was able to bring the country into the modern age as a single nation. He established the sacred Islamic law, the Sharia, as the paramount law of the land, and so it continues to this day, along with most of the other features of his theocentric monarchy.

Khalid was educated along with his brothers in a manner befitting a desert prince. Religious scholars took him through a complete study of the Koran and the conservative religious and social precepts of the Wahhabi sect, while he also acquired proficiency in martial combat and in the Arab sports of camel racing and falconry, which remained consuming passions for the rest of his life. From earliest childhood he was especially close to his half brother Faisal, and once they were of age their father sent them together on several foreign missions. Each was once the leader of the Saudi delegation to the United Nations. In 1958, when Faisal was named to the post of prime minister, Khalid became his chief advisor, and Khalid's support was crucial in March 1964 when the family decided to depose King Saud, Ibn Saud's eldest son and first successor, for incompetence and waste. When Faisal became king, he immediately named Khalid as crown prince, as Khalid's elder brother Muhammad had abandoned his right to succeed based on seniority. Faisal was a great success as king—vigorous, intelligent, and able to command the loyalty of the tribes—but dissent within the royal family was impossible to subdue completely. On 25 March 1975, a disgruntled nephew, Prince Faisal ibn Masaid, shot and killed the king during a public audience. Khalid succeeded, named his half brother Fahd as crown prince, and as one of his first acts, once the absence of a conspiracy was proved in his brother's murder, ordered the assassin beheaded.

In government, Khalid proved somewhat less rigid in his conservatism than his brother had been, promoting his country as a moderate force in the Arab world and as a mediator in the many disputes between his neighbors. As to Israel, however, he nearly equaled any Arab leader in the fanaticism of his opposition, never deviating in the slightest from his hard-line stand despite years of expensive persuasion by several Western nations, particularly the United States. In March 1979, Khalid broke relations with his former moderate ally, Pres. Anwar Sadat, when Egypt signed a peace treaty with Israel. In national defense matters Khalid's reign produced some notable successes: in May 1978 the United States sold Saudi Arabia 60 F-15 jet fighters, the most modern warplanes in the world, and in 1981 the Reagan administration pushed through Congress an $8.5-billion sale of advanced military equipment which included five airborne warning and control system planes, or AWACS, which represent the state of the art in radar technology. Although the official explanations from both countries stressed the Saudis' need for modern arms to counter "Communist expansion" in the Middle East, everyone knew that the big ultimate loser in the deals could well be Israel.

By far the most serious event in Khalid's reign—indeed, the gravest threat to the Saudi monarchy since its creation—came on 20 November 1979, when a group of several hundred heavily armed Bedouins seized the Grand Mosque in Mecca and held it for more than a week against repeated assaults by the Saudi army. Although the gravity of the seizure was not appreciated in the West, throughout Islam it was clearly perceived as a political and moral challenge to the worthiness of the House of Saud to continue as guardian of Islam's holiest shrines. The revolt was punished in typical Saudi style: in early January 1980 all the 63 survivors, having been quickly tried and convicted of treason and sacrilege, were publicly beheaded in eight cities around the country.

Prince Khalid had first begun to show signs of heart trouble in 1970, and underwent open-heart surgery in Cleveland, Ohio, in 1972 and again in 1978. He was also afflicted with a particularly severe form of degenerative osteoarthritis. His private plane reportedly had a fully equipped operating room, and he was followed by an extensive medical retinue in all his travels, even on his month-long visits to the desert tribes, when, as his father had done before him, he would hunt the oryx and gazelle and officiate at camel races.

He took more foreign trips as king than all his predecessors combined, making state visits to West Germany, Spain, France, and most notably to Britain, where, to the consternation of many, he was showered with almost every imaginable honor. This dearly bought friendship was severely tested by the distribution in the West of an anti-Saudi film made in Britain. Called *Death of a Princess,* it described the beheading of a Saudi royal princess for adultery with a commoner, and also purported to describe the sordid life in the royal harem in Riyadh. Britain abjectly apologized for the affair, but Arab royal tempers were scarcely cooled.

Khalid's successor, King Fahd, who also has serious health problems, is generally regarded as belonging to a somewhat more liberal, more Westernized, branch of the family. It was he who, in the mid-1970s, along with some relatives, lost some $6 million at the gambling tables in Monte Carlo, which earned him a stern rebuke from the king. Fahd is also master of several European languages (Khalid spoke only Arabic) and is reportedly fond of lengthy holidays at his opulent palace in

Spain. Fahd's half brother Abdullah, one of the most conservative and un-Westernized members of the family, was named crown prince under orders of the family council.

A.K.

Parents Abdul Aziz Ibn Saud, founder and king of Saudi Arabia, and Aljoharah Bint Mousaaid. **Married** 1919; eight children. **Religion** Muslim. **Education** Private tutoring in religion and traditional Bedouin skills, sports, and martial arts. **Career** Viceroy of Hejaz 1932; asst. to his brother Prince Faisal 1934–ca. 62; interior minister 1934–40s; Saudi rep. to various intl. conferences 1930s–50s; occasional Saudi rep. to U.N. 1940s–50s; v.p., council of ministers 1962–75; deputy prime minister 1964; crown prince 1965–75; minister of foreign affairs 1975; king of Saudi Arabia and pres. of council of ministers since 1975. **Honors** U.N. Gold Medal for Peace 1977; many other intl. honors and awards.

Further reading David Holden, "A Family Affair," in *New York Times Magazine,* 6 July 1975; David Holden, *The House of Saud,* 1981; Robert Lacey, *The Family,* 1981.

ART(HUR EDWARD) PEPPER
Jazz saxophonist
***Born* Gardena, California, USA, 1 September 1925**
***Died* Panorama City, California, USA, 15 June 1982**

Art Pepper was a musician of great style and originality whose long drug addiction and consequent prison terms did not prevent him from being one of the most admired saxophonists of modern jazz. Unlike many of his contemporaries, he came to take his status very seriously, and at the close of his career was convinced that he was the best jazz artist in the world. "I'll be like Trane [John Coltrane]," he said in 1977. "There was Pres [Lester Young], then Bird [Charlie Parker], and then Trane. And then there's going to be Pepper. I've felt that way all my life. I've never doubted it."

He had an unhappy, fearful, and loveless childhood, admiring only his father, a brutal seaman whom he rarely saw, and hardly knowing his dissolute mother, who refused to keep him with her. He was brought up by his paternal grandmother, a cold and distant woman by his description, who nevertheless paid for his clarinet lessons from the time he was nine. By the age of 12 he had switched to the alto saxophone, and by 16 had begun jamming in the fast-paced jazz scene on Central Avenue in the black ghetto of Los Angeles. His fellow players at that time—Dexter Gordon, Charlie Mingus, Joe Mondragon, and others—were soon to become well known as pioneers of modern jazz. Pepper joined a band led by the drummer Lee Young, Lester Young's brother, then played for a while as the only white musician in Benny Carter's big band, but had to quit in 1943 when the band went on a tour of the South, where interracial groups were not accepted. He always claimed that this was his first exposure to racial prejudice. He then played for three months with Stan Kenton's orchestra before being drafted into the Army, where he served for two years. He rejoined the Kenton orchestra after the war and played with them for the next five years, during which time he established himself as one of the leading saxophonists of post-bebop jazz, with a swinging style and a distinctively smooth cool tone, a sophisticated melodic understanding, and a thorough grasp of jazz technique and idiom. In a famous poll in *Downbeat* magazine in 1951, he received only 16 fewer votes than Charlie Parker for best alto saxophonist.

Pepper discovered heroin in 1950 and became hooked almost immediately. A highly promising solo career with his own band was just beginning, but his addiction fed his self-destructiveness, and in 1953 he was arrested for the first time. For the next 15 years he was in and out of institutions, including the Los Angeles County Jail, the U.S. Public Health Service Hospital in Fort Worth, Texas, and

San Quentin, perhaps the most notorious of American prisons. Finally, in 1969, after suffering a ruptured spleen as a result of drug use, he entered Synanon, the California center for drug-addiction cures, and there he was able at last to kick his habit. At Synanon, he met his third wife, Laurie Miller, a reformed junkie like himself. (His previous marriages had been disastrous failures.) She became his manager, confidante, and complete helpmate, and gave him the selfless love he had been seeking all his life. She was also the editor of his scathingly honest oral life story, *Straight Talk* (1979).

His comeback, beginning in 1975, was a great success. Although he had not played seriously for many years, his famous tone and technique seemed more brilliant and moving than ever. He was invited to conduct a clarinet clinic at the University of Denver, and spent a year with Don Ellis's band, a demanding and confidence-building experience. He recorded extensively and toured widely with his own group, always under his wife's watchful eye, and was highly praised wherever he went: in Europe, Japan, and even New York, where he had not played since the 1950s. "If I can last till I'm 65," he said in 1977, "there's no question that I'll be the new voice. I'll be *the* person—the first time a white guy has been the inspiration for the whole jazz world." He died at 56, after lingering for days in a coma following a series of massive strokes, a few weeks before he was scheduled to play Carnegie Hall as part of the Kool Jazz Festival.

A.K.

Father a seaman. **Married** (1) . . . (div.). (2) Diane (div.). (3) Laurie Miller: Patricia. **Education** Clarinet lessons from age 9, alto saxophone lessons from age 12. **Mil. service** U.S. Army 1944–45. **Career** Entered L.A. jazz world at age 16; with Gus Arnheim's big band 1942; with bands of Lee Young, Benny Carter, and Stan Kenton 1943; with Stan Kenton 1947–52, Earle Spencer's group 1949, Innovations in Modern Music group 1950–51; led combo on West Coast 1952. • Began recording 1952; frequent prison terms for drug possession 1953–68, including 1961–66 in San Quentin; with Lighthouse All-Stars 1956, led quintet 1959–60, with Buddy Rich band late 1960s; in Synanon detoxification program, CA 1969–72; worked in bakery and other nonmusical jobs 1972–75; teacher in clarinet clinic at Univ. of Denver 1975; with Don Ellis group 1976–77; toured Europe and Japan and played jazz festivals in U.S. late 1970s–early 80s. **Albums** *The Art Pepper Quartet; Art Pepper Meets the Rhythm Section; Art Pepper Plus Eleven; Intensity; Gettin' Together; Modern Jazz Classics; Surf Ride; Living Legend; The Omega Man; Smack Up; The Early Show; The Late Show; Discoveries; Early Art; The Way It Was; The Trip; Black California; Two Altos; Art Pepper with the Sonny Clark Trio; The Art Pepper Quintet; The Artistry of Pepper; The Return of Art Pepper; Pepper Pot; Like Wow; Modern Art; Buddy DeFranco/Art Pepper;* (with Chet Baker) *Playboys;* (with Bill Perkins and Richie Kamuca) *Just Friends;* also played on albums by Stan Kenton, Shorty Rogers, Shelly Manne, Howard Incraft, Henry Mancini, Marty Paich, Miles Davis, others. **Author** *Straight Talk* (autobiography), 1979.

Further reading Gary Giddins, "Art Pepper: The Whiteness of the Wail," in *Village Voice,* 4 July 1977.

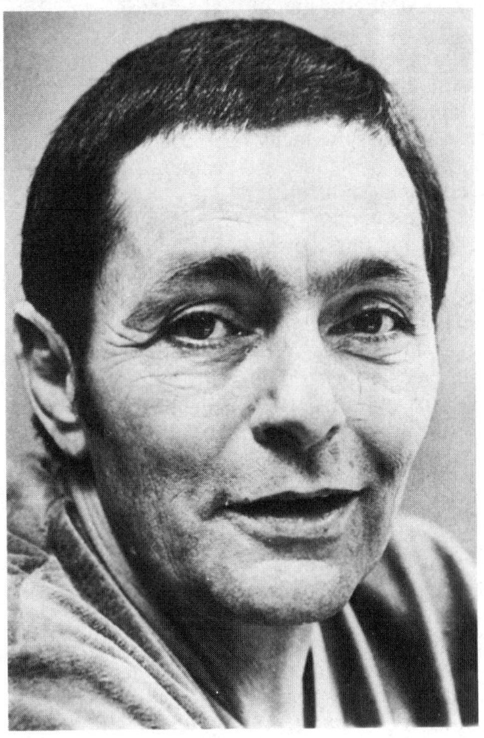

ROBERT J(OSEPH) KIBBEE
Chancellor of the City University of New York
***Born* New York City, USA, 19 August 1921**
***Died* New York City, USA, 16 June 1982**

City University of New York, the third largest university in the United States, was established in 1961 to administer the city's vast system of colleges and community colleges. Its chief mission, inherited from its oldest institution, City College (founded in 1897), is to make higher education available to the city's poor, many of whom are immigrants or the children of immigrants. As New York's population changed in the postwar years, with Jews, Italians, and other European ethnic groups moving out to the suburbs, and blacks, Hispanics, and Asians moving in, the university was called on to serve students whose educational needs could no longer be met by traditional college programs. In 1970 CUNY adopted an "open admissions" policy by which all graduates of the city's high schools, no matter how well or ill prepared, were guaranteed a place in one of its colleges. The chancellor of the university during the difficult period of adjustment that followed was Robert J. Kibbee, a career administrator with little experience in public urban education but with the imperturbable coolness and gift for diplomacy necessary to keep the system functioning despite faculty demoralization, radical student violence, government interference, and fiscal disaster.

The son of movie actor Guy Kibbee, he was born and raised on Staten Island, a borough of New York City, and was educated in Catholic schools and at Fordham University. He served with an antiaircraft unit in New Guinea and the Philippines during World War II, then earned a master's degree in educational administration from the University of Chicago, after which he was appointed dean of a small state college in Arkansas. From 1955 to 1958 he was dean of students at Drake University in Iowa. In 1957 he received his Ph.D. from the University of Chicago and the next year went to Pakistan to assist the government in reorganizing and modernizing the country's schools.

Kibbee joined the administrative staff of the Carnegie Institute of Technology in Pittsburgh in 1961 and as vice president for planning helped to oversee its merger with Mellon University in 1965. Just prior to his appointment to the chancellorship of CUNY he had a year's apprenticeship in the politics of urban education management as head of Pittsburgh's Board of Education, which was then undergoing a desegregation crisis and the unionization of its teachers.

Courtesy of City University of New York

Kibbee took over at CUNY in 1971. Open admissions had begun the previous year with a freshman class of 35,000, of whom half needed remedial reading and math. (The total student population in 1981 was about 200,000.) During the New York City budget crisis of 1975–76, the university lost millions of dollars of government funding. In addition to firing 5,000 employees, including 2,000 teachers, and closing the university for two weeks, Kibbee agreed to impose tuition charges for the first time in 129 years and eventually negotiated a new financing arrangement that prevented a takeover of CUNY by the state university system.

Kibbee underwent cranial surgery in the spring of 1981 and died of a brain tumor two weeks before his scheduled retirement. J.P.

Parents Guy B. K., actor, and Helen (Shay) K. **Married** (1) Katherine Kirk (div. 1973): Robert Joseph; Katherine Paterson; Douglas Alan. (2) Margaret Tracey Rockwitz, coll. teacher, 1980. **Religion** Roman Catholic. **Edu-**

cation Our Lady of Good Counsel Elementary Sch., Staten Island, NYC; Xavier High Sch., NYC; Fordham Univ., NYC, A.B. 1943; Univ. of Chicago, M.A. 1947, Ph.D. in higher educational admin. 1957. **Mil. service** U.S. Army, New Guinea and Philippine Islands 1943–45. **Career** Asst. dir. of statewide survey, Arkansas Commn. on Higher Education 1949–50; asst. dean 1950–52 and academic dean 1952–55, Southern State Coll., Magnolia, AR; dean of students, Drake Univ., Des Moines, IA 1955–58; educational advisor to govt. of Pakistan 1958–61; assoc. prof., Univ. of Chicago 1958–61; asst. for planning to Pres., Carnegie Inst. of Technology, Pittsburgh 1961–65; v.p. for planning 1965–68 and v.p. for admin. and planning 1968–71, Carnegie-Mellon Univ., Pittsburgh; bd. member 1968–71 and pres. 1970–71, Pittsburgh Bd. of Education; chancellor, City Univ. of New York since 1971. **Officer** V.P., Cttee. on Urban Program Univs. • Trustee: exec. cttee., Assn. of Colls. and Univs. of State of New York; New York State Higher Education Services Corp.; Inst. of Intl. Education; New York Interface Development Projects, Inc.; Urban Acad. for Management, Inc. • Member, bd. of dirs.: Mt. Sinai Sch. of Medicine, Medical Center, and Hosp.; Children's Medical Relief Intl. **Member** Exec. cttees. of Div. of Urban Affairs, Cttee. on Federal Legislation, Natl. Assn. of State Univs. and Land-Grant Colls.; Cttee. on Federal Relations, Amer. Assn. of State Colls. and Univs. **Honors** Hon. advisor, natl. advisory bd., Exec. High Sch. Internships of America; hon. degrees from Fordham and Hofstra univs. and from Polytechnic Inst. of Brooklyn. **Contributor** of articles on higher education to professional jrnls.

Further reading Michael Harrington, "Keep Open Admissions Open," in *New York Times Magazine,* 2 Nov. 1975.

REBEKAH (WEST) HARKNESS
Ballet patron and philanthropist
Born **St. Louis, Missouri, USA, 17 April 1915**
Died **New York City, USA, 17 June 1982**

Rebekah Harkness was a prominent benefactor of American dance and the founder of the Harkness Ballet, which performed from 1964 to 1974 amid a series of controversies over its artistic direction.

Born into a St. Louis banking family, Harkness—then Rebekah Semple West—was educated at private schools in St. Louis and South Carolina and was presented as a debutante. Her first marriage, to an advertising executive, ended in divorce. Her second, in 1947, was to the attorney William Hale Harkness, heir to the Standard Oil fortune, who died in 1954. Rebekah Harkness took over as president of his philanthropic foundation.

Harkness had been interested in the arts since her school days and was a serious sculptor and composer, studying with Nadia Boulanger in France and at the Dalcroze School and Mannes College of Music in New York. Many of her compositions were suites for ballet. In 1959 she founded the Rebekah Harkness Foundation to support American dance companies. The foundation's first beneficiaries were Jerome Robbins's Ballet USA and the Pearl Primus dance troupe, whose tours of Europe in 1961, and of Africa in 1962, respectively, were both made possible by Harkness grants. In 1962 Harkness opened her estate at Watch Hill, Rhode Island, to a 12-week summer dance workshop that produced new ballets by Alvin Ailey, Gerald Arpino, Brian Macdonald, and Robert Joffrey. For the next two years, she was the main sponsor of the Joffrey Ballet and sent the company on a State Department tour of the Middle East, Europe, and Russia.

In April 1964 the Harkness-Joffrey partnership ended in a quarrel over artistic direction, and Harkness established her own troupe with 14 of Joffrey's dancers. A five-story mansion on West 75th Street in Manhattan was converted into an elegant home for the company and its school. The company, however, was plagued by frequent changes of director (four in five years), the result of Harkness's constant intervention, and was disbanded in 1970. A year later she reconstituted it and merged it with her Harkness Youth Dancers (founded in 1968) to form a new Harkness Ballet, with herself as artistic director; it disbanded for good four years later. The company produced some notable dancers, including Helgi Tomasson, but its productions were an uneasy amalgam of classical and modern styles and received a mixed reception from the critics.

The Rebekah Harkness Foundation, which was renamed the Harkness Ballet Foundation in 1974, funded, in addition to the Harkness Ballet, the establishment of a dance department at Southern Methodist University in Dallas, the donation of a dance stage to the White House, and seven seasons of outdoor dance concerts at the Delacorte Theater in New York's Central Park. It also financed the renovation of a Broadway movie house into the opulent Harkness Theater, the first theater in the city designed specifically for dance productions, which opened in 1974 and was demolished two years later. Through her husband's charitable foundation, Harkness contributed several million dollars to medical research.

Harkness was the recipient of numerous honors, including New York City's Handel Award. She died at the age of 67 of cancer.

J.P.

Born Rebekah Semple West. **Parents** Allen Tarwater W., bank official, and Rebekah (Semple) W. **Married** (1) Dickson Pierce, advertising exec., 1938 (div. 1944): Allen West; Anne Terry McBride. (2) William Hale Harkness, atty. and philanthropist, 1947 (d. 1954): Edith Hale; Anne Harkness Mooney (stepdaughter). (3) Benjamin Harrison Kean 1961 (div. 1965). **Education** Rossman and John Burroughs Schs., St. Louis; Fermata Sch., Aiken, SC; Boulanger Sch. of Composition, Fontainebleau, France, late 1940s; Dalcroze Sch., NYC; Mannes Coll. of Music. **Career** Debutante, St. Louis; dancer 1930s, sculptor since 1930s, composer since 1940s; worked in ad agency, NYC, mid-1940s. • Pres., William Hale Harkness Foundn. since mid-1950s; founder 1959 and pres. since 1959, Rebekah Harkness Foundn. (renamed Harkness Ballet Foundn. 1974); founder 1964, and pres. and artistic dir. 1970–74, Harkness Ballet, NYC; founder 1964 and pres. since 1964, Harkness House for Ballet Arts, NYC; founder, Harkness Youth Dancers 1968; founder, Harkness Theater, NYC 1972. **Officer** Founder and pres. of bd. of dirs., Soc. for a More Beautiful Natl. Capital; trustee, Kennedy Center for Performing Arts, Wash. DC. **Member** River Club, NYC; Lyford Cay, Bahamas; Pres.'s Council on Youth Opportunity, Wash. DC. **Honors** Bronze Medal of Appreciation, NYC 1965; Marquis de Cuevas Prize, Univ. de la Dance, Paris 1965; Congressional Record citations 1965, 1966; Handel Award, NYC 1967; Shield Award, Amer. Indian and Eskimo Cultural Foundn. 1967; White House citations 1968; officer of Cultural and Artistic Merit, France 1966; Ballet des Jeunes Award 1975; hon. degrees from Franklin Pierce and Lycoming colls.; others. **Compositions** include ballet suites *Journey to Love,* [*Voyage vers l'amour*], 1958; *Barcelona Suite,* 1960; *Macumba,* 1965.

DJUNA BARNES
Novelist, playwright, poet, and painter
***Born* Cornwall-on-Hudson, New York, USA, 12 June 1892**
***Died* New York City, USA, 18 June 1982**

Djuna Barnes, the last surviving member of the legendary group of American expatriate writers of the 1920s and 1930s, spent the last four decades of her life in virtual obscurity in a Greenwich Village apartment. She had been a close friend of Gertrude Stein, and her name is familiar to students of the literary avant garde, but her work remains unread by the general public. T. S. Eliot wrote an admiring preface to her second novel, *Nightwood* (1936), and Edwin Muir described her verse play *The Antiphon* (1958) as "one of the greatest things that has been written in our time," but newspaper reviewers generally regarded her work as willfully obscure and pretentious. "Nothing ages so cruelly as unconventionality," wrote Anatole Broyard in a *New York Times* review of her *Selected Works* (1980). Denied a large popular audience for her fiction, she shunned the kind of celebrity she might have achieved as a literary gossip, remarking to an interviewer in 1971: "People's memoirs are so disgusting . . . why should I want to add to it?"

Barnes, whose father changed the original family name of Budington, was educated at home, and studied art at the Pratt Institute and the Manhattan Art Students League. At the age of 21 she joined the staff of the *Brooklyn Eagle* as a reporter and illustrator. She remained a free-lance journalist until 1931, contributing feature articles to the *New York Press,* the *World,* and *McCall's* magazine, and often providing her own illustrations. Her book of short stories, *The Book of Repulsive Women,* was published by a small Greenwich Village press in 1915, and she also became a regular contributor to little magazines and literary reviews such as the *Dial* and the *Transatlantic Review*. Her one-act plays *Three from the Earth, An Irish Triangle,* and *Kurzy of the Sea,* written in 1919, were produced in 1920 by Eugene O'Neill's Provincetown Players, with whom she also appeared on the stage. A founder member of the Theatre Guild, she was also a regular contributor to its magazine.

During the early 1920s, on assignment for *McCall's,* she visited Paris where she soon became a prominent figure in literary bohemia. Peggy Guggenheim became a close friend. Late in life, Barnes dismissed her part in this milieu offhandedly: "I was rather gay and silly and bright and all that sort of stuff, and wasted a lot of time." Something of her

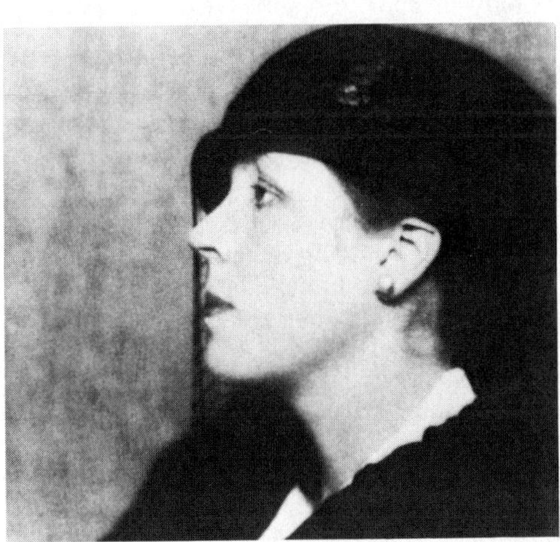

Courtesy of Man Ray

charm, wit, and beauty can be gathered from Peggy Guggenheim's memoirs, *Out of This Century* (1979), in which she is described as "handsome with her white skin, magnificent red hair and beautiful body." Another friend was Natalie Barney, a notorious lesbian *savante* who presided over the literary salon that Barnes satirized anonymously in *The Ladies' Almanack* (1928), privately printed in Dijon at the same press as Joyce's *Ulysses.* Her talent for ridicule is also evident in *Ryder* (1928), a parodic novel in which Wendell Ryder, a conceited and pompous polygamist who collects adoring women, emigrates to a log cabin in North America to found a community composed of his mother, wife, mistress, and numerous children. The book is interesting as a demonstration of its author's cleverness and familiarity with a wide range of English classics that she is adept at mimicking. It sold well in its first edition, but puzzled reviewers when reissued in 1979.

It is on *Nightwood* (1936), a psychopathological study of five people living in Paris, that Djuna Barnes's reputation chiefly rests. In his introduction to the American edition, T. S. Eliot praised her for "the great achievement of a style, the beauty of phrasing, the brilliance of wit and characterization, and a quality of horror and doom very nearly related to that of Elizabethan tragedy." Edwin Muir, writing many years later apropos of her verse play, went even further in paying tribute to her style, which he thought the equal of Joyce's: "Her prose has the closeness and precision of poetry yet is a workable prose medium." Aside from encomia such as these, most criticism of Barnes's work betrays the reader's confusion. Kenneth Rexroth, whose essay in *Contemporary Novelists* is one of the few attempts to define her style and subject, associates her not with the literary set in which she moved, but with "subversive bohemia" and "*fin de siècle* literary decadence." Her "special métier," he adds, was an "atmosphere of inescapable nightmare." Rexroth's observation that Barnes was at least as influential as an energetic, beautiful, emancipated woman as she was as a writer is borne out by the frequency of allusions to her in the memoirs of those who knew her. Had she chosen to do so, she would undoubtedly have told an interesting tale, but what attracted her in the lives of her contemporaries is probably preserved in *Nightwood.*

Not long after its publication, she took up an almost monastic existence, but did not abandon writing. *The Antiphon,* her verse drama, was published in 1958 and, in a translation by Dag Hammarskjöld, was produced in Stockholm in 1961. In 1943 she made a brief appearance as an artist in a show of paintings and drawings at Peggy Guggenheim's Manhattan Gallery. Her early stories were reissued by English and American publishers, and a posthumous volume of poems, *Creatures in an Alphabet,* is scheduled for publication in the fall of 1982. H.B.

Also wrote as Lydia Steptoe. **Parents** Wald B. (changed name from Henry Budington) and Elizabeth (Chappell) B. **Education** Private tutors; Pratt Inst. and Art Students League, NYC. **Career** Reporter, illus., feature writer for *Brooklyn Eagle, New York Press, World, McCall's,* other mags. and newspapers 1913–31; actress and dramatist, Provincetown Players, MA 1920s; full-time writer since 1931; co-founder, Theatre Guild, and columnist for its mag. **Officer** Trustee, New York Cttee., Dag Hammarskjöld Foundn. **Member** Natl. Inst. of Arts and Letters; Authors Guild; League of Dramatists, U.K. **Honors** Sr. fellowship, Natl. Endowment for the Arts 1981. **Novels** *Ryder,* 1928; *Nightwood,* 1936. **Short-story collections** *The Book of Repulsive Women,* 1915; *A Book* (stories, poems, and plays), 1923, rev. ed. as *A Night Among the Horses* (in U.K. as *The Spillway),* 1929; *Vagaries Malicieux: Two Stories,* 1975. **Plays** *Three from the Earth,* 1919; *Kurzy of the Sea,* 1919; *An Irish Triangle,* 1919; *To the Dogs,* 1923; *The Dove,* 1923; *She Tells Her Daughter,* 1923; *The Antiphon,* 1958. **Poetry** *Creatures in an Alphabet,* 1982. **Other** *The Ladies' Almanack,* 1928; *Selected Works,* 1962. **Stage actress** *Power of Darkness,* NYC 1920; *The Tiding Brought to Mary,* NYC 1922. **Contributor** to *Dial, Vanity Fair, Little Review, Transatlantic Review,* other mags. **Exhibition** of drawings and paintings, Manhattan Gall., NYC 1943. **Manuscript collection** Univ. of Maryland, College Park.

Further reading Edwin Muir, *The Present Age from 1914,* 1939; Joseph Frank, *The Widening Gyre,* 1963; Ellen Moers, *Literary Women,* 1976; Peggy Guggenheim, *Out of This Century,* 1979.

JOHN CHEEVER
Short-story writer and novelist
Born **Quincy, Massachusetts, USA, 27 May 1912**
Died **Ossining, New York, USA, 18 June 1982**

More diligently than any other writer of his time, John Cheever observed and expressed the disappointments and fears of a generation of secular, affluent Americans. A man of strong moral conviction, he frequently alluded to the possibility of renewal and redemption, but was better known for his somber evocations of despair and emptiness. Cheever's characters are frequently nostalgic for spiritual values that they have never experienced, and their condition is aptly summarized by a sentence from his last book: "He seemed to have been hurled bodily from the sanctuary of some church, although he had never committed himself to anything that could be called serious prayer."

Cheever was the second son of Frederick Cheever, a descendant of Massachusetts shipowners who traced his ancestry back to Ezekiel Cheever, who arrived in the Bay Colony in 1637. Frederick Cheever became prosperous as a shoe manufacturer, but lost his fortune in the stock market collapse of 1929. His English-born wife Mary then opened a gift shop, to the embarrassment of her family. John Cheever, following a family tradition, attended the Thayer Academy in South Braintree, Massachusetts, until he was expelled for smoking at the age of 16. With perverse resourcefulness, he described the incident in his first published story, "Expelled," which appeared in the *New Republic* when he was 17. After living briefly in Boston with his elder brother, Cheever went to Manhattan, where he lived in a cold-water flat and supported himself by writing stories, as well as synopses of current fiction for Metro-Goldwyn-Mayer. Thereafter, apart from four years of military service in the infantry and the signal corps, and brief spells of teaching at Barnard College (1956–57) and Boston University (1974–75), he did nothing but write fiction. He remembered announcing his vocation at the age of 12 to his parents, who told him that they did not object "so long as you are not seeking fame or wealth." Neither, Cheever reported, took the slightest interest in his career, which was well established by the time he was 25. He said on receiving the National Medal for Literature in April 1982 that he had always been devoted to the creation of "a page of good prose."

After selling his first story to the *New Yorker* when he was 22, he became a regular contributor to that magazine and did much to create a genre of short fiction that is now known, sometimes disparagingly, as "the *New Yorker* story." Cheever's stories usually take place in what his friend Walter Clemons, writing in *Newsweek,* described as "a recognizable landscape called Cheever country." At first, this was the Upper East Side of Manhattan, but as Cheever's subjects became older and wealthier his territory expanded to take in the fictional Westchester and Connecticut suburbs of Shady Hill, Bullet Park, and Proxmire Manor. From these affluent communities Cheever's characters journey daily to Manhattan, frequently with hangovers, and always haunted by the vague sense that although they are blessed by prosperity, they are damned by spiritual emptiness.

John Leonard's description of Cheever as "the Chekhov of the suburbs" is not unjust to his somber ironies and his ability to evoke moral and physical decline. Like Chekhov, Cheever punctuated mundane daily life with moments of grim comedy and unexpected violence: when Aunt Justina dies, her body remains in the living room because the zoning laws prohibit doctors from signing death certificates in the neighborhood; a rejected, crazed woman follows her seducer aboard the 5:48 train with a gun. But the association of Cheever stories with a suburban landscape and a range of domestic emotions obscures his true interests, which often reached toward the transcendent and mystical and used the language of myth and fairy tale. Cheever had enacted much of what he described, but he was not a documentary realist, and his literal landscape was sometimes the setting for allegories.

In one of his most famous stories, "The Swimmer" (later made into a movie starring Burt Lancaster), a middle-aged man sets out to swim across the county through his neighbors' pools. As he passes through a succession of gardens and cocktail parties, he feels the air grow chill and his strength wane. Arriving home, he finds his wife and children gone, his house abandoned and derelict. The story's diffident tone and familiar setting disguise its allegorical import: that the narrator's life, like Rip Van Winkle's, has passed while he was sleeping. Another minor masterpiece, "The Death of Justina," comes as close as Cheever ever gets to explicit statement of his subject. The speaker, an advertising copywriter, has written a commercial praising the virtues of Elixircol, an "age retardant": "Does your face in the morning seem rucked and seamed with alcoholic and sexual excesses . . .?" Going home on the train he stares out "onto a half-finished civilization . . . wondering why, in this most prosperous, equitable, and accomplished world . . . everyone should seem to be disappointed."

The strain of moral questioning was present in Cheever's writing from the first, but only in his later work does he approach a mystical intensity and a sense of Christian transcendence. It is characteristic of Cheever's writing, however, that such elements arise from the most commonplace settings. Farragut, the fratricidal hero of *Falconer* (1977), stands outside a laundromat and sees, through the glass door of a washing machine, the "clothes tossed and falling . . . like falling souls or angels." In earlier work, such as the much-praised story "The Enormous Radio," moral commentary seems inadequately assimilated within the dramatic fabric of the narrative. As if conscious of this failing, Cheever wrote in the preface to his collection *Stories:* "The constants that I look for . . . are a love of light and a determination to trace some moral chain of being. Calvin played no part at all in my religious education, but his presence seemed to abide in the barns of my childhood and to have left me with some undue bitterness."

Cheever's reputation as a short-story writer hindered recognition of his novels, in which much of his most daring and original work is to be found. With a virtually unanimous voice, reviewers of his novels berated his failure to master the longer form, and accused him of lacking intellectual power. Apparently unaware of the variety of forms that novels have taken, writers such as Maxwell Geismar, Joyce Carol Oates, and Benjamin DeMott la-

Courtesy of Nancy Crampton

mented Cheever's tendency to write episodic narratives. Cheever's readers, however, did not agree, and his novels, with the exception of *Bullet Park,* sold extremely well. *The Wapshot Chronicle* (1957) and *The Wapshot Scandal* (1964) trace the fortunes of a Massachusetts family not unlike Cheever's own through a succession of comic and moving episodes set in a small Massachusetts town, a missile base, and a New York suburb. *Bullet Park* (1969), an openly allegorical narrative whose central characters are called Hammer and Nailles, is a less assured novel that concludes with the attempted sacrifice of a child on the altar of the local church.

The poor reception of this novel marked the beginning of a low point in Cheever's fortunes. A heavy drinker for many years, he suffered a near-fatal heart attack in 1972 and then almost succumbed to alcoholism. With his wife and three children he lived in an eighteenth-century house in the Westchester County town of Ossining, where he spent his spare time engaged in the physical activities that he often depicted in fiction: walking with his dogs, riding horses, cutting firewood, and gardening. In 1975, he began a courageous and successful attempt to overcome his addiction to alcohol.

Falconer (1977), although not an autobiographical novel, suggests both the depths to which its author had sunk, and his newfound confidence and hope. Farragut, the hero, finds religious faith in prison, from which he escapes with the resolution to "settle for the stamina of love, a presence he felt like the beginnings of some stair." This book too had mixed reviews, but Walter Clemons wrote that while reading its final pages he had "the ecstatic confidence of finishing a masterpiece." In the following year, Cheever's career was crowned by the publication of *The Stories of John Cheever,* a collection of 61 stories that won the Pulitzer Prize and brought him the critical and commercial success that had long eluded him. Cheever's largest gift, wrote Richard Locke of this collection in the *New York Times,* is "the power to present a sensuous detail that effortlessly carries intense emotional and symbolic force."

By 1979, Cheever was suffering from the cancer that finally killed him, but he completed *Oh What a Paradise It Seems,* a 100-page novella that displays, more confidently than his earlier writing, the assurance that redemption can be achieved through "the great benefice of living here and renewing ourselves with love." His sense of irony and futility notwithstanding, Cheever seems, finally, to have embraced the counsel that Leander Wapshot, in *The Wapshot Chronicle,* gave to his sons: "Stand up straight. Admire the world. Relish the love of a gentle woman. Trust in the Lord." H.B.

Parents Frederick Lincoln C., shoe manufacturer, and Mary Deveraux (Liley) C., businesswoman. **Married** Mary M. Winternitz, coll. instr., 1941: Susan Cheever Tomkins, writer, b. 1944; Benjamin Hale, *Reader's Digest* ed., b. 1949; Frederico, b. 1958. **Religion** Episcopalian. **Education** Thayer Acad., South Braintree, MA, expelled 1928. **Mil. service** Infantry gunner for four years, then Signal Corps member, Philippines, U.S. Army, WWII. **Career** Writer since ca. 1929; instr., Barnard Coll., NYC 1956–57; visiting prof. of creative writing, Boston Univ. 1974–75; English instr., Sing-Sing Prison, Ossining, NY 1970s. **Member** Cultural exchange program with USSR 1964; Natl. Inst. of Arts and Letters; Amer. Acad. of Arts and Letters; Century Club, NYC. **Honors** Guggenheim Fellowship 1951; Benjamin Franklin Award, for story "The Five-Forty-Eight," 1954; literature award, Amer. Acad. of Arts and Letters

1956; O. Henry Award 1956, for story "The Country Husband," and 1964, for story "The Embarkment for Cythera"; Natl. Book Award, for *The Wapshot Chronicle,* 1958; Howells Medal, Amer. Acad. of Arts and Letters, for *The Wapshot Scandal,* 1965; editorial award, *Playboy,* for story "The Yellow Room," 1969; MacDowell Medal, MacDowell Colony 1979; Pulitzer Prize, Natl. Book Critics Award, and Amer. Book Award, all for *The Stories of John Cheever,* 1979; Natl. Medal for Literature, 1982; hon. degree, Harvard Univ. **Novels** *The Wapshot Chronicle,* 1957; *The Wapshot Scandal,* 1964; *Bullet Park,* 1969; *Falconer,* 1977; *Oh What a Paradise It Seems,* 1982. **Short-story collections** *The Way Some People Live: A Book of Stories,* 1943; *The Enormous Radio and Other Stories,* 1953; (jtly.) *Stories,* 1956; *The Housebreaker of Shady Hill and Other Stories,* 1958; *Some People, Places and Things That Will Not Appear in My Next Novel,* 1961; *The Brigadier and the Golf Widow,* 1964; *Homage to Shakespeare,* 1965; *The World of Apples,* 1973; *The Stories of John Cheever,* 1978. **Television scripts** "Life with Father," 1950s; "The Kidnapper of Shady Hill," 1980. **Contributor** to *O. Henry Prize Stories* 1941, 1951, 1956, 1964, and many other anthologies; also stories in *New Yorker, New Republic, Collier's, Story, Playboy, Atlantic,* other mags.

Further reading Lynne Waldeland, *John Cheever,* 1979; Christina Robb, "Cheever's Story," in *Boston Globe Magazine,* 6 July 1980; interview in *Writers at Work: The Paris Review Interviews,* 5th series, 1981; Francis J. Bosha, *John Cheever: A Reference Guide,* 1981.

GRANVILLE HICKS

Writer and literary critic

***Born* Exeter, New Hampshire, USA, 9 September 1901**

***Died* Franklin Park, New Jersey, USA, 18 June 1982**

During the course of a literary career that spanned four decades, Granville Hicks was frequently the focus of controversy and even denunciation. During the 1930s he was among the best-known apologists for communism in America and wrote *The Great Tradition* (1933), a much-discussed interpretation of post–Civil War American literature. He carefully plotted the subsequent changes in his political course in several memoirs and semi-autobiographical novels.

Born to Yankee parents of modest means, Hicks attended public schools in New Hampshire and Massachusetts, then entered Harvard University in 1919. His four years in Cambridge were filled with hard study and frugality, and he graduated in 1923 with highest honors in English and as a member of Phi Beta Kappa. After two years at Harvard Theological School, he abandoned what he later called his "somewhat inexplicable plan of entering the ministry," and moved to Northampton, Massachusetts, where he taught (1925–28) biblical literature at Smith College. He returned to Harvard in 1928–29 for an M.A. in English and began regularly to write articles and reviews for such magazines as *Nation, American Mercury,* and *Forum.* In 1929 he was appointed assistant professor of English at Rensselaer Polytechnic Institute in Troy, New York, and three years later bought a farm in the small town of Grafton, New York, that served as his home and center of creativity almost until the end of his life.

When he started work on *The Great Tradition* in 1931 he was not a Communist, but "passed for a radical because I disliked Roosevelt and had no respect for a business civilization." But the sight of the Hoovervilles beside the railroad tracks and of starving people sleeping on the streets of New York during his visits there appalled him. "I knew as well as I had ever known anything that I could not ignore all this. Something had to be done, and the voices were asking, more and more insistently, 'Why not Communism?'" He joined the party in 1934, the year after his literary history was published. His judgments of the great writers of late nineteenth- and early twentieth-century American literature were based on one primary criterion: their understanding of the economic conditions of the time, of the growing disparity between the rich and the poor. His heroes were Whitman, Emerson, Thoreau, Howells, Sinclair, London, and Dos Passos, creators of "the great tradition" and sharp critics of "greed, cowardice, and meanness." To these he opposed such writers as Henry James and Emily Dickinson, isolated aestheticists or regionalists who ignored the social abuses inherent in unbridled capitalism. Although the book was widely praised as a great and comprehensive work of systematic analysis, many critics, even leftists such as his friend Malcolm Cowley, editor of the *New Republic,* found it "much too schematic and dogmatic," in Cowley's words. His employers at Rensselaer and their businessmen supporters reacted by dismissing him from his teaching post in 1935, an assault on academic freedom that provoked a nationwide outcry. It was far from the end of Hicks's academic career, however, for he later taught at Harvard (1938–39), the New School for Social Research (1955–58), and New York, Syracuse, and Ohio universities.

His literary career flourished during his years as a Communist. In 1936 he published the first biography of John Reed, the American radical who wrote the earliest study of the Russian revolution, *Ten Days that Shook the World.* His *I Like America* (1938) was a kind of prophecy of what the United States would be like under communism. He edited a popular anthology, *Proletarian Literature in the United States* (1935), and co-edited *The Letters of Lincoln Steffens* (1938), the pioneering muckraker. He also wrote, while a Guggenheim Fellow in 1936–37, *Figures in Transition* (published in 1939), a study of contemporary British literature. He served as literary advisor to Macmillan, the publishers, from 1930, and was a member of the editorial staff of *New Masses* (1934–39), America's best radical literary publication.

Hicks resigned from the Communist Party in August 1939, as soon as he heard of the Hitler-Stalin nonaggression pact, and explained in a letter to the *New Republic* that he had become disillusioned with the party's American leadership, which he characterized as "strong in faith and weak in intelligence." His break with communism led him to regard with suspicion much of his work of the 1930s, in particular *The Great Tradition,* whose economic analysis he came to see as a "hopelessly narrow way of judging literature." Over the next few years he developed into a typical American liberal, still concerned with social justice, yet ultimately tolerant of other political opinions, willing to compromise, and more self-involved than ever. "If I had had my years of comforting certainty," he wrote in his autobiography *Part of the Truth* (1965), "when Marxism seemed to answer every question, I had long since had to learn how to live with doubts of every kind. . . . I had decided some time before that I was not personally responsible for saving the world; now it became clear that I could not save the world even if I put my mind to it." He attributed his learning of tolerance to his association with his neighbors in Grafton, who "taught me that people of many sorts could be right in their own ways, even when their ways were not my ways." This turnabout in political and social views culminated, in February 1953, in an appearance as a "cooperative witness" before the House Committee on Un-American Activities to testify about his knowledge of a Communist group at Harvard in the late 1930s. His popular novel, *Only One Storm* (1942), treats the political and social forces, including communism, confronting an American intellectual in the 1930s. His other novels were *The First To Awaken* (1940), *Behold Trouble* (1944), and *There Was a Man in Our Town* (1952).

Hicks worked as literary consultant to the *New Leader* from 1951 to 1958 and was contributing editor of *Saturday Review* from 1958 to 1969. He continued writing and teaching until incapacitated by a stroke in 1975. In 1979 he moved from Grafton to central New Jersey to be near his daughter and only child, and died there in an old people's convalescent home. A.K.

Parents Frank Stevens H. and Carrie Weston (Horne) H. **Married** Dorothy Dyer 1928 (d. 1981): Stephanie Craib. **Education** Public schs., Exeter, NH, and Framingham, MA; Harvard Univ., A.B. (Phi Beta Kappa) 1923, M.A. 1929; Harvard Theological Seminary 1923–24. **Career** Critic and writer since mid-1920s; literary ed., *Universalist Leader* mag. 1924–27; instr. in biblical literature, English literature, and composition, Smith Coll., Northampton, MA 1925–28; asst. prof. of English, Rensselaer Polytechnic Inst., Troy, NY 1929–35; literary advisor, Macmillan Co., NYC 1930–65; editorial staff member, *New*

Masses mag., NYC 1934–39; counselor in Amer. civilization, Harvard Univ. 1938–39; chmn., *Speaking of Books* radio program 1941–43; lectr., Pacific Northwest Writers Conference, Seattle 1948; literary consultant, *New Leader* mag., NYC 1951–58; writing instr., New Sch. for Social Research, NYC 1955–58; contributing ed., *Saturday Review* mag., NYC 1958–69; Berg Visiting Prof., New York Univ., NYC 1959; visiting prof., Syracuse Univ., NY 1960; McGuffey Visiting Prof., Ohio Univ., Athens 1967–68 and Chatham Coll., Pittsburgh, PA 1973; books ed., *American Way* mag., San Antonio, TX since 1973. **Officer** Chief air raid warden, Grafton Defense Council, Grafton, NY 1941–45; acting exec. dir., Corp. of Yaddo, Saratoga Springs, NY 1970–71. **Member** Amer. Communist Party 1934–39; Union for Democratic Action. **Honors** Guggenheim Fellowship 1936; Rockefeller Fellowship 1945; Day Award, Amer. Library Assn. 1968; hon. degrees from Skidmore and Siena colls. and Ohio Univ. **Criticism** *The Great Tradition: An Interpretation of American Literature since the Civil War,* 1933, rev. ed. 1935; *Figures in Transition: A Study of British Literature at the End of the Nineteenth Century,* 1939; *James Gould Cozzens,* 1958; (jtly.) *Literary Horizons: A Quarter Century of American Fiction,* 1970; Jack Alan Robbins, ed., *Granville Hicks in "The New Masses,"* 1974. **Novels** (jtly.) *The First To Awaken,* 1940; *Only One Storm,* 1942; *Behold Trouble,* 1944; *There Was a Man in Our Town,* 1952. **Poetry** (Jtly.) *New Light,* 1932. **Essays and biographies** *Eight Ways of Looking at Christianity,* 1926; *One of Us: The Story of John Reed,* 1935; (jtly.) *John Reed: The Making of a Revolutionary,* 1936; *I Like America,* 1938; *Small Town,* 1946; *Where We Came Out,* 1954; *Part of the Truth* (autobiography), 1965. **Editor** *Proletarian Literature in the United States: An Anthology,* 1935; (jtly.) *The Letters of Lincoln Steffens,* 1938; *The Living Novel: A Symposium,* 1957. **Contributor** to *American Mercury, Nation, Forum,* and other mags.

Further reading Robert J. Bicker, *Granville Hicks: An Annotated Bibliography, February, 1927 to June, 1967, with a Supplement to June, 1968,* 1968; Daniel Aaron, *Writers on the Left,* 1974; Vivian Gornick, *The Romance of American Communism,* 1978; Malcolm Cowley, *Dream of the Golden Mountains,* 1980.

ROSCOE H(ENRY) HILLENKOETTER

Director of the Central Intelligence Agency
***Born* St. Louis, Missouri, USA, 8 May 1897**
***Died* New York City, USA, 18 June 1982**

Roscoe H. Hillenkoetter's career as an intelligence officer in the U.S. Navy spanned four decades and included service in both world wars. His most important assignment occurred in the late 1940s under Pres. Harry S. Truman, when he served as the first director of the Central Intelligence Agency (CIA) as it is presently constituted.

Hillenkoetter entered the U.S. Naval Academy at Annapolis in 1916, and while still a midshipman served in 1918 aboard the U.S.S. *Minnesota* with the Atlantic fleet. The following year he graduated from the academy with distinction, 20th in a class of 467. Over the next 20 years he was assigned to a large number of varied tours of duty, notable among which was an instructorship in modern languages at Annapolis (1929–31) and positions as naval attaché in Paris (1933–35, 1938) and in Madrid and Lisbon (1938–40). In 1940–41 he served as attaché at the embassy in Vichy, France, where he worked closely with the French underground to effect the escape of people wanted by the Nazis.

He had been executive officer of the U.S.S. *West Virginia* for only two weeks in 1941 before being slightly wounded when the ship was sunk at Pearl Harbor. He was soon transferred to the U.S.S. *Maryland* as executive officer, then to Washington as intelligence chief on the staff of Adm. Chester Nimitz, the commander in chief of the Pacific theater. Later in the war, as commander of the U.S.S. *Dixie,* he was awarded the Bronze Star for meritorious service during the taking of the Solomon Islands, and during another tour of duty in Washington received the Legion of

Merit for his work as director of planning and control in the Bureau of Naval Personnel. He was given the command of the U.S.S. *Missouri* shortly after the Japanese surrendered on her flight deck, and in the spring of 1946 commanded the battleship under escort on a goodwill cruise of the Mediterranean. After another nine months' tour as naval attaché in Paris, Hillenkoetter, by then a rear admiral, was appointed on 1 May 1947 director of the Central Intelligence Group, succeeding Gen. Hoyt S. Vandenberg of the Air Force. When the CIA was established the following September, Hillenkoetter continued as director of central intelligence until October 1950, when he was succeeded by Gen. Walter Bedell Smith of the Army.

The CIA in its early years was far less autonomous in exercising its power than it later became. The National Security Council, within the Executive Office of the President, decided most of its policy and priorities, and there was also at this time a running dispute over intelligence authority between the Army's G-2, Naval Intelligence, and the State Department. As director of central intelligence, Hillenkoetter had to submit to the first public investigation of the CIA after the agency's surprising failure to forewarn U.S. participants of the violence that broke out at the Inter-American Conference in Bogotá, Colombia, in March 1948. He admitted before the House Executive Expenditures Subcommittee that the agency "did know of unrest in Colombia" but did "not want to alarm delegates unduly" by issuing warnings. In June 1950, very shortly after the outbreak of the Korean War, Hillenkoetter was called before the Senate Appropriations Committee to explain why the United States had been caught unawares by the North Korean invasion of the south. He stated that the CIA had known of the buildup of Communist forces on the border over the previous year and that an invasion had been expected, but that the agency had been unable to predict the "zero hour." Two months later the White House announced that Gen. Bedell Smith, commander of the First Army and a former ambassador to Moscow, would take over as director of central intelligence, and that Hillenkoetter would return to sea duty as he had requested.

His two subsequent assignments were of short duration: from November 1950 until September 1951 he was commander of the heavy cruiser U.S.S. *St. Paul* and of the Seventh Task Force, which provided cover for the advance and subsequent retreat of South

Korean land forces; then he was for nine months commander of the Brooklyn Navy Yard. From 1952 to 1956 he was commandant of the Third Naval District with headquarters in New York City, and finally became inspector general of the Navy until his retirement in 1957. He was created a vice admiral in April 1956.

After leaving the Navy, Hillenkoetter was named executive vice president of American Banner Lines, a short-lived entrant in the North Atlantic passenger trade. From 1962 he was vice chairman of Hegeman-Harris Co., a New York construction firm. He died at the age of 85. A.K.

Parents Alexander H. and Olinda (Denker) H. **Married** Jane E. Clark 1933: Jane Saar. **Education** U.S. Naval Acad., Annapolis, MD, B.S. 1919; submarine instruction, Submarine Base, New London, CT 1922. **Career** With U.S. Navy: Served on various battleships and submarines 1919–23; assigned to 15th Naval District, Balboa, Canal Zone 1923–25; aide to Comdr. Destroyer Squadrons, Scouting Fleet 1925–27; aide and flag lt., Comdr., Special Service Squadron 1927–29; instr., dept. of modern language, U.S. Naval Acad. 1929–31; with U.S.S. *Memphis* 1931–32; exec. and engineering officer, U.S.S. *Bainbridge* 1932; attaché to electoral mission, Nicaragua 1932; aide and flag lt., then aide and flag secty., Comdr. Special Service Squadron 1933; asst. U.S. naval attaché, U.S. Embassy, Paris 1933–35; assignment 1935–37 and gunnery officer 1937–38, U.S.S. *Maryland;* with Office of Chief of Naval Operations, Dept. of Navy, Wash. DC 1938, 1942; asst. U.S. naval attaché, U.S. Embassies, Paris and Madrid, and U.S. Legation to Lisbon 1938–40; naval attaché for air, Paris 1940–41 and Vichy 1941; exec. officer, U.S.S. *West Virginia* (wounded) 1941; exec. officer, U.S.S. *Maryland* 1941–42; officer in charge of intelligence, Comdr. in Chief, Pacific Ocean Area 1942–43; comdr., U.S.S. *Dixie,* Solomon Islands and New Hebrides, and rep. for Comdr., Destroyers, Pacific Fleet, South Pacific, 1943–44; asst. dir. of training 1944 and dir. of planning and control 1944–45, Bureau of Naval Personnel, Dept. of Navy; comdr., U.S.S. *Missouri* 1945–46; naval attaché, U.S. Embassy, Paris 1946; promoted to rear adm. 1946; special duty, Office of Secty. of Navy 1947; dir., Central Intelligence Agency 1947–50; comdr., Cruiser Div. ONE, 7th Task Force, Formosa 1950–51; comdr., Naval Base, Brooklyn, NY 1951–52; commandant, 3rd Naval District, NYC 1952–56; promoted to vice adm. 1956; navy inspector gen., Dept. of Navy 1956–57; retired 1957. • Exec. v.p. 1957 and chief exec. officer 1958–59, Amer. Banner Lines; vice chmn., v.p., and treas., Hegeman-Harris Co., Inc., NYC from 1962; dir., Electronics and Missile Facilities, Inc. **Member** U.S. Naval Inst. **Honors** Legion of Merit; Bronze Star; Purple Heart; Victory Medal, Atlantic Fleet Clasp; 2nd Nicaraguan Campaign Medal; Amer. Defense Service Medal, Base Clasp; Asiatic-Pacific Campaign Medal; Amer. Campaign Medal; World War II Victory Medal; Natl. Defense Service Medal; Korean Service Medal; United Nations Service Medal; Korean Presidential Unit Citation Badge; officer, Légion d'Honneur, and Order of Maritime Merit, France; Order of the Phoenix, Greece; Order of St. Maurice and St. Lazarus, Italy; Medal of Merit, Nicaragua.

CURT JURGENS
Actor
***Born* Munich, Germany, 13 December 1912**
***Died* Vienna, Austria, 18 June 1982**

Curt Jurgens enjoyed a successful international acting career that comprised more than 150 films and numerous stage roles. His pale, tall, Germanic appearance and somewhat impassive demeanor equipped him perfectly for parts as the Continental villain or seducer.

His father was a German businessman who met his mother, the daughter of French peasants, when she was teaching French to aristocrats in St. Petersburg, Russia. He trained to be a journalist, but switched to acting in the mid-1930s and began a long series of unmemorable roles at a time of profound disarray in the German and Austrian film industries. His career on the Berlin stage was more important, and he was among several dozen actors chosen to continue the operation of Vienna's famous Burgtheater during World War II; toward the end of the war he was sent to a camp in Hungary for political unreliables, escaped, and spent several months in hiding.

The first part to bring Jurgens international recognition was that of a vicious Nazi in *Des Teufels General* (1955; *The Devil's General),* which was popular throughout Western Europe and was imported into the United States in a dubbed version. Thereafter several significant roles came his way, in particular the male lead opposite Brigitte Bardot in her first noteworthy film, Roger Vadim's *Et Dieu créa la femme* (1956; *And God Created Woman),* and the wily U-boat commander in Dick Powell's *The Enemy Below* (1957), co-starring his friend Robert Mitchum. He appeared in a few film comedies—with Danny Kaye in *Me and the Colonel* (1958) and in an early Blake Edwards work, *This Happy Feeling* (1958)—and co-starred with Ingrid Bergman in the sentimental story of missionaries in China, *The Inn of the Sixth Happiness* (1958). His stay in Hollywood came to an end after the disastrous critical reception accorded Edward Dmytryk's remake of *The Blue Angel* (1959), in which he played Unrath, a timid professor undone by love (the role created by his old mentor Emil Jannings in the original version, which catapulted Marlene Dietrich to international stardom). His portrayal of the German rocket pioneer Werner von Braun in J. Lee Thompson's vapid *I Aim at the Stars* (1960) did nothing to improve his standing at the U.S. box office, and he returned to work primarily in German and Austrian films from the early 1960s. Thereafter his appearances in English-language films were much less frequent: he was the ship's captain in Richard Brooks's *Lord Jim* (1965), and had supporting roles in Guy Hamilton's epic *The Battle of Britain* (1969) and Franklin Schaffner's *Nicholas and Alexandra* (1971). Among his last appearances was as Stromberg, the archvillain, in the James Bond film directed by Lewis Gilbert, *The Spy Who Loved Me* (1977).

Jurgens considered himself principally a stage actor, and played the parts of some notable Americans on the German, Austrian,

Courtesy of German Information Center

and Swiss stages: he had the lead in David Rintels's *Clarence Darrow* (1976) and portrayed Ernest Hemingway (1977) in a lesser play by Rolf Hochhuth, author of *The Deputy.* He appeared once on Broadway, as an anti-Semitic German in the short-lived *The Great Indoors* (1966), and occasionally in Paris, where in 1953 he played Freud in the Henri Denker play *Le fil rouge.*

He lived in the luxurious style of an international film star, with houses in Vienna, Zurich, the French Riviera, the Bavarian Alps, southern Spain, and the Bahamas. He married five women and was divorced four times, sometimes amid great fanfare in the German-language press. His autobiography, *Sixty and Not Yet Wise* (English ed. 1976), was very popular in his homeland. He had suffered from heart disease since the mid-1960s, and underwent several serious operations in the United States. A.K.

Born Curd Jürgens. **Parents** Father a tradesman; mother a French teacher. **Married** (1) Lulu Basler, operetta singer, ca. 1934 (div.). (2) Judith Holzmeister, actress, 1947 (div.). (3) Eva Bartok, actress, 1955 (div.). (4) Simone Bicheron, model, 1958 (div. 1977). (5) Margie Schmitz 1978. **Education** Herder Sch., Berlin; Gymnasiums, Munich and Berlin; studied drama, Berlin. **Career** Newspaper reporter 1930s. • Stage and film actor since mid-1930s: Metropole Theater, Theater am Kurfürstendamm, and Komödie Theater, Berlin 1937–42; Deutsche Volkstheater, Vienna 1938–41; Vienna Burgtheater, Salzburg Festival, other playhouses in Germany, Austria, Paris from 1940s. • Imprisoned in Nazi detention camp, Hungary 1944, escaped; prof. of art, Austrian Acad. 1976. **Honors** Graf Volpi Pokal, Venice Biennale 1955; Ciné-Revue Award 1956; Josef Kainz Medal 1966; Sorrento Prize, Naples 1973. **Films** More than 50 films, Germany 1935–50; more than 60 films internationally since 1950, including: (also dir. and co-scenarist) *Pramien auf Tod,* 1950; (also dir. and co-scenarist) *Gangsterpremiere,* 1951; *Der letzte Walzer* (rel. as *The Last Waltz),* 1953; *Rummelplatz der Liebe* (rel. as *Circus of Love),* 1954; *Des Teufels General* (rel. as *The Devil's General),* 1955; *Les héros sont fatigués* (rel. as *Heroes and Sinners),* 1966; (also dir.) *Ohne dich wird es Nacht,* 1956; *Et Dieu créa la femme* (rel. as *And God Created Woman),* 1956; *The Enemy Below,* 1957; *Tamango,* 1957; *This Happy Feeling,* 1958; *Me and the Colonel,* 1958; *The Inn of the Sixth Happiness,* 1958; *The Blue Angel,* 1959; *Le vent se lève* (rel. as *Time Bomb),* 1959; *Ferry to Hong Kong,* 1959; *Katia* (rel. as *Magnificent Sinner),* 1960; *I Aim at the Stars,* 1960; *Three Moves to Freedom,* 1960; *Gustav Adolfs Page,* 1960; (also dir.) *Bankraub in der Rue Latour,* 1961; *The Longest Day,* 1962; *Die Dreigroschenoper* (rel. as *The Threepenny Opera),* 1963; *Chateau en Suède* (rel. as *Nutty Naughty Chateau),* 1963; *Hide and Seek,* 1964; *Psyche '59,* 1964; *Lord Jim,* 1965; *Dalle Ardenne all'Inferno* (rel. as *Dirty Heroes),* 1968; *The Assassination Bureau,* 1969; *The Battle of Britain,* 1969; *The Invincible Six,* 1970; *Hello-Goodbye,* 1970; *The Mephisto Waltz,* 1971; *Nicholas and Alexandra,* 1971; *The Vault of Horror,* 1973; *Soft Beds Hard Battles* (also rel. as *Undercovers Hero),* 1974; *Auch Mimosen wollen blühen,* 1976; *The Spy Who Loved Me,* 1977; *Schöner Gigolo—armer Gigolo* (rel. as *Just a Gigolo),* 1978; *Sergeant Steiner* (rel. as *Breakthrough),* 1979; *Goldengirl,* 1979. **Stage** *Le fil rouge,* 1953; *The Glass Menagerie,* 1963; *Richter in eigener Sache,* 1965; *Galileo Galilei,* 1966; *The Great Indoors,* 1966; *Clarence Darrow,* 1976; *Hemingway,* 1977; many others. **Author** . . . *Und kein bisschen weise* (autobiography, trans. as *Sixty and Not Yet Wise,* 1976).

RICHARD (ORSON) LOCKRIDGE

Writer of mystery and detective fiction

***Born* St. Joseph, Missouri, USA, 25 September 1898**

***Died* Tryon, North Carolina, USA, 19 June 1982**

Richard Lockridge was a master of the old-fashioned, urbane mystery novel, in which character and plot carry the story and violence is kept to a minimum. Alone and in collaboration with his first wife, Frances Davis, he published nearly 100 books, including the very popular Mr. and Mrs. North detective series.

The son of a salesman and a schoolteacher, Lockridge attended Kansas City Junior College and the University of Missouri at Columbia. After spending the last year of World War I scraping paint off battleships for the U.S. Naval Reserve, he studied journalism at George Washington University in Washington, D.C., while supporting himself as a carnival roustabout and a letterpress printer with the Postal Service. He landed his first job as a reporter and rewriter for the *Kansas City Kansan,* then worked for the *Kansas City Star,* where he met Frances Davis, a reporter and drama critic. They were married in 1922 and moved to Greenwich Village in New York City to make their living as writers. Lockridge covered murder trials and the theater for the *New York Sun* starting in 1928, while his wife worked on charity publicity.

In the early 1930s, Lockridge began publishing in the *New Yorker,* a series of humorous, semiautobiographical short stories (none of them mysteries) about the urban misadventures of Jerry and Pam North; these were later collected and made into a novel under the title *Mr. and Mrs. North* (1936). In *The Norths Meet Murder* (1940), he turned the couple into amateur detectives, modeled somewhat after Nick and Nora Charles in Dashiell Hammett's *The Thin Man.* The book was an instant success. Forty-seven more North mysteries followed at the rate of about three per year, all written by Lockridge from Frances's story outlines. Lockridge prided himself on his writing speed and claimed that he regularly produced 1,500 words between breakfast and lunch. Although the North series proved immensely popular for its solid characterizations (particularly of the daffy but intuitive Pam), melodramatic plots, and affectionately detailed New York settings, some critics complained that the later books were repetitive and the writing style so smooth as to be flat. In 1941, *Mr. and Mrs. North,* with a new mystery plot added, was adapted for the stage, and was shortly followed by a movie version with Gracie Allen. A television series appeared in the early 1950s. The last North mystery, *Murder by the Book,* was published in 1963, the year of Frances's death.

Lockridge continued to work on other detective series that he and his wife had started, notably those featuring Captain/Inspector Merton Heimrich of the New York State Police and Homicide Lt. Nathan Shapiro, a self-doubting New York policeman. These and other characters often appeared in one another's books, teaming up to solve crimes and compare detection styles. In the typical Lockridge mystery, the hero is happily married, highly competent, and completely honest, with a minor weakness of personality that is more endearing than troublesome. Crime is treated as an aberration within a well-ordered society, and no effort is made to understand the criminal mind, except insofar as it is necessary for the solution of the crime. The books are essentially novels of manners in mystery form.

In 1965 Lockridge married Hildegarde Dolson, also a mystery novelist. His last novel, *The Old Die Young,* a Lt. Shapiro mystery, was published in 1981. He died at the age of 83 after suffering a series of strokes.

D.T./S.A.

Parents Ralph David L., traveling salesman, and Mary Olive (Notson) L., schoolteacher. **Married** (1) Frances Louise Davis, reporter and mystery writer, 1922 (d. 1963). (2) Hildegarde Dolson, writer, 1965 (d. 1981). **Education** Kansas City Jr. Coll. 1916–18; Univ. of Missouri, Columbia 1920; George Washington Univ., Wash. DC ca. 1919–20. **Mil. service** Joined USNR 1918, lt. 1942–45. **Career** Census taker, carnival roustabout, post-office worker, and other odd jobs ca. 1919–21; reporter and rewriter, *Kansas City Kansan* 1921–22; reporter, *Kansas City Star* 1922; reporter 1922–28 and drama critic 1928–43, *New York Sun;* writer for *New Yorker* and other mags. 1930s–40s; mystery and crime novelist and short-story writer since ca. 1940. **Officer** Co-pres., Mystery Writers of America 1960. **Member** Authors League; PEN Intl.; Players Club. **Honors** Poe Award 1945, for radio play *Mr. and Mrs. North,* and special award 1960, Mystery Writers of America. **Novels** *Mr. and Mrs. North,* 1936; *Death in the Mind,* 1945; *A Matter of Taste,* 1951; *Murder Can't Wait,* 1964; *The Empty Day,* 1965; *Squire of Death,* 1965; *Encounter in Key West,* 1966; *Murder Roundabout,* 1966; *Murder for Art's Sake,* 1967; *With Option to Die,* 1967; *Murder in False-Face,* 1968; *A Plate of Red Herrings,* 1968; *Die Laughing,* 1969; *A Risky Way To Kill,* 1969; *Troubled Journey,* 1970; *Twice Retired,* 1970; *Inspector's Holiday,* 1971; *Preach No More,* 1971; *Death in a Sunny Place,* 1972; *Something Up a Sleeve,* 1972; *Write Murder Down,* 1972; *Not I, Said the Sparrow,* 1973; *Death on the Hour,* 1974; *Or Was He Pushed?,* 1975; *Dead Run,* 1976; *A Streak of Light,* 1976; *The Tenth Life,* 1977; *The Old Die Young,* 1981. **Novels co-authored with Frances Lockridge** *The Norths Meet Murder,* 1940; *Murder Out of Turn,* 1941; *A Pinch of Poison,* 1941; *Death on the Aisle,* 1942; *Hanged for a Sheep,* 1942; *Death Takes a Bow,* 1943; *Killing the Goose,* 1944; *Payoff for the Banker,* 1945; *Death of a Tall Man,* 1946; *Murder Within Murder,* 1946; *Untidy Murder,* 1947; *Think of Death,* 1947; *I Want To Go Home,* 1948; *Murder Is Served,* 1948; *The Dishonest Murder,* 1949; *Spin Your Web, Lady!,* 1949; *Foggy, Foggy Death,* 1950; *Murder in a Hurry,* 1950; *Murder Comes First,* 1951; *A Client Is Cancelled,* 1951; *Death by Association* (in U.K. as *Trial by Terror),* 1952; *Dead as a Dinosaur,* 1952; *Stand Up and Die,* 1953; *Death Has a Small Voice,* 1953; *Curtain for a Jester,* 1953; *A Key to Death,* 1954; *Death and the Gentle Bull,* 1954 (as *Killer in the Straw,* 1955); *Burnt Offering,* 1955; *Death of an Angel,* 1955 (as *Mr. and Mrs. North and the Poisoned Playboy,* 1957); *Practice to Deceive,* 1955; *Murder! Murder! Murder!* (collection), 1956; *The Faceless Adversary,* 1956 (as *Case of the Murdered Redhead,* 1957); *Voyage into Violence,* 1956; *Let Dead Enough Alone,* 1956; *The Tangled Cord,* 1957; *Catch as Catch Can,* 1958; *Accent on Murder,* 1958;

The Long Skeleton, 1958; *The Innocent House,* 1959; *Murder and Blueberry Pie,* 1959 (as *Call it Coincidence,* 1962); *Murder Is Suggested,* 1959; *The Golden Man,* 1960; *The Judge Is Reversed,* 1960; *Show Red for Danger,* 1960; *With One Stone* (in U.K. as *No Dignity in Death),* 1961; *The Drill Is Death,* 1961; *Murder Has Its Points,* 1961; *And Left for Dead,* 1962; *Night of Shadows,* 1962; *The Ticking Clock,* 1962; *First Come, First Kill,* 1962; *The Distant Clue,* 1963; *Murder by the Book,* 1963; *The Devious Ones* (in U.K. as *Four Hours to Fear),* 1964; *Quest for the Bogeyman,* 1965. **Juvenile** (jtly. with F. L., except as noted) *The Proud Cat,* 1951; *The Lucky Cat,* 1953; *The Nameless Cat,* 1954; *The Cat Who Rode Cows,* 1955; (sole author) *One Lady, Two Cats,* 1967. **Other** *Darling of Misfortune: Edwin Booth, 1833–93* (biography), 1932; *Cats and People,* 1950; (co-ed.) *Crime for Two,* 1955; *Sgt. Mickey and General Ike* (biography). **Radio play** "Mr. and Mrs. North," 1945. **Contributor** of short stories and articles to mags.

Further reading Jane Filstrup, "Murder for Two," in *New Republic,* 22 July 1978.

BOHUMÍR LOMSKÝ
Czechoslovak minister of defense
***Born* Budapest, Hungary, 22 April 1914**
***Death announced* Prague, Czechoslovakia, 22 June 1982**

Bohumír Lomský was defense minister of Czechoslovakia during the presidency of Antonin Novotný, which came to an inglorious end in the spring of 1968 following a series of reforms which brought to power progressive forces led by Alexander Dubček. He resigned his post in disgrace in April of that year, which was seen at the time as a victory for the progressives, although he strongly condemned the Warsaw Pact invasion of the country the following August.

A Slovak and the son of an engine driver, he attended the Hranice Military Academy from 1933 to 1936, then served during World War II as a lieutenant in Poland with the anti-Nazi Czechoslovak Legion and in the Soviet Union with Czechoslovak army units that he had helped to found. He studied in the Soviet Union from 1944 to 1947 at the Voroshilov Higher Military Academy, winning the lifelong friendship and respect of Soviet military leaders. In 1950 he joined the Czechoslovak Communist Party, and from 1951 to 1953, as a brigadier general, commanded the Brno Military-Technical Academy. From 1954 to 1956 he was deputy defense minister, and from April 1956 was defense minister, being named to the Central Committee of the Communist Party in 1958 and as a deputy to the National Assembly in 1960. He was made a full general late that same year.

Lomský, although indisputably a conservative, attempted to keep the armed forces out of the fierce power struggles that raged in Prague in late 1967 and throughout the first quarter of 1968. In late December, after the Presidium decided that Novotný could no longer hold both the presidency and the first secretaryship of the party, a plot came to light under which Novotný would be restored to full power and more than a thousand reformers would be arrested. The planned coup was undone by Novotný's reluctant orders, but the press, newly freed of censorship, began to conduct a full investigation of those who were behind the illegal plot. Scandals came to light involving misappropriation of government funds, theft of government property, blackmail, sexual orgies, and assorted illegalities. Colonel Gen. Vladimír Janko, a deputy defense minister, committed suicide in February, and Maj. Gen. Jan Šejna, deputy chief of the general staff, defected to the United States in early March. Lomský firmly protested his innocence of any illegal activity. In one speech of personal exculpation, he said that he had told Novotný: "The army may not be misused in the present situation by either side. . . . We are not, after all, somewhere in Africa!" Yet the progressive forces were winning the day everywhere, and he was forced to resign in April 1968. Even so, in his speech of resignation, he announced that he was in favor of the post-January reforms, and was

praised by a leading progressive, Josef Smrkovský, chairman of the National Assembly. He was succeeded by his deputy, Lt. Gen. Martin Dzúr.

Lomský's brave action in condemning the Soviet-ordered Warsaw Pact invasion was highly commended by the progressives' radio and newspapers. It was by that time far too late to call off the intervention, even if the Soviet commanders had been willing to listen to their old friend. He was appointed in early 1969 to a seat in the Federal Assembly (the reconstituted National Assembly, which had been stripped of most of its authority). His last years were spent in quiet retirement and increasing ill health. A.K.

Father an engine driver. **Education** Secondary sch.; Hranice Military Acad. 1933–36; Voroshilov Higher Military Acad., Moscow 1944–47. **Career** Lt., Czechoslovak Legion, Poland late 1930s; 1st lt. in Air Force and cofounder of Czechoslovak Army units, USSR 1939; 1st lt. and comdr. of defense district admin., Czechoslovakia 1947; div. (brig.) gen. and comdr., Brno Military-Technical Acad. 1951–53; lt. gen. 1954; col. gen. 1956; gen. of army 1960–68; staff member, Inst. of Military History, Prague since 1968. • Member since 1950, and member of Central Cttee. 1958–68, Czechoslovak C.P.; deputy minister of natl. defense 1954–56; minister of natl. defense 1956–58; deputy 1960–68 and member of Cultural Cttee. and of Defense and Security Council 1968, Natl. Assembly; member, Chamber of the People, Federal Assembly since 1969. **Honors** Order of White Lion 1948; Order of Labor 1964; Order of Red Star; Order of Red Banner; others.

Further reading H. Gordon Skilling, *Czechoslovakia's Interrupted Revolution,* 1976.

BARON BOURNE OF ATHERSTONE
Geoffrey Kemp Bourne
General in the British Army
***Born* England, 5 October 1902**
***Died* England, 26 June 1982**

Lord Bourne, one of Britain's most experienced generals, was commander of the British sector of Berlin during the 1948–49 airlift, and was director of military operations in Malaya while that country was recovering from civil war in the mid-1950s. He saw extensive service in World War II and in Ceylon and the Mideast.

The son of a colonel in the British Army, Geoffrey Kemp Bourne attended Rugby School and the Royal Military Academy at Woolwich. In 1923 he was commissioned into the Royal Artillery and posted first to Hong Kong, then to Gibraltar. After two years of study at the General Staff College (1935–36), he was assigned to the War Office in London, where he demonstrated considerable skill as a planning and staff officer.

Bourne held a variety of commands during World War II, but, because of his proven ability as a staff officer and because he had lost an arm in an accident as a young man, he saw active field service for only a few months in 1944 as commander of an artillery regiment in Italy. After the war he was posted to Java, India, and Burma. In early 1949, now a major general, he was appointed commander of the British zone in Berlin. He helped maintain and expand "Operation Vittles," the massive Allied airlift that brought millions of tons of food to the city during the Soviet blockade of 1948–49.

After serving as commander in chief of the Eastern Command, Bourne was sent to Malaya, at that time still under British military rule. As director of military operations, he overpowered Malayan Communist insurgents, using helicopters and advanced jungle fighting tactics, and founded the Malayan Army. In 1957 he was briefly commander in chief of Britain's Middle East Defence Forces, then returned to England as commandant of the Imperial Defence College. He retired in 1960 and later was a director general of the Aluminum Federation and a chairman of the National Building Agency.

Bourne was made KBE in 1954 and a life peer in 1964. He died at the age of 79.

S.A.

Courtesy of M. Bourne

Parents Walter Kemp B., army col., and Eveleyn B. **Married** Agnes Eveleyn Thompson 1928: Elizabeth Anne McKay Robertson; Michael Kemp, banker. **Religion** Church of England. **Education** Rugby Sch., Warwickshire; Royal Mil. Acad., Woolwich; Gen. Staff Coll., Camberley 1935–36. **Career** With British Army: commissioned into Royal Artillery 1923; in Hong Kong 1930–32, Gibraltar 1933–34, Colchester 1937; gen. staff officer 3rd grade, War Office, London 1938–41; maj., then col., Jt. Planning Staff, London 1941–42; brig. gen. staff, Jt. Staff Mission, Wash. DC 1942–43; comdr., 21st Anti-Tank Regiment, Guards Armored Div. ca. 1943; with Planning HQ, Ceylon ca. 1943–44; comdr., 152nd Field Artillery Regiment, Ayrshire Yeomanry, Italy 1944; brig. gen. staff, Airborne Corps, Belgium 1945; comdr., 5th Indian Div., Java and India 1946; head, British Services Mission, Burma 1947–48; maj. gen. 1948; gen. officer comdg., British sector, Berlin 1949–51; gen. officer comdg., 16th Airborne Div., Territorial Army 1951–52; gen. officer comdr. in chief, Eastern Command 1953; lt. gen., gen. officer comdg., and dir. of operations, Malaya 1954–56; col. commandant, Royal Artillery 1954–67; comdr. in chief, Middle East Land Forces 1957; gen. since 1957; commandant, Imperial Defence Coll. 1958–59; aide-de-camp gen. to the Queen 1959–60. • Dir. gen., Aluminum Fedn. 1960–63; chmn., Natl. Building Agency 1967–73. **Officer** Chmn. and pres., Officers' Pension Soc. **Member** Army and Navy Club. **Honors** Duncan Essay Gold Medal, Royal Artillery Instn. 1935; OBE 1942; Silver Star and Legion of Merit, U.S. 1944; CBE 1947; C.B. 1949; CMG 1952; KBE 1954; KCB 1957; GCB 1960; hon. col., 10th Battalion, Parachute Regiment, Territorial Army 1960–65; created Baron Bourne of Atherstone, life peer, 1964.

CHAIM GRADE
Novelist and poet
***Born* Vilna, Lithuania, 5 April 1910**
***Died* New York City, USA, 26 June 1982**

For 400 years, the Lithuanian city of Vilna (now Vilnius in the Lithuanian Soviet Socialist Republic) was the most productive cultural center of Eastern European Jewish life. Since the sixteenth century, it was a locus of outstanding Talmudic scholarship. Since the eighteenth, it was also the home of the Maskilim, those who sought an intellectual partnership between rabbinic Judaism and the Enlightenment, and of the Mitnagdim, the rationalist Orthodox opponents of Chassidism. In the early twentieth century, a group of avant-garde Yiddish writers and artists, known collectively as Young Vilna, flourished there, together with headquarters of the Zionist and socialist movements. In 1943, this historic community, known as "the Jerusalem of Lithuania," was destroyed by the Nazis.

Chaim Grade, a member of Young Vilna who survived the Holocaust as a refugee in the Soviet Union, devoted the rest of his life to the imaginative resurrection of Jewish Vilna in novels, stories, and poems of the highest literary standard. He alone among the last generation of secularized Yiddish writers was educated in yeshivas and could describe from experience the emotional and intellectual complexities of European Orthodox life. His writing is full of concern for the delineation of moral issues and for the ordeal of doubt and self-renewal that those who survived the Nazi attack were forced to undergo.

Grade's childhood was touched by almost every aspect of Vilna's history. One of his great-grandparents was a grenadier in Napoleon's army who found shelter in Jewish Vilna during the retreat from Moscow and eventually married into the community. Grade's father, a Hebrew teacher, was a Maskil with strong secularist and Zionist leanings; his mother, an apple seller, was a pious woman who sent her son to study in yeshivas (religious academies). In one of these yeshivas, young Grade came under the influence of Musar, a spiritual movement that demands strenuous self-purification, asceticism, and adherence to a rigid ethical code. He also developed an intense, almost filial devotion to his teacher, a rabbi known as the Khazon Ish ("Vision of Man," after the title of his best-known book). The unresolvable conflict between the Enlightenment ideals of his father and the religious ideals of his teacher generated a creative tension that informed all his later work.

In 1932, the year of his rabbinic ordination and of the departure of his teacher for the Holy Land, Grade gave up Orthodox Judaism and began to write poetry and to immerse himself in the socialist politics and secularist culture of Young Vilna. His first book, a collection of poems entitled *Yes,* was published in 1936. His second, the long narrative poem *Musarnikes* (1939), described the ascetics of his yeshiva days. Though no longer completely observant, he worked out a faith based on the pantheistic principles of the Jewish rationalist philosopher Baruch Spinoza and on the transcendent possibilities of art. "It is impossible to find a poet who is not religious," he once said.

The USSR annexed Lithuania in 1940 and suppressed all Hebrew and Zionist groups and the Yiddish press. The following year, the Nazis invaded Vilna, immediately killed 35,000 of its Jewish inhabitants at the field of Ponary, and enclosed the rest in a ghetto from which they rounded up individuals from time to time for deportation to forced-labor and death camps. Grade succeeded in escaping from the city with the withdrawing Soviet Army, but his wife and widowed mother were trapped inside and murdered. Until the end of the war he remained in Russia, living on rations from the Writers Union. He later published five volumes of poems written during these years. Of the many Yiddish writers who befriended him in Moscow, including some who were ardent supporters of Stalin, virtually every one was executed during Stalin's anti-Semitic persecutions of the early 1950s.

By that time, Grade had emigrated to the United States with his second wife, Inna Hecker, the daughter of a surgeon who had been executed by the Germans as a partisan. On leaving Russia in 1948, he had returned for a brief time to Vilna, then had gone to Paris, where he headed the Yiddish literary club for two years. In 1948 he settled in New York, choosing to go there rather than to Israel in order to avoid a confrontation with the aged Khazon Ish, whose claims on his loyalty had grown even more intense after the events of the Holocaust. The theological problem posed by the Holocaust—how to account for so awful a degree of suffering in a world ruled by a God of justice and compassion—was the subject of Grade's first prose work, the celebrated story "My Quarrel with Hersh Rasseyner" (1950). It took the form of an argument between Grade's literary alter ego, Chaim Vilner, and a Musarist rabbi for whom the Holocaust, far from being a disproof of God, is the final proof that only religious faith, not politics or philosophy, can save humans from their own evil.

Grade, whose early years as a writer were spent in questioning traditional Jewish values and customs, now took up the task of memorializing the Jews of Vilna in fiction. He published his short stories and serialized his novels in New York's secular Yiddish newspapers (of which, by the 1970s, only the *Jewish Daily Forward* remained). His was a small but devoted readership for whom he published many of his own books. His prose style is dense and descriptive—far more so than that of either Sholem Aleichem or Isaac Bashevis Singer, the two writers of Yiddish best known to American readers—and his Yiddish, because of its religious content, is heavily flavored with Hebrew. Critics of Yiddish fiction have been almost unanimous in their praise for the skill with which he caught the details of everyday life, his attention to moral and philosophical issues, and his ability to convey the subtleties of Jewish legal scholarship and the tensions that threatened to split the Jewish community apart at the same time that they held it together. His translator, Curt Leviant, observed: "Chaim Grade has written about one people in its entirety. He thereby joins that rare company of writers whose art is national in that it touches every fibre—religious, historic, societal, linguistic and folkloristic—of a complete civilization." For many years he lectured on Jewish literature and culture to Yiddish-speaking audiences in the U.S., Canada, Latin America, Africa, and Israel.

Although Grade's work received frequent translations into Hebrew, he remained virtually unknown to readers of English until 1974, when his novel *The Agunah* was published in an English translation by Leviant. An agunah, in Jewish law, is a woman whose husband is missing and who cannot remarry lest she unknowingly commit adultery. In the novel, this appalling predicament (which continues to afflict Orthodox women to this day) results in a violent confrontation between two rabbis, one bent on upholding the law despite the suffering it causes and the other willing to subvert it for humanitarian reasons, with the Jewish community split between them.

The Agunah was followed in 1976–77 by a translation of Grade's epic two-volume novel *The Yeshiva.* Set in the Musarist school of his youth, it re-created the singularly dedicated and obsessive world of the Talmudic academy. Its main character, the rabbi Tsemakh Atlas, a man tortured by desire and lack of faith, was, it has been suggested, an image of what the author might have become had he sacrificed his creativity and embraced the ultra-Orthodox life of the Khazon Ish. In the process of bringing this character to a renunciation of extremist piety and toward a temperate and healing faith, Grade constructs a panoramic view of the milieu in which Jewish religious scholarship was carried on for centuries.

No further translation of Grade's work reached the English-speaking public until after his death of a heart attack at the age of 72. Both *Rabbis and Wives,* a collection of novellas, and *My Mother's Sabbath Days,* a

Courtesy of Aaron Broches

memoir, were scheduled for posthumous publication. Arrangements were also being made to publish in Yiddish and English two more novels, *The Old House* and *From Beneath the Ground.* J.P.

Parents Shlomo-Mordecai G., rabbi and Hebrew teacher, and Vella (Blumenthal) G., apple peddler. **Married** (1) Fruma-Lieba Klepfich, nurse, 1936 (d. 1943). (2) Inna Hecker, writer. **Religion** Jewish. **Emigration** Refugee in USSR 1941–46; in Paris 1946–48; emigrated to U.S. 1948, naturalized 1960. **Education** Yeshivas in Vilna, Valkenik, and Bialystok; received rabbinic ordination 1932. **Career** Poet since 1932; member of Young Vilna literary group 1930s; head of Yiddish PEN club, Paris 1946–48; novelist and memoirist since 1950s; lectr. on literature, philosophy, and Hebrew culture, North and South America, Africa, Israel. **Honors** Lamed Prize, for *My Mother's Sabbath Days,* 1955; Epstein Fiction Award, for *The Well,* Jewish Book Council, Natl. Jewish Welfare Bd. 1968; Remembrance Award, for *The Seven Little Lanes,* World Fedn. of Bergen-Belsen Assns. 1969; Manger Prize, Israel 1970; Jewish Heritage Award for Excellence, 1976, and special award for *The Yeshiva,* B'nai B'rith; Bimko Prize, for *My Mother's Testament;* Leivick Prize; special prize in literature, Amer. Acad. for Jewish Research; hon. degrees from Jewish Theological Seminary, Hebrew Union Coll./Jewish Inst. of Religion, and Yeshiva Univ. **Poetry** *Yo* [*Yes*], 1937; *Musarnikes* [*Followers of Musar*], 1939; *Has* [*Hatred*], 1943; *Doyres* [*Generations*], 1945; *Mit dayn guf oyf mayne hent* [*With Your Body on My Hands*], 1946; *Oyf di khurves* [*On the Ruins*], 1947; *Pleytim* [*Refugees*], 1947; *Farvaksene vegn* [*Overgrown Paths*], 1947; *Der mames tsvoe* [*My Mother's Testament*], 1949; *Di shayn fun farloshene shtern* [*The Light of Extinguished Stars*], 1950; *Der mentsh fun fayer* [*The Man of Fire*], 1962; *Elegiye oyf di sovetish-yidishe shraybers*, 1962 (trans. as *Elegy for the Soviet-Yiddish Writers*, 1969); *Parmetene erd* [*Parchment Earth*], 1968. **Short stories and story collections** "Mayn krig mit Hersh Rasseyner," 1950 (trans. as "My Quarrel with Hersh Rasseyner," in Irving Howe and Eliezer Greenberg, eds., *A Treasury of Yiddish Stories*, 1954); *Di kloyz un di gas* [*Synagogue and Street*], 1974; *Der shtumer minyan* [*The Silent Minyan*], 1976. **Novels** *Der shulhoyf* [*The Synagogue Courtyard*] (novellas), 1958; *Der brunem* (novella), 1958 (trans. as *The Well*, 1967); *Di agune*, 1961 (trans. as *The Agunah*, 1974); *Tsemakh Atlas*, vol. 1, 1967, vol. 2, 1968 (trans. as *The Yeshiva*, vol. 1, 1976, vol. 2, 1977); *Rabbis and Wives* (novellas), 1982; *The Old House* (forthcoming); *From Beneath the Ground* (forthcoming). **Memoirs** *Der mame's shabbosim,* 1959 (partial trans. as *The Seven Little Lanes,* 1972; trans. as *My Mother's Sabbath Days* [forthcoming]).

Further reading S. Liptzin, *The Maturing of Yiddish Literature,* 1970; Curt Leviant, "The Prose of Chaim Grade," in *Midstream,* Nov. 1974; Ruth R. Wisse, "In Praise of Chaim Grade," in *Commentary,* Apr. 1977; Morton A. Reichek, "A Writer in Search of an Audience," in *Present Tense,* Summer 1978; Inna Hecker, "Chaim Grade: The Challenge to God," and "Chaim Grade: A Portrait of the Man," in *Judaica Book News,* Spring-Summer 1979.

ALEXANDER MITSCHERLICH
Psychoanalyst and physician
***Born* Hof, Bavaria, Germany, 20 September 1908**
***Died* Frankfurt-am-Main, West Germany, 26 June 1982**

Alexander Mitscherlich, a doctor and psychoanalyst who constantly sought to integrate those two disciplines, was the person most responsible for bringing the study and practice of psychoanalysis back to Germany after it had been banned during the Nazi regime. His most important accomplishment lay in his unremitting effort to force his fellow Germans to confront the horrors of the Hitler years and to accept their personal and collective responsibility and guilt.

He attended the University of Munich in the late 1920s, where he was active in left-wing politics. His vocal opposition to the rise of Nazism caused his doctoral dissertation—on Martin Luther—to be rejected, and he moved to Berlin, where he opened a bookstore. This was forcibly closed when the Nazis came to power in 1933, and he went into exile in Switzerland, beginning his medical studies in Zurich in 1935. In 1937 he returned to Germany to arrange for the legal defense of his political comrade Ernst Niekisch, was arrested, and spent eight months in jail in Nuremberg; once released, he was made to report to the Gestapo twice a day until the end of the war. He worked during the war at the clinic of the University of Heidelberg, and in late 1945, after the collapse of the Third Reich, he was finally admitted to the practice of medicine.

In 1946, Mitscherlich was named to head the German Medical Commission to the Nuremberg Military Tribunal, and he observed the trial of 23 doctors who were charged with conducting inhuman medical experiments for the SS on concentration-camp and prison inmates. Fifteen were convicted, seven were hanged, and none showed any remorse. With Fred Mielke he wrote an account of the trial to show his fellow Germans, who were extremely reluctant to accept the fact that atrocities had been committed in their name by their government over the previous decade. The book made a considerable impact: more than 100,000 copies were sold and extracts were eventually incorporated into school textbooks. The book appeared in the United States in 1949 under the title *Doctors of Infamy*. In a revised and expanded version the work won the Peace Prize of the West German book trade in 1969, a prize that had previously been given to Martin Buber and Albert Schweitzer.

Mitscherlich began an intensive study of psychoanalysis when at last permitted to do so, although he had been secretly learning the subject since the late 1930s. Psychosomatic medicine, a subject also banned under the Nazis, was a particular interest. In 1948 he founded the first German psychosomatic clinic, at the University of Heidelberg Medical School, and directed it until 1967. He was appointed professor of psychosomatic medicine at Heidelberg in 1952, and in 1959 the University of Frankfurt-am-Main named him professor of psychology and director of the Sigmund Freud Institute for Psychoanalysis and Psychosomatic Medicine, where he remained until his retirement in 1976. That year, he gave the annual Freud Anniversary Lecture before the New York Psychoanalytic Society. His best-known work in this field is *Illness as Conflict* (1966), a strong advocacy of a holistic (mind-and-body) approach to human health.

Again and again during his career, Mitscherlich returned to what he considered the central problem of German society: its unwillingness to confront the past. He was convinced that virtually all sectors of society "had given the regime their definite and enthusiastic support; but with its failure they regarded themselves as automatically absolved from personal responsibility." This "intensive defense against guilt, shame, and anxiety" required "a very considerable expenditure of psychic energy" and could in no way be ultimately successful. The definitive statement of his ideas on collective behavior is *The Inability to Mourn* (1967; English ed. 1969), which he wrote with his third wife, the Danish-born physician Margarete Mitscherlich-Nielsen.

His later works were often wide-ranging in their themes. The disappearance of the father-dominated family and its gradual replacement by a technology-dominated consumer society was the subject of *Society Without the Father* (1967; English ed. 1969); *The Idea of Peace and Human Aggression* (1969) emphasized his belief that destructive behavior is caused primarily by such social factors as collective consciousness; and in *The Desolation of Our Towns* (1965) he sharply criticized the utter lack of human-centered planning as the cause of the anomie of postwar German society.

Mitscherlich died at the age of 73 after a long illness. A.K.

Married (1) . . . (2) . . . (3) Margarete Neilsen, psychoanalyst. **Children** Two sons and three daughters from first two marriages; one son from third marriage. **Education** Gymnasium, Hof, Bavaria; Univs. of Prague, Berlin, and Freiburg; Univ. of Munich early 1930s; Univ. of Zurich 1935–37; Univ. of Heidelberg, medical degree 1946; studied psychoanalysis late 1940s. **Career** Bookseller early 1930s; active in leftist anti-Nazi resistance late 1930s; imprisoned, Nuremberg 1937; neurologist from 1945, later psychoanalyst; position in postwar govt.; head observer, German Medical Commn., Nuremberg War Crimes Trials 1946–48. • With Medical Sch., Univ. of Heidelberg: worked at clinic, WWII; founder 1948 and dir. 1948–67, Psychosomatic Clinic; extraordinary prof. of psychosomatic medicine 1952–58. • Founder 1959 and dir. 1959–76, Freud Inst. for Psychoanalysis and Psychosomatic Medicine, and prof. of psychology 1967–76, Univ. of Frankfurt; Freud Anniversary Lectr., New York Psychoanalytic Soc. 1976; lectr., Downstate Medical Center, NYC 1976. **Honors** Hon. member, Amer. Psychoanalytic Soc. 1952; Peace Prize for *Doctors of Infamy,* West German Book Trade 1969. **Author** (Jtly.) *Freier Sozialismus* [*Free Socialism*], 1946; *Freiheit und Unfreiheit in der Krankheit* [*Freedom and Slavery in Illness*], 1946; *Vom Ursprung der Sucht* [*On the Origin of Passion*], 1947; *Endlose Diktatur?* [*Endless Dictator?*], 1947; (jtly.) *Das Diktat der Menschenverachtung,* 1947 (trans. as *Doctors of Infamy,* 1949); (jtly.) *Wissenschaft ohne Menschlichkeit,* 1949, reissued as *Medizin ohne Menschlichkeit,* 1960 (trans. as *The Death Doctors,* 1962); (ed.) *Entfaltung der Psychoanalyse: das Wirken Sigmund Freuds in die Gegenwart* [*Development of Psychoanalysis: The Work of Sigmund Freud Today*], 1956; *Auf dem Weg zur vaterlosen Gesellschaft,* 1963 (trans. as *Society Without the Father,* 1969); *Die Unwirtlichkeit unserer Städte* [*The Desolation of Our Towns*], 1965; *Krankheit als Konflikt* [*Illness as Conflict*], 2 vols., 1966–67; (with Margarete Mitscherlich) *Die Unfähigkeit zu trauern,* 1967 (trans. as *The Inability To Mourn,* 1975); (ed.) *Der Kranke in der modernen Gesellschaft* [*Illness in Modern Society*], 1967; *Die idee des Friedens und die menschliche Aggressivität* [*The Idea of Peace and Human Aggression*], 1969; *Bis hierher und nicht weiter* [*To Here and No Further*], 1969; *Versuch, die Welt besser zu bestehen* [*Experiment to Better the World*], 1970; (with M. M.) *Eine deutsche Art zu lieben* [*A Germany to Love*], 1970; *Heimat/Nation* [*Homeland/Nation*], 1971; *Thesen zur Stadt der Zukunft* [*The Future City*], 1971; (co-ed.) *Hauptworte, Hauptsachen* [*Essential Points*], 1971; *Die Zähmung menschlicher Aggression im Dienste des Friedens* [*The Domestication of Human Aggression in the Service of Peace*], 1971; *Psycho-Pathographien* [*Psychopathographies*], 1972; *Wege in die städtische Zukunft* [*Loss in the Urban Future*], 1972; *Über Treue und Familie* [*On Loyalty and Family*], 1972; *Massenpsychologie ohne Ressentiment* [*Psychology of a People Without Remorse*], 1972; *Über Eigentum und Gewalt* [*On Property and Power*], 1972; *Utopie oder Wirklichkeit* [*Utopia or Actuality*], 1973; *Toleranz* [*Tolerance*], 1974; *Der Kampf um die Erinnerung* [*Struggle of the Memory*], 1975; (jtly.) *Glück, Gerechtigkeit* [*Luck, Justice*], 1976; *Das Ich und die Vielen* [*The I and the Many*], 1978. **Contributor** to professional jrnls.

PIERRE (ALEXANDRE CLAUDIUS) BALMAIN
Couturier
Born Saint-Jean-de-Maurienne, Savoy, France, 18 May 1914
Died Neuilly-sur-Seine, Paris, France, 29 June 1982

Pierre Balmain, designer of timelessly elegant clothes and one of the leading figures in Parisian haute couture since his first independent show in 1945, was among those responsible for creating the postwar "new look," a softly contoured style that replaced the severe, angular lines of the women's clothing of the 1930s and 1940s. In a profession associated with rapidly changed modes and flamboyance, Balmain was noted for luxurious simplicity and restraint, qualities that made him the favorite designer of many titled women, including Princess Anne of Denmark, Queen Sirikit of Thailand, and the Duchess of Windsor. He shunned self-conscious innovation, and strove for continuity, criticizing the press for demanding a new line for every year's collection: "Fashion is not planned. It must impose itself on the designer. We cannot sit down and decide to create longer skirts. New trends in clothes are not just plucked out of the air." The director of Balmain's workshop, Ginette Spanier, said in 1960: "We dress the most elegant private clientele, who do not care to look dated when they wear a suit they like the second year." The hallmark of the house of Balmain was luxurious ballgowns with wide, bouffant skirts that evoked the formal, traditionally "feminine" styles of the early years of the twentieth century.

The son of a wholesale merchant, Balmain was educated at the Lycée Chambéry and went to Paris at the age of 18 to study architecture at the École des Beaux Arts. His inclinations had already turned to clothing design, however, and when his mother, who was widowed in 1921, found herself unable to pay for his education, he took his sketches to the leading Paris designers of the day—Lelong, Lanvin, Piguet, and Molyneux. It was from Molyneux, for whom he worked until 1939, that Balmain learned his expertise in tailoring and his taste for understated elegance.

At the outbreak of war, Balmain was drafted into a pioneer regiment and sent to his native province of Savoy. There he met Gertrude Stein and Alice B. Toklas, who remained his lifelong friends and supporters. In

Courtesy of French Embassy

his autobiography *My Years and Seasons* (1964), Balmain relates that, during visits to his mother in wartime and during the German occupation, he took Stein and Toklas supplies of Parisian delicacies and warm clothes that he had made himself. They repaid his kindness by helping him promote his designs during his first visit to the United States in 1946. Gertrude Stein wrote in *Vogue* magazine at the time of the showing of his first collection in 1945: "I suppose there at the opening we were the only ones who had dressed all those long years in Pierre Balmain's clothes; we were proud of it. It is nice to know the young man when he is just a young man . . . [whom] nobody knows, and now, well, I guess very soon anybody will know."

After his release from the Army in 1940, Balmain joined the house of Lucien Lelong, where one of his colleagues was Christian Dior. Both intended to found their own houses, but Balmain was the first to become an independent designer, working out of a building on the rue François Ier that remains the headquarters of the Balmain company. With 16 employees and a small amount of capital provided by his mother, who sold some of her jewelry, Balmain put together his first collection, shown on 12 October 1945. His clothes were an instant success with a French public weary of austerity, who immediately propelled Balmain to the height of his profession—a position in which he remained for the rest of his life. Alice B. Toklas wrote of this event: "Suddenly there was the awakening to a new understanding of what mode really was, the embellishment and the intensification of women's form and charm."

The "new look" of postwar Paris couture is generally credited to Balmain, Cristobal Balenciaga, Jacques Fath, and Christian Dior. Balmain was the first of these to acquire a reputation outside France, at first through a commission to design for the wedding of Lady Ednam's daughter to the Argentine ambassador to the Court of St. James, and later through his astute marketing of ready-to-wear clothing based on haute couture designs in the United States, South America, and Japan, where he opened a boutique in 1968. In 1947 he was the first couturier to visit Australia, and his role as self-appointed ambassador for what *Le Monde* called "good taste and Parisian elegance" did much to reinstate Paris to its prewar position as the center of fashion. By the time of his death, Balmain had licensed 130 manufacturers to make more than 60 products bearing his name, including clothes

Courtesy of French Embassy

and accessories for men. The Balmain perfume business, inaugurated by "Vent Vert" in 1946, grew rapidly to include two more popular scents, "Jolie Madame" (1953) and "Miss Balmain" (1967). The line of perfumes was sold to Revlon in 1960. By the late 1960s, Balmain's clients included many film stars, including Marlene Dietrich, Joan Fontaine, Katharine Hepburn, Ingrid Bergman, and Sophia Loren.

Having begun as an innovator whose designs appealed primarily to the young, Balmain came to be noted as a designer of refined, unostentatious clothes for older women, and often used his mother as a model. When, in the 1960s, skirts became shorter and styles for women reflected new ideas of femininity, Balmain declined to change the approach that had proved so successful, and thus retained his wealthy, conservative clients, who grew older with him. An accomplished, charming, and cosmopolitan man who spoke English and Italian fluently, Balmain was a member of the Polo Club of Paris and a chevalier (later an officer) of the Légion d'Honneur; he maintained houses in Morocco, Elba, and Normandy, and led a social existence that was in perfect harmony with the distinctive aura of his couture business. His acceptance in the social milieu of the women

Courtesy of French Embassy

who purchased his dresses seems to have served as model for the careers of younger designers such as Oscar de la Renta, but Balmain's distinction was matched among his contemporaries only by Cecil Beaton, the leading example of what society columnists call "a confirmed bachelor."

Balmain was working in Japan on his fall collection when he became ill, and completed his designs for the show only days before his death from cancer of the liver. The Balmain show in the Grand Hotel, Paris, on 26 July 1982, was directed by Eric Mortenson, an assistant and friend of Balmain's for more than 25 years, who will continue to produce Balmain clothes. H.B.

Parents Maurice B., wholesale merchant, and Françoise (Ballinari) B., dressmaker. **Religion** Roman Catholic. **Education** Lycée, Chambéry, bachelier ès sciences; architecture sect., École des Beaux Arts, Paris 1933. **Mil. service** 440th Pioneer Regiment, Savoie 1939. **Career** Dress designer with fashion house of Capt. Edward Molyneux, Paris 1934–39; dress designer with fashion house of Lucien Lelong, Paris 1940–45; couturier, Maison Pierre Balmain, Paris since 1945, branches opened in NYC 1951–55, Caracas 1954, Tokyo 1960;

perfumer 1946–60; dir. gen., Pierre Balmain S.A. since 1977; also designer for stage and cinema; advisor to Govt. of France on foreign commerce. **Officer** V.P., Comité Colbert. **Member** Rotary Club, Automobile Club, and Polo Club, all Paris. **Honors** Officer, Légion d'Honneur 1961; kt., Order of Dannebrog, Denmark 1963; cavaliere ufficiale, Order of Merit, Italy 1966; Médaille de Vermeille, City of Paris; chevalier, Order of Saints Maurice and Lazare. **Author** *My Years and Seasons* (memoirs), 1964.

HENRY KING
Film director
***Born* Christiansburg, Virginia, USA, 24 January 1888**
***Died* San Fernando Valley, California, USA, 29 June 1982**

Few American filmgoers recognize the name of Henry King, yet he was one of the most prolific and versatile directors in the history of the art. Of his 103 pictures, most of which he made for Darryl Zanuck at Twentieth Century–Fox, a dozen have become classics, from the silents *Tol'able David* and *Stella Dallas* to *The Song of Bernadette* and *Twelve O'Clock High*. He was a follower of D. W. Griffith in his use of innovative camera work and editing to convey nuances of meaning and to guide the audience's imagination. More than Griffith, he had a knack for coaxing remarkably convincing performances out of his players. He regarded film as a craft and a business, and during his years at Fox was relied on to direct all kinds of routine projects, many of which he managed to make into much better films than their screenplays deserved.

King, of old Southern stock (his grandfather was an officer on Robert E. Lee's general staff), grew up on his father's farm near Christiansburg, Virginia, and attended a private school in Roanoke. For a time he was a combustion engineer with the Norfolk and Western Railroad, but he soon gave that up to tour the South as an entertainer with stock companies, circuses, and vaudeville troops. In 1912 he was signed as a film actor with the Lubin Co., and shortly afterward moved to the Balboa Amusement Co., where, in addition to acting, he wrote scenarios and began to direct short features. Between 1915 and 1919 he directed more than 30 pictures for the General Film Co., American Mutual, and Pathé. Fired by Famous Players–Lasky for exceeding his budget for *23½ Hours Leave* (1919), his first big success, he went to Robertson Cole studios, and after that company went bankrupt in 1921 helped to form Inspiration Pictures with financing provided by Averell Harriman.

The first film produced by Inspiration was *Tol'able David* (1921), an adaptation of a Joseph Hergesheimer short story about a poor boy from a peaceful mountain village and his confrontation with an invading gang of outlaws. The film, which starred his partner Richard Barthelmess, was shot in Virginia, close to King's childhood home; in later years he was often to return to the theme of traditional life in rural America. The Soviet film

Courtesy of Culver Pictures

director V. I. Pudovkin cited *Tol'able David* as an example of good scene construction through the intercutting of shots and of the proper manipulation of "plastic material" (incidental details that subtly reveal character). Most critics consider it to be one of the masterpieces of the silent era.

During the 1920s King tried his hand at a variety of genres, mostly for Sam Goldwyn's studio. His *The White Sister* (1924), which starred Lillian Gish as an Italian woman who takes the veil and Ronald Colman as her lover, was the first major U.S. film shot on location in Italy. For *The Winning of Barbara Worth* (1926) King gambled successfully on a taciturn cowboy from Montana, Gary Cooper, to play the lead. The most impressive of his 1920s films was undoubtedly *Stella Dallas* (1925), a surprisingly affecting melodrama about a scheming woman who gives up everything for her daughter.

In 1930 King switched to talkies and began his 30-year association with Twentieth Century–Fox. He was more concerned with the technical problems of making good, salable movies than with the demands of "art" and hence fit into the all-controlling studio system better than other directors who got their more ambitious wings clipped. His notable films of the decade included *State Fair* (1933), another sympathetic glimpse of rural Americana that was very popular (though Dwight MacDonald accused it of making light of the terrible conditions besetting farmers in Depression times); *Alexander's Ragtime Band* (1938), for which King received the first of his five Oscar nominations; and *In Old Chicago* (1938), the predecessor of the modern disaster movie, in which the historically dubious plot is compensated for by a costly but magnificent re-creation of the Chicago Fire of 1871.

King received two consecutive Academy Award nominations in 1944 and 1945 for a pair of biographies, *The Song of Bernadette,* a tactful and sensitive account of the Lourdes peasant girl who became a saint, and *Wilson,* a historical drama about the U.S. president; two unknowns, Jennifer Jones and Alexander Knox, were featured in the lead roles. During World War II King served in the Civilian Air Patrol, an auxiliary to the Army Air Corps that he had helped to found, and made *A Bell for Adano* (1945), after John Hersey's novel, and the sweetly nostalgic *Margie* (1946). He continued his long series of Tyrone Power swashbucklers with *The Black Swan* (1942), *Captain from Castile* (1946), *Prince of Foxes* (1949), and *King of the Khyber Rifles* (1953). With Gregory Peck he made two outstanding films, *Twelve O'Clock High* (1949), about the breakdown of a hard-nosed Air Force commander, which won King his fourth Oscar nomination, and *The Gunfighter* (1950), a psychological western that was not fully appreciated until years later.

In the 1950s, King continued to churn out pictures in whatever genre was called for—rural charmers *(I'd Climb the Highest Mountain,* 1951), biblical spectacles *(David and Bathsheba,* 1951), romances *(Love is a Many-Splendored Thing,* 1955, his fifth Oscar nomination), musicals *(Carousel,* 1956), and film biographies *(Beloved Infidel,* 1959). He also adapted two Hemingway novels, *The Snows of Kilimanjaro* (1956) and *The Sun Also Rises* (1957), both of which got mixed reviews, and F. Scott Fitzgerald's *Tender Is the Night* (1961), which turned out to be his last movie. Soon after it was made, King's mentor Zanuck lost his job in a power shuffle and King was retired.

Despite the popularity of so many of his films (which form the very backbone of the late-night television repertoire) and the respect in which he was held by other filmmakers, King received very little in the way of serious critical attention in the last 20 years and had to be rediscovered by the Museum of Modern Art in New York, which put together a seven-week retrospective of his films in 1978. In retirement he logged some 12,000 miles each year in his private plane, and when he died, at the age of 94, he was the oldest licensed pilot in U.S. history. J.P./M.T.

Father a farmer and lawyer. **Married** (1) Gypsy (d. 1952): Henry; John; Martha Ellen Creber. (2) Ida King Davis 1959. **Religion** Raised a Protestant; converted to Roman Catholicism. **Education** Roanoke Coll., VA. **Mil. service** Lt. col. and co-founder, Civil Air Patrol, WWII. **Career** Combustion engineer, Norfolk and Western Railroad, VA; actor in stock cos. and vaudeville troops early 1910s; film actor 1912–20. • Film dir.: various Hollywood studios 1915–30; (also co-founder) Inspiration Pictures 1921–25; 20th Century-Fox 1930–61. **Member** Founding member, Directors Guild of America. **Honors** Academy Award nominations 1939, for *Alexander's Ragtime Band,* 1944, for *The Song of Bernadette,* 1945, for *Wilson,* 1950, for *Twelve O'Clock High,* and 1956, for *Love Is a Many-*

Splendored Thing; D. W. Griffith Award, Directors Guild of America 1956; Medal of Honor, George Eastman House; retrospectives at MOMA 1978, Univ. of California at Los Angeles, British Film Inst. **Films** Forty-five short subjects and features 1915–21; *23½ Hours Leave,* 1919; *Tol'able David,* 1921; *The Seventh Day,* 1922; *Sonny,* 1922; *Bond Boy,* 1922; *Fury,* 1923; *The White Sister,* 1924; *Romola,* 1925; (also producer) *Any Woman,* 1925; (also producer) *Sackcloth and Scarlet,* 1925; *Stella Dallas,* 1925; *Partners Again,* 1926; *The Winning of Barbara Worth,* 1926; (also producer) *The Magic Flame,* 1927; (also producer) *The Woman Disputed,* 1928; (also producer) *She Goes to War,* 1929; (also producer) *Hell Harbor,* 1930; *Lightnin',* 1930; (also producer) *The Eyes of the World,* 1930; *Merely Mary Ann,* 1931; *Over the Hill,* 1931; *The Woman in Room 13,* 1932; *State Fair,* 1933; *I Loved You Wednesday,* 1933; *Carolina,* 1934; *Marie Galante,* 1934; *One More Spring,* 1935; *Way Down East,* 1935; *The Country Doctor,* 1936; *Lloyds of London,* 1936; *Ramona,* 1936; *Seventh Heaven,* 1937; *In Old Chicago,* 1938; *Alexander's Ragtime Band,* 1938; *Jesse James,* 1939; *Stanley and Livingstone,* 1939; *Little Old New York,* 1940; *Maryland,* 1940; *Chad Hanna,* 1940; *A Yank in the RAF,* 1941; *Remember the Day,* 1941; *The Black Swan,* 1942; *The Song of Bernadette,* 1943; *Wilson,* 1944; *A Bell for Adano,* 1945; *Margie,* 1946; *Captain from Castile,* 1947; *Deep Waters,* 1948; *Twelve O'Clock High,* 1949; *Prince of Foxes,* 1949; *The Gunfighter,* 1950; *I'd Climb the Highest Mountain,* 1951; *David and Bathsheba,* 1951; *Wait Till the Sun Shines, Nellie,* 1952; (episode) *O. Henry's Full House,* 1952; *The Snows of Kilimanjaro,* 1952; *King of the Khyber Rifles,* 1953; *Untamed,* 1955; *Love Is a Many-Splendored Thing,* 1955; *Carousel,* 1956; *The Sun Also Rises,* 1957; *The Bravados,* 1958; *The Old Man and the Sea* (uncredited), 1958; *This Earth is Mine,* 1959; *Beloved Infidel,* 1959; *Tender Is the Night,* 1961.

Further reading Roy Pickard, "The Tough Race," in *Films and Filming,* Sept. 1971.

(LEONARD) MALCOLM SAVILLE

Writer of children's books

***Born* Hastings, Sussex, England, 21 February 1901**

***Died* Hastings, Sussex, England, 30 June 1982**

Malcolm Saville was a prolific author of mystery and adventure novels for children. In the tradition of Arthur Ransome's Swallows and Amazons books, they provided lessons in idealism as well as action, and were very popular with several generations of young readers. In all, he wrote more than 80 books of fiction and nonfiction.

Saville was born in Sussex, the son of a bookseller, and attended the Richmond Hill School in Surrey. From 1920 to 1942 he worked in the publicity and sales promotion departments of a succession of publishers, including the Amalgamated Press (1922–36) and the George Newnes Company (1936–40). During World War II he served as controller with an Air Raid Prevention unit while his wife and children were evacuated to Shropshire. To entertain them, he wrote a novel about a secret society, the Lone Pine Club, whose youthful members share adventures and promise to "be true to each other whatever happens." It was published by Newnes in 1943. Saville eventually wrote a total of 20 Lone Pine novels that sold more than 2 million copies. The first and second books were serialized on BBC radio's "Children's Hour" program.

After the war, Saville, while continuing to write fiction, was associate editor of *My Garden* magazine until 1952 and a writer for Kemsley Newspapers from 1952 to 1955, when he returned to Newnes as general books editor. After his retirement in 1966 he wrote full-time. He created other juvenile series—Susan and Bill, Michael and Mary, the Buckinghams, the Jillies—to cover both sexes and all age groups. For preadolescents he wrote the Marston Baines thrillers, in which a sporty secret agent and his spy companions pursue sinister individuals and menacing organizations in exotic locales. Most of his books for younger children were set in the English countryside, which he vividly re-created.

In addition to the adventure books, he wrote, particularly in the 1970s, nonfiction books about country life, London's sights, nature exploration, and gardening; *King of Kings,* a retelling of the life of Jesus; two stories for the Children's Film Foundation, and one for BBC television.

Saville's numerous readers were a loyal lot and he kept in touch with them by speaking in schools, publishing a newsletter about his activities, and answering each of the 3,000 fan letters he received each year. His last Lone Pine novel, *Home to Witchend,* was issued in 1978; the following year he published *Words for All Seasons,* an anthology of religious verse and prose. L.F.

Parents Ernest Vivian S., bookseller, and Fanny Ethel (Hayes) S. **Married** Dorothy May McCoy 1926: two sons; two daughters. **Religion** Christian. **Education** Richmond Hill Sch., Richmond, Surrey; other schs. **Mil. service** Controller, Air Raid Prevention unit, WWII. **Career** With publicity dept., Cassell & Co., publishers, London 1920–22; sales promotion mgr. 1936–40 and gen. books ed. 1957–66, George Newnes Co., publishers, London; assoc. ed. and writer, *My Garden* mag., London 1947–52; writer, Kemsley Newspapers, London 1952–55. • Children's book writer since 1943. **Member** Soc. of Authors; Savage Club, London. **Partial list of juvenile fiction** In Lost Pine series: *Mystery at Witchend* (in U.S. as *Spy in the Hills),* 1943; *Seven White Gales,* 1944; *The Gay Dolphin Adventure,* 1945; *The Secret of Grey Walls,* 1947; *Lone Pine Five,* 1949; *The Elusive Grasshopper,* 1951; *The Neglected Mountain,* 1953; *Saucers over the Moor,* 1955; *Wings over Witchend,* 1956; *Lone Pine London,* 1957; *The Secret of the Gorge,* 1958; *Mystery Mine,* 1959; *Sea Witch Comes Home,* 1960; *Not Scarlet but Gold,* 1962; *Treasure at Amorys,* 1964; *The Man with Three Fingers,* 1966; *Rye Royal,* 1969; *Strangers at Witchend,* 1970; *Where's My Girl?,* 1972; *Home to Witchend,* 1978. • In Marston Baines series: *Three Towers in Tuscany,* 1963; *The Purple Valley,* 1964; *Dark Danger,* 1965; *White Fire,* 1966; *Power of Three,* 1968; *The Dagger and the Flame,* 1970; *Marston—Master Spy,* 1978. **Nonfiction and religious** *Country Scrap Book,* 1944; *Open-Air Scrap Book,* 1945; *Seaside Scrap Book,* 1946; *Coronation Gift Book,* 1952; *King of Kings,* 1958; *Small Creatures,* 1959; *Malcolm Saville's Country Book,* 1962; *Malcolm Saville's Seaside Book,* 1962; *Strange Story,* 1967; *Come to London,* 1967; *Come to Cornwall,* 1969; *Come to Devon,* 1969; *Come to Somerset,* 1970; *Eat What You Grow,* 1975; *Portrait of Rye,* 1977; *Discovering the Woodland,* 1978; *Countryside Quiz,* 1978; *Wonder Why Book of Exploring a Wood,* 1978; *Wonder Why Book of Exploring the Seashore,* 1979; *Words for All Seasons,* 1979; *Wonder Why Book of Wild Flowers Through the Year,* 1980.

Courtesy of Collins Publishers

IGOR GOUZENKO
Soviet defector
***Born* USSR, 1919**
***Died* near Toronto, Canada, June 1982**

Igor Gouzenko was a cipher clerk who on 5 September 1945 defected from the Soviet embassy in Ottawa, Canada, with 109 documents that exposed the successful Soviet penetration of Western atomic bomb secrets. His revelations, which at first were not believed, eventually led to the unmasking of several British, Canadian, and American spies. He lived the rest of his life in constant and growing fear of assassination by the NKVD (now the KGB).

Gouzenko studied at the Moscow Architectural Institute before attending the Military Intelligence School. He was a Red Army lieutenant when he was posted to Ottawa, where he worked under the military attaché, Col. Nikolai Zabotin, decoding orders from and encoding messages to the Directorate of Military Intelligence in Moscow. After two years in Canada, just before he was due to be returned to the Soviet Union, he decided to defect. He stole the most revealing documents he could lay his hands on from Colonel Zabotin's safe, and walked out of the embassy. Then began 36 hours of panic: he went first to the *Ottawa Journal,* where the inexperienced, provincial journalists told him they were not interested in his story and, in any case, could not understand the Russian of the proffered documents; he was subsequently turned away by the Royal Canadian Mounted Police and by the Justice Ministry. Finally a neighbor agreed to shelter him and his family, just before NKVD agents smashed into his apartment, only to find it empty. At last the Canadian authorities began to take him seriously, and started to study the contents of his cache of documents.

Their revelations were sensational. Although World War II had been over for only a month, the Soviets had been hard on the heels of their Western allies' most closely guarded secrets for more than three years. The British and Canadian governments quickly set up a royal commission of inquiry to investigate the espionage charges. The first spy to fall was Dr. Alan Nunn May, a Cambridge-trained physicist, and former employee at Canada's Chalk River atomic research establishment. Then Dr. Klaus Fuchs, a German-born British subject and another atomic physicist, was convicted, as was the most famous Canadian spy, Fred Rose, a Communist-Progressive member of the Canadian federal parliament. In the United States the Gouzenko papers led the FBI to expose the spy ring centering on Harry Gold, David Greenglass, and Julius and Ethel Rosenberg.

Gouzenko published his memoirs and the story of his escape in 1948 in *The Iron Curtain* (published in Canada as *This Was My Choice).* A film version was released later that year, with Dana Andrews as Gouzenko. His novel *The Fall of a Titan* appeared in 1954. Highly praised for its literary craftsmanship, the book had nothing to do with espionage or atomic secrets, but was the thinly disguised story of the betrayal and murder by Stalinist agents of the great Soviet writer Maxim Gorky.

Awarded British citizenship by King George VI, Gouzenko and his family lived a furtive life, frequently on the move and always under close police protection. He was never photographed without a sack over his head. He gradually grew convinced that the Western powers were not doing enough to track down Soviet espionage cells, and continually pressed for new laws that would make it easier for Soviet spies to defect to the West and live in safety and relative comfort. One of his most famous accusations has not, to this day, been cleared up: he was interviewed by a high-ranking officer of MI5, the British Intelligence Service, just after his defection in 1945. The man showed little interest in his revelations and apparently even made a false report to London of what Gouzenko told him. It seems likely that the man in question was either Kim Philby, later a famous defector to the USSR, or the late Sir Roger Hollis, from 1956 to 1965 director of MI5. Neither the British nor the Canadian government has admitted who the "mole" was, although Prime Minister Margaret Thatcher announced in Parliament in 1981 that an investigation several years before had cleared the name of Sir Roger.

Gouzenko was blind from diabetes for five

years before his death. He is survived by his wife and their two children, who for most of their lives were unaware of their parents' true identity. A.K.

Mother a schoolteacher. **Married** Svetlana Gousev, artist, 1942: Andrei, b. 1943; Anna, b. 1945. **Emigration** Defected to Canada 1945; granted British citizenship. **Education** Moscow Architectural Inst. 1938–41; Kuibishev Military Engineering Acad. ca. 1941–42; Military Intelligence Acad., Moscow, grad. with rank of lt. 1943. **Career** Member of GRU (Soviet military intelligence) 1941–45; cipher clerk, GRU HQ, Moscow ca. 1941–43; code officer, Soviet Embassy, Ottawa 1943–45; defected 1945; testified on Soviet spy network to special Royal Commn. of Inquiry on Espionage 1946; writer since 1947; industrial designer and farmer under various false names, Canada since late 1940s. **Author** *The Iron Curtain* (in Canada as *This Was My Choice),* 1948; *The Fall of a Titan* (novel), 1954.

Further reading Charles Wighton, *The World's Greatest Spies,* 1962.

JULY

JOHN WATTS
Composer and conceptual artist
***Born* Cleveland, Tennessee, USA, 16 July 1930**
***Died* New York City, USA, 2 July 1982**

The avant-garde composer John Watts was a specialist in electronic music, a virtuoso manipulator of the ARP synthesizer. As founder and director of Composers Theatre, a New York-based cooperative, he did much to bring contemporary music to a wider public. Many of his works were written to accompany dances by his wife, the choreographer Laura Foreman, with whom he also collaborated on a number of conceptual artworks.

A native of Cleveland, Tennessee, Watts became interested in music when he was a child—a certain piano chord fascinated him endlessly—but was discouraged by his family from serious study. He began taking lessons secretly in his early teens, became a clarinetist, and by the age of 19 had decided to become a composer. He received his bachelor's degree in 1949 from the state university and his master's degree in music in 1953 from the University of Colorado, then did doctoral work at the University of Illinois and at Cornell. His composition teachers, at these schools and elsewhere, included Cecil Effinger, Roy Harris, John Krueger, Robert Palmer, Burrill Phillips, David Van Vactor, and Karel Husa. Until the mid-1960s he taught music and directed children's theater at a succession of public and private schools, and from 1964 to 1967 was editor in chief of the weekly newspaper *Manhattan East.*

In 1964, Watts was awarded a six-week residency at the Yaddo artists' colony, during the course of which he realized the need for a nonprofit organization to produce, promote, and distribute the works of contemporary composers, many of them neglected by established orchestras and by traditional sources of funding. The result was Composers Theatre, a cooperative enterprise of which Watts became the director and chief fund raiser. It was administered in conjunction with Choreographers Theatre, a similar organization headed by his wife. By 1982 it had presented works by some 250 American composers, including 150

Courtesy of Laura Foreman

premieres, had established an archive, and had sponsored a recording series on the Trilogy label with Watts as producer. In 1969, Composers Theatre became affiliated with the New School for Social Research, where it offered, again under Watts's direction, a program of study in electronic music and audio engineering, the first of its kind in the country.

In addition to his work with Composers Theatre and its education branch, Watts continued as a prolific and award-winning composer with a particular genius for combining the synthesizer, live and taped, with other instruments. His works number more than 100 and include scores for dances, documentary and feature films, video installations, Off Broadway plays, and television. A recording of *The Music of John Watts* on the Serenus label, volume one of a projected series, contains his *Elegy to "Chimney": In Memoriam*

(1972), for live trumpet, 18-track synthesizer tape, and optional live synthesizer; *Piano for Te,* a chamber concerto for piano, tape, and 13 brass instruments; and the choral work *Mots d'Heures, Gousses, Rames,* with lyrics based on a fractured-French version of Mother Goose. This playfulness is characteristic of much of his work, as is a tendency toward mysticism. Donal Henahan, in a *New York Times* review of Watts's *Laugharne,* a memorial for the Welsh poet Dylan Thomas (Watts was of Welsh ancestry), said: "The over-all mood, established and sustained by long-held, slowly changing chords, is that of a requiem being celebrated somewhere in interstellar space. The tape, produced by a synthesizer, suspends a gentle jangling, rather like the tabla in an Indian raga, over the piece, enhancing the contemplative atmosphere." Another critic, writing in Stockholm's *Dagens Nyheter,* said, "There is a wide range of deft sophistication and wit [in his work], but with undertones and colorations almost too subtle for words." His compositions for dancers included the hypnotic *Mas,* based on eleventh-century Japanese court music, and numerous scores for Laura Foreman.

Watts and his wife also collaborated on a number of examples of conceptual art, of which the best known was the "media fantasy" *Wallwork,* organized in May 1981 in Lower Manhattan and repeated in Stockholm and Paris. Regarded by some as a hoax, by others as a witty inquiry into the relationship of audience to art and art to publicity, it consisted entirely of a publicity campaign for a nonexistent dance concert. Their three-part video piece *TimeCoded Woman,* in which a confessional monologue by Foreman was matched with a tape accompaniment by Watts, won medals at three successive Houston International Film Festivals from 1979 to 1981.

Watts spent much of his time as a guest soloist and workshop teacher at universities and music festivals in the United States, Canada, and Europe. During the summer of 1981 he was a resident fellow at La Cité des Arts in Paris. He died at the height of his career, a few days short of his 52nd birthday. J.P.

Married (1) . . .: Elizabeth, b. 1961. (2) Laura Foreman, choreographer and video artist. **Education** Univ. of Tennessee, B.A. 1949, grad. study 1949–50; Univ. of Colorado (grad. scholarship), M.Mus. 1953; Univ. of Illinois (grad. fellowship) 1955–56; Cornell Univ. (grad. fellowship) 1958–60. **Mil. service** Clarinetist, U.S. Army Special Services. **Career** Composer since 1949; grad. teaching asst. in theory, Univ. of Tennessee 1949–50; instr. of theory, Army-Navy Music Sch. 1951; assoc. prof. and resident in univ. theater, Univ. of Colorado 1953; dir. of music, Eagle and Minturn public schs., CO 1953–54; instr. in music and assoc. in children's theater, North Dakota State Coll., Fargo 1956–57; grad. asst. in orchestra, Cornell Univ., Ithaca, NY 1959–60; instr. of woodwinds, Waltann Sch. of Creative Arts, Brooklyn 1963–64; head of music and art, Eron Prep Sch., NYC 1963–64; ed. in chief, *Manhattan East* weekly newspaper 1964–67; founding dir., Composers Theatre, NYC since 1965; founding dir. of Electronic Music Program, coordinator of music workshop, and artist in residence, New Sch. for Social Research, NYC since 1969; ed., *CCT Review* 1974–77; soloist, resident composer, and lectr. at numerous univs., workshops, concerts, and festivals; producer, Composers Theatre Series, Trilogy Records; conceptual artist. **Member** Broadcast Music, Inc.; Amer. Music Center, NYC; Amer. Soc. of Univ. Composers; MENSA; Local 802, Amer. Fedn. of Musicians; Coll. Music Soc. **Honors** Berry Prize for Music Composition, Univ. of Tennessee 1950; Yaddo Fellowship 1964; citation, Intl. Conference of Weekly Newspaper Editors 1966; share in gold medal, for *War,* New York Intl. Festival 1968; Ford Foundn. grants 1970–72; (with Laura Foreman) bronze medal 1979 and silver medals 1980 and 1981 for *TimeCoded Woman I–II–III,* Houston Intl. Film Festival of the Americas; grant, Natl. Endowment for the Humanities 1979; study grant to La Cité Internationale des Arts, Coll. Center of the Finger Lakes 1981. **Instrumental, orchestral, and choral works** *Sonata for Piano,* 1956; *Signals,* 1970; *Elegy to "Chimney": In Memoriam,* 1973; *Piano for Te,* 1973; *Laugharne,* 1974; *Mots d'Heures: Gousses, Rames,* 1974; *Gallery Piece,* 1974; *Piano for Te Tutti,* 1975; *Mecox,* 1977; *Maxiconcerto,* 1977; *Le Match de Boxe,* 1978; *Eutectics,* 1978; *Processional,* 1978; *Canonades,* 1978; *Keepsakes,* 1978; *Timespace,* 1979; *Night Remembrance,* 1979; *A Little Night Music,* 1979; *Barbro Variations,* 1979; *Blue Notes,* 1980; *Ach!,* 1980; *Time Codes,*

1980; many others. **Dance scores** *City of Angels,* 1974; *Mas,* 1976; *Heirlooms,* 1977; *#SS,* 1977; *Ups,* 1977; *Entries,* 1978; *Go,* 1978; many others. **Film scores** *War* (documentary), 1968; *Daisies,* 1972. **Stage scores** *Faust,* NYC 1973; scores for children's theater. **Television** Theme for "Station Exchange," NBC-TV. **Video and conceptual art** "   ", 1970; *TimeCoded Woman, I–III,* 1979–81; *Avant-garde,* 1980; *Wallwork,* 1981; *Roomwork,* 1981; *M* U* S* I* C for "Table of Noon/Mat of the Moon,"* 1981. **Author** of articles in jrnls. and mags. **Collection** of music, tapes, and records in Amer. Music Center, NYC.

Further reading Sheldon Bart, *21st Century Five Star Final,* 1980.

(SYLVESTRE) ANTONIO GUZMÁN (FERNÁNDEZ)

President of the Dominican Republic
Born **La Vega province, Dominican Republic, 12 February 1911**
Died **Santo Domingo, Dominican Republic, 4 July 1982**

Pres. Antonio Guzmán's death from a single gunshot wound in the head occurred under mysterious circumstances that have not been entirely clarified even by his own government. During his term in office, which began in 1978, he was the prime mover behind the maturation of democracy in the Dominican Republic, and he was due to transfer the presidency to his duly elected successor and fellow socialist, Salvador Jorge Blanco, on 6 August 1982, marking the country's first peaceful transition of power in this century. The recent discovery of corruption among high-level members of his government, including some of his own aides, apparently drove him to suicide—or so said officials of his party.

Born into a landed family in the region of Santiago, in the north of the country, Guzmán was trained as an agronomist at the University of California. Like many of his fellow citizens, he was a sincere believer in democracy who kept strictly silent during the repressive, 31-year-long dictatorship of Gen. Rafael Trujillo Molina, which came to an end in 1961. In that year he joined the Dominican Revolutionary Party (PRD), then radical leftist in orientation but now affiliated with the Socialist International. When the PRD's leader, the exiled poet Juan Bosch, was elected president in 1963, Guzmán became minister of agriculture, a key cabinet post in a country largely dependent on sugar and other agricultural products for its export earnings. Seven months later, the Bosch government was brought down by a military coup, and Guzmán returned to his successful cattle and coffee farms.

During the civil war of 1965, which culminated in armed U.S. intervention, he put forward a plan, subsequently known as the "Guzmán formula," providing for eventual free elections after a period of rule by a transitional civilian government, which was headed by Hector García-Godoy. Guzmán was the PRD candidate for vice president in the election of 1966 when Bosch lost to the conservative candidate, Joaquin Balaguer, formerly a minister under the Trujillo dictatorship. He was nominated for president in 1974, but the center-left coalition backing him finally decided that it would be dangerous to oppose Balaguer's second reelection. In 1978, however, he ran against Balaguer as the PRD candidate and was winning an overwhelming victory when the military intervened, halting the vote counting and setting the stage for a coup d'état in favor of Balaguer. At that point the Carter administration insisted that the result of the vote be respected by the rightist generals, and threatened severe economic reprisals if it were not. Guzmán was sworn in on 16 August 1978, in the presence of Pres. José López Portillo of Mexico and a 27-member U.S. delegation headed by Secretary of State Cyrus Vance and U.N. Ambassador Andrew Young. After the inauguration, Guzmán kept all visiting dignitaries waiting while he completely and unexpectedly changed the entire top leadership of the armed forces, ousting all the antidemocratic generals who had nearly succeeded in making another Trujillo out of Balaguer.

Guzmán's administration began as a model of democracy: he quickly freed all political prisoners, abolished state censorship, continued the depoliticization of the armed forces, and made a start at land reform, under

which large U.S. corporations, principally Gulf+Western, were to be forced to give up many of their thousands of unused acres to their workers. He survived an attempted military coup in early 1979, but the ravages of Hurricane David, which killed 1,200 people in the country in September of that year, worsened an already stressful economic situation by diminishing sugar production at a time of declining prices on the world market. In 1982 Guzmán was informed that some of his own aides had hurt the economy still further by stealing millions of dollars from the government, largely through kickback schemes in public works contracts. Reportedly, he killed himself in order to avoid the humiliation of an investigation and the dishonoring of his name.

Immediately after Guzmán's death, his vice president, Jacobo Majluta, was sworn in as president, and the military commanders reaffirmed their support for the peaceful transfer of power to the government of president-elect Blanco, which was expected to continue the process of democratization begun by Guzmán. A.K.

Parents landowners; owned fabric store. **Married** Renee Klang: Sonia Hernández, govt. admin. subsecty.; Ivan (d.). **Religion** Roman Catholic. **Education** Elementary and high sch. in La Vega; agronomy and agriculture courses at Univ. of California and in FL. **Career** Cattle rancher, dairy farmer, and coffee, fruit, and rice planter, Santiago; exec. of Productos Dominicanos C. por A. • Joined Dominican Revolutionary Party (Partido Revolucionario Dominicano; PRD) 1961, elected to PRD natl. exec. cttee. and political commn. 1964; minister of agriculture 1963; member, mediating commn., to oversee free elections 1965; candidate for v.p. 1966; pres. of Dominican Republic since 1978.

SIR GEOFFREY (LANGDON) KEYNES

Surgeon and scholar

Born **Cambridge, England, 25 March 1887**

Died **Brinkley, near Newmarket, Suffolk, England, 5 July 1982**

Sir Geoffrey Keynes's two equally brilliant careers, as revolutionary surgical pioneer and meticulous literary scholar, were never meant either to intersect or wholly to diverge from one another. "My friends," he wrote, "had often thought that literature and bibliography were my first loves, with surgery as a background. In reality it had been the other way round." Over a lifetime of intensive work in both fields, with a myriad of publications to show for his efforts, he became the epitome of an English ideal, the scientific man of letters.

He was brought up in Cambridge, the son of John Neville Maynard Keynes, for many years the registrar of Cambridge University. His elder brother was John Maynard Keynes, Baron Keynes (1883–1946), the best-known and most influential economist of the twentieth century. At Rugby School he was the exact contemporary of Rupert Brooke, who became one of his closest friends and a strong influence on his developing literary taste. He won a foundation scholarship to Pembroke College, Cambridge, where he was a founding member of the literary Baskerville Club and continued to enlarge his already considerable private library. He read natural science, took a first-class degree, and in 1910, on a scholarship, entered St. Bartholomew's Hospital, London, the most eminent teaching hospital in Britain. His medical brilliance was quickly recognized: he won the Brackenbury Surgical Scholarship and the Willett Medal for operative surgery in 1913, the year of his medical qualification, upon which he became house surgeon. His first book, a John Donne bibliography, was published by Cambridge University Press in 1914. (Its fourth edition appeared in 1973.)

In 1914, Keynes left for the front, where he served first in the Royal Army Medical Corps, then as a surgeon with the British Expeditionary Force, in which he attained the rank of major and was mentioned in dispatches. In the course of treating hundreds of gravely wounded soldiers he first discovered the efficacy of routine blood transfusion, then an unheard-of practice, and later, in 1922, published the first monograph on the subject. His other medical breakthroughs were in the cure of breast cancer (he was years ahead of his time in championing limited excision over the Halsted radical mastectomy); in hernia operations; in thyroid disorders; and in surgery of the thymus (in 1942 he was the first in Britain to effect a cure for myasthenia gravis by means of thymectomy). Much of his work caused controversy when it was first discussed and found acceptance only after decades of dispute, yet his medical career was filled with honors. At the Royal College of Surgeons he was Hunterian Professor three times, in 1923, 1929, and 1945, and Thomas Vicary Lecturer in 1948. He won the RCS's Sims Commonwealth Travelling Fellowship in 1956, the Joll Prize in 1953, and the gold medal in 1969. At the Royal College of Physicians he was Harveian Orator and the first Oslerian Orator, and at the Royal Society he was Wilkins Lecturer. During World War II, with the rank of acting air vice marshal, he served as chief consulting surgeon in the Royal Air Force. He retired from full-time clinical work in 1947, after two years in the much-coveted post of senior surgeon at St. Bartholomew's, but retained his large private and National Health Service practices. His knighthood was conferred in 1955 "for surgical distinction."

Keynes's first-rate medical skill frequently informed his literary study, and he published distinguished works on the great seventeenth-century writer-scientists Sir Thomas Browne, author of *Religio Medici;* Robert Hooke, the biologist and natural philosopher; and William Harvey, his illustrious predecessor at St. Bartholomew's and the discoverer of the circulation of the blood. *The Life of William Harvey* (1966) was widely praised and represented the condensation of years of scholarly effort. His best-known literary studies, however, are undoubtedly those on the Romantic poet-engraver William Blake, whom he first encountered as a student in 1907. His Blake bibliography (1921) was a landmark in the reevaluation of the poet and in 1949 he founded the William Blake Trust to ensure the proper publication of the poet's illuminated prophetic books, then almost unknown to the general public. He brought out valuable scholarly works on Jane Austen, Rupert Brooke, Siegfried Sassoon, John Ray, George Berkeley, Thomas Gray, John Evelyn, William Hazlitt, Samuel Butler, and Izaak Walton, among others.

Keynes was also very well known as a designer and collector of books. With his friend Francis Meynell he edited and designed more than a dozen volumes for the much-praised Nonesuch Press, among which *Poetry and Prose of William Blake* (1961) was a famous and valuable edition. His own holdings of Evelyn, Browne, Hooke, Ray, Austen, Blake, and Hazlitt were second to none in private hands.

In the arts, too, Keynes was greatly honored. He was a trustee of the National Portrait Gallery from 1942 and chairman from 1958 to 1966, president of the Bibliographical Society in 1953, and at the age of 94 was elected an honorary fellow of the British Academy. His autobiography, *The Gates of Memory* (1981), full of precise medical and literary reminiscences, was highly praised in both scientific and literary journals.

His retirement was spent at Lammas House, his home in Suffolk near Cambridge, where he expertly practiced gardening and tree-planting and extended his long list of publications. His wife, the granddaughter of Charles Darwin, died in 1974. He died of pneumonia at the age of 95. A.K.

Parents John Neville Maynard K., registrar, Cambridge Univ., and Florence Ada (Brown) K. **Married** Margaret Elizabeth Darwin 1917 (d. 1974): Richard Darwin, prof. of physiology, b. 1919; Quentin George, photographer,

b. 1921; William Milo, surgeon, b. 1924; Stephen John, merchant banker, b. 1927. **Education** Rugby Sch., Warwickshire; Pembroke Coll., Cambridge (Foundation Scholarship), 1st Class Honors in natural science tripos 1909, B.Ch. 1914, M.A., M.D. 1918; St. Bartholomew's Hosp. (Entrance Scholarship 1910; Willett Medal Operative Surgery Scholarship 1913; Brackenbury Scholarship in Surgery 1913), London 1910–13; MRCS and LRCP 1913. **Mil. service** Maj., RAMC, and surgeon-specialist, British Expeditionary Force, France 1914–18; sr. consulting surgeon, with rank of acting air vice-marshal, RAF 1939–45. **Career** With St. Bartholomew's Hosp., London: house surgeon 1913; 1st asst., surgical directorate, then asst. surgeon, 1920; chief asst. until retirement 1947; consulting surgeon since 1947. • Surgeon: Mt. Vernon Hosp.; Radium Inst.; London County Council Thyroid Clinic, New End Hosp.; City of London Truss Soc. • With Royal Coll. of Surgeons: Hunterian Prof. 1923, 1929, 1945; council member 1944–52; Vicary Lectr. 1948; Joll Lectr. 1953; Moynihan Centenary Lectr. 1965; chmn., library cttee. • With Royal Coll. of Physicians: Harveian Orator 1958; Fitzpatrick Lectr. 1966; Oslerian Orator 1968. • Sir Arthur Sims Commonwealth Travelling Prof. 1956; Wilkins Lectr., Royal Soc. 1967; Blair Bell Lectr. and council member, Royal Coll. of Obstetricians and Gynaecologists. • Editor and bibliographer of English literature; biographer, book collector, sculptor, poet, painter, ornithologist; associated with Nonesuch Press 1920s. **Officer** Trustee 1942–66 and chmn. 1958–66, Natl. Portrait Gall., London; gov., St. Bartholomew's Hosp. since 1947; founder 1949 and chmn., William Blake Trust; pres. 1952–54 and member since 1914, Bibliographical Soc., London; dir., Rupert Hart-Davis Ltd.; Hunterian Trustee. **Fellow** FRCS, England 1920, Canada 1956; FRCOG 1950; FRCP 1953. **Member** Baskerville Club; Roxburghe Club. **Honors** Mentioned in dispatches, WWI; Joll Prize 1953, hon. gold medal 1969, and hon. librarian, Royal Coll. of Surgeons; kt. bachelor 1955; hon. freeman, Soc. of Apothecaries 1964; hon. member, Modern Language Assn. 1966; James Tait Black Memorial Prize, for *The Life of William Harvey,* 1967; Osler Gold Medal, Royal Coll. of Physicians 1968; gold medal, Bibliographical Soc. 1981; hon. foreign corresp. member, Grolier Club, NYC; hon. fellow of Pembroke Coll., Cambridge 1965, Royal Soc. of Medicine 1966, Darwin Coll., Cambridge 1976, British Acad. 1981, Royal Coll. of Physicians (London), Royal Coll. of Obstetricians and Gynaecologists, Amer. Surgical Assn., and Harvey Soc.; hon. degrees from univs. of Sheffield, Birmingham, Reading, Oxford, Cambridge, and Edinburgh. **Medical works** *Blood Transfusion,* 1922; *The Early Diagnosis of Malignant Disease,* 1935; (ed.) A.A. Bowlby, *Surgical Anatomy and Morbid Anatomy,* 8th ed., 1930; (ed.) H.F. Brewer et al., *Blood Transfusion,* 1949. **Bibliographies** *A Bibliography of the Works of Dr. John Donne, Dean of St. Paul's,* 1914; *A Bibliography of William Blake,* 1921; *A Bibliography of Sir Thomas Browne, Kt., M.D.,* 1924; *William Pickering, Publisher: A Memoir and a Hand-List of His Editions,* 1924, rev. as *William Pickering, Publisher: A Memoir and a Check-List of His Editions,* 1969; *A Bibliography of the Writings of William Harvey, M.D., Discoverer of the Circulation of the Blood,* 1928, as *A Bibliography of the Writings of Dr. William Harvey, 1578–1657,* 1953; *Jane Austen: A Bibliography,* 1929; *A Bibliography of William Hazlitt,* 1931; *John Evelyn: A Study in Bibliophily and a Bibliography of His Writings,* 1938; *John Ray: A Bibliography,* 1951, as *The Bibliography of John Ray,* 1973; *A Bibliography of Rupert Brooke,* 1954; *A Bibliography of Dr. Robert Hooke,* 1960; *A Bibliography of Siegfried Sassoon,* 1962; *Dr. Timothie Bright, 1550–1615: A Survey of His Life with a Bibliography of His Writings,* 1962; *A Bibliography of Sir William Petty and of "Observations on the Bills of Mortality" by John Graunt,* 1971; *A Bibliography of George Berkeley, Bishop of Cloyne: His Work and His Critics in the Eighteenth Century,* 1976; *A Bibliography of Henry King, Bishop of Chichester,* 1979. **Biography and literary studies** *The Commonplace Book of Elizabeth Lyttleton, Daughter of Sir Thomas Browne,* 1919; *The Illustrations of William Blake for Thornton's Virgil,* 1937; *Blake Studies: Notes on His Life and Works,* 1949, as *Blake Studies: Essays on His Life and Work,* 1971; *The Personality of William Harvey,* 1949; *The Portraiture* *of William Harvey,* 1949; *Engravings by William Blake, the Separate Plates: A Catalogue Raisonnée,* 1956; *Bibliotheca Bibliographici: A Catalogue of the Library Formed by Geoffrey Keynes,* 1964; *A Study of the Illuminated Books of William Blake, Poet, Printer, Prophet,* 1964; *The Life of William Harvey,* 1966; *Drawings of William Blake: Ninety-Two Pencil Studies,* 1970; (commentary) William Blake, *Songs of Innocence and of Experience,* 1970; *The Life of William Blake,* 3rd ed., 1971; (commentary) *Water-Colours Illustrating the Poems of Thomas Gray,* 1972; *William Blake's Water-Colour Designs for the Poems of Thomas Gray,* 1972; *The Marriage of Heaven and Hell,* 1975; *William Blake's "Auguries of Innocence,"* 1976; (contributor) *The Complete Portraiture of William and Catherine Blake,* 1977. **Editor** By William Blake: *Letters from William Blake to Thomas Butts, 1800–1803,* 1926; *The Note-Book of William Blake, Called the Rossetti Manuscript,* 1935; *William Blake's Engravings,* 1950; (jtly.) *William Blake's Illuminated Books: A Census,* 1953; *Pencil Drawings: Second Series,* 1956; *Illustrations to the Bible,* 1957; *Poetry and Prose of William Blake,* 1961; *The Complete Writings of William Blake,* 1966; *The Gates of Paradise: For Children, For the Sexes,* 3 vols., 1968; *"On the Morning of Christ's Nativity": Milton's Hymn with Illustrations by William Blake,* 1977. • Also works by John Evelyn, Rupert Brooke, William Hazlitt, William Harvey, John Donne, Sir Thomas Browne, Izaak Walton, Samuel Butler, Ambroise Paré, John Maynard Keynes, and Edward Gibbons. **Contributor** of articles to medical and scholarly jrnls.

Further reading John Stallworthy, "A Fortunate Man," in *British Medical Journal,* 19–26 Dec. 1981.

RAÚL ROA (GARCÍA)

Foreign minister of Cuba

Born **Havana, Cuba, 18 April 1907**

Died **Havana, Cuba, 6 July 1982**

An intellectual and a professor of social sciences, Raúl Roa served as Cuban foreign minister from shortly after Fidel Castro's successful overthrow of Fulgencio Batista's dictatorship in 1959 until 1976, when increasing ill health forced him to take over the largely ceremonial vice presidency of the National Assembly. Although he was but little involved in the making of foreign policy, which was always in the hands of Castro and his closest associates, he was one of the most intelligent and respected members of the government and a passionate and effective spokesman for the Cuban revolution in world forums.

Born into a wealthy family in Havana, he became involved in leftist politics while a student at Havana University, which he entered in 1925. In 1930 he was elected to the University Students Directorate, which fought against the dictatorship of Gerardo Machado, and the following year was imprisoned for the first time for antigovernment agitation. He strongly supported Gen. Batista's coup d'état against Machado in 1933 but was removed by Batista from the following provisional government. Two years later he helped organize a general strike against the Batista regime, and went into exile in the United States when it failed. In New York he was active in Cuban revolutionary politics and attended Columbia University and the New School for Social Research. In 1945–46 he was awarded a Guggenheim Fellowship to study the New Deal.

In 1948–52, during one of the few intervals of democratic government in twentieth-century Cuba, Roa, who was then dean of social sciences at Havana University, served as director of culture in the government of Pres. Carlos Prío Socarrás. When Batista returned to overthrow the Prío regime, Roa was arrested along with much of the rest of the government, and following a brief period of imprisonment went again into exile, this time to Mexico, where he lectured at the universities of Mexico City and Monterrey. He was again imprisoned after his return from exile in 1957.

Following immediately upon Castro's dramatic victory of 1 January 1959, Roa, a respected member of the leftist opposition but an avowed anti-Communist, was appointed ambassador to the Organization of American States. When in May the agrarian reform law was promulgated, involving large-scale expropriation and redistribution of land, much of it owned by U.S. citizens and corporations, a cabinet crisis ensued. On 12 June 1959, Roa was named foreign minister to replace Roberto Agramonte, who favored good relations with the United States.

These relations became increasingly strained, with Pres. Eisenhower, at the end of his second term, seeming to go out of his way to antagonize the new rulers in Havana. For their part, Castro and his ministers needed U.S. aid, particularly the favorable sugar quota, but as leftist nationalists with a long history of condemning U.S. economic hegemony, they had to appear to be freeing Cuba from that domination. Roa at first made the appropriate signs of conciliation: "Traditionally and historically," he said in Washington in September 1959, "and because of our ties of friendship, Cuba belongs to the Western group of nations." Yet the following May, after Eisenhower virtually eliminated Cuba's sugar quota in retaliation for Cuba's expropriation of the Esso and Texaco oil refineries,

Roa made the first of a long series of violently worded attacks on the United States and its Latin American allies. "Is it necessary," he asked in a famous speech before the United Nations Security Council, "in order to preserve hemispheric unity, democratic principles, and continued security, to lower one's head like a submissive bull to the butcher in the abattoir? Better honor without quota than quota without honor!" Later that year, strongly defending the Cuban-Soviet mutual defense treaty, he said before the OAS, "The most serious problem faced by the Americas today is not a hypothetical extracontinental intervention, but the actual and present threat of aggression by the government of the United States." Cuba, he went on, was convinced of an "imminent U.S. military attack," and he angrily walked out of the OAS meeting "because Cuba could not find protection" there. On 3 January 1961, the Eisenhower administration broke diplomatic relations with Cuba. In 1962, the United States engineered Cuba's expulsion from the OAS.

As it transpired, Roa's fears of military attack were well founded. On 17 April 1961, as U.N. Ambassador Adlai Stevenson, himself gravely misled by his superiors in the State Department, was fervently denying before the Security Council any thought of U.S. intervention, a large group of CIA-trained Cuban exiles and non-Cuban mercenaries, supported by U.S. air cover, landed at the Bay of Pigs. After three days of intense fighting the invasion force was totally routed. Roa was in New York at the time, and in an agitated speech before the Security Council said, "The Cuban people . . . are suffering from American bombs. . . . These crimes . . . have been sanctified, paid for, and blessed by the State Department, the Pentagon, and the CIA."

Roa had no part in defusing the Cuban missile crisis of October 1962, in reality a bluffing showdown between the United States and the Soviet Union, which the superpowers themselves resolved without Cuban participation. Cuban-American relations were by then in ruins, but the mutual anger gradually lessened and the antagonism grew more restrained. Roa had much to do with this lowering of dangerous tensions: although he continued in public to fulminate against American imperial dominance of the hemisphere (he called Argentina's Pres. Arturo Frondizi, for example, a staunch supporter of the United States, "a viscous concretion of all human excrescences" and "the villain of a badly composed tango"), in private negotiations he was somewhat more accommodating. He negotiated and signed a stern antihijacking agreement with Washington in 1973 which, by promising to extradite and prosecute all airplane hijackers, drastically reduced the incidence of such seizures from then on. Yet he continued to insist, even in 1974 before the General Assembly, that Cuba would never negotiate with the United States until its "criminal, arbitrary, anachronistic, and contradictory blockade" was lifted.

A slightly built man with a small mustache, Roa was the author of many books on international relations, Cuban history, and social justice. He married Ada Kouri, a physician, the daughter of a famous Cuban medical pioneer. Their only child, Raúl Roa-Kouri, is Cuba's permanent representative to the United Nations. Roa died at the age of 75 after a long illness. A.K.

Married Ada Kouri, physician: Raúl Roa-Kouri, Cuban rep. to U.N. **Emigration** In exile in U.S. mid- to late 1930s, in Mexico late 1950s. **Education** Havana Univ., doctorate in public and civil law 1934; Columbia Univ. and New Sch. for Social Research, NYC mid-1940s. **Career** Co-founder, Univ. Students Directorate 1930; arrested and imprisoned for antigovt. agitation 1931; active in provisional govt. 1933; ed., *El Mundo* and *Bohemia;* helped organize gen. strike against Batista regime 1935, went into exile in U.S., organized Cuban revolutionary assn. in NYC; named prof. of history of social doctrines and social philosophy 1940, and dean of social sciences 1948–59, Havana Univ.; dir. of culture, Ministry of Education, Cuba 1948–52; arrested and imprisoned 1952; lectr., univs. of Mexico City and Monterrey, Mexico 1950s; imprisoned 1957–59; ambassador to Org. of American States 1959; foreign minister 1959–76; member, Central Cttee. of Cuban C.P. from 1965; member, Council of State; v.p., Natl. Assembly 1976–81. **Honors** Guggenheim Fellowship 1945–46; natl. journalism award Justo de Lara 1954. **Author** *Viento Sur* [*South Wind*], 1953; *15 años después* [*Fifteen Years After*], 1950; *En pie* [*Afoot*], 1959; *Cuba en la ONU* [*Cuba in the U.N.*], 1961; (ed.) Pablo de la Torriente-Brau, Aventura del soldado desconocido cubano [*Adventure of the Unknown Cuban Soldier*], 1962; *Retorno a la alborada* [*Return at Dawn*] (2 vols.), 1964; *Escaramuza en las vísperas, y otros engendros* [*Skirmish in the Evenings, and Other Monstrosities*], 1966; *La revolución del 30* [*The Revolution of '30*], 1969; *Aventuras, venturas y desventuras de un mambí en la lucha por la independencia de Cuba* [*Adventures, Hazards, and Misfortunes of a Mambi in the Struggle for Cuba's Independence*], 1970; *Evocación de Pablo Lafargue* [*Evocation of Pablo Lafargue*], 1973; numerous published speeches and articles.

MARIA JERITZA

Opera singer

***Born* Brünn, Moravia, Austria-Hungary, 6 October 1887**

***Died* Orange, New Jersey, USA, 10 July 1982**

Maria Jeritza was a prima donna assoluta of opera's golden age, a star whose regal bearing, golden hair, and lustrous soprano voice entranced listeners in Vienna and New York. In her day she was worshiped by her fans, criticized by temperamental rivals, and was the subject of numerous romantic novels linking her name with those of famous composers. She was sometimes accused of scooping up to notes and of allowing a strident tone to creep into her singing, but even in her 60s she could move an audience to a three-minute standing ovation.

The daughter of a concierge, Jeritza (whose original name was Jedlicka) enrolled at the age of 11 at the conservatory of her native city, Brünn in Moravia (now Brno, Czechoslovakia), and two years later was accepted by Prof. Auspitzer of Prague University as a private pupil. The thought of singing before an audience—or even of auditioning—petrified her. One day in 1910, however, after practicing several arias in Auspitzer's studio, she was surprised to see the director of the Olmütz Opera emerge from behind the draperies. He hired her immediately and she made her debut as Elsa in Wagner's *Lohengrin.* She was also hired by the Vienna Volksoper and added a substantial number of operas to her repertoire during her two seasons as an understudy there.

Jeritza's long friendship with Richard Strauss began in October 1912 when she created the title role in his *Ariadne auf Naxos* during a guest appearance at the Stuttgart Royal Opera House; she was frequently invited to sing major roles in his operas, notably the world premiere of *Die Frau ohne Schatten* in Vienna in 1919. Early in 1912 she sang Rosalinda in Johann Strauss's *Die Fledermaus* at an Austrian summer spa to an audience that included the Emperor Franz Josef. "Why isn't that ravishing creature singing at the court opera?" he asked. "Must I always listen to fat, elderly women?" Later that year she made her debut at the Vienna Royal Opera in *Aphrodite,* written for her by Max von Oberleithner, and created a sensation by appearing in a scandalously diaphanous costume. The following year the Royal Opera (which became the Vienna State Opera) bought out her Volksoper contract.

Thereafter, Jeritza became one of Europe's most glamorous stars, idolized not only in Vienna but in all the cities where she made guest appearances. Her repertoire was eclectic and ranged from Bizet to Erich Korngold, from Wagner to Puccini. Her striking golden beauty, flamboyant acting, and dramatic soprano voice brought audiences to their feet night after night. Word of her talents reached the United States in 1915, but she refused to leave Europe in wartime; it was not until November 1921—when she was 34 years old and at the peak of her career—that she made her debut at the New York Metropolitan Opera House as Marietta in the American premiere of Korngold's controversial *Die tote Stadt.* When, a few days later, she thrilled the audience with her most famous role, that of the imperious diva Floria Tosca in Puccini's opera, the *New York Times* critic Olin Downes judged her performance "gloriously sung" and a "sweeping triumph," adding: "Those whose privilege it was to behold her performance will have memories. When great artists arise in future years, they will say: 'But I heard Maria Jeritza in *Tosca.*'"

By this time Jeritza had mastered 60 operatic roles. Between 1921 and 1932 she sang 348 performances in 20 operas with the Met, of which six were American premieres. In 1924 she introduced New York audiences to Leos Janáček's *Jenůfa,* whose title role she had created in Vienna in 1918. The writer Ernest de Weerth considered that, as the Princess in Puccini's *Turandot,* a role she first sang in 1926, she "reigned supreme, putting her stamp on it with an aplomb never rivaled." (Jeritza had studied the part with the composer and was bitterly disappointed when Rosa Raisa was chosen to sing the world premiere at La Scala, Milan, earlier the same year.) She also introduced two now-forgotten operas: Korngold's *Violanta* in 1927 and Alfano's *Madonna Imperia* in 1928. She was lauded for her interpretation of Helen of Troy in the American premiere of Richard Strauss's *Die aegyptische Helena* in 1928, but the opera itself was not a success.

Jeritza took the leading roles in the first Metropolitan productions of Franz von Suppé's *Boccaccio* and *Donna Juanita* and appeared as Malliela in Wolf-Ferrari's *The Jewels of the Madonna* in 1925. The company revived for her Massenet's *Thaïs* in 1922, Puccini's *Girl of the Golden West*—a great success—in 1929, and Wagner's *Der fliegende Holländer* in 1930. She was not a success in Bizet's *Carmen* in spite of the fact that she sang the seduction of Don José flat on her back. Wagner was her specialty: she was an enchanting Elsa in *Lohengrin* and a stylish, graceful Elizabeth in *Tannhäuser.* As Senta in *Der fliegende Holländer* she lacked a certain necessary spiritual quality, but she was outstanding as Sieglinde in *Die Walküre.*

Puccini himself coached Jeritza for many of her roles in his operas, including Giorgetta in *Il Tabarro,* which she learned in only 48 hours. She studied the leading role in *Turandot* with him until just a few weeks before his death; and for the part of Tosca they worked long hours together in an effort to make a show-stopper out of the aria *Vissi d'arte.* Nothing pleased him until, during the final rehearsal, the singer playing the villain Scarpia threw her to the floor with such force that she was unable to rise and had to sing the aria prone, to Puccini's delight. This celebrated bit of business became part of her legend and was adopted by other Toscas.

In addition to her operatic work, Jeritza was an impressive concert artist and toured the United States twice, the second time in 1934 with Rudolf Friml's operetta *Music Hath*

Courtesy of John H. Popper, photographer

Charms (originally titled *Annina*). She appeared in several movies and between 1908 and 1930 made numerous recordings for Odeon and Victor which did not do justice to her voice.

After her marriage to the movie executive Winfield Sheehan in 1935, Jeritza retired to their vast estate in Hollywood, where she bred the famous Imperial White horses of Vienna. Her third husband was an opera lover who saw her perform in 1910 and waited for 38 years until she agreed to marry him. At the age of 63 she returned to Vienna to give two performances of *Tosca* and *Cavalleria Rusticana;* ecstatic fans besieged her hotel to catch a glimpse of her. Vocally she was still superb, her voice rich with thrilling high C's—and once again she sang *Vissi d'arte* from a prone position. The following year she sang *Die Fledermaus* in English to benefit the Metropolitan Opera Fund. As an octogenarian she lived in Newark and was often invited by Cardinal Spellman of New York to be the hostess at his social functions. She died after a long illness at the age of 94. B.D.

Born Maria Jedlicka (some sources Mimi Jedlitzkova.) **Father** a concierge. **Married** (1) Baron Leopold von Popper de Podhurgen, businessman, 1919 (div. 1934). (2) Winfield Sheehan, film exec., 1935 (d. 1945). (3) Irving B. Seery, businessman and lawyer, 1948 (d. 1966). **Religion** Roman Catholic. **Emigrated** to U.S. 1921; naturalized. **Education** Entered Brünn Musikschule, Moravia, at age 11; private studies, Prague ca. 1900–10; Royal Acad. of Music, Vienna. **Career** Debut with Olmütz Opera 1910; understudy, Vienna Volksoper 1911–13; soprano, Vienna Royal Opera (later Vienna State Opera) 1912–32, 1949–52; soprano, Metropolitan Opera House, NYC 1921–32, 1951; concert tours in U.S. and Europe; guest appearances in Stuttgart, Prague, Budapest, Odessa, Berlin, Bremen, Stockholm, London, other cities; made recordings and appeared in several films. **Honors** Hon. member, Vienna Royal Opera 1923; Order of Knighthood, 1st Class, Austria 1935; hon. medal, City of Vienna 1950; Golden Ring of Honor, City of Vienna 1967; lady, Grand Cross of Holy Sepulchre, Austria; awards from the Vatican, France, and Italy. **Author** *Sunlight and Song* (autobiography), 1924.

Further reading Ernest de Weerth, "Opera's Golden Girl," in *Opera News,* 18 Feb. 1961.

(GUSTAV HEINRICH) RALPH VON KOENIGSWALD
Paleoanthropologist
***Born* Berlin, Germany, 13 November 1902**
***Died* Bad Homburg, Germany, 10 July 1982**

Ralph von Koenigswald, one of the world's foremost experts in hominid fossils, once wrote, "If you love fossils, fossils love you. This has been my secret." His careful and expert comparisons of the teeth and skulls of the confusing variety of early human species were instrumental in clarifying the evolutionary relationship between Java Man, Solo Man, Peking Man, and the Australopithecines. His own discoveries in Java in the 1930s and 1940s lent credence to his view that Asia, as well as Africa, may have been a birthplace of humanity.

Von Koenigswald was born and raised in

Germany, though he had Danish citizenship through his mother. He attended the Odenwaldschule south of Frankfurt and began collecting fossils in the area as a teenager with the encouragement of Rudolf Martin, a noted physical anthropologist who was the father of one of his friends. After studying geology and paleontology at Berlin, Tübingen, and Cologne, he graduated from the University of Munich in 1928 and became Martin's assistant at the university's Geological Institute. In 1930 he was hired as a paleontologist for the Dutch Geological Survey, which was then drawing up a geological map of Java. His task was to identify and date mammalian fossils discovered by the survey so that its geologists could determine the age of the rocks in which they were found and establish a chronological stratigraphic sequence for the island as a whole.

Java had been the site of paleontological investigation since the early 1890s, when the Dutch doctor and fossil hunter Eugene Dubois, digging at Trinil in central Java, found the partial remains of a human-like creature, whom he named *Pithecanthropus erectus*—the upright apeman. Successive expeditions to Java found no further trace of *Pithecanthropus* or any other human ancestors until 1931, when a rich fossil bed containing 11 human skulls was discovered at Ngandong, in the Solo River valley near Trinil. Von Koenigswald prepared, classified, and catalogued these remains at his headquarters in Bandung. He also photographed the excavation of the best-preserved skull; it was his first human disinterment. The Ngandong site proved to be some 600,000 years younger than that at Trinil, and "Solo Man," now usually called *Homo sapiens soloensis,* was not Dubois's *Pithecanthropus,* as von Koenigswald's careful anatomical comparison revealed.

Cutbacks by the Dutch government brought a halt to the geological survey in December 1934, forcing von Koenigswald to curtail promising work at Sangiran and Modjokerto in east Java. In 1936 he assigned a fossil skull from Modjokerto to a new species, *Homo* (or *Pithecanthropus) modjokertensis.* (This skull was later proven to be 1.9 million years old.) Also in 1936 he received a visit from Pierre Teilhard de Chardin, the French Jesuit and paleontologist, who urged him to seek financial support from the Carnegie Institution in Washington, D.C. Von Koenigswald traveled to the United States the following year and returned with adequate funding as a Carnegie research associate.

Courtesy of German Information Center

The Sangiran site soon yielded the long-awaited second skull of *Pithecanthropus erectus.* The validity of this and other remains which were claimed by von Koenigswald to possess distinctly human characteristics was debated bitterly by Dubois, then in his 80s, who maintained that *Pithecanthropus* was not human and indirectly accused von Koenigswald of faking his results. In 1939, at the invitation of Franz Weidenreich, von Koenigswald brought his finds to the Rockefeller Medical Center in Peking. There the two paleontologists compared the Javanese fossils with those of "Peking Man," *Sinanthropus pekinensis,* discovered a decade before. So closely did the two forms correspond that the term "Sinanthropus" was dropped from the scientific vocabulary, and both forms were subsumed under the species *Homo erectus.* The comparison left little doubt that these early humans had once ranged across eastern Asia.

Still older fossils emerged from the black clay at Sangiran, including further fragments of *Pithecanthropus modjokertensis* and a hominid jaw of immense size, found in 1941. Von Koenigswald dubbed this giant *Meganthropus paleojavanicus;* its exact classification is still a matter of dispute. With war approaching, von Koenigswald acted to protect his fossils, replacing the most important ones with plaster casts and entrusting the originals to friends of neutral nationality (he had taken Dutch citizenship in 1935). Unlike the Peking fossils, which disappeared within days of the Japanese occupation of the city, the Java fossils were almost intact when the war ended. (One was later discovered in Emperor Hirohito's personal museum.)

Von Koenigswald himself survived 32

months in a Japanese prisoner-of-war camp. In 1946 he moved to New York to work with Weidenreich at the American Museum of Natural History. Two years later he joined the faculty of the University of Utrecht in the Netherlands. In the following years he published descriptions of fossil teeth he had collected in Chinese drug stores from Java to New York City, where they are sold as medicinal "dragon bones." His book *Meeting Prehistoric Man,* written for the general public, was published in 1956. He also made study trips to fossil-rich areas in Africa, the Philippines, and Pakistan.

During the 1960s, von Koenigswald wrote an important series of studies on tektites, the glass meteorites found throughout southeast Asia. In 1964 he took his Javanese fossils to Cambridge University to compare them with those collected by the Leakeys at Olduvai Gorge in Kenya, and noted numerous parallels between the two sets of bones. In 1968, he and his collection were given a home at the Senckenburg Research Institute and Natural History Museum in Frankfurt, where, as curator of the division of paleoanthropology, he reconstructed aspects of the social behavior of the australopithecines on the basis of their fossil remains. He died at the age of 79.

P.D.

Parents Gustav Adalbert von K., ethnologist, and Martha Jacobi. **Married** Luitgarde S.L. Beyer; one daughter. **Citizenship** Danish national at birth; Dutch citizen since 1935. **Education** Odenwaldschule, Heppenheim, Germany; univs. of Berlin, Tübingen, and Cologne; Univ. of Munich, grad. 1928. **Career** Asst., Geological Inst., Univ. of Munich 1928–30; paleontologist, Geological Survey for the Dutch East Indies, Bandung and other locations, Java 1930–48; research assoc., Carnegie Instn., Java 1937–41; in Japanese POW camp, Java 1941–ca. 1944; research assoc., Amer. Mus. of Natural History, NYC 1946–48; prof. 1948–68 and emeritus prof. since 1968, State Univ., Utrecht; curator, div. of paleoanthropology, Senckenberg Mus., Frankfurt-am-Main since 1968. **Field expeditions** Hong Kong 1935; Bandung, Sangiran, Jetis, Trinil, and Ngandong, Java early 1930s, 1936–41; Peking 1939; North Africa 1951; South Africa 1952; Philippines, Thailand, and Borneo 1957; Pakistan and China 1966–67. **Member** (Foreign assoc.) Natl. Acad. of Sciences, U.S.; Royal Netherlands Acad. of Sciences; Austrian Acad. of Sciences; other scientific assns. and acads. **Honors** Rockefeller/Viking Fund Grant ca. 1946; Golden Anandale Medal, Royal Asiatic Soc., Calcutta 1954; Darwin Medal, Akademie Leopoldina 1959; Huxley Medal, Anthropological Inst., U.K. 1964; Werner-Reimars Foundn. Prize ca. 1966; hon. member, New York Acad. of Sciences; hon. degree from Gadjah Mada Univ., Indonesia. **Author** *Beitrag zur kenntnis der fossilen wirkel tiere Javas* [*A Contribution to Knowledge of Mammalian Fossil Works in Java*], 1933; *Neue* Pithecanthropus-*funde, 1936–38* [*New* Pithecanthropus *Findings, 1936–38*], 1948; *Begenungen mit dem Vormenschen,* 1956 (trans. as *Meeting Prehistoric Man,* 1956); *Die Geschichte des Menschen,* 1960 (trans. as *The Evolution of Man,* 1962). **Contributor** of some 220 papers on paleoanthropology, geology, and ethnology to scientific jrnls., textbooks, and festschrifts.

Further reading P.V. Tobias, "The Life and Times of Ralph von Koenigswald: Paleontologist Extraordinary," in *Journal of Human Evolution,* vol. 5, no. 5, 1976.

KENNETH (GILBERT) MORE
Actor
***Born* Gerrards Cross, Buckinghamshire, England, 20 September 1914**
***Died* London, England, 12 July 1982**

For most of the 1950s, Kenneth More was the top British film star—in Britain; he never succeeded in becoming an international figure. Then, in the 1960s, both Britain and the cinema changed, and More was suddenly no longer in demand. His career slumped almost as abruptly as it had boomed. Ironically, it was television—that supposedly parochial medium—that not only rescued him, but gave him the international recognition that he had not been able to achieve in films.

Kenneth Gilbert More was born in Gerrards Cross, Buckinghamshire; his father was an engineer and unsuccessful inventor. The boy spent a comfortable and happy childhood in southern England and the Channel Isles. When he was 17, his father contracted kidney disease, and More was obliged to leave school and look for work. He spent two years as an engineering apprentice, but had evidently inherited little aptitude for the work. After several other unsuccessful jobs, he sailed with two friends for Canada, planning to become fur trappers. The immigration authorities at Quebec, finding the three had £10 between them, sent them ignominiously back on the same boat. In desperation, More applied to an old friend of his father's, Vivian van Damm, proprietor of the Windmill Theatre in London.

The Windmill specialized in nude revue, then considered daring; More's job, as stagehand, entailed re-enrobing the nudes between sketches. Van Damm's advice ("You must never, *ever* become a bloody actor. Acting is the end") went unheeded. More gradually took to stooging and understudying, and was eventually featured in sketches. In 1937 he left the Windmill and spent two years in provincial repertory companies before joining the Navy when war broke out. Demobilized as a lieutenant, he returned to acting, taking small parts in the West End, in films, and on television (which in those days reached only a tiny audience).

His breakthrough to stardom came almost simultaneously on stage and in the cinema. In 1952 he landed the male lead in Terence Rattigan's *The Deep Blue Sea,* playing a cheerfully feckless ex-RAF pilot, and during the play's long and successful West End run, took one of the four leading roles in *Genevieve* (1953). This was a light, charming, and witty comedy in the Ealing tradition, built around the London-to-Brighton Veteran Cars Rally, and was rapturously received by the public. More portrayed a tweed-jacketed smoothie with an abrasive laugh, and followed up with a similar role in *Doctor in the House* (1954), in which he and Dirk Bogarde played medical students. This was another box-office smash, and won More the British Film Academy Award as Best Actor.

More collected another Best Actor award, at Venice, for the film version of *The Deep Blue Sea* (1955), although he was disappointed with the picture, feeling that Vivien Leigh was miscast. His greatest success came with *Reach for the Sky* (1956), in which he portrayed Douglas Bader, the legless amputee who became a war hero flying fighter planes. The film was hugely acclaimed in Britain, where More was voted Star of the Year; but it did poorly elsewhere, and today makes rather embarrassing viewing.

Courtesy of Zoë Dominic

He was now firmly established in the public mind as—in his own words—"either the stiff-upper-lip war hero, or the hearty, back-slapping, beer-drinking idiot." However, his comic timing was excellent, and he put it to good use in *The Admirable Crichton* (1957). There followed good roles in *A Night to Remember* (1958), about the sinking of the Titanic; *The Sheriff of Fractured Jaw* (1958), a comedy western; *North-West Frontier* (1959), Imperial heroics with Lauren Bacall; and *Sink the Bismarck* (1960). Then his career fell apart.

Man in the Moon (1960), a dismal comedy, was his first flop. He quarreled with the head of J. Arthur Rank, to whom he was under contract, and was banned from *The Guns of Navarone* (1961)—the part went to David Niven. In *The Comedy Man* (1963) he played a middle-aged actor on the skids, dangerously close to home; it was his favorite role, but was unenthusiastically received. William Wyler gave him a substantial role in *The Collector* (1965), but it was completely cut from the final release.

In 1967, the BBC came to the rescue, with the key role of Young Jolyon in their 26-part adaptation of Galsworthy's *The Forsyte Saga.* The series was immensely popular, in Britain and all over the world; More's performance was reckoned as the finest thing in it. Further television work followed, including a series as G.K. Chesterton's *Father Brown* (1974), and some excellent stage roles, notably in *The Secretary Bird* (1968), Rattigan's *The Winslow Boy* (1970), and as a Labour M.P. in Alan Bennett's *Getting On* (1971). More's film career also revived, though only with cameo parts. His days as a cinematic leading man were over.

More was made a CBE in 1970. He retired from public view in 1981, after it was confirmed that he was suffering from Parkinson's disease. P.K.

Parents Charles Gilbert M., gen. mgr. of Jersey Eastern Railways, and Edith Winifred (Watkins) M. **Married** (1) Beryl Johnstone 1940 (div.): one daughter. (2) Mabel Edith Barkby 1952 (div.): one daughter. (3) Angela McDonagh Douglas, actress, 1968. **Education** Victoria Coll., Jersey. **Mil. service** Lt., Royal Naval Volunteer Reserve 1940–45. **Career** Engineering apprentice; employed by Sainsbury's; stagehand, understudy, and acting debut 1935, Windmill Theatre, London; actor in provincial repertory theaters, Newcastle, Wolverhampton, and Birmingham to 1939; film and TV actor since mid-1940s. **Honors** Best-actor award, for *Doctor in the House,* British Film Acad. 1954; Venice Volpi Cup for best actor, for *The Deep Blue Sea,* Venice Film Festival 1955; Star of the Year award, *Picturegoer* gold medal for best male performer, and Prix Femina of Belgium, all for *Reach for the Sky,* 1956; CBE 1970; theater named for him in Ilford, Essex. **Member** Clubs: Garrick; Green Room; Stage Golfing Soc. **Stage** (all London except as noted) *And No Birds Sing,* 1946; *Power Without Glory,* 1947; *Peace in Our Time,* 1948; *The Way Things Go,* 1950; *The Deep Blue Sea,* 1952; (co-producer and dir.) *The Angry Deep,* Brighton 1961; *Out of the Crocodile,* 1963; *Our Man Crichton,* 1964; *The Secretary Bird,* 1968; *The Winslow Boy,* 1970; *Getting On,* 1971; *Signs of the Times,* 1973; *On Approval,* 1977. **Films** *Look Up and Laugh,* 1935; *Windmill Revels,* 1937; *Carry On London,* 1937; *Scott of the Antarctic,* 1948; *Man on the Run,* 1949; *Now Barabbas,* 1949; *Stop Press Girl,* 1949; *Morning Departure,* 1950; *Chance of a Lifetime,* 1950; *The Clouded Yellow,* 1950; *The Franchise Affair,* 1950; *No Highway,* 1951; *Appointment with Venus,* 1951; *The Galloping Major,* 1951; *Brandy for the Parson,* 1952; *The Yellow Balloon,* 1952; *Never Let Me Go,* 1953; *Genevieve,* 1953; *Our Girl Friday,* 1953; *Doctor in the House,* 1954; *Raising a Riot,* 1954; *The Deep Blue Sea,* 1955; *Reach for the Sky,* 1956; *The Admirable Crichton,* 1957; *A Night to Remember,* 1958; *Next to No Time,* 1958; *The Sheriff of Fractured Jaw,* 1958; *The 39 Steps,* 1959; *North-West Frontier,* 1959; *Sink the Bismarck,* 1960; *Man in the Moon,* 1960; *The Greengage Summer,* 1961; *Some People,* 1962; *We Joined the Navy,* 1962; *The Longest Day,* 1962; *The Comedy Man,* 1963; *The Mercenaries,* 1967; *Fraulein Doktor,* 1968; *Dark of the Sun,* 1968; *Oh! What a Lovely War,* 1969; *The Battle of Britain,* 1969; *Scrooge,* 1970; *The Slipper and the Rose,* 1976; *Journey to the Center of the Earth,* 1977; *Leopard in the Snow,* 1978; *The Spaceman and King Arthur,* 1979; *A Tale of Two Cities,* 1980. **Television** "Silence of the Sea," 1946; "Heart to Heart," 1963; "The Forsyte Saga," 1966–67; "Six Faces," 1973; "Father Brown," 1974; "An Englishman's Castle," 1978; "A Tale of Two Cities," 1980; "The White Rabbit"; "The Rocking Horse Winner"; "The Pump"; others. **Author** *Happy Go Lucky* (autobiography), 1959; *Kindly Leave the Stage,* (memoirs), 1965; *More or Less* (autobiography), 1978.

DAVID (ALAN) BROWN
Anglican bishop of Guildford
***Born* 11 July 1922**
***Died* London, England, 13 July 1982**

The Right Rev. David Brown, bishop of Guildford since 1973, was known for his work in encouraging the leaders of the Church of England to open new dialogues with members of other religions, especially Islam, of which he had special knowledge from his years as a missionary and teacher in the Sudan. His death followed soon after the rejection by the Anglican General Synod of a proposal, which he had championed, to establish a covenant with three of England's Free Churches.

Brown had an outstanding academic career at the London College of Divinity and the University of London's School of Oriental and African Studies, taking a B.D. with first-class honors in 1946, an M.Th. in Hebrew, Arabic, and Syriac in 1947, and a B.A. with first class honors in Classical Arabic in 1951. The following year he left for the Sudan, where he was from 1955 to 1961 principal of Bishop Gwynne College in Mundri. In 1966, after two years' study of Muhammad's life, in Arabic, with Muslim teachers, he returned to England to become assistant curate in Bromley and then vicar of Herne Bay in Kent. He was consecrated bishop of Guildford, Surrey, in 1973.

Brown's direct encounter with Islam convinced him that harmonious relations between religious groups could be achieved only in an atmosphere of mutual respect. Most of his books and booklets dealt with that theme, including *A Guide to Religions* (1975) and *All Their Splendour: World Faiths: A Way to Community* (1982). He chaired British Council of Churches committees on Islam in Britain and interfaith relations and in 1977 became chairman of the General Synod's Board for Mission and Unity. As leader of the Anglican delegation to the Churches Council for Covenanting he helped construct the arrangement that would have linked the Church of England in a covenantal relationship with three of the country's independent Protestant churches. This move for church unity was narrowly voted down in the General Synod on 7 July 1982, after which the Churches Council dissolved itself. Brown became ill on his way to its last meeting and died on his way to the hospital. He was 60 years old. C.M.

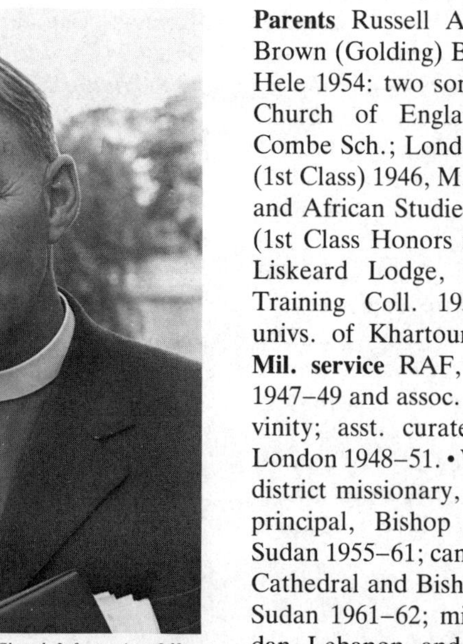
Courtesy of Church Information Office

Parents Russell Alan B. and Olive Helen Brown (Golding) B. **Married** Elizabeth Mary Hele 1954: two sons; one daughter. **Religion** Church of England. **Education** Monkton Combe Sch.; London Coll. of Divinity, B.D. (1st Class) 1946, M.Th. 1947; Sch. of Oriental and African Studies, Univ. of London, B.A. (1st Class Honors in Classical Arabic) 1951; Liskeard Lodge, Church Missionary Soc. Training Coll. 1951–52; studied Islam at univs. of Khartoum and Amman 1962–65. **Mil. service** RAF, WWII. **Career** Jr. tutor 1947–49 and assoc. 1948, London Coll. of Divinity; asst. curate, Immanuel, Streatham, London 1948–51. • With Church Mission Soc.: district missionary, Yambio, Sudan 1952–54; principal, Bishop Gwynne Coll., Mundri, Sudan 1955–61; canon missioner at Khartoum Cathedral and Bishop's Commissary (South), Sudan 1961–62; missionary, Diocese of Jordan, Lebanon, and Syria 1965–66. • Asst. curate, St. John the Evangelist, Bromley, Kent 1966–67; vicar, Christ Church, Herne Bay, Kent 1967–73; rural dean, Reculver, Kent 1972–73; bishop of Guildford, Surrey since 1973. **Officer** Chmn.: Canterbury Diocesan Council for Mission and Unity 1972–73; Working Party on Islam in Britain 1974–78 and Cttee. for Relations with People of Other Faiths since 1978, British Council of Churches; Bd. for Mission and Unity, Gen. Synod, Church of England since 1977; Consultative Cttee. on Islam in Europe, Conference of European Churches since 1980. • Warden, St. Augustine's Coll., Canterbury 1975–78; Church of England delegate to Churches Council for Covenanting since 1977. **Member** Royal Commonwealth Soc. **Author** *A Manual of Evangelism,* 1958; *The Way of the Prophet,* 1960; *Mission Is Living,* 1972; *A Guide to Religions,* 1975; *God's To-morrow,* 1977; *Meet the Bible,* 1978; *All Their Splendour,* 1982; others. **Contributor** to *Theology* and *New Fire.*

GIUSEPPE PREZZOLINI
Critic and journalist
Born **Perugia, Italy, 27 January 1882**
Died **Lugano, Switzerland, 14 July 1982**

Giuseppe Prezzolini's 80-year career as a writer spanned the development of Italy from a recently unified state, through the rise and fall of Fascism, into an industrialized democracy. When he came on the scene in the early years of the century, an earnest, self-educated bohemian with a passionate disdain for bourgeois values, there had recently been an upheaval in European social thought and philosophy, typified, for him, by Bergson, Croce, and Sorel. As founding editor of the journal *La Voce* from 1908 to 1914, Prezzolini assumed the role of spokesman for his generation and made himself the most prominent iconoclast of his day. He summarized the dissatisfactions of his period, and by resolutely rejecting the values of his time succeeded in transforming some of them. Filippo Donini, reviewing Prezzolini's *Journal 1942–1968* (1982) in the *Times Literary Supplement,* wrote that "if the renaissance of Italian culture started by Croce at the beginning of the century developed into a vast movement which really transformed and modernized Italian cultural life, most of the credit must be given to *La Voce.*"

The main interests of Prezzolini and his fellow *Vociani* were not, however, literature and the arts, but sociology, politics, and moral philosophy. "Our moral conditions," Prezzolini wrote in the journal, "would be much better if there were more young people who could read and understand a budget or a blueprint, rather than producing mediocre stories or silly poems by the dozen." His enthusiasm for technology, industrial development, and political reform resembled the creed of futurist painters and sculptors such as Boccioni and Carrà, and also, in political terms, allied him with Mussolini and Amendola, leaders of the

Courtesy of Columbia University

incipient Fascist movement. He was singled out by a critic writing in *Il Popolo d'Italia* in 1914 as a leading representative of "the new Italy which is rising—fresh, courageous, daring, and strong." Prezzolini joined with Mussolini in calling for Italian intervention in World War I, in which he served as an infantryman, and described in essays the battles of Caporetto and Vittorio Veneto. The ignominious failure of Italian arms did not quench his enthusiasm for the resurgence of his country: he described Italy's defeat as a moment of national self-knowledge, and in *La Voce* remarked that "war is a general exam to which, from time to time, history calls all people."

Such outspoken, direct commitment to a cause or course of action is, however, rare in Prezzolini's writing, which is characterized by sardonic detachment. In his memoir *Uomo finito* (1913), Prezzolini's friend and collaborator Giovanni Papini described how, as two impoverished bohemians, he and Prezzolini would meet in cafés to exchange sneers at the bourgeois. Later, in works like *Code of Italian Life* (1921), Prezzolini continued to describe his compatriots as ignorant and stupid; in *The Legacy of Italy* (in English, 1948), he characterized them as incapable of organization, boasting, arrogant, and, although addicted to swaggering, incompetent in war. In his negative attitude toward the status quo and his attraction to the positivist ideals of scientific and educational progress, he displayed a kind of inverted romantic idealism and defensive superciliousness that seems to have been prompted by frustration with human inadequacies. Not only Italians, but all peoples and institutions aroused his predilection for satire. In his preface to the Italian (but not the English) edition of *Machiavelli Antichrist* (1954; English ed. 1966), he apologizes for the superficiality of the book by explaining that it originated as a course of lectures at Columbia University: "Democracy is not merely an electoral parade, but a sincere effort to keep in step with the slowest soldier in the battalion. I had to begin with the alphabet of politics and philosophy, especially in the matter of Machiavellianism, which is foreign to the spirit of American schools, which are excellent for children, but tend to keep adults in a mental climate of infantilism."

Like many satirists, Prezzolini had a deep attraction to authoritarianism. He admired this quality in Machiavelli as much as he did in Mussolini, for both were men who represented the doctrine of *virtù,* a moral and physical strength and capacity to govern that claims independence from the distinction between good and evil. Prezzolini's ideal was to ally the brute strength of nations with their capacity for rational thought, and most of his efforts as a writer were directed toward this end. He wrote in *Friends* (1922): "At a certain point in my life, having buried the romantic turmoils and aspirations, I decided to become a useful man for others; to clarify certain ideas to Italians, to indicate their inferiorities in order to overcome them, to characterize foreign people and foreign movements . . . to point out hidden greatness; that is what one calls the work of culture."

Prezzolini was largely self-educated, but grew up in a literary household. His father, Luigi Prezzolini, was a government official, but maintained friendships with several writers, including the poet Giosuè Carducci. On his father's death in 1899, Prezzolini left school and took up a career as a reviewer and critic with the encouragement of Giovanni Papini, then a student at the University of Florence. Papini's literary character and social views were remarkably similar to those of Prezzolini—both were violently prejudiced, rigorously subjective and pragmatic in philosophical temperament, and took great pleasure in anticlerical and antiestablishment invective. Together they founded *Leonardo,* a radical journal, in 1903, and its successor, *La Voce,* in 1908. They also collaborated on a book, *Italian Culture* (1906). Prior to World War I Prezzolini also published his first study of Machiavelli, *The Art of Persuasion* (1907), and his most notable early work, *Benedetto Croce* (1909). The essay on Croce was reissued, along with studies of Benito Mussolini, Giovanni Amendola, and his friend Papini, as *Four Discoveries* (1964).

After his release from the army, Prezzolini turned *La Voce* into the publishing house Libreria della Voce, and also began contributing reports to an American press agency. He worked for the League of Nations from 1925 to 1929 as head of the information section of the International Institute on Intellectual Cooperation in Paris. From 1930 to 1950 he taught Italian literature at Columbia University, becoming an American citizen after World War II. As head of the Casa Italiana, Columbia University's center for Italian cultural activities, from 1930 to 1940, Prezzolini was often charged with being an agent of the Italian government. He denied these charges when they appeared in the *Nation,* and made an extensive rebuttal in a pamphlet in English, *The Case of the Casa Italiana* (1976). His major work of the years immediately before and during the war was his massive four-volume *Bibliographical Repertory of Italian Literature from 1903 to 1942,* published in 1946. His later work was largely devoted to producing a record of his early career. He published a two-volume edition of his correspondence with Papini entitled *Story of a Friendship* (1966, 1968).

In 1962 he returned to Italy but, seeing no reason to revise his low opinion of the Italian national character, moved to Lugano, Switzerland, in 1968. He continued to write prolifically, publishing several volumes of diaries, four studies and miscellanies related to *La Voce,* and an inquiry into mystical idealism, *God is a Risk* (1969). Some of his occasional writings, many of which had appeared in Italian newspapers after World War II, were collected in *The Useless Italian* (1953).

According to Filippo Donini, his "anti-conformism and desire to shock" did not lessen with age. He continued to pour scorn on both historical and contemporary people and institutions, but his passionate nature was not, it seems, unlikeable, or devoid of a sense of humor. In 1955 he published *Spaghetti Dinner*, a book that Craig Claiborne praised as "one of the most amusing books on pasta," and in 1948, in *The Legacy of Italy*, he paid this uncharacteristic tribute to his native country: "There must be something pleasing and easy-going in a civilization which without any organization, without a theoretical plan, without resorting to force, endures, spreads, and attracts." He died six months after his hundredth birthday. H.B.

Also wrote under pseudonym Giuliano il Sofista. **Parents** Luigi P., govt. prefect, and Emilia (Pianigiani) P. **Married** (1) Dolores Faconti 1905: Alessandro, b. 1911; Giuliano, b. 1915. (2) Gioconda Savin 1962 (d. 1981). **Emigrated** to U.S. 1930, naturalized; returned to Italy 1961, lived in Switzerland since 1968. **Education** Govt. schs. to 1899; then self-educated. **Mil. service** Infantry, Italian Army, WWI. **Career** Co-founder, jrnl. *Leonardo* 1903; collaborator on nationalist review *Il Regno* and other periodicals in late 1900s; co-founder 1908 and ed. 1908–14, jrnl. *La Voce,* Florence; political corresp., Rome office, *Il Popolo d'Italia* 1914–15, also corresp. for *Rivoluzione Liberale;* founder, Libreria della Voce publishing house 1919; corresp., Foreign Press Service early 1920s; Italian rep. and dir. of information sect., Inst. for Intellectual Cooperation, League of Nations, Paris 1925–29; dir. of Casa Italiana 1930–40 and prof. of Italian literature 1930–50, Columbia Univ.; ed., writer, and literary critic, NYC 1940–61, Italy 1961–68, and Lugano, Switzerland since 1968. **Honors** Cavaliere di Gran Croce, 1971; Penna d'Oro, Italy 1982. **Author** (Jtly.) *La cultura italiana* [*Italian Culture*], 1906; *L'arte di persuadere* [*The Art of Persuasion*], 1907; *Il sarto spirituale: mode e figurine per le anime della stagione corrente* [*The Spiritual Tailor: Fashions and Fashion Plates for the Current Season's Soul*], 1907; *Cos'è il modernismo?* [*What is Modernism*?], 1908; *Il cattolicismo rosso* [*Red Catholicism*], 1908; *Benedetto Croce*, 1909; *La teoria sindicalista* [*Syndicalist Theory*], 1909; *Studi e capricci sui mistici tedeschi* [*Studies and Fancies on German Mystics*], 1912; *La Francia e i francesi nel secolo XX osservati da un italiano* [*Twentieth Century France and Frenchmen Through the Eyes of an Italian*], 1913; *Vecchio e nuovo nazionalismo* [*Old and New Nationalism*], 1914; *Almanacco della Voce* [*The La Voce Almanac*], 1915; *Discorso su Giovanni Papini* [*A Discourse on Giovanni Papini*], 1995; *Manualetto italo-sloveno* [*Italian-Slovene Handbook*], 1915; *Tutta la guerra: antologia del popolo italiano sul fronte e nel paese* [*The Entire War: An Anthology of the Italian People in the Trenches and at Home*], 1918; *Paradossi educativi* [*Educational Paradoxes*], 1919; *Uomini 22 e citta 3* [*Men 22 Cities 3*], 1920; *Codice della vita italiana* [*Code of Italian Life*], 1921; *Amici* [*Friends*], 1922; *Mi pare* [*It Seems to Me*], 1923; *La cultura italiana* [*Italian Culture*], 1923; *Io credo* [*I Believe*], 1923; *I maggiori: antologia per le scuole medie* [*The Major Writers: A High School Anthology*], 6 vols., 1923–30; *L'aguzzingegni: esercizi per i ragazzi* [*Mindsharpeners: Exercises for Children*], 3 vols., 1923; *Giovanni Papini,* 1924; *Benito Mussolini*, 1924; *Le fascisme*, 1925 (trans. as *Fascism*, 1927); *Giovanni Amendola,* 1925; (jtly.) *Marte: antologia militare* [*Mars: A Military Anthology*], 1925; *La vita di Niccolò Machiavelli fiorentino*, 1928 (trans. as *Niccolo Machiavelli, The Florentine*, 1928); *Come gli americani scoprirone l'Italia, 1750–1850* [*How the Americans Discovered Italy*],

1933, enlarged ed. 1971; *Repertorio bibliografico della storia e della critica della letteratura italiana* [*Bibliographical Repertory of the History and Criticism of Italian Literature*], 4 vols., 1937–42; *The Legacy of Italy*, 1948; *America in pantofole* [*America in Bedroom Slippers*], 1950; *L'italiano inutile* [*The Useless Italian*] (autobiography), 1953; *America con gli stivali* [*America in Riding Boots*], 1954; *Machiavelli anticristo,* 1954 (trans. as *Machiavelli*, 1966); *Spaghetti Dinner*, 1955; *Saper leggere* [*Knowing How to Read*], 1956; *Il meglio di Prezzolini* [*The Best of Prezzolini*], 1957, 2nd. rev. ed. 1971; *Tutta l'America* [*All America*], 1958; *Il tempo della Voce* [*The Time of La Voce]*, 1960; *Dal mio terrazzo, 1946–59* [*From My Terrace*], 1960; *Diari (con Soffici) 1939–1945* [*Diaries (with Soffici's) 1939–45*], 1962; *I trapiantati* [*The Transplanted*], 1963; *Quattro scoperte: Croce, Papini, Mussolini, Amendola* [*Four Discoveries . . .*], 1964; *Storia di un'amicizia: Papini-Prezzolini* [*The Story of a Friendship*], vol. 1, 1966, vol. 2, 1968; *Ideario* [*Idearium*], 1967; *Dio è un rischio* [*God Is a Risk*], 1969; *Carteggio Boine-Prezzolini* [*Boine-Prezzolini Correspondence*], 1971; *Cristo e/o Machiavelli* [*Christ and/or Machiavelli*], 1971; *Gobetti e La Voce* [*Gobetti and La Voce*], 1971; *Il manifesto dei conservatori* [*The Conservative Manifesto*], 1972; *Amendola e la Voce,* 1973; *Italia fragile* [*Fragile Italy*], 1974; (jtly.) *La Voce 1908–13. Cronaca, antologia e fortuna di una rivista* [*La voce 1908–13: Chronicle, Anthology, and Fortune of a Review*], 1975; *Carteggio Giuseppe De Luca-Prezzolini 1925–1962,* 1975; *Prezzolini sul Fascismo* [*Prezzolini on Fascism*], 1975; *Mussolini e La Voce*, 1976; *Storia tascabile della letteratura italiana* [*Pocket History of Italian Literature*], 1976; *Soffici e La Voce*, 1977; *The Case of the Casa Italiana*, 1976; *Prezzolini alla finestra* [*Prezzolini at the Window*], 1977; *Carteggio di Prezzolini-Ardengo Soffici*, 1977; *Diario 1900–1941* [*Journal*], 1978; *Intervista sulla destra* [*Interview on the Right*], 1978; *Diario 1941–1968,* 1982; (with Alberto Moravia) *Lettere* [*Letters*], 1982.

COURTLANDT S(HERRINGTON) GROSS

Aircraft industry executive

***Born* Boston, Massachusetts, USA, 21 November 1904**

***Died* Villanova, Pennsylvania, USA, 15 July 1982**

Courtlandt S. Gross was a leading officer of the Lockheed Aircraft Corporation from the time of its acquisition in 1932 by his elder brother, Robert Ellsworth Gross (1896–1961), until his own retirement as chairman of the board in 1967. He led the company through its best years, when it was reaping huge profits from U.S. defense contracts during the buildup for the Vietnam War.

Born into a wealthy Massachusetts family, he followed his brother to St. George's School in Newport, Rhode Island, and then to Harvard, where he majored in English, graduating in 1927. As his brother had done, he first went to work as a salesman for Lee Higginson & Company, Boston (1927–29), but then joined a fledgling aircraft concern, the Viking Flying Boat Company of New Haven, where he remained until 1932, eventually becoming treasurer and director. After his brother and two partners bought Lockheed—founded in 1926 but never profitable, and by 1932 foundering in receivership—Gross left Viking and became Lockheed's New York-based director of East Coast operations.

Although he often seemed to relish working in the shadow cast by his brother's dynamism ("I'm just the dumb kid brother," he told an interviewer in 1946), Gross was appreciated throughout the industry as a hard-nosed manager and was greatly respected by his colleagues at Lockheed. He was responsible for several early successes, including the $25 million sale to Britain in the late 1930s of 250 Hudson bombers, then the largest aircraft contract ever awarded a U.S. firm. During World War II, as general manager of the Vega Company in California, a Lockheed subsidiary, he oversaw the production of the P-38 Lightning, a high-performance fighter and pursuit plane that operated in all theaters of the war. In cooperation with Boeing and Douglas, Vega also manufactured the B-17 Flying Fortress, the principal U.S. bomber.

Gross pushed for the development of a new airliner, the Lockheed Constellation, as defense spending waned just after the war. He pursued his belief in diversification during his tenure as president (1956–61), and then, after his brother's death, as chairman. Lockheed was thus well placed to enter the aerospace industry at the top, and won contracts for construction of both national-defense satellites and the Polaris missile. The two principal U.S. cargo planes, the C-130 Hercules and its even larger successor, the C-5A Galaxy, were both Lockheed creations and together filled nearly all military-transport needs throughout the 1960s and 1970s. By 1965, Gross saw the company's profits rise to $52 million on sales of $1.75 billion. Lockheed took sizable percentages of each year's Defense Department outlay: Gross's management of the company's interest in the complex military-procurement business was considered brilliant by Robert McNamara's Pentagon policymakers.

Gross left the company in 1967 to live in retirement in Villanova, an affluent suburb of Philadelphia, with his wife, Alexandra Van Rensselaer Devereux, who was closely related to several of the wealthiest and most influential families in Main Line society. The couple built and furnished a mansion of considerable size and spent much time traveling. Gross continued to serve on the boards of several corporations in the Philadelphia area. He was not involved in the creation of Lockheed's later troubles: the drift toward bankruptcy and subsequent federal bailout, or the international influence-buying scandal.

On 16 July 1982, the bodies of Courtlandt and Alexandra Gross and their 69-year-old housekeeper, Catherine VanderVeur, were found in their home. Each had been shot once in the head. In January 1983, a habitual criminal, Roger Buehl, 22 years old, was convicted of murdering them during the commission of a burglary. A.K.

Courtesy of Lockheed Corporation

Parents Robert Haven G., coal industrialist, and Mabel (Bowman) G. **Married** Alexandra Van Rensselaer Devereux 1939: Alexandra Devereux (d.); Courtlandt Devereux; Mary Lobel Walsh Wanamaker Watriss (stepdaughter). **Religion** Episcopalian. **Education** Public schs., Boston; Fassendon Sch., West Newton, MA; St. George's Sch., Newport, RI 1919–23; Harvard Univ., A.B. 1927. **Career** Clerk, salesman, Lee Higginson & Co. banking and investment firm, Boston 1927–29; buyer, asst. mgr., and treas., Viking Flying Boat Co., New Haven, CT 1929–32. • With Lockheed Aircraft Co.: eastern rep., NYC office 1933–40; gen. mgr., Vega Aircraft Co., subsidiary of Lockheed, Burbank, CA 1940–43; v.p. and gen. mgr., Burbank office 1943–52; member, bd. of dirs. 1943–77; exec. v.p. 1952-56; pres. 1956–61; chmn., bd. of dirs. and exec. cttee. 1961–67. **Officer** Dir.: Penn Mutual Life Insurance Co.; Girard Trust Bank; Smith, Kline, and French Labs.; Atlantic Richfield Co.; Philadelphia Contributorship for Insurance of Houses Against Loss by Fire. • Overseer and chmn., overseer's visiting cttee., Div. of Engineering and Applied Physics, Harvard Univ. 1960–65; head, United Way campaign, L.A.

PATRICK DEWAERE
Actor
***Born* Saint-Brieuc, Brittany, France, 26 January 1947**
***Died* Paris, France, 16 July 1982**

Patrick Dewaere played losers. Not exclusively, of course. Following his cinematic debut in 1970 he appeared in some two dozen pictures, becoming one of the leading young French actors; and in some of those films his roles were more carefree. But the archetypal Dewaere performance—as in Alain Corneau's *Série Noire* (1979), perhaps his best film—was as a *paumé,* one of life's born losers, sad-eyed and taciturn, crushed by unfeeling forces. He was fully aware of the danger, for an actor, of being possessed by the parts he played. In his last interview, shortly before his death, he complained: "I'm fed up with being taken over by unhappy roles. I want to play some happy parts!" He had, perhaps, come to that realization too late.

He was born Patrick Maurin in Saint-Brieuc, Brittany, into a theatrical family—a circumstance that initially he strongly resented. He had five older siblings, all already on the stage, and was considered the least gifted of his family. "When I played in Montherlant or Molière, in *Wuthering Heights,* or in television plays, it wasn't by vocation. I was just following the family trade." He failed his *baccalauréat* four times, and left home planning on some quite different career. But he was caught up in the vibrant excitement of Paris in May 1968, and found himself first helping to build, and then (under his grandmother's name of Dewaere) acting at the Café de la Gare, which rapidly became the foremost improvisational theater company in France.

Dewaere's first film was *Les mariés de l'an II* (1970). He landed a larger role in Claude Faraldo's anarchic comedy *Themroc* (1972), then achieved fame with Bertrand Blier's black farce *Les valseuses* (1974; released as *Going Places* and *Making It*), in which he starred with two other promising newcomers, Gérard Depardieu and Miou-Miou. This account of small-time crooks on the spree was genitally obsessed to a fault—Dewaere's character gets shot in the groin, and the film's title is slang for "testicles." Despite some critical disapproval, it was a huge success.

Along with his co-stars, Dewaere was now greatly in demand. Among the best of his subsequent films were Maurice Dugowson's *Lily, aime-moi* (1974), in which he played an ill-fated boxer; Claude Miller's *La meilleure façon de marcher* (1976; *The Best Way To Walk*), in which he was cast against type as an aggressively macho summer-camp monitor; *La marche triomphale* (1976), for the Italian director Marco Bellochio, as a conscript; *F comme Fairbanks* (1976), for Dugowson again, as an out-of-work dreamer who wants to be Douglas Fairbanks. For this film, he also composed the music.

Courtesy of French Embassy

Despite some well-publicized drug problems, Dewaere's career continued to prosper. He was reunited with Depardieu for *Préparez vos mouchoirs* 1978; (*Get Out Your Handkerchiefs*), another of Bertrand Blier's bad-taste comedies, which achieved international success and a critic's award in the United States. Most recently, he had completed *Paradis pour tous* (1982), in which he played a suicide, for Alain Jessua, and was about to start work on Claude Lelouch's *Edith et Mar-*

cel, as the boxing champion Marcel Cerdan, whose relationship with Edith Piaf was the subject of the film. He seemed enthusiastic about the project.

Dewaere's wife and young daughter were away on holiday, and he was alone in his Paris apartment. It was there that his body was found. He had shot himself through the head.

P.K.

Born Patrick Maurin. **Parents** Father a singer; mother an actress. **Married;** one daughter. **Education** Conservatoire, Paris. **Career** On stage and TV as child actor from age seven; comedian and actor with Paris café theaters late 1960s; co-founder, Café de la Gare experimental theater group, Paris 1968; film actor since 1970; also film composer. **Films** *Les mariés de l'an II,* 1970; *La maison sous les arbres,* 1971; *Themroc,* 1972; *Au long de la rivière Fango,* 1973; *Les valseuses* (rel. as *Going Places* and *Making It*), 1974; *Lily, aime-moi,* 1974; *Pas de problème,* 1975; *Catherine et Cie,* 1975; *Adieu Poulet,* 1975; *La meilleure façon de marcher* (rel. as *The Best Way to Walk),* 1976; *La marche triomphale,* 1976; *F comme Fairbanks* (rel. as *F as in Fairbanks),* 1976; *Le Juge Fayard, dit le shérif,* 1977; *La chambre de l'évêque,* 1977; *Préparez vos mouchoirs* (rel. as *Get Out Your Handkerchiefs),* 1978; *Coup de tête* (rel. as *Hothead),* 1978; *Série noire,* 1979; *Le grand embouteillage* (rel. as *Bottleneck),* 1979; *La clé sur la porte* (rel. as *A Singular Woman*), 1979; *Paco l'infaillible* (rel. as *Paco the Infallible),* 1979; *Un mauvais fils* (rel. as *A Bad Son),* 1980; *Plein sud,* 1980; *Psy,* 1980; *Mille-milliards de dollars* (rel. as *A Thousand Billion Dollars),* 1981; *Beau-Père,* 1981; *Hôtel des Amériques* (rel. as *Hotel of the Americas),* 1981; *Paradis pour tous* (rel. as *Paradise for All),* 1982.

CHARLES R(OBBERTS) SWART
State president of South Africa
***Born* Morgenzon, Orange Free State, 5 December 1894**
***Died* Bloemfontein, South Africa, 16 July 1982**

From 1961, when South Africa became a republic and left the British Commonwealth, Charles Swart served for one seven-year term in the largely ceremonial office of state president. Despite his deep roots in Afrikaner nationalism, he was accepted by the British as the last governor general of the Union of South Africa. As justice minister from 1948, the date of his National Party's accession to power, he was responsible for drafting the country's harsh laws concerning race and political dissent.

Born on a farm in the Orange Free State, then an Afrikaner republic, Swart was interned in 1902 along with his mother in a British concentration camp during the Boer War; his father died in a British prison. At the age of 13 he entered Grey University College in Bloemfontein, at which he earned his B.A. and LL.B. degrees. After teaching for a few years, he was jailed briefly in 1914, at the beginning of World War I, for taking part in a pro-German revolt against the Union government's decision to enter the war on the Allied side. Shortly thereafter he traveled to the United States, where he took a special diploma in journalism from Columbia University, worked briefly as a reporter in New York and Washington, and even won bit parts in a few Hollywood westerns and horror films. After returning home he was a columnist for Daniel F. Malan's Capetown daily, *Die Burger.*

"Blackie" Swart (his surname means "black" in Afrikaans) began his political involvement at a high level as private secretary to Gen. James B. M. Hertzog in 1919, a year after being admitted to the Free State bar. Hertzog, a republican and advocate of apartheid, had founded the National Party in 1913, and Swart soon became an active and influential member. He was the party's organizational secretary for the Free State from 1919, and was a member of its chief executive from 1928 and of its federal council from 1931.

In 1923, the year before Hertzog became prime minister for the first time, Swart was elected to parliament from Ladybrand in the

Courtesy of South African Information Service

Free State, a secure seat in the National Party heartland. He was defeated in 1938, but in 1940 won election as state party leader, and the next year was returned to parliament from his home area of Winburg, an even safer seat which he held until his appointment as governor general in 1959. He took an extensive part in parliamentary affairs almost from the start, serving on numerous committees and frequently as party whip, but gained no power in government until 1948, when Malan's Nationalists and their Afrikaner Party allies won a narrow victory over the United Party of Prime Minister Jan Smuts. In Malan's "all-Afrikaner" cabinet, Swart was made minister of justice.

His first priority was to give the Nationalists' pet theory of apartheid the force of law. Under his direction, legislation was drafted and pushed through parliament to restrict black people's freedom of movement, employment, and assembly; to strengthen police control over all citizens, particularly by means of the Pass Laws; and generally to ensure the continued ascendancy of white Afrikaner society. In 1950 he created the Suppression of Communism Act, under which he, as minister, was empowered to "name" and hence proscribe suspected subversives. He abolished legal appeals of criminal cases to the Privy Council, and initiated the penal custom of farming out state prisoners to private employers, who were allowed to make them work and keep them in private jails. He was an ardent champion of severe corporal punishment for many offenses, introducing the Flogging Bill to parliament in 1952 by brandishing a cat-o'-nine-tails. To opposition suggestions for reducing the number of lashes per flogging from 15 to 10, he is reported to have remarked, "What are five strokes among friends?"

Swart retained the justice portfolio in every government until 1959, and was simultaneously minister of education, arts, and science (1949–50) and deputy prime minister and leader of the House (1954–59). In 1958 he served as acting prime minister for a couple of weeks before losing to Hendrik Verwoerd, the powerful minister of native affairs, in a bitter contest for leadership of the National Party. His elevation to the suprapolitical office of governor general was the natural course for a defeated senior politician, but his past was severely criticized in the British press. His post-independence election (1961) as state president was expected, and his quiet tenure of that post aroused little public comment.

A dour man 6 feet 7 inches tall, Swart was the recipient of several honorary degrees from South African universities, and published a couple of novels in Afrikaans. From 1950 to 1976 he was chancellor of the Orange Free State University. A.K.

Parents Hermanus B. S. and Aletta (Robberts) S. **Married** Nellie de Klerk 1924: one son; one daughter. **Education** Grad. high sch. at age 13; Grey University Coll. (now Univ. of Orange Free State), Bloemfontein, B.A. 1911, LL.B. 1914; Univ. of South Africa; Sch. of Journalism, Columbia Univ., NYC. **Career** Jailed by British for participating in pro-German revolt 1914; teacher, Ficksburg High Sch., Orange Free State (OFS) 1914–15; secty., OFS examination bd. ca. 1916; lectr. in law, Univ. of Orange Free State 1917–18; admitted to bar, OFS 1918; advocate, Supreme Court of South Africa 1919–48; visiting lectr. in agricultural legislation, Glen Agricultural Coll., Bloemfontein 1920–23; legal asst., Bloemfontein County Council, and member of legal commn., Dutch Reformed Church, early 1920s; reporter, newspapers in NYC and Wash. DC; bit-part actor, Hollywood; journalist, *Die Burger* and other South African newspapers 1938–41; novelist and short-story writer. • With Natl. Party of OFS: secty. to leader 1919; organizing secty. 1919–28; named member of chief exec. 1928; named member of federal council 1931; leader and chief whip 1940–59. • Natl. M.P. for Ladybrand, OFS 1923–38, and for Winburg, OFS 1941–59; member, parliamentary cttees.; minister of justice 1948–59; minister of education, arts, and science 1949–50; deputy prime minister and leader of House of Assembly 1954–59; acting prime minister 1958; gov. gen., Union of South Africa 1959–61; state pres., Republic of South Africa 1961–67. **Officer** Patron: Durban Men's Choir; Cultural Open-Air Mus., Pretoria; Nederlands-Suid-Afrika Werkgemeenshap. • Founder: Fedn. of Afrikaans Cultural Socs.; Die Afrikaanse Handelsinstitut; Voortrekker Youth Movement. • Chancellor, Univ. of Orange Free State 1950–76. **Member** (Life) South African Agricultural Union; War Mus. Council. **Honors** Hon. v.p., Natl. War Fund 1939–45; Order of Honour, Voortrekker Youth Movement 1952; hon. col. of East Free State Regiment 1953 and Orange Free State Regiment 1962; hon. fellow of Coll. of Physicians, Surgeons, and Gynaecologists of South Africa 1963 and of Inst. of South African Architects 1967; Decoration for Meritorious Service 1972; Justice Medal 1972; hon. pres., Automobile Assn. of South Africa; hon. member, South African Acad. of Science and Art since 1960, Natl. Parks Bd., and Natl. Women's Memorial Commn.; hon. freeman of Johannesburg, Durban, Bloemfontein, and five other cities; hon. degrees from Univ. Coll. of Orange Free State, Rhodes Univ., and Potchefstroom Univ. **Author** *Kinders van Suid-Afrika* [*Children of South Africa*], 1961.

Further reading John Gunther, *Inside Africa,* 1955.

ROMAN (OSIPOVICH) JAKOBSON
Founder of modern linguistics
***Born* Moscow, Russia, 11 October 1896**
***Died* Boston, Massachusetts, USA, 18 July 1982**

Although linguists, unlike scientists in other disciplines, rarely win public fame, Roman Jakobson's name is familiar even to casual students of language and literature. He ranks, along with Ferdinand de Saussure, the originator of structuralism, and with his own student and disciple Noam Chomsky, as one of the giants of modern linguistics. Fluent in six languages, and able to read 25, Jakobson was a polymath whose major interests, according to a biographical article by his colleague Morris Halle in the *International Encyclopedia of Social Sciences,* encompassed "studies on the theory of linguistics, especially phonology and linguistic geography, contributions to the historical phonology of various Slavic languages, synchronic descriptions of phonological phenomena in different languages, including also their prosody, inquiries into morphology, investigations of medieval Slavic culture and literatures, especially Old Church Slavonic and medieval Czech, studies in folklore, sociolinguistics, poetics (especially metrics), literary criticism, and essays on the film, painting, and the theater." He was particularly renowned for his demonstration that all languages, no matter how apparently dissimilar, share certain universal phonemic properties, and that these properties can be classed according to the ways in which they are spoken and heard.

Jakobson was born in Moscow of Jewish parents and educated at the Lazarev Institute of Oriental Languages at Moscow University, from which he graduated in 1918. As founder and president of the Moscow Linguistic Circle from 1915 to 1920, he fell under the influence of the poet Vladimir Mayakovsky, whose Futurist school of writing maintained that the meaning of a word is intimately related to its sound, and that a new poetic diction should be created to communicate emotion phonetically, thus avoiding the semantic ambiguities of ordinary language. Jakobson, writing under the pseudonym Alyagrov, contributed several poems to the Futurist publication *Zaumnaya*

Gniga. His brief career as a poet was undoubtedly an important basis for his later work, which was marked by its extraordinary sensitivity to literary form.

Jakobson's earliest critical writing concerned other Futurist poets, and his first book, *Contemporary Russian Poetry* (1921), remains an important study of the Futurists. By 1930, he had become the leading critic of revolutionary Russian verse and had allied himself with the formalist school of literary analysis, which rejected historical and biographical criticism in favor of technical appreciation of form. These interests pointed the way to his later emphasis on the form and structure of language rather than its meaning.

Jakobson taught Slavic languages at the University of Moscow from 1918 to 1920, but completed his doctorate in 1930 at Charles University in Prague, where he went in 1920 as a member of the Russian Red Cross mission to Czechoslovakia. He mastered Czech with extraordinary rapidity, and soon became a prominent member of the Prague intelligentsia. In 1926 he was instrumental in founding the Prague Linguistic Circle, which first met under the chairmanship of Vilém Mathesius, and included the scholars Nicolai Trubetskoy and René Wellek. The work of the circle was made public at the first international conference of Slavic linguists in Prague in 1929. Jakobson and his colleagues questioned the value of the primarily historical and grammatical studies of nineteenth-century linguists and, basing their approach on the structuralism of Saussure, proposed a synchronic method of linguistic analysis whose central tenet was the theory that all languages pass through the same stages in the course of their development. In order to define and identify these stages in living speech, Jakobson began to analyze phonemes. This method enabled the members of the Prague Circle to describe languages both synchronically, accounting for their present structure, and diachronically, tracing their evolution through time. Their assumption, derived from Saussure, that language is a system of sounds that serve as arbitrary symbols for meaning, led them to concentrate on phonetics, the distinct acoustic elements of meaning, rather than grammar or syntax.

Working with ideas advanced by Saussure and the American linguist Edward Sapir, Jakobson and his colleagues developed their theory that each language is distinguished from all others by its inclusion or omission of particular phonemes from the set of all phonemes available to human speech and by the contrasts heard among the included phonemes (for example, between the sounds of *b* and *p*, or of *zh* and *ch*). In 1938 he suggested that each phoneme, contrary to accepted theories, consists of a substructure of component features that are utilized differently in different languages, and proposed a binary model by which phoneme usage within a language system could be defined. The empirical thoroughness of his investigations was confirmed by his studies of the ways in which children speak, and on the reversal of this process in aphasia, a cerebral illness that results in loss of speech. In *Child Language, Aphasia and Phonological Universals* (1940; English ed. 1968) he claimed that all children acquire the distinctive phonemic features of their languages in the same way, and that sufferers from aphasia undergo identical processes of speech dissolution.

This search for the very basis of language gained attention throughout Europe, and reached the height of its influence immediately after World War II. By that time, Jakobson, preceded by his growing fame, had left Masaryk University in Brno, where he had been professor of Russian philology from 1933 to 1939, to take visiting professorships in Copenhagen, Oslo, and Uppsala. He arrived in New York in 1942, one of many Jewish refugees from the Nazis. The following year he was appointed a visiting professor to the chair of Czechoslovak studies at Columbia University and became a founder member of the Linguistic Circle of New York. In 1949 he became Cross Professor of Slavic language and literature at Harvard University and, in 1957, institute professor at the Massachusetts Institute of Technology. Many of the linguists and Slavic scholars now teaching in American colleges and universities were trained by him. In 1952 he published, in collaboration with Halle and Gunnar Fant, a monograph on the system of interrelationships between speech sounds and the physical production of speech that prepared the way for Chomsky's generative phonology.

During the latter part of his career, Jakobson was revered not only as a linguist, but also as a pioneer in the application of linguistic knowledge to literary form. After World War II, American and European scholars became increasingly interested in the question of whether poetry should be regarded as a distinct form of language or as a heightened mode of ordinary speech. Jakobson's work as poet, critic, and linguist placed him in the forefront of the effort to unite the disciplines of linguistics and literary criticism. In discussing the poetry and prose of Boris Pasternak in 1936, he offered the insight that the structure of lyric poetry is characteristically metaphoric, whereas that of prose (and realistic literature in general) is characteristically metonymic, depending on the close association of physical attributes. Jakobson also wrote on Russian oral literature, and published numerous studies of poetic structure in Baudelaire, Shakespeare, Du Bellay, Dante, and Blake. He summarized his views in a paper given at Indiana University in 1958: "The poetic resources concealed in the morphological and syntactic structure of language . . . have been seldom known to critics and mostly disregarded by linguists, but skilfully mastered by creative writers. . . . All of us realize, however, that a linguist deaf to the poetic function of language and a literary scholar indifferent to linguistic problems . . . are equally flagrant anachronisms."

Jakobson's work had important applications to almost every field of study touching on communications, from the humanities

Courtesy of MIT Museum

(philosophy, structural anthropology, semiotics, and art as well as literary criticism) to the sciences (mathematical analyses of language, neurolinguistics, computer and information theory, and even the study of the genetic code). Three festschriften, published in honor of his 60th, 70th, and 80th birthdays, pay tribute to the remarkable range of his interests, and his work is currently being collected and reprinted by a Dutch publisher. He was the recipient of innumerable honors, including the Légion d'Honneur and 25 honorary degrees. A bibliography of his writings published in his 75th year includes more than 600 books and articles in six languages. *Dialogues,* a volume of conversations with his wife, Krystyna Pomorska, a professor of Russian literature at MIT, was scheduled for publication in September 1982. H.B.

Parents Osip J., chemist, and Anna (Volpert) J. **Married** (1) . . . (2) Svatava Pirkova. (3) Krystyna Pomorska, prof. of Russian literature, 1962. **Religion** Jewish. **Emigrated** to Czechoslovakia 1920; lived in Scandinavia 1939–41; emigrated to U.S. 1942, naturalized 1952. **Education** Lazarev Inst. of Oriental Languages, Moscow, B.A. (silver medal) 1914; Moscow Univ., M.A. 1918; Charles Univ., Prague, Ph.D. 1930. **Mil. service** Member of USSR Red Cross mission to Czechoslovakia 1920. **Career** Founding pres., Moscow Linguistic Circle 1915–20; instr. and research assoc., Univ. of Moscow 1918–20; prof. of orthoepy, Moscow Dramatic Sch. 1920; cofounder, Prague Linguistic Circle 1920s; asst. prof. 1933–34, visiting prof. 1934–37, and assoc. prof. of Russian philosophy and old Czech literature 1937–39, Masaryk Univ., Brno, Czechoslovakia; visiting lectr. in phonology, Univ. of Copenhagen 1939; visiting lectr. in linguistics 1939–40, Univ. of Oslo; visiting lectr. in Russian, Univ. of Uppsala 1940–41; prof. of linguistics, École Libre des Hautes Études, NYC 1942–46; visiting prof. of gen. linguistics, Inst. de Philologie et d'Histoire Orientales et Slaves 1943–46, and Masaryk Prof. of Czechoslovak Studies 1946–49, Columbia Univ.; Cross Prof. of Slavic Languages, Literatures, and Gen. Linguistics 1949–67 and prof. emeritus since 1967, Harvard Univ.; visiting inst. prof. 1957–60, inst. prof. 1960–70, and prof. emeritus since 1970,

Massachusetts Inst. of Technology, Cambridge, MA. • Fellow, Center for Advanced Study in Behavioral Sciences 1959, 1961; visiting fellow, Salk Inst. for Biological Studies, San Diego, CA 1966–69; fellow, Center for Cognitive Studies 1967–69; visiting prof. at Yale Univ. 1967 and 1971, Princeton Univ. 1968, Brown Univ. 1969–70, Brandeis Univ. 1970, Coll. de France 1972, Catholic Univ. of Louvain 1972, New York Univ. 1973, and Bergen Univ. 1976; consultant to UNESCO; co-ed., *International Journal of Slavic Linguistics and Poetics;* co-ed., Technology Press series on books in communications. **Officer** Pres.: Intl. Council for Phonetic Sciences 1948–61; Linguistic Soc. of America 1957. • V.P.: Intl. Cttee. of Slavists 1958–76; Intl. Assn. for Semiotic Studies since 1969; Intl. Soc. of Phonetic Sciences since 1970. • Chmn.: intl. council, Acta Linguistica. **Fellow** Amer. Acad. of Arts and Sciences. **Member** Amer. Anthropological Assn.; Acoustic Soc. of America; Mediaeval Acad.; New York Acad. of Sciences. • Foreign member: Norwegian Acad. of Sciences; Royal Danish Acad. of Sciences and Letters; Serbian Acad. of Sciences; Polish Acad. of Sciences; Royal Netherlands Acad. of Sciences; Irish Acad. of Sciences; Italian Acad. of Sciences, Bologna; British Acad.; Finnish Acad. of Sciences. **Honors** Chevalier, Légion d'Honneur 1947; award, Amer. Council of Learned Socs. 1960; award, Natl. Slavic Honor Soc. 1967; hon. pres., Tokyo Inst. for Advanced Study of Languages 1967; gold medal, Slovak Acad. of Science 1968; award, Amer. Assn. for Advancement of Slavic Studies 1970; centennial scholar, Johns Hopkins Univ. 1975; presidential bicentennial award, Boston Coll. 1976; Feltrinelli Intl. Prize for Philology and Linguistics, Accademia dei Lincei, Rome 1981; Hegel Prize, Intl. Hegel Soc. and City of Stuttgart 1982. • Hon. member: Acad. of Aphasia; Center for Byzantine Studies; Finno-Ugric Soc., Helsinki; Royal Soc. of Letters, Lund; Italian Assn. of Semiotic Studies; Czechoslovak Soc. of Arts and Letters; Sicilian Semiologic Circle; Phonetic Soc. of Japan; Royal Anthropological Inst. of Great Britain and Ireland; Natl. Assn. for Armenian Studies and Research; Philological Soc., England; Intl. Phonetic Assn. • Hon. degrees from univs. of Cambridge, Oslo, Chicago, Uppsala, Michigan, New Mexico, Grenoble, Nice, Rome, Yale, Charles, Purkyne, Ohio State, Zagreb, Brno, Tel Aviv, Louvain, Clark, Harvard, Columbia, Liège, Copenhagen, Georgetown, Ruhr-Bochum, and Oxford. **Author** *Noveyshaya russkaya poeziya* [*Contemporary Russian Poetry*], 1921; *O cheshskom stikhe preimushchestvenno v sopostavlenni s russkim* [*Czech Verse as Compared with Russian*], 1923; *Remarques sur l'évolution phonologique du russe comparée à celle des autres langues slaves* [*Remarks on the Phonological Evolution of Russian as Compared with That of Other Slavic Languages*], 1929; *Kindersprache, Aphasie und allgemeine Lautgesetze,* 1940 (trans. as *Child Language, Aphasia, and Phonological Universals,* 1968); (jtly.) *La geste du Prince Igor,* 1948; (jtly.) *Preliminaries to Speech Analysis: The Distinctive Features and Their Correlates,* 1952; (jtly.) *Fundamentals of Language,* 1956, 2nd rev. ed. 1971; *Paleosiberian Peoples and Languages: A Bibliographic Guide,* 1957; (co-ed.) *Description and Analysis of Contemporary Standard Russian,* 1959; (jtly.) *Low German Manual of Spoken Russian,* vol. 1, 1961, vol. 2, 1970; (co-ed.) *Poetics-Poetyka-Poetika, II: Problems of General Metrics and the Metrics of Slavonic Languages,* 1966; *Studies on Child Language and Aphasia,* 1971; *Studies in Verbal Art: Texts in Czech and Slovak,* 1971; *Roman Jakobson: A Bibliography of His Writings,* 1971; *Main Trends in the Science of Language,* 1973; *Form und Sinn* [*Form and Meaning*], 1973; *Questions de poétique* [*Questions of Poetics*], 1973; (ed.) *N.S. Trubetzkoy's Letters and Notes,* 1975; *Pushkin and His Sculptural Myth,* 1975; *Aufsatze zur Linguistik und Poetik* [*Contributions to Linguistics and Poetics*], 1976; *Six lectures sur le son et le sens,* 1976 (trans. as *Six Lectures on Sound and Meaning,* 1978); *Hölderlin-Klee-Brecht: Zur Wertkunst dreier Gedichte* [*Hölderlin-Klee-Brecht: The Verbal Art of Three Poems*], 1976; *Der grammatische aufbau der Kindersprache* [*The Grammatical Structure of Children's Language*], 1977; *The Sound Shape of Language,* 1978; *The Framework of Language,* 1980; *Brain and Language,* 1980; (with Krystyna Pomorska) *Poesie und Grammatik—Dialoge,* 1982 (trans. as *Dialogues,* 1982); many other books, essays, and articles. • *Selected Writings: Vol. I, Phonological Stud-*

ies, 1962; *Vol. II, Word and Language,* 1971; *Vol. III, The Poetry of Grammar and the Grammar of Poetry,* 1981; *Vol. IV: Slavic Epic Studies,* 1966; *Vol. V, Verse: Its Masters and Explorers,* 1979; *Vol. VI, Early Slavic Paths and Crossroads,* 1982; *Vol. VII, Studies in Comparative Mythology,* forthcoming.

Further reading *For Roman Jakobson: Essays on the Occasion of his Sixtieth Birthday* (festschrift), 1956; *To Honor Roman Jakobson: A Collection of Essays* (festschrift), 3 vols., 1967; Elmar Holenstein, *Roman Jakobson's Approach to Language: Phenomenological Structuralism,* 1976; Ladislav Matejka, ed., *Sound, Sign, and Meaning,* 1976; Linda R. Waugh, *Roman Jakobson's Science of Language,* 1976; Daniel Armstrong and C. H. van Schooneveld, eds., *Roman Jakobson: Echoes of His Scholarship,* 1977.

OKOT p'BITEK
Poet
Born **Gulu, Uganda, 1931**
Died **Kampala, Uganda, 19 July 1982**

Okot p'Bitek was among the most accomplished and respected of African poets, equally at home in English and Lwo, the language of his people, the Acholi. The stubborn persistence and even flourishing of traditional folkways among the Acholi, despite decades of Westernizing influence, is one of the important themes of his work, which includes, besides books of poetry and folktales, essays on the preservation and protection of African religion and culture.

The son of a schoolmaster, p'Bitek was born in Gulu, the main city of the Acholi district, and was educated at Gulu High School and King's College, Budo. In 1954 he was accredited as a teacher after two years of study at the government Training College, Mbarara, and began to teach near Gulu. He had become a champion football (soccer) player, and was selected for the Ugandan national team that attended the Olympic Games in London in 1956. He remained in Britain to study after the rest of his team returned home, earning a certificate of education from the University of Bristol, then a bachelor of law degree from the University of Wales at Aberystwyth, and finally a B.Litt. in 1963 from the Institute of Social Anthropology at Oxford with a thesis on Acholi oral literature.

p'Bitek returned to Uganda in 1963 and became affiliated with the sociology department at Makerere University, Kampala, one of the best universities in East Africa. In 1966, at the beginning of the presidency of Milton Obote, he was appointed director of the Uganda National Theater and Cultural Center. He brought a great deal of energy to the post, founding the successful Gulu Arts Festival in 1966, but political pressures forced him to relinquish it in 1968 and to go into exile in Kenya, where he remained throughout the dictatorship (1971–79) of Idi Amin. Employed during most of this time by the University of Nairobi, he founded the Kisumu Arts Festival, lectured widely (at the universities of Texas in 1969 and Iowa in 1971), and produced most of his best-known work.

p'Bitek's first published work, in Lwo, was the novel *Are Your Teeth White? Then Laugh!* Appearing in 1953, during his football career, it demonstrated the warm, slightly ironic sympathy for Acholi language and customs that marked all the rest of his work. He found a much wider public when his English translation of his *Song of Lawino* appeared in 1966 (it was published in the United States in 1969). Arranged in verse of deceptive simplicity, this "poetic novel" is an account of the reactions of Lawino, a proud and angry Acholi woman, to the spurious changes she sees happening around her, especially the desire of her estranged and partly educated husband to ape Western cultural values. In a similar vein, *Song of Ocol* (1970) purports to be the culturally dead husband's smug reply to Lawino's passionate denunciations. *Two Songs* (1971), consisting of *Song of Malaya* and *Song of a Prisoner*—the former about a prostitute, the latter a meditation on the death of p'Bitek's friend, the Kenyan politician Tom Mboya—won the 1972 Kenyatta Prize for Literature. His other poetry appeared in *The*

Horn of My Love (1974), a miscellany of poems in English and Lwo with p'Bitek's appended commentaries.

After the bitter civil war, severe famine, and total disruption that followed Amin's downfall, p'Bitek returned to Uganda. For five months before his death he held the professorship of creative writing in the literature department of Makerere University. In his last years he published little poetry, but *Hare and Hornbill* (1978), a selection of translated Acholi folktales, and his collected essays, *Africa's Cultural Revolution* (1973), both enjoyed wide readership. A.K.

Courtesy of Heinemann Educational Books, Ltd.

Father a schoolteacher. **Married** twice. **Emigration** In exile in Kenya and Nigeria 1970s. **Education** Gulu High Sch.; King's Coll., Budo; Govt. Training Coll., Mbarara, teaching certificate 1954; Univ. of Bristol, England, certificate in education; Univ. of Wales, Aberystwyth, LL.B.; Inst. of Social Anthropology, Oxford Univ., B.Litt. 1963. **Career** Teacher, Gulu area 1954–ca. 56; player on natl. football team mid-1950s; lectr. in sociology 1964 and prof. of creative writing 1982, Makerere University, Kampala; dir., Uganda Natl. Theater and Uganda Natl. Cultural Center, Kampala 1966–68; visiting lectr., Univ. of Texas 1969; fellow, intl. writing program 1969–70, and writer in residence 1971, Univ. of Iowa; sr. research fellow at Inst. of African Studies and lectr. in sociology and literature, Univ. of Nairobi 1971–78; prof., Univ. of Ife, Nigeria 1978–82. • Founder: Gulu Arts Festival, Uganda 1966; Kisumu Arts Festival, Kenya 1968. **Honors** Kenyatta Prize for Literature, for *Two Songs,* 1972. **Novel** *Lak tar miyo kinyero wi lobo?* [*Are Your Teeth White? Then Laugh!*], 1953. **Prose poems** *Wer pa Lawino,* 1969 (trans. as *Song of Lawino,* 1966); *Song of Ocol,* 1970; *The Song of a Prisoner,* 1971; *Two Songs: The Song of a Prisoner, The Song of Malaya,* 1971; (comp., trans., and commentator) *The Horn of My Love* (Acholi traditional songs), 1974; (comp. and trans.) *Hare and Hornbill* (Acholi folktales), 1978. **Essays** *African Religions in Western Scholarship,* 1970; *Religion of Central Luo,* 1971; *Africa's Cultural Revolution,* 1973. **Recording** *Okot p'Bitek of Uganda,* Voice of America 1968.

Further reading G. A. Heron, *The Poetry of Okot p'Bitek,* 1976.

WALWORTH BARBOUR
U.S. ambassador to Israel
***Born* Cambridge, Massachusetts, USA, 4 June 1908**
***Died* Gloucester, Massachusetts, USA, 21 July 1982**

Walworth Barbour was ambassador to Israel from 1961 to 1973, handling the highly sensitive post with great skill and discretion during three U.S. administrations. His appointment initiated the continuing practice of sending career diplomats rather than political appointees to the Tel Aviv embassy.

Barbour attended Phillips Exeter Academy

and Harvard University, joining the Foreign Service soon after his graduation in 1930. His early assignments were to Naples (1931–33), Athens (1933–36), Baghdad (1936–39; 1942), and Sofia (1939–41). He spent World War II as director of the Greek and Yugoslavian desk at the Cairo embassy (1943–44), then returned to Athens as second secretary (1944–45).

Back in Washington, Barbour was appointed assistant chief, then chief, of the State Department's Division of Southeastern European Affairs (1945–49). After two years in Moscow as counselor with the rank of minister (1949–51), he returned to the State Department to serve as director of Eastern European affairs (1952–54), then deputy assistant secretary for European affairs (1954–55), normally the highest career post in the department. From 1955 until his posting to Tel Aviv he was in London, first as deputy chief of mission (1955–56), then as minister and counselor (1956–58), and finally as career minister (1958–61).

Pres. Kennedy's decision, early in his administration, to depoliticize the Tel Aviv embassy was received with alarm in many quarters in Israel, where it was feared that the new ambassador would be just another "State Department Arabist" with limited access to the administration. Barbour eased all apprehension: he quickly took complete control of the embassy, which eventually became one of the best run in the world; carefully cultivated lasting intimacy with all important Israeli policymakers; and most of all, by his quiet determination and unobtrusive staying power, came to seem indispensable to everyone he dealt with. He managed relations during the 1967 Arab-Israeli war, and during many difficult moments over economic and military aid. He was often required to express official U.S. displeasure at Israeli moves, but reportedly always did so without alienating his hosts.

Pres. Nixon, early in his first term, was on the point of offering him the ambassadorship to Moscow, but Barbour let it be known that he was not interested in moving, and managed to stay on in Tel Aviv. At the end of his 12-year tenure, one of the longest on record for any U.S. ambassador, the *Jerusalem Post* called him "the professional's professional," and "a sagacious political intelligence who could continuously and precisely define for his own country and for his hosts the political aims of both, and more specifically the limits of tolerance of both." In 1973 he retired to

Courtesy of US State Department

Gloucester, Massachusetts, where he lived near his sister, who had served as hostess at his infrequent embassy receptions and dinners. He died of pneumonia at the age of 74.

A.K.

Parents Samuel Lewis B. and Clara (Hammond) B. **Education** Phillips Exeter Acad., Andover, MA; Harvard Univ., A.B. 1930. **Career** Joined U.S. Foreign Service 1930; vice consul, Naples 1931–33 and Athens 1933–36; 3rd secty., Baghdad 1936–39 and Sofia 1939–41; 2nd secty., Sofia 1941, Cairo 1941, and Baghdad and Cairo 1942; 2nd secty. to govt. of Greece and Yugoslavia in Egypt 1943–44; 2nd secty., then consul, Athens 1944–45; acting asst. chief 1945–47 and chief 1947–49, Div. of Southeastern European Affairs, State Dept., Wash. DC; counselor with rank of minister, Moscow 1949–51; dir., Office of Eastern European Affairs, State Dept. 1952–54; deputy asst. secty. of state for European affairs 1954–55; deputy chief of mission 1955–56, minister and counselor 1956–58, and career minister 1958–61, London; ambassador to Israel 1961–73. **Member** Diplomatic and Consular Officials, Retired. • Clubs: University; American; Swinley Forest, Surrey; Chevy Chase, MD. **Honors** Hon. fellow,

Weizmann Inst. of Science, Israel; Distinguished Service Award, State Dept. 1971; hon. degrees from Tel Aviv Univ., Hebrew Univ. of Jerusalem, Dropsie Univ., and Hebrew Union Coll.

DAVE GARROWAY
Television personality
***Born* Schenectady, New York, USA, 13 July 1913**
***Died* Swarthmore, Pennsylvania, USA, 21 July 1982**

Dave Garroway was the founding father of morning television, whose "Today" show attracted a large and devoted audience from the time of its first appearance on 14 January 1952. An amiable, intelligent man who never seemed uncomfortable on camera, he still personifies for many who remember him the great promise, as yet unfulfilled, of television's beginning years.

His early youth was spent moving almost constantly from place to place: he was the only child of a roving troubleshooting engineer for General Electric, and had been enrolled in 21 different public schools by the age of 14. The family finally settled down in St. Louis, where Garroway graduated from University High School and, in 1935, from Washington University. After an unpromising start as a salesman, he was hired in New York by NBC as a page and subsequently attended the company's announcing school, where he was eventually rated 23rd in a class of 24. He then worked as a special-events announcer with radio station KDKA in Pittsburgh, leaving in September 1940 for a similar job with WMAQ in Chicago, to which he returned in 1945 after serving in Hawaii as an ensign in the Navy during World War II. His radio jazz show, "11:60 Club," where his pleasant and unpretentious style was first evident, made him popular throughout the Chicago area. NBC signed him for a network radio show in 1947, then backed "Garroway at Large," a successful low-key variety show and his first foray into television, from 1949 to 1951.

When he heard that the network was planning to enter the then-unoccupied field of morning television and was casting about for someone to do a news and interview show, Garroway quickly went after the job. "They didn't want a lean-against-the-ladder, go-to-sleep-standing-up guy like me," he said later. But Sylvester L. (Pat) Weaver, NBC's vice president for programming, hired him anyway, and after an extraordinarily lavish advertising campaign, Garroway was launched as the "communicator" on the "Today" program in early 1952.

The show started slowly, with ungenerous critical notices and sparse backing from sponsors, but it quickly became habitual viewing for millions of early-rising Americans and within 18 months was turning huge profits for the network. Broadcast live from a street-level studio in Rockefeller Center, "Today" offered a mélange of frequent news and weather, plus information of the most disparate nature, all held together by the affable, unobtrusive courtesy of its star. Garroway was never condescending or flippant, whether interviewing V. K. Krishna Menon, Frank Lloyd Wright, or Miss Doughnut, delivering one of his carefully rehearsed and quietly effective commercials, or engaging in a subdued, one-sided conversation with J. Fred Muggs, a chimpanzee and the show's popular "animal-story editor." Garroway became one of the highest paid stars in television, and from 1955 to 1959 simultaneously served as narrator of "Wide Wide World" on Sunday afternoons.

He left "Today" in 1961, after the suicide of his second wife, in order to spend more time with his family. His frequent attempts to come back to the medium were all unhappy failures; they included a network show for CBS (1964–65), a local morning interview show in Boston (1969–70), and a summer replacement variety show, "Newcomers," on CBS in 1971. He was last on screen in January 1982, during the 30th-anniversary celebrations for "Today," and gave his famous signoff, right palm facing the audience: "This is Dave Garroway. Peace."

His death, by self-inflicted gunshot wound, occurred while he was suffering postoperative complications following open-heart surgery.

A.K.

Courtesy of NBC Photo

Born David Cunningham Garroway, Jr. **Parents** David Cunningham G., Sr., mechanical engineer, and Bertha (Tanner) G. **Married** (1) Adele Dwyer 1939 (div. 1946): Paris Newrock. (2) Pamela Wilde (d. 1961): David; Michael (stepson). (3) Sarah Lee Lippincott, astronomer. **Education** University High Sch., St. Louis, grad. 1931; Washington Univ., St. Louis, B.A. 1935; NBC Student Announcers' Class, NYC 1938. **Mil. service** Lt. (s.g.), on mine sweeper, then teacher of radio technicians and officer in charge of yeoman sch., Pearl Harbor, HA, USNR 1942–45. **Career** Asst. lab instr., Harvard Observatory 1935; salesman of piston rings, New England, and pronunciation textbooks, NYC, 1935–37; guide, NBC studios, NYC 1937; special feature announcer, radio sta. KDKA, Pittsburgh 1938; staff announcer 1940–42 and disc jockey of "11:60 Club" 1946–49, radio sta. WMAQ, Chicago; host, "Garroway at Large," WNBQ-TV, Chicago 1949–51. • With NBC, NYC: host, "Today Show," NBC-TV 1952–61; host, "The Dave Garroway Show," NBC-TV 1953–54; host, "Friday with Garroway," NBC radio 1954–56; narrator, "Wide Wide World," NBC-TV 1955–59. • Worked with U.S. Information Agency 1961; producer, "Exploring the Universe" TV show, 1961–62; host, "Garroway A.M. and P.M.," CBS 1964–65; host, "Tempo Boston," RKO Gen. TV 1969–70; host, radio show, KFI, L.A. 1971; host, "Newcomers," CBS 1971; made public service commercials 1970s. **Officer** Gov., Natl. Acad. of Arts and Sciences 1968; member, bd. of dirs., Federal Union. **Honors** City golf champion, St. Louis, and winner of Chicago Open Golf Tournament; gold medal award, Poor Richard Club of Phila. 1949; outstanding new male personality, Critics' Honor Roll 1950; most original in TV, *Look* mag. 1951. **Author** "I Lead a Goofy Life," in *Saturday Evening Post,* 11 Feb. 1956; *Fun on Wheels,* 1960.

Courtesy of NBC Photo

Further reading Thomas Whiteside, "The Time is Twenty-One After," in *New Yorker,* 5 Sept. 1959; Max Wilk, *The Golden Age of Television,* 1976.

B(ISHESWAR) P(RASAD) KOIRALA
Prime minister of Nepal
***Born* Biratnagar, Nepal, 8 September 1914**
***Died* Katmandu, Nepal, 21 July 1982**

B. P. Koirala was the only democratically elected prime minister in Nepal's history. He held the office just 18 months before being deposed and imprisoned by order of King Mahendra, an assertive absolute monarch jealous of the powers he had delegated to Koirala's government. For the rest of his life, which was spent largely in prison or exile and in steadily deteriorating health, "B. P." (as he was everywhere known) never ceased to call for the restoration of democratic freedoms in his country.

Koirala was the son of a Nepalese follower of Gandhi who died in a Nepalese prison. He was educated first at Benares Hindu University, then took a law degree at Calcutta University in 1937 and practiced law for several years in Darjeeling. While still a student he became involved in the Indian nationalist movement, and in 1934 he joined the Congress Party. During World War II he was interned by the British in Hyderabad for two years (1942–44). Following his release, with Indian independence imminent, he set about trying to bring change to Nepal. In 1947 he founded from India the solidly socialist Nepali Democratic Party, which in 1952 became the Nepali Congress Party. He was imprisoned in Nepal in 1947–48 after returning to his home city of Biratnagar to lead a labor demonstration. A year later he was arrested again, but was soon released following a 27-day hunger strike, popular protests, and the intervention of the Indian prime minister, Jawaharlal Nehru.

Courtesy of Jayaraj Acharya

Nepal had been governed for generations by the Ranas, a narrow, family-based oligarchy permitted by successive acquiescent kings to exercise all real power. The last Rana prime minister was dismissed in 1951, to be followed by the country's first "commoner" government, led by M. P. Koirala, B. P.'s elder half-brother, in which B. P. served for nine months as home secretary. He left the government to concentrate on the developing Nepali political structure: although not fully officially tolerated, political parties were increasing in importance, and the king was being pushed by events to offer some concession to growing democratic aspirations. Mahendra responded with a new constitution enabling free parliamentary elections to take place in early 1959. Only a fragmented parliament was expected, but Koirala's Nepali Congress scored a landslide, taking nearly three-quarters of the seats in the lower house. After several weeks of significant hesitation, Mahendra asked Koirala to form a government, which took office in May 1959.

Viewed from abroad, Koirala's debut as prime minister was a great success. He led his country's delegation to the United Nations and made carefully poised visits to China and India, then increasingly at odds over territorial disputes. Yet he was in trouble at home almost from the beginning. His land-reform measures, especially the revision of the tenancy laws so easily passed by parliament, deeply offended the landed aristocracy which had long dominated the army. His long-promised reform of the central bureaucracy outraged thousands of entrenched and powerful bureaucrats. And the king and court saw even their residual powers being eroded with amazing speed. The new government, the nation's first democratic experiment, thus managed to alienate simultaneously all the traditional centers of power. Mahendra acted quickly, brutally, and finally: on 15 December 1960, he suspended the constitution, dissolved parliament, dismissed the cabinet, imposed direct rule, and for good measure imprisoned Koirala and his closest government colleagues. The others were released after a few months, but Koirala, though he was suffering from throat cancer, was kept imprisoned without trial until 1968, when he was finally permitted to go and live in exile in Benares.

King Birendra, educated in England and the United States, succeeded his father in 1972, and the political climate was believed to be gradually improving. Koirala, however, was arrested immediately upon his return from exile in 1976 and charged with the capital offense of attempting armed revolution. Considerable international pressure secured his release on parole and enabled him to travel to the United States for medical treatment. He was arrested again on his return from New York in late 1977, but in March 1978 was finally cleared of all treason and sedition charges. After returning from a further medical visit to the United States he had a series of audiences with the king, and he later professed himself a believer in "national reconciliation." Even after a period of house arrest following student demonstrations in 1979, he praised Birendra's call for a national referendum the following year on the best form of monarchy for Nepal. The referendum was won by the king's party amid widespread charges of vote rigging, whereupon Koirala demanded a boycott of the 1981 elections.

Despite obviously failing strength, B. P. could still draw an enthusiastic crowd. He spoke to one of Nepal's largest public meetings in recent years in Katmandu's Ratna Park in January 1982. In addition to years of wide political adulation, Koirala was also popular as a novelist and short-story writer, and did much to enhance the literary acceptance and viability of Hindi, a minority language in Nepal. A.K.

Parents Krishna Prasad K. and Divya K., social workers. **Married** Sushila 1937: Prakash, social worker, b. 1946; Harsha, physicist, b. 1951; Shashanka, physician, b. 1955; Chetana Dikshit, b. 1959. **Emigration** In voluntary exile, Benares 1968–76. **Education** Gurjar Pathsala, Benares, grad. 1930; Harishchandra Coll., Benares, grad. 1932; Benares Hindu Univ., B.A. 1934; Calcutta Univ., LL.B. 1937. **Career** Member, Congress Party, India 1934; law practice, Darjeeling late 1930s; secty., Bihar sect., Congress Party 1939; interned by British, Hyderabad 1942–44; founder, Nepali Democratic Party (later Nepali Congress Party) 1947; led labor demonstration, Biratnagar 1947; imprisoned 1947–48, 1949; comdr. in chief, revolutionary army 1950–51; home secty. 1951; pres., Nepali Congress Party 1952 and since 1954; prime minister of Nepal 1959–60, leader of Nepalese delegation to U.N. 1960; imprisoned 1960–68; in exile in Benares 1968–76; imprisoned for treason and sedition 1976–77, 1977–78; under house arrest 1979. • Poet and short-story writer. **Member** Asian Socialist Org. since 1949; Socialist Intl. since 1959. **Political writings** *Rajatantra ra Lokatantra* [*Monarchy and Democracy*], 1960; *Thichieka Janata Jagisake* [*The Oppressed People Rise*], 1969; *Kranti ek anivaryata* [*Revolution: An Absolute Necessity*], 1970; *Panchayati Vyavastha Prajatantrik Chaina* [*The Panchayat System Is Not Democratic*], 1978; *Prajatantra ra Samajvad* [*Democracy and Socialism*], 1979; *Rastrya Ekata ko nimti Ahwan* [*A Call for National Unity*], 1980. **Novels** *Teen Ghumti* [*Three Turns*], 1968; *Narendra Dai* [*Brother Narendra*], 1969; *Sumnima,* 1970; *Modiaen* [*The Wife of a Grocer*], 1980. **Short-story collection** *Doshee Chashma* [*Defective Glasses*], 1947.

Further reading Leo E. Rose and M. Fisher, *The Politics of Nepal,* 1970; Leo E. Rose, *Nepal: Strategy for Survival,* 1971; Bhola Chatterji, *Portrait of a Revolutionary: B. P. Koirala,* 1982.

SIR ROBERT BIRLEY
Educator
***Born* Midnapore, Bengal, India, 14 July 1903**
***Died* Somerton, Somerset, England, 22 July 1982**

Sir Robert Birley was for many years one of the most liberal and energetic figures in British education. He was headmaster of two eminent public schools, Charterhouse and Eton, and a constant advocate of educational excellence and equality of educational opportunity.

He was born in India, where his father was a member of the Indian Civil Service assigned to the province of Bengal. Educated first at Rugby School, he then had a brilliant career at Balliol College, Oxford, where he took a first in modern history and won the Gladstone Memorial Prize. He first went to Eton in 1926 as assistant master and history tutor, and quickly gained a reputation as an inspiring teacher and a man with a burning interest in public causes. He was an effective member of the Eton Urban District Council, and worked hard to alleviate the heavy unemployment in Slough, a nearby industrial city.

In 1935, Birley was named headmaster of Charterhouse, where he remained through the difficult years of World War II, when many schools saw their enrollments and incomes severely reduced. By the time he left, however, in 1947, the school was again flourishing. He had been an influential member of the Fleming Committee in 1944, which recommended enlarging the opportunities for private education in Britain, a goal he always considered of the highest importance. A sabbatical visit in 1945 to Germany, then just defeated and beginning to experience the Allied occupation, led to his appointment as educational advisor to the military governor of the British Zone from 1947 to 1949. In that crucial post, he quickly realized that the occupiers' role could only be to assist the traditional excellence of German education to reassert itself after the ruinous educational program of the Nazi years, and his warmth, courtesy, and informed concern were widely appreciated and long remembered by the many German educators he dealt with.

His appointment as headmaster of Eton in 1949 was a foregone conclusion, and his tenure there was happy and productive for him. By this time he was well known as a liberal intellectual activist; his many civic activities, especially his involvement with the Workers Educational Association in Slough, gained him the secret nickname "Red Robert" among the boys at Eton, yet he always showed great respect for the college's five centuries of tradition.

Birley retired as headmaster at the age of 60 in 1963, but clearly had no intention of leaving education. In 1964 he went as visiting professor of education to the English-speaking University of the Witwatersrand in Johannesburg, South Africa. He knew he was unwelcome to the government, but extended his stay there to three years, encouraging the antiapartheid movement in the English-speaking universities and even persuading suspicious Afrikaner administrators to soften somewhat the harshness of the Bantu Education Act, especially as it applied to the understaffed and underfinanced African university colleges. "My strength," he said to friends who wondered at his success, "is that I am so immensely respectable." He also regularly taught history at the Orlando High School in the black township of Soweto.

On his return to Britain in 1967 he immediately took up the post of professor and head of the humanities and social sciences department at the new City University of London. There he was successful in broadening the curriculum of what was primarily intended as an engineering institution. He also joined the councils of the Institute of Race Relations, Voluntary Service Overseas, and the Minority Rights Group.

Birley was the BBC's Reith Lecturer in 1949, gave the Clark Lectures in 1961, and was Chichele Lecturer at All Souls College, Oxford, in 1967. He had a lifelong interest in book collecting and the history of printing, and was president of the Bibliographical Society in 1979. He held honorary degrees from universities in Britain, Germany, and South Africa. His knighthood was conferred in 1967.

A.K.

Parents Leonard B., in Indian civil service, and Grace Dalgleish Maxwell (Smyth) B. **Married** Elinor Margaret Frere 1930: Julia Rees, b. 1931; Rachel, b. 1935. **Religion**

Church of England. **Education** Rugby Sch., Warwickshire; Balliol Coll. (Brackenbury Scholarship), B.A. (1st Class Hons. in history) 1925, M.A. 1935. **Career** Asst. master, Eton Coll. 1926–35; headmaster, Charterhouse, Godalming, Surrey 1935–47; educational advisor to British military gov., Occupied Germany 1947–49; headmaster, Eton Coll. 1949–63; visiting prof. of education, Univ. of Witwatersrand, South Africa 1964–67; prof. and head of dept. of social sciences and humanities, City Univ., London 1967–71; chmn., Central Council, Selly Oaks Colls. 1969–80. • Lectr.: Burge Memorial 1948; Reith 1949; Clark 1961; Chancellors', Univ. of Witwatersrand 1965; Chichele, All Souls Coll., Oxford 1967; Gresham Prof. of Rhetoric since 1967. **Officer** Chmn.: Headmasters' Conference 1950s; Anglo–German Königswinter Conferences, Deutsch-Englische Gesellschaft; Witon Park Academic Council. • Pres.: Bibliographic Soc. 1979–80; Slough branch, Workers Education Assn. **Fellow** Soc. of Antiquaries. **Member** Eton Urban District Council early 1930s; Fleming Cttee. on Public Schs. 1944; Inst. of Race Relations; Voluntary Service Overseas; Atlantic Coll.; Minority Rights Group; Athenaeum; Travellers' Club. **Honors** Gladstone Memorial Prize 1924 and hon. fellow 1969, Balliol Coll.; CMG 1950; comdr., Order of Merit, West Germany 1955; KCMG 1967; hon. degrees from univs. of Oxford, Aston, Edinburgh, Leeds, Liverpool, Witwatersrand, City (London), Frankfurt, and from Technical Univ., Berlin. **Author** *The English Jacobins from 1789 to 1802,* 1924; *Czechoslovakia,* 1939; (ed.) *Speeches and Documents in American History,* 4 vols., 1944; *The German Problem and the Responsibility of Britain,* 1947; *School, Society, and the Delinquent,* 1951; *The Undergrowth of History,* 1955; *Sunk without Trace,* 1962.

SONNY STITT
Jazz saxophonist
Born **Boston, Massachusetts, USA, 2 February 1924**
Died **Washington, D.C., USA, 22 July 1982**

Of all the saxophonists to vie for Charlie (Bird) Parker's preeminence after his death in 1955, Sonny Stitt was always closest to the great originator's style and force. Yet he always insisted that his style was his own, independently developed, and he continued to perfect it during a distinguished performing career covering nearly four decades.

Stitt was born into a musical family: his father was a college music professor, his mother a piano teacher, and his brother later became a concert pianist. He grew up in Saginaw, Michigan, where his father was teaching, and learned to play the piano, clarinet, and saxophone from the age of seven. When barely a teenager, he was drawn to the lively, fast-developing jazz scene in Detroit, and at 17 he began traveling with bands. He heard his first Parker recording when he was 19 and touring with the Tiny Bradshaw band; when the group played Kansas City he went to meet Parker, who said, after jamming with Stitt for an hour at Chauncey Owenman's, "You sure sound like me." In 1945, when Parker was ill, Stitt was hired from New York by Dizzy Gillespie to replace Bird with his band in California. Shortly thereafter, perhaps eager to avoid the constant comparisons, Stitt switched his main instrument from alto to tenor saxophone. Yet stylistic comparisons continued to be made, and he later often recalled that just before Parker died he told Stitt, meeting him by chance one day in the street, "Man, I'm handing you the keys to the kingdom."

Stitt's association with tenor saxophonist Gene Ammons in their own band during the late 1940s and early 1950s marked the beginning of his reputation as a formidable jammer. Their "battles"—each trying to outdo the other in the number, brilliance, and invention of their choruses—became wildly popular with jazz fans, and led Stitt into a series of memorable musical confrontations with other saxophonists, including Eddie Davis, Ricky Ford, Paul Gonsalves, Red Holloway, and Zoot Sims. In his autobiography, *Straight Talk,* Art Pepper described in detail his long and grueling tenor duel with Stitt.

Courtesy of Muse Records

Among the most frequently recorded of jazz musicians, Stitt was felt by many to have entered a period of uninspired rote production during the 1960s, but any lack of inspiration was short-lived, for in 1971 his international tour with Gillespie and Thelonious Monk as the Giants of Jazz was an enormous success and found him once more in top form.

Stitt worked with many other famous bands—he was with Miles Davis in the early 1960s and subsequently played for a short time with J. J. Johnson, Zoot Sims, and Clark Terry—but is remembered best as a single, the solitary genius who traveled alone to every gig, picked up sidemen on the spot, and laid down the musical law to an audience that had come to see only him. His final performance came in early July 1982, when he was called in to replace Art Pepper, who had just died, at the Kool Jazz Festival in New York. Appearing in a set with Richie Cole, Stitt completely dominated the opening blues number, playing dozens of choruses to a delighted audience, completely oblivious of his accompanists or his partner. He died of cancer three weeks later. A.K.

Born Edward Stitt. **Parents** Father a music prof.; mother, Claudine Tibou, a piano teacher. **Married** Pamela W. Gilmore 1960: Katea Denise; Jason Cesaré. **Religion** Baptist. **Education** Piano lessons from age seven, later clarinet and alto saxophone lessons. **Career** Jazz instrumentalist since adolescence; toured with Tiny Bradshaw band 1940s; played with Dizzy Gillespie, NYC 1945–46, 1958; co-leader of band with Gene Ammons late 1940s–early 50s, led his own combo 1950s–60s; JATP tour, London 1958–59; played with Miles Davis early 1960s; toured Japan with Clark Terry, J. J. Johnson, and Zoot Sims group 1964; played Sweden 1966; world tour with Giants of Jazz 1971–72; played with Musical Life of Charlie Parker, Newport Jazz Festival, NYC and European tour 1974; clubs and theaters in NYC mid-1970s; Kool Jazz Festival 1982. • Ellington Fellow, Yale Univ. 1973. **Honors** New Star Award 1947, and All-Amer. Award, *Esquire;* All-Star Award, *Playboy;* Jazz Poll winner; awards from Amer. Legion and Cook County Dept. of Corrections; Artists and Models Greater Music Award. **Documentary film** *Jazz on a Summer's Day,* 1960. **Recordings** More than 75 albums, including *Constellation; 12!; Tune Up; Genesis; The Bebop Session; In Walked Sonny; Sittin' In; Soul Summitt;* (with Gene Ammons) *Together Again for the Last Time; Night Work; Two Sides of . . .; The Champ; . . . Plays Bird; Mellow Muse; Parallel-A-Stitt; Sonny Stitt with Art Blakey and the Jazz Messengers; Pow; Giants of Jazz; Newport in New York, the Jam Sessions, Vols. 3 and 4.*

VIC MORROW
Actor
***Born* New York City, USA, 14 February 1932**
***Died* Indian Dunes Park, Saugus, California, USA, 23 July 1982**

Actor Vic Morrow was best known for his starring role in the television series "Combat!" during the 1960s. He was killed along with two Vietnamese child actors in an accident during the filming of a movie called *The Twilight Zone.* Their deaths resulted in public inquiries into safety conditions in American film production.

Morrow grew up in the Bronx and dropped out of high school at the age of 17 to enlist in the navy. After his discharge he earned his diploma in night school and took prelaw and drama courses at Florida State College under the G.I. Bill. He spent a few years in regional theater groups before being accepted for two years of study at Paul Mann's Actors Workshop in New York City, where he made a living driving a cab. In the early 1950s he acted in an Off Broadway production of *A Streetcar Named Desire* and directed Jean Genet's *Deathwatch* and *The Maids.*

In 1954 Morrow was signed to his first screen role, that of the unregenerate juvenile delinquent in *The Blackboard Jungle* (1955). In subsequent westerns and war films, including *Tribute to a Bad Man* (1956), *Men in War* (1957), and *Cimarron* (1961), he was typecast as a troubled or violent youth. After a string of small supporting parts in television, he landed a starring role in the ABC series "Combat!" as the hardheaded career soldier Sgt. Chip Saunders, and led his troop of hardy G.I.s across the European battlefields of World War II for four seasons (1962–66). The series was praised for its solid ensemble acting, and Morrow, who also directed several episodes, was nominated for an Emmy for best actor in 1963. In 1965 he filmed his own screen adaptation of *Deathwatch,* and in 1970 directed *A Man Called Sledge* with James Garner and Laura Antonelli.

During the 1970s Morrow still appeared occasionally in television, notably in *Roots,* but his film career slumped; apart from the popular *The Bad News Bears* and a Disney adventure, *Treasure of Matecumbe* (both 1976); he worked mainly in low-budget Roger Corman productions (*Message from Space* and *Humanoids from the Deep*) and in Italian films. His role in an episode of *The Twilight Zone,* a screen version of the old television series, was his first appearance in a major motion picture in six years.

The accident, in which several crew members were injured (including the director, John Landis), occurred early in the morning of the final day of shooting for the first episode. Morrow, carrying the children in his arms, was running across a set of a Vietnamese village with a helicopter flying above him and explosions going off nearby. Debris from an explosion severed the tail section of the helicopter, and the broken rotor blade struck Morrow and the children. Some observers claimed that the explosives used on the set were out of control, that safety measures were inadequate here and in American stunt filming in general, and that the producers had violated California child-labor laws. Work on the film was suspended while an investigation was made by the Federal Aviation Agency and the National Transportation Safety Board. C.M.

Married Barbara Turner, actress, 1957 (div. 1964): Carrie, b. 1958; Jennifer, b. 1962. **Education** Public schs., NYC; took night sch. courses for high sch. diploma; Florida State Coll.; Mexico City Coll.; Actors Workshop, NYC. **Mil. service** USN 1949. **Career** Soda jerk, delivery boy, other odd jobs late 1940s; actor, Erie Playhouse, PA, and Hilltop Theater, Baltimore, early 1950s; cab driver, NYC 1950s; film actor since 1955; TV actor since late 1950s; also stage, film, and television dir. and writer. **Films** *The Blackboard Jungle,* 1955; *Tribute to a Bad Man,* 1956; *Men in War,* 1957; *God's Little Acre,* 1958; *Cimarron,* 1961; *Portrait of a Mobster,* 1961; (dir. and adaptor) *Deathwatch,* 1965; (dir.) *A Man Called Sledge,* 1970; *Dirty Mary, Crazy Larry,* 1974; *The Bad News Bears,* 1976; *Treasure of Matecumbe,* 1976; *Message from Space; Target: Harry; The Evictors; Humanoids from the Deep; Great White; 1990: The Bronx War-*

riors; The Twilight Zone (unfinished), 1982. **Television** (Also occasionally dir.) "Combat!" series 1962–66; "Bonanza"; "The New Breed"; "The Untouchables"; "The Rifleman"; "The Outlaws"; "G.E. Theater"; "The Glass House"; "Roots"; "Captains and the Kings"; "The Last Convertible"; "The Seekers"; (dir.) "The Evil Touch," Australia. **Stage actor** *A Streetcar Named Desire,* NYC 1950s; also stock productions in NYC, Baltimore, Hollywood, and Erie, PA. **Stage director** *Deathwatch,* NYC and Hollywood; *No Exit,* Hollywood; *La Ronde,* Hollywood; *The Maids,* NYC and Hollywood; *The Firstborn,* Hollywood. **Libretto writer** *Willie Loved Everybody* (unproduced musical), 1964.

BETTY PARSONS
Gallery owner and artist
***Born* New York City, USA, 31 January 1900**
***Died* Southold, New York, USA, 23 July 1982**

In the heyday of Abstract Expressionist painting, roughly 1948 to 1960, the Betty Parsons Gallery on West 57th Street in Manhattan was the leading showcase for the best new American art. Its owner, a sculptor and painter herself, had an unerring eye for what was artistically vital, fresh, and exciting, and was among the first to show the work of Jackson Pollock, Mark Rothko, Barnett Newman, and Clyfford Still when these artists were far from well known and almost universally rejected by the critics and the public. When her stellar attractions deserted her for better-paying, more aggressive dealers like Sidney Janis and Sam Kootz (she was sometimes an indifferent saleswoman), Parsons seemed able to tap an inexhaustible supply of innovative new talent on which to lavish her enthusiasm. "Always identify with the art," she said, "never identify with the artist."

The daughter of a wealthy New York stockbroker, she was born Betty Bierne Pierson, a descendant of Abraham Pierson, the first president of Yale. At the age of 13, she saw the great New York Armory show, where America got its first outraged taste of European modernism. In 1919, as a debutante just graduated from Mrs. Randall McKeever's finishing school, she met socialite Schuyler Livingston Parsons at the Astor estate in Bermuda, and married him a few weeks later. They were divorced in 1921 in France—"in those days one was under the thumb of the male," she said, "and I didn't like that much"—and she stayed on in Paris, studying with the sculptor Antoine Bourdelle at the Grande Chaumière and mixing with the American expatriate community, which included Gertrude Stein, Man Ray, Alexander Calder, and Hart Crane. Her first show of paintings, at the Galerie des Quatre Chemins in 1927, was a modest success.

In the 1930s Parsons moved to California. She befriended Garbo, Marlene Dietrich, and Robert Benchley, studied sculpture with Alexander Archipenko, and made a meager living as a wine selector (her family had lost most of its money in the stockmarket crash of 1929). Returning to New York in 1937, she exhibited at the Midtown Gallery and was invited to arrange exhibitions for the gallery on a free-lance basis. In 1939 she worked out a similar arrangement with the Wakefield Bookshop, where she opened a small basement gallery in which she showed the work of Walter Murch, Joseph Cornell, and Adolph Gottlieb, among others. After a brief stint handling modern art sales for dealer Mortimer Brandt, she opened the Betty Parsons Gallery in 1946 with an inaugural show of Northwest Coast Indian art organized by her friend Barnett Newman. By then, she had established a reputation as one of the very few dealers in the country who both understood and was sympathetic to Abstract Expressionism. The next year, Pollock, Rothko, Still, and Newman came to her from Peggy Guggenheim's gallery, which had recently closed.

From 1947 to 1951, these four formed the nucleus of a kind of academy of the New York School, using her gallery as a base; they hung one another's shows, wrote one another's catalogues, and advised Parsons on other artists. The gallery was the perfect place to show their sometimes unwieldy paintings. "The floor was uncarpeted," wrote critic and art historian Lawrence Alloway in a 1963 article in *Vogue,* "the paintings were unframed, the lighting never schmaltzy. It became a place where painters showed one another their work and saw their work fresh, in a new setting. The hanging of shows was an occasion for self-discovery and discussion, for camaraderie and analysis, and not merely preparations for a selling operation. . . . It was a fortunate coincidence that Betty Parsons and her gallery were available at the time when the American artists were discovering the power and resources of the big picture."

In 1951, the Abstract Expressionist group dissolved in a welter of personal, aesthetic, and legal disagreements; some of its members, like Pollock, moved to other galleries; Newman withdrew his art completely from public view. This was a blow to the gallery, but not a fatal one. During the 1950s, Parsons developed an impressive stable of artists that included Saul Steinberg, Bradley Tomlin, Robert Rauschenberg, Lee Krasner, Kenzo Okada, and Richard Lindner; in the 1960s and 1970s, she exhibited Agnes Martin, Hedda Sterne, Ann Ryan, Alexander Lieberman, Ellsworth Kelly, Richard Pousette-Dart, and Jack Youngerman. Of the great art movements since the 1950s, she missed only Pop, thinking it downbeat and too literary, and of the best postwar artists she failed to show only Jasper Johns. From 1958 to 1961, she ran a small second gallery, Section Eleven, devoted primarily to new artists.

Parsons showed her own work, sculptural assemblages of painted driftwood and found objects that critic John Russell called "provocative in shape, vivid in color, and epigrammatic in their concision," at numerous galleries in the United States, London, and Paris. Major retrospectives of her paintings and sculptures were mounted at the White Chapel Gallery in London in 1968, the Montclair Art Museum in New Jersey in 1974, and posthumously at her own gallery (she never showed there while she was alive) in 1982. She died of a stroke while working in her studio in Southold, Long Island. S.A.

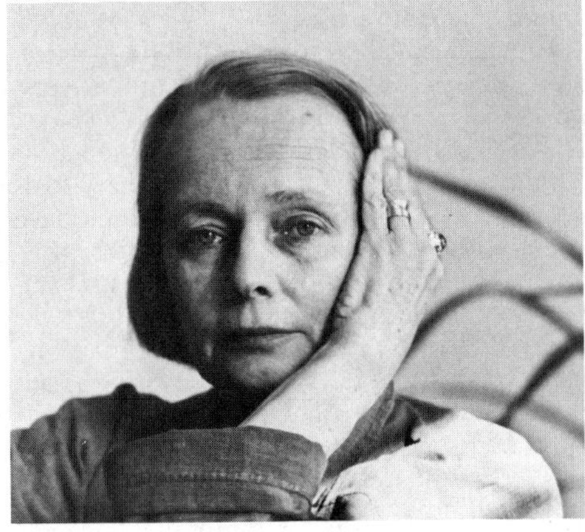

Courtesy of Alexander Liberman

Born Betty Bierne Pierson. **Parents** J. Fred P., stockbroker, and Suzanne (Miles) P. **Married** Schuyler Livingston Parsons, socialite, 1919 (div. 1921). **Education** Private schs., NYC; Acad. de la Grande Chaumière, Paris 1921–27; studied watercolor with Arthur Lindsey, France, and sculpture with Alexander Archipenko, U.S., ca. 1927–33. **Career** Artist since ca. 1920s; wine selector for liquor store, CA 1930s. • Art dealer and gall. dir., NYC: Cornelius Sullivan Gall. 1936–39; Wakefield Bookshop Gall. 1939–43; Mortimer Brandt Contemporary Gall. 1943–46; Betty Parsons Gall. since 1946; Section Eleven Gall. 1958–61; Parsons-Truman Gall. mid-1970s. • Juror, art exhibitions: Smithsonian Instn. 1976; Art 500, Indianapolis 1977; Acad. of the Arts, MD 1977; Whitney Mus., NYC 1977; New Sch. for Social Research, NYC 1977; Natl. Assn. of Women Artists 1979; Zaner Gall., Rochester, NY 1981; others. **Member** Subud meditative org. **Honors** Creative arts award, Brandeis Univ. 1980; Mayor's Award of Honor for Arts and Culture, City of New York 1981; Athena Award, Rhode Island Sch. of Design 1982; hon. degrees from Mt. Holyoke and Southampton colls. and Parsons Sch. of Design, NYC. **Solo exhibitions** Galerie des Quatre Chemins, Paris 1927; Midtown Gall., NYC, 10 shows 1936–57; Georgia Mus. of Art, Atlanta 1958; Miami Mus. of Modern Art 1963; retrospective, White Chapel Gall., London 1968; Studio Gall., Wash. DC 1971, 1973, 1975; retrospective, Montclair Art Mus., NJ 1974; Kornblee Gall., NYC 1977–80; Rhode Island Sch. of Design Mus., Providence 1977; Barbara Fiedler Gall., Wash. DC 1980; Nigel Greenwood Inc., London 1980; Amer. Center, Paris 1980; Newspace, L.A. 1980; Robert L. Kidd

Associates, Birmingham, MI 1980; Virginia Miller Galls., Miami 1981; retrospective, Betty Parsons Gall. 1982; other galls. **Group exhibitions** New Chenil Gall., London 1927; Midtown Gall., 1945, 1952–59; Whitney Mus. 1956; MOMA 1964, 1966; Heckscher Mus., Huntington, NY 1964, 1970; Amer. Acad. of Arts and Letters, NYC 1979; other galls. and museums in U.S. and U.K. **Collections** Rockefeller Univ., NYC; Montclair Art Mus.; Carnegie Inst.; Natl. Collection of Fine Arts; Phillips Collection, Wash. DC; CIBA-GEIGY Collection; Mortimer Brandt Gall., NYC; Whitney Mus.; also numerous private collections.

Further reading Calvin Tomkins, "A Keeper of the Treasure," in *New Yorker,* 6 Sept. 1975; Grace Glueck, "Betty Parsons: The Art Dealer's Art Dealer," in *Ms.,* Feb. 1976; Grace Lichtenstein, "Betty Parsons," in *ARTnews,* March 1979.

TATYANA GROSMAN

Printmaker and publisher

Born **Ekaterinburg, Siberia, Russia, 30 June 1904**

Died **New York City, USA, 24 July 1982**

Tatyana Grosman belonged to that very select group of people whose vocation has been to encourage the creation of works of art. It is a group whose members, frequently honored with the title "patron," have almost invariably been wealthy, but it was her indomitable energy rather than a personal fortune that Grosman devoted to the service of her artistic ideal.

Courtesy of ULAE

Changes in the nature of artistic expression are often brought about by a collaboration, or mutual sympathy, between a group of young artists and a collector or dealer who promotes their work in the face of public indifference. The unprecedented flourishing of fine-art lithography in the United States during the late 1950s and early 1960s had, to outward appearances, less momentous beginnings. In the garage of her modest suburban house in West Islip, Long Island, Grosman founded, in 1956, Universal Limited Art Editions (ULAE). Using two old lithographic stones that she had discovered in her garden path, she set out to revive a forgotten craft and to publish books illustrated with prints by the finest American artists.

Her first collaborators were Barnett Newman, Robert Motherwell, and Larry Rivers, but soon she was joined by Jasper Johns, Helen Frankenthaler, James Rosenquist, Robert Rauschenberg, and many other artists whose careers as printmakers would not have begun without Grosman's aid, or rather, insistence. It was impossible, wrote Calvin Tomkins in his study of Rauschenberg, *Off the Wall* (1980), to avoid her "gentle fury." She would pester those artists whose work she admired, telephoning and even haunting their apartments, until they decided that the only way to escape her was to submit, go to West Islip, and draw on a stone. Once the edition was printed she would use the same methods on curators and collectors, sitting in their offices for hours and enduring their indifference to gain her ends. Her achievement, Tomkins wrote in her *New Yorker* obituary, "is as mysterious as any great artist's. She changed the conditions under which art is made, and opened the way to others." Printmaking, formerly regarded as the least important (and least lucrative) aspect of a painter's work, or as a commercial craft designed for reproduction purposes, was not only revived by Grosman, but also established as a medium for major artistic expression.

Grosman, née Tatyana Aguschewitsch, was born and grew up in the Siberian town of Ekaterinburg, where her father edited the local newspaper. When, in 1918, the Czar and his family were executed by the Bolsheviks, her father was instructed not to publish the news by the local revolutionary committee. Shortly afterward, the family moved to Japan, where Tatyana attended a Catholic school in Tokyo, and then to Venice, Munich, and Dresden, where she studied for eight years at the Academy of Applied Arts. In 1931 she married Maurice Grosman, a painter, and moved to Paris. In 1940, when the Nazis began interning Jews, they fled to Marseilles and in 1942 walked across the Pyrenees to Barcelona and escaped to New York. Maurice Grosman supported them by printing silkscreen reproductions of famous paintings and giving art lessons until he was crippled by a heart attack in 1956. Tatyana, searching for a livelihood, founded ULAE with two worn stones and a second-hand lithographic press that she bought for $15. Her first book, *Stones* (1957), was a collaboration between the painter Larry Rivers and the poet Frank O'Hara, but what began as an effort to marry word and image gradually evolved, as her printing facilities and skill improved, into a primarily visual enterprise.

The invention of photolithography during the 1890s had led to the virtual disappearance of craftsman printers capable of performing the exacting task of making a lithographic image manually. First an image is drawn on a smooth stone with a greasy substance; the stone is then treated with acid and washed with plain water. Finally, the stone is covered with ink, which sticks to the grease but is repelled by the water. A sheet of paper pressed to the stone then receives an inverted impression of the artist's drawing. Grosman spared no efforts to accommodate the demands of her artists as they learned and developed the technique: special paper was made, and a succession of master printers worked, sometimes all night, to achieve intricate effects. In the hands of Robert Rauschenberg the process became even more complex: he applied newsprint, leaves, and magazine photographs to the stone to produce collages and, in one of his most famous series of prints, *Accident* (1963), made impressions from a broken stone. "For me," Grosman said to Calvin Tomkins, "graphics is neither a means of supplying art to young collectors nor a reproduction of an artist's work but, rather, the creative expression of an artist through lithographic stones or plates. What matters is that the print be alive, with the heartbeat of the artist in it." The results are now regarded as major works and major investments. One of the most celebrated ULAE prints, Jasper Johns's *Ale Cans,* sold at a 1980 New York auction for $22,000, perhaps 50 times what a similar print would have cost only two decades earlier.

Shortly before Grosman's death, the Museum of Modern Art paid tribute to her with the exhibition "For 25 Years: Prints from ULAE." The Art Institute of Chicago has also shown a selection of her work. She received an honorary doctorate from Smith College in 1977, and in 1981 an award from Brandeis University for outstanding achievement in the arts. In poor health for several years, she entrusted much of the responsibility for running her press to Bill Goldston, a young printer who continues to produce limited editions. Her husband died in 1976; they had one child, who died in infancy. H.B.

Born Tatyana Aguschewitsch. **Parents** Simeon A., newspaper publisher, and Anna (de Chochor) A. **Married** Maurice Grosman, artist, 1931 (d. 1976): Larissa, b. 1933 (d. 1935). **Religion** Jewish. **Emigrated** to France 1931; to U.S. 1943. **Education:** Gymnasium, Ekaterinburg, Russia to 1917; Convent of the Sacred Heart, Tokyo 1918–19; Hohere Mädchen Schule, Dresden; Acad. of Applied Arts, Dresden. **Career** Founding pres., Universal Limited Art Editions, Inc., West Islip, NY since 1956; pres., Telamon Editions Limited since 1970; pres., ULAE, Inc. since 1981. **Honors** Natl. Endowment for the Humanities grant 1966; Creative Arts Award, Brandeis Univ., Waltham, MA 1981; notable achievement proclamation, Suffolk County, NY 1981; certificate of appreciation, City of New York 1981; hon. degrees from Dowling and

Smith colls. **Exhibitions** 25th anniversary exhibitions of Universal Limited Art Editions prints, MOMA and galls. in NYC, Chicago, Wash. DC, and Düsseldorf, 1982.

Further reading Calvin Tomkins, *Off the Wall,* 1980; Calvin Tomkins, "Tatyana Grosman," in *New Yorker,* 9 Aug. 1982.

RICHARD (HAROLD) LAWLER
Surgeon
Born **Chicago, Illinois, USA, 12 August 1895**
Died **Chicago, Illinois, USA, 24 July 1982**

Richard Lawler made his mark in surgical history when he led a team that performed what was probably the earliest transplant of a human organ. His patient was a 49-year-old Chicago housewife, Ruth Tucker, who was suffering from bilateral polycystic kidney disease, a condition in which growths encrust the kidneys and prevent the flow of urine. At that time the disease was usually fatal.

On 17 June 1950, a decade before the introduction of immunosuppressive drugs (which decrease the risk of tissue rejection), Lawler and a team of surgeons at the Little Company of Mary Hospital near Chicago removed Mrs. Tucker's nonfunctioning left kidney and grafted in its place a kidney from an unnamed woman of the same age who had just died from cirrhosis of the liver. Though the donor was of the same blood group as Mrs. Tucker, she was not related to her and not an ideal donor. However, Mrs. Tucker's right kidney was functioning at only ten percent of capacity, and Lawler seized the chance to save her life. The operation was successful, but the grafted organ functioned for only a few months. In April 1951 it was found to have shrunken to the size of a golf ball and to be no longer excreting urine; nevertheless, because the kidney was still alive it was left in place. Mrs. Tucker died four years later of a coronary attack and pneumonia. Doctors are still debating what kept her alive for so long after she lost virtually all kidney function, and what effect, if any, Lawler's transplant had on her survival.

Lawler was born and raised in Chicago and worked there all his life. After two years as an ensign in the U.S. Navy's aviation unit in World War I, he transferred to the naval reserve and returned to Chicago to attend Loyola University, where he gained his M.D. degree in 1931. He served on the surgical faculty of Loyola's Stritch Medical School for nearly 50 years, from 1932 to 1979, and held long-term appointments as professor of surgery at Cook County Graduate School of Medicine and as senior attending surgeon at Cook County Hospital. He was on the staff of the Little Company of Mary Hospital for 42 years until his retirement, at age 84, in 1979.

Courtesy of Little Company of Mary Hospital

In 1970 Lawler was nominated for the Nobel Prize in medicine. His pioneering transplant operation was acknowledged by his colleagues at the first annual Lawler Symposium on Transplantation in 1974. Plaques commemorating his achievement are housed in the Smithsonian Institution, Washington, D.C., and outside the operating room where the transplant was performed. B.D.

Parents James L. and Margaret (Griffin) L. **Married** Charlotte Andersen 1936 (d.): Christine Nagle; Rosemary Wong. **Religion** Roman Catholic. **Education** Loyola Univ., Chicago, B.S. 1929, M.D. 1931; intern, Mercy Hosp., Chicago 1931–32; Cook County Grad. Sch. of

Medicine, IL 1937–40; Temple Univ., Phila. 1940; licensed in IL. **Mil. career** Ensign, USN aviation unit 1917–19; lt. (j.g.), USNR aviation 1919–31. **Career** Instr. 1932–38, and asst., then assoc., then clinical prof. of surgery 1938–79, dept. of surgery, Stritch Medical Sch., Loyola Univ.; surgeon, Little Company of Mary Hosp., Evergreen Park, IL 1937–79; sr. attending surgeon, Cook County Hosp., Chicago 1940–79; prof. of surgery, Cook County Grad. Sch. of Medicine; post surgeon, Amer. Legion Red Cross, Chicago. **Officer** Treas., Illinois Surgical Soc. **Fellow** Amer. Coll. of Surgeons since 1943; Amer. Physical Soc. since 1964; Amer. Coll. of Physicians; Intl. Coll. of Surgeons; AMA. **Member** Intl. Soc. of Univ. Colon and Rectal Surgeons; Chicago Medical Soc.; Illinois Medical Soc. **Honors** Transplant symposium held in his honor, Little Company of Mary Hosp. since 1974; hon. plaques at Smithsonian Instn. and Little Company of Mary Hosp. **Author** *Thigh Amputation,* U.S. Army medical bulletin. **Contributor** of articles to medical jrnls.

HAL FOSTER

Comic-strip artist

***Born* Halifax, Nova Scotia, Canada, 16 August 1892**

***Died* Spring Hill, Florida, USA, 25 July 1982**

The work of Hal Foster, creator of *Prince Valiant,* marked the zenith of the American adventure comic strip. His superb draftsmanship, skillful use of cinematic compositions, meticulous research, and literate writing produced a cartoon strip that was, in the words of comics historian Stephen Becker, "beautiful to look at, exciting to read, and educational in its ultimate effect." *Prince Valiant,* with its detailed depiction of medieval England, has remained popular for more than 40 years and is currently syndicated in some 320 newspapers worldwide.

Harold Rudolf Foster grew up in Halifax, Nova Scotia, and began drawing at the age of 16. "I'd stand nude in front of a mirror," he wrote, "and sketch myself until I'd turn blue from the cold. We couldn't afford many luxuries at the time." When his family moved to Winnipeg in 1906, he briefly took up fur trapping and hunting, then began his career as a commercial artist illustrating mail-order catalogues for the Hudson Bay Company. In 1921 he bicycled to Chicago to study at the Chicago Art Institute and the Chicago Academy of Fine Arts. By the mid-1920s he had built a solid reputation as a poster artist and catalogue illustrator, and in 1928 he was hired to draw the first series of episodes in a comic-strip adaptation of Edgar Rice Burroughs's *Tarzan of the Apes* (January–March 1929). After a brief return to advertising work while Rex Maxon took over the daily and Sunday strip, Foster penned the *Tarzan* Sunday page from 1931 to 1936.

Most comic-strip historians credit Foster with inventing, in *Tarzan,* the first truly modern adventure strip. His style, somewhat awkward and hesitant in the beginning, quickly grew assured and powerful; his draftsmanship was smooth and professional, his backgrounds richly detailed, and his compositions exciting

BACK IN THE ROOM, VALIANT TRIES TO CALM THE HYSTERICAL MAIDEN. "I SAW NOTHING," SHE CRIES. "IT HAPPENED SO QUICKLY." LAMBERT IS DEAD, AND VAL ASSURES THE LASS THAT SHE IS SAFE. SUDDENLY, LAMBERT'S BROTHER, BRIAN, BURSTS INTO THE ROOM.

© 1980 King Features Syndicate, Inc.

and well-balanced. "Under the pen of this incomparable artist," wrote one admirer, "Tarzan attained the most noble and most serene of his incarnations." Foster also replaced the traditional speech balloon with a narration block in the corner of each panel, an innovation he would carry over to *Prince Valiant.*

In the mid-1930s Foster was approached by William Randolph Hearst, who, inspired by the success of *Tarzan,* asked him to create a new strip for the Hearst-owned King Features Syndicate. Foster relinquished *Tarzan* to the talented Burne Hogarth, and in February 1937 published the first installment of *Prince Valiant.* Inspired by medieval legend and folklore, the strip recounts the adventurous life of the noble and romantic Val, son of the exiled King of Thule, who joins King Arthur's court, becomes a knight, fights a succession of usurpers, thieves, and magicians, marries the beautiful Princess Aleta, and raises a family. Foster modeled Val after himself. "I deleted what I disliked," he said. "He's sort of my body with muscles. He's all the things I would have loved to have been." The strip's storyline has the continuity of a historical novel; the drawings, which took Foster some 40 or 50 hours a week to research and prepare, are crammed with authentic period costumes, architecture, weaponry, heraldic devices, and landscape details. He borrowed from film the use of high and low views, close-ups, and panoramic horizontal and vertical frames. Among the strip's many enthusiastic fans was the Duke of Windsor, who called it "the greatest contribution to English literature in the past 100 years." Henry Hathaway directed a film version with Robert Wagner and Janet Leigh in 1954.

From 1971 to 1979, Foster collaborated on *Prince Valiant* with his assistant, John Cullen Murphy, who took over the job of illustrating Foster's stories. Some critics detected a slow but steady decline in the strip's energy and imagination thereafter. Foster was 89 when he died at a retirement home in Spring Hill, Florida. S.A.

Born Harold Rudolf F. **Parents** Edward Lusher F. and Janet Grace (Rudolf) F. **Married** Helen Lucille Wells 1915: Edward Lusher; Arthur James. **Emigrated** to U.S. 1921; naturalized 1934. **Education** Chicago Art Inst. 1922–24; Chicago Acad. of Fine Arts 1925–26; Natl. Acad. of Design. **Career** Prizefighter, fur trapper, wilderness guide, gold prospector, other jobs ca. 1910–20. • Commercial artist: Hudson Bay Co., Winnipeg, Manitoba; Stovals Co., Winnipeg 1911–13; T. Eaton Co., Winnipeg 1913–15; Buckley Studios, Winnipeg 1915–21; Jahn & Ollier Engraving Co., Chicago 1921–27; Paleske-Yount Co., Chicago 1921–36. • Illus. of Edgar Rice Burroughs's *Tarzan,* Famous Books and Players series ca. 1929; writer and cartoonist, *Tarzan of the Apes* comic strip, United Feature Syndicate 1929, 1931–36; writer 1937–79 and cartoonist 1937–71, *Prince Valiant* comic strip, King Features Syndicate; writer and cartoonist, *The Medieval Castle* comic strip 1944–45. **Fellow** Royal Acad. of Arts, London. **Member** Natl. Cartoonists Soc. **Honors** Banshees Silver Lady, King Features Syndicate 1952; Reuben Award 1957, plaque for best short strip 1964, plaques for best special feature 1966 and 1967, Gold Key Award 1977, and Segar Award 1978, Natl. Cartoonists Soc.; Sam Statuette, Swedish Acad. of Cartoons 1969; admitted to Hall of Fame, Mus. of Cartoon Art, Port Chester, NY. **Exhibition** of original *Prince Valiant* pages, Mus. of Cartoon Art 1975. **Author and illustrator** *Prince Valiant and the Three Challenges,* 1960; *Prince Valiant on the Island Sea,* 1968; *Prince Valiant in the New World,* 1968; *Prince Valiant and the Golden Princess,* 1968; *Prince Valiant in the Days of King Arthur,* 1969.

Further reading Stephen Becker, *Comic Art in America,* 1959.

SIR RICHARD (NELSON) GALE

Commander of airborne forces
***Born* London, England, 25 July 1896**
***Died* Kingston-on-Thames, Surrey, England, 29 July 1982**

General Sir Richard Gale was one of the most successful and popular British commanders of World War II. He led the 6th Airborne Division during the Allied invasion of Normandy, and later served for two years as deputy supreme Allied commander in Europe.

Born to well-to-do parents, he was brought up in Australia until the age of ten, then was sent to England to a succession of schools, including the Merchant Taylors' School and Aldenham. He attended the Royal Military College, Sandhurst, passing out in 1915 to a commission with the Worcestershire Regiment. During World War I, he served with the Machine Gun Corps on the Western Front, where his bravery won him the Military Cross.

Stationed in India continuously from 1919 until 1936, Gale rose through the ranks of the British Army, serving for many years as divisional master of foxhounds in Delhi while he was attached to Army Headquarters. In 1938, as a major in his new regiment, the Royal Inniskilling Fusiliers, he was ordered home and set to work on the planning staff of the War Office in London. When, in 1941, it was decided to form the 1st Parachute Brigade, Gale was ordered to raise and command the unit, and was accordingly promoted to brigadier, his rank until the end of the war. He immediately went through complete training as a parachutist.

On D-Day—6 June 1944—in a daring forward action four hours ahead of the main Allied assault on the Norman beaches, Gale and his men of the 6th Airborne were dropped behind German lines. Their objective, to establish a bridgehead on the Orne River, south of Caen, was fulfilled after many hours of fierce battles with the surprised enemy. Gale's own valor on that occasion—he rode in an open jeep, wearing his beret instead of a helmet, from one forward position to the next, constantly exhorting and inspiring his men—was so impressive that his staff wrote specially to the War Office on his behalf to recommend him for a decoration. He was soon thereafter awarded the DSO.

Gale commanded the 1st Division in Palestine in 1946–47 and was commander of British troops in Egypt during 1948. From 1949 until 1952 he was in Britain as director general of military training, then was sent to Germany as commander of British forces in Northern Europe, a post he held until he retired in 1957. The following year, however, he was recalled to active duty to succeed Viscount Montgomery as deputy supreme Allied commander in Paris, where he served with great distinction until his final retirement in 1960.

Tall and square-shouldered, with a ruddy complexion and bristling mustache and eyebrows, Gale looked every inch the popular image of a British officer. He was a frequent commentator on military history and strategy both before and after his retirement. His memoirs, *Call to Arms,* appeared in 1968, and were soon followed by two popular illustrated histories, *Great Battles of Biblical History* (1969) and *Kings at Arms* (1971), the latter a study of the great Oriental conquerors. He was aide-de-camp to Queen Elizabeth II (1954–57), and was created KBE (1950), KCB (1953), and GCB (1954). He also served as honorary commander of the Worcestershire Regiment (1950–61) and the Parachute Regiment (1956–61). A.K.

Parents Wilfred G., insurance exec., and Helen Webber Ann (Nelson) G. **Married** (1) Ethel Maude Larnack Keene 1924 (d. 1952). (2) Daphne Mabelle Eveline Blick 1953. **Education** King Edward VII Sch., Stratford-on-Avon; Merchant Taylors' Sch.; Aldenham; Royal Military Coll., Sandhurst, grad. 1915; Quetta Staff Coll., India. **Career** Second lt., Worcestershire Regiment 1915; with Machine Gun Corps, Western Front, WWI; subaltern in India 1919–36, on staff at Army HQ and Master of Delhi Foxhounds; promoted capt., Duke of Cornwall's Light Infantry 1930; maj., Royal Inniskilling Fusiliers 1938; lt. col. 1939; brig. 1941; raised and commanded 1st Parachute Brigade 1941; staff member 1938–42, and deputy dir., then dir., for air ca. 1942–43, War Office; comdr., 6th British Airborne Div. 1944; deputy comdr., 1st Allied Airborne Army 1945; comdr., 1st British Airborne

Corps 1945; maj. gen. 1946; gen. officer comdg., 1st Infantry Div., Palestine 1946–47; gen. officer comdg., British Troops, Egypt and Mediterranean Command 1948–49; dir. gen. of military training, War Office 1949–52; comdr. in chief, Northern Army Group, Allied Land Forces Europe, and comdr. in chief of British Army of the Rhine, Germany 1952–57; ADC (gen.) to the Queen 1954–57; retired 1957; recalled to duty as deputy supreme Allied comdr. of Europe, Paris 1958–60. **Officer** Chmn: council, Central Asian Soc.; exec. cttee., Army League. **Member** Army and Navy Club. **Honors** M.C. 1918; OBE 1940; DSO 1944; C.B. 1945; hon. col., Worcestershire Regiment 1950–61; KBE 1950; KCB 1953; GCB 1954; hon. col. commandant, Parachute Regiment 1956–61; comdr., Legion of Merit, U.S.; comdr., Légion d'Honneur, and Croix de Guerre with Palm, France; grand officier de la Couronne, Belgium. **Author** *With the 6th Airborne Division in Normandy,* 1948; *Call to Arms* (autobiography), 1968; *Great Battles of Biblical History,* 1969; *The Worcestershire Regiment,* 1970; *Kings at Arms,* 1971.

LUCILLE (VOORHEES) PARKER (WRIGHT) MARKEY

Owner of thoroughbred racing stable

***Born* Maysville, Kentucky, USA, 14 December 1896**

***Died* Miami, Florida, USA, 25 July 1982**

For 51 years, Lucille Parker Markey was an owner of Calumet Farm, a nursery and stable for thoroughbred racehorses on 846 acres in Lexington, Kentucky. Calumet reigned supreme in racing from 1941 to 1961, producing seven Kentucky Derby winners, including two winners of the Triple Crown, and collecting record-setting purses.

Born Lucille Parker, the daughter of a wealthy tobacco grower, she arrived at Calumet through her marriage in 1919 to Warren Wright, president of the Calumet Baking Powder Company, who inherited the farm from his father in 1931. It was then a nursery for trotters. The Wrights decided to raise and train thoroughbreds instead. Their first years in the business were unprofitable, and they were on the point of selling the farm in 1939 when Mrs. Wright hired Ben Jones as trainer. Within five years Calumet had a Triple Crown winner in Whirlaway, the first horse to earn a half million dollars, whose track record at the Kentucky Derby lasted 21 years. In 1948, its second Triple Crown winner, the legendary Citation, won a full million and made racing history by finishing in the money 44 times in 45 starts. Calumet's other Derby champions of those years were Pensive (1944), Ponder (1949), Hill Gail (1952), Iron Liege (1957), and Tim Tam (1958); an eighth, Forward Pass, won in 1968. Two of its fillies, Wistful (1949) and Real Delight (1952), took the Filly Triple Crown.

After Wright's death in 1950, his widow inherited Calumet and continued to operate it with her second husband, Gene Markey, a retired rear admiral and movie producer whose previous wives were the actresses Joan Bennett, Myrna Loy, and Hedy Lamarr. The Calumet program of retiring racehorses to stud at the top of their careers, usually successful, be-

Courtesy of Courier-Journal and Louisville Times

gan to fail in the 1960s—Citation was among the horses whose foals were disappointing—and Calumet's colors, devil's red and blue, were less and less seen in the winner's circle. The stable began a comeback in 1977 under trainer John Veitch, with a new generation of horses that included Alydar, Our Mims, and Davona Dale, winner of both the National and New York Triple Crowns. By 1982 the stable had 16 Eclipse Award divisional champions, with 35 titles among them, and its total winnings from racing totaled $26.4 million.

Mrs. Markey was afflicted with arthritis and was confined to a wheelchair in her later years. She died of bronchial pneumonia two years after the death of her husband. The ownership of Calumet Farm passed to five of her relatives, only one of whom had experience in breeding and racing. A cancer center at the University of Kentucky, built with a $4.6 million donation from Mrs. Markey, bears her name. C.M.

Born Lucille Parker. **Parents** John Winslow P., tobacco grower, and Sarah Belle (Owens) P. **Married** (1) Warren Wright, pres. of Calumet Baking Powder Co., 1919 (d. 1950): Warren, Jr., b. 1920 (d. 1978). (2) Gene Markey, rear adm., 1952 (d. 1980): Melinda Markey Bena Joseph (stepdaughter). **Religion** Christian Scientist. **Education** Weston Schs., St. Joseph, MO. **Career** Owner, Calumet Farm thoroughbred racehorse nursery and stable, Lexington, KY since 1931. **Member** Republican Party; Bath Club and Indian Creek Club, Miami Beach; Idle-Hour Country Club, Lexington.

Further reading William Leggett, "The Derby is Old Hat at Calumet," in *Sports Illustrated,* 17 Apr. 1978.

KENZO OKADA
Painter
***Born* Yokohama, Japan, 28 September 1902**
***Died* Tokyo, Japan, 25 July 1982**

Kenzo Okada was a Japanese-born painter who was active in the United States from the 1950s. Though he was often classed with the New York School of Abstract Expressionists, his work is calm and meditative in a distinctively Japanese manner, in contrast to the vivid, brashly energetic work of Jackson Pollock or Willem de Kooning.

A native of the port city of Yokohama, Okada studied traditional Japanese painting at the Tokyo University of Arts. In the mid-1920s he lived in Paris, where he first encountered Picasso, Matisse, and Braque. Returning to Japan, he developed an abstract geometrical style of painting and built a lucrative career.

In 1950 Okada moved to New York, where he was soon labeled an Abstract Expressionist (for want of a better term) and began showing regularly at the Betty Parsons Gallery, then one of the foremost showcases for new American art. Under the influence of American painters, Okada's brushwork became freer and his compositions less rigidly geometric. At the same time, his links to traditional Asian painting became more apparent, particularly in *Noh Player* (1967), an abstract but recognizable portrait of an actor, and *Early Light* (1968), a typical Japanese landscape with mountains and lake. His perfectly balanced compositions of gray, black, and pastel planes have the weathered appearance of hand-made paper or old silk and resemble collages of torn paper.

By the late 1960s, Okada's paintings were sought by collectors for their tranquil, elegant simplicity. Wrote John Canaday in the *New York Times,* "Mr. Okada practices superlatively a quiet, poetic landscape painting that seems almost old-fashioned nowadays. But for viewers seeking a meditative retreat from works that hop, op, pop, jiggle, or rumble, time spent in the presence of these low-keyed canvases should be most rewarding."

Okada became a U.S. citizen in 1960. Since the 1970s he spent part of each year painting in Japan. He continued to exhibit at the Betty Parsons Gallery (his last show there was in 1978) and also represented the United States and Japan in international exhibitions. He died of a heart ailment in Japan a few months after a major retrospective of his work was mounted by the Seibu Museum in Tokyo and Fukuoka. S.A.

Courtesy of Gwyn Metz

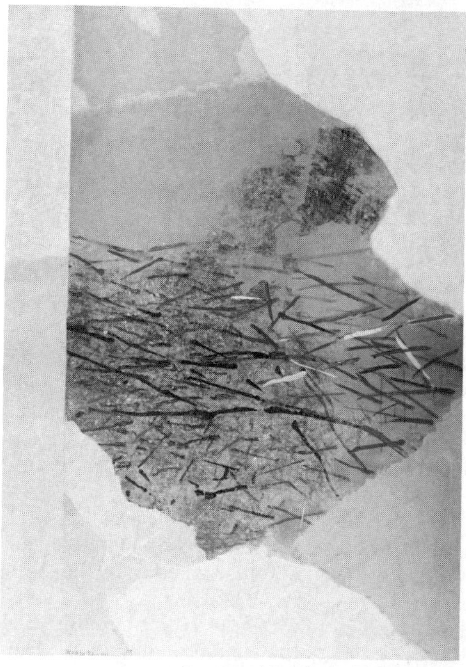

Courtesy of Sotheby Parke Bernet, Inc.

Parents Kazo O. and Yasu O. **Married** Kimi Kasono, dress designer, 1931. **Emigrated** to U.S. 1950; naturalized 1960. **Education** Meijigakuin Middle Sch., Tokyo; Tokyo Univ. of Arts; studied painting, Paris 1924–27. **Career** Artist since ca. 1927. • Art instr.: Nippon Art Coll. 1940–42; Musashino Art Inst. 1947–50; Tama Coll. of Fine Arts, Tokyo 1949–50. **Officer** Judge, Carnegie Intl. Exhibition. **Member** Nikakai art group, Japan since ca. 1938. **Honors** Nikakai Award 1936; Showa Shorie Award 1938; Yomiuri Press Award 1947; Campana Memorial Prize, Chicago Art Inst. 1954, 1957; Carnegie Inst. Exhibition Award 1955; Logan Prize 1955; award 1955, and Waite Award 1977, Amer. Acad. of Arts and Letters; 1st prize, Biennial, Columbia, SC 1957; award, Venice Biennale 1958; UNESCO award 1958; Ford Foundn. grant 1960; Dunn Intl. Prize 1963; Mainichi Art Award 1966; award poster, New York Council on the Arts 1969; other awards. **Solo exhibitions** Nichido Gall., Tokyo 1929–35; Hokuso Gall., Tokyo 1948, 1950; U.S. Army Education Center, Tokyo 1949, 1950, and Yokohama 1950; Betty Parsons Gall., NYC 1953, 1955, 1956, 1959, 1962, 1963, 1964, 1967, 1969, 1971, 1976, 1978; Corcoran Gall., Wash. DC 1955; Albright-Knox Gall., Buffalo, NY 1965; traveling retrospective, Tokyo, Kyoto, Honolulu, San Francisco, and Austin 1966–67; Columbus Gall., OH 1979; Univ. of Texas Gall. 1979; Galerie Mukai, Tokyo 1979; Phillips Collection, Wash. DC 1979; retrospective, Seibu Mus., Tokyo and Fukuoka 1982; other galls. and museums in Japan and U.S. **Group exhibitions** Salon d'Automne, Paris 1924–27; Nikakai group exhibitions, Japan since 1938; São Paulo Bienal 1955; Venice Biennale 1958; Tate Gall., London 1963; MOMA; Terry Dintenfass and Grace Borgenicht Galls., NYC 1982; other galls. and museums in Japan, Paris, and U.S. **Collections** Metropolitan Mus. of Art, NYC; MOMA; Art Inst. of Chicago; Guggenheim Mus., NYC; Whitney Mus., NYC; Carnegie Inst., Pittsburgh; Albright-Knox Gall., Buffalo; Phillips Gall., Wash. DC; Brooklyn Mus.; New York Univ.; Boston Mus. of Fine Arts; Santa Barbara Mus., CA; Yale Art Gall.; Rockefeller Inst., NYC; Chase Manhattan Bank, NYC; Equitable Life Assurance Soc.; Honolulu Acad. of Arts; Univ. of Colorado; Philharmonic Hall, NYC; Baltimore Mus.; Reynolds Metals Building, Richmond, VA; San Francisco Mus.; Portland Art Mus.; Denver Art Mus.; Osaka Kosukai Mus.; Neuberger Mus., Purchase, NY; Intl. Mus. of Art, Tokyo; Toyama Modern Art Mus., Tokyo; Gall. Nazionale d'Arte Moderna, Rome; Kagoshima Ibusuki Iwasaki Mus., Japan; Indianapolis Mus. of Art; Tougaloo Coll., MS; St. Lawrence Mus., NY; Wadsworth Atheneum, Hartford, CT; Smithsonian Instn.; Fukuoka Shi Art Mus., Japan; Toledo Mus. of Art; Intl. Mus. of Art, Kyoto; St. Louis City Art Mus.; Columbia Mus., SC; Brooks Memorial Art Gall.; others.

VLADIMIR K(OZMA) ZWORYKIN

Electronics engineer and inventor of television
Born **Mourom, Russia, 30 July 1889**
Died **Princeton, New Jersey, USA, 29 July 1982**

The Scottish theoretician A. A. Campbell Swinton, the American inventor Philo T. Farnsworth, and David Sarnoff of the Radio Corporation of America all made important contributions to the development of television technology, and all have been called, at one time or another, the "father" of television. But the credit for inventing the key components of the modern, all-electronic television system belongs to the visionary Russian scientist Vladimir K. Zworykin. In the mid-1920s, working for Westinghouse in the United States, Zworykin demonstrated the first effective television camera and a picture tube essentially the same as that found in today's television receivers. At the time, Zworykin had little idea of the extraordinary impact his inventions would have. "I was seeking something extrasensory, some new sense of vision," he said. "Television as home entertainment was not mine nor the early pioneers' dreams. We wanted to reproduce the human eye."

Zworykin came from an aristocratic Russian family that operated a fleet of boats on the Oka River, a tributary of the Volga. At the St. Petersburg Institute of Technology he studied electrical engineering and worked in the laboratory of Boris Rosing, a television pioneer. The experimental cameras of the day used a variety of mechanical methods—whirling disks, oscillating mirrors, and rotating selenium drums—to scan the scene to be televised, one section at a time. The sequence of light and dark areas thus produced was converted by a photocell into a varying electric current. Fed into a lamp in the receiver, the current created an illuminated pattern that was projected onto the receiver's screen by a second mechanical scanner. Mechanical television was fragile, low in sensitivity, and slow to form an image, and ultimately proved a dead end.

Rosing was one of the first to realize this. In 1907 he patented an improved receiver based on the recently invented cathode-ray tube (CRT), a glass vacuum tube in which was generated a powerful electron beam. With Zworykin's assistance, Rosing modified the CRT so that the strength of the beam varied with the fluctuations of the electric current from a mechanical camera. The beam was then directed toward a small fluorescent screen within the tube. Magnets on either side of the tube pulled the electron beam back and forth in a scanning motion that generated an image with sufficient resolution to reproduce geometrical shapes.

After receiving his degree in 1912, Zworykin attended the Collège de France in Paris and studied radiation and x-rays with the physicist Paul Langevin. When World War I began, he returned to Russia to serve in the

Courtesy of RCA News

army. He requested an assignment to a radiation research team, but was ordered into the Signal Corps as an inspector of radio equipment—"a mistake that changed my whole career," since it gave him a thorough knowledge of electronics. After the Revolution he left Russia, went to the United States, and in 1920 joined the Pittsburgh research laboratory of the Westinghouse Electric and Manufacturing Company, determined to develop a completely electronic television system.

In 1923, he filed his first patent, for the iconoscope, an electronic camera tube. Its lens projected an image of the subject onto a photosensitive mosaic made up of hundreds of thousands of tiny silver and cesium droplets deposited on a sheet of mica. Wherever a bright light fell on the mosaic, the droplets emitted electrons freely; droplets left in darkness lost proportionately fewer electrons. The result was a pattern of positive charges that matched the pattern of light and shade in the image of the subject. The amount of charge at each point increased steadily as the light continued to fall on it, a phenomenon known as "charge storage." An electron beam periodically scanned the surface, striking each point in turn and dissipating its positive charge. Behind the mica was a charged metallic plate that responded to each fluctuation in charge with a corresponding change in voltage. This, amplified, was transmitted to the receiver as the picture signal.

The iconoscope differed radically from previous television cameras in its use of electron scanning and in the unusual nature of the photosensitive surface. Its unique charge-storage feature, which increased the brightness and sharpness of the picture manyfold, made the iconoscope far more sensitive than its nearest competitor, the mechanical camera built by Philo T. Farnsworth. In 1924 Zworykin patented the kinescope, a vastly more sophisticated version of Rosing's CRT receiver. All the elements of an all-electronic television system had now been developed. However, Westinghouse executives were not impressed by the first demonstration of the iconoscope in 1923—Zworykin apparently overemphasized the research problems that still remained—and urged him to do "something more useful."

Over the next six years, Zworykin, who earned his doctorate from the University of Pittsburgh in 1926, worked on photocells, amplifiers, and scanning devices for use in motion-picture soundtrack and facsimile reproductions. At the same time he improved his iconoscope, obtaining a second patent in 1928. His first patent for color television was granted in 1929, the year he convinced David Sarnoff, then vice president of the Radio Corporation of America, to let him develop his television system as director of RCA's electronics research center in Camden, New Jersey. Zworykin blithely estimated that $100,000 would be adequate to develop a commercial system; RCA ultimately spent more than $50 million before seeing a profit. Improved versions of the iconoscope were used for the first high-quality television broadcasts in the United Kingdom (1936) and the United States (1941).

During the 1930s, Zworykin also worked on the design of secondary emission multipliers, which enable weak particles to generate strong flows of electrons. A multiplier of his design was incorporated into the scintillation counter, a highly sensitive radiation detector. He was also responsible for a number of improvements in the image orthicon tube, the tube most widely used in today's television cameras. During World War II, two military devices for seeing in the dark—the Snooperscope and the Sniperscope—were equipped with infrared-sensitive image tubes of his design. In 1934 Zworykin proposed that television cameras be installed in the noses of guided missiles to help direct them to their targets; such guidance systems did not come into common use for more than two decades. In 1940 he sponsored the development of an early version of the electron microscope.

The RCA laboratories were moved to Princeton in 1942. Zworykin was promoted to vice president five years later. In 1951 he married his second wife, a physician. After his official retirement from RCA with the rank of honorary vice president in 1954, he worked at RCA and at the Medical Electronics Research Center of Rockefeller Institute (now Rockefeller University) in New York City, encouraging cooperation between electronics engineers and medical professionals. He developed two other important inventions in 1957: the radio endosonde, a transmitter small enough to be swallowed, which can broadcast information on internal pressure changes from within the alimentary canal, and the ultraviolet color-translating television microscope, a device that provides color pictures of ongoing chemical reactions within the living cell. In 1966 he received the National Medal of Science, the nation's highest scientific award. In his last years he continued his research at Princeton University and the University of Miami, working on projects as diverse as nuclear fusion, solar energy, and electronic acupuncture.

Zworykin was by no means happy with the exploitation by the entertainment industry of the medium he had done so much to develop. In 1975, he said: "I had visions of the thrilling educational, cultural, and scientific applications of television. It could have been the golden medium. But it failed. . . . From the beginning, American television networks acceded to the public taste for trivia because of commercialism." Now, he added, "it's contaminating our society." P.D./S.A.

Parents Kozma Z., owner of riverboat fleet, and Elaine Z. **Married** (1) Tatiana Vasilieff 1916 (div.): Nina (d.); Elaine Z. Knudsen. (2) Katherine Polevitsky, physician, 1951. **Emigrated** to U.S. 1919; naturalized 1924. **Education** St. Petersburg Inst. of Technology, degree in electrical engineering 1912; Coll. de France, Paris 1912–14; Univ. of Pittsburgh, Ph.D. 1926. **Mil. service** Officer and communications equipment inspector, Signal Corps, Russian Army, WWI. **Career** Bookkeeper for financial agent, Russian Embassy, Wash. DC 1919–20. • Electronics researcher, Westinghouse Electric and Manufacturing Co., Pittsburgh 1920–ca. 1922, 1923–29; researcher, electronics development firm, Kansas ca. 1922–23. • With Radio Corp. of America: dir., electronics research lab., Camden, NJ 1929–42; assoc. research dir. 1942–45 and dir. of electronic research 1946–54, RCA Labs., Princeton, NJ; v.p. and technical consultant 1947–54; hon. v.p. and consultant since 1954. • Dir., Medical Electronics Research Center, Rockefeller Inst. (now Rockefeller Univ.), NYC since ca. 1954; researcher, Princeton Univ. 1970s; visiting prof., Inst. for Molecular and Cellular Evolution, Univ. of Miami since 1970. **Officer** Natl. chmn., Professional Group on Medical Electronics, Inst. of Radio Engineers; founder and pres., Intl. Fedn. for Medical Electronics and Biological Engineering; officer of the Acad., French Ministry of Education; gov., Intl. Inst. for Medical Electronics and Biological Engineering, Paris. **Fellow** Amer. Assn. for Advancement of Science; Amer. Inst. of Physics; Amer. Physical Soc.; Inst. of Electrical and Electronics Engineers. **Member** Amer. Acad. of Arts and Sciences; Amer. Philosophical Soc.; (charter member) Electron Microscope Soc. of America; Natl. Acad. of Engineering; Natl. Acad. of Sciences; (charter member) Soc. of Television Engineers; (charter member) Soc. of Television Pioneers; Sigma Xi. **Honors** Liebman Memorial Prize 1934, Medal of Honor 1951, and establishment of Television Prize in his name 1952, Inst. of Radio Engineers; Overseas Award 1939 and Faraday Medal 1965, British Instn. of Electrical Engineers; Modern Pioneer Award, Natl. Assn. of Manufacturers 1940; Rumford Medal, Amer. Acad. of Arts and Sciences 1941; War Dept. Certificate of Appreciation 1945; Navy Certificate of Commendation 1947; Potts Medal, Franklin Inst. 1947; Presidential Certificate of Merit 1948; chevalier, Légion d'Honneur 1948; Lamme Medal 1949 and Edison Medal 1952, Amer. Inst. of Electrical Engineers; Gold Medal of Achievement, Poor Richard Club 1949; Progress Medal Award, Soc. of Motion Picture and Television Engineers 1950; gold medal, Union Française des Inventeurs 1954; Trasenster Medal 1959 and Medical Electronics Medal 1963, Univ. of Liège; Christoforo Columbo Award and Order of Merit, Italy 1959; Broadcast Pioneers Award 1960; Sauveur Award, Amer. Soc. of Metals 1963; De Forest Audion Award 1966; Natl. Medal of Science 1966; Golden Plate Award, Amer. Acad. of Achievement 1967; Founders Medal, Natl. Acad. of Engineering 1968; named to Natl. Inventors Hall of Fame 1977; ring, Eduard Rhein Foundn. 1980. • Hon. fellow, Inst. Internazionale delle Comunicazione, Italy, and Television Soc., England; hon. member of British Inst. of Radio Engineers, Société Française des Électriciens et des Radioélectriciens, and Television Engineers of Japan; eminent member, Eta Kappa Nu Assn.; hon. degree from Polytechnic Inst., Brooklyn. **Patents** More than 120 patents on electronic devices, including iconoscope, kinescope, color TV system, radio endosonde, ultraviolet color-translating TV microscope, TV guidance systems for missiles and automobiles, others. **Author** *Photocells and Their Applications,* 1932; *Television,* 1940, rev. ed. 1954; *Electron Optics and the Electron Micro-*

scope, 1946; *Photoelectricity and its Application,* 1949; *Television in Science and Industry,* 1958. **Contributor** of papers on electronics to scientific jrnls.

Further reading G. Garratt and A. Mumford, "The History of Television," in *Proceedings of the Institution of Radio Engineers,* vol. 99, 1952; Irving Wolff, "Vladimir K. Zworykin," in *Proceedings of the Institution of Radio Engineers,* vol. 45, 1957; "Merchant of Vision," in *Saturday Review,* June 1957.

YEFET BEN-AVRAHAM TSEDAKA

Leader of the Samaritan community in Israel
***Born* Nablus, Palestine, Ottoman Empire, 1895**
***Died* Holon, near Tel Aviv, Israel, 30 July 1982**

Yefet Tsedaka was for some 50 years the leader of the Samaritan community in what is now Israel. The Samaritans, known to most Westerners only through the parable of the Good Samaritan in the New Testament, are, according to their own records, the descendents of those Israelites who remained in Samaria when part of the population was driven into exile by the Assyrian conquerors in 721 B.C. Although their religion, scriptures, and customs are similar to those of the Jews, they do not accept any other sacred texts beyond the Five Books of Moses, their Torah differs in significant details from the Jewish Torah, they write Hebrew in the original Canaanite script rather than in the square script introduced by the priest Ezra in the fifth century B.C., and their holy place is not Jerusalem but Mount Gerizim, to which the entire community makes a pilgrimage three times a year. At the beginning of the Common Era there were some three-quarters of a million Samaritans living in their ancient town of Shechem, but repression by a series of hostile or indifferent rulers—Romans, Christians, and Muslims—reduced their number to only 146 by the end of World War I.

Their escape from extinction has been credited in large part to Yefet Tsedaka, who, in cooperation with sympathetic Zionists, particularly Itzhak Ben-Zvi, the future president of Israel, managed to establish a flourishing offshoot community in Jaffa. His family had moved there in 1907, the first Samaritans to leave Shechem (now Nablus in the West Bank) since the eighteenth century. Other families followed, and Tsedaka became the leader of the group in the 1920s. One of their greatest problems was the disproportion of men to women—a ratio of about five to three. In 1924 Tsedaka broke precedent by marrying a Russian Jewish woman who had agreed to convert. His example was followed by other Samaritan men, and within five decades there were some 600 Samaritans living near Tel Aviv in the village of Holon, whose construction Tsedaka had helped to arrange. After Israel was founded in 1948, Tsedaka successfully petitioned the government to grant the Samaritans full citizenship under the Law of Return. The original Samaritans of Shechem came under Israeli jurisdiction when Jordan lost the West Bank territories in the 1967 war.

Tsedaka died at the age of 87, leaving eight children who are also leaders of the community. J.P.

Father Avraham Tsedaka, merchant. **Married** . . . 1924 (d. 1954): Binyamin; Yefet; six daughters. **Religion** Samaritan. **Education** Traditional Samaritan religious training. **Career** Leader of Samaritan community in Israel (formerly Palestine) since 1920s; religious teacher.

Further reading James Kraus, "The Good Samaritans," in *Present Tense,* Summer 1979.

AUGUST

CATHLEEN NESBITT

Actress

Born **Liskeard, Cheshire, England, 24 November 1888**

Died **London, England, 2 August 1982**

Cathleen Nesbitt was never—quite—a star. Though she was beautiful, talented, and versatile, and seldom lacked work throughout her long career, ultimate fame always eluded her. Many of her roles were beneath her merits; and as she ruefully remarked, if she really enjoyed a part, it was sure to be in a brief run. But for over 70 years she brought a rare grace and intelligence to the stage—and, less frequently, to the screen—and added in old age a dignity that was never overbearing.

She was born in Liskeard, Cheshire, and brought up in Belfast. Her mother was Welsh, and her father, an Ulsterman, was a merchant seaman who, as captain of the S.S. *Antrim,* took his daughter around the world. Before she was ten, she had seen South America, Egypt, and St. Petersburg; between voyages, she was educated in Belfast, graduating from the Queen's University in 1908. In 1910 she moved with her family to London, and trained for the stage under Rosina Filippi. At the invitation of Lady Gregory, a family friend, she joined the Irish Players for their American tour, with a small role in J. M. Synge's *Playboy of the Western World.* The play was widely held to constitute an insulting depiction of Irish life, and gave rise to violent rioting in New York; in Philadelphia, the entire company was prosecuted for performing an "obscene and blasphemous" work.

Courtesy of Mark Ramage

Back in London, Cathleen Nesbitt had her first major role as Perdita in Granville-Barker's production of *The Winter's Tale* (1912) at the Savoy Theatre. Later that year she met the young poet Rupert Brooke. From then until his death in 1915 they were passionately, though platonically, in love. "He would come and sit on my bed and talk until dawn, but strange as it may seem to anyone of this generation, we never actually 'became lovers.'" After his death, though, she regretted not having had a child by him. Brooke described her as "incredibly, inordinately, devastatingly, immortally, calamitously, hearteningly, adorably beautiful."

In 1915 Nesbitt sailed for America, and stayed there for four years, acting in plays by Shaw, Chesterton, and Galsworthy. She returned to England in 1919, and during the next two decades appeared in some of her most memorable roles, beginning with Jessica in *The Merchant of Venice* (1919) at the Court. In 1920 she played Cleopatra in an Oxford University production; her Antony was Cecil Ramage, and in 1921 they were married. Ramage became a Liberal M.P., but returned to the stage after losing his seat. Their marriage was dissolved in the late 1940s.

In the West End, Nesbitt played Margaret in Galsworthy's *Loyalties* (1922) and Mrs. Dubedat in Shaw's *The Doctor's Dilemma* (1923). That same year she appeared on stage with a live leopard in *The Eye of Siva,* "both promenading with equal grace," as a critic observed, and created the role of Yasmin in James Elroy Flecker's *Hassan.* In *Spring Cleaning* (1925) she was cast against type as a streetwalker. Other notable stage roles were in *A Bill of Divorcement* (1929); *Children in Uniform* (1932); Kate in *The Taming of the Shrew* (1935); Gertrude in *Hamlet* (1939); and Goneril in Granville-Barker's production of *King Lear* (1940).

Nesbitt's film career was more sporadic. She never played a leading role on screen, but lent distinction to supporting parts in more than 30 films, including *Fanny by Gaslight* (1943), *Nicholas Nickleby* (1947), *Three Coins in the Fountain* (1954), *Separate Tables* (1958), *Staircase* (1964), *The French Connection II* (1975), strikingly convincing as a drug addict, and Hitchcock's last film, *Family Plot* (1976). Her own last film was *Julia* (1977).

In 1950 she returned to the Broadway stage as Julia Shuttlethwaite in Eliot's *The Cocktail Party* (a role she had created for the Edinburgh premiere), and stayed mainly in America for the next 20 years. "One of the pleasures of the life that begins at 60," she remarked, "is that you begin to play mother roles." Most famously, she was Mrs. Higgins in the original production of *My Fair Lady* (1956). She also "mothered," among others, Richard Burton, Nicol Wiliamson, Joseph Cotten, and (when he played Napoleon in *Desirée* [1954]) Marlon Brando, and as Audrey Hepburn's great-aunt dispensed worldly wisdom in *Gigi* (1951).

Old age saw her as active as ever, happily accepting roles on stage and for television. She was awarded a CBE in 1978. In 1980 she played Juliana Bordereau in *The Aspern Papers* at Chichester, and was gratified the next year to be offered her old role in the revival of *My Fair Lady.* (Her initial reaction was, "Oh no, I'm much too young to be Rex Harrison's mother now!") After a highly successful tour, which took in New Orleans and San Francisco—and during which she celebrated her 93rd birthday—Cathleen Nesbitt returned to her London home, where she died a few months later of heart failure. P.K.

Parents Thomas H. N., merchant seaman, and Mary Catherine (Parry) N. **Married** Cecil Beresford Ramage, actor, politician, and lawyer, 1922 (div. late 1940s): Mark, advertising exec.; Jennifer, psychiatrist and writer. **Education** Victoria Coll.; Queen's Univ., Belfast, B.A. 1908; Lisieux, France; Sorbonne, Paris; studied drama with Rosina Filippi, London. **Career** Stage actress since 1910; with Irish Players acting troupe 1911–12; govt. censor and interpreter, London 1915; film actress since 1922; TV actress since 1950s. **Honors** Two Emmy Awards, for TV play "A Mask of Love," 1973; CBE 1978; Monte Carlo Award, for TV play "Abide with Me." **Stage** (all London except as noted) *The Cabinet Minister,* 1910; *The Master of Mrs. Chilvers,* 1911; *The Playboy of the Western World,* NYC 1911; *The Winter's Tale,* 1912; *Twelfth Night,* Paris 1913; *Quality Street,* 1913; *Quinneys,* Liverpool and NYC 1915; *Justice,* London and NYC 1916; *The Duchess of Malfi,* 1919; *The Merchant of Venice,* 1919; *The Grain of Mustard Seed,* 1920; *Antony and Cleopatra,* Oxford 1920; *Loyalties,* 1922, 1932; *The Doctor's Dilemma,* 1923; *The Eye of Siva,* 1923; *Hassan,* 1923; *The Madras House,* 1925; *Spring Cleaning,* 1925; *A Bill of Divorcement,* 1929; *The Case of the Frightened Lady,* 1931 and tour 1944; *Children in Uniform,* 1932; *The Taming of the Shrew,* 1935; *Hamlet,* European and Egyptian tour 1939; *King Lear,* 1940; *The Shop at Sly Corner,* 1945; *Medea,* 1948; *The Cocktail Party,* Edinburgh 1949 and NYC 1950; *Gigi,* NYC 1951; *The Uninvited Guest,* 1953; *Sabrina Fair,* NYC 1953, London 1954, and U.K. tour 1972; *Anastasia,* NYC 1955; *My Fair Lady,* NYC 1956 and U.S. tour 1980; *The Sleeping Prince,* NYC 1956; *The Chalk Garden,* U.S. tour 1957 and Chicago 1972; *The Claimant,* 1964; *The Royal Family on Broadway,* Chicago 1971; *Uncle Vanya,* NYC 1973; *The Aspern Papers,* Chichester Festival 1978, 1980; many others. **Films** *The Faithful Heart,* 1922; *The Case of the Frightened Lady,* 1932; *The Passing of the Third Floor Back,* 1936; *Pygmalion,* 1938; *Fanny by Gaslight* (in U.S. as *Man of Evil*), 1943; *Nicholas Nickleby,* 1947; *So Long at the Fair,* 1950; *Three Coins in the Fountain,* 1954; *Desirée,* 1954; *An Affair to Remember,* 1957; *Separate Tables,* 1958; *Staircase,* 1964; *Promise Her Anything,* 1966; *The Trygon Factor,* 1967; *Villain,* 1971; *The French Connection II,* 1975; *Family Plot,* 1976; *Julia,* 1977; others. **Television** More than 40 productions in the U.S. alone; "The

Mother," 1954; "The Playwright and the Star," 1957; "The Farmer's Daughter" series, 1962–65; "The Crucible"; "Abide with Me"; "The Old Crowd"; "Upstairs, Downstairs"; many others. **Author** *A Little Love and Good Company* (autobiography), 1974.

NIKOLAI (ALEKSEYEVICH) PILYUGIN

Automation and control-systems engineer

***Born* Krasnoye Selo, St. Petersburg region, Russia, 18 May 1908**

***Died* Moscow, USSR, 2 August 1982**

Nikolai Pilyugin died in the 25th anniversary year of the USSR's launching of Sputnik I, the world's first artificial satellite. The rocket booster that carried Sputnik aloft used a guidance system that he designed. Because much of his work is still classified, little information has been made public on his life and specific contributions to the Soviet space program, but the number and variety of his official honors indicate that he was held in high esteem by the Soviet leadership.

Pilyugin was born into a peasant family and was apprenticed to a mechanic. After working some years at this trade, he attended the Bauman Higher Technical School in Moscow, graduating in 1935. He served on the staff of the Zhukovsky Central Institute of Aerohydrodynamics until the German invasion of the Soviet Union in 1941, when he began to design aircraft for the war effort. He joined the Communist Party in 1940.

Beginning in 1946, Pilyugin worked under Sergey Korolev, a prewar rocket pioneer and the chief engineer of the Soviet space program in the 1950s, on the design of automatic control systems for rockets and missiles. After the launching of Sputnik, Pilyugin became the chief designer of guidance systems for more advanced boosters, manned spacecraft, and interplanetary robot probes. Much of the success of the USSR's program of automated planetary landers, an area in which the USSR has outstripped the United States, can be traced to Pilyugin's sophisticated and reliable designs. In the early 1960s he became head of a major research institute. He was made a full member of the USSR Academy of Sciences in 1966, the year of Korolev's death, and the following year was elected to the academy's presidium.

In 1969, Pilyugin was named to a chair at the Institute of Radiotechnology, Electronics, and Automation in Moscow, which he had joined the previous year as head of a subdepartment. There he trained much of the present generation of Soviet space scientists and engineers in automation and remote-control technology. He was made a Hero of Socialist Labor twice and was awarded the Lenin Prize, the State Prize, and five Orders of Lenin, among other awards. His obituary was signed by Leonid Brezhnev and 64 other Soviet dignitaries—an unusual sign of distinction. P.D.

Parents peasants. **Education** Bauman Higher Technical Sch., Moscow, grad. 1935. **Mil. service** Designed aircraft for Soviet air force, WWII. **Career** Apprentice mechanic, then mechanic, various research insts. ca. 1926–35; staff member, N.K. Zhukovsky Central Inst. of Aerohydrodynamics 1934–41; engineer and dir., research insts. since 1935; designer since ca. 1946 and chief designer since ca. 1957 of automated control systems for aircraft and spacecraft; head of major research inst. 1960s; subdept. head since 1969 and prof. since 1970, Moscow Inst. of Radiotechnology, Electronics, and Automation. • Member since 1940 and delegate to 23rd through 26th party congresses, CPSU; deputy to USSR Supreme Soviet since 1966. **Member** Corresp. member 1958–66, member since 1966, and member of presidium since 1967, USSR Acad. of Sciences; various commns. on industry, trade, and communications, Soviet of Nationalities. **Honors** Hero of Socialist Labor 1956, 1961; Lenin Prize 1957; USSR State Prize 1967; Order of the October Revolution; Order of Lenin five times; other medals. **Author** of books and articles on automation, control, and guidance systems for industry, communications, aircraft, and spacecraft.

(HUGH) DAVID (GRAHAM) CARRITT
Art historian, dealer, and critic
***Born* England, 11 April 1927**
***Died* London, England, 3 August 1982**

Since World War II, more major discoveries of lost Old Master paintings were made by the art dealer and historian David Carritt than everyone else put together. He had the seemingly miraculous ability to sleuth out unsuspected Dürers, Caravaggios, Fragonards, and Tiepolos in the recesses of backyard sheds, on ceilings, and even under the noses of his fellow dealers at auctions. His numerous coups excited the admiration, and just as often the envy, of the art world. "He has made art dealing seem the arena for discoveries, for glamour, for excitement," wrote critic Marina Vaizey in the *Tatler*. "His air of amused cultivation fits the glamorised idea too of the highly cultivated gentleman, or rather, aristocrat, the Scarlet Pimpernel of the art world, rescuing neglected masterpieces from obscurity, releasing them from dusty prisons into the sunlight of the world's great collections."

As a child, Carritt was determined to become an architect, and thoroughly familiarized himself with the interiors of Britain's great houses through the pages of *Country Life* magazine. He was educated at Rugby School, from which he visited nearby manor houses on his bicycle. At Christ Church, Oxford, where he earned a degree in history, he met the eminent art historian Sir Karl Parker, who encouraged his interest in art, and Benedict Nicholson, the editor of *Burlington* magazine, who took him to Florence to meet Bernard Berenson, the world-famous authority on Italian Old Masters. Berenson was impressed by Carritt's already formidable knowledge, the product less of scholarship than of devotedly, obsessively, looking at works of art, and predicted his success. Of that meeting, Carritt remarked that he "had been able to correct a few of Berenson's attributions."

After his graduation from Oxford, Carritt ran a modest business selling Old Master drawings from his London flat. When he was 25, he made his first major discovery, of Caravaggio's long-lost *The Musicians,* at the Lake District cottage of a retired naval surgeon. A few years later, while poking about in a Dublin dealer's back shed, he found, rolled up in a corner, six large decorative panels by one or both of the fifteenth-century Guardi brothers.

Although more established dealers found Carritt something of an upstart, the London auction house Christie's hired him in 1962 and quickly promoted him to director. The aggressive advertising of its main competitor, Sotheby Parke-Bernet, had given Christie's a setback, and Carritt's discoveries helped renew its fortunes. One of his notable finds was a much-sought-after ceiling mural by Tiepolo, which he tracked down to the Egyptian Embassy in London, the former home of a rich collector. "The general assumption is that things have vanished," he later remarked, "but generally they are simply still there—especially if they are fixed to the ceiling." Another find was a previously unknown portrait of St. Ivo by the Flemish master Rogier van der Weyden, valued at more than one million dollars, which decorated the mantelpiece in a country home in Bray. His greatest coup occurred in 1977, when, before an auction room full of dealers, he successfully bid £8,000 for a painting credited to a minor eighteenth-century French artist. He alone had recognized it as an early Fragonard, worth 70 times more.

Carritt's success was partly a matter of knowing the artists—he identified a misattributed Dürer etching because he had once seen Dürer's sketch for a lion that figures in it—and partly a matter of keeping himself informed about the histories of Britain's landed families, on whose manor-house walls great paintings were likely to have been hung and forgotten. Carritt had access to such houses through a carefully built-up network of social contacts; he also watched the obituaries column for news of deaths and inheritances. His sudden appearances at country estates to announce the presence of valuable paintings made him something of a legend, and less affluent aristocrats were said to yearn for the day when the butler would announce, "A Mr. Carritt to see you, sir."

Carritt considered himself a "midwife to masterpieces" and was satisfied to be a connoisseur and not a collector. He left Christie's in 1970 to become a director of Artemis, a London-based international art dealership financed by a consortium of bankers, and to head his own subsidiary, David Carritt, Ltd. During the 1970s he organized small but impressive Old Master exhibitions in London. He died of cancer at the age of 55. L.F.

Education Rugby Sch., grad. 1944; Christ Church Coll., Oxford, degree in history. **Mil. service** Air Training Corps, youth skywatching org., WWII. **Career** Private art dealer, London early 1950s–60s; art critic, *Evening Standard,* London early 1960s; dealer and dir., Christie's auction house, London 1962–70; dir. and bd. member, Artemis S.A. and subsidiaries since 1970; founding dir., David Carritt, Ltd., London since 1970. **Member** Travellers Club. **Contributor** of articles on art dealing, art collecting, and art history to newspapers and mags.

Further reading John Russell, "David Carritt: A Sleuth for All Seasons," in *ARTnews,* Feb. 1974; Marina Vaizey, art column, *Tatler,* Aug. 1978.

SIR JOHN CHARNLEY

Orthopedic surgeon and biomechanical engineer
***Born* Bury, Lancashire, England, 29 August 1911**
***Died* Manchester, England, 5 August 1982**

The outstanding achievement of Sir John Charnley, a pioneer in orthopedic surgery, was the perfection of total prosthetic hip replacement, a procedure that has brought mobility and freedom from pain to thousands of people.

Charnley lived and worked entirely in his native district, Lancashire, except for military service in the Mideast during World War II. He earned his medical degrees from the University of Manchester and was a resident at Manchester Royal Infirmary and Salford Royal Hospital. His teacher at the Manchester Infirmary was Sir Harry Platt, himself a major figure in clinical and surgical orthopedics, who had a decisive influence on the development of Charnley's engineering-oriented approach to orthopedic research. While a surgeon at the Manchester Infirmary (1947–52), he published his first book, *The Closed Treatment of Common Fractures* (1950), in which he argued for a nonsurgical approach to fracture treatment. "It demands much less inherent skill to operate on a fracture," he wrote, "than to treat a case successfully from beginning to end conservatively."

Charnley began his research on hip replacement in 1954, first in his own home and then at the biomechanical laboratory at Wrightington Hospital, where he was a consulting surgeon, financing the experiments with patent royalties from his other inventions, which included a "walking" caliper that he developed for the use of wounded soldiers in World War II. Existing models of artificial hip joints were ill-fitting and poorly lubricated, and quickly wore out. His first step was to analyze the composition of the body's own joint lubricant, synovial fluid, and its action in coating the head of the femur and the hip socket. He then tested the lubricative abilities of synovial fluid on various metals and plastics that were candidates for use in new prosthetic designs. His attempts to replace both the hip-socket and femur-head surfaces with Teflon failed because the material wore away rapidly and became covered with a brown, fibrinous material that impeded the movement of the joint.

Eventually, Charnley made several important discoveries. He found that the strength of the joint is enormously increased when large amounts of methyl-methacrylate cement are applied as a grout to fix the artificial ball and socket firmly to their underlying bones. In 1962, he discovered that high-density polyethylene gives better results than Teflon. Tests showed that the frictional properties of polyethylene, unlike those of other plastics or of metal sliding on metal, were decidedly improved by synovial fluid. After years of experimentation, Charnley found that the most effective combination of materials was a thick-walled plastic socket used in conjunction with a femoral head of highly polished metal with the smallest possible diameter.

Since 1961, surgeons using Charnley's improved hip prostheses have achieved a success rate of 90 percent. Problems with the remaining cases were ascribed to the body's rejection of the prosthesis material or bacterial infection during surgery. To combat the latter problem, Charnley designed an airtight glass chamber, with its own supply of sterilized air, to enclose the surgeon, his assistant, and the lower half of the patient. This reduced postoperative complications by half.

In 1962, Charnley opened the Centre for Hip Surgery at Wrightington, where his methods are taught to orthopedic surgeons from all over the world. Today more than 50,000 Charnley hip-replacement operations are performed annually, mostly on people suffering from severe arthritis.

Charnley was professor of orthopedic surgery at the University of Manchester from 1972 to 1976 and became a fellow of the Royal Society in 1975, the first orthopedist to be thus honored. In 1974 he won the prestigious Lasker Clinical Medical Research Award. He was made CBE in 1970 and was knighted in 1977. B.D.

Married Jill Margaret Heaver 1957: one son; one daughter. **Education** Bury Grammar Sch., Lancs.; Univ. of Manchester, B.Sc. 1932, M.B. and Ch.B. 1935; resident, Manchester Royal Infirmary and Salford Royal Hosp. **Mil. service** Maj., RAMC, Mideast, WWII. **Career** With Univ. of Manchester: lectr. in orthopedics 1947–76; hon. lectr. in clinical orthopedics 1959–76; hon. lectr. in biomechanical engineering, Inst. of Science and Technology 1966–72; prof. of orthopedic surgery 1972–76; emeritus prof. since 1976. • Hon. asst. orthopedic surgeon 1947–52 and consulting orthopedic surgeon since 1952, Manchester Royal Infirmary; staff orthopedic surgeon, Park Hosp., Davyhulme, Lancs. 1950s; consultative orthopedic surgeon since 1950 and founder and dir. of Centre for Hip Surgery since 1962, Wrightington Hosp., Wigan, Lancs.; clinician, King Edward II Memorial Hosp., Midhurst since 1969; Robert Jones Lectr., Hosp. for Joint Diseases, NYC 1974; Hunterian Prof., Royal Coll. of Surgeons. **Fellow** FRS 1975; FRCS; Amer. Coll. of Surgeons; British Orthopedic Assn. **Honors** Olof Af Acrel Medal, Swedish Surgical Soc. 1969; CBE 1970; gold medal, Soc. of Apothecaries 1971; Gairdner Foundn. Intl. Award 1973; Lasker Clinical Medical Research Award 1974; Freedom of County, Borough of Bury 1974; Cameron Prize, Univ. of Edin-

Courtesy of University of Manchester

burgh 1974; Lister Medal, RCS 1975; Buccheri-La Ferla Prize, Italy 1977; kt. 1977; Alber Medal, Royal Scottish Acad. 1978; hon. member of Amer. Acad. of Orthopedic Surgeons, South African Medical Assn., and Amer., French, Belgian, Swiss, Brazilian, and French-Canadian Orthopedic Socs.; hon. degrees from univs. of Manchester, Belfast, Liverpool, Uppsala, and Leeds. **Inventor** of walking caliper, hip prosthesis, other medical devices. **Author** *The Closed Treatment of Common Fractures,* 1950; *Compression Arthrodesis,* 1953; *Acrylic Cement in Orthopaedic Surgery,* 1970; *Low Friction Arthroplasty of the Hip,* 1979. **Contributor** of articles on hip replacement to medical jrnls.

SIR HUGHIE (IDWAL) EDWARDS
Royal Air Force pilot and war hero
Born **Fremantle, West Australia, 1 August 1914**
Died **Sydney, Australia, 5 August 1982**

Sir Hughie Edwards, Australia's most decorated World War II hero, led daring commando-like bomber raids on German military and industrial installations during the early years of the war. His military honors included the Victoria Cross, the Distinguished Flying Cross, the Distinguished Service Order, and the Order of the British Empire.

The son of Welsh immigrants, Edwards was a professional football (soccer) player before joining the Australian Army in 1934. He soon transferred to the RAAF, was chosen for advanced flight training in Britain, and by 1941 was a wing commander with the RAF's 105th Squadron, a force of Blenheim fighter-bombers equipped with onboard radar.

On 15 June 1941, Edwards, though suffering from injuries received in a flying accident, led a daylight raid against German shipping off the Dutch coast. Despite heavy antiaircraft fire, he boldly flew in at mast height to bomb and strafe one 4,000-ton vessel, causing extensive damage. Two weeks later, he led 15 Blenheims against the heavily defended coastal factories at Bremen, without benefit of cloud cover. All 15 bombers were hit as the squad came in at low altitude, flying beneath power and telegraph cables and through a massive balloon barrage; they released their bombs and withdrew with a loss of four planes. Edwards received the Distinguished Flying Cross and the Victoria Cross for leading these attacks. Later in the war, he commanded a Mosquito squadron and headed bomber stations in Lincolnshire and in Chittagong, Australia.

Edwards was named commandant of the Central Fighting Establishment in 1958 and in 1960 was appointed aide-de-camp to the Queen. His last post in the RAF was as director of establishments in the Air Ministry. In 1974, the year he was made KCMG, he was appointed governor of West Australia, but retired after a year owing to ill health and returned to his former job as a director of the Australian Selection Trust, Ltd. He died at his home outside Sydney at the age of 68.

S.A.

Father Hugh E. **Married** (1) Cherry Kyrle Beresford 1942 (d. 1966): one son; one daughter. (2) Dorothy Carew Berrick 1972. **Education** Fremantle Boys Sch., West Australia. **Career** With South Fremantle Football Club early 1930s. • Joined Australian Army 1934; cadet, Royal Australian Air Force 1935–36. • With RAF: advanced flight training 1936; pilot, 139th Squadron late 1930s–early 40s; wing comdr., 105th Squadron 1942–43; bomber-station comdr., Binbrook, Lincs. 1943–44; bomber-station comdr., Chittagong, Australia 1945; also commanded Mosquito squadron, WWII; commandant, Central Fighter Establishment 1958–60; ADC to the Queen 1960–63; dir. of establishments, Air Ministry 1962–63. • Resident dir., Australian Selection Trust, Ltd.. 1964–74, late 1970s; gov., West Australia 1974–75. **Member** Clubs: White's; RAF; M.C.C.; Union and Imperial Service, Sydney. **Honors** Mentioned in dispatches, WWII; V.C. 1941; DFC with Bar 1941; DSO 1942; OBE 1947; C.B. 1959; kt. of Grace of Order of St. John 1947; KCMG 1974.

SAMUEL M. KOOTZ
Art dealer
***Born* Portsmouth, Virginia, USA, 23 August 1898**
***Died* New York City, USA, 7 August 1982**

Samuel Kootz, who operated a well-known gallery in New York City from 1945 to 1966, was an early advocate of Abstract Expressionist painting. His was the first gallery to put on group shows of works by Jackson Pollock, Willem de Kooning, Robert Motherwell, Hans Hofmann, and other artists of the New York School; he also promoted the postwar careers of Picasso, Léger, and Miró. A forceful, sometimes blunt salesman, his motto was: "Show as good pictures as can be provided — and get rid of them as fast as you can."

Kootz worked as a lawyer after graduating from the University of Virginia in 1921; he moved to New York City in 1923 to become an advertising executive and did promotional work for Hollywood on the East Coast in the mid-1920s. In 1934 he became a dealer in silk and made important contacts in the New York art world commissioning fabric designs from well-known American painters, including Stuart Davis and Arthur Dove. It was a small step from selling artist-designed fabrics to selling art. By the 1940s, Kootz was running a private art dealership and organizing exhibitions, notably a massive survey of recent American art for Macy's, the department store, in 1942.

In 1945 he opened the Kootz Gallery, in partnership with his first wife, Jane Ogden, and showed the works of Carl Holty, William Baziotes, the French artist Fernand Léger, Fritz Glarner, and Robert Motherwell (whom he supported in a Florida studio with a small stipend). He soon added Adolph Gottlieb, Byron Browne, Hans Hofmann, and Romare Bearden to his roster of artists. Later in the decade he exhibited Joan Miró, Piet Mondrian, Jean Arp, and several other important European artists, most of them Surrealists.

Kootz flew to Paris early in 1947 to meet Pablo Picasso, who had not shown new work in the United States for nearly a decade, and convinced him to allow the Kootz Gallery to mount his first postwar American show later that year. It was a great success, launched the gallery in earnest, and resulted in Kootz's becoming Picasso's worldwide dealer for a time. The considerable capital he acquired from his Picasso sales enabled him to bankroll a series of exhibitions by young American artists when the gallery reopened on Madison Avenue in 1949. One of them was the first collective exhibition by the Abstract Expressionists, whom Kootz called the Intrasubjectivists (they are also known as Action Painters, Abstract Impressionists, and the New York School). Starting in 1950, he sponsored yearly New Talent shows; the first was chosen by critic Clement Greenberg, one of the most vocal champions of the new American art, and the second by Greenberg and art historian Meyer Schapiro. The gallery soon ranked with that of Betty Parsons in prestige among artists and dealers.

By the early 1960s, Kootz's most profitable artist was Hans Hofmann, a late-blooming Abstract Expressionist. Although Kootz considered him a "great American painter," few critics or buyers agreed at first. It was largely due to Kootz's adroit and tenacious salesmanship that Hofmann's paintings increased in price from $1,000 to $18,000 apiece from the mid-1950s to 1965. Today Hofmann is hailed as a major painter and his works sell for about $200,000.

Kootz closed his gallery shortly after Hofmann's death in 1966, claiming that "it just wasn't much fun anymore. . . . Back in the early days at the start of the [Abstract Expressionist] movement, you couldn't give pictures away. Toward the end there, though, anything we hung—even if it had nothing to do with the kind of art we'd always stood for—would be snapped up indiscriminately just because *we* were showing it." He retired to his home in Easthampton, Long Island, where he worked on his memoirs, which had not been published at the time of his death.

He was the author of two books on American art, two detective novels (including one dealing with the art world), and a play about returning G.I.s, *Home is the Hunter,* that had a seven-week run in New York in 1946. He died of cancer at the age of 83. S.A.

Married (1) Jane Ogden, art dealer (d. 1970). (2) Joyce Lowinson, psychiatrist. **Education** Univ. of Virginia, LL.B. 1921. **Career** Lawyer, VA ca. 1921–23; advertising exec., NYC 1923–34; silk converter and design commissioner, NYC 1934–40s; art dealer since ca. 1944; dir., Kootz Gall., NYC 1945–48, 1949–66; dealer and agent for Pablo Picasso 1948–49. **Author** *Modern American Painters,* 1928; *Puzzle in Paint* (novel), 1943; *New Frontiers in American Painting,* 1944; *Puzzle in Petticoats* (novel), 1944; *Home is the Hunter* (play), 1946.

Further reading Dore Ashton, *The New York School: A Cultural Reckoning,* 1972; Gwen Kinkead, "The Spectacular Fall and Rise of Hans Hofmann," in *ARTnews,* Summer 1980.

CARL (BJORN) BRAESTRUP
Radiological physicist
***Born* Copenhagen, Denmark, 13 April 1897**
***Died* Middletown, Connecticut, USA, 8 August 1982**

Carl Braestrup was one of the first scientists to warn against needless exposure to radiation in factories, hospitals, and homes. The safety standards he proposed and the devices he invented to minimize radiation risk are still in use today.

The youngest son of a Danish naval officer, Braestrup emigrated to America at the age of 21. He attended Carnegie Tech in Pittsburgh and received his B.S. from the Massachusetts Institute of Technology in 1922, then joined Bell Laboratories in New York as a development engineer (1922–23). After working with several other engineering-development firms, he began, in 1928, a long association with Columbia University, teaching part-time and doing research at the university's Postgraduate Medical School. From 1929 he directed the physics laboratory of the New York Department of Hospitals.

Braestrup's task at the physics laboratory was to oversee the safe use of radiation and radioactive materials used in medical treatment. Seeking an accurate way to measure doses of radiation, he developed a film badge, to be worn by workers on their clothing, that recorded the amount and type of radiation in the local environment. The film badges later used by the Atomic Energy Commission were based on the same principle.

During World War II, Braestrup worked with the Columbia University staff of the Manhattan Project, the secret effort to develop the atomic bomb, helping to determine the radiological health hazards of atomic weapons and atomic energy. After the war, the federal government hired him as a consultant for the atomic bomb tests on Bikini Atoll and for the office of the army's surgeon general. From 1952 to 1963 he worked with the AEC's national laboratory in Oak Ridge, Tennessee, investigating the radiation-shielding properties of building materials and inspecting plants that processed radioactive substances. In 1955 he joined the civil-defense program in New York City, where he had set up a radiation-safety laboratory in the Empire State Building, to train firemen in radiation-detection and decontamination procedures.

Braestrup's work in nuclear medicine also dated from the early 1950s, when he demonstrated that cancer patients and hospital medical staff were receiving high doses of radiation—often thousands of roentgens—from radium applicators used in the destruction of tumors. The Theratron, a machine that directs a focused beam of cobalt radiation on deep-seated tumors, minimizing the damage to healthy tissue nearby, was patented by Braestrup and the Canadian engineer D.T. Green in 1953 and is still widely used.

With Richard T. Mooney, Braestrup investigated the levels of x-rays emitted by television sets; their study was instrumental in bringing about stricter federal regulatory standards. Braestrup's 1958 book *Radiation Protection,* written for users of cathode-ray tubes, electron microscopes, and other sources of radiation, made available to the public, for the first time, the results of recent experiments on methods of shielding.

After his retirement, Braestrup continued to work as a radiation consultant at Lenox Hill Hospital in New York City. He died at the age of 85 of complications following a stroke.

P.D.

Father Danish naval officer. **Married** Elsebet Kampmann 1928: Peter, ed.; Mrs. Daniel B. Strickland. **Emigrated** to U.S. 1919; naturalized. **Religion** Congregationalist. **Education** Carnegie Inst. of Technology, Pittsburgh; Massachusetts Inst. of Technology, B.S. 1922. **Mil. service** Columbia Univ. research team, Manhattan Project, WWII; consultant on atomic tests, U.S. govt. 1946. **Career** Development engineer, Bell Laboratories, NY 1922–23; designer and chief engineer, development firms 1923–28; researcher and instr. at Postgraduate Medical Sch. 1928–32 and research assoc. in radiology 1947–67, Columbia Univ.; dir., physics services, New York City Dept. of Hospitals, New York Univ., then Columbia Univ., 1929–50, and Delafield Hosp. 1950–67; assoc. prof. in physics, New York Univ. 1948–49. • Consultant: Surgeon Gen.'s Office, U.S. Army 1945–69; U.S. Veterans' Hosps. 1946–67; AEC, NY 1947–63; Oak Ridge Inst. for Nuclear Studies, TN 1952–63; (also head of advisory cttee., and instr.) Civil Defense Project, NYC 1955; Lenox Hill Hosp., NYC since 1967. **Officer** Chmn., commn. on shielding design, Natl. Council on Radiation Protection. **Fellow** Coll. of Amer. Radiologists. **Member** Expert advisory panel on radiation, WHO; Intl. Commn. on Radiological Protection; Amer. Physical Soc.; Amer. Radium Soc.; Radiation Research Soc.; (emeritus) Radiological Soc. of North America; (emeritus) Amer. Assn. of Physicists in Medicine; Cosmos Club. **Honors** Hon. member: Natl. Council on Radiation Protection; Sigma Xi. **Patents** Radiation-detecting film badge; Theratron cobalt-therapy machine; other devices. **Author** (Jtly.) *Radiation Protection,* 1958; (jtly.) *World Health Organization Manual of Radiation Protection in Hospitals.* **Contributor** of more than 50 articles on radiation protection to mags. and jrnls.

ANTON BRUEHL
Photographer
***Born* Australia, 1900**
***Died* San Francisco, California, USA, 10 August 1982**

Anton Bruehl, a pioneer of the modernist aesthetic in photography, was one of the most prominent fashion and advertising photographers of the 1930s. His commercial success followed the appearance of his series of advertisements for the Weber and Heilbroner Company, which were published in *The New Yorker* in 1929. In this series, Bruehl used his skill in arrangement, choice of angle, and lighting to accentuate the shapes and textures of familiar objects such as hats and cotton reels, calling attention to their form rather than function—an innovative approach at the time, though common in current advertising. During the 1930s, Bruehl worked for *Vogue, Vanity Fair,* and *House and Garden* as a fashion photographer, becoming celebrated for the excellence of his color photography, a medium he was among the first to use and which he developed in collaboration with Fernand Bourges, a printing technician working for Condé Nast who perfected a superior process of reproducing color negatives. His photograph *Dancers,* depicting swirling figures against a dark background, originally commissioned as a cover for *Esquire* in 1931, was republished by *ARTnews* in April 1978 and described as a classic of early color photography.

Bruehl, who was born in Australia of German parentage, trained as an electrical engineer and came to the United States in 1919 to work for General Electric. In 1923 he saw an exhibition at the New York Art Center of photographs by students of Clarence White, and joined White's school of photography shortly afterwards. There he met Paul Outerbridge, whose success as an advertising photographer prompted him to take up similar work in 1926, after he had worked for six months in the portrait studio of Jessica Tarbox Beals.

Bruehl joined White's school at a time when many photographers in the United States had become aware of European artistic movements, especially Cubism, that questioned photography's alliance with impressionistic art. Pictorial photographers of the first decade of the 20th century had tried to emancipate the photographic print from the stigma of a machine-made object by stressing the need for the photographer to manipulate the negative and so alter the impression received by the lens. By 1920, however, Charles Sheeler, Paul Strand, and Edward Weston had begun to decry the pictorialist aesthetic as a travesty of photography's true expressive potential, which, they felt, lay in its unrelenting realism and fidelity to appearances. As early as 1916, Strand and Sheeler had made photographs of buildings and interior scenes that recalled Cubist painting in their emphasis on intersecting lines and planes. Bruehl was influenced by the modernists and paid close attention to the composition rather than the subjects of his photographs. His earliest work shows an interest in the interplay of two-dimensional design and three-dimensional space, and it was this style that led to his success as an advertising photographer.

Unlike earlier leaders of photographic movements such as Alfred Stieglitz, Bruehl did not regard art and commerce as separate fields. During the period of his greatest commercial success he remained a member of the Pictorial Photographers of America and helped run their New York exhibitions. Like Edward Steichen, also a successful advertising photographer, he did a great deal to enhance the quality of commercial photography, and his work has now achieved recognition as art. His photographs are in the collections of the International Museum of Photography at George Eastman House in Rochester, New York, the Museum of Modern Art in New York City, and the Art Institute of Chicago. In later years Bruehl lived in Delray, Florida, and in San Francisco, where he died at the age of 82. H.B.

Married Sarah Barnes (d.): Anton, Jr.; David; Stephen. **Emigrated** to U.S. 1919; naturalized. **Education** Studied electrical engineering, Australia 1910s; Clarence White Sch. of Photography, NYC 1924. **Career** Electrical engineer, General Electric Co. 1919–ca. 24; photographer and teaching asst. 1924–25 and dir. 1925–26, Clarence White Sch. of Photography; photographer, Jessica Tarbox Beals portrait studio, NYC ca. 1925; advertising and commercial photographer, NYC 1926–ca. 40; chief color photographer, Condé Nast Publications, NYC mid-1930s. **Member** Exec. and jury cttees., Pictorial Photographers of America, NYC. **Honors** Gold medal eight times, Art Directors Club, NYC. **Exhibitions** Stuttgart 1929; Julien Levy Gall., NYC 1932; MOMA 1932; Witkin Gall., NYC 1978; others in U.S. and France. **Collections** Center for Creative Photography, Univ. of Arizona, Tucson; MOMA; Art Inst. of Chicago; Intl. Mus. of Photography, Rochester, NY. **Photographer** (Also author) *Mexico,* 1933; Lowell Thomas, *Magic Dials: The Story of Radio and Television,* 1939; other books. **Contributor** of fashion photographs to *Vanity Fair, Vogue, House and Garden, Esquire,* other mags.

Further reading Nancy Hall-Duncan, *The History of Fashion Photography,* 1979.

SIR GEOFFREY (STANLEY) de FREITAS
Labour politician and diplomat
***Born* 7 April 1913**
***Died* 10 August 1982**

Sir Geoffrey de Freitas served three different constituencies over three decades as Labour member of Parliament. He was named high commissioner to Ghana in 1961 by the Conservative government, and remained in Africa three years before returning to electoral politics. A committed European for many years, he was successively chairman of the Labour Committee for Europe (1965–72) and then, once Britain joined the European Community, vice president of the European Parliament (1975–79).

He was the son of Sir Anthony de Freitas, a distinguished barrister and judge. Educated first at Haileybury School, he then attended Clare College, Cambridge, where he won a full blue in athletics and was president of the Cambridge Union in 1934. He was awarded a Mellon Fellowship and spent two years studying international law at Yale University. On his return he was called to the bar at Lincoln's Inn (1937), where he held the Cholmeley Scholarship.

In 1936, de Freitas won the first of the many elections he contested, as Labour member of the Shoreditch Borough Council in London's East End. He had joined the Labour Party in 1931. With two other young men of means he turned an abandoned factory in Hoxton into a youth settlement house, and lived on the premises for two years. He was adopted as prospective Labour parliamentary candidate for Nottingham Central in 1939, but abandoned all his plans when war came and volunteered for the Royal Artillery. From 1940 until the end of the war he served with the Royal Air Force, rising to the rank of squadron leader. In the general election of 1945 he was elected to Parliament for the first time.

His quick intelligence was soon remarked in Westminster, and in August 1945 he was named parliamentary private secretary to the prime minister, Clement Attlee. He held this insider's post for only eight months, learning enough to proceed to a junior ministry, and he was undersecretary of state for air until 1950. In that year's general election, which returned the Labourites with only a fragile majority, he left his constituency at Nottingham Central to stand for Lincoln, which he won and represented until 1961. During the short period of Attlee's second ministry (1950–51), de Freitas was undersecretary of state at the Home Office.

In 1961, de Freitas, who had just been appointed shadow minister of agriculture, was offered the post of high commissioner to Ghana, the equivalent of an ambassadorship. Ghana was the first British colony in Africa to achieve independence, and it was experiencing considerable economic and political difficulties; the Conservative government felt that a high commissioner with political expertise was required, and de Freitas, after securing his constituents' and Hugh Gaitskell's blessing, accepted the post. He had a successful two-year tour of duty in Accra, and the Foreign Office, eager to keep him in the diplomatic service and perhaps away from parliamentary politics, offered him the high commissionership to the then-evolving East African Federation. In the meantime he was sent in 1963 as high commissioner to Kenya, at that time about to achieve independence. The East African Federation, however, was a British conception which found no favor with the African states involved. It never became a reality, and de Freitas, by then somewhat weary of diplomacy, resigned to return to British politics.

He contested the general election of 1964 for Kettering and won the seat, holding it until his retirement from Parliament in 1979. Although he was given no ministry in any of the Labour governments after 1964, he was nevertheless in constant demand as a spokesman in favor of the British move toward Europe. In 1965–66 he led the British delegation to the Consultative Assembly of the Council of Europe in Strasbourg, where he was elected assembly president. In 1966 he led a delegation to the NATO Parliamentary Conference.

De Freitas was a forceful member of a large number of organizations, including the North Atlantic Assembly, of which he was president from 1976 to 1978; La Gauche Européenne, of which he was chairman from 1966 to 1978; the Attlee Foundation (1967–76); the Society of Labour Lawyers; the Nature Conservancy; the British Council; the Churches Social Responsibility Committee; and the Churchill Trust. He was made KCMG in 1961 and a privy councillor in 1967. A.K.

Parents Sir Anthony Patrick de F., barrister and judge, and Lady de F. (Maud Short). **Married** Helen Graham Bell 1938: three sons; one daughter. **Religion** Church of England. **Education** Haileybury; Clare Coll., Cambridge; Mellon Fellow in intl. politics, Yale Law Sch.; Lincoln's Inn (Cholmeley Scholarship), barrister-at-law 1937. **Mil. service** Royal Artillery 1939; squadron leader, RAF 1940–45. **Career** Joined Labour Party 1931; co-founder and operator, boys' club, Hoxton, London, and barrister on Midland Circuit, late 1930s; Labour member, Shoreditch Borough Council, London 1936–39. • Labour M.P. for Central Nottingham 1945–50, Lincoln 1950–61, and Kettering, Northants., 1964–79. • Parliamentary private secty. to Prime Minister 1945–46; undersecty. of state, Air Ministry 1946–50; undersecty. of state, Home Office 1950–51; shadow minister of agriculture 1960–61; British high commnr. in Ghana 1961–63 and Kenya 1963–64. • Chmn.: Labour parliamentary party cttees. on housing 1951–54, air 1955–60, agriculture 1960–61, defense 1964–71 and 1974–76; Labour Cttee. for Europe 1965–72; Select Cttees. on Privileges 1964–67 and Overseas Development 1974–79. • British delegate to U.N. 1949, 1964; member of British delegation 1951–54, leader of delegation 1965–66, assembly v.p. 1965–66, and assembly pres. 1966–69, Consultative Assembly, Council of Europe; member 1955–60 and leader 1965–66, British delegation to NATO Parliamentary Conference; founder member 1955 and pres. 1976–78, North Atlantic Assembly; v.p., European Parliament 1975–79; pres., Intl. Social Service, Geneva since 1979; chmn., European Consultants Ltd. since 1979. • Farmer, Bourn, Cambs. 1953–69. **Officer** Chmn.: Soc. of Labour Lawyers 1955–58; Gauche Européenne 1966–78; Attlee Foundn. 1967–76; Annual Atlantic Community Seminar, Univ. of East Anglia since 1978. • Vice chmn.: Nature Conservancy 1954–58; Churches Social Responsibility Cttee. 1956–61; British Council 1964–68. • Pres.: Cambridge Union 1934; Notts Ramblers' Assn. ca. 1948; Inland Waterways Assn. since 1978. • Dir., Laporte Industries 1968–78; gov., Haileybury. **Member** Natl. cttee., British Workers' Sports Assn. 1930s; Gen. Council of the Bar 1939; council, Agricultural Cooperative Assn. 1964–69 and Churchill Trust 1967–77; Royal Inst. of Intl. Affairs; Intl. Juridical Assn. • Clubs: Reform; Garrick; Hawks, Cambridge; (liveryman) Guild of Air Pilots. **Honors** Full blue in high jump, Cambridge Univ. Athletic Club; KCMG 1961; P.C. 1967; hon. fellow, Clare Coll., Cambridge.

GORDON (WADE) RULE

U.S. Navy cost controller

Born **Washington, D.C., USA, 29 December 1906**

Died **Arlington, Virginia, USA, 10 August 1982**

Gordon Rule was a maverick civil servant who insisted on telling the truth in public about the morass of waste, corruption, and conflict of interest that he discovered in his position as chief civilian controller of naval procurement. His military and political superiors in the Defense Department tried once to muzzle and demote him, yet many of them came, in the end, to admire him as a scrupulously honest watchdog who knew more about the complex business of military-supply contracting than anyone in Washington.

After attending George Washington University and its law school, Rule joined Washington's most prestigious law firm, Covington, Burling, in 1935. He left to serve in the Navy during World War II, rising to the rank of captain. He worked briefly as a foreign aid negotiator for the State Department during the years of the Marshall Plan just after the war, but left in 1948 to form his own law firm, where he remained until he was persuaded to join the Navy Department as director of procurement in 1963.

Rule's expert negotiating skills and mastery of contract law were quickly appreciated at the Pentagon, and he was given the Superior Civilian Service Award in 1967 (for "courage in challenging the status quo [and] absolute integrity") and the Distinguished Civilian Service Award, the navy's highest civilian decoration, in 1971 (for "extraordinary acumen, judgment, initiative and integrity"). He made a name for himself on Capitol Hill in the late 1960s as the only Pentagon official willing to testify openly about waste in naval procurement and against the expensive federal bailout of foundering military contractors, such as Lockheed. Such companies, he thought, should be allowed to go bankrupt. He was particularly outspoken in his criticism of some large contractors, especially Grumman Aircraft and Litton Industries, which habitually demanded hundreds of millions of dollars beyond every contract for purported cost overruns.

In 1972, when the Nixon Administration was trying to curb bureaucratic independence, Rule told a Senate subcommittee of the Joint Economic Committee, in response to a direct question, that Nixon's appointment of Roy L. Ash, president of Litton, to be director of the Office of Management and Budget was "a mistake." "Old General Eisenhower must be twitching in his grave," he said. "He was the one who first called attention to the so-called military-industrial complex, and I frankly think . . . it is almost a military-industrial-executive department complex." The following day, Rule's superior, Adm. Isaac C. Kidd, chief of the Naval Matériel Command, demanded that he sign a letter of resignation, which Rule refused to do. Although he could not be demoted, he was then immediately transferred, over loud protests from members of Congress, to a nonsensitive job 30 miles from Washington. He returned to his old Pentagon position after Nixon's downfall.

Rule lost a skirmish in 1976 with Adm. Hyman G. Rickover over what he insisted were built-in cost overruns in the contract to build the first Trident nuclear submarine, but was eventually proved right; the Trident lagged years behind schedule and was one of the most costly ships ever built. After his retirement in 1977 as chief of the navy's Procurement Control and Clearance Division, he continued to speak out against procurement waste. Only two months before his death of cancer, he attacked Defense Secretary Caspar Weinberger for ordering the Pershing II missile into production before testing had been completed. Here again he was vindicated: in its widely publicized but long-delayed first test, on 22 July 1982, the Pershing exploded 17 seconds after launching. A.K.

Married Margaret M. **Education** Western High Sch., Georgetown, DE; George Washington Univ., Wash. DC, LL.B. 1935, LL.M. and M.P.L. 1936. **Mil. service** Capt., USN 1942–46; deputy dir., then acting dir., Contract Div., Bureau of Ships, Korean War. **Career** Lawyer, Covington, Burling law firm, Wash. DC 1935–42, 1947; private law practice, Wash. DC 1948–63. • With U.S. Govt.: negotiator, State Dept. 1946–48; chief negotiator for Defense Dept. on U.S. bases in Europe under NATO agreement 1952–53; dir., Procurement Control and Clearance Div., Naval Matériel Command 1963–76; head, Contract Claims Control and Surveillance Group, USN 1969–71; consultant on procurement, Logistics Management School, USN 1972–74. **Member** Metropolitan Club, Wash. DC since 1940. **Honors** Commendation medal, Secty. of Navy, for Korean War service; Superior Civilian Service Award, USN 1967; Distinguished Civilian Service Award, USN 1971. **Author** *The Art of Negotiation,* 1962.

Further reading Brit Hume, "Admiral Kidd vs. Mister Rule," in *New York Times Magazine,* 25 Mar. 1973.

HENRY (JAYNES) FONDA
Actor
***Born* Grand Island, Nebraska, USA, 16 May 1905**
***Died* Los Angeles, California, USA, 12 August 1982**

Back in the days when Ronald Reagan was first running for the Republican nomination, Jack Warner encountered someone wearing a "Ronald Reagan for President" badge. The old movie mogul peered at the badge, shaking his head. "No, no, no," he growled. "Henry Fonda for the President. Ronald Reagan for his best friend."

Warner's casting instinct was sound. Over the years, Henry Fonda built up a screen, and stage, persona which embodied something near the theoretical ideal of an American president, possessed of all the quietly heroic virtues: a man of decency, integrity, and reason, stubbornly determined to uphold justice and do the right thing; slow to anger; aiming always to overcome his opponents by persuasion rather than force, if humanly possible. Quite early in his career, he had played *Young Mr. Lincoln;* by general consent, it remains the definitive performance.

There was a darker side which rarely appeared on screen, although he was occasionally cast in unsympathetic roles, and even—late in his career—as a villain. Four of his five marriages failed, and his second wife committed suicide. He was reputedly a harsh and difficult parent, emotionally repressed and remote. Fonda himself was fully aware of this dichotomy. "I don't really like myself. Never have. People mix me up with the characters I play." This may explain why he was only really happy, by his own admission, when he was working. "Acting to me is putting on a mask. The worst torture that can happen to me is not having a mask to get in back of."

Henry Jaynes Fonda was born in Grand Island, Nebraska, and grew up in Omaha, where his father owned a printing company. His early ambition was to be a writer; at the age of ten, he wrote a short story called "The Mouse," told from the mouse's point of view, which was published in a local newspaper. When he was 14 his father, a liberal, took him to witness the lynching of a black man, an experience that made a deep impression on the boy.

After graduating from Omaha Central High School in 1923, Fonda enrolled at the University of Minnesota to study journalism, taking part-time jobs to supplement his allowance. The routine proved too strenuous; after two years he dropped out and returned to Omaha, where a family friend, Dorothy Brando, mother of Marlon Brando, was helping to run the Community Playhouse. She persuaded the shy Fonda to audition for the juvenile lead in their current production, and to his surprise he found acting enjoyable. Taking the lead in *Merton of the Movies,* he later recalled, was "like being ten years old and playing cops and robbers." He stayed with the company for three seasons, doubling as assistant director, before leaving to try his luck in the East. In Falmouth, Massachusetts, he joined the newly formed University Players Guild. Among his fellow players were Joshua Logan, Bretaigne Windust, Mildred Natwick, Margaret Sullavan, and James Stewart.

At first, Fonda's acting skills were found less than impressive. "Bretaigne Windust told me, 'Let's face it, Hank. You're a scenic designer.' But I wanted to be an actor." He persisted, gradually getting better roles and an occasional walk-on part on Broadway. In 1931 he married Margaret Sullavan; they separated after two months, but remained on friendly terms. Fonda achieved fame in 1934, when he played the title role in *The Farmer Takes a Wife* on Broadway to laudatory notices, and signed a Hollywood contract with Walter Wanger. His first film (1935) was a screen version of his Broadway hit, with Janet Gaynor.

Fonda married his second wife, Frances Seymour Brokaw, in 1936. Their daughter Jane was born in 1937, and their son Peter in 1939.

The Trail of the Lonesome Pine (1936) was the first outdoor Technicolor film, and the first appearance of the Fonda persona, idealistic and quietly resolute. (His performance was the inspiration for Al Capp's Li'l Abner.) He was a criminal on the run in Fritz Lang's *You Only Live Once* (1937), a role he rendered totally sympathetic. Wanger had loaned him to Warners for that film, and he stayed there to squire Bette Davis in *That Certain Woman* (1937) and *Jezebel* (1938), in which he valiantly attempted a Southern accent.

Ironically, since he disliked guns and felt profoundly insecure about horses, many of Fonda's films were westerns. *Jesse James* (1939) was his first, as brother Frank (Tyrone Power played Jesse). Then he made his first film with John Ford, *Young Mr. Lincoln* (1939), and established himself as a star. The story line was trivial, but Fonda's performance exuded an unmistakable craggy authority. Two more films with Ford followed: *Drums Along the Mohawk* (1939), a handsome pioneer western, and *The Grapes of Wrath* (1940), from Steinbeck's novel of dispossessed migrants trekking to California. In the latter, as Tom Joad, Fonda brought to his performance an unpretentious nobility and emotional power which were—and are—intensely moving. He was nominated for an Academy Award, but the Oscar went to Jane Darwell, who played his mother.

Fonda was now at the peak of his career. Critics praised his performances for their sincerity and naturalness, commending the honesty of his portrayals. This naturalness was exactly what he was aiming for. "My goal is that the audience must never see the wheels go round, not see the work that goes into this. It must seem effortless and real."

In order to play Tom Joad, a part he greatly coveted, Fonda was obliged to sign a seven-year contract with Twentieth Century-Fox, a deal he came to regret. "I made all kinds of movies I hated. My gorge rises when I think of them." He was relieved to be loaned to Paramount for Preston Sturges's *The Lady Eve* (1940) with Barbara Stanwyck—a rare chance to play comedy, which he did with delicious solemnity. But after that his assignments were mediocre, or worse, until William Wellman's *The Ox-Bow Incident* (1943), which offered him a classic role as the sole protestor against a lynching. James Agee referred scathingly to "rigor artis," but most reviewers were enthusiastic.

Courtesy John Springer Associates, Inc.

Escaping to the navy, Fonda saw active service on board a destroyer in the Pacific, and was awarded a Bronze Star and Presidential Citation. He was discharged as a lieutenant, and returned to Hollywood to play Wyatt Earp in *My Darling Clementine* (1946), John Ford's radiant celebration of frontier mythology, built around the heroic serenity of Fonda's performance. He took the Jean Gabin role in *The Long Night* (1947), Anatole Litvak's ill-advised remake of Marcel Carné's *Le jour se lève,* and then played a priest in his only failure with Ford, *The Fugitive* (1947), a simpleminded version of *The Power and the Glory* by Graham Greene. For Ford again, he was cast against type as an inflexible martinet in *Fort Apache* (1948), a cavalry western, with John Wayne as his easygoing subordinate.

"The theatre was my first love. It was. It is." In 1948 Fonda turned his back on Hollywood and returned to Broadway and live theater, making no more films for seven years. "In the theatre, the actor does a complete job at each performance, inspired by the audience, whose response prevents his job from becoming tiresome. While in pictures the same director is the only audience and the sole judge of the performance. I prefer acting for a lot of different people rather than for one man." Joshua Logan's *Mister Roberts,* a comedy-drama set on a World War II supply vessel in the Pacific, opened on Broadway in February 1948 with Fonda in the title role. It proved a huge critical and popular success, and ran for years. Fonda stayed with it for 1,670 performances and "never got tired of it." In 1950, during the play's run, his wife Frances committed suicide in a sanitarium after suffering a nervous breakdown.

After *Mister Roberts,* Fonda starred in two more long-running hits, *Point of No Return* (1951) and *The Caine Mutiny Court Martial* (1954), the latter directed by Charles Laughton. He left this after a year in order to appear in the screen version of *Mister Roberts* (1955). It was his seventh film with John Ford, who had insisted on casting him in preference to William Holden or Marlon Brando. Ironically, they disagreed vehemently over interpretation, and finally came to blows. Ford, who was ill, handed the direction over to Mervyn Le Roy, and Fonda announced that he would never again work with the director of his finest pictures. The film was the hit of the year.

As Pierre in King Vidor's visually striking but culturally inept *War and Peace* (1956), Fonda was miscast, but he was the only cast member (as *Time* remarked) "who seemed to have read the book." He was ideally cast, though, as the wrongly accused innocent in Hitchcock's downbeat, documentary-style *The Wrong Man* (1957), and equally so in *Twelve Angry Men* (1957). This was Sidney Lumet's first film (produced by Fonda himself after seeing a TV version), in which he played the lone juror in a murder trial who gradually talks round the other 11. It was a critical success in Europe, but flopped in America, much to Fonda's disappointment, since he thought it one of the best things he had done. In retrospect, he was right.

From then on Fonda divided his career equally between films and stage work, plus some television. On Broadway, he had a year's run in *Two for the Seesaw* (1958), followed by leads in *Silent Night, Lonely Night* (1959), Ira Levin's *Critic's Choice* (1960), and Garson Kanin's *A Gift of Time* (1962). In the late 1950s he appeared in a western series for NBC-TV, "The Deputy." There was no shortage of film work, but roles of any substance were becoming rare. He was generally offered cameos as authority figures—politicians or police chiefs. He played a secretary of state in Preminger's *Advise and Consent* (1961); a presidential candidate in *The Best Man* (1964); and the president in Lumet's *Fail Safe* (1964), a thoughtful doomsday drama overshadowed by Kubrick's jokey *Dr. Strangelove*.

In 1965, Fonda married for the fifth and last time. His third marriage, to Susan Blanchard, and fourth, to Countess Afdera Franchetti, had both ended in divorce. During the 1960s, his relationship with his children came under strain; though politically liberal, he found himself out of sympathy with Jane's radicalism and Peter's identification with drug culture. There were no problems, though, with his daughter Amy, adopted during his third marriage. Fonda used to call her "the white sheep of the family."

He played the police chief to Widmark's honest cop in *Madigan* (1968)—a good film, but a minor role—and then made two interestingly offbeat westerns. Sergio Leone's *Once Upon a Time in the West* (1968) gave him the most villainous role of his career, gunning down defenseless nine-year-olds; he played it with relish, and the film was highly successful, especially with younger audiences. In Joseph L. Mankiewicz's cynical *There Was a Crooked Man* (1969) he was the prison governor, underplaying wittily against Kirk Douglas's cheerful rogue. For the rest of the 1970s, though, his films were unremarkable.

Courtesy of Harvard Theater Collection

Fonda's solo performance as the great liberal lawyer Clarence Darrow opened on tour in 1974 and then moved to Broadway, to great critical acclaim. Shortly before the end of the run, he collapsed in his dressing room with a heart attack. With a pacemaker installed, he returned to the show, transferring to Los Angeles and then to London. He had also undergone surgery for cancer, but continued to work without respite in plays, films, and television.

In 1981, Fonda received a special Academy Award, for his life's achievement. But his long-delayed best-actor Oscar finally came with his last film, his first good screen role in years, *On Golden Pond* (1981). As a crotchety old professor painfully coming to terms with his estranged daughter and his approaching death, Fonda was playing very close to home—a resemblance stressed by the casting of Jane Fonda as his film daughter. The dignity of his performance, and that of his co-star, Katharine Hepburn, rescued the film from what threatened to become gross sentimentality. He completed filming with difficulty, and was too ill to attend the Oscar ceremony. A few months later, he succumbed to chronic heart disease. P.K.

Parents William Brace F., print-shop owner, and Herberta (Jaynes) F. **Married** (1) Margaret Sullavan, actress, 1931 (div. 1933). (2) Frances Seymour Brokaw, socialite, 1936 (d. 1950): Jane, actress and political activist, b. 1937; Peter, actor, b. 1939. (3) Susan Blanchard, actress, 1950 (div. 1956): Amy. (4) Afdera Franchetti, countess, 1957 (div. 1962). (5) Shirlee Mae Adams, model, 1965. **Education** Omaha Central High Sch., grad. 1923; Univ. of Minnesota 1923–25; Navy Indoctrination Sch., Quonset, RI, and Quartermaster Sch., Naval Training Base, San Diego, CA WWII. **Mil. service** Quartermaster 3rd class and lt. (s.g.) with Air Combat Intelligence Office, U.S. Navy, Pacific 1942–45. **Career** Sports instr. at settlement house and troubleshooter for Northwestern Bell Telephone Co. 1923–25; actor and asst. dir., Omaha Community Playhouse 1925–28; actor, University Players, Falmouth, MA, summers 1928–32, Baltimore season 1931–32; professional stage actor since 1929; film and TV actor since 1935. **Member** Actors Equity; SAG. **Honors** Tony Award, for *Mister Roberts,* 1949; Bronze Star and presidential citation, WWII; award for outstanding performances of characters of truth and justice in the Amer. theater, Amer. Civil Liberties Union 1974; Life Achievement Award, Amer. Film Inst. 1978; special Tony Award 1979; hon. Oscar for career achievement 1981; Acad. Award for best actor, for *On Golden Pond,* 1982; hon. diploma from Lincoln Square Acad., NYC; hon. degrees from Ursinus Coll. and Nebraska Univ. **Stage** (all NYC unless otherwise noted) *The Game of Life and Death,* 1929; *I Loved You Wednesday,* 1932; *Forsaking All Others,* 1933; *New Faces,* 1933; *The Farmer Takes a Wife,* 1934; *Blow Ye Winds,* 1937; *Mister Roberts,* 1948; *Point of No Return,* 1951; *The Caine Mutiny Court Martial,* 1954; *Two for the Seesaw,* 1958; *Silent Night, Lonely Night,* 1959; *Critic's Choice,* 1960; *A Gift of Time,* 1962; *Generation,* 1965; (also dir.) *Our Town* and *The Front Page,* L.A. 1968; (dir.) *The Caine Mutiny Court Martial,* L.A. 1970; *Fathers Against Sons Against Fathers* (solo show), U.S. tour 1970–71; *The Time of Your Life,* L.A. 1971; *The Trial of A. Lincoln,* tour 1971; *Clarence Darrow* (solo show), U.S. tour 1974 and London 1975; *First Monday in October,* Wash. DC and NYC 1978; *The Oldest Living Graduate,* 1980. **Films** *The Farmer Takes a Wife,* 1935; *Way Down East,* 1935; *I Dream Too Much,* 1935; *The Trail of the Lonesome Pine,* 1936; *The Moon's Our Home,* 1936; *Spendthrift,* 1936; *You Only Live Once,* 1937; *Wings of Morning,* 1937; *Slim,* 1937; *That Certain Woman,* 1937; *Jezebel,* 1938; *I Met My Love Again,* 1938; *Blockade,* 1938;*The Mad Miss Manton,* 1938; *Spawn of the North,* 1938; *Jesse James,* 1939; *Let Us Live,* 1939; *The Story of Alexander Graham Bell,* 1939; *Young Mr. Lincoln,* 1939; *Drums Along the Mohawk,* 1940; *The Grapes of Wrath,* 1940; *Lillian Russell,* 1940; *The Return of Frank James,* 1940; *Chad Hanna,* 1940; *The Lady Eve,* 1940; *Wild Geese Calling,* 1941; *You Belong to Me,* 1941; *The Male Animal,* 1942; *Rings on Her Fingers,* 1942; *The Magnificent Dope,* 1942; *Tales of Manhattan,* 1942; *The Big Street,* 1942; *The Immortal Sergeant,* 1943; *The Ox-Bow Incident,* 1943; *My Darling Clementine,* 1946; *The Long Night,* 1947; *The Fugitive,* 1947; *Daisy Kenyon,* 1947; *A Miracle Can Happen,* 1948; *Fort Apache,* 1948; *Jigsaw,* 1948; *Mister Roberts,* 1955; *War and Peace,* 1956; *The Wrong Man,* 1957; *The Tin Star,* 1957; (also co-producer) *Twelve Angry Men,* 1957; *Stage Struck,* 1958; *Warlock,* 1959; *The Man Who Understood Women,* 1959; *Advise and Consent,* 1961; *Stranger on the Run,* 1962; *Spencer's Mountain,* 1962; *How the West Was Won,* 1963; *The Longest Day,* 1963; *Fail Safe,* 1964; *The Best Man,* 1964; *Sex and the Single Girl,* 1964; *The Rounders,* 1964; *The Battle of the Bulge,* 1965; *The Dirty Game,* 1966; *A Big Hand for the Little Lady,* 1966; *Welcome to Hard Times,* 1967; *Firecreek,* 1968; *Yours, Mine, and Ours,* 1968; *Madigan,* 1968; *The Boston Strangler,* 1968; *Once Upon a Time in the West,* 1968; *Too Late the Hero,* 1969; *There Was a Crooked Man,* 1969; *The Cheyenne Social Club,* 1969; *Sometimes a*

Great Notion, 1970; *The Serpent,* 1972; *Ash Wednesday,* 1973; *The Last Days of Mussolini,* 1974; *My Name Is Nobody,* 1974; *Midway,* 1976; *Rollercoaster,* 1977; *Tentacles,* 1977; *The Great Smoky Roadblock,* 1977; *The Swarm,* 1978; *Fedora,* 1978; *Meteor,* 1978; *The Greatest Battle,* 1978; *City on Fire,* 1979; *On Golden Pond,* 1981. **Television** "The Deputy" (series), NBC 1959–60; "The Good Years," 1962; "The Smith Family" (series), ABC 1971–72; "The Red Pony," 1973; "America's Romance with the Land," 1973; "Clarence Darrow," 1974; "Collision Course," 1976; "The Fonda Legacy," 1976; "Home to Stay," 1978; "The Henry Fonda AFI Special," 1978; "The Oldest Living Graduate," 1980; "Gideon's Trumpet," 1980; "Summer Solstice," 1981; "America and Americans"; "Travels with Charley"; others. **Exhibitions** (With Henry Miller) Windsor Gall., Beverly Hills, CA 1974; guest artist, Los Angeles City Fedn. of Labor Exhibition, California Mus. of Art and Industry 1974. **Author** (Jtly.) *My Life,* 1981.

Further reading Lillian and Helen Ross, *The Player,* 1962; John Springer, *The Fondas,* 1970.

SALVADOR SÁNCHEZ
Boxer
Born **Santiago Tianguistenco, Mexico, 26 January 1959**
Died **Querétaro, Mexico, 12 August 1982**

Salvador Sánchez, the World Boxing Council featherweight champion, was 23 years old and in the prime of his career when he was killed in an automobile crash. Sánchez had a career record of 43 wins, one loss, and one draw. He gained the featherweight title by defeating Danny (Little Red) Lopez in early 1980.

Born to a family of 11 children in the small town of Santiago Tianguistenco, near Mexico City, where his father owned a construction company, Sánchez started fighting as a schoolboy. "Trouble would start when the other guys would look me over and see how little I was and then steal my books and pencils," he recalled. "I could take that but when they began to call me *niña* or little girl then I would have to show them I had the tools. . . . I liked to defend myself. I also like to hit others. Sure, sure, mostly to hit others."

At the age of 16, after two years as an amateur boxer during which he was undefeated in 14 bouts, Sánchez left school and turned professional, despite the disapproval of his family. He was an aggressive fighter but not a showy one, playing on his opponent's weaknesses and wearing him down rather than trying for a knockout in the early rounds. With a Mexico City lawyer as his manager and his own physician as his trainer, Sánchez compiled a record of 32–1–1 by February 1980, when he challenged Lopez for the WBC featherweight crown and knocked him out in the thirteenth round. He successfully defended his title against nine challenges, one of them a rematch with Lopez, who retired from boxing after Sánchez knocked him out again in the

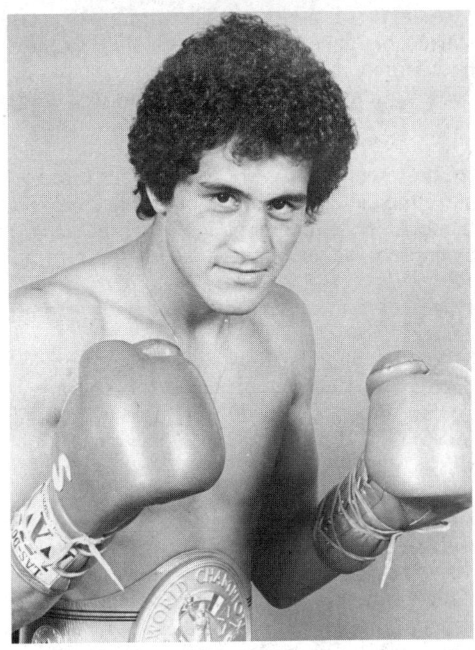

Courtesy of Hollis Stein

fourteenth round. In August 1981 he knocked out Wilfredo Gómez, the previously undefeated superbantamweight champion who had moved up to the featherweight division, and in July 1982 he knocked out Azumah Nelson of Ghana. His earnings from boxing, reportedly about $2 million, were invested in real estate, securities, and a fleet of expensive automobiles.

Sánchez, who was married and had two infant sons, expected to retire from boxing at the end of 1983 and had mentioned an interest in studying medicine. He was training in Mexico for an upcoming bout with Juan LaPorte when his Porsche 928 collided with a truck early in the morning of 12 August. J.R.

Father Felipe, owner of construction co. **Married** Maria Teresa: Cristián Salvador, b. 1981; Omar, b. 1982. **Education** Schs. in Santiago Tianguistenco, Mexico, left at age 16. **Career** Amateur boxing 1973–75; professional boxer since 1975; World Boxing Council featherweight champion since 1980.

CHARLES WALTERS

Film director and choreographer
Born **Pasadena, California, USA, 17 November 1911**
Died **Malibu, California, USA, 13 August 1982**

Though never as well known as his MGM colleagues Vincente Minnelli, Busby Berkeley, Gene Kelly, and Stanley Donen, Charles Walters directed movie musicals whose lightheartedness and verve made them classics of the genre. A dancer himself, he made use of crane shots and tracking shots to produce the physical sensation of movement in the audience.

A native of Pasadena and a graduate of the University of Southern California, Walters started his dancing career with the Fanchon and Marco road shows. He soon arrived in New York and appeared in a series of Broadway shows, the last of them *Du Barry Was a Lady* (1939). When *Du Barry* was transferred to the screen by MGM, Walters was hired to stage the dance sequences for Lucille Ball and Gene Kelly. Other films for which he served as choreographer in the next few years were *Presenting Lily Mars* (1943), *Girl Crazy* (1943), *Meet Me in St. Louis* (1944), and *Ziegfeld Follies* (1946).

After Walters had acquired some experience photographing his own choreography, Arthur Freed, his producer at MGM, tried him out as a director on *Good News* in 1947. It was a hit, and Walters was given *Easter Parade,* with Judy Garland, Fred Astaire, and Ann Miller, and *The Barkleys of Broadway,* with Astaire and Ginger Rogers, for his next assignments. During his 19 years as an MGM director, he made 20 movies, some of them straight dramas and comedies *(The Tender Trap* [1955], *Don't Go Near the Water* [1957], *Ask Any Girl* [1959], *Please Don't Eat the Daisies* [1961]) but most of them airy, tuneful musicals *(Three Guys Named Mike* [1951], *Dangerous When Wet, Lili,* and *Torch Song* [all 1953], *Billy Rose's Jumbo* [1962]). Walters had a particularly close relationship with Judy Garland, whom he directed in *Good News, Easter Parade, Summer Stock* (1950; U.K. title *If You Feel Like Singing),* and *High Society* (1957). In 1951 he staged and danced in her famous show at the Palace in Los Angeles.

Walters had the rare ability to choreograph for the camera as well as the dancers. He began *Easter Parade* with a long tracking shot that follows Fred Astaire's feet through the streets of New York and into a shop for the first dance number, "Drum Crazy." He could create a feeling of intimacy for a quiet solo by having the camera circle in from behind like a sympathetic eavesdropper, as in Debbie Reynolds's "Little Girl Blue" solo in *Jumbo,* or send the audience sailing through a window from outside, as he did in *Summer Stock.* "What makes a Walters musical different," wrote John Kobal in his book *Gotta Sing! Gotta Dance!,* "is an intuitive sense of rhythm, which controls the picture from the shooting, through the cutting stages." The result, even when the script was weak or the star miscast, was an exuberant piece of entertainment with the air of complete spontaneity.

Walters's last film for MGM was *The Unsinkable Molly Brown,* with Shirley MacLaine, in 1964. He left the studio the same

year, displeased by the attitude of a new group of executives who showed no appreciation for the fine art of the movie musical. After making *Walk, Don't Run* for Columbia—it was Cary Grant's last film as well—he went into retirement. In the 1970s he directed situation comedies and two Lucille Ball specials for television. He died at the age of 70 of mesothelioma, a rare lung cancer. C.M.

Child Joseph (adopted). **Education** Univ. of Southern California. **Career** Dancer, with Fanchon and Marco stage shows 1934–39, with dance team at Versailles Club 1935; dancer in and dir. of stage musicals, NYC 1939–42; choreographer 1942–47 and film dir. 1947–66, MGM, Hollywood; dir., Columbia Pictures, Hollywood 1966; guest lectr. in directing, Univ. of Southern California 1980. **Stage dancer** *The Tale of the Wolf,* 1925; *Strange Interlude,* 1928; *No More Frontier,* 1931; *Musical Parade,* 1935; *Jubilee,* 1935; *So Proudly We Hail,* 1936; *The Show Is On,* 1936; *Between the Devil,* 1937; *I Married an Angel,* 1938; *Du Barry Was a Lady,* 1939; (also choreographer) Judy Garland Show, L.A. 1951. **Stage director** *Let's Face It,* 1941; *Banjo Eyes,* 1941; *St. Louis Woman,* 1946. **Film choreographer** *Seven Days Leave,* 1942; *Presenting Lily Mars,* 1943; *Du Barry Was a Lady,* 1943; *Girl Crazy,* 1943; *Best Foot Forward,* 1943; *Broadway Rhythm,* 1944; *Meet Me in St. Louis,* 1944; *The Harvey Girls,* 1945; *Ziegfeld Follies,* 1946; *Summer Holiday,* 1947. **Film director** *Good News,* 1947; *Easter Parade,* 1948; *The Barkleys of Broadway,* 1949; *Summer Stock* (in U.K. as *If You Feel Like Singing),* 1950; *Three Guys Named Mike,* 1951; *Texas Carnival,* 1951; *The Belle of New York,* 1952; *Dangerous When Wet,* 1953; *Lili,* 1953; *Torch Song,* 1953; *Easy to Love,* 1953; *The Glass Slipper,* 1955; *The Tender Trap,* 1955; *High Society,* 1956; *Don't Go Near the Water,* 1957; *Ask Any Girl,* 1959; *Please Don't Eat the Daisies,* 1960; *Two Loves/Springtime,* 1961; *Billy Rose's Jumbo,* 1962; *The Unsinkable Molly Brown,* 1964; *Walk, Don't Run,* 1966. **Television director** "Here's Lucy"; "The Governor and J.J."; two Lucille Ball specials. **Interview** John Cutts, "On the Bright Side: An Interview with Charles Walters," in *Films and Filming,* Aug. 1970.

Further reading Douglas McVay, "Charles Walters: A Case for Reassessment," in *Focus on Film,* no. 27, 1977.

PATRICK MAGEE
Actor
Born **Armagh, Northern Ireland, 1926**
Died **London, England, 14 August 1982**

The Irish-born actor Patrick Magee, a player in some of the Royal Shakespeare Company's most adventurous productions, possessed an unusual voice that was described by a *New Statesman* drama critic as "a strange, sandpapery wail." "Once you have fallen victim to it," wrote Harold Hobson in the *Sunday Times* of London, "you will never escape. There is something unearthly about it." Hearing this voice for the first time in 1957, when Magee

Courtesy of Zoë Dominic

performed in a radio broadcast of his play *All That Fall,* the existentialist playwright Samuel Beckett was astonished to discover that it was the same voice in which he imagined his male characters speaking. Magee became one of the best interpreters of Beckett's tortured, fragmented dramas, and Beckett wrote a number of works for him, notably *Krapp's Last Tape.* His other major roles included the Marquis de Sade in the stage and film versions of Peter Weiss's *Marat/Sade* and McCann in the stage and film versions of Harold Pinter's *The Birthday Party.*

Magee grew up in Armagh, Northern Ireland, and learned acting as an apprentice with a touring company led by Anew McMaster, after which he joined the Northern Ireland Festival Company. He made his London debut in a production of Eugene O'Neill's *The Iceman Cometh* in 1958. That was also the year in which he performed *Krapp's Last Tape,* a one-act play in which an old man listens to the taped reminiscences of his younger self. The following year he was in *Embers,* a radio play that Beckett wrote for him and actor Jack MacGowran. He played Words in Beckett's *Words and Music* (1961), then the blind cripple Hamm in a 1963 Paris production of *Endgame,* repeating the role in London in 1964 after he joined the Royal Shakespeare Company. Later in the season he appeared in *The Birthday Party* and David Rudkin's *Afore Night Come.*

In 1965 the Royal Shakespeare Company mounted Peter Brooks's production of *Marat/Sade,* one of the most controversial and powerful plays in modern theater history. As the Marquis de Sade, who directs the inmates of the insane asylum in which he is confined in a play about the murder by Charlotte Corday of the Jacobin Marat, Magee was cold, intense, elegant, and defiantly egoistic. He won a Tony Award when the play was moved to Broadway later in the year. The film version came out in 1967, by which time he had gone on to play Matti in Brecht's *Puntila,* Schwitter in Dürrenmatt's *The Meteor,* Leeds in *Staircase* opposite Paul Scofield, and Frank Brady in *Keep It in the Family* in New York. During the 1970s he returned to Beckett twice, as the sole character in the autobiographical *That Time* (1974), written for him by Beckett, and as Hamm in a production of *Endgame* given as part of a Beckett festival at the Royal Court (1976). He also gave a much-praised solo show of readings from Beckett's prose works in 1975.

Magee entered films in 1960 and made nearly 40, including *Seance on a Wet Afternoon* (1964), *The Birthday Party* (1968), and two Stanley Kubrick films, *A Clockwork Orange* (1971) and *Barry Lyndon* (1975); generally he was cast in roles that required more than a touch of subtle malice. His last film appearance was in *Chariots of Fire* in 1981. In 1980 he was a world-weary Mephistopheles in a London stage production of Marlowe's *Dr. Faustus,* and in 1981 played the lead in Brian Friel's *Faith Healer.* He was 56 when he died.

C.M.

Married Isabel: twin children. **Education** St. Patrick's Coll., Armagh, Northern Ireland. **Career** Apprentice actor, Anew McMaster's stage troupe, and actor with Northern Ireland Festival Co., 1950s; assoc. artist, Royal Shakespeare Co., London since 1964; in films since 1960; also in TV and radio. **Honors** Tony Award, for *Marat/Sade,* 1965. **Stage** (all London except as noted) *The Iceman Cometh,* 1958; *Krapp's Last Tape,* 1958; *The Buskers,* 1959; *Cock-A-Doodle-Dandy,* 1959; *A Whistle in the Dark,* 1961; *Words and Music,* 1961; *Endgame,* Paris 1963, London 1964 and 1976; *The Birthday Party,* 1964; *Afore Night Come,* 1964; *Marat/Sade,* London and NYC 1965; *Squire Puntila and his Servant Matti,* 1965;

Hamlet, Stratford 1965; *The Meteor,* 1966; *Staircase,* 1966; *Keep It in the Family,* NYC 1967; *Dutch Uncle,* 1969; *The Battle of Shrivings,* 1970; *A Touch of the Poet,* Brighton 1970; *The Rough Field,* 1973; *The Master Builder,* 1974; *That Time,* 1974; *Beckett Evening,* 1975; *The White Devil,* 1976; *Dr. Faustus,* 1980; *The Faith Healer,* 1981; others. **Films** *The Criminal,* 1960; *Never Back Losers,* 1961; *Rag Doll,* 1961; *The Boys,* 1962; *A Prize of Arms,* 1962; *The Servant,* 1963; *Dementia 13,* 1963; *The Young Racers,* 1963; *Ricochet,* 1963; *The Very Edge,* 1963; *Zulu,* 1964; *Masque of the Red Death,* 1964; *Seance on a Wet Afternoon,* 1964; *The Skull,* 1965; *Monster of Terror,* 1965; *Marat/Sade,* 1967; *Decline and Fall,* 1968; *The Birthday Party,* 1968; *Hard Contract,* 1969; *King Lear,* 1970; *Cromwell,* 1970; *You Can't Win Them All,* 1971; *The Fiend,* 1971; *A Clockwork Orange,* 1971; *The Trojan Women,* 1971; *Young Winston,* 1972; *Asylum,* 1972; *Pope Joan,* 1972; *Beware of the Brethren,* 1972; *Lady Ice,* 1973; *And Now the Screaming Starts,* 1973; *The Final Programme,* 1974; *Luther,* 1974; *Demons of the Mind,* 1974; *Galileo,* 1975; *Barry Lyndon,* 1975; *Telefon,* 1977; *Rough Cut,* 1980; *Sir Henry at Rawlinson's End,* 1980; *Chariots of Fire,* 1981; others. **Television** "Who Pays the Ferryman"; "You Never Can Tell"; "Churchill and the Generals"; "The Greeks"; "Kidnapped"; "The Flip Side of Dominic Hyde"; "Horace." **Radio plays** *All That Fall,* 1957; *Embers,* 1959; also broadcasts of readings of works by Beckett.

Courtesy of NEMS Management

Further reading Deirdre Bair, *Samuel Beckett: A Biography,* 1977.

ERNIE BUSHMILLER
Cartoonist
***Born* New York City, USA, 23 August 1905**
***Died* Stamford, Connecticut, USA, 15 August 1982**

Nancy, for four decades one of the most popular of newspaper comic strips, was the creation of veteran cartoonist Ernie Bushmiller. Carried in some 600 newspapers daily, it features the antics of a round-faced, cheerful little girl, her aunt Fritzi, and her friend Sluggo. Simply drawn, with plain backgrounds, little dialogue, and a dependence on crude sight gags, it was scorned by sophisticated comics aficionados, but every suggestion to newspaper editors that it be replaced with something more interesting was invariably met with outrage by its many fans, not all of whom are children.

A native of the Bronx, Bushmiller went to work right out of grammar school as a copy boy for the now defunct *New York Evening World* newspaper, where he soon became an illustrator. He got first-hand instruction in cartooning by observing Milt Gross, Rudolph Dirks, and other top comic-strip artists at the *World*'s offices, meanwhile taking night classes at the National Academy of Design. In 1925 he took over *Fritzie Ritz,* a strip about an adventurous flapper, from Larry Whittington, and showed such expertise as a visual gagman that comedian Harold Lloyd brought him out to Hollywood for a year to write material for his films.

In 1931 the *World* folded and *Fritzi Ritz* was taken over by the United Feature Syndicate. Nancy, Fritzi's niece, was introduced as a peripheral character in the mid-1930s and quickly eclipsed Fritzi in popularity. In 1940 Bushmiller gave her her own comic strip, which was an immediate success. *Fritzi Ritz* was absorbed by *Nancy* soon after. Collections of *Nancy* strips are published monthly.

Bushmiller moved to Stamford, Connecticut, in the late 1950s. The National Cartoonists Society named him its cartoonist of the year in 1978. He continued to draw seven

© 1982, United Features Syndicate, Inc.

© 1982, United Feature Syndicate, Inc.

strips a week until his death at the age of 76. *Nancy,* drawn by other artists, continues in syndication. S.A.

Parents Ernest George B. and Elizabeth (Hall) B. **Married** Abby Bohnet 1930. **Education** Public schs., NYC; Natl. Acad. of Dcsign, NYC 1920s. **Career** Copy boy and illus., *Red Magic* mag. supplement ca. 1919–25, and cartoonist, *Fritzi Ritz* comic strip 1925–31, *New York Evening World;* comedy writer for Harold Lloyd, Hollywood, CA 1920s; cartoonist for *New York Graphic,* other newspapers 1930s; cartoonist, *Fritzi Ritz* 1931–38, *Phil Fumble* 1930s, and *Nancy* since 1940, United Feature Syndicate. **Member** Soc. of Illustrators; Natl. Cartoonists Soc.; advisory bd., Salvation Army; Artists and Writers Assn.; Dutch Treat Club; Banshees Club. **Honors** Cartoonist of year, Natl. Cartoonists Soc. 1978.

(AXEL) HUGO (TEODOR) THEORELL

Biochemist

***Born* Linköping, Sweden, 6 July 1903**

***Died* Stockholm, Sweden, 16 August 1982**

Forced to abandon his career as a doctor after he was partially paralyzed by an attack of polio, Hugh Theorell became a scientific researcher. Under the Nobel Prize-winning biochemist Otto Warburg, he began a four-decade study of enzymes, those substances that make life possible by speeding the chemical reactions of the cell. His discoveries concerning oxidation enzymes were basic to the elucidation of the chemistry of cellular metabolism and won him the Nobel Prize in physiology or medicine in 1955.

Theorell, the son of a Swedish military surgeon, completed secondary school in Linköping in 1921, then moved to Stockholm to study medicine at the Karolinska Medico-Surgical Institute, from which he took his bachelor's degree in 1924. After three months' study of bacteriology at the Pasteur Institute in Paris, he joined Stockholm's Institute of Medical Chemistry, where he discovered in 1926 that blood plasma contains lipoproteins.

Before he had completed his M.D. degree, Theorell was stricken with polio in both legs. After many months, he learned to walk again, albeit with difficulty. Only by obtaining special permission from the Swedish government (there were strict legal definitions of the physical fitness required of medical doctors) was Theorell able to defend his thesis and earn his M.D. in 1930. Later that year he was appointed a lecturer in physiological chemistry at the Karolinska Institute.

At the Institute of Physical Chemistry of the University of Uppsala Theorell began to study the red muscle protein myoglobin. He determined its molecular weight by spinning it in the ultracentrifuge recently invented by the institute's director, The Svedberg. By 1932, Theorell had obtained such pure samples of myoglobin that he was able to crystallize it for the first time. Observing its reactions with oxygen and carbon monoxide, he concluded that myoglobin acts as an oxygen reservoir, a source of the "second wind" we experience during physical exertion.

In 1933, Theorell joined the laboratory of Otto Warburg and Walter Christian at Berlin-Dahlem on a Rockefeller Fellowship. Warburg and Christian had recently discovered a yellow enzyme in yeast that catalyzes a stage in the breakdown of glucose, thus clearly playing a part in oxidation, the process by which cells use oxygen to produce energy from food. They were able to determine that an essential part of the enzyme was a small yellow flavinoid pigment—it was, in fact, riboflavin, a B vitamin—but the nature of the remainder of the enzyme remained unknown. Theorell set out to clarify its composition through electrophoresis, a separation process then being developed at Uppsala, in which an electric current is passed through a conducting liquid, causing dissolved ions (electrically charged particles) to be attracted to the electrode of opposite charge. He devised a method for scooping up the ions once they had become separated, and in 1934 succeeded in purifying and crystallizing the enzyme.

Theorell then gently separated the enzyme into two parts. He found that the larger portion is a protein—reinforcing the growing suspicion that all enzymes are proteins—and that the smaller, yellow portion is a modified riboflavin attached to a phosphate group. This component, later named flavin mononucleotide, was the first coenzyme to be clearly defined. Neither the protein nor the coenzyme by itself is capable of a chemical reaction, but when Theorell joined the split sections together again, the enzyme regained its function. Theorell further demonstrated that the coenzyme's phosphate group served to link it to the protein, and that two particular nitrogen atoms on the flavin made up the enzyme's active site. Many coenzyme-protein partnerships were discovered in the following years using Theorell's reversible splitting technique, and other B vitamins besides riboflavin were eventually shown to be present in coenzymes.

Impressed by Theorell's achievements, which occurred within a 15-month period, the usually critical Warburg bestowed on him the epithet of "the master of enzyme research." Soon after his return to Stockholm in 1936, the Nobel Foundation established a research institute in biochemistry of which he served as director until 1970, conducting studies on a variety of oxidation and reduction enzymes.

One subject of investigation was cytochrome c, which, like hemoglobin and myoglobin, was known to contain both protein and a heme, a molecular structure consisting of iron and a porphyrin ring. By 1938 Theorell had shown that the porphyrin and protein were chemically linked in two places, accounting for the molecule's stability. Many other proteins were subsequently shown to have such "prosthetic groups" (firmly attached coenzymes). Theorell resumed his study of cytochrome c with Anders Ehrenberg during the 1950s. In 1955 they suggested that an atom of iron lay at the center of the molecule within the porphyrin ring, with the helical chains of the protein surrounding this core. The iron atom was centrally located, they believed, to protect it from oxidizing agents. Later x-ray studies of the molecule's shape confirmed Theorell's model.

Courtesy of Nobel Foundation

His main activity after World War II was the study of alcohol dehydrogenases, which play a vital part in the metabolism of alcohol. In 1948, workers at the institute crystallized alcohol dehydrogenase from horse liver. The researchers were puzzled by its presence, since horses do not drink alcohol. Decades passed before other scientists discovered that the intestines of all mammals constantly produce small amounts of alcohol from sugar.

Describing the chemical action of hydrogenase proved to be difficult. Enzymes are quite specific, causing only certain chemicals to react. However, as Theorell showed, if they catalyze a particular reaction, they will also catalyze its reverse. This is the case with alcohol dehydrogenase, which helps yeast cells make alcohol from aldehyde and assists liver cells to oxidize alcohol to aldehyde. The direction in which a reaction proceeds depends on such factors as the speed of the reaction and the presence of other enzymes in the metabolic chain. To add to the complexity of the situation, alcohol dehydrogenase contains a protein and a coenzyme, while the coenzyme and the substance acted on can occur in both oxidized and reduced forms.

In 1946, Theorell was joined by Britton Chance of the Johnson Research Foundation at the University of Pennsylvania, who had developed sensitive spectrophotometric equipment suitable for observing enzyme reactions in living cells. By the early 1950s, the chemical equations and reaction speeds had been completely worked out for the liver enzyme and much had been learned about the yeast enzyme. The mode of action of alcohol dehydrogenase is still referred to as the Theorell-Chance mechanism. A sidelight of this work was the development of a highly specific test for measuring blood-alcohol content, which was adopted by Swedish and West German law-enforcement agencies.

After receiving the Nobel Prize in 1955, Theorell continued to work on the metabolism of alcohol. In 1963, his team began to use the synthetic compound pyrazole to inhibit the activity of alcohol dehydrogenase, which by then had been studied more thoroughly than any similar substance. With the enzyme temporarily out of action, the alcohol in the system was slowly broken down by catalase, another enzyme. This technique showed some promise as a medical treatment for reducing the danger of cirrhosis in alcoholics, although the researchers feared that longer persistence of alcohol in the bloodstream might injure other organs.

As he neared retirement, Theorell served tenures as president of both the Swedish Royal Academy of Science and the International Union of Biochemistry; he was also head of the Stockholm Philharmonic and Academic Orchestra societies. In the early 1970s he joined a group of distinguished scientists to warn of the dangers posed to the body by constant exposure to drugs, pesticides, food additives, and other chemicals. He died at the age of 79; his autobiography, published in 1977, has not yet been translated into English.

P.D.

Parents Ture T., military physician, and Armida (Bill) T. **Married** Margit Alenius, musician and harpsichord teacher, 1931: three sons. **Education** Linköping State Secondary Sch., grad. 1921; Pasteur Inst., Paris 1924; Karolinska Medico-Surgical Inst., Stockholm, bachelor of medicine 1924, M.D. 1930. **Career** With Karolinska Inst.: assoc. asst. and asst. 1924–28; temporary assoc. prof. 1928–29; docent and lectr. in physiology and chemistry 1930–32; researcher, Chemical Inst. 1936. • Asst. prof. of biochemistry, Univ. of Uppsala 1932–36; research asst., Kaiser Wilhelm Inst. für Zellphysiologie, Berlin-Dahlem ca. 1933–35; founding dir. and prof., dept. of biochemistry 1936–70, and prof. emeritus since 1970, Nobel Medical Inst., Stockholm; chief ed., *Nordisk Medicin* jrnl. since 1954. **Officer** Secty. gen. 1940–45, and chmn. 1946–47 and 1957–58, Swedish Soc. of Physicians and Surgeons. • Chmn.: Swedish Chemists' Assn. 1947–49; Stockholm Philharmonic Soc. 1951–73; Wenner-Gren Soc.; bd. of dirs., Wenner-Gren Center Foundn.; Bergvall Foundn.; Stockholm Concert Soc.; Mazer Quartet Soc.; Academic Orchestra Soc., Stockholm. • Pres.: Intl. Union of Biochemistry 1967–73; Swedish Royal Acad. of Science 1967–69. **Fellow** Royal Soc. since 1959. **Member** State Research Center for Natural Sciences, Sweden 1950–54; State Research Center for Medical Science 1958–64; Royal Soc. of Sciences, Uppsala; Swedish Soc. of Medical Research; Swedish Acad. of Engineering Science; Royal Acad. of Music; Royal Danish Acad. of Arts and Letters; Norwegian Acad. of Science and Letters; Royal Norwegian Soc. of Arts and Sciences; Amer. Acad. of Arts and Sciences; (assoc.) Natl. Acad. of Sciences, Wash. DC; Amer. Philosophical Soc., Phila.; New York Acad. of Sciences; Acad. Nazionale dei Quaranta, Rome; Polish Acad. Nauk, Warsaw; Indian Acad. of Sciences; Belgian Medical Acad.; Acad. Royale de Belgique; Bayerische Akad. der Wissenschaften; Leopoldina Acad., Halle. **Honors** Rockefeller Foundn. grants 1932, 1940s; Jubilee Prize, Swedish Medical Soc. 1935; Björkén Prize 1938; Trafvenfeldt Gold Medal 1947; Dubb Medal 1948; Pasteur Medal, Soc. de Chimie Biologique, Paris 1948; Alvarenga Prize 1951; Nobel Prize in physiology or medicine 1955; Scheele Medal, Swedish Biological Soc. 1958; hon. member, Swedish Soc. of Physicians and Surgeons 1958; Jubilee Medal, Karolinska Inst. 1960; comdr., Légion d'Honneur, France 1962; officer, Order of the Southern Cross, Brazil 1962; Paterno Medal, Italian Chemical Soc. 1962; comdr., Royal Norwegian Order of St. Olav 1963; Karrer Medal, 1965; comdr., 1st Class, Order of the North Star 1966 and Order of the Finnish Lion 1967, Finland; Ciba Medal 1971; Semmelweiss Medal, Budapest 1971; tercentenary gold medal, Swedish Soc. of Physicians; hon. member, Soc. de Chimie Biologique; hon. degrees from univs. of Sorbonne, Louvain, Brazil, Pennsylvania, Michigan, Kentucky, and Libre, Brussels. **Contributor** of more than 220 papers on protein analysis and synthesis to scientific jrnls.

Further reading C.W. Carter et al., *Biochemistry in Relation to Medicine,* 1959; *Nobel Lectures, Physiology or Medicine, 1942-1962,* 1963; Dorothy M. Needham, *Machina Carnis,* 1971.

RUTH FIRST
Writer and revolutionary
Born Johannesburg, South Africa, 1925
Died Maputo, Mozambique, 17 August 1982

Dr. Ruth First was a brilliant and unrelenting opponent of the Afrikaner Nationalist regime that has run South Africa since 1948. As a sociologist, lecturer, widely published writer, and political activist, she was for 35 years an effective crusader against apartheid and became a prime irritant to the all-powerful South African Bureau of State Security, which was almost certainly responsible for her murder.

Born to Jewish immigrants from the Baltic states who were members of the International Socialist League, she was educated at the University of the Witwatersrand, where she joined the Communist Party. She was also secretary of the Young Communist League and the Progressive Youth Council.

During the widespread mine strike in 1946, First was one of the most active whites in the black cause, and served for a time as secretary of the Communists' central offices in Johannesburg. She became an editor for a succession of radical periodicals, including the *Guardian* and the *New Age,* both eventually banned, and *Fighting Talk,* a literary magazine. In 1947, she helped expose the appalling oppression on the farms of Bethal, where the condition of the African workers was little better than slavery.

She married in 1949 Joe Slovo, a lawyer and labor organizer and, like her, a Communist. They were defendants, along with many others, at the notorious Treason Trial of 1956, at which, despite the feverish efforts of the prosecution and much perjured evidence by government witnesses, all were acquitted. Their home was a central meeting place for radical South Africans, black as well as white, and they counted among their close friends Walter Sisulu and Nelson Mandela, leaders of the African National Congress, a banned organization of which the Slovos were among the few white members.

In 1963, First was arrested and held in solitary confinement without trial for 117 days under the so-called 90-Day detention law. On her release she immediately left South Africa with her family, never to return. Her book, *117 Days* (1965), is an account of her arrest and interrogation. The family settled in North London, and from 1973 for six years she lectured at Durham University on the sociology of underdevelopment.

In 1979 she went to the Eduardo Mondlane University in Maputo, Mozambique, on a year's sabbatical to study the lives of Mozambican migrant laborers, particularly the miners who leave their villages to endure the hardships of the South African gold and diamond mines. *The Mozambique Miner,* the results of her study, will be published in 1983. She was persuaded to remain in Maputo at the Center for African Studies of the university, and was in her office there when she opened the letter bomb that killed her on 17 August. The South African government denied any involvement in her death, but there is no doubt of Pretoria's guilt in the minds of most informed observers. Several other African National Congress members in exile have met violent deaths in similar fashion.

Among First's published works were *South West Africa* (1963), *The South African Connection: Western Involvement in Apartheid* (1973), and *Libya: The Elusive Revolution* (1974). In 1980 she published, with co-author Ann Scott, a universally praised biography of Olive Schreiner, the early twentieth-century Boer author of *Story of an African Farm.*

A.K.

Parents Julius F., furniture manufacturer, and Matilda F. **Married** Joe Slovo, advocate, 1949: Shawn; Gillian; Robyn. **Religion** None professed; of Jewish birth. **Emigration** In exile since 1964; deported from Kenya 1964; lived in U.K. and Mozambique. **Education** Univ. of Witwatersrand, B.A. **Career** Joined Communist Party of South Africa as student, later secty. of Johannesburg Office; secty., Young Communist League and Progressive Youth Council; member, African Natl. Congress of South Africa; ed. 1940s–60s of a succession of periodicals, including *Fighting Talk, Spark, The Guardian* (Johannesburg ed.), and *New Age* (Transvaal ed.); tried for high treason 1956, acquitted 1958; arrested and held in solitary confinement for 3 months, 1963; Simon Research Fellow, Univ. of Manchester 1972–73; lectr. in sociology of underdevelopment, Univ. of Durham 1973–80; dir. of research, Centre of African Studies, Eduardo Mondlane Univ., Maputo, Mozambique since 1979. **Author** (Co-ed.) *South West Africa: Travesty of Trust,* 1963; *117 Days,* 1965; *The Barrel of a Gun: A Study of Military Rule in Africa* (in U.S. as *Power in Africa: The Politics of Coup d'Etat),* 1970; (jtly.) *The South African Connection: Western Involvement in Apartheid,* 1972; *Libya: The Elusive Revolution,* 1974; (jtly.) *Olive Schreiner,* 1981; *Black Gold: The Mozambican Miner, Proletarian and Peasant,* 1983. **Contributor** to *Ramparts, New Statesman, International Affairs,* other jrnls. and mags.

LORD CROMWELL
David Godfrey Bewicke-Copley
Senior government broker
***Born* England, 29 May 1929**
***Died* Coventry, West Midlands, England, 18 August 1982**

As senior government broker, Lord Cromwell advised the British government and the Bank of England on how best to finance the national debt through the sale and purchase of stock and securities on the London Stock Exchange. Although he occupied this important office for only a little over a year before dying of injuries sustained during a riding accident, Cromwell is credited with introducing new stock-selling methods that enabled the government to get a consistently favorable rate on its transactions, thus reducing government expenditures.

David Godfrey Bewicke-Copley came from an old noble family; three of his ancestors held the title of keeper of the King's purse in the fifteenth century. His father, for whom the barony was reactivated after a period of abeyance, was a career army officer. Educated at Eton and Magdalene College, Cambridge, he was called to the bar by the Inner Temple in 1954, but instead of practicing law he joined the London Stock Exchange. In 1960 he became a partner of Mullens & Company, the brokerage house for the government and the Bank of England since the 1780s, where he had charge of gilt-edged securities (blue-chip stocks). In 1973 he was promoted to second partner and deputy government broker, and in 1981 he succeeded Thomas Gore Browne in the senior post.

As the government's financial agent to the Stock Exchange, Lord Cromwell (he had succeeded his father in 1966) was privy to confidential financial information—how, when, and at what price the government planned to buy or sell stock—that would have considerable effect on the market if it were widely known. He skillfully managed to keep professional investors from second-guessing the government's intentions and undercutting its profits. In addition to raising funds for the national debt commissioners and generally "keeping an orderly market," as he called it, Cromwell helped devise innovative "tap" stock plans to attract big investors into buying excess government stock, and was involved in planning foreign debt repayments and municipal and industrial refinancing.

Cromwell was an enthusiastic farmer, gardener, and horseman and was a member of the Pytchley and Fernie Hunts. On 14 August, at his family farm at Cotesbach, Leicestershire, he was thrown twice onto his head from a horse that was only partly trained. He died of head injuries at a Coventry hospital four days later. S.A.

Succeeded his father as Baron Cromwell 1966. **Parents** Baron C., mil. officer, and Lady C. (Freda Constance Cripps). **Married** Vivian Penfold 1954: Anne Elizabeth Runciman, b. 1955; Davina Mary, b. 1958; Godfrey John Bewicke-Copley, b. 1960; Thomas David, b. 1964. **Education** Eton Coll.; Magdalene Coll., Cambridge; called to bar, Inner Temple 1954. **Career** Member of London Stock Exchange since 1956; partner since 1960 and second sr. partner since 1973, Mullens & Co., London since 1960; 2nd govt. broker 1973–81; sr. govt. broker since 1981; owner of farm in Leicestershire. **Member** Pytchley and Fernie Hunts.

L(AWRENCE) QUINCY MUMFORD

Librarian of Congress
***Born* Hanrahan, North Carolina, USA, 11 December 1903**
***Died* Washington, D.C., USA, 15 August 1982**

L. Quincy Mumford was the 11th librarian of Congress and the only one trained as a professional librarian. During his 20-year tenure, which started during the presidency of Dwight Eisenhower and lasted through that of Gerald Ford, he oversaw the expansion of the library's collection and services and the introduction of new technology that made the expansion possible.

One of ten children of a North Carolina tobacco farmer, Mumford started school in a one-room schoolhouse and helped in the harvesting and curing of tobacco until his departure in 1921 for Trinity College (later Duke University) in Durham. He earned his bachelor's degree with honors and went on for a master's in English while working full-time in the university library. In 1928 he turned down an offer of a job with a tobacco company to enter the School of Library Science at Columbia University, from which he was hired in 1929 by the New York Public Library. After two years as a reference assistant in the NYPL's General Information Division, one of the busiest information centers in the country, he joined the administrative staff and was named chief of the preparations division in 1936 and coordinator of general services in 1943.

Mumford's skill at helping to manage the vast holdings and operations of the NYPL brought him to the attention of the trustees of the public library of Cleveland, Ohio, of which he became assistant director in 1945. He took over as director five years later. He was active in Cleveland's civic affairs and developed a rapport with state and local legislators. In 1954 he was chosen to succeed Luther Evans as head of the Library of Congress and began a year's term as president of the American Library Association.

The role of the national library was then undergoing a reconsideration and was the subject of some controversy. The federal legislators who controlled its funds wanted the greater part of its resources devoted to serving the information needs of senators, congressmen, and other government officials. Research librarians were anxious to see it take the lead in solving bibliographic, acquisitions,

Courtesy of Fabian Bachrach

organizational, and technical problems raised by the sudden influx of scientific and other materials after World War II. Mumford cultivated the good will of Congress with well-planned budget presentations, evidence of careful management, and the establishment, under the Legislative Reorganization Act, of the new Congressional Reference Service, while cautiously beginning projects aimed at assisting research libraries. Between 1954 and 1974, the library's appropriations jumped 1,000 percent, from $9.4 million to $96 million; its staff grew from 1,600 to 4,500; its collections were increased from 33 million items to 74 million; and at Mumford's urging a third building was added to the library complex. Major projects undertaken during these years included the establishment of the Cataloging in Publication program for domestic imprints, the publication of the 610-volume *National Union Catalog, Pre-1956 Imprints,* studies leading to the revision of the copyright law, the introduction of automated systems for information storage and retrieval, the preservation and restoration of books and early films, the extension of services to the handicapped, and the acquisition of foreign books and serials and of the Rosenwald Collection of rare books.

At the request of Pres. Ford, Mumford remained in office a year beyond the mandatory retirement age, despite poor health. He was succeeded in 1974 by the present librarian, historian Daniel Boorstin. He died of a heart ailment at the age of 78. J.P.

Parents Jacob Edward Q., tobacco farmer, and Emma Luvenia (Stocks) Q. **Married** (1) Permelia Catherine Stevens, librarian, 1930 (d. 1961): Kathryn Deane. (2) Betsy Perrin Fox 1969: three stepchildren. **Education** Grifton High Sch., NC, grad. 1921; Trinity Coll. (later Duke Univ.), Durham, NC, A.B. (Phi Beta Kappa) 1925, A.M. 1928; Columbia Univ., B.S. in library science 1929. **Career** Student asst. 1922–25, staff member 1925–26, head of circulation 1926–27, and acting chief of reference and circulation 1927–28, Duke Univ. library; student asst., Columbia Univ. library 1928–29; gen. reference asst. 1929–32, gen. asst. in charge of Director's Office 1932–35, exec. asst. and chief of Preparation Div. 1936–43, on leave as dir. of Processing Dept. at Library of Congress 1940–41, and exec. asst. and coordinator of Gen. Services Div. 1943–45, New York Public Library; asst. dir. 1945–50 and dir. 1950–54, Cleveland Public Library; lectr., Sch. of Library Science, Western Reserve Univ. 1946–54; librarian of Congress 1954–74. **Officer** With American Library Assn.: member since 1932; chmn., Cttee. on Photographic Reproduction of Library Materials 1944–46; chmn., Cttee. on Federal Relations 1950–52; chmn., Audiovisual Bd. 1952–53; pres. 1954–55. • Pres.: Ohio Cleveland Library Club 1946–47; Ohio Library Assn. 1947–48; library cttee., Ohio Post-war Planning Commn. 1947–48; exec. cttee., Cleveland Occupational Planning Commn. 1950–51; Manuscript Soc. 1968–70. • Chmn.: (ex officio) Permanent Cttee. for Oliver Wendell Holmes Devise 1954–74; Federal Library Commn.; bd. of visitors, Duke Univ. • Trustee: (ex officio) Kennedy Center for Performing Arts to 1974; Wilston Intl. Center for Scholars; Great Lakes Historical Soc. • Dir.: Films Council of America; Great Books Foundn. • Secty. (ex officio), Library of Congress Trust Fund Bd. 1954–74. **Fellow** Benjamin Franklin Fellow, Royal Soc. **Member** Ex officio: bd., Historic Amer. Bldgs. Survey, Natl. Park Service 1954–74; Science Information Council 1965–74; Bd. of Regents, Natl. Library of Medicine to 1974; Federal Council on Arts and Humanities to 1974; Natl. Commn. on Libraries and Information Science. • Cttee. for Survey of Army Medical Library, WWII; Lincoln Sesquicentennial Commn. 1958–60; (corresp.) UNESCO Intl. Advisory Cttee. on Bibliography; (corresp.) Massachusetts Historical Soc.; advisory commn. on publication, Papers of George Washington; sponsors cttee., Papers of Woodrow Wilson; advisory bds. of Dumbarton Oaks Research Library and Collection and the Cafritz Foundn.; natl. advisory cttees. of Amer. Antiquarian Soc., British Mus. Soc., and U.S. Cttee. for Amer. Library in Paris; Natl. Book Cttee.; Natl. Trust Historic Preservation; Carolina Charter Corp.; Omicron Delta Kappa; Beta Phi Mu; Cosmos Club, Wash. DC; Explorers Club, NYC. **Honors** Hon. fellow, Truman Library Inst.; hon. trustee, U.S. Capitol Hill Historic Soc.; hon. degrees from univs. of Duke, Rutgers, Bucknell, Notre Dame, Pittsburgh, Michigan, and from four colls.

Further reading Charles A. Goodrum, *The Library of Congress,* 1974; Benjamin E. Powell, "Lawrence Quincy Mumford, Twenty Years of Progress," in *Librarians of Congress, 1802–1974,* 1977.

ALFRED S(CHIFFER) BLOOMINGDALE

Businessman and presidential advisor
***Born* New York City, USA, 15 April 1916**
***Died* Santa Monica, California, USA, 20 August 1982**

Alfred S. Bloomingdale was the founder and longtime head of Diners Club, the first of the major credit-card operations. He helped finance the presidential campaign of his close friend Ronald Reagan and was a member of Reagan's unofficial advisory group, the "kitchen cabinet," along with a dozen other businessmen.

Bloomingdale was the grandson of Lyman Bloomingdale, the founder of Bloomingdale's department store in New York City, and he went to work there in 1938 after graduating from Brown University, where he played football. In the early 1940s he was a theatrical producer and agent (Frank Sinatra and Judy Holliday were among his clients, and the *Ziegfeld Follies* of 1943 was one of his more successful shows). He then spent some years as an executive of Columbia Pictures in Hollywood.

In 1950, after trying a number of business ventures, including the sale of a lint-free dust-mop, he began a small credit-card business in Los Angeles called Dine and Sign. It quickly merged with an East Coast rival, Diners Club, of which Bloomingdale became vice president. ("I'm not a gourmet at all," he once remarked, "I'm more of a banker.") As president from 1955 to 1968 and chairman of the board from 1964 to 1969, he directed the company's acquisition of a collection agency, a credit-checking firm, and the Fugazy Travel Bureau. Diners Club, however, was outstripped by American Express, and then by BankAmericard and Mastercharge, and was acquired in 1969 by the Continental Corporation, an insurance group.

Courtesy of Robert R. Bloomingdale

After his retirement, Bloomingdale headed a number of real-estate ventures, including Marina Bay Resort in Fort Lauderdale, Florida. Following Reagan's election in 1980, he was given special access to the White House as a member of the so-called kitchen cabinet, which advises Pres. Reagan on government policy and on appointments to government posts. Their mission, Bloomingdale said, was "surrounding Ronnie with the best people—the ones we'd hire for our own businesses." Other members of the group, most of whom had been business associates in California, were Joseph Coors, the brewery owner; Jack Wrather, an oilman and owner of radio and television stations; Charles Wick, a film producer and commodities speculator; and Justin Dart, a drugstore magnate. Bloomingdale also worked for the Reagan Coalition Conference, another group of wealthy friends involved in persuading the public to support the administration's budget-cutting program, and reportedly donated $10,000 to Nancy Reagan's campaign to restore the upstairs White House. He was appointed by Reagan to the Foreign Intelligence Advisory Board and the Advisory Commission on Public Diplomacy.

Bloomingdale died of cancer a few weeks after he was sued for breach of contract by a young woman who claimed to have been his sexual companion and confidante for 12 years and who charged that he had reneged on an oral promise of lifetime support. The dismissal of the suit in late September 1982 left unresolved the status of a written contract between the two. J.P.

Parents Hiram C. B. and Rosalind (Schiffer) B. **Married** Betsy Lee Newling 1946: Lee

Geoffrey; Elisabeth Lee; Robert Russell. **Education** Riverdale Country Day Sch., NYC; Westminster Sch., CT; Brown Univ., Providence, RI, grad. 1938. **Career** Asst. merchandise mgr., Bloomingdale Bros., NYC 1938–41; theatrical agent and producer, NYC 1941–46; exec., Columbia Pictures, Hollywood 1946–50; co-founder 1950, v.p. 1950–55, pres. 1955–68, chmn. of bd. 1964–69, and consultant since 1970, Diners Club; active in Republican politics since 1964; unofficial presidential advisor since 1980. **Officer** Pres. and dir., Marina Bay Resort, Ft. Lauderdale, FL since 1972; pres. 1970–76 and v.p. since 1977, Alfred S. Bloomingdale Enterprises, Inc. • Chmn. of bd.: Surfside 6 Floating Homes, Ft. Lauderdale 1970–80; Quadrox Corp., L.A. since 1974; Journey's End Hotel, Marietta, GA since 1978; 15th St. Fisheries since 1978. • Dir.: Lyman G. Realty, Inc., B. Bros. Realty, Inc., and Bloomingdale Properties, all NYC; Beneficial Standard Corp., Kintec, Inc., and Continental Airlines, all L.A.; California Inn Management, Lawrence, KS; Los Angeles Rams, Anaheim, CA; Intl. Rescue Cttee. • Trustee emeritus, Brown Univ. **Member** Bd. of regents, St. John's Hosp., Santa Monica, CA, and Loyola Marymount Univ., L.A.; Foreign Intelligence Advisory Bd. since 1981; U.S. Advisory Commn. on Public Diplomacy since 1981; Acad. of Motion Picture Arts and Sciences; Republican Party; Westminster Alumni; Brown Univ. Club; Delta Kappa Epsilon. **Honors** Papal kt. comdr., Order of St. Gregory.

GEORGE D(AVID) WOODS
President of the World Bank
Born **Boston, Massachusetts, USA, 27 July 1901**
Died **near Lisbon, Portugal, 20 August 1982**

George D. Woods, an investment banker, was chairman of the First Boston Corporation in 1962 when Pres. Kennedy named him to the presidency of the International Bank for Reconstruction and Development, popularly known as the World Bank. During his tenure, which lasted until 1968, the bank liberalized its loan policies to third-world countries and pressed for greater contributions from industrialized nations to the loan fund.

Woods was the son of a shipyard worker and grew up in Brooklyn, where his father was employed at the Brooklyn Navy Yard. He never went to college, and after graduating from Brooklyn Commercial High School went to work on Wall Street in 1918 as an office boy at Harris, Forbes & Company. He rose steadily in the employ of the company, which merged into the First Boston Corporation in 1934, and he finally became chairman of First Boston, by then one of the largest investment banks in the world, in 1951.

Woods was drawn into the affairs of the World Bank by Eugene R. Black, president from 1949 to 1962 and a former colleague at Harris, Forbes. Acting as an unpaid consultant, Woods adjudicated in 1956 the compensation to be paid by Egypt for the nationalization of the Suez Canal; helped India in 1955 set up the Industrial Credit and Investment Corporation, a private development bank, which functioned as a conduit for World Bank investment in private industry; and in 1960 implemented the World Bank's decision to finance joint construction of storage dams by Pakistan and India. He was therefore thoroughly familiar with World Bank operations when he was picked to succeed Black. The United States, contributing 30 percent of the bank's capital, had until 1981 the right to nominate its president.

His first priority was to obtain increased capitalization for the International Development Association, the affiliate of the World Bank responsible for "soft" loans to underdeveloped countries for educational and agricultural projects. Loans of this type, where repayment was less sure, had been less favored by bank officials than "hard" loans for such purposes as dams and industrial plants, on which the bank could expect repayment within a fixed period. Woods succeeded in changing the bank's course on loan policy, and the new course has remained in effect to the present day.

In 1968, on his retirement from the bank,

Courtesy of Fabian Bachrach

Woods was succeeded as president by Robert McNamara, secretary of defense in the Kennedy and Johnson administrations and a chief architect of the Vietnam War. Woods assumed the chairmanships of the Executive Service Corps and the Henry J. Kaiser Family Foundation. While at First Boston he had arranged for the $1.5 billion financing of Kaiser Industries, one of the largest business deals in U.S. history.

He had a lifelong interest in the New York theater, and was a principal backer of several Broadway productions, including the hits *Dead End* and *Sailor Beware.* A friend of John Ringling North, he was for a time treasurer and director of Ringling Brothers, Barnum and Bailey Circus. He also served as director of Lincoln Center for the Performing Arts in New York. A.K.

Parents John W., naval shipyard worker, and Laura A. (Rhodes) W. **Married** Louise Taraldson 1935. **Education** Brooklyn Commercial High Sch., grad. 1918; night courses, Amer. Inst. of Banking 1920–23; New York Univ. **Mil. service** Col., U.S. Army Gen. Staff Corps, and Army rep. on War Production Bd. cttees., 1942–45. **Career** Office boy, then investment banker, Harris Forbes & Co. (later Chase Harris Forbes & Co.), NYC 1918–34; dir. 1934–62 and 1968–76, chmn. of exec. cttee. 1947–51, and chmn. of bd. 1951–62, First Boston Corp., NYC; special assignments with World Bank 1950s and co-founder of development banks in India 1955, Pakistan 1956, and Philippines 1962; pres. and chmn. of bd., Intl. Bank for Reconstruction and Development 1963–68; pres. ex officio and chmn. of exec. dirs., Intl. Development Agency 1963–68; pres. ex officio and chmn. of bd., Intl. Finance Corp. 1963–68; chmn. and trustee, Henry J. Kaiser Family Foundn. 1968–80; chmn. 1968–74, chmn. of exec. cttee. 1974–77, and dir. since 1977, Intl. Exec. Service Corp.; pres. 1971–77 and dir. since 1977, Foreign Bondholders Protective Council, Inc.; dir., First Boston Corp. 1976–77. **Officer** Dir.: Kaiser Foundn. Hosps.; Pittsburgh Plate Glass Co.; Campbell Soup Co.; Schenley Industries; New York Times Co.; Lincoln Center for Performing Arts, Inc., NYC. • Trustee: Ochs Trust; New York Foundn.; Rockefeller Foundn.; Kennedy Library; Amer. Shakespeare Festival Theater and Acad. • Bd. chmn., Repertory Theater, Lincoln Center; bd. chmn., treas., and dir., Ringling Bros., Barnum and Bailey Circus. **Member** Clubs: Links, Pinnacle, Players, Racquet and Tennis, World Trade Center, Bonds, Recess, all NYC; Duquesne, Rollins, and Rock, all Pittsburgh; Federal City, City Tavern, F Street, and Intl., all Wash. DC. **Honors** Legion of Merit, 1945; hon. degrees from Univ. of Notre Dame, Allegheny Coll., Bowdoin Coll.; hon. trustee, Univ. of Notre Dame; hon. dir., Lincoln Center for Performing Arts, Inc.

KING SOBHUZA II
Ngwenyama and head of state of Swaziland
***Born* Swaziland, 22 July 1899**
***Died* Mbabane, Swaziland, 21 August 1982**

Sobhuza II, Ngwenyama (Lion) of Swaziland, reigned over his small country for 82 years, longer than any other monarch in the world. An assertive and indomitable autocrat who wanted nothing to do with parliamentary democracy or constitutional monarchy, whatever he accomplished for his nearly 600,000 people—who were for the most part intensely devoted to him and the traditions he embodied—depended on his own wily diplomatic skills. He left his country wholly independent, with a flourishing agricultural base and considerable export earnings from officially encouraged exploitation of iron and asbestos deposits.

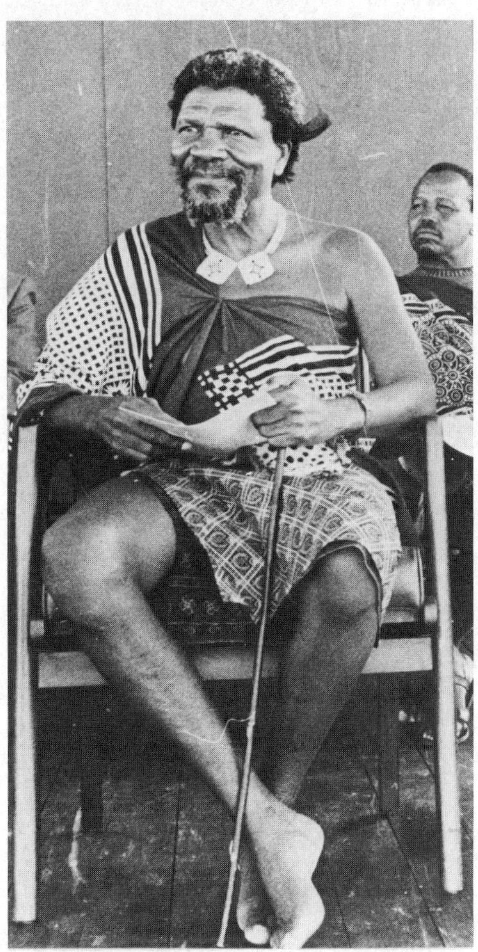

Sobhuza was born during the Boer War, only a few months before the death of his father, King Ngwane V. During a regency led by the queen mother, which lasted until he assumed full powers at age 22, he attended the country's first primary school at Zombodze and then the Lovedale Institute in South Africa's Cape Province. The British government, in the meantime, made a protectorate of Swaziland, which it ruled through a high commissioner. In 1922, shortly after becoming paramount chief, Sobhuza traveled to London to explain to the British that the vast grants of land his ancestors had been forced to make to Boer and English settlers were only temporary, and that any notion of sale in perpetuity was completely unacceptable to him and alien to Swazi tradition. Though not immediately successful, his claim marked the beginning of a steady series of appeals to the primacy of tradition, made over a lifetime of artful diplomatic and political maneuvering. At his death the Swazi nation controlled two-thirds of the country's land, and in 1982 his government began intensive negotiations with South Africa to regain other land, including an outlet to the sea, which the landlocked Swazis claim was unjustly seized in the late 19th century.

Sobhuza's relations with his much larger neighbors, South Africa and Mozambique, were careful and correct, with frequent royal visits to Pretoria and Maputo, and a constant reluctance to criticize either country in international forums. Many member states of the Organization of African Unity have condemned Swaziland for not speaking out against South Africa's institutionalized racism, but the king realized that such defiance would almost surely mean the end of the nation's independence. South Africa has become Swaziland's principal trading partner, and since the discovery of major iron-ore deposits near Mbabane in the late 1950s Swaziland has used Mozambique's railways and the port facilities at Maputo. During the 1970s many South African tourists found in Swaziland a liberal haven from their puritanical country, flocking in to spend money in Mbabane's casino, dance halls, and pornography shops.

After decades of wrangling with the British over the extent of his authority, Sobhuza won independence for Swaziland in 1969. The country became the 28th independent member of the British Commonwealth and the 125th member of the United Nations. The British left behind a constitution, not at all to the king's liking, which provided for general elections within a parliamentary system. When, in 1972, the tiny opposition won 3 out of 30 seats and began making speeches demanding more freedom and less centralization of authority, Sobhuza decided that he had had enough of democracy. Early in 1973, declaring that the parliament was filled with "hyenas urinating upwind to stampede the cattle below," he abrogated the constitution, dismissed the parliament, jailed the opposition leader, and began to rule by decree with the assistance of his close advisors, who were mostly members of his own family, the Dlamini. His actions drew no protest from his people.

Sobhuza spent much of his time away from his palace in Mbabane, staying in the royal kraal outside the capital with his wives, who were thought to number more than 100. By his marriages he cemented kinship ties throughout his ethnically homogeneous country. The number of his children was never officially announced, but popular estimates ranged up to 600.

Although there was no one alive in Swaziland who remembered the last royal succession, the aftermath of Sobhuza's death produced neither uncertainty nor crisis. One of his senior wives, Dzeliwe, whom he had chosen as Ndlovukazi (She Elephant), or queen mother, will head the regency until the new king (who was not immediately named but is almost certainly one of Sobhuza's youngest sons) comes of age. There is no tradition of crown prince or heir apparent in Swaziland's royal family, and palace intrigue over the succession has therefore been limited.

A.K.

Member of Dlamini clan. **Parents** King Ngwane V, also called Bhunu, and Queen Lomawa. **Married** many wives, reportedly as many as 100: possibly 600 children. **Education** Primary sch., Zombodze, Swaziland; Lovedale Inst., Cape Province, South Africa. **Career** Chosen Ngwenyama (paramount chief) by inner council of royal family at age 4 months, 1899; mother regent until his installation as constitutional ruler under British High Commnr. 1922; officially recognized as head of state and king 1967; became constitutional monarch after Swaziland achieved independence 1968; abolished British-style constitution and assumed absolute powers 1973; head of Imbokodvo (Royal) Party. **Officer** Chancellor: Univ. of Botswana and Swaziland 1975–76; University Coll. of Swaziland 1976–79. **Honors** KBE.

Further reading Hilda Kuper, *Sobhuza II: Ngwenyama and King of Swaziland,* 1978.

ALBERTO (de ALMEIDA) CAVALCANTI
Filmmaker
Born **Rio de Janeiro, Brazil, 6 February 1897**
Died **Paris, France, 23 August 1982**

Alberto Cavalcanti was a pioneering and prolific filmmaker whose career spanned four decades and several countries and languages. For many years he made silent films in France, then documentaries and fictional films in England. After writing and directing several Portuguese-language features in his native Brazil, he fled the country to work in Austria, Israel, and finally France. Except for a few features, such as *Dead of Night* (1945), of which he directed two segments, his films are rarely seen today.

Cavalcanti was educated at the École des Beaux Arts in Geneva, where he studied architecture and interior design. His first contact with the world of film was in France, where just after World War I he began working as an art director on experimental and avant-garde films. Although he became less famous than his contemporaries and competitors René Clair and Jean Renoir, several of the silent works of his French period are well remembered, including *Rien que les heures* (1926), which he directed, produced, and co-wrote; *En rade* (1927); and *Le capitaine Fracasse* (1928), an adaptation of the Balzac novel. He made a relatively easy transition to directing talking pictures, but was deeply unsatisfied with the quality of the romantic boulevard comedies he was assigned to direct for the Paramount studios in Paris during the early 1930s.

By the time he arrived in England in 1934, Cavalcanti was a figure of considerable renown in filmmaking circles. At the urging of John Grierson, the guiding spirit behind the incipient British documentary-film movement, he went to work at the film unit of the General Post Office, at that time a small-scale producer of inventive documentaries, both long and short, on all sorts of subjects. There he joined a talented group of young English filmmakers that included Basil Wright, Harry Watt, Humphrey Jennings, and Robert Hamer. Cavalcanti's best films for the GPO, among the dozen he directed and produced there, were *Coalface* and *Night Mail* (both 1936), with scripts by W.H. Auden and music by Benjamin Britten. After Grierson's resignation in 1938, Cavalcanti became the effective director of the film unit, but left a year later because of pressure from the government over his foreign nationality. In 1941 he went to work at Ealing Studios, then run by producer Michael Balcon, and until 1944 continued the propaganda-documentary work he had done for the GPO, producing *Yellow Caesar* (1941), *Greek Testament* (1942), *Find, Fix and Strike* (1943), and *The Foreman Went to France* (1941).

Finally, near the end of the war, Cavalcanti began to make the sort of commercial feature films he had long dreamed of doing. For the polished and macabre *Dead of Night,* Balcon employed four directors, each assigned different segments; Cavalcanti's two were "The Christmas Story" and the famous "Ventriloquist's Dummy" scene starring Michael Redgrave. He also made *Nicholas Nickleby* (1947), a faithful adaptation of Dickens that suffered by being compared with David Lean's rival and highly successful *Great Expectations,* released the same year, and *They Made Me a Fugitive* (1947), starring Trevor Howard.

Cavalcanti returned to Brazil in the early 1950s and there made several Portuguese-language films, including *O canto do mar* (1954) and *Mulher de verdade* (1954). At a time of great political unrest he was suspected of being a Communist, and was forced to flee his native country and return to Europe. He worked with Bertolt Brecht in Austria on *Herr Puntila und sein Knecht Matti* (1955) and with Joris Ivens on *Die Windrose* (1956). In his later years he did some stage direction, including a production in Spain of García Lorca's *Blood Wedding,* made a film about Theodor Herzl entitled *The Story of Israel* (1967), and worked extensively for French television. He had lived in Paris for several years before his death. A.K.

Born Alberto de Almeida-Cavalcanti. **Father** a mathematician. **Emigration** Moved to Switzerland 1910s; to France 1920s; to U.K. 1934–48, 1960–68; to Brazil 1948–53; to Europe 1954–60 and since mid-1970s; to U.S. 1968–mid-70s. **Education** Law studies 1913; architecture studies, École des Beaux Arts, Geneva. **Career** Avant-garde artist and film set designer, Paris 1920s. • Film dir., producer, and writer: Paris 1925–34; with GPO Film Unit, England 1934–ca. 40; with Crown Film Unit, England 1940–42; with Ealing Studios, London ca. 1941–48; head of production, Vera Cruz film co., Brazil 1949–53; then joined Kino Film briefly; with production units in Europe and Israel 1953–mid-60s. • Stage dir., Europe and Israel; dir. for French TV since late 1960s; lectr., Univ. of California at Los Angeles 1968 and Film Study Center, Cambridge, MA 1973. **Member** Garrick Club. **Film director** (also scriptwriter and producer in some cases) *Le train sans yeux,* 1926; *Rien que les heures,* 1926; *En rade,* 1927; *Yvette,* 1927; *La p'tite Lilie,* 1927; *La jalousie de barbouillé,* 1927; *Le capitaine Fracasse,* 1928; *Le petit chaperon rouge,* 1929; *Vous verrez la semaine prochaine,* 1929; *Toute sa vie,* 1930; *Les vacances du diable,* 1930; *À mi-chemin du ciel,* 1930; *Dans une île perdue,* 1931; *En lisant le journal,* 1932; *Le jour du frotteur,* 1932; *Revue montmartroise,* 1932; *Nous ne ferons jamais de cinema,* 1932; *Le truc de brésilien,* 1932; *Le mari garçon,* 1932; *Coralie et cie,* 1933; *Plaisirs défendus,* 1933; *Tour de chant,* 1933; *Pett and Pott,* 1934; *SOS Radio Service,* 1934; *New Rates,* 1934; *Line to Tschierva Hut,* 1936;

We Live in Two Worlds, 1937; *Who Writes to Switzerland?,* 1937; *Message from Geneva,* 1937; *Four Barriers,* 1937; *Men of the Alps,* 1939; *Midsummer's Day's Work,* 1939; *Yellow Caesar,* 1941; (comp.) *Film and Reality,* 1942; *Alice in Switzerland,* 1942; *Went the Day Well?,* 1942; *Watertight,* 1943; *Three Songs About Resistance,* 1943; *Champagne Charlie,* 1944; (episode) *Dead of Night,* 1945; *The Life and Adventures of Nicholas Nickleby,* 1947; *They Made Me a Fugitive,* 1947; *The First Gentleman,* 1947; *For Them That Trespass,* 1948; *Simao o coalho,* 1952; *O canto do mar,* 1954; *Mulher de verdade,* 1954; *Herr Puntila und sein Knecht Matti,* 1955; (supervising dir.) *Die Windrose,* 1956; *Castle in the Carpathians,* 1957; *La prima notte,* 1958; *The Monster of Highgate Ponds,* 1960; *The Story of Israel: Thus Spake Theodor Herzl,* 1967. **Film producer** *Calendar of the Year,* 1934; *Book Bargain,* 1935; *Big Money,* 1935; *BBC: The Voice of Britain,* 1935; *Rainbow Dance,* 1935; *Roadways,* 1936; *Coalface,* 1936; *Night Mail,* 1936; *The Saving of Bill Blewitt,* 1937; *Money a Pickle,* 1937; *N. or NW.,* 1938; *Happy in the Morning,* 1938; *Forty Million People,* 1938; *North Sea,* 1938; *Men in Danger,* 1938; *The City,* 1938; *Speaking from America,* 1939; *Spare Time,* 1939; *Spring Offensive,* 1939; *Squadron 992,* 1939; *The First Days,* 1940; *Men of the Lightships,* 1940; *The Foreman Went to France,* 1941; *Mastery of the Sea,* 1941; *Guests of Honour,* 1941; *The Big Blockade,* 1941; *Greek Testament,* 1942; *Find, Fix and Strike,* 1943; *Halfway House,* 1944; *Caicara,* 1950; *Terra sempere terra,* 1951; *Painel,* 1951; *Santuario,* 1952; *Volta redonda,* 1952. **Stage director** *Blood Wedding,* Spain; other plays. **Author** *Film e realidad* [*Film and Reality*]. **Interviews** *Screen,* Summer 1972; "Alberto Cavalcanti on *Nicholas Nickleby,*" in *Literature and Film Quarterly,* Winter 1978.

N(EIL) R(IPLEY) KER
Paleographer and medievalist
Born London, England, 28 May 1908
Died near Pitlochry, Perthshire, Scotland, 23 August 1982

N. R. Ker is generally considered the foremost British expert on paleography, the study of ancient and medieval transcripts, calligraphy, and scribal practices. A methodical researcher with an encyclopedic knowledge of medieval authors, scripts, texts, and languages, he was also an innovator who introduced to the field studies on the general history of bookmaking, book collecting, and libraries ancient and modern.

The son of a British Army officer, Ker prepared at Reigate and Eton. At the age of 15, he published his first scholarly work, a catalogue and description of 301 tombstone inscriptions in the churchyard of Upton-cum-Chalvey. In 1927 he went up to Magdalen College, Oxford, to study philosophy, politics, and economics. With the encouragement of C. S. Lewis, one of his instructors, he switched to English language and literature, became interested in paleography after reading faulty and incomplete translations of Old English manuscripts, and produced a B.Litt. thesis (1933) on the tenth-century *Aelfric's Homilies.* In 1936 he was appointed to lecture on the subject at Oxford. After service as a conscientious objector at Oxford's Radcliffe Infirmary during World War II, he was elected a fellow of Magdalen in 1945 and appointed a university reader in paleography. On the retirement in 1955 of C. T. Onions, the distinguished philologist and one of Ker's early mentors, he became the librarian of Magdalen as well.

Ker's first major work, *Medieval Libraries of Great Britain: a List of the Surviving Books* (1941), immediately established him as an important paleological and bibliographical authority. In a review of Ker's *Pastedowns in Oxford Bindings* (1954), a catalog of medieval manuscript fragments that were used as bindings for later books, the medieval historian Noel Denham-Young cited his "incomparable skill in using bibliographical technique to supplement an unrivalled memory for scripts. He has thus broadened the scope of paleography to an extent that would have astounded the nineteenth century."

Traditional paleography was chiefly concerned with classifying the various styles of script within a manuscript and identifying the handwriting of individual authors. Ker went beyond this to study every detail of the scribe's and the bookmaker's arts. "With him," wrote C. R. Cheney in a contribution to Ker's 1978 festchrift, "no part of a book, no pressmark, medieval or modern, no chainmark—one may even say, no wormhole—passes unnoticed." Through historical detective work and the examination and comparison of widely scattered sources, he traced the provenance of many medieval books, often buried on the shelves of obscure parish libraries, and with as many as 20 different anonymous items bound within a single codex, that had never before been seriously studied. The work was time-consuming but fundamentally important for making these primary sources available to scholars. From 1941 onward, he devoted considerable effort to cataloguing and describing the manuscript collections of libraries such as those of All Souls College at Oxford, Lambeth Palace, and various parochial libraries of the Church of England. Ker also wrote introductions to five facsimile editions of Old and Middle English texts, including J. R. R. Tolkien's edition of the *Ancrene Wisse*.

After an early retirement from Oxford in 1968, Ker devoted himself to the most ambitious of his compilations, a four-volume catalogue of medieval manuscripts in British libraries. Two volumes had been published and the second two were nearly completed when Ker, a lifelong outdoorsman and mountain climber, fell to his death while bilberrying with his wife. P.D.

Parents Robert Macneil K., army officer, and Lucy Winifred (Strickland-Constable) K. **Married** Jean Frances Findlay 1938: one son; three daughters. **Education** Reigate Sch.; Eton Coll. 1921–ca. 27; Magdalen Coll., Oxford, B.A. 1931, B.Litt. 1933, M.A. 1939. **Mil. service** Conscientious objector; hosp. porter, Radcliffe Infirmary, Oxford, WWII. **Career** With Oxford Univ.: univ. lectr. in paleography 1936–46; univ. reader in paleography 1946–68; Lyell Reader in Bibliography 1952–53; librarian 1956–68 and v.p. 1962–63, Magdalen Coll.; reader emeritus since 1968; emeritus fellow since 1969; curator, Bodleian Library. • Sandars Reader in Bibliography, Cambridge Univ. 1955; Edwards Lectr., Univ. of Glasgow 1960; visiting prof., Univ. of Illinois 1967 and Yale Univ. 1971. **Officer** Pres., Mountaineering Club, Magdalen Coll. 1929–30. **Fellow** Magdalen Coll. 1945–68; British Acad. since 1958; Soc. of Antiquaries since 1965; Royal Historical Soc.; corresp. fellow, Medieval Acad. of America. **Member** Bayerische Akademie der Wissenschaft since 1977; council member and consultant, Early English Text Soc. **Honors** Gollancz Memorial Prize, British Acad. 1959; gold medal, Bibliographical Soc. 1975; hon. fellow, Magdalen Coll., Oxford since 1975; CBE 1979; hon. degrees from univs. of Reading, Leyden, and Cambridge. **Author and editor** *Medieval Libraries of Great Britain: A List of the Surviving Books,* 1941, rev. ed. 1964; (co-ed.) *Catalogus librorum manuscriptorum bibliothecae Wigorniensis made in 1622–23,* 1944; *Pastedowns in Oxford Bindings,* 1954; *Oxford College Libraries in 1556,* 1956; *Catalogue of Manuscripts containing Anglo-Saxon,* 1957; (ed.) *The Parochial Libraries of the Church of England,* 1959; *English Manuscripts in the Century After the Norman Conquests,* 1960; *Records of All Souls College Library, 1437–1600,* 1971; *Catalogue of Manuscripts in Lambeth Palace,* 1972. • *Medieval Manuscripts in British Libraries: Vol. I, London,* 1969; *Vol. II, Abbotsford-Keele,* 1977; vols. III and IV in preparation. **Contributor** of more than 50 articles on paleography, bibliography, and the history of libraries to *Medium Ævum* and other scholarly jrnls.; also numerous introductions to facsimile eds. of medieval manuscripts.

Further reading M.B. Parks and A.G. Watson, eds., *Medieval Scribes, Manuscripts, and Libraries: Essays Presented to N.R. Ker,* 1978.

STANFORD MOORE
Biochemist
***Born* Chicago, Illinois, USA, 4 September 1913**
***Died* New York City, USA, 23 August 1982**

Stanford Moore shared the 1972 Nobel Prize in chemistry for the first elucidation of the amino acid sequence of an enzyme and for fundamental discoveries on how enzymes work. Together with his longtime collaborator William H. Stein and the Danish researcher Christian Anfinsen, he determined the structural formula of pancreatic ribonuclease, which is composed of a chain of 124 amino acids totaling 1,876 atoms, and made predictions concerning the structural basis of the enzyme's catalytic activities that were borne out by later research. Commenting on the importance of this work in his Nobel Prize lecture, Moore stated, "The human body is half protein, in terms of its solid constituents. Yet as of today we know the chemical and physical structure of only a small percent of these. . . . If we are ever really to understand the host of reactions in which proteins participate in living cells we need to know the structures of thousands of proteins of different origins and different functions. . . . Such information is fundamental to a rational approach to the repair of many a biological malfunction."

A native of Chicago, Moore grew up in Nashville, Tennessee, where his father taught law at Vanderbilt University and from which he graduated summa cum laude with a B.A. in chemistry in 1935. He did his doctoral work in organic chemistry on a graduate fellowship at the University of Wisconsin; then, at the urging of his thesis advisor, biochemist Karl Link, he joined the internationally renowned biochemistry laboratory headed by the German emigré Max Bergmann at New York's Rockefeller Institute (now Rockefeller University).

During World War II Moore was on leave with other members of the laboratory administering chemical projects for the wartime Office of Scientific Research and Development. On his return, he and Stein began their study of enzymes, which are specialized proteins that act as catalysts in the breakdown of other chemicals. Their experiments were made on bovine ribonuclease, a relatively small, stable enzyme available in a pure crystalline preparation at low cost from Armour, Inc., the Chicago meat-processing company. Ribonuclease, which is produced by the pancreas, facilitates the breakdown of ribonucleic acid (RNA) in the digestive tracts of animals, but little was known about the structure and functioning of this or any other enzyme.

The first step in determining the structure of ribonuclease was to determine its chemical composition by breaking it down into its constituent amino acids and then measuring the quantity of each acid. Breaking down the enzyme was easily accomplished by the process known as hydrolysis, the dissolution of the chemical links in the protein chain by the application of acid. The effort to isolate and measure the various amino acids, however, took years. Moore and Stein used column chromatography, an elegant separation technique invented in 1906. They poured a solution of the hydrolyzed enzyme down a tall glass column packed with potato starch. The starch impeded the downward progress of each amino acid at a different rate; when the solution finally began trickling out of the bottom of the column several days later, the amino acids emerged one by one at well-spaced intervals. To avoid the tedious task of replacing the test tubes under the column by hand, Moore and Stein arranged the test tubes on a mechanized carousel. They eventually cut down the time needed to produce a chromatogram from two weeks to one by replacing the potato starch in the column with more efficient polymethacrylic resins. In 1958 they added an automated process to analyze the presence and concentration of amino acids in each tube. In the end, they had a fully automated amino-acid analyzer that could analyze hydrolyzed proteins overnight. It is now standard equipment in academic and industrial biochemistry laboratories around the world and has made possible rapid advances in biochemistry that otherwise would have taken years to achieve.

In 1951 Moore served as a visiting investigator at Cambridge University, where he met Frederick Sanger, who published the first analysis of a protein, insulin, in 1954. On his return to New York, Moore set out to determine the exact sequence of the amino acids in

Courtesy of Ingbert Grüttner

ribonuclease. Rather than completely hydrolyze the enzyme as they had done before, the research team used digestive enzymes to break it down into large pieces. Separating these fragments by chromatography, they studied the sequence of amino acids in each piece and tried to deduce their place in the original molecule. This procedure, which can be compared to dropping a pile of plates on the floor and then trying to reassemble them, occupied Moore, Stein, and their graduate assistants until 1959, when they published a two-dimensional formula for ribonuclease. The functional structure of the enzyme was still a mystery, however. The molecule, they knew, is composed of a peptide chain folded into a complex three-dimensional shape, of which a relatively small proportion accounts for its useful chemical activity, the breaking down of RNA. "The whole molecule may perhaps be something like a precision lathe," they wrote, "where a ton or more of machinery is required to bring a few ounces of metal in the cutting tool to bear accurately on the work." After further study, they identified as the enzyme's active components the 12th and 119th amino acids in the peptide chain. That these acids had to operate in conjunction, yet were at opposite ends of the chain, was good evidence that at least some of the chain takes the form of a coil or helix. This was later confirmed by x-ray crystallographic studies. The peptide chain is now thought to create a form-fitting cavity in which RNA molecules are broken down by various amino acid residues.

Since the late 1950s, structural and functional analysis of proteins has become a major part of molecular biology. "It is fundamental to medicine," Moore explained in an interview, "to know the structure of 2,000 enzymes by the year 2000." With the recent development of DNA sequencing, whereby the blueprints for protein molecules are read directly from the genetic code, it is likely that Moore's goal will be met.

Since the mid-1970s, Moore suffered from amyotrophic lateral sclerosis (Lou Gehrig's disease), a degenerative and ultimately fatal disease of the nerves and muscles. He carried on research at Rockefeller University until the summer of 1982, when he apparently poisoned himself after writing farewell notes to his friends. P.D.

Parents John Howard M., law prof., and Ruth (Fowler) M. **Religion** Roman Catholic. **Education** Vanderbilt Univ., Nashville, TN, B.A. (summa cum laude) 1935; Univ. of Wisconsin, (Alumni Research Foundn. Fellow), Ph.D. in organic chemistry 1938. **Mil. service** Technical aide, Office of Science Research and Development, Natl. Defense Research Cttee., Wash. DC 1942–45; with Operational Research Sect., U.S. Armed Forces HQ, Hawaii 1945. **Career** With Rockefeller Inst. for Medical Research (now Rockefeller Univ.), NYC: asst. 1939–42; assoc. 1942–49; assoc. member 1949–52; member and prof. of biochemistry since 1952; John D. Rockefeller Prof. since 1981. • Consultant, Army Chemical Corps 1945–58; member, editorial bd., *Journal of Biological Chemistry,* Amer. Soc. of Biological Chemists 1950–60; visiting prof., Univ. of Brussels 1950–51; visiting investigator, Cambridge Univ. 1951; visiting prof. of health sciences, Sch. of Medicine, Vanderbilt Univ. 1968. **Officer** Chmn., panel on protein, cttee. on growth, Natl. Research Council 1947–49; secty., commn. on proteins, Intl. Union of Pure and Applied Chemistry 1953–57; treas. 1956–59 and pres. 1966–67, Amer. Soc. of Biological Chemists; chmn., organizing cttee., 6th Intl. Congress of Biochemistry 1964;

chmn., sect. on biochemistry, Natl. Acad. of Science 1969–72; pres., Fedn. of Amer. Socs. for Experimental Biology 1970–71; trustee, Vanderbilt Univ. 1974. **Member** Natl. Acad. of Sciences since 1960; Amer. Chemical Soc.; Biochemical Soc., U.K.; Harvey Soc., U.K.; Amer. Assn. for the Advancement of Science; Amer. Acad. of Arts and Sciences; Phi Beta Kappa; Sigma Xi. **Honors** Founders Medal, Vanderbilt Univ. 1935; chromatography award 1963 and Richards Medal 1972, Amer. Chemical Soc.; Linderstrøm-Lang Medal, Copenhagen 1972; (jtly.) Nobel Prize in Chemistry 1972; hon. member, Belgian Biological Soc. and Belgian Royal Acad. of Medicine; hon. degrees from univs. of Brussels and Paris. **Contributor** of papers on protein and carbohydrate chemistry to scientific jrnls.

Further reading "The 1972 Nobel Prize in Chemistry," in *Les Prix Nobel en 1972,* 1973.

CALVIN (EUGENE) SIMMONS
Conductor
Born **San Francisco, California, USA, 27 April 1950**
Died **Lake Placid, New York, USA, 23 August 1982**

The death of Calvin Simmons in a boating accident deprived the American music world of one of its most promising young conductors. At 32, he had been, for three years, the music director of the Oakland Symphony and the main force behind its revitalization, and was known for his vibrant readings and effortless technique. His success had been an encouragement to black students seeking careers in classical music.

Simmons's father was a San Francisco longshoreman and his mother a nurse, gospel singer, and church pianist from whom he took his first piano lessons when he was five years old. At nine he auditioned for the San Francisco Boys Chorus, a department of the San Francisco Opera. Madi Bacon, its director, was impressed by the fact that he accompanied himself and readily accepted him, even though his voice was none too strong. He had his first taste of conducting at the Chorus and later conducted his high-school orchestra, in which he played French horn. At Bacon's recommendation he entered the Cincinnati College of Music to study with the conductor Max Rudolf, whom he followed in 1969 to the Curtis School of Music in Philadelphia, where Rudolf Serkin was among his piano teachers. During his vacations, he worked with the Merola Opera Summer Program and the Western Opera Theater, both training grounds for San Francisco's young singers, and with the latter group toured the West Coast. In 1970, Kurt Herbert Adler, conductor of the San Francisco Opera, offered him a position on the staff, but Simmons asked for time to finish his education. When, in 1972, he made his professional debut with the Western Opera as the conductor of Humperdinck's *Hansel and Gretel,* predictions of a bright future were universal. In addition to his work as assistant conductor with the San Francisco Opera from 1972 to 1975, he spent four summers in England as the youngest conductor, and only American, on the staff of the Glyndebourne Festival Opera.

Courtesy of Oakland Symphony

In 1975 Simmons joined the Los Angeles

Philharmonic as assistant to the conductor, Zubin Mehta, under the auspices of the Exxon Arts Endowment, and in 1977 inherited from Pierre Boulez and Michael Tilson Thomas the summer music directorship of the Ojai Festival. Two years later he was appointed music director of the Oakland Symphony, which had lost its old audience and was in search of a new approach. "Oakland is an orchestra that wants to do things, and I'm a conductor who wants to do things. It is a large enthusiastic community, exactly the right place to 'do my time.'" By the end of his first season he had won over the reviewers, the symphony management, the musicians, and the public. The orchestra began offering free admission to elderly and handicapped people through a ticket-sponsorship project, enlarged its education program and its series of neighborhood concerts, and found more funds for its fellowship program for minority students. In addition to traditional fare, Simmons introduced Sibelius, Bartók, Shostakovich, and a good selection of the modern British composers he had grown to love at Glyndebourne—Benjamin Britten, Gustav Holst, Thea Musgrave, Sir William Walton, and Sir Michael Tippett, who gave him permission to present the West Coast premiere of his *Fourth Symphony*.

During the years at Oakland, Simmons was much in demand nationwide as a guest conductor for orchestral and operatic music. He gave the world premiere of Gian Carlo Menotti's opera *La Loca* with Beverly Sills at San Diego, conducted Bizet's *Les Pêcheurs de Perles* at the New York City Opera, and conducted an intensely dramatic performance of Shostakovich's *Lady Macbeth of Mtsensk* at the San Francisco Opera, all to great acclaim. A performance at New York City's Mostly Mozart Festival in August 1980 elicited these comments from critic Andrew DeRhen in *Hi Fi/Musical America:* "It was conductor Calvin Simmons who proved the hero of the evening. The 30-year-old Californian has the valuable talent of knowing how to turn out a polished performance with a minimum of visible effort. His gestures were clean and directed, and his readings balanced freshness and spontaneity with dignified musicianship. . . . The elegant counterpoint in the slow movement of the Mozart Symphony No. 16 in C seemed almost to dance into the ear."

In August 1982 Simmons went to Lake Placid, New York, for a brief vacation. He had just completed a very successful guest appearance in St. Louis as conductor of Mozart's *Cosí fan Tutte* in an innovative production directed by Jonathan Miller, and was slated to conduct *The Magic Flute* at the New York City Opera in September, at the beginning of his fourth season at Oakland. On 24 August he disappeared after taking a fiberglass canoe out on Connery Pond in gusty weather. His body was recovered by divers 11 days later.

B.D.

Parents Henry Calvin S., longshoreman, and Mattie Pearl S., nurse, gospel singer, and church pianist. **Religion** Baptist. **Education** Piano lessons from age five, French horn from age 12; Balboa High Sch., S.F.; Cincinnati Coll. of Music (scholarship) 1967–69; Curtis Inst. of Music, Phila. 1969–72. **Career** With San Francisco Opera: chorister from age nine, San Francisco Boys Chorus; rehearsal pianist during high-sch. years, and assoc. music dir. 1972, Western Opera Theater; asst. conductor, Merola Opera Summer Program 1970; asst. conductor, San Francisco Opera 1972–75. • Member of conducting staff, Glyndebourne Festival Opera, Sussex, England, summers 1974–77; asst. conductor, Los Angeles Philharmonic Orch., and music dir., Young Musicians Foundn. Debut Orch., L.A. 1975–78; music dir., Ojai Festival, CA since 1977; music dir. and conductor, Oakland Symphony Orch., CA since 1979. • Guest conductor with numerous orchs. and opera houses, including New York Philharmonic, New York City Opera, Metropolitan Opera, San Diego Opera, Buffalo Philharmonic, London Philharmonic, Mostly Mozart Festival. **Honors** Adler Award, San Francisco Opera 1972; Exxon Arts Endowment Conductor 1975–78; Stokowski Conducting Award, Amer. Symphony Orch.

KAZUO IWAMA

President of Sony Corporation

Born **Anjo City, Aichi prefecture, Japan, 7 February 1919**

Died **Tokyo, Japan, 24 August 1982**

The giant multinational Sony Corporation, now a household name in high-quality electronics, began just after World War II as a tiny firm that repaired radios and manufactured vacuum tubes in an upper floor of a bombed-out Tokyo department store. Kazuo Iwama, who joined the company three weeks after its incorporation, helped launch Sony into a period of unprecedentedly rapid growth by spearheading its development of the first Japanese transistor radio. He was one of Sony's three main directors and was president of the corporation since 1976 and of its American subsidiary from 1971 to 1973.

Born in Anjo City near Nagoyo in southern Honshu, Iwama studied geophysics and worked as a seismologist at Tokyo Imperial University during and immediately after World War II. Masaru Ibuka and Akio Morita, co-founders of Tokyo Telecommunications Engineering Company, Ltd., Sony's predecessor, persuaded him to work for the fledgling firm in 1946 and put him in charge of tape-recorder production, although he had no experience in electronics. That year, he married Morita's sister, Kikuko.

In the early 1950s Ibuka set out to develop the first transistor radio. The company had never built a radio before and no Japanese firm had produced a single transistor or showed any interest in producing one. "I had no knowledge of semiconductor devices whatsoever," Iwama later said, "but volunteered to head up a task force to study the transistor. I was very, very young." He visited the United States in 1954 to study semiconductor technology with Western Electric, which held the patents. Within a few months, Tokyo Telecommunications had produced its first transistor, and by August 1955 it was marketing its first radio, the TR-55. (An American firm had managed to put a transistor radio on the market a few months before, but Tokyo Telecommunications captured the Japanese market.) In 1960, Sony (the name was changed in 1958) introduced the world's first transistorized television, which Iwama also helped develop.

Iwama was made Sony's senior managing director in 1966, a few years before the corporation embarked on an ambitious global marketing strategy and a program of establishing manufacturing plants abroad. Iwama, whose cool urbanity was an asset in dealing with Western businessmen, was placed in charge of the newly formed Sony Corporation

Courtesy of SONY Corporation

of America in 1971 and oversaw the opening in San Diego of the first Japanese color-television factory in the United States. Returning to Japan in 1973, he was made deputy president and in 1976 succeeded Morita as Sony's president and chief operating officer.

Iwama was awarded the medal of honor with blue ribbon by Emperor Hirohito in 1979 for his services to Japan's electronics industry. He died in Tokyo of colonic cancer at the age of 63. S.A.

Parents Shin-emon I. and Suma I. **Married** Kikuko Morita 1946: Noria; Hiroko; Tomoko. **Education** Tokyo Imperial Univ., grad. 1942; studied transistor technology, U.S. 1954. **Career** Seismology researcher, Earthquake Research Inst., Tokyo Imperial Univ. 1945. • With Sony Corp. (known as Tokyo Telecommunications Engineering Co., Ltd., until 1958), Japan and U.S.: electronics researcher 1946–50s; head, transistor development team 1953–55; sr. managing dir. 1966–71; co-founder 1971, pres. and chief operating officer 1971–73, and bd. chmn. since 1978, Sony Corp. of America; deputy pres. and rep. managing dir. 1973–76; pres. and chief operating officer since 1976. **Honors** Blue ribbon medal of honor, Japan 1979.

Further reading Nick Lyons, *The Sony Vision,* 1976.

JOHN J(EROME) TEAL
Ecologist and arctic researcher
Born **New York City, USA, 7 February 1921**
Died **Huntington Center, Vermont, USA, 26 August 1982**

The musk ox *(Ovibos),* a member of the goat family native to the Canadian tundra that resembles a cross between a sheep and a bison, is one of the very few large mammals to be successfully domesticated in modern times. The establishment of small but thriving herds of musk oxen to provide meat, milk, and wool to North American Eskimos was the work of ecologist and arctic enthusiast John J. Teal, who first began breeding them on his farm in northern Vermont.

The son of an engineer and a speech teacher, Teal developed a love of nature and the far north at an early age and kept a collection of more than 2,000 birds, fish, and mammals at his childhood home in Greenwich, Connecticut. Six foot three and 220 pounds, he played football for Harvard and earned his B.S. in anthropology in 1944. During World War II he earned the Distinguished Flying Cross, three Bronze Stars, and the Air Medal with four Oak Leaf Clusters for his service as a command pilot on bomber missions over Germany. On his days off he flew his B-17 on aerial tours of England's neolithic ruins.

In 1946 Teal received a master's degree in anthropology and human relations from Yale and set out on a long-dreamed-of solo exploration of the Alaskan wilderness. On a traveling fellowship from the Arctic Institute of North America, he and his wife, Penelope Holden, trekked through northern Scandinavia in two expeditions from 1951 to 1953, studying the vast reindeer herds of the Lapps and investigating archeological remains in the Orkney and Shetland islands. Teal had his first encounter with wild musk oxen while traversing a glacier on the island of Spitzbergen, some 400 miles north of Norway.

Convinced that the musk ox could be a boon to impoverished Eskimos, Teal obtained a special trapping license from the Canadian government. (The musk ox has been under government protection since 1926 after it was hunted almost to extinction by Eskimos, Indians, and whites.) In 1954–55 he led two expeditions to Canada's Barren Grounds, above the Arctic Circle, and captured three male and two female calves. They proved to be intelligent, adaptable, and easy to breed in captivity. "The meat is better than beef," wrote Teal, "the wool is the lightest and softest known, and the milk is as good as cow's milk." In 1954 he founded the Institute for Northern Agricultural Research, which later financed breeding programs in Alaska, Canada, Greenland, Iceland, and northern Scandinavia, with grants and assistance from the Ford and Carnegie foundations, the Canadian government, and McGill University. The most successful program to date is in Alaska, where some 250 Eskimos from 22 villages run a profitable business making knitted goods from the wool, called *qiviut.*

In all, Teal led 14 geographical, anthropological, and trapping expeditions above the Arctic Circle. From 1964 to 1977 he taught at the University of Alaska and helped to found a reindeer-breeding industry on the MacKenzie Delta. In the late 1970s he returned to his 300-acre farm in Huntington Center, Vermont, where he died of cancer at the age of 61. S.A.

Parents John Jerome T., engineer and businessman, and Isabelle D. (O'Sullivan) T., speech and phonetics instr. **Married** Penelope Holden 1950 (div. 1971): Pamela G. Nunavik, b. 1951; Ptarmigan Pyrie, b. 1953; John Alden, b. 1955; Lansing Holden, b. 1964. **Education** Brunswick Sch., Greenwich, CT; Newman Sch., Lakewood, NJ, grad. 1938; Harvard Univ., B.S. 1944; aviation training, West Point, NY ca. 1943; Yale Univ., A.M. 1946. **Mil. service** Capt. and acting command pilot, 388th Bomber Group, 8th U.S. Army Air Force, Germany 1944–45. **Career** Scrap-iron collector, Lehigh Valley Railroad, NJ ca. 1939–44; utility hand, then rep., Tower Co., Canada and Wash. DC 1949. • Anthropological and ecological researcher, Canada, Alaska, Scandinavia, and Arctic Circle since 1946; established musk-ox breeding programs, Canada, Greenland, Alaska, and Norway 1950s–70s; research assoc., McGill Univ., Montreal 1951–52; staff member, Tromsø Mus., Norway; founder and pres., Inst. of Northern Agricultural Research, Huntington Center, VT since 1954; assoc. prof. of anthropology and geography, Univ. of Vermont 1957–59; consultant and dir., Canadian reindeer industry, MacKenzie Delta, Alaska since 1960; prof. of human ecology, Univ. of Alaska, Fairbanks 1964–77. **Officer** Chmn.: Fairbanks Sister City Cttee. 1965–66; Interior Alaska chapter, Amer. Scandinavian Foundn. 1966–67; Fairbanks Parent-Teacher Assn. 1966–68; bicentennial cttee. 1976 and sch. bldg. cttee., Huntington, VT. **Fellow** Carnegie Corp. Traveling Fellow, Svalbard, Norway, and northern Scandinavia 1950–51; 1st sr. fellow, Arctic Inst. of North America, McGill Univ. 1951–52; Lithow Osborne Traveling Fellow 1966–67. **Member** Amer. Assn. for Advancement of Science; Amer. Anthropological Soc.; Fedn. of Amer. Scientists; Amer. Soc. of Mammologists; New York Acad. of Sciences; Connecticut Acad. of Sciences; Soc. for Amer. Archaeology; Council on Foreign Relations; Norsk Polarklubb; Tromsø Mus., Norway; Harvard Travellers Club; Sigma Xi. **Honors** DFC, Air Medal with four Oak Leaf Clusters, and Bronze Star three times, WWII; Ford Foundn. fellowship 1958; traveling grant, Ohio State Univ. Research Foundn., Scandinavia. **Film** *Arctic Roundup,* short film on musk-ox ecology and domestication. **Author** *Gift of Dominion,* 1966. **Contributor** of articles on anthropology, geography, and northern agriculture to textbooks and professional jrnls.

Further reading Robert Lewis Taylor, "The Friend of the Musk Ox," in *New Yorker,* 4 Oct. and 11 Oct. 1958.

LORD EVANS OF HUNGERSHALL

Benjamin Ifor Evans
University administrator
***Born* London, England, 19 August 1899**
***Died* 28 August 1982**

Lord Evans, a literary scholar by training, was the able and energetic provost of University College of London University from 1951 until 1966. He was an expert at the friendly persuasion of people of wealth, and managed to raise vast sums of money for the college's postwar building program by appealing to trusts, foundations, and private industry.

Born Benjamin Ifor Evans, he attended the Stationers' Company School and University College, London. In 1921 he was hired as a lecturer in the department of English literature at Manchester University, where he remained until 1925, when he was appointed to the first of a series of professorships. He headed the English departments, successively, at Southampton (1925–26), Sheffield (1926–33), and finally Queen Mary College, London (1933–44). In 1944 he was elected principal of Queen Mary College, serving until his election as provost of University College in 1951.

Writing under the name Ifor Evans, he was a prolific and facile literary critic. *A Short History of English Literature* (1940) was a much-needed compendium that attracted a wide student audience in its Pelican edition. *A Short History of British Drama* (1948) was rather less popular. In *Literature between the Wars* (1948), he argued that a loss of moral certainty had produced a literature of disillusionment, with much unsatisfactory formal experimentation. He discovered a lost Tudor play, *The Commody of Susanna,* which he edited in 1937 with W. W. Greg, the great editor and bibliographer. Among his other literary studies were those on William Morris, John Keats, and Shakespeare. His three novels, *In Search of Stephen Vane* (1946), *The Shop on the King's Road* (1947), and *The Church in the Markets* (1948), were thin on plot and character and rich in personal musings about London, a city he knew thoroughly, and famous figures of the past.

Courtesy of Linguaphone Institute

University College in 1951 faced severe crises on several fronts: the buildings were, by and large, either dilapidated or damaged from wartime bombing; there was an acute lack of lodging and classroom facilities for the students, who had grown considerably in number after the war; and the government had very little money to allocate for maintenance of the academic status quo and none at all for building and expansion. Evans realized he had to go outside the normal avenues of financing, and immediately launched an appeal to private industry, which within four years yielded £400,000 for a new engineering building. This pace was too slow, however, so he expanded his fund-raising horizons to include such well-heeled private corporations and foundations as Marks & Spencer, the Wolfson Foundation, the Wellcome Trust, and the Max Rayne Foundation. From these and other sources he managed the extraordinary feat of raising about £200,000 each year he was provost, thus setting University College for the first time in its history on a firm financial footing. Lord Goodman, head of the Arts Council and an old friend, once remarked admiringly that Evans was "probably the most successful university beggar."

He was knighted in 1955, then made a life peer in 1967, the year after his retirement as provost. As a Labour member of the House of Lords, he often spoke out against the deadening effect of government financial control over the universities. His maiden speech on 13 December 1967 attacked the government's decision not to build a unified national library in Bloomsbury. In addition to his primary duties, Evans was also educational director of the British Council (1940–44), vice chairman of the Arts Council (1946–51), vice president of the Royal Society of Literature in 1974 and its chairman from 1975 to 1977. He was the recipient of several honorary degrees and foreign decorations. A.K.

Parents Benjamin E. and Ann (Powell) E. **Married** Marjorie Ruth Measures 1923: Mary Ann, b. 1931. **Education** Stationers' Co. Sch.; University Coll., London, B.A. 1920, M.A. 1922. **Career** Lectr. in English literature, Univ. of Manchester 1921–24; prof. of English language and literature, University Coll., Southampton 1925–26; prof. of English literature, Sheffield Univ. 1926–33. • With Univ. of London: univ. prof. of English language and literature 1933–44 and principal 1944–51, Queen Mary Coll.; public orator 1947–52; provost, University Coll., London 1951–66. • With Ministry of Information 1939–41; educational dir., British Council 1940–44; consultant, Wates Foundn.; literary critic and historian. **Officer** Chmn.: *Observer* Trust 1957–66; Natl. Insurance Advisory Cttee. since 1957; (also v.p. 1974) Royal Soc. of Literature 1975–77; Educational Advisory Council, Thames Television; Linguaphone Inst.; Rediffusion Educational Council; Cassell Trust. • Vice chmn., Arts Council 1946–51; pres., Anglo-Israel Assn.; trustee, British Mus. **Fellow** FRSL; Queen Mary's Coll.; University Coll., London. **Member** Executive, British Council 1950–54; Athenaeum Club. **Honors** Kahn Travelling Fellowship 1924; kt. bachelor 1955; created Baron Evans of Hungershall of the Borough of Royal Tunbridge Wells, life peer, 1967; officer, Légion d'Honneur, France; chevalier, Order of Crown, Belgium; comdr., Order of Oranje-Nassau, Netherlands; comdr., Order of Dannebrog, Denmark; hon. degrees from University Coll., London, and univs. of Manchester and Paris. **Author** *Encounters,* 1926; *English Poetry in the Later Nineteenth Century,* 1933; *The Limits of Literary Criticism,* 1933; *Keats,* 1934; (co-ed.) *The Commody of Susanna,* 1937; (co-ed.) *Jack Juggler,* 1937; *Tradition and Romanticism,* 1940; *A Short History of English Literature,* 1940; *English Literature,* 1944; *In Search of Stephen Vane* (novel), 1946; *The Shop on the King's Road* (novel), 1947; *Literature Between the Wars,* 1948; *A Short History of English Drama,* 1948; *The Church in the Markets* (novel), 1948; (jtly.) *The Arts in England,* 1948; *The Use of English,* 1949; (jtly.) *A Victorian Anthology,* 1949; *The Language of Shakespeare's Plays,* 1951; *Science and Literature,* 1954; *English Literature: Values and Traditions,* 1962; *Portrait of English Literature,* 1979.

INGRID BERGMAN
Actress
***Born* Stockholm, Sweden, 29 August 1915**
***Died* London, England, 29 August 1982**

The story of Ingrid Bergman's career is not unlike a movie script. A gawky Swedish orphan afflicted with clumsy shyness, chosen at the age of 18 to play a leading film role, she became an instant success in her native country before going to Hollywood, where, within eight years, she eclipsed Garbo and became the world's most popular actress. Then, in 1948, she left her husband and daughter to follow her lover, the Italian director Roberto Rossellini. Her reputation ruined by scandal, and branded in the U.S. Senate as "a powerful influence for evil," she seemed to have forfeited her career, but she won back her public with *Anastasia* (1956) and again rose to the top of her profession, giving her most complex performance in Ingmar Bergman's *Autumn Sonata* (1978).

Her various talents were never displayed in a single film: she was the vulnerable, demure girl of *Intermezzo* (1939), the tragic, dignified wife of *Casablanca* (1942), the saintly, baseball-playing nun of *The Bells of St. Mary's* (1945), the suffering spy of *Notorious* (1946), and the self-sacrificing missionary of *The Inn of the Sixth Happiness* (1958). At first her extraordinary beauty overshadowed her acting ability, just as her image as the embodiment of pure womanhood concealed the complexities of her private life, but eventually she outgrew all attempts to typecast her, playing the tough-minded Israeli politician Golda Meir in "A Woman Called Golda" (1981).

Ingrid Bergman's childhood was saddened by bereavement. Her German mother died when she was three, and her father, a painter turned commercial photographer, when she was 13. The unmarried aunt with whom she went to live after her father's death died only six months later. She was then brought up by an uncle, who allowed her to study acting at the Royal Dramatic Theater School in Stockholm only under protest. Although shy and awkward, she was capable, then as in later life, of remaining perfectly composed in performance, and her determination to succeed secured her a part in the film *Monkbrogreven* (1934) after only a year at the academy. In 1935, after her appearance in *Branningar,* she was voted Sweden's most promising young actress and signed a five-year contract with Gustav Molander, director of her best-known early film, *Intermezzo* (1936). Frequently cast opposite Gösta Ekman, the reigning Swedish star of the day, Bergman was soon regarded as a rival to Greta Garbo, and began to acquire a following in Nazi Germany, where she made a film for UFA studios in 1938. The wholesome image of the demure maiden that she presented to her public was mirrored in the domestic serenity of her private life. While still a drama student she had met Petter Lindstrom, a confident and handsome dentist whose austere personality complemented her own insecurity and lack of worldly experience. They were married in July 1937 and settled in Stockholm, where their daughter Pia was born.

Despite her growing European fame, Bergman remained virtually unknown in the United States until the release of *Intermezzo,* which the *Los Angeles Daily News* described as the best Swedish film ever shown in the United States. The critic had high praise for its star: "Miss Bergman not only has beauty . . . but she is endowed with an emotional intensity which is extremely rare. . . . Hollywood producers ought to form a pool to bring her out to this country, if only to keep her out of Swedish pictures, which are getting altogether too good." These qualities were also noticed by an agent working for David Selznick, who was then looking for foreign films that he could remake in Hollywood. He persuaded Bergman to go to Hollywood in 1938 to make an American version of *Intermezzo* with Leslie Howard. Breaking all Hollywood custom, Selznick allowed her to appear under her own name, which then had an unattractively German association, and without using any makeup. This strategy, forced on him by Bergman's refusal to do anything but follow the dictates of her own nature, was immensely successful. Selznick told a *Look* interviewer in 1958: "We deliberately built her up as a normal, healthy, non-neurotic career woman, devoid of scandal and with an idyllic home life." The American public, satiated with exotic European sirens such as Garbo and Dietrich, took Bergman's unaffected naturalness to their hearts. Graham Greene, then film critic of the *Spectator,* wrote of her performance in *Intermezzo* in 1940: "The film is most worth seeing for the new star Ingrid Bergman, who is as natural as her name. What star before has made her entrance with a highlight gleaming on her nosetip? The gleam is typical of a performance which doesn't give the effect of acting at all but of living—without make-up."

Her first stay in the United States was brief, but at her husband's urging she returned there with her daughter shortly before the outbreak of war. By this time, the press, falling for Selznick's ploy, was ready to welcome her in appropriate terms. Bosley Crowther wrote in the *New York Times* on her arrival: "Picture the sweetheart of a Viking freshly scrubbed with Ivory soap, eating peaches and cream from a Dresden china bowl on the first warm day of spring atop a sea-scarred cliff, and you have a fair impression of Ingrid Bergman." Although under contract to Selznick, she did not appear in any of his productions until the following year. In 1940, when her husband came to join her, she appeared with Burgess Meredith in Ferenc Molnar's play *Liliom* at the 44th Street Theatre in New York, despite her rudimentary knowledge of English. She had been mistaken by the producer for another Swedish actress, Signe Hasso, whose American career had begun some years earlier. Selznick then loaned her to the director Gregory Ratoff for his film *Adam Had Four Sons* (1941), which was followed by her appearance as a barmaid in Victor Fleming's *Dr. Jekyll and Mr. Hyde* (1941).

In a four-year period—1942 to 1945—she made *Casablanca* with Humphrey Bogart, *For Whom the Bell Tolls* and *Saratoga Trunk* with Gary Cooper, *Gaslight* with Charles Boyer, *The Bells of St. Mary's* with Bing Crosby, and *Spellbound* with Gregory Peck. Her performances won her an Academy Award for *Gaslight* in 1944 and the New York Film Critics award as the best actress of 1945. Six years after her arrival in the United States she was a superstar, although the films in which she had appeared were more distinguished by her than she was by them. *Spellbound,* however, marked the beginning of her collaboration with Alfred Hitchcock, for whom she made *Notorious* (1946) and *Under Capricorn* (1949), two of her finest, most complex roles.

As Andrew Sarris noted in the *Village Voice* after her death, Bergman's appeal in *Casablanca* and *The Bells of St. Mary's* was to the hearts of would-be male protectors, for whom she represented an ideal, beautiful, passive, and noble woman. When, in *Casablanca,* her sense of duty triumphs over her passion and she leaves Humphrey Bogart standing in the rain to fly off with her dull husband, both the melancholy romantics and the admirers of moral rectitude are satisfied—erotic desire has been aroused, but then suppressed. Her life, however, took a different course. In 1948, having seen two films by Roberto Rossellini, *Open City* and *Paisan,* she wrote to the director begging him to let her appear in his next production. According to the Hollywood gossips, her marriage to Lindstrom had been foundering for some years and, furthermore, she longed for artistic recognition. Her autobiography implies that both theories were true, and adds that she had been having an affair with the photographer Robert Capa for some years before her departure for Rome in 1949. In 1950 she gave birth to Robertino, her son by Rossellini, and a storm of abuse was heaped on her in the American press. Edwin Johnson, a senator from Colorado, spoke on the floor of the Senate for an hour, denouncing her as "Hollywood's apostle of degradation," and the chorus of denunciation was joined by thousands of American women, members of roundtables and junior leagues, who boycotted her films. It was a testimony to the power of the image that Selznick had created, because what her detractors were complaining of was not that such things happen, but that they happen to the heroine of *The Bells of St. Mary's.*

Courtesy of Culver Pictures

She made six films with Rossellini, none successful at the time but now gaining favor, and bore twin daughters in 1952 after their marriage, by proxy, in Mexico (the Italian courts considered both their divorces invalid). The passing of the beautiful wholesome Ingrid Bergman was followed by a complete eclipse of her reputation, but by the mid-1950s, when Rossellini left her for another married actress and she made *Anastasia* (1956), the American public was ready to welcome her back. Her second Academy Award, for *Anastasia,* and her marriage to the Swedish producer Lars Schmidt completed her rehabilitation, after which she remained a sought-after performer for the rest of her career. Her new image, that of a mature woman who had conquered numerous troubles, was recognized by Kenneth Tynan in 1958: "Her fullest performance has been as herself, the heroine of a sad, sincere novelette written in disapproving headlines. . . . Bergman is the average sensual woman . . . whose life has little in common with the nuns and saints and patient wives she has played on the screen."

Tynan also observed that her talent was for sweetness and suffering, that she would never play tragic or comic roles successfully. In this he was proved wrong; Bergman's later career revealed an enormous range of acting ability. In *Indiscreet* (1958) and *Cactus Flower* (1969) she mastered comedy, and in the theater and on television belied her early persona in *Hedda Gabler* (1962) and *Captain Brassbound's Conversion* (1972). She won a third Academy Award, for best supporting actress, for her role in *Murder on the Orient Express* (1974), but her finest late performance is commonly agreed to be the role of the neurotic, embittered pianist reunited with her family in Ingmar Bergman's *Autumn Sonata* (1978). By then she had been struggling against cancer for four years, and announced that she had made her last film. She returned from retirement, however, to play Golda Meir in the television film "A Woman Called Golda" (1982), a performance for which she was posthumously awarded an Emmy in September 1982. She died on her 67th birthday. H.B.

Parents Justus B., painter, photographer, and camera-store owner, and Friedel (Adler) B. **Married** (1) Petter Lindstrom, dentist and neurosurgeon, 1937 (div. 1950): Pia, TV reporter, b. 1938. (2) Roberto Rossellini, filmmaker, 1950 (div. 1958): Robertino, real-estate salesman, b. 1950; Isabella, actress and model, b. 1952; Ingrid, sociologist, b. 1952. (3) Lars Schmidt, theatrical producer, 1958 (div. 1975). **Emigrated** to U.S. 1939; to Italy 1950; lived in Europe and U.K. since 1960s. **Education** Lyceum For Flickor, Stockholm; Royal Dramatic Theater Sch., Stockholm 1933–35. **Career** Actress, in films since 1935, on stage since 1940, on TV since 1950. **Officer** Pres. of jury, Cannes Film Festival 1973. **Honors** Academy Awards 1944, for *Gaslight,* 1956, for *Anastasia,* and 1974, for *Murder on the Orient Express;* New York Film Critics Awards 1945, for *The Bells of St. Mary's,* 1956, for *Anastasia,* and 1978, for *Autumn Sonata;* Tony Award, for *Joan of Lorraine,* 1946; Emmy Awards 1959, for "The Turn of the Screw," and 1982, for "A Woman Called Golda"; Sylvania Award, for "The Turn of the Screw," 1959; award for best supporting actress, Amer. Soc. of Film and Television Critics, for *Murder on the Orient Express,* 1974; Donatello Award, for *Autumn Sonata,* Italy 1979; Order of Vasa. **Films** *Munkbrogreven,* 1934; *Branningar,* 1935; *Swedenhielms,* 1935; *Valborgsmassoafton,* 1935; *Pa Solsidan,* 1936; *Intermezzo* (Swedish version), 1936; *Dollar,* 1938; *En Kvinnas Ansikte,* 1938; *Die vier Gesellen,* 1938; *En enda Natt,* 1939; *Intermezzo* (remake in English), 1939; *Juninatten,* 1940; *Adam Had Four Sons,* 1941; *Rage in Heaven,* 1941; *Dr. Jekyll and Mr. Hyde,* 1941; *Casablanca,* 1942; *For Whom the Bell Tolls,* 1943; *Swedes in America* (documentary), 1943; *Gaslight,* 1944; *Saratoga Trunk,* 1945; *Spellbound,* 1945; *The Bells of St. Mary's,* 1945; *Notorious,* 1946; *Arch of Triumph,* 1948; *Joan of Arc,* 1948; *Under Capricorn,* 1949; *Stromboli,* 1950; *Europa '51* (rel. as *The Greatest Love),* 1952; *Siamo donne,* 1953; *Giovanna d'Arco al rogo,* 1954; *Un viaggio in Italia* (rel. as *Journey in Italy),* 1954; *Fear,* 1955; *Anastasia,* 1956; *Elena et les hommes* (rel. as *Paris Does Strange Things),* 1957; *Indiscreet,* 1958; *The Inn of the Sixth Happiness,* 1958; *Aimez-vous Brahms?* (rel. as *Goodbye Again),* 1961; *The Visit,* 1964; *The Yellow Rolls-Royce,* 1965; *Stimulantia,* 1967; *Cactus Flower,* 1969; *A Walk in the Spring Rain,* 1970; *From the Mixed-Up Files of Mrs. Basil E. Frankweiler,* 1973; *Murder on the Orient Express,* 1974; *A Matter of Time,* 1976; *Autumn Sonata,* 1978. **Stage** *Liliom,* NYC 1940; *Anna Christie,* Santa Barbara, CA 1941; *Joan of Lorraine,* NYC 1946; *Joan of Arc at the Stake* (oratorio), Naples 1953; *Tea and Sympathy,* Paris 1956; *Hedda Gabler,* Paris 1962; *A Month in the Country,* Guildford, England 1965; *More Stately Mansions,* NYC 1967; *Captain Brassbound's Conversion,* Wash. DC 1972; *The Constant Wife,* NYC 1975; *Waters of the Moon,* London 1979. **Television** "The Turn of the Screw," 1959; "24 Hours in a Woman's Life," 1961; "Hedda Gabler," 1963; "The Human Voice," 1967; "A Woman Called Golda," 1981. **Author** (Jtly.) *Ingrid Bergman: My Story,* 1980.

Further reading Joseph Henry Steele, *Ingrid Bergman,* 1959; Richard Schickel, *The Stars,* 1962; Lillian Ross and Helen Ross, *The Player,* 1962; Rudy Behlmer, ed., *Memo from David O. Selznick,* 1972.

(A.) LEHMAN ENGEL

Conductor, composer, and teacher
Born **Jackson, Mississippi, USA, 14 September 1910**
Died **New York City, USA, 29 August 1982**

Lehman Engel was an important contributor to the development of the American musical theater, conducting more than 100 musicals, including some of Broadway's best-known hits. He was also a composer of incidental music for serious plays and of concert works, operas, and dance scores.

The son of a clothing and shoe salesman, Engel spent a somewhat uncomfortable childhood in Jackson, Mississippi, where his was one of the few Jewish families. He began studying the piano at an early age and took up conducting in high school. He enrolled at the Cincinnati Conservatory, but, according to his autobiography, learned more about music in Mother Haacke's boarding school than in his formal classes. The cacophony of students practicing their instruments taught him, he said, "the colors of the orchestral mosaic. In time I began to know the entire orchestral family intimately without tuition." After a year he transferred to the Cincinnati College of Music, where he composed and conducted *The Pierrot of the Minute,* the first of several operas.

When he was 19, Engel turned down an offer of a teaching job, went to New York City, and spent some months studying music theory with a private teacher in order to qualify for a graduate fellowship to the Juilliard School. His composition teachers at Juilliard included Rubin Goldmark; later he studied with Roger Sessions. He organized an amateur chorus, produced Kurt Weill's children's opera *Der Jasager,* wrote criticism for the *Musical Leader,* and helped found the *Dance Observer.* He also began writing scores for such modern-dance pioneers as Martha Graham and Charles Weidman.

In 1934 Engel was hired by Melvyn Douglas to conduct the music for a production of Sean O'Casey's play *Within the Gates,* which Douglas planned to direct. The score, it turned out, was not good enough to use, and Engel offered to replace it. Overnight, he completed five choruses, four songs, and the incidental music. His score was a success, though the play was not, and Engel's Broadway career was launched. In 1936 he conducted Kurt Weill's *Johnny Johnson* for its entire New York season and the following year was in the pit for the world premiere of Aaron Copland's opera for children, *The Second Hurricane.*

During the Depression, Engel organized, under a grant from the Works Projects Administration, the Madrigal Singers, who performed concerts of early American folk and medieval choral music, long before either was in vogue. He later worked with Orson Welles and John Houseman on Federal Theater Project productions, among them T. S. Eliot's *Murder in the Cathedral* (1936). As an enlisted man during World War II he conducted a military orchestra at the Great Lakes Naval Training Station, then was appointed chief composer of the Navy's film division.

Engel's career as a conductor reached its height in the late 1940s, the golden years of the American lyric theater. He oversaw the musical direction of such classics as *Brigadoon, Annie Get Your Gun, Carousel,* and *Guys and Dolls*—all shows whose success depended greatly on the timing and technique of the orchestra. He also made numerous cast recordings. He won two Tony Awards for conducting, the first in 1950 for Gian-Carlo Menotti's opera *The Consul,* and the second three years later for *Wonderful Town* and a series of Gilbert and Sullivan operettas. Of the more than 40 plays for which he wrote incidental music, the most famous included *Hamlet* and *Macbeth* for Sir Maurice Evans, Robert Ardrey's *Thunder Rock,* Maxwell Anderson's *Anne of the Thousand Days,* and Tennessee Williams's *A Streetcar Named Desire.* Writing for the theater, he insisted, requires steady professionalism and the ability to adjust one's creativity to the requirements of the show, qualities he attributed to Mozart, who, he said, "had no time for the muse to belt him."

Beginning in 1960, Engel taught workshops for theater composers and lyricists under the sponsorship of Broadcast Music, Inc.; many of Broadway's hit musicals of the 1970s and 80s, including *Nine, A Chorus Line, Little Shop of Horrors* and *The Best Little Whorehouse in Texas,* were the work of his students.

Courtesy of Broadcast Music, Inc.

He was the author of seven books on the history and theory of theater music and of a multivolume history of Renaissance and baroque music. He was working on an oral history of the American theater at the time of his death of cancer at the age of 71. B.D.

Parents Ellis E., shoe salesman, and Juliette (Lehman) E. **Religion** None professed; of Jewish birth. **Education** Cincinnati Conservatory of Music 1926–27; Cincinnati Coll. of Music 1927–29; Juilliard Sch., NYC (fellowship), grad. 1934; private studies with Roger Sessions in composition. **Mil. service** Conductor of military orch. at Great Lakes Naval Training Sta., then chief composer for film div. and lt., U.S. Navy 1942–46. **Career** Composer of concert music, dance scores, and instrumental music for theater and films; conductor of music for lyric theater, films, television, radio, and recordings; co-founder, *Dance Observer;* writer on music. • Founding conductor, Madrigal Singers, WPA 1936–39; assoc. with Federal Theater Project, WPA late 1930s; pres., Arrow Music Press, Inc., since 1938; dir. of workshops for composers and lyricists, Broadcast Music, Inc. since 1960; dir. of music dept., Amer. Musical and Dramatic Theater Acad. 1962–65; lectr. at Salzburg Seminar in Amer. Studies 1968 and at orgs. and univs. throughout U.S.; exec. dir., musical theater development, Columbia Pictures-Screen Gems. **Officer** V.P., Composers and Lyricists Guild. • Member, bd. of dirs.: Henry St. Settlement music sch., NYC; Everyman Assn., Inc.; Foundn. of Theatre and Music Collection, Mus. of City of New York. **Member** Advisory bd., New York High Sch. of Performing Arts; composers commn., League of Composers; Authors Guild; Concert Artists Guild; Players Club; Sigma Alpha Mu. **Honors** Award, Soc. for Publication of Amer. Music 1946; Tony Awards 1950, for music direction of *The Consul,* and 1953, for music direction of *Wonderful Town* and of Gilbert and Sullivan repertory; gold medal, Jackson, MS 1958; Bellamann Award 1964; scroll of honor, Consular Law Soc. 1968; award of merit, Cultural Div., Austria 1968; grant, Natl. Endowment for Humanities ca. 1981; citation, Hartford Conservatory; hon. degrees from Cincinnati Conservatory Coll. of Music, Millsaps Coll., and Boguslawski Coll. of Music. **Composer of incidental music** (all NYC) *Within the Gates,* 1934; *Murder in the Cathedral,* 1936; *A Hero Is Born,* 1937; *The Shoemaker's Holiday,* 1938; *Hamlet,* 1938; *Everywhere I Roam,* 1938; *Thunder Rock,* 1939; *Family Portrait,* 1939; *The Time of Your Life,* 1939; *Heavenly Express,* 1940; *The Trojan Women,* 1941; *Macbeth,* 1941; *A Kiss for Cinderella,* 1942; *Henry VIII,* 1946; *John Gabriel Borkman,* 1946; *Yellow Jack,* 1947; *A Streetcar Named Desire,* 1947; *Me and Molly,* 1948; *A Temporary Island,* 1948; *Anne of the Thousand Days,* 1948; *Uniform of Flesh,* 1949; *The Mikado,* 1949; *The Wisteria Trees,* 1950; *Saint Joan,* 1951; *The Strong Are Lonely,* 1953; *Fanny,* 1954; *Julius Caesar,* 1955; *Middle of the Night,* 1956; *The Ponder Heart,* 1956; *There Was a Little Girl,* 1960; many others. **Musical director** (all NYC) *Second Hurricane,* 1937; *Johnny Johnson,* 1937; *Heavenly Express,* 1940; (also dir.) *The Beggar's Opera,* 1941; *Carousel,* 1945; *Annie Get Your Gun,* 1946; *Call Me Mister,* 1946; *Showboat,* 1946; *Mr. Winkle's Holiday,* 1946; *Brigadoon,* 1947; *Dear Judas,* 1947; *Macbeth,* 1948; *Uniform of Flesh,* 1949; *The Pirates of Penzance,* 1949; *Trial by Jury,* 1949; *H.M.S. Pinafore,* 1949; *The Consul,* 1950; *The Liar,*

1950; *Bless You All,* 1950; *The Mikado,* 1952; *Iolanthe,* 1952; *Wonderful Town,* 1953; *Goldilocks,* 1958; *Destry Rides Again,* 1959; *Take Me Along,* 1959; *Do Re Mi,* 1960; *I Can Get It For You Wholesale,* 1962; *What Makes Sammy Run?* 1964; *Bajour,* 1964; *La Grosse Valise,* 1965; many others. **Operas** *The Pierrot of the Minute,* 1929; *Medea,* 1935; *The Soldier,* 1956. **Ballets** *Scientific Creations,* 1932; *Traditions,* 1938; *The Shoe Bird,* 1968. **Orchestral, vocal, and instrumental works** *Piano Sonata,* 1937; two symphonies, 1939 and 1945; *Cello Sonata,* 1945; *Violin Concerto,* 1945; others. **Composer, films for U.S. Navy** *The Fleet Came to Stay; Report to Judy; Well Done; Fury in the Pacific.* **Recorded** more than 60 albums as conductor. **Author** *Renaissance to Baroque,* 7 vols., 1931; *Music for the Classical Tragedy,* 1953; *Planning and Producing the Musical Show,* 1957, rev. ed. 1966; *The American Musical Theatre: A Consideration,* 1968, rev. ed. 1975; *Words with Music,* 1972; *Getting Started in the Theater,* 1973; *This Bright Day* (autobiography), 1973; *Their Words are Music,* 1975; *The Critics,* 1976; *The Making of a Musical,* 1977; (comp.) *Folk Songs.* **Contributor** to *World Book Encyclopedia,* 1973.

NAHUM GOLDMANN

Zionist leader

***Born* Wisznewo, Lithuania, 10 July 1895**

***Died* Bad Reichenhall, West Germany, 29 August 1982**

In his influence and accomplishment, Nahum Goldmann ranks with the greatest leaders in the history of Zionism. Although he had many enemies among the leaders of Israel, a country he repeatedly criticized for military adventurism, he was universally respected as a diplomat of skillful compromise and brilliant improvisation and a fighter for Jewish rights and ideals everywhere, both in Israel and in the Diaspora.

He was born in Lithuania into a rabbinical family; his father was a teacher and writer. When he was six the family moved to Frankfurt-am-Main, where he received his primary education. He attended the universities of Marburg and Berlin, then worked during World War I in the Jewish section of the German Foreign Ministry, and finally took a law degree from Heidelberg University in 1920 and a Ph.D. the following year.

Goldmann had been an active Zionist for several years before he first visited Palestine in 1913. *Eretz Israel,* a passionate account of his travel experiences and beliefs, appeared in 1914. After the war he briefly (1921–22) published a weekly, *Freie Zionistische Blätter,* then in 1925 joined with his partner in that enterprise, Jacob Klatzkin, in founding a publishing house, Eshkol, to produce a German-language Jewish encyclopedia. The first volumes of *Encyclopaedia Judaica* appeared in 1928, and by 1932, when the Nazis ordered publication halted, ten volumes in German and two in Hebrew had been published. In the early 1960s Goldmann was instrumental in reestablishing the project, and the publication of the English-language *Encyclopaedia Judaica* was completed in 1972.

Goldmann became a member of the Radical Zionist faction in the early 1920s, and was elected the faction's representative on the Zionist Action Committee in 1926. At first he opposed Chaim Weizmann's plan to include non-Zionist Jewish movements in the Jewish Agency and in 1931 formed a majority coalition that denied Weizmann reelection as president of the Zionist organization. The two leaders were reconciled by 1933, and worked as close allies thereafter. Along with his insistence that a Jew could be properly politically involved only as a Zionist, Goldmann also believed that any future Jewish state could accommodate only a portion of world Jewry. The Diaspora would always exist, and its cultural and political needs had to be met.

Forced to flee Germany in 1933, Goldmann was in the same year elected president of the Committee of Jewish Delegations. In 1935, the year Germany convicted him in absentia of high treason and deprived him of citizenship, he was appointed representative of the Jewish Agency at the League of Nations in

Geneva, which had become his home. In 1936, with Rabbi Stephen Wise, he set up a new organization, the World Jewish Congress, of which he was executive chairman until Wise's death in 1951, then president until 1977.

Goldmann moved to the United States in 1940, and during World War II he served as chief Zionist lobbyist in Washington and New York. He had come strongly to support the idea of partition in Palestine as the best way to guarantee Jewish sovereignty in the coming state, and set about trying to persuade Allied governments of his point of view. The eventual United Nations decision in favor of partition owed much to his tough yet engaging diplomacy. He attempted to postpone the proclamation of the state of Israel in May 1948, however, believing that a few more weeks of negotiations would win peaceful concessions from the surrounding hostile Arab states and so avoid the first Arab-Israeli war, which immediately followed independence. He was elected co-chairman of the World Zionist Organization in 1948 and then its president in 1956, 1961, and 1965. He was also offered a portfolio in David Ben-Gurion's first cabinet, which he refused.

One of his most important accomplishments was initiating and presiding over the Conference on Jewish Material Claims against Germany in 1951. Negotiating with his friend Konrad Adenauer, the West German chancellor, Goldmann in September 1952 won major monetary reparations from the young West German state. As of 1982 more than $36 billion had been received by the families of victims and survivors of Nazi persecution. He then set up the Memorial Foundation for Jewish Culture to continue the Claims Conference's work. Smaller payments were agreed to by Austria, but East Germany refused to pay anything.

Goldmann had frequent and acerbic disagreements with Israeli policymakers, particularly over the militarism that led to ever wider and bloodier wars with the Arabs. He concluded that Israel could be at peace with its neighbors only as a neutral state guaranteed by the great powers, for only in that way could his Zionist dream of "a spiritual and inspirational center for the Jewish people throughout the world" be achieved. Twice, in 1956 and 1970, Israeli leaders undercut his efforts at private diplomacy with Pres. Gamel Abdel Nasser of Egypt. He was strongly critical of Labor government leaders, especially Ben-Gurion and Golda Meir, but his finest scorn was saved for Menachem Begin's Likud government, which he accused of aggravating anti-Semitism throughout the world. In 1964, the year he finally accepted Israeli citizenship, Goldmann declared that Zionists "do not owe any legal or political loyalty to Israel." Frequently in interviews he called himself a goy, or Gentile, explaining in 1977 "that what I meant was that I am not stubborn, I am not a fanatic, I am flexible, I understand the other fellow's point of view, I am tolerant, and that's not the Jewish character." Among his last acts was to join in July 1982 with Pierre Mendès France, former premier of France, and Philip Klutznick, president of the World Jewish Congress, in calling for an end to the Israeli invasion of Lebanon and peaceful coexistence between the Israeli and Palestinian peoples.

A man of great culture and urbanity who was fluent, even to the point of oratory, in six languages, Goldmann stayed only rarely in Israel after his citizenship, preferring life in Paris, where he lived for many years in an elegant private hotel on the Avenue Montaigne. He was the author of several books, including an extensive autobiography, first published in Germany in 1970 as *Statesman without a State,* then revised as *My Life as a German Jew* (1980) and *My Life: U.S.A.–Europe–Israel* (1982). His more general com-

Courtesy of World Zionist Organization

mentaries on Zionism and its history and goals were contained in *Where Is Israel Going?* (1975) and *The Jewish Paradox* (1976; English ed. 1978).

In 1978, Beth Hatefutsoth, the Museum of the Diaspora on the campus of Tel Aviv University, was named for Goldmann, who had helped found it the year before. After his death in the small Bavarian spa of Bad Reichenhall, where he had gone for a cure, it was announced that he would be buried on Mount Herzl in Jerusalem alongside other great Zionist leaders. This right was disputed by some Israeli politicians, who believed he had forfeited it because of his years of opposition to government policies. Most Israeli published notices of his death were bitterly critical; Menachem Begin, as head of government, said no public word in his memory. A.K.

Parents Salomon Zvi G., writer and Hebrew teacher, and Rebecca (Kwint) G. **Married** Alice Gottschalk 1934: Michael; Guido. **Religion** Jewish. **Emigration** Brought to Germany as a child; convicted of treason and deprived of German citizenship 1933, became citizen of Honduras; lived in Europe, U.S., and Israel; citizen of Israel since 1964, of Switzerland since 1968. **Education** Schs. in Frankfurt-am-Main; Univ. of Marburg 1914; Univ. of Berlin 1915; Heidelberg Univ., J.D. 1920, Ph.D. 1921. **Career** Staff member, Information Office, German Foreign Ministry, WWI; publisher, *Freie Zionistische Blätter,* Zionist periodical 1921–22; founder 1922 and head 1922–34, Eshkol Publishing Co.; co-ed. and publisher, German ed. of *Encyclopaedia Judaica* to 1934. • Zionist since ca. 1910; member, HaPoel HaTzair Zionist political party early 1920s, left to join Zionist Radical group early 1920s; member 1926–34 and acting chmn. 1934, Zionist Action Cttee., Germany; member, political commn. to negotiate with MacDonald govt.; chmn., political cttee., 17th Zionist Congress 1931; chmn., Cttee. of Jewish Delegations, Paris 1936. • With Jewish Agency for Palestine (later Jewish Agency for Israel): member, exec. cttee. 1934; liaison with League of Nations, Geneva 1934–40; dir., Wash. DC office 1941–46; chmn. 1951–56; pres. 1956–68. • With World Zionist Org.: joined 1934; co-chmn. of exec. 1951; pres. 1956–68. • With World Jewish Congress: founder 1936; exec. chmn. 1936–51; chmn., admin. cttee. 1945–51; acting pres. 1949; pres. 1951–77. • Pres., Conference on Jewish Material Claims Against Germany since 1950; chmn., Cttee. for Jewish Claims on Austria since 1953; chmn., 1st intl. conference for Soviet Jewry, Paris 1960. • Founder: (also pres. since 1965) Memorial Foundn. for Jewish Culture; Beth Hatefutsoth, Nahum Goldmann Mus. of Jewish Diaspora, Tel Aviv Univ. 1978; World Council of Jewish Education; Conference of Presidents of Major Amer. Jewish Orgs. for Israel. **Honors** Hon. pres., *Encyclopaedia Judaica,* NYC since 1960; Légion d'Honneur, France; hon. degrees from Weizmann Inst., Tel Aviv Univ., Brandeis Univ. **Author** *Eretz Israel—Reisebriefe aus Palästina* [*Eretz Israel—Travel Letters from Palestine*], 1914; *Dor shel Khurban u-Geulah* [*Generation of Holocaust and Redemption*], 1968; *Be-Darkhei Ami* [*On the Paths of My People*], 1968; *The Autobiography of Nahum Goldmann*, 1969; *Memories,* 1970; *Staatsmann ohne Staat* [*Statesman without a State*] (autobiography), 1970; *Où va Israël?* [*Where is Israel Going?*], 1975; *Community of Fate* (collection), 1976; *Le paradoxe juif*, 1976 (trans. as *The Jewish Paradox*, 1978); *Mein Leben als deutscher Jude* [*My Life as a German Jew*] (autobiography), 1980; *Mein Leben: U.S.A.-Europa-Israel* [*My Life: U.S.A.—Europe—Israel]* (autobiography), 1982. **Interview** *Moment,* Sept. 1977.

Further reading William Frankel, "The Rebel," in *Present Tense,* Winter 1978.

SEPTEMBER

SIR CLIFFORD (MICHAEL) CURZON
Pianist
***Born* London, England, 18 May 1907**
***Died* London, England, 1 September 1982**

The virtuoso pianist Sir Clifford Curzon was renowned for his vast repertory, beauty of tone, and an intuitive sense of style supported by thoughtful study. Early in his career he was known as a master of the Romantic concerto and as a sensitive interpreter of contemporary British music. More recently, as Max Loppert noted in *The New Groves Dictionary of Music,* "a unique combination of nervous energy and Olympian calm has earned him the virtually undisputed title of 'greatest living Mozartian.'" Harold C. Schonberg wrote in the *New York Times* that Curzon's "tensile strength, so necessary to Mozart, is the secret of only a few living musicians."

Curzon's uncle was the composer Albert Ketelbey; his mother and his father, a dealer in antiques, were both amateur musicians, and they introduced him to the violin when he was five. He switched to piano a year later and took his first lessons from his mother's voice coach. At 12 he entered the Royal Academy of Music in London, the youngest pupil ever to be admitted up to that time. At 14 he entered the senior school, where he studied with Charles Reddie (whose teacher had been a pupil and companion of Franz Liszt); there he won two scholarships and every prize open to pianists, including the prestigious McFarren Gold Medal. He later studied with Tobias Matthay and Katharine Goodson.

Courtesy of Fritz Curzon

When he was 16, Curzon was invited by Sir Henry Wood, conductor of the Promenade Concerts at Queen's Hall, London, to appear as one of the three soloists in Bach's *Triple Concerto*. The following year he gave the world premiere of Germaine Tailleferre's ballade for piano and orchestra, *Les jeux de plein air*. (In his enthusiasm he invited Tailleferre to a rehearsal, then had to renege when Sir Henry refused to meet a woman composer.) Sir Henry's interest greatly helped his career; they toured Britain several times together, and Curzon made ten appearances in a single season of the Proms.

Curzon's father fell ill in the mid-1920s, leaving the family destitute. The blow fell at a bad time for young Curzon, who had hoped to be able to study with Schnabel in Berlin but instead had to take a subprofessorship at the Royal Academy. Fortunately, the mother of a colleague at the Academy bequeathed him enough money to enable him to go to Berlin in 1928. (He still could not afford an overcoat or gloves, and his fingers showed the effects of frostbite to the end of his life.) After two years of intensive work he traveled to Paris to study with Wanda Landowska and Nadia Boulanger. In 1931, he married the Chicago-born harpsichordist Lucille Wallace, who had also studied with Schnabel. The two occasionally appeared in concert together until 1954, when they adopted the orphaned sons of the singer Maria Cebotari and Mrs. Curzon retired from performing to mother them.

During the 1930s, Curzon gained recognition throughout Europe as a star performer. He made his New York debut in 1939 to great acclaim and returned in 1947 for the first of many tours. Of his performance of the Tchaikovsky First Piano Concerto, Jerome D. Boehm wrote in the *Herald Tribune*: "This writer can remember only one previous performance, that of Rachmaninoff, which approached Mr. Cuzon's incandescent intensity, technical perfection, and beauty of tonal investiture." Curzon gave the world premiere of Alan Rawsthorne's Piano Concerto No. 2 in London in 1951, and the following year formed the Edinburgh Festival Piano Quartet with Joseph Szigeti, William Primrose, and Pierre Fournier. He performed as a soloist at virtually all the important European festivals, including those at Edinburgh, Zurich, Bergen, Munich, Salzburg, and Prades.

Curzon's practice schedule was four to eight hours a day. He did not record much, telling one record-company executive, "The trouble with you fellows is that you want stuffed butterflies rather than catching the bird on the wing." Between concert tours, he took long breaks for study and refreshment, especially gardening, at one of his three homes (near Hampstead Heath in London, at Cumberland in England's Lake District, and on the Attersee in Austria). He took no students. "If ever I fall on hard times," he once said, "I would rather trim a hedge than teach."

Curzon, a fellow of the Royal Academy of Music since 1939, was made CBE in 1958 and was knighted in 1977. He died at the age of 75 of a blood disease. B.D.

Parents Michael C., antiques dealer, and Constance (Young) C. **Married** Lucille Wallace, harpsichordist, 1931 (d. 1977): two sons, adopted 1954. **Education** Violin and piano lessons in childhood; Royal Acad. of Music (Thalberg Scholar and Potter Exhibitioner), London 1919–26; studied with Katharine Goodson and Tobias Matthay in England, with Artur Schnabel in Berlin 1928–30, and with Wanda Landowska and Nadia Boulanger in Paris 1930. **Career** Prof., Royal Acad. of Music 1926–32; U.K. debut 1923, U.S. debut 1939; co-founding member, Edinburgh Festival Quartet 1952; frequent tours of U.K., Europe, and U.S. as soloist and guest pianist with major orchs., including New York Philharmonic, Philadelphia, Pittsburgh, Toronto, Berlin, Cincinnati, Detroit, Los Angeles, and the BBC Promenade Concerts; performed at Holland, Zurich, Bergen, Beethoven, Salzburg, Edinburgh, Prades, Aldeburgh, Snapes, other major festivals; occasional recordings. **Fellow** Royal Acad. of Music 1939. **Honors** McFarren Gold Medal, Royal Acad. of Music; CBE 1958; kt. 1977; gold medal, Royal Philharmonic Soc. 1980; hon. fellow, St. Peter's Coll., Oxford 1981; hon. degrees from univs. of Leeds and Sussex. **Interview** "Clifford Curzon Talks to Alan Blyth," in *Gramophone*, May 1971.

WŁADYSŁAW GOMUŁKA

Head of Polish Communist Party
***Born* Krosno, Austro-Hungarian Empire, 6 February 1905**
***Died* Warsaw, Poland, 1 September 1982**

Władysław Gomułka directed the Polish Workers Party from 1943 to 1948 and the Polish United Workers Party from 1956 until 1970, when his government's bloody repression of worker revolts in the Baltic ports forced him to resign. He was unusual among Soviet-bloc statesmen in that he had a modicum of personal appeal; he arrived in office in 1956, a firm anti-Stalinist and a proven Polish nationalist, on one of those waves of popular anticipation, even exultation, that periodically recur in Poland. The hope he engendered was dead before very long, however, crushed by the weight of the Communist regime's bureaucratic inertia and absolute resistance to reform. The disgrace of his failure and resignation was followed by 12 years of obloquy and oblivion, although a minor rehabilitation effort was mounted on his behalf in the last months of his life.

He was born to a poor family in Lwów Province in what is now southern Poland. Before his birth, his parents had returned, disillusioned and destitute, to their native Krosno after several unhappy years working in mining and factory jobs in the United States. Although he was a promising student, his family had no means of keeping him in school beyond the age of 14, and he was sent away from home on an apprenticeship. Two years later he was already involved in union organizing, at first as a member of the Socialist Party, then as a clandestine member of the illegal Communist Party. He was arrested and briefly imprisoned in 1926 for distributing a leftest pamphlet in Krosno. After his release he moved to Warsaw, where he became regional secretary for the chemical workers' union, and then to the Dabrowa Gornicza industrial region of Silesia, where he held a similar position. As a member of the trade-union section of the Communist Party Central Committee, he was frequently involved in illegal strikes, which were usually brutally put down. In 1931, leading a protest by streetcar workers in Warsaw, he was permanently injured by a police gunshot wound in the leg, and was again arrested and sentenced to prison. Released in 1934, he traveled to the Soviet Union, where he was enrolled in Moscow's International Lenin School. He became friendly with one of the school's political warfare instructors, Josip Broz, called Tito.

In 1936, on his return to Poland, Gomułka was rearrested and given a seven-year sentence. This stay in prison undoubtely saved his life, for in 1938, in the midst of the Great Purge in the Soviet Union, virtually the entire Polish Communist leadership was summoned to Moscow and executed for deviationism, after which the Comintern officially dissolved the party. By 1939 he was out of prison, and in September of that year he fought against the Nazis in the futile defense of Warsaw. After the fall of the city, he and the tiny Communist underground made their way to Lwów, then under Soviet occupation.

When, in January of 1942, the Comintern finally allowed the formation of a new party in Poland, to be called the Polish Workers Party, Gomułka was appointed first secretary of the Warsaw branch. He was active in the People's Guard, a leftist, locally directed, partisan guerrilla organization, quite distinct from the more numerous and influential Home Guard, which was directed by the exile government from London. The People's Guard was responsible for the famous attack on the Café Club, a casino frequented by Nazi officers, in reprisal for the Germans' hanging of 50 Polish hostages.

Gomułka continued to move up within the party. In November 1943, after the Gestapo arrested Paweł Finder, the national first secretary, he was appointed to the supreme leadership post. He remained in Warsaw until the beginning of the popular uprising against the Nazi occupation in mid-1944, when he moved to Lublin, where the Soviet-dominated Polish Committee of National Liberation was being formed into a provisional government. In January 1945, with Gomułka as first deputy premier and Communists occupying key cabinet positions, the National Unity government moved to Warsaw. In his first experience in government, Gomułka proved himself competent and ruthless. As minister responsible for the "recovered territories"—those formerly German areas east of the Oder-Neisse line annexed to Poland by the Soviet victors—he efficiently arranged for the wholesale deportation of the indigenous German-speaking population, many of whom had been there for generations. As party leader, he was charged with establishing the Communists as dominant in the government at the expense of their principal coalition partner, the Polish Peasants Party. By means of a campaign of violence, intimidation, and murder that was fully supported by the Soviet occupiers, the Peasant leader, Stanisław Mikołajczyk, who had returned from London to become deputy premier for agriculture, was forced back into exile after the fraudulent 1947 general election.

Signs of tension were soon apparent between Gomułka and an important part of the Communist leadership—those men who had spent much of the war in Moscow. He spoke often of "the Polish road to socialism," rejected outright any thought of agricultural collectivization, resisted the imposition of the Cominform, and was notably supportive of Tito's insistence on independence from Moscow. Given Stalin's increasing demands for subservience from the Soviet-bloc parties, such singular positions were sure to lead to trouble for Gomułka. He was indispensable so long as the party was contending with bourgeois organizations for national dominance; once that was achieved, however, he was seen as an obstinate burden to be got rid of. On 31 August 1948, before the Central Committee, Bolesław Bierut, the chief Moscow hardliner, accused him of "rightist deviationism." Three days later he lost the party leadership, the fol-

lowing month he was relieved of his government posts, and in November 1949 he was removed from the Central Committee. He held a powerless government office until his arrest in August 1951, after which he was interned without trial and incommunicado, accompanied only by his wife, in a government villa near Warsaw. He was able to obtain his release only in July 1954, 15 months after Stalin's death.

In June 1956 the secret police fired on striking workers in Poznań, killing dozens and wounding hundreds. The outrage epitomized the thorough popular discontent with the regime, and demands for a change in the Stalinist leadership became overwhelming; Gomułka, still regarded as the Stalinists' principal victim, was the natural recourse. A plenary session of the Central Committee was called to elect a new leadership, the meeting to begin on 19 October, but before Gomułka could be voted back in, the session was interrupted by the unannounced arrival from Moscow of a planeload of agitated Russians, the most powerful of Stalin's heirs: Nikita Khrushchev, Vyacheslav Molotov, Anastas Mikoyan, Lazar Kaganovich, and Marshal Ivan Konev. The secret confrontation that followed gave rise to years of gossip and speculation in Poland. It is possible that Gomułka had only a minor role in the all-night discussions, but the most commonly repeated story is that the blustering Khrushchev, after denouncing the Polish Communists as traitors, demanded to know the identity of his chief antagonist. "I am Gomułka," came the answer, "formerly first secretary of the party, and because of Stalin and you yourselves I have spent three years in prison." The Soviets were finally satisfied that Gomułka's resurgence meant no threat to their hegemony, and returned to Moscow on 21 October, after which the Central Committee elected Gomułka first secretary.

The following month, after engineering the dismissal of Konstantin Rokossovsky, a Soviet Army marshal "on loan" as Polish defense minister, Gomułka led a delegation to Moscow that won several important concessions: Soviet troops stationed in Poland would henceforth be maintained by the USSR; Polish wartime debts of some 2 billion rubles were canceled; and 1.4 million tons of grain and 700 million rubles in credits were granted to Poland. Clearly, the Kremlin was convinced that Gomułka was not about to lead Poland into a disaster similar to the one that had just befallen Hungary. The powerful Catholic Church was accommodated in early November, when Stefan Cardinal Wyszyński was released from years of house arrest and permitted to resume office as primate of Poland. An explosion of films, novels, and publications of all sorts followed. The Poles called their newly recovered freedoms "the October springtime." Gomułka's address to the Central Committee at year's end seemed to confirm his ascendancy and to promise even more consultation and change: "The working class has recently taught a heavy lesson to party and government leaders. . . . The working class has never lightly resorted to the weapon of the strike. . . . The truth had to be told yesterday, and it must be told today."

It soon became clear, however, that Gomułka's anti-Stalinism was not synonymous with reformism, but only with nationalism. Although he surely sensed the strength of national popular support for him, as a complete realist he knew that he had few close followers in the party hierarchy; he had to depend increasingly on the tolerance of the bare centrist majority that had recalled him from oblivion. He realized furthermore that the Communists would never be able to govern Poland democratically, and that he would have to rely continually on secret-police coercion to maintain them in power. The endemic stagnation of the party and government bureaucracy quickly reasserted itself and overcame all calls for change, as the great majority of Poles settled back into their habitual sullen dissatisfaction. The consensus among them was that Gomułka, blinded by power, had lost his hold on Polish reality.

The last years of Gomułka's rule were almost unrelievedly grim. All talk of economic reform was abandoned, and aridity and stagnation were palpable everywhere. Official anti-Semitism was again encouraged against the tiny remnant of Poland's Jewish community, and Gomułka, although his wife was Jewish, did nothing to stop the vicious attacks directed by his security chief, Gen. Mieczysław Moczar. He was also among the most strident opponents of the liberal regime of Alexander Dubček in Czechoslovakia, firmly supporting the Warsaw Pact invasion of August 1968. In December 1970, as he was signing a peace treaty with West Germany that legitimized the Oder-Neisse line as the Polish-German border, his government was preparing to announce food-price increases of up to 30 percent. On 15 December, workers in Gdańsk and Szczecin who had taken to the streets in protest were fired upon by the militia, and several were killed. The authorities blamed the unrest on "hooligans," which only made the protests spread. On 20 December the Central Committee accepted Gomułka's resignation "for reasons of health." He was succeeded by Edward Gierek, a powerful Politburo member and party secretary in Katowice Province.

For the next dozen years, Gomułka lived in complete obscurity in the Warsaw suburb of Konstancin. At first, he and his regime were the objects of strident attacks by their successors, but these gradually ceased as Gierek and his men encountered ever graver economic difficulties. In 1976 he was reported to be working on his memoirs, which would almost certainly never be published in Poland. The irony was widely remarked that this man, always so intolerant of intellectuals and of such bourgeois ideas as freedom of speech, should in the end be so eager to justify his actions in a book. His reputation underwent a partial rehabilitation at the very end of his life. In 1980, Gierek, himself about to be swept from power, published a 75th-birthday tribute to Gomułka in *Trybuna Ludu*, and in March 1982 Gen. Wojciech Jaruzelski, head of the martial-law regime, visited Gomułka in a Warsaw hospital, where he was dying of throat cancer. In late spring a number of articles appeared in *Zdanie*, an organ of the Kraków party, attempting a more realistic reappraisal of the Gomułka years.

He was given a hero's funeral, with full military honors, by the martial-law authorities, in an apparent attempt to confer a measure of continuity and legitimacy on the military government. An official eulogy praised his "warnings against Western credits," an allusion to the $26 billion in foreign debts incurred by Gierek. In contrast to the corruption and arrogance rampant under his immediate successor, his honesty and simplicity were also invoked. His plain pine coffin was carried by an honor guard, followed by soldiers carrying more than a hundred wreaths and dozens of satin pillows with his many decorations.

A.K.

Also known as Comrade Duniar and Comrade Wiesław. **Father** Jan, oil worker and miner. **Married** Zofia, statistician: Ryszard, engineer. **Education** Elementary sch., Krosno, grad. 1915; vocational sch. ca. 1915–19; Intl. Lenin Sch., Moscow. **Mil service** Member, People's Guard, and organizer, People's Army, sub-Carpathian region 1942–ca. 45. **Career** Blacksmith and mechanic, Krosno 1920s; organized Sila, socialist worker youth party 1920s; member and organizer 1920s–38 and member of trade-union sect. of Central Cttee. 1930s, Communist Workers' Party; imprisoned for leftist activities, Krosno 1926; secty. to various trade union orgs., Warsaw and Silesia 1927; imprisoned 1931–34, 1936–39; organizer and fighter, workers' defense battalion, Warsaw 1939. • With Polish Workers' Party: member 1942–48; 1st secty., Warsaw branch 1942; secty., Central Cttee. 1943; secty. gen. and party leader 1943–48. • Deputy premier, Polish Cttee. of Natl. Liberation 1945; deputy premier and minister for regained territories, Polish Govt. of Natl. Unity 1945–49; deputy to Sejm (parliament) 1947–49, 1957–72; member, United Workers' Party ca. 1948–49; v.p., Supreme Natl. Control Chamber 1949; imprisoned 1951–54; 1st secty. and party leader, Central Cttee., Polish United Workers' Party 1956–70; member, Council of State 1957–71. **Honors** Many Polish and intl. decorations and honors. **Author** (Jtly.) *Walka o jeunośc̀ narodu* [*Struggle for the Unity of Nations*], 1946.

Further reading Konrad Syrop, *Spring in October: The Polish Revolution of 1956*, 1957;

M.K. Dziewanowski, *The Communist Party of Poland*, 1959; Flora Lewis, *The Polish Volcano*, 1959; Richard F. Staar, *Poland, 1944–1962*, 1962; Hans Roos, *A History of Modern Poland*, 1966; Rodger Swearingen, ed., *Leaders of the Communist World*, 1971; Nicholas Bethell, *Gomułka: His Poland and His Communism,*, 1969, rev. ed. 1972.

CARLO ALBERTO DALLA CHIESA
Chief of Italian anti-Mafia operations
***Born* Saluzzo, Italy, 1920**
***Died* Palermo, Sicily, 3 September 1982**

Carlo Alberto Dalla Chiesa was well known throughout Italy as a hero of World War II, as a smart and effective police officer who led a surprisingly successful national mobilization against the Red Brigades and other urban terrorist groups, and finally as the widely respected director of the first important anti-Mafia operation in recent Italian history. After only four months as police prefect of Palermo, he was assassinated in his car, along with his wife of six weeks, by a group of gunmen—almost certainly Mafiosi—in the center of the city. His murder occasioned outrage and apprehension throughout Italy, where there have always been strong doubts about the ability of the authorities to protect public order and citizens' lives.

Dalla Chiesa was born in Saluzzo, a town in Piedmont south of Turin. His family had a long military tradition, and he was given an upbringing in accordance with its strong principles of personal rectitude and service to the state. He was an officer in the Italian Army at the start of World War II, but left it to join the Resistance in 1943. He entered the Carabinieri, the national police, after the war, and as a young lieutenant was sent to Sicily as part of an anti-Mafia brigade. This was in 1948, during the rule of Salvatore Giuglino as chief of the Mafia; on this tour of duty Dalla Chiesa earned the respect of his superiors and subordinates as incorruptible, strict, and absolutely determined.

He then spent several years in Milan, in his native North, where, while rapidly moving up in the ranks, he efficiently reorganized the police station and the officers' quarters. Once again he went to Palermo, this time as a colonel, to be commander of the city's detachment of Carabinieri. While there, he played an important part in the arrest of Frank Coppola, the Sicilian-American gangster. In the 1970s, with urban terrorism beginning to reach alarming proportions in northern Italy, he was returned to Turin as brigadier general. He was notably successful directing the investigation that led to the arrest of Renato Curcio, one of the earliest leaders of the Red Brigades. With this exploit, he began to be associated in the public mind with antiterrorist operations.

In 1978, following the kidnapping and assassination of Aldo Moro, a former prime minister, Dalla Chiesa was appointed to head a special antiterrorist unit, one with extraordinary powers to cut through the many conflicting and overlapping bureaucratic, police, and judicial areas of responsibility that have long impeded effective law enforcement in Italy. He ordered his men to infiltrate the Red Brigades' elaborate command structure, and within 18 months had smashed the organization's two foremost cells, in Milan and Genoa, and severely weakened the one in Turin. In 1979, promoted to general of division, Dalla Chiesa was named head of the Carabinieri's 20,000-member northern command. In 1981 he became deputy commander in chief of the Carabinieri. Although he was extraordinarily reticent in public pronouncements and interviews, he was popularly regarded as the country's best policeman, a thorough professional who knew how to get results, even from a bureaucracy notoriously resistant to efficiency of any kind.

His move back to Palermo as prefect of police was by far his most difficult and dangerous assignment. It was a civil post rather than a military one, so he was obliged to resign his commission in the Carabinieri; the traditional and constitutional restrictions on the office impeded him from the very beginning. His demand for renewed extraordinary powers got him into a public fight with the energetic and respected interior minister of the central government, Virginio Rognoni. "A prefecture in itself," the general said, "does not interest me. The struggle against the Mafia interests me, as well as the means and powers to conquer it in the interests of the state." To this widely supported demand Rognoni was constrained to reply, "The powers of the prefect of Palermo will be those assigned him by law." Dalla Chiesa was futher hampered in that he was not allowed to bring his chief aides with him, but was forced to choose his closest subordinates from the ranks of the Palermo police force, a highly unreliable and even suspect organization. By midsummer, however, he had achieved a somewhat precarious working relationship with the ministry, and had received from the financial administration a preliminary report on the monetary dealings of some 3,200 people with suspected Mafia ties.

Dalla Chiesa knew that in order to defeat the Mafia he would have to strike hard at many powerful people. In particular, he would have to dismantle the mutually supportive network that linked the Mafia with senior members of political organizations, notably the Christian Democratic Party. Over the last decade the Mafia's enormous profits from narcotics trafficking have produced a chaotic boom in many parts of Sicily and southern Italy; its penetration into the region's economic and political life has been so deep that a cure would require radical, even destructive, surgery.

In the first nine months of 1982, nearly 250 murders or disappearances were committed by the Mafia in the Palermo area alone. On 30 April, the very day before Dalla Chiesa's arrival, Pio La Torre, an anti-Mafia Communist deputy, was gunned down in the city. Nevertheless, the assassination of Dalla Chiesa and his wife seemed to many Italians a singular outrage, an indisputable sign of the Mafia's utter disdain for the rule of law and the popular will. The deep anger that pervaded the general's funeral, however, was directed more at the government—so little concerned for his safety that he was not even provided with a bulletproof car—than at the Mafia itself. Dalla Chiesa's funeral eulogy was spoken by the archbishop of Palermo, Salvatore Cardinal Pappalardo, who condemned "the actions and decisions, slow and uncertain, of those who should provide for the security of ordinary citizens, government servants, and state officials." Pres. Sandro Pertini and Prime Minister Giovanni Spadolini, who attended the funeral, were roundly booed as they left the church.

The Italian parliament immediately passed a law making it illegal for anyone to have any connections with the Mafia, and a successor to Dalla Chiesa as prefect, Emanuele de Francesco, soon arrived from Rome with significantly enhanced powers. It is considered highly unlikely, however, especially after the return (November 1982) of the Christian Democrats to power in the central government, that there will be any meaningful purging of the senior ranks of that party to eliminate Mafia sympathizers. It is even less likely that the murderers of Dalla Chiesa and his wife will ever be brought to justice.

A.K.

Father a carabiniere. **Married** (1) . . . : Nando. (2) Emanuela Setti Carraro, nurse, 1982 (d. 1982). **Religion** Roman Catholic. **Education** Studied law and political science. **Career** Infantry officer, Italian Army ca. 1919–43; joined Resistance unit 1943. • With Carabinieri natl. police: joined 1946; lt., anti-Mafia brigade, Sicily 1948; officer, Milan detachment 1950s; col. and comdr., Palermo detachment 1960s; brig. gen., Turin 1970s; in charge of natl. prisons late 1970s; head of anti-terrorist campaign 1978–81; gen of div. and head of nothern command 1979; deputy comdr. in chief 1981; resigned commn. 1981. • Police prefect of Palermo 1982.

FREDERIC DANNAY

Writer and editor of mystery fiction
***Born* Brooklyn, New York, USA, 20 October 1905**
***Died* White Plains, New York, USA, 3 September 1982**

The development of high-quality mystery fiction in the United States was the work of two cousins, Frederic Dannay and Manfred B. Lee. Under the pseudonym of Ellery Queen, they collaborated on a series of sophisticated and popular crime novels, written in classic style, which gave rise to several radio and television series. *Ellery Queen's Mystery Magazine*, edited by Dannay, introduced scores of new writers, raised the literary standards of the genre, and created an unexpectedly large market for mysteries.

Both cousins were born in Brooklyn, New York, to Jewish parents. Lee, the older by nine months, changed his name from Manfred Lepofsky. Dannay took his first name from Frédéric Chopin and his last from the combined first syllables of his original name, Daniel Nathan. He spent his childhood in upstate New York and returned to the city when he was 12. That summer, an aunt brought him *The Adventures of Sherlock Holmes* to entertain him during an illness, and he was hooked.

After graduating from high school, Lee became a publicist for a movie company and Dannay became a copywriter and art director for an advertising agency. They often discussed the possibility of joining forces to write a mystery novel in the manner of such best-selling authors as S. S. Van Dine. The offer of a $7,500 prize in a mystery-writing contest sponsored by *McClure's Magazine* and the publishing house of Frederick A. Stokes finally set them to work on *The Roman Hat Mystery*, featuring a tall, prim detective named Ellery Queen—a melodious and memorable name that they also used as a pseudonym. They won the contest, but *McClure's* folded before the prize could be awarded. The book was published by Stokes to much acclaim, and after two more equally successful collaborations Dannay and Lee were able to quit their jobs for full-time careers as mystery writers. Their output eventually included 35 Ellery Queen novels, 4 novels under the pseudonym Barnaby Ross that featured an aged actor-detective named Drury Lane, 8 short-story collections, and countless half-hour radio scripts.

Like Van Dine's hero, Philo Vance, Queen is a brainy sleuth who solves unusual crimes by dint of wide knowledge and mental concentration, much in the manner of Sherlock Holmes. Often he assists his father, a police inspector. The first nine books, wrote critic Francis M. Nevins, Jr., in his account in *Crime and Mystery Writers*, were "richly plotted specimens of the Golden Age deductive puzzle at its zenith, full of bizarre circumstances, conflicting testimony, enigmatic clues, alternative solutions, fireworks displays of virtuoso reasoning and a constant crackle of intellectual excitement. . . . Most of Queen's distinctive story motifs—the negative clue, the dying message, the murderer as Iagoesque manipulator, the patterned series of clues deliberately left as scenes of crimes, the false answer followed by the true and devastating solution—originated in these early novels." The second-period novels of the late 1930s were less stylized; one of them, *The Four of Hearts* (1938), contained a well-drawn picture of contemporary Hollywood, where Dannay and Lee worked for a time as scriptwriters.

The first Ellery Queen radio show was aired by CBS in 1939. Dannay and Lee were paid $25 per script. CBS did not think sleuthing a serious subject and did not try to find a sponsor for the show until a power failure kept it off the air one night and the switchboard was jammed with complaints. There were two Ellery Queen television series in the 1950s and another in 1975–76, but none of the screenplays was written by Dannay and Lee, though some were based on their novels. Pilot episodes for the other proposed series—one in 1971, with the unlikely combination of Peter Lawford as Queen and Henry Morgan as the Inspector, and the second in 1975—were failures. The producers of the second pilot went on to create the long-running Columbo series. To the knowledgeable viewer, it was evident that the murderer and victim in the first episode were based on Dannay and Lee.

In 1941, while recovering from a serious car accident, Dannay persuaded the magazine publisher Lawrence E. Spivak to start *Ellery Queen's Mystery Magazine*, now the largest-selling magazine of its kind in the world. It was under Dannay's sole editorship for 41 years, since the first issue, and was dedicated to publishing the best in mystery stories, including those by writers not usually thought of as "crime" writers, among them Mark Van Doren, Sinclair Lewis, and Arthur Miller. Newcomers to the genre were sought out and encouraged. Anthony Boucher, writing in the *New York Times* in 1961, credited Dannay with rescuing American detective fiction from the pulps and restoring its reputation as high-quality literature appreciated by an educated readership, as it had been in the days of Poe. Dannay also edited more than 100 anthologies of stories culled from the magazine and from his vast private collection.

The most productive period of the Dannay and Lee collaboration was the 16 years from 1942 to 1958, during which the partners wrote 12 novels, most of them specializing, according to Nevins, in "in-depth character studies, magnificently detailed evocations of place and mood . . . and explorations into historical, psychiatric and religious dimensions." *Calamity Town* (1942), *Ten Day's Wonder* (1948), *Cat of Many Tails* (1949), and *The Origins of Evil* (1951) are usually cited as the best of the group. *The Finishing Stroke*, published in 1958, was apparently intended to be the last Queen novel, but the authors decided to bring him back for one last series, beginning with *The Player on the Other Side* (1963) and ending with *A Fine and Private Place* (1971). Lee died of a heart attack soon afterward. Dannay continued to edit the magazine and the anthologies until his own death, following a brief illness, in 1982.

The collaboration between the two was by all accounts one of amicable belligerence. "It's worse than marriage," Lee told Israel Shenker of the *New York Times* in 1969. "Clash of personalities is good for the ultimate product," Dannay added. "We're not so much collaborators as competitors. It's produced a sharper edge." The address of the Manhattan office where they hammered out plots and characterizations was kept a secret even from their wives and families. In the early years, before their identities were revealed, they sometimes appeared at lectures as Ellery Queen (masked) and Barnaby Ross—either one could play Queen, since they resembled each other—to match wits in the construction and solution of intricate plots. Both them of were certain that the mystery story would continue to hold its own as

Courtesy of Ellery Queen Magazine

first-rate literature. "In 20 or 30 years," Dannay told Shenker, "the literary historians will go back to the good mystery novels to find out what was really going on. Our books are as much a canvas of their time as the books by Proust were of his time." B.D./J.P.

Born Daniel Nathan; name legally changed. **Parents** Meyer H. N. and Dora (Walerstein) N. **Married** (1) Mary Beck 1926 (d.): Douglas; Richard. (2) Hilda Wisenthal 1947 (d. 1972): Stephen (d.). (3) Rose Koppel 1976. **Education** Boys' High Sch., Brooklyn. **Career** Copywriter, art dir., account exec., and typographic consultant, advertising agencies, NYC to 1931. • As Ellery Queen: writer of detective fiction since 1929, full-time since 1931; co-ed., *Mystery League* mag. 1933–34; co-scriptwriter, "The Adventures of Ellery Queen" radio series 1939–48; ed., *Ellery Queen's Mystery Magazine* since 1941; compiler of anthologies; lectr. on detective fiction. • Visiting prof., Univ. of Texas, Austin 1958–59. **Officer** Co-founder and co-pres., Mystery Writers of America. **Member** Crime Writers' Assn., London; Baker St. Irregulars. **Honors** (jtly., as Ellery Queen, except as noted) Edgar Allan Poe Annual Awards from Mystery Writers of America: best radio drama, for "The Adventures of Ellery Queen," 1945; best short story 1947, 1949; special awards 1951, for *Queen's Quorum,* and 1968, for fortieth anniversary of *The Roman Hat Mystery*; best novel, for *The Glass Village*, 1954; Grand Master Award 1960. • Silver Gertrude and Gold Gertrude, Pocket Books; citation for meritorious service, Natl. War Fund 1945; Youth Oscar Award, Youth United 1949; 3rd place, Best Mystery Writers of All Time, Gallup Poll 1950; Poe Ring, Mystery Writers of Japan 1956; Columba Prize in Mystery, Iona Coll. 1968; Grand Prix de Littérature Policière, for *And On the Eighth Day,* 1978; hon. degree from Carroll Coll. 1979; many others. **All works** written jtly. as Ellery Queen, except as noted. **Novels** *The Roman Hat Mystery*, 1929; *The French Powder Mystery*, 1930; *The Dutch Shoe Mystery*, 1931; *The Greek Coffin Mystery*, 1932; *The Egyptian Cross Mystery*, 1933; *The American Gun Mystery*, 1933, as *Death in the Rodeo*, 1951; *The Siamese Twin Mystery*, 1933; *The Chinese Orange Mystery*, 1934; *The Spanish Cape Mystery*, 1935; *Halfway House*, 1936; *The Door Between*, 1937; *The Devil to Pay*, 1938; *The Four of Hearts*, 1938; *The Dragon's Teeth*, 1939, as *The Virgin Heiress*, 1954; *Calamity Town*, 1942; *There Was an Old Woman*, 1943, as *The Quick and the Dead,* 1956; *The Murderer Is a Fox*, 1945; *Ten Days' Wonder*, 1948; *Cat of Many Tails*, 1949; *Double, Double*, 1950, as *The Case of the Seven Murders*, 1958; *The Origin of Evil*, 1951; *The King is Dead*, 1952; *The Scarlet Letters*, 1953; *The Glass Village*, 1954; *Inspector Queen's Own Case*, 1956; *The Finishing Stroke*, 1958; *The Player on the Other Side*, 1963; *And on the Eighth Day*, 1964; *The Fourth Side of the Triangle*, 1965; *A Study in Terror* (novelization of screenplay), 1966, as *Sherlock Holmes Versus Jack the Ripper*, 1967; *Face to Face*, 1967; *The House of Brass*, 1968; *Cop Out*, 1969; *The Last Woman in His Life*, 1970; *A Fine and Private Place*, 1971. • Jtly., as Barnaby Ross: *The Tragedy of X*, 1932; *The Tragedy of Y*, 1932; *The Tragedy of Z*, 1933; *Drury Lane's Last Case*, 1933. • As Daniel Nathan: *The Golden Summer*, 1957. **Omnibus volumes** *Ellery Queen's Big Book*, 1938; *Ellery Queen's Mystery Parade*, 1944; *The Case Book of Ellery Queen*, 1949; *The Wrightsville Murders*, 1956; *The Hollywood Murders*, 1957; *The New York Murders*, 1958; *The Bizarre Murders*, 1962. • Jtly., as Barnaby Ross: *The XYZ Murders*, 1961. **Short-story collections** *The Adventures of Ellery Queen*, 1934; *The New Adventures of Ellery Queen,* 1940; *More Adventures of Ellery Queen*, 1940; *The Case Book of Ellery Queen*, 1945; *Calendar of Crime*, 1952; *QBI: Queen's Bureau of Investigation*, 1954; *Queens Full*, 1965; *QED: Queen's Experiments in Detection,* 1968. **Editor** (solely, as Ellery Queen) More than 100 anthologies, including *Challenge to the Reader,* 1938; *101 Years' Entertainment: The Great Detective Stories, 1841–1941*, 1941 rev. ed. 1946; *Sporting Blood: The Great Sports Detective Stories*, 1942, as *Sporting Detective Stories,* 1946; *The Misadventures of Sherlock Holmes,* 1944; *Best Stories from Ellery Queen's Mystery Magazine*, 1944; *Rogues' Gallery: The Great Criminals of Modern Fiction*, 1945; *To the Queen's Taste*, 1946; *Murder by Experts*, 1947; *20th Century Detective Stories*, 1948, rev. ed. 1964; *The Literature of Crime: Stories by World-Famous Authors*, 1950, as *Ellery Queen's Book of Mystery Stories*, 1957; *12*, 1964; *Lethal Black Book*, 1965; *Poetic Justice: 23 Stories of Crime, Mystery and Detection by World-Famous Poets from Geoffrey Chaucer to Dylan Thomas*, 1967; *Minimysterics*, 1969; *Murder—In Spades!*, 1969; *Shoot the Works!*, 1969; *Mystery Jackpot*, 1970; *The Golden 13*, 1971; *Best Bets*, 1972; *Japanese Golden Dozen,* 1978; editions of works by Dashiell Hammett, O. Henry, Margery Allingham, Erle Stanley Gardner, Stanley Ellin, Julian Symons, others. **Literary criticism** *The Detective Short Story: A Bibliography*, 1942; *Queen's Quorum: A History of the Detective-Crime Short Story as Revealed by the 106 Most Important Books Published in This Field Since 1945*, 1951, rev. ed. 1969; *In the Queen's Parlor, and Other Leaves from the Editors' Notebook*, 1957. **Plays** (With others) *Danger, Men Working*, 1936; more than a dozen others; many radio scripts. **Manuscript collection** in Humanities Research Center, Univ. of Texas at Austin.

Further reading Jacques Barzun and Wendell Hertig Taylor, *A Catalogue of Crime*, 1971; Julian Symons, *Mortal Consequences: A History from the Detective Story to the Crime Novel*, 1972; Francis M. Nevins, Jr., *Royal Bloodline: Ellery Queen, Author and Detective*, 1973.

JACK TWORKOV
Painter
Born **Biała, Poland, 15 August 1900**
Died **Provincetown, Massachusetts, USA, 4 September 1982**

During 60 years of painting, Jack Tworkov never ceased to question the basis of his art. An admirer of Cézanne, he first worked in a naturalistic style modified by Cubism but, in company with de Kooning, Gorky, Kline, and other members of the New York School, he made an abrupt and thorough transition to Abstract Expressionism soon after World War II. In retrospect, both these modes seemed mere stages in his discovery of a unique personal style that was not fully revealed until the showing of his last works at the Guggenheim Museum a few months before his death. In these late paintings, which are chiefly geometric compositions of harmonious colors applied with painterly strokes, he resolved the tension between the opposing tendencies of his work—toward premeditated organization on the one hand, and spontaneous self-expression on the other.

Tworkov was uncomfortable with realism, and recalled his six years working on public murals with the Federal Art Project of the Works Progress Administration as "dreary and dull." But he was equally dissatisfied with the wilder excesses of Abstract Expressionism, whose self-conscious radicalism and rejection of tradition were alien to his thoughtful, measured temperament. De Kooning and other leading figures of the movement were champions of the notion that painting should be an expression of nothing more than the creator's tortured state of mind. Beside their work, Tworkov's paintings seemed detached and dry. According to Emily Genauer, writing in the *New York Herald Tribune* in 1964, "Tworkov's hand is too deliberate, his mind too analytic, his personality too modest to find their most effective projection in an idiom like Abstract Expressionism, whose essence is spontaneity, audacity, automatism." This judgment, made when Abstract Expressionism was at the height of its vogue, defines Tworkov's strengths by negation, and names his virtues as faults.

Courtesy of Nancy Hoffman Gallery

Born in Poland, Tworkov was one of five children of a Jewish tailor who remarried in middle age. "Our house was a precarious place for me," he recalled in a memoir printed in *Art in America.* Hence his turning inward: "I have known alienation all my life. It holds no romance for me. My striving is not for the far-off or far-out landscape, but for the naturalization of a home ground." His family emigrated to the United States when Tworkov was 12, but their life, he explained, did not improve, and he missed the milieu in which he had been brought up. He studied technical drawing at Stuyvesant High School, but when he went to Columbia University he majored in English literature, his principal pleasure. Soon after graduating in 1923 he left his parents' home and began an independent existence in Greenwich Village. His first encounter with the paintings of Cézanne and Matisse led him into art school, where he studied with conservative painters such as Charles Hawthorne and Guy Pène du Bois and developed a style of subdued, thoughtful realism. His first solo show was at the A.C.A. Gallery in New York City in 1940. During the early years of World War II he worked for the WPA, but abandoned this in 1941 to work as a tool designer. He did not paint again until 1945, by which time his work was directed both toward automatic expression and toward the resolution of difficulties in still-life painting.

He was first attracted to Abstract Expressionism while working for the WPA with a fellow painter, Walter Quirt, who was experimenting with automatic drawing. Tworkov showed his own automatic drawings to his Freudian analyst, but finding them too "painful" and "unpleasant" to exhibit publicly, he also worked on a series of still lifes that appeared in his solo show at the Egan Gallery in New York City in 1947. It was not until 1948, when he rented a studio adjacent to that of Willem de Kooning, that he decisively adopted the style of painting—wraithlike forms in vivid colors—that allied him with Abstract Expressionism. Thereafter he exhibited regularly in New York City and with increasing frequency elsewhere in the United States. He taught at Queens College from 1948 to 1955 and took part in numerous summer schools, including that of Black Mountain College. In 1963 he was appointed to the prestigious post of chairman of the art department at Yale University, where he acquired a reputation for being an excellent teacher with an eye for promising students. His pupils included several artists who later became prominent members of the avant garde, such as Richard Serra and Chuck Close. An exhibition of his work at the Whitney Museum in 1964 confirmed his position as a leading abstractionist, despite the dissenting opinions of those critics who found his work lacking in expressionist force. Not until his second Whitney show, in 1971, was his style generally recognized as a significant departure from the mainstream of Abstract Expressionism.

From 1969, when he resigned his post at Yale, he and his wife spent the winters in New York City, where they occupied two floors of an industrial building in Chelsea, and summers in Provincetown, where Tworkov had studied as a young man and had bought a small studio. In an interview given to *Art in America* shortly before his death at the age of 82, he said, "I am tired of the artist's agonies, whether in painting or in poetry. . . . I wanted something outside myself, something less subjective." His late paintings are an assertion that images, shapes, and colors in abstract painting are self-justifying and need bear no reference to the painter's state of mind.

Courtesy of Nancy Hoffman Gallery

Tworkov was an articulate man who, had he not been a painter, might have made his way as a writer. His copious journals, and the many interviews that he gave, are ample evidence of his continual effort to assess the value of his profession and its place in a world that, in his estimation, paid little attention to the values of art. Explaining his own development, he said in 1977: "By the end of the 1950s I felt that the automatic aspects of Abstract Expressionist painting of the gestural variety, to which my painting was related, had reached a stage where its forms had become predictable and automatically repetitive. Besides, the exuberance that was a condition of the birth of this painting could not be maintained forever without pretense." His writing reveals a man who was a perceptive critic of his own work and therefore bore the double burden of creation and judgment. H.B.

Parents Hyman T., tailor, and Esther (Singer) T. **Married** Rachel Wolodarsky 1935: Hermine Ford Moskowitz; Helen. **Religion** Jewish. **Emigrated** to U.S. 1913; naturalized 1928. **Education** Stuyvesant High Sch., NYC; Columbia Coll., NYC, grad. 1923; studied painting, Provincetown, MA, summers 1923–25; Natl. Acad. of Design, NYC 1923–25; Art Students League, NYC 1925–26. **Mil. service** Tool designer for war industry, WWII. **Career** Painter since 1920s; designer, Remo Bufano puppet theater 1920s; designer, Playwrights' Theater, NYC 1928–30; artist, Federal Art

Project, Works Progress Admin. 1935–41; Leffingwell Prof. of Art and chmn. of art dept. 1963–69 and prof. emeritus since 1969, Yale Univ. • Visiting artist and instr.: Queens Coll. 1948–55; Amer. Acad. in Rome 1972; Dartmouth Coll., Hanover, NH 1973; Royal Coll. of Art, London 1974; Cooper Union Sch. of Art, NYC 1975; Univ. of California, Santa Barbara 1976; California State Coll., Long Beach 1979; also Black Mountain Coll., Indiana Univ., Tulane Univ., Univ. of Illinois, Univ. of Minnesota, Univ. of Missouri, Univ. of Wisconsin, Pratt Inst., American Univ., others. **Member** Amer. Acad. and Inst. of Arts and Sciences. **Honors** Clark Prize and 28th Biennial Gold Medal, Corcoran Gall. of Art, Wash. DC 1963; Guggenheim Fellowship 1970; Painter of the Year, Skowhegan Sch. of Art, NY 1974; hon. degrees from Maryland Inst. of Art, Columbia Univ., and Rhode Island Sch. of Design. **Solo exhibitions** A.C.A. Gall., NYC 1940; Egan Gall., NYC 1947–54; Baltimore Mus. of Art 1948; Stable Gall., NYC 1954; Walker Art Center, Minneapolis 1957; Yale Univ. Art Gall. 1963; retrospective, Whitney Mus. of Art, NYC, and U.S. tour 1964–65; Castelli Gall., NYC 1965–68; Toledo Mus. of Art, OH 1971; Whitney Mus. 1971; Nancy Hoffman Gall., NYC 1974, 1975, 1977, 1982; Denver Art Mus. 1974; retrospective, U.K. tour 1979–80; Guggenheim Mus., NYC 1982; many other shows in U.S. galls. **Group exhibitions** Amer. Vanguard, Paris 1952; Kassel, West Germany 1958; MOMA and European tour 1958–60; Amer. Vanguard tour, Austria and Yugoslavia 1961–62; Whitney Mus. 1972, 1973, 1981; Mus. of Art, Rhode Island Sch. of Design, Providence 1973, 1976; Cleveland Mus. of Art 1974; Indianapolis Mus. of Contemporary Art 1974; Mus. of Contemporary Art, Cincinnati 1974; Krannert Art Mus., Champaign, IL 1974; Nancy Hoffman Gall., 1974, 1977, 1978; Virginia Mus. of Art, Richmond 1974; Corcoran Biennial, Wash. DC 1975; Brooklyn Mus., NYC 1976, 1980; Guggenheim Mus. 1976, 1979; Hirschhorn Mus., Wash. DC 1976; Art Inst. of Chicago 1977; Worcester Art Mus., MA 1978; Montclair Art Mus., NJ 1978; Yale Univ. Art Gall. 1978; Rockland Center for the Arts, West Nyack, NY 1979; Betty Parsons Gall., NYC 1980; Aldrich Mus., Ridgefield, CT 1981; Summit Art Center, NJ 1981; Root Art Center, Hamilton Coll., Clinton, NY; many others. **Collections** Albright-Knox Gall., Buffalo, NY; Baltimore Mus. of Art; Brooklyn Mus. of Art; Chase Manhattan Bank, NYC; Cleveland Mus. of Art; Detroit Inst. of Arts; Fort Wayne Mus. of Art, IN; Honolulu Acad. of Arts; Wadsworth Atheneum, Hartford, CT; Kent State Univ. Art Galls., OH; Metropolitan Mus. of Art, NYC; MOMA; Natl. Gall. of Art, Wash. DC; Phillips Collection, Wash. DC; Portland Mus. of Art, OR; Mus. of Art, Rhode Island Sch. of Design; Rockefeller Univ., NYC; San Francisco Mus. of Art; Guggenheim Mus., NYC; Storm King Art Center, Mountainville, NY; Univ. Art Mus., Santa Barbara, CA; Huntington Art Gall., Univ. of Texas, Austin; Elvehjem Mus., Univ. of Wisconsin, Madison; Whitney Mus. of Amer. Art, NYC; Yale Univ. Art Gall.; other public and private collections in the U.S. and Europe. **Contributor** of articles on painting to art jrnls. **Interview** Steven W. Kroeber, "An Interview with Jack Tworkov," in *Art in America,* Nov. 1982.

Further reading Edward Bryant, *Jack Tworkov,* 1964; Kasha Linville Gula, "The Indian Summer of Jack Tworkov," in *Art in America,* Sept. 1973; April Kingsley, "Jack Tworkov," in *Art International,* 1974; Lois Fichner Rathus, "Jack Tworkov: A Retrospective View," in *Arts,* Sept. 1982.

SIR DOUGLAS (ROBERT STEUART) BADER
Royal Air Force pilot and war hero
***Born* London, England, 21 February 1910**
***Died* London, England, 5 September 1982**

Sir Douglas Bader, a hero of the Battle of Britain, was one of the most influential aerial tacticians of World War II and an outstanding pilot whose bravura was tempered by a cool, logical mind. He was only the third man in British history to win bars to both the Distinguished Service Order and the Distinguished Flying Cross. During his three and a half years as a prisoner of war in Germany he made four escape attempts and was finally confined to a maximum-security prison. His achievements were all the more remarkable for having been made by a man with two artificial legs.

The son of a Royal Engineer who died of injuries suffered in World War I, Bader was educated at St. Edward's School, Oxford, where he was a top athlete. He went to the Royal Air Force College at Cranwell on a cadetship and upon his graduation in 1930 was given an above-average rating for flying and a recommendation as a "plucky, capable, headstrong" pilot. He was posted to the 23rd Squadron at Kenley, where he played for the cricket and rugby teams and became a star aerial acrobat. His performance at an air show at Hendon was described by a writer in the London *Times* as "ten minutes of the cleanest trick flying, synchronised to a fraction of a second."

On 14 December 1931, while on a brief visit to Woodley, near Reading, he accepted a dare to "beat up" the airfield, though his plane, a Bulldog, was not as maneuverable as his usual Gamecock, and though it was against regulations. But a snide comment about his being "chicken" sent him up in an angry mood to begin a low run across the field. As he went into a roll, one wingtip hit the ground and the plane crashed, leaving Bader with his left shin crushed and his right leg nearly severed at the knee. He survived a double amputation because he was physically fit and because he resented suggestions that he might be dying. He was 21 years old.

After several months on a pegleg and crutches, Bader was fitted with artificial legs. Despite the skepticism of his doctors, he insisted that he did not need a cane, saying, "I'm going to make these bloody legs do what I want." He learned not only to walk and drive a car, but to play tennis, squash, and golf, though not without pain. (In 1948 he was to win a 36-hole challenge cup with a scorecard of 79 and 82.) Eventually he learned to fly again, but the RAF declined to give him anything but ground duties; so in 1933 he resigned his commission and went to work for the Asiatic Petroleum Company.

When the Nazis invaded Poland, Bader petitioned the Air Ministry for a pilot's job, was accepted, and in November 1939 flew solo again for the first time in eight years. He covered the beaches during the British evacuation of Dunkirk in May-June 1940. The following June he was given command of the 242nd Squadron, the only Canadian squadron in the RAF. The squadron had lost half its men and most of its equipment at Dunkirk, but Bader proved to be a natural leader and quickly restored morale.

Bader's controversial strategy was to attack incoming Nazi planes head on with as many British fighters as possible and to position his planes high between the sun and the enemy, in exactly the spot preferred by the German pilots. So outstanding were his results that he was soon leading 60 fighters in the 12th Group Wing, which scored a record of 152 kills in exchange for 30 losses in the Battle of Britain. In March 1941 Bader commanded three Spitfire squadrons that made daily offensive sweeps over France. He was credited with 22 enemy planes destroyed; his own private total was 30. Those flying alongside on return trips were often astonished to see him calmly smoking his pipe with his oxygen mask unclipped and his cockpit top flipped back, despite the danger of lighting a match in a Spitfire.

On 9 August 1941, Bader collided with a Messerschmidt over Béthune, France. One of his artificial legs caught in the wreckage and held him upside down as the plane plunged 19,000 feet; just in time he fell away and parachuted to safety. He was captured by the Germans and imprisoned in the hospital in St. Omer while he recovered from two broken ribs. After his leg was found and returned to him (a replacement leg was also dropped in by the RAF), he escaped from his third-floor room by climbing down a rope of knotted sheets, with his legs hung around his neck. Although he was betrayed and recaptured, he bedeviled the Germans by trying to escape again and again, and was moved to progressively more secure prisons until he reached the Colditz fortress, where his guards confiscated his legs every night. Toward the end of the war he was offered the chance to be invalided home, but chose to stay with his fellow prisoners until the fortress was liberated by the Americans in April 1945. In September he led a victory flypast of 300 aircraft over London.

Bader retired from the RAF in 1946 to rejoin the Aviation Department at his old firm (now known as Shell Petroleum), refusing all suggestions that he enter politics. In 1958 he was appointed managing director of Shell Aircraft Ltd. After his retirement from Shell in 1969, he served on the Civil Aviation Authority (1972–78) and was a salesman of aviation equipment. Throughout Britain he was regarded as a symbol of the nation's grit in standing up to the Nazis. He was also a symbol of hope to people with similar disabilities, and his activities on their behalf earned him the CBE in 1956 and a knighthood in 1976. A movie version of Paul Brickhill's biography of Bader, *Reach for the Sky,* with Kenneth More in the lead role, was released in 1957.

Bader died of a heart ailment while returning home from a speaking engagement at an RAF Association dinner. B.D.

Parents Frederick Roberts B., Royal Engineer, and Jessie (Scott-Mackenzie) B. **Married** (1) Olive Thelma Exley Edwards 1933 (d. 1971). (2) Joan Eileen Murray 1973. **Education** Colet Court; Temple Grove, Eastbourne; St. Edward's Sch., Oxford (scholarship), grad. 1928; RAF Coll., Cranwell (cadetship), grad. 1930; Central Flying Sch. **Career** Commissioned in RAF and posted to 23rd Squadron 1930; invalided out of RAF 1933 after loss of both legs in flying accident; joined Aviation Dept., Asiatic Petroleum Co. Ltd. (later Shell Intl. Petroleum Co.); rejoined RAF 1939; posted to Gen. Duties Branch; posted to 19th Squadron 1940; flight lt. with 222nd Squadron 1940; squadron leader comdg. 242nd Canadian Fighter Squadron 1940–41; wing comdr., 12th Group Wing 1940; wing comdr., Tangmere Wing 1941; POW, Germany 1941–45; group capt., Essex Sect. 1945, and comdr. 1945–46, 11th Group; retired from RAF 1946. • Rejoined Aviation Dept. 1946 and mgr. of aircraft operations 1952–58, Shell Petroleum Co.; managing dir., Shell Aircraft Ltd. 1958–69; salesman of aircraft equipment since 1970; part-time newspaper columnist; opened Bader Arms public house, Tangmere 1981. **Officer** Chmn., Flight Time Limitations Bd. 1974–78. • Dir.: Trafalgar Offshore Ltd.; Patrick Barthropp. **Fellow** Royal Aeronautical Soc. 1976; **Member** Civil Aviation Authority 1972–78; Buck's Club; Royal Air Force Club. **Honors** DSO 1940 and Bar 1941; DFC 1940 and Bar; mentioned in dispatches three times; chevalier, Légion d'Honneur, and Croix de Guerre with Palm, France 1947; CBE 1956; kt. 1976; deputy lt., Greater London; hon. degree from New Univ. of Ulster. **Author** *Fight for the Sky: The Story of the Spitfire and the Hurricane,* 1973.

Further reading Paul Brickhill, *Reach for the Sky,* 1956; Laddie Lucas, *Flying Colours: The Epic Story of Douglas Bader,* 1981.

Courtesy of Shell Photographic Service

NORMAN (RICHARD) COLLINS

Novelist, publisher, and broadcasting executive
***Born* London, England, 3 October 1907**
***Died* London, England, 6 September 1982**

Norman Collins was prominent both as a publisher and as a broadcasting executive; he was also the author of several popular novels, including the best seller *London Belongs To Me.* In the 1940s Collins recognized the great potential of television and as an energetic administrator at the BBC fought hard for improvements and innovations in the field. Later he fought even harder for a British television network that would be independent of the BBC and supported by strictly controlled advertising. It was largely because of his efforts that the government passed the Independent Television (ITV) Act. For the last 20 years of his career he served as vice chairman of Associated Television, one of ITV's franchised stations.

Collins was born in London; his father was an artist of Huguenot descent. His interest in publishing was apparent from an early age: when only eight years old he was producing his own magazine. After primary school he gained admission to the William Ellis School in Hampstead, but instead of going on from there to university—his family was unable to support him—he joined the Oxford University Press as a publicity assistant. He later worked for the literary editor of the *News Chronicle* (1929–33).

Collins was 27 when he achieved his first executive position, as deputy chairman of the London publishing house Victor Gollancz. That same year (1934) his first novel, *Penang Appointment,* was published: this was followed in 1937 by *Flames Coming Out of the Top.* He quickly gained a reputation as an entertaining writer, able to capture with sympathy and wit the characters and the details of ordinary life. Collins continued to write in his spare time throughout the war years and published his best seller, *London Belongs To Me,* in 1945. More than 30 years later the novel was made into a very successful series by Thames Television. He wrote a number of well-received novels in the postwar years; the last one, published in 1978, was *The Husband's Story,* about an unglamorous Admiralty spy and his London suburban life. Selina Hastings, reviewing the book in the *Telegraph Sunday Magazine,* observed: "In spite of Norman Collins' rather patronising approach, his attention to minute detail and sheer narrative skill make this suburban spy story wholly absorbing."

Collins's broadcasting career began in 1941 when he left Gollancz to become a radio producer in charge of the BBC's North American Service. His experience as an executive and his natural enthusiasm and forcefulness proved invaluable in the growing field of wartime radio. Three years later he was called upon by the Director-General of the BBC, William Haley, to put into practice the plans for a General Overseas Service. This was to be the model for the Corporation's postwar alternative to the Home Service, the Light Programme. In 1946, Collins was named controller of the "Light," and under his imaginative leadership it quickly surpassed the "Home" in popularity.

As wartime stringencies lifted there was a revival of interest in television, a medium still in its infancy. Within little more than a year, Collins switched jobs to become controller of television. He moved to the BBC's television center at Alexandra Palace in north London and soon discovered that some of the staff saw him as an intruder and resented his somewhat maverick style. William Haley also had reservations about Collins's style of leadership, and although Haley himself was an innovator, he did not share his television controller's ambitious plans for the medium's future. The slower pace at which Collins was obliged to proceed did not suit him at all, and by the time the BBC hierarchy realized that television was quickly becoming broadcasting's most vital form, Collins was out of favor. He was passed over in 1950 for the newly created post of director of television and promptly resigned.

Collins then devoted himself to promoting the idea of a commercial television network. He worked vigorously from cramped quarters in Covent Garden and supported himself on his royalties and by running the small electronic components company he had formed. Supporters of his campaign included many business people and a small majority of the Conservative Party. The entire Labour Party and Conservative traditionalists such as Lord Hailsham were totally against the idea. Many Britons were proud of the BBC's record and did not want the country's broadcasting future to follow the American pattern. Collins spearheaded his movement with style and humor. He devised the title "independent" television, thus avoiding the negative connotations of the word "commercial." Much of the opposition was stifled by his insistence that advertisers would have no control of program content and, most important, that the number of commercial interruptions and the time allotted to them would be strictly limited. Not always on the defensive, Collins lost no time in pointing to the unfairness and potential danger of the BBC's monopoly of so vital a form of communication.

When a Conservative government passed the Independent Television Act, Collins's company, Associated Television (ATV), gained one of the new network's franchises and commenced broadcasting. Collins paid little heed to Labour threats that the act would be repealed when they were next in office. By the time they were, ITV had become a distinctive and permanent feature of British broadcasting. However, the newly franchised stations had a hard time of it in the very early days, as the public was disinclined to switch over from the BBC channel they had come to know and love. Collins's company solved its financial problems by bringing in a rival group from the entertainment world—Val Parnell, Prince Littler, and Lew (now Lord) Grade—who had not secured a franchise of their own. Grade became the new chairman and Collins the deputy chairman. With the showman Grade in charge, Collins lost his precious chance of becoming a full-fledged television impresario. Nevertheless he remained with ATV and grew wealthy. He retired in 1977. In December 1981, suffering from cancer, he resigned from the board of Independent Television News and the following April relinquished his directorship of the Associated Communicatons Corporation.

In the later years of his life, Collins dabbled in Conservative politics and gave valuable service to the Adoption Committee for Aid to Displaced Persons, to the Council for Nature, and to the National Playing Fields Association. As well, he was involved in the work of the National Book League, the English Stage Society, and the Sadler's Wells Foundation. He also found time to conduct an investigation of the Loch Ness Monster. R.T.

Father Oliver Norman C., artist. **Married** Sarah Helen Martin, actress, 1931: one son; two daughters. **Education** William Ellis Sch., Hampstead, London. **Career** Publicity asst., Oxford Univ. Press 1926–29; asst. literary ed., *News Chronicle,* London 1929–33; deputy chmn., Victor Gallancz Ltd., publishers, 1934–41. • With BBC, London: mgr., North Amer. Service 1941; mgr., Empire Talks 1941–44; dir., Gen. Overseas Service 1944–46; controller of Light Programme 1946–47; controller of television 1947–50. • Founder, Associated Broadcasting Co. 1951; deputy chmn. 1954–77 and dir. 1977–82, Associated Television Corp. (Associated Communications Corp. since 1979); dir., Independent Television News Co. 1955–81; dir., UPITN Corp. 1971–73; gen. commnr. of income tax since 1967. **Officer** Chmn.: Age Action Year 1976; British Foundn. for Age Research 1977; Hyde Park Films; Watergate Productions Ltd.; Central Sch. of Speech and Drama, Industrial Broadcast Services, Ltd.; (also gov. 1965–69) Natl. Book League; Loch Ness Investigation Bureau. • Gov.: British Film Inst. 1949–51; Atlantic Inst. 1965–69; Sadler's Wells Foundn. • Pres.: Radio Industries Club 1950; Pitman Fellowship 1957; Regent Advertising Club 1959–66; Adoption Cttee. for Aid to Displaced Persons 1962–70; Lifeline 1962–70; appeals cttee., Natl. Playing Fields Assn. 1967–69. • V.P., Council for Nature 1963–66. **Member** Council, English Stage Soc. 1964–78; Conservative Party. • Clubs: Carlton; Turf; Beefsteak; M.C.C. **Novels** *Penang Appointment,* 1934; *The Three Friends,* 1935; *Trinity Town,* 1936; *Flames Coming Out of the Top,* 1937; *Love in Our Time,* 1938; *I Shall Not Want* (in U.S. as *Gold for My Bride*), 1940; *Anna* (in U.S. as *The Quiet Lady*), 1942; *London Belongs To Me* (in U.S. as *Dulcimer Street*), 1945; *Black Ivory,* 1947; *Children of the Archbishop,* 1951; *The Bat that Flits,* 1952; *The Bond Street Story,* 1958; *The Governor's Lady,* 1968; *The Husband's Story,* 1978. **Other** *The Facts of Fiction,* 1932; *The Captain's Lamp* (play), 1938.

SIR GERALD (GRAY) FITZMAURICE
Judge of the World Court and the European Court of Human Rights
***Born* Storrington, Sussex, England, 24 October 1901**
***Died* London, England, 7 September 1982**

Sir Gerald Fitzmaurice, a noted international lawyer and specialist in the law of the sea, served for almost 20 years as an international judge, first as a member of the International Court of Justice (World Court) and later as British representative at the European Court of Human Rights.

Born in Sussex, the son of Vice Admiral Sir Maurice Fitzmaurice, Gerald Gray Fitzmaurice was educated at Malvern College and then went up to Caius College, Cambridge, where he achieved distinction as a student of law. He was called to the bar of Gray's Inn at the age of 24 and remained there for four years, then became an assistant legal advisor at the Foreign Office. Over the next ten years he gained a reputation as a highly skilled and meticulous lawyer. With the outbreak of war he moved to the Ministry of Economic Warfare, where he worked on ingenious methods of hampering Germany's ocean commerce. By 1943 he was back at the Foreign Office and became closely involved with the drafting of Britain's proposals for the International Civil Aviation Conference in Chicago and for the San Francisco conference on the United Nations charter.

Fitzmaurice was also concerned with the peace conferences with Japan and Italy and served as counsel for the United Kingdom in several cases before the International Court of Justice. One of the most contentious of these was Britain's dispute with France over the ownership of the Ecrehos and Minquiers rocks off the south and east shores of Jersey in the Channel Islands. The court's 1953 ruling in Britain's favor owed much to Fitzmaurice's careful and detailed testimony. Soon thereafter he was appointed principal legal advisor at the Foreign Office and awarded a knighthood (KCMG). He was appointed a Queen's Counsel in 1957. In the mid-1950s he was heavily involved in the international conventions that led to significant decisions being taken at the first United Nations Conference on the Law of the Sea in 1958. Fitzmaurice also reported on the law of treaties to the International Law Commission, where he was well known for his painstaking explication of lengthy, complex material. His talent for sound analysis was equally evident in his numerous articles on international law and in his series of papers on the case law of the World Court.

Fitzmaurice was elected to the World Court on the death of Sir Hersch Lauterpacht in 1960. Numerous honors followed, including a GCMG and election to the Gray's Inn bench. In the main his opinions as a judge of the World Court were in line with the majority; even so, he usually produced fastidious, stylishly written explanations of his reasons for concurrence. His most significant dissension came in 1962, when Ethiopia and Liberia asked the Court to rule in a case alleging South African violation of its mandate of South West Africa. Fitzmaurice and the court's president, Sir Percy Spender of Australia, issued a joint minority opinion that the Court was not legally competent to rule in the case. Four years later, the court ruled that Ethiopia and Liberia had no legal right to bring the South West African matter before its judges. This surprising reversal, in line with Fitzmaurice's thinking and brought about by Spender's casting vote, was not at all popular and further contributed to the almost universal frustration at South Africa's behavior. The issue also created a rift in the court, and had this not occurred it is generally thought that Fitzmaurice would have succeeded to its presidency.

In 1971 Sir Gerald was named president of the tribunal for the Beagle Channel; he continued this work well after the expiration of his term at the World Court. Some islands in the Beagle Channel, which is slightly to the north of Cape Horn between Chile and Argentina, were claimed by both of the bordering countries. The tribunal, through its examination of historical documents and maps and a visit to the area, unanimously decided in 1977 that the islands in question—Picton, Nueva, and Lennox—belonged to Chile. On that basis, Chile claimed sovereignty over some southerly outlying rocks, the Evout and Barnevelt islands. If Chile's interpretation were sound, then, in Fitzmaurice's phrase, it would "automatically involve jurisdiction over the appurtenant waters and continental shelf and adjacent submarine areas." Argentina declared the court's award of the islands to Chile null and void and continued to exercise its fleet in the area.

Fitzmaurice was elected to the European Court of Human Rights at Strasbourg in 1974. On numerous occasions he dissented from the court's findings. One of the issues that interested him most was that of Britain's alleged torture in Northern Ireland of 14 suspected members of the IRA. Earlier, the European Commission for Human Rights had unanimously agreed that methods of interrogation involving sensory deprivation—prolonged standing, hooding, subjection to loud noise, and deprivation of food, water, and sleep for long periods—constitute torture. During the Strasbourg Court's deliberations, Fitzmaurice argued that these techniques should not be placed in the same category with such barbarous practices as impaling prisoners on a stake through the rectum. In January 1978, the court overturned the commission's findings by 13 votes to 4, but found Britain guilty of "inhuman and degrading" techniques. Fitzmaurice was the only one of the 17 judges to dissent from that verdict.

Fitzmaurice retired from the European Court in 1980 but remained active in international law until his death. R.T.

Parents Sir Maurice F., admiral, and Mabel Gertrude (Gray) F. **Married** Alice Evelina Alexandra Sandberg 1933: two sons (one d. 1979). **Education** Malvern Coll.; Gonville and Caius Coll., Cambridge, B.A., LL.B. (1st Class in Law Tripos) 1924; called to the bar by Gray's Inn 1925. **Mil. service** Legal advisor, Ministry of Economic Warfare 1939–43. **Career** Private law practice 1925–29 and since 1973. • 3rd legal advisor 1929–30s, 2nd legal advisor 1945–53, and principal legal advisor and deputy undersecty. 1953–60, Foreign Office, London. • Legal advisor, U.K. delegations: Intl. Civil Aviation Conference, Chicago 1944; U.N. Charter Conference, S.F. 1945; Paris Peace Conference 1946; U.N. Assembly 1946, 1948–59; Japanese Peace Conference, S.F. 1951; Berlin and Manila Conferences 1954; Law of the Sea Conferences 1958, 1960. • U.K. counsel 1950s and judge 1960–73, Intl. Court of Justice, The Hague; member 1955–60, pres. 1959, and special rapporteur for treaty law, Intl. Law Commn., U.N.; member, Permanent Court of Arbitration 1954–80; bencher, Gray's Inn 1961; pres., Beagle Channel arbitration tribunal 1970s; judge, European Court of Human Rights, Strasbourg 1974–80. **Officer** Pres., Grotius Soc. 1956–60; pres., Inst. of International Law 1967–69. **Member** Clubs: Athenaeum, and United Oxford and Cambridge Univ., London. **Honors** CMG 1946; KCMG 1954; Q.C. 1957; GCMG 1960; hon. fellow, Gonville and Caius Coll. 1961; hon. degrees from univs. of Edinburgh, Cambridge, and Utrecht. **Contributor** to *British Journal of International Law, American Journal of International Law, Hague Recueil, Yearbook of the International Law Commission,* other legal jrnls.

SHEIK MUHAMMAD ABDULLAH
Chief minister of Jammu and Kashmir
Born Soura, near Srinagar, Kashmir, India, British Empire, 5 December 1905
Died Srinagar, Kashmir, India, 8 September 1982

Sheik Muhammad Abdullah, the Lion of Kashmir, was from the early 1930s the principal figure in the political life of Kashmir, the only state in the Indian union with a non-Hindu majority. He was a close follower of Mahatma Gandhi from 1937 and one of the last surviving leaders of the Indian independence movement. Although his preeminence in his homeland and the absolute devotion of his people have never been questioned or threatened, several Indian central governments reacted strongly against his independent and autocratic style, and he spent almost all the years from 1953 to 1968 as a political prisoner. In 1975 he was again permitted to take up the post of chief minister of the joint state of Jammu and Kashmir.

Abdullah was born into a poor but not destitute family of shawl makers. The title of sheik was inherited from his father, who died soon after his son's birth. Educated at the Muslim universities of Lahore and Aligarh, in present-day Pakistan, he returned to Srinagar and became a schoolteacher.

Political activism, usually of an intensely sectarian sort, was then second nature to all educated Kashmiri Muslims. The princely state was governed by a Hindu, Maharajah Sir Hari Singh, in a harshly partisan manner that gained him the deep hatred of his Muslim subjects, who formed over two-thirds of the population. On 13 July 1931 the all-Hindu army fired on a group of Muslim protesters, killing 14. Abdullah, one of the leaders of the demonstration, was arrested, and from prison, along with a group of colleagues, formed the Muslim Conference, which functioned at first as a kind of employment agency for educated Muslims but gradually expanded its base of action to join forces with the much larger Indian independence movement led by Gandhi and his chief lieutenant, Jawaharlal Nehru, himself a Kashmiri Hindu. Failing to persuade the other founders of the Muslim Conference to follow his lead in denouncing communalism and sectarianism and in opening their membership to Hindus and Sikhs, Abdullah formed in 1939 a new, secular organization, the National Conference, which immediately became the central political force of Kashmir. He already enjoyed the complete adulation of his people, who acclaimed him as Sher-i-Kashmir (Lion of Kashmir), a title he wore proudly throughout his career. In 1946 he was again arrested and imprisoned for actions against the maharajah.

He was released a year later in the midst of a raging political storm. With partition between India and Pakistan imminent, Kashmir

had become the most central focus of concern. Muslim Pathan tribesmen, encouraged by the Pakistanis, invaded the Vale of Kashmir from the Northwest Frontier Province, and other uprisings against the maharajah were spreading. Hari Singh came under great pressure from Nehru and Lord Mountbatten, the last British viceroy and new governor general, to come to an immediate modus vivendi with Abdullah, and the sheik was accordingly named to the state's emergency administration. The accession of Kashmir to a progressive, secular India was clearly the preferable course to Abdullah, but he continued to cherish the dream, shared by many of his countrymen, of Kashmiri independence.

In early 1948, Nehru sent Abdullah with the Indian delegation to Lake Success, New York, to argue India's case against Pakistani aggression before the United Nations Security Council. When he returned home after two months, he was named prime minister of Kashmir. During the negotiations over the evolving Indian constitution, he won unique concessions for Kashmir that avoided its complete integration into the union; but his rule, never quieting down after its stormy beginning, began to seem an increasing burden to the central government. He started speaking frequently about independence, expressing misgivings about secularism and the accession to India. Corruption and a repressive one-party rule by the National Conference were widely noted defects in his government.

Finally, in August 1953, he was dismissed from office and imprisoned without trial. He was released in early 1958, but reimprisoned four months later; released again in April 1964, he was at precarious liberty for only 13 months before being returned to detention. Throughout his ordeal he never agreed to make the one statement that would have secured his instant release—a promise of future loyalty to India. Yet shortly after his final release, in 1968, when on his return to Srinagar he was rapturously received by hundreds of thousands of Kashmiris, he confessed that his views had somewhat softened. Seven years later, after much hard negotiating, a settlement was reached between Abdullah and the central government that allowed him to return to power as chief minister. Under the terms of this agreement, Abdullah abandoned his insistence on a plebiscite to settle the sovereignty question and in effect acknowledged that Kashmir was irrevocably part of India. New Delhi secured his limited support at a time of strong Kashmiri dissatisfaction with direct rule by the central government.

Little changed in Kashmir during Abdullah's second administration: rampant corruption and coercive rule by the resuscitated National Conference continued as if nothing had interrupted them. His relations with Prime Minister Indira Gandhi, whom he had known from her childhood, steadily improved, although he refused to curtail civil liberties in Kashmir during her declaration of national emergency in 1975–77. He continued to make frequent attacks on the central government, but they no longer caused the same bitterness and elicited no further reprisals against him.

News of his death of a heart attack was received with incredulity by his people, many of whom accorded him semidivine status. Indian armed forces were put on alert along the border with Pakistan, and the state government quickly named as new chief minister Abdullah's eldest son, Farooq, a 45-year-old physician who had been brought into the government only a month before as minister of health. Although he subsequently reformed the cabinet, the new Sheik Abdullah, with little of his father's charisma, faced an unstable and even dangerous future in office. A.K.

Father Sheik Muhammad Ibrahim, shawl maker. **Married** Begum Akbar Jahan 1932: Farooq Abdullah, physician and politician; Mustafa Kemal; one other son; two daughters. **Religion** Muslim. **Education** Grammar schs., Srinagar and Jammu; Kashmir Coll.; Univ. of Lahore, grad. with distinction; Univ. of Aligarh, Uttar Pradesh, M.Sc. 1930. **Career** Science teacher, state high sch., Srinagar, Kashmir ca. 1930; led political movement against maharajah of Kashmir and imprisoned 1931; founding pres., Muslim Conference 1931–39; political activist with Indian independence movement 1937–ca. 38, imprisoned 1938; founding pres., Natl. Conference, Kashmir 1939–50s; founder, Quit Kashmir movement 1946; imprisoned for sedition 1946–47; pres., All-India State Peoples' Conference 1946–47; organizer of "peace brigade" militia and head of interim state admin., Jammu and Kashmir 1947; member, Indian delegation to U.N., Lake Success, NY 1948; prime minister, Jammu and Kashmir 1948–53; member, Indian Constituent Assembly 1949; member for Kashmir, Indian parliament 1949–52; imprisoned 1953–58, 1958–64; goodwill ambassador to Pakistan and pilgrimage to Mecca 1964; goodwill ambassador to Europe, Mideast, and U.S. 1964–65; imprisoned 1965–68; founded Kashmir Plebiscite Front 1968; in exile 1971–72; allowed to reenter Kashmir 1972; chief minister, Jammu and Kashmir since 1975; leader, State Congress Party 1975–77; leader of reformed Natl. Conference Party since 1977.

Further reading Dilip Hiro, *Inside India Today,* 1976; Yuri Nasenko, *Jawaharlal Nehru and India's Foreign Policy,* 1977.

WILFREDO (OSCAR DE LA CONCEPCIÓN) LAM (Y CASTILLA)
Painter
Born **Sagua la Grande, Cuba, 8 December 1902**
Died **Paris, France, 11 September 1982**

The painter Wilfredo Lam, the only non-European member of the School of Paris, became associated with the Surrealists after illustrating a poem by André Breton, the French poet whose theories gave rise to the Surrealist movement. "Although a master of technique, and quickly aroused by the social issues of his time," said Breton, "Lam was intensely drawn to the treasure of primitive vision." His characteristic style, which was based on the forms of grotesque animals and plants, owed its inspiration to the self-conscious primitivism of Picasso, but drew its subject matter from the religious rites and landscapes of Lam's Cuban and African heritage. Although he lived the greater part of his

Courtesy of Gimpel & Weitzenhoffer

life in Spain and France, he remained a distinctly Cuban painter and maintained close ties with his native country before and after the revolution.

Wilfredo Oscar de la Concepción Lam y Castilla was the oldest son of an 84-year-old Chinese merchant who had eight more children before he died at the age of 108. His mother was of Caribbean Indian and Negro ancestry. Lam studied painting at the Academie San Alejandro in Havana from 1920 to 1923 and then settled in Madrid, where his teacher was Fernando Alvarez de Sotomajor. He first saw Picasso's work in the mid-1930s, by which time the Spanish artist had been incorporating primitive motifs such as African masks into his paintings and drawings for some 20 years. Lam, encouraged by this example, immediately modified his style to resemble that of Picasso, who, untroubled by Lam's frank imitation of his own work, enthusiastically championed the younger painter after their first meeting in Paris in 1938. Through this friendship, Lam became a member of the avant-garde circle that included André Breton, Paul Éluard, Yves Tanguy, and Tristan Tzara.

Like many other artists of his generation, Lam supported the Spanish Republican cause and fought against Franco during the unsuccessful defense of Madrid in 1938. He moved to Paris at the end of that year, but continued to visit Cuba regularly until 1952, when Paris became his permanent home. His paintings of the 1940s were partially influenced by the Surrealists, but Picasso continued to provide his main inspiration, especially after the completion of *Guernica,* whose monochromatic tones, distorted figures, and animal imagery were echoed in Lam's work throughout his career. Despite this strong dependence on a stylistic model, Lam evolved subject matter that was uniquely his own, placing ever greater stress on symbols that are unmistakably non-European. The tropical plant forms and spiky, aggressive creatures, half bird, half horse, that appear in his later work—especially *Jungle,* a large canvas owned by the Museum of Modern Art in New York—are thought to have been inspired by the Cuban voodoo cults with which he became acquainted during visits to Cuba in 1946–47. According to Sheldon Williams, writing in *Contemporary Artists,* Lam "has refashioned voodoo elements and the lush forbidden fruit of jungles in the Western hemisphere while at the same time portraying these in a contemporary style acceptable to cultured Western eyes." However, in a lengthy profile of Lam published in *ARTnews* in September 1950, Geri Trotta denies this basis for Lam's art, asserting that Lam had attended voodoo ceremonies only rarely, and then as a sightseer. If his paintings do contain symbolic or mystical significance, this is probably personal and owes its force to Lam's imagination rather than any external source. Other critics have named the paintings of El Greco and Henri Rousseau as analogues for Lam's twisted forms and plant motifs. His style borders on Surrealism and Cubism in its use of recurring symbols and its sparse, linear quality, but its final effect is unique and cannot be associated with either movement.

Lam, who was married three times and had

Courtesy of Gimpel & Weitzenhoffer

four children, one of whom died at birth, exhibited regularly in Europe, the United States, and Latin America from the 1940s to the early 1970s. Although relatively little known in the United States, in Europe Lam is considered a modern master and is ranked with Picasso, Léger, Matisse, and Ernst. One of his last public appearances was in 1980, when he was invited to the May Day ceremonies in Havana by the Cuban government. He died in Paris at the age of 79. H.B.

Father a trader. **Married** (1) Eva Piris 1929 (d. 1931): one son (b., d. 1931). (2) Elena Holzer, cancer researcher, 1944 (separated 1950). (3) Lou Laurin 1959: Eskil Soren, b. 1961; Ian Erik Timour. b. 1962; Jonas, b. 1969. **Emigrated** to Spain ca. 1924; went to Paris ca. 1939; lived in Cuba, Martinique, NYC, Italy, and Paris ca. 1941–52; in Paris since 1952. **Education** Acad. San Alejandro, Havana 1920–23; studied painting with Fernando Alvarez de Sotomajor, Madrid 1924–28. **Mil. service** Fighter for Republican cause, Spanish Civil War 1936–39. **Career** Painter since mid-1920s; joined Surrealist movement late 1930s. **Member** Graham Foundn. of Advanced Study in Fine Arts, Chicago 1958. **Honors** First prize, Salon Nacional, Havana 1951; Premio Lissone, Rome 1953; prize, Guggenheim Intl. Award Exhib., NYC 1964; Premio Marzotto, Milan 1965. **Solo exhibitions** Sagua la Grande, Cuba 1923; Galerie Pierre Loeb, Paris 1939, 1945; Galerie Pierre Matisse, Paris 1941–46, 1957–60, 1982; Galerie Maeght, Paris 1953; Salon de Mai, Paris, yearly 1954–70s; Palacio de Bellas Artes, Maracaibo, Venezuela 1957; Museo de Arte Moderna, Havana 1965; retrospective, traveling to Kunsthalle, Basel 1965, Kestner Gesellschaft, Hanover 1967, Stedelijk Mus., Amsterdam 1967, Moderna Museet, Stockholm 1967, Palais des Beaux-Arts, Brussels 1967, and Musée National d'Art Moderne, Paris 1968; Galerie Krugier, Geneva 1970; Gimpel Fils, London 1970; Gimpel & Weitzenhoffer, NYC 1970; Galerie Gimpel & Hanover, Zurich 1971; retrospective, Ordrupgaardsamlingen, Copenhagen 1978. Many other exhibitions in Havana, Paris, Rome, Venice, Milan, NYC, Haiti, and Venezuela. **Group exhibitions** Perls Galls., NYC 1939; Galerie Maeght 1947; Carnegie Instn. 1959; Kassel, West Germany 1959; Musée d'Art Moderne de la Ville, Paris 1966; other exhibs. in Paris, NYC, Havana, West Germany, Brussels, and Mexico City. **Collections** Musée National d'Art Moderne, Paris; Musée, Grenoble; Moderna Museet, Stockholm; Tate Gall., London; Art Inst. of Chicago; MOMA; Guggenheim Mus., NYC; Rhode Island Sch. of Design, Providence; Musée d'Art Moderne de la Ville, Paris; also museums in Malmö, West Berlin, Rotterdam, Vienna, Indianapolis, Oslo, Hanover, Caracas, Havana, Yugoslavia, Denmark, and the Netherlands.

Further reading Geri Trotta, "Wilfredo Lam Paints a Picture," in *ARTnews,* Sept. 1950.

MARCUS WALLENBERG
Banker
***Born* Stockholm, Sweden, 5 October 1899**
***Died* Stockholm, Sweden, 13 September 1982**

For more than 40 years Marcus Wallenberg exercised a dominant influence in Sweden as the country's most powerful banker, a close friend and supporter of socialist prime ministers, and a canny industrialist who knew how to make capitalists prosper under socialism. At the height of his career he was a member of the board of directors of no less than 60 Swedish companies, as well as head of the Wallenberg Group, a conglomerate centered on the country's largest bank and controlling such firms as Saab-Scania, the automaker; SKF, the largest manufacturer of ball bearings in the world; Electrolux home appliances; and L. M. Ericsson, the world's second largest maker of telephone equipment. He was a founder of SAS, the Scandinavian Airline System.

At the time of his birth his family had been a force in Swedish finance and diplomacy for two generations. His grandfather, Anders Oskar Wallenberg, had founded the Stockholms Enskilda Bank in 1856, which eventually became the country's largest. His uncle, Knut Agathon, was Swedish foreign minister from 1914 to 1917. He was educated at the Royal Institute of Technology in Stockholm and the Stockholm School of Economics before being sent abroad to foreign financial capitals—Geneva, Paris, New York, London, and Berlin—in order to learn banking first hand. He was at this time a world-class tennis player, winning the Swedish indoor championship in 1920 and 1926 and representing his country in the Davis Cup and at Wimbledon, where he was the first Swede to play on center court.

He began work as an assistant manager in his grandfather's bank, mastering the entire operation before becoming vice chairman in 1958 and chairman in 1969. In 1971, against the publicly expressed wishes of his equally influential older brother Jacob, he engineered the merger of the Stockholms Enskilda Bank with the Skandinaviska Bank to form the Skandinaviska Enskilda Banken. The new bank became the largest and most powerful commercial bank in the country, the principal bank for 15 of Sweden's 18 largest companies. He was its chairman until his retirement in 1976, then was honorary chairman until his death.

Wallenberg was one of the foremost proponents of Sweden's famous "middle way"—the kind of welfare-state socialism, involving little outright nationalization of industries, that was practiced by a succession of Social Democratic governments from 1932 to 1976. These governments exacted high corporation and estate taxes in order to finance expensive social programs, but left industrial ownership and control in the hands of the capitalists. Most Swedish businessmen were far less complacent about socialism than Wallenberg, who maintained excellent relations with Sweden's socialist leaders; he was particularly friendly with Tage Erlander, prime minister from 1946 to 1969, the era of greatest prosperity for Swedish capitalists. At the time of his death his personal fortune was estimated at $17 million, and his family was worth perhaps three times that amount.

During World War II, Wallenberg served as trade delegate in talks with Britain (1939–43), Finland (1940–44), and Britain and the United States (1943–44). Thereafter he was named to numerous national and international financial organizations, including the Swedish Banks Association, the Federation of Swedish Industries, the Council of European Industrial Federations, and the International Chamber of Commerce. From 1968 to 1976 he was a trustee of the Nobel Foundation. In his later years he provided some financial assistance to the organization that was trying to rescue his cousin, the Swedish diplomat Raoul Wallenberg, who had saved tens of thousands of Hungarian Jews from the Nazis at the end of World War II by distributing false passports and who was later arrested by the Russians, imprisoned in the Soviet Gulag, and abandoned by the West.

A week after Wallenberg's death, Swedish voters returned the Social Democrats under Olof Palme to power following six years of a conservative coalition, the country's first non-leftist government since 1932. Wallenberg did not contribute to the expensive antisocialist advertising campaign mounted by several prominent businessmen: he believed capitalists would continue to thrive, despite Palme's determination to lessen their dominance of the country's economy. A.K.

Parents Marcus W., district judge, and Amalia (Hagdahl) W. **Married** (1) Dorothy Helen MacKay 1923 (div. 1935): Marc (d. 1972); Peter, business exec., b. 1926; Ann-Mari. (2) Baroness Marianne de Geer of Leufsta 1936 (d. 1978). **Religion** Protestant. **Education** Stockholm Sch. of Economics, grad. 1920; Royal Inst. of Technology, Stockholm; studied economics and banking, Geneva, Paris, NYC, London, and Berlin 1920–25. **Career** Professional tennis player 1920s. • With Stockholms Enskilda Bank: asst. mgr. 1925–27; deputy mgr. and dir. 1927–46; managing dir. 1946–58; vice chmn. 1958–69; chmn. 1969–71. • Bd. chmn.: L. M. Ericsson 1933–77; ASEA 1930–76; Saab-Scania 1937–80; Stora Kopperberg Bergslag & Papyrus A.B. 1944-80; (also founder) Scandinavian Airlines System 1951–76; (also founder) Incentive since 1963; (also founder) ADELA Investment Co. SA 1964–67; Skandinaviska Enskilda Banken 1972–76 (hon. chmn. since

Courtesy of Skandinaviska Enskilda Banken

1976); many other Swedish and foreign cos. • Swedish trade negotiator, with U.K. 1939–43, with Finland 1940–44, and with U.K. and U.S. 1943–45. **Officer** Chmn.: Swedish Lawn Tennis Assn. 1934–53 (hon. chmn. since 1953); Swedish Banks Assn. 1949–51, 1956–57 (hon. chmn. since 1975); Industrial Inst. for Economic and Social Research 1950–75 (hon. chmn. since 1975); Swedish natl. cttee., Intl. Chamber of Commerce 1951–64 (hon. chmn. 1964–76); Royal Swedish Lawn Tennis Club since 1953; (also founder) British-Swedish Chamber of Commerce in Sweden 1954–57; (also vice chmn.) Fedn. of Swedish Industries 1959–64; Council of European Industrial Fedns. 1960–63; (also founder) Business and Industrial Advisory Cttee., Org. for European Cooperation and Development 1962–64; economic consultative cttee., Intl. Chamber of Commerce-U.N. Gen. Agreement on Tariffs and Trade 1969–71.; other Swedish and intl. orgs. • Pres.: Inst. Intl. d'Études Bancaires 1955–56; Intl. Chamber of Commerce 1965–67. • Trustee: World Wildlife Fund Intl. since 1966; (also founder) Swedish Natl. Appeal since 1971. • Bd. member: Knut and Alice Wallenberg Foundn. since 1920s; Nobel Foundn. 1968–76. **Member** Natl. Bd. of Civil Aviation, Sweden 1945–66; Stabilization Council 1955–57 and Economic Planning Council 1962–64, Swedish Govt. **Honors** Swedish indoor tennis champion 1920, 1926; Order of Seraphim; KBE, U.K; Légion d'Honneur, France; Grand Crosses, Orders of Vasa, Polar Star, Lion of Finland, and Italian Order of Merit; Grand Band, Order of Star of Africa, Liberia; comdr., 1st Class, Order of Dannebrog, Denmark; Order of St. Olav, 1st Class, Norway; Order of Mexican Eagle, 1st Class; Order of Cruzeiro do Sul, Brazil; Order of White Rose, Finland; Order of Falcon, Iceland; hon. paramount chief, Sannequilie Mah Chiefdom, Liberia; hon. degrees from Royal Inst. of Technology, Stockholm Sch. of Economics, and Georgetown Univ.

Further reading Kati Marton, *Wallenberg,* 1982.

KRISTJÁN (THÓRARINSSON) ELDJÁRN
President of Iceland
Born **Eyjafjördur, Iceland, 6 December 1916**
Died **Cleveland, Ohio, USA, 14 September 1982**

The archeologist and historian Kristján Eldjárn served three consecutive terms as president of Iceland. He was only the third person to hold that office since Iceland became a parliamentary republic in 1944.

Born in Eyjafjördur, in the nothern part of the island, Eldjárn studied Icelandic history, literature, and archeology at the University of Copenhagen and received his Ph.D. from the University of Iceland. He joined the staff of the National Museum of Iceland in Reykjavík in 1945 and within two years was appointed its curator and the official state antiquary. He led numerous archeological expeditions in Iceland, Sweden, Greenland, and Newfoundland, published several books on early pagan and Christian ruins, and edited the journal of the Icelandic Archeological Society.

Eldjárn, an excellent speaker and lecturer, captured public attention in the 1960s as the host of a popular television series about archeology. He decided to run for office and, campaigning on an anti-NATO platform, defeated Gunnar Thoroddsen of the Independence Party by a margin of nearly two to one in the 1968 presidential elections. He was returned unopposed in 1972 and 1976. In the latter years of his third term, with inflation running well above 50 percent, the deputies to the Althing, Iceland's parliament, had increasing difficulty forming a stable ruling coalition. Following the inconclusive general elections of late 1979, Eldjárn called three times for a new government before Thoroddsen managed to patch together a shaky coalition of progressives, agrarians, and Communists in early 1980.

Eldjárn suffered from heart trouble and left the presidency in 1980. He died in a Cleveland hospital of a pulmonary embolism following open-heart surgery for coronary sclerosis.

C.M.

Courtesy of Ólöf Eldjárn

Parents Thórarinn E., farmer and teacher, and Sigrún Sigurhjartardottir. **Married** Halldóra Ingólfsdottir 1947: Ólöf, bookseller, b. 1949; Thórarinn, writer, b. 1949; Sigrún, graphic artist, b. 1954; Ingólfur, b. 1960. **Religion** Evangelical Lutheran Church. **Education** Akureyri Grammar Sch., Iceland, grad. 1936; Univ. of Copenhagen 1936–39; Univ. of Iceland, magister artium 1944, Ph.D. 1957. **Career** Teacher, Akureyri Grammar Sch. 1939–41; curator 1945–47 and dir. and state antiquarian 1947–68, Natl. Mus. of Iceland, Reykjavík; ed., *Journal of the Archeological Society*, Icelandic Archeological Soc. since 1949; editorial cttee. member, *Acta Archaeologica* since 1957; editorial bd. member, *Cultural-Historical Lexicon of the Nordic Middle Ages* 1957–78; host of TV series on archeology 1960s; pres. of Iceland 1968–80; prof., Univ. of Iceland since 1981; writer, lectr., and trans. • Dir., numerous archeological expeditions to Iceland, Sweden, Greenland, and Newfoundland. **Officer** With Icelandic Archeological Soc.: bd. member since 1945; ed. of yearbook since 1947; pres. since 1979. • Pres., Soc. of Grad. Students, Reykjavík 1948–49; chmn., Icelandic Topographical Cttee. 1959–68. • Bd. member: (also member since 1950) Icelandic Acad. 1956–59; humanities div., Icelandic Scientific Fund 1958–68; Icelandic Literary Soc. 1961–68. **Member** Soc. of Icelandic Writers since 1956; Nature Conservation Cttee., Reykjavík 1958–68; permanent cttee., Union Intl. des Sciences Préhistoriques et Protohistoriques since 1962; Royal Nordic Manuscript Soc. since 1963; official cttee. for honors and decorations, Iceland 1966–68; Royal Historical and Antiquities Acad. since 1971; Royal Gustav Adolf Acad., Uppsala since 1977. • Corresponding member: Tromsø Mus., Norway since 1950; Intl. Inst. of Arts and Letters since 1957; Jutland Archeological Soc. since 1962. **Honors** Hon. member: Norwegian Folk Mus. since 1961; Norwegian Acad. of Sciences since 1971; Swedish Archeological Soc. since 1973; Icelandic Writers Union since 1977; Gesellschaft für Früh- und Vorgeschichte, Germany since 1980; Soc. of Antiquaries, Scotland since 1980. • Grand Cross, Order of North Star, Sweden; Grand Cross with Chain of Order of Falcon, Sweden, Order of St. Olav, Norway, and Order of White Rose, Finland; kt., Order of Elephant, Denmark; other decorations from Iceland; hon. degrees from univs. of Aberdeen, Lund, Odense, Bergen, Leningrad, and Leeds. **Author** of *Rústirnar í Stöng* [*The Ruins at Stöng*], 1947; *Gegið á reka* [*Twelve Archeological Articles*], 1948; *Um Hólakirkju* [*On Hólar Cathedral*], 1950; *Um Grafakirkju* [*On Gröf Church*], 1954; *Kuml og haugfé úr heiðnum sið á Íslandi* [*Graves and Antiquities from the Heathen Period in Iceland*], 1956; *Íslensk list frá fyrri öldum*, 1957 (trans. as *Ancient Icelandic Art*, 1957); *Stakir steinar* [*A Collection of Essays*], 1959; *Hundrað ár í Thjóðminjasafni* [*One Hundred Years of the National Museum of Iceland*], 1962; *Hageliksverk Hjálmars í Bólu* [*The Art of Hjálmar in Bola*], 1975; *Arngrímur Gíslason Málari* [*The Painter Arngrímur Gíslason*], 1983. **Translations** Poul Nörlund, *Fronar byggðir á hjara heims* [*Habitation in Greenland in Former Times*], 1972; Petter Dass, *Norð urlandstrómet* [*The Trumpet of the North Country*], 1977; Helgi Finsen and Esbjörn Hiort, *Steinhúsin gömlu á Íslandi* [*The Old Stone Houses in Iceland*], 1978; Wilhelm Busch, *Max og Morits* [*Max and Moritz*], 1981. **Contributor** of articles on Icelandic history and archeology to scholarly jrnls.

For additional honors see *Addendum*.

JOHN (CHAMPLIN) GARDNER

Novelist, teacher, and critic
Born **Batavia, New York, USA, 21 July 1933**
Died **Susquehanna, Pennsylvania, USA, 14 September 1982**

John Gardner's death in a motorcycle accident at the age of 49 cut short the career of one of the most effusive American novelists. He became famous with startling rapidity after the publication of *Grendel* (1971), a retelling of the Old English epic *Beowulf* from the point of view of the monster, and then, in book after book, displayed an extraordinary ability to give fictional life to theories about the moral and intellectual condition of modern humanity.

Reviewers of Gardner's fiction consistently expressed the reservation that his books, though replete with invention, were betrayed by thinness of texture, and overly concerned with notions drawn from the work of other writers. Admitting his technical virtuosity, Morris Dickstein, reviewing his epic poem *Jason and Medeia* (1973), accused Gardner of having "little power of judgment or depth of inspiration. Like another superb technician, Ezra Pound, he needs to hang his hat on another man's rack . . . always the clever student, full of boyish bravado, he sets tough tasks for himself . . . and polishes them off effortlessly, without really pondering if they were worth doing at all." Even in *Grendel*, probably his most accomplished and satisfactory book, Gardner is caught between his own inventiveness and the demands of literary convention. The result is something like a bravura literary exercise based on the proposition "What if the monster could talk?"

Courtesy of Joel Gardner

Gardner, who was described in a *New York Times* profile as "looking something like a pregnant woman trying to pass for a Hell's Angel," cut a strange figure on the Binghamton campus of the State University of New York, where he taught creative writing from 1979 until his death. He was a small, fair-haired, potbellied man who talked excitedly, was addicted to pipes and motorcycles, and strongly disliked urban life. He grew up in Batavia, New York; his father was a dairy farmer and lay preacher, and his mother, a teacher of English, read Shakespeare aloud in the barn at milking time. He began writing and telling tales when he was 12 to help himself recover from the trauma of having caused the death of a younger brother in a tractor accident. (The incident resurfaced many years later in the short story "Redemption.") He received his undergraduate education at DePauw University in Indiana and Washington University in St. Louis before completing a Ph.D. in classical and medieval literature in 1958 at the University of Iowa, which allowed him to submit his dissertation in the form of a novel, *The Old Men*.

Gardner's teaching career began at Oberlin College and continued at Chico State College, San Francisco State College, Southern Illinois University, and Binghamton. Although none of his fiction was accepted for publication until 1966, he was extremely active as a critic and translator of Old and Middle English texts, aiming his commentaries primarily at the general reader rather than his fellow specialists. It was largely for this reason that his most ambitious work in this field, *The Life and Times of Chaucer* (1977), received a cool reception from reviewers, who found Gardner's approach to his subject careless, fanciful, and too concerned with creating an impression of Chaucer as a protomodern writer, plagued by uncertainties similar to those that troubled Gardner himself. The critical biography is, however, one of the most successful attempts to introduce Chaucer to a general audience. One respected Chaucerian, Charles Muscatine, praised it for its enthusiasm and felt that its liveliness more than made up for its questionable assertions.

Gardner's first novel, *The Resurrection* (1966), established a pattern for his fiction that was preserved in his last, *Mickelsson's Ghosts* (1982). In both, a college professor searches through the stock concepts of Western philosophy and literature in order to discover what Chandler, hero of the earlier novel, calls an "unreasonable affirmation," an "aesthetic theory" that will justify and explain life's contingencies. *The Resurrection*, heavily loaded with philosophical tags, attracted little notice in the press, and *The Wreckage of Agathon* (1970), a satire set in ancient Sparta during the reign of the dictator Lycurgus, did little to increase the size of Gardner's audience. In the second novel, however, the philosophical content is more successfully assimilated to narrative and characters: Agathon, an elderly philosopher, and Peeker, his young disciple, imprisoned for their anarchic views and resistance to the dictatorship, ruminate on such questions as the survival of culture and humane values in a military state. It was only in his third novel, *Grendel* (1971), that Gardner was able to develop a powerful idea within an adequate vehicle. Grendel the monster, seen in *Beowulf* only as an evil, destructive force, is portrayed as a sentient creature who longs to be accepted by the very people it attacks. *Grendel* made Gardner into a best-selling writer, but it did not prove to be a solid base from which his subjects or technique developed. The ten works of fiction that he published before his death exhibit an extraordinary diversity of styles and purposes, from *Jason and Medeia* (1973), a retelling in verse of the legend of the Argonauts, to a children's story, *In the Suicide Mountains* (1977).

If *Grendel* is Gardner's most successful work, *The Sunlight Dialogues* (1972) is his most ambitious. This sprawling panorama, containing more than 80 well-defined characters, is set in Gardner's childhood hometown, which he employs both as a naturalistic setting and as an allegorical representation of Everytown, USA. The Sunlight Man, half madman, half sage, is the kind of wise idiot familiar from works as disparate as Dostoyevsky's *The Idiot* and Ken Kesey's *One Flew Over the Cuckoo's Nest*. His dementia and impassioned monologues question the values of the town's solid citizens, especially those of the police chief, Fred Clumly, who stands for experience, tolerance, and finally compassion. Jan Hokenson, in *Contemporary Novelists,* notes Gardner's interest in "dualisms" and compares the Sunlight Man with the figure of the medieval jester, "a professional disturber of the moral peace." Like all Gardner's commentary on contemporary life, the Sunlight Man's wisdom is borrowed from a host of literary antecedents, and estimates of the novel's worth depend on whether the critic admires, forgives, or abhors works that smell of the lamp. What prevents *The Sunlight Dialogues* from being merely a tedious farrago of threadbare philosophical tags and literary devices is Gardner's ability to set his philosophical speculations in the naturalistic setting of an upstate New York town. Just as Saul Bellow's unrivaled ability to describe Chicago and New York City is able to carry his obtrusive intellectual baggage, so does Gardner's interest in living characters and their fates sustain his college professor's addiction to ideas. His next novel, *Nickel Mountain*, published in 1973 but written much earlier in his career, retained the somber rural setting but was far less philosophical; it was a study of the moral development of a middle-aged man who marries a pregnant teenager.

October Light (1976), according to Jan Hokenson, is "the violent, raging counterweight" to *Nickel Mountain*, the story of a brother and sister finally unleashing old hatreds and guilts at each other at the end of their lives. Interspersed with the main narrative and forming almost a third of the book is the text of the cheap adventure novel read by the sister in her bedroom, where her brother has imprisoned her. Wrote critic Robert Towers: "Gardner's work gives the impression of having proceeded from a too well-stocked mind, a mind that cannot resist the temptation, arising from its own cultivation, that must bring to bear the whole weight of Greek mythology, Western philosophy from Plato to the present, medieval allegory, English literature, and Protestant theology upon the quotidian lives of farmers, police chiefs and piano teachers." Nonetheless, *October Light* won the National Book Critics Circle award and was named one of the best books of 1976 by *Time* and the *New York Times*. Gardner tried the book-within-a-book experiment again in *Freddy's Book* (1980); this time, a freakish writer is locked in a bedroom, and the book on which he works, *King Gustav and the Devil*, eventually takes over the narrative as another character begins to read it.

By the time he wrote *Mickelsson's Ghosts*, which was published a few months before his death, Gardner had left his wife of 23 years to marry a fellow teacher at Binghamton. Partly a ghost story, partly a murder mystery, and partly a conventional story of an academic's midlife crisis, the book, though skillfully told and nicely chilling in places, was nearly sunk by its freight of philosophical discussions, many of them of the hopeless classroom variety.

Since he died before he had completed his work, one cannot know how Gardner might have fulfilled the promise of his finest books, and the sum of judgments on his fiction is therefore bound to seem unfairly negative. The course he might have taken is suggested in *On Moral Fiction* (1978), a critical tract in which Gardner examined the nature and objectives of his own craft, comparing his novels favorably with those of his American contemporaries, which he found for the most part "short on significant belief." Observing that we live in "an age of mediocre art," he attributed this decline to the corrosive teachings of Sartre, Wittgenstein, and Freud, who have promulgated pessimism, caution, and determinism—all habits of mind that Gardner, following Tolstoy, saw as inimical to endorsement of life, the true purpose of art. "Great art," he wrote, "celebrates life's potential, offering a vision unmistakably and unsentimentally rooted in love." Most contemporary American writers of fiction, he said, have abandoned the struggle to produce art in order to indulge themselves in the fashionable pursuits of playing intellectual games with their readers and flirting with despair and cynicism. "Real art," he insisted, "creates myths a society can live instead of die by." It is difficult, however, to see how Gardner's fiction exemplifies his own critical principles, and all that these two aspects of his writing appear to have in common is a sentimental nostalgia for a mythical bygone age when writing was founded on firm principles and beliefs.

Many readers of Gardner's critical manifesto were troubled not by his admittedly commonplace ideas but by the vehemence of his attacks on his fellow novelists, including Barth, Bellow, Vonnegut, Barthelme, Coover, Heller, and Mailer. John Barth, questioned by a *New York Times* interviewer in 1979, summed up Gardner's attack on him as follows: "There's something very self-serving about his argument. He's making a shrill pitch to the literary right wing that wants to repudiate all of modernism and jump back into the arms of their nineteenth-century literary grandfathers." Alfred Kazin, however, reviewing the book in *Esquire*, said that the issues raised by Gardner "are more urgent than the way Gardner handles them," noting that Gardner, though "talented, serious, and eagerly affirmative . . . lacks the intense originality that would make his argument personal, delightful, and more persuasive."

In 1977, Gardner was diagnosed as having cancer of the colon; the disease went into remission after surgery, and the following year he moved to Binghamton, where he directed the creative-writing program. With his second wife he was the editor of *MSS*, a magazine for new writers. He died less than a week before he was to marry for a third time. His *On Becoming a Novelist*, and *Tengu Child*, a volume of stories by the Japanese writer Kikuo Itaya that he helped translate, will be published posthumously. H.B.

Parents John Champlin G., dairy farmer and

lay preacher, and Priscilla (Jones) G., high-sch. literature teacher. **Married** (1) Joan Louise Patterson, pianist, composer, and music teacher, 1953 (div. 1979): Joel; Lucy. (2) Elizabeth M. Rosenberg, English prof., 1980 (div. 1982). **Education** DePauw Univ., Greencastle, IN 1951–53; Washington Univ., St. Louis, A.B. 1955; Univ. of Iowa, Iowa City (Woodrow Wilson Fellowship), M.A. 1956, Ph.D. in classical and medieval literature 1958. **Career** Instr., Oberlin Coll., OH 1958–59; instr., Chico State Coll., CA 1959–62; asst. prof. of English, San Francisco State Coll. 1962–65; prof. of English, Southern Illinois Univ., Carbondale 1965–76; visiting prof., Northwestern Univ., Evanston, IL 1973; visiting prof., Bennington Coll., VT 1975–76; prof. of English, Skidmore Coll., Saratoga Springs, NY 1976–77; prof. of English, Williams Coll., Williamstown, MA 1976–77; visiting prof., George Mason Univ., Fairfax, VA 1977–78; dir., creative writing program, State Univ. of New York, Binghamton since 1979; co-ed., *MSS* literary mag. 1981; ed., Southern Illinois Univ. Press Literary Structures Series. • Novelist, short-story writer, poet, librettist, critic, and trans. since 1950s. **Member** Modern Language Assn.; PEN; Amer. Assn. of Univ. Professors. **Honors** Danforth Foundn. Fellow 1970–73; best fiction award, for *Grendel*, *Time* and *Newsweek* 1971; award, Natl. Endowment for the Arts 1972; Guggenheim Fellow 1973–74; award, Amer. Acad. of Arts and Letters; fiction award, for *October Light*, Natl. Book Critics Circle 1976. **Novels** *The Old Men: A Novel* (diss.), 1959; *The Resurrection*, 1966; *The Wreckage of Agathon*, 1970; *Grendel*, 1971; *The Sunlight Dialogues*, 1972; *The Censor* (limited ed.), 1972; *Jason and Medeia* (epic poem), 1973; *Nickel Mountain: A Pastoral Novel*, 1973; *October Light*, 1976; *Freddy's Book*, 1980; *Mickelsson's Ghosts*, 1982. **Short-story collections** *The King's Indian: Stories and Tales*, 1974; *The Art of Living and Other Stories*, 1981; (ed. and co-trans.) Kikuo Itaya, *Tengu Child*, 1982. **Fiction for children** *Dragon, Dragon and Other Timeless Tales*, 1975; *Gudgekin the Thistle Girl and Other Tales*, 1976; *The King of the Hummingbirds and Other Tales*, 1977; *In the Suicide Mountains*, 1977; *Vlemk, the Box-Painter*, 1980. **Poetry** *A Child's Bestiary*, 1977; *Poems*, 1978. **Libretti** *William Wilson*, 1978; *Three Libretti*, 1979; several others. **Literary criticism** (Co-ed.) *The Forms of Fiction*, 1961; (ed.) *The Complete Works of the Gawain-Poet in a Modern English Version*, 1965; (co-ed) *Papers on the Art and Age of Geoffrey Chaucer*, 1967; (ed.) *The Alliterative Morte Arthure, The Owl and the Nightingale, and Five Other Middle English Poems in A Modernized Version*, 1971; *The Construction of the Wakefield Cycle*, 1974; *The Construction of Christian Poetry in Old English*, 1975; *The Poetry of Chaucer*, 1977; *The Life and Times of Chaucer* (biography), 1977; *On Moral Fiction*, 1978; *On Becoming a Novelist*, 1983. **Radio plays** "The Temptation Game," 1971; several others. **Contributor** to Matthew Bruccoli and C. E. F. Clark, Jr., eds., *Pages*, vol. 1, 1976; also essays, articles, and short stories in numerous literary reviews and popular mags. **Interview** Joyce Renwick and Howard Smith, *John Gardner: An Interview*, 1980.

Further reading Stephen Singular, "The Sound and the Fury over Fiction," in *The New York Times Magazine*, 8 July 1979; John M. Howell, *John Gardner: A Bibliographical Profile*, 1980.

BASHIR (PIERRE) GEMAYEL
President-elect of Lebanon
Born **Beirut, Lebanon, 10 November 1947**
Died **East Beirut, Lebanon, 14 September 1982**

The legislative election of Bashir Gemayel, leader of the Maronite Christian Phalangists, to the presidency of Lebanon exactly coincided with the realization of his greatest military goal: the defeat—primarily at the hands of the Israelis—and departure from Beirut of his principal enemies, the Palestine Liberation Organization. Although he was the only announced candidate for president and had begun to speak of uniting the country behind his leadership, he was passionately hated by most Lebanese Muslims and even by the members of several rival Christian groups. He died when a remote-controlled bomb blast leveled the Phalangist headquarters in East Beirut while he was presiding at a meeting there; it is unclear which of his enemies arranged his assassination. In the immediate aftermath of his murder, and before he was succeeded as president-elect by his elder brother, Amin, his followers, apparently with Israeli acquiescence, invaded two Palestinian camps south of Beirut and for 48 hours conducted a massacre of hundreds of refugees, most of them women and children.

At the time of Bashir's birth in Beirut, his father, Pierre Gemayel, was head of the Phalangist Party (Kataeb), which he had founded in 1936 on German, Italian, and Spanish fascist models. The family power center was located in Bikfayya, in central Lebanon east of the capital. Bashir, the youngest of six children, was given military training by the Phalangists from the age of 11. He was educated in Beirut at the Lycée Franco-Libanais, received a law degree from St. Joseph's University, an institution run by French Jesuits, and in 1972 went to the United States to study political science and law at Southern Methodist University in Dallas, Texas. After working briefly for a law firm in Washington, D.C., he returned home to master the complex political and military structures of the Phalange, which he was already destined to lead.

When civil war began in Lebanon in 1975, Gemayel gave up his legal career and other political activities to fight. After the commander of the militia was killed in action in 1976, Gemayel was chosen to succeed him. The civil war effectively destroyed the fragile polity, the balance between Christian and Arab and between left and right, that had cohered to govern Lebanon since the country's independence in 1943. It also confirmed the Phalangists as the most powerful—and most ruthless—of the Christian factions. The new elements in the Lebanese equation were the Syrian army of occupation and their nominal allies, the PLO. The latter, with thousands of heavily armed members, had seized a power base in Beirut and to the south after having been driven out of Jordan by King Hussein in the early 1970s.

For Gemayel, overcoming the Arab left entailed first uniting his own Christian right, and he proceeded to accomplish this by force. In June 1978, Phalangist militiamen ambushed and killed, together with his wife and child, Tony Franjieh, the son and heir of Suleiman Franjieh, a former president and head of a powerful Christian fiefdom centered in Zhgarta, in northern Lebanon. It was widely believed that the two assassination attempts survived by Gemayel, including one in February 1980 that killed his 18-month-old daughter Maya, were the work of Franjieh's militia. In early July 1980 the Phalange made a surprise attack on the armed supporters of the National Liberal Party, which was headed by Camille Chamoun, another former president and the leader of a faction whose power base was in central Lebanon, alongside that of the Gemayel family. In intense fighting that included tank and artillery barrages, the Phalange destroyed the military power of the NLP and seized control of East Beirut, in the process killing hundreds of people, including the wife of Dany Chamoun, son of Camille and a deputy in the Lebanese parliament.

Gemayel emerged from these bloody confrontations as the de facto head of all Christian forces in Lebanon and the only candidate strong enough to contest the presidency. He became the principal recipient of Israeli aid in the region, receiving from them American arms and ammunition, military clothing, and money. He welcomed the Israeli invasion of

Courtesy of Lebanese Information Center

Lebanon on 4 June 1982, and during Israel's ensuing two-month siege of the PLO in West Beirut his forces contributed heavily to the massive artillery strikes that virtually destroyed the Muslim sector of the capital.

On 23 August, in the midst of the PLO evacuation of Beirut under the supervision of U.S., French, and Italian troops, the Lebanese parliament met to elect a successor to Elias Sarkis, a Maronite Catholic like all Lebanon's presidents but a mere bureaucrat with no landed base and no personal militia. Sarkis's main supporters, the Syrian occupation forces, had long since abandoned him, and his reelection was out of the question. Despite the boycott of the parliamentary session by nearly all the Muslim deputies, Gemayel was elected on the second ballot. (The two Muslims who did attend had their houses blown up in West Beirut.) News of his election caused delirious celebrations among his supporters in East Beirut, with much firing of rifles into the air, but the rest of the country, weary of the incessant killing, had little hope that the greatly feared Gemayel could unite the country as he promised to do.

Over the next three weeks he nevertheless made considerable strides in the direction of unity. He proclaimed himself determined to disband all the private militias and to strengthen the Lebanese Army. Despite numerous reports of a secret meeting near Beirut with Menachem Begin immediately after his election, he soon issued a call for the withdrawal of all foreign forces from Lebanon, pointedly including the Israelis. There were signs that he was moving to patch up old quarrels: he made peace with Camille Chamoun and was on the point of persuading Saed Salam, the popular Sunni Muslim leader from West Beirut, to return as prime minister. Suleiman Franjieh, however, would not be won over. He predicted that Gemayel would not live to take office.

Whoever placed the 300-pound bomb on the top floor of the heavily guarded Phalange headquarters in the Ashrafieh district of East Beirut—Israeli, Syrian, Lebanese Muslim, or Lebanese Christian—it was almost certainly not a Palestinian. Yet these people, rendered newly defenseless by the evacuation, became the almost instantaneous victims of the Phalangists' revenge. On the night of the assassination the militia crossed over into West and Southwest Beirut and were permitted by Israeli guards to enter the Shatila and Sabra refugee camps, ostensibly to seek out PLO soldiers in hiding. For two days and nights they indiscriminately killed all the Palestinians they could find. From his summer palace in Ehden, northern Lebanon, Franjieh pronounced Gemayel's death an "agreeable surprise," but denied responsibility for it, and claimed that he still could not bury the bodies of his son, daughter-in-law, and granddaughter, dead four years, because they remained unavenged.

Amin Gemayel was easily elected president in his brother's place and took office on schedule on 23 September. He had worked for years in the Phalange's political office, and was widely believed to be less fanatic than Bashir, but because he had no reputation as a military strongman with which to win the respect of the violent clansmen, his prospects for pacifying Lebanon were considered exceedingly dim. A.K.

Parents Pierre G., leader of Phalangist Party, and Geneviève G. **Married** Solange Tutunji 1977: Maya, b. 1978 (d. 1980); Youmna; Nadim. **Religion** Maronite Catholic. **Education** Military training, Phalangist Party ca. 1958–69; Jamhour Secondary Sch., Ashrafieh; Inst. Moderne du Liban, baccalaureate; Lycée Franco-Libanais, Beirut, baccalaureate; St. Joseph Univ. Law Sch., Beirut, lic. en droit 1971; postgrad. seminar in intl. law, Southern Methodist Univ., Dallas 1972; admitted to Beirut bar. **Career** With law office, Wash. DC 1972; lawyer, Albert Laham law firm, Beirut 1972–75; leader, Maronite Catholic Community. • With Phalangist Party (Kataeb): political dir., Ashrafieh district 1972; member, political bureau; militia leader, Lebanese civil war 1975–76; comdr. in chief, Military Council (later Security Council) from 1976; comdr. in chief, United Lebanese Front from 1976. • Elected pres. of Lebanon 1982. **Honors** Order of Cedar 1982.

GRACE (PATRICIA) KELLY
Princess Grace of Monaco
Actress and member of the Monégasque royal family
Born Philadelphia, Pennsylvania, USA, 12 November 1929
Died Monte Carlo, Monaco, 14 September 1982

In 1955, Grace Kelly, a cool honey-blonde from a newly rich Philadelphia family, ranked second only to James Stewart as America's most popular film star. But within a year she had married, turned her back on Hollywood, and devoted herself to family life, raising three children and presiding over her local Red Cross. This unremarkable routine would surely have relegated the beautiful and dutiful Grace Kelly to the "Whatever became of . . . ?" columns were it not for the fact that on her wedding day she assumed the title of Her Serene Highness Princess Grace of Monaco. For many of her admirers, the royal nuptials signified a fairy tale come true, and over the years the popular press did all it could with the myth of her magical life. Her untimely death in an automobile accident robbed it of the expected happy ending.

Grace Patricia Kelly was the third of four children born to John Brendan (Jack) Kelly and his wife Margaret. Jack was the son of an Irish immigrant and as a young man won Olympic medals for sculling. He started his career in the bricklaying trade and went on to become a multimillionaire construction contractor. He also became an influential Democrat and earned himself a reputation as a playboy. Two of Jack Kelly's brothers were well known in the theater, George as a Pulitzer Prize-winning playwright and Walter as a vaudeville trouper and film actor. Grace's mother, of German descent, had a successful career as a magazine model in the early 1920s; she later coached the women's athletics team at the University of Pennsylvania.

Grace was a shy, skinny young girl who suffered from asthma. She certainly did not fit the athletic, outgoing Kelly mold and seemed almost to enjoy her confinements in the sickroom. It was here that her interest in theater first became apparent. She would spend long hours in sober conversation with her dolls, inventing for each a distinctive character and voice. As she grew up she could never quite decide whether she would train to become an actress or a ballet dancer. Neither possibility particularly pleased her parents; they hoped she might pursue something more secure.

Like her brother and sisters, Grace was educated privately in Germantown, the Philadelphia suburb in which the family lived. Upon graduating from high school in 1947 she applied to Bennington College but, failing to gain admission, commenced a two-year course at the Academy of Dramatic Arts in New York, where she was soon able to support herself by modeling for photographers and appearing in television commercials. Her professional debut came in July 1949 when she appeared in a revival of her uncle's comedy, *The Torch Bearers*, at the Bucks County Playhouse in New Hope, Pennsylvania. That season she also appeared in the Playhouse's production of *The Heiress*. Local reviewers were rather more interested in her family connections than in her acting abilities, but she was impressive enough to win a Broadway role, as the Captain's daughter in August Strindberg's *The Father*. The production ran from November 1949 until the spring of 1950.

Throughout her period in New York, the actress appeared in many television series, including "Philco Television Playhouse," "Hallmark Hall of Fame," and "Somerset Maugham Theater." This brought her to the notice of Hollywood and she secured a small part in *Fourteen Hours* (1951), a 20th Century-Fox film shot in New York. The film's sole claim to fame is that it is the one in which Grace Kelly made her movie debut.

For the summer season of 1951, the actress joined the Elitch Gardens Theatre in Denver, Colorado, where she played major roles in *Detective Story, The Man Who Came to Dinner, The Cocktail Party, Ring Around the Moon*, and *For Love or Money*. By the end of the season she had been offered a part in a United Artists western and went to Hollywood. The film was Fred Zinnemann's masterful *High Noon* (1952), and in it she played the prim Quaker bride of Gary Cooper. Her limited role was easily overshadowed by the film's suspensefulness and Cooper's towering performance. Lacking further Hollywood offers, she returned to Broadway to appear in the short-lived *To Be Continued*. From there she went back to Philadelphia to star in *For*

Love Or Money and *Accent on Youth* at the Playhouse in the Park, which was renamed for her father, who had sponsored it, after his death in 1960.

Her real Hollywood break came when she took a screen test for the part of an Irish wench in 20th Century-Fox's *Taxi*. She didn't get the part, but her agent showed the test to some directors. Alfred Hitchcock was interested in her, but so was John Ford and his MGM boss Dore Schary. The actress signed a seven-year contract with MGM and was soon on her way to Africa to make *Mogambo* (1953), in which she played a cool, aristocratic Englishwoman embroiled in an illicit romance with Clark Gable. The performance brought her an Oscar nomination for best supporting actress, and it brought her once again to the attention of Alfred Hitchcock.

Hitchcock had little use for the overtly sexual "blonde bombshell" actresses of the 1950s, believing that sex on screen, like his plots, should unfold enigmatically. Kelly's "sexual elegance," as he called it, was perfect for his purposes. He borrowed her from MGM for his *Dial M for Murder* (1954), casting her as an unlucky adulteress for whom Ray Milland, as her tennis-champion husband, plans an intricate and bloody demise. Hitchcock borrowed her again the same year for *Rear Window*. Her portrayal of an impeccably bred Park Avenue fashion editor, not above a bit of sexual enticement to get her photographer fiancé James Stewart to settle down, was one of the high points of her short career. Both she and Stewart deftly caught the light thriller's charm as well as its deeper nuances.

Kelly's third and final Hitchcock movie was *To Catch A Thief* (1955); it is almost certainly her most captivating work. Her gently mocking seduction of Cary Grant, as an urbane former jewel thief, outside her hotel room, catches him, and the audience, breathless. As with *Rear Window*, Kelly's debonaire performance was a perfect vehicle for Hitchcock's romantic themes and a wonderful foil for his more sinister undercurrents. "I didn't discover Grace," Hitchcock once said, "but I saved her from a fate worse than death. I prevented her from being eternally cast as a cold woman."

The only other actress to star in three Hitchcock movies was Ingrid Bergman, who died just two weeks before Grace Kelly. Both women—elegant, beautiful, suggesting hidden depths—were the director's most successful female leads. But while Bergman went on to perform a number of memorable roles with other directors, Kelly will be remembered, first and foremost, as a Hitchcock star. Oddly enough, her major accolades were for her atypical role as the careworn but resolute wife of an alcoholic singer (Bing Crosby)—a part turned down by Greta Garbo—in a very different kind of movie, *The Country Girl,* for which she received both the Academy Award for best actress and the New York Film Critics Award.

Prior to her performance in *To Catch A Thief*, Kelly honored her contract with MGM by appearing in the jungle melodrama *Green Fire* (1954) with Stewart Granger. MGM, hoping to cash in on the actress's great popularity, touted the film as the "thrilling climax" of Kelly's career. Unhappily, it was her nadir; the movie was a terrible flop. The already tense relationship with MGM worsened when Kelly, understandably wary, rejected the next role they offered her and was suspended. After *To Catch A Thief* she was suspended again for refusing another role.

The years 1953 and 1954 were extremely busy ones for Kelly: she made four box-office hits—her three Hitchcock movies and *The Country Girl*—as well as *Green Fire* and *The Bridges at Toko-Ri* (1955), an adaptation of

James A. Michener's Korean War novel in which she played a supporting role. In *The Great Movie Stars: The International Years* (1972), David Shipman writes: "She was tinsel town's new golden girl, and it was impossible to flick the pages of any magazine without coming across her name." But despite her ascendant position, the prize she most wanted—the starring role in *Giant*—eluded her.

In 1955, MGM gave her a new contract and promised her some livelier movies. Tennessee Williams's *Cat On A Hot Tin Roof* was bought with Kelly in mind, and she was to star in remakes of *The Swan* and *The Philadelphia Story*. But by this time Prince Rainier III of Monaco, having made her acquaintance in the spring of 1955 at the Cannes Film Festival, was looking for a way to meet her again. He managed to secure invitations for himself, his priest, and his doctor to share Christmas dinner with the Kellys in Philadelphia. A lightning romance ensued, and within two weeks of their second meeting the engagement of the prince and the actress was formally announced. At the same time the prince let it be known that his future wife would be giving up her film career just as soon as her contract would allow.

The Swan (1956) was delicate tale of a young woman's romantic entanglements with a crown prince. Made before Kelly's sudden engagement, but released in the wake of the royal wedding, the film did poorly at the box office; it had been upstaged by the real thing. *High Society*, the 1956 musical starring Kelly, Frank Sinatra, Celeste Holm, and Bing Crosby, with music by Cole Porter, was a big hit, especially in Britain. But the musical was not in the same league as the classic *Philadelphia Story* on which it was based. Kelly's performance, her last professional role and good as ever, could not compare with the original Katharine Hepburn interpretation.

The 32-year-old Rainier, a member of the Grimaldi family, which had ruled Monaco for 650 years, was in a hurry to marry, not least because his throne, to which he had ascended in 1949, needed an heir. If he failed to produce one, his state would be subsumed by France under a pact devised in the aftermath of World War I. So on 19 April 1956, Kelly's Hollywood commitments completed, the couple were married in Monaco.

The groom, a half inch shorter than his bride, who was five feet six, encountered some difficulty in getting the wedding ring over her knuckle. But once the gold band was in place, the celluloid princess was suddènly a real one, albeit of a pocketbook principality with a distinctly Ruritanian air. The fantasy of her "enchanted life" was played up by the press and eagerly consumed by the public. Statistics concerning the lavish quantities of silk and lace required by her bridal gown were faithfully reported. Even the cake, a 200-pound edifice of seven tiers, received many column inches of attention. When the festivities were over, the couple set sail for their honeymoon aboard the royal yacht, onto which 15,000 carnations were jettisoned from a plane courtesy of Aristotle Onassis.

The following year, Princess Grace gave birth to a daughter, Caroline. The infant princess was heiress apparent to the Monégasque monarchy for 14 months until her brother Albert was born. Stephanie, a second daughter, was born in 1965. Apart from being a busy mother, Princess Grace involved herself in numerous organizations, charities, and affairs of state. She became president of the Monégasque Red Cross and of the Princess Grace Foundation, which supports local artists. She also served as the honorary president of the Girl Guides of Monaco and the Association Mondiale des Amis de l'Enfance. Her work for the Red Cross and on behalf of young people earned her the United Nations Food and Agriculture Organization's Ceres Medal in 1977.

In her spare time, Princess Grace enjoyed needlepoint and making collages of dried flowers, some of which were exhibited at a Paris gallery. She also became a keen amateur astrologist and handwriting analyst. But her abiding interest was in motherhood. She was an active proponent of breastfeeding and held

Courtesy of Culver Pictures

traditionalist views about the role of women: "With animals, you don't see the male caring for the offspring. It is a woman's prerogative and duty, and a privilege." On another occasion, she said: "Women's natural role is to be a pillar of the family. . . . Emancipation of women has made them lose their mystery."

The princess was reported to be hopping mad when her oldest daughter married a French playboy in 1978, but Grace later denied this. "The truth is," she said, "that the prince and I felt that Caroline was too young to marry *anyone*." Caroline's marriage broke up shortly thereafter. The newspapers, which had so assiduously promoted the image of Grace's charmed life, were just as unremitting in their speculation on problems within the royal household. Celebrity-followers of her own generation avidly read gossip columns for the latest Monaco tidbits, but for those who had grown up in the 1960s and 1970s, and for those who preferred to remember Grace as a screen idol, the ups and downs of the conservative princess, now bespectacled and a little matronly, were of little consequence.

Of even less consequence—except to the playboy set—was her adopted state. Grace's arrival as Monaco's first lady increased tourism and replenished its nearly empty coffers, but it remained essentially what it had long been—a tax and gambling haven for the very rich. The princess worked hard to improve its image, initiating an annual international arts festival and making documentaries to extol its virtues as a vacation spot and cultural center. Somerset Maugham had once described Monaco as "a sunny place for shady characters." Now under Rainer III and Grace, it became a bustling resort full of skyscrapers, sometimes unkindly referred to as an amusement park.

Apart from her tourist documentaries, Princess Grace gave a number of poetry readings and narrated two films, one about the Kirov ballet school, *The Children of Theater Street* (1977), the other about the Nativity (1982). She always maintained her interest in the film industry and in 1976 joined the board of 20th Century-Fox Film Corporation. But the nearest the princess came to returning to Hollywood was in 1962, when she expressed an interest in Hitchcock's *Marnie*. Her husband reluctantly agreed, but apparently the Monégasque politicos did not. Eventually the part was played by Tippi Hedren.

On 13 September 1982, while driving back to Monte Carlo from the family summer home in the French hills overlooking Monaco, Princess Grace suffered a stroke and lost control of her car. Her daughter Stephanie, the only passenger, tried to apply the handbrake, but could not reach it in time. The car plunged down a hillside and landed upside down in a garden. Stephanie suffered from fractures and shock but was not badly hurt. At first it was reported that Princess Grace had sustained only minor injuries, but in fact her condition was very grave. She died of a cerebral vascular hemorrhage the next day. Her funeral, attended by many celebrities, took place in the Cathedral of Monaco, where she and Rainier had been married 26 years earlier. R.T.

Parents John Brendan K., athlete, building contractor, and politician, and Margaret (Majer) K., model and athletic coach. **Married** Prince Rainier III of Monaco 1956: Caroline Louise Marguerite, b. 1957; Albert Alexandre Louis Pierre, b. 1958; Stephanie Marie Elizabeth, b. 1965. **Religion** Roman Catholic. **Emigrated** to Monaco 1956; jt. U.S. and Monégasque citizenship. **Education** Studied ballet; Ravenhill Acad. of the Assumption, Germantown, PA; Stevens Sch., Germantown, grad. 1947; Amer. Acad. of Dramatic Arts, NYC ca. 1947–48. **Career** Model and TV-commercial actress ca. 1947–49; stage actress 1949–50s; film and TV actress 1951–56. • Princess of Principality of Monaco since 1956. **Officer** Pres.: Monégasque Red Cross since 1958; Princess Grace Foundn. since 1965; Garden Club of Monaco; (also founder) Monaco Intl. Arts Festival. • Chmn., organizing cttee., Centennial of Monte Carlo 1966; member, bd. of dirs., 20th Century-Fox Film Corp. **Member** Intl. council, Salk Inst., San Diego. **Honors** Academy Award and New York Film Critics Award, for *The Country Girl*, 1954; Ceres Medal, U.N. Food and Agriculture Org. 1977; Grand Cross, Order of St. Charles; Grand Cross, Order of Greece; Grand Cross, Equestrian Order of Greece; Grand Cross, Equestrian Order of Holy Sepulchre of Jerusalem; Lady of Sovereign Order of Malta; gold medals from French, Italian, and Austrian Red Cross; Distinguished Daughter of Pennsylvania; hon. degree from Duquesne Univ. • Hon. pres.: (also founding member) Assn. Mondiale des Amis de l'Enfance 1963; Monaco-U.S.A.; Girl Guides of Monaco; Irish-American Cultural Inst. **Stage** *The Torch*

Bearers and *The Heiress,* New Hope, PA 1949; *The Father*, NYC 1949–50; *Alexander*, Albany, NY 1950; summer stock, including *The Cocktail Party, Accent on Youth, The Man Who Came to Dinner,* and *Ring Round the Moon*, Denver, CO 1951; *To Be Continued,* NYC 1952; other productions in NYC, NY, and Phila. **Television** "Philco Television Playhouse," "Studio One," "Hallmark Hall of Fame," "Somerset Maugham Theater," other dramatic series 1950s; also narrator of religious and children's programs 1960s–70s. **Film** *Fourteen Hours*, 1951; *High Noon*, 1952; *Mogambo*, 1953; *Dial M for Murder*, 1954; *Rear Window*, 1954; *The Country Girl*, 1954; *Green Fire*, 1954; *The Bridges at Toko-Ri*, 1955; *To Catch a Thief*, 1955; *The Swan*, 1956; *High Society*, 1956; (narrator) *The Children of Theater Street*, 1977; *The Nativity,* 1982. **Author** *My Book of Flowers*, 1980.

Further reading Gwen Robyns, *Princess Grace: A Biography,* 1976; *The Story of Princess Grace: Once Upon a Time Is Now* (TV documentary), NBC 1977; Phyllidia Hart-Davis, *Grace: The Story of a Princess*, 1982; Trevor Hall, *Her Serene Highness: Princess Grace of Monaco*, 1982.

SADEGH GHOTBZADEH
Foreign minister of Iran
***Born* Iran, 1936**
***Died* Teheran, Iran, 15 September 1982**

Sadegh Ghotbzadeh was in most respects quite unlike his fellow leaders of the Iranian revolution. Worldly, Westernized, well-tailored, and fluent in English and French, he made little pretense to devoutness as a Muslim and came to be regarded with deep suspicion by the zealous mullahs and their followers who gradually turned the revolution to their fundamentalist course. His tenure as foreign minister coincided with the early stages of the crisis surrounding the U.S. hostages imprisoned in the Teheran embassy, and he became internationally famous as a blunt advocate of his country's right to hold them. His closeness to the Ayatollah Ruhollah Khomeini. the republic's omnipotent *faghi,* or spiritual leader, shielded him for a time from his enemies' attacks, but their triumph over him was inevitable. He was convicted in August 1982 of plotting to kill Khomeini and was executed by firing squad in Teheran's Evin Prison. There was no reprieve from his former mentor, who had often said that he considered Ghotbzadeh to be like a son to him.

The son of a moderately well-to-do lumber merchant, Ghotbzadeh was brought up in Teheran and became involved at a young age in the complex antishah intrigue that developed after the overthrow in 1953, with the connivance of the U.S. Central Intelligence Agency, of the leftist-nationalist government of Mohammad Mossadegh. In common with many young intellectuals, he belonged to the National Front, which was directed primarily by Mossadegh's secularist followers, but he was also deeply influenced by Mehdi Bazargan's Movement for the Liberation of Iran, an organization with a strongly Islamic base. He left Iran at the age of 22 for the United States to study political science at Georgetown University in Washington, D.C., but devoted so much time to antishah politics that his studies were neglected, and the university expelled him. He continued his political organizing, however, and in 1962, after he disrupted a meeting organized by Ardeshir Zahedi, the shah's ambassador to Washington, his visa was revoked and he was ordered to leave the country.

SAVAK, the shah's dreaded secret police force, was well aware of the subversive danger posed by Ghotbzadeh and others like him, and he was forced to live a clandestine existence in exile, first in Canada, then France. By 1971, when he went to join the exiled Khomeini in Najef, Iraq, Ghotbzadeh was among the best-known antishah militants in the West. He began to serve as the ayatollah's primary emissary to sympathetic Arab governments and organizations, including Libya, Syria, Algeria, and the Palestine Liberation Organization. He is said to have persuaded Khomeini to move to France, rather than to another Arab country, when Pres. Saddam Husayn expelled him from Iraq in the autumn of 1978. Along with Abolhassan Bani-Sadr, a young economist and the son of a wealthy and respected ayatollah, and Ibrahim Yazdi, a former cancer researcher at Baylor University in Texas, Ghotbzadeh handled all Khomeini's contacts with the French authorities and the press, first in Paris and then in Neauphle-le-Château, a village to the southeast. All three were members of the ayatollah's secret Revolutionary Council.

It was abundantly clear to most observers by late 1978 that the shah's regime was tottering, and when the monarch abdicated and fled the country in January 1979 there was no question that Khomeini would replace him. The secular National Front, led by Prime Minister Shahpur Bakhtiar, had been left in control of the government by the shah, but it was swept away after the ayatollah's return on 1 February, accompanied by Bani-Sadr, Yazdi, and Ghotbzadeh. On 11 February, Bakhtiar resigned and was replaced as premier by Mehdi Bazargan, who immediately named Bani-Sadr minister of foreign affairs and the economy and Ghotbzadeh head of Iranian radio and television.

At first Ghotbzadeh got along well with the fundamentalist clerics, who along with the merchant class formed the core of Khomeini's political strength. He was ruthless in purging all opposition from the media's central offices, banning all Westernized programming and generally toeing the strict Islamic line on every question, from attacking the secular left to insisting that all women, especially those of the relatively liberated middle class, resume wearing the veil in public. Yet he was known to retain, even to flaunt, his own Western lifestyle. This self-indulgent bachelor, with his tailored French suits, silk ties, and autocratic ways, gradually came to seem a grievous scandal to the pious, ever-zealous mullahs, some of whom began to attack him openly. Still, he retained both his seat on the powerful Revolutionary Council and Khomeini's obvious favor.

Soon after the fundamentalist students attacked the U.S. embassy in Teheran in November 1979 and seized as hostages nearly all the members of the U.S. mission, Ghotbzadeh made a bold and calculating move nearer the center of power. By quickly and unequivocally supporting the militants and all their actions, he fatally undermined the position of his principal rival, Foreign Minister Bani-Sadr, who had taken a more conciliatory approach toward the strongly hostile reaction of the United States and its Western allies. When Bani-Sadr agreed to go to New York to plead Iran's case before the United Nations Security Council, Ghotbzadeh persuaded Khomeini to forbid the trip, and Bani-Sadr was forced to resign. In late November 1979, Ghotbzadeh was named foreign minister.

Once in office, he seemed to turn gradually from total confrontation to attempted compromise with the United States. In interview after interview, he failed to revive his earlier demands that the hostages be tried and executed for espionage and refused to close the door to negotiations to end the impasse. Once he even flew to Paris for two secret meetings with Hamilton Jordan, chief of Pres. Carter's White House staff. By Jordan's account, Ghotbzadeh openly suggested that the United States government could respond most easily to the Iranians' demand for the return of the shah by simply arranging his murder. "Perhaps the CIA can give him an injection or do something to make it look like a natural death," Ghotbzadeh reportedly said. (Jordan said that he rejected the proposal out of hand.)

Ghotbzadeh's newfound flexibility only gained him the mullahs' intensified enmity. They preached against him and his candidacy when he ran for president in January 1980. He gained only one percent of the vote, which was won overwhelmingly by Bani-Sadr. His poor showing in that relatively open election was due as much to his being little known in Iran as to the fundamentalists' antipathy. He remained in office through the bungled U.S. rescue attempt of April 1980, in the aftermath of which he was notably restrained in his recriminations. But the rapid ascendancy of the Islamic Republican Party (IRP), which counted among its leaders all his most powerful enemies, spelled the early end of his tenure at the Foreign Ministry. He resigned on 18 August 1980, sending a letter to the Majlis, or parliament, that enumerated all the difficulties involved for Iran in the continued detention of the hostages.

The following 7 November, after a speech in which he attacked the Islamic Republican Party for excesses in its operation of the state radio and television, Ghotbzadeh was arrested. Khomeini soon intervened, however, and he was released three days later. He made no further public statements from that time on, and lived a quiet life in northern Teheran, pursuing his family's business interests and studying Islamic law. Unlike Bani-Sadr, who had also been removed from office by the triumphant IRP and who later fled to France, Ghotbzadeh made no known attempt to flee the country.

His second arrest in early April 1982 marked the beginning of the end. He was accused of plotting to kill Khomeini and members of the Revolutionary Council, and after two weeks of interrogation appeared on television to confess his guilt. He made the sensational admission that he had accepted money and encouragement in his plotting from Ayatollah Qazem Shariat-Madari, the widely respected Azerbaijani spiritual leader and Khomeini's principal rival. Shariat-Madari was quickly placed under house arrest, but has not so far been brought to trial or had his religious authority revoked, as IRP spokesmen had threatened. Ghotbzadeh claimed that he had balked at killing Khomeini because of his "special sentimental loyalty" to him, but supported nonetheless the violent overthrow of the government. After declaring "I am shamed before the nation. Free me or execute me," he was returned to prison.

His trial, in August 1982, was secret and swift. The country's chief prosecutor, Hojatolislam Muhammad Reyshahri, and Ayatollah Sadegh Khalkhali, the revolution's bloodthirsty and widely feared "hanging judge," had both spoken out frequently against him in the Majlis and on television. He was convicted on his own admission, and although the court pronounced no sentence, his execution was expected at any time. It came a month later, after the High Judicial Court upheld the verdict against him. A.K.

Father a timber merchant. **Religion** Muslim. **Education** Georgetown Univ., Wash. DC, expelled 1962. **Career** Co-leader of student branch of natl. antishah resistance movement and member of Natl. Front mid-1950s, jailed twice for political activities; founder, Iranian Students Assn., Wash. DC 1959; antishah activist, U.S. 1959–62, and in exile in Canada, Algeria, Syria, Iraq, and France 1962–78; member, Revolutionary Council 1979–80; dir., Natl. Iranian Radio and Television Agency 1979; minister for foreign affairs 1979–80; member, cttee. of Islamic Conference on Afghanistan 1980; defeated in presidential election Jan. 1980, left govt. Aug. 1980, arrested and released Nov. 1980; businessman, Teheran 1980–82; arrested and convicted of treason 1982.

Further reading M. Ledeen and William Lewis, *Debacle,* 1981; Hamilton Jordan, *Crisis: The Last Year of the Carter Presidency,* 1982.

DAVID DUBINSKY
Union leader
***Born* Brest-Litovsk, Byelorussia, Russian Empire, 22 February 1892**
***Died* New York City, USA, 17 September 1982**

Under David Dubinsky's energetic presidency (1932–66), the International Ladies Garment Workers Union (ILGWU) rose from near bankruptcy to great prosperity and became one of the most admired and progressive organizations in the U.S. labor movement. His influence extended well beyond his own union, and he was a much-heeded voice in both major U.S. labor federations, as well as the founder and mentor of two New York-based political parties, the American Labor Party and the Liberal Party.

He was born David Dobnievsky in czarist-controlled Poland, the son of a baker. When he was a small child, his family moved to Łódź, where he received an excellent primary education, learning to read and write Polish, Russian, and Yiddish. He left school after his thirteenth birthday, and after a year became a master baker in his father's shop. At the age of 15 he was elected, primarily because of his knowledge of languages, as secretary of his local of the bakers' union. He soon led his members out on strike, an action that affected his father's business as well as many of the other bakeries in Łódź.

At 16, because of his continued involvement in union organizing, he was arrested and interrogated by the Russian secret police, who sent him into exile to Chelyabinsk, Siberia. In the course of his 18-month journey there he was interned in several prisons, but eventually managed to escape and made his way back to Łódź, where for a time he again worked for his father.

In 1910 his brother, who had gone to New York, sent Dubinsky a steamship ticket to come and join him. He had earned enough to bring along his older brother, and in January 1911 the two young men, David not yet 19, arrived in New York. He decided almost immediately to switch trades, quickly qualifying as a cutter in the ladies' dress industry, and at the same time joined Local 10 of the ILGWU, a fledgling union founded in 1900, which was attempting to bring some order and progress to the squalid and oppressed working lives of garment workers. The appalling fire in the sweatshop run by the Triangle Shirtwaist

Courtesy of ILGWU

Company, which killed 145 immigrant garment workers, occurred only two months after his arrival. The disaster caused enormous popular revulsion, and marked the beginning of a serious effort on the part of key state officials to improve working conditions.

Dubinsky became a naturalized U.S. citizen in 1916. Two years later, after a steadily increasing involvement in the affairs of Local 10, he was elected to its executive board, and in 1921 became its managing secretary. He was a member of the Socialist Party, as was much of the rest of his union, and denounced the Bolshevik Revolution, which had a growing appeal to many segments of the U.S. left. When the U.S. Communist Party came into being, formed in large part by dissident Socialists, Dubinsky and other democratic-leftist union leaders began a concerted attack on the Communists that intensified over the next four decades.

His move to the top of the ILGWU hierarchy continued. In 1922, he was elected a vice president of the national union, a post he held concurrently with the manager's job in

Local 10; in 1929 he became secretary-treasurer of the national; and in 1932, after standing in as chief executive for several years during the last illness of the union's president, Benjamin Schlesinger, Dubinsky was elected to the presidency, to which he was regularly reelected.

The ILGWU had made few gains during the early part of the Great Depression. The nearly insolvent union claimed fewer than 40,000 members, representing only a fraction of the employment in the huge ladies' apparel industry. The industry, moreover, was gradually falling under the control of organized crime, which was attracted by the high profits to be made from sweatshop conditions. Even when the union was able to get a contract, the manufacturers could usually violate it at will. The New Deal proved a boon to unions in general, for its legislative centerpiece, the National Industrial Recovery Act of 1933, mandated collective bargaining in all industries engaged in interstate commerce. Using this law to the ILGWU's advantage, Dubinsky was able to organize large parts of the industry: within three years he had increased membership by more than five times and had amassed nearly a million dollars in assets. By that time he was also a vice president of the American Federation of Labor, and joined John L. Lewis, the miners' leader, in 1935 to found the Committee for Industrial Organization, which later became the Congress of Industrial Organizations. He resigned from the AFL executive council in 1936 when it voted to suspend the CIO unions, but the following year, disturbed by what he saw as growing Communist influence within the CIO, withdrew the ILGWU from that federation as well. His union remained independent of both federations until 1940, when it rejoined the AFL, of which Dubinsky was reinstated as vice president in 1945.

Dubinsky always claimed that his greatest achievement for his members was bringing a standard 35-hour week to the unstable, exploitive industry. "When we banished the sweatshops," he said in one of his reelection acceptance speeches, "when we reduced the hours of work, when we increased wages, when we provided health centers, when we established Unity House [an 850-acre union vacation center], when we participated in community life, when we eliminated worry, torture, hunger, and starvation, we performed a service for the future of America." By 1966, when he decided not to stand for reelection, the ILGWU had 450,000 members and assets of $500 million. The membership slipped to 350,000 over the course of the next 15 years, however, as large numbers of new immigrants were forced into nonunionized sweatshops and unchecked foreign competition in women's wear kept U.S. wages and benefits low.

Dubinsky, who supported the Progressive candidacy of Sen. Robert La Follette in 1924, resigned from the Socialist Party in 1928. He backed Franklin Roosevelt in 1932 and 1936, the last time as a leader of the New York-based American Labor Party, which he had formed with Sidney Hillman, president of the ILGWU's sister organization, the Amalgamated Clothing Workers Union. In 1944, when the ALP appeared to be shifting toward Communist control, he left to form, with Adolf A. Berle, Alex Rose, and others, the Liberal Party. As vice chairman, Dubinsky saw the Liberals become an important power in New York politics, particularly in the election of John Lindsay as mayor in 1965 and 1969. The ILGWU left the party in 1969, but Dubinsky remained a member until his death. He was also a co-founder in 1947 of Americans for Democratic Action.

A diminutive man with a loud voice, strong Yiddish accent, and charismatic speaking style, D.D., as he was known to his members, never wavered in his strong support of Israel. From 1933 he was an influential member of the Jewish Labor Committee, a refugee-relief organization, and was outspoken in support of the Histadrut, Israel's General Federation of Labor. The David Dubinsky Hospital in Beersheba was paid for by the ILGWU. He was awarded the Presidential Medal of Freedom by Pres. Lyndon Johnson in 1969. His autobiography, *David Dubinsky: A Life with Labor* (1977), was written with A. H. Raskin, longtime labor correspondent for the *New York Times*. He died at the age of 90 after a long illness. A.K.

Born David Dobnievsky. **Parents** Bezalel D., baker, and Shaine (Wishingrad) D. **Married** Emma Goldberg 1915 (d. 1974): Jean Appleton. **Religion** Jewish. **Emigrated** to U.S. 1911; naturalized 1916. **Education** Zionist and Konshtadt schs., Łódź, Poland; night sch., NYC. **Career** Baker's apprentice, then master baker, ca. 1903–08; member ca. 1905–09 and secty. 1907, Bakers' Union, Łódź; imprisoned, then exiled to Chelyabinsk, Siberia, 1908, escaped 1909, amnestied 1910; kneepants operator and cloak and suit cutter, NYC garment factories 1911–20s. • With Intl. Ladies Garment Workers Union: member since 1911, exec. bd. member 1918, vice chmn. 1919, chmn. 1920, and managing secty. 1921–29, Cutters' Local 10, NYC; v.p. and bd. member 1922–29; gen. secty. and treas. 1929–32; pres. 1932–65; admin., retiree service dept. and special assistance fund 1966; hon. pres. since 1966; delegate to many labor councils and intl. conferences. • With Amer. Fedn. of Labor (AFL): v.p. and exec. council member 1934–36 and 1945–55; founder, Labor Chest 1934; rep., governing body, Intl. Labor Org., Geneva 1935; co-organizer, Cttee. for Industrial Orgs. 1935; member, postwar planning cttee. 1942; rep., various management and labor councils 1945; rep. and consultant, U.N. Economic and Social Council 1946; delegate, intl. trade union conference on Marshall Plan, London 1948; delegate and gen. council member, founding conference, Intl. Conference of Free Trade Unions, London 1949; member and rep., other AFL conferences and cttees. 1930s–50s. • With AFL-CIO: member, unity cttee. 1954–55; v.p. and exec. council member 1955–66. • Co-founder, Jewish Labor Cttee. 1934; member, conference on workers' education, Intl. Fedn. of Trade Unions, London 1936; member, Intl. Clothing Workers Fedn. Conference 1936; member, wage and hour commn., Ladies' Apparel Industry 1938–41; member, special wage and hour commn., P.R. 1940; vice chmn., Amer. Labor Conference on Intl. Affairs 1940s; labor rep., Natl. Coat and Suit Industry Recovery Bd. 1942; founding member, Labor League for Human Rights 1942; member, other labor councils and cttees. 1930s–60s. • Political and govt. positions: member, Amer. Socialist Party 1912–28; labor advisor, Natl. Recovery Admin. Code Authorities 1933–35; founding member, Amer. Labor Party 1936–44; presidential elector, Amer. Labor Party and Democratic Party 1936; member, trade union advisory cttee. on intl. labor affairs, U.S. Dept. of Labor 1940s; member, War Dept. Bd. 1941; dir., Natl. War Fund 1941–45; founding vice chmn., Liberal Party, NY since 1944; co-founder, Americans for Democratic Action 1947; presidential advisory cttee. on labor-management policy 1961; member, Democratic Party. **Officer** Member, bd. of dirs.: Greater New York Fund 1942; Amer. Overseas Aid—U.N. Appeal for Children ca. 1945; Willkie Memorial 1945; Franklin D. Roosevelt Memorial Fund 1948; Joint District Court, NY. **Fellow** Amer. Acad. of Arts and Sciences since 1952. **Member** Exec. cttee., Citizen's Cttee. to Support the Marshall Plan 1947; Greater New York for United Negro Coll. Fund 1948; natl. sponsors cttee., Amer. Heart Assn.; natl. labor council, Natl. Conference of Christians and Jews; Inter-American Advisory Cttee.; many other civic and charitable orgs. **Honors** King's Medal of Service, U.K. 1946; Humanitarian Service Award, Eleanor Roosevelt Cancer Foundn. 1961; Golden Door Award, Amer. Council of Nationalities Service 1965; Freedom Award, Intl. Rescue Cttee. 1966; Medal of Grand Cavalier of the Republic, Italy 1966; foundn. created in his honor, gen. exec. bd., Intl. Ladies Garment Workers Union 1967; Presidential Medal of Freedom 1969; Sr. Citizen of the Year, NY 1970; hosp. named for him, Beersheba, Israel; hon. degrees from Bard Coll. and Temple, Brandeis, Roosevelt, and Columbia univs. **Author** (Jtly.) *David Dubinsky: A Life with Labor* (autobiography), 1977.

Further reading John Dewey, *David Dubinsky: A Pictorial Review,* 1951; Max D. Danish, *The World of David Dubinsky,* 1957; Charles A. Madison, *American Labor Leaders: Personalities and Forces in the Labor Movement,* 1962; "David Dubinsky, the ILGWU, and the American Labor Movement," special issue, *Labor History,* Spring 1968; Boyle S. Neidle, *Great Immigrants,* 1973.

VERA STRAVINSKY

Painter and costume designer
***Born* St. Petersburg, Russia, 25 December 1888**
***Died* New York City, USA, 17 September 1982**

For 30 years Vera Stravinsky was the wife, amanuensis, and muse of the twentieth century's greatest composer, but it is a measure of her strength of character that their marriage always seemed an alliance of equals. An actress, set designer, and painter of some note, she was celebrated above all as an extraordinarily beautiful and gracious woman in whose presence many of the more significant artistic events of the century took place.

Thomas Mann, a frequent visitor to her house in Hollywood, described her as "a specifically Russian beauty," but though she was born and raised in Russia, she was not of Russian descent. She was the only child of a Swedish mother, Henriette Malmgren, and Artur de Bosset, a Frenchman whose Huguenot ancestors had emigrated to Russia during the eighteenth century. Her father, a wealthy manufacturer of electrical equipment, had socialist beliefs and named his daughter for the heroine of Goncharov's novel *The Precipice*. She was brought up in the provincial town of Kudinova, where her father's factory was situated, and attended a boarding school in Moscow, where she became an accomplished pianist and an enthusiastic amateur actress under the spell of Sarah Bernhardt and Eleonora Duse. Her parents were divorced in 1917, after which her father fled from the Bolsheviks to Chile, where he died in 1937.

After graduating from school in 1908, Vera was sent to the University of Berlin by her father, who regarded Paris, the fashionable resort of many young Russians of the time, as too frivolous for his daughter, who was already feted as a beauty. In Berlin she enrolled as a student of philosophy, science, and anatomy, but switched to art in her second year and attended the lectures of Heinrich Wölfflin. At some point in her early 20s she was briefly married to a man named Lury, but the marriage lasted only a few days. In 1912 she married again, having returned to Moscow to study at the Nelidova Ballet School. Her second husband, whose name was Robert Shilling, is hardly less obscure than her first; she left him almost immediately for Sergey Yurievich Sudeikin, a painter and close associate of Sergey Diaghilev, the impresario and founder of the Ballet Russes. Although she did not meet Stravinsky until 1921, she certainly knew the music he had already written for Diaghilev, as Sudeikin had designed the set for the first production of *Le sacre du printemps*. Her intention in studying ballet, she later said, was not to become a dancer but "to acquire poise" and be able "to move gracefully" in the theatrical roles she played at the Kamerny Theater. By 1916, when she and Sudeikin moved to St. Petersburg, she had also appeared in several film comedies and starred as Elena in Protozanov's silent film version of *War and Peace* (1915).

Her career, and the wealthy, cultured life of the Russian intelligentsia in general, was abruptly ended by the Bolshevik revolution of 1917, which forced Vera and Sudeikin to move to Yalta in the Crimea, where they were married in 1918. Two years later, when the Red Army invaded the Crimea, they were forced to flee again to Tiflis in the Caucasus, and from there to Paris, where they joined the group of émigrés that gathered around Diaghilev. Vera recalled that during the voyage to France all the passengers were robbed by a group of thieves, and that the leader of the group, struck by her beauty, not only let her go unharmed, but presented her with a purse full of gold coins.

In Paris she assisted Diaghilev as a set designer, and took small parts in the productions of the Ballet Russes. She worked with Georges Rouault on the set for *Le fils prodigue,* and danced the Queen in Diaghilev's famous revival of *The Sleeping Beauty* in 1921. The costume that she wore in that part is now in the collection of the Metropolitan Museum of Art. With a fellow émigrée, Tula Danilova, she also ran a fashion boutique. Her first meeting with Stravinsky, which took place in a Montmartre restaurant in February 1921, was the beginning of their mutual attraction. She parted from Sudeikin later that year, but her liaison with Stravinsky was not widely known until 1925, when Stravinsky and Sudeikin, visiting New York for a production of *Le sacre du printemps,* refused to speak to each other and became the subject of gossip in the American press. Between 1922 and 1926, Vera continued her work in the ballet and shared an apartment with Gabrielle Picabia, wife of the painter. She played the role of the bride in *Les noces* in 1923, and the following year designed sets and costumes for *L'histoire du soldat.*

In January 1940, Vera joined Stravinsky in the United States, where they were married in March. They eventually settled in Hollywood, which remained their home until 1969, when they moved to New York City in order to be closer to the medical facilities on which the composer relied during his last years. The Stravinskys' house became a refuge for numerous expatriates, including Thomas Mann, Christopher Isherwood, and Aldous Huxley. Vera attributed the happiness of their marriage to the fact that they followed different artistic impulses: "I didn't interfere in his music and he didn't tell me how to paint." She had dabbled in art at earlier periods in her life, but didn't apply herself seriously until the late 1940s, by which time she had encountered a great deal of modern painting through her work as the proprietor of the art gallery La Boutique on Cienega Boulevard in Hollywood. There she exhibited and sold pre-Columbian sculptures, works by modern French painters, and her own constructions and collages. During the 1950s she began to paint in gouache in a style that is neither abstract nor representational, but uses color and shape to allude to forms in nature. Robert Craft wrote in *Igor and Vera Stravinsky: A Photograph Album* (1982): "She does not copy and does not sketch, or even take notes except for verbal reminders of the colors of a composition of nature. To her, color *is* composition, and her greatest gifts are an infallible color sense and skill in color manipulation."

Her work was exhibited for the first time in Yalta in 1918 and during the next 20 years was also shown in Rome, Venice, Milan, at the art museums of Pasadena and Santa Barbara, and in Mexico City. Stuart Preston paid tribute in the *New York Times* to her "smart, mysterious, metropolitan semi-abstracts." Her work won even warmer praise from those who knew her. Christopher Isherwood, contributing to a catalogue issued for a New York exhibition in the late 1950s, asserted that her pictures "have the authority of absolute sincerity and genuine visionary experience." Both he and Aldous Huxley, writing in the same publication, singled out a quality of joyfulness that pervaded both her painting and her life. "Hers," Huxley wrote, "is a happy art."

Although successful as a painter, Vera Stravinsky's later life was troubled by the controversy surrounding the copious flow of publications edited by herself and Robert Craft and purporting to have been written by the composer. In addition, Stravinsky's children by his earlier marriage sued her for a large share of the royalties on his music, and after her death there was legal wrangling between them and Craft over the fate of his archives, Vera having willed Craft half the stock in the corporation formed to manage them. H.B.

Born Vera de Bosset. **Parents** Artur de B., electrical equipment manufacturer, and Henriette Malmgren. **Married** (1) Lury (div.). (2) Robert Shilling 1912 (div.) (3) Sergey Yurievich Sudeikin, painter and set designer, 1918 (div.). (4) Igor Stravinsky, composer, 1940. **Emigrated** to France 1920; to U.S. 1940. **Education** Privately educated, Kudinova to 1904; boarding sch., Moscow, grad. 1908 with gold medal and certificate to teach mathematics; Univ. of Berlin; Nelidova Ballet Sch., Moscow. **Career** Dancer, Kamerny Theater, Moscow, and actress in Russian films, including *War and Peace,* 1910s; painter from 1917; costume and set designer and dancer, Ballets Russes, and co-owner of Tuli-Vera atelier, Paris 1920–39; owner of La Boutique art gall., Hollywood 1940–ca.1945. **Exhibitions** of paintings in Yalta 1918, London, Rome, Venice, Milan, NYC, Santa Barbara, Houston, Santa Fe, L.A., Pasadena, Taxco, and Mexico City. **Author** (Jtly.) *Stravinsky, in Pictures and Documents,* 1978; *Fantastic Cities and Other Paintings,* 1979.

Further reading Igor Stravinsky, *Igor Stravinsky, An Autobiography,* 1962; Robert Craft, *Stravinsky: Chronicle of a Friendship, 1948–1971,* 1972; Robert Craft, *Igor and Vera Stravinsky: A Photograph Album, 1921–71,* 1982.

EMMET JOHN HUGHES

Speechwriter to President Eisenhower
***Born* Newark, New Jersey, USA, 26 December 1920**
***Died* Kingston, New Jersey, USA, 19 September 1982**

Emmet John Hughes, though a lifelong Democrat, served as speechwriter and political advisor to two prominent Republicans—first for Pres. Dwight Eisenhower, for whom he wrote the "I shall go to Korea" speech, decisive in the 1952 campaign; and then for Gov. Nelson Rockefeller of New York during two of his runs for the presidency. When not assisting politicians, he also worked for many years as a magazine writer, chiefly for Time Inc., and as a professor of political science.

The son of a county court judge, he graduated summa cum laude from Princeton in 1941 and began graduate work in history at Columbia, working with Prof. Carlton J. H. Hayes. When Hayes became ambassador to Spain in 1942, he took Hughes along as embassy press attaché, a job the young man held until 1946, simultaneously serving as an Army private and junior operative in the Office of Strategic Services, forerunner of the CIA. While in Madrid, he was offered the choice job of chief of *Time* magazine's bureau in Rome (1947–48), then was transferred to the same position in Berlin (1948–49), where he served during the airlift. He then returned to New York to be articles editor for *Life* until 1952, when he took a leave of absence to work for Eisenhower's election.

Hughes believed that the Democratic administration in 1952 was "a prisoner of its critics," unable to take foreign-policy initiatives for fear of being denounced as soft on Communism. Only a moderate Republican like Eisenhower could, once in office, enter into meaningful negotiations with the Soviet Union. Hughes drafted the "Korea" speech, the most important in Eisenhower's campaign, and was the chief writer of Eisenhower's first inaugural address. By far his most momentous work, however, was the speech to the American Society of Newspaper Editors on 16 April 1953, a month after Stalin's death, which pledged the new administration to seek peaceful coexistence through negotiations with the Communists.

Hughes left the White House before the end of 1953, returning to *Life* as special European correspondent. In 1956 he again temporarily abandoned journalism to work as chief speechwriter in Eisenhower's reelection campaign. He was chief of foreign correspondents for Time-Life from 1957 to 1960, when, after publishing *America the Vincible* (1959), a scathing attack on the Eisenhower-Dulles foreign policy, he was hired by Nelson Rockefeller, who was then seeking the Republican nomination, as speechwriter and principal strategist. He always abhorred Rockefeller's victorious opponent Richard Nixon, "a divisive, not a unifying, political figure," in Hughes's view. "I am dismayed by the obscurity of his political principles."

He remained with Rockefeller until 1963 as the governor's special assistant, then worked for five years (1963–68) as columnist for *Newsweek* magazine. After two further years (1968–70) on the Rockefeller staff, and another loss to Nixon, he accepted an appointment as researcher and professor at the Eagleton Institute of Politics at Rutgers University, the post he held until his death from heart disease.

Hughes's other books were *The Church and the Liberal Society* (1944), a reworking of his senior thesis at Princeton in which he examined the democratic challenges facing the Roman Catholic Church; *Report from Spain* (1947), an anti-Franco polemic that urged the Western democracies to ostracize the Spanish dictatorship; *The Ordeal of Power* (1963), widely considered the most vivid and comprehensive memoir of the Eisenhower presidency; and *The Living Presidency* (1973), a study of the institution itself, which the American historian Henry Steele Commager considered "the most thoughtful and the most perspicacious book on the presidency that I have ever read." A.K.

Parents John L. H., judge, and Grace (Freeman) H. **Married** (1) Marifrances (div.): John. (2) Eileen Lanouette, researcher (div.): Mary Larkin; Kathleen Freeman. (3) Katherine Nouri (div.): Caitlin; Johanna. **Religion** Roman Catholic. **Education** Princeton Univ., A.B. (summa cum laude; Phi Beta Kappa)

1941; Columbia Univ. 1941–42. **Mil. service** Pvt., U.S. Army WWII; agent for Office of Strategic Services, State Dept., and Office of War Information, Spain and North Africa 1942–46. **Career** Press attaché, U.S. Embassy, Madrid 1942–46. • With Time Inc.: Rome bureau chief 1947–48 and Berlin bureau chief 1948–49, *Time;* text ed. 1949–52 and special European corresp. 1953–56, *Life;* ed., *Fortune* 1956–57; chief foreign corresp., Time-Life Intl. 1957–60. • Columnist, *Newsweek* 1963–68; editorial consultant, *Washington Post* 1963–68; researcher and prof. of politics, Eagleton Inst., Rutgers Univ., New Brunswick, NJ since 1970. • Speechwriter, Dwight Eisenhower presidential campaigns 1952, 1956; admin. asst. to Pres. Eisenhower 1953; speechwriter, Nelson Rockefeller presidential primary campaign 1960; special asst. to Gov. Rockefeller and sr. advisor on public affairs to Rockefeller family 1960–63; special asst. to Gov. Rockefeller 1968–70. **Officer** Member, bd. of dirs., Lambert Intl. Corp. from 1962. **Author** *The Church and the Liberal Society,* 1944; *Report from Spain,* 1947; *War in Spain* (film script), 1958; *America the Vincible,* 1959; (ed.) *Education in World Perspective,* 1962; *The Ordeal of Power: A Political Memoir of the Eisenhower Years,* 1963; *The Living Presidency: The Resources and Dilemmas of the American Presidential Office,* 1973. **Contributor** to *Look,* other mags.

IVAN KHRISTOFOROVICH BAGRAMIAN

Soviet Army leader in World War II

***Born* Yelisavetpol, Azerbaijan, Russia, 2 December 1897**

***Died* USSR, 21 September 1982**

Ivan Bagramian was the only Armenian among the Soviet Union's 36 marshals. From 1920 his life was entirely devoted to the Soviet Army, and during World War II he was an effective commander on several fronts, particularly the one comprising the Baltic states. He also distinguished himself at the Battle of Kursk and Orel and at the taking of Königsberg (now Kaliningrad).

He was born in Yelisavetpol (now Kirovabad), Azerbaijan, the son of a railroad worker, and began attending military academy at an early age. During World War I, as an officer cadet, he served first in the czarist army, then with the independent Armenian army that attempted to set up independent republics in the Transcaucasus just after the fall of the czar. Once Soviet forces had established control over Armenia, Georgia, and Azerbaijan, he joined the Red Army (December 1920) and began to move up in the ranks.

Bagramian began advanced military training just after the civil war, graduating successively from the advanced commanders' cavalry training course (1925), the advanced course for general officers (1931), the Frunze Military Academy (1934), and the General Staff Academy (1938). In the autumn of 1940 he was named chief of the department of operations of army and district headquarters. At the beginning of World War II, as a colonel, he was transferred to a similar assignment on the Southwestern Front, where he was also chief of the general staff. Here he became friendly with Nikita Khrushchev, then first secretary of the Communist Party in the Ukraine. He was a lieutenant general by the end of 1941, and assistant chief of staff to Marshal Semyon Timoshenko.

His first army command came in July 1942, and he performed well during the arduous Soviet winter offensive of 1942–43. In November 1943, promoted to full general, he was given command of the 1st Baltic Front and the assignment of driving the Nazis out of Estonia, Latvia, and Lithuania. In a few months, together with the forces of Gen. I. D. Chernyakovsky, commander of the 1st White Russian Front, he drove the Germans from Vitebsk and threatened to destroy the German 3rd Panzer Army. In July 1944, with German attention diverted by the Allied landings in Normandy, his troops captured the junction of Šiauliai, Lithuania, on the rail line connecting East Prussia with the German armies to the north, effectively cutting them off. By October 1944, with the Germans in retreat before the numerically superior Soviets,

Bagramian led the 1st Baltic Army into East Prussia, cradle of German militarism, and seized Reichsmarshal Hermann Göring's estate in the Rominten Forest. Late in the war he commanded the 3rd Byelorussian Front.

After the war, Bagramian was commander of the Baltic Military District until 1954, overseeing the Sovietization of the three formerly independent countries. He attained marshal's rank in 1955. From 1954 until 1956 he served as chief inspector of the Ministry of Defense and deputy defense minister, then for two years headed the Voroshilov General Staff Academy. In 1958 he was again deputy defense minister, and in 1968 was named inspector general for the Ministry of Defense.

Bagramian was a candidate member of the Communist Party Central Committee from 1952 to 1961 and a member from 1961. He was also a deputy to the second through the seventh meetings of the USSR Supreme Soviet. His decorations included five Orders of Lenin, the Order of the October Revolution, three Orders of the Red Banner, two Suvorov Orders, First Class, and various medals. He died after a long illness at the age of 84. A.K.

Father a railroad worker. **Education** Technical sch.; officers' sch., grad. 1917; advanced cavalry training course, grad. 1925; advanced training course for gen. officers, grad. 1931; Frunze Military Acad., grad. 1934; Gen. Staff Acad., grad. 1938. **Career** Railroad technician to 1915; officer cadet, czarist and Armenian armies 1915–20. • With Soviet Army: cavalry regiment 1920; squadron comdr. 1922; regimental comdr. 1924; instr., Frunze Military Acad. 1938–40; chief of Dept. of Operations of Army and District HQ 1940; lt. gen. and asst. chief of staff to Marshal Semyon Timoshenko 1941; chief of staff and operations command, Southwestern and Western Fronts 1941–43; col. gen., then gen., 1943; comdr., 1st Baltic Front 1943–45; comdr., 3rd Byelorussian Front 1945; comdr., Baltic Military District 1945–54; chief inspector and deputy defense minister, Ministry of Defense 1954–56; marshal 1955; dir., Voroshilov Gen. Staff Acad. 1956–58; chief of rear admin. and supply services and deputy defense minister 1958–68; inspector gen., Ministry of Defense since 1968. • Member of CPSU since 1941; deputy to USSR Supreme Soviet since 1946; candidate member 1952–61 and member since 1961, CPSU Central Cttee.; member, Youth Affairs Commn., Soviet of Nationalities since 1974. **Honors** Order of Kutuzov, 1st Class, 1943; Hero of Soviet Union 1944; Order of Lenin five times; Order of Suvorov, 1st Class, twice; Order of Red Banner three times; Order of October Revolution; Polish and Mongolian orders; military medals. **Author** [*Warrior City on the Dnieper*], 1965; [*Fighting Trends of the Soviet Armed Forces*].

SIR MAXWELL JOSEPH

Business executive and hotelier
***Born* London, England, 31 May 1910**
***Died* London, England, 22 September 1982**

Sir Maxwell Joseph, sometimes referred to as Britain's last great tycoon—and certainly one of the toughest and shyest—built a massive commercial empire by working only a 16-hour week. With no taste or talent for management, he left day-to-day affairs to others and concentrated on a few bold moves. As chairman of the Grand Metropolitan group, he wrested control of key companies in the hotel, entertainment, betting, and catering industries, and at one point, with his boldest bid ever, almost bankrupted his group. But he and a few well-chosen top executives nursed the ailing giant back to health. Its shares, which had once sunk to 18.5 pence each, were topping £2.70 at the time of Sir Maxwell's death.

Joseph was born into a lower-middle-class Jewish family in London's East End. A quiet, slightly built boy, he did well at his local primary school and in 1921 gained entrance to a grammar school. He left school in 1926 when he was 16 to work as a clerk in Ernest Ewers & Williams, a Hampstead real-estate agency. Five years later, with the help of a £100 loan from his father, who dealt in property, he set up his own estate agency, Connaught Hooper & Company, in Golders Green, North London. At the age of 21 he was, by all accounts, the youngest estate agent in the country. A year later he married Sybil Nedas, sister-in-law of property dealer—and eventually tycoon—Harold Samuel; they had two children.

Courtesy of Grand Metropolitan

Shortly before World War II, Joseph's small fortune dwindled as property prices collapsed. After war service as a lance corporal in the Royal Engineers, he returned to his real-estate business, solidified his position once again, and starting in 1948 gradually began to buy up small hotels in the London area. His first important acquisition was the war-torn Mandeville Hotel close to London's West End shopping center, which he bought with some of his own money and a loan of £25,000. In 1957, with plenty of backing, his £1 million bid for the Mount Royal hotel at Marble Arch was successful. As British property boomed in the 1960s, his profits soared, and he quickly gained a reputation as an instinctively smart financier. Institutional investors recognized the logic and farsightedness of his acquisitions strategy.

Joseph formed his hotels into the Grand Metropolitan (GrandMet) group, went public, and saw his group's sales rise from £50 million in 1969 to £625 million by the early 1970s. In addition to its British hotels, GrandMet now owned a chain of public houses and industrial catering companies, the Express Dairy chain of small stores, the Mecca leisure concerns and betting shops, Berni Inns, and numerous hotels and other properties in France.

In 1971 he surprised the City financial establishment by seeking a £50-million controlling interest in Truman Hanbury Buxton, the London brewing company. After a tense eight-week battle, he won, and immediately went after an even larger brewery, Watney Mann. He dazzled the City by getting control of it, despite much acrimony and cries of "merger mania" from within the industry. It was Britain's largest takeover ever, but the price that Joseph's group paid—£400 million—together with the subsequent rapid rise in interest rates, the essential modernization of many of its companies, and slumping property prices, created severe financial problems. GrandMet's shares plummeted, and the many investors who had taken off in Maxwell Joseph's beautiful balloon bit their nails.—Would they all come crashing down? They didn't, mainly because some of the less vital ballast was unloaded and the pilots kept calm.

Back on an even keel by the end of the decade, Joseph was ready for more mergers. He chose to invest in the United States, and in another bitterly fought contest, involving a 1980 court battle, his group acquired Liggett & Myers, the North American tobacco and liquor conglomerate. GrandMet's management set about the task of restructuring their international interests while Joseph took a cool look at Coral Leisure, the British bookmaking concern that owned Pontin's holiday camps. He put in a bid, but withdrew it after the Monopolies Commission began an investigation to determine whether ownership of Coral might give GrandMet an unduly large share of London's profitable casino business.

Joseph's next foray was once again in America: he purchased the InterContinental Hotel chain from the financially squeezed Pan American World Airways. This further internationalized GrandMet and gave it a total of almost 200 hotels. Joseph's hotel collection, which had always been his prime interest, now included the Mayfair and Europa in London, the Carlton in Cannes, the Amstel in Amsterdam, and the Angleterre in Copenhagen. When the London Ritz came on the market in 1976, Joseph wanted to buy it and make it his flagship hotel. But the GrandMet board, in a rare dissent, voted against the purchase.

In 1981, the year in which Joseph finally accepted a knighthood, GrandMet was the employer of 130,000 people, had pretax profits of £186.6 million, a market capitalization of £1.3 billion, and a turnover of more than £3 billion.

It is not surprising that a man who made his fortune gambling on companies also enjoyed gambling at the racetrack. But it was the Labour Party dark horse on which he put his money in 1964: although he had little sympathy with their policies, he bet that they would win the general election. They did, and he became £50,000 richer. His other hobbies included gardening and antiques, and he built up a very fine collection of stamps.

Although Joseph lived apart from his first wife for more than 30 years, he did not get divorced until 1981. He then married Eileen Olive, his companion for the last 20 years, who had changed her name to Joseph by deed poll. In July 1982, he announced that he would hand over the chairmanship of the group in March 1983 to Stanley Grinstead, the man who had been in charge of GrandMet's financial management for the past 25 years. Joseph underwent a throat operation for cancer in 1981 but maintained that this had not affected his decision to retire. However, his health deteriorated badly in August 1982 and he died in September at the age of 72. R.T.

Father real-estate agent. **Married** (1) Sybil Nedas 1932 (separated 1953; div. 1981): Stephen, business exec.; one daughter. (2) Eileen Olive, interior designer, 1981. **Religion** Jewish. **Education** Hampstead Grammar Sch., London, left at age 16. **Mil. service** Lance corp., Royal Engineers, WWII. **Career** Clerk, Ernest Ewers & Williams real-estate agency, London 1926–30; founder and agent, Connaught Hooper & Co. real-estate agency, London 1931; hotel buyer since 1948; chmn., Mount Royal Marble Arch, Ltd. 1957; founding chmn., Grand Metropolitan, Ltd. since 1957. • Chmn.: Norfolk Capital, Ltd. since 1969; Truman Hanbury Buxton, Ltd. since 1971; Liggett & Myers since 1980; Intercontinental Hotels since 1981; Lombard Banking Co.; Gittspur Co.; other subsidiaries of Grand Metropolitan. • Dir.: Express Dairy Co., Ltd. since 1969; Watney Mann & Truman Holdings, Ltd. since 1977; Mecca, Ltd.; Fraser Ansbacher, Ltd.; Intl. Distillers and Vintners, Ltd.; Cunard Steamship Co.; others. **Officer** Gen. council member since 1972 and chmn. of natl. council 1977–78, British Hotels, Restaurants, and Caterers Assn. **Honors** Kt. 1981; Cape of Good Hope Gold Medal.

FLEMMING B(RUUN) MUUS
Resistance leader and writer
***Born* Copenhagen, Denmark, 21 November 1907**
***Died* Copenhagen, Denmark, 23 September 1982**

The Secret Operations Executive (SOE) was founded by the British to supply training, arms, and intelligence support to resistance movements in countries occupied by the Nazis. From 1943 to 1945, its Danish unit was led by Flemming B. Muus, an unusually daring and capable agent who increased the unit's effectiveness tenfold. Just after the war, he was convicted by the Danish government of embezzling funds from the SOE, and hence was never honored publicly for his service by his countrymen. Maj. George Taylor, the Danish liaison at the London SOE headquarters, wrote of him: "No one cognizant of the history of 1943 and 1944 will venture to deny that Muus displayed many touches of brilliance, but most of those who knew him well will admit just as readily that he was an adventurer, to be true a most charming and lovable adventurer."

The son of a consular official, Muus embarked early on a business career. In 1931 he left Denmark, by some accounts because of accusations of financial improprieties, to work for the Elder Dempster shipping firm in Cape Palmas, Liberia. When the Germans invaded Denmark in 1940, he wrote to London and Washington volunteering his services, but was turned down on the grounds that Denmark had declared its neutrality. In 1942, after a roundabout journey through Africa, he made his way to England, where he joined the Buffs Regiment, a unit open to foreign nationals. He quickly advanced to the rank of major and enlisted as a trainee in the SOE. His personable manner, intelligence, knowledge of languages, and organizational ability made him the obvious choice for a new Danish SOE leader.

Muus parachuted into Jutland in 1943 and set up headquarters in a women's boarding house in Copenhagen, using the code name Jørgen. Capitalizing on progress made by his predecessors, he reorganized the SOE circuit and forged links with the three main resistance groups, the Ringen, the Dansk Samling, and the Communists. He established a network of safe houses and drop zones for Allied supplies and personnel and increased the number of successful SOE sabotage operations from 122 in 1942 to 969 in 1943. After the Germans took the king hostage and put the country under the authority of a Reichskommissioner, Muus, together with 12 others, founded an underground government known as the Frihedsraad (Free Council), which worked closely with the Allies.

The Gestapo's capture of several key SOE agents in mid-1944 forced Muus and his associates to remove to the islands in the south of Denmark. In October the Gestapo began a massive manhunt for Muus, who fled to Sweden with his wife in December, using the escape route for POWs and Jewish refugees that he had organized the year before. Upon his arrival in London in January 1945, Muus was received by King George VI and congratulated by his chiefs at the SOE. He was asked to provide records of all SOE funds that had passed through his hands, but was unable to account for a large sum. A Danish commission of inquiry found him guilty of embezzlement and sent him to prison. Some historians, claiming that no Resistance leader working under constant danger in an occupied country could be expected to keep accurate books, charged that Muus was framed by his enemies.

After his release in 1947, Muus worked for a gold-mining concern in South Africa. He returned to Denmark in 1949 to begin a new career as a writer. His first book, *The Spark and the Flame* (1950), described his exploits with the Resistance. He also wrote a series of children's adventure stories and several biographies, including one of his mother-in-law, Monica Wichfeld, a Resistance leader executed by the Nazis. Muus later served on the board of the Danish Resistance Museum and edited its magazine. He died in Copenhagen at the age of 74. S.A.

Code name Jørgen. **Parents** Kai Bruun M., Danish consul gen., and Agnete (Zahle) M. **Married** Varinka Wichfeld, Resistance worker and author, 1944. **Education** Øster Borgerdydskole; Sch. of Commerce, Copenhagen; Patriotic Sch. for Resistance Workers and Secret Operations Exec. (SOE) training 1942–43. **Career** With shipping firms 1920s: Elias B. Muus, Inc., Kerteminde, Denmark; L. Späth, Berlin; Gen. Motors, Copenhagen. • With Elder Dempster Lines, Ltd., Cape Palmas, Liberia 1932–42. • Maj., Buffs Regiment, British Army 1942; leader, SOE network, Danish Resistance 1943–45; founding member, Frihedsraad (Freedom Council), Denmark 1943–45; imprisoned for embezzlement ca. 1945–47, Denmark. • With New Consolidated Gold Fields, Ltd., Johannesburg 1947–49; writer, Denmark since 1949; ed., *Veterans of the Liberation Movement* newsletter 1973. **Officer** Member, bd. of dirs. 1973, v.p. 1974, and secty. since 1975, Danish Resistance Mus. **Member** Special Forces Club, London; Veterans of Danish Fight for Freedom. **Honors** Lundgreens Award 1962; DSO. **Author** *Ingen tænder et lys,* 1950 (trans. as *The Spark and the Flame,* 1956); *Solsiden vender mod nord* [*South to North*], 1951; *Det begyndte under Sydkorset* [*It Began Under the Southern Cross*], 1952; *Der kom en dag* [*There Came a Day*], 1953; (with Varinka Wichfeld Muus) *Monica Wichfeld,* 1954 (trans. as *Monica Wichfeld, A Very Gallant Woman,* 1955); *Over 23 grænser* [*Across 23 Borders*], 1955; (with V.W.M.) *Skik & Brug* [*Customs*], 1956; *Mange er kaldede* [*Many are Called*], 1966; *Jam—en hund* [*Jam—A Dog*], 1967; *Gjort Gerning* [*Finished Deed*], 1979; *Elias B. Muus 1829–1979, En Familie og dens virksomhed gennem 150 år* [*Elias B. Muus 1829–1979, A Family and its Achievements Through 150 Years*], 1979. **Juvenile books** *Bo redder A-bomben* [*Bo Saves the A-bomb*]; *Bo og gestapochefen* [*Bo and the Gestapo Commander*]; *Bo på sporet af Sputnik* [*Bo on the Trail of Sputnik*]; eight others.

Further reading E.H. Cookridge, *Inside S.O.E.,* 1966; Richard Petrow, *The Bitter Years,* 1974.

SARAH (MILLICENT HERMIONE) CHURCHILL
Lady Audley
Actress and writer
***Born* London, England, 7 October 1914**
***Died* London, England, 24 September 1982**

If Britain's wartime leader, Sir Winston Churchill, had not been one of the most famous statesmen of his time, his daughter Sarah's private life would almost certainly have passed unnoticed. As it was, the actress's much-publicized "wild period" provided the tabloids with material enough to label her "a fiery redhead," and worse, "a notorious woman." But her family and friends knew her to be sensitive and artistic, a complex woman with deep family commitments and a distressing drink problem.

Sarah Millicent Hermione Churchill was born in 1914, the third of Sir Winston and Lady Clementine Churchill's four children. Her brother Randolph, who became a Conservative M.P., and her sister Diana, who married one, are both deceased; her younger sister Mary, a writer, is married to Lord Soames. She was a frail child, and at the age of five or six she had to have tubercular glands removed from her neck. Her sister Mary, in her biography *Clementine Churchill,* wrote: "Sarah panicked when the chloroform mask was held over her face; becoming hysterical, she . . . ran round and round the operating theatre until she was caught and subdued by sheer force. . . . The operation left a scar on Sarah's neck . . . and . . . a deep impression on her inner being, making her dread all forms of physical restraint."

When she was 13, she transferred from Notting Hill High School in London to North Foreland Lodge, a boarding school on the Kent coast at Broadstairs, where she grew into a strong young woman. From Broadstairs, she was sent for a year to a finishing school in Paris (1933), then made her debut into the London social set. Shy and dreamy, she was a reluctant debutante, but a striking one: tall, with a pale complexion, auburn hair, and green eyes. Her mother confided to a friend: "Sometimes she looks absolutely lovely—but on the other hand she can look like a moping raven."

Once she had suffered through the convention of "coming out," Churchill attended a dancing school, then shunned further ladylike pursuits and became a chorus girl in a revue, *Follow The Sun,* which opened in Manchester in December 1935. By the time the show had reached London, she had fallen in love with its male lead, a twice-married Austrian-born comedian named Vic Oliver, who was 17 years her senior. Her parents were aghast when she announced her intention of marrying him—which she did, in New York, on Christmas Eve 1936.

After *Follow The Sun,* Churchill switched to straight roles—much to the relief of Sir Winston—and enjoyed modest success on the London stage. Early in 1941 she played in *Outward Bound,* then performed the title role in J. M. Barrie's *Mary Rose;* from there she went into repertory for a summer season at the London Coliseum. She left the stage in October 1941 to help in the war effort, serving in the photointelligence section of the Women's Auxiliary Air Force (WAAF) and accompanying her father, then prime minister of the wartime coalition, as his aide-de-camp at the 1943 strategy-planning conference with Pres. Roosevelt in Teheran; she also went with her father to Yalta in 1945 for the postwar policy meeting with Roosevelt and Josef Stalin.

After demobilization in 1945, Churchill and her husband were divorced and she resumed her acting career. Her British stage appearances included the popular *Gaslight* (1946) and *The Barretts of Wimpole Street* (1948). She made her American stage debut at Princeton, New Jersey, in June 1949, playing Tracy Lord in *The Philadelphia Story*. A critic described her performance as "constantly gay and charming." Also in that year she married a society photographer, Anthony Beauchamp. Her Broadway debut came in 1951, when she appeared in *Gramercy Ghost.* During the 1950s the actress was a frequent guest on American television shows, played in a number of Hollywood television dramas, and for two years hosted "The Hallmark Hall of Fame." She returned to London in 1958 to play the title role in *Peter Pan* and in the early 1960s appeared in a succession of roles on the British stage, notably as Eliza in the 1960 touring production of *Pygmalion* and as Rosalind in *As You Like It.* In September of 1966 she co-starred in *A Matter of Choice,* a collection of sketches, songs, and poems. Her final stage appearance was at the Hayloft Dinner Theater in Manassas, Virginia, in February 1976, when she played in a musical based on her own short story, *The Boy Who Made Magic.*

Churchill's first film role was in the 1940 production *He Found a Star.* Her later films include *When in Rome* (1952), *All Over Town* (1947), *Royal Wedding* (1951), and *Serious Charge* (1959).

Anthony Beauchamp's suicide in 1958 marked the beginning of Churchill's most difficult period. She was arrested for drunkenness in Malibu, California, following a complaint about a rowdy party in her apartment; reportedly, she subjected the sheriff's deputies to a volley of obscene abuse. Her family and friends were relieved when she found happiness with her third husband, Lord Audley, whom she married in 1962; but he died less than a year after their wedding. In 1968 she created another minor scandal when she was arrested for being drunk and disorderly in London's expensive Belgravia district and spent several nights in Holloway Prison. That same year, her landlord took out an injunction to prevent her from breaking bottles outside the door of her apartment.

In later life, Churchill took up painting, just as her father had done in his retirement. At the time of her death, of an undisclosed illness, some of her work was on display, along with Sir Winston's, at a London gallery. Her published writings include two books of verse and a memoir, *A Thread in the Tapestry,* which is chiefly about her father. Her autobiography, *Keep On Dancing,* appeared in 1981. R.T.

Parents Sir Winston Spencer C., prime minister of Britain, soldier, and author, and Lady Clementine Ogilvy (Hozier) C. **Married** (1) Vic Oliver, comedian, 1936 (div. 1945). (2) Anthony Beauchamp, photographer, 1949 (d. 1958). (3) Lord Audley 1962 (d. 1963). **Education** Notting Hill High Sch., London; North Foreland Lodge, Broadstairs, Kent; finishing sch., Paris; De Vos Sch. of Dancing, London. **Mil. service** With photographic intelligence sect., Women's Auxiliary Air Force 1941–45; ADC to Winston Churchill, Teheran 1943 and Yalta 1945. **Career** Stage actress and dancer since 1936, film actress since 1940, TV actress since 1950s; poet, painter, and writer. **Stage**

(all London except as noted) *Follow the Sun,* 1935; *Mandragola,* 1939; *Misalliance,* 1940; *Outward Bound,* 1941; *Mary Rose,* 1941; *Squaring the Triangle,* 1945; *Gaslight,* 1946; *The Barretts of Wimpole Street,* 1948; *House in the Sand,* 1949; *The Philadelphia Story,* Princeton, NJ, and U.S. tour 1949; *Gramercy Ghost,* NYC 1951; *Peter Pan,* 1958; *Night Life of the Virile Potato,* 1960; *Pygmalion,* U.K. tour 1960; *As You Like It,* 1961; *From this Hill,* 1963; *Fata Morgana,* 1964; *A Matter of Choice,* 1966; *The Idiot,* 1970; (also co-writer) *The Boy Who Made Magic,* 1976; other plays in repertory seasons. **Films** *He Found a Star,* 1940; *All Over Town,* 1947; *Royal Wedding,* 1951; *When in Rome,* 1952; *Serious Charge,* 1959; others. **Television** Host, "Hallmark Presents Sarah Churchill," 1951, "Hallmark Hall of Fame," 1952–54; "Hamlet," 1953; "Richard II," 1954; others. **Recording** *A Matter of Choice,* 1980. **Author** *A Thread in the Tapestry* (memoirs), 1967; *Unwanted Statue and Other Poems,* 1969; *Keep On Dancing* (autobiography), 1981; one other book of poems.

Further reading Mary Soames, *Clementine Churchill,* 1979; Mary Soames, *Family Album,* 1982.

VALERIE BETTIS
Modern dancer and choreographer
Born **Houston, Texas, USA, 20 December 1919**
Died **New York City, USA, 26 September 1982**

Valerie Bettis, a modern dancer and choreographer of uncommon energy and dramatic intensity, broke new ground in 1947 when she choreographed a modern-dance work for a ballet company, the first time such a combination had ever been tried. She also had a successful career as a dancer and actress on Broadway and was the first to create experimental dances for television.

The daughter of a wealthy dealer in oil-rig equipment, Bettis grew up in Houston, Texas, where she attended the public schools and was presented as a debutante. She was a dance student from the age of ten. At 18 she left the University of Texas to study in New York City with Hanya Holm, the most famous disciple of the modern-dance pioneer Mary Wigman. After appearing in the "Railroads on Parade" exhibit at the New York World's Fair in 1939–40, she made her solo debut in 1941 at the Carnegie Chamber Music Hall, and in 1942 made her first major attempt at choreography with *And the Earth Shall Bear Again,* set to the music of John Cage. The following year she danced in her own solo *The Desperate Heart,* for which John Malcolm Brinnin wrote the accompanying poetry and her first husband, the Brazilian pianist and composer Bernardo Segall, wrote the music. For the next several years she toured the Americas, with her husband as her accompanist, and in 1944 organized a dance company, the first of several she led over the years. Critic John Martin of the *New York Times* wrote that she possessed "a stunning technique, a speed without precedent in the modern field, and a temperament that can make the atmosphere fairly sizzle."

Like many dancers and choreographers, Bettis soon realized that the audience for serious artistic dance was too small to offer constant employment, and found an equally appreciative audience in the commercial theater. Her performance as the bloodthirsty temptress Tiger Lily in the 1948 revue *Inside U.S.A.* was a show-stopper. She took up singing and acting in *Great To Be Alive!* and *Bless You All* (both 1950), played the Serpent in George Bernard Shaw's *Back to Methuselah* (1958), and replaced Lotte Lenya in *The Threepenny Opera* in 1955 and *Brecht on Brecht* in 1962. She began choreographing for the stage in 1944 with *Glad To See You* and went on to do productions of *Beggar's Holiday, Ulysses in Nighttown,* and the Actors Studio version of *Peer Gynt,* meanwhile branching out into television with her own show in 1946 and with "The Paul Whiteman Revue" series and variety shows. During the 1950s, the heyday of televised drama, she choreographed "Our Town," "The Women," "The Sound and the Fury," George

Gershwin's "135th Street," and Stravinsky's "Histoire du soldat" for commercial and educational networks. In 1952 she went to Hollywood to devise simple dances for Rita Hayworth, including the celebrated "Dance of the Seven Veils" for *Salome.*

To aficionados of modern dance, Bettis is best known for her powerful dance-dramas based on literary works, including *Yerma,* from the play by Federico Garcia Lorca, *The Golden Round,* a solo for Lady Macbeth, and *Winesburg, Ohio,* from the story collection by Sherwood Anderson. The finest, by general consensus, was *As I Lay Dying* (1949), an adaptation of William Faulkner's novel, in which Bettis danced the central role of the mother. John Martin wrote in the *Times* that *As I Lay Dying* "took dance farther from its own medium into drama than ever before without getting lost." Bettis's adventurous attempt to create a rapprochement between modern dance and ballet (*Virginia Sampler,* 1947) failed because the Ballet Russe de Monte Carlo was unable to adapt to the new technique or to the composition's distinctively American idiom. Her version of Tennessee Williams's *A Streetcar Named Desire,* staged in 1952 for the Slavenska-Franklin Ballet, was incorporated into the repertory of American Ballet Theater and was revived in 1982 by the Dance Theater of Harlem.

During her 35-year career, Bettis often had stage, television, and concert productions going concurrently; she also taught and performed at universities, dance festivals, and her own Greenwich Village studio. Her last work, completed shortly before her death of cancer, was an adaptation for a liturgical dance troupe of W. H. Hudson's *Green Mansions.* E.W.

Parents Royal Holt B., oil-rig equipment supplier, and Valerie Elizabeth (McCarthy) B. **Married** (1) Bernardo Segall, pianist and composer, 1943 (div. 1955). (2) Arthur A. Schmidt 1959 (d. 1969). **Education** Studied dance from age ten; San Jacinto High Sch., Houston, TX; Univ. of Texas, Austin; studied dance with Hanya Holm, NYC 1937–40. **Career** Dancer since mid-1930s: with Hanya Holm Dance Co. 1937–40; solo debut 1941; organized first group 1944; frequent solo and group performer in concert, in musical comedies, on tour. • Choreographer since 1942; actress since 1950s; stage dir. and teacher since 1960s; founder 1964, Valerie Bettis Theatre/Dance Company, NYC; founder 1964, artistic dir., and pres., Dance Studio Foundn., Inc.; teacher at Jacob's Pillow and other dance festivals; artist in residence, Univ. of California at Los Angeles 1968–69, also taught at other colls. **Honors** John Martin Award, for *The Desperate Heart,* 1943; Donaldson Awards for best danseuse and best musical-comedy debut, for *Inside U.S.A.,* 1948; Mademoiselle Award, for *Inside U.S.A.,* 1948; Critics Award, for "The Paul Whiteman Revue," 1949; Natl. Endowment for Arts Choreographer's Fellowship 1981. **Modern-dance choreographer** *Prairie Barn,* 1941; *And the Earth Shall Bear Again,* 1942; *The Desperate Heart,* 1943; *Dramatic Incident,* 1945; *Virginia Sampler,* 1947; *As I Lay Dying,* 1949; *A Streetcar Named Desire,* 1952; *The Golden Round,* 1955; *Winesburg, Ohio,* 1960; *Early Voyages,* 1960; *On Ship,* 1970; *Echoes of Spoon River,* 1976; *Next Day,* 1978; *Green Mansions,* 1982; *Domino Furioso Columbine; Yerma;* others. **Musical-comedy choreographer** (all NYC except as noted) *Glad To See You,* Boston and Phila. 1944; *Beggar's Holiday,* 1946; *Peer Gynt,* 1951; *Ulysses in Nighttown,* 1958; *Pousse-Café,* 1966; *Final Solutions,* 1968; others. **Stage dancer and actress**

(all NYC except as noted) *Glad To See You,* Boston and Phila. 1944; *Inside U.S.A.,* 1948; *Great To Be Alive!,* 1950; *Bless You All,* 1950; *The Frogs of Spring,* tour 1953; *The Threepenny Opera,* 1955; *Back to Methuselah,* 1958; *Ulysses in Nighttown,* London 1959 and European tour; *Brecht on Brecht,* 1962; *America Dances,* 1963; others. **Stage director** *If Five Years Pass,* NYC 1962; *Adam and Eve* (opera), NYC 1974; *The Corner,* NYC 1975; others. **Film choreographer** *An Affair in Trinidad,* 1952; *Salome,* 1952; *Let's Do It Again,* 1953; *Athena,* 1954; others. **Television choreographer and dancer** "Valerie Bettis Dancers," 1946; "Paul Whiteman Revue," 1949; "The Women," 1955; "Your Show of Shows," "Studio One," "Omnibus," other dramatic productions and variety shows.

PAUL KOLLSMAN

Aeronautics engineer

***Born* Freudenstadt, Germany, 22 February 1900**

***Died* Los Angeles, California, USA, 26 September 1982**

By transforming the aircraft altimeter into a precision instrument, Paul Kollsman helped make flying possible in any kind of weather. His altimeter, developed in 1928, replaced four different instruments—the ordinary altimeter, the landing altimeter, the level flight indicator, and the climb indicator—and was part of the equipment used by James Doolittle when he made the first "blind" flight (without visibility through the windshield) in aviation history. It is still standard equipment on virtually all aircraft built today.

Kollsman, who was born in the Black Forest area of Germany, studied science and engineering at technical schools in Stuttgart and Munich. In the early 1920s he designed a new kind of automobile engine. Unable to sell it in Germany, he emigrated to the United States in 1923 in the vain hope of interesting an American automobile manufacturer. He eventually took a job as a parts inspector for the Pioneer Instrument Company in Queens, New York, which produced altimeters accurate to between 50 and 100 feet, not nearly enough to make "blind" flying possible. When Kollsman made suggestions for improvements, he was fired.

In 1928, Kollsman and his brother Otto started their own instrument company in an attic workshop in Brooklyn. Their first product was Kollsman's altimeter. It was sensitive to minute changes in barometric pressure, which decreases with altitude, and converted these changes to altitude readings accurate to within five feet, an order of magnitude greater than any competing design. Word of the improved altimeter soon reached the aerial acrobat James Doolittle, who was working with the Daniel Guggenheim Fund for the Promotion of Aeronautics to develop safe techniques for all-weather flight. Impressed by the responsiveness and accuracy of the altimeter and the clarity of its display dials, which were moved by gears made by Swiss watchmakers, Doolittle had one installed in the fund's training plane, a Consolidated NY-2, which he piloted on his historic flight in September 1929 at Mitchel Field, Long Island.

During the 1930s, Kollsman perfected other devices, including improved rate-of-climb and airspeed indicators. When he sold his company in 1940, his altimeter was in almost universal use. Until recently, it was common practice for pilots to radio the airport's control tower before takeoff and landing in order to obtain the correct atmospheric pressure, or "Kollsman number," by which to set their altimeters. Radar determination of altitude, which is accurate down to a foot or less, has now begun to supplant the Kollsman altimeter, but the device is still installed in most aircraft as a safety measure.

In his later years, Kollsman became interested in membrane technology. He received a number of patents for membranes used in cheese processing and in the desalinization of seawater. In 1979 he and Doolittle attended a reenactment of the first all-instrument flight on its 50th anniversary. P.D.

Married (1) Luli Deste, author (d. 1951). (2) Eva Franzen 1957. **Emigrated** to U.S. 1923. **Education** Technical schs., Stuttgart and

Munich. **Career** Parts inspector, Pioneer Instrument Co., NYC, ca. 1924–28; founding pres., Kollsman Instrument Co., NYC 1928–40; consultant and v.p., Square D Co., Detroit 1940s; membrane-technology researcher 1960s–70s; established aeronautics library, Inst. of Aeronautical Sciences. **Patents** Barometric altimeters, 1928 and 1929; positive compass; rate-of-climb indicator; electric altimeter; heated pitot tube for airspeed indicator; cheese-separation membrane; desalinization membrane; slip-resistant surface for showers and baths; many other devices.

H(ORST) W(OLDEMAR) JANSON

Art historian

***Born* St. Petersburg, Russia, 4 October 1917**

***Died* Italy, 30 September 1982**

If sales figures are an accurate measure of fame, H. W. Janson, author of the best-selling textbook *History of Art* (1962), was the world's most celebrated art historian. His "survey of the major visual arts from the dawn of history to the present day" had sold more than 2.5 million copies by the time of his death, making Janson the most influential teacher of his subject in the United States and a respected authority in other countries, where his work was known in ten translations. Janson's preeminence was challenged only by that of the English art historian and television personality Kenneth Clark, whose urbane manners contrasted strikingly with Janson's brusque, Germanic enthusiasm. Whereas Clark takes the role of a charming host conducting a tour of his private collection, Janson was a born pedagogue who seized the attention of his audience by continually relating the art he described to everyday concerns. Anyone who takes on the task of describing the history of art from paleolithic times to Abstract Expressionism in a single volume is vulnerable to the charge of glibness, but Janson did all he could to forestall this danger, revising his opinions in successive editions (the last in 1977), and choosing works from outside the familiar pantheon of masterpieces.

Although Horst Woldemar Janson was born in St. Petersburg, his parents were of Swedish and German descent and lived in Latvia. Shortly after their son's birth they fled from the Russian Revolution to Finland, and thence to Hamburg, where Janson received his preparatory and undergraduate education. He was delighted to recall that his scholarship to Harvard University, from which he received an M.A. in 1938 and a Ph.D. in 1942, was paid for by the Nazi government. He began teaching at the Worcester Art Museum, and worked at Iowa State University and Washington University, St. Louis, before joining the faculty of New York University in 1949. Encouraged by the example of Heinrich Wölfflin and Erwin Panofsky, who had trained many of the scholars who inaugurated the study of art history in the United States, Janson sought to bring his field into the mainstream of academic life by pointing out the importance of visual symbolism to the study of culture. At NYU, under his influence, art history assumed a central role in the curriculum, having formerly been a subject reserved for practicing artists.

Janson's first major study, *Apes and Ape Lore in the Middle Ages and the Renaissance* (1952), was prompted by an etching, given him by his wife as a birthday present, that depicted apes among classical ruins. The book was an exploration of apes as objects of fascination to pre-Darwinian thinkers, who, he speculated, regarded apes as descendants of man or as disturbingly imperfect parodies of the human condition. The work on which his scholarly reputation chiefly rests, however, was the comprehensive study *The Sculpture of Donatello* (1957). Both these books won College Art Association awards for the most distinguished work of art historical scholarship by an American or Canadian scholar.

While making these contributions to scholarship, Janson was also writing textbooks, often in collaboration with his wife, Dora Jane Heineberg, for the growing number of American undergraduate art students. In 1952 he published *The Story of Painting for Young People,* and in 1957 *The Picture History of Painting,* which sustained the H. N. Abrams publishing house for many years. He repeated

Courtesy of Harry N. Abrams, Inc.

this success with *Key Monuments in the History of Art,* the first work of art history to become a best seller in the college market. *History of Art,* which first appeared in 1962, quickly became a standard text in thousands of American colleges and universities, earning Janson a fortune in royalties.

Both in his scholarly works and his popularizing textbooks, Janson was at pains to show that the concerns of the artist are closer to those of everyday life than is commonly accepted. The most important business of the art educator, he told the editor of *ARTnews,* "is to train the art patrons of the future." By patrons he meant not wealthy collectors and connoisseurs, but consumers presented with a choice between good and bad design. Although he did otherwise in the *History of Art,* Janson saw nothing wrong with "starting a course with the present and working your way back. You can start with the here and now on the assumption that however little a student may understand what's going on today, at least he is more likely to have been exposed to it." The main thesis of his teaching was that art history is not a succession of avant-gardes that rise from neglect to constitute the establishment, but a more chaotic process in which artistic creation is closely allied to other human endeavors, especially technology. Some great works of art of the future, he predicted, would be made by computers and photocopiers.

Janson, who chaired NYU's art department until 1975, was named professor emeritus in 1979. Some of his important essays were collected in the volume *Sixteen Studies* in 1974. Shortly before his death, which took place while he was traveling by train between Milan and Zurich, he was working on *Nineteenth-Century Sculpture Revisited* and *Art in the Nineteenth Century,* the latter a volume of essays on which he collaborated with his colleague Robert Rosenblum. H.B.

Parents Friedrich J. and Helene (Porsch) J. **Married** Dora Jane Heineberg, art historian, 1941: Anthony Frederick; Peter; Josephine; Charles. **Emigration** Brought to Finland and Germany as a child; emigrated to U.S. ca. 1937. **Education** Public schs., Hamburg, Germany; Univ. of Hamburg; Harvard Univ. (German govt. grant), M.A. 1938, Ph.D. in medieval and Renaissance art 1942. **Career** Asst., fine arts dept. 1936–37 and visiting prof. 1967, Harvard Univ.; lectr. in art, Worcester Art Mus., MA 1936–38; instr., Iowa State Univ., Iowa City 1938–41; asst. prof. and curator of art collection, Washington Univ., St. Louis 1941–48; • With New York Univ.: prof. of arts and chmn. of fine art dept., Wash. Sq. Coll., and prof., Inst. of Fine Arts, 1949–79; prof. emeritus since 1979. • Ed. in chief, *Art Bulletin,* Amer. Studies Assn. 1962–65; Mellon Lectr., Natl. Gall. of Art, Wash. DC 1974; consulting ed., Time-Life Library of Art, Time, Inc. **Officer** Pres., Coll. Art Assn. 1970–72; v.p., Renaissance Soc. of America; v.p., Intl. Cttee. for History of Art in Paris. **Fellow** Amer. Acad. of Arts and Sciences; Natl. Humanities Inst. **Member** Amer. Studies Assn.; council, Swiss Inst. for Art History, Zurich; council, Inst. for Study of Art of Lombardy. **Honors** Guggenheim Foundn. Fellowship 1948–49, 1955–56; Morley Prize 1952, for *Apes and Ape Lore in the Middle Ages and the Renaissance,* and 1957, for *The Sculpture of Donatello,* Coll. Art Assn.; hon. degree, New York Univ. **Author** *Apes and Ape Lore in the Middle Ages and the Renaissance,* 1952; (with D. J. Janson) *The Story of Painting for Young People,* 1952; *The Sculpture of Donatello,* 2 vols., 1957; (with D. J. J.) *The Picture History of Painting,* 1957; *Key Monuments in the History of Art,* 1959; (with D. J. J.) *History of Art,* 1962, 3rd rev. ed. 1977; (ed.) *The Library of Art History,* 1967; (jtly.) *A Basic History of Art,* 1971; *Sixteen Studies,* 1974; (ed. and comp.) *Catalogues of the Paris Salon, 1673–1881,* 1977; (jtly.) *The Romantics to Rodin,* 1980; (jtly.) *Art of the Nineteenth Century,* 1983; *Nineteenth-Century Sculpture Revisited,* forthcoming. **Contributor** of papers on art history to professional jrnls. **Interview** Milton Esterow, "A Conversation with H. W. Janson," in *ARTnews,* Feb. 1982.

OCTOBER

MUKTANANDA PARAMAHANSA

Hindu spiritual leader

Born **Mangalore, Mysore, India, British Empire, 15 May 1908**

Died **Ganeshpuri, near Thana, Maharashtra, India, 2 October 1982**

Swami Muktananda Paramahansa was revered as a saint, a man who had achieved perfect realization of his divine nature, by half a million followers from San Francisco to Australia. At his religious community at Ganeshpuri, in southwestern India, and on speaking tours throughout the world, he taught techniques of meditation intended to rouse the kundalini, the latent power that is considered by Hindu mystics to lie dormant at the base of the spine. He demanded from his followers neither belief in Hindu theological doctrines nor any material sacrifice; his message was "Honor and worship your own inner being. God dwells within you, as you." A look or touch from him, it was said, could produce in its recipient a feeling of ecstasy and wholeness.

Muktananda was 15 years old when, inspired by a meeting with the mystic Swami Nityananda, he left his well-to-do family to become a wandering religious seeker. In 1947, when he was nearly 40, he encountered Nityananda again, underwent a revelatory experience, and became his disciple, living with him in his jungle retreat and spending his time gardening and meditating. After Nityananda's death in 1961, Muktananda inherited the title of swami and began to acquire disciples of his own. "He seemed to be in an ecstatic state all the time, even when he was cooking or reading the newspaper," recalled one. The community quickly grew into a small town covering 50 acres, with thousands of visitors, many of them Westerners, passing through every year. He was much sought after by prominent members of the Indian government and became spiritual advisor to Prime Minister Indira Gandhi.

In 1970, Muktananda, who was known to his followers as Baba, "father," made the first of three world tours. In the United States, his students, who eventually numbered 100,000, established ashrams (sanctuaries) in most of the major cities, with their national headquarters in a converted resort hotel in the Catskills. In California, he was consulted by groups of psychotherapists and paid respectful visits by Gov. Jerry Brown, Werner Erhard, the founder of est, and poet Allen Ginsberg. Elsewhere, he was met with skepticism and ridicule for the quaint figure he cut in his brightly colored socks and wool caps. The travel writer Paul Zweig was one of the many listeners who found themselves unexpectedly touched by him. In an article for *Harper's,* Zweig wrote: "I don't think I will ever understand why, after sitting with him for a few minutes, I experienced a surge of emotions so powerful and so profound that it left me exhausted. I wept uncontrollably, although, at the same time, I found that I was unaccountably happy, for I had a sense of having seen myself for the first time." Muktananda, he said, was "someone who could 'infect' you with that experience of ecstasy, and who could then help you to control it, and to integrate it into your life. . . . His power lay precisely in his lack of mystery. If he was a wizard, he was a wizard of the ordinary."

Muktananda died while meditating in his temple at Ganeshpuri; he was 74. C.M.

Parents landowners. **Religion** Hindu. **Career** Religious seeker and student of various meditation teachers, India early 1920s–1947; disciple of Swami Nityananda, Ganeshpuri, Maharashtra, India 1947–61; teacher of meditation and Siddha Yoga since 1961; founder of Gavdevi ashram, Ganeshpuri, and of religious communities in U.S., Europe, Australia, other countries. **Author** of more than 35 books, including *Citśakti vilāsa,* 1970 (trans. as *Chitshakti vilas: The Play of Consciousness,* 1972); *Bhagawan Nityananda: His Life and Mission,* 1972; *Satsang with Baba,* 4 vols.,

1974–78; Paul Zweig, ed., *Selected Essays,* 1976; *God Is with You,* 1978; *I Welcome You All with Love,* 1978; *Perfect Religion,* 1980. **Recording** *Inner Stages of Sadhana,* 1970.

Further reading *Swami Muktananda Paramahansa: Sixtieth Birthday Commemoration Volume,* 1968; Paul Zweig, "The Master of Ganeshpuri," in *Harper's,* May 1977.

VIVIEN MERCHANT

Actress

Born **Manchester, England, 22 July 1929**

Died **London, England, 3 October 1982**

Actress Vivien Merchant was best known for her work in the opaque dramas of her husband, the English playwright Harold Pinter. Dark and intense, with the grace and physical control of a dancer, she was equally adept at portraying sensuality and remoteness, the two most important qualities—often displayed simultaneously—of Pinter's female characters.

Born Ada Thomson, Merchant studied ballet with her mother, a dance teacher, and took elocution and diction lessons in preparation for an acting career. At the age of 13 she left the Bury Convent School in Manchester to join Harry Hanson's touring repertory company and appeared as Adele in an adaptation of *Jane Eyre.* She debuted in London as a dancer in Noel Coward's revue *Sigh No More,* then for the next six years toured England with the companies of Hanson and Donald Wolfit, doing Shakespeare in repertory. Merchant never saw herself as a glamorous actress and came to prefer the relative obscurity of regional repertory theater; throughout the 1950s and early 60s she played in and around London and in the provinces in half a dozen companies and in a great variety of roles, from Lady Macbeth to a small singing part in Coward's musical *Ace of Spades* (1950).

While a member of Barry O'Brien's repertory company in Bournemouth, she married Pinter, a struggling actor in the same troupe. They had a son, Daniel, in 1958, while they were still living in the acutest poverty. Merchant's income as an actress enabled Pinter to concentrate on playwriting. She appeared in his first play, *The Room,* in 1957, and continued to be, as he said, the "ideal interpreter" of his work, starring in *The Lover* (1963), *The Homecoming* (1965), *The Tea Party* (1970), and *Old Times* (1971). Pinter also directed her—unsuccessfully, she felt—in the television version of *The Lover,* for which she was named best actress of the year.

The Homecoming, produced by the Royal Shakespeare Company in London and New York City (her only U.S. appearance), was her biggest stage success. As Ruth, the enigmatic wife who manipulates the psychosexual obsessions of her husband's family, Merchant was alternately smoldering and sphinxlike, to the amazed delight of the critics. She also appeared in a television production of *The Homecoming* and was named best television actress in 1963. Her film performances, few but memorable, included *Alfie* (1966), Joseph Losey's *Accident* (1967, from a screenplay by Pinter), Hitchcock's *Frenzy* (1972), and the screen version of *The Homecoming* (1974).

In August 1975, on the opening night of Pinter's *Otherwise Engaged,* Merchant sparked a minor scandal by announcing that she was suing him for divorce on grounds of adultery with the biographer and socialite Lady Antonia Fraser. She died, two years after Pinter's remarriage, of severe jaundice and internal bleeding caused by alcoholism.
C.M.

Born Ada Thomson. **Parents** William T., and Margaret (MacNaughton) T., dance teacher. **Married** Harold Pinter, actor and playwright, 1956 (div. 1980); Daniel, b. 1958. **Education** Studied ballet with her mother, also elocution and diction; Bury Convent Sch., Manchester, left at age 13. **Career** Stage actress with repertory cos. of Harry Hanson, Donald Wolfit, Royal Shakespeare, and others since 1943; film actress since 1944; TV actress since 1960s. **Member** Ronnie Scott's Club. **Honors** TV Actress of the Year, for "The Lover," Guild of British Television Producers and Directors, 1963. **Stage** (all in London except as noted) *Jane Eyre,* Peterborough 1943; *Sigh No More,* 1945; *As You Like It,* 1947, 1953; *Ace of Spades,* 1950; *The Merchant of Venice,* 1953; *Macbeth,* London 1953 and tour of U.K. and eastern Europe 1967–68; *Weekend at Woodcote,* 1955; *Motive for Murder,* Harrow 1955; *The Room,* 1957, 1960; *Judith,* 1962; *The Lover,* 1963; *The Homecoming,* 1965 and NYC 1967; sketch *We Who Are About To . . .* (also called *Night*), in *Mixed Doubles,* 1969; *Sweet Bird of Youth,* Watford 1968; *Flint,* 1970; *Mary Stuart, Queen of Scots,* Edinburgh 1970; *The Tea Party,* 1970; *Exiles,* London 1970 and Stratford 1971; *Old Times,* Stratford 1971; *The Man of Mode,* Stratford 1971; *The Maids,* 1974; *Gaslight,* 1974; *Death of a Salesman,* 1975; *The Vortex,* 1975; *Love's Old Sweet Song,* 1976; *All Over,* Brighton and U.K. tour 1976; *The Father,* 1977. **Films** *The Way Ahead,* 1944; *Alfie,* 1966; *Accident,* 1967; *Alfred the Great,* 1969; *Under Milkwood,* 1972; *Frenzy,* 1972; *The Offense,* 1973; *The Homecoming,* 1974; *The Maids,* 1974; others. **Television plays** "A Slight Ache," 1959; "A Night Out," 1960; "Night School," 1960; "The Collection," 1961; "The Lover," 1963; "The Tea Party," 1965; "The Common," 1973; "The Man in the Iron Mask," 1976; "Breakaway," 1980; "A Tale of Two Cities," 1980; "The Homecoming"; "Weather in the Streets"; "A Month in the Country"; "Don Juan in Hell"; "War of the Children"; "Focus"; others.

AHMAD HASSAN AL-BAKR

President of Iraq
***Born* Tikrit, Iraq, 1914**
***Died* Baghdad, Iraq, 4 October 1982**

Gen. Ahmad Hassan al-Bakr was the unelected president of the Republic of Iraq from 1968 to 1979, a time of relative quiet and prosperity compared to the bloody and chaotic preceding years. He was a prominent leader of the Ba'ath (Resurrection) Party, a predominantly socialist, fiercely nationalist grouping that has been a powerful force in Iraq since the antimonarchist revolution of 1958.

Born to a traditionally devout farmer's family in Tikrit, a village that has given Iraq a considerable number of Ba'athist military men, Bakr decided first to be a teacher, graduating from a teachers' training college in 1932. He taught in Baghdad until 1938, when he quit his profession to enter the military academy. He participated in the unsuccessful revolt of Rashid Ali in 1941 against the pro-Western, monarchist government of Nuri as-Said, and was imprisoned and cashiered as an officer in its aftermath. He was reinstated only in 1957.

The following year, as commander of the 1st Infantry Brigade, Bakr occupied Habbaniya Air Base, 40 miles west of Baghdad, in support of the brutal coup d'état by Gen. Abdel Karim Qasim, in the course of which the bloody bodies of Premier Said, King Faisal II, and the rest of the royal family were displayed, hung upside down by the heels, to the press and people. In April 1959 he was arrested by Qasim on suspicion of complicity in the revolt at Mosul, which was bloodily suppressed with Communist and Kurdish assistance, but was soon released and again placed on the retirement list. He is believed at that point to have become a Ba'athist.

In February 1963 he was the prime mover behind the coup that ended the Qasim regime and brought the Ba'athists to power for the first time. Pres. Qasim was summarily executed at the state television studios. The new president, Marshal Abdul Salam Arif, named Bakr as prime minister. Arif soon found himself at odds with radical Ba'athists and seized total power in November 1963, keeping a few moderate Ba'athists at his side; Bakr was allowed to remain as vice president for a few months before being dismissed. He was given the honorary title of ambassador, but was expected to disappear from political life.

On Pres. Arif's death in a helicopter crash in 1966, the presidency went to his brother, Gen. Abdul Rahman Arif, who proved weak and indecisive in office. Bakr had meanwhile regrouped his Ba'athist military colleagues, who between them represented all strains of Iraqi nationalism. On 17 July 1968 he seized power, eventually assuming the offices of president, prime minister, commander in chief of the armed forces, head of the Revolutionary Command Council, and secretary general of the Ba'ath Party.

His rule was not without its difficulties, though Iraq's economic development, spurred by greatly increased petroleum revenue after 1973, was very impressive. The Ba'ath Party had no great popularity in the country as a whole, and was actively opposed by powerful elements in the Army. In 1969, primarily to divert national attention from such dissention, he ordered a series of mass show trials in Baghdad against a purported pro-Israeli spy ring. Many prominent and respected civilian figures were executed in this charade, which was certainly the nadir of Bakr's presidency. Trouble with the Kurds, an important ethnic minority, followed during the 1970s, but by persuading the Shah of Iran, an old enemy of the Ba'athists, to cease supporting the Kurdish rebels, Bakr managed largely to subdue them by 1975.

In 1976 the president suffered a stroke, which caused his gradual withdrawal from the center of affairs in favor of his dynamic vice president, Saddam Hussayn, chief of the civil, radical faction of the Ba'ath and like him a native of Tikrit. He resigned the presidency on 16 July 1979, exactly 11 years after assuming it. A.K.

Father a farmer. **Married** . . . (d. 1974): Muhammad Hassan (d. 1978); two other sons; six daughters. **Religion** Sunni Muslim. **Education** Teachers Coll., Baghdad, grad. 1932; Military Coll., Baghdad 1938. **Career** Teacher 1932–38; joined Iraqi Army 1938; imprisoned and cashiered for revolutionary activities 1941; reinstated, 1957; comdr., 1st Infantry Brigade 1957; participated in coup d'état 1958, arrested 1959, dismissed from army 1959; joined Ba'ath Party 1959; reinstated in army 1961; comdr., 19th Brigade 1961; participated in coup d'état 1963; prime minister of Iraq, Feb. and Nov. 1963; vice premier 1963–64; named hon. ambassador 1964; participated in coup d'état 1968; chmn. of Revolutionary Command Council, pres. of Iraq, prime minister, and comdr. in chief of armed forces 1968–79; named field marshal 1969; minister of defense 1973–77; resigned 1979. • Gen. secty., regional leadership since 1968, and deputy secty. gen., natl. leadership since 1977, Ba'ath Party.

Further reading Hanna Batutu, *The Old Social Classes and the Revolutionary Movements of Iraq,* 1978.

GLENN (HERBERT) GOULD
Pianist
Born **Toronto, Ontario, Canada, 25 September 1932**
Died **Toronto, Ontario, Canada, 4 October 1982**

The world of modern piano performance boasts several great virtuosi, some of whom are also celebrated eccentrics, but none like Glenn Gould. He was, unique among contemporary pianists, the possessor of an analytic intelligence that understood music as architectonic structure, of which he sought to produce the perfect articulation, changing tempi and drawing out voices with a cool disregard of the composer's instructions. Because of his disrespect for orthodox musical tradition, and also because he was a recluse who shunned performing in public, he was often treated with ridicule and resentment by the music establishment. Yet his genius, especially in the interpretation of Bach, was admired throughout the world, and his recordings sold more than 1.25 million copies during his lifetime.

Gould lived most of his life in Toronto, where he was born in 1932, the son of a well-to-do furrier. He was gifted with absolute pitch and at the age of three began to take piano lessons from his mother, a singer who was a distant cousin of the composer Edvard Grieg. At ten he entered the Royal Conservatory of Music, from which he earned the associate diploma two years later; in 1945 he made his performing debut on the organ and the following year became the youngest graduate in the history of the school. He made his formal piano debut with the Toronto Symphony Orchestra in 1947 playing the Beethoven Fourth Concerto, which he had learned from a recording by Artur Schnabel, one of his idols (another was the harpsichordist Roslyn Tureck). During his high-school years he made only a handful of appearances and radio broadcasts; he refused to enter piano competitions—the usual route to a career—on the grounds that they distract students from attending to the real problems of musicianship.

From 1952 to 1955, Gould shut himself up in his parents' cottage on Lake Simcoe, where he had the solitude "to rethink the way in which the piano ought to be played." The task of the pianist is to create, by conveying pressure from his or her muscles and bones to the mechanism of the instrument, a series of vibrations arranged in relation to one another according to a set of organizing principles determined by the composer. The exact amount of force exerted by the fingers, and the exact response of the keys, hammers, and strings—what he called "tactilia"—were therefore matters of vast concern to Gould, whose overriding passion was the achievement of the finest possible degree of control over the physical circumstances of making music. In his view, the standard posture of most modern pianists—tall and upright, with most of the force coming from the upper arms—is perhaps appropriate for the tidal waves of sound demanded by the Romantic composers of the late nineteenth century (by whom Gould was unimpressed), but not for the crystalline counterpoint of Bach or the gem-like delicacies of Mozart. Nor are modern pianos, with heavy actions and overused sustaining pedals, sufficiently responsive; Gould rebuilt his pianos to give a secco, harpsichord-like action.

Gould's U.S. debut took place in Washington, D.C., in January 1955, with an unusual program that combined the G Major Partita and five Three-Part Inventions by Bach with Beethoven's Sonata in E Major, Webern's *Variations,* the Berg Sonata, and works by the Renaissance composers Gibbons and Sweelinck. The day after he played his first New York recital he was signed to a recording contract by Columbia Masterworks (now CBS Masterworks). His first recording, made in June 1955, was of Bach's *Goldberg Variations,* an exuberant interpretation that became an instant classic.

Courtesy of Don Hunstein

For the next nine years Gould toured the United States, Europe, and Israel as a recitalist and soloist with major orchestras. He was the first North American pianist to play in the Soviet Union (1957), where he startled the audiences by playing the forbidden music of Schoenberg. His reputation for virtuosity was soon rivaled by his reputation for eccentricity, for Gould had no interest at all in observing the codes of behavior and dress favored by the classical-music establishment. A hypochondriac with a dread of drafty halls, he played, even in summer, in an overcoat, galoshes, and cut-off gloves, with a rug under the piano and a supply of warm spring water handy. He refused to sit on anything but his own 14-inch custom-made stool, which had separately adjustable legs, and on which he sat crosslegged and hunched over with his face nearly level with the keyboard. In his complete absorption with the music he often hummed aloud and beat time with a free hand.

It was not these idiosyncracies that most bothered his critics, however, but the liberties he took with tempo, direction of chords, and other details of composition considered nearly sacred by most musicians. The result of this slavish obedience to convention, Gould insisted, was a general uniformity of style that makes contemporary musicians sound like so many clones of one another. His changes were made for the most cogent musical reasons, but were still considered scandalous. At a famous performance of the Brahms D Minor Concerto with the New York Philharmonic, the conductor, Leonard Bernstein, with whom Gould often collaborated, made an announcement politely dissociating himself from his soloist's interpretation.

In 1964, after nine years of playing concerts and recitals, Gould retired from public performance. This was in accordance with a life plan he had formed years earlier, which called for him to perform until he was 30 and spend the next 20 years learning his chosen repertoire and composing. Playing before spectators was an exhibition that made him feel, he told an interviewer, "like a vaudevillian." He was much more at home in the recording studio, where he was able to concentrate on producing a perfect realization of a piece of music with the aid of splicing, remixing, and other electronic advantages shunned by purists. Of every hour he spent in the studio, he estimated that only eight minutes were spent in actual playing; the rest was all production work. In all, he made nearly 80 recordings for CBS, including most of the Bach keyboard repertoire and works by Mozart, Beethoven, Byrd, Schoenberg, Hindemith, Krenek, and Sibelius. "When he plays a Bach fugue," wrote critic Edward Rothstein of the *New York Times,* "every voice is articulated as if by a different hand, with scrupulous clarity and refined attention to detail. . . . Repeated playings of a recording reveal a condensation of thought in the most minute elements of sound, a sensation of compressed meaning rarely accessible in a concert hall. . . . Paradoxically, this intense spareness finally speaks to the listening body. It can be difficult to sit still for this playing. Its compression and tensile strength make much of it seem like an ecstatic dance."

Once he left the stage, Gould withdrew into a hermitlike existence in his Toronto apartment, where he lived on a single meal a day and an assortment of vitamin pills. As had always been his custom, he rarely practiced more than an hour a day, since most of his work consisted of listening and thinking. He wrote articles and reviews for *High Fidelity* and other magazines and produced a series of documentaries for the Canadian Broadasting Corporation in which he blended speaking voices and musical excerpts contrapuntally. One of these, *The Idea of North,* was an exploration of that "heroic solitude" he considered necessary for creative effort—a physical and spiritual landscape free of distractions and encumbrances, bleak but limitless. He continued to work at composing and transcribed a number of orchestral works for piano and for chamber orchestra, notably Wagner's *Siegfried Idyll.* He also devised the soundtracks for a number of films, including *Slaughterhouse Five* (1974) and the forthcoming *Wars.* By 1982 he was ready to try conducting, and after some successful experiments formed a chamber orchestra, a move that excited his admirers, since his conducting was expected to be as enlightening as his playing.

Although he rarely recorded the same piece twice, he broke his custom in April 1982 when he made a second version of the *Goldberg Variations,* more introspective and yet more ecstatic than the first. The disc was released in time for the celebration on 25 September of Gould's fiftieth birthday. On the 27th he suffered a massive stroke; he sank into a coma and died a week later without regaining consciousness. He left no students or disciples who could continue his remarkable union of imagination, intellect, and technique.

J.P.

Parents Russell Herbert G., furrier, and Florence (Grieg) G. **Education** Williamson Road Public Sch., Toronto; studied piano with mother to age ten; Royal Conservatory of Music, Toronto, associate diploma with highest honors 1946, continued private lessons with Alberto Guerraro to 1952; Malvern Collegiate Inst., Toronto 1945–51. **Career** Pianist and composer from childhood; debut as organist, Toronto 1945; debut as pianist, Toronto 1946; radio performer from 1950, recording artist from 1955; U.S. debut 1955; U.S. tours annually 1956–59; toured USSR and Germany 1957, Israel 1958; recitalist and soloist with major orchs., including Berlin, New York, Pittsburgh, Vancouver, San Francisco, and Toronto; co-dir., Stratford Music Festival, Ontario 1961; final concert tour and lectr. at Univ. of Cincinnati 1962; retired from performing 1964 to record, compose, write, and broadcast; founder and conductor of chamber orch. 1982. **Member** Toronto Musicians Assn.; Composers, Authors, Publishers Assn. of Canada. **Honors** Bach Medal, Cohen Music Awards, London 1959; Molson Prize, Canada Council 1968; hon. degree from Univ. of Toronto. **Radio documentaries** "Arnold Schoenberg: The Man Who Changed Music," 1962; "Dialogues on the Prospects of Recordings," 1965; "The Art of Glenn Gould," 1966–67; "The Idea of North," 1971; "The Latecomers," 1971; "Glenn Gould on the Moog Synthesizer," 1972; "Arnold Schoenberg: The First 100 Years," 1974; "The Quiet in the Land," 1975; others. **Television** "The Subject is Beethoven," 1961; "Glenn Gould and the Music of the USSR," 1962; "Glenn Gould on Bach," 1962; "Glenn Gould Features Richard Strauss," 1962; "The Art of Fugue," 1963; "Glenn Gould's Toronto"; others. **Films** *Glenn Gould Off the Record, On the Record,* 1960; *Conversations with Glenn Gould,* 1966; *Glenn Gould Plays Bach,* 3 films, 1980–81. **Soundtracks** *Spheres,* 1969; *Slaughterhouse Five,* 1972; *The Terminal Man,* 1974; *The Wars,* 1983. **Recordings** of works by Anhalt, Bach, Beethoven, Berg, Bizet, Brahms, Byrd, Gibbons, Gould, Grieg, Handel, Haydn, Hetu, Hindemith, Krenek, Morawetz, Mozart, Prokofiev, Schoenberg, Schumann, Scriabin, Shostakovitch, Sibelius, Richard Strauss, Tanayev, Wagner, others. **Compositions** *String Quartet No. 1,* 1956; *Cadenzas to Beethoven's Piano Concerto No. 1,* 1958; *So You Want to Write a Fugue?*, 1964; *A Letter from Stalingrad,* 1964. **Contributor** of articles to *High Fidelity, Saturday Review,* other periodicals. **Recorded interviews** Vincent Tovell, *At Home with Glenn Gould,* 1959; John McClure, *Glenn Gould: Concert Dropout,* 1968. **Printed interview** Jonathan Cott, *Forever Young,* 1977.

Further reading Geoffrey Payzant, *Glenn Gould, Music and Mind,* 1978; Samuel Lipman, "Glenn Gould's Dissent," in *Commentary,* Nov. 1979; Mark Czarnecki, "Glenn Gould, 1932–1982," in *Maclean's,* 18 Oct. 1982.

LEROY R(ANDLE) GRUMMAN

Founder of Grumman Aerospace Corporation

***Born* Huntington, New York, USA, 4 January 1895**

***Died* Manhasset, New York, USA, 4 October 1982**

The unprecedented demand for large numbers of military aircraft during World War II was the single greatest factor in the growth of the giant aerospace industry. Leroy R. Grumman, a former Navy test pilot and aeronautics engineer, captured lucrative military contracts for his rugged and dependable carrier-based fighters and built the Grumman Aircraft Engineering Corporation from an undercapitalized aircraft-repair firm with 16 employees to a manufacturing giant producing hundreds of planes a month for the war effort. Today Grumman Aerospace employs some 20,000 workers and is the ninth largest defense contractor in the United States and the single largest employer on Long Island.

Grumman, the son of a Long Island carriage-store owner, worked his way through Cornell University, earning a B.S. in mechanical engineering in 1916. After graduation, he worked briefly for the New York Telephone Company, then enlisted in the naval reserve as a machinist's mate when the U.S. entered World War I. He trained as a test pilot and aircraft engineer and was assigned to the Naval Air Factory in Philadelphia, where he met the aviation pioneers Grover and Albert Loening, who were then building two-seater biplanes for the Navy. They convinced Grumman to retire his commission in 1920 in order to test aircraft for them and manage their New York plant.

When the Loening company came under new management in 1929, Grumman, now general manager, decided to form his own aircraft-repair and design firm with two Loening engineers, Leon A. Swirbul and Bill Schwendler. In 1930 they set up shop in a 11,500-square-foot garage in Baldwin, Long Island, repairing amphibious private planes made by Loening. Grumman strove to acquire Navy contracts, and by the end of the year he had landed one for the design and construction of two prototype aluminum floats with retractable landing gear that could convert Navy biplanes to amphibious use. Grumman's design was so revolutionary that he and Swirbul had to make the first test flight themselves to convince skeptical Navy engineers. The same skeptics were sufficiently impressed by Grumman Aircraft's experimental XFF-1 fighter to order 60 between 1931 and 1933.

A polite, unpretentious, shy man who wasted few words, Grumman let the forceful, fast-talking Swirbul handle the company's day-to-day management while he devoted himself to aircraft design. Probably his best-known invention was the first safe method of folding back the wings of fighter planes. This permitted a 50 percent increase in the number of aircraft that could fit on the deck of a carrier. A believer in simplicity, Grumman worked out his folding wing using an ordinary eraser with a paper clip stuck in either side.

At the beginning of the war, the Navy was buying as many aircraft as Grumman's firm could produce. Grumman F4F-4s, Hellcats, Wildcats, and Avengers—all fast, maneuverable, heavily armed craft with fat, cigar-shaped fuselages (copied, as Grumman freely admitted, from the Messerschmidt design)—were sent by the thousands to combat Japan's Zeros and were credited with downing more than half of all enemy planes destroyed in the Pacific. The company, which Grumman had always envisioned as a small outfit, hired some 22,000 workers in the last year of the war and set an all-time American production record in March, rolling 664 planes off the assembly line. In all, Grumman Aircraft produced more than 17,500 Navy fighters and torpedo-bombers, with General Motors producing an additional 13,500 from Grumman designs. In 1945 Grumman was awarded the Presidental Medal for Merit for his company's exceptional war record. "The name Grumman on a plane or a part," said Rear Adm. John McCain in 1942, "has the same meaning to the Navy that sterling on silver has to you."

Courtesy of Grumman Aerospace Corp.

In 1946, Grumman, now 51, was blinded by a severe allergic reaction to a shot of penicillin administered during treatment for pneumonia. He relinquished the presidency of the company to Swirbul but stayed on as chairman of the board until 1966, when the company was building the Lunar Module that was flown to the moon by the Apollo astronauts, and as a director until 1972, when Grumman Aerospace was submitting plans for the wings of the space shuttle. In 1981 he successfully opposed a takeover bid by the LTV Corporation of Dallas. He died of complications from diabetes and heart ailments at the age of 87.

S.A.

Parents George Tyson G., carriage-store owner, and Grace Ethel (Conklin) G. **Married** Rose Marion Werther 1921: Marion Elinor Phillips; Florence Werther Hold; Grace Caroline Nelson; David Leroy. **Religion** Presbyterian. **Education** Huntington High Sch., NY, grad. 1911; Cornell Univ., Ithaca, NY, B.S. 1916. **Mil. service** With USNR: machinist's mate 2nd class 1917; studied gasoline engines, Columbia Univ. 1917; training in aeronautics engineering and flight, Massachusetts Institute of Technology and Naval Air Stations at Miami and Pensacola 1918; ensign and pilot 1918; lt. j.g., test pilot, and engineer, Naval Air Factory, Phila. ca. 1919–20. **Career** Engineer, New York Telephone Co., NYC 1916–17; test pilot and aeronautics engineer, then gen. mgr., Loening Aeronautical Engineering Corp., NYC 1920–29. • With Grumman Aircraft Engineering Corp. (now Grumman Aerospace Corp.), Bethpage, NY: founding pres. 1929–46; bd. chmn. 1946–66; dir. 1946–72; hon. chmn. since 1966. **Officer** Trustee emeritus, Cornell Univ. **Fellow** Inst. of Aeronautical Sciences. **Member** Soc. of Automotive Engineers. • Clubs: North Hampstead Country, Manhasset Bay Yacht, Locust Valley Creek, and Hicksville Aviation, NY; Riomar and Vero Beach Country, FL. **Honors** Presidential Medal for Merit 1945; Daniel Guggenheim Medal 1948; Hawks Memorial Award 1958; Hunsaker Medal, Natl. Acad. of Sciences 1968; named to Aviation Hall of Fame, Dayton, OH 1972; named to Long Island Hall of Fame; aeronautics engineering bldg. named for him, Cornell Univ.; hon. fellow, Inst. of Aeronautical Sciences; hon. degrees from Brooklyn Polytechnic Inst. and Adelphi Coll. **Inventions** Retractable landing gear for amphibious aircraft; folding-wing design for Navy fighters; many other aircraft designs.

Further reading Richard Thruelson, *The Grumman Story,* 1976.

HOWARD SACKLER
Playwright and director
***Born* New York City, USA, 19 December 1929**
***Died* Santa Eulalia del Rio, Ibiza, Spain, 4 October 1982**

Howard Sackler won the Pulitzer Prize for the best play of 1969, *The Great White Hope,* based on the tragic, ruined career of Jack Johnson, the first black heavyweight boxing champion. The play, Sackler's Broadway debut, also won the two other major dramatic honors of its season, the Tony and the New York Drama Critics Circle awards.

The son of a real-estate agent, Sackler was born in Manhattan and attended Brooklyn College, graduating in 1950. He began writing screenplays while still in college, and saw the first one, *Desert Padre* (1950), a documentary, made into a film by Stanley Kubrick, then just beginning his career. He wrote two other original screenplays for Kubrick, *Killer's Kiss* (1952) and *Fear and Desire* (1953). He received grants from the Rockefeller and Littauer foundations in 1953–54.

Sackler's first stage venture, *Uriel Acosta* (1954), gained him the Maxwell Anderson Award; his second, *The Yellow Loves* (1959), won the Sergei Award. He had several one-act plays produced in various regional theaters around the United States during the 1960s, including *Mr. Welk and Jersey Jim, The Nine O'Clock Mail, A Few Enquiries,* and *Skippy. The Pastime of Monsieur Robert* (1966), concerning a French aristocrat under the Reign of Terror, was seen in London and San Francisco.

The Great White Hope was first produced in 1967 at the Arena Stage in Washington, D.C., directed by Edward Sherin. Sackler paid for the major part of the Broadway production himself out of the proceeds from his sale of the film rights, and received 75 percent of the net earnings from an extended run. Written in passionate, tumbling blank verse, the play sympathetically follows its prizefighter-hero from his early triumph in 1908, when he first won the heavyweight title, through his subsequent humiliation and victimization at the hands of his racist enemies, who were furious and unforgiving that a black man should expose the sham of white supremacy, to his tragic disillusionment and ignominious loss of the title to a white man in 1915. Although the principal stars, James Earl Jones as the boxer and Jane Alexander as his mistress, received rave reviews, the play itself was not to the taste of all critics, some of whom found it superficial and histrionic, drawbacks that its four-hour length and 25 highly stylized scenes did little to correct. The film, which appeared in 1970 with the same stars, had a script only lightly revised by Sackler from its theater version. It was not a success.

Of his subsequent plays, only one reached Broadway. *Goodbye Fidel* (1980), directed by Sherin and starring Jane Alexander, the director's wife, concerned the plight of upper-class exiles from Castro's Cuba. Considered prosaic and dull, it closed after a very few performances. A more promising vehicle, *Semmelweiss* (1977), a treatment of the pioneering nineteenth-century Hungarian physician Ignaz Philipp Semmelweiss, received a successful performance at the Studio Arena in Buffalo, New York, and a controversial one the following year at Washington's Kennedy Center. A widely publicized fight over rewriting and recasting between Sackler and Sherin on one side and the producers, Roger L. Stevens and Robert Whitehead, on the other resulted in the abandonment of plans to take the play to Broadway.

Sackler's directorial career started early. From 1953 to 1968 he was a production director of Caedmon Records, New York and London, and was responsible for some 200 recorded productions of world drama, many including the best British acting talent. He was director of a 1964 NBC television special, "Shakespeare, Soul of an Age," starring Michael Redgrave, and in the mid-1960s took an acclaimed production of Samuel Beckett's *Krapp's Last Tape* on a European tour. His poetry, published in little magazines, appeared in collected form as *Want My Shepherd* (1954).

His other screenplays were for *Bugsy* (1973), *Jaws II* (1978), *Gray Lady Down* (1978), and, with Paul Theroux, for Peter Bogdanovich's *Saint Jack* (1979). At the time of his death he was working on a play, *Klondike,* about the Alaska-Yukon gold rush. He was found dead in his studio in Ibiza, where he had made his home for several years. A.K.

Parents Martin S., real-estate agent, and Ida (Rapaport) S. **Married** Greta Lynn Lungren 1963: Molly; Daniel. **Education** Brooklyn Coll., NYC, B.A. 1950. **Career** Playwright, screenwriter, and stage dir. since 1950s; production dir., Caedmon Records, NYC 1953–68. **Honors** Rockefeller Grant 1953; Littauer Foundn. Grant 1954; Maxwell Anderson Award, for *Uriel Acosta,* 1954; Sergei Award, for *The Yellow Loves,* 1959; Pulitzer Prize, New York Drama Critics Circle Award, and Tony Award, for *The Great White Hope,* 1969. **Plays** *Uriel Acosta,* 1954; *Mr. Welk and Jersey Jim,* 1960; *The Yellow Loves,* 1960; *A Few Enquiries,* 1965; *The Nine O'Clock Mail,* 1965; *The Pastime of Monsieur Robert,* 1966; *The Great White Hope,* 1968; *A Few Enquiries* (collection), 1970; *Semmelweiss,* 1977; *Goodbye Fidel,* 1980. **Screenplays** *Desert Padre* (documentary), 1950; *Fear and Desire,* 1955; (dir. and adaptor) *A Midsummer Night's Dream,* 1961; *The Nine O'Clock Mail* (TV play), 1965; *The Great White Hope,* 1970; *Bugsy,* 1973; (jtly.) *Gray Lady Down,* 1978; (jtly.) *Jaws II,* 1978; *Saint Jack,* 1979. **Poetry** *Want My Shepherd,* 1954. **Stage director** (all NYC except as noted) *King John,* 1953; *The Family Reunion,* 1954; *Women of Trachis,* 1954; *Purgatory,* 1955; *The Words Upon the Windowpane,* 1955; *Hamlet,* Dublin 1957; *Krapp's Last Tape,* Ireland and European tour 1960; *Chin-Chin,* London 1960; *Susanna Andler,* Guildford 1971, 1972, London 1973; *The Duchess of Malfi,* L.A. 1976. **Television director** "Shakespeare: Soul of an Age," 1964. **Contributor** to *Poetry, Hudson Review, Commentary,* other mags. **Manuscript collection** in Univ. of Texas, Austin.

STEFANOS STEFANOPOULOS
Prime minister of Greece
***Born* Pyrgos, Ilía, Greece, 1899**
***Died* Athens, Greece, 4 October 1982**

The Greek politician Stefanos Stefanopoulos, a minister in several cabinets since the 1930s, served as prime minister of an interim government for 15 months just prior to the 1967 coup d'état that put Greece under martial law for seven years. Born into a prominent family from Ilía, in the northwestern Peloponnese, he studied law, politics, and economics at the University of Athens and the Sorbonne. In 1930, as a member of the conservative Populist Party, he was elected a parliamentary deputy for Ilía, a seat to which he was regularly returned. During the early 1930s he served as undersecretary and then minister for national economy. In 1936, the monarchy, abolished 12 years earlier, was restored by the Populist-controlled National Assembly; new elections resulted in a stalemate between republicans and royalists, and Gen. Ioannis Metaxas, with the support of King George II, took control of the country.

After parliamentary government was reinstated in late 1944, Stefanopoulos, who had been active in the anti-Nazi resistance movement, served as minister of communications (1944) and of economic coordination (1946–50). In 1950, together with 27 other deputies, he defected from the Populists to form the Popular Unitive Party, which was absorbed the following year into Field Marshal Alexandros Papagos's Greek Rally Party. Stefanopoulos served as foreign minister and then as deputy prime minister during Papagos's government (1952–55). After Papagos died, Stefanopoulos, passed over for the premiership in favor of Konstantinos Karamanlis, left the Greek Rally and founded the Communal Party, on whose ticket he lost the Ilía by-election of 1956. He was reelected in 1958, and three years later helped form the Center Union Party, which came to power under Georgios Papandreou in 1963 with Stefanopoulos as deputy prime minister (1963–64) and minister of economic coordination (1964–65).

In 1965, King Constanine II, charging that the government was being taken over by Communists, dismissed Papandreou and assembled a coalition cabinet consisting of members of the Central Union, with Stefanopoulos as the prime minister. His government, known as "the Government of Apostates," lasted barely 15 months amid increasing demonstrations of parliamentary impotence. Four months after its fall, a military junta under Col. Giorgios Papadopoulos staged a coup d'état.

Courtesy of Greek Press & Information Service

With the return of democracy in 1974 under his old rival Karamanlis, Stefanopoulos, now in his 70s, formed the rightist National Rally Party, which gained seven percent of the vote in the 1977 elections. Stefanopoulos, however, failed to win a seat, and the party later dissolved. In his last years he lived in retirement in Ilía. He died of heart and lung ailments at the age of 83. S.A.

Father Christos S., politician, and Fani S. **Religion** Greek Orthodox. **Education** Univ. of Athens; Sorbonne, LL.D. **Mil. service** With Greek Resistance, WWII. **Career** Prof., Industrial Coll. • Parliamentary deputy for Ilía 1930–56, 1958–77; Greek rep. to U.N., NATO Council of Ministers, Belgian Pact, other intl. orgs. and conferences; member, Populist Party 1930–50; co-founder, Populist Unitive Party 1950; member, Greek Rally Party 1951–55; co-founder, Populist Socialist Party (Communal Party) 1956; co-founder, Center Union Party 1961; founder, Natl. Rally Party 1975. • Undersecty. of state for natl. economy 1932–34; minister for natl. economy 1934–35; minister of communications 1944; minister of finance 1946; minister of labor and supplies 1946; minister of economic coordination 1946–50; foreign minister and deputy prime minister 1952–55; deputy prime minister 1963–64 and minister of economic coordination 1964–65; prime minister 1965–66. **Honors** Grand Cross, Order of Phoenix, Greece, and Order of Dannebrog, Denmark. **Author** [*Money and the Currency Crisis*], 1930; [*Social Security*], 1932; [*Economic and Social Studies*], 1935; [*Reconstruction in Greece*], 1936; [*Philosophy and Social Systems*], 1936; other books on Greek economics and politics.

WALTER TERRY
Dance critic
Born **New York City, USA, 14 May 1913**
Died **New York City, USA, 4 October 1982**

Walter Terry, dance reviewer for the *New York Herald Tribune* from 1939 to 1966 and for the *Saturday Review* from 1967 to 1981, deserves much of the credit for the American public's acceptance of dance as an art form and for the development of a critical vocabulary with which to explain and describe it. When he began his career, in the mid-1930s, the great dance pioneers had only very small audiences for their work. The present fascination with dance grew up over the past quarter-century, during which time Terry proselytized constantly in print, in speaking tours, and on radio and television.

Born in Brooklyn, Terry grew up in Connecticut and was educated at the University of North Carolina, a center of dance study, where he was a member of the student company. After his graduation he took lessons in ballet, modern, ethnic, and popular dance. The choreographer and dancer Ted Shawn was just then leaving a job as a dance reviewer for the *Boston Herald*; Terry replaced him, at the same time turning down an invitation to join Shawn's troupe as a performer, and three years later moved to the *Herald Tribune* at a salary of $11.67 a week, reviewing, he said, "anything that moved." During his wartime service in the army, from 1942 to 1945, he was stationed in Cairo, where he taught dance at the American University.

Courtesy of Martha Swope

The postwar years brought great gains for American dance, which came to be widely appreciated through the mass-culture forms of film, television, and the Broadway show. Terry's instructive criticism came to be relied on not only by dance enthusiasts but by choreographers and performers as well. He recognized quality and was quick to assist it: he was the only prominent New York City newspaper critic to report on Rudolf Nureyev's debut in Brooklyn in 1962, and his descriptions of the Royal Danish Ballet helped win that company the popularity that has made it a source of star performers for prominent New York dance theaters. In addition to his writing, he undertook numerous lecture tours (including tours abroad for the State Department), organized dance festivals, supported regional American ballet, and presided over the dance world in general with avuncular benevolence. Despite his interest in dance of all kinds, he did not like undisciplined experimentation or overproduced spectacles. "If all you're selling is physical virtuosity," he told *Ballet News* in 1980, "the ladies who hang by their teeth at the circus have a better act. . . . I want works that disturb the mind, because virtuosity for its own sake leads to boredom."

Terry was the author of 22 books, including biographies of Isadora Duncan, Ruth St. Denis, Ted Shawn, and August Bournonville, the founder of the Danish style of ballet. His last book, on Richard Cragun, was published in Germany a few weeks after his death of cancer at the age of 69. L.F.

Parents Walter Matthews T. and Frances Lindsay (Gray) T. **Education** Private and public schs., New Canaan, CT; Univ. of North Carolina, Chapel Hill, A.B. 1935; private dance lessons. **Mil. service** Master sgt., U.S. Army, Africa and Mideast 1942–45. **Career** Dance critic, *Boston Herald* 1936–39; dance critic and ed., *New York Herald Tribune* 1939–42 and 1945–66, *World Journal Tribune* 1966–67, and *Saturday Review* 1967–82; dance critic, *Dance Magazine* 1982. • Lectr.: Adelphi Univ. 1942, Southern Connecticut State Coll. 1974–75, Yale Univ. 1975, Connecticut Coll., other colls. and univs.; U.S. Information Agency tour of eastern Europe and U.K. 1976; many other speaking tours. • Consultant: Cultural Exchange Program, U.S. State Dept.; Fulbright Fellowships; New York State Council on Arts; Connecticut Commn. on Arts; Maine Council on Arts; Rockefeller, Guggenheim, and Ford Foundns.; TV shows. • Scriptwriter, Voice of America; numerous guest appearances on radio and TV; host, "Invitation to Dance" radio show 1940. • Artistic dir., Jacob's Pillow Dance Festival 1973; organizer of numerous dance festivals and judge of numerous dance competitions; advisor-contributor, Dance Collection Library and Mus. of Performing Arts, New York Public Library. **Officer** V.P., U.S. chapter, Intl. Dance Council, UNESCO. **Member** Newspaper Guild, NYC; advisory commn., High Sch. of Performing Arts, NYC. **Honors** Kt., Order of Dannebrog, Denmark 1976; Capezio Dance Award 1980; fellowship, Amer. Univ., Cairo; hon. degree from Ricker Coll. **Author** (Contributor) *Dance: A Basic Educational Technique*, 1941; *Invitation to Dance*, 1942; *Star Performance: The Story of the World's Great Ballerinas*, 1945; (jtly.) *Ballet in Action*, 1954; *The Dance in America*, 1956, rev. ed. 1971; *Ballet: A New Guide to the Liveliest Art,* 1959; *On Pointe! The Story of Dancing and Dancers on Toe*, 1962; *Isadora Duncan: Her Life, Her Art, Her Legacy*, 1963; *The Ballet Companion,* 1968; *Ballet: A Pictorial History*, 1969; *Miss Ruth: The "More Living Life" of Ruth St. Denis*, 1969; *Careers for the Seventies: Dance*, 1971; (jtly.) *100 Years of Dance Posters*, 1975; *Ballet Guide*, 1975; *Frontiers of Dance: The Life of Martha Graham*, 1975; *Ted Shawn: Father of American Dance*, 1976; *I Was There*, 1978; *Great Male Dancers of the Ballet*, 1978; *The King's Ballet Master: A Biography of Denmark's August Bournonville*, 1979; *Alicia and Her Ballet Nacional de Cuba*, 1981; *How to Look at Dance*, 1982; *Richard Cragun*, 1982. **Contributor** to *Encyclopaedia Britannica, Compton's Encyclopedia, The Dance Encyclopedia, Enciclopedia dello Spettacolo, The Dancing Times, Ballet News, Dance Magazine, Horizon, Ballet Annual*, other reference books and periodicals.

FERNANDO LAMAS
Film and television actor and director
Born Buenos Aires, Argentina, 9 January 1915
Died Los Angelos, California, USA, 8 October 1982

The Argentine-born actor Fernando Lamas was one of the best-known of Hollywood's stereotyped "Latin lovers" of the 1950s. Tall, dark, suave, and athletic, he starred in dozens of forgettable films, usually in the kind of role that required him to have, he said, "a sword in one hand, a blonde in the other, and a horse outside." In the early 1960s he embarked on a successful career as a film and television director.

The son of an electrical engineer, Lamas was orphaned at the age of four and was raised by his aunt and paternal grandmother. He began acting in school productions when he was 12, studied law and drama in college, and became an expert swimmer, boxer, and fencer. In 1934 he made his professional stage debut with a Buenos Aires repertory company and also found work as a nightclub singer and entertainer. When he won the South American freestyle swimming championship in 1937 he was offered a regular dramatic role in a popular Argentine radio series. He broke into films in 1939, and with his fifth picture, *Lady Windermere's Fan* (1942), became a star in South America. In 1949, after 14 more Spanish-language films, he went to Hollywood to dub the Spanish version of an American film, was spotted by talent scouts for MGM, and was quickly signed to a contract. The next year he moved permanently to the United States.

Courtesy of Culver Pictures

MGM cast him in a string of routine westerns and period romances, including *The Law and the Lady* (1951), *The Girl Who Had Everything* (1953), *Sangaree* (1953), *Jivaro* (1954), and *The Girl Rush* (1955), always as the romantic Latin, a role for which he had no particular relish. "I was the technicolor boy," he recalled. "When I was brought to Hollywood, I was to fill the shoes of Valentino and John Gilbert. All I saw were horses, girls, and guitars." After a well-publicized affair with Lana Turner, he married in 1954 his third wife, Arlene Dahl, his co-star in *Sangaree* and *Diamond Queen* (1953). He divorced her in 1960 and a few years later married Esther Williams, MGM's swimming actress, whom he had outswum in *Dangerous When Wet* (1953).

By the end of the 1950s, Lamas turned to television directing. Starting with a few episodes of the "Run for Your Life" series, he developed a fast, competent style well suited to action series and later to prime-time soap operas such as "Falcon Crest" (in which his son Lorenzo appears) and "Flamingo Road." He also directed two little-seen theatrical features, *The Magic Fountain* (1961) and *The Wild Ones* (1967). He still appeared occasionally on screen; his last film was *The Cheap Detective* (1978).

In 1982 Lamas agreed to his first regular television acting role, in the series "Gavilan," playing yet another smooth Latin ladies' man. He had finished several episodes when he was hospitalized in September for back pains and was discovered to have inoperable cancer. He died two weeks later at the age of 67.

C.M.

Parents Emelio L., electrical engineer, and Maria L. **Married** (1) Pearla Mux, actress (div.). (2) Lidia Babachi 1946 (div. 1952): Alexandra, b. 1947. (3) Arlene Dahl, actress, 1954 (div. 1960): Lorenzo. (4) Esther Williams, actress and swimmer, 1967. • One other daughter, Christina. **Emigrated** to U.S. 1950; naturalized 1955. **Education** Studied law and acting, schs. in Argentina, Spain, France, and Italy; Teatro Experimental, Buenos Aires. **Career** Amateur athlete 1930s, stage actor and nightclub performer 1934–50, radio actor 1937–50, and film actor 1939–50, Argentina; film actor since 1951 and TV actor since mid-1950s, U.S.; also film and TV dir. and writer; formed his own production co. mid-1950s. **Member** Acad. of Motion Picture Arts and Sciences; Directors Guild; AFTRA; SAG; AEA. **Honors** Intercollegiate boxing champion, Argentina; freestyle swimming champion, South America 1937; International Film Award, for *A Place Called Glory*, 1967. **Films** *En el ultimo piso*, 1942; *Frontere sur*, 1942; *Lady Windermere's Fan*, 1942; *Evasion*, 1947; *Navidad de los pobres*, 1947; *El tango vuelve a Paris*, 1947; *La otra y yo*, 1948; *La rubia mireya,* 1948; *Historia de una mala mujer,* 1948; *Vidalita*, 1949; *De padre desconocido*, 1949; *La historia del tango*, 1949; *The Avengers*, 1950; *The Law and the Lady*, 1951; *The Merry Widow*, 1952; *The Girl Who Had Everything*, 1953; *Dangerous When Wet*, 1953; *Sangaree*, 1953; *Diamond Queen*, 1953; *Rose Marie*, 1954; *Jivaro*, 1954; *The Girl Rush,* 1955; *The Lost World*, 1960; (also dir.) *La fuente magica* (rel. as *The Magic Fountain),* 1961; *Duel of Fire*, 1962; *Revenge of the Musketeers*, 1963; *Die Hölle von Manitoba* (rel. as *A Place Called Glory*), 1966; (also dir.) *The Wild Ones*, 1967; *Valley of Mystery*, 1967; *Kill a Dragon*, 1967; *The Savarona Syndrome*, 1969; *Backtrack*, 1969; *100 Rifles*, 1969; *Powder Keg*, 1971; *The Cheap Detective,* 1978; many other films in Argentina and the U.S. **Stage** *Happy Hunting*, NYC 1956; other productions in Argentina and the U.S. **Television actor** Episodes of "Burke's Law," "Run for Your Life," "Hondo," "The Mod Squad," "McCloud," "It Takes a Thief," "Gavilan," many other series. **Television director** Episodes of "Run for Your Life," "The Bold Ones," "S.W.A.T.," "Mannix," "The Rookies," "Starsky and Hutch," "Falcon Crest," "Flamingo Road," "House Calls," "Code Red," "Maverick," many other series.

BARON NOEL-BAKER OF DERBY
Philip John Noel-Baker
Labour cabinet minister and winner of Nobel Peace Prize
Born London, England, 1 November 1889
Died London, England, 8 October 1982

Philip Noel-Baker, in his youth an accomplished scholar and athlete, served his country and the Labour Party with distinction as a longtime M.P. and cabinet minister, but is best known internationally as a tireless worker for world peace through disarmament. His career was crowned by the award of the Nobel Peace Prize in 1959.

He was the son of Joseph Allen Baker, a Liberal M.P. who had come from Canada to establish an engineering business in Willesden, London, becoming a member of the London County Council and also, as a prominent Quaker, an influential voice in the World Alliance of Churches. His six children were educated in a sober Quaker manner, made acutely aware from their earliest years of their social responsibilities. Philip attended the Bootham School, York, then Haverford College, a Quaker institution in Pennsylvania, and finally King's College, Cambridge, where he gained a first in economics and the University Whewell Scholarship in International Relations and was the first to combine the presidencies of the University Athletic Club and the Cambridge Union. He was exceptionally gifted in athletics, and qualified as a runner on the British Olympic team that competed at Stockholm in 1912, his last year at Cambridge. He was later captain of the British running team at the Olympic Games at Antwerp in 1920, where he won the silver medal in the 1,500 meters, and at Paris in 1924. He was commandant of the entire British team at Helsinki in 1952.

Upon leaving university, Baker became vice principal of Ruskin College, Oxford, an institution whose primary purpose was educating workmen and artisans. The following year King's College, Cambridge, elected him to a fellowship. He could not, because of his Quaker beliefs, enlist in the army when World War I broke out, but he organized the first Friends' Ambulance Unit, which he took first to France and Belgium, then to Italy, always performing with exemplary bravery. Italy awarded him the Silver Medal for Military Victory and the Croce di Guerra.

Even before the end of the war, Noel-Baker (he had adopted the name Noel in 1915 on his marriage to Irene Noel, a cousin of Lord Byron) had been thinking seriously about disarmament and an international organization to protect the peace. In 1919 he was part of the League of Nations section of the British delegation to the Paris Peace Conference and was a member of the League's secretariat until 1922. As principal assistant to Sir Eric Drummond, first secretary general of the League, he was one of the framers of the Geneva Protocol and the author of a book on that subject (1925), as well as of *Disarmament* and *The League of Nations at Work* (both 1926). In 1924, the year he first stood, unsuccessfully, for Parliament, he was appointed to the Sir Ernest Cassel Chair of International Relations at London University.

His career in Parliament began with his election as Labour member for Coventry in 1929. For two years he served as Parliamentary private secretary to the foreign minister, Arthur Henderson, but then was defeated in the general election of 1931. He won reelection from Derby in 1936 and held that seat, the name of which was changed to Derby South in 1950, until his retirement in 1970. He was joint parliamentary secretary to the Ministry of War Transport in Churchill's wartime coalition; after the Labour victory of 1945 he served as minister of state at the Foreign Office (1945–46), chairman of the Labour Party (1946–47), secretary of state for air (1946–47) and commonwealth relations (1947–50), and finally, in the last year of Attlee's government, head of the Ministry of Fuel and Power. He was a member of the Privy Council from 1945.

Noel-Baker never lost an opportunity to speak up for disarmament, although he always objected to being labeled a unilateralist. His book, *The Arms Race: A Programme for World Disarmament* (1958), a meticulous analysis of the possibilities for world peace, won the Albert Schweitzer Prize in 1960. His Nobel Peace Prize the year before was a great surprise to him; he donated the money to be used in the cause of world disarmament, principally through the United Nations Association. He spent his retirement in the service of this cause, and was an indefatigable letter writer to the *Times* and traveler to every international disarmament conference. In 1981, when he was 91, he wrote and recorded a pop song on the subject. He was created a life peer in 1977.

Noel-Baker received numerous foreign decorations as well as honorary degrees from British, Commonwealth, and U.S. universities. His only child, Francis Noel-Baker, was a Labour M.P. from 1945 to 1970. A.K.

Born Philip John Baker. **Parents** Joseph Allen B., politician and businessman, and Elizabeth B. (Moscrip) B. **Married** Irene Noel 1915 (d. 1956): Francis Edward, politician and writer, b. 1920. **Religion** Quaker. **Education** Bootham Sch., York; Haverford Coll., PA; King's Coll., Cambridge (Univ. Whewell Scholar in Intl. Relations), M.A. (2nd Class in Historical Tripos, Part 1, 1910, 1st Class in Economics Tripos, Part 2, 1912); Univ. of Munich; Sorbonne. **Mil. service** Co-organizer and 1st commandant, Friends' Ambulance Unit, France, Belgium, and Italy 1914–15; officer, 1st British Ambulance Unit, Italy 1915–18. **Career** Vice principal, Ruskin Coll., Oxford 1914; Cassel Prof. of Intl. Relations, Univ. of London 1924–29; Dodge Lectr., Yale Univ. 1934. • With League of Nations: League of Nations sect., British delegation to peace conference 1919; member, Secretariat, and principal asst. to secty. gen. 1919–22; member, British delegation, 10th Assembly 1929–30. • Principal asst. to pres., Disarmament Conference, Geneva 1932–33. • With U.N.: member, British delegation to Preparatory Commn. 1945; chmn., subcttee. for Gen. Assembly agenda 1945; member, British delegation to Gen. Assembly 1946–47; other posts in U.N. cttees. • Delegate, Colombo Conference on Economic Aid 1950. • Political and ministerial posts: Labour M.P. for Coventry 1929–31, for Derby 1936–50, and for Derby South 1950–

70; parliamentary private secty. to Secty. of State for Foreign Affairs 1929–31; member, advisory cttee., council on aliens 1940–42, and minister of state 1945–46, Foreign Office; jt. parliamentary secty., Ministry of War Transport 1942–45; secty. of state for air 1946–47; vice chmn. 1946, chmn. 1946–47, and chmn. of Foreign Affairs Group 1964–70, Labour Party; secty. of state for commonwealth relations 1947–50; minister of fuel and power 1950–51. • In Olympic Games: capt. of British running team 1920 and 1924; competitor 1928; commandant of British team 1952. **Officer** Pres.: Cambridge Univ. Athletic Club 1910–12; Cambridge Union 1912; Intl. Council on Sports and Physical Education since 1956; Intl. Council on Sports and Physical Recreation, UNESCO since 1960; British Vietnam Cttee.; Socialist Campaign for Multilateral Disarmament; other cttees. and orgs. **Fellow** King's Coll., Cambridge. **Member** Labour Party since ca. 1920s; U.N. Assn. **Honors** Mons Star ca. 1916; Silver Medal for Valor, Italy 1917; Croce di Guerra, Italy 1918; silver medal, Olympic Games, Antwerp 1920; Howland Prize, Yale Univ. 1934; P.C. since 1945; Nobel Peace Prize 1959; Schweitzer Book Prize, for *The Arms Race*, 1960; hon. fellow, King's Coll. since 1961; Olympia Diploma of Merit 1975; officer, Légion d'Honneur 1976; papal kt., Order of St. Sylvester 1977; created Baron of the City of Derby, life peer, 1977; hon. degrees from univs. of Birmingham, Nottingham, Manchester, Colombo, Queen's (Ontario), Brandeis, Loughborough, and from Haverford Coll. **Author** *The Geneva Protocol for the Pacific Settlement of International Disputes*, 1925; *Disarmament*, 1926, rev. ed. 1970; *The League of Nations at Work*, 1926; *Disarmament and the Coolidge Conference*, 1927; *The Juridical Status of the British Dominion in International Law*, 1929; *The Private Manufacture of Armaments*, vol. 1, 1936; *The Arms Race: A Programme for World Disarmament*, 1958; *The First World Disarmament Conference, 1932–1933, and Why it Failed*, 1979; (jtly.) *J. Allen Baker, M.P., a Memoir*; also pamphlets and articles. **Contributor** Storm Jameson, ed., *Challenge to Death*, 1934; *Poland's Martyrdom: The German Invasion in Photographs and Facts*, 1940; *Underground Poland Speaks*, 1941.

ANNA FREUD

Psychoanalyst and pioneer in child psychology
***Born* Vienna, Austria, 3 December 1895**
***Died* London, England, 9 October 1982**

A preeminent psychoanalyst and the author of seminal works in the field, Anna Freud devoted 60 years of her life to the scientific study of children's behavior and to the treatment of emotional disorders in the young. The acuity of her research into the effects of childhood experience on adult pathological behavior, together with her pioneering work in the field of ego psychology, was quickly recognized and highly valued, even by the most fractious members of her profession. In recent years, her demonstration of the importance of the "psychological" parent has had far-reaching effects within the field of family law.

Sigmund Freud, the founder of the science Anna practiced, was her father, her teacher, and her professional mentor. He was also, surprisingly and against his own best advice, her psychoanalyst. Anna Freud became a most articulate exponent of her father's radical theories, but she was never doctrinaire. She recognized that psychology is a human science and a young one, in which open-mindedness is as important as clinical thoroughness.

Anna, Martha and Sigmund Freud's sixth and last child, was born in Vienna in 1895. That same year, her 39-year-old father, together with the Viennese physiologist Josef Breuer, published *Studies in Hysteria*, an historic work that signified the beginning of psychoanalysis as a discipline in its own right. Although the book was poorly received in the medical world, Freud's practice as a neurologist began to improve, and his youngest child was raised in comfortable surroundings. But by the time she was attending the Cottage Lyceum, she, like all Jews in the city after the turn of the century, was becoming increasingly aware of anti-Semitism within the Viennese establishment.

Very few details of Anna's childhood are documented, and she always remained reticent on the subject. On one occasion she did confess that from an early age she had little or no interest in anything "unrealistic or supernatural." "As soon as animals began to talk, or fairies or witches, or ghosts to appear . . . my attention flagged and disappeared. To my own surprise, I have not altered much in this respect." A letter from her father, written when Anna was 17 and convalescing away from home, suggests that she was a restless and serious-minded adolescent: "Your plans for school can easily wait till you have learned to take your duties less seriously. . . . It can only do you good to be a little happy-go-lucky and enjoy having such lovely sun in the middle of winter." In the event, Anna's school plans did not materialize. Instead, she gained first-class experience for her future career by teaching in an elementary school, working as secretary of Helene Deutsch's new Vienna Psychoanalytic Institute, attending her father's lectures at the university, and helping him with his correspondence. By the time she was 27, she had delivered her first paper before the Vienna Psychoanalytic Society and had become a practicing analyst.

From the start, Anna Freud was an innovator. She was one of the first to use psychoanalytic techniques in the treatment of childhood neurosis. By patiently scrutinizing and interpreting the play, paintings, and dreams of neurotic children—research that had hitherto been virtually ignored—she began to understand the fears and obsessions of the young. Her papers, describing in detail how children's mental suffering could be alleviated, were eagerly read by other young researchers, notably Dorothy Burlingham, Marianne Kris, and Erik Erikson. Recognizing their need for training, Freud instituted her *Kinderseminar*, where it soon became apparent that she was as gifted a teacher as she was an analyst. At about the same time she established Vienna's first day nursery and an elementary school that catered to the particular educational needs of her young patients. The *Kinderseminar* group, a few of whose members taught in the school, recognized in Freud some of the character traits of her famous father. Although far less irascible than he, she possessed some of his driving spirit and ability to generate enthusiasm and loyalty in others. But the quality which most inspired her colleagues was her inexhaustible patience and attentiveness, both as a teacher and as an analyst.

In the 1920s and early 1930s, Anna Freud wrote a number of papers, many of which were delivered before the Vienna Psychoanalytic Society, which she served as chairman from 1925 to 1928. These papers were later revised and collected as Volume I (1974) of *The Writings of Anna Freud*. Her prose style, as well as the substance of her work, much impressed her colleagues: she managed to explain complex procedures and theories in crystal-clear, graceful language. Unfortunately, admiration for her work—and indeed for the work of other psychoanalysts—did not extend far beyond small scholarly groups and societies. Leading physicians and educators, and parents as well, expressed outrage at the psychologists' apparently consuming interest in sexual etiology. Another more insidious reason for hostility lay in the fact that most of the foremost analysts were Jewish. However, on a day-to-day basis, the pioneer child psychologists were more aware of an internal controversy: while Anna Freud was developing her theories and practice in Vienna, Melanie Klein was busy formulating a quite different approach in Berlin. Klein's thesis was that a child's behavior is rooted in the first year of its life and that it is necessary to confront the patient directly with his or her earliest, most

Courtesy of Austrian Consulate General

primitive fantasies and emotions. But Freud, a believer in her father's theory that emotions evolve sequentially through a number of distinct sexual phases, contended that the probing of a child's psychosis should be gentle and very gradual. She felt that a bond of trust between analyst and patient must be well established before pathological behavior can be properly identified and effectively treated. This central conflict between the two women, and other methodological differences between the "Kleinians" and the "Anna Freudians," continued for many years, with considerable animosity on both sides.

Anna Freud's *The Ego and the Mechanisms of Defence* was published in 1936 (English ed. 1937) and had an immediate and significant impact upon the profession. Earlier, psychoanalysts had largely concentrated on aspects of the patient's primitive biological urges (libido), and on his or her unconscious desires, obsessions, and pathological development—essentially "id analysis." By the time Anna Freud was established in her career, her father had published his conceptions about the tripartite division of the psyche. He defined the id as the source of unconscious, instinctual drive; the ego as a part of the id influenced by external sources, i.e., the conscious self; and the superego as the partly conscious internalization of parental and societal attitude, the source of conscience, moral belief, and guilt. His daughter's book systematically examined the particular ways in which the ego, interacting with the id and the superego, could rationalize and repress or suppress, and thereby act as a defensive agent against anxiety and fear. Her text ably demonstrated how the defense mechanisms a child employs vary according to the nature of the fear or danger. For example, a young girl with an "anal impulse"—an internal drive for uncleanliness and disorder—may "defend" herself by being spotlessly clean and meticulously well organized. Her ego effectively reverses a threatening emotion.

By going beyond the bounds of id analysis and explaining and advocating "ego psychology"—utilization of the appropriate defensive functions of the conscious self—Anna Freud made a landmark contribution to her field. In a January 1972 *New York Times* review of the revised edition of *The Ego and the Mechanisms of Defence* (it had appeared as Volume II of *The Writings of Anna Freud*), Robert Sussman Stewart wrote: "By holding our defensive functioning under the microscope, Anna Freud produced one of the most refined tools analysts had ever had; the 'analysis of the defenses' opened up a whole series of innovations in psychoanalytic technique. One could see now the structure of the total personality: the way in which our character traits are formed. How our ego chooses to defend itself gives us our mannerisms, our temperaments—our attitude toward life and to the people around us."

Anna Freud's book appeared two years after the assassination of Engelbert Dollfuss, the Austrian chancellor, by Nazi infiltrators. The political situation was deteriorating almost daily, but it was not until well after Austria was forcibly absorbed by the German Reich that Sigmund Freud finally agreed to leave Vienna. The family moved to London in June 1938 and he died there of cancer 15 months later. Anna Freud, together with her close friend and colleague Dorothy Burlingham, decided to open a war nursery in Hampstead for children whose lives had been disrupted, often tragically and violently, by the Nazi air raids. The Hampstead War Nursery served another function as well; it was the women's laboratory. They recorded their researches into the behavior of their uprooted children in *Young Children in War-Time* (1942) and *Infants Without Families* (1943), both of which became textbooks in Britain and the United States.

The old rivalries between Melanie Klein's followers—known as the "English Group" since Klein's move to London in 1925—and the "Anna Freudians" or "Continental Group" were renewed by Anna Freud's arrival in London. Both groups belonged to the British Psychoanalytic Society and up to the early 1950s it often appeared as if the society would split down the middle. However, by the time of Klein's death in 1960 the two camps had moved into rather different territories: the English School concentrated almost exclusively on serious psychotic disturbances in children, delving ever deeper into the unconscious, while Anna Freud and her colleagues began to observe children's defensive behavior more in terms of its potential to make them wholesome, fully functioning individuals rather than as a means of conquering severe psychosis. Freud always remained wary of attaching too much importance to the necessarily highly speculative interpretation of preverbal behavior.

After the Hampstead Nursery closed in 1945, Anna Freud and a number of her collaborators instituted teaching sessions in Hampstead. Out of this grew the Hampstead

Child-Therapy Course and Clinic, a center for psychoanalytic training, research, and treatment, which Freud directed from 1952 until the time of her death. At Hampstead, a new method of recording work was established through the maintenance of "development profiles" for each child. These profiles systematically and exhaustively identified and assessed the stages of emotional development or regression, and served as an important tool in diagnosing the precise etiology of pathological behavior. Her work at the Hampstead Clinic, which remains the largest and most comprehensive institute of its kind in the world, resulted in a number of publications, since collected as Volumes IV through VIII of *The Writings of Anna Freud.*

In the 1960s and 1970s Freud displayed increasing interest in the application of child psychology to the general welfare of the young. Her lectures at the Yale Law School and at the Yale Child-Study Center led to her collaboration with two Yale professors, Joseph Goldstein and Albert Solnit. Their books, *Beyond the Best Interests of the Child* and *Before the Best Interests of the Child* (both 1973), expressed Freud's firm belief in the importance of the "psychological" parent, who is not necessarily the biological one usually accorded legal preference in family court cases. The Yale professors also advocated separate legal counsel for children in court cases to protect both their physical and their psychological welfare. The books were translated into a number of languages and have had a major impact on family law. Many countries have since revised their divorce laws and have effected important changes in the areas of child custody, adoption, and foster care.

Throughout her career, Freud approached her work with an open mind, but she held some precepts from which she never deviated. Believing strongly in her father's tripartite system of the psyche, she eschewed the behaviorists' doctrine that psychology's concern should be with the objective evidence of behavior and not with research based, at least in part, on theoretical propositions. Although she took criticism well, and answered it succinctly, she was sometimes troubled by the way in which her ideas, expressed with such clarity, were repeatedly vulgarized. While there may have been a grain of truth in allegations from parents and teachers that certain psychologists preach almost total permissiveness in child-rearing and believe that virtually all children are in need of analysis, it was not a fair criticism to level against Anna Freud. She was certainly progressive but always recognized the need for a reasonable mixture of discipline and latitude in the home and at school. And far from encouraging parents to submit their children to analysis, she often advised against it, preferring to employ psychoanalytic treatment only in instances of specific pathological behavior.

Anna Freud's life as an analyst, teacher, researcher, writer, and administrator was a very busy one indeed, but she nevertheless found time to serve on several professional bodies, collaborate with scientists from around the world, deliver many lectures, and receive innumerable awards and honorary degrees. Since she was devoted to the study of the mind and its emotions, it is not surprising that many were interested to learn something of her own emotional life. On that subject Anna Freud was unforthcoming and did not once grant a personal interview. She never married, and died in her Hampstead home at the age of 86. R.T.

Parents Sigmund F., founder of psychoanalysis, and Martha (Bernays) F. **Religion** Jewish. **Emigrated** to U.K. 1938; naturalized. **Education** Cottage Lyceum, Vienna; private training in psychoanalysis from her father. **Career** Elementary-sch. teacher, Vienna; children's psychoanalyst, Vienna 1923–38 and London since 1938; founder, *Kinderseminar*, day nursery, and elementary sch., Vienna; founding dir., Residential War Nursery for Homeless Children, Hampstead, London 1940–45; co-founder 1947 and dir. since 1952, Hampstead Child-Therapy Course and Clinic; co-ed., *Psychoanalytic Study of the Child* since 1945; lectr. at Yale Law Sch., Yale Child-Study Center, many other instns. **Officer** Chmn. 1925–38 and member 1922–38, Vienna Psychoanalytic Soc.; secty., Vienna Psychoanalytic Inst.; v.p., Intl. Psychoanalytic Assn. since 1938. **Member** British Psychoanalytic Soc. and Inst. since 1938; London Inst. of Psychoanalysis since 1938. **Honors** Dolly Madison Award for outstanding service to children, Hillcrest Children's Center 1965; CBE 1967; Grand Decoration of Honor in Gold, Austria 1975; hon. degrees from univs. of Clark, Sheffield, Chicago, Yale, Columbia, Harvard, and Frankfurt, and from Jefferson Medical Coll. **Author** *Einführung in die Technik der Kinderanalyse*, 1927 (trans. as

Introduction to the Technique of Child Analysis, 1928); *Einführung in die Psychoanalyse für Pädagogen*, 1930 (trans. as *Introduction to Psycho-Analysis for Teachers*, 1931, in U.S. as *Psychoanalysis for Parents and Teachers of Young Children*, 1931); *Das Ich und die Abwehrmechanismen*, 1936 (trans. as *The Ego and the Mechanisms of Defence*, 1937); (jtly.) *Young Children in War-Time*, 1942; (jtly.) *War and Children*, 1943; (jtly.) *Infants Without Families*, 1943; *The Psycho-Analytical Treatment of Children*, 1946; (co-ed.) *The Standard Edition of the Complete Works of Sigmund Freud*, 24 vols., 1953–56; (jtly.) *The Enrichment of Childhood*, 1962; (jtly.) *Children in Hospitals*, 1966; *Normality and Pathology in Childhood*, 1966; *Indications for Child Analysis, and Other Papers, 1945–1956*, 1969; *Research at the Hampstead Child-Therapy Center, and Other Papers*, 1970; *Problems of Psychoanalytic Technique and Therapy*, 1973; (jtly.) *Beyond the Best Interests of the Child*, 1973; *Before the Best Interests of the Child*, 1973; (jtly.) *Psychoanalytic Assessment: The Diagnostic Profile,* 1977; *Psychoanalytic Psychology of Normal Development, 1970–1980*, 1981; *The Writings of Anna Freud*, 8 vols., 1966–81. **Recording** *On Aggression*, 1974. **Contributor** to *Intl. Jrnl. of Psychoanalysis*. **Interview** Joseph Sandler, *The Technique of Child Psychoanalysis: Discussions with Anna Freud*, 1980.

Further reading J. G. Howells, ed., *Modern Perspectives in Child Psychiatry*, 1965; Franz Alexander et al., eds., *Psychoanalytic Pioneers*, 1966; Seymour L. Lustman, "The Scientific Leadership of Anna Freud" in *Journal of the American Psychoanalytic Association*, vol. 12, 1967; Paul Roazen, *Freud and His Followers*, 1975.

CLINTON T(RUMAN) DUFFY

Warden of San Quentin Prison

Born **San Quentin, California, USA, 24 August 1898**

Died **Walnut Creek, California, USA, 11 October 1982**

From 1940 until 1952, Clinton T. Duffy was the widely admired reforming warden of San Quentin State Prison in California, then the largest and most notorious penitentiary in the United States. Although he presided over the executions of 90 inmates, he was an articulate, lifelong opponent of capital punishment.

The son of a guard at the prison, Duffy grew up in Prison Town in the shadow of San Quentin, which is located on San Francisco Bay just north of the Golden Gate Bridge in Marin County. Aside from service in the Marine Corps during World War I and a few years working for the Northwestern Pacific Railroad, his entire career was spent in the California prison system, mostly at San Quentin itself. Duffy started as a clerk, became secretary to the warden in 1929, prison historian in 1936, and the following year was appointed secretary to the California Adult Authority, the state parole board, and assistant secretary to the Board of Prison Directors.

Abominable conditions prevailed at San Quentin at that time. Inmates were routinely tortured for even minor infractions of discipline, were fed rotten food, and were often thrown naked into windowless dungeons. Public disgust at such revelations forced Gov. Culbert Olson to dismiss the prison's entire governing board and to demand the resignation of the warden, Court Smith. The governor then named Duffy as an interim replacement for Smith while he searched for a tougher, more experienced successor, but Duffy's reforming zeal produced immediate results, and he remained in the job 12 years.

His major accomplishments, all widely reported and discussed at the time, included eliminating the "holes," as the dungeons were called, and the "spots"—small circles on which prisoners were forced to stand for 12 hours at a stretch—as well as all forms of corporal punishment. He fired brutal guards and broke the power of the victimizing "bosses" among the inmates. He hired a dietician to improve the quality of the food, provided all prisoners with radio headsets, and established a prisoners' radio station and newspaper. He encouraged inmates to participate in athletics and adult education, let them sell whatever handiwork they made, and abolished mandatory head shaving and numbered uniforms. He believed that alcohol was behind the commission of most serious crimes, and started the country's first prison chapter of Alcoholics Anonymous. "I never knew a convict's number or his crime," he said after his retirement, "but I knew the men and I treated them like men." He was the first warden of San Quentin to be able to walk freely throughout the prison, unarmed and without a bodyguard.

In one of his three books, *88 Men and 2 Women* (1962), Duffy described in general terms arranging for and carrying out the executions of the 90 prisoners killed during his tenure as warden. He objected to capital punishment on both moral and practical grounds. "Killing is as wrong for all," he wrote, "as it is for the few. And it is as wrong for the state as it is for the individual. Who are the people of any state to say that a person, no matter how horrible his crime, deserves to die?" He described asking all prisoners on death row whether capital punishment had in any way deterred them. "All they ever thought of, they said, was jealousy or hatred or revenge." His other books were *The San Quentin Story* (with Dean Jennings, 1950) and *Sex and Crime* (with Al Hirshberg, 1965).

Duffy was required to resign as warden when Gov. Earl Warren appointed him to the board of the Adult Authority, now the Board of Prison Terms, from which he retired in 1962. His wife, Gladys, the daughter and granddaughter of San Quentin guards, published a colorful account of their life in *Warden's Wife* (with Blaise Whitehead, 1959).

A.K.

Father a San Quentin prison guard. **Married** Gladys Carpenter: John, physician. **Education** Grammar sch., San Quentin, CA; San Rafael High Sch., CA. **Mil. service** With U.S. Marine Corps, WWI. **Career** Clerk, Northwest Pacific Railroad, CA 1920s. • With California state correctional system: clerk 1920s, secty. to warden 1929–40, prison historian ca. 1936–40, and temporary warden, then warden 1940–52, San Quentin State Prison; asst. secty., Bd. of Prison Dirs. 1937–40; secty. 1937–40 and bd. member 1952–62, California Adult Authority. **Officer** Dir., Clinton Duffy Fellowship. **Author** (Jtly.) *The San Quentin Story*, 1950; *88 Men and 2 Women*, 1962; (jtly.) *Sex and Crime*, 1965.

Further reading Gladys Duffy and Blaise Whitehead, *Warden's Wife*, 1959.

EDITH H(INKLEY) QUIMBY
Radiological physicist
Born **Rockford, Illinois, USA, 10 July 1891**
Died **New York City, USA, 11 October 1982**

Although radiotherapy offered new hope for cancer patients when it was first introduced at the beginning of this century, it also posed new dangers, since radiation kills healthy cells along with diseased cells. Edith H. Quimby's work on dosage measurement, as well as her later investigation of radioactive isotopes, promoted the safe use of radiation in medical treatment and research.

Born Edith Smaw Hinkley, she was raised in Illinois and Idaho, and majored in physics and mathematics at Whitman College in Walla Walla, Washington, from which she graduated in 1912. After teaching high school in Oregon for two years, she went to the University of California at Berkeley on a teaching fellowship to study for her master's degree. In 1918, her husband, who was also a physicist, joined the faculty of Columbia University. The following year, Quimby joined the staff of New York's Memorial Hospital for Cancer and Allied Diseases, where Gioacchino Failla was developing one of the country's first radiological research laboratories.

Over the following decades, Quimby became one of Failla's chief collaborators. She measured the amount of radiation emitted by radium and x-rays and tested live patients and cadavers to determine how much radiation reaches the surface of the skin and how much

Courtesy of Columbia University

penetrates to different points within the body. The 50 articles she wrote between 1920 and 1940 provided the first practical guidance for physicians on dosage specifications for radiotherapy. In 1940 she became the first woman to receive the prestigious Janeway Medal of the American Radium Society, and in 1941 she was awarded the gold medal of the Radiological Society of North America.

After teaching at Cornell University Medical College from 1941 to 1942, Quimby followed Failla to Columbia University's College of Physicians and Surgeons, where she was appointed associate professor of radiology. While working part-time on the medical effects of radiation exposure for the Manhattan Project, the secret effort to develop the atomic bomb, she also began to do research on radioactive isotopes, investigating the effects of radioactive sodium, which had recently been produced in the university's cyclotron, on leukemia in mice. It soon became clear that the new radioisotopes would play an increasingly important role in medicine as therapeutic agents and as "tracer" elements in diagnosis and research. In addition to recommending safety measures for medical personnel and researchers using isotopes, Quimby established procedures for disposing of radioactive wastes, for handling the bodies of deceased patients who had been treated with radioisotopes, and for dealing with accidental spills. The results of her work appeared in two books in 1958 and 1960.

Quimby became a full professor at Columbia in 1954 and professor emeritus in 1961. She died at her Greenwich Village home at the age of 91. P.D.

Born Edith Smaw Hinkley. **Parents** Arthur Sealy H., farmer and architect, and Harriet (Hinkley) H. **Married** Shirley Leon Quimby, physicist, 1915. **Religion** Episcopalian. **Education** Grammar sch., Rockford, IL, grad. 1904; Boise High Sch., ID; Whitman Coll., Walla Walla, WA (tuition scholarship), B.S. 1912; Univ. of California (teaching fellowship), M.S. 1916; postgrad. study, Columbia Univ.; diplomate, Amer. Bd. of Radiology in Physics. **Mil. service** With Manhattan Project, NYC, WWII. **Career** High-sch. science teacher, Nyssa, OR 1912–14; science teacher, Antioch High Sch., CA 1916–18; asst., then assoc. physicist, Memorial Hosp. for Cancer and Allied Diseases, NYC 1919–42; asst. prof. of radiology, Cornell Medical Coll., Ithaca, NY 1941–42; assoc. prof. 1943–54, prof. of radiology 1954–61, and prof. emeritus 1961–78, Columbia Univ., NYC; radiology consultant, U.S. Veterans Admin.; examiner, Amer. Bd. of Radiology. **Officer** Pres., Amer. Radium Soc. 1954. **Fellow** Amer. Physical Soc. **Member** Natl. Council on Radiation Protection and Measurements since 1936; advisory commn. on medical uses of isotopes, AEC 1946–66; Radiation Research Soc.; Radiological Soc. of North America; Phi Beta Kappa; Sigma XI; Democratic Party; League of Women Voters. **Honors** Janeway Medal, Amer. Radium Soc. 1940; gold medal, Radiological Soc. of North America 1941; medal for achievement, Intl. Women's Exhib. 1947; Amer. Design Award, Lord and Taylor 1949; Jagadish Bose Memorial Gold Medal, Indian Radiological Soc. 1952; medal, Amer. Cancer Soc. 1957; gold medal, Interamerican Coll. of Radiology 1958; Judd Award, Memorial Hosp. for Cancer and Allied Diseases 1962; gold medal, Amer. Coll. of Radiology 1963; Scientific Achievement Award, AMA 1973; Distinguished Service Award, Radiological and Medical Physics Soc. 1976; Coolidge Award, Amer. Assn. of Physicists in Medicine 1977; medal for achievement, NYC; hon. degrees from Rutgers Univ. and Whitman Coll. •

Hon. member: Amer. Roentgen Ray Soc.; James Ewing Soc.; Soc. of Nuclear Medicine; Chilean Radiological Soc.; Peruvian Radiological Soc.; Brazilian Cancer Soc. **Author** (Jtly.) *Radioactive Isotopes in Clinical Practice,* 1938; (jtly.) *Physical Foundations of Radiology,* 1944; (jtly.) *Radioactive Isotopes in Medicine and Biology,* vol. 1, 1958; *Safe Handling of Radioactive Isotopes in Medical Practice,* 1960. **Contributor** of more than 75 papers on radiology and radiation protection to scientific jrnls.

MARIO DEL MONACO
Tenor
***Born* Florence, Italy, 27 July 1915**
***Died* Mestre, near Venice, Italy, 16 October 1982**

At the height of his career, Mario Del Monaco was acclaimed as one of the greatest dramatic tenors of his generation, notably in heroic Italian and French roles. He was not much of an actor, relying on stock gestures and stagy athletics, but the intensity and brilliance of his voice delighted audiences at La Scala and the Met.

Del Monaco's decision to become an opera singer was made before he reached the age of eight. He was encouraged by his mother, a trained singer, and his father, a government official and avid opera buff. He disliked formal lessons, however, and abandoned them after a few months, preferring to teach himself from recordings and by memorizing opera scores. He also studied painting and sculpture at the academy of art in his hometown of Pesaro, on the Adriatic coast. At the age of 13 he made his nonprofessional debut in a production of Massenet's cantata *Narcisse* at the Teatro Beniamino Gigli in nearby Mondolfo. He made one further attempt at formal voice training when he was 19, at Pesaro's Rossini Conservatory, but left after six months. A year later, at the invitation of conductor Tullio Serafin, he competed against 80 other students for a place in the studio attached to the Teatro dell'Opera in Rome and came in first, but by most accounts he never studied there.

Del Monaco made his professional debut in Pesaro in 1939 as Turiddu in Mascagni's *Cavalleria Rusticana.* During his six and a half years of service in the Italian army in World War II he did more singing than fighting. On New Year's Day of 1941 he sang the role of Lt. Pinkerton in Puccini's *Madama Butterfly* at the Teatro Puccini in Milan; it was his first oustanding success. After the war his career took off in spectacular fashion. At La Scala in Milan he mastered 33 leading tenor roles, mainly in the Italian repertory. He appeared also in Rome, Naples, Barcelona, Lisbon, Stockholm, and at London's Covent Garden, and early in 1946 he sang in Buenos Aires, Rio de Janeiro, and Mexico City. Back in Italy that summer his inspired singing as Radames in Verdi's *Aïda* created a sensation at Verona, and later that year he brought down the house in Trieste with his portrayal of the heroic poet Andrea Chénier in the Giordano opera of that name. By 1948 he was internationally famous.

Del Monaco made his U.S. debut in *Aïda* in September 1950, on the opening night of the season at the San Francisco Opera. Rudolf Bing, general manager of the New York Metropolitan Opera Company, was in the audience and asked him to make a guest appearance at the Met. His interpretation there of des Grieux in Puccini's *Manon Lescaut* was well received; the *New York Herald Tribune* noted that he was "the proud possessor of a fresh and powerful voice" and that he had "the added asset of an animated and by no means reticent personality, and not least of all, uncommonly good looks." The following year Del Monaco joined the Met's regular roster of singers, an association that was to last almost a decade. Those roles which demanded a powerful and brilliant top register brought him the greatest praise. *Time* magazine in 1954 described his Chénier thus: "He stood back, heaved an enormous breath, spread his arms and let fly with a stunning high B flat that he held until it began to sound as if a phonograph needle was stuck in a groove." He sang Radames with an impact, wrote Olin Downes in the *New York Times,* "that shattered the rafters and brought down the house." His most brilliant interpretation was the title role in Verdi's *Otello,* which he sang more than 250 times. His recording of the work was one of the most eagerly sought of all operatic albums.

Though his voice, especially the glorious top register, was generally praised by public and critics alike, some took exception to his *stilo declamato* and ridiculed his tendency to sing at an unrelenting *mezzo-forte.* The soprano Joan Sutherland judged him "far too noisy a tenor" and refused to sing with him. Even in his early days his middle and lower registers exhibited a certain tightness, causing his voice to sound forced. The critic Irving Kolodin went so far as to complain that his Otello was "screamed rather than sung, ranted rather than acted," and added that though Del Monaco had an impressive voice he showed "less evidence of brain than any tenor since Lauri-Volpi."

But this was a minority view. Del Monaco was acclaimed everywhere as one of the best Italian tenors since World War II. His stentorian tones continued to delight audiences until 1973. By then his powers were failing, leaving only enough of the former magic to remind his devotees, as Christopher Norton Welsh wrote in a review in *Opera,* "how much poorer our operatic life is without such gargantuan personalities." After his retirement he painted and taught singing. He was for many years a kidney-dialysis patient and died of a heart attack at the age of 67.

B.D.

Parents Father a govt. official; mother a singer. **Married** Rina Fedora Filippini, singer: Giancarlo, opera dir.; Claudio. **Education** Scuola d'Arte, Pesaro; Rossini Conservatory, Pesaro 1934; self-taught in singing. **Mil. service** Italian Army, WWII. **Career** Opera singer since 1941, U.K. debut 1946, U.S. debut 1950; principal tenor, Metropolitan Opera House, NYC 1951–59; sang at major opera houses in Europe, U.S., and South America; toured USSR 1960, Germany 1961–62; painter and singing teacher from 1973; many recordings. **Honors** Arena d'Oro 1955; Orfeo d'Oro 1957; Maschera d'Oro 1958; gold medal, City of Paris; Academic Order of Lenin, USSR. **Films** (Voice) *Young Caruso,* 1953; *Cavalleria Rusticana,* 1953; several others.

HANS (HUGO BRUNO) SELYE
Medical researcher, endocrinologist, and physician
Born **Vienna, Austria, 26 January 1907**
Died **Montreal, Quebec, Canada, 16 October 1982**

"In my life," wrote endocrinologist Hans Selye in his 1977 autobiography, "I shall have accomplished only one thing: a better understanding of stress." When he entered on his research career in the early 1930s, the word "stress" was not even in use as a medical term. Today, stress, defined by Selye as "the nonspecific response of the body to any demand made upon it," is understood to cause or contribute to heart disease, kidney disease, arthritis, and a host of other ailments. Selye was a tireless proselytizer for stress management, which he explained to the public in books and frequent lecture tours. His work, according to medical psychologist Frank Engel, "has permeated medical thinking and influenced medical research in every land, probably more rapidly and more intensely than any other theory of disease ever proposed."

Selye was the son of a surgeon with the Austro-Hungarian Imperial Army, and learned French and English from his governesses before entering the College of the Benedictine Fathers in his home town of Komárom in Hungary. When, at the end of World War I, Komárom was annexed by Czechoslovakia, Selye was arrested at a protest demonstration and brought before a military court. In 1925, despite an undistinguished academic record, he was accepted by the school of medicine at the German University of Prague, from which he earned his M.D. in 1929, graduating first in his class. He received his Ph.D. in organic chemistry two years later.

In 1931 Selye went to Johns Hopkins University in Baltimore on a Rockefeller Research Fellowship; the following year he transferred to McGill University in Montreal, where he became a lecturer in biochemistry and a member of the research group of James B. Collip, one of the discoverers of insulin, who was then investigating the little-understood field of sex hormones. Selye was assigned to inject extracts of cow ovaries into rats. Autopsies of the rats showed surprising results: their sex organs, against all expectation, had not been affected, but the adrenal glands atop the kidneys were swollen, the lymphatic system and the thymus gland had shrunk, and the rats had developed peptic ulcers. Further experiments showed that these same symptoms could be produced by a variety of toxic chemicals, by exposure to freezing cold, and by extreme muscle fatigue. In a 1936 paper in *Nature,* Selye proposed that the three symptoms constitute a "general adaptation syndrome" by which the body responds to any harmful agent.

The idea that an organism reacts in the same way to a variety of dangers flew in the face of orthodox medical opinion, which holds that the diagnosis of disease is possible only because specific symptoms are associated with each. Selye's concept of the stress syndrome

Courtesy of Blackstone-Shelburne NY

was compared disparagingly to homeopathic medicine, osteopathy, and chiropractic. Although Collip tried to discourage him from continuing his line of research, he received funding and encouragement from the 1923 Nobel laureate Sir Frederick Banting (another discoverer of insulin), and within five years was able to demonstrate that the stress syndrome is produced by the action on the adrenal glands of adrenocorticotropic hormone, or ACTH, which is secreted by the pituitary. When stimulated by ACTH, the adrenals produce another class of hormones, the corticoids, which bring about the characteristic reactions that Selye had noted. By the late 1940s, other researchers had synthesized one of the corticoids, cortisone, in enough quantity for experimental use. When Selye administered cortisone or ACTH to patients suffering from any of 30 unrelated diseases, all experienced marked relief from their symptoms. These findings, which seemed to point toward a unified theory of disease, caused great excitement in the medical world. Even the usually staid *Scientific American* responded with enthusiasm: "It is clear that the pages of history have turned a new chapter in man's long search for the mechanism of disease."

Selye, who from 1945 to 1976 was professor and director of the Institute of Experimental Medicine and Surgery at the University of Montreal, seemed to have found just such a unified theory. By subjecting rats to moderate levels of stress over long periods, he had identified three stages of the general adaptation syndrome. In the first, which he called the "alarm reaction," the adrenals and thymus swelled in the manner he had observed. In the second, the "stage of resistance," they returned to normal, and the rats seemed to bear up well under continuing stress; but eventually they spent their "adaptation energy," entered a final "stage of exhaustion," and died. Selye noted that the symptoms of the exhausted rats—ulcers, hypertension, cardiovascular disease—are identical to those of human beings under constant stress. "The apparent cause of illness," he wrote, "is often an infection, an intoxication, nervous exhaustion, or merely old age, but actually a breakdown of the hormonal adaptation mechanism seems to be the most common ultimate cause of death in man."

By 1950 the field of human stress research was launched in earnest. While scientists sought a more detailed picture of the effects of stress on the endocrine system, psychologists found Selye's ideas helpful in understanding how physical illness affects mental health. Selye was showered with dozens of awards and honors; he set forth his ideas in several popular books, including *Stress* (1950), dedicated "to those who are under the exhausting nervous strain of pursuing their ideal," and *The Stress of Life* (1956).

However, further research in the 1960s and 1970s indicated that Selye's work, although important, was incomplete. His three-stage model of stress reaction could not be verified experimentally. Nor could his theory explain why the same source of stress produced widely different reactions in different people. Hormone treatment with cortisone and ACTH was proven to cause undesirable side effects and did not turn out to be the all-curing panacea that Selye had expected. In the mid-1970s a major challenge to his theory was proposed by a group of researchers led by John W. Mason of the Walter Reed Army Hospital Institute of Research. They claimed that stress, far from being a nonspecific reaction, is often a specific neurohormonal reaction to adverse psychological stimuli. This called into question much previous stress research, in which psychological factors had been downplayed or ignored. The differences between Selye and Mason's group are still unresolved.

In 1976 Selye founded the International Institute of Stress at the University of Montreal; the international team of first-rate researchers that he assembled included Roger Guillemin and Andrew Schally, who shared the 1977 Nobel Prize in Medicine for discovering the brain hormones secreted by the hypothalamus. Even after the replacement of his cancerous hips by prostheses (one metal, one plastic), Selye kept up a 12-hour-a-day, seven-day-a-week schedule of research, lectures, writing, and exercise. In his later popular books he outlined his program of stress management in everyday life. He differentiated between bad stress and good stress (which he called "eustress"). "Stress is the spice of life," he said. "People could live past 100 by understanding and conquering stress. . . . Our aim shouldn't be to completely avoid stress, which at any rate would be impossible, but to learn how to recognize our typical response to stress and then to try to live in accordance with it."

Selye died of heart disease two months after he gave up working at his laboratory. He was 75. P.D.

Parents Hugo S., military surgeon, and Maria Felicitas (Langbank) S. **Married** (1) Frances Rebecca Love 1936 (div.): Catherine. (2) Gabrielle Grant 1949 (div.): Michel; Jean; Marie; André. (3) Louise Drevet 1978. **Religion** Roman Catholic. **Emigrated** to Canada 1932; naturalized. **Education** College of the Benedictine Fathers, Komárom. Czechoslovakia 1916–24; Univ. of Paris 1925–26; Univ. of Rome 1926–27; German Univ. of Prague, M.D. 1929, Ph.D. in organic chemistry 1931; diplomate, Royal Coll. of Physicians and Surgeons, Canada. **Career** Asst. in experimental pathology, German Univ. of Prague 1929–31; Rockefeller Research Fellow, biochemical hygiene dept., Johns Hopkins Univ., Baltimore 1931. • With McGill Univ., Montreal: Rockefeller Research Fellow 1932–33; lectr. in biochemistry 1933–34; asst. prof. of biochemistry 1934–37; asst. prof. of histology 1937–41; assoc. prof. of histology 1941–45. • With Univ. of Montreal: prof. and dir. 1945–76 and prof. emeritus since 1977, Inst. of Experimental Medicine and Surgery; founding pres. 1976 and ed. of jrnl. *Stress* since 1980, Intl. Inst. of Stress. • Expert consultant, Surgeon Gen., U.S. Army 1947–57. • Grieve Memorial Lectr., Canadian Assn. of Orthodontists 1972; Armstrong Lectr., Aerospace Medical Assn. 1972; Bell Memorial Lectr., Univ. of Michigan 1973; Rennebohm

Lectr., Univ. of Wisconsin, Madison 1973; other lectureships. • Editorial bd. member: *Revue Canadienne de Biologie; American Journal of Cardiology; American Journal of Proctology; Biochemical Clinics; Experimental Medicine and Surgery; M.D. Medical Newsmagazine; Medical Digest; World-wide Abstracts of General Medicine;* many other medical and scientific jrnls. in North and South America and Europe. **Officer** Pres., Montreal Physiological Soc. 1943–44; pres., Soc. de Biologie de Montreal 1951–52; (also fellow) North America chmn., endocrinology sect., Pan American Medical Assn. **Fellow** Royal Soc. of Canada; Amer. Assn. for Advancement of Science; New York Acad. of Sciences; Amer. Geriatrics Soc. **Member** Canadian Natl. Soc. for Medical Research; Canadian Soc. for Study of Allergy; Amer. Soc. for Study of Arteriosclerosis; Amer. Assn. for Cancer Research; Aerospace Medical Assn.; Canadian Medical Assn.; Ohio Hungarian Soc.; Canadian Physical Soc.; (charter member) Pharmacological Soc. of Canada; (also founder) science council, Amer. Heart Assn.; (also founder) Soc. for Endocrinology, U.K.; Assn. of Physicians from Slovakia; Canadian Authors Assn.; Phi Delta Epsilon; Alpha Omega Alpha; Club Richelieu, Montreal; other orgs. in North and South America, Europe, and Asia. **Honors** Casgrain and Charbonneau Prize, McGill Univ. 1946; Wilson Medal, Amer. Clinical and Climatological Assn. 1948; medal, Acad. Medico Fisica Fiorentina, Italy 1950; Heberden Research Medal 1950; hon. citizen of Verona 1955; award, Amer. Coll. of Angiology 1959; award, Western Soc. of Periodontology 1960; Miller Memorial Award 1960; Humanitarian Award, Canadian B'nai B'rith 1961; Vishnevski Medal, Soviet Acad. of Medical Sciences 1962; Henderson Gold Medal, Amer. Geriatrics Soc. 1964; Mendel Medal, Acad. Scientarium Bohemoslavejica 1965; medal, Swedish Medical Soc. 1965; Pirquet Gold Medal, Pirquet Soc. of Clinical Medicine 1966; medal, Faculty of Medicine, Univ. of Nancy 1966; Canada Centennial Medal 1967; Bernard Medal, Univ. of Montreal 1967; Washington Medal, Amer. Hungarian Studies Foundn. 1967; Norris Prize, Sir George Williams Univ. 1968; Markusovsky Medal, Szombathely, Hungary 1968; Savaria Medal, Szombathely City 1968; medal, Debrecen Univ., Hungary 1968; Centennial Medal, Faculty of Medicine, Univ. of Graz 1968; gold medal, Amerikai Magyar Szoveteg 1968; gold medal, Arpad Akad. 1968; C.C. 1969; Virchow Gold Medal 1970; medal, Medical Soc., WHO 1971; commemorative plate, Paul D. White Symposium, Amer. Coll. of Cardiology 1971; Starr Medal, Canadian Medical Assn. 1972; Prix de l'Oeuvre Scientifique, Assn. des Médecins de Langue Française 1974; distinguished service award, Amer. Soc. of Abdominal Surgeons 1974; Killam Prize 1974; Man of the Year, Assn. des Assureurs de Vie de Montreal 1974; Kittay Award 1976; Order of Flag, Hungary 1977; Queen's Silver Jubilee Medal, Canada 1977; life achievement award, Encyclopaedia Britannica 1977; Literary Award, for *The Stress of My Life,* Canadian Authors Assn. 1977; medal, Univ. of Calcutta 1979; Semmelweiss Medal, NYC; other hons. and awards. • Hon. pres.: Hungarian Medical Assn. of America; Austrian Soc. of Canada. • Hon. fellow: Hebrew Univ. of Jerusalem since 1977; Univ. of Haifa since 1978; Alpha Encyclopaedia, Montreal; Acad. of Pharmacological Sciences; Soc. Médicale Polonaise. • Hon. member: Intl. Coll. of Surgeons; Amer. Clinical and Climatological Assn.; Aesculapian Soc., Univ. of Ottawa; Pathological and Anatomical Soc., Essex Cty., NY; many other socs. in North and South America, Europe, and Asia. • Hon. degrees from univs. of McGill, Windsor, Assumption, Argentina Natl., Montevideo, San Carlos, Westphalia, Wilhelms, Cagliari, Karl-Franzens, Purkyne, Guelph, Laval, Haifa, Alberta, and from Hahnemann Medical Coll. and Hosp., Philadelphia Coll., and Catholic Univ. of Chile. **Author** *The Steroids,* 1943; (jtly.) *Encyclopaedia of Endocrinology,* sect. 1, 4 vols., 1943, sect. 4, 2 vols., 1946; *The Ovary,* 1944; *Textbook of Endocrinology,* 1947; (jtly.) *On the Experimental Morphology of the Adrenal Cortex,* 1950; *Stress,* 1950; (jtly.) *Annual Reports on Stress,* 1951–56; *The Story of the Adaptation Syndrome,* 1952; (jtly.) *Symbolic Shorthand System for Physiology and Medicine,* 1956; *The Stress of Life,* 1956, rev. ed. 1976; *The Chemical Prevention of Cardiac Necroses,* 1958; *The Pluricausal Cardiopathies,* 1961; *Calciphylaxis,* 1962; *From Dream to Discovery: On Being a Scien-*

tist, 1964; *The Mast Cells,* 1965; *Thrombohemorrhagic Phenomena,* 1966; *In Vivo: The Case for Supramolecular Biology,* 1967; *Anaphylactoid Edema,* 1968; *Experimental Cardiovascular Diseases,* 2 vols., 1970; *Hormones and Resistance,* 2 vols., 1971; *Stress Without Distress,* 1974; *Stress in Health and Disease,* 1976; *The Stress of My Life: A Scientist's Memoirs,* 1977; (co-ed.) *Cancer, Stress, and Death,* 1979; *Selye's Guide to Stress Research,* vol. 1, 1980. **Contributor** *Reflections on Biologic Research,* 1967; *Endocrinological Aspects of Disease Processes,* 1968; Alan Monet and Richard Lazarus, eds., *Stress and Coping,* 1982; also more than 1,700 papers to medical jrnls. **Interview** Lawrence Cherry, "On the Real Benefits of Eustress," in *Psychology Today,* Mar. 1978.

Further reading Waldemar Kaempffert, "Cortisone and ACTH: An Assay," in *New York Times Magazine,* 16 Dec. 1951; Robert J. Trotter, "Stress Confusion and Controversy," in *Science News,* 31 May 1975.

BARON ALAIN (JAMES GUSTAVE JULES) DE ROTHSCHILD

Banker and Jewish leader

***Born* Paris, France, 7 January 1910**

***Died* New York City, USA, 17 October 1982**

Alain de Rothschild was a senior member of the French branch of the Rothschild family, whose name has for two centuries been nearly synonymous with European banking. He was partner and officer of the Rothschild banking establishments and other interests in Paris, but was even better known as the principal leader and spokesman for an important and influential sector of France's Jewish community.

He was the son of Baron Robert de Rothschild, a banker, and was educated at the Lycée Louis-le-Grand and in the law faculty of the University of Paris, earning a law degree as well as a diploma from the École Libre des Sciences Politiques. He and his younger brother, Élie, were mobilized as officers in the French Army in 1939, and were among the thousands of troops guarding the Maginot Line. They were captured during the German offensive in the spring of 1940—Alain in an army hospital where he was recovering from a wound—and were interned until 1945 in prisoner-of-war camps, primarily at Lübeck, where both were transferred after attempting escapes from other camps. The fact that they were officers, as well as Rothschilds, allowed them to escape the murderous fate that befell other French Jews. Both were awarded the Croix de Guerre.

In 1946, Rothschild Frères, a private investment bank founded in 1817, was reestablished in Paris, with Alain and Élie each holding a quarter interest, and their elder cousin Guy a half share. In 1967 the organization was expanded and reconstituted as a commercial bank, Banque Rothschild, with Alain as vice president, and was one of the many similar establishments nationalized by the Socialist government in early 1982. The Rothschilds, forbidding their name to be used by the bank they were leaving, received nearly $100 million in compensation, much of which was channeled to a family enterprise in New York, New Court Securities, which changed its name in 1982 to Rothschild Inc. Other French-based family companies, unaffected by nationalization, in which the three senior Rothschilds held important interests included the Société d'Inventissement du Nord, the Compagnie du Nord, and the Société Française d'Inventissements Pétroliers.

Alain de Rothschild's leadership in French Jewish affairs fulfilled another part of the family tradition. He became a member of the Jewish Consistory of Paris in 1946 and its president in 1949. He took a leading role in the resettlement in France of nearly 200,000 Jews of North African origin during the 1950s and 1960s. In 1967 he was elected president of the Jewish Consistory of France, and from 1976 headed the Representative Council of French Jews, becoming the principal public spokesman for Jewish concerns. Though frequently criticized in this role by more militant Jews for excessive restraint and politeness in protesting the increasing pro-Arab policies of successive French governments, he generally performed ably as a unifier and conciliator, and his family's influence gave him comprehensive access to those at the highest levels of power. As anti-Semitic terrorism increased in Paris, he became ever more forthright in his denunciations of the "passivity" and "inexplicable impotence" of the police and the "indifference of our political leaders," particularly after the two most notorious attacks—at the synagogue in the Rue Copernic in October 1980 and at the Jewish restaurant in the Rue des Rosiers in August 1982.

The baron, who in his youth was a handsome and dashing yachtsman, explorer, and inveterate party-giver, gradually adopted the colorless, uncontroversial, and highly conservative manner characteristic of the higher reaches of the French establishment. From 1959 he was mayor of Chamant, in the Oise department, where he maintained a country house. He died of a massive heart attack while on a business trip to New York. A.K.

Parents Baron Robert de R., banker, and Nelly (Beer) de R. **Married** Mary Chauvin de Treuil 1938: Beatrice Rosenberg; Eric, businessman; Robert. **Religion** Jewish. **Education** Lycée Louis-le-Grand; Univ. of Paris, lic. en droit; École Libre des Sciences Politiques, diplôme. **Mil. service** Officer, French Army 1939–45; POW, Germany 1940–45. **Career** Partner, Rothschild Frères, Paris 1946–67; v.p., Banque Rothschild, Paris 1968–82; partner, New Court Securities (now Rothschild Inc.), NYC 1982. • Pres.: Soc. d'Investissement du Nord 1963–67; Soc. Française d'Investissements Pétroliers 1963–70; Compagnie du Nord 1968–70; Discount Bank of France. • Bd. member: Banque Lambert, Brussels since 1949; Five Arrows Fund N.V., Curaçao; Paris–Orleans Railroad; Rothschild-Expansion Co.; Second Continuation Ltd., London; Parfums Caron; Château Lafite Rothschild; other companies. • Mayor, Chamant, Oise, France since 1959. **Officer** Pres.: Assn. Consistoriale Israélite de Paris 1954–67; Central Consistory of French Jews since 1967; Rep. Council of Jewish Instns. of France since 1976. **Member** Automobile Club of France; Polo de Paris. **Honors** Officer, Légion d'Honneur, and Croix de Guerre, WWII.

Further reading Frederick Morton, *The Rothschilds,* 1962.

PIERRE (ISAAC ISIDORE) MENDÈS FRANCE

Premier of France

***Born* Paris, France, 11 January 1907**

***Died* Paris, France, 18 October 1982**

Although he was president of the council of ministers, or premier, for only 7 months and 17 days during 1954–55, Pierre Mendès France came to seem to many in France and abroad the epitome of the principled politician and the very soul of the French left. He was the first to undertake French decolonialization, thereby proving himself one of the few genuine statesmen in the discredited Fourth Republic, a man who told the truth and kept his promises with complete consistency. Yet he gave no quarter to his opposition, which was numerous, and he seemed to cultivate the art of displeasing the electorate, a gift which kept him in power only a short time. The shadow cast by his government was a long one, and his intellectual and political heirs, in power from May 1981, have fully recognized their debt to him.

He was born into a moderately prosperous family; his father sold women's clothing—*confections pour dames.* The Mendès Frances were of Sephardic Jewish origin, having lived in Bordeaux since at least the seventeenth century, but were originally from Spain or Portugal. The name, he often speculated, came about through an ancient linking by marriage of the Mendoza and Franco families. He had a brilliant student career: he was the youngest pupil in his lycée to pass the *baccalauréat,* the youngest graduate of the prestigious École Libre des Sciences Politiques, where he was first among 800 students, and at the age of 21 he was the youngest lawyer in France. His first book, *The Fiscal Accomplishment of the Poincaré Government* (1928), so impressed the leaders of the Radical Socialist Party, which he had joined at 16, that an Assembly seat was soon found for him at Louviers, in the Eure department in Normandy, and in 1932 he became the youngest deputy in the chamber. He was first elected mayor of Louviers in 1935.

Primarily a theoretical economist by training, Mendès France was an unqualified supporter of Léon Blum's Popular Front government. In 1938, at the start of Blum's second administration, he was named undersecretary of the Treasury, the youngest government member of the Third Republic. This government, however, lasted only four weeks, falling on the Senate's rejection of Mendès France's plan for economic mobilization to meet the war that nearly everyone thought was likely.

He abandoned politics in 1939 to join the French Air Force, serving briefly in Syria. The following year, faced with the Nazi onslaught, he moved his family first to Bordeaux, then to Morocco. He was among the many deputies who, believing that the government's removal to North Africa was imminent, wanted to be first on the scene; but these loyalists had not counted on the Vichy collaborationists. He was arrested as a military deserter in Casablanca and returned to prison in Clermont Ferrand, France, where he was tried and sentenced. On 21 June 1940 he escaped from prison, and after eight months with the Resistance in both the occupied and unoccupied zones he eventually reached London, the seat of the Free French government in exile. He joined the Free French Air Force, attached to the British RAF, and as a captain and navigator in the Lorraine squadron flew many bombing raids over France and Germany.

He first met Charles de Gaulle, the charismatic Free French leader, in February 1942, and managed to resist for a time the general's request that he join the headquarters staff. In the fall of 1943, however, at the urging of Gaston Defferre, a political ally of Mendès France and a close advisor to de Gaulle, Mendès France took up the economics portfolio of the Liberation Committee of Algiers. In September 1944, after the Liberation, the de Gaulle government was established, and Mendès France served as minister of the national economy, sharing responsibilities for fiscal affairs with René Pleven, minister of finance, a far more conservative politician. The greater traditional power of the Finance Ministry quickly proved too much even for Mendès France's brilliance, and his rather austere solutions to the grave disequilibrium of supply and demand then facing France—closing down the black market and restricting the money supply—found no favor with either the people, the press, or de Gaulle, who chose instead Pleven's more conformist, laissez-faire plan. He left office in April 1945, retaining de Gaulle's thorough approbation: "He [resigned] with dignity. And so I kept my esteem for this exceptionally valuable collaborator. In sum, if I do not adopt the policy on which he insists, I in no way exclude the possibility of making it mine one day, circumstances having changed" (*War Memoirs,* vol. III). De Gaulle himself left office in January 1946, already disgusted with the fractiousness of Fourth Republic politics, to enter a 12-year exile on his country estate, during which he and Mendès France remained on polite terms, but they were never to be political allies.

Out of power for the next nine years, Mendès France became a voice of somewhat caustic wisdom in the Assembly, as incompetent

Courtesy of French Embassy

governments succeeded disreputable governments to the alternate fascination, bewilderment, and impatience of the people. The economy was stagnating next to West Germany's already evident recovery, and the war in Indochina, which had been going on since 1946, seemed more obviously unwinnable with each passing year. In May 1953, Pres. Vincent Auriol asked Mendès France to form a government, but the Assembly refused to invest him. Thirteen months later, however, six weeks after the disastrous French defeat at the Battle of Dienbienphu, in which 15,000 officers and men were lost in just one week, the Assembly accepted a government headed by Mendès France, and did so morever by the remarkably one-sided vote of 462 to 13. He was the fourteenth premier, and his was the twentieth government, since World War II. He promised the Assembly to end the war within a month, and to resign if he could not. He took over from the colorless, time-serving Joseph Laniel, and his forthrightness and evident integrity brought an immediate change to the complexion of French politics. He took, exceptionally, both the offices of prime minister and foreign minister.

Within days he left for Geneva, where he negotiated at great length with Zhou Enlai, foreign minister of the Chinese People's Republic, and Ho Chi Minh and Pham Van Dong of the Vietminh, the victors at Dienbienphu. On 21 July, one month and one day after his deadline, Mendès France presented the peace treaty to the Assembly. "I wish no one to be under any illusions about the content of the agreement just signed in Geneva. The text is cruel in parts, because it attests to facts that are cruel. It could not be otherwise." Vietnam was divided on the seventeenth parallel, and the French pulled out entirely from the country, although the Americans quickly took their place in the south.

The bustling energy and enthusiasm of "PMF"—as he soon came to be called by his supporters, in conscious reference to FDR—were heartening and infectious. Working out of the foreign minister's suite in the Quai d'Orsay, he drew to his side some of the country's most brilliant young people, notably his chief of staff, Jean-Jacques Servan-Schreiber, Françoise Giroud, and Michel Rocard, all now prominent political figures. His interior minister was François Mitterrand, future president of France. He also emulated the Roosevelt custom of radio fireside talks (which he called Saturday night chats), but these only inflamed the latent animosity against him in the Assembly, where it was feared he was aspiring to personal power.

In late July he visited Tunisia, where anti-French agitation, rioting, and killing had intensified since 1952. He signed an agreement to confer internal autonomy on the insurgent nationalist regime headed by Habib Bourguiba, who led the country later to full independence. In late August he brought before the Assembly a bill for French participation in the European Defense Community, an idea for a European army that was firmly supported by the United States and Britain, but for which, it had long been evident, there was no Assembly majority. In permitting a free vote on the bill, however, Mendès France ensured the defeat of the EDC and earned the furious ire of its internationalist adherents. He immediately entered negotiations to accomplish many of the aims of the EDC; the Paris Agreements, permitting a measure of German rearmament, secured a bare majority in the Assembly in November with full government backing. The same month also marked the beginning of the Algerian revolt, with 30 terrorist acts in one day against French establishments. His initial move to placate the revolutionaries met strong Assembly resistance, and his eventual appointment of Jacques Soustelle, the archconservative advocate of Algérie Française at any price, as governor general came too late to save his government.

By the end of 1954 it was clear that his government's days were numbered. Mendès France's popularity, so high after the Geneva Agreement, had steadily declined; even with all his energy, he was unable to counter the inevitable political disillusionment that eventually capsized all governments under the Fourth Republic. A nonsmoker and practically a teetotaler, he was ridiculed and vilified throughout the country for his campaign to increase milk consumption and decrease alcoholism, which he carried to the extent of actually drinking milk at state dinners. Even his Norman constituents—big producers and consumers of dairy products—were said to be enraged at such un-French behavior: many of them had for years made Calvados for sale from private stills. Yet abroad, Mendès France had a popularity and renown of no French politician since de Gaulle. On a successful tour of the United States in November, he was widely lionized and photographed. British newspapers and politicians of all parties always praised him highly. "Your vitality and your courage," Churchill wrote him in January 1955, "have given me the impression that France is led in a way that I have not known since Clemenceau."

International adulation was not to save him. On 6 February 1955 the government lost a routine budget vote, then, demanding a vote of confidence, lost by 319 to 273, with 22 abstentions. Mounting the podium for the last time as premier after the result was announced, Mendès France attempted to address the Assembly. In one of the Fourth Republic's most disgraceful scenes, deputies throughout the chamber screamed insults, pounded their desks, and shook their fists at him, refusing to let him speak. Yet he would not be drowned out. "Something has changed in men's and women's hearts," he said. "What has been done in these 7 months and 17 days will remain. How can the nation forget the hopes that have been rekindled?"

From 1 February to 23 May 1956, Mendès France was minister of state in the Republican Front government of Guy Mollet. He had originated the front, along with Mollet, Mitterrand, and the leftist Gaullists led by Jacques Chaban-Delmas, as an electoral alliance before the January 1956 Assembly elections. When the front did well enough to attempt forming a government, Pres. René Coty, no admirer of Mendès France, sent for Mollet. In great disagreement from the start over Algerian policy and ill at ease in a clearly secondary position, Mendès France resigned the ministry on 23 May 1956. It was his last position of government responsibility. He strongly opposed de Gaulle's return to power in 1958, which he considered tantamount to a coup d'état; he held to this position throughout the campaign for the Assembly elections of 1958, in which he lost his seat. He never afterward wavered in his opposition to the Gaullist regime. "There is no example in history of a regime founded on a single man which did not end in disaster." He was a deputy once again, from March 1967 to May 1968, representing Grenoble, in the Isère. Gaston Defferre, running for president against Georges Pompidou in 1969, announced that he would appoint Mendès France as his prime minister. He won only 5 percent of the vote in the first round, however, and was forced to withdraw. During the profound civil disruptions of May 1968, Mendès France was one of the few politicians trusted and listened to by the student leaders.

Mendès France's interest and expertise in economic administration easily coexisted with the great demands of his political life. For many years he was a professor at the prestigious École Normale d'Administration. He also held the highly respected posts of governor of the International Monetary Fund (1947–58), adjutant governor of the International Bank for Reconstruction and Development in Washington (1946–58), and president of the National Economic Commission (1952–60). Among the more popular of his 13 books were *The Pursuit of Freedom* (1943; English ed. 1956), *Encounters* (with Aneurin Bevan and Pietro Nenni, 1958), *A Modern French Republic* (1962; English ed. 1963), and *Face to Face with Asia* (1972; English ed. 1974).

After a retirement full of activity, mostly divided between his country house in Louviers and his large Paris apartment in Auteuil, always crowded with visitors, Mendès France had the great pleasure of seeing the left triumphant once again, when Mitterrand won both the presidency in May 1981 and a Socialist Assembly and Senate the following month. On 21 May, during the investiture reception at the Élysée Palace, Pres. Mitterrand gave him a formal accolade. "Without you," said the president, "this would not have been possible." Though increasingly ill, Mendès France continued to speak out on important issues. In July 1982, in his last public statement, he joined with other Western Jewish leaders, among them Nahum Goldmann, in a widely reported call for peaceful coexistence between Israel and the Palestine Liberation Front. His death occasioned an outpouring of unanimously fond and extraordinarily emotional recollections from people of all walks of life, not excluding some of his lifelong political adversaries. A.K.

Parents Cerf M. F., clothes designer and cloth dealer, and Palmyre (Cahn) M. F. **Married** (1) Lily Cicurel 1933 (d. 1967): Michel; Bernard. (2) Marie-Claire Servan-Schreiber de Fleurieu 1971. **Religion** Jewish. **Education** Public schs.; Coll. Turgot; École Libre des Sciences Politiques, diplôme; Univ. of Paris, dr. en droit; certificates in history and geography; admitted to Paris bar at 21. **Mil. service** Lt., French Air Force, Syria and France 1939; imprisoned by Vichy govt., Clermont Ferrand, France (escaped 1940); with Resistance units 1940; capt., Lorraine bomber group, Free French Air Force, Germany and North

Africa 1940–43. **Career** Joined Radical Socialist Party age 16; mayor 1935–58 and gen. councilman 1937–58, Louviers; deputy for Louviers, Eure, 1932–40 and 1946–58 and for Grenoble, Isère, 1967–68, Natl. Assembly; chmn., tariff cttee., Chamber of Deputies 1936; member, county council, Pont-de-l'Arche 1937–58; pres., county council, Eure 1945–58. • Undersecty. of state for treasury 1938; finance commnr., Cttee. of Liberation, Algiers 1943–44; minister of natl. economy 1944–45; head, French financial missions to Wash. DC and Bretton Woods conferences 1944; adjutant gov., Intl. Bank for Reconstruction and Development, Wash. DC 1946–58; gov., Intl. Monetary Fund 1947–58; named permanent rep. of France to U.N. Economic and Social Council 1947; pres., Commn. for Natl. Accounts and Economic Budgets 1952–60; pres., commn. of finances, Natl. Assembly, 1953; prime minister and minister of foreign affairs 1954–55; minister of state without portfolio 1956. • Leader, Radical Socialist Party 1955–75; co-founder, Republican Front 1956; member, independent commn. on intl. development issues 1977–80; head, PSU (Socialist Party); prof., École Normale d'Administration. • Pres., editorial bd., *Les Cahiers de la République* to 1963; dir., *Courrier de la République.* **Honors** Officer, Légion d'Honneur; Croix de Guerre; Rosette de la Résistance; Médaille des Évadés; grand officer, Order of Léopold, Belgium; hon. dr. of laws. **Author** *L'oeuvre financière du gouvernement Poincaré* [*The Fiscal Accomplishment of the Poincaré Government*], 1928; *Histoire de la stabilisation du franc* [*History of the Stabilization of the Franc*], 1928; *La banque internationale* [*The International Bank*], 1930; *Liberté, liberté chérie* (memoirs), 1943 (trans. as *The Pursuit of Freedom,* 1956); *Roissy-en-France* (memoirs), 1946; (jtly.) *La science économique et l'action,* 1954 (trans. as *Economics and Action,* 1955); *Gouverner c'est choisir* [*To Govern is To Choose*], 1953; *Sept mois et dix-sept jours* [*Seven Months and Seventeen Days*], 1955; *La politique et la vérité* [*Politics and Truth*], 1958; (jtly.) *Rencontres* [*Encounters*], 1958; *La république moderne,* 1962 (trans. as *A Modern French Republic,* 1963); *Pour préparer l'avenir* [*To Prepare for the Future*], 1968; *Dialogues avec l'Asie d'aujourd'hui,* 1972 (trans. as *Face to Face with Asia,* 1974); (jtly.) *Science économique et lucidité politique* [*Economic Science and Political Lucidity*], 1973; *Choisir* [*Choose*], 1974; *La vérité guidait leurs pas* [*Truth Guided Their Steps*], 1977. **Contributor** to *L'étude du problème des États-Unis d'Europe,* 1930.

Further reading Donald McCormick, *Mr. France,* 1955; Sanche de Gramont, "Re-enter: Mendès-France, Hoping," in *New York Times Magazine,* 16 Apr. 1967.

BESS TRUMAN
First lady of the United States
***Born* Independence, Missouri, USA, 13 February 1885**
***Died* Independence, Missouri, USA, 18 October 1982**

Bess Truman, the wife of U.S. president Harry S Truman, had a well-deserved reputation for taciturnity and reserve when in the White House, refusing all requests for interviews and giving no news conferences. Yet she was greatly respected by the American people for her firm sense of self-worth, her independence, and her absolute devotion to the best interests of her husband. Pres. Truman always insisted that his wife, whom he often referred to as "the Boss," was an indispensable element in his political success. "She was my chief advisor always," he said after his retirement. "She always helped me in everything. She was a full partner in all my transactions—politically and otherwise."

Elizabeth Virginia Wallace, always known as Bess, was born into one of the most prominent families in Independence, a medium-sized town in western Missouri near Kansas City. Her birthplace, on Delaware Avenue, was a rambling Victorian structure called the

Gates Mansion, built in 1865 by her grandfather, George Porterfield Gates, a miller, soon after he arrived in Missouri from Vermont.

She met the future president, whose family's social and financial position was considerably lower than hers, when they were both in the second grade. They attended Sunday school, grade school, and high school together, graduating from Independence High School in 1901. They saw little of one another, however, over the next dozen years, as Truman worked at a succession of jobs away from Independence and she was sent to the Barstow Finishing School for Girls in Kansas City. They began courting about 1914, according to some reports against the wishes of her mother, and became engaged only in 1917, before Truman went off to war in France. Finally, in June 1919, when she was 34 and he 35, they were married.

The couple moved into the Gates Mansion with Mrs. Wallace, as Truman, with the help of a friend from the army, started a haberdashery business, which failed in 1921. The next year, backed by the powerful Kansas City political machine of Thomas Pendergast, he was elected judge for Jackson County. In 1926 he was elected presiding judge of the county court, an office he held until 1934, when he was the Pendergast machine's successful candidate for the U.S. Senate. He was barely reelected in 1941.

In Washington, the Trumans lived entirely on his $10,000 salary in a modest apartment. Mrs. Truman's main interests were caring for their home and raising their only child, Margaret, who was born in 1924. Pres. Franklin Roosevelt's choice of Truman as his running mate in 1944—replacing Henry Wallace—was a surprise to almost everyone in the country, but not so great a shock as occurred 82 days after their inauguration, when Roosevelt's death made Truman president.

Mrs. Truman quickly understood that she was entirely unequipped to replace Eleanor Roosevelt, undoubtedly the most active and outspoken first lady in U.S. history. Her first official engagement was a fiasco: invited to launch a hospital plane, she was unable, after more than a dozen tries, to smash the champagne bottle, then became soaked when a mechanic broke it with a wrench. The newsreels ran pictures of the ceremony, which most of the country found amusing, but Mrs. Truman saw the whole affair as a personal embarrassment, and shortly thereafter canceled her first news conference as first lady. She never af-

terwards met the press en masse; in her occasional written responses to reporters' questions, her most frequent answer was a terse "No comment." She was the last president's wife to escape intensive and intrusive media coverage, a feat she accomplished by sheer force of will.

Her years as first lady, however, were hardly devoid of activity. After wartime austerity, the country expected an increase in the number of social events at the White House, and Mrs. Truman obliged, averaging three social engagements a day, plus directing the domestic staff and serving as hostess at countless luncheons and dinners. "One of the biggest contributions she made," said the president in 1963, "was to see that the feminine part of the White House was run properly. She made sure that the snooty women were well treated. That's something I wouldn't do—I wouldn't talk to them." The president often had to protect his wife against unkind remarks from the press and other politicians. Both Rep. Adam Clayton Powell and Clare Boothe Luce were banished from all White House social functions for making comments against her. When her hairstyle or taste in clothes was criticized, Truman sprang to her defense: "She looks exactly like a woman who has been married for 25 years should look."

She was reported as not wanting her husband to run for a new term in 1948. Once he made the decision to run, however, she backed him fully, even joining him on his famous whistle-stop campaign around the nation. "Harry is so sure he is right," she remarked to a friend during the campaign, "so sure that people will know he is right, that I hope he wins." Yet four years later her counsel prevailed. When the president made his announcement that he would not run again at a Jefferson-Jackson Day dinner, Mrs. Truman, seated at the head table, seemed quite unable to hide her happiness and satisfaction. "When you made your announcement," Harry Vaughan, one of the president's poker-playing cronies, reported to him, "Mrs. Truman looked the way you do when you draw four aces."

They returned to the mansion on Delaware Avenue in Independence, where they lived for the rest of their lives. Mrs. Truman supervised the household budget, did her own shopping, and generally enjoyed her retirement. Their trips away from home were infrequent, sometimes back to Washington, more often to New York to visit their daughter and four grandsons. After the president died at Christmas 1972, he was buried on the grounds of the Truman Memorial Library in Independence. "I would like to be buried out there," he had told her, "so that I can get up and walk to my office if I want to. And when the time comes, you'll be there beside me, probably saying, 'Harry, you oughtn't!'" Mrs. Truman was indeed buried there almost exactly a decade after her husband's death. At 97, she was the longest-lived first lady in U.S. history.
A.K.

Born Elizabeth Virginia Wallace. **Parents** David Willock W., businessman and customs officer, and Madge (Gates) W. **Married** Harry S Truman, politician, later pres. of U.S., 1919 (d. 1972): Mary Margaret Truman Daniel, singer, author, b. 1924. **Religion** Episcopalian. **Education** Independence High Sch., MO, grad. 1901; Barstow Finishing Sch. for Girls, Kansas City, MO. **Career** Clerk, secty., and personal asst. to Harry Truman; first lady of U.S. 1945–52. **Member** Democratic Party; Congressional Club, PEO Sisterhood, H Street United Service Org., and Senate Wives Club, Wash. DC 1930s–40s; many other natl. and charitable orgs. **Honors** Hon. chmn., English Classics Collection of Books, Russian War Relief 1945; hon. comdr., Amer. Cancer Soc. 1947; hon. pres. of Girl Scouts, Women's Natl. Democratic Club, Home Hospitality Cttee. of War Recreation Services; hon. member of Amer. Newspaper Women's Club, Daughters of Colonial Wars, Red Cross Motor Club, Women's Natl. Farm and Garden Assn.; hon. officer and member of many other orgs.

Further reading Marianne Means, *The Woman in the White House,* 1954; Harry S. Truman, *Memoirs,* 2 vols., 1955–56; Margaret Truman Daniel, *Souvenir,* 1956; G. B. West, *Upstairs at the White House,* 1973; J. Robbins, *Bess and Harry: An American Love Story,* 1980.

SIR SIEGMUND (GEORGE) WARBURG

International banker

***Born* Tübingen, Germany, 30 September 1902**

***Died* London, England, 18 October 1982**

Siegmund Warburg was the thoughtful and soft-spoken founder and longtime chairman of S. G. Warburg & Company, one of the most respected and influential of British merchant (investment) banks, though by no means among the City's oldest or most establishment-oriented. His gentlemanly demeanor masked an aggressive dynamism that did much to modernize British merchant banking. Though frequently an underdog, he is believed never to have lost a takeover battle or a proxy fight.

From the sixteenth century the Warburg family was prominent in many fields in Germany, but was probably best known as bankers. M. M. Warburg & Sons, the family firm, was established in Hamburg in the late eighteenth century. Siegmund's father, Georg, never joined the bank, but became a noted gentleman farmer in Swabia. The boy, an only child, was educated at the Humanistisches Gymnasium in Reutlingen and the Evangelisches Seminar in Urach, the latter a fifteenth-century Protestant establishment that admitted him as its first Jewish student. He excelled in Classical Greek and Latin and was able to quote from both languages all his life.

After an initial apprenticeship in the family bank in Hamburg, Warburg was sent to London to train at N. M. Rothschild & Sons and thence to the United States, where he worked first for an accounting firm, then for the International Acceptance Bank, and finally for Kuhn, Loeb & Company, where two of his uncles were partners. He returned to Germany in 1930 and became a partner in M. M. Warburg, starting up the bank's first branch office in Berlin.

Warburg was a close friend and advisor to Baron von Neurath, a neighbor of his father's in Swabia, who, though not a Nazi, became Hitler's first foreign minister. After the violent anti-Jewish rioting that followed the Reichstag fire of February 1933, Warburg insisted that Neurath intercede with President von Hindenburg to get Hitler dismissed. The foreign minister refused, warning his young advisor that no one then in Germany had the power to oppose the Nazis. Warburg immediately took his family to England, arriving with less than £5,000. He became a British subject in 1939.

Courtesy of International Investor—Yves de Bain

His first British venture was the New Trading Company Ltd., founded with family-connected Dutch capital, to which he gave his own name in 1946, when he returned from serving with British intelligence during the war. After a decade of steady growth, the firm took over an old City banking house, Seligman Brothers, and took a seat on the all-important London Accepting Houses Committee. In the long-running battle of 1957–59 for the control of British Aluminium, Warburg was almost alone in backing the insurgent, Reynolds Metals Company, against the bid of the Aluminum Corporation of America, which was supported by virtually the entire merchant-banking establishment. Warburg & Company's decisive victory forced modernization on the older banks of the City, which in turn produced a rebirth of efficiency and effectiveness in British banking. Siegmund Warburg became an internationally respected name in banking circles, and his boldness, inventiveness, and prudence were soon legendary. He was quickly accepted by the very establishment he had so successfully contended against, receiving a knighthood in 1966. The firm's corporate clients eventually included British Petroleum, Grand Metropolitan, Trust Houses Forte, Unilever, and Imperial Chemical Industries; it was the leading British underwriter of Eurobonds and served in an advisory capacity to the government of Indonesia.

Warburg was an urbane conversationalist who could happily spend hours discussing subjects far removed from finance, but was also reputed to be a hard taskmaster (bankers at Warburg worked the longest hours in the City) as well as a devotee of graphology, insisting that all prospective employees agree to an analysis of their handwriting. His philanthropic activities were extensive, particularly in Israel, but he always insisted on strict anonymity.

In 1964 he resigned the chairmanship of his firm, and five years later resigned as partner. He was prevailed upon to serve as president from 1970 to 1978, after which he became chairman of the advisory council. He did much of his work by telex and telephone from his home in Lausanne, Switzerland. He died at the age of 80 on a visit to London. A.K.

Parents Georg Siegmund W., farmer and agriculturalist, and Lucie (Kaulla) W., pianist and composer. **Married** Eva Marie Philipson 1926:

George Siegmund, accountant and banker, b. 1927; Anna M. Biegun, b. 1930. **Religion** Jewish. **Emigrated** to England 1933; naturalized 1939. **Education** Humanistisches Gymnasium, Reutlingen, Germany; Evangelisches Seminar, Urach, Germany 1920–30. **Mil. service** With British intelligence, WWII. **Career** Trainee ca. 1920–25, partner 1930–38, and mgr. of Berlin branch 1931–34, M. M. Warburg & Co., Hamburg; asst. and trainee, N. M. Rothschild & Sons, London 1925, Lybrand Ross Bros. & Montgomery, Boston mid-1920s, and Intl. Acceptance Bank, NYC late 1920s; asst. late 1920s and dir. 1956–64, Kuhn, Loeb & Co., NYC; dir., New Trading Co., Ltd., London 1938–46. • With S. G. Warburg & Co., London: founding chmn. 1946–64; dir. 1946–69; chmn., Mercury Securities (holding co. for S. G. Warburg & Co.) 1950s–64; pres. 1970–78; chmn., advisory council since 1978. **Officer** Dir., Weizmann Inst. of Science, Israel; founder and endower, Foundn. of Graphological Science and Application, Univ. of Zurich. **Member** London Accepting Houses Cttee. **Honors** Kt. 1966; Order of Sacred Treasure, 1st Class, Japan 1978; Grand Cross of Merit, Germany.

Further reading Joseph Wechsberg, *The Merchant Bankers,* 1968; David Farrer, *The Warburgs,* 1975.

KORCZAK ZIOLKOWSKI
Sculptor
***Born* Boston, Massachusetts, USA, 6 September 1908**
***Died* Sturgis, South Dakota, USA, 20 October 1982**

In 1939, Korczak Ziolkowski, an assistant sculptor working on the Mount Rushmore National Memorial, was asked by Sioux Chief Henry Standing Bear "to caress a mountain so that the white man will know that the red man had great heroes, too." Seized by the vision of creating a monumental memorial to American Indian life and culture, Ziolkowski set himself the largest sculpting task in history: carving a 563-foot-high, 600-foot-long equestrian figure of Crazy Horse, the Sioux chief who led the massacre of Gen. George Armstrong Custer's troops at the Battle of the Little Big Horn, out of a solid granite mountain. "They think I'm a screwball and I tell them they're right," said Ziolkowski. "You have to be a screwball to get anything big done in this world."

Orphaned at the age of three in a boating accident, Ziolkowski was adopted by an Irish prizefighter and contractor who beat him frequently but who also taught him the basics of wood and steel working. "He made me cut steel I-beams with a hacksaw, and God help me if a broke a blade." At the age of 16, Ziolkowski left home and found work as a carpenter and pattern maker in the East Boston shipyards, where he began carving ships' figureheads, eagles, and the like in his spare time. His first real sculpture commission was a marble bust of the judge who had administered his case at family court. By the age of 25, Ziolkowski was making his living as a portrait sculptor. His style of heroic realism, which gave all his portraits an air of fierce nobility and independence whether the subject warranted it or not, proved to be quite popular. Among his better-known works of the 1930s were a 14-foot statue of Noah Webster, presented free of charge to Webster's hometown of West Hartford, Connecticut, and a bust of Polish composer and statesman Ignacy Paderewski that won first prize at the 1939 New York World's Fair. Yet Ziolkowski's work attracted no attention in official art circles, and he often boasted that he had never taken an art class.

During his brief stint as an assistant to Gutzon Borglum at Mount Rushmore, Ziolkowski became skilled at explosives and learned to handle a jackhammer and rock-cutting torch. But Borglum and Ziolkowski, both men of strong ego and volatile temper, did not get on well together, and Borglum soon dismissed him, saying, "I think it would be better for you to pursue your creative career efforts where you are not hampered by any other way of doing things."

After a hitch with the U.S. Army during

Courtesy of Crazy Horse Foundation

World War II, Ziolkowski moved his wife and adopted child out to the Black Hills of South Dakota, where he had purchased the 600-foot Thunderhead Mountain in order to carry out his promise to Standing Bear. In 1948, with the approval of Sioux leaders, he began work on the monument, which he purposely scaled to dwarf Mount Rushmore. He was then 40 years old.

His second marriage, to Ruth Ross, one of his assistants on the Noah Webster monument, produced ten children. Ziolkowski's obsession quickly became a family enterprise: the sons assisted him on the mountain while Ruth and the daughters ran the nonprofit Crazy Horse Memorial Foundation museum and led tourists around the grounds. By the 1970s, the monument had attracted considerable media attention and Ziolkowski had become something of a national folk hero. Admission fees, donations, and the sale of souvenir Crazy Horse statuettes financed the project. Ziolkowski refused to accept federal aid, though it was offered twice, in order to protect his plan from outside interference.

Ziolkowski often claimed that carving the monument was more a mining-engineering job than it was art, and that a "competent engineer" could complete the work from his detailed plans. Using tons of dynamite, several massive drilling rigs, tractors, bulldozers, and dump trucks (most donated by the manufacturers in return for Ziolkowski's endorsement), he almost singlehandedly removed more than seven million tons of granite. The labor was dangerous: he overturned Jeeps and tractors several times on the steep roads he had bulldozed up the mountain, had six discs removed from his spine in four separate operations after being struck by a 300-pound cable, suffered two heart attacks, and underwent open-heart surgery in mid-1982, by which time the rough outlines of the figure, after 34 years of work, were just becoming visible.

Ziolkowski died at the age of 74 and was buried under the mountain in a tomb he had blasted for himself years before. His family and the Crazy Horse Memorial Foundation intend to finish the monument, which will probably take a decade or more, and to establish an American Indian university and medical center on the site. S.A.

Indian name Shooting Star. **Parents** unknown; raised by foster father, a prizefighter and contractor. **Married** (1) Dorothy Brewster Comstock ca. 1933 (div. ca. 1949): one child. (2) Ruth Ross 1950: Adam, b. 1951; Casimir, b. 1954; Monique; Jadwiga; Dawn; Marinka; Mark; three other children. **Education** Rindge Technical Sch., Boston. **Mil. service** U.S. Army, Europe, WWII. **Career** Pattern maker and carpenter, Bethlehem Steel shipyards, East Boston 1920s–ca. 32; sculptor since 1930s; asst. to Gutzon Borglum, Mt. Rushmore Natl. Memorial project, SD 1939; occupied in carving monumental figure of Chief Crazy Horse into Thunderhead Mountain, Custer, SD since 1948; founding bd. chmn., Crazy Horse Foundn. since 1948. **Member**

Courtesy of Crazy Horse Foundation

Natl. Sculpture Soc. **Honors** 1st prize in sculpture, for bust of Paderewski, New York World's Fair 1939; Trustee Award, Natl. Western Heritage and Cowboy Hall of Fame 1974; hon. degree, Fairfield Univ. **Collections** San Francisco Art Mus.; Judge Baker Guidance Center, Boston; Symphony Hall, Boston; Vassar Coll., Poughkeepsie, NY; public monuments and statues in West Hartford, CT, Deadwood, SD, other towns.

Further reading Roy Bongartz, "The Mountain Versus Korczak Ziolkowski," in *Esquire,* Mar. 1971; Robb DeWall, *Crazy Horse and Korczak: The Story of an Epic Mountain Carving,* 1982.

RICHARD (FRANKLIN) HUGO
Poet
***Born* Seattle, Washington, USA, 21 December 1923**
***Died* Seattle, Washington, USA, 22 October 1982**

The American poet Richard Hugo was the master of what Helen Vendler, writing in the *New York Times Book Review,* called "the sure and deliberate exploitation of drabness." His subject was the bleak expanse, physical and spiritual, of the Pacific Northwest, where he spent nearly all his life, and the bleakness of soul in which most people (as he saw it) labor to survive. His poems, conversational but not casual, are thick with detail, yet the cumulative effect of his descriptive writing is less the evocation of a particular place than the distillation of a kind of epic sadness toward which all human effort tends.

Hugo's first book of poems, *A Run of Jacks,* was published in 1961, when he was 38. Most of the poems were set in Seattle, where he had attended public school and (after service as a bombardier in the Army Air Corps during World War II) the state university, and where he spent 13 years working for the Boeing Company. In 1964, just before the publication of his second book, *Death of the Kapowsin Tavern,* he joined the English faculty at the Missoula branch of the University of Montana. He remained there for the rest of his career, becoming director of the creative-writing program and taking occasional leaves of absence to teach at other universities and to give readings on the college poetry circuit. In 1977 he succeeded Stanley Kunitz as head of the Yale Younger Poets Series.

Poets, Hugo said in an essay in his collection *The Triggering Town* (1979), write out of their own feelings of worthlessness and their sense of being "a wrong thing in a right world." "We sweat through poem after poem to realize what dumb animals know by instinct and reveal in their behavior: My life is all I've got." This predication of creativity on the alienation and emotional distress of the poet came into play in his fourth book, *The Lady in Kicking Horse Reservoir* (1973), in which the author appears often as a maudlin bar-hopper, and even more in his fifth, *What Thou Lovest Well, Remains American* (1975), in which he risked a plunge into sentimentality in order to taste fully the dreariness and poverty of Montana's squalid towns and empty spaces. Vernon Young, reviewing the book in the

Courtesy of Thomas Victor

Hudson Review, wrote: "Hugo is writing American gothic . . . the visible is compelling, the invisible remains supreme." In *31 Letters and 13 Dreams* (1977) he tried out a loose, direct, epistolary form that enabled him to move more freely into other personas and to relieve his poems of their sometimes oppressive uniformity.

Hugo's last volumes of poetry, both published in 1980, were *White Center* and *The Right Madness on Skye.* The latter, the product of a visit to that remote island on a Guggenheim Fellowship, proved wrong those critics who thought Hugo a regional poet, for he easily transplanted to Scotland his sense of bleakness and of the perversion of the natural order by human venality. In 1981 he published his only work of fiction, a well-written, traditional murder mystery entitled *Death and the Good Life,* whose hero, a one-time poet turned deputy sheriff, believes that "we are asked to endure more than we can ever bear." He died of leukemia at the age of 58. J.P.

Parents Herbert Franklin James H., naval officer, and Esther Clara (Monk) H. **Married** (1) Barbara Williams 1951 (div. 1966). (2) Ripley Schemm 1974: Melissa Merrifield Hansen; Matthew Ferdinand Hansen (stepchildren). **Education** Public schs.; Univ. of Washington, Seattle, B.A. 1948, M.A. 1952. **Mil. service** First lt. and bombardier, USAAC, Mediterranean theater 1943–45. **Career** Storekeeper, budget coordinator, documents writer, and documents supervisor, Boeing Co., Seattle 1951–63. • With Univ. of Montana, Missoula: visiting lectr. 1964–65; asst. prof. of English 1965–69; assoc. prof. 1969–70; prof. and dir. of creative-writing program since 1971. • Visiting poet, Univ. of Iowa 1970–71; Roethke Chair, Univ. of Washington 1971; visiting prof., Univ. of Colorado 1974–75; Visiting Distinguished Prof. Chair, Univ. of Arkansas, Little Rock 1980. • Ed., Yale Younger Poets Series since 1977; participant in numerous writers' conferences and workshops. **Honors** DFC, 5 Bronze Battle Stars, and Air Medal with 3 Oak Leaf Clusters, WWII; Roethke Prize 1964 and Bullis Award 1966 and 1972, *Poetry Northwest;* Northwest Writers Book of the Year Award 1965; Pacific Northwest Booksellers Assn. Poetry Award 1965; Rockefeller Fellowship 1967–68; Guggenheim Fellowship 1977–78; Cane Prize, Poetry Soc. of America 1980; fellowship, Acad. of Amer. Poets 1981. **Poetry** *A Run of Jacks,* 1961; *Death of the Kapowsin Tavern,* 1965; *Good Luck in Cracked Italian,* 1969; *The Lady in Kicking Horse Reservoir,* 1973; *What Thou Lovest Well, Remains American,* 1975; *Rain Five Days and I Love It,* 1975; *31 Letters and 13 Dreams,* 1977; *Selected Poems,* 1979; *White Center,* 1980; *The Right Madness on Skye,* 1980. **Criticism and anthologies** (Co-ed.) *Five Poets of the Pacific,* 1964; *The Triggering Town: Lectures and Essays in Poetry and Writing,* 1979. **Novel** *Death and the Good Life,* 1981. **Manuscript collection** in Univ. of Montana, Missoula.

CYNTHIA PROPPER SETON

Novelist

***Born* New York City, USA, 11 October 1926**

***Died* Northampton, Massachusetts, USA, 23 October 1982**

Cynthia Propper Seton was the author of five novels about the decline and revitalization of love and marriage, written with a tart perceptiveness, deft wit, and gentle irony reminiscent of the nineteenth-century comedy of manners. She did not have a large audience, the public taste for such novels being limited, but reviewers had begun to recommend her work with increasing enthusiasm.

Seton, who was descended from a Huguenot family, was born in New York City, attended the Fieldston School for Ethical Culture in the Bronx, and married a psychoanalyst in 1949, soon after her graduation from Smith College. During the 1950s and 1960s, while she was raising her five children, she wrote a column of social commentary for the *Berkshire Eagle.* A selection of her col-

Courtesy of W.W. Norton & Co. Inc.

umns was published in 1962 under the title *I Think Rome is Burning.* When she reached her fortieth year she had, she said, "the experience of suddenly growing up," entailing a reevaluation of herself from "secondary and derivative" to "primary and autonomous." At the same time she produced two books, *A Special and Curious Blessing* (1968) and *The Mother of the Graduate* (1970), that examined marriage, family relationships, and the rapid change in sexual and social mores of the 1960s. She continued to work with these themes when she took up fiction writing. Her first novel, *The Sea Change of Angela Lewes* (1971), was followed by *The Half Sisters* (1974), *A Fine Romance* (1976), which was nominated for the National Book Award, *A Glorious Third* (1979), and *A Private Life* (1982).

In her first four novels, Seton explored the theme of the educated middle-aged woman—well-to-do, with a professional husband and grown children—who finds herself questioning the assumptions on which her married life is based. The temptation to abandon marriage entirely is overcome because her women prove capable of reorganizing their lives on new principles. Seton's was a temperate feminism: her object was to generate understanding and reconciliation rather than rejection, and her male characters, though not as well drawn as the women, were not excluded from her sympathy. "I want to write about husbands who may be obtuse, but who are *not* brutes, and remind their wives that there is a great deal to hang in there for," she told an interviewer for *Publishers Weekly* in 1976. "And I want to take the middle-aged woman and evoke her refusal to be demeaned, to honor it with a serious acknowledgment."

Seton was little concerned with plot; what distinguishes her books is not action, but her precise and elegant prose style, which she modeled on the prose of Gibbons, George Eliot, and Proust. Her characters are exceedingly well-read, and their conversations are embellished with literary references. Her last novel, *A Private Life,* about a New York journalist who goes to Europe to write a feature about an aunt with a scandalous past, was published to favorable reviews only a few months before Seton's death of leukemia at the age of 56. C.M.

Born Cynthia Propper. **Parents** Karl P., lawyer, and Charlotte (Janssen) P. **Married** Paul H. Seton, psychoanalyst, 1949: Anthony M., TV news producer, b. 1950; Julia Meredith, art restorer, b. 1953; Margaret Propper Seton-Jacobson, physician, b. 1954; Jennifer R., lawyer, b. 1957; Nora Janssen, press secty., b. 1961. **Religion** Dutch Reformed. **Education** Fieldston School for Ethical Culture, NYC; Smith Coll., Northampton, MA, A.B. 1948. **Career** Columnist, *Berkshire Eagle,* Pittsfield, MA 1956–68; columnist, *Washington Post* 1959–60; novelist since 1971; teacher, Indiana Writers Conference 1982 and other conferences; lectr. **Member** Authors Guild since 1968. **Novels** *The Sea Change of Angela Lewes,* 1971; *The Half Sisters,* 1974; *A Fine Romance,* 1976; *A Glorious Third,* 1979; *A Private Life,* 1982. **Social commentary** *I Think Rome is Burning,* 1962; *A Special and Curious Blessing,* 1968; *The Mother of the Graduate,* 1970. **Interview** John F. Baker, "Cynthia Propper Seton," in *Publishers Weekly*, 12 July 1976.

GIOVANNI CARDINAL BENELLI
Archbishop of Florence
***Born* Poggiole di Vernio, near Pistoia, Italy, 12 May 1921**
***Died* Florence, Italy, 26 October 1982**

Cardinal Benelli, the conservative archbishop of Florence, was considered a prominent candidate for the papacy during the two conclaves of 1978. He had been a powerful church administrator, one of the principal aides to Pope Paul VI during most of his reign.

Born to middle-class parents in Tuscany, he attended the diocesan seminary in Pistoia and was ordained in October 1943. He then went to Rome for further study, attending the French Seminary, the Pontifical Gregorian University, which awarded him a doctorate in canon law, and finally the Pontifical Ecclesiastical Academy, the training ground for the Vatican's foreign service. In 1947 he began his service in the Curia when he met and became private secretary to Monsignor Giovanni Battista Montini, the future Paul VI, who had been undersecretary of state since 1937 and who was one of the most influential figures in the church. In 1950, Benelli began his work in diplomacy, serving in junior posts in Dublin, Paris, Rio de Janeiro, and Madrid. In 1965–66 he was the chief Vatican observer at UNESCO's Paris headquarters, where he first became involved with problems of illiteracy and basic education, concerns he retained throughout his career.

Paul VI, who succeeded to the papacy in 1963, named his protégé titular archbishop of Tusuro in 1966 and sent him to Senegal as apostolic pro-nuncio for West Africa. A year later he was recalled to Rome and appointed *sostituto* (undersecretary) of the Vatican Secretariat of State, the same position the pope had held when they met. He began almost immediately to function as de facto secretary of state, first because he had intimate Curial experience as well as the pope's confidence, then because his superior, Amleto Cardinal Cicognani, was over 80 and very ill. Two months after the appointment the pope issued "On Ruling the Universal Church," his plan for reforming the Curia along lines laid down by Vatican Council II, which had concluded its work in 1965. The plan called for regrouping the Curial congregations, including the all-powerful Holy Office, around the Secretariat of State, which was historically only the private office of the pope. The church's primary

levers of power and lines of communication, as well as all right of access to the pope, were consequently placed in Benelli's eager, tireless, and competent hands.

Although Paul called him "our friend, collaborator, and treasure," his relative youth, impatience to see results, and above all his brusque and authoritarian manner made Benelli numerous enemies among the church's upper hierarchy. Progressives, for their part, came to see him as no friend of reform, but rather as a cautious centralizer of authority who would do his best to resist the council's demands for change. The appointment in 1969 of a new secretary of state, Jean Cardinal Villot, only enhanced Benelli's authority, as Villot ceded him vast areas of control. The undersecretary was an incessant worker who had few close friends and no interests or hobbies apart from church concerns. His intelligence was considered more intuitive than analytic or contemplative, but his mastery of languages—he knew English, French, Spanish, Portuguese, and German, as well as Latin and Italian—made him an effective communicator.

In June 1977 the pope, though extremely reluctant to lose his services, named Benelli archbishop of Florence and at the same time conferred on him a cardinal's hat. In order to participate in the next conclave, or perhaps even to succeed to the papacy himself, some pastoral experience was necessary for a priest who had spent his lifetime in church administration. He proved to be a rather rigid and dogmatic archbishop, even by the highly conservative standards of the Italian hierarchy. Although his see was in the middle of the so-called Red Belt of Communist-run northern Italian cities, he refused all requests by Eurocommunists for a dialogue, saying, "Christians who vote communist either don't know Marxism or don't know Christianity." He led the unsuccessful fight to repeal the law permitting divorce and demanded excommunication for anyone taking advantage of the liberal abortion law.

Benelli was popularly considered *papabile,* or likely to be elected pope, after Paul's death in 1978, but most qualified observers considered his chances less than good, again because of his youth and the considerable lingering resentment from his time in the Curia. Yet he became the unexpected power broker of the conclave, managing to get his candidate, Albino Cardinal Luciani, patriarch of Venice, elected as pope. When John Paul I died after a reign of only 33 days, Benelli was thought much more likely to succeed, but a deadlock between him and Giuseppe Cardinal Siri of Genoa was broken by the election of a Pole, Karol Cardinal Wojtyła of Kraków, as John Paul II.

The last four years of Benelli's life were spent in the relative obscurity of the archepiscopal palace in Florence. His death, from complications following a heart attack, resulted, according to his doctors, from "his absolute refusal to be promptly hospitalized." About two hours before the end, waking from a coma, he asked to be taken back to the palace to die in his own bed. His death reduced the membership of the College of Cardinals to 120, of whom only 105, being under 80 years of age, are eligible to vote in a papal conclave.

A.K.

Religion Roman Catholic. **Education** Diocesan Jr. Seminary, Pistoia, Italy; French Seminary, Rome; Pontifical Gregorian Univ., Rome, licentiate in theology and laureate in canon law; ordained to the priesthood 1943; Pontifical Ecclesiastical Acad., Rome, grad. 1946. **Career** Private secty. to Vatican Undersecty. of State 1947–50; chargé d'affaires ad interim, Apostolic Nunciatures, Dublin 1950, Paris 1953, Rio de Janeiro 1960, and Madrid 1962; Vatican permanent observer, UNESCO 1965–66; Vatican delegate, World Conference for Elimination of Illiteracy and Conference for Harmonization of Programs of Basic Education in Central and South America 1965–66; titular archbishop, Tusuro, and apostolic pro-nuncio, Senegal 1966–67; apostolic delegate to West Africa 1966–67; Vatican undersecty. of state 1967–77; archbishop of Florence since 1977; elevated to cardinal 1977. • Consultor: Congregation for Doctrine of Faith; Congregation for Bishops; Commn. for Revision of Canon Law; Pontifical Commn. for Pastoral Care of Migrants and Tourists. **Member** Pontifical Commn. for Russia; Pontifical Commn. for Ecclesiastical Archives of Italy; Papal Household.

Further reading Gary MacEoin, *The Inner Elite,* 1978.

See *Addendum* for further information.

SYBIL LEEK
Writer on witchcraft and the occult
Born **Stoke-on-Trent, Staffordshire, England, 22 February 1917**
Died **Melbourne, Florida, USA, 26 October 1982**

Sybil Leek, a practitioner of the ancient pre-Christian religion known as Wicca, or witchcraft, made a comfortable living as an author and lecturer on occult subjects. Although her publishers did their best to make her books appear tantalizingly lurid, she was, on the contrary, an accomplished writer with an engaging style and a matter-of-fact attitude toward the supernatural.

Leek was born to a well-to-do Staffordshire family that had been active in witchcraft since the twelfth century, and was educated at home until her teens. After the death of her first husband, a concert pianist, she lived for a time with gypsy tribes in the New Forest, then opened the first of several antique stores and went to work as a journalist for the BBC. During World War II she served as a nurse with the Red Cross in London. When England's witchcraft laws were abolished in 1966 she began to write and speak in defense of the Old Religion. Benevolent or "white" witches, she explained to an interviewer, believe that earthly events are controlled by divine beings who can be invoked by a sustained concentration of mental energy; black magic is only a debased form of the art. In her long robes and with her pet jackdaw riding on her shoulder she cut a pleasantly eccentric figure, and was soon a media personality on both sides of the Atlantic.

Leek moved to the United States in 1964 and lived in Hollywood before settling near Cape Canaveral in Florida. She turned out books on reincarnation, numerology, telepathy, and similar subjects at the rate of three or four a year, wrote a column for the *Ladies' Home Journal,* and was the official medium on the ghost-hunting expeditions of Hans Holzer. She was also a sought-after psychic healer and astrologer, and with the assistance of her two sons by her second marriage she operated an astrological service for businessmen and an astrology school in St. Louis, Missouri. Her death, at the age of 65, was of cancer.

J.P.

Born Sybil Fawcett. **Father** engine fitter. **Married** (1) . . ., concert pianist, ca. 1940 (d. ca. 1942). (2) Brian Leek (d.): Stephen B., photographer, b. 1950; Julian, photographer, b. 1951. **Religion** Wicca. **Emigrated** to U.S. 1964. **Educated** at home and boarding sch. **Mil. service** Nurse, Red Cross, London, WWII. **Career** Astrologer and journalist since 1939; formerly owner of antiques stores, documentary filmmaker for BBC, and pres. of Witchcraft Research Assn.; ed. and publisher, Twin World Publications 1969–72; founder, astrology sch., St. Louis, MO 1972; assoc. ed., Macfadden Women's Group; columnist, *Ladies' Home Journal;* ghost hunter and lectr. on astrology and reincarnation. **Author** *A Shop in the High Street,* 1962; *A Fool and a Tree,* 1964; *The Jackdaw and the Witch,* 1966; *The Astrological Cookbook,* 1968; *Diary of a Witch,* 1968; *Numerology: The Magic of Numbers,* 1969; *The Tree That Conquered the World* (novel), 1969; *The Sybil Leek Book of Fortune-Telling,* 1969; *Cast Your Own Spell,* 1970; *Sybil Leek's Astrological Guide to Successful Everyday Living,* 1970; *Phrenology,* 1970; *How to Be Your Own Astrologer,* 1970; *Telepathy: The Respectable Phenomenon,* 1971; *The Complete Art of Witchcraft,* 1971; *Guide to Telepathy,* 1971; *Pictorial Encyclopedia of Astrology,* 1971; *Astrological Guide to Financial Success,* 1972; *Astrological Guide to the Presidential Candidates,* 1972; *ESP: The Magic Within You,* 1972; *My Life in Astrology,* 1972; (jtly.) *The Bicycle: That Curious Invention,* 1973; *Sybil Leek's Book of Herbs,* 1973; *The Story of Faith Healing,* 1973; *The Best of Sybil Leek,* 1974; *Reincarnation: The Second Chance,* 1974; *Sybil Leek's Zodiac of Love,* 1974; *Tomorrow's Headlines Today,* 1974; *Driving Out the Devils* (in U.K. as *Sybil Leek on Exorcism: Driving Out the Devils*), 1975; (jtly.) *Astrological Guide to Love and Sex,* 1975; *Herbs: Medicine and Mysticism,* 1975; *The Night Voyagers: You and Your

Dreams, 1975; *Star Speak: Your Body Language From the Stars,* 1975; *Sybil Leek's Book of Curses,* 1975; (jtly.) *The Assassination Chain,* 1976; (jtly.) *Inside Bellevue,* 1976; (jtly.) *A Ring of Magic Islands,* 1976; *Sybil Leek's Book of the Curious and the Occult,* 1976; *Moon Signs,* 1977; *Astrology and Love,* 1977.

See *Addendum* for further information.

ABBA P(TACHYA) LERNER
Economist
***Born* Bessarabia, Russia, 1903**
***Died* Tallahassee, Florida, USA, 27 October 1982**

Abba P. Lerner was a theoretical economist whose many publications exerted a wide influence in his field, though he was little known to the public at large. His principal contributions to economic thought were in the areas of welfare economics, theory of inflation and capital, and analysis of socialist economic systems.

Lerner was born to Jewish parents in Bessarabia, also called Russian Moldavia. The family moved to England when he was a child, and he grew up in London's East End, a social cauldron where he got first-hand knowledge of all forms of socialism and Zionism, an intimate appreciation of the effects of poverty and unemployment, and a thorough command of English to add to his knowledge of Yiddish, Hebrew, and Russian. He had to leave school at 16, going to work as a cap maker, and for the next ten years had no fixed career, spending time as a rabbinical student, Hebrew-school teacher, and small businessman. By means of his obvious linguistic and analytical abilities, he managed in 1929 to gain admission to the London School of Economics. After studying under J. R. Hicks, Friedrich August von Hayek, and especially Lionel Robbins, who, Lerner later said, "made me an economist," he obtained his B.Sc. in 1932. His Ph.D. came 11 years later.

Lerner won many of the endowed prizes at the LSE, and from 1932 was publishing well-received articles on international trade theory in such influential journals as *Economica, Review of Economic Studies,* and *Economic Journal.* In 1934–35 he went on a fellowship to Cambridge, where John Maynard Keynes was completing his greatest work, *The General Theory,* parts of which were discussed at seminars and tutorials. Lerner wrote the earliest important article on the theory in 1936, a kind of review, read and approved beforehand by Keynes himself, that managed not only to clarify the essence of the book with admirable terseness, but also to make some original theoretical additions.

After teaching several terms at the LSE, Lerner moved to the United States in 1937. Columbia University offered him the first of his many U.S. teaching posts in 1939–40, after which he went to the University of Kansas (1940–42), the New School for Social Research in New York City (1942–47), Roosevelt University in Chicago (1947–59), Michigan State (1959–65), and finally the University of California at Berkeley, where he was professor from 1965 to 1971 and emeritus professor thereafter. He was distinguished professor of economics at Queens College of the City University of New York from 1971 to 1978, then was a full-time member of the Florida State faculty at Tallahassee until his death at the age of 79. He was frequently a visiting scholar at universities in the United States and abroad, notably at the Hebrew University and Tel Aviv University in Israel.

Lerner became one of the foremost explicators and exponents of Keynes, publishing more than 30 articles by 1944. In that year appeared what many consider his most important work, *The Economics of Control,* a prescriptive analysis of the state's duty to meet human needs and promote human welfare by economically coherent and rational means. He demonstrated the necessity for equal income distribution as the sanest way to full employment, price stability, and the optimum level of "welfare"—defined by Lerner as simply the greatest benefit for the greatest number.

He was considered an authority on the economics of collectivist societies, believing that profit maximization within a competitive corporate structure was the only way for such societies to maintain economic balance. This "market socialism," which has been tried in Hungary and Yugoslavia with great success and in Poland with no success at all, is an idea highly unattractive to doctrinaire communists, although it has always appealed to the more resourceful socialists in Western Europe.

In his work on inflationary theory, which was spurred by the heavy worldwide inflation following World War II, Lerner anticipated as early as 1948 the phenomenon of stagflation, the modern and somewhat un-Keynesian situation under which inflation recurs in a sluggish rather than a booming economy. He also held that stable prices, and hence optimum welfare, were gravely threatened by unrestricted collective bargaining, and that monetary value could only be maintained by means of a policy of income restriction. His other important books were *The Economics of Employment* (1951), *Everybody's Business* (1961), and *Flation* (1972).

Lerner was a distinguished fellow of the American Economic Association and was its vice president in 1963. He was also a fellow of the American Academy of Arts and Sciences and a member of the National Academy of Sciences. A.K.

Parents Morris Isaac L. and Sofie (Buchman) L. **Married** (1) Alice Sendak 1929: Lionel John; Marion Lerner Levine. (2) Dalia Goldfarb 1960. **Religion** Jewish. **Emigration** Brought to U.K. as a child; emigrated to U.S. 1937; naturalized 1949. **Education** Left sch. at age 16; rabbinical student; London Sch. of Economics, B.Sc. 1932, Ph.D. 1943; Cambridge Univ. (Leon Post Grad. Fellowship) 1934–35; Univ. of Manchester 1935. **Career** Cap machinist, Hebrew-sch. instr., and small businessman, London 1919–29; asst. lectr., London Sch. of Economics 1935–37; lectr., Columbia Univ. 1939–40; asst. prof., Univ. of Kansas City, MO 1940–42; assoc. prof. 1942–46 and prof. of economics 1946–47, New Sch. for Social Research, NYC; Hillman Prof. of Economics, Roosevelt Univ., Chicago 1947–59; prof. of economics, Michigan State Univ., East Lansing 1959–65; prof. of economics 1965–71 and prof. emeritus since 1971, Univ. of California, Berkeley; distinguished prof. of economics, Queens Coll., City Univ. of New York 1971–78; prof. of economics, Florida State Univ., Tallahassee since 1978; visiting prof. at Amherst Coll., Univ. of Virginia, Hebrew Univ., Univ. of Hawaii, Univ. of Tel Aviv, Johns Hopkins Univ., Univ. of California at Los Angeles, and Univ. of Rio de Janeiro; Ely Lectr. 1966. • Managing ed., *Review of Economic Studies* 1933–37; consultant to Rand Corp. 1949, Economic Commn. for Europe 1950–51, and Economic Inst. for Mediterranean Affairs 1958–59; advisor to Govt. of Israel 1953–56 and Bank of Israel 1955–56. **Officer** Pres. 1973 and co-founder, Univ. Center for Rational Alternatives, Queens Coll.; v.p. 1963 and distinguished fellow, Amer. Economic Assn. **Fellow** Center for Advanced Study of Behavioral Science 1960–61; Econometric Soc.; Amer. Acad. of Arts and Sciences. **Member** Natl. Acad. of Sciences; Royal Economic Assn. **Honors** Rockefeller Fellowship 1938–39; Natl. Science Foundn. grant 1975–76; Rockefeller residency, Bellagio Study and Conference Center, Italy 1976; hon. degree from Northwestern Univ. **Author** *The Economics of Control,* 1944; (jtly.) *Planning and Paying for Full Employment,* 1946; *The Economics of Employment,* 1951; *Essays in Economic Analysis,* 1953; *Everybody's Business,* 1961; *Flation,* 1972; (jtly.) *Kalkala Yelila* [*Efficient Economics*], 1974; (jtly.) *The Economics of Efficiency and Growth: Lessons* *from Israel and the West Bank,* 1975. **Contributor** of articles to *American Economic Review, Journal of Political Economics, Quarterly Journal of Economics, Review of Economic Studies, Social Research,* others.

Further reading William Breit and Roger L. Ransom, *The Academic Scribblers: American Economists in Collision,* 1971; Irvin Sobel, "Abba Lerner," in *Challenge,* Mar.-Apr. 1980.

J(OYCE) C(LYDE) HALL
Founder of Hallmark Cards, Inc.
***Born* David City, Nebraska, USA, 29 August 1891**
***Died* Kansas City, Missouri, USA, 29 October 1982**

J. C. Hall built Hallmark Cards, Inc., from a tiny postcard-jobbing firm into the largest manufacturer of greeting cards in the United States, with worldwide sales of about $1 billion a year. A conservative man who sought to promote what he saw as the traditional Midwestern virtues—common sense, civic responsibility, and sentimentality—Hall was remarkably successful in creating a similar public image for his company, whose advertising slogan is "When you care enough to send the very best."

Hall grew up in a poor Nebraska family. While he was still in elementary school he began working for a stationer selling perfume and imported postcards door to door. In 1910 he dropped out of high school to open a wholesale postcard-jobbing firm based in Kansas City, Missouri. His older brother joined him the next year and in 1913 they began marketing Christmas cards. When their small plant was destroyed in a fire in 1914, they purchased a Kansas City engraving shop to print their own line of tasteful greeting cards—"the art of the masses," Hall called them—which were an immediate success. World War I gave considerable impetus to the business as people bought cards to send to soldiers overseas. By the mid-1920s, the Hall Brothers Company, with J. C. Hall as president and chairman and his brothers as vice presidents, employed more than 100 workers, and its cards were distributed nationwide.

Courtesy of Hallmark Cards, Inc.

The company entered a period of rapid growth in the 1930s and 40s thanks to Hall's management innovations, which included the first display rack and efficient reorder system for retailers and intensive advertising campaigns on radio and, later, television. The company, known as Hallmark Cards, Inc. since 1954, was the first to use art by Norman Rockwell, Grandma Moses, Walt Disney, and even Winston Churchill on its cards, in addition to illustrations by staff artists of the standard waifs, puppies, kittens, and flowers. A well-tended network of small distributors throughout the country helped make Hallmark a household name.

Hall, who was described as a benevolent patriarch by his employees, controlled every detail of his company's operation, from card designs and color choice to office decor and cafeteria menus, and introduced some unusual employee benefits, including group discussions and in-house income-tax counseling. Not being responsible to stockholders or to a strong board of directors, he was able to gamble with the company's money in ways the executive of a public corporation could not. Beginning in the 1950s he sponsored several radio and television programs, including "Hallmark Hall of Fame," a critically praised but unprofitable drama showcase. In the mid-1950s he authorized the construction of Crown Center, a slum-clearance project to restore the area around Hallmark's headquarters in Kansas City, paid for entirely by the company. The project, originally estimated to cost $115 million, had cost $227 million by 1980 and was expected to cost nearly that much again before completion.

In 1966 Hall handed over the presidency to his son Donald, but stayed on as chairman to oversee the expansion of Hallmark's product lines to include books, candles, jewelry, crystal and pewter figurines, and other gift items. In addition to Crown Center, the company bought considerable local real estate in the 1970s, becoming one of Kansas City's major property owners. Although Hallmark donated a part of its profits to charities and encouraged its employees to do volunteer work by allowing them flexible schedules, its reputation for community responsibility was severely compromised in July 1981 when more than 100 people were killed in the collapse of two concrete walkways in the newly built, Hallmark-owned Hyatt Regency Hotel.

Hall died after a long illness at the age of 91, leaving most of his personal fortune—over $100 million—to charity. C.M.

Parents George Nelson H., lay preacher, and Nancy Dudley (Houston) H. **Married** Elizabeth Dilday 1922 (d. 1976): Elizabeth Ann Reid; Barbara Louise Marshall; Donald Joyce, business exec. **Religion** Christian. **Education** Norfolk High Sch., NB, left 1910; business coll. night classes, Kansas City, MO. **Career** With stationery store, Norfolk ca. 1901–05; co-founder, Norfolk Post Card Brokerage Co. 1907–10; postcard jobber, Kansas City, MO 1910–16; founding pres., Hall Brothers Paper Craft Co., Kansas City 1916–23; founding pres. and chmn., Hall Brothers Co., Kansas City 1916–54; pres. 1954–66 and bd. chmn. since 1954, Hallmark Cards, Inc., Kansas City. **Officer** Member, bd. of dirs.: 1st Natl. Bank of Kansas City; People to People; Eisenhower Foundn.; Midwest Research Inst.; Johnson County Bank; Univ. of Kansas City; Pembroke Country Day Sch.; Helping Hand Inst.; Drake Univ. • Pres., Kansas City Rotary Club; trustee, Kansas City Art Inst.; chmn., Safeway Federal Savings and Loan, Kansas City. **Member** Natl. Assn. of Greeting Card Publishers; Republican Party; Shriners. • Clubs: Kansas City Country, River, and Saddle and Sirloin, Kansas City. **Honors** King's Medal, U.K. 1946; Légion d'Honneur 1949; CBE; DeForest Award, Natl. Assn. for Better Radio and Television 1953; Horatio Alger Award, Amer. Schs. and Colls. Assn. 1957; Mr. Kansas City Award, Kansas City Chamber of Commerce 1961; Trustees' Sponsors Award, Natl. Acad. of Television Arts and Sciences 1961; trustee's citation, Midwest Research Inst. 1972; hon. degrees from univs. of Missouri, Kansas State, and Nebraska. **Author** *When You Care Enough* (autobiography), 1979.

NOVEMBER

KING (WALLIS) VIDOR

Film director

Born **Galveston, Texas, USA, 8 February 1894**

Died **Paso Robles, California, USA, 1 November 1982**

In January 1920, the young King Vidor, just embarking on his career as a director, published an announcement in *Variety*. Grandiosely headed "Creed and Pledge," it began: "I believe in the motion picture that carries a message to humanity"—a statement that reflects, in its candid idealism as in its sententiousness, both the strengths and the defects of Vidor's output. The films he made deal with large themes and vivid emotions, characters in dynamic conflict with nature and society; it was hardly surprising, then, that even his finest pictures were prone to sentimentality and melodrama. Vidor, Andrew Sarris has commented, "created more great moments and fewer great films than any other director of his rank."

King Wallis Vidor was born in Galveston, Texas, the son of a prosperous lumber merchant of Hungarian descent. As a boy, he was sent to Peacock Military Academy in San Antonio, which he hated. His first exposure to the cinema was a showing of Georges Méliès's *A Trip to the Moon;* fascinated, he took a vacation job as a ticket taker and assistant projectionist at Galveston's first motion-picture theater. He was soon inspired to make films of his own, starting with newsreel scenes of a hurricane, and graduating to two-reel comedies and sponsored documentaries. With the proceeds from these, Vidor made the down payment on a Model T Ford, and in 1915 he, his wife Florence Arto, and a friend set out across the desert for Hollywood. The journey was precariously financed by the sale of footage of their travels to the Ford Motor Company.

Courtesy of Culver Pictures

In Hollywood, Florence rapidly found work as a bit player, and soon rose to be a major star. (Her career ended with the coming of the talkies.) For Vidor, success came more slowly. Taking whatever was offered at the studios, he worked as an extra, and as a studio clerk at Universal, while writing scenarios. After directing a number of independent two-reelers, he made his first feature, *The Turn in the Road* (1919). Improbably, since Vidor's scenario was strongly imbued with his own Christian Science beliefs, his backers were a group of local doctors, who had formed the Brentwood Film Corporation. This, and his three subsequent films for Brentwood (featuring a newcomer he had discovered, Zasu Pitts), were successful enough for him to establish his own small studio, Vidor Village.

Releasing through First National, Vidor produced eight modest but increasingly assured movies, often starring his wife, before joining Metro, soon to become MGM, in 1923. Even in these early films, Vidor's charged sense of landscape, especially in its more threatening aspects, is clearly apparent. At MGM, though, he found himself tagged as a reliably competent staff director, assigned to light romantic comedies and society melodramas. After two years, he complained to MGM's boy wonder, Irving Thalberg, that he was tired of making "ephemeral films," and wanted to tackle a big subject. "Such as?"

asked Thalberg. Vidor suggested three—war, wheat, and steel—and Thalberg, with unerring box-office instinct, chose war.

The Big Parade (1925) made Vidor's name. Starting out as the first picture "to show the War from the viewpoint of ordinary soldiers and privates," it was gradually expanded, as Thalberg realized its potential, into a major spectacular, with lavish scenes of troops marching through wooded landscapes. Today, the film can scarcely maintain its former reputation as an antiwar movie—its soft-focus view of war seems distinctly romanticized—but the love scenes between John Gilbert and his French sweetheart are sensitively handled, and Vidor's instinct for pictorial composition is unfailingly effective.

Vidor directed two more John Gilbert vehicles—*La Bohème* (1925), with Lillian Gish, and a swashbuckler, *Bardelys the Magnificent* (1926)—before making the finest of his silent films, *The Crowd* (1928). Starring Vidor's second wife, Eleanor Boardman, and a young unknown, James Murray, the film presents a bleak commentary on the American Dream, much influenced by contemporary German cinema. Impressive in its technical virtuosity and downbeat realism, this account of the decline of a fecklessly optimistic everyman and his disillusioned wife, amid the harsh indifference of the big city, was received with widespread critical enthusiasm, and has increased its reputation ever since.

Now both successful and intellectually respectable, Vidor was chosen by William Randolph Hearst to further the acting career of his mistress, Marion Davies. Despite on-set interference from the great man (Hearst firmly vetoed any attempts to have Miss Davies hit by a custard pie), Vidor turned in some creditable work, making the most of Davies's pleasant but limited talent in three comedies, of which the best was *Show People* (1928), a mild satire on Hollywood.

Hallelujah (1929), Vidor's first sound film, was remarkable both for its impressionistic use of sound and for being the first feature with an all-black cast—a commercially risky venture at that period. Though marred by the patronizingly sentimental view of blacks then current, the film retains considerable emotional impact, especially in the climactic chase through the swamp. Notwithstanding the cumbersome early sound equipment, Vidor's camera work remained notably fluid; even more so in *Street Scene* (1931), the first of several films for Sam Goldwyn, with the camera roaming and craning around the huge urban set.

After some routine assignments for MGM, Vidor cut free from the studio in order to make *Our Daily Bread* (1934), the "wheat" section of his chosen trilogy. Unable to interest Thalberg, or any major studio, in a story of unemployed workers making good on a collective farm, Vidor mortgaged his house and acted as his own producer, co-scripting with his third wife, Elizabeth Hill. Despite some naivety of treatment, the film's vigorous optimism carries it through. As always, the theme of humanity's struggle with natural forces involved Vidor deeply, and the famous final sequence of the cutting of an irrigation channel is exhilarating in the pace of its Soviet-influenced montage.

For the rest of the 1930s, Vidor's films were largely unremarkable, though he received an Academy Award nomination for *The Citadel* (1938), directed in England for MGM. He hit form again with *Northwest Passage* (1940), his first film in color. Shot mainly on location in Idaho, this account of an arduous trek across country by a band of British irregulars, in pre-Revolutionary America, allowed Vidor to indulge to the full his sense of nature as vast, beautiful, and implacably hostile. Spencer Tracy starred, and Vidor also offered him the lead in *An American Romance* (1944), the "steel" film that completed his trilogy. Tracy, however, backed out, and the film suffered badly from weak casting and from drastic and insensitive cutting by MGM, though some powerful industrial sequences survived.

With *Duel in the Sun* (1946), a vast, sprawling and (in every sense) highly colored western, David Selznick made an unashamed bid at repeating the success of his greatest production, *Gone With the Wind.* If he failed, it was no fault of Vidor, who directed *Duel* with (in the words of one critic) "that Wagnerian authenticity of emotional excess which gives his films a genuine mysticism, a Nietzschean pantheism." Equally grandiose was *The Fountainhead* (1949), taken from Ayn Rand's overblown novel, with Gary Cooper uncomfortably cast as the Lloyd Wright-ish architect, constructor of blatantly phallic skyscrapers. For Selznick again, Vidor returned to the swamplands of the South with *Ruby Gentry* (1952); in the title role, Jennifer Jones reprised her *Duel in the Sun* performance as the sultry incarnation of destructive sexuality.

Perhaps inevitably, *War and Peace* (1956) presented a much-diminished rendering of

Tolstoy's mighty novel, although the major set pieces, especially the Battle of Borodino and the retreat from Moscow, were impressively staged. Vidor's last film, the biblical epic *Solomon and Sheba* (1959), was beset by production problems, including the death of its star, Tyrone Power, midway through filming. Vidor was unhappy with Power's replacement, Yul Brynner, whose shallow, one-dimensional performance matched that of his co-star, Gina Lollobrigida. The film's critical and commercial disaster impelled Vidor's retirement from filmmaking.

During the 1960s, Vidor taught a graduate cinema class at the University of California at Los Angeles, and in 1973 published a perceptive and practical book on his craft, *King Vidor on Film Making*. He had earlier written a likeable autobiography, *A Tree Is a Tree* (1953). In 1979 he received an honorary Oscar—his first, though he was five times nominated as best director—for "his incomparable achievements as a cinematic creator and innovator." The later years of his retirement were spent on his California ranch, where he died of heart failure. P.K.

Parents Charles Shelton V., lumber manufacturer, and Kate (Wallis) V. **Married** (1) Florence Arto, actress, 1915 (div. 1924): Suzanne. (2) Eleanor Boardman, actress, 1926 (div. 1931): Antonia; Belinda. (3) Elizabeth Hill, screenwriter, 1932 (div. 1953). **Religion** Christian Scientist. **Education** Galveston High Sch., TX; Peacock Mil. Acad., San Antonio, TX; Jacob Tome Inst., Port Deposit, MD. **Career** Ticket taker and asst. projectionist, movie theater, Galveston; freelance news cinematographer and reporter, Mutual Weekly, Ford Weekly, and Pathé Exchange newsreel cos. ca. 1910–15; actor, then dir., Vitagraph Co. of America, Santa Monica, CA 1915; clerk, then film dir. and screenwriter, Universal Studios 1915–18; cofounding dir., Vidor Village film studio, Hollywood early 1920s; dir., producer, and screenwriter, Metro Studios (later MGM) 1923–40s; dir., United Artists, Paramount, and Warner Brothers studios 1940s–59; grad. instr. in film, Univ. of California at Los Angeles 1960s. **Member** Acad. of Motion Picture Arts and Sciences; Bel Air Country Club; Beverly Hills Town Club. **Honors** Special award, for *Our Daily Bread,* League of Nations 1934; best film award, for *The Citadel,* New York Film Critics 1938; award, Screen Directors Guild 1950; Christopher Award, for *War and Peace,* 1956; special prize for life's work, Edinburgh Film Festival 1964; hon. Academy Award for film achievements 1979. **Director** (also scriptwriter and/or producer in some cases) *The Turn in the Road,* 1919; *Better Times,* 1919; *The Other Half,* 1919; *Poor Relations,* 1919; *The Jack-Knife Man,* 1919; *The Family Honor,* 1920; *Love Never Dies,* 1921; *The Sky Pilot,* 1921; *Woman, Wake Up,* 1922; *The Real Adventure,* 1922; *Dusk to Dawn,* 1922; *Wild Oranges,* 1922; *Conquering the Woman,* 1923; *Alice Adams,* 1923; *Peg o' My Heart,* 1923; *The Woman of Bronze,* 1923; *Three Wise Fools,* 1923; *Happiness,* 1923; *His Hour,* 1924; *Wine of Youth,* 1924; *Wife of the Centaur,* 1924; *Proud Flesh,* 1925; *The Big Parade,* 1925; *La Bohème,* 1925; *Bardelys the Magnificent,* 1926; *The Crowd,* 1928; *Show People,* 1928; *The Patsy,* 1928; *Hallelujah,* 1929; *Not So Dumb,* 1930; *Billy the Kid,* 1930; *Street Scene,* 1931; *The Champ,* 1931; *Cynara,* 1932; *The Stranger's Return,* 1933; *Our Daily Bread,* 1934; *The Wedding Night,* 1935; *So Red the Rose,* 1935; *The Texas Rangers,* 1936; *Stella Dallas,* 1937; *The Citadel,* 1938; *Northwest Passage,* 1940; *Comrade X,* 1940; *H. M. Pulham, Esq.,* 1941; *An American Romance,* 1944; *Duel in the Sun,* 1946; *A Miracle Can Happen* (also rel. as *On Our Merry Way*), 1948; *The Fountainhead,* 1949; *Beyond the Forest,* 1949; *Lightning Strikes Twice,* 1951; *Japanese War Bride,* 1952; *Ruby Gentry,* 1952; *Man Without a Star,* 1955; *War and Peace,* 1956; *Solomon and Sheba,* 1959. **Author** *A Tree Is a Tree* (autobiography), 1953; *King Vidor on Film Making,* 1973.

Further reading John Baxter, *King Vidor,* 1976; Clive Denton, *The Hollywood Professionals,* vol. 5, 1976.

E(DWARD) H(ALLETT) CARR
Historian
***Born* London, England, 28 June 1892**
***Died* Cambridge, England, 3 November 1982**

Before commencing his major occupation, the multivolume *History of Soviet Russia,* at the age of 55, E. H. Carr had gained considerable experience in three quite separate fields. He spent two decades with the British Foreign Office, was Wilson Professor of International Relations at Aberystwyth, and for six of his eleven years in that position he also worked as assistant editor of the *Times* of London. In addition to his *History of Soviet Russia,* which A. J. P. Taylor described as a "monument of erudition and analysis," Carr wrote biographies of Feodor Dostoevsky and Mikhail Bakunin, several volumes of European intellectual history of the nineteenth and twentieth centuries, and a controversial work, *What Is History?,* based on his Trevelyan Lectures.

Perhaps more than any other Western European, Carr recognized the tremendous significance of the Russian Revolution—not so much as the destruction of a system that no longer satisfied the masses, but rather as the commencement of a radical new style in the art of state affairs. His primary interest in Lenin, Trotsky, and other revolutionaries had to do with their roles, not as ideologues or nihilists, but as master builders—the creators of a vast new governmental structure and of a twentieth-century superpower. And since the Soviets' ambitions were so grand, Carr was hardly surprised by their tyranny and failures along the way; indeed, through his *Times* editorials he urged the West not to use the terrible bloodiness of Soviet history as an excuse for cold war. Carr believed that it was highly unrealistic to hope that the League of Nations or other international bodies could somehow impose a morality on the world. But the world would profit, he maintained, by continuing dialogue and hard bargaining between the mighty nations of the East and West.

Edward Hallett Carr was born in 1892 and educated in London at Merchant Taylors' School. He was a Craven Scholar at Trinity College, Cambridge, and after obtaining a double first in Classics in 1916 joined the Foreign Office. His work at the Paris Peace Conference in 1919 earned him a CBE when he was only 28. After working with the Paris Conference of Ambassadors in 1920–21, Carr returned to the Foreign Office in London, and except for a four-year stint as second secretary at the British Legation in Riga, Latvia (1925–29), remained at headquarters. He worked as assistant advisor on League of Nations affairs from 1930 until 1933, when he became a first secretary.

During his period in Latvia, Carr developed an interest in the Russian language and Russian literary scholarship that was reflected in his first book, *Dostoevsky* (1931). Avrahm Yarmolinsky commented in the *New York Times:* "While this life of Dostoevsky has serious limitations it is nevertheless the best book on the man that has been offered to the public in any language." Carr's second work, *The Romantic Exiles* (1933), an illuminating portrayal of the intertwining lives of Mikhail Bakunin, Aleksandr Herzen, and George Herwegh and their wives, was also well re-

ceived. He published in 1934 *Karl Marx: A Study on Fanaticism,* and three years later published *Michael Bakunin,* which remains the standard biography of the nineteenth-century anarchist and archrival of Marx. Edmund Wilson in the *New Republic* complained that while it was the best of Carr's biographies, "it has the faults of his other books—the dependence on clichés, which makes impossible any vividness of evocation; the never intermitting British chill, which is always putting Bakunin in his place."

Carr resigned from the Foreign Office in 1936 to take up his appointment as Wilson Professor of International Politics at the University College of Wales in Aberystwyth. During World War II he returned briefly to government service in the Ministry of Information as director of foreign publicity, and from 1941 to 1946 he was assistant editor of the London *Times.* His realistic view of changes in the balance of world power and of the need to cooperate with the USSR to beat the Nazis and organize the peace upset many of the *Times*'s readers, as did his acceptance of the inevitability of Soviet influence in Eastern Europe. For the home front, Carr stressed the need to reduce unemployment and keenly promoted improvements in the social-welfare system. Many of the measures advocated by Carr and by *Times* editor Robert Barrington-Ward were adopted by the postwar Labour government. Carr left the *Times* in 1946, but continued for some years to write for the *Times Literary Supplement.*

While at Aberystwyth, he wrote a number of texts, including *International Relations Since the Peace Treaties* (1937), covering the years 1919 to 1936, and *Britain: A Study of Foreign Policy from Versailles to the Outbreak of War* (1939). These and Carr's other works on political and diplomatic history of the period were generally well received as careful and sound analyses, particularly *Conditions of Peace* (1942) and *The Soviet Impact on the Western World* (1946). The *History of Soviet Russia* was begun in 1947, when Carr relinquished his Wilson Professorship. Part I minutely records the events of the Bolshevik revolution from 1917 to 1923; Part II of the work covers the period 1923 to 1924; Part III examines the years 1924 to 1926 and documents Stalin's rise to power and the beginnings of a planned economy and of the development of Soviet foreign policy. Part IV, *Foundations of a Planned Economy, 1926–1929,* which Carr wrote with R. W. Davies, was completed in 1978. To a large extent, the critical reception of the entire ten-volume work was impressive, and Carr's fluent, forthright style appealed to almost all reviewers. But some expressed regret that the volumes adhered too closely to official sources and virtually ignored all other Western scholarship on the subject.

During the writing of *History of the Soviet Union,* Carr found time for some teaching and tutored in politics at Balliol College, Oxford, from 1953 to 1955, at which time he became a fellow of Trinity College, Cambridge. He also wrote a number of other books while *History* was in progress. His *Studies in Revolution* (1950) was a collection of essays, most of which had appeared in the *Times Literary Supplement.* In a scathing review, A. J. P. Taylor wrote in the *Manchester Guardian:* "His new collection . . . demonstrates afresh the advantages and disadvantages of Mr. Carr's philosophic approach. . . . To write about evil with detachment is to be on the side of evil. Hence Mr. Carr, with his cool reason, arrived before the war at conclusions favourable to Hitler; and now arrives at conclusions favourable to Stalin." Another *Guardian* reviewer, Geoffrey Barraclough, was almost as critical in his review of Carr's *What Is History?* (1961): "The pessimism which afflicts historians today is not all due (as Mr. Carr too lightly suggests) to the fact that they belong to a declining middle class in a declining society. . . . Mr. Carr is perilously near to the doctrine that history exists to fulfil a social need. If so, he is confusing history and myth." But David Caute, writing in the *Spectator,* called it "a remarkable book, a classic, and quite free from jargon. Mr. Carr is a radical: his concept of progress comprises a devastating assault on heavily defended academic bastions."

Some of Carr's fellow historians believed that he was a little too dry and detached in his analysis of international relations, and rather more interested in documents than in people. But his colleagues also recognized his deep concern for peace and social advancement, and acknowledged his massive and important contribution to historical scholarship. He died after a long illness at the age of 90. R.T.

Married Anne Ward Howe 1925: one son. **Education** Merchant Taylors' Sch., London; Trinity Coll., Cambridge (Craven Scholarship), double 1st Class in Classics 1916. **Ca-**

reer With Foreign Office: temporary clerk, London 1916; with British delegation, Peace Conference, Paris 1919; temporary secty., Conference of Ambassadors, British Embassy, Paris 1920–21; 3rd secty., Paris 1922; 3rd secty., London 1922–25; 2nd secty., British Legation, Riga, Latvia 1925–29; staff member, London 1929–30; asst. advisor on League of Nations affairs 1930–33; 1st secty. 1933–36. • Historian and biographer since 1930s; Wilson Prof. of Intl. Politics, University Coll. of Wales, Aberystwyth 1936–47; dir. of foreign publicity, Ministry of Information 1939–40; asst. ed., *Times,* London 1941–46; tutor in politics, Balliol Coll., Oxford 1953–55. **Fellow** Trinity Coll., Cambridge since 1955; FBA 1956. **Member** Oxford Club; Cambridge Club. **Honors** CBE 1920; hon. fellow, Balliol Coll., Oxford; hon. degrees from univs. of Manchester, Cambridge, Sussex, and Gröningen. **Author** *Dostoevsky 1821–1881: A New Biography,* 1931; *The Romantic Exiles: A Nineteenth-Century Portrait Gallery,* 1933; *Karl Marx: A Study in Fanaticism,* 1934; *International Relations Since the Peace Treaties,* 1937, rev. as *International Relations Between the Two World Wars, 1919–1939,* 1947; *Michael Bakunin,* 1937, rev. ed. 1975; *Britain: A Study of Foreign Policy from the Versailles Treaty to the Outbreak of War,* 1939; *Propaganda in International Politics,* 1939; *The Twenty Years' Crisis, 1919–1939: An Introduction to the Study of International Relations,* 1939, rev. ed. 1946; *The Future of Nations: Independence or Interdependence?,* 1941; *Conditions of Peace,* 1942; *Nationalism and After,* 1945; *The Soviet Impact on the Western World,* 1946; *The Moral Foundations of World Order,* 1948; *Studies in Revolution,* 1950; *The New Society,* 1951, rev. ed. 1957; *German-Soviet Relations Between the Two World Wars, 1919–1939,* 1951; *What Is History?,* 1961; *1917: Before and After* (in U.S. as *The October Revolution: Before and After*), 1969; *The Russian Revolution: From Lenin to Stalin,* 1979; *From Napoleon to Stalin,* 1980. • *A History of Soviet Russia:* Part I, *The Bolshevik Revolution, 1917–1923,* 3 vols., 1950–53; Part II, *The Interregnum, 1923–1924,* 1954; Part III, *Socialism in One Country, 1924–1926,* 3 vols., 1958–64; (jtly.) Part IV, *Foundations of a Planned Economy, 1926–1929,* 3 vols., 1969–78. **Contributor** of articles on current history and politics to newspapers and jrnls.

Further reading C. Abramsky and Beryl J. Williams, eds., *Essays in Honor of E. H. Carr,* 1972.

JACQUES TATI

Comedian and film director

***Born* Le Pecq, near Paris, France, 9 October 1908**

***Died* Paris, France, 5 November 1982**

Each of the great film comedians created a persona—an immediately recognizable screen personality, with stylized dress and mannerisms—that recurs almost unaltered from film to film. Chaplin became the baggy-trousered, resilient tramp; Harold Lloyd was horn-rimmed, studentish, zanily optimistic; Harry Langdon acted the overgrown baby; Keaton was dignified, deadpan, resourceful in adversity. And Jacques Tati was Monsieur Hulot.

Hulot is tall and gangling, in a long, shabby raincoat and a nondescript hat. His pipe sticks out one way, his meticulously rolled umbrella another. His loping walk is unique: high on the toes, leaning forward at an improbable angle, he seems about to topple over, or perhaps take off. There is no malice in Hulot; unfailingly courteous and helpful, he creates chaos around him with sublime unconsciousness. Adults, especially officials, view him with alarmed mistrust, but children and dogs like him. He has a wistful eye for pretty young women, though far too polite and diffident to do anything about it. His relationship with machinery is complex and disastrous; he prods at a gadget with bemused curiosity, upon which it generally goes berserk, or breaks.

Jacques Tati was born Jacques Tatischeff at Le Pecq, on the outskirts of Paris, where his paternal grandfather, a Russian count, had

Courtesy of French Embassy

served as a diplomat. Intended to join the family picture-restoration business, Tati was sent to a college of art and engineering, and was then apprenticed to a firm in England, where the son of the family imparted a taste for rugby football. Back in France, he played rugby professionally for a season before his growing skills as a mime led him, in 1931, to choose the music halls as a career. His father was scandalized. "I would be cut off without a *sou,* he said, if I wanted to do such a thing. Well, I am without the *sou* still and I am perfectly happy."

Tati soon achieved success with an act in which he mimed the prominent sporting figures of the day. Colette was among those who admired him. "He is both the football and the goalkeeper, the boxer and his opponent, the bicycle and its rider," she wrote. "He makes you see invisible partners, and objects in his empty hands." Several of his routines were preserved in the short films he made, to his own scripts, during the 1930s: *Oscar, champion de tennis* (1931); *On demande une brute* (1934); *Gai dimanche* (1935); *Soigne ton gauche* (1936), the first film directed by René Clément; and *Retour à la terre* (1938). In 1944, he married Micheline Winter—a happy marriage, which lasted until his death.

After acting roles in two films by Claude Autant-Lara—*Sylvie et le fantôme* (1946), as the ghost, and *Le diable au corps* (1947)—Tati directed another short, *L'école des facteurs* (1947), in which he played a postman. This proved so successful that his producer persuaded him to expand it into a full-length feature, *Jour de fête* (1949; *The Big Day*). The film is set in a lovingly observed French village, on the day of its annual fair; the arrival and departure of the fairground horses frame the action. There is little plot, as such; the humor derives from the disruption caused to the quiet life of the village by the arrival of the traveling fairground folk, and in particular from its effect on François, the village postman. At the fair's mobile cinema, a documentary is shown on the high-speed methods of the U.S. Post Office. Spurred into action, François leaps on his ancient bicycle and hurtles feverishly off on his rounds, at one point using the tailboard of a passing truck to sort his mail.

Already, the characteristic elements of Tati's cinematic style are in evidence. Almost all the action is filmed in medium or long shot; Tati disliked close-ups, finding them unnatural and unsubtle. "It is up to the spectator to discover what there is to see." Dialogue is unimportant, and often indeed unintelligible, but the soundtrack plays a vital role, as in the famous sequence where François is tormented by an invisible, but highly audible, wasp. The humor is gentle, unforced, even at times unobtrusive, and largely visual. As François, Tati acts with his whole expressive body, placing little reliance on facial expression.

Jour de fête was a critical and commercial success, and won an award for best script at the Venice Film Festival. However, Tati, resisting suggestions for a sequel (*François se marie,* or the like), took four years before directing his next film. The delay stemmed partly from difficulty in finding financial backing, but mainly from the unhurried, painstaking care with which Tati invariably worked. "I'm not a baker," he once remarked. "I can't manufacture films like bread rolls."

Les vacances de M. Hulot (1953; *Mr. Hulot's Holiday*) marked the first appearance of Tati's alter ego, and proved his masterpiece. Hulot, in his decrepit car, arrives at a family hotel in a small, sleepy seaside resort in Brittany, where his benign, pipe-smoking presence succeeds in disrupting both the staff and the other holiday makers. Once again, the humor is predominantly visual—Hulot himself uses only one word: "Hulot"—and aural; words carry little meaning in themselves, but are used merely as contributory noises on the carefully composed soundtrack. The film consists largely of a series of endlessly inventive comic episodes, derived from close, ironic observation of human idiosyncracies. Perhaps the most famous are the tennis match, in which Hulot's eccentric service devastates all his opponents, and a funeral at which a spare inner tube inadvertently becomes a wreath. Tati chose this last sequence to illustrate the difference between his work and that of Chaplin. "Hulot just wanted to take out his car tyre, and without his doing anything about it, the leaves stick to it and make a wreath. If this had happened to Chaplin he would have deliberately put the leaves on the tyre, and presented it, twirling his cane, in order to leave the cemetery decently. Hulot does not get out, he stays until the end, shaking hands with everybody."

With *Vacances,* Tati achieved international recognition, winning awards in New York and Cannes. Again he ignored proposals for facile sequels, preferring to work in his own meticulous, independent fashion on his own project. *Mon oncle* (1958; *My Uncle*), his first film in color, contrasted two worlds: that of Hulot, living in a cheerful, ramshackle Parisian *quartier,* and that of his sister and brother-in-law, the Arpels, in their sterile, ultramodern, mechanized home. The humor stems largely from the havoc caused by the malfunctioning, unwittingly set off by the gentle, shambling Hulot, of various gadgets in the Arpel house and in M. Arpel's equally soulless factory. Much of the film is hilarious, but some critics detected an ominously didactic note creeping into the comedy. *Mon oncle* won an Oscar as best foreign film of the year.

Tati himself was a kindly man, of great personal charm, with an aristocratic incomprehension of financial matters. Hitherto, despite his perfectionist approach, his films had been made on small budgets, and showed handsome profits. Now, however, turning down several offers from Hollywood, Tati embarked on a massive new project that would eventually cost over $3 million. *Playtime* (1967) took three years to film, and involved the construction, on the outskirts of Paris, of a lavish, futuristic set covering six acres (inevitably dubbed "Tativille"). The film, in which Hulot took a more peripheral role, satirized packaged tourism, the sterile uniformity of modern buildings, and the monstrous impersonality of bureaucracy; it culminated in a superbly orchestrated, hour-long sequence in which a pretentious new restaurant gradually self-destructs. But for all the complexity and ingenuity, the film's satiric intent worked to the detriment of its humor, and much of *Playtime* seemed cold and remote. The picture was poorly received, and achieved only limited distribution.

Now deeply in debt, Tati had extreme difficulty in raising finance for his next film, *Trafic* (1971; *Traffic*), in which Hulot is commissioned to drive a newly devised camping vehicle from Paris to a show in Amsterdam. The satire, directed against self-defeating motormania, had acquired a lighter touch, and several episodes—notably an elegantly choreographed multiple pileup—worked well; but the overall effect, especially beside Tati's earlier work, was thin. *Trafic* failed to make enough to recoup Tati's debts, and the bank thereupon impounded all his previous films.

Deprived of revenue, Tati was now unable to make films, and directed only one further work. "Parade" (1974), a slight but charming circus picture, was made for Swedish television, and allowed Tati to reprise several of his old music-hall numbers. In 1977 his debts were paid off by a Paris distributor, and his films were re-released. At the time of his death, of a pulmonary embolism, he was working on a new film. It was to have been called *Confusion.* P.K.

Born Jacques Tatischeff. **Father** a picture restorer. **Married** Micheline Winter 1944: Sophie, b. 1947; Pierre, b. 1949. **Education** Lycée St.-Germain; art training, trade sch., Paris ca. 1924–25; apprenticed to picture framer, England. **Mil. service** 16th Dragoons, St. Germain; French Army, WWII. **Career** Rugby player, Racing Club team 1920s; stage and circus performer since 1930s; filmmaker and actor since 1931; co-dir., Gêrant De Cady-Films 1933–38. **Honors** Linder Award for best comic short subject, for *L'école des facteurs,* 1949; prize for best screenplay, Venice Film Festival 1949, and Grand Prix du Cinéma, France 1950, for *Jour de fête.* • For *Les vacances de M. Hulot:* Intl. Critics Prize, Cannes Film Festival 1953; Delluc Prize 1953; Prix Femina 1953; Algerian Film Critics Prize 1953; New York Film Critics Award 1954; 2nd prize for best foreign film, Swedish Film Critics Assn. 1954; best film, Cuba 1956; Golden Laurel Award, Edinburgh Film Festival 1958. • For *Mon oncle:* Jury Grand Prize, Cannes Film Festival 1958; prize, Commn. Supérieure

Technique du Cinéma 1958; gold medal, Federazione Italiana del Circolo del Cinema 1958; diploma of honor, Resena Mundiál de los Festivales Cinematográficos, Mexico 1958; Méliès Prize, French Cinema Critics Assn. 1958; best foreign film, New York Film Critics 1958; best French film, Assn. de la Presse Cinématographique Suisse 1958; Academy Award for best foreign film 1958; San Jorge Prize, Film Critics of Barcelona 1958; special jury award, Czechoslovakian Workers' Festival 1958; two gold and two silver plaques, French Film Festival, Rio de Janeiro 1958; Kunniakirja Award, Finland 1958; best foreign film, Spain 1958; special jury prize, Mar del Plata Festival 1959; best film, best score, and best cinematography, Assn. of Brazilian Film Critics 1959. • For *Playtime:* Scandinavian Oscar 1968; grand prize, Acad. du Cinéma, France 1968; silver medal, Moscow Festival 1969; grand prize, Inter-Clubs 1969; best film, Austria 1969; Kunniakirja Award, Finland 1969. • For *Trafic:* European Natl. Prize, Italy 1972; outstanding film, London Festival 1972; Kunniakirja Award, Finland 1972; Valdotaine Gold Cup 1973. • Grand prize for life's work, Maison Intl. du Cinéma 1969. **Films** (director, actor, and writer, unless otherwise noted) *Oscar, champion de tennis,* 1931; (actor and co-screenwriter) *On demande une brute,* 1934; *Gai dimanche,* 1935; (actor and screenwriter) *Soigne ton gauche,* 1936; *Retour à la terre,* 1938; *L'école des facteurs,* 1947; (actor) *Sylvie et le fantôme,* 1946; (actor) *Le diable au corps,* 1947; *Jour de fête* (rel. as *The Big Day*), 1949; *Les vacances de M. Hulot* (rel. as *Mr. Hulot's Holiday*), 1953; *Mon oncle* (rel. as *My Uncle*), 1958; *Playtime,* 1967; *Trafic* (rel. as *Traffic*), 1971; *Confusion* (unfinished). **Television director** "Parade" (documentary), 1974.

Further reading Penelope Gilliatt, *Jacques Tati,* 1976; Stuart Byron and Elizabeth Weis, eds., *The National Society of Film Critics on Movie Comedy,* 1977; Brent Maddock, *The Films of Jacques Tati,* 1977; Gerald Mast, *The Comic Mind,* 1979.

FRANK (ARTHUR) SWINNERTON
Novelist, critic, and journalist
Born **Wood Green, Middlesex, England, 12 August 1884**
Died **Cranleigh, Surrey, England, 6 November 1982**

Frank Swinnerton, who published his first novel in 1909, was a survivor of the Georgian age of English writing. He had numbered Arnold Bennett, H. G. Wells, and A. A. Milne among his friends, and as a manuscript reader at the firm of Chatto & Windus had recommended Lytton Strachey's *Eminent Victorians* for publication. But despite his age he remained a prolific creator of fiction into the 1970s, and could look back on a career that spanned more than 70 years, having begun before that of D. H. Lawrence. His first popular success, *Nocturne* (1917), was his seventh novel: by the time of his death he had published more than 40 works of fiction, 20 critical studies, and an autobiography.

His output, although large, was not varied, and there is no reason to revise the judgment of H. G. Wells, made more than 60 years ago, that Swinnerton "sees life and renders it with a steadiness and detachment and patience . . . . He has no underlying motive. . . . He does not want you or anyone to do anything." Swinnerton was a realist who resolutely avoided taking up any position in relation to his subjects and who offered, in the words of his obituary in the *Times* of London, "precise and truthful testimony to what people were like, and what went on in their hearts and minds during the first quarter of this century." Swinnerton himself predicted, with a modest air that was characteristic of him, that after a hundred years had passed he would have "sunk without trace from every record of the Georgian era." If this does indeed happen it will be because Swinnerton avoided seeing, or perhaps did not see, any significance in the actions and thoughts of his characters beyond the contingency of everyday life. In a statement that he contributed to *Contemporary*

Novelists (1976) he described his "two fundamental assumptions" as "character is Fate" and "in life there are neither rewards nor punishments; there are consequences."

It is precisely this quality, John Lucas argues in *Contemporary Novelists,* that marks Swinnerton as a Georgian writer. A "true disciple of Meredith and true contemporary of Forster," he "enjoys that sense of eager . . . secularism that is so marked a feature of the novelists of the opening decades of the 20th century." In Forster, the major writer of the period, this secularism is sometimes abandoned in favor of whimsies about pagan myth, or, in his major works, such as *Howard's End* or *Passage to India,* becomes the basis of a humanitarian morality that vies with religion. Swinnerton, by contrast, not only "believes in the holiness of carnal love," as John Lucas writes, but is content to seek no further than this for his fictional inspiration. What Wells characterized as "steadiness and detachment and patience," Lucas describes as an "unemphatic liberal moral position."

Swinnerton, the son of an English father and a Scottish mother, had a childhood that, although unsettled and marred by serious illness, he remembered as happy. At the age of 14, hoping to become a journalist, he joined the newspaper firm of Hay, Nisbet & Company as an office boy, but left after two years to work at the publishing company of J. M. Dent. By 1907, when he became a proofreader at Chatto & Windus, he had begun to write, and his fourth novel, *The Merry Heart,* was accepted in 1909 by his employer. It was not a popular success, but it won him esteem at Chatto & Windus, where he was promoted from proofreader to literary advisor, or editor, a position he retained for 17 years while continuing to write in his spare time. It was his seventh novel, *Nocturne* (1917), that made him famous, but his other early works were praised by the London *Times* for their "great charm and skill." By 1926, when he resigned from Chatto & Windus to devote himself to his own writing, Swinnerton had built up an extensive acquaintance in London publishing circles that was to stand him in good stead in his later critical writing, especially *The Georgian Scene* (1934), whose major protagonists, Wells, Bennett, Galsworthy, and Forster, were all his friends. His move in the late 1920s to the quiet Surrey village of Cranleigh, where he bought a sixteenth-century cottage, was made in order to avoid literary cliques, but he nonetheless continued to be an active reviewer for the *Observer* and *John O'London's Weekly.* From 1962 to 1966 he was president of the Royal Literary Fund, an important source of support for young authors.

Courtesy of Mark Gerson

Despite the aftereffects of childhood illness, Swinnerton became a robust, portly man whose kindly manner, fondness for conversation and cats, and tendency to reminisce were elements of a genteel air of literary eccentricity. He is said to have celebrated the completion of each of his books by eating a hot plum pudding, no matter what the season. His acknowledgment of laziness notwithstanding, he was devoted to his craft, sustaining an active writing schedule into his ninety-fifth year. In his later years, however, his very fidelity to his work seems to have isolated him from the events of his time and made him into a literary survivor rather than a contemporary novelist.

H.B.

Parents Charles S. and Rose (Cottam) S. **Married** (1) . . . 1919: one daughter. (2) Mary Dorothy Bennett 1924 (d.): Olivia. **Education** Grammar sch., left at age 14. **Career** Office boy, Hay, Nisbet & Co. newspaper firm, London 1899–1900; reception clerk, then confidential clerk to Hugh Dent, J. M. Dent &

Co., publishers, London 1902–07; proofreader 1907–09 and ed. 1909–26, Chatto & Windus Ltd. publishers, London; novelist and short-story writer since 1909; critic since early 1910s; drama critic, *Truth* and *Nation,* London 1919–21; literary critic, *Evening News,* London 1929–32; novel critic, *Observer,* London 1937–43; critic and columnist, *John O'London's Weekly,* London 1949–54. **Officer** Pres., Royal Literary Fund 1962–66. **Honors** Hon. life member, Reform Club. **Novels** *The Merry Heart: A Gentle Melodrama,* 1909; *The Young Idea: A Comedy of Environment,* 1910; *The Casement: A Diversion,* 1911; *The Happy Family,* 1912; *On the Staircase,* 1914; *The Chaste Wife,* 1916; *Nocturne,* 1917; *Shops and Houses,* 1918; *September,* 1919; *Coquette,* 1921; *The Three Lovers,* 1922; *Young Felix,* 1923; *The Elder Sister,* 1925; *Summer Storm,* 1926; *A Brood of Ducklings,* 1928; *Sketch of a Sinner,* 1929; *The Georgian House: A Tale in Four Parts,* 1932; *Elizabeth,* 1934; *Harvest Comedy,* 1937; *The Two Wives,* 1940; *The Fortunate Lady,* 1941; *Thankless Child,* 1942; *A Woman in Sunshine,* 1944; *English Maiden: Parable of a Happy Life,* 1946; *Faithful Company: A Winter's Tale,* 1948; *The Doctor's Wife Comes to Stay,* 1949; *A Flower for Catherine,* 1950; *Master Jim Probity* (in U.S. as *An Affair of Love*), 1952; *A Month in Gordon Square,* 1953; *The Sumner Intrigue,* 1955; *The Woman from Sicily,* 1957; *A Tigress in Prothero* (in U.S. as *A Tigress in the Village*), 1959; *The Grace Divorce,* 1960; *Death of a Highbrow,* 1961; *Quadrille,* 1965; *Sanctuary,* 1966; *The Bright Lights,* 1968; *On the Shady Side,* 1970; *Nor All Thy Tears,* 1972; *Rosalind Passes,* 1973; *Some Achieve Greatness,* 1976. **Criticism and reminiscences** *George Gissing: A Critical Study,* 1912; *Robert Louis Stevenson: A Critical Study,* 1914; *Women,* 1918; *Tokefield Papers,* 1927, rev. as *Tokefield Papers, Old and New,* 1949; *A London Bookman,* 1928; *Authors and the Book Trade,* 1932; *The Georgian Scene: A Literary Panorama* (in U.K. as *The Georgian Literary Scene 1910–1935*), 1934, rev. eds. 1938, 1950, 1969; *Swinnerton: An Autobiography,* 1936; *The Reviewing and Criticism of Books,* 1939; *The Cats and Rosemary* (juvenile), 1948; *Arnold Bennett,* 1950, rev. ed. 1961; *The Bookman's London,* 1951, rev. ed. 1969; *Londoner's Post: Letters to Gog and Magog,* 1952; *Authors I Never Met,* 1956; *The Adventures of a Manuscript, Being the Story of "The Rugged Trousered Philanthropists,"* 1956; *Background with Chorus: A Footnote to Changes in English Literary Fashion Between 1901 and 1917,* 1956; *Figures in the Foreground: Literary Reminiscences 1917–1940,* 1963; *A Galaxy of Fathers,* 1966; *Reflections from a Village,* 1969; *Arnold Bennett: A Last Word,* 1978. **Editor** *An Anthology of Modern Fiction,* 1937; Arnold Bennett, *Literary Taste,* 1937; William Hazlitt, *Conversations of James Northcote,* 1949; *The Journals of Arnold Bennett,* 1954. **Manuscript collection** at Univ. of Arkansas, Fayetteville.

LEONID (ILYICH) BREZHNEV
Soviet head of state and Communist Party leader
***Born* Kamenskoje, Ukraine, Russia, 19 December 1906**
***Died* Moscow, USSR, 10 November 1982**

As chairman of the Presidium of the Supreme Soviet of the USSR from June 1977 and general secretary of the Soviet Communist Party from March 1966, Leonid Brezhnev was unquestionably the most powerful man in the world. He was only the fourth paramount leader in Soviet history, after V. I. Lenin, Joseph Stalin, and Nikita Khrushchev, and he came to preside, stolidly and with everflagging energy, over a regime of thorough political, economic, and ideological inertia. Although the country over the past generation has experienced a welcome period of relative internal stability, as well as a greatly increased military power, the enormous dead weight of the state bureaucracy, the increasing failure of the system to meet the basic material needs of the people, the rampant corruption at all levels of the party and government, and above all the absolute resistance of the regime to any change and reform have become far more salient parts of Brezhnev's domestic political legacy. In foreign affairs, he came to see his pet policy of détente, which he had taken much time and care to enunciate, largely rejected in the West, where the leadership saw only aggression and deceit behind the Soviet treatment of Czechoslovakia, Afghanistan, and Poland. He was sometimes perceived as a master apparatchik, a man who, for all the delight he took in flattery and honors, actually led the Politburo, for the first time in Soviet history, by consensus rather than by bullying force.

He was born in the Ukrainian industrial city of Dneprodzerzhinsk, which was called Kamenskoje until 1936. His parents were Great Russians; his father, a native of Kursk province, was a steelworker. His first job after primary education was as a manual laborer in Kamenskoje Zavod, the same steel mill his father worked in, but he did not remain long in factory work. In 1923 he moved to Kursk, where he began to study agriculture and first joined the Komsomol, the Communist youth organization. He entered the Kursk Technicum for Land Organization and Reclamation, graduating as a surveyor in 1927, but pursued that profession for only a year, in the Kursk area and in Byelorussia, before being sent to the Urals for three years of work as a land-use specialist. There he eventually became, successively, director of the district land department, deputy chairman of the Bisert district soviet executive committee, and deputy chief of the Urals regional land administration. Soviet land policy in the late 1920s was particularly brutal and exploitative: under Stalin's system of forced agricultural collectivization, all private land, arable or not, had to be taken away from the kulaks, or landed peasants, and added to the local collectives. The kulaks who refused—there were millions of them—were simply eliminated. Brezhnev was undoubtedly good at this work, earning particular commendation from his superiors for excellence in administration and organization. In 1930–31, as a reward and further advancement, he was allowed to attend the Timiryazev Academy in Moscow, an elite agricultural institution. In 1931 he was also accepted as a full member of the Communist Party.

Another career change ensued, perhaps connected to his success in the party. He returned to Dneprodzerzhinsk, his hometown, to work as a fitter and stoker at the steel mill, now renamed the Feliks E. Dzerzhinsky Metallurgical Factory after the founder of the Cheka, the forerunner of the KGB. At the same time, from 1931 to 1935, he studied at the local metallurgical institute. He was elected chairman of the factory's trade-union committee and secretary of the institute's party cell. He graduated in 1935 with a degree in metallurgical engineering.

From November 1935, Brezhnev spent a year in military service, primarily in the Trans-Baikal military district, where he was political commissar in a tank company. His political activities grew in importance upon his return to Dneprodzerzhinsk in 1936. After serving for several months as director of the metallurgical institute, he became in 1937 deputy chairman of the city soviet, then in May 1938 was named to head a department of the party regional committee in Dnepropetrovsk, the chief city of the area. He remained in this committee until the Nazi invasion of 1941, becoming secretary for propaganda in early 1939, secretary for agriculture in late 1940, and, on the eve of the war, secretary for the defense industry, responsible for conversion of factories to military production. Stalin's Great Purge passed him by, either because of his evident value as a loyal apparatchik or because of the protection of Khrushchev, party first secretary in the Ukraine from 1938 to 1949 and the man primarily responsible for carrying out the purge in the vast province.

Brezhnev served as commissar during World War II, first on the Southern Front as deputy chief of the political directorate, then as chief commissar with the 18th Army and on the 4th Ukrainian Front. Entering the war as a colonel, he was promoted to major general in 1943. Although political officers generally avoided close combat, Brezhnev is described in his official biography as having been involved in the hard fighting to establish the Black Sea beachhead at Novorossijsk. He also participated in planning the Red Army's move into Czechoslovakia and at the end of the war, before leaving the military in 1946, he was commander of the Carpathian military district. The career military officers Brezhnev came to know during the war formed an important sector of his support during his years in power.

The exact nature of Brezhnev's connection with Khrushchev from the time of the purges has been the subject of intense speculation among Soviet specialists since the 1950s, but no solid evidence survives. Their careers, however, became increasingly closely connected after the end of the war. Brezhnev returned to the Ukraine to be first secretary of the Zaporozhye regional party committee, where he directed the rapid reindustrialization of the devastated area. In November 1947 he returned again to his home region, becoming first secretary in Dnepropetrovsk and a member of the Central Committee of the Ukrainian Communist Party. He held this post until mid-1950, when he was called to Moscow for a few months of indoctrination, then sent to be party first secretary in the Moldavian SSR, formerly the Rumanian province of Moldavia, southwest of the Ukraine, which had been annexed by the Soviet Union after the war as one of 16 quasi-autonomous republics. His task in Kishinev was to introduce agricultural collectivization everywhere and simultaneously to entrench party control throughout the formerly Nazi-occupied area. Party membership greatly increased as he swiftly accomplished the sovietization of the republic.

Brezhnev stayed in Moldavia for two years, then returned to Moscow and was for the first time appointed to the central (national) leadership of the party. At the 19th Party Congress in October 1952, five months before Stalin's death, he was elected a member of the Central Committee, one of its ten deputy secretaries, and a candidate member of the newly enlarged Politburo, the highest party body. He was dropped from the Politburo and the Secretariat immediately following Stalin's death, probably because he was not a close associate of Georgi Malenkov and Vyacheslav Molotov, the most powerful of the dictator's immediate successors. Until February 1954 he was chief commissar of the Soviet Navy, having been granted an honorary promotion to lieutenant general, then was sent as party second secretary to Kazakhstan, a republic in Soviet Central Asia. He succeeded to the first secretaryship in August 1955 and held this post until February 1956, when at the 20th Party Congress he was restored to his positions as candidate member of the Politburo and secretary of the Central Committee. While in Kazakhstan he was charged with the local administration of Khrushchev's Virgin Lands agricultural development program, a scheme under which enormous tracts of steppe on both sides of the Urals—87 million acres by one estimate—were brought under cultivation for the first time. Though ultimately a disaster both for Khrushchev and for Soviet agriculture, the plan worked well at first and Brezhnev received part of the credit for the relatively successful harvests of 1955 and 1956.

Brezhnev supported his mentor Khrushchev in the struggle against the so-called antiparty group, which culminated in the downfall of Malenkov, Molotov, and their allies in June 1957 and in the elevation of Brezhnev the following month to full membership in the Presidium (Khrushchev's new name for the Politburo). In 1958 he received the added duties of deputy chairman of the Central Committee's office overseeing party affairs within the Russian Federation (RSFSR). He attended to his assignments carefully, but was nearly invisible—distinctly a second-level functionary—to Kremlin watchers both in and out of the Soviet Union. This situation changed abruptly in May 1960, when he was chosen to succeed Marshal Kliment Voroshilov as chairman of the Presidium of the Supreme Soviet—the prestigious and ceremonial but nearly powerless office of head of state. He was forced to give up his secretaryship on the Central Committee—a position of real power—but managed, as so often in his career, to turn an apparent reversal into a strategic success. He came to be mentioned for the first time as a possible successor to Khrushchev, and he was able to travel widely, cementing domestic ties and cultivating international ones. He was reelected chairman of the Presidium in April 1962 and reappointed as secretary of the Central Committee in June 1963. On 15 July 1964, Brezhnev was succeeded as Presidium chairman by Anastas Mikoyan.

By this time Khrushchev was in serious trouble with his colleagues, who laid the blame for the disasters in agricultural planning and for the bungled Cuban missile crisis squarely on him. He was furthermore accused of indulging in the same glorification of his own person and position that he had so stridently condemned in Stalin. This flagrant violation of the principle of collegial leadership—always a cherished article of faith within the Soviet hierarchy—would be tolerated no longer. It is not known to what extent Brezhnev participated in (or even instigated) the Kremlin discussions that led to Khrushchev's ouster on 14 October 1964. Widespread speculation since has identified the key figure behind the plot as Mikhail Suslov, the party's chief ideologist, who chose Brezhnev to take the first secretaryship because he seemed the least likely to usurp his colleagues' prerogatives and power. Khrushchev's other post, that of chairman of the Council of Ministers, or prime minister, was given to Aleksei Kosygin. The new leadership, including Nikolai Podgorny as chairman of the Presidium, appeared together for the first time on 18 October atop the Lenin Mausoleum, during a celebration for the return of three cosmonauts. In his address for the occasion, Brezhnev promised improvement in the economy and the standard of living, and pledged continued efforts at peaceful coexistence with the West.

Subtle changes in style and substance were perceptible in the Brezhnev-Kosygin regime almost from the very beginning. Wages were raised, restrictions on private farming were eased, and there was for a time a marked increase in the availability of consumer goods. With his background in land-use analysis, Brezhnev claimed the same overlordship of agricultural policy that Khrushchev had exercised, and in his first major statement on the matter, before a plenary session of the Central Committee in March 1965, he reversed several of his predecessor's policies. During his next 18 years in power, Soviet agricultural production officially increased by 50 percent, yet the country receded ever further from its goal of self-sufficiency in food, and the old ideal of the Soviet Union serving as the breadbasket of the entire Communist world was simply no longer mentioned. After disastrous crop failures in the early 1970s, the Soviet Union became the world's largest purchaser of grain, much of it from the United States. Brezhnev had a practically negligible impact on the entrenched agricultural bureaucracy, the single factor most responsible, in the opinion of every qualified observer, for the dismal past and present performance of Soviet agriculture and for its extremely precarious future.

As Khrushchev's deputy, Brezhnev had often displayed a flair for personnel management. Once in power, he demonstrated a circumspect handling of the monumental egos of his Kremlin colleagues that came to be among the most successful facets of his reign, as party and government functionaries became gratefully accustomed to more secure tenure of their positions. Although the costs of this policy were high—institutionalization of incompetence in some cases and an inevitable tendency to keep people in office well past their primes, thus blocking the way of younger and perhaps more innovative talents—the benefits to the regime in terms of stability and continuity were undeniable. Brezhnev moved very slowly against his adversaries, waiting until mid-1967 to rid himself of two particular critics, the hard-line neo-Stalinists Aleksandr Shelepin and Vladimir Semichastny (the latter replaced as head of the KGB by Yuri Andropov). Not until 1972 did he remove Khrushchev's old protégé Pyotr Shelest from the post of Ukrainian party secretary and put in his own man, Vladimir Shcherbitsky. Brezhnev brought his men to the fore with great deliberation over many years. It was often remarked near the end of his life how many of his closest colleagues came from the industrial area near the Dnepr bend—this "Dnepropetrovsk mafia" was composed of those he had come to know and trust during his days in the Ukraine, and they formed the core of his support in the party and among the armed forces.

At the 23rd Party Congress in 1966, the title of Brezhnev's office was changed from first secretary to general secretary and the name of the Central Committee's Presidium reverted to Politburo, its name under Stalin. In May 1977 he promulgated a new constitution, geared to "developed socialism," which, among other measures, strengthened the power of the chairman of the Presidium of the Supreme Soviet, a position he took away from Podgorny the following month. In May 1976 he was promoted to marshal of the Soviet Union, the country's highest military rank. He also held the titles of supreme commander of the armed forces and chairman of the Defense Council.

Internal dissent, whether from intellectuals, would-be emigrants, religious minorities, or human-rights advocates, was probably the Brezhnev era's most notorious problem. Brezhnev opposed the mass arrests of earlier periods, favoring instead the more selective sanctions adopted by Andropov and the KGB: dismissal of dissenters from work, occasional psychiatric internment, general harassment, internal exile, and even emigration, the last a solution unheard of until the early 1970s, when Jews began to be allowed to leave the Soviet Union for Israel. Forced emigration was even tried in several intractable cases, including the famous one of the anti-Communist writer Aleksandr Solzhenitsyn, an international figure of great moral force and probably Russia's greatest twentieth-century novelist, who was exiled and stripped of his citizenship (a penalty forbidden by the constitution) in February 1974. One of the country's greatest scientists, the physicist and academician Andrei Sakharov, a fearless spokesman for human rights and an inspiration to millions throughout the world, was effectively silenced by forcible removal from Moscow to Gorky. Although the KGB's victims probably numbered in the thousands under Brezhnev, rather than in the millions as under Stalin, the greater publicity received by each case and the shrewd ruthlessness of the secret police have turned the dissident problem into a continuing international embarrassment of major proportions. In late 1982, Vitaly V. Fedorchuk, Andropov's successor as head of the KGB, began a renewed crackdown on dissident activity.

Soviet foreign policy under Brezhnev frequently seemed unfocused and even schizophrenic. There was no more of Khrushchev's overt bellicosity and little inclination to intervene directly in far-off disputes, and great store was officially set by détente, which Brezhnev often claimed as his greatest accomplishment. Yet he presided over a gigantic arms buildup, covering all areas of the military, and showed himself quick to intervene with crushing force when Soviet hegemony was threatened. The Warsaw Pact invasion of Czechoslovakia in August 1968, which deposed the liberal Communist regime of Alexander Dubček and caused an upheaval in world Communism, was widely believed to be Brezhnev's responsibility. Out of it came the so-called Brezhnev Doctrine, which held that any threat to the establishment of Communism in one country would be taken as a direct threat to all Communist countries. The doctrine evidently applied to Poland in 1981, when a liberal groundswell occasioned by the success of Solidarity, the independent trade-union movement, was effectively stifled by military action, though without the need for invasion by the Soviet Army. The invasion that befell Afghanistan in late 1979, probably seen by the Kremlin initially as little more than a strengthening of the fraternal government of a neighbor, caused international indignation, undermined the 1980 Moscow Olympic Games, and deeply involved the Soviet Army in a war showing every sign of being unwinnable. Relations with Communist China, which had badly deteriorated under Khrushchev, grew even worse under Brezhnev when fighting broke out in 1969 along the Amur River, the Sino-Soviet border.

The selling of détente afforded Brezhnev the opportunity to appear before the world as a statesman, offering peace in exchange for guaranteed security. His greatest success came in the early 1970s, when he enjoyed a cordial relationship with the two most influential Western leaders, Chancellor Willy Brandt of West Germany and Pres. Richard Nixon. In 1970 he negotiated a treaty with West Germany that recognized the post–World War II borders of East and West Germany and Poland. He received Nixon on a visit to the Soviet Union in May 1972, during which they signed the Anti-Ballistic Missile Treaty and the Interim Agreement on Offensive Missiles and agreed to establish a joint U.S.-USSR Commercial Commission. The following October the U.S.-USSR Trade Agreement was signed in Washington (it was abrogated by the Soviets in January 1975). In June 1973 Brezhnev arrived in the United States for an eight-day visit, during which he initialed with Nixon no fewer than 13 treaties and agreements, including the Agreement on the Prevention of Nuclear War. Nixon visited Moscow and Yalta in June 1974 and Pres. Gerald Ford went to Vladivostok the following November.

In the summer of 1975 Brezhnev headed the Soviet delegation to the Helsinki Conference on Security and Cooperation in Europe, where he was successful in winning acceptance

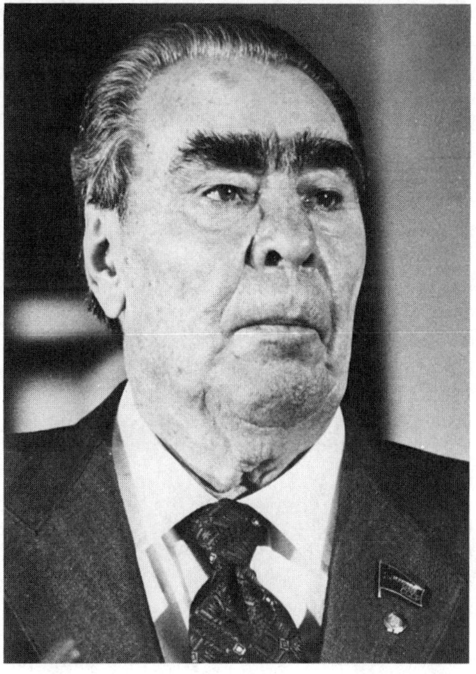

of the territorial status quo established after World War II—a major objective of Soviet foreign policy since the 24th Party Congress in 1971. The Final Act of the Helsinki accords, however, included agreements on human rights and access to information that the Soviets were loath to accept, only doing so, in the end, because the success of the Helsinki talks was so vitally important to Brezhnev. His last summit with the leader of the Western alliance was his meeting with Pres. Jimmy Carter in Vienna in late 1979 to sign the second agreement to limit nuclear weapons (SALT II). This treaty was in trouble in the U.S. Senate from the start, and its prospects for ratification vanished after the Soviet invasion of Afghanistan. Soviet relations with the United States, and to a lesser extent with Western Europe, cooled even further after the conservative, deeply anti-Soviet administration of Pres. Ronald Reagan came to power in 1981.

During his final years there was a steady and remarkable decline in Brezhnev's physical strength. Yet in the face of countless news stories in the West that had him suffering from one incurable illness after another, he continued at the helm of the Kremlin, his frequent absences from official functions alternating with equally frequent public appearances, parade reviews, and speeches. His hold on his posts seemed more secure than ever when his close friend Nikolai Tikhonov took over as prime minister on Kosygin's retirement in 1980. Clearly, there was no one left in the hierarchy with the will or the power to challenge Brezhnev. Yet it appears, at least in retrospect, that the death of Suslov in January 1982 marked the beginning of the end of the Brezhnev era. The dour old Stalinist had been Brezhnev's unstinting supporter since 1964 and together they seemed to have enough leverage with their colleagues to prevail at every turn. Andropov's lightning-quick advancement into Suslov's post of party watchdog, coupled with the arrest, in the spring, of close friends of Brezhnev's daughter Galina on corruption charges, strongly suggest that the supreme leader's position was being undermined.

Brezhnev's family was marginally more conspicuous than those of other Soviet leaders. His wife, Viktoria Petrovna, said to be of a Jewish family, stayed resolutely out of the limelight, but his children were more visible. His son Yuri held the post of deputy minister for foreign trade from 1976 and his daughter Galina's third husband, Lieut. Gen. Yuri Churbanov, was an obscure police officer until his marriage, whereupon he was named first deputy minister for internal affairs. The removal of both men from office was expected early in the Andropov regime. Brezhnev and his wife lived in a relatively modest five-room apartment on Kutuzovsky Prospect and had a dacha in Kolchuga, a village just outside Moscow. He was known to appreciate all forms of material flattery, expensive gifts, and especially costly Western automobiles, of which he owned dozens even though he was a notoriously poor driver. His heavy smoking of American filter cigarettes and his impressive capacity for vodka were both sharply curtailed by his physicians during his last years. He was a surprisingly emotional man, easily moved to tears, but unlike his predecessor he never allowed his emotions to get the better of his political judgment.

The announcement of his death came as a surprise to many in Moscow. Everyone had seen him on television only three days before, as he stood for two hours in subfreezing temperatures on the Lenin Mausoleum reviewing a military parade for the sixty-fifth anniversary of the Bolshevik Revolution. The official statement said nothing about the cause of death, but confirmed for the first time that he had been suffering from abdominal aneurysm, as well as coronary insufficiency, arrhythmia, and tissue scarring.

Brezhnev's funeral was the largest in the Soviet Union since Stalin's. All of downtown Moscow was sealed off by the police and militia as millions of citizens waited in line, three abreast, to pass before the body, which lay in state, surrounded by flowers and medals, in the House of Trade Unions. Only a day after his death the Politburo chose Andropov to succeed him as party general secretary, an unexpectedly quick choice that was confirmed the very next day by the full Central Committee, who were summoned to vote in the heavily guarded Council of Ministers building. Andropov was nominated by Konstantin Chernenko, Brezhnev's right-hand man and probable first choice as successor. It was widely noted in the West that Andropov had for months been the subject of a KGB campaign depicting him as the most liberal of the potential successors, though many doubted this was a true portrayal. No successor to Brezhnev as head of state was immediately named; Andropov was expected to consolidate his power further before assuming that office.

Brezhnev held a large number of Soviet

decorations, including five Orders of Lenin (more than any Soviet citizen has ever received), two Orders of the Red Banner of Labor, the Lenin Peace Prize, the Order of the Patriotic War, First Class (the highest military decoration), the Order of the Red Star, and designations as a Hero of the Soviet Union and twice as a Hero of Socialist Labor. He also frequently received the decorations of fraternal Communist countries, including, in the last year of his life, the Afghan Order of the Golden Palm. For his slim volumes of highly selective memoirs he was given in 1979 the Lenin Prize for Literature, an award that caused much rueful amusement in the Union of Soviet Writers. After his death the Central Committee proceeded to rename several towns, streets, squares, ships, and schools after him, honors previously accorded only to Lenin among the nation's supreme leaders.
A.K.

Parents Ilya Yakovlevich B., steelworker, and Natalya Denisovna B. **Married** Viktoria Petrovna, possibly metallurgist or gynecologist, ca. 1932: Galina; Yuri, trade minister; Mikhail, journalist. **Education** Klassicheskaya Gymnaziya, Kamenskoje 1915–21; metallurgical vocational sch., Kamenskoye; Technicum for Land Organization and Reclamation, Kursk, grad. 1927; Timiryazev Acad., Moscow ca. 1930–31; Inst. of Metallurgy, Kamenskoye, degree in metallurgical engineering 1935. **Mil. service** Political commissar, tank co., Red Army, Trans-Baikal mil. district 1935–36; col. ca. 1941–43; deputy chief, Southern Front political directorate 1941–42; chief, political dept., 18th Army, northern Caucasus 1942–45; chief, political directorate, 4th Ukrainian Front 1942–45; maj. gen. 1943; saw action in Caucasus, Black Sea, Crimea, Poland, Hungary, and Czechoslovakia; comdr. and chief, political directorate, Carpathian mil. district, Chernovtsy 1945–46; lt. gen. and 1st deputy chief of main political directorate, Soviet Navy 1953–54; named marshal of Soviet Union 1976; supreme comdr. of armed forces and chmn. of Council of Defense of USSR 1970s. **Career** Manual laborer, Kamenskoje Zavod steel mill ca. 1921–23; joined Komsomol (All-Communist Youth League), Kursk 1923; surveyor, Kursk region and Byelorussia, and land-use specialist, Ural region, late 1920s; head of district agriculture dept. and deputy chmn. of exec. cttee., Bisert District Soviet of Workers' Deputies late 1920s–early 30s; deputy head, agricultural admin., Sverdlovsk region late 1920s–early 1930s; steelworker, Dzerzhinsky Metallurgical Factory, Dneprodzerzhinsk 1931–37. • With CPSU: member since early 1930s; chmn. of trade union cttee. 1931–33 and dir. of workers' faculty 1933–35, Dzerzhinsky Metallurgical Factory; dir. and party secty., Inst. of Metallurgy, Dneprodzerzhinsk 1936–37; deputy chmn., exec. cttee., City Soviet of Workers' Deputies, Dneprodzerzhinsk 1937–38. • With Dnepropetrovsk Regional Cttee., Ukrainian C.P.: deputy chief 1938–39; propaganda secty. 1939–41; agriculture secty. 1940; defense secty. 1940; 1st secty., Central Cttee. 1947–50. • First secty., Zaporozhye Regional Cttee. 1946–47; 1st secty., Central Cttee., Moldavian C.P. 1950–52; 2nd secty. 1954–55, and 1st secty. and Central Cttee. bureau member 1955–56, Kazakh C.P. • With Supreme Soviet of USSR: deputy 1950, 1954, 1958, 1964; member since 1960; chmn. of Presidium 1960–64 and since 1977. • With Central Cttee., CPSU: member since 1952; member of Secretariat 1952–53, 1956–60, and since 1963; candidate member 1952–53 and 1956–57, and member since 1957, Presidium (Politburo since 1966); deputy chairman of RSFSR political bureau 1958–60; first secretary 1964–66; gen. secty. since 1966. • Chmn., USSR Constitutional Commn. since 1964. **Honors** Hero of Socialist Labor 1961, 1966; Gold Star Medal 1966, 1976, 1978; Lenin Peace Prize 1972; Karl Marx Gold Medal, Acad. of Sciences, USSR 1977; Lenin Prize for Literature, for autobiographical trilogy, 1979; Gold Star, Vietnam 1980; Order of Golden Palm, Afghanistan 1982; Gold Medal of Peace, U.N.; Order of Victory; Hammer and Sickle Gold Medal; Intl. Dmitrov Peace Prize; Intl. Gold and Mercury Prize for Peace and Cooperation; Hero of Soviet Union twice; Order of Khmelnytsky, 2nd Class; Order of Patriotic War, 1st Class; Order of Red Star; Golden Peace Medal, World Peace Council; Order of Lenin five times; Order of Red Banner of Labor twice; Order of October Revolution twice; many other decorations from USSR, Poland, Czechoslovakia, other socialist countries. **Author** *Piatdesiat let velikykh pobed sotsialisma,* 1967 (trans. as

Fifty Years of Great Achievements of Socialism, 1967); *KPSS v borbe za edinstvo vsekh revolyutsionnykh i mirolyubivykh sil,* 1972 (trans. as *The CPSU in the Struggle for Unity of All Revolutionary and Peace Forces,* 1975); *Leninskym kursom,* 1975 (trans. as *Following Lenin's Course: Speeches and Articles, 1972–1975,* 1975); *Vozrozhdenie,* 1978 (trans. as *Rebirth,* 1978); *Tselina,* 1978 (trans. as *The Virgin Lands,* 1978); *Malaya Zemlya,* 1978 (trans. as *Little Land,* 1978); *How It Was: The War and Postwar Reconstruction in the Soviet Union,* 1979; *Selected Speeches and Writings on Foreign Affairs,* 1979; *Peace, Détente, and Soviet-American Relations: A Collection of Public Statements,* 1979; *Trilogy: Little Land; Rebirth; The Virgin Lands* (memoirs), 1980; *Peace, Détente, Cooperation,* 1981; *Socialism, Democracy, and Human Rights,* 1981; *Vospominaniya* [*Reminiscences*], 1981; many other collections of speeches and reports of the Central Committee of the CPSU, in Russian and English translation.

Further reading George W. Simmonds, ed., *Soviet Leaders,* 1967; Michel Tatu, *Power in the Kremlin,* 1969; Rodger Swearingen, ed., *Leaders of the Communist World,* 1971; John Dornberg, *Brezhnev: The Masks of Power,* 1974.

ELIO PETRI

Film director and scriptwriter
***Born* Rome, Italy, 29 January 1929**
***Died* Rome, Italy, 10 November 1982**

During the 1960s a number of European directors, working independently rather than as a "school" in any formal sense, began to produce a new kind of film, one in which overtly political messages were conveyed through the formats and conventions of popular cinema. Notable among these filmmakers, all of whom were politically left-wing, were Costa-Gavras (*Z* and *State of Siege*), Yves Boisset (*L'attentat*), Gillo Pontecorvo (*Battle of Algiers*), Francesco Rosi (*Hands over the City*), and—the earliest practitioner of this approach—Elio Petri. Petri strongly maintained that no excuse was needed for aiming his films at the widest possible audience. "There are those who reproach us for reaching a huge audience; for them success is a kind of corruption. But I find that a moralistic, and ultimately a reactionary attitude. A single film, admittedly, can't do much to change opinions, but a whole lot of films can change overall attitudes."

Elio Petri was born into a working-class family and studied literature at the University of Rome. After graduating, he entered journalism, becoming weekly film critic of *L'Unità,* the official newspaper of the Italian Communist Party. Giuseppe de Santis's film *Roma Ore 11* (1952; *Rome 11 O'Clock*) was based on Petri's account of a disaster in which a staircase collapsed under 200 women workers waiting to apply for a single job. The picture was well received, and Petri, who had collaborated on the screenplay, went on to script 14 more films for de Santis and other neorealist directors before starting to direct on his own account.

His first film, apart from two documentary shorts, was *L'assassino* (1961), in which Marcello Mastroianni played a rich dilettante accused of murder. Critical and public response was enthusiastic; *Il Giorno* commended the film's "polish, detail, and a certain macabre cheerfulness." Petri directed two more films before making his first international success, *La decima vittima* (1965; *The Tenth Victim*), a futuristic thriller with Mastroianni and Ursula Andress. (In conformity with his popular approach, Petri preferred to cast famous stars whenever possible.) In *A ciascuno il suo* (1967; *We Still Kill the Old Way*) he courageously attacked the power of the Mafia. But his expressive cinematic style and scathing view of "respectable" society were most effectively combined in his finest picture, *Indagine su un cittadino al di sopra di ogni sospetto* (1969; *Investigation of a Citizen Above Suspicion*), which won an Academy Award as best foreign film and received several awards at Cannes. *Investigation* starred Gian Maria Volonté, one of Petri's favorite actors, as a right-wing police chief who tests his own invulnerability by deliberately leaving clues that implicate him as the murderer of his mistress. No other Italian filmmaker had dared to expose the corruption and arrogance of the police, who are protected by law from public ridicule. A reviewer for *Corriere della Sera* wrote that "it is the first time . . . that the censors have cheered."

La classe operaia va in Paradiso (1971; *The Working Class Goes to Heaven,* or *Lulu the Tool*), which won first prize at Cannes, starred Volonté as a bewildered worker caught up in a strike. Petri continued his satirical assault on middle-class convention in *La proprietà non è più un furto* (1972; *Property Is No Longer Theft*) and poked savage fun at Italy's ruling Christian Democrats in *Todo modo* (1976). In 1978 he directed Sartre's "Les mains sales" for Italian television, starring Mastroianni; the last of his 11 feature films was *Buone notizie* (1979; *Good News*). Elio Petri died of cancer in a Rome hospital. P.K.

Education Technical sch.; Univ. of Rome, degree in literature. **Career** Film critic for C.P. newspaper *L'Unità,* and journalist, early 1950s; scriptwriter since 1952; dir. of documentaries 1954–57; dir. of feature films since 1961. **Member** Italian C.P. to 1956. **Honors** Academy Award for best foreign film, for *Indagine su un cittadino al di sopra di ogni sospetto,* 1970; special jury prize 1970, for *Indagine su un cittadino,* and grand prize 1972, for *La classe operaia va in Paradiso,* Cannes Film Festival. **Film director and scriptwriter** *Nasce un campione* and *I sette contadini* (documentaries), mid-1950s; *L'assassino* (rel. as *The Lady Killer of Rome*), 1961; *I giorni contati,* 1962; *Il maestro di Vigevano,* 1963; (episode) *Altà infedelta* (rel. as *High Infidelity*), 1964; *La decima vittima* (rel. as *The Tenth Victim*), 1965; *A ciascuno il suo* (rel. as *We Still Kill the Old Way*), 1967; *Un tranquillo posto di campagna* (rel. as *A Quiet Place in the Country*), 1968; *Indagine su un cittadino al di sopra di ogni sospetto* (rel. as *Investigation of a Citizen Above Suspicion*), 1969; *La classe operaia va in Paradiso* (rel. as *The Working Class Goes to Heaven* and as *Lulu the Tool*), 1971; *La proprietà non è più un furto* (rel. as *Property Is No Longer Theft*), 1972; *Todo modo,* 1976; *Buone notizie* (rel. as *Good News*), 1979. **Television director** "Les mains sales," 1978. **Interview** Joan Mellen, "Cinema Is Not for an Elite but for the Masses," in *Cineaste,* vol. 6, no. 1, 1973.

Further reading Joan Mellen, *The Cinema of Rebellion,* 1974.

BABETTE DEUTSCH
Poet, literary critic, and translator
***Born* New York City, USA, 22 September 1895**
***Died* New York City, USA, 13 November 1982**

Most good or great poets who are also good or great critics usually have something in common: they tend to see literary history—particularly the contemporary scene—as contested ground, and they instinctively defend the kind of verse they wish to write themselves. This was not the case, however, with Babette Deutsch. As an astute critic, she remained sensitive for a great many years to whatever seemed to be happening at the moment; but as a good if fairly limited poet she never went beyond the concerns and techniques of the Imagist poets who were briefly in fashion when she began to publish her own verse shortly after the end of World War I.

Deutsch was born in New York and educated at the Ethical Culture School and at Barnard College, from which she took her A.B. in 1917. Her first book of poems, *Banners,* was published two years later. In 1921 she married Avrahm Yarmolinsky, a literature scholar and the head of the Slavonic Division of the New York Public Library, with whom she had two sons. She began teaching

Courtesy of Sam Tamashiro

at the New School for Social Research in 1933 and was for a time secretary to Thorstein Veblen. In 1944 she joined the faculty of Columbia University, where she taught for 27 years, and where a scholarship was established in her name in 1977, six years after her retirement.

Three times Deutsch engaged in what is probably the most vulnerable kind of critical enterprise, the attempt to write what amounts to instant literary history, to sort out and define what new poets of every conceivable persuasion are trying to achieve. What compelled her to take the risk was her intense conviction that poetry matters in the modern world. "Poetry is important," she maintained at the opening of her 1935 survey *This Modern Poetry*. "No less than science it seeks a hold upon reality, and the closeness of its approach is the test of its success." There are strong echoes here and elsewhere in her criticism of I. A. Richards's influential argument that complex imaginative approximations of experience are indispensable aids for coping with a complex and shifting world. "Modern poetry," Deutsch continues, "addresses itself to the modern mind"; the reader must become "acclimated to his time: to the ideas about the psyche, about the physical universe, about the social order, which modern poetry breathes . . . . He must be willing to learn the language with which the poet creates awareness of a changed world." And at the same time she recognized that "the once enormous domain" of true poetry has shrunk to a "small if intensely cultivated region, subject of late years to frequent raids by dramatist and novelist"—and subject as well, of course, to the same dangers Richards had warned against, the gross oversimplification of experience that mass culture offers as sufficient equipment for living. The very title of this book has a rhetorical dimension: it suggests the need for education, the need to help the untrained reader who wonders what this modern poetry is, with its complexities and demands and unfamiliar turns of speech, and why it matters. *This Modern Poetry* is an earnest attempt to answer the reader's questions, to make intelligible even the strangest new voices. Her sympathies here are as broad as her curiosity about every manifestation of poetry: she is as open to the poetry of Kipling and Robinson as she is to the much different work of Eliot or Wallace Stevens. If she does finally have a preference, it is for the kind of poetry Eliot also championed, in which thought and feeling are co-equal and fused rather than kept separate. But the book is never partisan or dogmatic.

The dangers that such criticism entails are considerable: the critic has to be right about which poets are worth listening to (here Deutsch's score is high, even after more than 40 years); and, paradoxically, the sounder his tentative generalizations, the quicker they are likely to be superseded. The just observations Deutsch made about the poetry of Yeats and Auden when it was truly new became, in the most honorable sense, commonplaces, points of departure for later critics who had the leisure for extended analysis. Of great value when they first appeared, *This Modern Poetry* and *Poetry in Our Time* (which incorporates large sections of the earlier book) are inevitably dated.

Deutsch's own poetry is another matter. She is by definition a modern poet, writing in the twentieth century, but her verse is barely modern in the sense of confronting modern complexities or even the everyday objects of modern living. Save for the presence of electric lights rather than candles and the occasional offstage hum of an airplane engine, there is virtually nothing in her poetic world that would be out of place in the poetic worlds of Thomas Hardy or Emily Dickinson (and technically there is nothing in her verse early or late that would seem out of place in, say, Ezra Pound's 1914 anthology *Des Imagistes*). The scenes in which her short lyrics take place are usually alike: a quiet natural landscape caught at a moment when a season or the time of day is perceptibly shifting. The action is usually the same as well: a sensitive observer—often the poet herself, speaking in her own voice—looks at the processes of change and reflects on the changes that human life also must submit to. In "Ephemeris," for example (the title is typical and significant), a lover momentarily at peace with the world around him observes

> Golden the haze is, from whose
> abundance we weave
> A summer fugue:
> Music that grieves for nothing.
> Quietly
> Day falls, the grass darkens.
> A widening hush
> Allows barely for the shadow of an alas.
> We stay only to watch the wimpling river
> flowing greyly on.

Deutsch's tone as a poet is never really tragic or despairing. What gives life some meaning is the power of memory, the power of the mind to understand its position, and especially the power of art—of poetry in its broadest sense—to fix the valuable moments of being. In this way poetry and criticism become part of the same enterprise, if we realize that poetry is the art of fixing experience and criticism the appreciative attempt to see what art has made permanent.

Although Deutsch did not herself know Russian, she assisted her husband on a number of translations of Russian poetry; their collaborations included *The Twelve Chairs* by Aleksandr Blok (1920), an edition of Aleksandr Pushkin's *Eugene Onegin* (1943), and the anthologies *Modern Russian Poetry* (1921) and *Two Centuries of Russian Verse* (1962). Deutsch also made translations from the German and French and was the author of four novels and several books for children. She was secretary of the National Institute of Arts and Letters, chancellor of the Academy of American Poets, and a member of the American Academy of Arts and Letters. She died in her sleep in her Manhattan apartment at the age of 87. E.B.

Parents Michael D. and Melanie Fisher. **Married** Avrahm Yarmolinsky, writer and literary scholar, 1921 (d. 1976): Adam, lawyer and govt. official, b. 1922; Michael B., microbiologist, b. 1928. **Education** Ethical Culture Sch., NYC 1901–13; Barnard Coll., NYC, A.B. 1917. **Career** Lectr., New Sch. for Social Research, NYC 1933–35; secty. to Thorstein Veblen 1930s; lectr. in poetry 1944–60 and sr. lectr. 1960–71, Columbia Univ.; poet, trans., and literary critic; lectr., Poetry Center, 92nd St. YM/YWHA, NYC. **Officer** Secty. from 1969 and member from 1958, Natl. Inst. of Arts and Letters; chancellor, Acad. of Amer. Poets. **Member** Advisory bd., Natl. Book Cttee. since 1964; Amer. Acad. of Arts and Letters; Civic Club; PEN; Cttee. for Cultural Freedom. **Honors** Poetry prize, for "Thoughts at the Year's End," *Nation* 1926; gold pin, New York State Fedn. of Women's Clubs 1933; Julia Ellsworth Ford Foundn. Prize, for *Walt Whitman: Builder for America,* 1941; Benét Memorial Award 1957; hon. consultant to Library of Congress 1960–66; Distinguished Alumna Award and scholarship named in her honor, Barnard Coll. 1977; hon. degree from Columbia Univ. **Poetry** *Banners,* 1919; *Honey out of the Rock,* 1925; *Fire for the Night,* 1930; *Epistle to Prometheus,* 1931; *One Part Love,* 1939; *Take Them, Stranger,* 1944; *Animal, Vegetable, Mineral,* 1954; *Coming of Age: New and Selected Poems,* 1959; *Collected Poems 1919–1962,* 1963; *The Collected Poems of Babette Deutsch,* 1969. **Novels** *A Brittle Heaven,* 1926; *In Such a Night,* 1927; *Mask of Silenus: A Novel about Socrates,* 1933; *Rogue's Legacy: A Novel about François Villon,* 1942. **Literary criticism** *Potable Gold: Some Notes on Poetry and This Age,* 1929; *This Modern Poetry,* 1935; *Poetry in Our Time,* 1952, rev. ed. 1963; *Poetry Handbook: A Dictionary of Terms,* 1957, 4th rev. ed. 1974; (ed.) *Poems of Samuel Taylor Coleridge,* 1967. **Translator** (With Avrahm Yarmolinsky) Aleksandr Blok, *The Twelve Chairs,* 1920; A.Y., ed., *Modern Russian Poetry,* 1921, rev. as *Russian Poetry,* 1922; (with A.Y.) *Contemporary German Poetry,* 1923; K. I. Chukovsky, *Crocodile,* 1931; (contributor) A.Y., ed., *The Works of Aleksandr Pushkin,* 1936; Solomon Blumgarten, *Rosh Hashanah L'Ilanoth,* 1940; Rainer Maria Rilke, *Poems from The Book of Hours,* 1941, rev. ed. 1969; A.Y., ed., Aleksandr Pushkin, *Eugene Onegin,* 1943; (with A.Y.) Nikolai Leskov, *The Steel Flea,* 1943, rev. ed. 1964; (verse trans.) *Selected Writings of Boris Pasternak,* 1949; (contributor) A.Y., ed., *A Treasury of Russian Verse,* 1949, rev. as *An*

Anthology of Russian Verse 1812–1960, 1962, and as *Two Centuries of Russian Verse: An Anthology from Lomonosov to Voznesensky,* 1966; Yvan Goll, *Jean sans terre,* 1958; Yvan Goll, *Elegy of Ihpetonga,* 1962. **Juvenile** *Heroes of the Kalevala, Finland's Saga,* 1940; *It's a Secret!,* 1941; *Walt Whitman: Builder for America,* 1941; *The Welcome,* 1942; *The Reader's Shakespeare,* 1946; (with A.Y.) *Tales of Faraway Folk,* 1952; (with A.Y.) *More Tales of Faraway Folk,* 1963; *I Often Wish,* 1966; (trans.) Elisabeth Borchers, *There Comes a Time,* 1969. **Other** *Only the Living,* 1943.

VINOBA BHAVE

Philosopher and social worker

Born **Gagoda, Maharashtra, India, British Empire, 11 September 1895**

Died **Paunar, Maharashtra, India, 15 November 1982**

Acharya Vinoba Bhave was one of the principal spiritual heirs of Mohandas Gandhi. An ascetic teacher, a lifelong celibate who never formed any worldly attachments or held any political office, he preached renunciation of worldly goods—especially land—as the best way to achieve the aims of the nonviolent Indian revolution. Although his movement's millennial goals were never fully realized, he had a great and continuing impact on the conscience of the country and many considered him to be, in fact, the most practical of the Mahatma's disciples.

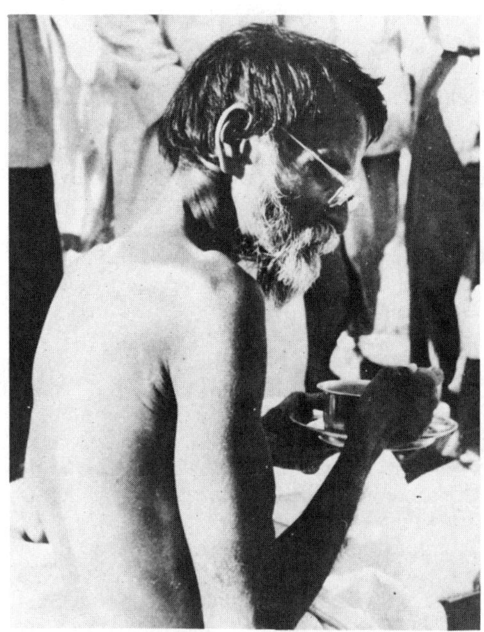

He was born Vinayak Narahari Bhave to a Brahmin family, the eldest of five children. His father, a painter and musician, wanted him to go to England to study science, but he remained in India. Educated at Government High School, Baroda, he proved to be a brilliant student, and was well on his way toward a secular career when a spiritual mandate caused him to abandon that path and turn instead to the thorough study of Sanskrit and the Hindu scriptures, which he undertook in Benares. Sanskrit was only the first of many languages he learned throughout his life. In addition to English, French, Arabic, and Persian, he mastered no fewer than ten major Indian languages.

In 1916, knowing that Gandhi had returned from South Africa the previous year, Bhave traveled to the Mahatma's principal ashram at Sabarmati, near Ahmadabad, and wrote a letter asking for admittance, being too shy to approach the great man directly. In reply, Gandhi asked him to join, changed his first name from Vinayak to the diminutive form Vinoba, and wrote the young man's father, "Your Vinoba is with me. His spiritual attainments are such as I myself attained only after a long struggle." Bhave went away again for a year's further study of Sanskrit, and on his return remained a committed and tireless supporter until the Mahatma's death. In 1921 a wealthy follower of Gandhi offered to build a second ashram, and Bhave was sent to accomplish the task. The new holy center, at Sevagram, near Wardha, later became Gandhi's main headquarters. "He is one of the ashram's rare pearls," said Gandhi of his disciple, "one of those who have come not to be blessed but to bless, not to receive but to give."

Bhave became one of the movement's foremost militants, particularly respected for his ability to implement solutions to the basic social and economic problems of village life. He was a vigorous proponent of the home industries, chiefly the spinning and weaving of cotton, a crucial part of Gandhi's plan for Indian self-sufficiency. He also worked constantly throughout his life to eliminate the caste system and to counter its evil effects. During the 1920s he organized several campaigns by untouchables to gain entry to the Hindu temples that were closed to them. Brahmin priests, regarding Bhave as a traitor to his caste and no better than the untouchables he led, once beat him so badly that he was left permanently deaf in one ear.

Bhave was in the front lines of the civil-disobedience campaign against British rule. During the famous salt satyagraha in 1930, he was jailed for the first of six times, and eventually spent a total of two years in British custody. Gandhi chose him to lead the campaign against Indian entry into World War II, which resulted in his longest sentence. He spent his years in jail proselytizing his fellow prisoners, speaking to them of the coming independence and lecturing on the *Bhagavad Gita,* for him the holiest Sanskrit text. He was popularly acclaimed as an *acharya,* or teacher by example.

His period of greatest renown began in 1951, three years after Gandhi's assassination. Hearing of the bloodshed in the Telengana district of Hyderabad state between landless peasants and brutal landlords, a situation exploited by the Communist Party, he set off on foot for the area, accompanied by a few followers. Speaking in his characteristically soft yet powerful voice, he converted countless thousands to Gandhi's way of *ahimsa* (nonviolence), including many of the most bloodthirsty guerrillas and not a few of the biggest landlords. From this triumph came the movement called *bhoodan yajna* (land-gift sacrifice), which attracted international attention over the next several years. Traveling from village to village, always on foot, he would conduct prayer meetings, hear local complaints, then appear before the largest landowner of the area, saying, "I have come to loot you with love. Consider me as one of your sons, and give me my share of land, so I may give it to the landless." In three years he had collected more than four million acres, which, though only a fraction of his goal of 50 million acres (one-sixth of the country's arable land), was enough to make people believe that one of the most profound revolutions in Indian history was under way. In 1952, in response to a plea from Prime Minister Jawaharlal Nehru, Bhave walked nearly 800 miles to New Delhi to discuss his campaign with the National Planning Commission. On the way he collected additional thousands of acres; at the end of his journey many members of Parliament contributed land, and the president of India, Rajendra Prasad, gave his entire estate in Bihar.

When in the mid-1950s the *bhoodan* movement seemed to falter—much of the land given was of no agricultural value and the new tenants were often harassed by litigation—Bhave began to preach *gramdan,* or "village gift," a larger concept involving parceling out an entire village's land among all its inhabitants. In 1960 he led a partially successful campaign to convert the *dacoits,* or outlaws, of the Chambal Ravines in central India to the ways of *ahimsa.*

Bhave retired from the world in the mid-1960s to live permanently in his ashram at Paunar, not far from the Gandhi ashram at Sevagram that he had founded. He emerged in 1976 to lead a national seminar on the state of emergency declared by Prime Minister Indira Gandhi, in which he was joined by Jaya Prakash Narayan, another of Gandhi's leading disciples and a close friend of many decades. In 1979 he began a fast to death to ban the slaughter of cows, breaking it only after Prime Minister Morarji Desai promised a constitutional amendment on the subject. He ate nothing but curds and unrefined sugar during most of his life, suffered from several diseases, including malaria and duodenal ulcer, and usually weighed less than 100 pounds. In early November 1982 he suffered a heart attack. Seeing the end approaching, he gave up all food and medical treatment, refusing even the request of Indira Gandhi, who went to his bedside, to resume nourishment and medication. He died the following week. A.K.

Born Vinayak Narahari B. **Parents** Narahari Shambhurao B., musician, painter, and textile technologist, and Rukminibai B. **Child** Shrimati Mahadevi Tai (adopted). **Religion** Hindu. **Education** Govt. High Sch., Baroda, Gujarat; Baroda Coll., left at age 21; studied Sanskrit, Hindu theology, and philosophy, Benares. **Career** Joined Indian nationalist movement ca. 1916; co-worker and disciple of Mohandas Gandhi 1916–48; founder, Sevagram ashram, Maharashtra 1921; led numerous satyagrahas, including first satyagraha against India's involvement in WWII, 1920s–40s, and was jailed six times for civil disobedience; founding leader, *bhoodan yajna* (land-gift sacrifice) movement since 1951; leader, *shanti sena* (peace volunteers) and *gramdan* (village gift) movements since 1950s; leader, discussion seminar on natl. state of emergency 1976; spiritual leader and founder of numerous ashrams. **Author** *Bhoodan Yajna,* 1953 (trans. as *Land Gifts Mission,* 1953); *From Bhoodan to Gramdan,* 1957; [*Talks on the Gita*], 1960; [*The Essence of the Quran*], 1962; [*Democratic Values*], 1963; [*Steadfast Wisdom*], 1966; [*The Essence of Christian Teachings*], 1966; (jtly.) [*School of Non-Violence, A Handbook*], 1969; [*Women's Power*], 1975; (trans.) *Bhagavad Gita.* **Contributor** Shriman Narayan, ed., *Letters from Gandhi, Nehru, Vinoba,* 1968.

Further reading Hallam Tennyson, *Saint on the March: The Story of Vinoba Bhave,* 1955; J. J. Lanza del Vasto, *Gandhi to Vinoba: The New Pilgrimage,* 1956; Shriman Narayan, *Vinoba: His Life and Work,* 1970.

HEINAR KIPPHARDT

Playwright

***Born* Heidersdorf, Upper Silesia, Germany, 8 March 1922**

***Died* Munich, West Germany, 18 November 1982**

The West German playwright Heinar Kipphardt was one of the foremost practitioners of the documentary drama, a style of playwriting popular in the 1960s in which pieces of recorded history (transcripts, tapes, publications) are creatively adapted to illuminate issues of social and moral concern. A Marxist and a Brechtian, he was known in the United States for a single play, *In the Matter of J. Robert Oppenheimer,* one of the successes of the 1968 New York season.

Kipphardt was born in Upper Silesia; his father, a dentist, was an opponent of the Nazis who spent five years in a concentration camp (and, by some accounts, died there). In 1942 Kipphardt was drafted out of medical school to serve on the Russian front in a Wehrmacht panzer division, from which he is said to have deserted. He finally earned his medical degree at Düsseldorf and became a staff psychiatrist at the Charité Neurological Clinic in East Berlin, also joining the Deutsches Theater as literary advisor. His first play, *Shakespeare Urgently Sought,* which lampooned the East German taste for Socialist Realist theater of the worst kind, was produced there in 1953 and won the National Prize.

Throughout the decade of the 1950s Kipphardt alternated between treating mentally ill individuals at the clinic and satirizing a morally ill society on stage. When his play *Mr. Szmil's Chairs,* an adaptation of the novel *The Twelve Chairs* by the Russian comic writers Ilya Ilf and Yevgeny Petrov, was banned by the state censor in 1959, he departed for West Germany, eventually settling in Munich, where he began writing the kind of hard-hitting documentary theater practiced by Rolf Hochhuth (*The Deputy*) and Peter Weiss (*The Investigation*). He wrote one minor piece in this style, *The General's Dog* (1962), about the inability of Germans to acknowledge the shameful past, before writing *In the Matter of J. Robert Oppenheimer.* It was first staged at Erwin Piscator's Free People's Theater in West Berlin in 1964 and played throughout West Germany before its arrival in New York in 1968.

Oppenheimer was the brilliant physicist who headed the team that developed the atomic bomb. After Hiroshima and Nagasaki, in remorse at having given the world so terrible a weapon, he tried to prevent the development of the yet more powerful hydrogen bomb. He was accused of disloyalty to the United States and in 1954 had his security clearance withdrawn by the Atomic Energy Commission. Kipphardt's play, adapted from the 3,000-page transcript of the AEC hearings and from other documents, raises the troublesome issues of whether scientists bear a moral responsibility for the consequences of their creations and of whether a nation, in the name of patriotism, can compel its citizens to act in

Courtesy of German Information Center

ways they deem detrimental to humanity as a whole. Whatever emotions the play gave rise to in German audiences, in the United States it was recognized as having a direct bearing on the Vietnam War, organized opposition to which was just then getting under way. *Oppenheimer,* wrote Catharine Hughes in her book *Plays, Politics, and Polemics,* "was easily one of the most significant American theatrical events of the 60s, even if it did require a European to confront us with ourselves."

Oddly, no other play of Kipphardt's received an American production or even a translation into English. His next, *Joel Brand* (1965), was a documentary drama about the Hungarian Jew who was forced by the Nazis to negotiate a business deal involving the exchange of one million Hungarian Jewish lives for ten thousand British trucks. (The British refused, and the Jews were killed.) Kipphardt's later works, some of which were written while he was chief dramatist at the Munich Kammerspiele, included *The Night the Boss Was Slaughtered* (1967), a satire about bourgeois West Germans; *Soldiers* (1968), an adaptation of a play by the eighteenth-century Romantic poet J. M. R. Lenz; and a film script, play, and novel about a schizophrenic poet. He published two collections of short stories and a volume of verse.

Kipphardt died in Munich at the age of 60, during preparations for the production of his last play, *Brother Eichmann.* J.P.

Father a dentist. **Emigrated** to West Germany 1959. **Education** Univs. of Bonn, Königsberg, Breslau, and Würzburg; Medical Acad., Düsseldorf, M.D. **Mil.. service** Panzer div., Wehrmacht, Russian front 1942–44 (deserted). **Career** Asst. doctor, Charité Neurological Clinic, East Berlin 1950–59; literary advisor and chief dramatist, Deutsches Theater, East Berlin 1950–59; chief dramatist, Kammerspiele, Munich 1969–71; dramatist, short-story writer, novelist, and poet. **Member** German Acad. of Representational Arts; West German PEN Center. **Honors** East German Natl. Prize, for *Shakespeare dringend gesucht,* 1953; Schiller Memorial Prize 1962; Gerhart Hauptmann Prize 1964; Adolf Grimme Prize 1965; TV prize, German Acad. of Representational Arts 1975; film prize, Soc. of German Doctors 1976; Prix Italia 1976; Bemer Literature Prize 1977. **Plays** *Shakespeare dringend gesucht: Ein satirisches Lustspiel in drei Akten* [*Shakespeare Urgently Sought: A Satirical Comedy in Three Acts*], 1954; *Der Aufstieg des Alois Piontek: Eine tragikomische Farce* [*The Rise of Alois Piontek: A Tragicomic Farce*], 1956; *Esel schreien im Dunkeln* [*Donkeys Bray in the Night*], 1958; *Die Stühle des Herrn Szmil* [*Mr. Szmil's Chairs*], 1961; *Bartleby,* 1962; *Der Hund des Generals: Schauspiel* [*The General's Dog: Drama*], 1962; *Joel Brand: Die Geschichte eines Geschäfts* [*Joel Brand: The Story of a Deal*], 1965; *Der Nacht in der der Chef geschlachtet wurde* [*The Night the Boss Was Slaughtered*], 1965; *In der Sache J. Robert Oppenheimer,* 1966 (trans. as *In the Matter of J. Robert Oppenheimer,* 1967); (adaptor) J. M. R. Lenz, *Die Soldaten* [*The Soldiers*], 1968; *Sedanfeier,* 1970; *Leben des schizophrenen Dichters, Alexander März* [*Life of the Schizophrenic Poet Alexander März*] (film scenario), 1976; *Stücke* [*Plays*], 2 vols., 1973–74; *Theaterstücke I,* 1978; *März, ein Kunstler Leben* [*März, An Artist Life*], 1979; *Bruder Eichmann* [*Brother Eichmann*], 1983. **Short-story collections** *Die Ganovenfresse: Zwei Erzählungen* [*The Ganoven Mouth: Two Sto-*

ries], 1964; *Der Mann des Tages und andere Erzählungen* [*The Man of the Day and Other Stories*], 1977. **Novel** *März,* 1976. **Poetry** *Angelsbrucker Notizen: Gedichte* [*Notes from Angelsbruck: Poems*], 1977.

Further reading Catharine Hughes, *Plays, Politics, and Polemics,* 1973; R. Hinton Thomas and Keith Bullivant, *Literature in Upheaval: West German Writers and the Challenge of the 60's,* 1974.

WILLIAM P(ETER) McGIVERN

Suspense writer and novelist

***Born* Chicago, Illinois, USA, 6 December 1922**

***Died* Palm Desert, California, USA, 18 November 1982**

In a career as a mystery writer that began in earnest soon after the end of World War II, William P. McGivern published 25 novels, several children's books, and more than 300 short stories, many of which appeared in the *Saturday Evening Post, Cosmopolitan,* and *Collier's.* He also wrote more than 100 episodes for television series such as "Kojak" and "San Francisco International Airport" and a number of screenplays, some of them adapted from his own novels. In all, 14 of the author's stories have been made into films; *The Big Heat,* generally regarded as McGivern's most exciting work, earned him a Mystery Writers of America Edgar Allan Poe Award as the best novel to be screened in 1953.

McGivern was born and raised in Chicago.

Courtesy of Arbor House

His mother was a dress designer and his father the president of a bank, but the family suffered during the Depression and he left school after the tenth grade to work in a railroad yard. He sold his first story shortly before entering the U.S. Army in 1942. Sergeant of a 15-man artillery group, he saw action in Normandy, Belgium, and Central Europe during World War II and received five military decorations, including a Soldier's Medal for saving the life of an army colleague. He studied for a year at the University of Birmingham in England (1945–46), then worked for a time as a reporter for the *Philadelphia Evening Bulletin,* becoming a full-time fiction writer in 1951. He and his wife, the novelist Maureen Daly, wrote and traveled in Europe and North Africa; their collection of travel essays from this period, *Mention My Name in Mombasa,* was published in 1958.

By the end of the 1950s, when McGivern had settled in Hollywood, he had published 14 novels and had a firm reputation as a highly competent mystery writer of the "hard school." Critics identified his work with that of W. R. Burnett and Raymond Chandler. *The Big Heat* (1953) is the story of an honest detective, Dave Bannion, who relentlessly seeks answers and then revenge in the sleazy world of crooked politicians, extortionists, and policemen on the take. A reviewer for the *Times Literary Supplement* wrote: "Another notably fresh and interesting story. . . . The earnest denunciation of municipal corruption which is put into Bannion's mouth has nothing like the laconic force of [John D.] Macdonald's writing, but the background of police work is particularly well done, and Bannion, rather surprisingly, comes through some patches of woolly writing as a sympathetic and interesting character."

The theme of a policeman's crusade against

big-city corruption reappeared in McGivern's 1954 novel *Rogue Cop:* two brothers commence their police careers with high ideals; one maintains them, the other, compromised, becomes an underworld lackey. But the memory of his good father and his belief in God remain vital forces in the rogue cop's life and he manages to escape his snare and regain self-respect; in the process, however, he loses his brother. *Odds Against Tomorrow* (1957) concerns two of the participants, one black and one white, in a botched bank heist. They find refuge in a lonely Pennsylvania farmhouse, where, cut off from the environments that fed their respective prejudices, friendship begins to replace their mutual distrust.

McGivern's only espionage novel, *Caprifoil* (1972), is, for the most part, an exciting story, but the intrigue wanes when a group of Arab revolutionaries who are holding hostage the egotistical and reactionary French president propose that they exchange him for ten U.S. atomic devices, sufficient to obliterate Israel if it refuses to renounce its nationhood and "disperse"—a demand too farfetched to sustain the plot. There is also an unevenness in McGivern's character portrayals: most are intelligently written, but a few, especially his thumbnail portraits, are unconvincing stereotypes. McGivern is often noted by critics as a writer of considerable sensitivity, but just beneath the slick surface of his prose, some readers might detect streaks of misogyny and homophobia.

Caprifoil was followed by two tense and popular melodramas, *Reprisal* (1973) and *Night of the Juggler* (1975). In 1979 McGivern realized his long-term desire to write about his experiences as an artillery sergeant during the Battle of the Bulge: *Soldiers of '44* focuses on Sergeant Docker and his team of gunners, who are protecting a strategic hill in the wintry Ardennes. McGivern sees many similarities between Docker's men and the Nazi aggressors whose duty it is to capture the hill: racism, cruelty, and guilt exist on both sides. The author maintained in a *Publishers Weekly* interview that his novel is about "the absolute terror of occupation and the physical realities of that terrain, not the moral question. You could get trapped in a mental labyrinth if you started thinking about moral questions, and besides, nobody had the time." Nevertheless, McGivern displays great interest in the "meaning" of the war and its significance in the lives of those who fought it. Paul Fussell, writing in *New Republic,* complained that *Soldiers of '44* is a "creaky, leaden American melodrama" that "misrepresents . . . the emotional conditions of the war," but P.-L. Adams commented in his *Atlantic* review: "Mr. McGivern has created a war novel with believable characters, varied action, continuous suspense and a conclusion that shifts, unexpectedly but with good reason, from physical action to a moral confrontation with implications that carry beyond its military setting."

McGivern, who also wrote scripts for adventure films and television series, died shortly before his sixtieth birthday after a long battle with cancer. His recent suspense epic, *Summitt,* was published five months before his death. R.T.

Also wrote under pseudonym Bill Peters. **Parents** Peter Francis M., banker, and Julia Frances (Costello) M., clothes designer. **Married** Maureen Daly, writer, 1948: Megan Shaw; Patrick. **Education** Loyola Acad., Chicago; Univ. of Birmingham, England 1945–46. **Mil. service** Master sgt., artillery unit, U.S. Army, Europe 1943–46. **Career** Laborer, railroad yard, Chicago 1930s; reporter and book reviewer, *Philadelphia Evening Bulletin* 1949–51; short-story writer and novelist since 1940s, TV scriptwriter 1970s; guest lectr., Univ. of North Carolina 1961; co-owner, KOWN radio sta., Escondido, CA. **Officer** Pres., Mystery Writers of America 1980. **Member** Television Acad. of Arts and Sciences; Crime Writers of Great Britain; Writers Guild of America; Authors League; Democratic Party. • Clubs: Players, NYC; Garrick and Savage, London; Indian Wells Country, Palm Desert, CA. **Honors** Soldier's Medal 1944; Bronze Star; three other mil. decorations, WWII; Edgar Award, for *The Big Heat,* Mystery Writers of America 1952. **Novels** *But Death Runs Faster,* 1948, as *The Whispering Corpse,* 1950; *Heaven Ran Last,* 1949; *Very Cold for May,* 1950; *Shield for Murder,* 1951; *Blondes Die Young,* 1952; *The Crooked Frame,* 1952; *The Big Heat,* 1953; *Margin of Terror,* 1953; *Rogue Cop,* 1954; *The Darkest Hour,* 1955, also as *Waterfront Cop,* 1956; *The Seven File* (in U.K. as *Chicago-7*), 1956; *Night Extra,* 1957; *Odds Against Tomorrow,* 1957; *Savage Streets,* 1959; *Seven Lies South,* 1960; *The Road to the*

Snail, 1961; *Police Special* (omnibus), 1962; *A Pride of Place,* 1962; *A Choice of Assassins,* 1963; *The Caper of the Golden Bulls,* 1966; *Lie Down, I Want to Talk to You,* 1967; *Caprifoil,* 1972; *Reprisal,* 1973; *Night of the Juggler,* 1975; *Soldiers of '44,* 1979; *Summitt,* 1982; *War Games,* 1983. **Screenplays** *I Saw What You Did,* 1965; *Chicago 7,* 1969; *The Wrecking Crew,* 1968; *The Man from Nowhere,* 1968; *Lie Down, I Want to Talk to You,* 1968; *Caprifoil,* 1973; *Joe Battle,* 1974; (jtly.) *Brannigan,* 1975; *Night of the Juggler,* 1975; *Hell on Frisco Bay;* others. **Television scripts** "The Young Lawyers," 1970; "San Francisco International Airport," 1970; "Banyon," 1972; "Kojak," 1973–77; other series. **Other** (With Maureen Daly McGivern) *Mention My Name in Mombasa: The Unscheduled Adventures of an American Family Abroad,* 1958; *Killer on the Turnpike* (short stories), 1961. **Contributor** of more than 300 short stories to *Saturday Evening Post, Collier's, Cosmopolitan,* other mags. **Manuscript collection** at Mugar Memorial Library, Boston Univ. **Interview** in *Publishers Weekly,* 12 Mar. 1979.

ERVING GOFFMAN

Sociologist

***Born* Manville, Alberta, Canada, 11 June 1922**

***Died* Philadelphia, Pennsylvania, USA, 19 November 1982**

Erving Goffman was one of the most original and stimulating thinkers in contemporary sociology and social anthropology. His acute observations and analyses of the minute details of human interaction, and of the social arrangements that conventions of interactive behavior protect and promote, opened to scholarly inquiry (and also for the instruction of interested laymen) an area of behavior that had been considered too commonplace to be of significance. In this respect some of his supporters went so far as to compare him with Freud. His protean work influenced nearly every branch of the social sciences and was the object of great admiration and great controversy. Although his prose style is not easy, it is enlivened by the frequent use of anecdotal illustrations and of metaphors invented for his purposes (frontstage/backstage; role distance; supportive and remedial interchanges; self-talk; frames, keyings, and fabrications). This fluidity of language placed him somewhat outside the limits of usual academic sociological discourse and gave rise to a plethora of conflicting interpretations of his work.

Goffman was born in Alberta, Canada, and earned his A.B. from the University of Toronto in 1945. After taking his M.A. at the University of Chicago, he spent three years teaching at the University of Edinburgh and doing ethnographic field research in the Shetland Islands for his doctoral degree (Chicago, 1953). Until 1958, when he joined the faculty of the University of California at Berkeley, he worked on research projects for the University of Chicago and the National Institute of Mental Health. Since 1968 he was Benjamin Franklin Professor of Anthropology and Sociology at the University of Pennsylvania.

Goffman's early books, beginning with *The Presentation of Self in Everyday Life* in 1959, were influenced by Émile Durkheim's pioneering studies of the phenomena of day-to-day existence and by the occupation studies of the Chicago School of sociology. In his first book he developed his idea of the face-to-face encounter as a piece of theater in which the participants function as performers, trying, by choice of clothing, mannerism, and speech, to put across desirable self-images, and signaling by verbal mechanisms their willingness to support, for the duration, one another's proffered identities—in his phrase, to "defer" to one another's "demeanors." In later books (*Behavior in Public Places,* 1963; *Relations in Public,* 1971) this analysis of self-presentation—what Goffman called "impression management"—was refined to such an extent that the individual appeared to be reduced to a set of roles, with no authentic self at base. Identity is said to be "diffusely located in the flow of events in the encounter," and to be "something that resides in the arrangements prevailing in a social system for its members." This led some of Goffman's leftist critics, especially in the 1960s, to attack him for supposedly contradicting their Rousseauian axiom that each person has a true and good self that is subject to corruption by the very social conventions Goffman describes.

While social conventions work, in most instances, to make coexistence smoother and more orderly, to everyone's benefit, such orderliness requires a high level of conformity. In *Asylums* (1961) and *Stigma* (1963) Goffman analyzed the processes by which "total," or custodial, institutions (including mental hospitals, prisons, monasteries, and orphanages) enforce conformity among their inmates by suppressing their "unacceptable" self-images, the responses of the inmates to this suppression, and the ways in which people marked as "different" deal with social encounters. Both books grew out of Goffman's experience (1956–57) at St. Elizabeths Hospital in Washington, D.C., where he posed undercover as a recreation therapist. *Asylums* became a standard text of the movement to reform psychiatric treatment and led to Goffman's appointment in 1971 to a government committee investigating institutional life.

During the late 1960s Goffman studied interactive behavior in the context of group-sustaining rules and norms (*Interaction Ritual,* 1967) and through the application of game theory, especially to such consciously role-playing situations as espionage (*Strategic Interaction,* 1969). In *Frame Analysis* (1971) he isolated and explicated a set of "frames of reference" (play, fantasy, dream, everyday reality) by which people organize and make sense of their experiences. His last two books dealt with communications—specifically, the forms by which cultural assumptions and individual and group self-images are communicated to their respective publics. Both books found an audience among laymen as well as sociologists. *Gender Advertisements* (1979) demonstrated the ways in which the makers of advertising art sell not only their products but a particular view of gender roles (the dominance of men over women), encoded in the postures, facial expressions, and spatial relations of the models. *Forms of Talk* (1981), which was nominated for a National Book Critics Circle Award, offered particularly acute and engaging analyses of the academic lecture (with its displays of authority, rituals of flattery and respect, and atmosphere of institutional self-congratulation) and of "response cries" (the exclamations by which people restore their mental equilibrium after making mistakes, indirectly solicit attention, or feign emotion).

Goffman's presidency of the American Sociological Association, to which he was elected in 1981, was cut short by his serious illness. A widower with one son by his first wife, he had recently remarried and was the father of an infant daughter. J.P.

Parents Max G. and Anne G. **Married** (1) Angelica Schuyler Choate 1952 (d. 1964): Thomas Edward. (2) Gillian Sankoff, linguist: Alice. **Emigrated** to U.S. 1945. **Education** Univ. of Toronto, A.B. 1945; Univ. of Chicago, M.A. 1949, Ph.D. in sociology 1953. **Career** Instr., dept. of social anthropology, Univ. of Edinburgh, and field researcher in Shetland Islands, Scotland 1949–51; research asst. 1952–53 and research assoc. 1953–54, Div. of Social Sciences, Univ. of Chicago; research assoc., Visiting Scientist Program, Lab. of Socioenvironmental Studies, Natl. Inst. of Mental Health 1954–57; asst. prof. 1958–59, assoc. prof. 1959–62, and prof. 1962–68, dept. of sociology, Univ. of California, Berkeley; Benjamin Franklin Prof. of Anthropology and Sociology, Univ. of Pennsylvania since 1968. **Officer** Pres., Amer. Sociological Assn. 1981–82. **Fellow** Amer. Acad. of Arts and Sciences. **Member** Cttee. for Study of Interaction 1971; Amer. Anthropological Assn. **Honors** MacIver Award 1961 and Mead-Cooley Award in Social Psychology 1979, Amer. Sociological Assn.; Guggenheim Fellowship 1977–78; "In Medias Res" Intl. Prize for Communication 1978; hon. degree from Univ. of Manitoba. **Author** *The Presentation of Self in Everyday Life,* 1959; *Encounters: Two Studies in the Sociology of Interaction,* 1961; *Asylums: Essays on the Social Situation of Mental Patients and Other Inmates,* 1961; *Stigma: Notes on the Management of Spoiled Identity,* 1963; *Behavior in Public Places: Notes on the Social Organization of Gatherings,* 1963; *Interaction Ritual: Essays on Face-to-Face Behavior,* 1967; *Strategic Interaction,* 1969; *Relations in Public: Microstudies of the Public Order,* 1971; *Frame Analysis: An Essay on the*

Organization of Experience, 1971; *Gender Advertisements,* 1979; *Forms of Talk,* 1981. **Contributor** of articles and reviews to *British Journal of Sociology, Psychiatry, American Journal of Sociology, American Anthropologist, Human Relations, New Society,* other jrnls.

Further reading Jason Ditton, ed., *The View From Goffman,* 1981.

ABRAHAM L(OUIS) POMERANTZ
Lawyer
***Born* New York City, USA, 22 March 1903**
***Died* New York City, USA, 20 November 1982**

Abraham L. Pomerantz, an expert on shareholders' derivative suits, an unusual form of lawsuit in which minority stockholders of a corporation sue its directors or officers for mismanagement on behalf of the corporation itself, became something of a dreaded figure in the boardrooms of America's largest corporations during his five-decade career. A quick-moving, bearlike man with a rabbinic style of courtroom oratory, Pomerantz relished a good legal battle and won most of his; at his retirement he was one of the richest lawyers in America.

Born in Brooklyn of Russian Jewish immigrant parents, Pomerantz graduated from Brooklyn Law School. After a brief stint as a legal assistant, he started a private practice, but business was so poor that he spent most of his time playing rummy with other lawyers. All through the 1920s Pomerantz's earnings were less than $2,000 a year. In 1933, just at the point of desperation, he received a phone call from the widow of his high-school gym teacher, asking if he could help her recoup the heavy losses she had sustained when her National City Bank of New York shares had plummeted in value from $400 each to about $20 after the Crash of 1929. National City Bank was then under investigation by the Senate Banking Committee. It was revealed that the bank's officers had paid themselves a large percentage of its profits in incentive bonuses; the draining away of so much of the bank's income had caused stock prices to drop. This was the opening Pomerantz sought. He filed a minority shareholders' derivative suit, then little known and rarely used, on the widow's behalf and, with a prominent New York lawyer presenting the case in court, won a $1.8 million decision for the bank, forcing the officers to return their bonuses. Pomerantz's income from the case was $60,000, three times his total previous earnings as a lawyer. Two equally successful actions followed against Chase Bank and William Randolph Hearst's Hearst Consolidated Publications. By the 1940s, Pomerantz was occupied full-time in prosecuting minority shareholders' suits. "To be honest," he said, "it was easy for me to go down that road. I didn't have any other practice. My alternative was knock rummy."

Pomerantz was active in liberal politics and in 1945 ran unsuccessfully for the New York State Supreme Court. The following year he was appointed deputy chief prosecutor of German industrialists at the Nuremberg Trials, but after eight months he quit in disgust at what he considered the U.S. Government's reluctance to prosecute the trials vigorously. On his return to the United States he was dismayed to learn of the promulgation of the anticommunist Executive Loyalty Order, which he called "the most Nazi-like and terrifying law since the Alien and Sedition Acts." He served as campaign treasurer for Henry Wallace's bid for the U.S. presidency on the Progressive ticket in 1948. In 1950, in one of the most sensational and controversial spy trials of the postwar years, he defended Valentin A. Gubitchev, a Soviet diplomat, and Judith Coplon, an employee of the U.S. Justice Department, who were accused of passing military secrets to the USSR.

Pomerantz emerged at the top of his field in the 1960s and 1970s, winning four out of every five shareholders' suits he brought against the likes of Jack Warner of Warner Brothers Pictures, Royal Little of Textron, the directors of Fairchild Camera, and the managers of 13 of the nation's biggest mutual funds. In the late 1970s he instituted a large number of suits against managers who blocked lucrative takeover bids, disregarding the best interests of the stockholders, in order to hold on to their

own positions. Many of the executives whom he defeated in court turned around and retained him as defense counsel in shareholders' suits brought by other lawyers. But his main interest was always with the small investor. "With the money I've made I haven't forgotten that it's a hard, cruel world, and when it's a question of the rich against the poor, I'm for the poor." He continued to be active in liberal causes until his death in New York City at the age of 79. S.A.

Parents Louis P., apartment builder, and Lena (Betz) P. **Married** Phyllis Cohen 1926: Daniel; Charlotte. **Religion** Jewish. **Education** Brooklyn Boys High Sch., grad. 1920; Brooklyn Law Sch., LL.B. (cum laude) 1924; admitted to New York State bar 1924. **Career** Asst. to Milton C. Weisman, lawyer, NYC 1924; private law practice, NYC since 1924; founding partner, Pomerantz, Levy, Haudek & Block law firm, NYC since 1940; deputy chief prosecuting attorney, German industrialists, Nuremberg Trials 1946. • Law instr., Brooklyn Law Sch. 1925; lectr., Columbia Univ., Univ. of Pennsylvania, Harvard Law Sch., Yale Law Sch., Northwestern Univ. Law Sch., Univ. of London, other schs. **Officer** Treas., Henry Wallace presidential campaign 1948. **Member** Advisory cttee. on rules of practice and procedure, U.S. Supreme Court; cttee. on qualifications to practice before U.S. courts, Judicial Council, U.S. 2nd Circuit Court; Anglo-Amer. Exchange; Amer. Bar Assn.; Amer. Law Inst.; Practicing Law Inst.; *New York Law Journal;* Democratic Party.

Further reading Spencer Klaw, "Abe Pomerantz is Watching You," in *Fortune,* Feb. 1968; Neal Goff, "Takeover Backlash: The Shareholders Sue," in *Financial World,* 15 June 1979.

BARON REDCLIFFE-MAUD OF THE CITY AND COUNTY OF BRISTOL
John Primatt Redcliffe Maud
Civil servant, diplomat, and college principal
Born **Bristol, England, 3 February 1906**
Died **Oxford, England, 20 November 1982**

Lord Redcliffe-Maud, a leading British civil administrator of the postwar period, held key positions during periods of radical change. His tenure as permanent secretary at the Ministry of Education followed almost immediately after the mammoth, far-reaching Education Act of 1944, and at the time of the Suez Crisis, when there was an acute shortage of gasoline in Britain, he was permanent secretary at the Ministry of Fuel and Power. Redcliffe-Maud was subsequently appointed high commissioner to South Africa and his years as a diplomat there were beset by the rancorous issues of apartheid and of South Africa's separation from the British Commonwealth. Later, as chairman of the Royal Commission on Local Government, he was again at the center of a contentious issue. His commission's sweeping recommendations, welcomed by experts in the field, proved too radical for the Conservative government responsible for implementing the reforms.

John Primatt Redcliffe Maud was born in 1906, the son of a former bishop of Kensington. He was educated at Eton, went on to New College, Oxford, as a classics scholar, and then went to Harvard to study politics. In 1929 he was appointed a fellow of University College, Oxford, and remained there for ten years; he was college dean from 1932 to 1939 and became the university's first full-time lecturer in politics. His first book, *Local Government in Modern England,* appeared in 1932 and was well received; his third, *City Government: The Johannesburg Experiment* (1938), was the result of his year's study in South Africa as a Rhodes Travelling Fellow. Maud was appointed master of Birkbeck College, London, in 1939, then during World War II served in the Ministry of Food. In 1944 he became second secretary in the Office of the Minister of Reconstruction and a year later was appointed secretary of the office of the Lord President of the Council.

As permanent secretary at the Ministry of Education (1945–52), Maud was one of the main implementers of the Labour Government's 1944 Education Act. The age of leaving school was raised to 15, secondary education became obligatory for all children, and provisions for teacher training were significantly expanded. Maud, who was a contributor to *Education in a Changing World* in 1951, acquired a formidable reputation as an administrator while at the Ministry of Education and in 1952 was given the even more challenging job of permanent secretary at the Ministry of Fuel and Power, a post he retained until 1959. During this period, under the Minister, Geoffrey Lloyd, he instituted the conversion of trains from steam to diesel power and changed many coal-burning power stations to oil, as a means of reducing the demand for coal, which had been in short supply since the war. Maud was also greatly involved with Britain's adoption of a nuclear-power program to further alleviate its fuel shortage. The Suez crisis made many demands on Maud's administrative skills; with little warning he had to institute gasoline rationing and insure that the crisis would not cripple the nation's major industries and transportation networks.

Maud became high commissioner to South Africa in 1959. While he abhorred apartheid, he was a firm believer in the Commonwealth ideal, and felt that South Africa, a leading member, should at all costs remain within the international body. However, despite the best efforts of Maud and his colleagues, South Africa could not be persuaded to significantly change its racist policies. Upon the nation's departure from the Commonwealth, Maud's title changed from high commissioner to ambassador, but he remained, at his own insistence, high commissioner of Swaziland and Basutoland and of the Bechuanaland Protectorate.

After leaving Africa in 1963, Maud returned to University College, Oxford, as master. He remained there until his retirement in 1976. In 1966, a year before he was appointed a life peer, he was named chairman of the Royal Commission to consider the structure of local government in England outside London. After three years the commission proposed that 58 "unitary" authorities should replace the many smaller local authorities, with Liverpool, Manchester, and Birmingham becoming "metropolitan" authorities which, unlike the "unitary" ones, would comprise a number of smaller authorities—somewhat similar to the scheme of city councils within the Greater London Council. One of the main aims of the commission was to reduce the differences in quality between urban and rural administrations, and to some extent this was achieved with the passage of the Local Authorities Act in 1972. But the Conservative government, aware of grassroots opposition in its traditionally strong areas, failed to implement a number of the commission's radical proposals.

Lord Redcliffe-Maud's book *English Local Government Reformed* appeared in 1974, while he was serving as chairman of the Prime Minister's Committee on Local Government Rules of Conduct. His other books include a volume of memoirs, *Experiences of an Optimist.* He died in Oxford at the age of 76.

R.T.

Parents John Primatt Maud, bishop of Kensington, and Elizabeth Diana (Furse) Maud. **Married** Jean Hamilton, concert pianist, 1932: one son; three daughters (one d.). **Religion** Church of England. **Education** Eton Coll. (King's Scholarship and Newcastle Medal); New Coll., Oxford (Open Classical Scholarship), double 1st Class in Moderations and Greats; Harvard Coll. (Davison Scholarship from Oxford Univ.), A.B. 1929. **Career** Jr. research fellow 1929, and fellow and dean 1932–39, University Coll., Oxford; Rhodes Travelling Fellowship, Africa ca. 1938; councilor, Oxford City 1930–36; tutor, Colonial Administrative Services Course, Oxford 1937–39; Univ. Lectr. in Politics, Oxford 1938–39; master, Birkbeck Coll., Univ. of London 1939–43; panelist, "Brains Trust" TV program, BBC early 1940s. • Deputy secty., later 2nd secty., Ministry of Food 1941–44; 2nd secty., Office of Minister of Reconstruction 1944–45; secty., Office of Lord Pres. of Council 1945; permanent secty., Ministry of Education 1945–52; member, Economic Planning Bd. 1952–58; permanent secty., Ministry of Fuel and Power 1952–59; British high commnr. 1959–61 and ambassador 1961–63, South Africa; British high commnr. for Basutoland, Bechuanaland Protectorate, and Swaziland 1959–63. • Member, U.K. delegations: Conferences on Food and Agriculture, Hot Springs 1943; U.N. Rescue and Relief Admin., Atlantic City, NJ 1943; UNESCO 1946–51. • Master, University

Coll., Oxford 1963–76; high bailiff of Westminster since 1967. **Officer** Pres.: (also member 1946–50) exec. bd., UNESCO 1949–50; Royal Inst. of Public Admin. 1969–79; British Diabetic Assn. since 1977. • Chmn.: Local Govt. Management Cttee. 1964–67; council, Royal College of Music 1965–73; Royal Commn. on Local Govt. in England 1966–69; Prime Minister's Cttee. on Local Govt. Rules of Conduct 1973–74; appoints commn., Press Council 1973–75. **Fellow** (Sr. fellow) Royal Coll. of Art 1961; FRCM 1964; Eton Coll. 1964–76; (assoc.) Jonathan Edwards Coll., Yale Univ. 1968. **Member** (Foreign assoc.) Venezuelan Acad. of Sciences 1973; Savile Club; Eton Ramblers. **Honors** CBE 1942; KCB 1946; GCB 1955; created Baron Redcliffe-Maud of City and County of Bristol, life peer, 1967; hon. fellow of New Coll. 1964 and University Coll. 1976, Oxford; Pres.'s Medal, Inst. of Public Relations 1974; hon. degrees from univs. of Witwatersrand, Natal, Leeds, Nottingham, and Birmingham. **Author** *Local Government in Modern England,* 1932; *Johannesburg and the Art of Self-Government,* 1937; *City Government: The Johannesburg Experiment,* 1938; *Local Government in England and Wales,* 1953; (jtly.) *English Local Government Reformed,* 1974; *Support for the Arts in England and Wales,* 1976; *Experiences of an Optimist* (memoirs), 1981. **Contributor** *Oxford and the Groups,* 1934; *Personal Ethics,* 1935; *Education in a Changing World,* 1951.

JOHN HARGRAVE

Writer, inventor, and leader of Social Credit Party

***Born* 1894**

***Died* 21 November 1982**

John Hargrave was the eccentric founder of two small but moderately influential organizations, the Kibbo Kift and the Greenshirts, that functioned in Britain between the world wars; the former promoted nature lore and woodcraft, and the latter promoted the ideas of the Social Credit Party, of which Hargrave was a leader. He was also a novelist, the inventor of an automatic aircraft navigator, a lexicographer, and a cartoonist.

The son of Quaker parents, Hargrave left school at the age of 14 to work as an illustrator of children's books, and at 17 became the chief cartoonist of the *London Evening Times.* During World War I he served in the Royal Army Marine Corps at Gallipoli and Salonika; he was invalided out in 1916 and became art manager at a publishing firm. He left that job after three years to freelance as a journalist. At the same time he also broke with the Boy Scouts, with whom he had long been active, telling its founder, Lord Baden-Powell, that the organization had fallen into the hands of "old soldiers and vicars." The Kibbo Kift Kindred, which he founded in 1920, was, like the Boy Scouts, a camping organization, but with a far more mystical bent. Its members wore a uniform of shorts, hooded jerkin, and cloak, engaged in pseudo-tribal woodland rituals, and were urged by Hargrave, who was called White Fox, to practice self-discipline and work for the brotherhood of man. H. G. Wells and Julian Huxley were among the group's advisors.

By 1929 Hargrave had turned all his energies to furthering C. H. Douglas's Social Credit movement, which demanded a complete reform of banking to produce a debt-free economy, no matter what the cost in unemployment. His followers, the Greenshirts, many of whom were alumni of the Kibbo Kift, were intended by Hargrave to be a company of "life-urgent" visionaries attuned to the power of the Sun and the other nature deities of old England. In his newsletter, *The Message from Hargrave,* he exhorted them with such slogans as "Whelm on Me, ye Resurrected Men!" and "Social Credit is Solar Magick!" The movement did not survive the 1937 law prohibiting the wearing of political uniforms, and after World War II Hargrave had no success in trying to revive it. The Social Credit Party remains strong in Alberta, Canada, where it ruled from 1935 to 1971, and where Hargrave was honorary advisor to the Government Planning Committee in 1936–37.

Hargrave wrote six novels between 1924 and 1935; in the last of them, *Summer Time*

Ends, he tried to give the illusion of simultaneous action by using neither capitalization nor punctuation. His nonfiction books include several works of Social Credit propaganda, two critical accounts of the Suvla Bay landing in the Gallipoli campaign of World War I, a dictionary, and a biography of Paracelsus, the sixteenth-century doctor and magician. Hargrave himself was a practitioner of psychic healing. In the late 1940s he and a colleague invented an optical display for aircraft that projected an image of the ground below onto the instrument panel. It was patented as the Hargrave Automatic Navigator. When, 20 years later, a similar device was patented by a government-backed inventor, Hargrave sued, unsuccessfully, for £8 million in compensation. One of his ancestors was Lawrence Hargrave, the inventor of the box kite.

Hargrave died at the age of 81. A rock musical based on his life played in Edinburgh in 1976. J.P./C.B.

Known in Kibbo Kift as White Fox. **Father** Gordon H., landscape painter. **Married** (1) Ruth Clark 1919 (div. 1952): one son. (2) Gwendolyn Gray, actress, 1968. **Religion** Raised a Quaker. **Education** Wordsworth's Sch., Hawkshead. **Mil. service** 10th Irish Div., RAMC, Turkey and Greece 1914–16. **Career** Illus. and cartoonist since age 14; chief cartoonist, *London Evening Times* ca. 1911–14; artist 1914 and art mgr. 1917–20, C. Arthur Pearson Ltd. publishing co., London; freelance writer and journalist since early 1920s; founding leader, Kibbo Kift Kindred 1920–29 and Greenshirts 1929–37; leader of Social Credit Party 1920s–30s; inventor, novelist, and psychic healer. **Officer** Commnr. for woodcraft and camping, Boy Scouts, U.K. 1910s–20. **Honors** Hon. advisor 1936–37 and publisher of *Alberta Report* 1937, Govt. Planning Cttee., Alta., Canada. **Novels** *Harbottle,* 1924; *Young Winkle,* 1925; *And Then Came Spring,* 1926; *The Pfenninger Failing,* 1927; *The Imitation Man,* 1931; *Summer Time Ends,* 1935. **Other** *Lonecraft,* 1913; *At Suvla Bay,* 1916; *Tribal Training,* 1919; *The Great War Brings It Home,* 1919; *The Confession of the Kibbo Kift,* 1927; *Professor Skinner Alias Montagu Norman,* 1939; *Propaganda the Mightiest Weapon of All; Words Win Wars,* 1940; *Social Credit Clearly Explained,* 1945; *The Life and Soul of Paracelsus,* 1951; *The Paragon Dictionary,* 1953; *The Suvla Bay Landing,* 1964; *The Facts of the Case Concerning the Hargrave Automatic Navigator for Aircraft,* 1969; other books and pamphlets on woodcraft and politics. **Contributor** to *Encyclopaedia Britannica,* newspapers, and mags.

BURTON B(ERNARD) TURKUS

Prosecutor of organized crime and labor-management arbitrator
Born **New York City, USA, circa 1902**
Died **New York City, USA, 22 November 1982**

The death in the electric chair of the gangster and labor racketeer Louis (Lepke) Buchalter, head of the Brooklyn-based Murder, Incorporated, in March 1944 marked the first time that American law enforcers succeeded in executing a leader of organized crime. The testimony of former accomplices at his trial revealed to the public the existence of a nationwide crime syndicate that had infiltrated industries in all major cities, operated by murdering its opponents, and was everywhere protected by corrupt politicians. Two of Lepke's prosecutors, Thomas E. Dewey and William O'Dwyer, were able to exploit his notoriety in their campaigns for public office, Dewey becoming governor of New York State (and nearly winning the presidency in 1948) and O'Dwyer becoming mayor of New York City. Another prosecutor was Burton Turkus, known in gangland circles as Mr. Arsenic, chief of the Brooklyn district attorney's homicide division from 1940 to 1945, whose capable investigation and court presentation helped convict Lepke and eight other mobsters on first-degree murder charges.

Turkus was born in Brooklyn to immigrant Jewish working-class parents. After graduating from Manual Training High School, he worked nights as a telegraph operator for Western Union and studied law at New York University, entering the bar in 1925. For the next 15 years he had a private practice in criminal law, saving 17 murder defendants from the death penalty. In 1940, when William O'Dwyer was appointed to reform the Kings County (Brooklyn) district attorney's office, one of the most corrupt in the country, he brought in Turkus as his assistant.

The Williamsburg, Brownsville, and East New York sections of Brooklyn were the headquarters of Lepke and his partner Jake (Gurrah) Shapiro, who together had been running protection rackets since the 1920s and who controlled nearly every highly competitive industry in New York City, including the needle trades, the construction trades, and fish and produce selling. Their staff of professional murderers was recruited mainly from the Jewish and Italian slums of Brooklyn and lower Manhattan. In August 1939, Lepke, in a double-cross by other mob leaders, was persuaded to surrender to the FBI to face a narcotics-selling charge; once convicted, he was turned over to Dewey, then New York State's special prosecutor for organized crime, who convicted him of racketeering in the baking industry. While Lepke was in custody, Turkus and other members of the Brooklyn prosecutor's team secured the help of an informant, Abe (Kid Twist) Reles, a high-ranking member of Murder, Incorporated, and built a case against Lepke for ordering the death of a former truck driver who had threatened to complain to Dewey after being forced out of business by Lepke's racketeers. Six associates of Lepke's, all of them sadistic killers responsible for scores of murders, went to the electric chair before Lepke exhausted his appeals.

Turkus's account of the investigation, *Murder, Inc.* (1951), written with journalist Sid Feder, was the basis for a 1960 movie of the same name in which Henry Morgan played Turkus. He was also the model for Humphrey Bogart's character in *The Enforcer* (1950). In 1952 he was briefly the host of a television show called "Mr. Arsenic."

Turkus lost a race for a Brooklyn county judgeship in 1942—although he was an independent Democrat, he ran as a Republican—and thereafter stayed clear of politics. He was named chief assistant district attorney in 1945, but left that job in the same year to work as a labor-management mediator for the upholstered-furniture and retail-drug industries, joining the State Mediation Board in 1948 by appointment of Gov. Dewey. In 1957 he was jointly chosen by the International Longshoremen's Association and the New York Shipping Association to act as impartial arbitrator for the Port of New York; his arbitration settled a 1968 dockworkers' walkout that had paralyzed the waterfront for 11 days. He never retired from his law practice and died in his office at the age of 80. J.P.

Parents Father a watchmaker; mother a seamstress. **Married** Naomi Herman 1944: Donald. **Religion** Jewish. **Education** Manual Training High Sch., NYC; New York Univ., law degree; admitted to New York bar 1925. **Career** Telegraph operator, Western Union; criminal lawyer, Brooklyn 1925–40; asst. district attorney and chief of homicide div. 1940–45, and chief asst. district attorney 1945, Kings County (Brooklyn), NYC. • In private practice in labor arbitration since 1945: member, New York State Mediation Bd. 1948–57; appointed arbitrator, Port of New York 1957; panel member of Federal Mediation and Conciliation Service, Natl. Mediation Bd., Amer. Arbitration Assn., New Jersey Bd. of Mediation; arbitrator for airline, retail-drug, automobile, upholstered-furniture, and other industries. • Expert examiner, New York State Dept. of Civil Service; lectr., bar assns. and trade unions; technical consultant and scriptwriter for radio, TV, films; host, "Mr.

Arsenic" TV series 1952. **Member** Natl. Acad. of Arbitrators; Amer. Arbitration Assn.; Intl. Acad. of Law and Science; Amer. Judicature Soc.; District Attorneys Assn.; Friars Club; Honor Legion, Police Dept. of New York City; Detective Endowment Assn.; bar assns. of Brooklyn, New York City, and New York State. **Author** (Jtly.) *New York Law of Alimony,* 1932; (jtly.) *Murder, Inc.,* 1951.

HUGH HARMAN
Animator
Born **Colorado, USA, circa 1903**
Died **Chatsworth, California, USA, 25 November 1982**

Few animators from the early days of theatrical cartoons received the public recognition accorded Max Fleischer, Walter Lantz, and, above all, Walt Disney. The name of Hugh Harman, a collaborator of Disney's from his days in Kansas City and later the founder of MGM's excellent cartoon studio, is known only to students of animation, but his imaginative work with Rudolf Ising on the original *Looney Tunes* and *Merrie Melodies* series was often on a par with the best from the Disney studio (still considered the pinnacle of traditional animation), and sometimes, as in Harman's antiwar short *Peace on Earth* (1939), surpassed it.

Harman was still a high-school student in Kansas City, Missouri, when his older brother Fred, the creator of the *Red Ryder* comic strip, introduced him to Disney. In 1922 he joined Disney's ill-fated Laugh-O-Grams Company, where he met Ising and taught himself the rudiments of cartoon animation. Disney moved to Hollywood the next year, and Harman and Ising, after failing to make it as independent animators in Kansas City, followed him there in 1925. They worked on Disney's *Alice* comedies, a mixture of live-action and animated figures, and the *Oswald the Rabbit* series. In 1928 they were lured away from Disney's studio by George Winkler, the financier of the Oswald cartoons, to do the Oswald series on their own. (This forced Disney to come up with a new character called Mickey Mouse.) When Walter Lantz edged them out of the Winkler studio, they signed up with another distributor, Leon Schlesinger, who sold the first of their *Looney Tune* cartoons (the name was a play on Disney's *Silly Symphonies*) to Warner Brothers. Most of the *Looney Tunes,* and many of the *Merrie Melodies* series that followed, featured Bosko the Clown, a creature who looked at first rather like a wide-mouthed, earless Mickey Mouse and who was transformed in later cartoons into a small black boy. Harman and Ising constantly battled with Schlesinger over budgets, and ultimately broke with him to start MGM's cartoon studio in 1934. At last, with adequate funds and facilities, they set out to attain the technical excellence that distinguished the Disney cartoons. They did their first two-color cartoon, *The Discontented Canary,* in 1934 (Disney still had exclusive rights to the three-color Technicolor process) and steadily improved their work throughout the mid-1930s.

The cartoons made by Harman and Ising after MGM let them go in 1938 are remarkably similar to Disney's: they feature cute, appealing animal characters, broad sight gags, tight coordination of music, dialogue, and movement, and skillful draftsmanship. Harman was especially adept at animating rapid movements and odd perspectives. In 1940 the Harman-Ising short *The Milky Way,* a kitten story, won an Academy Award; the partners shared six other Oscar nominations between them. Harman was nominated for a Nobel Peace Prize for his 1939 cartoon *Peace on Earth.* For all their popularity they never reached their full artistic potential. They were unable to find a sympathetic studio to fund them for long, and on their own they never developed a roster of strong, recognizable characters on which they could depend for regular income, as did Disney with Mickey Mouse and Donald Duck.

In 1942 the Harman and Ising team broke up; Harman went into business doing training films for industry and Ising made animated instructional shorts for the military. Although they worked together after the war on a variety of projects, mostly for television, they never made another theatrical cartoon. Harman died at the age of 79. S.A.

Child Michael. **Education** High sch., Kansas City, MO. **Military service** ca. 1922. **Career** Animator since 1922; with Laugh-O-Grams Co., Kansas City 1922–23; with Disney studios, Hollywood 1925–28; with Winkler studios, Hollywood 1928–29; independent producer and animator, Warner Brothers Pictures, Hollywood 1930–33; with MGM cartoon studio, Hollywood 1934–38; independent producer and animator 1938–42; made industrial training films, TV commercials, other films since 1940s. **Honors** (Jtly.) Academy Award, for *The Milky Way,* 1940. **Theatrical cartoons** *Looney Tunes* series, 1930–32; *Merrie Melodies* series, ca. 1932–33; *Happy Harmonies* series and other cartoons, 1934–43; *Peace on Earth,* 1939.

Further reading Mike Barrier, "The Careers of Hugh Harman and Rudolf Ising," in *Millimeter,* Feb. 1976.

QUEEN HELEN OF RUMANIA

Regent and royal advisor
***Born* Athens, Greece, 2 May 1896**
***Died* Lausanne, Switzerland, 28 November 1982**

Although she was married to the deposed King Carol II of Rumania only during his years as crown prince, and not during his kingship, Queen Helen served as regent while her son Michael was a minor, and advised Michael throughout his two reigns before the royal family was permanently exiled to make way for the establishment of a Communist republic in 1947.

Born with the title Princess of Greece and Denmark, the daughter of Crown Prince Constantine of Greece (later King Constantine I) and Princess Sophia of Prussia, Helen was descended on both sides of the family from Catherine the Great and on her mother's side from Queen Victoria. She and her sister and three brothers were given a strict English upbringing. In 1921 a double marriage was arranged between Helen and Crown Prince Carol, the son of King Ferdinand of Rumania, and between Helen's brother George and Carol's sister Elizabeth. These marriages had been eagerly sought by the royal house of Rumania, which was anxious to improve ties with other Balkan states and, more particularly, to curb the excesses of Carol, a playboy whose elopement with the daughter of a Rumanian army officer had been annulled a short time before. A son, Michael, was born to Helen and Carol later in the year.

From the beginning the marriage seemed destined to fail. The reserved, proud Helen preferred a quiet home life to the ostentatious vitality of the Rumanian court. Carol soon took up openly with Magda Lupescu, a renowned beauty. Pressed by his father and the council to give her up, Carol in a fit of pique angrily renounced the throne and left the country in 1925. The abdication was quickly made official, and Michael, then only three years old, was appointed successor designate. He was crowned king two years later, on the death of Ferdinand, and his mother was made one of three regents. In 1928, Helen and Carol were divorced.

Although generally liked by the Rumanians, Helen had little political influence. Opposition forces in the council succeeded in bringing back Carol in 1930; with him came Lupescu. He was crowned within two days of his arrival and immediately sent Helen into exile in Florence, allowing her to see her son, who had reverted to the status of crown prince, only once a year. Carol's reign lasted a decade, during which he was constantly occupied in trying to crush the pro-Nazi Iron Guards, who demanded that he ally himself with Hitler and were infuriated by his liaison with Lupescu, the daughter of a Jewish businessman. In 1939, after he established a dictatorship, they assassinated his prime minister, Armand Călinescu. When the Soviet

Union and then the Axis powers seized Rumanian territory in 1940, they rioted, forcing Carol to abdicate in favor of Michael, now 18, who thus became one of the very few kings to rule both before and after his father.

Helen returned from Florence and became her son's principal advisor. His sovereignty was no more than titular: real political power was held by a Fascist government led by Marshal Ion Antonescu. Helen spent much of World War II nursing wounded soldiers from the eastern front, where several Rumanian divisions were fighting alongside the Germans at Odessa and Stalingrad. In August 1944, on the eve of a Russian invasion, she helped plan the coup d'état that returned Michael to power and aligned Rumania with the Allies. (The king personally arrested Antonescu and his guards at the palace and imprisoned them in the fireproof room that held the royal stamp collection.)

Two years after the war ended, Helen and Michael were forced out of the country by Rumania's new Russian-backed Communist government. Michael became a stockbroker in Geneva and Helen settled in Florence and then in Lausanne. She died there at the age of 86. C.M.

Born Princess of Greece and Denmark. **Parents** King Constantine I of Greece and Princess Sophia of Prussia. **Married** King Carol II of Rumania 1921 (div. 1928): Michael, king of Rumania, later stockbroker, b. 1921. **Emigrated** to Rumania 1921; in exile, Italy 1930–40 and Italy and Switzerland since 1947. **Career** Consort of Crown Prince Carol of Rumania 1921–27; regent of Rumania 1927–30; advisor to King Michael 1940–47.

Further reading Arthur S. Gould Lee, *The Royal House of Greece,* 1948; A. S. G. Lee, *Helen, Queen Mother of Rumania,* 1956.

DECEMBER

MARTY FELDMAN

Comedian and comedy writer
***Born* Canning Town, East London, England, 8 July 1934**
***Died* Mexico City, Mexico, 2 December 1982**

Marty Feldman was able to make comic capital from a face that seemed to have been pieced together from spare parts. With his broken nose and popping eyes, he looked, said a writer for the *Daily Express* of London, "like something that had fallen off the roof of Notre Dame Cathedral in a thunderstorm." Most American moviegoers knew him as one of Mel Brooks' band of loonies, but in Britain he was best known for his 1970 television show "Marty" and his work as a comedy writer.

The son of Polish-Russian Jewish immigrants—his father was a pushcart peddler who became a dress manufacturer—Feldman grew up in the East End of London and dropped out of school at 15 to go to work as a messenger boy and play trumpet in a jazz band. By the time he was 17 he had been an assistant to a sideshow act, a racetrack tipster, a shill for a tourist-trapping Parisian portrait sculptor, and a book thief. (His education, he once said, consisted of reading these stolen books.) Ejected from France for vagrancy, he worked the music halls for a time and toured in a comedy trio, Morris, Marty and Mitch, then joined the BBC as a staff writer in 1957, when he was 23. His collaboration with Barry Took on the radio series "Round the Horne" (1965–69) won the Writers Guild Award in 1967. That year he was also chief writer for BBC-TV's "The Frost Report" and was subsequently hired to write and perform in David Frost's "At Last The 1948 Show," together with Tim Brooke-Taylor and two future members of Monty Python, Graham Chapman and John Cleese. Audience reaction to him was so positive that he was soon given his own show, "Marty," which had 15 million viewers weekly. He also appeared in *Every Home Should Have One* (1969) and other movies, and did some directing at London's Fringe Theatre.

The success of "Marty" led to Feldman's first appearance in the United States, as a regular on "Dean Martin Presents the Golddiggers," a 1970 summer series, which was followed by "Marty Feldman's Comedy Machine." In 1974 he left England for Hollywood, where he quickly became a member of the Mel Brooks team, along with Gene Wilder, Madeline Kahn, and Peter Boyle. He was Eye-gore, the cheerful hunchback, in Brooks' *Young Frankenstein* (1974), the honest Sergeant Sacker in Wilder's *The Adventures of Sherlock Holmes' Smarter Brother* (1976), and Marty Eggs in Brooks' *Silent Movie* (1976). He made his directing debut in 1977 with *The Last Remake of Beau Geste*, in which he played the identical twin of Michael York; it was a modest success, unlike his second film, *In God We Trust* (1979), about a fallen monk.

Feldman offscreen was low-key and gentle, a vegetarian (since the days of his wartime

Courtesy of Michael Maslansky

evacuation to a farm area) who married the daughter of a butcher. "I would not willingly eat anything that had intelligent life," he said, "but I would willingly eat a producer." His comedy, more visual than verbal, was in the clowning tradition of Buster Keaton and Stan Laurel and was enhanced by his misshapen features, which carried an expression of pleasant melancholy. (The broken nose was acquired in a boxing match; the straying eyes, which could look in two directions at once, were the result of a thyroid condition brought on by a boating accident.)

He died of a heart attack in Mexico City on the day that he finished filming *Yellowbeard,* a pirate spoof written by Graham Chapman. *Slapstick,* a Jerry Lewis picture, had not yet been released at the time of his death.

C.M.

Parents Father a pushcart peddler, later dress manufacturer; mother Cecilia. **Married** Lauretta Sullivan, secty., later assoc. film producer, 1959. **Religion** Jewish. **Education** Left sch. at age 15. **Career** Trumpeter in jazz group at age 15; various odd jobs 1950s, including sideshow asst., touring comedian, and sculptor's shill; comedy writer for radio from 1957, for TV from 1960s, for films from 1970s; comedy actor on TV from 1967, in films from 1969; also stage, film, and TV dir. **Honors** (Jtly.) award for TV writing, for "Bootsie and Snudge" and "The Army Game," *Daily Mirror* 1961; Writers Guild Award for best radio comedy series, for "Round the Horne," 1967; Light Entertainment Personality of the Year, for "Marty," Guild of Television Producers and Directors 1969–70; BBC Television Personality of the Year, Variety Club of Great Britain 1970; Royal Television Soc. Personality of the Year Award 1970; Montreux Silver Rose, for "Marty," 1970; Montreux Golden Rose and City of Montreux Trophy, for "The Best of the Comedy Machine," 1971. **Radio writer** "Educating Archie," 1957; "Round the Horne," 1965–69; others. **Television writer** "Bootsie and Snudge," 1961; "The Army Game," 1961; "The Walrus and the Carpenter" and other scripts, "Comedy Playhouse," 1960s; "Frost Report," mid-1960s; others. **Television writer and performer** "At Last The 1948 Show," 1967; "Marty," 1970; "Dean Martin Presents the Golddiggers," 1970; "The Marty Feldman Comedy Machine," 1972; also specials "Marty Amok," "Marty Abroad," "Marty—Back Together Again," others. **Television actor** "The Man Who Came to Dinner," 1972; "Bonjour Monsieur Lewis" (documentary); "The Sixth Day"; "The Compartment"; "Playmates"; guest appearances on variety and comedy shows; (dir.) episodes, "When Things Were Rotten," 1975. **Film comedian** *Every Home Should Have One* (in U.S. as *Think Dirty*), 1969; *The Bed Sitting Room,* 1969; *Young Frankenstein,* 1974; *The Adventures of Sherlock Holmes' Smarter Brother,* 1976; *Silent Movie,* 1976; *Sex With a Smile,* 1976; (also dir. and co-scriptwriter) *The Last Remake of Beau Geste,* 1977; (also dir. and co-scriptwriter) *In God We Trust, or Gimme That Prime-Time Religion,* 1979; (co-scriptwriter only) *The Secret Policeman's Other Ball,* 1982; *Slapstick,* 1983; *Yellowbeard,* 1983.

GEORGE B(OGDAN) KISTIAKOWSKY

Chemist, government advisor, and nuclear-disarmament advocate
***Born* Kiev, Ukraine, Russia, 18 November 1900**
***Died* Cambridge, Massachusetts, USA, 7 December 1982**

The explosives expert George B. Kistiakowsky played key roles in the creation of the atomic bomb during World War II and in the establishment by the United States of a network of intercontinental ballistic missiles during the 1950s. In later life, convinced that nuclear annihilation was all but inevitable, Kistiakowsky, like so many other scientists who worked on the bomb, called for an end to atomic testing and a reduction in the world's stockpiles of nuclear weapons.

Kistiakowsky was born into a Ukrainian Cossack family that had acquired a strong academic tradition: his father, grandfather, and great-grandfather were all professors at the University of Kiev. After attending private schools in Moscow and Kiev, he joined the White Army in 1918 to fight the Communist revolutionaries, but, he recalled, "I spent most of my time running away from the Bolsheviks and changing generals." When the Red Army occupied the Crimea in 1920 he fled to Istanbul, where he was briefly interned in a concentration camp, and then made his way to Berlin; an émigré uncle paid for his education at the university there. He received a doctorate in physical chemistry in 1925 and the following year emigrated to the United States to work at Princeton University as an International Education Board Fellow. From 1930 he was a member of the faculty of Harvard University, becoming Lawrence Professor of Chemistry in 1938.

In 1940, with war imminent, Kistiakowsky joined the National Defense Research Committee to conduct research on explosives. By 1942 he had become chairman of the NDRC's explosives division, with laboratories in Bruceton, Pennsylvania, and Woods Hole, Massachusetts, under his supervision. One of his first tasks was to devise an explosive that could safely be smuggled into Japanese-occupied China for use by saboteurs. His team at Bruceton developed a powdered explosive that, at his suggestion, was made to resemble ordinary flour. Known by the code name "Aunt Jemima," the powder could be made into dough and even baked into bread without losing its power. "To test it," Kistiakowsky said, "we chewed some of it and then took it out and blew up a bridge with it." Tons of the explosive reached the Chinese resistance forces packed into flour bags.

Beginning in 1943, Kistiakowsky worked with the Manhattan Project to develop the atomic bomb. Two designs were under consideration: a uranium bomb and a plutonium bomb. In each case, a triggering device was needed to compress the fissionable material rapidly into a critical mass, initiating a chain reaction. Finding a trigger for the plutonium bomb posed technical problems. Enriched plutonium explodes prematurely just as it reaches critical mass, expending only a tiny fraction of its energy. Some method had to be devised to bring a loosely packed plutonium core together with sufficient rapidity to reach a supercritical mass before the chain reaction was well under way. Several scientists proposed that the plutonium core be imploded by an outer layer of ordinary chemical explosives. In February 1944, Kistiakowsky was called to Los Alamos to develop such a device.

Courtesy of Harvard University

His main difficulty was delivering a perfectly spherical shock wave to the plutonium, so that it would be compressed uniformly and not blasted out of the core to one side or the other. It took more than a year before Kistiakowsky's group solved all the attendant problems. The bomb test at Alamogordo, New Mexico, on 16 July 1945, code-named "Trinity," was held primarily to verify that the implosion mechanism worked. It did. Kistiakowsky, standing 10,000 yards away from ground zero, was knocked into a trench by the force of the blast. "I am sure," he said later, "that at the end of the world—in the last few milliseconds of the earth's existence—the last human will see what we saw." On 9 August 1945 a plutonium bomb was dropped on Nagasaki.

At Harvard, where he chaired the chemistry department from 1947 to 1950, Kistiakowsky continued his research on shock waves, molecular spectroscopy, and the kinetics of chemical reactions. He was a member of several governmental consulting bodies, including the Air Force's Ballistic Missile Advisory Committee (1953–58), which successfully urged the development of intercontinental ballistic missiles, especially solid-fueled rockets launched from submarines, to counter the threat—largely imaginary at that time—of Soviet nuclear attack. In 1957 he was appointed to the President's Science Advisory Committee, a group formed in reaction to the Soviet launching earlier that year of Sputnik I, the world's first artificial satellite. Two years later he became chairman of that group and special assistant for science and technology to Pres. Dwight Eisenhower. The president, who foresaw and feared the nuclear-arms race, came to value the independent advice Kistiakowsky offered him on weapons testing and space-vehicle development. Kistiakowsky's memoir, *A Scientist in the White House* (1976), provides a record of how the U.S. government arrived at a set of nuclear-weapons policies with virtually no public input or debate.

By the 1960s Kistiakowsky had joined those who consider nuclear weapons more a threat to world survival than a deterrent to Soviet aggression. He was a member of the advisory board of the Arms Control and Disarmament Agency from 1962 to 1969, but soon realized that neither side was willing to give up its ability to wage atomic war. He opposed Pres. Johnson's escalation of the Vietnam War and in 1967 resigned his post as foreign-policy advisor. Throughout the 1970s he spoke out on defense issues, calling for a halt to the development of antiballistic missiles and other weapons systems. In 1977 he became chairman of the Council for a Livable World, a Boston- and Washington-based group advocating arms control.

Kistiakowsky's last public statement was an editorial in the November 1982 issue of the *Bulletin of the Atomic Scientists,* published a few weeks before his death of cancer. "The political leaders of powerful nations continue offering pious words about their love of peace," he wrote, "but the arsenals keep growing, the stability of nuclear peace is being undermined, and the proposals for arms controls negotiations on both sides are so unbalanced as to be obviously non-negotiable. As one who has tried to change these trends, working both through official channels and, for the last dozen years, from outside, I tell you as my parting words: Forget the channels. There is simply not enough time left before the world explodes. Concentrate instead on organizing, with so many others who are of like mind, a mass movement for peace such as there has never been before." P.D.

Parents Bogdan K., law prof., and Mary (Berenstam) K. **Married** (1) Hildegard Moebius 1926 (div. 1942): Vera Fischer, physicist. (2) Irma E. Shuler 1945 (div. 1962). (3) Elaine Mahoney 1962. **Emigrated** to Germany ca. 1921; to U.S. 1926, naturalized 1933. **Education** Private schs., Moscow and Kiev to 1918; Univ. of Berlin, D.Phil. 1925 and postgrad. study 1925–26. **Mil. service** Infantryman and tank officer, White Army, Russia 1918–20; consultant 1940, sect. chief 1941, and div. chief and dir. of Explosives Research Labs. 1942–43, Explosives Div., Natl. Defense Research Cttee.; consultant 1943, member 1944, and chief of explosives div. 1945–46, Manhattan Project, Los Alamos, NM. **Career** Intl. Education Bd. Fellow 1926–28 and staff member 1928–30, chemistry dept., Princeton Univ. • With Harvard Univ.: asst. prof. of chemistry 1930–33; assoc. prof. 1933–38; Lawrence Prof. of Chemistry 1938–71; chmn., chemistry dept. 1947–50; emeritus prof. since 1971; member of Harvard Coll. admissions cttee. and of faculty cttee. on athletics. • Visiting scholar, Center for Intl. Studies, Massachusetts Inst. of Technology 1973. • Member of Ballistic Missile Advisory Cttee. 1953–58 and special foreign-policy advisor 1960s, U.S. Dept. of Defense; member, Pres.'s Science Advisory Cttee. 1957–64; member, U.S. delegation, Conference for Prevention of Surprise Attack, Geneva 1958; special presidential advisor for science and technology 1959–61; member, gen. advisory cttee., U.S. Arms Control and Disarmament Agency 1962–69; member, research advisory cttee. on chemical engineering, NASA; chmn., Federal Council for Science and Technology. **Officer** Member of Cttee. on Atomic Energy 1941, chmn. of Cttee. on Science and Public Policy 1962–65, and v.p. 1965–73, Natl. Acad. of Sciences; chmn., Council for a Livable World since 1977. • Chmn. of science bd. and dir., Itek Corp. since 1961; dir., Cabot Corp. **Fellow** Amer. Acad. of Arts and Sciences. **Member** (Foreign) Royal Soc. since 1959; Amer. Philosophical Soc.; Amer. Chemical Soc.; Amer. Physical Soc.; Faraday Soc.; Sigma Xi. **Honors** From Amer. Chemical Soc.: Nichols Medal, New York sect. 1947; Gibbs Medal, Chicago sect. 1960; Parsons Award 1961; Marshall Award, Huntsville sect. 1963; Debye Award 1968; Richards Medal, New England sect. 1968; Priestly Medal 1972. • Army and Navy ordnance awards 1946; Medal for Merit

1946; King's Medal, U.K. 1948; exceptional service award, USAF 1957; Priestly Award, Dickinson Coll. 1958; Medal of Freedom 1961; Ledlie Prize 1961 and chemistry lectureship established in his honor 1971, Harvard Univ.; Lewis Medal, Combustion Inst. 1961; Natl. Medal of Science 1967; Lehman Award, New York Acad. of Sciences 1968; Franklin Medal, Franklin Inst. 1972; hon. fellow, Chemical Soc., London; hon. member, Phi Lambda Upsilon and Phi Beta Kappa; hon. degrees from univs. of Harvard, Oxford, Pennsylvania, Rochester, Princeton, and Columbia, and from Williams Coll., Case Inst., and Carnegie Inst. of Technology. Author *Photochemical Processes,* 1929; *A Scientist in the White House,* 1976. **Contributor** of more than 200 papers on kinetics of chemical reactions, macromolecular structure, thermochemistry of organic compounds, and physics of high explosives to science jrnls.

Further reading James Phinney Baxter, *Scientists Against Time,* 1947; John Finney, "Key Strategist in the Science War," in *New York Times Magazine,* 12 June 1960; Daniel Kevles, *The Physicists,* 1978.

MARTY ROBBINS

Country-and-western singer and songwriter
***Born* Glendale, Arizona, USA, 26 September 1925**
***Died* Nashville, Tennessee, USA, 8 December 1982**

Marty Robbins, author of the 1959 hit song "El Paso," was a country-and-western star who branched out into gospel, blues, Hawaiian, and Caribbean music and had a substantial rock and pop following during the 1960s. His smooth voice was well suited to the sentimental ballads in which he specialized. Many of his songs looked back with nostalgia to the gunfighter era, and typically carried a dash of Mexican mariachi.

Courtesy of Country Music Foundation

A Gene Autry fan, Robbins grew up in the Arizona desert, one of nine children in a poor family, and learned music from his father, a harmonica player, and his grandfather, Texas Bob Heckle, a traveling medicine man and storyteller. After Navy service in the Pacific, he returned to Phoenix and held a series of odd jobs, including ditchdigging, amateur boxing, and truck driving, before finding a place as a guitarist in a roadhouse band. Discovering that he could sing, he organized his own group, the K-Bar Cowboys, to perform in local clubs and radio stations, and by the late 1940s was host of a television show, "Western Caravan." In 1953 he was signed as a regular by the Grand Ole Opry in Nashville and had his first Top Ten hits with "I'll Go On Alone" and "I Couldn't Keep From Crying." His "Singing the Blues" topped the country charts in 1956, and from then on hardly a year went by without his turning out at least one best seller—in all, 43 Top Ten records and 18 number ones.

Beginning in 1957, Robbins's songs began selling to rock 'n' roll audiences as well. "A White Sport Coat and A Pink Carnation" (1957), "She Was Only Seventeen" (1958), "Stairway of Love" (1958), "Big Iron" (1960), and "Devil Woman" (1961) were all

Courtesy of Country Music Foundation

international successes among fans of rock 'n' roll and pop. Most successful of all was "El Paso," a Mexican-flavored ballad about jealousy and violent death in a Texas saloon that sold two million copies in six months and was the first country song to be awarded a Grammy. His best-selling songs of the 1960s and 1970s included "Ruby Ann" (1962), "Begging to You," 1963, "Ribbon of Darkness" (1965), "Tonight Carmen" (1967), "I Walk Alone" (1968), "My Woman, My Woman, My Wife" (1970, his second Grammy winner), and "El Paso City" (1976). He made frequent television and concert appearances, acted in half a dozen gunslinger movies, and had a cameo role in Clint Eastwood's *Honkytonk Man* in 1982. From 1965 he was also a cattle rancher and stock-car racer—he survived several disastrous accidents—and later owned music-publishing and movie-production companies and two record labels.

Robbins was inducted into the Country Music Hall of Fame in October 1982. He died two months later of a heart attack—his third—following an eight-hour quadruple-bypass operation. He was 57. J.P.

Born Martin David Robinson. **Parents** Jack Joe R. and Emma (Heckler) R. **Married** Marizona Baldwin 1945: Ronnie, singer; Janet K. Robinson. **Education** Glendale, AZ; high sch., Phoenix, AZ. **Mil. service** USN, Pacific 1944–48. **Career** Guitar player, singer, and songwriter since 1940s; singer, K-Bar Cowboys, Phoenix, AZ late 1940s; host of radio show and "Western Caravan" TV show, KPHO, Phoenix late 1940s; recording artist, CBS Records 1952–72, MCA Records 1972–74, Columbia Records since 1975; regular performer, Grand Ole Opry, Nashville, TN since 1953; frequent concert tours and guest appearances on TV variety shows; star of syndicated TV show "Marty Robbins' Spotlight" 1977. • Film actor since 1960s; stock-car racer since 1965; operator of cattle farm, Franklin, TN since 1965. **Officer** Pres.: Mariposa Music, Maricopa Music, and Maricana Music since 1960, and Charger Records since 1970, Nashville. **Member** Natl. Assn. of Stock-Car Racers; Amer. Fedn. of Music; Country Music Assn.; Acad. of Country Music; AFTRA; SAG. **Honors** Grammy Awards 1960, for song "El Paso," and 1971, for song "My Woman, My Woman, My Wife"; Man of the Decade, Acad. of Country Music 1970; elected to Nashville Songwriters Hall of Fame 1975; Gold Trustees Award, Natl. Country Hall of Fame 1979; best male singer, *Music City News* 1982; elected to Country Music Hall of Fame 1982; Million Performance Award, for "El Paso," and 23 citations of achievement, BMI; four trophies, *Music City News;* Gold Guitars, gold and platinum records, and ASCAP awards. **Albums** More than 75, including *Song of Robbins,* 1957; *Marty Robbins,* 1958; *Song of the Islands,* 1958; *Greatest Hits,* 1959; *Gunfighter Ballads,* 1959; *More Gunfighter Ballads,* 1960; *More Greatest Hits,* 1961; *Just Sentimental,* 1961; *Portrait of Marty Robbins,* 1961; *After Midnight,* 1961; *Devil Woman,* 1962; *Hawaii's Calling Me,* 1963; *Return of Marty Robbins,* 1963; *Island Woman,* 1964; *R.F.D.,* 1964; *Turn the Lights Down,* 1965; *Tonight Carmen,* 1967; *I Walk Alone,* 1969; *My Woman, My Woman, My Wife,* 1970; *The World of Marty Robbins,* 1971; *All-Time Greatest Hits,* 1972; *Marty Robbins Today,* 1972; *Come Back To Me,* 1982. **Writer** of more than 500 songs. **Film actor** *Buffalo Gun,* 1962; *Ballad of a Gunfighter,* 1963; *Honkytonk Man,* 1982; *The Gun and the Gavel; The Badge of Marshal Brennan;* others. **Author** *Small Man* (novel), 1966.

NATHAN (S.) PINE
Bookseller
***Born* Russia, 17 April 1892**
***Died* New York City, USA, 7 December 1982**

One of the venerable institutions of the New York literary world is Dauber & Pine, the secondhand bookshop on lower Fifth Avenue, on the edges of Greenwich Village, where rare bargains and rare love of books are both available in quantity. Nathan Pine, its co-owner for 57 years and a bookseller for nearly 80, knew almost all the major contemporary American writers and was, in turn, much beloved by them. His voice, wrote Gilbert Millstein in an appreciation in the *New York Times,* "sounds like the dry rustling of good paper and the turning of pages. . . . There are probably only half a dozen or so bookstores like Dauber & Pine left in New York City and, I will swear, no booksellers of the age, tenacity, or enthusiasm of Nat Pine."

Pine came to the United States from Russia with his family when he was 12 and immediately went to work at his uncle's bookstore, earning three dollars a week. For the next 20 years he sold books in New York, Chicago, and San Francisco. In 1925 he returned to New York and went into partnership with Sam Dauber in a shop on Fourth Avenue, the traditional street for secondhand bookstores in Manhattan. The following year they moved to their present location on Fifth. The shop, full of dusty leatherbound volumes and Old World serenity, was a favorite haunt of writers and scholars, including Thomas Wolfe, Sinclair Lewis, Carl Van Doren, Louis Untermeyer, and Saul Bellow. In some cases Pine and Dauber helped writers build entire book collections, only to buy them back in the end from the writers' estates. "The nicest thing about the book business is the people you buy from or sell to," said Pine. "Without the printed word, there would not be a civilization, and there's something special about people who are interested in the printed word. They are a species all their own—learned, kind, knowledgeable, and human." An attempt at eviction by the New School for Social Research, the owners of their building, in 1977 was thwarted by a storm of outrage from the literary community.

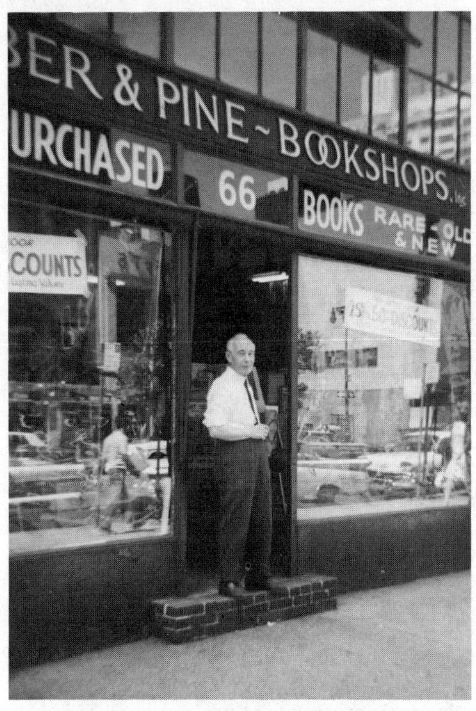

Courtesy of Tillie Pine

Since the 1960s Pine worked with Murray Dauber, the son of his original partner. He was 90 years old when he retired from bookselling in early 1982. He died eight months later of a heart attack. J.P.

Married Tillie S., teacher and writer of children's books, 1924: Mona Pine Monroe, teacher, b. 1930. **Religion** Jewish. **Emigrated** to U.S. at age 12. **Education** Evening courses, New York Univ. **Career** Worked in bookstores from age 12, NYC, Chicago, S.F.; co-owner, Dauber & Pine Bookshops, Inc., NYC 1925–82.

LEON JAWORSKI

Lawyer and Watergate special prosecutor
***Born* Waco, Texas, USA, 19 September 1905**
***Died* Wimberley, Texas, USA, 9 December 1982**

Leon Jaworski was a politically well-connected Texas corporation lawyer who achieved international prominence in 1973–74 as director of the Special Prosecution Force, the large group of lawyers and investigators looking into the Watergate affair. Pres. Richard Nixon was forced by the publication of incriminating evidence to resign during Jaworski's tenure, and later the special prosecutor was widely viewed as remiss in not pressing for Nixon's indictment on charges of criminal malfeasance in public office.

Jaworski was born to a poor family in central Texas. His mother had been born in Austria; his father was from Poland, and earned a meager income as an itinerant Evangelical minister. After education in the Waco public schools, where he excelled in debating, he attended Baylor University, a Baptist institution in Waco, receiving his LL.B. degree in 1925, the same year he became the youngest person ever admitted to the Texas bar. In 1926 he took an LL.M. at George Washington University, Washington, D.C. In his first case, he successfully defended a man accused of operating an illegal still. Another early case, which gained him statewide attention, was his unsuccessful defense of a black man accused of murdering a white couple.

In 1931, Jaworski joined a prominent Houston law firm, Fulbright, Crooker, Freeman & Bates, and became a partner three years later. During his 50 years of association with the firm he helped it attract a large number of wealthy corporations as clients. Fulbright & Jaworski, as it is known today, employs more than 300 lawyers and has become one of the country's largest and most prestigious firms.

As a colonel in the Army's Judge Advocate General's Corps during World War II, Jaworski proved an effective prosecutor under military law. Before leaving the Army in 1946 he was chief of the war crimes trial section of the JAGC at the War Crimes Tribunal at Nuremberg. He returned to his old firm in Houston, becoming senior partner in 1951.

One of the firm's most famous clients during this time was Rep. Lyndon Johnson. In 1948, Jaworski helped Abe Fortas defend Johnson, the disputed winner of the Democratic primary for the U.S. Senate, in an election-fraud case brought by his opponent. Johnson's political career was saved when he won the case and later the election. In 1960, Jaworski again represented Johnson, overseeing the complex litigation that allowed him to run simultaneously for vice president and senator.

Jaworski, a lifelong Democrat, was known to be conservative on most social issues. Although he opposed wiretaps and other forms of electronic surveillance except in cases affecting national security, he was outspokenly against several of the Supreme Court's decisions, notably *Miranda* v. *Arizona* (1966), which protected suspects' rights. He also favored curbs on civil disobedience and opposed all gun-control laws. In the matter of racial justice, Jaworski was only slightly more enlightened than most of his fellow Texans. He served under Archibald Cox as special assistant to the U.S. attorney general, Robert Kennedy, from 1962 to 1965, and helped to press criminal contempt charges against the governor of Mississippi, Ross R. Barnett, for refusing to obey a federal judge's order to desegregate the state university. Yet he also appeared in court in 1963 for the University of Texas, defending its asserted right to run segregated dormitories, and two years later led the fight against including poor people on the board of Houston's antipoverty agency.

It was undoubtedly the unprogressive aspects of Jaworski's record that made the nationally known lawyer—he was president of the American Bar Association in 1971–72—seem to the Nixon White House an attractive candidate for a successor to Archibald Cox as special prosecutor. Cox, a Harvard law professor, had held the office since 25 May 1973, and had pressed the White House unrelentingly for the release of nine tape recordings of presidential conversations. He was dismissed on 20 October 1973 during the famous "Saturday night massacre," and the office of special prosecutor was abolished. Nixon was then forced by public and Congressional outrage to seek out another man for the post, and Gen. Alexander Haig, then White House chief of staff, telephoned Jaworski and offered him the job. In his Watergate memoir, *The Right and the Power* (1976), Jaworski recalled telling Haig, "I've taken a public position since this affair started that it should be very thoroughly investigated and publicized. And I feel that every person criminally involved should be prosecuted. If I take this job, I'm going to work that way."

The U.S. public and press, by and large, were skeptical about Jaworski's independence and doubted whether he could equal Cox's dogged determination. Yet as soon as he was convinced of Nixon's criminal responsibility—which, he admitted, greatly surprised him—he won over the Special Prosecution Force, the press, and much of public opinion by pursuing the president through the courts with calm and orderly zeal. In April 1974 he persuaded John J. Sirica, chief judge of the Federal District Court for the District of Columbia, who had jurisdiction over the entire Watergate investigation, to subpoena 64 tapes of presidential conversations. When the White House refused, Jaworski asked the Supreme Court to rule on the subpoena. A few days before, he had publicly accused Nixon of making a "farce" of the Special Prosecution Force and of attempting to "undercut" him as an independent prosecutor. Despite Gen. Haig's guarantees, Jaworski received almost no cooperation from the White House, which once even refused him entry.

On 8 July, Jaworski went before the Supreme Court to argue his case. His opponent, James D. St. Clair, a prominent Boston attorney appearing for the president, held that the constitutional doctrine of separation of powers gave Nixon the right not to honor the subpoena. Jaworski directly denied this assertion, saying, "This nation's constitutional form of government is in serious jeopardy if the president, any president, is to say that the Constitution means what he says it does, and that there is no one, not even the Supreme Court, to tell him otherwise." The Court ruled unanimously on 24 July that the subpoena was justified and upheld at the same time its traditional right "to say what the law is."

Three articles of impeachment were voted by the House Judiciary Committee in late July, charging Nixon with obstruction of justice, abuse of power, and failure to comply with lawful subpoenas. Before the president could be tried in the Senate, however, the White House released the tapes demanded by Jaworski. Among them was the so-called smoking-gun tape, recorded on 23 June 1972, only a few days after the Watergate burglary, which proved that Nixon had from the very beginning masterminded the cover-up of evidence of criminal wrongdoing by his staff. The president, realizing that conviction in the Senate and removal from office were imminent, resigned on 8 August 1974.

Jaworski's conduct of his office over the next two months became the subject of intense controversy. He was almost alone among the members of the Special Prosecution Force in his reluctance to prosecute Nixon. He wrote later that he doubted whether a fair trial, untainted by adverse prior publicity, could be guaranteed anywhere in the country, and believed in any case that such a trial would divide and shock the nation even further. He was not consulted by the White House before Pres. Gerald Ford granted Nixon a full pardon on 8 September, but refused to challenge the pardon's legality in the courts, believing that the power to pardon was a presidential prerogative under the Constitution.

He resigned effective 25 October 1974, claiming that most of his work was done, and returned to his firm in Houston. His successor, Henry S. Ruth, Jr., still had a great deal of litigation to oversee before the force could be disbanded. In 1978, Jaworski returned once again to Washington in an official capacity when he became special counsel to the House Ethics Committee during the investigation into influence buying among members of Congress by the South Korean rice dealer Tongsun Park.

A dapper man just under six feet tall with wavy gray hair and a bulbous nose, Jaworski served on the board of directors of several large Texas corporations and was always active in state and national lawyers' organizations. He spent much time during his final years on his 400-acre ranch near Wimberley, Texas, 35 miles southwest of Austin. He was diagnosed as suffering from cancer of the pancreas in February 1982, but his death resulted from a heart attack as he was cutting wood at the ranch. A.K.

Parents Joseph J., Evangelical minister, and Marie (Mira) J. **Married** Jeannette Adam 1931: Joan Moncrief; Claire Draper; Joseph III. **Religion** Presbyterian (elder). **Education** Waco High Sch., TX, grad. at age 15; Baylor Univ., Waco (scholarship), LL.B. 1925; admitted to TX bar 1925; George Washington Univ., Wash. DC, LL.M. 1926. **Mil. service** Col. 1942–46 and chief of war crimes trial sect., Judge Advocate Gen.'s Corps, U.S. Army. **Career** Assoc. 1931–34, partner 1935–51, and sr. partner since 1951, Fulbright, Crooker, Freeman & Bates (now Fulbright & Jaworski), Houston; special asst. to U.S. Attorney Gen. 1962–65; special counsel to Attorney Gen. of Texas 1963–65, 1972–73; presidential advisor 1964–69; special prosecutor, Watergate Special Prosecution Force, Office of the White House 1973–74; special counsel, House Cttee. on Standards of Official Conduct 1977–78. • Member, Pres.'s Commn. on Law Enforcement and Admin. of Justice 1965–67; U.S. member, Permanent (Intl.) Commn. of Arbitration, The Hague 1965–69; arbitration member, Intl. Centre for Settlement of Investment Disputes 1967; member, Commn. on Marine Science, Engineering, and Resources 1967–69; Pres.'s Commn. on Causes and Prevention of Violence 1968–69; chmn., Gov.'s Cttee. on Public Sch. Education; member, Natl. Citizens Cttee. for Community Relations. **Officer** Pres.: Houston Bar Assn. 1949; Texas Civil Judiciary Council 1950–52; Rotary Club, Houston 1955–56; Houston Chamber of Commerce 1960; (also regent 1958–66) Amer. Coll. of Trial Lawyers 1961–62; State Bar of Texas 1962–63; (also member of standing cttee. on federal judiciary 1960–63) Amer. Bar Assn. 1971–72; Leon Jaworski Foundn.; Baylor Medical Foundn.; M.D. Anderson Foundn.; (also dir.) Houston chapter, Amer. Red Cross. • Chmn.: (Protestant chmn.) Houston chapter, Natl. Conference of Christians and Jews 1955–61; Democrats for Reagan Steering Cttee. 1980; jt. admin. cttee., Texas Medical Center and Baylor Univ. Coll. of Medicine; bd., Southwest Bancshares Inc., Houston; (also member of legal cttee.) bd. of trustees, Southwestern Legal Foundn. • V.P., Natl. Space Hall of Fame. • Dir.: Anderson Clayton & Co., Houston; Benjamin Franklin Savings & Loan Assn., Houston; Intercontinental Natl. Bank; Coastal States Gas Producing Co.; Gulf Publishing Co.; Gulf Printing Co.; (also chmn. of exec. cttee.) Bank of Southwest, Houston. • Trustee: United Fund 1958; Natl. Conference of Christians and Jews 1966; Natl. Coll. of District Attorneys; Texas Medical Center; Baylor Univ. Coll. of Medicine; Houston Symphony Soc. **Fellow** Amer. Bar Foundn.; Amer. Coll. of Trial Lawyers. **Member** Amer. Law Inst.; Democratic Party. • Clubs: Houston; Houston Country; International; Coronado; Headliners; Warwick; Metropolitan. **Honors** Legion of Merit, WWII; Brotherhood Award, Houston chapter, Natl. Conference of Christians and Jews 1961; distinguished alumnus award, Baylor Univ. Sch. of Law 1964; alumni achievement award, George Washington Univ. 1965; medal, Amer. Bar Assn. 1975; hon. pres., Canadian Bar Assn.; hon. member, Phi Delta Phi and Order of Coif; hon. degrees from Baylor Univ. and 14 other instns. **Author** (all memoirs) *After Fifteen Years,* 1961; *The Right and the Power,* 1976; (jtly.) *Confession and Avoidance,* 1979; (jtly.) *Crossroads,* 1981.

Further reading Brock Brower, "The Conscience of Leon Jaworski," in *Esquire,* Feb. 1975; James Doyle, *Not Above the Law,* 1977.

FREEMAN F(ISHER) GOSDEN
Radio comedy writer and performer
***Born* Richmond, Virginia, USA, 5 May 1899**
***Died* Los Angeles, California, USA, 10 December 1982**

"Amos 'n' Andy," the most popular series in radio history and the first situation comedy, was the single most important factor in the success of radio broadcasting as a medium of mass entertainment in the United States. Derived from the nineteenth-century minstrel show, which featured white performers doing comic parodies of stereotyped black characters and black speech, it recounted the hardships and misadventures of two Southern blacks—one honest, hardworking, and churchgoing, the other easygoing and gullible—trying to make a living running a down-at-heels taxicab company in Harlem. "Amos 'n' Andy" ran for 35 years, but blackface humor was no longer considered acceptable by the 1950s, and the show did not survive the transition to television.

All the writing and acting—more than 100 parts, most of them black—were done by Freeman F. Gosden (Amos) and Charles J. Correll (Andy), the show's creators, both of whom were descended from white Southern families. Gosden, the younger by ten years, grew up in Richmond, Virginia; his father had been a soldier in Mosby's Raiders, the Confederate cavalry unit that refused to surrender at the end of the Civil War. As a child, he did impersonations and was a clog dancer and ukulele player in minstrel shows. In 1919, after wartime service as a radio operator in the Navy and brief jobs as a tobacco and car salesman, he became a traveling producer for the Joe Bren Company, a supplier of scripts and talent for amateur theatricals. Here he made the acquaintance of Correll, who had joined the company the year before. The two developed a harmony act and within a few years were performing regularly on Chicago radio stations. At the request of the management of station WGN, they worked out an idea for a comedy show to be done in Southern black dialect. It was a runaway success. When WGN refused to allow Gosden and Correll to syndicate it using prerecorded discs, they moved the show in 1928 to a rival station, changing its name from "Sam 'n' Henry" to "Amos 'n' Andy." By 1929 they had killed all competition in their time slot and were signed for network distribution by NBC. The immediate result was a 35 percent increase in sales of radio sets. The country was experiencing its first nationwide entertainment craze.

An estimated 40 million people—nearly one third of the population—tuned in each night in the early years of the Depression. During the broadcast there was a noticeable drop in the use of phones, toilets, taxis, and buses; movie theaters interrupted the feature in order to keep the crowd from going home; auto theft increased. Factories scheduled work shifts around the show, and ministers and editorial writers drew sermons from "Amos 'n' Andy" episodes. Gosden and Correll attained the status of celebrities and were invited to the White House. This enormous popularity was the result of Gosden and Correll's success in transcending the flagrant racial stereotyping on which the show was based and allowing the listeners to empathize with the characters' problems while briefly forgetting their own. Gosden, who had been raised by a black servant and had grown up alongside black children, took care to make the characters amusing but not ridiculous. Blacks were divided over the question of whether this kind of ethnic humor was acceptable. The show had many black listeners, but there were perennial complaints from others who thought it insulting, demeaning, and exploitative—a criticism that Gosden and Correll were at pains to deny.

By the end of the decade, "Amos 'n' Andy" had begun to drop in the ratings. In 1943 it was switched to a half-hour format and additional writers and actors were brought in. Gosden and Correll sold the show to CBS for \$2.5 million in 1948 and continued to write and perform in it until 1954, when its sponsor canceled it because it was losing money. A music-hall show hosted by Amos, Andy, and their friend, the notorious Kingfish, ran from 1954 to 1960, when Gosden and Correll retired. The television version of "Amos 'n' Andy," which had an all-black cast, began broadcasting in 1951, but soon became the target of criticism from the NAACP and was taken off the air.

Gosden was a golfing partner of Pres. Eisenhower and during his retirement served as a trustee of the Eisenhower Medical Center in Palm Desert, California. He was ill with a heart ailment for some years before his death of heart failure at the age of 83. Correll died in 1972. J.P.

Father Walter G., Confederate soldier. **Married** (1) Leta Marie Schreiber 1927 (div.): Freeman, Jr.; Virginia Marie Jackson. (2) Jane Elizabeth Stoneham 1944: Craig; Linda. **Education** Mil. acad., Atlanta; schs. in Richmond, VA. **Mil. service** Radio operator and electrician, USN, WWI. **Career** Amateur actor and singer from childhood; traveling salesman, American Tobacco Co., and car salesman, 1910s; producer of amateur theatricals 1918–24 and mgr. of circus div. 1924–25, Joe Bren Co., Chicago; entertainer 1925 and writer and actor for "Sam 'n' Henry" 1926–27, radio sta. WGN, Chicago. • Writer and actor, "Amos 'n' Andy" radio series: WMAQ, Chicago 1928–29; NBC 1929–48; CBS 1948–54. • Co-writer, "Amos 'n' Andy" TV show 1951–53; host, "The Amos 'n' Andy Music Hall," CBS radio 1954–60. **Officer** Founder and lifetime trustee, Eisenhower Medical Center, Palm Desert, CA. **Films** *Check and Double Check,* 1930; *The Big Broadcast of 1936,* 1935. **Author** (Jtly.) *Sam 'n' Henry,* 1926; (jtly.) *All About Amos 'n' Andy,* 1929. **Collection** of "Amos 'n' Andy" material in Doheny Library, Univ. of Southern California, LA.

Further reading Jim Harmon, *The Great Radio Comedians,* 1970; J. Fred MacDonald, *Don't Touch That Dial!,* 1979; Arthur Frank Wertheim, *Radio Comedy,* 1979.

CLARA (GOLDSCHMIDT) MALRAUX
Writer and memoirist
***Born* Magdeburg, Germany, 1897**
***Died* Paris, France, 15 December 1982**

Clara Malraux was the first wife of André Malraux (1901–76), the renowned French writer, political activist, and philosopher of art who was minister of culture under Charles de Gaulle. After nearly two decades of self-denying dedication to her husband's career, she separated from him, lived bravely through World War II as a member of the Resistance, and finally achieved independent fame as a writer and memoirist.

She was the daughter of a wealthy German Jewish industrialist and lived from 1915 with her mother and brothers in Paris, where she was privately educated. In 1921 she met Malraux, a brilliant young man of little formal education who yet showed a remarkable range of knowledge and sophistication. To their parents' horror, the couple soon eloped to Italy. In Florence they decided to marry, but only as an experiment: they would divorce after six months if it failed. She remembered how early in their marriage "we lived here and there, sometimes in Paris, wonderfully free in our movement, conquering each day one aspect of this earth, delighting in our bodies and minds, challenging each other with the knowledge we had acquired from our travels, from reading, from long walks in museums and galleries, from hours passed in the cinema and nightclubs, from the ballets russes (the authentic company), from the theater (rather seldom), from our walks in the streets, under vaults and colonnades. . . ." They visited Italy, Germany, Austria, Greece, Tunisia, and Belgium. They speculated in the stock market, at first with some success, using mostly Clara's money.

Each had a taste for adventure. In 1923, Malraux devised an elaborate scheme that involved their traveling to Cambodia to visit and catalogue ancient Khmer temples, then stealing their stone carvings and other decorations to sell to American art dealers. He was arrested and imprisoned by the French colonial authorities, but his wife was allowed to return to France. She organized a formidable legal defense to free him and induced many prominent intellectuals to campaign for his release. On his return to Paris he attributed his freedom not to the support of his wife and friends, but to the Annamese people. His book *The Royal Way* (1930) describes his temple-hunting adventures in the Khmer jungles, touching only lightly on his crass motives for going there.

As her husband progressed to literary eminence during the 1930s, Clara Malraux felt herself becoming less and less a part of his life. She was with him for a time in Spain, while he was a pilot in the Republican air force during the civil war, but he was often absent from her and their daughter for long periods.

They separated in 1939, but postponed divorce until after the German occupation, during which she lived in Toulouse and continued, as she had before the war, to help German Jews escape Nazi persecution. They divorced in 1946, just after Malraux's service as information minister in Charles de Gaulle's postwar government. "Keep my name," he said to her at the time. "You have earned it." She never gave it up.

Her friends reported that in later life she gradually recovered much of her youthful gaiety, independence, and openness. She found again her Jewish identity, as well as her German one, and began to write books that were increasingly well received: a collection of Persian tales, an account of an Indonesian journey, a study of the Israeli kibbutz system, translations of Virginia Woolf. Her best-received work was a six-volume series of memoirs, *The Noise of Our Steps* (1963–75), of which two volumes, *Learning To Live* (1963) and *Our 20 Years* (1966), were translated into English under the title *Memoirs* and published in 1967. She was unsparing of Malraux, but he never publicly criticized her account of their life together.

Her only immediate survivor is their daughter, Florence (named for the city of their elopement), the wife of the film director Alain Resnais. A.K.

Born Clara Goldschmidt. **Father** a businessman. **Married** André Malraux, writer and statesman, 1921 (div. 1946): Florence, screenwriter, b. 1933. **Religion** Jewish. **Education** Privately educated, Paris. **Career** Trans., *Action* mag. early 1920s; staff member, *L'Indochine* and *L'Indochine Enchaînée* newspapers, Saigon 1925; active with French Resistance, WWII; writer and memoirist since 1940s. **Author** *Le bruit de nos pas* [*The Noise of Our Steps*], 6 vols. (vols. 1 and 2 abridged and trans. as *Memoirs,* 1967): Vol. 1, *Apprendre à vivre* [*Learning To Live*], 1963; Vol. 2, *Nos vingt ans* [*Our Twenty Years*], 1966; Vol. 3, *Les combats et les jeux* [*Fights and Games*], 1969; Vol. 4, *Voici que vient l'été* [*Here Comes the Summer*], 1973; Vol. 5, *La fin et le commencement* [*The End and the Beginning*], 1967; Vol. 6, *Et pourtant j'étais libre* [*And Yet I Was Free*], 1969. • *Portrait de Grisélidis,* 1945 (trans. as *A Second Griselda,* 1947); *La maison ne fait pas crédit* [*The House Does Not Give Credit*], 1947; *Contes de la Perse* [*Tales from Persia*], 1947; *Par de plus longs chemins* [*By Longer Roads*] (novel), 1953; *La lutte inégale* [*The Unequal Struggle*] (novel), 1958; *Java, Bali,* 1963; *Civilisation du kibboutz* [*Civilization of the Kibbutz*], 1964; *Vénus des quatre coins de la terre: Douze rencontres en Israël* [*From the Four Corners of the Earth: Twelve Encounters in Israel*], 1971; *Rahel, ma grande soeur: un salon littéraire à Berlin au temps du romantisme* [*Rahel, My Older Sister: A Literary Salon in Berlin in the Romantic Age*] (biography), 1980; trans. of works by Virginia Woolf.

Further reading Robert Payne, *A Portrait of André Malraux,* 1970; Pierre Galante, *Malraux,* 1971; Axel Madsen, *Malraux,* 1976.

(ANTHONY) COLIN (BRUCE) CHAPMAN

Racing-car designer and sports-car manufacturer
Born **Richmond, Surrey, England, 19 May 1938**
Died **Norfolk, England, 16 December 1982**

Colin Chapman created a revolution in auto racing when he introduced the Lotus to the Formula One (Grand Prix) circuit in the late 1950s and to the Indianapolis 500 in 1963. His ingenious designs, which stressed lightness, maneuverability, and aerodynamic stability over brute power, and which were almost always one step ahead of the competition, helped ensure Britain's domination of motor racing in the 1960s and 1970s and made the Lotus team the most successful in history.

Chapman studied engineering at London University, financing his education partly through the resale of the secondhand cars that he bought and repaired as a hobby. In 1947 he converted an unsalable 1930 Austin 7 to a lightweight trials car. In partnership with his future wife, Hazel Williams, he raced a second version on the club circuit and racked up a series of impressive wins, then started the Lotus Engineering Company in an old garage in North London to manufacture a limited line of similar cars for other drivers. He left his job as a development engineer with the British Aluminium Company in 1955 to devote all his time to the business. By the late 1950s, Lotus cars, driven by the likes of Mike Hawthorn and Stirling Moss, reigned on the Formula Junior circuit. Stirling Moss brought Lotus its first Grand Prix win, at Monaco, in 1960.

In 1959, the year that Lotus opened its first factory, in Hertfordshire, Chapman introduced the Lotus Elite, a two-seater road car with a fiberglass body. Sales of the Elite and later models, which topped 3,000 units in 1979, paid for the development and maintenance of the racing team. Group Lotus, as the firm was called after it went public in 1969, diversified into speedboat design and plastics research, and was considered the heir to Porsche as an engineering innovator, design consultant, and builder of prestige roadsters.

Not satisfied with beating Porsche and Ferrari on their own ground with the revolutionary Lotus 25, in which the engine formed an integral part of the chassis (the monocoque design), Chapman entered the Indianapolis 500 in 1963 with a slim, low, rear-engined car. Jimmy Clark, Lotus's top driver and one of the best in the world, took second place that year and first place in 1965. By then, American racing teams were hurrying to copy the Lotus design. Chapman stayed ahead of them, coming out in 1968 with a wedge-shaped gas turbine with four-wheel drive. The car broke all qualifying records and dominated the race until the last few minutes, when its power unit failed. The Lotus team's success was more consistent on the Grand Prix circuit, where five of Chapman's drivers won world championships: Clark in 1963 and 1965, Graham Hill in 1968, Jochen Rindt in 1970, Emerson Fittipaldi in 1972, and Mario Andretti in 1978. Clark and Mike Spencer, another driver, were both killed racing Lotuses in 1968.

Chapman was responsible for two other major Formula One innovations. In the mid-1970s he built the first car to utilize "ground effects." Its aerodynamic shape created a downforce on the upper body and a low-pressure area underneath the chassis, producing better road adhesion. All Formula One cars now use this design. For the 1981 Grand Prix season he came up with an even more radical idea: the dual-suspension Lotus 88, with a stiff suspension for the chassis and a softer one for the driver capsule. In trials, it proved to be almost impossible to pass. The car was banned by the Grand Prix authorities at the last minute on unspecified grounds, but modifications of the design are being slipped around the regulations by several manufacturers.

In 1981, Group Lotus, hard hit by the world recession and heavily in debt, cut back production of road cars to less than 500 units. Its involvement as an engineering subcontractor with the bankrupt DeLorean sports-car manufacturing project did its financial situation no good. Chapman's death of a heart attack at the age of 54 left the future of the company very much in doubt. S.A.

Father S. F. Kennedy C., publican. **Married** Hazel Patricia Williams 1954: Jane; Sarah; Clive. **Education** Stationers' Co.'s Sch., Hornsey, North London; London Univ., B.Sc. **Mil. service** Pilot, RAF 1950. **Career** Builder, designer, and dealer of sports and racing cars since late 1940s; structural and civil engineer 1951–52; development engineer, British Aluminium Co., London 1952–55; founding pres., Lotus Engineering Co. (now Group Lotus Cars, Ltd.) since 1953; manager and owner, Lotus Grand Prix racing team; automotive design consultant, Ford Motor Co. and DeLorean Car Co. **Fellow** FRSA 1968; University Coll., London 1972. **Member** Clubs: British Racing Drivers; British Auto Racing; British Racing and Sports Car. **Honors** Formula One World Constructors Championship 1963, 1965, 1968, 1970, 1972, 1978; CBE 1970; Young Businessman of the Year, *Manchester Guardian* 1970; Ferodo Trophy in perpetuity since 1978; Royal Designer for Industry, Royal Soc. of Arts 1979; hon. degree from Royal Coll. of Arts.

Further reading Leo Levine, "The Strange Story of the Man Who Shook Indy," in *Mechanix Illustrated,* May 1969; Innes Ireland, "Formula 1 Cars for the Year 2000: Colin Chapman Forecasts the Shape of Things to Come," in *Road and Track,* June 1982.

LEONID (BORISOVICH) KOGAN
Violinist
Born **Yekaterinoslav, Ukraine, USSR, 14 November 1924**
Died **USSR, 17 December 1982**

Leonid Kogan, the "aristocrat of the violin," was for 30 years a leading virtuoso on the international circuit, second only to the legendary David Oistrakh among contemporary Soviet violinists. A *New York Times* reviewer, writing on the occasion of his first U.S. tour in 1958, said of his playing that it was "remarkable for its purity of sound, the grace of its melodic outlines and its beautiful balance between restraint and feeling."

Kogan took his first violin lessons from his father, a photographer and amateur violinist, when he was seven, and made such progress that the family moved from Yekaterinoslav (now Dnepropetrovsk) in the Ukraine to Moscow so that he could be enrolled in the Central Music School, one of 25 schools in the Soviet Union for musically gifted children. He studied with Abram Yampolsky, a disciple of Leopold Auer, made his debut at the age of 16, and in 1943 passed the tough audition for the Moscow Conservatory. At the 1947 World Festival of Democratic Youth in Prague he shared first prize, and four years later he won the Queen Elisabeth International Competition in Brussels. Immediately after his completion of postgraduate studies he was appointed to the faculty of the Moscow Conservatory, where he became a full professor in 1963. He also organized a trio with the pianist Emil Gilels, whose sister Yelizaveta he married, and the cellist Mstislav Rostropovich.

From the mid-1950s, when he began making concert tours of Europe, Kogan was acknowledged as one of the world's greatest living masters of the violin. His performance of the Brahms Violin Concerto at the Athens Festival in 1957 earned an ovation that lasted 18 minutes. He made his American debut with the concerto at Carnegie Hall in January 1958, drawing rapturous reviews. "He is wholly an individual as an instrumentalist, an interpreter, and a platform personality," wrote Irving Kolodin in *Saturday Review.* "The marks of his art, as they have been conveyed by numerous recordings, are purity of sound and refinement of musicianship. To those the actuality added a tone of soaring lyric beauty . . . , a boldness of style, and a warmth of spirit that made every note count in the total design." Howard Taubman of the *New York Times* called him a performer of "exceptional subtlety" and "uncompromising delicacy of taste" whose "performances are as supple and probing as his mind is perceptive." He made frequent return visits to the United States on cultural exchange programs and toured Europe, South America, China, and Australia.

Within the USSR, Kogan was known as one of the best interpreters of contemporary music, the first Soviet violinist to play and record Alban Berg's Violin Concerto. Among the composers who wrote works for him were Tikhon Khrennikov, Kara Karayev, Aram Khachaturian, Moissei Vainberg, and Yuri Levitin. Both Kogan's wife and their son Pavel are also violinists—Franco Mannino's *Concerto for Three Violins* (1965) was written for the family—and his daughter Nina is a pianist who accompanied Kogan on his 1975 U.S. tour.

Kogan was admitted to the Communist Party in 1954 and was never anything but a loyal Soviet citizen. In 1970 he was one of six Jewish musicians who signed a statement declaring the Soviet Union free of anti-Semitism. In January 1971 he and the conductor Maksim Shostakovich withdrew from an engagement with the Pittsburgh Symphony because one of the cellists was a Russian defector. (Kogan's brother-in-law Gilels had performed with the same orchestra only a few weeks before.) When the Soviet government began its campaign to discredit the physicist and humanitarian Andrei Sakharov in 1973, Kogan was among the many artists and intellectuals who publicly denounced him. Many of Kogan's performances in the United States were disrupted by demonstrators protesting the USSR's refusal to allow Jews to emigrate. Kogan called them "hooligan renegades" motivated by "unseemly political considerations." "I always think," he said,"that people come to my concerts so that together we can visit the world of the beautiful and the spiritual."

The Soviet Union awarded Kogan the Lenin Prize in 1965 and named him a People's Artist in 1966. The official announcement of his death by the news agency Tass gave no details of the cause or place. B.D.

Father Boris, photographer and amateur violinist. **Married** Yelizaveta Gilels, violinist: Pavel, violinist, b. 1952; Nina, pianist. **Religion** Jewish. **Education** Violin lessons with father from age seven; Central Music Sch., Moscow 1934–43; Moscow Conservatory, grad. 1948, postgrad. studies 1948–51. **Career** Recital debut, Moscow 1941; soloist debut, Moscow Philharmonic Orch. 1944; Canadian debut 1954, London and Paris debuts 1955, South American debut 1956, NYC debut 1957; frequent concert tours of USSR, U.S., Western Europe, China, Australia; guest soloist with major orchs.; numerous recordings. • Lectr. 1952–63 and prof. of violin since 1963, Moscow Conservatory; member, CPSU since 1954; juror, Tchaikovsky Competition. **Honors** Co-winner, 1st prize, World Festival of Democratic Youth, Prague 1947; 1st prize, Queen Elisabeth Intl. Competition, Brussels 1951; Honored Artist of RSFSR 1955; Lenin Prize 1965; People's Artist of USSR 1966; Order of Red Banner of Labor; medals.

DWIGHT MACDONALD
Author, critic, and editor
***Born* New York City, USA, 24 March 1906**
***Died* New York City, USA, 19 December 1982**

Dwight Macdonald was a lively and witty controversialist and one of the most original and respected critics of the century. Because of his humane leftism and the incisive critical intelligence he applied to U.S. culture and society, he was sometimes called America's George Orwell. He knew almost everyone on the American left, but rarely adhered to any creed or movement for long. Concerning his inability to follow party lines, Irving Howe said: "Sober or drunk, Macdonald could not walk a straight one." Yet he never drifted into neoconservatism along with other radicals from the 1930s, but kept his basic principles and his integrity intact.

He was born in Manhattan to a family of comfortable means. His father was an attorney, his mother the daughter of a wealthy Brooklyn merchant. He attended Collegiate School in New York, Barnard School for Boys in the Bronx, then Phillips Exeter Academy in Massachusetts, which he called "my big educational experience." At Yale, from which he graduated in 1928, he was managing editor of the *Yale Literary Magazine.*

Macdonald hoped for a career as a literary critic, but his father's death in 1926 and the dwindling of his mother's inheritance meant that he would have to find a better-paying job on graduation. After six months as an executive trainee at Macy's, he decided that the world of retail merchandizing was not where he belonged. In late 1929 a Yale classmate helped him get a job as associate editor of *Fortune* magazine, a glossy business monthly then about to begin publication that was owned by another Yale graduate, Henry R. Luce. He learned the journalist's trade at *Fortune* over seven years, finally quitting in 1936 in protest over what he considered high-handed editing of a four-part article he had written that was critical of the United States Steel Corporation.

It was only in the mid-1930s, after a reading of the Marxist classics, that Macdonald became a political radical. He was never deceived by Stalinism, however, but almost from the beginning favored the more liberal brand of Communism propounded by Trotsky. He joined with Philip Rahv, William Phillips, F. W. Dupee, and others in 1937 to restart *Partisan Review,* an influential leftist magazine that in its first incarnation (1934–36) had been a hard-line Stalinist literary monthly and that was now to be anti-Stalinist but decidedly in favor of revolutionary socialism. In 1938, Macdonald began contributing to *New International,* a somewhat ponderous Trotskyist periodical. He was a member of the Socialist Workers Party from 1939 to 1941, and in 1940 wrote a pamphlet, *Jobs not Battleships,* published by *New International,* that objected to the coming war as an international capitalist sham. He left *Partisan Review* in 1943 in fundamental disagreement with the other editors about the true nature of the war and the Axis menace.

Macdonald started *Politics,* a classic left-wing "little magazine," on a shoestring in 1944. Its subscribers never exceeded 5,000, but they were loyal, vociferous, and politically highly sophisticated. At first published as a

Courtesy of Nancy Crampton

monthly, it later became a bimonthly, suspended publication for a while in 1947–48, then was revived briefly as a quarterly before shutting down definitively in 1949. When *Politics* was reprinted in full in 1968, Hannah Arendt, in an introduction to the edition, wrote of its continued "astounding relevance," adding, "Praise is due exclusively to the editor of this one-man magazine, to his extraordinary flair for significant fact and significant thought, from which followed his flair in the choice of contributors." These consisted of anti-Stalinist leftist intellectuals on both sides of the Atlantic, and included Albert Camus, Simone Weil, Victor Serge, Bruno Bettelheim, James Agee, Mary McCarthy, John Berryman, and Marianne Moore, of whom the first three were published in English for the first time in the pages of *Politics.*

In 1948, Macdonald published his first book, *Henry Wallace: The Man and the Myth,* a highly critical account of the "opportunist" who had been editor of the *New Republic,* secretary of agriculture, vice president during Roosevelt's third term, and who was in 1948 running for president under the Progressive Party banner.

Many of Macdonald's articles appeared, after *Politics* closed, in the *New Yorker,* and in 1951 he became a full-time staff writer on that weekly magazine. His periodical work became less concerned with political theory and more with the sociocultural topics the *New Yorker* specialized in, although his second book, *The Root Is Man: Two Essays in Politics* (1953), was an attempt at distinguishing between radicalism and progressivism and an appeal for radical humanism. He won a fellowship from the Ford Foundation and began writing a critical, debunking study of that philanthropic institution, which he published in serial form in the *New Yorker* and then as a whole under the title *The Ford Foundation: The Men and the Millions* (1956). His next book was *Memoirs of a Revolutionist: Essays in Political Criticism* (1957), a collection of pieces that had appeared in the *New Yorker, Encounter, Partisan Review,* and particularly *Politics.*

Macdonald was *Esquire*'s film critic from 1960 to 1966, while still on staff at the *New Yorker.* He had high standards and liked relatively few films, a fact he ascribed to Hollywood's continual failure to take creative advantage of "*the* great modern art form." He described watching the remake of *Ben-Hur* as "like waiting at a railroad crossing while an interminable freight train lumbers past, often stopping completely for a while." His best pieces from *Esquire* were collected in *Dwight Macdonald on Movies* (1969).

The first essay in *Against the American Grain* (1962) is generally considered Macdonald's most famous. The theme of "Masscult and Midcult" is "the influence of mass culture on high culture," the way in which American popular culture, "manufactured for the market," taints everything it touches, inhibiting the development of works of true merit and encouraging middlebrow attitudes in many artists, critics, and scholars. The products of the "tepid ooze" of midcult received his most withering scrutiny. Among his best-known targets, treated in other essays in the book, were the Revised Standard Version of the Bible ("like finding a parking lot where a great church once stood"), *Webster's Third New International Dictionary,* whose editors he thought ridiculously permissive, "Great Books of the Western World," and James Gould Cozzens's *By Love Possessed,* a widely praised best seller of the 1950s that Macdonald showed to be dull, pretentious, and convoluted.

Like many critics, he received more attention for the things he disliked than for the things he admired, and there were many more of them. In *Discriminations* (1974), his last essay collection, he explained this: "I've always specialized in negative criticism—literary, political, cinematic, cultural—because I've found so few contemporary products about which I could be 'constructive' without hating myself in the morning."

He returned to political involvement during the 1960s, supporting the occupation of part of Columbia University by radical students and encouraging draft-age men to refuse to serve in the army. For the latter action the Justice Department named him and others in 1969 as unindicted co-conspirators of Dr. Benjamin Spock, charging them with counseling draft evasion. Invited to a White House reception in 1965, he circulated an antiwar petition among the other guests, and in 1967 was a prominent member of the Writers and Editors War Tax Protest. He described his politics in later years as "conservative anarchism" and himself as a Mugwump.

Macdonald's other books included *Parodies* (1960), a well-received anthology of great literary send-ups from Chaucer to Beerbohm, a lengthy introduction to his edition of *The Poems of Edgar Allan Poe* (1966), and an annotated abridgement of the memoirs of Alexander Herzen, *My Past and Thoughts* (1973). He was frequently a visiting professor at various U.S. universities, and from 1968 served as chairman of Spanish Refugee Aid. He divided his time between a house in East Hampton, Long Island, and an apartment on Manhattan's Upper East Side, where he died of heart failure at the age of 76. A.K.

Parents Dwight M., lawyer, and Alice (Hedges) M. **Married** (1) Nancy Gardiner Rodman, social activist and business mgr. of *Partisan Review* and *Politics,* 1935 (div. 1950): Michael Cary Dwight; Nicholas Gardiner. (2) Gloria Lanier Kaufman, art historian, 1950: Day; Sabina (stepchildren). **Religion** Baptized Presbyterian; later nonbeliever. **Education** Collegiate Sch. and Barnard Sch. for Boys, NYC; Phillips Exeter Acad., Andover, MA, grad. 1924; Yale Univ., B.A. 1928. **Career** Trainee exec., Macy's dept. store, NYC 1928–29; staff writer and assoc. ed., *Fortune,* NYC 1929–36; co-ed. and co-publisher, *Miscellany* literary review 1930–33; assoc. ed., *Partisan Review,* NYC 1937–43; writer, *New International* 1938–mid-40s; member, Socialist Workers Party 1939–41; co-founder (with Nancy Rodman), ed., and publisher, *Politics* mag., NYC 1944–49; assoc. ed., *Encounter,* London mid-1950s; staff writer, *New Yorker,* NYC 1951–71; film critic 1960–66 and political columnist 1966–68, *Esquire,* NYC; literary and cultural critic. • Visiting prof.: Northwestern Univ., Evanston, IL 1956; Bard Coll., Annandale-on-Hudson, NY 1960; Univ. of Texas, Austin 1966; Univ. of California, Santa Cruz 1969 and San Diego 1977; Hofstra Univ., Hempstead, NY 1969–70; Univ. of Wisconsin, Milwaukee 1970; Univ. of Massachusetts, Amherst 1971; Yale Univ. 1971; State Univ. of New York, Buffalo 1973–74; John Jay Coll., City Univ. of New York 1974–76. **Officer** Co-founding member of bd. of dirs. since 1953 and chmn. since 1968, Spanish Refugee Aid. **Fellow** Ezra Stiles Coll., Yale Univ. since 1967. **Member** Usage panel, *American Heritage Dictionary* 1965; Writers and Editors War Tax Protest 1967; elected 1970 and on award cttee. for literature, Amer. Inst. of Arts and Letters; Amer. Acad. of Arts and Sciences; Psi Upsilon; others. **Honors** Ford Foundn. Fellowship mid-1950s; Guggenheim Fellowship 1963; hon. degree, Wesleyan Univ. **Author** *Henry Wallace: The Man and the Myth,* 1948; *The Root Is Man: Two Essays in Politics,* 1953; *The Ford Foundation: The Men and the Millions,* 1956; *Memoirs of a Revolutionist: Essays in Political Criticism,* 1957; *The Responsibility of Peoples and Other Essays in Political Criticism,* 1957; *Masscult and Midcult,* 1961; *Our Invisible Poor,* 1962; *Against the American Grain: Essays on the Effects of Mass Culture,* 1962; *Dwight Macdonald on Movies,* 1969; *Politics Past,* 1969; *Discriminations: Essays and Afterthoughts 1938–1974,* 1974. **Editor** *Parodies: An Anthology from Chaucer to Beerbohm—And After,* 1960; *The Poems of Edgar Allan Poe,* 1966; Alexander Herzen, *My Past and Thoughts: An Annotated Abridgement of the Memoirs of Alexander Herzen,* 1973. **Translator** Albert Camus, *Neither Victims Nor Executioners,* 1968. **Contributor** to *Partisan Review, New Yorker, Commentary, Diogenes, New York Review of Books, Esquire, Nation,* other mags. and jrnls.

Further reading Christopher Lasch, *The New Radicalism in America,* 1965; James Gibbert, *A History of Literary Radicalism in America,* 1968; William L. O'Neill, *A Better World,* 1982; William Barrett, *The Truants: Adventures Among the Intellectuals,* 1982.

ARTUR RUBINSTEIN
Pianist
***Born* Łódź, Poland, 28 January 1887**
***Died* Geneva, Switzerland, 20 December 1982**

Although other performers, such as Vladimir Horowitz, played with more ostentatious virtuosity, and still others, such as Emil Gilels and Rudolf Serkin, played with a greater degree of emotional intensity, Artur Rubinstein had a strong claim to the title of the world's most respected pianist. He was certainly, having sold more than 10 million copies of his recordings, one of the most popular pianists who ever lived. There was no aspect of piano literature that he had not explored, and no composer that he did not play convincingly. In his early years a champion of Prokofiev, Stravinsky, Debussy, Ravel, Poulenc, and the great modern Spanish composers, he became one of the finest interpreters of the Romantics, especially Brahms and above all his countryman Chopin, whose music provided exactly the right vehicle for Rubinstein's cultivated sensibility and irrepressible *joie de vivre*. "The warmly outgoing and beneficent lyricism of his phrasing, expressed in tones of richest and most gorgeous hue," wrote Max Loppert in *The New Groves Dictionary of Music,* "has provided an ideal standard of Chopin interpretation—not necessarily flawless in virtuosity but imbued with an inimitable spirit of civilized yet passionate eloquence and aristocratic poetry."

Rubinstein's career as a concert pianist spanned 80 years, a virtually unbroken sequence of performances that began in 1898 and ended in 1976, when an attack of shingles left him almost completely blind. He always played with his head thrown back, rarely looking at the keys, but during his last years failing eyesight made this characteristic of his style into a necessity. "I like to look up over the piano," he told an interviewer, "so I can listen and follow the lines of a piece. Looking at your fingers for accuracy is too confusing. I'd rather miss a few notes than play by phrase instead of as a whole." This preference for exuberant performance over pedantic rendition of a score was the cornerstone of Rubinstein's reputation as a musician. A short, powerfully built man with long arms, huge hands, and a shock of white hair, he seemed to defy time with his energy and sheer love of his vocation. In his seventies he was still giving marathon performances, playing two concerts a week for extended periods, and often playing three concertos in a single evening. "No man has lived his life more fully than I have," he was fond of saying, and as if this needed further corroboration, he left his wife in 1980 and began living with his English secretary, who was 50 years younger than himself.

Until he was in his mid-forties, Rubinstein was content to indulge his flair for high living, getting by on his natural talent without bothering to develop it fully. Born in Łódź, Poland, he began to play the piano at the age of three, was immediately recognized as a prodigy, and gave his first public performance the following year. His father, a textile manufacturer, sent him to study at the Warsaw Conservatory. When he was about nine he was taken to Berlin to play for the Hungarian violin master and conductor Joseph Joachim, who arranged his studies with Heinrich Barth, a pupil of Lizst, and later with Ignacy Paderewski, the most eccentric and flamboyant of the great Romantic pianists. He made his formal debut in Berlin in 1900 playing Mozart's Concerto in A Major with Joachim con-

Courtesy of RCA Records

Courtesy of RCA Records

ducting, and thereafter became well known in Germany and Poland, particularly as a soloist with the Warsaw Symphony Orchestra under the direction of Emil Młynarski, whose daughter Aniela, as yet unborn, was to become Rubinstein's wife more than 30 years later.

His first American tour, in 1906, which included appearances with the Philadelphia Orchestra in Philadelphia and New York, was not an outstanding critical success. His style of playing was too direct to satisfy audiences who admired the more bombastic performers of an earlier generation. Moreover, he faced the difficulty experienced by all prodigies—that of acquiring a mature personality to support technical virtuosity. Following the disappointment of his American tour, he gave no public performances for four years. During this time he lived in Paris, forming important friendships with Picasso and Hemingway, enjoying numerous love affairs, and acquiring a taste for good food, wine, and cigars. His bohemian past was a central part of the legend he created. "It is said of me that when I was young I divided my time impartially among wine, women, and song. I deny this categorically. Ninety percent of my interests were women." His extremes of good fortune were matched by extremes of bad. At times he was reduced to sleeping on park benches and subsisting on coffee and rolls, and at 21, out of work and in debt, he attempted suicide in a Berlin hotel.

His reappearance in public in a Berlin concert in 1910 marked a turning point in his career. By 1914, when he moved to London and worked briefly as a military translator, he was no longer a prodigy. With Eugène Ysaÿe, the violinist, he gave a series of concerts for Allied troops in 1915. The following year he consolidated his growing reputation with a 125-concert tour of Spain, where he was received ecstatically. He became known as a leading interpreter of the composers Manuel de Falla, Enrique Granados, and Isaac Albeníz. Heitor Villa-Lobos dedicated a composition to him, as did Stravinsky. In 1917–18 he toured South America with great success, and was persuaded to undertake a second American tour. This, like the first, was a disappointment, and he returned to the European concert circuit. He told Harold Schonberg in a *New York Times* interview in 1961: "When I played in Latin countries . . . they loved me because of my temperament. But when I played in England and America, they felt that because they paid their money they were entitled to hear all the notes. I dropped too many notes in those days, and they felt they were cheated." It is doubtful, however, whether Rubinstein represented his own performing history correctly. His recordings do not show a marked change in his style or technique, and the *New York Times* review of his Carnegie Hall concert on 20 February 1919 was extremely favorable. All pianists have to wait for their day of public esteem; Rubinstein's was to come later, at a time when Hollywood and his own engaging personality had joined forces to create his public image.

His marriage to Aniela Młynarska in 1932 led to a profound change in his private and professional life. "I'm rather a patriarchal Jew who believes in the importance of a wife and children. Those who bear my name shouldn't suffer for my shortcomings. I didn't want my wife to meet someone who would say, 'What a pity your husband never developed his talent.' So I began working." Retiring to an Alpine village in 1934, he practiced laboriously for 12 to 16 hours a day, rethinking his technique and relearning the works he had already committed to memory. His third U.S. tour, which began at Carnegie Hall in November 1937, was an unqualified success and marked the beginning of Rubinstein's rise to the very top of his profession. "He simply cannot produce an ugly, forced or jagged sound no matter how heavily he comes down on the keyboard," wrote one critic. "As soon as his fingers touch the keys, one knows that the Old Master is at work; and the penetrating tone rolls out and fills the house." After 1938, when he became associated with RCA Victor, his recordings became steadily more numerous and more popular. There are very few major works for piano that he did not record,

Courtesy of RCA Records

and it is probable that his recordings are more numerous than those of any other pianist.

At the beginning of World War II, Rubinstein left Paris with his family and settled first in Hollywood, where he supplemented his work as a recitalist by recording piano music for films, and then in New York. In 1946–47 he was heard on the soundtracks of films about Schumann, Brahms, and Lizst, and he appeared in person in *Carnegie Hall* (1947) and *Of Men and Music* (1950). He became an American citizen in 1946, but continued to travel frequently, and maintained houses in Paris and in Marbella on Spain's Costa del Sol. During the war, his Paris house, on the Avenue Foch, was taken over by the Nazis, who also stole his art collection.

Much of his wealth was expended on behalf of charities and political causes. Among those he supported most vigorously were the Frédéric Chopin fund to provide help for European artists in the postwar years; the NAACP Legal Defense Fund; and the state of Israel, where he founded a piano competition. Despite his cosmopolitan style—he spoke eight languages fluently—he retained an affection for Poland and its suffering citizens (the six brothers and sisters he left behind were all killed by the Nazis). When he returned to Warsaw in 1958 for his first concert in 20 years, the audience demanded ten curtain calls. His visit in 1975 was the subject of a documentary film, *The Comeback.* Another documentary, *Arthur Rubinstein—Love of Life,* combining concert footage with the pianist's reminiscences—Rubinstein was famous as a raconteur—won an Academy Award in 1969.

Even in extreme old age, Rubinstein's stamina and memory surpassed those of nearly all his colleagues. He had total recall of hundreds of works and rarely practiced. Before his retirement from the stage he played more than 100 concerts annually in every part of the globe except Germany, where he refused to perform. He completed an autobiography, *My Early Years,* in 1973, 30 years after it was commissioned by Blanche and Alfred A. Knopf, and a second volume *My Many Years,* in 1980. He died at his home in Geneva at the age of 95. H.B.

Parents Ignace R., textile producer, and Felicia (Heyman) R. **Married** Aniela Młynarska 1932: Eva Coffin, b. 1933; Paul, b. 1935; Alina Anna, b. 1945; John Arthur, actor, b. 1946. **Religion** Jewish. **Education** Began piano lessons at age three; Warsaw Conservatory of Music to age eight; Berlin Acad. of Music; musical education supervised by Joseph Joachim from age ten; studied piano with R. M. Breithaupt, Heinrich Barth, Ignacy Paderewski, composition with Robert Kahn and Max Bruch. **Mil. service** Mil. interpreter, London, WWI. **Emigrated** to U.S. 1937; naturalized 1946. **Career** First public recital at age four; formal debut, Berlin at age 13, subsequently played concerts in USSR, Poland, Germany, Austria; debuts in Paris and London 1905, U.S. 1906, Spain 1915; worldwide tours to six continents. • Numerous recordings from 1930s; composer of chamber and piano music; several film and TV appearances and soundtracks. **Officer** Founder and pres., Frédéric Chopin Fund 1946. **Member** (Assoc.) Acad. des Beaux Arts from 1971. **Honors** Chair of musicology named in his honor, Hebrew Univ., Jerusalem 1964; Medal of Freedom, U.S. 1976; Musician of the Year, *Musical America* 1976; KBE 1977; comdr., Cross with Star, Order of Merit 1978, and Order of Polonia Restituta, Poland; distinguished service award, Kennedy Center, Wash. DC 1978; intl. piano competition named in his honor, Israel; gold medal, Royal Philharmonic Soc.; comdr., Légion d'Honneur; officer, Order of Santiago, Portugal; comdr., Chilean Republic; comdr. of crown and officer, Order of Leopold, Belgium; Order of Grand Cross of Alfonso XII, Spain;

Agnon Award; bronze medallion, City of New York; hon. citizen of Philadelphia, Chicago, Colombia; hon. member of Acad. of Brazil and Accademia di Santa Cecilia, Rome; hon. degrees from Yale, Brown, Northwestern, Rutgers, Columbia, and Hebrew univs. **Documentary films** *Arthur Rubinstein—Love of Life,* 1968; *The Comeback,* 1975. **Soundtracks** *I've Always Loved You,* 1946; *Night Song,* 1947; *Song of Love,* 1947; *Carnegie Hall,* 1947; *Of Men and Music,* 1950. **Recordings** of Chopin, Ravel, Liszt, Rachmaninoff, Beethoven, Mozart, Grieg, Schumann, Tchaikovsky, Brahms, Saint-Saëns, Dvořák, Schubert, Fauré, Mozart, Franck, other composers. **Author** *My Young Years,* 1973; *My Many Years,* 1980.

Further reading Aylesa Forsee, *Artur Rubinstein, King of the Keyboard,* 1969; Donal Henahan, "This Ageless Hero, Rubinstein," in *New York Times Magazine,* 14 Mar. 1976.

HANS-ULRICH RUDEL
World War II German air ace
***Born* Konradswaldau, Germany, 2 July 1916**
***Died* Rosenheim, West Germany, 21 December 1982**

Hans-Ulrich Rudel, known as the Eagle of the Eastern Front, was the most decorated German soldier of World War II. Flying 2,530 combat missions, mainly in Stuka dive bombers, he was credited by the Luftwaffe High Command with the destruction of 519 tanks, 150 bunkers and artillery emplacements, and 800 combat vehicles of various types. He became a leading neo-Nazi after the war.

He was the son of a Protestant pastor, and was known in childhood as a timid boy and an indifferent student. He enlisted in the Luftwaffe in 1936, and flew support missions during the Nazi invasions of Poland and France in 1939–40. His greatest success came against the Soviets on the Eastern Front, where he amassed all of his tank hits and in addition destroyed three major warships and 70 smaller seacraft and landing ships. He was responsible for thousands of deaths. His exploits were well known to Allied pilots, who were constrained, despite themselves, to admire his bravery. The most renowned French pilot of the war, Pierre Clostermann, later elected deputy in the National Assembly, once remarked, "What a pity he didn't wear our uniform."

On 1 January 1945, Adolf Hitler, calling Rudel "the greatest and bravest soldier the German people have ever known," conferred on him the country's highest military decoration, which no one else has ever won, the Golden Oak Leaf with Swords and Diamonds to the Knight's Cross of the Iron Cross. The following April, very near the time of Hitler's suicide, which took place a month before Germany's surrender, Rudel was shot down and had to have his right leg amputated below the knee. He was flying again before the amputation had healed. Captured at war's end, he was released in April 1946.

Rudel never admitted any guilt over his wartime deeds or beliefs; indeed, the latter remained unchanged. He went to live in Argentina for five years from 1948, working closely with other Nazis for the aviation contractor Kurt Tank in Córdoba. In this capacity he was instrumental in building up the Argentine Air Force. During this period he was the author of several books combining war memoirs and Nazi philosophy, including *In War and Peace, Between Germany and Argentina,* and *From Stukas to the Andes.* His memoirs appeared in English in 1953 under the title *Stuka Pilot,* with an astonishingly friendly foreword by Group Captain Douglas Bader, DSO.

In 1953 he returned to Germany and ran for a seat in the Bavarian state legislature as a candidate of the extreme-right German Reich Party. He lost, and returned to South America in 1956, living in Argentina and São Paulo, Brazil. In 1959 he ran for the Rheinland-Pfalz legislature under the same party's banner, but drew only a tiny percentage of the vote. He continued to participate in neo-Nazi affairs throughout the 1960s and 1970s, when he lived mainly in Austria, first in Kitzbühel and then in nearby Kufstein, both in the Tyrol. He died of a brain hemorrhage.

His funeral, in the German village of Dornhausen, was attended by 2,000 people and caused considerable embarrassment to the West German government. Many of the mourners wore their Iron Crosses and gave the Nazi salute, forbidden since the end of the war. The officially discouraged verses to "Deutschland über Alles," the national anthem, were sung at the graveside, and, most remarkable of all, a squadron of Air Force planes flew over and dipped their wings in an apparent gesture of respect and honor. Many of those present swore the planes flew in a swastika formation. Questions were immediately raised in the Federal Parliament over how such a demonstration of Nazi sympathies could have proceeded unhindered by the authorities, but no answers were forthcoming, not even from the Defense Ministry about the identity of the Luftwaffe pilots who participated in the flyby.

A.K.

Parents Johannes R., Protestant minister, and Martha R. **Emigration** Lived in Argentina 1948–53, Argentina and Brazil 1956–59, Austria from 1970s. **Education** Schs. in Schweidnitz and Görlitz. **Career** Joined Luftwaffe as cadet officer 1936; reconnaissance officer, Poland and France 1939–40; pilot, dive-bomber squadron, Eastern Front 1940–45; appointed wing comdr. of bomber squadron 1945. • Worked with Kurt Tank airplane manufacturing firm, Córdoba, Argentina ca. 1948–ca. 53; active in Deutschen Reichspartei (German Reich Party) and neo-Nazi movement from 1953. **Honors** Golden Oak Leaf with Swords and Diamonds to Knight's Cross of Iron Cross 1945; many other mil. hons. **Author** *Trotzdem,* 1949 (trans. as *Stuka Pilot,* 1952); *Aus Krieg und Frieden* [*In War and Peace*], 1954; *Zwischen Deutschland und Argentinien* [*Between Germany and Argentina*], 1954; *Von den Stukas zu den Anden* [*From Stukas to the Andes*], 1956.

JACK (RANDOLPH) WEBB

Actor, producer, and director

***Born* Santa Monica, California, USA, 2 April 1920**

***Died* Los Angeles, California, USA, 22 December 1982**

"Dragnet," undoubtedly the most popular television crime series ever shown in the United States, was the creation of Jack Webb, who starred as the taciturn, impassive detective Sgt. Joe Friday. In the 1960s and 1970s Webb was the executive producer of several television series based on law enforcement; the most successful of these, "Adam-12," was, like "Dragnet," based on actual cases drawn from Los Angeles police files.

Born in Santa Monica, a suburb of Los Angeles, Webb grew up in poverty with his mother and grandmother. Forced to pass up an art scholarship to the University of Southern California in order to support his family, he went to work in a men's clothing store while gradually becoming involved in local radio production. After a brief hitch as a bomber pilot and USO entertainer with the Army Air Corps during World War II, he returned to California in 1945 and landed a job with a San Francisco radio station, covering the San Francisco U.N. Conference and hosting an early-morning jazz show. He played a hard-boiled detective in the series "Pat Novak for Hire" for ABC before moving in 1947 to Los Angeles, where he continued to act in radio crime dramas while taking bit parts in films, helped by his first wife, the actress Julie London. Probably his best film role was as a paraplegic war veteran in Stanley Kramer's *The Men* (1950).

On the set of *He Walks by Night* (1949), in which Webb played a police detective, a police sergeant who was serving as the film's technical advisor suggested to him that a radio show be created with plots based on Los Angeles Police Department cases. Webb sold NBC on the idea and "Dragnet" premiered on national radio in mid-1949. The show's terse, matter-of-fact dialogue, realistic plots, and emphasis on actual police procedure set it apart from the violent gangster and private-eye dramas then common; by 1951 it was the most popular show on radio.

In December 1951 NBC brought "Dragnet"

to television, with Webb as producer, director, and star. A stickler for authenticity, he befriended real police detectives and studied the way they dressed, talked, and acted. He had an exact replica of the LAPD squad room—accurate down to the extension numbers on the telephones—built on the Disney lot, where episodes were shot, often on a hectic two-day schedule, for his production company, Mark VII, Ltd. Violence and bloodshed were kept to a bare minimum; Friday and his partner, Detective Frank Smith, played by Ben Alexander, dealt mostly with domestic and white-collar criminals, never with organized crime, psychotic mass murderers, or vicious cops (the incessant themes of most later crime programs). This proved to be a winning approach: the series ran until 1959 and again from 1967 to 1970, with Harry Morgan playing Friday's new sidekick, Detective Bill Gannon. At the height of its popularity, in the late 1950s, "Dragnet" attracted nearly 40 million viewers a week. Joe Friday's polite but businesslike warning—"just the facts, ma'am"—and the show's opening disclaimer—"only the names have been changed to protect the innocent"—entered the realm of the transcendent cliché and became grist for innumerable parodies. Even the ominous "dum-de-dum-dum" theme music became famous for signalling doom to miscreants. The show dealt disapprovingly with student radicalism and teenage sex and drug use and came to be a notorious symbol of self-righteous moralizing.

Webb continued to direct, produce, and act in films throughout the 1950s and 1960s, but he was most successful as an executive producer of television series. Nearly a dozen Mark VII series were on the air between 1968 and 1975, notably "Adam-12," a realistic portrayal of the daily rounds of two patrolmen that was sometimes shown in LAPD training classes, and "Emergency!," based on actual paramedical and fire cases. An enthusiastic fan of 1920s jazz, Webb also owned two music leasing companies, Mark VII Music and Pete Kelly's Music.

Webb died in his home in Los Angeles of a heart attack caused by arteriosclerosis. The Los Angeles police chief ordered precinct-house flags to be flown at half-staff. S.A.

Also wrote under pseudonyms John Farr and Tex Grady. **Parents** Samuel Chester W. and Margaret (Smith) W. **Married** (1) Julie London, actress and singer, 1947 (div. 1954): Stacy, b. 1950; Lisa, b. 1952. (2) Dorothy Towne 1955 (div. 1957). (3) Jackie Loughery, beauty queen, 1958 (div. 1964). (4) Opal. **Education** Belmont High Sch., L.A. **Mil. service** USO entertainer and bomber pilot, USAAC 1942–45. **Career** Clerk, men's clothing store 1940s; disc jockey and news announcer, radio sta. KSO, S.F. mid-1940s; radio actor and producer, S.F. and L.A. 1945–60s; film actor since late 1940s and dir. and producer since 1954; TV actor, producer, and dir. since 1951; founding owner of Mark VII, Ltd. since 1952 and of Mark VII Music Co. and Pete Kelly's Music Co. since mid-1950s; production exec., Warner Television Studios, Hollywood 1963. **Officer** Exec. bd. member, United Cerebral Palsy Fund. **Member** SAG; Screen Dirs. Guild; Amer. Soc. of Cinematographers; Amer. Fedn. of Radio Announcers; San Francisco Press Club. **Honors** Edgar Allan Poe Award, for "Dragnet," Mystery Writers of America 1950; best TV dir., *Look* 1953, 1954; best TV actor, *Billboard* 1954; hon. sgt., USMC; hon. chmn., United Cerebral Palsy Assn.; other hons. and awards. **Radio actor** "Pat Novak for Hire," 1945; "Johnny Modero—Pier 23," 1947; "The Whistler," late 1940s; "This Is Your FBI," late 1940s; (also creator, producer, and dir.) "Dragnet," 1949–55; (also creator, producer, and dir.) "Pete Kelly's Blues," 1950; (also creator) "True Series," 1961. **Television producer and director** (Also creator and actor) "Dragnet," 1951–59, 1967–70; "Noah's Ark," 1950s. **Television executive producer** "Adam-12," 1968–73; "The D.A.," 1970–71; "O'Hara, U.S. Treasury," 1970–71; "Emergency," 1971–75; "Chase," 1973; "The Rangers," 1974–75; "Hec Ramsey," 1975; "Mobile One," 1975; "Project U.F.O.," 1978; others. **Television movies** (Actor, producer, and dir.) "Dragnet '69," 1969; (narrator) "Escape," 1973; (exec. producer) "Little Mo," 1978. **Film actor** *Hollow Triumph,* 1948; *He Walked by Night,* 1949; *Dark City,* 1950; *The Men,* 1950; *Halls of Montezuma,* 1950; *Sunset Boulevard,* 1950; *Appointment with Danger,* 1951; *You're in the Navy Now,* 1951; (also producer and dir.) *Dragnet,* 1954 and remake 1966; (also producer and dir.) *Pete Kelly's Blues,* 1955; (also producer and dir.) *The D.I.,* 1957; (also producer and dir.) *Archie,* 1959; (also producer and dir.) *—30—,* 1959; (also producer) *All About Archie,* 1960; (also producer) *The Last Time I Saw Archie,* 1962; (exec. producer only) *The Man from Galveston,* 1963; (also producer and dir.) *Purple Is the Color,* 1964; others. **Novels** *The Brass Halo,* 1957; *The Deadly Sex,* 1959; *One for My Dame,* 1961; *The Gilded Witch,* 1963; *Make My Bed Soon,* 1963. **Nonfiction** *The Badge,* 1958.

LOUIS (MARIE ANTOINE ALFRED) ARAGON
Poet and novelist
***Born* Paris, France, 3 October 1897**
***Died* Paris, France, 24 December 1982**

Louis Aragon was throughout his career a passionate partisan of various literary and political movements, all revolutionary in nature, from Dada and Surrealism in the 1920s to Communism after 1930. He was not widely read in the West outside France, and even in his native country his literary reputation had declined by the time of his death, but for decades he has been (at least officially) the favorite French writer in most Communist countries. He was amazingly prolific: in addition to a full career as editor and political polemicist, he wrote ten major novels and hundreds of poems, of which several are universally regarded as classics.

Aragon was born in unfavorable circumstances in Paris's fashionable 16th *arrondissement.* He was the illegitimate son of Louis Andrieux, a 57-year-old anticlerical radical who had been in 1880 the Paris prefect of police, and Marguerite Toucas, a young woman of 24 who was living with and working for a local family. Andrieux, a married man, chose the child's name and suggested to the mother that she raise him as her very young brother. His earliest childhood was thus passed among three women who claimed him as their brother but were really his mother and aunts.

Even as a child he was a gifted and prolific writer, producing 60 "novels" by the age of nine. After studying at the Lycée St.-Pierre in the luxurious suburb of Neuilly, Aragon passed two *baccalauréats,* and in 1916, at 19, began medical studies. Military service intervened, however, and Aragon performed bravely at the front, winning the Croix de Guerre in August 1918 before taking part in the French occupation of the Rhineland and the Saar. He did not return to medicine after demobilization.

He had been friends with André Breton from their adolescence, then during the war had met Philippe Soupault. The three formed a kind of junior literary triumvirate, publishing from 1919 a review called *Littérature,* which soon became the principal organ of the Dada movement in France. The poet Paul Éluard and others joined the group in the early 1920s. Dada, the brainchild of the Rumanian-born poet-publicist Tristan Tzara, exalted antirationalism and such bizarre compositional forms as mechanical writing, while excoriating conventional behavior and political conformity. Aragon's first political tract, "Down with the Lucid French Genius," appeared in *Littérature* in March 1921. Two months before, with Breton, he had tried to join the French Communist Party but was rebuffed. He had already published his first collection of poems, *Fire of Joy* (1920), and his first novel, *Anicet, or The Panorama* (1921), was about to appear.

From 1921 to 1924 he was an active advocate of Dada, but gradually, led by Breton, drifted away from the movement's defiant and somewhat childish cult of meaninglessness. For their flirtation with Communism, the two were read out of Dada by Tzara (who joined the party himself in the early 1930s), but by that time they had already begun to identify with Surrealism. Breton published his "First Surrealist Manifesto" late in 1924. Aragon's works of the period, the poems in *Perpetual Motion* (1926) and the novel *Paris Peasant* (1926; English eds. 1970, 1971) sold very well and helped popularize the new movement. In both his first novels the dazzling absurd or surreal effects seem subordinate to his primary gifts—strong narrative drive, intensely close observation, and fluent, contemporary language. These strengths always remained with his fiction, whichever political or literary movement he might be following.

Breton and Aragon led a small group of Surrealists into the Communist Party in January 1927. They were at first mistrusted by their new comrades, but eventually, because of the increasing radicalism of the Comintern, came to replace the old-guard official party intelligentsia led by Henri Barbusse. In 1928, after having attempted suicide at the end of a disastrous affair with Nancy Cunard, Aragon met the Russian writer Elsa Triolet, the sister-in-law of the poet Vladimir Mayakovsky. From the beginning, their relationship became the most important thing in Aragon's life; she was his confidante, his teacher, his lover, his muse, his unifier. With her and another Surrealist, Georges Sadoul, Aragon traveled to the Soviet Union for the first time in November 1930, after Mayakovsky's suicide, and there he underwent a spiritual transformation. They attended the Revolutionary Writers Congress in Kharkov, where Aragon and Sadoul wrote a long self-criticism, confessing their past errors and disavowing everything about Surrealism that was incompatible with dialectical materialism, in particular Freudian psychology. "Our only desire," they wrote, "is to work as efficaciously as possible according to the directives of the party, to whose discipline and control we promise to subordinate our literary activity." This marked the beginning of Aragon's break with Breton and Surrealism, which became final in 1932 when Aragon publicly rejected Breton's defense of *Red Front* (1931; English ed. 1933), a collection of incendiary poems that Aragon had written while in the USSR ("I sing," went one verse, "of the proletariat's violent domination over the bourgeoisie").

Aragon's period of greatest work was just then beginning, accompanied by a more reasonable, less self-consciously crazy public persona. He spent a year in the Soviet Union from April 1932, working on the French edition of *International Proletarian Literature,* and on his return to Paris became a general reporter and columnist for *L'Humanité,* the party newspaper. In mid-1933 he joined the editorial board of *Commune,* the influential review published by the Association of Revolutionary Writers and Artists. His books continued to be well received, including the poems in *Hurrah the Urals* (1934) and the novel *The Bells of Basel* (1934; English ed. 1936), the latter being the first in his series of fine realistic novels called *The Real World,* a title meant to underline his break with Surrealism. These novels, all very different from one another, represent the zenith of his fictional art. They are *The Residential Quarter* (1936; English ed. 1938), winner of the Prix Renaudot in the year of the Popular Front, *Travelers on the Impériale* (1942; English eds. 1941, 1947), and *Aurélien* (1944; English ed. 1947).

In late 1934, Aragon represented his association of writers and artists at the 1st Congress of Soviet Writers in Moscow, and the following June organized in Paris the 1st Congress of Writers in Defense of Culture, a group of Communist and anti-Fascist intellectuals. He had officially taken over from Barbusse the role of chief party cultural spokesman. At the Paris congress he made a speech announcing his fully finished conversion to Communism: "The man I was seems to me now a shadowy being. I see again the long stages of his reeducation. Ah, it was not without pain, he had his about-faces, his backslidings. But here he is today, cured of his social sickness. Look at him, comrades, and tell me: don't I have reason to be proud of myself?"

The self-satisfied tone of one who is convinced of his rightness began frequently to reappear in Aragon's political writings. Having given so much of his soul to Communism, he could not countenance the possibility of the new religion leading him and other true believers astray. In June 1936 he returned to the Soviet Union for the funeral of Maxim Gorky, remaining there six months and sending back to *Commune* paeans to the Soviet system, including a lengthy article on Stalin's new Soviet constitution, which he called "a new and true Declaration of the Rights of Man. . . . These phrases are not at all the precious utopia of a generous heart, but the flesh and blood of a real world." He was still in Moscow in October 1936, the beginning of mass executions under the Great Purge. "The Supreme Court has spoken," he reported in *Commune.* "Death to the 16 adjudged guilty. The country would not have understood any other verdict." (Bukharin, Kamenev, and Zinoviev had been executed for treason earlier in the year.) In March 1937 he launched *Ce Soir,* a new Communist daily, and was soon applauding the second great Moscow purge trial and dismissing Stalin's critics. "Let them shut up, the scandalous advocates of Trotsky and his accomplices. . . . Here are the consequences of these gentlemen's 'anti-Stalinist' passions. . . . They are in fact the advocates of Hitler and the Gestapo." As late as July 1939, Aragon was denouncing in *Ce Soir* "the well-orchestrated campaign that dares even declare that Stalin wants an entente with Hitler." A month later, after the signing of the Hitler-Stalin nonaggression pact, he wrote, "The USSR shows once more, and with a flourish, its desire for peace with everyone. Silence to the anti-Soviet conspiracy!" Two days later, on 25 August, *Ce Soir* was banned. Statements like these stuck to Aragon for the rest of his life and made suspect all of his subsequent political judgments in the eyes of most of his countrymen.

He was drafted in 1939 into the medical corps, where he invented a method of freeing wounded men trapped in tanks, for which he received the congratulations of the minister of war. He participated in the English evacuation of Dunkirk, again received a Croix de Guerre, took part in underground operations from the Eure to the Dordogne, was captured by the Nazis (but escaped after only an hour), and was again decorated, this time with the prestigious Military Medal. It was during this period of national peril that Aragon wrote his best poetry—patriotic, defiant, loving, beautifully and naturally expressed. From 1940 to 1942 he lived in secret with Elsa in Nice, a part of France technically under the Vichy collaborationists but in reality relatively free of control. From 1942 until the Liberation he remained in hiding, the Communist intellectual leader of the Southern Zone. His poetry appeared in *Heartbreak* (1941), *Elsa's Eyes* (1942), *Brocéliande* (1942), *Grévin Museum* (1943), and *The French Diana* (1945). He was often considered, even by those opposed to his politics, the poet laureate of the Resistance. Many of his poems of the war years have been set to music and recorded by the best popular singers of the day.

Atter the war he and Elsa were the best-known members of the National Writers' Committee, a leftist group whose "blacklist" of collaborationist writers—thought by many to have been compiled by Aragon himself—occasioned a national scandal and lengthy recriminations. (In 1941 he had authorized publication of part of *Aurélien* in the *Nouvelle Revue Française,* then a Nazi-sanctioned journal run by the archfascist Pierre Drieu La Rochelle.) He was the willing focus of the adulation of dozens of young poets and prose writers. He was once again, from late 1944 to late 1946, editor of *Ce Soir.*

Aragon's Communism became even more defiant after the start of the cold war. He was an ardent defender of Zhdanovism, the tenets of Socialist Realism or "party art" imposed on the international Communist movement from late 1947. He began, in accordance with the doctrine, to write a series of novels, *The Communists* (6 vols., 1949–51), an account of the tumultuous party experience in France in 1939–40, novels that were notably unsuccessful and that even he eventually disowned. From 1948 he was associated with *Les Lettres Françaises,* the intellectual Communist review, becoming its editor in 1953. In its pages he continued his obeisance to Stalinism, defending the ridiculous "philosophical theses" of Lysenko on the existence of two sciences, one bourgeois and the other proletarian, and participating in the "personality cult" surrounding party first secretary Maurice Thorez, an old friend, whose permitted return to France in late 1952 was the occasion for one of Aragon's most vilified poems, "He Returns." He ordered a portrait from his friend Picasso to commemorate Stalin's death in *Les Lettres Françaises,* but the nonrealistic picture, published on page one, caused scandal and outrage in the party. Yet his position on the party's central committee, to which he was elected in 1950, was not put in jeopardy by such reversions to avant-garde taste; he remained on the committee until his death.

Aragon declared himself "overwhelmed" by the revelations of brutality that accompanied the Soviet Union's de-Stalinization campaign after 1956. From this point one may see the beginnings of a certain liberality of thought in Aragon's political life. Although he approved the Soviet crushing of the Hungarian revolt in 1956, he spoke up forcefully for the writers Andrei Sinyavsky and Yuli Daniel, convicted of crimes against the Soviet state at the beginning of the Brezhnev era, and cautioned the Soviet Union in 1968 against abridging the freedom of Czechoslovak intellectuals. For the latter heresy he was punished by the Soviets, who canceled all East-bloc subscriptions to *Les Lettres Françaises,* an act of vengeance that forced it to cease publication in 1972. Aragon's poetry of this period was mainly personal and lyrical: *Eyes and Memory* (1954), *Elsa* (1959), and *Elsa's Fool* (1963). Two of his best novels also date from these years: *Holy Week* (1958; English ed. 1961), about Napoleon's return from Elba, and *The Killing* (1965), about Aragon's wartime experiences. Two other novels, the difficult *Blanche or Forgetfulness* (1967) and *Henri Matisse* (1971; English ed. 1972), an homage to his friend, were less well received. In May 1968, Aragon was the only member of the central committee to take part in street debates at the University of Paris with the student leader, Daniel Cohn-Bendit.

After Elsa's death on 16 June 1970, Aragon entered a long period of mourning, which gradually ended as he began to oversee the publication of his complete works. His collected poetry, in 15 volumes, most with his own commentaries, finished publication only in 1981. *The True Lie* (1980) collected his stories, some of which had never been printed. He gave his and Elsa's papers in 1977 to the National Center for Social Research.

From the time of his conversion to Communism until the end of his life he remained a man of abstemious habits and of considerable personal reserve. He was noble in appearance and unfailingly eloquent, a master of colloquial French in his life as in his writing. Many who knew him remarked that he was in no sense a proletarian, yet he disdained all that was implied by class distinction, and particularly detested the subtle, all-pervasive, class-based hierarchization of French society.

On 19 September 1981, Aragon was named a chevalier of the Legion of Honor, with Pres. François Mitterrand himself conferring the accolade. The meagerness of this distinction was remarked in some quarters, but the state really had no other way to reward him: he had always refused to apply for membership in the French Academy, an absolute prerequisite for election. In September 1982 he was honored by *L'Humanité* with a large exhibition and reception. His death occasioned several violently anti-Communist comments from various members of the French right wing, which simply proved that his work and his life continue to inspire passion, discussion, and controversy. A.K.

Parents Louis Andrieux, police prefect, and Marguerite Toucas. **Married** Elsa Kagan Triolet, writer, 1939 (d. 1970). **Education** Lycée St.-Pierre de Neuilly 1908–14; faculty of medicine, Univ. of Paris 1916–17. **Mil. service** Medical auxiliary, 355th Infantry Regiment, French Army 1918; auxiliary dr., with rank of adjutant, labor regiment, then Tank Div., French Army, Belgium and France 1939–40 (captured; escaped); active with French Resistance and leader of intellectual Resistance 1940–45. **Career** Poet and novelist; co-founder, *Littérature* review 1919; active in Dada movement 1921–24; co-founding member, Surrealist movement 1924–32; joined Communist Party 1927; staff member, C.P. newspaper *L'Humanité* 1933–34; sub-ed., *Commune* review 1933–ca. 36; founder and co-dir., *Ce Soir* Communist newspaper 1937–

39; ed., *Étoiles* and *La Drome en Armes* clandestine periodicals, WWII; ed., *Ce Soir* 1944–46; staff member 1948–53 and dir. 1953–72, *Les Lettres Françaises;* founder 1949 and pres.-dir. gen., Éditeurs Français Réunis; member of Central Cttee. of French C.P. from 1950; member, advisory bd., *Europe* literary review from 1958. **Officer** Founder 1935 and secty. of French sect., Intl. Assn. of Writers for Defense of Culture; v.p., Assn. of Combatant Writers 1945–60; member from mid-1940s and pres. 1957, Natl. Writers' Cttee. **Member** Academie Goncourt 1967–68; Lenin Intl. Peace Prize Cttee. **Honors** Croix de Guerre 1918; Prix Renaudot, for *Residential Quarter,* 1936; Croix de Guerre, army citation, and Military Medal, WWII; Lenin Peace Prize, for "Ode to Stalin," USSR 1957; Order of October Revolution, USSR 1972; Order of People's Friendship, USSR 1977; chevalier, Légion d'Honneur 1981; hon. degrees from univs. of Prague and Moscow. **Poetry** *Feu de joie* [*Fire of Joy*], 1920; *Le mouvement perpétuel* [*Perpetual Motion*], 1926; *La grande gaîté* [*High Spirits*], 1929; *Persécuté persécuteur* [*Persecuted Persecutor*], 1931; *Front Rouge,* 1931 (trans. as *Red Front,* 1933); *Hourra l'Oural* [*Hurrah the Urals*], 1934; *Le crève-coeur* [*Heartbreak*], 1941; *Cantique à Elsa* [*Canticle to Elsa*], 1941; *Brocéliande,* 1942; *Les yeux d'Elsa* [*Elsa's Eyes*], 1942; (as François La Colère) *Le musée Grévin* [*Grévin Museum*], 1943; *France écoute* [*France Listens*], 1944; (as François Lacolère) *Neuf chansons interdites, 1942–1944* [*Nine Banned Songs*], 1945; *La Diane française* [*The French Diana*], 1945; *Le nouveau crève-coeur* [*The New Heartbreak*], 1948; *Les yeux et la mémoire* [*Eyes and Memory*], 1954; *Mes caravanes et autres poèmes* [*My Caravans and Other Poems*], 1954; *Le roman inachevé* [*The Unfinished Romance*], 1956; *Elsa,* 1959; *Poésies: Anthologie, 1917–1960* [*Poetry: Anthology*], 1960; *Les poètes* [*The Poets*], 1960; *Le fou d'Elsa* [*Elsa's Fool*], 1963; *Il ne m'est Paris que d'Elsa* [*For Me There Is no Paris but Elsa's*], 1964; *Le voyage de Hollande* [*The Voyage from Holland*], 1964; *Élégie à Pablo Neruda* [*Elegy to Pablo Neruda*], 1966; *Les chambres* [*The Rooms*], 1969. **Novels** In series *Le monde réel* [*The Real World*]: *Les cloches de Bâle,* 1934 (trans. as *The Bells of Basel,* 1936); *Les beaux quartiers,* 1936 (trans. as *Residential Quarter,* 1938); *Les voyageurs de l'Impériale,* 1942 (*Travelers on the Impériale;* trans. as *The Century Was Young,* 1941, and as *Passengers of Destiny,* 1947); *Aurélien,* 1944 (trans. 1947); *Les Communistes* [*The Communists*], 6 vols., 1949–51. • Others: *Anicet, ou le panorama* [*Anicet, or The Panorama*], 1921; *Les aventures de Télémaque* [*The Adventures of Telemachus*], 1922; *Le paysan de Paris,* 1926 (trans. as *Nightwalker,* 1970, and as *Paris Peasant,* 1971); *La semaine sainte,* 1958 (trans. as *Holy Week,* 1961); *La mise à mort* [*The Killing*], 1965; *Blanche ou l'oubli* [*Blanche or Forgetfulness*], 1967; (anonymously) *Irène,* 1968; *Henri Matisse,* 1971 (trans. 1972); *Théâtre/Roman* [*Theater/Novel*], 1974. **Short-story collections** *Servitude et grandeur des Français: Scènes des années terribles* [*Servitude and Greatness of the French: Scenes from the Terrible Years*], 1945; (as Saint Roman Arnaud) *Trois contes* [*Three Tales*], 1945; *Shakespeare,* 1965 (trans. 1966). **Plays** *L'armoire à glace un beau soir,* 1924 (trans. as *The Mirror-Wardrobe One Fine Evening,* 1964); *Au pied du mur* [*At the Foot of the Wall*], 1924; (jtly.) *Le trésor des Jesuites* [*The Treasure of the Jesuits*], 1929. **Nonfiction** *Traité du style* [*Treatise on style*], 1928; *Pour un réalisme socialiste* [*For a Socialist Realism*], 1935; *En français dans le texte* [*In French in the Text*], 1943; *L'homme communiste* [*The Communist Man*], vol. 1, 1946, vol. 2, 1953; *Chroniques du bel canto* [*Chronicles of Bel Canto*], 1947; *L'example de Courbet* [*The Example of Courbet*], 1952; *Le neveu de M. Duval* [*The Nephew of M. Duval*], 1953; *Journal d'une poésie nationale* [*Diary of a National Poetry*], 1954; *La lumière de Stendhal* [*The Light of Stendhal*], 1954; *Littératures soviétiques* [*Soviet Literature*], 1955; *J'abats mon jeu* [*I Lay Down My Cards*], 1959; (jtly.) *Histoire parallèle,* 4 vols., 1962, rev. as *Les Deux Géants: Histoire des États-Unis et de l'URSS de 1917 à nos jours,* 1962–64 (vols. 1 and 2 trans. as *A History of the USSR from Lenin to Khrushchev,* 1964); *Les collages* [*Collages*], 1965; *Je n'ai jamais appris à écrire, ou les incipits* [*I Never Learned How To Write*], 1969. **Editor** *Avez-vous lu Victor Hugo?* [*Have You Read Victor Hugo?*], 1952; *Introduction aux littératures soviétiques: Contes et nouvelles*

[*Introduction to Soviet Literature: Tales and Novellas*], 1956; *Elsa Triolet choisie par Aragon* [*Elsa Triolet, A Selection by Aragon*], 1960. **Translator** Lewis Carroll, *La chasse au snark,* 1928; *Cinq Sonnets de Pétrarque,* 1947; Tchinghiz Aitmatov, *Djamilia,* 1959. **Conversations** (With Jean Cocteau) *Entretiens sur la musée de Dresde,* 1957 (trans. as *Conversations on the Dresden Gallery,* 1982); *Entretiens avec François Crémieux,* 1964; *Aragon parle avec Dominique Arban,* 1968; *Fernand Séguin rencontre Louis Aragon,* 1969. **Collections** *Le Libertinage* (essays and play), 1924; Hannah Josephson and Malcolm Cowley, eds., *Aragon, Poet of the French Resistance,* 1945, as *Aragon: Poet of Resurgent France,* 1946; Claude Roy, ed., *Aragon,* 1959; *Oeuvres romanesques croisées d'Elsa Triolet et Aragon* [*Fictional Works of Triolet and Aragon*], 1964–74; George Sadoul, ed., *Aragon,* 1967; *Oeuvre poétique* [*Poetic Works*], 15 vols., 1974–81; *Le mentir vrai* [*The True Lie*] (collected stories), 1980. **Archives** in Natl. Center for Social Research.

Further reading Germaine Brée and Margaret Otis Guiton, *An Age of Fiction: The French Novel from Gide to Camus,* 1957; M. Adereth, *Commitment in Modern French Literature,* 1968; Lucille Becker, *Louis Aragon,* 1971.

JACK SWIGERT
Astronaut and politician
***Born* Denver, Colorado, USA, 30 August 1931**
***Died* Washington, D.C., USA, 27 December 1982**

Jack Swigert was a member of the three-man astronaut crew that piloted the disastrous Apollo 13 moon mission back to earth in 1970 after an explosion crippled the spacecraft's command and service modules. In 1982 he became the third astronaut to be elected to Congress, but he died of cancer one week before he was to take office.

The oldest son of a Denver opthalmologist, Swigert was interested in hot rods and motorcycles as a boy and earned his private flying license at the age of 16. He studied mechanical engineering at the University of Colorado, where he was a star football player, and upon graduation in 1953 joined the U.S. Air Force, flying jet fighters in Korea and Japan, and narrowly escaping death on one occasion when his fighter crashed and exploded on a Korean airfield. In 1956 he left the service to test planes for Pratt and Whitney in Connecticut, the world's largest maker of jet engines, and for North American Aviation (later North American Rockwell) in California. He first applied for NASA's astronaut program, the next and last logical step for an ambitious test pilot, in 1963 during the second round of enlistments, but was rejected because he lacked an advanced degree and sufficient flight experience. For the next three years he studied for an M.S. in aerospace science at Rensselaer Polytechnic Institute in Troy, New York, and worked for Rockwell test-flying the Rogallo Wing, an inflatable spacecraft-recovery system being developed for the Gemini capsules. In 1966 he reapplied to NASA and was accepted, along with 18 others, into the Apollo moon-exploration program, where he made something of a legend for himself among the astronauts as a high-living ladies' man.

His first major assignment was on the ground crew for Apollo 7, the first successful manned Apollo flight, in 1968. He was next named backup command-module pilot for Ken Mattingly on the Apollo 13 landing mission, and did intensive preparatory work on command- and service-module malfunction procedures. The launch was set for 11 April 1970. Seventy-two hours before takeoff, Mattingly was removed from the crew because he had been exposed to German measles. Swigert took his place.

The flight, plagued with minor problems from the beginning, turned into a major disaster on the third day. During a routine fluid-mixing procedure, a short-circuited switch caused a liquid-oxygen tank to explode, blowing out one side of the service module and cutting off electric power to the command module. Swigert and his crewmates James Lovell and Fred Haise were forced to spend much of their time in the cramped lunar module, which had its own power system, while the craft orbited the moon without landing and returned to earth. They transferred back to the cold, dark command module for reentry. Although the $40 million flight ended safely, it intensified the public debate over the costs of the space program and ultimately contributed to the loss of support for manned lunar exploration.

Courtesy of NASA

The flight turned out to be Swigert's last. He was assigned to the first joint U.S.-Soviet space mission in 1975, but was dropped from the flight crew for having lied about using his NASA connection for profit, according to the memoirs of astronaut Walter Cunningham. In 1977 he resigned from the space program to run for the U.S. Senate from Colorado, but was defeated by William Armstrong in the Republican primary. After a brief stint as vice president of two Denver industrial-research companies, he entered the 1982 race for Colorado's newly created sixth congressional district, promising strong support for Pres. Reagan's economic policies. Partway through the campaign, a malignant tumor was removed from his right nasal passage. The disease was considered to be under control and Swigert hardly slackened his pace, but by August the cancer had spread to his bone marrow. Voter sympathy for his medical problems, which Swigert made public in his television announcements, may even have helped his campaign; he won easily in November with 63 percent of the vote. He was hospitalized in mid-December when cancer was discovered in his lungs, and he died of respiratory failure a week later. S.A.

Born John Leonard S., Jr. **Parents** John Leonard S., opthalmologist, and Virginia S. **Religion** Roman Catholic. **Education** Blessed Sacrament Sch. and Regis High Sch., Denver; Denver East High Sch., grad. 1949; private pilot's license at age 16; Univ. of Colorado, B.S. 1953; pilot training program and gunnery sch., Nellis Air Force Base, NV 1953; Rensselaer Polytechnic Inst., Troy, NY, M.S. 1965; Univ. of Hartford, M.B.A. 1967. **Mil. service** Fighter pilot, USAF, Korea and Japan 1953–56; jet fighter pilot, Massachusetts Air Natl. Guard 1957–60 and Connecticut Air Natl. Guard 1960–65. **Career** Engineering test pilot, Pratt and Whitney Aircraft, CT 1957–64, and North American Aviation, Inc. (later North American Rockwell), CA 1957–66. • With NASA: astronaut 1966–78; member, support crew, Apollo 7, 1968; backup crew member, then command-module pilot, Apollo 13, 1970. • Staff dir., Commn. on Science and Astronautics, U.S. House of Representatives 1973–ca. 77; v.p., BDM Corp., Denver and VA, and Intl. Gold and Minerals Corp., Denver 1979–82; elected Republican rep. to Congress from CO 6th district 1982. **Fellow** Amer. Astronautical Soc.; (assoc.) Soc. of Experimental Test Pilots; (assoc.) Amer. Inst. of Aerospace and Astronautics. **Member** Quiet Birdmen; Republican Party; Phi Gamma Delta; Pi Tau Sigma; Sigma Tau. **Honors** Octave Chanute Award 1966, Flight Achievement Award 1970, and Haley Astronautics Award 1971, Amer. Inst. of Aerospace and Astronautics; Presidential Medal of Freedom 1970; distinguished service medal, NASA 1970; distinguished alumnus award, Univ. of Colorado 1970; gold medal, City of New York 1970; gold medal, City of Chicago 1970; medal for valor, City of Houston 1970; Antonian Gold Medal 1972; hon. degrees from Amer. International Coll. and univs. of Western Michigan and Western State.

Further reading Walter Cunningham, *The All-American Boys,* 1977.

(LEWIS) JOHN COLLINS
Clergyman and peace campaigner
***Born* Hawkhurst, Kent, England, 23 March 1905**
***Died* London, England, 31 December 1982**

John Collins, canon of St. Paul's from 1948 until his retirement in 1981, was one of the most active, committed, and progressive clergymen in the Church of England. He was the founder of Christian Action, which grew into a vigorous witness against apartheid in South Africa, and he was among the founders of the Campaign for Nuclear Disarmament, which during the 1960s was the most influential antinuclear movement in Britain.

The son of a contractor, he attended Cranbrook School and Sidney Sussex College, Cambridge. Upon graduation he entered Westcott House, Cambridge, to prepare for ordination. In 1928 he went to Whitstable, Kent, to serve as deacon in the parish church, and the next year, after his ordination to the priesthood, became chaplain of Sidney Sussex College. He was clearly singled out for future advancement in 1931 when he was made a minor canon of St. Paul's Cathedral in London and a deputy priest-in-ordinary to King George V. He lectured in theology at King's College, London, in 1932, and was promoted to priest-in-ordinary in 1934, the year he returned to Cambridge to become vice principal of Westcott House.

The rapid movements in Collins's career continued in 1937 when he went to Oriel College, Oxford, as fellow, lecturer in theology, and chaplain. He became dean of the college the next year. During World War II he remained in Britain as chaplain of the Royal Air Force Volunteer Reserve, and at Yatesbury, one of the air bases at which he was stationed, he inspired the formation of a group of Christians committed to spiritual renewal through social action. This was the prototype of Christian Action.

He returned to Oriel after the war, and in 1946 organized the first "call to Christian action in public affairs" at a public meeting at Oxford Town Hall on 5 December. A declaration issued later affirmed the meeting's "faith in the reality of God's providence in human history. . . . In all national and international affairs the rule of God's law, and not the self-interest of the stronger, is the ultimate determinant." Christian Action devoted its energies at first to promoting the ideal of a united Europe, a campaign that attracted influential politicians of both major parties, then from 1953 began to concentrate on supporting passive resistance to apartheid in South Africa. In 1956, when 156 opponents of apartheid were arrested and charged with treason, Christian Action established a Defence and Aid Fund to help the prisoners and their families.

In February 1958, Collins addressed a large public meeting in Central Hall, Westminster, out of which grew the Campaign for Nuclear Disarmament, which counted among its founders Bertrand Russell, Kingsley Martin, editor of the *New Statesman,* the writer J. B. Priestley, and the publisher Victor Gollancz. The best-known CND action was the yearly march from London to Aldermaston, site of the British nuclear-weapons research station. Collins was unable to persuade Christian Action to join the antinuclear campaign, but he divided his time between both causes. He was often vilified as a communist, fellow traveler, and worse. A firm believer in parliamentary democracy, he strongly opposed in 1960 Russell's formation, within the ranks of CND, of the Committee of 100, a group committed to civil disobedience to further the aims of disarmament. Convinced that leftist elements were gaining control of CND, Collins resigned as chairman in 1964. He remained, however, as president of Christian Action from 1959 until his death. He was also that organization's chairman from 1946 to 1973. He lived to see many of the positions he advocated on racism, sexual morality, and disarmament become the accepted ones of his church.

Collins's various extraecclesiastical involvements were undoubtedly the reason why he was never made a bishop but remained residentiary canon of St. Paul's until his retirement in October 1981. He was also the cathedral's chancellor (1948–53), precentor (1953–70), and treasurer (1970–81). He was awarded several foreign decorations, including, in 1978, the gold medal of the United Nations Special Committee against Apartheid. He was also nominated three times for the Nobel Peace Prize. His best-known contribution to theology was *The New Testament Problem* (1937). *A Theology of Christian Action* (1949) provided a rationale for the young movement, and his autobiography, *Faith under Fire* (1966), described his lifelong struggle to reawaken Britain's social conscience. He died of a heart attack at the age of 77.

A.K.

Parents Arthur C., building contractor, and Hannah Priscilla C. **Married** Diana Clavering Elliot 1934: four sons. **Religion** Church of England. **Education** Cranbrook Sch., Kent; Sidney Sussex Coll. and Westcott House, Cambridge; ordained deacon, Diocese of Canterbury 1928; ordained priest 1929. **Mil. service** Chaplain, RAF Volunteer Reserve 1940–45. **Career** Curate, Whitstable Parish Church, Kent 1928–29; chaplain, Sidney Sussex Coll. 1929–31. • With St. Paul's Cathedral, London: minor canon 1931–34; chancellor 1948–53; canon residentiary 1948–81; precentor 1953–70; treas. 1970–81. • Deputy priest-in-ordinary 1931–34 and priest-in-ordinary 1934–35 to King George VII; asst. lectr. in theology, King's Coll., London 1934; vice principal, Westcott House, Cambridge 1934–37; fellow, lectr., and chaplain 1937–48 and dean 1938–48, Oriel Coll., Oxford. • **Officer** Chmn.: (also pres. since 1959) Christian Action 1946–73; Campaign for Nuclear Disarmament 1958–64; Martin Luther King Foundn. 1969–73. • Co-pres., Western European Movement against Nuclear Weapons 1959–64; pres., Intl. Defence and Aid Fund since 1964. **Member** Labour Party from 1946. **Honors** Order of Grand Companion of Freedom, 3rd Div., Zambia 1970; comdr., Order of Northern Star, Sweden 1976; gold medal, U.N. Special Cttee. against Apartheid 1978. **Author** *The New Testament Problem,* 1937; *A Theology of Christian Action,* 1949; (jtly.) *Three Views of Christianity,* 1962; *Faith under Fire* (memoir), 1965; many pamphlets. **Contributor** to *Encyclopaedia Britannica, Hibbert Journal,* other books, mags., and jrnls.

Further reading C. W. M. Gill, "The Canon Collins Controversy," in *Fortnightly Review,* Nov. and Dec. 1954.

Addendum

GEORGES (CHARLES) BRASSENS

Poet and musician

***Born* Sète, Hérault, France, 22 October 1921**

***Died* Sète, Hérault, France, 30 October 1981**

Georges Brassens was one of the best-loved musicians of France, whose well-made, colloquial, ironic songs, full of verve and unconventionality—which he performed far better than anyone else—gained an exalted place in the immensely varied world of French popular music.

The son of a mason, he was born in a fishing village on the Gulf of Lions in the Mediterranean, reluctantly received an education at the local lycée, and arrived in Paris in early 1940 to seek his fortune, an anarchist to the core and already a poet. His first collection of poems, *By Chance,* appeared in 1942, but he had to struggle for another decade before being discovered. His other publications include a novel, *The Tower of Miracles* (1953), and the collection *Poems and Songs* (1973). In 1956 he wrote the music for and performed in René Clair's film *Porte des lilas.*

In 1952, Brassens was heard by Jacques Grello, a popular singer, who introduced him to the famous Patachou, chanteuse, impresario, and club owner. It was at Chez Patachou that Brassens enjoyed his first cabaret success, and over the following years other performances led to other triumphs, at the Alhambra, before huge audiences at the Palais de Chaillot and the Olympia, and at his favorite place, the venerable Bobino Music Hall, where he returned nearly every year until his last performances in Paris in March 1977.

Most of his 140-odd songs describe the lives and deaths of ordinary people: honest peasants, disillusioned soldiers, gravediggers, prostitutes, lovers on a park bench. His greatest influences were the troubadours, the poets of the Pléïade, and especially François Villon. There is nothing particularly extraordinary about his simple, unadorned music: it "adds to the verse," he said, "gives it a familiar quality, makes it more accessible." He was never accompanied on stage by anything other than his own guitar and a bassist. It is his words that count most, that bear all the passion of his songs, and they are almost untranslatable. Brassens has remained virtually unknown outside France.

A large, rumpled man with melancholy eyes (after meeting him, Jean-Paul Sartre described "his goodness—one sees it in his eyes"), Brassens was widely praised by large segments of the French establishment, and even Pres. Charles de Gaulle once quoted him in a speech. He was awarded the grand prize for poetry by the Académie Française in 1967, despite a tremendous flap over the lack of patriotism of his antiwar song "The Two Uncles," in which he declared that "it's crazy to die for ideas." Profits from the sales of 20 million records changed his life but little: he lived in a tiny, old-fashioned flat in Montparnasse, drove a battered Citroën, spent his time with old friends from the days before he became famous. When he learned that he had contracted an incurable, generalized cancer, he returned to die at his family home in Sète, where his best-known request, from his song "Request to be Buried on the Beach at Sète," was finally fulfilled:

> This tomb sandwiched between sky and sea
> Will cast no sad shadow on the scene,
> But an indefinable charm—
> The women will use it as a shelter
> To change into their bathing suits and the children
> Will say "Neat!" of this sand castle . . .
> Poor pharaoh kings, poor Napoleon,
> Poor great ones lying in the Panthéon,
> Poor ashes of consequence,
> You will envy a little the eternal man of summer
> Dreaming, his feet in the waves,
> Spending his death on vacation.

A.K.

Parents Jean B., stonemason, and Elvira (Dagrosa) B. **Education** Coll. Paul-Valéry,

Sète; Lycée de Montpellier, left at age 17. **Career** Poet and musician; odd jobs, Paris 1940–52; singer in cabarets and music halls, on radio and on records since 1952; contributor, *Libertaire.* **Member** Anarchist Fedn. **Honors** Grand prize for recording, Acad. Charles-Cros 1964 and other years; grand prize for poetry, Acad. Française 1967. **Songs** 500, including "The Bad Reputation," "The Gorilla," "The Two Uncles." **Recordings** *Georges Brassens Sings of the Birds and the Bees,* 1965; many others. **Film soundtrack** *Porte des lilas,* 1956. **Poem and song collections** *À la venvole* [*By Chance*], 1942; *La mauvaise réputation* [*The Bad Reputation*], 1954; *Georges Brassens,* 1963; *Georges Brassens, poète d'aujourd'hui* [*Georges Brassens, Poet of Today*], 1965; *Chansons* [*Songs*], 1967; *Poèmes et chansons* [*Poems and Songs*], 1973. **Novel** *La tour des miracles* [*The Tower of Miracles*], 1953. **Interview** *André Sève interroge Brassens: toute une vie pour la chanson* [*André Sève interviews Brassens: A Whole Life for Song*], 1975.

Further reading Elizabeth Peer, "Songs About . . . *Pardon?*," in *New York Times Magazine,* 18 Feb. 1968.

CLYDE T(HOMAS) HOLLIDAY

Aerospace engineer

***Born* Hermleigh, Texas, USA, 20 October 1911**

***Died* Arlington, Virginia, USA, 23 June 1982**

The first photographs of the earth from space were taken in 1946 by cameras housed in captured German V-2 rockets that had been launched as part of a government testing program by the Applied Physics Laboratory at Johns Hopkins University. The cameras had been designed by Clyde T. Holliday, an APL instrumentation engineer. Holliday's cameras have also been used by meteorologists, global-resource planners, and military-intelligence agents to photograph vast areas of the earth's surface from vantage points high in or above the atmosphere.

Holliday was educated at Texas A&M, Georgetown University, and the Rochester Institute of Technology, then worked for several years in Houston as a photographer and instrument-repair specialist. In 1942 he became an engineering staff assistant at the Carnegie Institution's department of terrestrial magnetism, helping to develop the radio proximity fuse for artillery shells. From 1943 to 1945 he worked on fire-control systems for antiaircraft weapons at the Applied Physics Laboratory, to which the proximity-fuse program had been transferred.

After the surrender of Germany in 1945, the U.S. Army seized 100 V-2 rockets at the Peenemünde launching grounds and shipped them to White Sands, New Mexico, for testing. The APL was charged with developing an experimental program in high-altitude photography using the V-2s, and Holliday was assigned to design, build, and install appropriate equipment. He adapted the compact and sturdy Fairchild K-25 camera to take one picture per second, with a shutter speed of one five-hundredth of a second and a lens aperture of *f*/5.6. The first test, a complete success, took place on 24 October 1946. Views taken from a distance of 100 miles, the height of the rocket's trajectory, clearly showed cloud patterns as well as the curvature of the earth. Testing continued through 1948, using V-2s and Navy Aerobee sounding rockets.

Starting in the 1950s, Holliday equipped missiles and satellites to record and transmit data through video systems. This was a definite improvement over film, which is sometimes lost or destroyed during reentry into the atmosphere. In July 1967, Holliday processed the first color pictures of the whole earth, taken at a height of 20,000 miles with a slow-scan television camera aboard DODGE, an APL satellite. The far-ultraviolet spectrometer that was used by the crew of Apollo 17 in 1971 to determine that no gases are leaking from the moon's interior had an optical system designed by Holliday. Another of his devices, carried by the joint Soyuz-Apollo orbital mission of 1975, provided information on the density of atmospheric gases at an altitude of roughly 130 miles.

From the mid-1970s, Holliday designed and tested electro-optical devices for the APL's Submarine Technology Division. He died at the age of 70 of complications following a stroke. P.D.

Married Lois Evans: Susan Ellen, b. 1950; Steven Evans, b. 1952; George Eric, b. 1960. **Education** Texas A&M Univ., College Station, TX; Georgetown Univ., Wash. DC; Rochester Inst. of Technology, NY. **Career** Photographer and instrument-repair specialist 1935–42, Houston, TX; engineering staff asst., dept. of terrestrial magnetism, Carnegie Instn., Wash. DC 1942–43. • With Applied Physics Lab., Johns Hopkins Univ., Laurel, MD: staff asst. 1943–45; assoc. engineer, Aerodynamic Research Group 1945–48; assoc. engineer and project supervisor, Research Center 1948–53; engineer and project supervisor with Ramjet Burner Lab. Group 1953–54, with Talos Missile Field Testing Group 1954–63, and with Fleet Systems Instrumentation Group 1963–65; principal engineer, Space Dept. Physics and Instrumentation Group 1965–76; engineer, Submarine Technology Div. since 1976. **Officer** Founding member, governing-bd. member, chmn. of Fiber Optics Working Group, and technical v.p., Soc. of Photo-optical Instrumentation Engineers. **Member** Soc. of Photographic Scientists and Engineers; Soc. of Motion Picture and Television Engineers; Natl. Capitol Area Council, Boy Scouts of America. **Honors** Ordnance Development Award, USN, and certificate of Merit, Office of Scientific Research and Development, WWII; Gov.'s Award, Soc. of Photo-optical Instrumentation Engineers; Silver Beaver, Luther Lamb Award, and Wood Badge, Boy Scouts of America. **Patents** Micrometer, 1950; firing-error recorder, 1956; short-duration, high-intensity spark-gap arrangement, 1958. **Contributor** of papers on aerospace instrumentation and optical systems to scientific and engineering jrnls.

JOSH MALIHABADI
Shabbir Hasan Khan
Poet
***Born* Malihabad, Oudh, India, British Empire, 5 December 1898**
***Died* Islamabad, Pakistan, 22 February 1982**

Shabbir Hasan Khan, better known as Josh Malihabadi, was an influential and widely respected poet who wrote in Urdu, an Indic language that is the principal tongue of Pakistan and of Muslims in India. A committed socialist all his life, he was the first to introduce modern political and economic ideas to Urdu poetry, whose themes had changed little over the centuries.

He was born in the kingdom of Oudh, located in the present-day Indian state of Uttar Pradesh. His aristocratic family had well-established connections in government and literature, but the boy began early to show signs of rebellion. He received a high-school education in Husainabad and Lucknow, but quit university—first in Aligarh and then in Agra—intending to devote his life to literature, and moved to Hyderabad, a princely state in southern India and a flourishing center of Islamic culture and Urdu learning. He absorbed a great deal about the highly technical craft of Urdu versification from his colleagues in the court of the nizam, or prince, but refused to produce the usual *qaseeda* (poems of praise) required of all poets in the nizam's employ, for he had ceased believing in princely privilege. The nizam, a man of great culture and generosity, granted him a "condemnation allowance" before banishing him from his realm.

Josh—the name he took for a nom de plume—then produced several unsuccessful literary magazines. He often wandered about the country, living off wealthy admirers of his poetry and local princes, accepting their largesse while denouncing their rule. As early as 1930 he was recognized as *shair-i-inqilab* (poet of the revolution), and this title stayed with him throughout the Indian struggle for independence from Britain. In book after book of verse he attacked the British for their selfish blindness, their inability to understand the aspirations of the people. During World War II he was especially angry that Britain had committed Indian lives to the fight against the Axis, a battle he believed was none of any Indian's business. "You are shouting," one of his best-known lines goes, "now that your own house is on fire." Radio Berlin broadcast several of his poems as proof that India was not behind the British war effort.

After independence, Jawaharlal Nehru, an old friend, offered Josh the editorship of *Aaj Kal,* the magazine published by All-India Radio. In this highly respectable post he continued his iconoclasm, privately attacking some of the prime minister's closest colleagues, and came to be seen as a curmudgeonly eccentric. He was awarded India's highest literary and cultural honor, the Padma Bhushan.

He frequently traveled to Pakistan after partition to attend the formal Urdu poetry-reading sessions called *mushairas,* and was always begged by the conferees to remain in the Muslim country. In 1956 he moved permanently to Pakistan, surprising and disappointing his friend Nehru, and lived there the rest of his life. In an interview in 1967, however, he said that he was not happy in Pakistan, for his friends and memories were all Indian. His utopian vision of the triumph of socialism on the subcontinent remained as strong as ever.

Josh's literary output included more than 15 books of poetry, three books of essays, and several scripts for Urdu films. He was also the guiding force behind the monumental attempt to produce a comprehensive Urdu dictionary. In his last years, as a special officer of the Pakistani National Council of the Arts, he received rent-free lodgings and a state pension of 4,000 rupees per month. He died in the Pakistani capital of cardiac arrest and pulmonary infection. A.K.

Born Shabbir Ahmad Khan. **Father** Nawab Bashir Ahmad, feudal lord and poet. **Married** Begum Ashraf Jahan 1917 (d.): Sajjad Hyder Kharosh; Saeeda Khatoon. **Religion** Muslim. **Emigrated** to Pakistan 1956. **Education** Sitapur High Sch., Husainabad; Jubilee High Sch. and Church Mission High Sch., Lucknow; MAO Coll., Aligarh 1913; St. John's Coll., Agra, sr. Cambridge diploma 1914. **Career** Marxist poet and journalist since 1920s; with Translation Bureau 1924–36, and official poet 1934–36, Hyderabad; publisher of literary mags., Delhi 1930s–40s; film lyricist, Poona 1940s; ed., *Aaj Kal* mag., All-India Radio, Delhi late 1940s–50s; literary advisor, Urdu Development Bd., Pakistan since late 1950s; officer, Pakistani Natl. Council of Arts. **Honors** Padma Bhushan literary prize, India. **Author** *Isharat* (essays), 1942; *Yadoon-ki-baraat* [*Procession of Memories*] (autobiography); more than 15 vols. of poetry and several collections of prose.

BARBARA (MARY CRAMPTON) PYM
Novelist
***Born* Oswestry, Shropshire, England, 2 June 1913**
***Died* Oxfordshire, England, 11 January 1980**

Before 1977, Barbara Pym was known as the author of six novels that were respectfully noticed but not widely read. In that year, she achieved an unexpected literary celebrity that raised her to the status of a remarkable and lionized writer. This abrupt turn in her fortunes had little to do with the merits of her fiction, which is neither as poor as her neglect implied nor as fine as her discoverers claimed. It was brought about by the *Times Literary Supplement,* which, to celebrate the seventy-fifth anniversary of its founding, asked eminent literary people to name those twentieth-century writers who, in their opinion, were most grossly overvalued or unfairly ignored. In the second category, Lord David Cecil and Philip Larkin both named Barbara Pym, who was then living in retirement in a small Oxfordshire village, unable to find a publisher for her work. Her seventh novel, *Quartet in Autumn,* was accepted by Macmillan on the same day that the *TLS* published its encomiums. Thereafter, reviews of her books were adulatory, and invariably invoked the spirit of Jane Austen. "Though this was nonsense," as the London *Times* obituary writer pointed out, "her exploration of her own fairly restricted milieu and her penchant for satirical observation did give a strength to her novels which their apparently fragile, almost fugitive quality, initially disguised." Her forte, the *Times* added, was the "subtle, penetrating observation of genteel milieux and her delicate treatment of the shy and retiring corners of the human character."

Pym was one of the two daughters of a Shropshire solicitor and was educated at Huyton College, a private school near Liverpool, and at St. Hilda's College, Oxford, where she read English literature and from which she graduated in 1934. She began to write at school, and had completed several apprentice novels before joining the Postal and Telegraph Censorship Office in Bristol at the beginning of World War II. From 1943 to 1946 she worked with the Women's Royal Naval Service. After the war she returned to London and found a job at the International African Institute, where she was first a research assistant for and later assistant editor of the anthropological journal *Africa.* She published her first novel, *Some Tame Gazelle,* in 1950, and during the next 11 years wrote 5 more, the last of which, *No Fond Return of Love,* came out in 1961. After *Quartet in Autumn* was rejected by more than 20 publishers, nothing more of her work appeared for 15 years, although she continued to write. In 1974 she retired to live with her sister near Oxford. Following her rediscovery in 1977 and the springing up of a cult of her admirers, several of her previous novels were reissued and two new novels were published.

The revival of interest in her writing intensified, if anything, after her death in 1980. Two years later, *A Few Green Leaves,* written during her last illness, and *An Unsuitable Attachment,* written in 1963 and found among her papers, were published to universal acclaim. In the United States, where she had become very popular, her books were made available in hardcover and paperback by E. P. Dutton.

The intimate, restricted tone that Pym's critics praise in her novels is achieved by her consistent use of a single narrator, but the scope of her fiction is usually broader than most reviews suggest. The reader is always conscious of social pressures that have shaped the context in which the narrator observes. This context changed perceptibly as Pym went on writing, widening to include, in *A Few Green Leaves,* an entire village. Many of her characters are anthropologists, professional observers of human life whose methods and concerns she both employs and mocks in her fiction. If her books may be said to be "about" anything, in the sense of having a persistent theme, they are about the falsity of romance and the disparity of its conventions from the lives that most people lead. Her distinction lay in the detailed, unsentimental scrutiny of subjects that other writers tackled only at the risk of falling into bathos. Within the confining intimacy of the society she describes—a country rector's household, a genteel but declining London neighborhood, an office where four elderly employees live out their lives—the most tenuous contacts take on the stature of momentous events.

Pym's women narrators are people who, for one reason or another, have chosen to accept the seclusion and detachment that society has forced upon them, and who have defenses and resources that allow them to lead single lives. The witty and charming Mildred Lathbury of *Excellent Women* (1952), "one of the last . . . of the great narrating English virgins," according to John Updike, decides to shun marriage on the basis of what she hears through the walls of her apartment building and of her observation of men. Other Pym heroines, like Jane in *Jane and Prudence* (1953) and Wilmet in *A Glass of Blessings* (1958), chose marriage at an early age but now find that their desire for emotional and intellectual fulfillment cannot be satisfied by their husbands. The opposite sex is often portrayed in Pym's novels as fatuous, presumptuous, and conspicuously less intelligent than the "excellent women" who are always there when they are needed, ready to dispense tea and sympathy. Little wonder then that her Jane Eyres are not eager to meet their Rochesters, but prefer solitary lives and seek consolation, like their creator, in "church, gardening, local history, and country walks."

Philip Larkin, considering what was the most permanent quality of her work, concluded that it is her sense of "the underlying loneliness of life" and "the virtue of enduring this." That is also the subject on which Larkin concentrates and it is surely likely that her novels and his poems will continue to be read as classics of mid-century irony. Their scale is small but their proportions are exact. As Larkin said, they are "miniatures that will not diminish." H.B.

Parents Frederick Crampton P., solicitor, and Irena (Thomas) P. **Religion** Church of England. **Education** Huyton Coll.; St. Hilda's Coll., Oxford, B.A. (hons.) 1934. **Mil. service** Postal and Telegraph Censorship Office, Bristol 1939–ca. 43; Women's Royal Naval Service, England and Naples 1943–46. **Career** Novelist since 1940s; research asst. 1946–58 and asst. ed. and editorial secty. 1958–74, *Africa,* Intl. African Inst., London. **Member** Soc. of Authors, U.K.; PEN. **Novels** *Some Tame Gazelle,* 1950; *Excellent Women,* 1952; *Jane and Prudence,* 1953; *Less Than Angels,* 1955; *A Glass of Blessings,* 1958; *No Fond Return of Love,* 1961; *Quartet in Autumn,* 1977; *The Sweet Dove Died,* 1978; *An Unsuitable Attachment,* 1982; *A Few Green Leaves,* 1982.

Further reading Philip Larkin, "The World of Barbara Pym," in *Times Literary Supplement,* 11 Mar. 1977; Karl Miller, "Ladies in Distress," in *New York Review of Books,* 9 Nov. 1978; John Updike, "Lem and Pym," in *New Yorker,* 26 Feb. 1979.

HERBERT QUANDT
Industrialist and financier
***Born* Pritzwalk, Brandenburg, Germany, 22 June 1910**
***Died* Bad Homburg, West Germany, 2 June 1982**

Industrialist Herbert Quandt, the scion of one of Germany's richest manufacturing families, took over Bayerische Motoren Werke (BMW) in the 1960s and turned it into a world-renowned builder of prestige automobiles and motorcycles.

His father, Günther Quandt, a textile manufacturer from Brandenburg, built the family industrial empire in the early 1900s, diversifying into potash refining, battery production (the Quandt-owned firm Varta Batterie A.G. is now one of the world's largest), mining, steel, and munitions, including Mauser firearms. Much of the business was destroyed or confiscated during and just after World War II, but in the postwar economic boom Günther was able to rebuild and even extend his operations.

Herbert, who suffered from an eye ailment, was privately educated from the age of ten. Since he could barely read, he trained his memory and was later able to keep the myriad details of his business in his head. Starting as an operator of a die-casting machine in the Varta battery factory, he rose through the ranks and assumed joint control, with his half brother Harald, of the family holding company when their father died in 1954. Like Günther, Herbert was secretive about the nature and extent of his business dealings and was rarely seen in public.

In the early 1960s, Quandt bought a 50 percent share of BMW, a financially ailing manufacturer of midget cars and motorcycles surviving on its past reputation as a supplier of aircraft engines to the Luftwaffe. He replaced the company's top management, forestalled a takeover bid by Daimler-Benz, the Mercedes manufacturers, and oversaw a public-relations effort aimed at creating a new image for the BMW car. The firm developed a line of luxurious, high-performance sedans that were an immediate success in the European market and later in the United States. Within a decade BMW was producing 200,000 cars yearly and earning a healthy profit.

In 1967 Harald Quandt was killed in a plane crash, leaving his half of the business to his wife and children. Herbert was in the midst of a large-scale reorganization and consolidation of the syndicate, with most of its subsidiaries being grouped under Varta A.G. and Industrie Werke Karlsruhe-Augsburg, a heavy-industry holding company. After successive divisions of stock between the two families, Herbert settled with Harald's heirs in 1975, in part with cash obtained by selling the families' 14 percent share of Daimler-Benz to Kuwait for one billion marks (about $600 million). By the 1980s, the Quandt empire employed some 70,000 workers, many on a profit-sharing plan that Quandt introduced in 1974, and grossed $1.5 billion a year.

The kidnapping of Quandt's youngest daughter in 1978 by a 14-member gang of terrorists seeking a ransom of $12 million was narrowly averted by the German police.

Quandt died at the age of 72. Leadership of the syndicate is expected to pass to his son, Sven. C.M.

Courtesy of German Information Center

Parents Günther Q., industrialist, and Antonie (Ewald) Q. **Married** (1) . . . : Silvia, b. 1939. (2) . . . : Sonja, b. 1951; Sabina, b. 1953; Sven, businessman, b. 1955. (3) Johanna Bruhn: Susanne, b. 1963; Stephan, b. 1966. **Education** Public sch. to 1920; then private tutoring. **Career** Machine operator and other jobs to 1940, dir. from 1940, and chmn. from 1954, Varta Batterie A.G., Hanover; managerial and exec. jobs with various family cos. to 1954; co-dir. 1954–67, dir. since 1967, and chmn. of supervisory bd., family holding co. Allgemeine Gesellschaft für Industrie-Beteiligung, Stuttgart-Zuffenhausen; principal owner and chmn. of supervisory bd., Bayerische Motoren Werke (BMW), Munich since early 1960s. • Chmn., supervisory bd., and major stockholder: Altana Industrie-Aktien und Anlagen A.G., Frankfurt; CEAG Industrie-Aktien und Anlagen A.G., Bad Homburg; Industrie Werke Karlsruhe-Augsburg A.G., Karlsruhe; Busch Jaeger Gesellschaft für Industrie-Beteiligungen, Munich; Byk Gulden Lomber Chemische Fabrik GmbH, Frankfurt; other firms. • Bd. member: Daimler-Benz to 1975; Deutsche Bank, Inc., Frankfurt; Gerling Konzern Allgemeine Versicherungs A.G., Cologne; Industrial Planning Corp., Karlsruhe; Rhein-Steel Co.; Wagon-Union Co., Berlin; Concordia Electricity Corp., Wintershall; other firms. **Honors** Bavarian Medal of Service 1968; Grand Medal of Honor in Gold with Star, Austria 1979; hon. degree, Univ. of Mainz.

MAX SCHERR

Newspaper editor

***Born* 1916**

***Died* Berkeley, California, USA, 31 October 1981**

Max Scherr was a combative radical who founded the *Berkeley Barb,* a tabloid of the counterculture, in 1965 and remained its proprietor and editor until 1973. The paper, which suffered a long and slow decline after a few flourishing years, finally expired in 1980.

Scherr was trained as a lawyer, worked as a union and civil-rights organizer, and by 1965 was the owner of a popular Berkeley bar, the Steppenwolf, which he sold to start the *Barb.*

For years each issue was assembled in his home with the assistance of an eager volunteer staff who were paid 65 cents an hour or 25 cents a column inch. He sold most of the first press run of 2,000 copies himself in the many bookstores and coffeehouses of the Bay Area.

The *Barb*'s style—feisty, iconoclastic, anarchistic—endeared it to its New Leftist readership, who pushed its circulation over 90,000 by 1969. Its favorite targets were Gov. Ronald Reagan, S. I. Hayakawa, president of San Francisco State College, and "the pigs," a label affixed to all authority figures, especially the police. The paper covered the major radical stories thoroughly: the revolution and all its manifestations; rock politics, especially the murder at the Rolling Stones' concert at Altamont, California; the police invasion of the Berkeley People's Park; the suppression of the Black Panthers; and multifarious experiments with sex, drugs, and life-styles. Its layout eschewed all elegance; some called the *Barb* the ugliest paper in the United States.

The beginning of the end came in mid-1969, when a rival paper, the satirically named *Berkeley Fascist,* reported Scherr's net profit from the *Barb* at over $5,000 a week. The staff struck the paper when the editor refused to consider their demands for a union and greater decision-making authority. Angry readers joined in picketing the paper's new offices, their signs calling Scherr "miser" and "pig."

Scherr relented for a time, offering to sell the paper to the staff for $140,000, but later changed his mind. Timothy Leary, the psychedelic-drug advocate, brought a millionaire friend to Berkeley who was thought to be willing to pay $250,000, but that deal fell through as well. The 40-odd staff members, who called themselves the Red Mountain Tribe, categorically rejected Scherr's patriarchal attitudes and set out to found an alternative to the alternative paper, which was first called the *Barb on Strike* and later the *Tribe.* The *Barb* was reduced to a skeleton of its former self with all its writers gone, while the ads for sexual services grew in number and prominence in the paper and its circulation began a steady decline.

Scherr remained adamant in his views. "I was for honest journalism," he recalled at the end of his life. "Everyone began voicing ideologies, advocating static points of view." He was generally intolerant of the movement's new currents, especially feminism. He disposed of his interest in the *Barb* in 1973 under circumstances that were never fully revealed, remaining as "editor emeritus" until the last issue, number 735, appeared in July 1980. By then even the sex ads had moved to another paper and the circulation was below 2,000, where it had begun.

Scherr suffered a heart attack in 1970 and died after a long battle with cancer. His common-law wife and two children had left him and he was still ostracized by many in the community.

"We were a lot of well-meaning fools," he reflected shortly before the end. "All of us were tainted by the environment we were brought up in. We had no revolutionary base, no real class consciousness. Along with the good, we developed a large rip-off philosophy." Yet his old leftist idealism persisted: "We broke down a lot of barriers to honest thought and opened up a whole visionary realm to the future, which has to be worked on yet."

A.K.

Married (common-law) Jane 1959 (separated): two children. **Education** Law sch. **Career** Lawyer; union and civil-rights organizer; owner, Steppenwolf Bar, Berkeley, CA 1958–65; founder 1965, publisher and ed. 1965–73, and ed. emeritus 1973–80, *Berkeley Barb.*

Further reading Robert J. Glessing, *The Underground Press in America,* 1970.

ADDITIONAL DATA ON ENTRANTS

Algren, Nelson (1981)

The Devil's Stocking, his last novel, was published in Frankfurt, West Germany, in 1982.

Benelli, Giovanni Cardinal (1982)

His parents were Luigi and Maria (Simoni) Benelli. He attended the Diocesan Seminary in Pistoia from 1932 to 1941, the Pontifical Gregorian University from 1941 to 1946, the French Seminary in Rome from 1941 to 1943, and the Pontifical Ecclesiastical Academy from 1943 to 1946; he held the degrees D.D., D.C.L., and S.T.L. He served with the Apostolic Nunciatures in Dublin from 1950 to 1953, Paris from 1953 to 1960, Rio de Janeiro from 1960 to 1962, and Madrid from 1962 to 1965, and represented the Vatican at numerous international conferences.

Bradley, Omar N. (1980)

A General's Life: An Autobiography, written in collaboration with Clay Blair, was published in 1983.

Douglas, Melvyn (1981)

He had roles in the film *Death Squad* (1974) and the television movie "Portrait of Grandpa Doc" (1982).

Eldjárn, Kristján (1982)

In addition to the honors already noted, he was a knight, first class, of the Order of Dannebrog, Denmark, and a knight of the Order of Seraphim, Sweden; the holder of the Grand Cross of the Order of Leopold, Belgium; and the recipient of honorary decorations from the Icelandic Red Cross and the Church of Skálholt, Iceland.

Hays, Lee (1981)

The Weavers' last concert was the subject of *Wasn't That a Time* (1982), a documentary film by Jim Brown.

Leek, Sybil (1982)

Her parents were Christopher Edwin and Louisa Ann Fawcett. Her second husband, Reginald Brian Leek, was an antiques dealer who died in 1975.

Longhair, Professor [Henry Byrd] (1980)

The Last Mardi Gras, a live album, was released in 1982.

Marley, Bob (1981)

The film *Reggae Sunsplash,* released in 1981, contained concert footage of Marley and the Wailers.

Monroney, A. S. Mike (1980)

The photograph on page 103 of the 1980 volume is not of A. S. Mike Monroney but of his son, Mike Monroney, who is also a politician.

Montale, Eugenio (1981)

The Second Life of Art, a collection of essays edited and translated by Jonathan Galassi, was published in 1982.

Piaget, Jean (1980)

In addition to the honors already noted, he received the following awards: Prix de la Ville, Geneva 1963; medal, University of

Moscow 1966; award, American Research Association 1967; citation, Council of Regents, Minneapolis 1968; gold medal, Centro Internazionale Pio Manzo 1969; Prix Foneme 1970; Hall Medal 1972; commander, Légion d'Honneur 1980. He was also an honorary member of the Federación Colombiana de Psicología, Bogotá.

Porter, Katherine Anne (1980)

Joan Givner's *Katherine Anne Porter: A Biography,* published in 1982, contradicted many of the details given in previous biographies and in reference books. The source of most of the facts that have been called into question was Porter herself.

Sellers, Peter (1980)

The last Inspector Clouseau film, *Trail of the Pink Panther* (1982), was pieced together by director Blake Edwards from outtakes and unused footage from previous films in the series. Sellers also played six roles, including Hitler, in a 1976 film, *Undercovers Hero.*

Thornton, Charles B. (1981)

He was awarded the Presidential Medal of Freedom, not the Medal of Honor.

de Villa, Luz Corral [Doña Lucha] (1981)

Doña Lucha was the first of Pancho Villa's three wives (he remarried twice without benefit of divorce). One of her successors, Soledad Seaez, is still living; the other, Austreberia Renteria de Villa, died in May 1982.

Voskovec, George (1981)

He appeared in *Barbarosa* (1982), a western directed by Fred Schepisi.

Waldock, Sir Humphrey (1981)

The International Court of Justice reports that his death occurred on 15 August 1981, not 17 August.

Wilkins, Roy (1981)

Standing Fast: The Autobiography of Roy Wilkins, written in collaboration with Tom Mathews, was published in 1982.

Wright, James (1980)

A collection of his poems, *This Journey,* appeared in 1982.

Wurf, Jerry (1981)

Jerry Wurf: Labor's Last Angry Man, by Joseph C. Goulden, based largely on interviews with Wurf and his colleagues, was published in 1982.

List of Abbreviations

A&I	Agricultural and Industrial
A&M	Agricultural and Mechanical
A.B.	Aktiebolaget (company)
ABC	American Broadcasting Company
acad.	academy; académie; academia
ACLU	American Civil Liberties Union
ADC	aide-de-camp
adm.	admiral
admin.	administration; administrative; administrator
AEA	Actors Equity Association
AEF	American Expeditionary Force
AFB	Air Force Base
AFC	Air Force Cross; Australian Flying Corps
AFL-CIO	American Federation of Labor–Congress of Industrial Organizations
AFTRA	American Federation of Television and Radio Artists
A.G.	Aktien Gesellschaft (joint stock company)
AIA	American Institute of Architects
AID	Agency for International Development
AK	Alaska
Akad.	Akademie
AL	Alabama
Alta.	Alberta
A.M.	Master of Arts
AMA	American Medical Association
Amer.	American
Apr.	April
AR	Arkansas
ASCAP	American Society of Composers, Authors, and Publishers
assn.	association
assoc.	associate
asst.	assistant
Aug.	August
AZ	Arizona
b.	born
B.A.	Bachelor of Arts
BBC	British Broadcasting Corporation
B.C.	British Columbia
B.Ch.	Bachelor of Surgery
B.Ch.E.	Bachelor of Chemical Engineering
B.D.	Bachelor of Divinity
bd.	board
Beds.	Bedfordshire
Berks.	Berkshire
B.F.A.	Bachelor of Fine Arts
bldg.	building
B.Litt.	Bachelor of Letters
B.M.	Bachelor of Medicine
BMI	Broadcast Music, Incorporated
brig.	brigadier
bros.	brothers
B.S.	Bachelor of Science; Bachelor of Surgery
B.Sc.	Bachelor of Science
Bucks.	Buckinghamshire
CA	California
ca.	circa
Cambs.	Cambridgeshire
Cantab.	of Cambridge University
capt.	captain
Carms.	Carmarthenshire
C.B.	Companion, Order of Bath
CBC	Canadian Broadcasting Corporation
CBE	Commander, Order of the British Empire
CBS	Columbia Broadcasting System
C.C.	Companion, Order of Canada
CENTO	Central Treaty Organization
C.H.	Companion of Honour
Ch.B.	Bachelor of Surgery
Ch.M.	Master of Surgery
chmn.	chairman
C.I.	Imperial Order of the Crown of India
CIA	Central Intelligence Agency

cia.	company
CIE	Companion, Order of the Indian Empire
cie.	company
C.M.	Master of Surgery
CMG	Companion, Order of St. Michael and St. George
CO	Colorado
co.	company
col.	colonel
coll.	college; collège
comdg.	commanding
comdr.	commander
commn.	commission
commnr.	commissioner
comp.	compiler
corp.	corporation; corporal
corresp.	correspondent; corresponding
C.P.	Communist Party
CPA	Certified Public Accountant
CPSU	Communist Party of the Soviet Union
CSI	Companion, Order of the Star of India
CT	Connecticut
cttee.	committee
cty.	county
CVO	Companion, Royal Victorian Order
d.	died
D.Arch.	Doctor of Architecture
DBE	Dame Commander, Order of the British Empire
D.C.	District of Columbia
D.Ch.	Doctor of Surgery
D.C.L.	Doctor of Civil Law; Doctor of Canon Law
DCMG	Dame Commander, Order of St. Michael and St. George
D.C.T.	Doctor of Christian Theology
DCVO	Dame Commander, Royal Victorian Order
D.D.	Doctor of Divinity
DE	Delaware
Dec.	December
D.Econ.	Doctor of Economics
D.Ed.	Doctor of Education
D.en D.	Doctor of Law
D.Eng.	Doctor of Engineering
D.ès L.	Doctor of Letters
D.ès S.	Doctor of Science
D.ès Sc.	Doctor of Science
D.ès Sc.Pol.	Doctor of Political Science
devel.	development; developing
D.F.A.	Doctor of Fine Arts
DFC	Distinguished Flying Cross
Dip.Arch.	Diploma in Architecture
dir.	director
diss.	dissertation
D.Iur.	Doctor of Jurisprudence
div.	division; divorced
D.Jur.	Doctor of Jurisprudence
DL	Deputy Lieutenant
D.Litt.	Doctor of Literature
D.Mus.	Doctor of Music
D.O.	Doctor of Ophthalmology; Doctor of Osteopathy
D. Phil.	Doctor of Philosophy
dr.	doctor
Dr.en Fil.y Let.	Doctor of Philosophy and Letters
Dr.Eng.	Doctor of Engineering
Dr.Ing.	Doctor of Engineering
Dr.Iur.	Doctor of Law
Dr.Pol.Sc.	Doctor of Political Science
Dr.rer.nat.	Doctor of Natural Science
Dr.rer.pol.	Doctor of Political Science
DSC	Distinguished Service Cross
D.Sc.	Doctor of Science
DSM	Distinguished Service Medal
DSO	Distinguished Service Order
D.V.M.	Doctor of Veterinary Medicine
ed.	editor; edition
educ.	education; educated
EEC	European Economic Community
exec.	executive
exhib.	exhibition
FBA	Fellow of the British Academy
FBI	Federal Bureau of Investigation
Feb.	February
fedn.	federation
FL	Florida
foundn.	foundation
FRCM	Fellow of the Royal College of Medicine
FRCOG	Fellow of the Royal College of Obstetricians and Gynaecologists
FRCP	Fellow of the Royal College of Physicians
FRCS	Fellow of the Royal College of Surgeons
FRS	Fellow of the Royal Society

FRSA	Fellow of the Royal Society of Art
FRSC	Fellow of the Royal Society of Canada
FRSE	Fellow of the Royal Society of Edinburgh
FRSL	Fellow of the Royal Society of Literature
FRSM	Fellow of the Royal Society of Medicine
FRSNZ	Fellow of the Royal Society of New Zealand
FSIAD	Fellow of the Society of Industrial Artists and Designers
ft.	fort
GA	Georgia
gall.	gallery
GATT	General Agreement on Tariffs and Trade
GBE	Knight/Dame Grand Cross, Order of the British Empire
G.C.	George Cross
GCB	Knight Grand Cross, Order of the Bath
GCE	General Certificate of Education
GCIE	Knight Grand Commander, Order of the Indian Empire
GCMG	Knight/Dame Grand Cross, Order of St. Michael and St. George
GCSI	Knight Grand Commander, Order of the Star of India
GCVO	Knight/Dame Grand Cross, Royal Victorian Order
gen.	general
Glam.	Glamorgan
GLC	Greater London Council
Glos.	Gloucestershire
GmbH	Gesellschaft mit Beschraenkter Hoftung (limited liability company)
GOP	Republican Party
gov.	governor
govt.	government
grad.	graduate
GRU	Glavnoe Razvedivatel noe Upravlenie (Soviet Army Intelligence)
Hants.	Hampshire
H.E.	His/Her Eminence; His/Her Excellency
Herts.	Hertfordshire
HI	Hawaii
H.M.	His/Her Majesty
HMS	His/Her Majesty's Ship (or Service)
hon.	honorable; honorary
hons.	honors
hosp.	hospital
HQ	Headquarters
HRH	His/Her Royal Highness
HSH	His/Her Serene Highness
IA	Iowa
IBM	International Business Machines
ID	Idaho
IL	Illinois
illus.	illustrated; illustration
IN	Indiana
inc.	incorporated
inst.	institute
instn.	institution
instr.	instructor
intl.	international
IRA	Irish Republican Army
ITA	Independent Television Authority
ITT	International Telephone and Telegraph
ITV	Independent Television
Jan.	January
J.B.	Bachelor of Jurisprudence
J.D.	Doctor of Jurisprudence
j.g.	junior grade
JP	Justice of the Peace
jr.	junior
jrnl.	journal
jt.	joint
jtly.	jointly
KBE	Knight Commander, Order of the British Empire
K.C.	King's Counsel
KCB	Knight Commander, Order of the Bath
KCIE	Knight Commander, Order of the Indian Empire
KCMG	Knight Commander, Order of St. Michael and St. George
KCSI	Knight Commander, Order of the Star of India
KCVO	Knight Commander, Royal Victorian Order
K.G.	Knight, Order of the Garter
KGB	Komitet Gossudarstvennoi Bezopastnosti (Committee of State Security)
KO	knockout
KS	Kansas

kt.	knight; knighted
KY	Kentucky
LA	Louisiana
L.A.	Los Angeles
lab.	laboratory
Lancs.	Lancashire
LCC	London County Council
lectr.	lecturer
Leics.	Leicestershire
L.I.	Long Island
Lic.	Licencié; Licentiate
Lic.en droit	Licentiate in Law
Lic.en fil.y let.	Licentiate in Philosophy and Letters
Lincs.	Lincolnshire
LL.B.	Bachelor of Laws
LL.D.	Doctor of Laws
LL.M.	Master of Laws
L.M.S.	Licentiate in Medicine and Surgery
LP	Long-playing record
LRCP	Licentiate of the Royal College of Physicians
LRCPE	Licentiate of the Royal College of Physicians of Edinburgh
LRCS	Licentiate of the Royal College of Surgeons
LRCSE	Licentiate of the Royal College of Surgeons of Edinburgh
lt.	lieutenant
ltd.	limited
MA	Massachusetts
mag.	magazine
maj.	major
Man.	Manitoba
Mar.	March
M.B.	Bachelor of Medicine
M.B.A.	Master of Business Administration
M.C.	Military Cross
M.Ch.	Master of Surgery
MD	Maryland
M.D.	Doctor of Medicine
ME	Maine
mfg.	manufacturing
MGM	Metro-Goldwyn-Mayer
mgr.	manager
MI	Michigan
mil.	military
Middx.	Middlesex
MN	Minnesota
M.L.S.	Master of Library Science
MO	Missouri
MOMA	Museum of Modern Art, New York City
Mon.	Monmouthshire
M.P.	Member of Parliament
MRCP	Member of the Royal College of Physicians
MRCVS	Member of the Royal College of Veterinary Surgeons
MS	Mississippi
M.S.	Master of Science; Master of Surgery
msgr.	monsignor
MT	Montana
mt.	mount
M.Th.	Master of Theology
mus.	museum
MVO	Member, Royal Victorian Order
NAACP	National Association for the Advancement of Colored People
NASA	National Aeronautics and Space Administration
natl.	national
NATO	North Atlantic Treaty Organization
N.B.	New Brunswick
NBC	National Broadcasting Company
NC	North Carolina
ND	North Dakota
NE	Nebraska
Nfld.	Newfoundland
NH	New Hampshire
NIH	National Institutes of Health
NJ	New Jersey
NKVD	Narodny Kommissariat Vnutrennikh Del (People's Commissariat of Internal Affairs, Soviet police agency)
NM	New Mexico
no.	number
Northants.	Northamptonshire
Notts.	Nottinghamshire
Nov.	November
N.S.	Nova Scotia
NSW	New South Wales
N.T.	Northern Territory
NV	Nevada
N.V.	Naamloze Vennootschap (limited liability company)
NWT	Northwest Territories

NY	New York State
NYC	New York City
N.Z.	New Zealand
OBE	Officer, Order of the British Empire
O.C.	Officer, Order of Canada
Oct.	October
OECD	Organization for Economic Cooperation and Development
OEEC	Organization for European Economic Cooperation
OH	Ohio
OK	Oklahoma
O.M.	Order of Merit
Ont.	Ontario
op.	opus
OPEC	Organization of Petroleum Exporting Countries
OR	Oregon
orch.	orchestra
org.	organization
Oxon.	Oxfordshire; of Oxford University
PA	Pennsylvania
PBS	Public Broadcasting System
P.C.	Privy Councillor
Pembs.	Pembrokeshire
PEN	Poets, Playwrights, Essayists, Editors, and Novelists
Ph.D.	Doctor of Philosophy
Phila.	Philadelphia
PLO	Palestine Liberation Organization
Polytech.	Polytechnical
postgrad.	postgraduate
POW	prisoner of war
PR	Puerto Rico
pres.	president
prof.	professor
pty.	proprietary
pvt.	private
Q.C.	Queen's Counsel
Qld.	Queensland
Que.	Quebec
RAAF	Royal Australian Air Force
RADA	Royal Academy of Dramatic Arts
RAF	Royal Air Force
RAMC	Royal Army Medical Corps
RCA	Radio Corporation of America
rep.	representative
rev.	revised; reverend
RI	Rhode Island
RIBA	Royal Institute of British Architects
ROTC	Reserve Officers' Training Corps
RSFSR	Russian Soviet Federated Socialist Republic
S.A.	South Australia; Sociedad Anónima
Salop.	Shropshire
SALT	Strategic Arms Limitations Talks
Sask.	Saskatchewan
SC	South Carolina
sch.	school
SD	South Dakota
SEC	Securities and Exchange Commission
sect.	section
secty.	secretary
sen.	senator
Sept.	September
S.F.	San Francisco
s.g.	senior grade
sgt.	sergeant
SHAEF	Supreme Headquarters, Allied Expeditionary Force
SHAPE	Supreme Headquarters, Allied Powers, Europe
soc.	society; société; sociedad
sr.	senior
SSR	Soviet Socialist Republic
St.	Saint
Sta.	Station
Staffs.	Staffordshire
S.T.B.	Bachelor of Sacred Theology
S.T.D.	Doctor of Sacred Theology
Ste.	Sainte
S.T.L.	Licentiate of Sacred Theology
supt.	superintendent
TN	Tennessee
trans.	translator; translated
treas.	treasurer
TUC	Trades Union Congress
TX	Texas
UAR	United Arab Republic
U.K.	United Kingdom
U.N.	United Nations
UNESCO	United Nations Educational, Scientific, and Cultural Organization
UNICEF	United Nations International Children's Emergency Fund

univ.	university; université; universität; universidad
UPI	United Press International
U.S.	United States
USA	United States of America
USAAC	United States Army Air Corps
USAF	United States Air Force
USAID	United States Agency for International Development
USN	United States Navy
USNR	United States Naval Reserve
USO	United Service Organization
USS	United States Ship (or Service)
USSR	Union of Soviet Socialist Republics
UT	Utah
VA	Virginia
V.A.	Veterans Administration; Royal Order of Victoria and Albert
V.C.	Victoria Cross
Vic.	Victoria
vol.	volume
v.p.	vice president
VT	Vermont
WA	Washington State
W.A.	Western Australia
Wash. DC	Washington, D.C.
WHO	World Health Organization
WI	Wisconsin
Wilts.	Wiltshire
Worcs.	Worcestershire
WPA	Works Progress Administration (formerly Work Projects Administration)
WV	West Virginia
WW	World War
WY	Wyoming
YMCA/YWCA	Young Men's/Young Women's Christian Association
YMHA/YWHA	Young Men's/Young Women's Hebrew Association

List of Obituary Writers

A.K.	Andrew Kimmens
B.B.	Barbara Bedway
B.D.	Betty Donaldson
C.B.	Catherine Barr
C.M.	Chloe Magen
D.T.	Daisy Taylor
E.B.	Elmer Borklund
E.W.	Elaine Weiss
H.B.	Howard Batchelor
J.P.	Janet Podell
J.R.	Jonathan Rogers
L.F.	Lisa Friedman
M.T.	Michael Tubridy
P.D.	Peter Desmond
P.K.	Philip Kemp
R.T.	Roland Turner
S.A.	Steven Anzovin

Cumulative Alphabetical Index

Numerals in italic type indicate the volume year in which the main entry appears (*80* is 1980). If further information on the entrant appears in the Addendum to a subsequent volume, the year of that volume is added in roman type.

Names prefixed with particles—*de, du, al, von,* etc.—are alphabetized as follows: if the particle begins with a letter in uppercase (for example, *De Lullo*), the name is alphabetized under the first letter of the particle. If the particle begins with a letter in lowercase (for example, *de Irujo* or *el-Sadat*), the name is alphabetized under the first letter of the main word. Asian names spelled with the surname first are so alphabetized, without a comma (e.g., *Soong Ching-ling*), but regular alphabetization is used if the entrant adopted the Western custom of placing the surname last (e.g., *Ling, Hung-hsun*).

Cumulative Index of Entrants by Profession

Numerals in italic type indicate the volume year in which the main entry appears (*80* is 1980). If further information on the entrant appears in the Addendum to a subsequent volume, the year of that volume is added in roman type.

Names prefixed with particles—*de, du, al, von,* etc.—are alphabetized as follows: if the particle begins with a letter in uppercase (for example, *De Lullo*), the name is alphabetized under the initial letter of the particle. If the particle begins with a letter in lowercase (for example, *de Irujo* or *el-Sadat*), the name is alphabetized under the first letter of the main word. Asian names spelled with the surname first are so alphabetized, without a comma (e.g., *Soong Ching-ling*), but regular alphabetization is used if the entrant adopted the Western custom of placing the surname last (e.g., *Ling, Hung-hsun*).

Teachers and writers who worked within a particular field of endeavor are grouped with those who practiced the profession. A teacher of ballet, for example, would be listed under "Dancers and Choreographers"; a professor of law would be listed under "Judges, Lawyers, and Criminologists"; and a writer who produced essays on architecture would be listed under "Architects and Planners."

The index is divided into the following categories:

Actors, Actresses, Mimes, and Entertainers

Anthropologists

Archaeologists

Architects and Planners

Art Historians, Collectors, Critics, and Dealers

Artists and Craftsmen

Arts Administrators

Astronomers

Aviators and Astronauts

Biographers and Memoirists

Biologists, Botanists, and Zoologists

Business Executives and Industrialists

Chemists

Children's Writers

Composers, Arrangers, and Songwriters

Criminals

Dancers and Choreographers

Designers

Diplomats

Directors

Dramatists and Scriptwriters

Earth Scientists
(including Geographers, Geologists, Meteorologists, and Oceanographers)

Economists, Financial Specialists, and Bankers

Educationists and Educational Administrators

Engineers and Technologists

Explorers

Farmers, Horticulturists, and Agricultural Researchers

Folklorists

Foundation Administrators

Heads of State, Presidents, Premiers, and Governors General

Historians

Illustrators, Cartoonists, and Animators

Intelligence Agents and Officers

International Affairs Officials

Inventors

Journalists and Editors (including Travel Writers)

Judges, Lawyers, and Criminologists

Labor Leaders

Librarians, Museum Curators, Archivists, and Antiquarians

Linguists, Philologists, and Lexicographers

Literary Scholars (including Critics and Translators)

Management and Industrial Relations Specialists

Mathematicians and Statisticians

Medical Practitioners and Researchers

Military Officers and Strategists

Musical Performers and Conductors

Naturalists

Novelists and Short Story Writers (including Humorists)

Performing Arts Critics and Scholars

Philanthropists

Philosophers

Photographers and Cinematographers

Physicists

Poets

Political Scientists

Politicians

Producers

Psychiatrists and Psychologists

Public and Government Officials

Publishers

Radio and Television Personalities

Religious Figures
(including Clergy, Scholars, and Occultists)

Royalty and Socialites
(including notable spouses of famous people)

Social, Political, and Human Rights Activists

Social Workers

Sociologists and Social Scientists

Sports and Games Figures